THE PARODY EXCEPTION IN COPYRIGHT LAW

The Parody Exception in Copyright Law

SABINE JACQUES

OXFORD
UNIVERSITY PRESS

OXFORD
UNIVERSITY PRESS

Great Clarendon Street, Oxford, OX2 6DP,
United Kingdom

Oxford University Press is a department of the University of Oxford.
It furthers the University's objective of excellence in research, scholarship,
and education by publishing worldwide. Oxford is a registered trade mark of
Oxford University Press in the UK and in certain other countries

First Edition published in 2019

Published in the United States of America by Oxford University Press
198 Madison Avenue, New York, NY 10016, United States of America

British Library Cataloguing in Publication Data
Data available

Library of Congress Control Number: 2018961850

ISBN 978–0–19–880693–6

Foreword

'The parody exception in copyright law' is probably a far too modest title for this comprehensive study, unless one emphasizes the broad scope of the title and sees it as a reference to the comprehensive nature of the exercise. Sabine Jacques looks at every angle of the parody exception and finishes her book with a case study of parody in the music industry.

I had the privilege to accompany the journey of this book right from the start. It started life as a very ambitious doctoral thesis that kept growing and that went ever more in depth. It would have been all too easy, but nevertheless very interesting, to merely offer a comparative study of the parody case law in a couple of jurisdictions and to try and draw a few conclusions concerning the options for the newly introduced parody exception in the UK. Instead, Sabine Jacques went back to basics and started by asking what parody really is.

There is no point in spilling the beans here or trying to summarize her in-depth analysis. Let me just suggest that there is potentially a world of difference between ridicule and mockery and that one needs to be clear what the shift from ridicule to mockery means. How broad is the concept of mockery? In any case, there seems to be a need for the parody to refer to the original work. Its roots need to be recognizable for the parody to work. That involves a degree of copying, of sorts, so there needs to be an exception, at least arguably. From there the lines become less clear and different options are open. Is it merely a case of putting the work in a different context? Is the key point the absence of confusion between the original work and its parody? Or is it rather the absence of competition between the original work and its parody? All these are crucial questions and I leave it to the reader to discover the answers and leads in the book itself.

It is needless to say that the answers are not merely black or white, but that their shade of grey also depends to a large extent of the place parody is given in culture and how that choice is reflected in copyright law.

Copyright brings with it the three-step test and moral rights and the intriguing question of how the parody exception fits in with both of them. Yet more questions for in-depth analysis, bringing the reader closer to the in-depth perspective. And all that is done in a comparative context, not merely in Europe, but taking in also Canada, Australia, and the US.

Parody also has a very strong link with human rights and particularly with the freedom of expression. Balancing rights in this context provides the final essential building blocks for the study of the parody exception.

With all those elements to hand there follows the case study of parody in the music industry.

What started as an ever more ambitious doctoral thesis has become a comprehensive study of the parody exception. Sabine Jacques was right to dedicate part of her research time at the start of her academic career at UEA to this project. This has become 'the' book on the parody exception and Sabine Jacques deserves to be congratulated for writing it and for offering us such a rich and enriching pallet.

Paul Torremans
Professor of Intellectual Property Law, School of Law,
University of Nottingham
Nottingham, 13 June 2018

Foreword

Acknowledgements

Combining my two passions, intellectual property law and music, this book constitutes my greatest intellectual journey to date. This project would have not been possible without the precious advice, support, and contributions of many people along the way, to all of whom I owe heartfelt gratitude.

First, I would like to thank and express my gratefulness to my PhD supervisors, Professors Estelle Derclaye and Paul Torremans. Your invaluable guidance, encouragement, and patience have been essential to my professional development. I would also like to thank both of my PhD examiners, Jonathan Griffiths and Nigel Gravells, for their challenging questions and useful advice which led to the present work.

I would also like to thank my friends and colleagues from the University of East Anglia, namely, Morten Hviid, Andreas Stephan, Rob Heywood, Claudina Richards, Avidan Kent, Joe Purshouse, Gemma Mitchell, John Street, Tola Amodu, Ian Edwards, Michael Hamilton, Nick Scharf, and Sally Broughton Micova. Your boundless support, patience, and friendship is invaluable to me. I am deeply indebted to my dear friend and colleague Angelika Reichstein who has supported me beyond words throughout the PhD and its conversion into a monograph.

This book would not have been possible without the invaluable encounters made throughout this journey which have provided me with helpful insights. In particular, I would like to thank Justice Pagone, Jean-Michel Bruguière, Carys Craig, Krzysztof Garstka, Bernd Justin Jütte, Florian Koempel, Vick Bain, Cédric Manara, Hugo Cox, and Trevor Cook for sharing their thoughts on this project with me. I am particularly grateful to my dear friend, Lynne Chave, who devoted her time to reading (too) many drafts of this work throughout the years.

These acknowledgements would be incomplete if I limited them to the people who have influenced and inspired me since the beginning of the PhD. Special appreciation goes to Anselm Kamperman Sanders, Ana Ramalho, and the teaching team at the University of Maastricht, where I undertook my LLM, and where I now have the pleasure to 'pay it forward' by delivering some classes to the new generations of the IPKM programme. Here, I would also like to show my gratitude to Mr Melchior Wathelet, whose passion for the European Union has been infectious and whose lectures at the University of Liège were the most memorable and influential to date. From my time at this institution, special thanks to Nicolas Petit, Alain Strowel, and Véronique Delforge who helped me pursue my enthusiasm for intellectual property law while being an undergraduate and masters student.

Mostly, I would like to express my deepest gratitude to my lifelong friends who relentlessly encourage me through times of need and new endeavours: Amélie Adam, Jérémy Dodeigne, Meelimari Guljavin, Vincent Colin, Alexandra Léonard, Francesca Mazzuchelli, Rossella Pulvirenti, Florelia Vallejo, David Alvarez, Céline Schnitzler, Stéphanie Paquet, Cécile François, Lara Kleynen, Sarah Corman, and Benjamin Vatovez.

Lastly, I am grateful to my parents for their love, patience, and trust in my choices. Heartfelt gratitude goes to Gauthier Dupont—I am sure you know way more about copyright than you ever wished to know but I am deeply grateful for your love, curiosity, and eternal support.

Finally, I dedicate this book to all the artists whose creativity can only thrive where diversity can continue to exist.

Norwich, United Kingdom
1 June 2018

Contents

Table of Cases

UNITED NATIONS HUMAN RIGHTS COMMITTEE

WTO PANEL

EUROPEAN COURT OF HUMAN RIGHTS/EUROPEAN COMMISSION OF HUMAN RIGHTS

EUROPEAN UNION

NATIONAL

Australia

Canada

France

Germany

United Kingdom

Table of Legislation

Regulations

Directives

NATIONAL

Australia

Canada

List of Abbreviations

A&M	Auteurs & Media
A.C.	Canadian Reports, Appeal Cases
ACHPR	African Commission on Human and Peoples' Rights
ADR	Alternative Dispute Resolution
AFPIDA	Branche française de l'Association littéraire et artistique internationale
AGO	Advocate-General Opinion
AGRIF	The General Alliance against Racism and for the respect of the French and Catholic Identity
ALAI	Association littéraire et artistique internationale
All ER	All England Law Reports
Ann. Prop. Ind.	Annales de la Propriété Intellectuelle
Ass plen.	Assemblée Plénière
AUSFTA	Australia–United States Free Trade Agreement
BCE	Before the Common/Current/Christian Era
BASCA	British Academy for Songwriters, Composers and Authors, UK
BBC	British Broadcasting Corporation
Berne	Berne Convention
BNP	British National Party
BSB	British Satellite Broadcasting
Bull.	Bulletin
C.A.F.	Federal Court of Canada: Appeal Division
CE	Common Era
C.F.	Canada Federal Court Reports
CA 1968	Australian Copyright Act 1968
CA 1985	Canadian Copyright Act 1985
Cah. Dr. D'auteur	Cahiers du droit d'auteur
CAIP	Canadian Association of Internet Providers
Canadian Charter	Canadian Charter of Rights and Freedoms 1982
Cass.	Cour de Cassation
CCE	Communication Commerce Electronique
CCLA	Canadian Copyright Licensing Agency
CDPA	Copyright, Patents and Designs Act 1988, as amended
CERD	International Convention on the Elimination of All Forms of Racial Discrimination
CFDT	Confédération française démocratique du travail
Ch D	Chancery Division
Ch	Chancery
Ch	Law Reports, Chancery Division
Charter	EU Charter of Fundamental Rights
Chron.	Chronique
Cir.	Circuit
CJEU	Court of Justice of the European Union
CLR	Queensland Crown Lands Law Reports
CLR	Commonwealth Law Reports, Australia
CLRC	Copyright Law Review Committee, Australia
C.P.R.	Canadian Patent Reporter
D.	Recueil Dalloz hebdomadaire, partie jurisprudence
D.L.R.	Dominion Law Reports

DSB	Dispute Settlement Body
ECDR	European Copyright and Design Reports
ECHR	European Convention of Human Rights
ECtHR	European Court of Human Rights
EMLR	Entertainment and Media Law Reports
ESAC	Entertainment Software Association and Entertainment Software Association of Canada
esp.	especially
Ets	Établissements
EU Charter	EU Charter of Fundamental Rights
EU	European Union
EWCA	England and Wales Court of Appeal, UK
EWHC	England & Wales High Court (Administrative Court)
Fasc.	Fascicule
FC	Canada Federal Court Reports
FCA	Federal Court of Australia
FCAFC	Federal Court of Australia: Full Court
FCR	Federal Court Reports, Australia
FCTD	Federal Court Trial Division, Canada
Fox Pat. C.	Fox's Patent, Trade Mark, Design and Copyright Cases, Canada
FSR	Fleet Street Reports
Gaz. Pal.	Gazette du Palais
GEMA	Gesellschaft für musikalische Aufführungs- und mechanische Vervielfältigungsrechte, Germany
HCA	High Court of Australia
HR	Human Rights
HRA	Human Rights Act 1998
Hub	The Copyright Hub
I.R.	Recueil Dalloz-Sirey: Informations Rapides
ICCPR	International Covenant on Civil and Political Rights
ICESCR	International Covenant on Economic, Social and Cultural Rights
ICJ	International Court of Justice
IHRR	International Human Rights Reports
InfoSoc Directive	The Information Society Directive 2001/29/EC
IP	Intellectual Property
IPC	French Intellectual Property Code
IPO	UK Intellectual Property Office
IPR	Intellectual Property Reports, Australia
IPR	Intellectual Property Rights
IRPI	Institut de Recherche en Propriété Intellectuelle
J.-CL. Marques	Jurisclasseur Marques
JCP	La Semaine Juridique: Juris Classeur Périodique
Jurispr.	Jurisprudence
L	Legislation
MCPS	Mechanical-Copyright Protection Society, UK
MPA	Music Publishers Association, UK
NF	National Front party, France
NLA	Newspaper Licensing Agency
O.R.	Ontario Reports
OAS	Organization of American States
Obs.	Observations
OED	Oxford English Dictionary

OHIM	Office for Harmonization in the Internal Market
OJ	Official Journal of the European Communities
OSCE	Organization for Security and Co-operation in Europe
PCC	Patents County Court
PPL	Phonographic Performance Limited, UK
Prop. Int.	Propriété Intellectuelles
PRS	PRS for Music, UK
RDPI	Revue du droit de la propriété intellectuelle
Réf.	Référé
Rép. pén. Dalloz	Répertoire de droit pénal et de procédure pénale Dalloz
Rev. trim. dr. comm.	Revue trimestrielle de droit commercial et de droit économique
RG	Rôle Général
RIDA	Revue Internationale du Droit d'Auteur
RIDC	Revue Internationale de Droit Comparé
RLDI	Revue Lamy Droit de l'Immatériel
RPC	Reports of Patent, Design and Trade Mark Cases
RTD com	Revue Trimestrielle de Droit Commercial et de Droit Economique
S.C.R.	Canada Supreme Court Reports
SABIP	Strategic Advisory Board for Intellectual Property Policy, UK
SACEM	La Société des auteurs, compositeurs et éditeurs de musique, France
SCC	Supreme Court of Canada
SGAE	Sociedad General de Autores y Editores de España
SOCAN	Society of Composers, Authors and Music Publishers of Canada
Somm.	Sommaire
STIM	Svenska Tonsättares Internationella Musikbyrå, Sweden
TGI	Tribunal de Grande Instance
Trib. Civ	Tribunal Civil
Trib. Comm.	Tribunal du Commerce
Trib. corr.	Tribunal Correctionnel
TRIPS	Agreement on Trade-related Aspects of Intellectual Property Rights
UDHR	Universal Declaration of Human Rights
UGC	User-Generated Content
UK	The United Kingdom
UKSC	UK Supreme Court
UN	United Nations
UNHCHR	United Nations High Commissioner for Human Rights
US	The United States of America
VCLT	Vienna Convention on the law of treaties of 1969
WLR	Weekly Law Reports
WCT	WIPO Copyright Treaty
WIPO	World Intellectual Property Organization
WPPT	WIPO Performances and Phonograms Treaty
WTO	World Trade Organization

1

Parody—Nature and Definition

1. What is a Parody?

Parodies have been created throughout times and cultures. Representing a particular form of comment, parodies have an important function in democratic societies as a catalyst in the development of art and discourse. This important social and cultural value is reflected in the judicial latitude generally afforded to this particular type of creative endeavour even prior to its codification. Parody, used here as an umbrella term for various related terms, is now legally permissible based upon a copyright defence within the United States ('US'), Australia, Canada, and the European Union ('EU').[1] Yet the exact meaning of terms such as parody, satire, caricature, and pastiche remains nebulous.

Legislators have shied away from carving definitions. The Court of Justice of the European Union ('CJEU') has superimposed EU-wide characteristics upon the pre-existing practices of the courts of EU Member States by interpreting the terms 'caricature, parody and pastiche' for the first time in *Deckmyn.*[2] The Court establishes 'parody' as an autonomous concept in the context of EU copyright law,[3] having regard to the ordinary meaning of the terms in everyday language, and taking into consideration the context in which the parody arises.[4] Here, the CJEU identifies a work as a 'parody' by its satisfaction of two requirements: firstly, it must 'evoke an existing work while being noticeably different from it' and secondly, it must 'constitute an expression of humour or mockery'.[5] By adopting these requirements, the CJEU decides that it is unnecessary to *distinguish* between works of parody, pastiche, or caricature, since it is better for copyright law to understand parody as a multivalent concept which *includes* forms of pastiche and caricature.[6]

To evaluate the potential impact of this construction, this chapter explores the contours of the concept of parody. It considers the wider historical context before focusing on the legal evolution of the genre in the five jurisdictions under scrutiny.[7]

[1] However, as explained in Chapter 2, the EU merely offers a possibility for EU Member States to introduce a parody exception in their national laws.

[2] C-201/13 *Johan Deckmyn and Vrijheidsfonds VZW v. Helena Vandersteen and Others* [2014] ECLI:EU:C:2014:2132 (hereafter *Deckmyn*).

[3] Meaning it must be interpreted uniformly throughout the EU: *Deckmyn* (n 2) [17]; Advocate General's Opinion in *Deckmyn* [2014] ECLI:EU:C:2014:458 (hereafter AGO in *Deckmyn*) [35].

[4] *Deckmyn* (n 2) [19]; AGO in *Deckmyn* (n 3) [45].

[5] *Deckmyn* (n 2) [20]; AGO in *Deckmyn* (n 3) [48].

[6] AGO in *Deckmyn* (n 3) [46]; see section 5.2.

[7] In this work, references to 'parody' encompass both parody, *sensu strictu*, and other related terms such as satire, caricature, and pastiche unless otherwise specified.

2. Origin and Historical Overview of Parody in Art Fields

2.1 Etymology of 'parody'

In Ancient Greece, *parodia* is seen as having two different meanings, as the prefix *para-* can mean either 'counter' or 'beside', while *-ode* translates as 'song'. Selecting which version has been adopted presents a hurdle. The first meaning seems to refer to a tension or contrast between the original and new work, while the second meaning suggests a neighbourly relationship, with the two works standing side-by-side.[8] The latter, once 'translated' into copyright language, might lead one to conclude that the new work is akin to an 'adaptation', one of the bundle of exclusive rights granted to right-holders.[9] However, based upon analysis of usage from Ancient times up to the present day,[10] scholars agree that the former meaning—a relationship of contrast between the new work and the original—dominates.[11]

2.2 Early uses of parody as a vehicle for political and social commentaries

The first use of *parodia*, dated at 335 BCE, is attributed to Aristotle in his poems referring to Hegermon.[12] In this literary context, *parodia* refers to a moderate length narrative poem which uses the meter and vocabulary of the then well-established form of epic poems. *Parodia* of this type are satirical, addressing mock-heroic topics and intended to create a comic effect.[13] However, parodic forms were not confined to poetry, and featured in plays including the works of Aristophanes.[14]

The analysis of the texts of these old comedies, which are still available today, reveals that two main characteristics can be assigned to parody. The first feature is the prevalent reference made to the coeval language of Athens. The second feature is the target of these critiques. The parody results from political and social commentaries which reference the earlier works of other writers.[15] The parodic concept is broad and includes satire within its scope. While a humorous element is generally present, it is not mandatory.

2.3 Early particularities of music parodies

Jumping forward to the first century C.E., Quintilianus, a popular Italian author, provides two definitions of parody. In Book VI, Quintilianus describes parody in these terms:

[8] L Hutcheon, *A Theory of Parody: The Teachings of Twentieth-Century Art Forms* (University of Illinois Press 1985) 32.

[9] Adaptation is an exclusive right of the original right-holder.

[10] The fields covered in this section are poetry, literature, plastic arts, music, cinematography, and drama.

[11] A Strowel, 'La parodie selon le droit d'auteur et la théorie littéraire' (1991) 26 *RIEJ* 23, 30.

[12] S Dentith, *Parody* (Routledge, 2000) 9.

[13] Ibid, 10.

[14] For example, Aristophanes liked to mock Cratinus in his plays (e.g. *Knights*). Cratinus, an eminent poet of Old Comedy, had the reputation of often being drunk and incontinent. Cratinus replied through *Pytine* which takes inspiration from his portrayal made in *Knights*. Z P Biles, 'Intertextual biography in the rivalry of Cratinus and Aristophanes' (2002) 123(2) *The American Journal of Philology* 169.

[15] Dentith (n 12) 45–54; Biles (n 14) 197.

What men call wisdom is a 'legacy', where 'legacy' replaces 'faculty'. Or again we may invent verses resembling well known lines, a trick called parody.[16]

In Book IX, he provides a specific definition in relation to musical works: 'Parody, a name drawn from songs sung in imitation of others, but employed by an abuse of language to designate imitation in verse or prose.'[17]

Later, Quintilianus underscores his preference for the second definition, which refers to singing the lyrics from one song to a different melody. This definition formed the basis for later music definitions of parody by scholars from the sixteenth century onwards. These all share the distinction that the requirement for any humorous element is set aside, focusing instead on a *degree of imitation* while simultaneously establishing *a distance* between the new and the original work.

2.4 Narrowing parody to its ridiculing or imitative function

Reference to parody in the literature is scarce from the fifth century until an apparent resurgence of the genre in the sixteenth century. This was accompanied by a growing interest from classical scholars in defining the phenomenon. It was at this time that the scope of parody narrowed to a *ridiculing* function, echoing the postmodern understanding of the genre. Scaliger, the Renaissance scholar often considered the first to devise the definition of parody for the literary genre, having rediscovered Quintilianus, determines that parody means 'to introduce in place of a serious thing another ridiculous one'.[18] The target of the parody remains undefined, permitting the mocking of the previous work *or* an unrelated subject.

Yet, Scaliger recognizes the complexity of defining parody. When discussing the figures of speech in literature, he circumscribes his basic definition by adding: 'parody, in which the serious is imitated, and by the imitation subverted'.[19] In doing so, the reference to ridicule is set aside and the focus is on *the imitative* feature of parody. This technique, which Scaliger also calls parody, sought to adapt texts to ensure they conformed to the religious sensibilities of the day. The same technique was used for originally secular songs to facilitate greater dissemination of religious texts.[20] Estienne, a contemporary of Scaliger, contributed most to defining parody in the musical field at that time. He chose to emphasize the imitation aspect in his definition of musical parody: 'a song or melody which I compose in imitation of another'.[21]

2.5 From ridicule to mockery

During the seventeenth century, parody featured prominently in drama and theatre. Here, to reinforce the criticism function of the genre, parody generally took the form of *mockery*, manifesting in grotesque gesturing and intonation by the actors, as well as the language used.[22] Present also in literature, parody was similarly used to mock previous works.[23] Ironically, while mockery was adopted in an attempt to provoke a

[16] Quintilianus translated in H E Butler, *The Institutio Oratoria of Quintilian* (4 vols II, Loeb Classical Library, 1953) 493.

[17] Ibid, 395.

[18] As cited in R Falck, 'Parody and contrafactum: a terminological clarification' (1979) 65 *The Musical Quarterly* 1, 3.

[19] Ibid. [20] Ibid, 4. [21] Ibid. [22] Dentith (n 12) 126. [23] See section 3.3.

change of style or genre, in using this tool, parodists perpetuated the very types of work that they sought to eradicate.[24]

This phenomenon, which later became known as the *parodic paradox*,[25] is exemplified by the novel *Don Quixote* by Cervantes, a work which contains all the traditional characteristics of a modern novel. In this piece, the author criticizes the chivalric romance through parody. While Cervantes aims to denigrate this genre so that literature may advance, his borrowing from this style seems only to have contributed to its proliferation.[26]

2.6 Persistence of music parodies' digression: referencing other works through alteration and distortion

In music, parody took a slightly different form. It referred either to a musical rearrangement to adapt a work for different musical registers, or a technique which transformed a song's lyrics or replaced them with an entirely different text.[27] In Rousseau's dictionary published in 1768, a musical parody is described as:

> An instrumental piece which is made into an aria by adjusting the words. In a well-made music, the melody is composed to words; in a parody, the words are composed to the melody; all the stanzas of a song except the first are a kind of parody.[28]

Essentially, Rousseau is describing parody as a musical technique in which lyrics are adapted to suit the music.[29] His definition is somewhat judgemental, since it contrasts 'well–made' music with a 'melody' in which the music seems compromised in its adaption to the words, and not vice versa. This is echoed by the German musician Schilling, who describes parody thus:

> The Greeks understood by this comic poems ... In music, parody is ... the alteration of the text of a vocal composition, whereby a new text is prepared for an existing vocal composition, which is itself unchanged.[30]

It is apparent that parody in music at that time, unlike in drama or literature, had little to do with ridicule or mockery,[31] and so lacked any specific target. Rather, parody is used to *imitate* and reference previous works *via alteration*. As in other artistic fields, however, parody was seen as serving a beneficial function.[32] For example, the seventeenth-century musician Couperin expressed his appreciation to those poets who reworked his own songs, because this increased the popularity and dissemination of his originals.[33]

[24] Dentith (n 12) 33.

[25] Ibid, 36.

[26] On the publications of the time: G R Hoekstra, 'An eight-voice parody of Lassus: André Pevernage's "Bonjour Mon Coeur"' (1979) 7 *Early Music* 367; M Ribon, *Parodies Bachiques sur les Airs et Symphonies des Opera* (Paris, 1695).

[27] Falck (n 18) 5. [28] Translation in ibid, 9.

[29] J Ward, 'The use of borrowed material in 16th-century instrumental music' (1952) 5(2) *Journal of the American Musicology Society* 88.

[30] Schilling translated in Falck (n 18) 10.

[31] It is only in the twentieth century that parody is generally defined in music in terms of a ridiculing function.

[32] D J Grout, 'Seventeenth-century parodies of French opera—Part I' (1941) 27(2) *The Music Quarterly* 211–19.

[33] Couperin actually thanked the poets directly in the preface of one of his books: F Couperin, *Pièce de Clavecin* (3rd book, preface, Paris, 1722) reprinted in *Le Pupitre* (Paris, 1969).

2.7 Downfall of the genre

With the Enlightenment, parody gained an increasingly negative reputation as being mediocre, derivative, and parasitical owing to the emerging 'genius' cult attributed to creative works.[34] The fact that parody might even constitute a criminal offence could explain its decrease in popularity during that period. The British culture of the time provides a good illustration. The popular works *Gulliver's Travels* and *Robinson Crusoe* both include limited parody or satire.[35] This is seen as demonstrating the authors' reluctance to rely upon these techniques because they were perceived to be an *obstacle* to creativity.[36] While parodies were considered derivative and unoriginal, satire was seen as creative and diverse. Most of the famous authors of the eighteenth century adopted satire as the literary tool of choice to reveal the social, political, and religious conflicts of the time.[37]

Parody's decline continued into the nineteenth century, and scholars document it being used predominantly to ridicule neoclassical speech or to express resentment towards particular poets or contemporary topics.[38] This lack of interest mirrored a more general disinterest in literature, which in turn has been linked to a gradual shift in audiences' habits with the emergence of film and other new forms of entertainment.[39]

2.8 Rebirth of the genre: multi-functionality of parodies

The twentieth century saw a renaissance of parody across different art forms. With this rebirth, parody becomes far more complex: its targets include specific established works and well-established artistic styles or conventions, often combined in single works, and intertwined with other related genres. Magritte's parody of David's portrait of *Madame Récamier* (Figure 1.1) provides an interesting example. Although Magritte parodies a specific earlier artistic work, the work's intricacy derives from the intermingling with elements of satire, pastiche, and caricature, making it problematic to categorize the work definitively in any one of these sub-genres.

As scholars rediscover the works of great authors, including Shakespeare, Swift, Proust, Verlaine, and Pope, all of which feature parody, the parodic genre's reputation is again on the rise, leading one commentator to label the twentieth century as 'an age of parodies'.[40]

This brief historical study illustrates how use of the term parody has evolved across art fields. It reveals that parody is *multi-functional*: provoking laughter, conveying criticism, providing (positive or negative) social or political commentary, paying homage, and developing or testing artistic or musical rules and techniques. Furthermore, the target of the parody may vary, to include the underlying work itself, other works, a style, or something completely unrelated. As the definitions examined here demonstrate how

[34] Further honed by concepts adopted in copyright law.

[35] C Rutz, 'Parody: a missed opportunity?' (2004) 3 *IPQ* 284, 286.

[36] D Macdonald, *Parodies: An Anthology from Chaucer to Beerbohm and After* (Random House, 1960) 563.

[37] P Dias da Silva and J Garcia, 'YouTubers as satirists: humour and remix in online video' (2012) 4 *JeDEM* 89, 91.

[38] S Chatman, 'Parody and style: rhetoric and film' (2001) 22(1) *Poetics Today* 25, 34; Dentith (n 12) 117; T Wright, *A History of Caricature and Grotesque in Literature and Art* (Chatto & Windus, 1985) 342; G D Kiremidjian, 'The aesthetics of parody' (1969) 28(2) *The Journal of Aesthetics and Art Criticism* 231–42; R Tuve, 'Sacred "parody" of love poetry, and Herbert' (1969) 8 *Studies in Renaissance* 249; W van O'Connor, 'Parody as criticism' (1964) 25(4) *College English* 241.

[39] Dentith (n 12) 118.

[40] R L Mack, *The Genius of Parody Imitation and Originality in Seventeeth-Century English Literature* (Palgrave Macmillan, 2007).

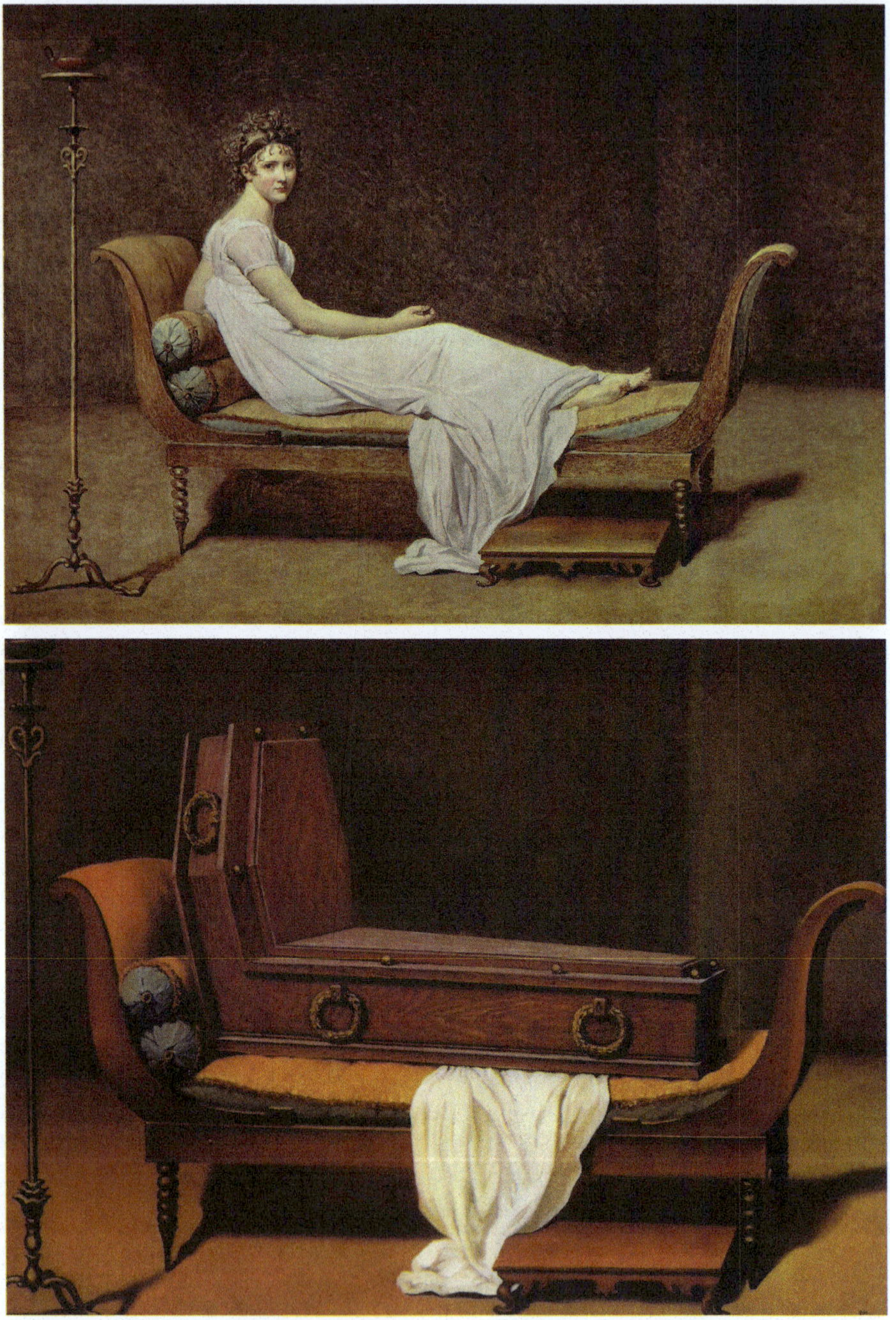

Figure 1.1 J-L David portrait of Madame Récamier (1800)

Magritte's parody (1951) (bottom): Building upon David's painting (top), Magritte aims to comment on well-regarded painting conventions, the mortality of humans, and create an homage to David's work.

Jacques-Louis David (1748–1825), *Madame Recamier*, 1800, oil on canvas, 174 × 244 cm. Paris, Musée Du Louvre. Photo © DEA PICTURE LIBRARY / De Agostini Editore / Age footstock.

René Magritte, *Perspective: Madame Récamier by David*, 1951, oil on canvas, 60.5 × 80.5 cm. National Gallery of Canada, Ottawa. © ADAGP, Paris and DACS, London 2018. Photo ©: Artepics / Alamy Stock Photo.

'parody' is open-textured and contextual, one might wonder how cultural theorists have defined parody as a concept.

3. The Relationship of Parody with Other Related Concepts

As has been seen, parody is often used interchangeably with terms such as pastiche, caricature, satire, irony, imitation, plagiarism, and burlesque. This section is a brief sketch of the main features of each of these terms to interrogate the boundaries of the genre overall. Ultimately, this section investigates how far this terminology will assist the assessment of which activities could fall under the parody exception in copyright law.

3.1 Parody and irony

Irony[41] is distinguishable from parody because irony does not constitute an artistic genre. However, the terms are related because irony can be used as an *instrument* within the parodic creative process.[42] Hutcheon goes as far as labelling irony as the best tool for parody.[43] Parody and irony are both forms of indirect and double-voiced discourse.[44] Neither are parasitic, since their objective is not to become a substitute of the earlier work.[45]

Literature teaches us that, in art, irony serves two functions: a semantic function and a pragmatic function.[46] The former is concerned with contrast, showing up the differences with the previous text. The latter is an evaluation from the author of the new work. When dealing with parody works, irony fulfils the *semantic* function, if we agree with Hutcheon's analysis.[47]

Put simply, parody and irony can both be described as a form of communication which relies upon an earlier work. Parody does not always rely upon irony, but irony is one instrument to achieve its aim.

3.2 Parody and satire

Scholars often imply that parody is a variant of the satirical genre.[48] If it is true that both parody and satire borrow from previous works, use irony, and adopt a critical

[41] Irony comes also from ancient Greek and means dissimulation, feigned ignorance, see H G Liddell, R Scott, G Crane, H S Jones, R McKenzie, and E A Barber, *A Greek-English Lexicon* (Clarendon, 2002).

[42] For common features between both terms see M Rose, *Parody//Meta-fiction: An Analysis of Parody as a Critical Mirror to the Writing and Reception of Function* (London, 1979) 51.

[43] Hutcheon (n 8) 31; Van O'Connor (n 38) 248.

[44] Double-voicing is usually attributed to Bakhtin's works. In his study of literature and the philosophy of language, Bakhtin defines this concept in relation to parody as meaning: 'it superimposes a voice doing the parodying over the voice of what is being parodied, because the very act of reproducing another's voice makes the other's words sound mocked, exaggerated, and gives them a derisive intonation.' W G Simon, 'Bakhtin: parody' (1990) 12(1–2) *Quarterly Review of Film & Video* 23.

[45] Hutcheon (n 8) xiv.

[46] C Kerbrat-Orecchioni, 'L'ironie comme trope' (1980) 41 *Poétique*, 108–27.

[47] Hutcheon (n 8) 56.

[48] For more information see R P Blackmur, 'Parody and critique: Mann's Doctor Faustus', in *Eleven Essays in the European Novel* (Harcourt, Brace & World, 1964) 97–116; W C Booth, *The Rhetoric of Fiction* (University of Chicago Press, vol. III); L Feinberg, *The Satirist: His Temperament, Motivation and Influence* (Iowa State University Press, 1963); Macdonald (n 36); R Paulson, *The Fictions of Satire* (Johns Hopkins University Press, 1967); M Rose (n 42); C Stone, *Parody* (Martin Secker, 1914).

distance from the original work, the departure is in the *way* they each rely on irony.[49] With satire, irony is used for its *pragmatic*, evaluative function[50] mostly to demonstrate the negative point of view of the satirist. It is mostly pejorative.

Hutcheon, thus, differentiates satire from parody because parody may pay tribute to the original work from which it borrows, whereas the satirist aims to ridicule the original work.[51] Chatman, however, stresses that it is hard to deny the ridiculing effect attached to the postmodern meaning of parody.[52] The difference is perhaps one of degree. Furthermore, Hutcheon argues that the difference between parody and satire lies in their focus: satire tends rather to be focused on moral and social subjects with an intention of amelioration.[53] The actual position seems less clear-cut, as parody can be used to this end too. For example, parody can lead to a new kind of art or bring a genre to an end.[54]

Rose emphasizes two differences between parody and satire.[55] She posits that parody necessarily includes an original work as an integral part of its structure, whereas satire does not have to use parts of an original work in order to achieve its aim. Secondly, parodies create a comic effect in contrast to a denigrating one, as is the case in a satire. This approach seems most familiar to the legal debates surrounding the parody exception in copyright law.

Ultimately, these genres are not hermetically separated from one another. Parody and satire can blend in a single work called a 'satiric parody'. Parody is either a vehicle for satire or a type of genre of parody which is satiric.[56] In English literature, there is also a mix of satires and parodies present in Swift's *Gulliver's Travels.*[57] Swift intended to parody previous tales of exploration, but also to satirize British politics and European society more generally. The song *Barbie Girl* by the Danish band Aqua is a more recent example. At one level, the song parodies the famous fashion doll manufactured by Mattel, but at the same time, it is a satiric commentary on the 'blond bimbo' image of women in today's society.[58]

Finally, the target of the respective works distinguishes them. While parody has rather an intramural target (the original work, the author of the original work, or the author of the parody), satire has an extramural target (values, traditions, politics, authority, or other third object).

3.3 Parody and burlesque (or travesty)

The word 'burlesque' comes from 'burlesco' which derives from the seventeenth-century Italian word 'burla', meaning 'to ridicule', 'to mock'. The latter may have older roots as

[49] Hutcheon (n 8) 52.

[50] See section 3.1 to understand the pragmatic and the evaluative function of irony.

[51] Macdonald (n 36) xiii. [52] Chatman (n 38) 33.

[53] Hutcheon (n 8) 16 and 43. This idea carries on today. See, for example, the quotation from P Martens as cited in B Mouffe, *Le droit à l'humour* (Larcier, 2011) 48 where it is said that humour and law contribute to the concept of justice. Both laughter and judging comprise a repressive function.

[54] See section 2.5. [55] Rose (n 42) 81. [56] Hutcheon (n 8) 62.

[57] Nevertheless, in literature, the distinction between parody and satire may refer to the object that parody aims to reach being the previous work or the style of an author, whereas satire aims towards something extramural such as another person or societal value. See Y-M Tran-Gervat, 'Pour une définition opérationnelle de la parodie littéraire: parcours critique et enjeux d'un corpus spécifique' (1996) 13 *Cahiers de Narratologie* 7.

[58] It is interesting to note that this song was the object of a lawsuit in the US, and the US Appeal Court eventually decided that this work was lawful under the fair use for the purpose of parody. *Mattel v. MCA Records*, 296 F.3d 894 (9th Cir. 2002).

'burra' means 'no sense' in Latin. However, this is speculation. Over time, burlesque was adopted in other countries. In France, it became synonymous with 'grotesque' or referred to the use of vulgar vocabulary in drama and poetry.[59] It is only later that the term entered the English language.

Genette considers burlesque to be different from parody because parody modifies the object but generally not the style of the work whereas burlesque modifies the style but not the object.[60] Dentith narrows the scope of burlesque by emphasizing that the textual transformation under the genre is mainly satirical, whereas in the case of parody, the transformation is playful.[61] Hence, under this definition, the intention underlying the new work is different. In parody, the intention is to adopt a critical distance from the target work, which may have a comic effect. The intention underlying a burlesque (also called travesty) work is merely to ridicule or to mock.[62]

Hence, parody and burlesque (or travesty) seem artificial synonyms, although the main difference is one of degree: burlesque focuses on the ridiculing aspect while parody's scope is wider to encompass a broader critical function. Humorous intent is only one of multiple facets of parody, whereas it seems more essential to burlesque. Moreover, burlesque tends to modify the style rather than the object, while parody modifies the object while retaining the style of the work.

3.4 Parody and caricature

Although caricature is recognized in the literary and musical fields, it is most frequently associated with graphic art. In terms of etymology, caricature is derived from the Italian word *caricare*, meaning 'to surcharge'. Indeed, caricature seems more akin to a *technique* than being a genre per se. The Baroque masters praised caricature in the eighteenth century, but it is possible to trace use of this technique in Ancient Egypt,[63] Greece, and later, in the works of Leonardo da Vinci. Consequently, the history of the term pre-dates parody.

More recently, English artists have used this technique in portraits of politicians and in social commentaries.[64] By virtue of its 'vicious' side, caricatures and caricaturists have been harshly treated. For example, in post-Revolutionary France, caricaturists could receive a custodial sentence.[65] In Germany, caricature was subject to censorship because it was illegal to caricature the Royal Family. Curiously, this was also the moment when caricature was most popular in France and in England. Here, there are echoes of the negative reputation associated with parody which arose because of its use of biting critique.

The invention of printing machines and newspapers marked a revival of interest in caricature.[66] Since then, caricature is still used in the daily press, and now in other

[59] Rose (n 42) 40. [60] G Genette, *Palimpsestes* (Paris: Le Seuil, 1982) 29.

[61] Dentith (n 12) 11. [62] Hutcheon (n 8) 40.

[63] In Egypt for example, humans were often represented as animals doing human activities which appear to be humorous. The Greeks used caricature humans as monsters. See Wright (n 38) 4–22.

[64] R Paulson, 'Pictorial satire: from emblem to expression' in R Quintero (ed.), *A Companion to Satire: Ancient and Modern* (Malden, Oxford, Victoria: Blackwell Publishing, 2007) 312.

[65] Da Silva and Garcia (n 37) 92; see the case of Charles Philipon who started a satirical newspaper after the French Revolution with caricatures inside. In one of his releases, he made a caricature of the King where the King's face was shaped into a pear because of its natural shape. It is relevant to understand that, at that time, calling somebody a pear meant the same as calling him a buffoon. Charles Philipon was sentenced several times to jail time.

[66] A Tunç, 'Pushing the limits of tolerance: functions of political cartoonists in the democratization process: the case of Turkey' (2002) 64 (1) *International Communication Gazette* 48.

media, to expose malpractice within an administration or political corruption, or simply to ridicule famous people.

Caricature is defined as the technique of exaggeration or oversimplification of idiosyncratic features of the subject.[67] This may be taken to such an extreme that the end result is grotesque to the audience. Caricature and parody are related because both may use irony to achieve their goal. But caricature may also be put alongside satire, since it also places the accent on the idiosyncrasy of morals, traditions, and behaviours meaning that its target is external to the subject on which it is based. The difference between parody and caricature is especially hard to grasp because the two terms are used interchangeably in plain language. However, caricatures focus primarily upon living people or other reality-based subjects, while this is not particularly the case for parodies, which can focus on non-living subjects.

In sum, both parody and caricature have lost popularity at some time because of the severity of their critique. Both utilize irony as a tool, although they use it differently to achieve their aim: caricature (like satire) focuses on the pragmatic function, while parody focuses on the semantic function of irony. In other words, caricature is the oversimplification or exaggeration of its object's characteristics whereas to parody is to adopt a critical distance from the original work which can be done through the exaggeration of characteristics of the object but can also be achieved by other means. Finally, most of caricature targets living beings whereas parody can target a person or an object.

3.5 Parody and pastiche

As with parody, there is no universal definition of 'pastiche'. The term is known to derive from the Italian term 'pasticcio', meaning a confused or mixed work. In simple terms, pastiche is typically defined as the imitation of another's style. For example, it was (and still is to some extent) usual literary practice for young writers to develop their writing skills by replicating 'the style of' a particular established author.

As Genette describes, and Dentith later confirms, pastiche differs from parody because pastiche emphasizes the similarity of elements rather than seeking to transform the original.[68] As pastiche is a stylistic imitation,[69] it lacks the ironic transcontextualization which is present in parody.[70] Also, as pastiche focuses on the idiosyncrasy of an author, a pastiche work will rarely be based on a single work but rather will draw on a collection of their works. Consequently, there is less contrast between the old and the new in pastiche than exists in parody. Pastiche is closer to imitation whereas parody can be seen as a continuance of the past. While it also relies upon a previous work, parody offers the possibility for change which pastiche in literature lacks.[71]

A pastiche work is a new work which relies on a previous work and which stays in the same genre as the original work, while the parody permits the new work to depart from the genre of the original work. A few scholars, including Jameson, consider that parody can be non-critical and associate parody to pastiche for this reason.[72] However, most scholars agree that while pastiche may include an element of criticism, this is ancillary whereas criticism is essential in parody.

[67] Kiremidjian (n 38) 235.
[68] Genette (n 60) 34; Dentith (n 12) 11.
[69] Genette (n 60) 30.
[70] Hutcheon (n 8) 12.
[71] Genette (n 60) 34.
[72] F Jameson, 'Postmodernism and consumer society' in Hal Foster (ed.), *The Anti-Aesthetic* (Bay Press, 1986) 127–45.

One similarity between parody and pastiche is that both signal their borrowing from the original work, i.e. neither aims to be a substitute for the original.[73] This is what separates these genres from plagiarism.

If we adopt Rose's definition, then pastiche is a form of forgery albeit that the author does not intend to create a hoax.[74] This seems a reasonable characterization, since pastiche is never intended to become the original.[75] Pastiche is common in popular culture. The *Austin Powers* films are a pastiche, featuring the worst clichés of the 'Swinging Sixties', while some artists even poke fun at their own art—Quentin Tarantino's films *Pulp Fiction* and *Kill Bill* borrow from popular novels[76] and kung fu films.[77] These examples demonstrate that pastiche can encourage creativity and embraces the birth of new works.

Overall, pastiche is close to parody, since both signal that a borrowing has been made, but pastiche relies more on imitation whereas parody aims to adopt a critical stance towards the original work.

3.6 Parody and imitation

Parody is often defined by reference to imitation.[78] According to Rose, the main difference between parody and imitation lies in the fact that parody acknowledges that a borrowing has been made, whereas this signal is missing in an imitation.[79] However, many other scholars beg to differ, considering an imitation which fails to signal the borrowing made to be plagiarism.

If we refer to Hutcheon, imitation has become linked to parody because of the modern meaning of the term parody.[80] In past centuries, imitation was used by writers to approve and perpetuate works of the past, i.e. the relationship between the new work and the original work being a relationship of *inclusion*. So, even though we can see some similarities with the intent involved in an imitation and in a parody, the major difference lies, once again, in the *critical distance* missing in mere imitation works.[81]

Imitation is an established way to pay tribute to the works which are imitated.[82] William van O'Connor describes it as the 'sincerest flattery' and it is in this light that parody is an imitation.[83] We can infer from the above, that the difference between imitation and parody can be very difficult to pinpoint in practice, since it is mainly a difference of intent.[84]

Therefore, although parody and imitation are close, what distinguishes them is that parody focuses on criticizing or mocking the original work whereas imitation merely pays tribute to the original work, thereby lacking the critical distance which is so important in a work of parody.

[73] Hutcheon (n 8) 38. [74] Rose (n 42) 43.

[75] It should be noted that 'original' is used here in the sense of 'new', rather than in a 'copyright' sense to imply the work contains enough creative content to be eligible for copyright protection. Indeed, a work of pastiche can borrow ideas from multiple sources and still be considered 'original' under copyright law.

[76] *Pulp Fiction* is a 1960 pastiche borrowing from these novels. [77] See *Kill Bill.*

[78] See section 2. [79] Rose (n 42) 25. [80] Hutcheon (n 8) 10.

[81] Ibid, 34. [82] Dentith (n 12) 105. [83] Van O'Connor (n 38) 243.

[84] In Federal Court of Australia, *TCN Channel Nine Pty Limited v. Network Ten Pty Limited (No 2)* [2005] FCAFC 53, the Australian judge, in defining parody and satire, first referred to the *Macquarie Dictionary*, then turned to the teachings of Margaret Rose for whom parody requires imitation while satire does not inevitably need it to fulfil its purpose; finally, the judge turned to *Copinger and Skone James on Copyright* for the test to apply. See section 5.4.

3.7 Parody and plagiarism

Parody should not be confused with plagiarism even though, colloquially, the terms are sometimes used interchangeably.[85] While parody and plagiarism both involve the reproduction of earlier works, the major difference between the two is foreshadowed earlier. Parodies acknowledge the borrowing which are made whereas plagiarism purposely does not.

The intention behind the work is different.[86] As discussed already, parody intends to create a distance from the work which it borrows, thereby acknowledging the borrowing. With plagiarism, the intent is to substitute or deceive the audience by passing off the borrowings as the plagiarist's own creation.[87] Parody uses irony and plays with the context in which the work evolves. Plagiarism does not change the context of the original and does not play with the original work through the use of irony. In essence, plagiarism is fraud whereas parody is creative.

3.8 Conclusion

While the preceding analysis may have failed to define clear boundaries which distinguish parody from related concepts, it has provided some insight into the relationships which exist between them. This is summarized in the following table (Figure 1.2) which is based upon Dyer's framework for the categorization of imitation.[88]

Concealed	Unconcealed

Not textually signalled	Textually signalled

Evaluatively open	Evaluatively predetermined

Plagiarism	Imitation	Pastiche	Parody	Burlesque	Caricature	Satire

Figure 1.2 Dyer's framework revisited*

*R Dyer, *Pastiche* (New York: Routledge, 2007) 24.

The first level confirms whether concealment of the imitative status is essential for the purpose of the genre or technique. The second level relates to the evidence of elements within the new work which recognizes the borrowings made. The third level reviews the public's perception of the author's judgement of the borrowings. The 'evaluatively predetermined' category identifies whether either a positive or negative

[85] H M Paull, *Literary Ethics* (Butterworth, 1928) 14; Rose (n 42) 41.

[86] Hutcheon (n 8) 40.

[87] P Jewell and J Louise, 'It's just a joke: defining and defending (musical) parody' (2012) 10 *Australian Review of Public Affairs* 8; M Klang and J Nolin, 'Tolerance is law: remixing homage, parodying plagiarism' (2012) 9 *SCRIPTed*, 159.

[88] R Dyer, *Pastiche* (New York: Routledge, 2007) 24.

judgement of the borrower is expressed. The 'evaluatively open' characterization relates to genres which either do not pass judgement, or may equally provide a positive or negative judgement on the borrowings. Once this framework is established, the place of each genre and technique can be studied.

Parody acknowledges its borrowings and depends upon the sharing of ciphers between the parodist and the public. Without this signalling of the borrowings, the public would be unable to recognize the work as a parody. Pastiche differs from parody because it relies more heavily upon imitation and features less detachment between the two works. Burlesque, caricature, and satire also expose and signal the imitation, but all three are evaluatively predetermined in the sense that they usually carry a negative judgement. Lastly, we have seen that parody *and* the three related concepts can all be distinguished from plagiarism and forgery. Plagiarism aims to hide its imitation. The only common feature with parody is its evaluative openness, i.e. without necessarily making a judgement on the elements copied.

4. Cultural Scholars' Definition of Parody

Constructing a comprehensive definition is a challenge. We have seen that not only is there a lack of any well-established definition which traverses the different art fields,[89] but also that scholars fail to agree on a definition which captures parody's many facets without blurring the frontiers between parody and other related concepts.[90] This section examines the various definitions devised by cultural theorists, to see whether these assist our quest. We may categorize these theorists as falling into one of two camps.

4.1 Linking parody to an art field or societal context

Kiremidjian belongs to a group of theorists who favour a limited definition of parody which links the definition to a specific art field or context.[91] He defines parody as:

> [A] kind of literary mimicry which retains the form of stylistic character of the primary work, but substitutes alien subject matter or content ... [and] thus establishes a jarring incongruity between form and content.[92]

From our historical account of parody,[93] we will note that this definition does not translate directly to other art fields because it is focused on *literature* alone. Additionally, for Kiremidjian, a parody's target is the work which it imitates. Yet, we have seen that this is not always the case. Also, a parody may be created by an exaggeration of existing features, not just by substituting 'alien' content.

Rather than linking parody to a particular art field, Bakhtin founds his definition by linking parody to its *context*. Focusing on late Medieval and Early Modern Europe, he concludes that as parody originates from carnival, its context is concerned with the defeat of authority, sacred institutions, official rituals, language, and values. All of these are apt targets for parody.[94] In Bakhtin's view, this social context both gives rise to grotesque, mimicries, and parodies, while also explaining why parody is more popular at some points in history than at others. Not all agree with this characterization. Dentith challenges this, by tracking parody relative to various historical events

[89] See section 2. [90] See section 3. [91] Like Bakhtin, discussed later.
[92] Kiremidjian (n 38) 232. [93] See section 2.
[94] M Bakhtin, *The Dialogic Imagination* (University of Texas Press, 1981) 79; Dentith (n 12) 22.

and by demonstrating that parody did not peak in the Medieval period.[95] Mack criticizes Bakhtin's definition as being unduly restrictive, and considers that 'the functions of parodies in modern times are narrow and unproductive',[96] even insignificant.

4.2 Defining parody through its functions

The second school of theorists endeavours to define parody through its *functions*, rather than based upon either context or field of art, but this school is itself sub-divided. The first focuses on the function of parody for humour or criticism, while the second attaches equal importance to its many facets.

Jameson, for example, focuses upon the comic element. He argues that parody should not be characterized by its function for critical review, since without the element of ridicule, parody melds into pastiche: i.e. a reworking 'in the style of' an original work or author. A contra-position considers that pastiche places emphasis on the similarities between two works, whereas parody's imitation is to *contrast* with the earlier work. Yet, based on the historical evolution of the term, a comic element does not seem decisive for a work to be classified as parody, rather than pastiche.

Unlike Jameson, Hutcheon considers that parody warrants a high social status and constructs her definition based upon its critique function. This emphasis leads to a parodic genre signalling an integration of discourse other than its own.[97] Hutcheon defines parody as 'a form of repetition with ironic critical distance, marking difference rather than similarity'.[98] Recognizing that this definition is broad, Hutcheon explains that it is sufficiently broad to encompass all kinds of hypertextuality,[99] because in the case of parody, the audience has a crucial role: both encoder and decoder must share the same code.[100]

Genette, in defining parody as the 'diversion with minimalistic transformation'[101] or a 'playful transformation of a particular text',[102] attempts to attribute equal weight to its critical and comedic functions. He also categorizes parody as one kind of hypertextuality, by placing reliance on two factors. The first concerns its function, in the sense of the effect on the audience—satiric, playful, or serious. The second is the relationship between the two works as one of transformation or imitation.[103] For Genette, parody is a playful transformation,[104] as its purpose is to entertain, but without mocking or being detrimental to the original text.[105] As a result, his definition is narrow. For example, he labels works such as *Don Quixote* as 'anti-novels', not parodies, because they target an entire genre, rather than a single work. Later scholars, such as Tran-Gervat, challenge such sub-categorization, since some of the elements which form the basis of the distinctions are recognized as being elements in modern parodies too.[106]

[95] Dentith (n 12) 37. [96] Mack (n 40) 4.

[97] Hutcheon qualifies irony as the best instrument to achieve parody and both terms are a form of indirect and double-voiced discourse (meaning there are two voices and two meanings within a single expression). Hutcheon (n 8) 31.

[98] Ibid, 6.

[99] i.e. 'any relationship uniting a text B (*hypertext*) to an earlier text A (*hypotext*) upon which it is grafted in a manner that is not that of commentary' Genette's definition cited in N Korkut, *Kinds of Parody from Medieval to Postmodern* (Middle East Technical University, 2005) 8.

[100] Hutcheon (n 8) 37. [101] Translation is mine. Genette (n 60) 40.

[102] Ibid, 202.

[103] Genette infers that there is a sharp distinction between transformation and imitation, which allows parody to differ from pastiche.

[104] Ibid, 34. [105] Ibid, 43. [106] Tran-Gervat (n 57) 3.

Rose aims at crafting a universal definition of parody: 'the comic refunctioning of preformed linguistic or artistic material'. Her use of 'comic refunctioning' identifies both the humour and the criticism functions of parody.[107] The target is also general, which reflects parody's practice across the fields of art. This simple definition is seemingly attractive, yet it sheds little light upon what is seeks to describe.

In contrast, Dentith concludes that it is impossible to encapsulate all forms of parody in a single definition.[108] Instead, an adequate definition is only possible from a particular focus, which in his case is the cultural politics of parody. He therefore suggests that this aspect of parody 'includes any cultural practice which provides a relatively polemical allusive imitation of another cultural production or practice'.[109]

4.3 Lessons for the legal interpretation of parody

Few theorists contest the difficulty of defining parody. There is a general consensus that parody embodies creativity, but beyond that a parody's target may vary from the underlying work, established artistic conventions or styles, the author of the original work, the parodist themselves, or more generally, to traditions, social values, or political standpoints.[110] Additionally, the nature of a parodist's borrowing varies greatly, too. This may range from a parody which relies upon a specific previous work, to a composite of several works, to established general styles and conventions. Also, the amount borrowed differs from one kind of parody to another. For example, we have seen that in music it is common for a parody to copy the musical notes directly, and only alter the lyrics. Finally, one of the most disputed aspects concerns the functions of parody. Cultural theorists either select the criticism or the comic function of parody as paramount, or view all possible functions as equally significant. The overall picture is confused. We might expect any attempt to craft a definitive 'legal' definition of parody to face the very same issues.

Despite all these aspects which present uncertainty, some common features can be identified. Firstly, there is consensus that parody requires an element of imitation irrespective of whether this is of an earlier work, works, style, or artistic convention. Secondly, the parodist adopts that element of imitation in order to make an observation, whether by way of criticism, commentary, or even homage. The essence of parody seems to be that it seeks to convey a message by making a creative reference to an earlier work, or body of works.

Finally, we can already appreciate that there may be no need for positive law to delve deeply into details of that which distinguishes parody from other related concepts, such as pastiche and caricature. Since these concepts are all so closely linked, they seem capable of fitting within the same legal doctrine. Hence, while distinctions will remain relevant for experts in those particular art fields, it seems likely that these should prove irrelevant to our enquiry, which is largely concerned with the activities of users.

5. Towards a Legal Definition of Parody

While none of the countries considered in this book has elected to incorporate a definition of parody within their national copyright law, national courts have crafted their own definitions on a case-by-case basis, and legal scholars have devoted attention to

107 Rose (n 42) 52. 108 Dentith (n 12) 6. 109 Ibid, 9.
110 This is a non-exhaustive list.

understanding the meaning of the term. Furthermore, stakeholders in the EU copyright system have voiced their own concerns about the appropriate framing of legislation, based upon possible overlap between parody and satire, or parody, pastiche, and caricature.[111] In a 'battle' between users and right-holders of copyright works, the former tend to favour a broad definition, whereas the latter prefer a narrow and precise definition to best secure their interests.

According to statutory interpretation rules and practices, the ordinary meaning of the terms is typically the starting point when trying to understand the legal meaning of any terms which the legal instrument does not itself define. This is the case with the parody exception. Since legislators have refrained from setting out a definition within the copyright legislation, this task falls to the judiciary to develop the legal meaning in particular cases. Often, a judge's first step is to consult a dictionary. As judicial interpretative practices may have recourse to different dictionaries, it is easy to envisage that the understanding of the same term may vary from one country to another. This seems especially likely in the case of parody (and its related terms) because we have traced parody's tumultuous history and reviewed how the term seems to have defied any precise definition.

Although the meanings of parody, pastiche, caricature, and satire may vary greatly from one dictionary to another, the *legal* definition should be shaped having regard to the purpose and context of the exception within the copyright paradigm. The legislator's intent should serve two purposes: it should act as guidance to ensure consistency and stability while allowing for a certain degree of flexibility to adapt to new circumstances. Otherwise, at a time when technological advancement enables numerous ways to rework previous copyright works, it may become tempting to stretch the meaning of the terms beyond what was intended.

Before turning to the analysis of judicial interpretation approaches in each jurisdiction, we first consider why a parody exception has been considered necessary in copyright law. This will reveal that the parody exception is situated within a wider context, meaning the existing international human rights framework may exert influence on the definition of parody in intellectual property law.

5.1 The origins of the parody exception and its basis in human rights values

As inferred earlier, a parody is a form of comment, which is seen to play an essential function in preserving and promoting the exercise of freedom of expression in a democratic society. Fostering the continuing development of art and discourse, parodies are protected under the fundamental right of freedom of expression which we will briefly outline here, while leaving the substantive discussion for Chapter 5.

Additionally, to understand the role of the parody exception within copyright law,[112] we must also consider the overarching goals of copyright protection. Traditionally, in civil law countries, copyright law merely recognizes the pre-existing natural rights of an author arising from the unique link between an author and their work. In contrast,

[111] S McCausland, 'Protecting "a fine tradition of satire": the new fair dealing exception for parody or satire in the Australian Copyright Act' (2007) 29(7) *EIPR* 287.

[112] We will see that Australia and Canada have preferred 'parody and satires' where the US remains silent. See sections 5.3, 5.4, and 5.5.

in common law countries where the utilitarian approach prevails, exclusive rights of authors are granted in recognition of their contribution to society.

Despite these distinct rationales, the lines are often blurred and policy makers typically advance both arguments.[113] For example, copyright is a tool which can be used to foster cultural diversity.[114] The more works that are created, the more likely it is that these will express a wide divergence of opinions. But copyright is used as an economic tool, which is mainly focused upon the incentive of remuneration. The predominant trend in copyright law over the last decade is ever-expanding the scope of protection afforded to right-holders by focusing on the economic aspect of copyright. One explanation of this is that an author only benefits from remuneration retrospectively, once their work has been exploited. Hence, copyright's emphasis has gradually shifted to preserve the investment made in the creation of works resulting in a corresponding down-playing of the cultural dimension in copyright. The parody exception permits greater consideration of copyright as a means of fostering creativity as protected under the right to freedom of expression.[115]

Generally, there are two ways to appraise the relationship between the parody exception and freedom of expression.[116] In the first, copyright is considered the principle to which freedom of expression (exercised through parody) is an exception. In this scenario, parodies might be expected to be upheld as lawful in limited cases.[117] Alternatively, freedom of expression is seen as the main 'rule' to which copyright, seen as an exception, should be strictly interpreted. From this perspective, it is the right-holder who must justify that their objection to a parody of their protected work is proportionate to the legitimate aim sought by copyright, as against the social need of a democratic society.

[113] D Gervais, 'Intellectual property and human rights: learning to live together' in P L C Torremans (ed.), *Intellectual Property and Human Rights* (3rd edn, Kluwer, 2008) 20. The Wittem project for a European Copyright Code enshrines the parody exception under the heading 'Uses for the purpose of freedom of expression and information' (article 5.2(1)(e)). For the time being, the decision from the CJEU. *Deckmyn* (n 2), removes all doubt for Member States, [27] and [34]. For examples of the use of freedom of expression as justification for the introduction of the parody exception for policy makers, as in the UK: UK Government, *Impact Assessment: Copyright Exception for Parody* (20 December 2012) 1, available at https://www.gov.uk/government/uploads/system/uploads/attachment_data/file/308746/ia-exception-parody.pdf (access date: 1 June 2018); *Digital Opportunity: A Review of Intellectual Property and Growth: An Independent Report by Professor Hargreaves* (IPO, 2011) 50; *Canada*: Bills Committee on the Copyright (Amendment) Bill 2011, *Copyright Exception for Parody; Australia*: 'A further exception promotes free speech and Australia's fine tradition of satire by allowing our comedians and cartoonists to use copyright material for the purposes of parody or satire.' P Ruddock, *Copyright Amendment Bill 2006: Bill and Explanatory Memorandum* (First and Second Readings, House of Representatives, 19 October 2006) 2; C Geiger, 'The Constitutional Dimension of Intellectual Property' in P L C Torremans (ed.), *Intellectual Property and Human Rights* (3rd edn, Kluwer, 2008) 122.

[114] C J Craig, 'Putting the community in communication: dissolving the conflict between freedom of expression and copyright' (2006) 56 *U. Toronto L.J. 75*, 110.

[115] Conceiving copyright as a traditional property right entails a judgement on particular forms of expression which is at odds with the right to freedom of expression. A Couto, 'Copyright and freedom of expression: a philosophical map' in A Gosseries, A Marciano, and A Strowel (eds), *Intellectual Property and Theories of Justice* (Palgrave Macmillan, 2008) 165.

[116] D Voorhoof, 'La Liberté d'expression est-elle un argument légitime en faveur du non-respect du droit d'auteur?' in A Strowel and F Tulkens (eds), *Droit d'auteur et liberté d'expression: regards francophones, d'Europe et d'ailleurs* (Larcier, 2006) 55.

[117] This would appear to be the approach taken by EU Member States due to the wording of the InfoSoc Directive which expressly states exclusive rights to be the rule to which exceptions must be interpreted strictly. See Chapter 3, section 2.2.

The most persuasive arguments reject both these approaches. Strowel and Tulkens[118] and Voorhoof[119] argue that international and European provisions protecting freedom of expression are limited by copyright. National copyright laws enshrine internal limits in order to respect the right of freedom of expression.[120] It is simply easier for freedom of expression to flourish where there is a specific legal exception.

The mere existence of a parody exception does not mean that the interests of parodists are prioritized over those of right-holders;[121] rather, a specific parody exception is simply more efficient than any general defence to balance those interests. After all, the purpose of copyright legislation weighs in favour of high level of protection of exclusive rights for right-holders whilst acknowledging that it must allow for permissible uses contributing to social and cultural development. Hence, a strict interpretation of exceptions prevails, tinting the definitions likely to be attributed to parody.[122] A word of caution is in order. Although it is tempting to encapsulate many peripheral activities, one should refrain from giving the terms a meaning so broad that it is likely to jeopardize the balance struck by legislators between the right-holders and users' interests. Such interpretation, whilst attractive to circumvent the limitations of certain legal traditions (e.g. the closed catalogue of exceptions prevailing in the EU) would go against legal history and probably set the country at odds with its international obligations.[123]

This may also explain why national courts, determining copyright disputes, are typically reticent to accept a defendant's argument which is based on freedom of expression directly. Courts perhaps fear they will jeopardize the balance which the legislator has elected to strike between freedom of expression and copyright.[124] However, enacting a parody exception maintains respect for the separation of powers between the legislative and the judicial branches,[125] since the legislator effectively legitimizes the courts to consider the proper balance of interests in any particular case. Ultimately, the introduction of a parody exception results from a balance achieved by legislatures between the goal of increasing the economy and fostering cultural diversity[126] and reinserts cultural values within the copyright paradigm.[127] As seen in what follows, this

[118] A Strowel and F Tulkens, 'Equilibrer la liberté d'expression et le droit d'auteur' in Strowel and Tulkens (eds), *Droit d'auteur et liberté d'expression* 17.

[119] Voorhoof (n 116) 54.

[120] This includes not only copyright exceptions but also the idea/expression dichotomy, subject matter, and term of protection. P B Hugenholtz, 'Copyright and freedom of expression' in N Elkin-Koren and N W Netanel (eds), *The Commodification of Information* (Kluwer, 2002) 351.

[121] Strowel and Tulkens (n 116) 22.

[122] For more, see Chapter 3, sections 1 and 2.

[123] See Chapter 2, sections 3 and 4.

[124] C-306/05 *SGAE v. Rafaël Hoteles* [2006] *SA* ECLI:EU:C:2006:764, [52]. This does not exclude that in exceptional circumstance, arguments based upon other fundamental rights outside copyright will not be applicable. See in common law countries, the public interest defence, and the theory of abuse of rights in France. Also in G B Dinwoodie, 'Copyright and free expression: engine or obstacle' in *Copyright and Freedom of Expression* (Huygens Editorial, 2008) 253–8, esp. 258.

[125] It suffices to examine the difficulty in recognizing the legality of parodies of trade marks despite the argument based on freedom of expression which has constitutional value. Given the absence of exception for the purpose of parody in trade mark law, courts have been reluctant to render uses for this purpose lawful.

[126] This is based on article 27 UDHR and article 15 ICESCR which preserve the right to participate in cultural life.

[127] For more on the crisis of the legitimacy of IP: C Geiger, 'Constitutionalising: intellectual property law? The influence of fundamental rights on intellectual property in the European Union' (2006) 37(4) *IIC* 371.

detour has consequences for the appreciation of the terms parody, pastiche, caricature, and satire within the legal sphere.

5.2 The European Union

EU copyright law requires parody to be an autonomous concept across the Union's territory.[128] Following a consistent line of jurisprudence of the CJEU, parody must be defined in relation to its ordinary meaning, in relation to the context in which it is used in the relevant Directive, and having regard to the objectives of that legislation.[129] In *Deckmyn*, the Court reviewed the dictionary definitions of the terms, and identified (agreeing with the Advocate General's Opinion—'AGO') that all parodies have two essential features: one 'structural' (a transformation which is, simultaneously, a copy and a creation); and one 'functional' aspect (it constitutes an expression of humour or mockery).[130] It seems that as the Court found no need to articulate any differences between parody, caricature, and pastiche, this should be understood to mean that the copyright provision merely lists three genres which derogate from the scope of the right-holder's exclusive rights.[131]

Several important points derive from this decision. Firstly, it is clear that legal regulation of parody is concerned with both 'parody of' and 'parody with'.[132] Secondly, although a humorous character is required, the nature of the humour is unspecified, leaving discretion to Member States.[133] It is worth noting that the Court includes 'mockery' under humour. This results in broadening the exception to non-comical expressions which comprise derision, ridicule, or even material which is 'insultingly inappropriate to the circumstances'.[134] This is rather unsurprising as the AGO already emphasized that parody is an artistic expression and the result of exercise of an individual's right of freedom of expression.[135] Therefore, it can be inferred that this link to human rights considerations should influence the interpretation of the exception.[136] Thirdly, parody has always been a permeable, evolving concept which should not be confined to music, literature, or drawings. It is also relevant to cinematographic works, works of craftmanship, and other types of artistic works. At the same time, attempts to link parody, pastiche, and caricature to particular artistic expressions impose

[128] *Deckmyn* (n 2) [17]; AGO in *Deckmyn* (n 3) [35].

[129] *Deckmyn* (n 2) [19]; AGO in *Deckmyn* (n 3) [45]; C-285/12 *Aboubacar Diakité v. Commissaire général aux réfugiés et aux apatrides* [2014] ECLI:EU:C:2014:39, [27]; C-549/07 *Friederike Wallentin-Hermann v. Alitalia* [2008] ECLI:EU:C:2008:771, [17]; C-119/12 *Josef Probst v. mr.nexnet GmbH* [2012] ECLI:EU:C:2012:748, [20] and C-49/11 *Content Services Ltd v. Bundesarbeitskammer* [2012] ECLI:EU:C:2012:419, [32].

[130] *Deckmyn* (n 2) [20]; AGO in *Deckmyn* (n 3) [48].

[131] On 28 July 2016, the German *Bundesgerichtshof* ('BGH') applied the *Deckmyn* teachings for the first time in file no. I ZR 9/15 ('Auf fett getrimmt'). This case dealt with the alteration of a photo of a famous German actor depicting her in a rather unflattering manner. The BGH confirmed the need to give a broad meaning to parody post-*Deckmyn*. Hence, the photo editing was sufficient to allow the recognition of the original while being noticeably different from it, [28]–[35].

[132] AGO in *Deckmyn* (n 3) [61]–[65]; *Deckmyn* (n 2) [21].

[133] The AGO confers a broad margin to Member States. AGO in *Deckmyn* (n 3) [69].

[134] See *Oxford English Dictionary*. The etymology of 'mockery' comes from the French verb 'se moquer' connoting a lack of respect or derision. It is often biting, bitter, or even hurtful. This is in line with the established case law under the ECHR. See Chapter 5, section 4.2.

[135] AGO in *Deckmyn* (n 3) [70].

[136] Chapter 7, section 2, explains that the greater the use of a humorous, political, or public interest character, the more likely it is that the expression will be lawful.

an unnecessary limitation which overlooks the existence of various forms of 'hybrid' parody, which include combined elements of text, images, and music altogether.

It seems reasonable to question whether the CJEU interpretation in *Deckmyn* is sufficient to achieve uniform interpretation of parody throughout the EU given the breadth of the Court's interpretation.

5.2.1 France

Prior to codification of copyright law, French courts exhibited latitude towards defendants' acts which carried an imprint of humour in recognition of a general freedom to critique, as well as humour's social function. Parodies were, therefore, afforded special treatment, long before a specific exception for the purposes of parody, pastiche, and caricature was incorporated into national copyright legislation in 1957.[137] Seen as derivative of the right of critique, parodies were praised for their dual social objectives: to entertain and to incite discourse within society.

Once copyright legislation was enacted, in the absence of a statutory definition, French courts defined the terms 'parody, pastiche and caricature' on a case-by-case basis. Although parody was most closely linked to a playful, ridiculing, mocking function prior to codification, consideration of decisions since codification demonstrates that the French courts have recognized that parody has a broader role in society.

5.2.1.1 Defining parody broadly as a change of context

The first notable decision, *Peanuts*,[138] concerned a parody of a copyright-protected comic strip, which featured the cartoon character *Snoopy* in a mildly pornographic scenario. This transposition of a children's character to an unexpected context is reflected in the first instance court's definition of a parody as: 'tending to provoke complicity of the reader and irony through the distorting imitation of the original work'.[139] This definition has the particularity of reflecting the main features of parody as consistently understood by theorists,[140] insofar as it includes the role of the audience's recognition of the underlying work in the parody, and the double-voiced discourse[141] arising from the transformation (here, a change of context) of the imitation. Noticeably, the court's definition does not place any reliance on humour. To the contrary, the court considered the work a parody (within the scope of the copyright exception) because of the critical comment it conveyed.[142]

This approach was soon confirmed and extended in *Tarzoon*.[143] In this case, a court of first instance was required to establish whether a satire of Tarzan fell within the copyright exception for parody. Citing human rights considerations,[144] the court reiterated that illustrations made to express critical opinions are as socially valuable as those which were simply humorous. Here, the court noted that the defendant used the

[137] H Schuermans, *Code de la Presse* (Larcier, 1861) 173; on the introduction of the French parody exception, see Chapter 2, section 4.1.

[138] TGI Paris, 19 janvier 1977, RIDA, 1977, n°92, pp. 167–9.

[139] Author's translation. Ibid. [140] See section 4. [141] See n 40.

[142] Yet the opposite result was reached in the pastiche of Calimero in light of sadomasochist situations: TGI Paris, 24 mars 2000, légipresse 2000 I, p. 71.

[143] TGI Paris, 3 janvier 1978, D., 1979, p. 99, obs. Desbois; see works mentioned in Chapter 6, section 4.3.2.

[144] Ibid.

Tarzan cartoon to highlight the irony that western society at that time criticized materialism, whilst simultaneously embracing it.[145] Consequently, the court accepted this particular satirical work as a parody.

5.2.1.2 Attempts at distinguishing parody from other related terms

Later in 1988, the French Supreme Court attempted to distinguish between the three terms adopted in statutory provision: parody, pastiche, and carticature.[146] Legal proceedings were commenced by the successor-in-title of Charles Trénet and Thierry Le Luron for rights in the song *Douce France*, against a parody—*Douces Transes*—which adopted new lyrics for the original tune. The court asserted that a parody requires immediate identification of the underlying work, which distinguishes it from pastiche and caricature. Here, the court understands 'caricature' as any mockery of a person[147] or character, while a 'pastiche' comments on the style or genre adopted by the original author.

In each case, the legal definition adopted by the Supreme Court defines the genre in relation to its target: a parody targets the underlying work, pastiche targets the style of a work,[148] and caricature targets a person or a character.[149] These restricted definitions impact upon the legal protection afforded to such works. For example, this legal definition of parody does not encompass a work where the target is unrelated to the underlying work, as is often the case in satire.

Given that this restriction is not a result of any statutory interpretation, scholars have attempted to rationalize the court's approach. Many adopt a similar stance as Desbois, who argues that the three terms identify a single category of socially valuable transformative works, but with each relating to a different art field: parody is relevant to music, pastiche to literary works, and caricature to plastic arts. However, his categorization seems unduly restrictive. For example, it fails to take account of any equivalent for motion pictures.

Françon revisits the *Tarzoon* case[150] to build upon Desbois's analysis, and defines a parodist as one who 'creates a satiric vision of a work which is not his, for the joy of the public'.[151] While this definition has the advantage of including satire (or 'parody with'—targeting something other than the underlying work) within the concept of parody, Françon seems to conflate the two terms into a single genre.[152] Despite this

145 Satire seems to be understood here as referring to something external to the original work it borrows from.

146 Cass., 12 janvier 1988, RIDA, n°137, p. 98; Paris (1ère ch.) 15 octobre 1985, D. 1986, somm. 1986, obs. Colombet.

147 Possibly raising image rights or other personality rights issues.

148 It must be remembered that a style belongs to the sphere of ideas which is not covered by copyright. Here, style must be understood as the style of a particular work. See section 3.5; Dalloz, 'Exception au droit d'exploitation' (2006) 9, [806]; F Delfour, *L'Imitation Créatrice* (University of Toulouse, 2000) 72.

149 A Berenboom, 'La parodie' in E Cornu (ed.), *Bande dessinée et droit d'auteur* (Larcier, 2009) 104; Mouffe (n 53) 20.

150 See n 143.

151 Translation is mine. A Françon, 'Questions de droit d'auteur relatives aux parodies et productions similaires' (1988) 6 *Droit d'Auteur* 302.

152 This is contested by experts in various art fields. Hutcheon's explanation is that people confuse parody and satire because of how these genres use irony. He considers that parody pays tribute to the original work from which it borrows, while the satirist aims to ridicule the original work. However, Chatman stresses that, according to its postmodern meaning, a ridiculing effect is integral to parody. The difference is thus one of degree. Chatman (n 38) 33; Macdonald (n 36) xiii; Hutcheon (n 8) 16 and 43.

flaw, the definition has some resonance within the literature. For example, Sangsue establishes a very similar definition in relation to literary works by defining parody as a playful, comic, or satiric transformation of a previous work.[153]

In sum, while French jurisprudence focuses on the target of the parody, French legal scholarship tends to focus on the art field in which the parody evolves. Overall, each approach appears equally unsatisfactory, as they both impose an apparently unnecessary limit on parody. While parody, pastiche, and caricature *may* represent different artistic concepts or terms of art which may vary with time and space, from a legal perspective all three relate to a transformation of an existing work into a new expression. Thus, it seems unnecessary to distinguish further between the three terms in order to regulate unauthorized use within a legal regime.[154]

On balance, the use of the three different terms simply aims to reflect the diversity of existing artistic expressions.[155] Had the French legislature intended the different terms to relate to specific authorial works, then it would have been straightforward to do this explicitly, by providing a specific regime for each.[156] In the absence of such precision, the better approach is to understand parody as encompassing caricature, pastiche, and even satire.[157] In turn, any requirement that each of the three styles must incorporate a humorous character requires 'humour'[158] to be understood more broadly than amusement or comedy, and encompass tribute or criticism as well.[159]

In the recent *Bauret v. Koons*,[160] the French tribunal of first instance endorsed the two main requirements set out in *Deckmyn*[161] as sufficient to define the purpose of parody. Consequently, previous approaches attempting to distinguish the terms in relation to particular art forms should be set aside post-*Deckmyn*.[162]

5.2.2 The United Kingdom[163]

In October 2014, UK copyright law introduced a new defence to infringment covering 'parody, caricature and pastiche'. As in France, the legislator refrained from any statutory definition, leaving the courts to interpret the terms on a case-by-case basis.[164]

[153] D Sangsue, *La Parodie* (Hachette Supérieur, 1994) 5.

[154] B Galopin, *Les exceptions à usage public en droit d'auteur* (IRPI, 2012) 303; P Tréfigny, 'Les conditions de licéité de l'imitation en droit d'auteur' in *l'Imitation: contribution à l'étude juridique des comportements référentiels* (PUS, 2000) 222; Strowel (n 11) 41.

[155] Strowel (n 11) 42.

[156] S Durrande, 'La parodie, le pastiche et la caricature' in *Mélanges en l'honneur de André Françon* (Dalloz, 1995) 133.

[157] As further supported by the human rights framework. See Chapter 5.

[158] *Deckmyn* (n 2) [20].

[159] *Saint-Tin*: TGI Evry, 9 juillet 2009, RG n°09/02410 confirmed Paris, 18 février 2011, RG n°09/19272, Propr. Int. 2011 n°39, p. 187.

[160] TGI Paris, 9 mars 2017, RG n°15/01086. [161] *Deckmyn* (n 2).

[162] Yet, recently Bruguière argued for the need to go back to the Supreme Court's stance. In doing so, this scholar argues that there is more margin for courts to determine what constitute the rules of the genre in each art field. J-M Bruguière, 'La réception du fair dealing britannique dans le système d'exception fermée français' (2018) *RIDA* (forthcoming).

[163] Reference to the UK jurisdiction in this book specifically means the courts of England and Wales and the UK Supreme Court, unless otherwise stated.

[164] Interestingly, parody cases prior to the introduction of a parody exception in UK copyright law already show a tendency to understand parody as a multivalent term: see *Hanfstaengl v. Empire Palace* [1894] 3 Ch 109; *Francis, Day & Hunter v. Feldman & Co* [1914] 2 Ch 728; *Glyn v. Weston Feature Film Co* [1915] 1 Ch 261; *Joy Music v. Sunday Pictorial Newspaper* (1920) [1960] 2 QB 60; *Twentieth Century Fox Film Corp. v. Anglo-Amalgamated Film Distributors* [1965] 109 SJ 107;

In the absence of any judicial decisions applying the new exception, some insight may be gleaned from non-binding documents, such as government releases and UK Intellectual Property Office ('IPO') guidance for creators. Very early in the consultation process, the IPO acknowledges the close relationship between the three associated terms. It initially attempted to distinguish the terms based on their ordinary meaning by referring to the *Oxford English Dictionary*[165] which defines the three terms as:

> Caricature: a grotesque usually comically exaggerated representation especially of a person or ridiculously poor imitation or version.
>
> Parody: humorous exaggerated imitation of an author, literary work or style, etc or feeble imitation, travesty.
>
> Pastiche: picture or musical composition from or imitating various sources or literary or other work composed in the style of a well-known author, etc.[166]

However, instead of delving further into the distinction, the IPO moves on and states:

> [T]he UK government recognised that whilst these terms may have different connotations and meanings, they 'all include an element of imitation, and may incorporate, to a greater or lesser extent, elements of the original work. The whole point of these types of works is that they should "conjure up" the original work upon which they are based.'[167]

This perhaps demonstrates a shift in the statutory interpretative practices and marks a willingness to recognize that the three terms are so closely related that defining clear boundaries between each term is counterproductive for its legal meaning.[168] Recalling the brief historical overview and the comparison of parody with other related terms, such a position appears to be correct. Interestingly, we can also appreciate the influence of other legal traditions. Whilst it remains unclear whether the UK governement has been influenced by the 'holistic' understanding of parody, the mention of the 'conjure-up test' seems to be a clear reference to US case law, which we shall consider shortly in the next section.

Although initially endorsing the position that the legal understanding of parody, pastiche, and caricature does not require the three terms to be distinguished, the IPO then seems to embark on a dangerous path. Instead of relying on the common denominators (imitation and incorporation) which are applicable to a wide range of uses, subsequently, the IPO's focus seems to limit the scope of parody to particular art fields. In a communication issued as part of the consultation process, the IPO recounts that parody has to be understood as 'a literary or artistic work that imitates the characteristic style of an author or a work for comic effect or ridicule'.[169] Here preferring the *American Heritage Dictionary*[170] to the *Oxford English Dictionary*, the IPO also limits the scope of the exception to 'target parodies' (also referred to as 'parody of'). Hence, the legal meaning of parody requires the use to comment on the work or its author.

Schweppes v. Wellington [1984] FSR 210; *Williamson Music v. The Pearson Partnership* [1987] FSR 97; *Allen v. Redshaw* [2013] EWHC 1312 (Pat).

165 Though this is not made explicit by the impact assessment, this definition coincides with the first indent of the definition found in the *American Heritage Dictionary of English Language*.

166 *Taking Forward the Gowers Review of Intellectual Property: Proposed changes to copyright exceptions* (Newport: Intellectual Property Office, 2008) para 188.

167 Ibid, para 189.

168 Ibid, para 190.

169 *Impact Assessment* (n 113) 3.

170 Though this is not made explicit by the impact assessment, this definition coincides with the first indent of the definition found in the *American Heritage Dictionary of English Language*.

The reliance on one dictionary instead of another can therefore have important consequences for the scope of the exception.

During the legislative process, there is a clear sign that the legislator intended the three terms to be taken as a whole, therefore constituting an argument against the distinction of the three terms.[171] Despite the fact that the ordinary meaning should constitute the starting point for defining parody, it seems inappropriate to use dictionary definitions to differentiate between each term, rather than to extract the commonalities between them. The latter approach affords a more comprehensive understanding which provides avenues for flexibility. This is essential if the parody exception is to adapt to new uses. Furthermore, the reliance on common features contributes to stability which is essential for parodists and right-holders.

After the introduction of the parody exception, the IPO released a guidance document for creators and right-holders. This guidance notes:

> In broad terms parody imitates a work for humorous or satirical effect, commenting on the original work, its subject, author, style or some other target. Pastiche is a musical or other composition made up of selections from various sources or one that imitates the style of another artist or period. A caricature portrays its subject in a simplified or exaggerated way, which may be insulting or complimentary and may serve a political purpose or be solely for entertainment.[172]

Here, while the IPO seeks to distinguish parody from pastiche or caricature, it also expands the meaning of parody, being either a comment on the original ('parody of') or on anything else outside the borrowing made ('parody with'). If anything, the different statements from the IPO demonstrate the difficulty in defining parody and its related terms.

The uncertainty surrounding the current meaning of the terms has led to a heated debate amongst scholars. The main discussion focuses on whether a holistic approach to parody should prevail over the distinction between parody, pastiche, and caricature. Emily Hudson, for example, has argued that each term should be understood separately, with the result that pastiche could be far-reaching in scope, extending uses such as mash-ups, fan fiction, sampling, collage, and other appropriation art forms.[173] While appreciating why some find this approach appealing, it seems to overlook the lessons learned from the historical account.[174] This established that pastiche focuses more on imitation than requiring any specific 'message' to be conveyed. By adopting 'pastiche' as a catch-all term for any potentially socially valuable use, there is a real risk of expanding the scope of the exception, rendering it void of substance, as well as extending it beyond the legislator's intent.[175]

[171] In addition to the documents already mentioned, one can refer to the government's response to the *Hargreaves Review of Intellectual Property and Growth* which said it would 'bring forward proposals in autumn 2011 for a substantial opening up of the UK's copyright exceptions regime […] This will include proposals […] to introduce *an exception for parody*' (author's emphasis) *The Government Response to the Hargreaves Review of Intellectual Property and Growth* (3 August 2011) 7.

[172] IPO, 'Exceptions to copyright: Guidance for creators and copyright owners' (October 2014) 7, available at https://www.gov.uk/government/uploads/system/uploads/attachment_data/file/448274/Exceptions_to_copyright_-_Guidance_for_creators_and_copyright_owners.pdf (access date: 22 May 2018).

[173] E Hudson, 'The pastiche exception in copyright law: a case of mashed-up drafting?' (2017) 4 *IPQ* 346.

[174] See section 2.

[175] The legislator's intention seems to be that curtailing the exclusive rights of right-holders is only welcomed in circumstances where the use amounts to a new expression, through the emphasis of 'comment' on either earlier works or a third object, extramural to the work it borrows from. See UK Government, *Impact Assessment: Copyright Exception for Parody* (20 December 2012) 3.

Stemming from the IPO's statements during the consultation process, there was an intention to understand the three terms as fitting within the parody umbrella. While Hudson's proposals represent an elegant solution for introducing flexibility and adaptability, it might also act like a Trojan horse within the copyright system by disrupting the copyright balance too heavily in favour of users. This would ignore the high level of protection for right-holders which the EU legislation mandates.

Additionally, this proposed expansion of the 'parody' exception to uses such a sampling would seem to create an English version of 'fair use' without proper scrutiny. Hudson herself acknowledges that her definition of 'pastiche' would bring the UK closer to an understanding of parody as adopted by the US Second Circuit in *Cariou v. Prince*.[176] However, as we shall see later,[177] this particular decision has itself been the subject of criticism for stretching the scope of fair use so far that there is a real risk that this is likely to impact on the normal exploitation of works by right-holders (and their ability to license for derivative uses). [178] Such a position would also weigh against the three-step test against which all copyright exceptions must be measured and would severely curtail the principle of strict interpretation currently prevailing.[179] This is also dangerous as fair use belongs to a different legal system in which stability is derived from a rich jurisprudence accumulated over approximately 150 years, which the UK does not have.

In essence, Hudson questions whether in *Deckmyn* the CJEU has actually interpreted the meaning of 'parody' per se, rather than 'parody' as the umbrella term including 'pastiche and caricature', and concludes in favour of the former. Indeed, a basis for this can be found in the EU Commission's position as per its written submission in *Deckmyn*.[180] *Deckmyn* arguably provides guidelines as to how one could construe the meaning of pastiche, i.e. that pastiche requires 'two key activities: imitation of the style of pre-existing works, and the utilisation or assemblage of pre-existing works in new works'.[181]

This definition is hard to reconcile with *Deckmyn*.[182] Firstly, the current trend amongst Member States to refer to the exception for 'the purposes of parody, pastiche and caricature' as 'the parody exception': if the CJEU did not intend 'parody' to be used as this shorthand, then it is reasonable to presume that the Court would have taken the opportunity to emphasize the importance of distinguishing between the terms. The Court's focus on 'parody' reflects the first question referred to by the Belgian court,[183] but while summarizing the facts in the national dispute, the CJEU refers to

[176] 714 F.3d 694 (2d Cir. 2013). [177] See Chapter 5, section 5.5.

[178] The scholar acknowledges that this reasoning would enable the UK to get away from the straightjacket of the limited exceptions listed in article 5.3 of the InfoSoc Directive. This is a huge leap likely to change the approach endorsed at EU and UK levels. If this amounts to introducing a wider fair use approach than the one currently enforced in the US, such a move surely requires further scrutiny and public consultation.

[179] See Chapter 3, section 2.2. [180] AGO in *Deckmyn* (n 3) [41].

[181] Hudson (n 173) 363.

[182] It is not denied that UK courts may adopt such a position in a post-Brexit world. However, current official documents from the UK government demonstrate a willingness to keep a certain influence of the CJEU in the UK. Additionally, once treated as a third country, it is reasonable to argue that the UK will have to enter into a trade agreement with the EU, in which case it is likely that the EU will seek the CJEU's interpretation being maintained in future relations between the UK and the EU.

[183] Before delivering his Opinion, it is good practice for the Advocate General to state the limits of that Opinion. Analysing the preliminary observations of the Opinion, there is nothing to suggest that the Advocate General intended to limit the Opinion to parodies only and that it does not extend to caricature and pastiche. Adopting a reasoning *a contrario*, I argue that what is not excluded is therefore included. See AGO in *Deckmyn* (n 3) [27]–[31].

the defendant's political *caricature*[184] within the context of the *parody* exception.[185] Thus, the Court's language suggests the three terms fit within the umbrella of parody.[186] Secondly, the CJEU agrees with the Advocate General's definition of parody by expressively referring to his Opinion.[187] Although the judgment does not repeat what the wording of Advocate General in full, it is credible that by adopting the Advocate General's solution, the Court endorsed its reasoning on this point. Here, the Opinion could not be clearer; there is no need to distinguish the three terms for the purpose of the parody exception in copyright law:

> The parody exception does not appear in isolation but rather, on the contrary, as part of a series of three categories in the form of a continuous list ('caricature, parody or pastiche'), I do not believe that a comparison with each of the concepts with which it coexists is of particular relevance for the present purposes. It may be difficult in a specific case to assign a particular work to one concept or another when those concepts are not in competition with one another. That being so, it does not seem to me to be necessary to proceed any further with that distinction, since, in short, all those concepts have the same effect of derogating from the copyright of the author of the original work which, in one way or another, is present in the—so to speak—derived work.[188]

This warning of the danger of delineating the boundaries of each term for the effectiveness of the exception appears equally applicable to the UK as to other EU Member States. Even if the UK decides to depart from the EU understanding of parody in a post-Brexit world (and should it be allowed to do so),[189] there are numerous hurdles ahead.[190] Perhaps least convincingly, early parody cases prior to the exception refrained from distinguishing the terms and refer to 'parody'.[191] However, as these were decided prior to the introduction of the exception, English judges may well want to depart from this position. Yet, distinguishing parody from pastiche and caricature seems to be against the legislator's intent. As explained earlier, the brief overview of the IPO's

[184] Interestingly, the 'caricature' is used in the French version of the judgment but not in the English version. The latter refers to 'political cartoon'. As French is the working language of the Court, one could argue that it is this version which carries more weight.

[185] *Deckmyn* (n 2) [11].

[186] Ibid, [12], where the CJEU refers to the provision as '*the* parody exception' and not the exception for parody, pastiche, or caricature. Furthermore, at [22] the CJEU refers to '*an* exception' when referring to article 5.3.k of the InfoSoc Directive. Adopting Hudson's understanding would essentially amount to three exceptions as each term would abide by different requirements. As she acknowledges, pastiche would not require humorous intent, for example.

[187] Ibid, [20].

[188] AGO in *Deckmyn* (n 3) [46].

[189] Resulting from the EU referendum of 24 June 2016, the UK is planning to leave the EU. While the negotiations are still ongoing, it is very hard to predict what the future holds for UK copyright law. Currently, the UK needs to abide by EU law at least until the end of the transition period. If the UK leaves the EU, there are likely to be two options: (1) the UK remains part of the EEA (e.g. Norway), (2) the UK enters association agreements or free trade agreements on particular matters with the EU. Both solutions cover intellectual property matters. If the UK remains part of the EEA, it will still be bound by EU copyright legislation as these instruments have EEA relevance. Similarly, association agreements or other free trade agreements include IP provisions but these have a more general, abstract character which would allow the UK a limited margin of manoeuvre. Here, the UK courts would be able to craft their definitions of parody.

[190] Given the recent introduction of the parody exception in UK copyright law and its proximity to the provision of the InfoSoc Directive, it is more likely that the UK will be influenced by EU developments in this area. See R Arnold et al, *The Legal Consequences of Brexit Through the Lens of IP Law* (2017) Oxford Legal Studies Research Paper No. 15/2017, 9; L McDonagh, 'UK patent law and copyright law after Brexit: potential consequences' in O Fitzgerald and E Lein (eds), *Complexity's Embrace: The International Law Implications of Brexit* (MQUP, 2018) 189.

[191] As exemplified in France, see n 164.

statements during the consultation preceding the amendment of the Copyright Act appears to refer to parody as encapsulating other uses such as parody and pastiche.

Finally, and most importantly, Hudson's approach would probably not only jeopardize the UK's compatibility with its international obligations—as it would be more far reaching than fair use to include any type of appropriation—but it would go beyond a well-rooted rejection of a fair use style exception in UK copyright law. As we will further cover in Chapter 2, with the UK's accession to the Berne Convention in 1887, the UK Copyright Act 1911[192] paved the way for a rejection of US fair use to bring the UK closer to its Europeancontinental neighbours.[193]

As the tradition is for courts to define the purpose of copyright exceptions on a case-by-case basis, future cases might shed some light on the exact meaning of 'parody' as well as on the importance of humour or the type of humour required. In the meantime and despite the uncertainties linked to the current political context,[194] some insight can be gleaned from the interpretation of the exception by the CJEU in *Deckmyn*. In which case, the latest IPO guidance definitions should be set aside in favour of a more comprehensive approach as per the government's documents published prior to the introduction of the new exception. Although for legal purposes the three styles belong arguably to the same (legal) genre, it is legitimate to question whether the legal recognition of three different styles of 'parody' has any impact, or indeed whether use of other similar terms, such as satire or burlesque, has any influence on the legal definition of parody. This will be better appreciated when contrasted with the Canadian and Australian parody exceptions.[195]

5.3 The United States

Early US cases demonstrate a wide understanding of parody which includes uses targeting both earlier copyright-protected works or having a subject unrelated to the works it reproduces. For example, in *Metro-Goldwyn-Mayer, Inc. v. Showcase Atlanta Cooperative Productions, Inc.*,[196] District Judge Evans defines parody and satire thus:

> A parody is a work in which the language or style of another work is closely imitated or mimicked for comic effect or ridicule. A satire is a work which holds up the vices or shortcomings of an individual or institution to ridicule or derision, usually with an intent to stimulate change; the use of wit, irony or sarcasm for the purpose of exposing and discrediting vice or folly.[197]

Building upon this definition, the judge adds:

> [P]arody must do more than merely achieve comic effect. It must also make some critical comment or statement about the original work which reflects the original perspective of the parodist thereby giving the parody social value beyond its entertainment function. Otherwise, any comic use of an existing work would be protected, removing the 'fair' aspect of the 'fair use' doctrine and negating the underlying purpose of copyright law of protecting original works from unfair exploitation by others.

192 Geo.6 5(1911) c.46.

193 Another possibility is that the UK's adoption of 'fair dealing' stems from the influence of the first Australian Copyright Act 1905 (s 28).

194 See sections 5. 195 Ibid. 196 479 F.Supp. 351 (1979) (N.D. Ga 1979).

197 Ibid, [357]. Here the judge cites an earlier parody decision in the area of trade marks, *Dallas Cowboys Cheerleaders v. Pussycat Cinema, Ltd* 467 F.Supp. 366 (S.D.N.Y. 1979) 376. This definition can be traced to *Webster's New International Dictionary* (2nd edn, 1960) where a parody is defined as '[a] writing in which the language and style of an author, or poem, or other work, is closely imitated or mimicked'. This definition is also present in *Berlin v. EC Publications, Inc.*, 219 F.Supp. 911 (S.D.N.Y. 1963) 915.

In essence, parody cannot be a shortcut to getting a licence for a use but requires the creation of a new expression having a particular social function.[198] Hence, there needs to be some critical bearing or comment made through the parodic or satiric use.

The landmark parody case which has caused the US approach to depart from other jurisdictions is undoubtedly the *Campbell* case.[199] In 1989, a popular rap group, 2 Live Crew, created a 'parody' by replacing the original lyrics of Roy Orbison and William Dees' rock ballad *Oh, Pretty Woman*. In considering whether the use fell under the parody fair use defence, the US Supreme Court created a clear distinction between parody and satire.[200]

Taking the definition directly from that decision a parody is 'the use of some elements of a prior author's composition to create a new one that, at least in part, comments on that author's works'.[201] Therefore, a 'parody needs to mimic an original to make its point, and so has some claim to use the creation of its victim's (or collective victims) imagination […]'.[202] A parody must reproduce enough copyright-protected elements to 'conjure up' with the earlier work to make its parodic commentary recognizable.[203] The Supreme Court limits the scope of the parodic purpose further by adding that, for fair use to apply, a parody needs to comment upon or criticize the work it borrows from, aiming at creating a new artistic work rather than 'superseding the objects of the original'.[204] Nevertheless, the Court agreed that the quality and tastefulness of the parody are irrelevant for detemining the fair use purpose.[205] Conversely, satire is defined as the use of a particular work for commenting on an unrelated object.[206] Here, the 2 Live Crew reproduction served as a vessel for a criticism of something other than the original and, consequently, would fall outside the fair use doctrine.[207] The case was remanded and the parties eventually settled out of court.

Subsequently, post-*Campbell* US courts have reinforced this binary distinction by attempting to categorize *all* transformative works as either parody or satire.[208] For example, *The Wind Done Gone,* retells the story of a literary classic, racist melodrama, *Gone With the Wind.* This use was considered as a legitimate parody because it is aimed at directly commenting on the novel's plot.[209] But the unauthorized rewrite of a song,

[198] In compliance with the freedom of expression justification.

[199] *Campbell v. Acuff-Rose Music Inc.* 510 US 569 (1994) (hereafter *Campbell*). The very first US case on parody seems to be the burlesque reworking of *Gaslight*, a British play. Here, the court held against the finding of fair use because the use was for the purpose of burlesque rather than parody. However, this holding was invalidated in *Campbell*. See *Benny v. Loew's, Inc.*, 239 F.2d 532 (9th Cir. 1956). See section 3.3 for an understanding of burlesque.

[200] Before this case, the US courts were using the terms parody and satire as synonyms. B P Keller and R Tushnet, 'Even more parodic than the real thing: parody lawsuits revisited' (2004) 94 *TMR* 979.

[201] *Campbell* (n 199) [580].

[202] Ibid, [580]–[581].

[203] *Campbell* (n 199) [588]. Therefore the removal of copyright notices on photographs is not a parody, see *Wilen v. Alt. Media Net, Inc.*, No. 03CIV2524 (RMB) (JCF) (S.D.N.Y. Jan. 26, 2005).

[204] This inherently explains why it is harder for fan fiction or mash-up works to meet the parody purpose for fair use to apply. *Campbell* (n 199) [583]; repeated in *Suntrust Bank v. Houghton Mifflin Company*, 268 F.3d 1257, 1268–9 (11th Cir. 2001) (hereafter *Suntrust*); *Salinger v. Colting et al*, 641 F.Supp.2d 250 (S.D.N.Y. 2009) [257]–[258] (hereafter *Salinger*); *Henley v. DeVore*, 733 F.Supp.2d 1144 (C.D. Cal. 2010).

[205] *Campbell* (n 199) [582].

[206] *Dr. Seuss Enters., L.P. v. Penguin Books, U.S.A., Inc.*, 109 F.3d 1394, p. 1401 (9th Cir. 1997) (hereafter *Dr. Seuss II*); *Leibovitz v. Paramount Pictures Corp.*, 137 F.3d 109, 114 (2d Cir. 1998).

[207] R A Posner, 'When is parody fair use' (1992) 21 *J. Legal Stud.* 67, 71.

[208] M McCrann, 'A modest proposal: granting presumptive fair use protection for musical parodies' (2009) 14 *Roger Williams U. L. Rev.* 96, 97; Keller and Tushnet (n 200) 979.

[209] *Suntrust* (n 204) [1268]–[1269].

Boogie Woogie Bugle Boy, to comment upon social customs was held not to be a lawful parody.[210]

More recently in *Bourne*,[211] a US district court was called upon to decide whether a parody of the author (as opposed to the author's work) could fit the purpose of parody as understood under US copyright law. The defendant reproduced the Disney musical work *When You Wish Upon A Star* in a song called *I Need A Jew* to allege that Walt Disney was racist. The court held in favour of the parodist because the use of the musical work reinforced the derivative's parodic nature by criticizing the original work.[212] In *Salinger v. Colting et al*,[213] the Swedish author, Fredrik Colting, published *60 Years Later: Coming Through the Rye* which reproduces substantial parts of J.D. Salinger's well-known *Catcher in the Rye* classic. Faced with a copyright lawsuit, Colting sought to rely on the parody exception for his new sequel to the classic. The same district court held that a tribute or sequel could not be understood as a parody unless the parodic or critical elements of the new work were the primary focus for the use.[214] Here, the underlying reasoning was that the parody exception should not become a means to legitimize any exploitation of existing copyright-protected works later claimed as comments made under the cover of parody.[215] If a parodist wishes to comment on something external using a copyright-protected work, a reference can be made by imitating the style of the original author, rather than reproducing their specific expressions. Nevertheless, a comment on the work should be made to qualify as parody under US copyright legislation. This has resulted in an arguably unnatural extension of the term satire to include many 'worthy' transformative uses of works which cannot fit within the parody category.[216]

Some have argued that more recent cases have paved the way to relinquish the strict parody/satire dichotomy.[217] In a fairly recent case,[218] the Second Circuit considered the borrowing of a pair of feet from a famous photograph by Jeff Koons in a work seeking to comment on the social and aesthetic power of mass media. Here, the court seems to have focused on the creative endeavour behind the use and on the creative added value enshrined in the parody work. Nonetheless, by relying heavily on the wording of the *Campbell* decision, the court maintains the distinction but allows for exceptions.[219]

[210] *MCA, Inc. v. Wilson*, 677 F.2d 180 (2d Cir. 1981). Similarly held, in *The Cat Not in the Hat* case, whereby the parodists aimed at commenting on O.J. Simpson's trial using Dr Seuss's work, *The Cat in the Hat. Dr Seuss Enters., L.P. v. Penguin Book USA, Inc.*, 924 F.Supp. 1559 (S.D. Cal. 1966) (hereafter *Seuss I*) upheld in *Dr. Seuss II* (n 206). Also, in *Columbia v. Miramax* whereby the defendant borrowed from *Men in Black* for the promotion of Michael Moore's film *The Big One. Columbia Pictures Indus. v. Miramax Films Corp.*, 11 F.Supp.2d 1179 (C.D. Cal. 1998).

[211] *Bourne Co. v. Twentieth Century Fox Films Corp.*, 602 F.Supp.2d 499 (S.D.N.Y. 2009).

[212] Though, interestingly, Disney was not the author of this song. But the popularity of the public figure was held to be so closely attached to this copyright-protected work that the parody was acknowledged as falling under fair use. A similar outcome was held in *Burnett .v Twentieth Century Fox Film Corp.*, 491 F.Supp.2d 962 (C.D. Cal. 2007).

[213] *Salinger* (n 204). [214] Ibid, [260]. [215] *Campbell* (n 199) [599].

[216] This is to ensure that these works benefit from a 'fair use' defence to an infringement claim, e.g. *Salinger* (n 204) [257]–[258]; *Suntrust* (n 204), [1268]; *Seuss I* (n 210) [1400]. See also R Kairalla, 'Works as weapon, author as target: why parodies that target authors (not just their works) should be fair uses' (2012) 2 *NYU J. Intell. Prop. & Ent. L.*, 234.

[217] A Lai, 'Copyright law and its parody defense: multiple legal perspectives' (2015) 4 *NYU J. Intell. Prop. & Ent. L.* 311.

[218] *Blanch v. Jeff Koons*, 467 F.3d 244 (2d Cir. 2006). Interestingly, the Second Circuit has the tendency to be more liberal compared to parody cases which went through the Ninth Circuit where a more conservative approach prevails.

[219] See Chapter 5, section 5.5.

5.4 Australia

While EU law adopts a copyright exception for 'parody, pastiche and caricature', the Australian legislature preferred to draft the exclusion in terms of 'parody and satire'. This section considers whether this different choice of words is likely to capture a different sub-section of transformative uses.

As in the case of France, the UK, and the US, there is no definition of either 'parody' or 'satire' within the Australian Copyright Act itself. According to statutory interpretation rules and, especially, section 15AA of the Acts Interpretation Act 1901 (Cth), '[i]n interpreting a provision of an Act, the interpretation that would best achieve the purpose or object of the Act (whether or not that purpose or object is expressly stated in the Act) is to be preferred to each other interpretation'. However, the Australian Copyright Act provides very little guidance and close to nothing to help with the understanding of parody and satire.

Nevertheless, a Government Factsheet released in 2006 identifies that:

> Satire often involves attacking an idea or attitude, an institution or a social practice, through irony, derision, or wit. Parody often involves the imitation of the characteristic style of an author or a work for comic effect or ridicule.[220]

Later updates[221] repeat this definition, and further identify that courts are likely to appraise the meaning of the terms in everyday language (e.g. by consulting dictionaries) before making a determination of the meaning within the context of the Act.

Building on definitions contained in the *Macquarie Dictionary*, the Australian Copyright Council notes that:

> A parody is an imitation of a work that may include parts of the original. In some cases, a parody may not be effective unless parts of the original are included. It seems that the purpose of a true parody is to make some comment on the imitated work or on its creator.[222]

'Satire', in turn, draws:

> attention to characteristics or actions—such as vice or folly—by using certain forms of expression—such as irony, sarcasm and ridicule. Thus, while a parody is not necessarily humorous, it seems that satire has two elements, based upon the object to which the audience's attention is drawn (vice or folly etc) and the manner in which it is done (irony, ridicule etc).[223]

Hence, a satire may be a style of parody.

Both these definitions, although not legally binding, also set the focus on the structural features of parody—a creative imitation—but with seemingly less weight allocated to any humorous aspect of parody. Uncertainty surrounding the legal meaning of parody and satire has given rise to four main schools of scholarly interpretation.

The first (and arguably least convincing) approach defers to the understanding of parody and satire according to US copyright law. This approach derives from the Amended Explanatory Memorandum and the second reading of the Copyright Act in the Australian Senate. These identify the US definitions of the terms as potentially relevant, because of the existence of a free trade agreement between Australia and the US

[220] Attorney-General's Department, *Copyright Amendment Act 2006—Fact Sheets: New Australian Copyright Laws: Parody and Satire* http://www.ag.gov.au.

[221] Australian Copyright Council, *Parodies, Satires & Jokes* (Information sheet G083v05, 2012) 2.

[222] Ibid; repeated in Australian Copyright Council, *Parodies, satires & jokes* (Information sheet G083v05, 12/2014) 3.

[223] Information sheet G083v05, 12/2014, 3.

('AUSFTA').[224] If the Australian courts adopt the same approach, a parody (or 'target parody'[225]) comments on the underlying work, whereas satire (or 'weapon parody'[226]) refers to the underlying work to comment on anything other than that work.[227] As we have just seen, post-*Campbell* US courts have tended to attempt to categorize *all* transformative works as either parody or satire which has resulted in an arguably unnatural extension of the term satire so that it captures 'worthy' transformative uses which cannot fit within the restricted parody category.[228]

During the consultation process, lobbyists for right-holders championed the US definitions to support their position that the meaning of the terms (and hence the scope of the exception) should be narrow. The introduction of an exception which listed parody and satire separately is seen by some as a position statement rejecting this US jurisprudential distinction between satire and parody.[229] At the time of enactment in 2006, its choice of wording for a 'parody' exception was unique.[230] While it is likely that the same arguments will be advanced again by right-holders before the courts during any litigation concerning unauthorized parodies,[231] it would seem counterproductive for Australian courts to adopt the US definitions for the following reasons.

The US definitions might lead to a confusing and unnecessarily complex situation in which works which would be termed as 'parody' according to the ordinary meaning of the word would be legally defined as 'satire'. A hypothetical example of this is The Ashes Tour songs of the Australian cricket supporters' club called The Fanatics.[232] These songs adapt the words of well-known songs to reflect the fans' support of their team. While ordinary Australians would consider these to be clear examples of parody, a US-style approach by Australian courts would see such uses as satire, simply because the target of the songs is cricket, and not the underlying copyright-protected work. While the characterization as 'parody' or 'satire' might not impact on the outcome of any legal determination, adopting legal definitions which are unnecessarily distinct from the ordinary meaning of the term seems more likely to be detrimental to, rather than benefit, the efficient operation of the exception.

A second school of thought argues that the Australian courts should adopt the definitions provided by relevant theorists. For example, in *TCN Channel Nine v. Network*

[224] Amended Explanatory Memorandum and Commonwealth of Australia, Parliamentary Debates, Senate, 30 November 2006 where the Minister of Justice mentions that those definitions might be relevant.

[225] 'Parody of' in the EU understanding of parody. *Campbell* (n 199) [580].

[226] 'Parody with' in the EU jargon. [227] *Campbell* (n 199) [581].

[228] This is to ensure that these works benefit from a 'fair use' defence to an infringement claim, e.g. *Suntrust* (n 204) [1268]; *Seuss I* (n 210) [1400].

[229] C Condren, J Milner Davis, S McCausland, and R A Phiddian, 'Defining parody and satire: Australian copyright law and its new exception (Part 1)' (2008) 13(3) *MALR* 273, 279; J McCutcheon, 'The new defense of parody or satire under Australian copyright law' (2008) 2 *IPQ* 163, 178.

[230] In 2012, Canada adopted the same wording. See section 5.5; Condren et al (n 229) 278.

[231] Amongst others, submissions to Commonwealth of Australia, Attorney-General's Department, *Issues Paper, Fair Use and Other Copyright Exceptions in the Digital Age* (May 2005) (Fair Use Inquiry) by the Copyright Agency Limited; Copyright Council (supported by Media Entertainment and Arts Alliance, Viscopy and the National Association for the Visual Arts), available at http://www.copyright.org.au/acc_prod/AsiCommon/Controls/BSA/Downloader.aspx?iDocumentStorageKey=7dbe6c97-6a51-410c-b0d2-462205d03531&iFileTypeCode=PDF&iFileName=Attorney-General%27s%20Department%20%E2%80%9CFair%20Use%20and%20Other%20Copyright%20Exceptions:%20An%20examination%20of%20fair%20use (access date: 22 May 2018).

[232] Examples of songs can be found at http://www.thefanatics.com/web_blog.view.php?web_blog_ID=24 (access date: 22 May 2018).

Ten,[233] a case which arose prior to the introduction of a specific exception, Conti J.'s definition of parody relied upon the scholarship of Rose. The facts in the case are very straightforward. The defendant used a number of short extracts from a Channel Nine television programme in its own light-hearted topical review show, *The Panel*. Network Ten ran two arguments in its defence. Firstly, it argued that extracts, averaging only forty seconds in length, could hardly constitute a 'substantial' copy. In the alternative, they argued that the use was permitted fair dealing, either for news reporting or for criticism/review. At first instance, Conti J. upheld Network Ten's main defence, considering that Channel Nine had failed to demonstrate that any substantial part of their work had been reproduced. The trial judge also considered the alternative defence. In his reasoning, Conti J. found it useful to draw a distinction between parody and satire: parody, in his view, requires imitation, and thus copying of earlier works whereas satire's aim is to pass comment on something, and does not necessarily require borrowing from an earlier work, although immediate recognition of the material is required. Accordingly, Conti J. concluded that reproducing short extracts for the purpose of satire, comedy, or light entertainment could be considered as legitimate.[234] Parodic use, however, which required copying of an earlier work, either requires permission, or it must fall within one of the categories of uses covered by the fair dealing defences, which then were concerned with uses such as for the purposes of criticism, review, or news reporting.[235]

Therefore, it is possible that Australian courts may consult the works of other theorists, outlined previously in section 3. As it has been demonstrated that the theorists are unable to reach any consensus between themselves, the scope of the terms would hinge upon which theorists are consulted, and varying outcomes may result for the same types of parodies.[236]

A third approach prefers the working definitions built by legal scholars who have engaged in evaluating the meaning of parody and satire within a copyright context. Based upon the ordinary meaning of the terms, the definitions established by Condren et al appear the most thorough to date.

These scholars label 'parody' as:

> [T]he borrowing from, imitation, or appropriation of a text, or other cultural product or practice, for the purpose of commenting, usually humorously, upon either it or something else;

while 'satire' is:

> [T]he critical impulse manifesting itself in some degree of denigration, almost invariably through attempted humour; the artistic results (usually humorous) of expression of such a critical impulse. [237]

In contrast, Jewell and Louise's conception of parody focuses less upon humour, defining it as 'the imitation of an artistic work or artist's style, sometimes for the sake

233 [2001] FCA 108 (trial) (hereafter *TCN*). 234 Ibid, [46].

235 ss 41–42 Australian Copyright Act 1968 ('CA 1968').

236 This seems to be the approach favoured in *Pokemon Company International, Inc. v. Redbubble Ltd* [2017] FCA 1541, where Pagone J. referred explicitly to the definitions noted in *TCN* before holding that there is likely to be an overlap between the purpose of the exception and the assessment of fairness. In doing so, the Australian court followed a similar path to the Canadian Supreme Court in *CCH* and collapsed the first step of the fair dealing assessment (defining the purpose of the use) with the first fairness factor. For more, see Chapters 2, 3, and 4.

237 C Condren, J Milner Davis, S McCausland, and R A Phiddian, 'Defining parody and satire: Australian copyright law and its new exception (Part 2)' (2008) 13 *MALR* 401, 402.

of ridicule, or perhaps as a vehicle to make a criticism or comment'.[238] It remains to be seen whether Australian courts will determine that parodies and satires require any humorous element, or whether a broader definition will be adopted.[239]

Finally, the approach which has gained most support[240] is the form of statutory interpretation[241] which consults dictionaries to derive the ordinary meaning of statutory terms.[242] Traditionally, Australian courts refer to the *Macquarie Dictionary*. This includes the following definitions:

Parody:

1. A humorous or satirical imitation of a serious piece of literature or writing.
2. The kind of literary composition represented by such imitations.
3. A burlesque imitation of a musical composition.
4. A poor imitation; a travesty.

Satire:

1. The use of irony, sarcasm, ridicule, etc., in exposing, denouncing, or deriding vice, folly, etc.
2. A literary composition, in verse or prose, in which vices, abuses, follies, etc., are held up to scorn, derision, or ridicule.
3. The species of literature constituted by such composition.

A common criticism of this approach to interpretation is that dictionary definitions can lag behind their contemporary usage.[243] Although when the practice was first adopted by courts, dictionary definitions aimed to be largely prospective, now dictionaries tend to adopt a more historical approach which captures all past usages of a term.[244] Indeed it was the recognition of the limitations of these dictionary definitions which actually motivated Conti J. to look to Rose's research instead.

Additionally, it seems legitimate to question the relevance of (historical) dictionary definitions to the purpose and objectives of a particular legislative provision.[245] Given that a legislator would aim for legislation to cover future evolution, any definition set too much in the past could be detrimental to the proper application of the parody exception. For example, although the Australian legislature was looking ahead to future uses of works in the digital age, the dictionary definitions have remained unchanged since 1981, a time when the internet barely existed,[246] and they can be traced back to

238 Jewell and Louise (n 87) 2.

239 Yet, as the definitions proposed also refer to a particular previous work, I wish to make a reservation that the court will understand these as allowing parodies or satires that result from the combination of different previous work without any further creation such as in mash-up works.

240 Fair dealing decisions prior to the parody exception already had recourse to the use of dictionaries to define the purpose of the exception. *Stevens v. Kabushiki Kaisha Sony Computer entertainment* [2005] HCA 58; *TCN* (n 233); *De Garis v. Neville Jeffresse Pidler* (1990) 37 FCR 99; *AGL Sydney Ltd v. Shortland County Council* (1989) 17 IPR 99, [105].

241 The Interpretation Act from 1901, applicable in the Commonwealth.

242 Ibid, ss 15AA and 15AB.

243 Which might explain why Australia is considering a move from the fair dealing to the fair use style of copyright exceptions, see Chapter 2.

244 See preface to the third edition of the *Oxford English Dictionary* available at http://public.oed.com/the-oed-today/preface-to-the-third-edition-of-the-oed/ (access date: 22 May 2018); Condren (n 229) 286.

245 This criticism can be broadened to other countries. While resorting to dictionaries is an obvious starting point, the over-reliance of judges upon dictionaries impairs the efficiency of the law.

246 The revolutionary impact of this technology is associated with the mid-nineties and was recognized as representing 99% of telecommunicated information in 2007. M Hilbert and P López, 'The

the definitions adopted by the *Oxford English Dictionary* in 1884, made available in a complete edition in 1933.[247]

Given the advent of new technologies and the substantial changes that occurred in media and the arts, including the advent of television, film, radio, and the internet, it would seem that definitions dating from 1884 may be of dubious value for judges needing to interpret whether a new form of critique arising in our digital age is a satire or parody. However, these definitions can constitute a valuable starting point.

While it is possible to find shortcomings with each of the approaches described here, it is apparent they are in agreement that parody requires a combination of imitation and creation.[248] The need for a humorous character is also present, but is less prominent than we have seen in the definitions adopted in the EU countries. Finally, there is no debate in Australia that the concept of parody extends to works which either comment upon the underlying work, or where the underlying work is used as a vehicle to comment upon something else.

This broad understanding is welcome, since any particular use can sit uneasily within a rigid framework of legal categories.[249] It seems to be rare that this type of work is either a parody or a satire in a strict sense. More often, works comprise both, and might be known colloquially as a 'satirical parody' or a 'parodic satire'. Television and radio provide good examples, including satirical news programmes, such as *The Daily Show* (presented by Stewart and Noah),[250] radio programmes, such as *The Blow Parade* (presented by Taylor and Hansen),[251] and in Hip Hop music, where songs such as Nas' *I Can* (which borrows from *Für Elise* as well as older works, including Sterne's book *Tristram Shandy*[252]).

5.5 Canada

Canada is no exception to the approach of the other countries mentioned, since Canadian copyright legislation does not define parody and satire either.[253] Given the current absence of established case law interpreting the exception, insight will be derived from judicial attempts to define parody prior to the introduction of a specific parody exception under the Copyright Act 1985 as well as from the first parody decision in *United Airlines, Inc. v. Jeremy Cooperstock*[254] since its introduction.

Firstly, to date, Canadian courts have rejected the definitions used in the US.[255] The *Michelin* case in 1996[256] considered a trade union parody of the Bibendum man logo in

world's technological capacity to store, communicate, and compute information' (2011) 332(6025) *Science (journal)* 60, available at http://www.martinhilbert.net/WorldInfoCapacity.html (access date: 10 November 2018).

[247] The difference being that the *Oxford English Dictionary* realized the limitation of these old definitions and redrafted them in 2005 to reflect a more recent meaning of parody.

[248] Adopting a wide definition of parody encompassing other genres.

[249] This is confirmed in *Pokemon Company International, Inc. v. Redbubble Ltd* (n 236).

[250] News satire including both parodies and satires. http://thedailyshow.cc.com/ (access date: 22 May 2018).

[251] https://www.wikivividly.com/wiki/The_Blow_Parade (access date: 23 November 2018).

[252] https://www.youtube.com/watch?v=RvVfgvHucRY (access date: 22 May 2018).

[253] Section 29 Copyright Act (1985); Commerce and Economic Development Bureau, *Bills Committee on the Copyright (Amendment) Bill 2011—Copyright Exception for Parody* (Intellectual Property Department, 2011) 1.

[254] (2017) FC 616 (hereafter *United Airlines*).

[255] Confirmed in *United Airlines* [108] and [116].

[256] *Compagnie Générale des Établissements Michelin-Michelin & Cie v. National Automobile, Aerospace, Transportation and General Workers Union of Canada* (1996) 71 C.P.R. (3d) 348 (hereafter *Michelin*).

which a leaflet depicted the well-known character crushing a Michelin worker. Although the Federal Court considered the US definitions established in *Campbell*,[257] it saw no reason to adopt either the definitions or a fair use defence from another legal regime, based upon different jurisprudence,[258] not least because Canada does not have any long tradition of accepting fair use for the purposes of parody.[259] Thus, the Canadian court preferred to adopt the ordinary meaning of the terms, and consulted the *Collins Dictionary of the English Language*.[260] This defined parody as 'a musical, literary or other composition that mimics the style of another composer, author, etc. in a humorous or satirical way'.

Secondly, in *Favreau*,[261] a case concerning a pornographic parody of the TV situation comedy show, *La Petite Vie*, the Court of Appeal constructed its own definition of parody, as: 'normally [involving] the humorous imitation of the work of another writer, often exaggerated, for purposes of criticism or comment'.[262] Yet, there seems to be no reason to cling to this particular definition for the purpose of the new exception, as its limited scope seems to reflect the fact that the court was only concerned with defining the term to suit the facts of that particular case. While the definition acknowledges that not all parodies are humorous, it seems to be restricted to works of literature and target parodies, in which the parodist's message is to comment upon the underlying work.

With the introduction of new law which specifically refers to 'parody and satire', it appears reasonable to assume that courts will seek to identify the ordinary meaning of the terms, to construct their definition, which may be different in scope from the definitions adopted in the cases prior the introduction of the new exception. This view is based upon Canadian principles of legal interpretation, including section 12 of the Canadian Interpretation Act.[263] The latter states that the law must be interpreted in a manner which ensures its objectives. One of the accepted principles of interpretation is the literal approach, which assumes that legislation adopts the ordinary meaning of words, unless a specific definition is provided.[264] As this is the case for parody and satire, we can presume that ordinary definitions will have to be considered.

Moreover, since 2004 in *CCH*[265] (and confirmed in 2012[266]), the Canadian Supreme Court has initiated a radical shift in the interpretation of copyright fair dealing

257 *Campbell* (n 199).

258 Several differences distinguish the US and Canada. First, the US has a fair use system. It is an open-ended list of exceptions which is not exhaustive. While in Canada, as the system is a fair dealing exception, the list in section 29 CA 1985 is exhaustive, requiring a change of legislation to amend it. Moreover, the fair use factors do not equate to the fair dealing factors as, for example, the US does not require mention of the source and the author for the fair use for the purpose of criticism while it is required under Canadian legislation.

259 *Michelin* (n 256) [61]–[67].

260 2nd edn, Collins (1986).

261 Teitelbaum J. Some indulgence can be found in *Productions Avanti Ciné-Vidéo Inc. v. Favreau*. The case dealt with the creation of a pornographic film called *La Petite Vie* relying on a well-known television series. The judge did not reject the parody exceptions as a copyright defence. Nevertheless, as in this particular case the defendant was trying to ride on the popularity of the earlier work rather than making a parody, the judge did not accept the defence: (1999) 177 D.L.R. (4th) 129, leave to appeal to S.C.C. refused, 27527 (25 May 2000) [574]–[575].

262 The court did have recourse to definitions established by scholars but eventually set them aside.

263 Section 12 of the Canada Interpretation Act 1985 is analogous to section 15AA of the Australian Act Interpretation Act.

264 L Lauzière, *L'interprétation des lois* (2012) 17, available at https://www.redactionjuridique.chaire.ulaval.ca/sites/redactionjuridique.chaire.ulaval.ca/files/lauziere-interpretation_des_lois_2012.pdf (access date 1 June 2018).

265 *CCH Canadian Ltd v. Law Society of Upper Canada* [2004] 1 S.C.R. 339 (hereafter *CCH*).

266 *Entertainment Software Association of Canada v. SOCAN* [2012] S.C.C. 34 (hereafter *SOCAN*).

provisions, which requires that these are given a broad interpretation of its purpose,[267] in recognition of the status of users' rights.[268] Although it remains to be seen how this principle of interpretation will impact on the understanding of 'parody and satire' by Canadian courts, it is reasonable to suggest that the terms should enjoy a 'large and liberal interpretation in order to ensure that users' rights are not unduly constrained'.[269]

The Canadian Federal Court has paved the way in *United Airlines* by endorsing the EU parody requirements as established in *Deckmyn.* According to the court, these two main requirements of humorous intent and absence of confusion adequately reflect the ordinary meaning of the terms.[270] By doing so, the court equally did not find it relevant to distinguish the terms parody and satire any further and confirmed that the comment can be directed at something external to the elements reproduced.[271]

6. Conclusion

Following the introduction of a specific parody exception in copyright legislation, there are some differences between the type of uses which can benefit from the exception in the US, Australia, Canada, and the European Union. Indeed, despite the inherently speculative nature of this enquiry, since courts in the UK have yet to have the opportunity to interpret the new exception, it is possible to draw the following observations.

The historical overview demonstrates that parody (understood as a single concept) is a form of criticism which is dependent upon the context in which it evolves. In order to respect this influence of the context, culture, art field, time, and space, any legal definition of parody must be sufficiently fluid and flexible for courts to be able to adapt as habits change. Without exception, legislators have elected to leave the particular meaning for the parody exception undefined.

In the US, this has led to the desire to limit the reach of the exception to uses which directly comment upon the work it borrows from (though the distinction is slowly fading). In doing so, the US system is characterized by an unnatural distinction between parody and satire. To avoid this fictional parody/satire dichotomy, the Australian and Canadian legislators expressly framed their copyright exception to include satire. Consequently, courts should allow the application of the parody exception to both uses which comment directly on the work they borrow from and uses which comment on a third subject, using the copyright-protected work as a vehicle for their expression.

The European approach is equally flexible. The terms used in the law indicate that uses of caricature, parody, or pastiche should be exempted from copyright infringement provided that the conditions for the exception's application are satisfied. Consequently, the CJEU's *Deckmyn* decision is welcomed, and it may resonate in Australia and Canada. By refusing to distinguish between the terms 'pastiche, parody, and caricature', it has been argued here that the Court established that all three types belong to the same genre. As such, to qualify as a parody under the exception, a work within the EU must display a humorous character, and must be recognizably different from the underlying work to avoid confusion with it, generally achieved through comment. As copyright cases are often concerned with where the line should be drawn between ideas and protectable expressions of ideas, a broad understanding of parody

[267] *CCH* (n 265) [48]. [268] See Chapter 3, section 2. [269] *CCH* (n 265) [51].
[270] *United Airlines* (n 254) [119].
[271] S Jacques, 'First application of the Canadian parody exception' (2017) 12(11) *JIPLP* 895.

should afford courts leeway to determine whether a use is a parody, or not, without the need to resort to fictitious definitions which confine what a parody is, as in the US since the *Campbell* case.[272]

The main difference between the various domestic definitions of parody concerns the appraisal of humour. While the CJEU interpretation requires humour as an essential element of parody, it is arguable that in Australia and Canada, equal weight is given to humorous and critical expressions. Does this mean that critical expressions may be judged a parody in Australia, but not within the EU? This is unlikely. Although copyright exceptions are interpreted strictly,[273] the CJEU indicates in *Deckmyn* that interpretation should not be so strict as to defeat the purpose of the exception.[274] By making plain that 'humour' includes mockery,[275] it seems that the term should be interpreted broadly enough to respect all different kinds of humour including acerbic and harsh criticism as long as these expressions are not intentionally harmful.[276] This is also supported by human rights considerations[277] as the parody exception is heavily anchored by recognition of the right to freedom of expression. In this arena, courts have already acknowledged that satire, and other less comic expressions, provide a valuable starting point for reflection and discussion in our society.[278] Therefore, EU and national courts within the EU may refer to decisions in cases concerning human rights violations to support a definition of humour which extends to non-comical expressions of criticism and comment.[279]

[272] Note that, post-*Campbell*, US courts only apply the parody exception to 'parody of' (target parodies) not 'parody with' (weapon parodies); *Campbell* (n 199).

[273] Except for Canada with the users' rights doctrine allowing for a broad interpretation of fair dealing. See Chapter 3, section 2.2.2.

[274] *Deckmyn* (n 2) [19] and [23].

[275] *Deckmyn* (n 2) [20].

[276] See Chapter 4, section 2.1.

[277] See Chapter 5, section 4.

[278] Ibid.

[279] See Chapter 7, sections 2 and 3.

2

Legality of the Parody Exception in Light of International Treaties and Domestic Copyright Laws

1. Introduction

A parody exception may only be introduced into national copyright law if it satisfies the three-step test enshrined in international treaties. This test, used to delineate the scope of copyright exceptions and limitations, ensures that national legislators do not render the reproduction right, recognized in the Berne Convenion, meaningless.[1] This chapter evaluates whether the parody exception, as crafted in each jurisdiction under scrutiny, passes this yardstick.

To evaluate whether the parody exception meets the three-step test, we first need to appreciate the context leading to the introduction of specific exceptions under copyright law in the first place. The underlying objective determines the exception's scope, i.e. the encroachment upon right-holders' exclusive rights which must be tolerated. This is relevant for the assessment of the three-step test.

2. Why is a Specific Parody Exception Needed in Copyright Legislation?

In this section, we consider whether copyright law requires a specific parody exception. This is best understood by briefly revisiting the history and evolution of copyright law leading up to the adoption of the three-step test by Berne signatory parties.

2.1 The birth of the copyright system

Historically, the development of creative endeavours and technologies have always been interlinked. Gutenberg's invention of mechanical printing and the propagation

[1] Note that there is no agreement whether 'exceptions' and 'limitations' are separate notions. While the WT/160/DS panel report distinguishes the terms, the literature tends to use the terms interchangeably. The TRIPS Agreement, WIPO Treaties, and the InfoSoc Directive have both terms next to each other without definition. The recitals of the Directive reinforce the interchangeability of the terms. It is argued that this is likely to be the result of a compromise between the different legal traditions. This book treats the terms synonymously to refer to specific defences, which prevent right-holders from exercising their exclusive rights in certain circumstances, i.e. leaving aside the idea/expression dichotomy, the originality requirement, the term of protection, and the first sale doctrine. B Galopin, *Les exceptions à usage public en droit d'auteur* (IRPI, 2012) 8; A Kur, *Of Oceans, Islands, and Inland Water—How Much Room for Exceptions and Limitations under the Three Step-Test?* (2008) Max Planck Institute for Intellectual Property, Competition & Tax Law Research Paper Series No. 08-04, 1–48; V Benabou and S Dussollier, 'Draw me a public domain' in P Torremans (ed.), *Copyright Law A Handbook of Contemporary Research* (Edward Elgar, 2007) 426; P El Khoury, *Les exceptions au droit d'auteur* (thèse Montpellier, 2007) 25.

of the Renaissance is a well-known illustration of this relationship. While Cavalli criticizes the overreliance on the mechanical press as a triggering event for the birth of copyright law,[2] it is very hard to deny that it was this very event which led to a collective awareness of the need for a legislative response.[3]

It was the invention of the printing press which led to the growth of the printing industry and the popularity of books. As a result, the British Monarchy assumed the right to grant royal printing privileges in return for payment to control the lawful printing of books. This practice not only enriched the Crown coffers, but created a legal instrument of control to censor which works were printed. Over time, the Crown delegated its authority by charter to The Stationers' Company,[4] a collective association for printers, and enacted law which required all printed works to be registered with this association.[5]

A turning point occurred when the charter of The Stationers' Company was not renewed. It was replaced by the Statute of Anne enacted by the UK Parliament in 1709.[6] This Act sought to end the grant of royal privileges and censorship, by vesting the exclusive right to print books in their authors for a limited period of time.[7] This first 'copyright' law[8] was the result of social, political, and economic considerations,[9] based upon newly emergent utilitarian principles.[10] Esssentially, it is in the public interest to encourage authors to disseminate their published works widely, and engage in new creative endeavours. Allocating private rights to control, and be remunerated for, commercial exploitation of works acknowledges the financial investment needed to create and publish new works. This stimulates further creativity,[11] simultaneously furthering social-based aspirations.

Similar printing privileges existed in mainland Europe.[12] These were abolished following the French Revolution, and replaced by what are termed 'authors' rights'.

[2] J Cavalli, *La Genèse de la Convention de Berne pour la protection des œuvres littéraires et artistiques du 9 Septembre 1886* (Lausanne, 1986) 13.

[3] On the history of copyright: J Hofman, *Introducing Copyright: A Plain Language Guide to Copyright in the 21st Century* (Commonwealth of Learning, 2009); R Deazley, *Rethinking Copyright* (Edward Elgar, 2006); P Goldstein, *Copyright's Highway: From Gutenberg to the Celestial Jukebox* (Stanford Law and Politics, 2003); G Davies, *Copyright and the Public Interest* (Thomson, 1994) 19–23; L R Patterson, *Copyright in Historical Perspective* (Vanderbilt University Press, 1968) 3–179.

[4] M Leaffer, *Understanding Copyright Law* (Matthew Bender, 1989) 2–5.

[5] W Copinger and J F Skone James, *On Copyright* (16th edn, Sweet & Maxwell, 2010) chapter 2.

[6] Statute of Anne 1709. This was not a clear break as described by L Bently, 'Introduction to Part I: the history of copyright' in L Bently, U Suthersanen, and P L C Torremans (eds), *Global Copyright: Three Hundred Years Since the Statute of Anne, from 1709 to Cyberspace* (Edward Edgar, 2010) 11.

[7] It is noteworthy to repeat that the Statute of Anne is not only the first copyright law but it had considerable influence on common law systems around the world such as the US, Canada, and Australia.

[8] Caution must be exercised when using the statement 'first copyright law'. The Statute of Anne is a milestone for British copyright and copyright in other countries but this does not mean it was the first one in the world. Bently (n 6) 7; S Vaidhyanathan, *Copyrights and Copywrongs: The Rise of Intellectual Property and How it Threatens Creativity* (New York University Press, 2001) 40.

[9] W Cornish, 'The Statute of Anne 1709: its historical setting' in Bently, Suthersanen, and Torremans (eds), *Global Copyright* 21.

[10] See section 2.2.

[11] This approach reflects Adam Smith's theories, i.e. exclusive rights granted through copyright to right-holders are necessary to circumvent market failure resulting from free-riders. Additionally, these private transactions within the market not only serve the needs of those individuals, but further society's goals too. For more: P Gaudrat, 'Les démêlés intemporels d'un couple à succès: le créateur et l'investisseur' (2001) 190 *RIDA* 70, 71; A Smith, *An Inquiry into the Nature and Causes of the Wealth of Nations* (5th edn, Methuen & Co., 1904).

[12] G Petri, 'Transition from guild regulation to modern copyright law (Sweden)' in Bently, Suthersanen, and Torremans (eds), *Global Copyright* 111; C Geiger, 'The influence (past and present)

Authors' rights are anchored primarily in natural law considerations, rather than being premised upon economic or utiliarian considerations. Pursuant to natural law principles,[13] positive law merely recognizes the natural rights an author has to control the uses of their work. Authors' rights enjoy a special status as inviolable and sacred because they derive from the unique bond connecting an author to their work, which is seen as representing a materialization of their own personality.[14]

The Statute of Anne's influence is perceptible in the US as well as in Australia and Canada. It is said that colonies already had their own variations of copyright legislations before the adoption of the well-known article I, section 8, clause 8 of the US Constitution in 1787.[15] While the scope of protection intended by the Founders of the Constitution remains speculative,[16] it is very clear that the protection sought had to be achieved through granting *economic rights* for a *limited period* of time to the *author*. Against this backdrop, the US adopted its first copyright legislation in 1790[17] modelled on the Statute of Anne.[18] From this point onward, US copyright legislation has undergone several major revisions until today, especially to comply with international treaties.[19]

A full history of copyright law is more complex than that of mechanical printing (and would require an interdisciplinary analysis incorporating legal theory, economics, philosophy, etc.), and the utilitarian/natural law dichotomy described has never been hermetic.[20] There are signs of purely economic considerations in authors' rights, just as there is clear evidence of the natural law within the common law.[21] Nevertheless, it can be appreciated that there are reasonable arguments which support the creation of exclusive rights for authors, based upon the underlying aim to promote public welfare using private market incentives to achieve that goal. By granting quasi-property[22] rights for intangible cultural goods, the law recognizes the importance of informational and cultural works which would be produced at sub-optimal levels without this specific legal regime. While it is clear that a paradigm which permits monopolies for

of the Statute of Anne in France' in Bently, Suthersanen, and Torremans (eds), *Global Copyright* 124; Cavalli (n 2) 14–16, 19.

[13] This is based on John Locke's theory that as an individual owns himself, a person is also the owner of his own work, which is a materialization of himself. This notion of property is philosophical, not legal, with the result that a person only has an exclusive right on their work, and not an absolute monopoly. See further S Dusollier, *Droit d'auteur et protection des oeuvres dans l'univers numérique* (Larcier, 2007) 219; J Locke, *Second Treatise of Civil Government* (1690) available at http://www.constitution.org/jl/2ndtreat.htm chapter 5, s 27.

[14] H Desbois, *Le droit d'auteur en France* (3rd edn, Dalloz, 1978) 538.

[15] M Leaffer, *Understanding Copyright Law* (Matthew Bender, 1989) 4.

[16] Probably the best illustration of this is the framer's reluctance to refer to copyright to focus on the promotion the progress of the useful art. Ibid.

[17] Act of May 31, 1790, Ch. 15, 1 Stat. 124.

[18] G J Yonover, 'Artistic parody: the precarious balance: moral rights, parody, and fair use' (1996) 14 *Cardozo Arts & Ent. L.J.* 79, 91.

[19] Most notably the adoption of the 1909 Act overhauling the US copyright paradigm (17 U.S.C.). Yet, this revision did not enable the US legislation to meet the minimum standards set out in the Berne Union. The US entry occurred later with the Berne Convention Implementation Act 1988. Pub. L. No. 100–568 (1988).

[20] Supporting this, see Mark Schultz's contribution at the Symposium on *Authors, Attribution and Integrity* organized by George Mason University (18 April 2016). The transcript was published as part of the summer issue in 8(1) *Journal of International Commercial Law* 1, 11.

[21] Dusollier notes that the editors referred to John Locke's theories to support their position at the time of the adoption of the Statute of Anne. Dusollier (n 13) 217.

[22] Non-rivalrous and non-excludable.

certain works of authorship interferes with free market ideals, this legal fiction is considered necessary to enable investment in creative labour to be recouped.

Modern copyright laws across the globe have now embraced this basic rationale by conferring a limited monopoly for cultural works.[23] The regimes incorporate a trade-off, by providing levels of protection which are, supposedly, an adequate incentive for creators to produce cultural goods whilst simultaneously limiting the monopoly using other legal doctrines, such as the idea/expression dichotomy, the originality requirement, copyright exceptions, and duration.

2.2 The impact of different political philosophies on shaping the copyright system

As outlined already, common law and civil law conceptions of copyright law are underpinned by different philosophical foundations. Copyright law in common law countries (UK, US, Australia, and Canada) traditionally relies upon utilitarian justifications,[24] granting exclusive rights to those who invest in creating and disseminating creative works because society at large benefits from having access to such works. In contrast, copyright laws in civil law countries (e.g. France) are founded upon natural law principles, which focus more on the unique relationship between the author and their work.[25] These differing philosophical foundations are also evident in the approach adopted in respect of copyright exceptions.

Accordingly, the common law approach is to construct a copyright system which grants exclusive rights which are as limited as possible, because these rights are merely instrumental in achieving the desired societal benefit. From this perspective, copyright exceptions provide a 'breathing space' to foster third-party uses of a protected work which are likely to afford *more* benefit to society than would be obtained by permitting right-holders to retain control.

This is generally realized through the adoption of exceptions for 'fair dealing' or 'fair use'.[26] The former, evident in UK, Australian, and Canadian copyright law, seeks to exclude certain unauthorized, but socially beneficial, uses of a protected work from infringement, provided that the use is objectively fair.[27] The latter, enshrined in US

[23] Monopoly here is understood as the fact that copyright protection inherently comprises a deadweight loss, given that the right-holder's enforcement of exclusive rights allows them to set the price for works at a level higher than the marginal cost of a copy. This leads to a situation where potential customers, valuing the work above its marginal cost but less than its monopoly price, will not buy the work, leading to the deadweight loss. In a way, by trying to remedy a particular type of market failure, copyright legislation can lead to another type of market failure by creating monopolies. For more, see N Elkin-Koren, 'Copyright policy and the limits of freedom of contract' (1997) 12 *Berkeley Tech. L.J.* 93, 99.

[24] On the utilitarian approach, see M Senftleben, *Copyright, Limitations and the Three-Step Test: An Analysis of the Three-Step Test in International and EC Copyright Law* (Kluwer, 2004) 12; L Guibault, *Copyright and Contracts: An Analysis of the Contractual Overridability of Limitations on Copyright* (Kluwer, 2002) 10.

[25] This follows Locke's theory where resources are free and abundant in the world (just like ideas) and if a person combines the resources with his personal efforts (his creativity), the result is something that he owns property in (copyright is a property right). The protection is acquired by the sole creation of the work and the law simply recognizes the property right in the work.

[26] It is important to note that not all copyright exceptions take the form of fair use or fair dealing. See, amongst others. ss 28A, 28B, 29A, 31, 31A, 31B, 31BA, 31BB, and 33 CDPA 1988.

[27] Galopin (n 1) 160; Kur (n 1) 9; C Geiger, *Droit d'auteur et droit du public à l'information* (IRPI, 2004) 246; A Lepage, 'Vue générale sur les exceptions et les limitations au droit d'auteur dans l'environnement numérique' (2003) *January–March e.Bulletin du droit d'auteur* 1, 3; Guibault (n 24) 15; A Lucas, *Droit d'auteur et numérique* (Litec, 1998) 173.

copyright law, seeks the same result but does not specify particular types of unauthorized use. Instead, case law has established the relevant factors which determine whether a certain use is deserving.[28] Consequently, the US 'fair use' approach prompts a plethora of judicial decisions to test its boundaries.

In contrast, as civilian copyright laws focus on the relationship between the author and their work,[29] exclusive rights are granted to protect the author's interests. In other words, the presumption is that the author should retain control over whether and how their own works are exploited for financial benefit (irrespective of whether an alternative scheme of ownership would further the interests of society better). Historically, copyright law as per the civil law tradition included few exceptions and required[30] these to be interpreted strictly to promote legal certainty.[31]

Hence, the typical picture presented that the author's interests prevail over the public interest in civil law countries, whereas the common law jurisdictions offset the author's interests more in favour of the public interest.[32] Yet, this image is an oversimplification.[33] Indeed, the public interest concerns underpin *all* copyright laws[34] irrespective of the underlying legal tradition. These are present in both utilitarian and natural law-based philosophies.[35]

Additionally, distinctions between common law and civil law jurisdictions have been eroded further by the adoption of international treaties and agreements which span across legal traditions.[36] Numerous amendments made to copyright laws at international and regional level have gone beyond what is needed simply to respond to technological changes.[37] As discussed further in what follows, these legislative changes have resulted in an expansion of works covered by copyright law's protection, extension to the term of protection, and an increase in the activities falling within the copyright owner's exclusive rights.[38]

All this has culminated in an increasing call for more copyright exceptions to preserve, or reinstate, the public interest[39] in light of copyright's expanded realm of exclusive rights.[40] Although copyright law grants these exclusive rights for a

[28] 17 US Code §§ 107–119 (fair use at § 107). [29] See n 25.

[30] Arguably, this is still the case: Chapter 3, section 1.

[31] C Caron, 'Les exceptions au regard du fondement du droit d'auteur en droit français' in A Lucas, P Sirinelli, and A Bensamoun, (eds), *Les exceptions au droit d'auteur: état des lieux et perspectives dans l'Union européenne* (Dalloz, 2012) 24; Galopin (n 1) 160; Dusollier (n 13) 215; Geiger (n 27) 224; Senftleben (n 24) 22; Guibault (n 24) 15; Lucas (n 27) 171–3.

[32] At least initially. We will see that the evolution of the law has perhaps disrupted this balance. See Chapters 3 and 4.

[33] Dusollier (n 13) 448.

[34] D J Gervais, 'Making copyright whole: a principled approach to copyright exceptions and limitations' (2008) *UOLTJ* 1, 5; C Geiger, J Griffiths and R M Hilty, 'Declaration on a balanced interpretation of the "three-step test" in copyright law' (2008) 39(6) *IIC* 707, 708; Geiger (n 27) 226.

[35] Senftleben (n 24) 7–10; Guibault (n 24) 8; G Davies, 'The convergence of copyright and authors' rights—reality or chimera?' (1995) 26(6) *IIC* 964–89. Yet, Geiger notes a drawback of natural law considerations: C Geiger, 'The constitutional dimension of intellectual property' in P L C Torremans (eds), *Intellectual Property and Human Rights* (3rd edn, Kluwer, 2008) 123.

[36] B Sherman and L Bently, *The Making of Modern IP Law* (Cambridge University Press, 1999).

[37] Vaidhyanathan (n 8); A Strowel, *Droit d'auteur et copyright: divergences et convergences* (Bruylant and L.G.D.J., 1993) 149.

[38] The scope of copyright therefore goes beyond the realm of commercial exploitation even in cases where copyright enforcement may not be possible or is undesirable as these conflict with fundamental values or result in high transaction costs.

[39] As recalled by Numa Droz at the first diplomatic conference at Berne. Actes 1884, 67 (closing speech to the 1884 conference).

[40] Caron (n 31) 21; S Ricketson, SCCR/9/7: WIPO Study on Limitations and Exceptions of Copyright and Related Rights in the Digital Environment (related) (2003) WIPO Study Committee on Copyright and Related Rights 1, 3; Lepage (n 27) 32; D J Gervais, 'Towards a new core international

time-limited period, these exceptions recognize that there are legitimate circumstances in which right-holders should be precluded from enforcing their rights, even though the legal protection remains in force.[41] Generally, copyright exceptions are motivated by the social, cultural, and economic needs of a particular jurisdiction,[42] such as to foster cultural diversity and new creative endeavours in the national public interest.[43] Exceptions also assist in defining the scope of exclusive rights with greater precision.

2.3 Reinstating legitimacy in the copyright paradigm through a specific parody exception

Changing times and the developing technologies, then, have led to multiple revisions of the copyright system. The last fifty years have seen a strengthening of the exclusive rights of right-holders, shifting the balance in favour of protecting industry interests at the expense of future authors.[44]

In this context, the parody exception is a legal mechanism introduced to strike a fairer balance: right-holders *should* receive a sufficent scope of protection to recoup their investment in creating new original works, but this should not be so comprehensive as to preclude the creation of all parodies of that work.

Like the challenges brought by technology, right-holders typically perceive the introduction of a parody exception as a threat, arguably overlooking that copyright's expansion has conferred upon them a strong and long monopoly. For example, the basic copyright term for original works currently lasts for the author's life plus seventy years whereas the Statute of Anne granted protection for a maximum of fourteen years since publication which could be renewed for another fourteen years if the author was still alive.[45]

Therefore, a parody exception in copyright law seeks to rectify the balance between right-holders, users, and subsequent authors. After all, copyright law should be crafted to permit others to appropriate existing, well-known works, provided that these are reworked to create new works which contribute to greater social welfare overall.[46] Additionally, it seems that right-holders are more reluctant to authorize use of their works for the purpose of parody compared with other types of use, perhaps fearing a negative criticism of their work or not wishing association with any particular sentiment expressed.[47] Hence, a specific exception appears to be justified, but this should not be without limits. Some appropriation made by a parodist may not provide social value because of, for example, the discriminatory nature of the comment being made.[48] In these instances, it may prove necessary to protect the interests of the author of the original work over those of the parodist. We shall now consider how this balancing is achieved within the three-step test.

copyright norm: the reverse three-step test' (2005) 9 *Marq. Intell. Prop. L. Rev.* 1–36; Kur (n 1) 4; also in *Théberge v. Galerie d'Art du Petit Champlain Inc.* [2002] S.C.C. 34, [30]–[31].

41 Lepage (n 27) 1.

42 In *WIPO 1886, Berne Convention Centenary 1986* (Geneva, 1986) 195; Preamble of WCT 1996.

43 Consideration also has to be given to the fact that limitations on absolute protection are dictated, quite rightly, by the public interest. The ever-growing need for mass instruction could never be met if there were no reservation of certain reproduction facilities, which at the same time should not degenerate into abuses. *WIPO 1886, Berne Convention, Centenary 1986* (Geneva, 1986) 195.

44 Desbois describes this as a new kind of censorship. Desbois (n 14) 322.

45 See n 38.

46 See Chapter 1, section 5.1.

47 See sections 3.2 and 4.

48 See further on this in Chapter 5, section 4.1.5.

3. What is the Three-Step Test?

The three-step test is an instrument of international copyright law. When first incorporated into the Berne Convention ('Berne'),[49] its aim was to guide national legislators by curtailing the exceptions which could be made to the reproduction right under national copyright law. It has now been incorporated into three subsequent international treaties: the TRIPS agreement ('TRIPS'),[50] the WIPO Copyright Treaty ('WCT'),[51] and the WIPO Performances and Phonograms Treaty ('WPPT').[52] As a result, the three-step test serves a fundamental role in the introduction of *any* new copyright exception in national law.[53]

More recently, the test has found its way into EU texts and national legislations. This has led to different interpretations creating uncertainties as to its scope, and attracting a wealth of commentaries. As a thorough study of the three-step test is a detailed and complex endeavour,[54] which goes beyond the scope of this book, the next sections summarize the aspects which are most pertinent to our task.

3.1 The origins and morphing of the three-step test

3.1.1 Protection of the reproduction right

The three-step test appeared in the Berne Convention for the first time following a revision arising from the Stockholm Conference in 1967. This revision sought to strengthen copyright by making the exclusive 'right of reproduction'[55] mandatory at

[49] Article 9(2) Berne Convention for the Protection of Literary and Artistic Works of September 9, 1886 as amended at Paris on 28 September 1979.

[50] Agreement on Trade-related Aspects of Intellectual Property Rights of 1994; Annexe 1C to the Agreement Establishing the World Trade Organization, 15 April 1994. This shift also had the consequence of departing from the influence of natural laws dominating the Berne Convention to utilitarian considerations, such as primarily economic justifications for copyright. It is through article 9(1) that part of Berne has been rejuvenated, as WTO member states have to comply with articles 1–21 Berne and with articles 13 (which expands the test to all exclusive rights), 17 (trade marks), 26(2) (industrial designs), and 30 (patents) TRIPS. This repetition of the test by reference to Berne and the specific provision in TRIPS led Senftleben to conclude that the test not only extends the tool to all exclusive rights but also functions as an *additional* safeguard for the exceptions admitted under Berne. Senftleben (n 24) 90, 121, and 155; Ricketson (n 40) 47, 49, and 52.

[51] Articles 1(4) and 10(1)–(2) WCT of 20 December 1996. Insofar as the three-step test is generally restrictive of the exceptions which satisfy the test, the three-step test in WCT is permissive to exceptions by noting that such exceptions are not limited to those complying with the test. A F Christie and R Wright, 'International review of intellectual property and competition law a comparative analysis of the three-step tests in international treaties' (2014) 45(4) *IIC* 409, 431; S Dusollier, 'L'encadrement des exceptions au droit d'auteur par le test des trois étapes' (2005) 2 *I.R.D.I.* 213, 215; Senftleben (n 24) 106; Ricketson (n 40) 57–63; M Ficsor, *The Law of Copyright and the Internet—The 1996 WIPO Treaties, their Interpretation and Implementation* (OUP, 2002) 60–1; Agreed Statements Concerning the WCT, *Statement Concerning Article 10*, WIPO Diplomatic Conference, WIPO Doc. No. CRNR/DC/96 (1996).

[52] Article 16(2) WIPO Performances and Phonograms Treaty of 20 December 1996.

[53] Kur (n 1) 16; Gervais (n 34) 25; H Sun, 'Overcoming the Achilles heel of copyright law' (2007) 5(2) *NJTIP* 264, 268; Gervais (n 40) 13; Senftleben (n 24) 67.

[54] This study has been done by others, including Senftleben (n 24).

[55] The reproduction right was already present but not fully recognized before 1967. C Geiger, D Gervais, and M Senftleben, 'Understanding the "three-step test"' in D Gervais (ed.) *International Intellectual Property* (Edward Elgar, 2015) 584.

international level.[56] The three-step test was introduced to support this right based upon concern that without limits in place, national legislators might adopt exceptions which would undermine the mandatory nature of this important right.

From the very beginning, the three-step test had a double objective: firstly, it needed to recognize exceptions already present in national legislation, which, in turn, reflected different approaches based upon different philosophical underpinnings; and secondly, it sought to direct future national legislators in terms of the types of copyright exception which could be permissibly introduced.[57] This dual role explains why the test itself, set out in what follows, was drafted in such an open manner:[58]

> [I]t shall be a matter for legislation in the countries of the Union to permit the reproduction of such works in certain special cases, provided that such reproduction does not conflict with a normal exploitation of the work and does not unreasonably prejudice the legitimate interests of the author.[59]

Time passed and while signatory parties felt the need for greater harmonization, as the number of signatories to Berne grew, the chances of reaching agreement grew increasingly remote. The adoption of TRIPS presented a solution, accompanied by a shift of forum from WIPO to WTO. While Berne's primary focus is protection of authors, TRIPS sought to establish international minimum standards of intellectual property protection based upon the WTO's market-related concerns of facilitating international trade.[60] Consequently, when the three-step test was incorporated into TRIPS, it was directed to protect the interests of right-holders (not authors) and it extended the test to all exclusive rights (not just the reproduction right). This first adjustment is not trivial because it shifts from securing the legitimate interests of *creators* to protecting the interests of those who exploit the copyright-protected works.[61]

Subsequently, the growth of the internet and its implications for copyright law led to the adoption of the WIPO Internet Treaties (WCT and WPPT). These sought to accommodate the digital environment by expanding the range of exclusive rights reserved to the right-holder. As these treaties also included the three-step test, national legislators were permitted to extend copyright exceptions to operate within this new environment.[62] During negotiations, some parties expressed concern that as the reach of the three-step test expanded, exceptions would cease to be effective in the digital context, perhaps only covering inconsequential uses rather than providing an effective counter-mechanism to the expansion of exclusive rights. As reassurance, an Agreed Statement regarding the three-step test was adopted to reflect the desired balance of interests between the rights of authors and the public interest. The Preamble in the statement[63] underlines that the same exceptions and limitations which Berne recognizes

[56] Many countries already had an exclusive reproduction right in their national systems but it was not yet acknowledged at international level. C Geiger, 'From Berne to national law, via the Copyright Directive: the dangerous mutations of the three-step test' (2007) 29(12) *EIPR* 486–91, esp. 486.

[57] Dusollier (n 13) 436.

[58] K J Koelman, 'Fixing the three-step test' (2006) 8 *EIPR* 407–12.

[59] Article 9(2) Berne Convention.

[60] This explains why moral rights are left outside the scope of the treaty, compared to the Berne Convention for example. For more: M T Sundara Rajan, *Copyright and Creative Freedom—A Study of Post-Socialist Law Reform* (Routledge Studies in International Law, 2006) chapter 1.

[61] Even outside copyright law, as traces of three-step tests can be found in relation to trade mark, design, and patent legislation. See TRIPS, articles 17, 26(2), and 30.

[62] Sun (n 53) 277; Sundara Rajan (n 60) 22–5.

[63] The statement notes: 'Recognizing the need to maintain a balance between the rights of authors and the larger public interest, particularly education, research and access to information, as reflected in the Berne Convention.'

in the 'analogue world' should extend into the digital world too, although interpreted in a manner appropriate to that digital environment.[64]

3.1.2 The EU variant

The European Union implemented the WIPO treaties via the InfoSoc Directive of 2001,[65] by partial harmonization of national copyright legislation in EU Member States. The wording of the InfoSoc Directive's operative provisions includes the text of the three-step test.[66] Whilst having a main objective of harmonizing the exclusive rights of reproduction,[67] communication to the public,[68] and distribution,[69] the InfoSoc Directive also sought to recognize national initiatives which introduced related exceptions, adding these to the *acquis communautaire*. This was considered necessary because operators might exploit differences between national copyright legislation, to harm the functioning of the internal market, in terms of cross-border exploitation of works.[70] In pursuing these aims, the InfoSoc Directive seeks to achieve a fair balance between the interests of right-holders and the public.[71]

Some seventeen years later, there is a general consensus that the InfoSoc Directive has failed to live up to its promise to harmonize copyright across the EU. There is

[64] Agreed Statements concerning the WIPO Copyright Treaty adopted at the Diplomatic Conference on 20 December 1996.

[65] The new Copyright Directive proposed by the Commission within the Digital Single Market Strategy will be set aside as it says nothing about the parody exception. *Proposal for a Directive of the European Parliament and of the Council on copyright in the Digital Single Market* (14 September 2016) COM(2016)593. However, the EU Parliament Culture and Education Committee ('CULT') published an opinion in favour of expanding the quotation exception in the proposed new directive to parody uses. CULT proposes to add recital 21(a), which seems to focus on short reproductions and mirrors the three-step test, recital 21(b), which suggests a user-generated content ('UGC') exception at EU level, and article 5(a), which expands the quotation exception to non-commercial parodies reproducing small parts of earlier works (and would require acknowledging the underlying copyright-protected work). Whilst inclusion of parody uses within the new directive is appreciated (should these amendments be adopted), the scope of the parody exception is likely to be reduced as it focuses on small amounts copied, non-commercial uses, and requires acknowledging the original. European Parliament, *Opinion of the Committee on Culture and Education for the Committee on Legal Affairs* (4 September 2017) COM(2016)0593 – C8-0383/2016 – 2016/0280(COD), Rapporteur: Marc Joulaud, Amendments 14, 15, and 60. The Committee for the Internal Market and Consumer Protection also tables a similar amendment. European Parliament, *Opinion of the Committee on the Internal Market and Consumer Protection for the Committee on Legal* (14 June 2017) COM(2016)0593 – C8-0383/2016 – 2016/0280(COD), Rapporteur: Catherine Stihler, Amendment 55. While this amendment is not limited to a certain amount reproduced it still requires identifying the earlier work. In addition, it provides an invitation for judges to consider fair practices in a particular sector. The latter is welcomed as it adds some flexibility in a closed system of exceptions. Yet, such provision is absent from the Council's revised presidency proposal. Council of the European Union, *Revised Presidency compromise proposal regarding Articles 2 to 9* (26 September 2017) 2016/0280 (COD).

[66] The preparatory works concerning the adoption of the Information Society Directive started in 1995 with the Green Paper on 'Copyright and Related Rights in the Information Society' COM (95) 382, the 1996 Followed Paper COM (96) 568, the initial proposal from the Commission COM (1997) 628, and finally, the 1999 amended proposal COM (1999) 250.

[67] Article 2 of the InfoSoc Directive.

[68] Article 3 of the InfoSoc Directive.

[69] Article 4 of the InfoSoc Directive.

[70] Recitals 6 and 7 of the InfoSoc Directive; initial proposal from the Commission COM (1997) 628, p. 8. Therefore, the harmonization had to facilitate the functioning of the internal market for copyright-protected works, recital 31.

[71] Preamble and recital 31 of the InfoSoc Directive; A Ramalho, 'Parody in trademarks and copyright' (2009) 5 *Cambridge Student Law Review* 59.

particular disenchantment in relation to exceptions,[72] which has arisen for two main reasons. Firstly, the InfoSoc Directive stopped short of mandating exceptions which might be necessary to respect the different cultural and legal traditions of its Member States. In fact, article 5 of the InfoSoc Directive requires only *one* exception (for temporary acts of reproduction)[73] to be mandatory, and contains an exhaustive list of *twenty optional* exceptions.[74] Secondly, the role and meaning of the three-step test incorporated within the InfoSoc Directive remains largely unclear,[75] resulting in a profusion of scholarly criticism.[76]

The three-step test is enshrined in article 5(5) of the InfoSoc Directive and has a slightly different wording to that adopted in international law. According to this provision:

> The exceptions and limitations provided for in paragraphs 1, 2, 3 and 4 shall only be *applied* in certain special cases which do not conflict with a normal exploitation of the work or other subject-matter and do not unreasonably prejudice the legitimate interests of the rightholder.[77]

But who is the addressee of this version of the test, legislators or national courts? Does the EU legislature intend Member States to incorporate this test within the national legislation which enacts this part of the InfoSoc Directive?[78] If so, then, as Galopin notes, repetition of the test would appear redundant. As all EU Member States are already signatories to the relevant international copyright treaties, they have already agreed to comply with the test when enacting copyright exceptions. Additionally, it seems reasonable to presume that as article 5 establishes an exhaustive list of permitted exceptions, the EU legislature has already had regard to the three-step test and considers that these (and only these) comply.[79] For these reasons, it seems that the InfoSoc Directive's repetition of the test should be understood as fulfilling a new role.

The wording used might imply that article 5(5) is concerned with *how* the exception is *applied in individual cases*, rather than how the exception should be implemented into national legislation.[80] Accordingly, some Member States, including France, have incorporated the text of article 5(5) within their legal order and require judges to determine whether, or not, the three-step test is satisfied when applied to the particular facts before them. Some see this approach as problematic.

Firstly, legal certainty is jeopardized owing to the lack of any consensus as to the proper interpretation of the test. As it is the defendant who must prove that the test is satisfied, it seems unlikely that users will be able to predict whether or not their intended use is permitted, or not.[81] Sheer fear of litigation is likely to deter the very

[72] See current discussions on the EU copyright reform and especially the Reda report available at https://juliareda.eu/copyright-evaluation-report/ (access date: 1 June 2018).

[73] Article 5(1) of the InfoSoc Directive.

[74] Recital 32, Article 5(2)–(3) of the InfoSoc Directive.

[75] Article 5(5) of the InfoSoc Directive.

[76] The various criticisms are summarized in what follows.

[77] The emphasis is the author's own.

[78] Some countries, such as Spain and Belgium, already had part of the three-step test in their national law while France, Greece, Ireland, Italy, Luxembourg, and Portugal introduced the test after the implementation of the InfoSoc Directive in their domestic law.

[79] Galopin (n 1) 386.

[80] Recital 44 of the InfoSoc Directive; G Mazziotti, *EU Digital Copyright and the End-user* (Springer, 2008) 85; Dusollier (n 13) 438; C Caron, 'Les exceptions: l'impact sur le droit français' (2002) 2 *Propriétés Intellectuelles* 25, 26; P-Y Gautier, 'De la transposition des exceptions: à propos de la directive "droit d'auteur dans la société de l'information" ' (2001) 25(19) *CCE* 10.

[81] P-Y Gautier, 'Les exceptions au regard du droit d'auteur de l'Union Européenne' in Lucas, Sirinelli, and Bensamoun (eds), *Les exceptions au droit d'auteur* 42; A Lucas, 'For a reasonable interpretation of the three-step test' (2010) 32(6) *EIPR* 277; Dusollier (n 13) chapter 4; Geiger (n 27) 262.

socially beneficial uses which the exception is there to protect. Secondly, the InfoSoc Directive's harmonization aims are thwarted by conflicting national decisions in the same or similar cases,[82] i.e. a use may be permitted in one Member State but held unlawful in another, merely because of inconsistent application of the test. Thirdly, it is doubtful that national courts are adequately equipped, in terms of the facts and resources available to them, to apply the test.[83] Thus, these concerns cast doubt that national judges are the intended target. Indeed, a third interpretation is that it is the EU courts which are the addressees of article 5(5), i.e. the InfoSoc Directive incorporates the three-step test so that the CJEU may determine the legality of the national law exception.[84]

Thus, presence of a three-step test within the InfoSoc Directive gives rise to two possibilities. First, it is there to direct national *legislators* when seeking to implement one of the permitted exceptions of article 5, as overseen by the CJEU. In this scenario, the test should be applied by the legislator to assess conditions under which any particular type of use is lawful, for example, whether use should be free, or whether a statutory licence scheme is needed for the country to meet its international obligations.[85] This approach implies that article 5(5) of the InfoSoc Directive simply echoes the international obligation of Member States, and is somewhat redundant.

Alternatively, if the test is *also* directed at national judges, then article 5(5) effectively imposes an additional condition before any *particular* use will benefit from the exception.[86] Faced with a copyright infringement claim, a national court needs to assess whether the unauthorized use meets the conditions of a defence provided by national law, and then further assess whether, given the particular surrounding circumstances of the case, the use also meets the requirements of the three-step test. Acting in this manner, judges acquire a larger margin of appreciation on whether any particular use should be permitted, and there is little legal certainty or hope for harmonization.

Just as Member States have taken different views as to their obligation to replicate article 5(5) within national copyright law, so the literature is divided on the proper addressee(s) of the test, and there is currently no settled answer.[87]

While awaiting a definitive interpretation from the CJEU of the test in relation to the parody exception, the Court's guidance in relation to other optional exceptions

[82] This is due to the direct effect of directives in certain cases where they are unconditional, sufficiently clear and precise. Galopin (n 1) 389. This is the case of the UK where some courts have made reference to the three-step test. See *Fraser-Woodward Ltd v. British Broadcasting Corporation* [2005] EWHC 472 (Ch), (Mann J.); *Hyde Park Residence Ltd v. Yelland* [2000] 3 WLR 215, CA, (Aldous L.J.). Additionally, some right-holders have tried to invoke the three-step test in front of courts to render a use illegitimate. Lucas (n 81) 277; J Griffiths, 'The "three-step test" in European copyright law—problems and solutions' (2009) 4 *IPQ* 428.

[83] Additionally, there are serious doubts that the three-step test is workable at all for the interpretation of exceptions beyond the introduction of a copyright exception.

[84] In favour of this interpretation: R Burrell and A Coleman, *Copyright Exceptions: The Digital Impact* (Cambridge University Press, 2005) 298.

[85] Recital 36 of the InfoSoc Directive and Dusollier (n 51) 26.

[86] This is supported by the verbs used in the drafting of article 5(1)–(4) and 5(5) of the InfoSoc Directive. While the earlier uses 'may' the latter uses 'shall'. Moreover, article 5(5) is also applicable to the mandatory exception enshrined in article 5(1) of the InfoSoc Directive. Finally, recital 44 infers that national judges are the addressees. M Senftleben, 'Overprotection and protection overlaps in intellectual property law—the need for horizontal fair use defences' in A Kur and V Mizaras (eds), *The Structure of Intellectual Property Law* (Edward Elgar, 2011) 152.

[87] The Wittem Project appears to extend the scope of the test to enable the adoption of new exceptions not already harmonized by the Code (article 5.5). The project is available at https://www.ivir.nl/copyrightcode/introduction/; Galopin (n 1) 398.

provides contradictory guidance as to the interpretation of article 5(5).[88] Some decisions indicate that the three-step test is to be considered at the stage that an exception is implemented by Member States.[89] Here, while national legislators should enjoy broad discretion, they must also respect other well-established EU principles of a high level of protection for authors,[90] proportionality,[91] legal certainty,[92] and strict interpretation.[93] Elsewhere, the CJEU seems to require national courts to construe an exception in light of the three-step test.[94] Going even further, the CJEU has also required a defendant's acts to be measured against the three-step test.[95] Yet, the CJEU has stated that provided an unauthorized use falls within an exception, then it is non-infringing and article 5(5) should be held satisfied.[96] Finally, and despite all the other inconsistency, CJEU jurisprudence is consistent in stating that the role of article 5(5) is not to broaden the scope of the listed exceptions.[97]

It will be appreciated that while the general role of the three-step test within the InfoSoc Directive remains unclear, its application to the parody exception is equally uncertain. *Deckmyn* has escalated debate among scholars,[98] all of whom are critical of the possibility that article 5(5) might further restrict the circumstances in which a parody exception would apply.[99] Another approach, which is gaining support, proposes that the role of the InfoSoc Directive's three-step test is concerned with proportionality to fine-tune the balance between right-holders and the public interest.[100]

Although in *Deckmyn* the CJEU (again) missed the opportunity to clarify the meaning of article 5(5),[101] the Court, nevertheless, directs that the parody exception

[88] C-463/12 *Copydan Båndkopi v. Nokia Danmark A/S* [2015] ECLI:EU:C:2015:144 (hereafter *Copydan*); C-201/13 *Johan Deckmyn and Vrijheidsfonds VZW v. Helena Vandersteen and Others* [2014] ECLI:EU:C:2014:2132 (hereafter *Deckmyn);* C-117/13 *Technische Universität Darmstadt v. Eugen Ulmer KG* [2014] ECLI:EU:C:2014:2196 (hereafter *Ulmer*); C-435/12 *ACI Adam BV and Others v. Stichting de Thuiskopie and Stichting Onderhandelingen Thuiskopie vergoeding* [2014] ECLI:EU:C:2014:254 (hereafter *ACI Adam*); C-360/13 *Public Relations Consultants Association Ltd v. Newspaper Licensing Agency Ltd and Others* [2014] ECLI:EU:C:2014:1195 (hereafter *PRCA*); C-162/10 *Phonographic Performance (Ireland) Limited v. Ireland* [2012] ECLI:EU:C:2012:141; C-145/10 *Eva-Maria Painer v. Standard Verlags GmbH and Others* [2011] ECLI:EU:C:2011:798 (hereafter *Painer*); C-302/10 *Infopaq International A/S v. Danske Dagblades Forening* [2012] ECLI:EU:C:2012:16 (hereafter *Infopaq II*); C-462/09 *Stichting de Thuiskopie v. Opus Supplies Deutschland GmbH and Others* [2011] ECLI:EU:C:2011:397 (hereafter *Opus Supplies*); C-403/08 *Football Association Premier League Ltd and Others v. QC Leisure and Others* and C-429/08 *Karen Murphy v. Media Protection Services Ltd* [2011] ECLI:EU:C:2011:631 (hereafter *FAPL);* C-5/08 *Infopaq International A/S v. Danske Dagblades Forening* [2009] ECLI:EU:C:2009:465 (hereafter *Infopaq I*); R Arnold and E Rosati, 'Are national courts the addressees of the InfoSoc three-step test?' (2015) 10(10) *JIPLP* 744–8.

[89] *ACI Adam* (n 88) [25]; *Painer* (n 88) [101]; *Opus Supplies* (n 88) [33].

[90] *Painer* (n 88) [107]. [91] Ibid, [105]–[106]. [92] Ibid, [108].

[93] Ibid, [109].

[94] *Ulmer* (n 88) [47]; C-351/12 *Ochranný svaz autorský pro práva k dílům hudebním o.s. v. Léčebné lázně Mariánské Lázně a.s.* [2014] ECLI:EU:C:2014:110, [40]; *Infopaq I* (n 88) [55].

[95] *Ulmer* (n 88) [56]; *PRCA* (n 88) [53]–[63]; *FAPL* (n 88) [180]–[181].

[96] *Infopaq II* (n 88) [55]–[57]; *FAPL* (n 88) [181].

[97] *Ulmer* (n 88) [47]; *Copydan* (n 88) [90]; *ACI Adam* (n 88) [26].

[98] The literature heavily criticizes the InfoSoc Directive to the point where scholars wonder whether adopting a fair use clause in EU law would solve this situation. However, academics are evenly split. In favour: Senftleben, Hugenholtz, Geiger; *contra*: Lucas, Janssens, Galopin.

[99] However, it is now clear from the jurisprudence of the CJEU that a national legislator cannot introduce an exception narrower than what is provided in the InfoSoc Directive. C-510/10 *DR and TV2 Danmark A/S v. NCB—Nordisk Copyright Bureau* [2012] ECLI:EU:C:2012:244, [36].

[100] C Geiger, D J Gervais and M Senftleben, 'The three-step test revisited: how to use the test's flexibility in national copyright law' (2014) 29(3) *Am U Int'l L Rev* 581, 626. Also supported by recital 3 of the InfoSoc Directive.

[101] Advocate General's Opinion in *Deckmyn* [2014] ECLI:EU:C:2014:458 (hereafter AGO in *Deckmyn*), [29]. This is because the Court is bound by what the national court asked and the Court

requires 'a fair balance between, on the one hand, the interests and rights of (rightholders), and, on the other, the freedom of expression of the user of a protected work'.[102] Since this statement is based upon the specific facts of the case, it seems possible to extrapolate and interpret the general role of the three-step test as extending further: i.e. to balance *all* the competing interests, including those of third parties in some particular circumstances where the parodic use is not clear cut.[103] This position finds support in recital 3 of the InfoSoc Directive which states that the harmonization sought through the Directive 'relates to compliance with the fundamental principles of law and especially of property, including intellectual property, and freedom of expression and the public interest'. This seems to envisage other third-party interests, such as the protection against discrimination or hate speech.[104]

3.1.3 Interim conclusion

The uncertainties surrounding the addressee of the three-step test in copyright supranational legislation led some national legislators to introduce this instrument directly within their national laws, thereby requiring its application in individual cases whereas others deliberately have not. For example, while the UK, Canada, and the US refused to introduce this test, France[105] and Australia[106] included the test in their national legislation. Doing so, national legislators definitely require national judges to verify compliance with the three-step test on a case-by-case basis each time the application of a copyright exception is sought (although not explicitly in the case of parodies as explained later). But the reach of the test goes beyond these jurisdictions (as pointed out by Geiger); traces of the application of the three-step test by the judiciary are to be found in countries where the legislator did not insert the instrument into its national legislation.[107] There is very little doubt that the three-step test will have a significant role in the application of copyright exceptions and, therefore, the parody exception in the future.

3.2 The interpretation of the three-step test

Whilst the wording of each form of the three-step test is similar, it is erroneous to believe that the different provisions carry the same obligations.[108] In this part, we outline the differing interpretations of this test which have emerged.[109]

But before we embark on an examination of the differences, it is worthwhile highlighting aspects which enjoy a wide degree of agreement as general remarks. For

of Appeal of Brussels focused its questions on the parody exception rather than including article 5(5) InfoSoc Directive.

[102] *Deckmyn* (n 88) [26]–[27].

[103] See Chapters 4 and 5.

[104] See Chapter 5, section 4.

[105] Law 2006-961 of 1 August 2006 concerning Copyright and Neighbouring Rights in the Information Society, published in the Official Gazette, 3 August 2006, 11529.

[106] Section 200 AB of the Australian Copyright Act of 1968, introduced into Australian law by the Copyright Amendment Act 2006 (No 158, 2006).

[107] Geiger (n 56) 486–91, esp. 489.

[108] A comparison undertaken led to the conclusion that there is not *one* three-step test but 'eight different stepped tests' at international level. Christie and Wright (n 51) 409–33.

[109] The same statement can be transferred to national decisions on the interpretation of the three-step test in the field of copyright. If one looked at the different national decisions, one would see that the decisions are far from speaking with one voice. National courts have adopted different interpretations over the years and these also depart from the panel copyright report.

example, there seems little doubt that the test comprises three distinctive steps, and that these are cumulative.[110] Furthermore, the test's open texture was a deliberate choice to cover the different approaches to copyright exceptions (i.e. enumerated list, fair dealing, and fair use). Lastly, we can obtain some guidance on the interpretation of the three-step test from the WTO Panel decision concerning section 110(5) of the US Copyright Code, but this is limited to the scope of the test according to TRIPS, and so it is not binding in relation to Berne.

3.2.1 Certain special cases

The first step of the three-step test requires that exceptions to exclusive rights remain confined to 'certain special cases'. The wording suggests that the step has two aspects. Firstly, it seems to require that national legislators ensure that any exception is directed to a limited number of situations only, i.e. a quantitative limit.[111] Secondly, there is a qualitative aspect: the 'special' purpose of an exception must be determined in advance.[112]

In the Berne context, it appears reasonable that the objectives for introducing a new copyright exception should be taken into consideration.[113] Yet, this is at odds with the WTO Panel decision under TRIPS,[114] which only took account of the quantitative dimension. Here, the Dispute Settlement Body ('DSB') is believed to have focused only on the quantitative assessment of the provision,[115] because consideration of the qualitative aspect might be seen as too much interference with the national sovereignty of its members.[116]

Given that the WTO is specifically economics-focused, this also suggests that the DSB approach should not become the definitive interpretation of this first step. Not only does a combined quantitative and qualitative approach find support from Berne, but the post-TRIPS WIPO Diplomatic Conference of 1996 emphasized the

[110] Records of the Intellectual Property Conference of Stockholm, *Report on the Work of Main Committee I (Substantive Provisions of the Berne Convention: Articles 1-20)*, (1967) 11 June 1967–14 July 1967, vol. II, p. 11456; C Geiger, 'The role of the three-step test in the adaptation of the information society' (2007) *January–March UNESCO e-copyright bulletin* 1, 5; Sun (n 53) 267; Dusollier (n 51) 214; Geiger (n 27) 253; Senftleben (n 24) 125; Ricketson (n 40) 21; Lepage (n 27) 6; J Reinbothe and S v. Lewinski, *The WIPO Treaties 1996—The WIPO Copyright Treaty and the WIPO Performances and Phonograms Treaty—Commentary and Legal Analysis* (Butterworths, 2002) 124. However, trying to insert some flexibility into the test, Geiger et al argue that the test should be 'considered together and as a whole in a comprehensive overall assessment' Geiger et al (n 34) 711. This is vividly criticized by Lucas. Lucas (n 81) 281.

[111] 'Certain' has two ordinary meanings. A qualitative sense: 'determined, fixed, settled; not variable or fluctuating' and a quantitative sense: 'of positive yet restricted (or of positive even if restricted) quantity, amount, or degree; of some extent at least'. Definitions from the *OED*. There is a common understanding that the latter meaning prevails. In addition to the ordinary meaning, this interpretation is supported by the intention of the drafters. Geiger (n 27) 253; Senftleben (n 24) 134–5; Ricketson (n 40) 63; Reinbothe and Lewinski (n 110) 124; Ficsor (n 51) 129.

[112] Through the ordinary meaning of 'special'.

[113] Against this position, see S Ricketson, *The Three-Step Test, Deemed Quantities, Libraries and Closed Exceptions* (Centre for Copyright Studies, 2002) 31.

[114] The decisions of the DSB are binding on the parties of the dispute but there are considerable doubts as to their authority beyond the dispute in hand. Dusollier (n 13) 446. This is not to underestimate the importance of study of the decisions. To the contrary, signatory parties may look to these decisions to understand the interpretation of the test resulting in a consolidated practice of how the test has to be understood. Kur (n 1) 33.

[115] WTO Panel WT/DS160/5 of 16 April 1999, para VI.146. In doing so, and facing the practical difficulty of calculating the number of cases likely to be relevant pursuant to the exception under scrutiny, the DSB relied upon estimates submitted by the parties to the dispute.

[116] Dusollier (n 13) 446–7.

importance of protecting societal values. Indeed, it seems that this condition cannot be 'policy blind', since it is implicit that any national legislator introducing a copyright exception will face opposing interests. These differing interests may only be reconciled by recourse to a clearly stated and specific public policy, so that the exception secures values which are important to the relevant society.[117]

What is agreed, however, is that the concept of 'certain special cases' does establish a quantative limit which circumscribes exceptions to apply to a minority of uses in the specific circumstances stated. In essence, copyright exceptions should be definite in scope and reach.

3.2.2 Conflict with the normal exploitation of the work

The second step mandates that any exception must not conflict with the normal exploitation of the work. Given the importance of this requirement, the scope of this second step still gives rise to animated debates among scholars and stakeholders. The main issue is whether policy arguments should be taken into consideration.[118]

Despite the market-based imprint of the Panel decision, the DSB did endorse a two-part normative and empirical approach to this second step:

> In our opinion, these definitions appear to reflect two connotations: the first one appears to be of an empirical nature, i.e., what is regular, usual, typical or ordinary. The other one reflects a somewhat more normative, if not dynamic, approach, i.e., conforming to a type or standard ... [W]e will attempt to develop a harmonious interpretation which gives meaning and effect to both connotations of 'normal'.[119]

Thus, an empirical approach seems to suggest that the market for the type of work which would benefit from the exception must be measured against that of the protected work, and then an assessment is made whether the exception is likely to cause significant harm to exploitation of the protected work, based upon actual or potential markets.[120] The qualitative aspect is concerned with 'norms' via a consideration of non-economic elements, including the public interest or fundamental rights concerns attached to certain exceptions.[121] Consequently, it is believed that this step should be assessed by balancing the likely economic impact of the exception on the market of the original with the significance of the values upon which the exception is based.[122]

This second step also needs evaluation within the context of the digital environment. Although Berne considers the exploitation of non-digital works only, it nevertheless provides context to guide an appreciation of this step within the digital environment. Firstly, Berne provides strong protection of the reproduction right.[123] Transposed to a

[117] Gervais (n 34) 25–7; Senftleben (n 24) 146; Ricketson (n 40) 25.

[118] For: Senftleben, Geiger, Griffiths, Hilty; *contra*: Bornkamm, Ricketson, Lucas.

[119] WTO Panel (n 115) para VI.199.

[120] Senftleben (n 24) 182 and 194.

[121] Also supported under TRIPS, see TRIPS Preamble recognizing 'the underlying public policy objectives of national systems for the protection of intellectual property, including developmental and technological objectives'. Additionally, see article 7 TRIPS for the extension to the digital environment and article 8 TRIPS for further interests to be considered.

[122] WTO Panel (n 115) para VI.211. Later, the diplomatic conference in relation to the WIPO internet treaties repeated the need for a fair balance between the interests of the right-holder and the public interest, which is even more important as the WCT deals directly with the challenges presented by the growth of internet; S Ricketson and J Ginsburg, *International Copyright and Neighbouring Rights* (OUP, 2005) para 13.21; Senftleben (n 24) 177–84.

[123] This is exemplified by the failure to harmonize a private copying exception, despite the social value which such an exception provides.

digital context, Senftleben argues that a reproduction right in the digital era enables right-holders to exploit and control *new* uses of protected works. Technological developments establish entirely new markets for right-holders, which would not have been envisaged at the time the work was created. Conversely, potential markets which never emerge because of opposition by right-holders fall outside the scope of this step.[124] Secondly, it is proposed that 'normal exploitation' is not so wide as to encompass any use which a right-holder can monitor.[125] Again, by analogy with the private copying exception, the study group at the Stockholm conference made special note that 'normal exploitation' only implies that an exception which captures a very large number of unauthorized copies will not be permitted.[126] It can be inferred that an exception which gives rise to a small number of unauthorized copies should pass this step.[127]

It seems reasonable to conclude, in both analogue and digital environments, that a conflict with the normal exploitation of a work occurs when a right-holder is deprived of an actual or potential market of significant economic importance. This is influenced by the likelihood that remuneration for an activity falling within the exception would constitute a considerable source of income, and thus forms part of the economic core of copyright.[128] Whether or not activities would provide a major source of income may be determined by studying the overall commercialization of works of a category affected by the income in question.[129] This matter is left for national legislation to decide.

3.2.3 Absence of unreasonable prejudice to the legitimate interests of the author/right-holder

Once the first two steps are satisfied, the third step requires some further balancing. This final stage precludes an exception which would unreasonably prejudice the legitimate interests of authors and/or right-holders.[130] Thus, we must consider three issues so that we may measure whether an exception is likely to satisfy this last step: firstly, whose interests are to be considered, secondly what interests are legitimate, and, finally, how might these interests be prejudiced unreasonably?[131]

Firstly, the interested parties depend upon the treaty concerned. While Berne and WCT refer to the 'author' specifically, it is commonly accepted that this reference extends to any subsequent right-holders. Conversely, pursuant to TRIPS, the test specifically considers the interests of right-holders, i.e. those that exploit, rather than create,

[124] Senftleben (n 24) 180. [125] Kur (n 1) 26; Senftleben (n 24) 181.

[126] See n 110.

[127] This echoes the conclusion reached in the Panel decision, [6.183]. Yet, the appreciation of this step in relation to specific exceptions may change with time. As this second step requires determination of whether the kinds of uses authorized by the parody exception are likely to be uses that right-holders might want to exploit for themselves, it may be that, one day, parody uses which were not deemed significant become an important source of revenue for right-holders.

[128] Senftleben (n 24) 193.

[129] Peukert argues that widely accepted exceptions such as the parody exception satisfy the second step in the digital era due to their normative justifications. A Peukert, 'A bipolar copyright system for the digital network environment' (2005) 28(1) *Hastings Communications & Entertainment Law Journal* 33, 34.

[130] While Berne and WCT refer to the author, TRIPS refers to right-holders.

[131] This step also offers the possibility for signatory parties to introduce equitable remuneration. It is the author's opinion that no equitable remuneration or compulsory licence should be provided for the parody exception. Such remuneration would have the negative consequence of putting a price on the exercise of fundamental freedoms. Therefore, equitable remuneration is not studied here.

the rights. This explains why author-only interests, such as moral rights, were not considered by the DSB in the Panel decision.[132]

Secondly, it is reasonable to conclude that this step aims at considering interests other than a work's normal exploitation (i.e. the subject of the second step), otherwise the second step would become redundant. From an economic perspective, any exception hampers the possibility to generate revenue to some extent, so potentially *all* sources of income should be considered.[133] But this third step, as per Berne and WCT, should also take account of non-economic interests, particularly moral rights.[134]

Thirdly, the fact that the prejudice caused must be 'unreasonable' indicates that some 'reasonable' level of prejudice must be tolerated. Hence, any harm created by an exception must be proportionate to the objectives sought. Here, uses which ought to be beyond right-holders' control—because the use protects a value which underpins the justification for copyright law, such as the preservation of freedom of expression—imply that the exempted area is not unreasonably prejudicing the legitimate interests of the author or right-holder.[135]

In conclusion, if a use must be allowed via the existence of an exception (as it responds to important social, cultural, and economic needs of a society), interests of right-holders must still be considered and weighed fairly[136] to ensure that the prejudice caused is not disproportionate.

3.2.4 What is the realm of the three-step test?

The introduction of the three-step test into the Berne Convention in 1968 established a template for exceptions and limitations which seeks to strike a fair balance between the protected interest of authors (including right-holders) and the public interest. Subsequently, we have seen that the three-step test has not only been incorporated into other international laws, but introduced into EU and national laws too. In doing so, the test has now become the concern of the judiciary, because the legislator has placed a greater responsibility on judges to interpret and apply the three-step test to particular facts.[137] Arguably, trial judges are ill-placed to assess compliance with the three-step test, not just because of ambiguity surrounding its meaning (leaning towards a strictly economic approach due to the WTO forum), but also owing to the sheer difficulty of striking a 'fair' balance between the numerous interests at stake.

While this test was originally implemented as a protective shield to allay concerns that national legislators might introduce new, unconstrained exceptions which might annihilate the right of reproduction, it has now morphed into a torpedo which might jeopardize any meaningful role for copyright exceptions. Under the current regime, owing to its repetition in numerous legal texts at different level, exclusive rights are

[132] Unless otherwise specified, 'right-holder' in this section encompasses both 'author' and 'right-holder'.

[133] This differs from the second step where only the major revenue stream is considered. See section 3.2.2.

[134] Except under TRIPS where moral rights are not part of the scope of the treaty, article 9(1) TRIPS. For a detailed analysis of moral rights in relation to the parody exception, see Chapter 6.

[135] Senftleben (n 24) 230; see Chapter 5.

[136] Gervais (n 40) 18–19; Ricketson (n 40) 27.

[137] Also inferred by the AGO in *Deckmyn* (n 101) [29].

likely to prevail in most cases over exceptions and limitations. It is likely to be rare that a defendant will be able to muster sufficient evidence to demonstrate that all three steps of the test are satisfied in respect of their use. Fearing litigation and lacking certainty whether the exception will apply, users seem more likely to seek the right-holder's permission as a default option, or simply elect not to use the work (whether socially valuable or not).

In light of these concerns, scholars have been vocal in calling for a re-interpretation of the test.[138] This is of particular concern for jurisdictions, such as EU Member States and Australia, where the three-step test has been incorporated into regional/national copyright legislation.[139] Against this backdrop, it appears that the recent *Deckmyn* decision may provide a way to balance the potentially economics-oriented approach of the three-step test to include social and cultural objectives for EU countries, at least.[140] Arguably, by requiring *all* competing interests to be weighed, including those of third parties, the CJEU is reminding national courts that the scope of copyright exceptions is not only subject to compliance with the three-step test, but that consideration must be given to fundamental rights too.[141] If the three-step test is to apply directly to individual cases, then national courts should also be more open to arguments based on the realization of human rights in the particular cases before them.[142] This may tip the balance in favour of the defendant more often than the current status quo would seem to suggest.

4. Compliance of the Parody Exception with the Three-Step Test

This section considers whether the current parody exceptions comply with the three-step test. This is an important line of inquiry, because it provides the yardstick against which every national version of the parody exception must be measured. We shall commence our inquiry by considering the French parody exception which is one of a list of well-established copyright exceptions. The fair dealing approaches (UK, Australia, and Canada) will then be reviewed, before finally turning to the fair use approach adopted in respect of copyright exceptions in the US.

[138] Geiger (n 56) 486–91, esp. 490; Geiger et al (n 34) 711; Max Planck Institute Declaration on the Three-step Test available at http://www.ip.mpg.de/fileadmin/ipmpg/content/forschung_aktuell/01_balanced/declaration_three_step_test_final_english1.pdf (access date: 10 November 2018); P B Hugenholtz and R L Okidiji, *Conceiving an International Instrument on Limitations and Exceptions to Copyright* (Report, 2008) available at http://www.eifl.net/sites/default/files/resources/201409/conceiving_an_international_instrument_on_limitiations_and_exceptions_to_copyright.pdf; Koelman (n 58) 407–12.

[139] Here, the UK is included within EU countries. The white paper states that the UK will implement all EU legislation prior to Brexit and that the CJEU will still have an influence on the interpretation of legislation until explicit repeal by the UK government (White Paper, 2 February 2017, available at https://www.gov.uk/government/publications/the-united-kingdoms-exit-from-and-new-partnership-with-the-european-union-white-paper (access date: 10 November 2018)).

[140] See Chapters 5 and 7.

[141] While this is not explicitly stated in the *Deckmyn* decision, it is more developed by the AGO in *Deckmyn* (n 101) [42].

[142] Traditionally, some national judges such as English judges have been more reluctant to hear arguments based on human rights law in copyright cases (aka external limits). This is because it is perceived as being the role of the legislator to strike a balance between property rights and other fundamental rights through internal limits of copyright legislation (e.g. duration, scope, subject matter, and exceptions).

4.1 France

Just as the UK is the home of common law, so France is the mother of the civil law tradition. France adopted a statutory parody exception with the implementation of the Intellectual Property Code in 1957.[143] The exception, therefore, precedes the introduction of the three-step test in Berne in 1967. Yet, as France is both an EU member and a signatory to the international copyright treaties discussed, the French legislator must still ensure that its exception remains compliant with its international and supranational obligations.

The parody exception was incorporated into the French Intellectual Property Code ('IPC') in recognition of accepted judicial practice.[144] Parodies and quotations were not considered to infringe authors' rights, in recognition of the right to criticize[145] upheld by the eighteenth-century revolutionaries.[146] Unfortunately, there is very little literature on these earlier practices. This may support an assumption that the introduction of a statutory parody exception was uncontentious, as it merely codified a well-established practice.[147]

Adopting the civil law author-oriented approach outlined earlier, French courts consider that exclusive rights must be interpreted broadly to protect the author's interests appropriately. The corollary is that any statutory exceptions limiting those rights must be interpreted strictly.[148] From this perspective, a judge has generally a fairly limited role;[149] as the balancing of interests has already been undertaken by the legislator, the courts merely apply the exception.[150]

With this in mind, the parody exception[151] reads: 'Once a work has been disclosed, the author may not prohibit: … [p]arody, pastiche and caricature, observing the rules of the genre.'[152]

It is reasonable to infer that the first step of the international three-step test is satisfied, as there seems little doubt that 'parody, pastiche and caricature' constitute 'certain special cases' in the sense of the treaties.[153] Additionally, as reference is made to the 'rules of the genre', French courts have a framework to meet the second and third steps

[143] Article 41, 4° of the law of 11 March 1957 (now article L122-5 4° IPC); for more on this law: R Savatier, 'Loi du 11 mars 1957 sur la propriété littéraire et artistique' (1957) 42(2) *JCP* 677.

[144] The parody exception already figured in revolutionary decrees in force between 1791 and 1957. Galopin (n 1) 3; A R Bertrand, 'Exceptions à la protection en matière de droit d'auteur qui figurent au CPI' in *Droit d'auteur* (Dalloz, 2012) 326; P El Khoury, *Les exceptions au droit d'auteur, étude de droit comparé* (University of Montpellier, 2007) 22. Jean-Michel Bruguière adds that, although the parody exception consists of a judicial creation, the 'rules of the genre' was a concept created by the legislator. J-M Bruguière, 'La réception du fair dealing britannique dans le système d'exception fermée français' (2018) *RIDA* (forthcoming).

[145] 'Droit de critique'; A Strowel, 'La parodie selon le droit d'auteur et la théorie littéraire' (1991) 26 *RIEJ* 44; M Buteau, *Le droit de critique en matière littéraire, dramatique et artistique* (L. Larose et L. Tenin, 1909).

[146] Decisions prior the codification of the exception: Trib. Comm. Seine, 26 juin 1934, gaz. Pal. 1934. 2. 594; Trib. Comm. Seine, 26 août 1886, Ann. 1889, p. 352; Trib. Civ. Seine, 12 juin 1879, Ann. propr. ind. 1879, p. 239; Trib. Corr. Seine, 20 mars 1877, Ann, 1877, p. 212; Trib. Civ. Seine, 23 février 1872, Ann. propr. ind. 1873, p. 162; Trib. Corr. Paris, 6 février 1834. Gaz. Trib. 8 février 1834.

[147] Geiger (n 27) 88.

[148] Galopin (n 1) 2; P Sirinelli, 'Le droit d'auteur à l'âge du numérique' in X Greffe and N Sonnac (eds), *Culture Web. Création, contenus, économie numérique* (Dalloz, 2008) 409.

[149] See section 2.2; P Malaurie, *L'ordre public et le contrat* (Paris, 1950) 603.

[150] See Chapter 4, section 2.

[151] The wording of the exception is the same today as in the Law of 1957.

[152] WIPO's translation of the French Intellectual Property Code, available at http://www.wipo.int/wipolex/en/details.jsp?id=16750 (access date: 1 June 2018).

[153] See Chapter 1, section 5.2.1.

of the three-step test. As Chapter 4 will explain in more detail, the 'rules of the genre' impose additional requirements on unauthorized use, thereby providing a framework which should enable the French parody exception to comply with the three-step test. The requirements include factors (resembling fair use and fair dealing, which we shall consider shortly) allowing a judge to assess the user's motivation, as well as taking account, for example, of the extent of the use and the impact on the market of the original. Additionally, and perhaps too often forgotten, Jean-Michel Bruguière reminds us that the rules of the genre also invite judges to consider fair practices developed in particular art fields.[154]

Prior to *Deckmyn*, French courts already weighed up the competing interests in particular cases as a matter of routine. Since its underlying rationale is as a right to critique, this has allowed judges to admit human rights-based arguments in parody cases.[155] The right to critique includes the right to create parody works without requiring authorization, since parody is heavily anchored in the tradition of fundamental rights, including freedom of expression. Indeed, the French legislator considered freedom of expression to be the most important justification for a parody exception.

Despite this apparent compliance, the French legislator responded to the InfoSoc Directive by amending article L.122-5 IPC to incorporate the wording of the three-step test into national law. While French courts have yet to apply the three-step test as an additional requirement of the parody exception, this test has been applied directly in cases involving other copyright exceptions.[156] The result of imposing the three-step test as an additional requirement before an exception applies is likely to restrict the scope of the narrowly construed exception.

In conclusion, by subjecting the unauthorized use to 'the rules of the genre', the French legislator considers the three-step test, as enshrined in international texts, satisfied. However, it seems to have considered that the EU harmonizing legislation has imposed further restrictions. As for all the other jurisdictions, this compliance is honed further by the need to respect the author's moral rights which will be covered in Chapter 6.

4.2 The United Kingdom

The newly introduced parody exception is a result of extensive consultation. Although copyright law was completely overhauled by the CDPA in 1988, it was enacted prior to both the digital revolution and most EU harmonization. The Gowers Review,

[154] Bruguière (n 144).

[155] See especially in trade mark cases: Riom, 15 septembre 1994 D. 1995, p. 429, note Edelman; TGI Nanterre, réf., 28 mai 2003: légipresse 2003, I, p. 118; Baud and Colombet, 'La parodie de marque: vers une érosion du caractère absolu des signes distinctifs?' D. 1998, chron. p. 227; *contra*: TGI Paris, 3e ch., 21 mars 2000, CCE 2000, Comm. 88, note Caron; TGI Paris, 3e ch., 4 juillet 2001: Expertises 2001, p. 395; or in relation to image rights: Reims, 9 février 1999: JCP G 1999, II, 10144, note Bigot; D. 1999, p. 449, note Edelman; Cass. 1ère Civ., 13 janvier 1998: RIDA mars 1998, p. 201, obs. Kéréver; JCP G 1998, II, 10082, note Loiseau; D. 1999, p. 120, note Ravanas.

[156] Cass. 1ère Civ., 28 février 2006, JurisData n°2006-032368; RIDA mars 2006, p. 323; JCP G 2006, II, 10084, note Lucas; CCE 2006, Comm. 56, note Caron; A&M 2/2006, p.177, note Dusollier; Propr. intell. 2006, p. 179, obs. Lucas; RTD com. 2006, p. 370, obs. Pollaud-Dulian; Appeal referral: Paris, 4e ch., 4 avril 2007: JurisData n°2007-329335; RIDA mars 2007, p. 379; CCE 2007, Comm. 68, note Caron; A&M 4/2007, p. 346, note Dusollier; Propr. intell. 2007, p. 320, obs. Lucas; RTD com. 2007, p. 357, obs. Pollaud-Dulian; second referral to the Supreme Court: Cass. 1ère Civ., 19 juin 2008: JurisData n°2008-044405; RIDA mars 2008, p. 299; RLDI juillet 2008, n°1322.

reporting in 2006, first drew attention to the need for a parody exception in UK copyright law.[157] This proposal was studied by the IPO, which undertook a two-stage public consultation in 2008[158] and 2009.[159] These consultations identified highly bifurcated opinions. Opponents argued that the existing legislation made adequate provision for parody already, that the exception would be open to abuse or countenance plagiarism, and that it would not give rise to litigation owing to uncertainty surrounding its intended reach.[160] In addition, right-holders protested that they would lose income because of the exception. In sum, the debate focused around whether an exception was needed, rather than concerning what form an exception should take. Ultimately, the evidence supporting an exception was deemed to be insufficient for a change to be warranted.[161]

A new review of UK copyright law was commissioned in 2010, following a change in government.[162] The Hargreaves Review was tasked with assessing how effectively the existing intellectual property framework supported economic growth and innovation. Reporting in 2011, Hargreaves reaffirmed the need for a parody exception within UK copyright law, as one of the factors needed to 'enhance the economic potential of the UK's creative industries',[163] while also recognizing the 'long and vibrant tradition' of British comedy and the emerging 'new forms of expression' which the internet facilitates.[164]

The government undertook further consultation on the proposal, and while the representations from opponents were consistent with those made a few years earlier, the economics-based arguments in favour of a parody exception seemed to prevail. While it was acknowledged that a parody exception is necessary to realize the right of freedom of expression,[165] it was also linked to improving the digital skills base of the population.[166] In adopting Hargreaves' proposal for a parody exception, the UK government attached importance to the anticipated economic growth opportunities that permitting parodies would allow. Comedy, for example, was identified as 'big business'.[167]

157 A. Gowers, *Gowers Review of Intellectual Property* (London: HM Treasury, November 2006) Recommendation 12.

158 UK-IPO, *Taking Forward the Gowers Review of Intellectual Property: Changes to Copyright Exceptions* (Newport: UK-IPO, 2008).

159 UK-IPO, *Taking Forward the Gowers Review of Intellectual Property: Second Stage Consultation on Copyright Exceptions* (Newport: UK-IPO, 2009).

160 Regarding the definition, scope, conditions, and the barrier between plagiarism and parody.

161 See n 159, 46.

162 A coalition between the Conservatives and Liberal Democrats replaced the former Labour government.

163 Quoting from Professor Hargreaves at http://www.bbc.co.uk/news/technology-13429217 (access date: 1 June 2018).

164 I Hargreaves, *Digital Opportunity. A Review of Intellectual Property and Growth* (Independent Report, 2011).

165 'Parody may be as old as Aristophanes but it has found new popularity in recent years with the development of online social media and digital technology. Modern parodies are as likely to be made at home by ordinary people as by professional writers, broadcasters and comedians. Parodies have become part and parcel of online social interaction, with parody works adorning Facebook walls and trending on Twitter. The modern public's response to an event is as likely to be expressed through Photoshop competitions and Downfall parodies as through traditional comment, argument, and debate.' HM Government, *Consultation on Copyright* (2011) para 7.103.

166 '[T]he most important issues in that area concern freedom of expression . . . there is an economic link. Video parody is today becoming part and parcel of the interactions of private citizens, often via social networking sites, and encourages literacy in multimedia expression in ways that are increasingly essential to the skills base of the economy.' See n 164, 50.

167 Ibid.

A parody exception would support a 'growing entertainment market worldwide' and permit comedy to 'reach wider audiences'.[168]

The parody exception to the economic right of reproduction finally came into force on 1 October 2014.[169] Pursuant to section 30A(1), there will be no infringement of copyright in a literary, dramatic, musical, or artistic work where there is a *fair dealing* with the original work *for the purposes of caricature, parody, or pastiche*.[170]

Before turning to a more detailed examination of section 30A(1) in light of the three-step test, it is important to note that, arguably, this provision does not limit itself to dealings by way of reproduction. Having its roots in sub-section 2(1)(i) of the Copyright Act 1911, 'dealing' is the legal term designating any use of a work which would otherwise constitute a copyright infringement. The only conditions imposed by the legislation for an unauthorized use to fall within the exception are that the use is: (1) fair; and (2) for the purposes of caricature, parody, and pastiche.

While there is no statutory definition of 'fair', its meaning has been developed in case law. In the landmark decision of *Hubbard v. Vosper*,[171] Lord Denning indicated that fairness is a 'question of degree'. [172] Most of the judicial consideration of fairness relates to the copyright exception for criticism, review, quotation, and news reporting.[173] Stemming from this case law, three factors seem to be decisive: the commercial nature of the use; the quantity copied; and whether the work had been previously published, or not.[174]

Does the UK parody exception comply with the three-step test? Firstly, while the language of section 30A(1) CDPA 1988 is broad, being applicable to all works and presumably to all exclusive rights, the legislator has limited this exception to dealings for 'purposes of caricature, parody and pastiche'. It might be questionable whether this amounts to 'certain special cases', as understood under the first step, given the lack of any statutory definition and coherent body of decisions of what parody, caricature, and pastiche entail.[175] However, the CJEU itself, in the *Deckmyn* case, refused to define parody, despite qualifying it as an autonomous concept under EU law favouring the judicial route.[176]

Here, the intepretation of the parody exception in *Deckmyn* does provide some certainty. By requiring all parodies to have a humorous character and evoke an existing work while being noticeably different from it,[177] the CJEU provides the over-arching criteria, thus permitting the exception to apply in 'certain special cases'.[178]

Secondly, fairness also permits compliance with the second step of the test that an exception must not conflict with 'the normal exploitation of the work'. While it remains uncertain whether UK courts will adopt the same fairness factors as under other fair dealing exceptions, it is reasonable to assume that these factors will be influential. In addition, it is arguable that any fairness factors will need to comply with the two requirements set out in *Deckmyn*, at least until express rejection of the

[168] See n 165, para 7.104.

[169] The Copyright and Rights in Performances (Quotation and Parody) Regulations 2014, SI 2014/2356.

[170] The parody exception is also available for performances, schedule 2, para 2B.

[171] *Hubbard v. Vosper* [1972] 2 QB 84, CA (Civ Div) 94 and 98.

[172] Ibid, 94.

[173] Section 30 CDPA.

[174] However, as argued in Chapter 4, the parody exception probably requires an adaptation of these factors.

[175] And the UK does not enjoy the same rich case law as in France since Revolutionary times.

[176] *Deckmyn* (n 88) [14]–[17].

[177] Ibid, [20].

[178] The UK does not yet enjoy the same long-standing experience as French courts have since the Revolutionary decrees and which inherently helps determine the outer boundaries of the exception.

CJEU's influence post-Brexit. Here, the CJEU rejected imposition of certain factors, such as the requirement that the parody must display an original character of its own, be explicitly attributed to the parodist (distancing it from the original author), comment only on the work on which it was based, or mention the source of the original. However, it is strongly believed that fairness factors enable the UK to pass the second step.

Finally, the exception should not 'unreasonably prejudice the legitimate interests of the author'. This suggests that the fair dealing parody exception should not impose a disproportionate prejudice to either the economic or non-economic interests of the author.[179] As the fair dealing factors already take account of commercial factors, the main question remaining is to determine the boundaries of the exception. In particular, does the UK parody exception provide restrictions to ensure that the author's moral rights are preserved? While there is no indication in section 30A(1), it is important to note that the UK parody exception is only an exception for economic rights. Therefore, the original authors retain the possibility to enforce their moral rights to secure their interests.[180]

To sum up, it seems reasonable to conclude that there is sufficient basis for the UK parody exception to satisfy the three-step test today. Of course, it remains to be seen how it will be interpreted in practice, pending further consideration and implementation by the courts.

4.3 Australia

Consistent with its common law tradition, Australian copyright exceptions, like those in the UK, also generally adopt a 'fair dealing' form.[181] The Copyright Act 1968 ('CA 1968') provides a flexible formula confined to certain limited purposes.[182] This leaves it to judges to determine which factors are pertinent to assess the fairness of any qualifying use.

A number of motivating factors seem to have led up to the introduction of a new fair dealing exception 'for the purpose of parody and satire' in 2006. This was introduced as new sections 41A and 103AA of the CA 1968. These include the need to counterbalance the increasing protection of right-holders within their copyright legislation,[183] as well as adapting the scope of the exclusive rights to take account of new technologies, and to provide additional legal certainty for users. [184] Aware that the EU Directive permitted Member States the option of providing a parody exception, Australia was keen to keep pace. During its Second Reading, Attorney-General Philip Ruddock justified the introduction of the new exception by the aim of protecting 'Australia's fine tradition of satire', noting:

[179] Yet, under article 13 TRIPS only economic interests are taken into account.

[180] See Chapter 6.

[181] Australia codified its own fair dealing provision in 1905; it appears to be very similar to the English provision as they share part of their legislative and common law history. Sims believes the Australians copied the provision from the cl. 4(5) of the UK's Copyright Bill 1900. A Sims, 'Strangling their creation: the courts' treatment of fair dealing in copyright law since 1911' (2010) 2 *IPQ* 192, 193.

[182] Ricketson (n 40) 73.

[183] Attorney-General's Department, *Issues Paper, Fair Use and other Copyright Exceptions in the Digital Age* (05/2005) (Fair Use Inquiry) by the Copyright Agency Limited, 8.

[184] N Suzor, 'Where the bloody hell does parody fit in Australian copyright law?' (2008) 13 *MALR* 220; M Sainsbury, 'Parody, satire and copyright infringement: the latest addition to Australian fair dealing law' (2007) 12 *MALR* 292; Commonwealth of Australia, Parliamentary Debates, House of Representatives, 19 October 2006, 2 (Philip Ruddock, Attorney-General).

Australians have always had an irreverent streak. Our cartoonists ensure sacred cows don't stay sacred for very long and comedians are merciless on those in public life. An integral part of their armoury is parody and satire—or, if you prefer, 'taking the micky' out of someone.[185]

The Minister of Justice also referred to 'Australia's fine tradition of poking fun at itself and others', adding that the exception would 'not be unnecessarily restricted'. [186]

The introduction of a parody exception attracted little controversy in Australia. Thus, the legislative process affords sparse insight on the approach to satisfying the three-step test. However, based upon preparatory materials, the legislator's primary aim was to recognize the value of humorous and critical expressions within a democratic society,[187] which required the exclusive rights of right-holders to be balanced against the value of parody as an artistic expression.[188] Accordingly, section 41A provides:

A fair dealing with a literary, dramatic, musical or artistic work, or with an adaptation of a literary, dramatic or musical work, does not constitute an infringement of the copyright in the work if it is for the purpose of parody or satire.[189]

Initially, the Attorney-General proposed that this new fair dealing exception would be added into existing section 200AB Act 1968, which already incorporates the three-step test into the Copyright Act.[190] As we have seen earlier, the reason for repeating the international test within the national legislation is to task the judiciary with compliance with international obligations.[191] Consequently, trial judges are required to assess whether the three-step test is satisfied in any particular case, based upon the evidence which the defendant has produced to the court.[192] Unlike the reiteration of the three-step test in the InfoSoc Directive, section 200AB(7) CA 1968 provides guidance as to the meaning of the test, insofar as its interpretation is required to be in compliance with article 13 of the TRIPS Agreement.

The proposed introduction of the parody exception within section 200AB encountered serious criticism from the Senate Legal and Constitutional Affairs Committee.[193]

[185] Attorney-General Philip Ruddock, 'Protecting Precious Parody', *Daily Telegraph*, 30 November 2006; Second Reading speech to the House of Representatives (Commonwealth of Australia, Parliamentary Debates, House of Representatives, 19 October 2006, 2 (Philip Ruddock, Attorney-General); Commonwealth of Australia, Parliamentary Debates, 29 November 2006, 112 (Chris Ellison, Minister for Justice and Customs).

[186] Commonwealth of Australia, Parliamentary Debates, House of Representatives, 19 October 2006, 2 (Philip Ruddock, Attorney-General).

[187] A distinctive feature of the Australian legislation is the absence of recognition of freedom of expression at constitutional level. Hence, the protection of freedom of expression derives from international texts. See Chapter 5, section 1.

[188] Australian Government Discussion Paper, *Proposed Moral Rights Protection for Copyright Creators* (Australian Government Printer, June 1994) 49, [3.66]–[3.67]; Commonwealth of Australia, Parliamentary Debates, House of Representatives, 19 October 2006, 2 (Philip Ruddock, Attorney-General); Attorney-General's Department, Submission No 69A to the Senate Standing Committees on Legal and Constitutional Affairs, Inquiry into the Provisions of the Copyright Amendment Bill 2006, 8 November 2006, 3.

[189] Section 103AA expands the parody exception to audio-visual content.

[190] This introduction of the three-step test in Australian copyright law derives from article 17.4.10 AUSFTA. The influence of the US on the Australian legal order is not to be underestimated. There are consultations of a possible reform to adopt a fair use formula instead of fair dealing. See discussion paper available at http://www.alrc.gov.au/publications/copyright-and-digital-economy-dp-79 (access date: 10 November 2018).

[191] C Bond, A Paramaguru, and G Greenleaf, 'Advance Australia Fair? The copyright reform process' (2007) 10(3/4) *The Journal of World Intellectual Property* 284, 295.

[192] Gervais (n 34) 36.

[193] Senate Inquiry, Parliament of Australia, Senate Legal and Constitutional Affairs Committee, Inquiry into the Provisions of the Copyright Amendment Bill 2006 (available at www.aph.gov.au), report dated 13 November 2006, [3.70]; S McCausland, 'New room to lampoon: the new fair dealing

Primarily, this arose because the three-step test was seen as being transmuted into a four-step test (the use was required to be both 'a special case' and 'for the purpose of parody'). Additionally, the additional stage was believed to create too much uncertainty for users, who would be unable to foresee whether their intended use would be permitted by the exception.[194] Consequently, the government adopted a free-standing fair dealing provision, assessing that its formula was adequate to comply with the international three-step test.[195]

Notwithstanding the assertions made at the time, we should still satisfy ourselves that the Australian parody exception is compliant with the three-step test. As with the UK provision, it is evident that the exception extends beyond the reproduction right, as section 41 applies to all copyright dealings, including adaptations. Ricketson has traced the origins of 'dealings' in CA 1968 back to the UK Copyright Act 1911.[196] Thus, its legal meaning, as in the UK, includes any use which would otherwise result in a copyright infringement. Therefore, the only limitations imposed on parodists under section 41 are that the dealing must be 'for the purposes of parody and satire', and 'fair'.

Does 'parody and satire' amount to 'certain special cases' as understood under international treaties? As mentioned, there is no statutory definition of the terms. The principal case in which these terms have been considered by an Australian court is the *TCN* decision, decided before the enactment of a specific parody exception. Here, Conti J. consulted the *Macquarie Dictionary* definitions and determined that the essence of parody is the imitation of the original, while satire is 'form of ironic, sarcastic, scornful, derisive or ridiculing criticism of vice, folly or abuses'[197] which does not require imitation to function. While the judge considered that a parody could be a fair dealing, he concluded that satire could not. Clearly, this is at odds with the wording of the new legislative exception which does envisage that certain 'satirical' uses (at least) can be fair dealing.

Based on the above, and pending further guidance from the Australian courts, it seems reasonable to assume that the terms parody and satire need to be interpreted broadly. While, like its UK counterpart, the Australian exception is framed as a fair dealing exception, the *TCN* case might suggest that fair dealing is being interpreted rather (too) restrictively. The application of fair dealing has always been a challenge for judges and, arguably, the new Australian provisions give little reassurance to defendants because there is no guidance as to how fairness is to be determined. While it is reasonable to assume that factors adopted under other fair dealing exceptions are likely to be influential, it is noteworthy that judges may depart from these and can even adopt new factors as long as these respect the three-step test and fundamental rights.[198] However, as noted by Weatherall, Australian judges seem to have put more

exception for parody or satire' (2007) 1 *Art+Law* 3; Weatherall's Law (available at http://weatherall.blogspot. com), post date: 5 July 2006; P Loughlan, 'Parody, copyright and the new four-step test' (2006) *December IPSANZ* 46; For a general critique of the importation of the three-step test into national copyright laws: Koelman (n 58) 407.

194 B Mee, 'Laughing matters: parody and satire in Australian copyright law' (2010) 20(1) *Journal of Law, Information and Science* 61, esp. 71.

195 Nevertheless, Loughlan wonders whether the new parody exception in the copyright legislation would survive if challenged under article 13 TRIPS without further limitation. The author of this book does not share her concerns. P Loughlan 'Parody, copyright and the new four-step test' (2006) *December IPSANZ* 46, 49. For a study of fairness factors, see Chapter 4, section 2.

196 Enacted in Australian law by section 2 of the Copyright Act 1912 (Cth).

197 *TCN* [17].

198 By analogy with Ricketson's reasoning regarding the compliance of sub-section 40(1) with the three-step test, it could be argued that fairness under section 41 is too uncertain and vague to meet the

emphasis on the purpose of the use rather than on the fairness factors to determine the lawfulness of a use.[199] This has the effect of reintroducing some legal certainty for the exception to respect this first step.

The second step of the three-step test considers whether, or not, a use conflicts with the normal exploitation of the work. The compliance of section 41 with this step depends heavily on how fairness of a particular use is contemplated. Similar to our assessment of the UK exception, the court should take account of the nature of the particular use, right-holders' usual manner of exploitation, and typical revenue streams, including whether right-holders create or license parodies and satires. To achieve this, it seems likely that Australian judges will consider the historical development of fair dealing and use comparative analysis to determine whether there is a conflict of economic interests in a particular case. Therefore, if fair dealing implies adopting similar factors to those mentioned under section 40(2), then it is believed that the parody meets the second step of the three-step test. As further developed in Chapter 4, these include the nature of the work, availability of a licence, effect of the dealing upon the market of the original, and the quality and quantity of the copied parts.

Assuming that the first two steps are met, the Australian version of the exception still needs to comply with the third step. This step should be easier to meet given that the exception only relates to copyright and does not exempt the parodies from being liable for violation of the author's moral rights.[200]

Overall, compliance of the Australian parody exception with the three-step test is possible, but dependent upon adoption of 'fairness factors' which take due account of the second and third steps of that test. Without suitable crafting, it is arguable that the parody exception might conflict with the normal exploitation of a work, so rendering the third step moot. Given how little attention this exception received during the legislative debates, at present, it is difficult to verify its compliance with the three-step test.[201]

4.4 Canada

Consistent with its common law tradition, Canada introduced a fair dealing formula for copyright exceptions in 1921.[202] As we are now familiar, an otherwise infringing use will benefit from a defence provided (i) the use falls within one of the specified categories, and (ii) is considered to be a fair dealing by courts. While the range of exceptions has expanded, 'fair dealing' remains a concept expounded in the case law.[203]

first step of the test. S Ricketson, 'The three-step test, deemed quantities, libraries and closed exceptions' (Centre for Copyright Studies Ltd, 2002) 63.

199 Intellectual Property Research Institute of Australia (IPRIA) and Centre for Media and Communications Law (CMCL), *Response to the Issues Paper: Fair Use and Other Copyright Exceptions in the Digital Age* (July 2005) 11.

200 See Chapter 6.

201 It is important to combine section 41 with section 5(2) CA 1968: 'Use made of a work in creating another work shall not make that other work an adaptation, provided such work constitutes an independent new work in relation to the work used.'

202 Copyright Act, 1921 S.C., ch. 24 (Can.); Y Gendreau, 'Synthèse possible ou impossible du droit civil et de la common law—l'exemple du Canada' in *La mise en oeuvre des droits d'auteur: Le rôle de la législation nationale en droit d'auteur* (ALAI, 1999) 363; S Plante, 'Les nouvelles exceptions en droit canadien: un faux débat' (1998) 11 *Cah. Prop. Intell.* 2; for more on the influence of the Statute of Anne on Canada: D J Gervais, 'A Canadian copyright narrative' in P L C Torremans (ed.), *Copyright Law: A Handbook of Contemporary Research* (Edward Elgar, 2009) 51.

203 S Beaulac, 'Legal interpretation in Canada: opening up legislative language as a means to internationalisation' (2010) 5/2010 *University of Edinburgh working papers series* 1–36.

The specific parody exception, introduced into the Copyright Act, experienced a lengthy gestation. It first featured in Bill C-60 of 2005. This marked the start of the major reform of Canada's Copyright Act required to implement the international obligations arising from the WIPO treaties. This Bill did not progress before Parliament was dissolved in November 2005.[204] Bill-61 re-introduced the same subject matter some three years later, but it suffered the same fate.[205] In 2010, Minister Tony Clement tabled a revised proposal, Bill C-32,[206] but it failed to be implemented before a further change of Parliament. Finally, new legislation was implemented by Stephen Harper's majority in the government. Based upon Bill C-11, which largely replicated Bill C-32, it introduced a fair dealing exception for the purpose of parody or satire. Bill C-11 received Royal Assent on 29 June 2012 and most of the provisions were brought into force on 7 November 2012.[207]

Unfortunately for our purposes, the parody exception was largely overshadowed by other topics in pre-implementation discussions. The general policy behind the complete new set of new copyright exceptions—of which the parody exception was only one—was to achieve a better balance between the right-holders' right to remuneration and the need for users to access protected works, as required to protect the public interest.[208] Accordingly, the government sought to protect freedom of expression, as well as the social benefits[209] associated with parodies and satires, by providing a copyright environment more amenable to fostering the creation of these particular types of expressions.

The newly introduced parody exception, incorporated into section 29 of the Copyright Act 1985, states: 'fair dealing for the purpose of research, private study, education, parody or satire does not infringe copyright.' Marking a departure from the other fair dealing provisions which we consider in this book, the Canadian legislator included parody and satire within an existing provision covering use for the purpose of research, private study, and education. By doing so, it is possible that this Canadian version of the parody exception complies more easily with 'certain special cases'. If courts still need to confirm the interpretation of parody and satire (although the first case since the introduction of the parody exception adopts the two main EU requirements), the fairness factors have already been developed under the other purposes mentioned in section 29, thereby providing more legal certainty.

As with the other common law jurisictions considered, Canadian courts have a proactive role in interpreting the provision by identifying which uses are likely to be 'fair'. In line with the Supreme Court ruling in *CCH*,[210] fair dealing is assessed 'holistically', based mainly upon six variables. Courts must consider the purpose and character of the dealing, the amount copied, whether the alleged infringer had alternatives to the

[204] Bill C-60: An Act to amend the Copyright Act, 38th Parl., 1st Sess., 53–54 Eliz. II (2004); see preamble of the Copyright Modernization Act, SC 2012, c20.

[205] Bill C-61: An Act to amend the Copyright Act, 39th Parl., 2nd Sess., 56–57 Eliz. II (2008).

[206] Bill C-32, cl. 21 (modifying § 29).

[207] The fair dealing exceptions for the purposes of parody or satire and the UGC have been in force since 7 November 2012.

[208] Plante (n 202); for more on the Canadian copyright reform: L J Murray, 'Copyright talk: patterns and pitfalls in Canadian Policy discourses' in M Geist (eds), *The Public Interest: The Future of Canadian Copyright Law* (Irwin Law, 2005) 15.

[209] M Ficsor, *Comments on the UGC Provisions in the Canadian Bill C-32* (2010) 9 http://www.copyrightseelaw.net/archive/?sw_10_item=31; J Bailey, 'Deflating the Michelin Man' in *In the Public Interest: The Future of Canadian Copyright Law* (Irwin Law, 2005) 125–66, esp. 127.

[210] *CCH Canadian Ltd v. Law Society of Upper Canada* [2004] 1 S.C.R. 339 (hereafter *CCH*); *Entertainment Software Association of Canada v. SOCAN* [2012] S.C.C. 34 (hereafter *SOCAN*).

dealing, the nature of the copied work, and the effect of the dealing on the work.[211] These six factors enable section 29 to pass the second step of the three-step text more easily in a similar way to other common law jurisdictions we covered earlier.

Having passed these two initial steps, the exception should not cause a disproportionate prejudice to non-economic interests of the original author. As typical of the common law tradition, the parody exception relates to economic rights only. The Canadian legislator left the author's moral rights untouched by the exception.[212]

4.5 The United States

While the US, like UK, Australia, and Canada, is a common law jurisdiction, copyright exceptions are based upon 'fair use' and not 'fair dealing'. Fair use might be seen as the reverse of fair dealing, since there is no statutory limit regarding the purpose of a permitted use, whereas the fairness factors are codified in section 107 of the United States Copyright Act 1976. Case law interpretation of the Act has determined that use of a protected work for the purposes of parody will not infringe copyright provided the use is 'fair' as per the statutory factors.[213] In determining the fairness of the use, US courts have particular regard to the purpose and character of the use, the nature of the copyright-protected work, the amount of what is being copied, and the effect of the use upon the market of the original.[214] Like fair dealing, the fair use doctrine is broad and flexible. Therefore, judges can take account of additional factors, if relevant, and attribute more weight to some of the factors than to others.[215] In addition, while section 107 makes mention of the right of reproduction, fair use is not limited to any specific exclusive right.

The main difference between fair use and other approaches to exceptions considered previously is the undefined, open-ended character of the unauthorized use. This enables copyright defences to adapt to technology changes and users' habits without requiring specific legislation. Here, courts take on an important role in shaping the scope and reach of copyright exceptions, but they also ensure its compliance with the three-step test on a case-by-case basis. However, as no clear-cut rules exist which distinguish permitted uses from those which may infringe based upon the reason for the use, the outcome in any litigation is unpredictable, meaning that users enjoy little legal certainty.

Despite its long standing, academic scholars still debate whether the open-ended fair use doctrine is compliant with the three-step test. This very point was considered in the DSB decision in which the European Community lodged a complaint with WTO based upon non-compliance with the TRIPS three-step test (art. 13 TRIPS) of certain exceptions included in section 110(5) of the US Copyright Code. The particular provision permits television and radio music to be played in public places (including retail establishments) without paying a royalty fee under certain conditions. In order for the fair use defence to be confined to 'certain special cases', the DSB held that the exception must be well-defined and narrow in scope.[216] Considering this interpretation, it is

[211] See analysis of parody factors in Chapter 4. [212] See Chapter 6.

[213] The fair use doctrine is older than that as it can be traced back to the *Folsom v. Marsh* decision of 1841. 9 F.Cas. 342 (C.C.D. Mass. 1841) as acknowledged in *Harper & Row Publishers, Inc. v. Nation Enters.*, 471 U.S. 539, 550 (1985).

[214] Section 107(1)–(4).

[215] Confirmed by Congressional intent: H.R. REP. No. 1476, 94th Cong., 2d Sess. 66 (1976); S. REK No. 473, 94th Cong., 1st Sess. 62 (1975).

[216] WTO Panel (n 115), [6.113].

reasonable to argue that the fair use doctine is unlikely to be narrow and clear enough to meet the threshold.[217] Furthermore, as the defence is available to any user following a finding of copyright infringement, the potential pool of users is unlimited.[218] For these reasons, it remains questionable whether the fair use doctrine can be qualified as 'limited' in reach and scope.

However, if we consider the application of US fair use to parodies, it becomes easier to argue that fair 'parodic' use does meet the first of the three steps in the test. As seen in Chapter 1, the US Supreme Court narrowed the scope of the fair use doctrine for this use in *Campbell v. Acuff-Rose Music, Inc.*[219] Requiring a permitted parody to pass comment or criticism *of* the original borrowed work,[220] this decision did not exclude *parody with* (i.e. using the borrowed materials as a vehicle for comments) provided that comments and criticisms of society at large per se. But later lower courts have noted the parody/satire distinction as determinative because parodists who rely upon a copyright-protected work merely as a vehicle for criticism of something else do not *need* to reproduce a protected work in order to achieve this goal.[221]

The second step is probably easier to assess. Indeed, as the three-step test has its roots in the Anglo-American tradition, it is hard to deny the link between the prohibition of conflict with the normal exploitation of the work and the fourth US factor, requiring examination of the effect of the use upon the market of the original.[222] As further developed in Chapter 4, US courts seem to look favourably on parodies which involve a comic element and some form of critical comment of the parodied work.[223] Here, it may be inferred that the *Campbell* decision broadens fair use by its reformulation of the first factor, since the US Supreme Court rephrased the question for the application of fair use as:

> [W]hether the new work merely supersedes the objects of the original creation, or whether and to what extent it is 'transformative,' altering the original with new expression, meaning, or message. The more transformative the new work, the less will be the significance of other factors, like commercialism, that may weigh against a finding of fair use.[224]

As section 106(2) of the US Copyright Code grants the copyright holder the exclusive right to produce derivative works, the Supreme Court's dictum appears to permit US courts to circumscribe this right and permit any transformation of copyright-protected works which convey a new expression building on the original.[225] Consequently, whilst older US decisions held that the fair use doctrine did not apply to uses which left the copied elements unchanged (especially where an artistic work was copied), decisions post-*Campbell* have permitted this type of use. For example, a reduction in size of copyright photographs for online purposes,[226] a reproduction of posters and tickets

[217] H C Jehoram, 'Restrictions on copyright and their abuse' (2005) 27(10) *EIPR* 359, 362; Sun (n 53) 291.

[218] WTO Panel (n 115), [6.126].

[219] 114 S. Ct 1164 (1994).

[220] Ibid, 578–9.

[221] This teaching was previously mentioned in: *Metro-Goldwin-Mayer v. Showcase Atlanta Cooperative Productions, Inc.* 479 F. Supp 351 (N.D. Ga. 1979), 357; *MCA, Inc. v. Wilson* 425 F. Supp. 443 (S.D.N.Y. 1976), aft'd, 677 F.2d 180 (2d Cir. 1981), 180 and 453; *Fisher v. Dees* 794 F.2d 432. (9th Cir. 1986), 436; *Rogers v. Koons*, 960 F.2d 301, 309–10 (2d Cir. 1992), 310.

[222] Senftleben (n 24) 184–7. This also explains why the fourth factor has often had a dominant weight in the courts' application of fair use. *Harper & Row, Publishers, Inc. v. Nation Enterprises*, 471 U.S. 539, 566 (1985).

[223] *Metro-Goldwin-Mayer v. Showcase Atlanta Cooperative Productions, Inc.* 479 F.Supp 351 (N.D. Ga. 1979).

[224] 114 S. Ct 1164 (1994) 569.

[225] And also perhaps of article 12 Berne.

[226] *Perfect 10, Inc. v. Amazon.com*, Inc. 487 F.3d 701 (9th Cir. 2007).

as illustrations in a book on a band's history,[227] the replication of photographs on canvas[228] and in paintings[229] have all been held to be permitted fair use, despite the commercial nature of that use, because there was a transformation in use from the original expressive purpose.[230]

Provided that the second step is satisfied, fair use for the purposes of parody should not unreasonably prejudice the right-holders' legitimate interests. This is probably the hardest step for US law to satisfy. With the expansion of fair use to transformative use, it is reasonable to argue for the introduction of some kind of financial compensation, such as a compulsory licence scheme. Equally, there are concerns that the fair use case law has stifled protection of authors' non-economic interests significantly. On its accession to Berne in 1989, the US was obliged to recognize the moral rights of paternity and integrity as prescribed under article 6bis Berne Convention.[231] As a result, the Visual Artists Rights Act of 1990 ('VARA') added a new section 106A into the US Copyright Code. However, this limits the rights of intergrity and attribution to visual arts alone.[232] As we shall see in Chapter 6, the courts' application of moral rights has eroded the level of protection granted to authors. The enforcement of moral rights is closely linked to an infringement action of economic prerogatives.[233] Therefore, it is arguable that the breadth of permitted use which courts have allowed based upon fair use transformativeness (adopting *Campbell* principles) cripples the non-economic interests of authors, jeopardizing its compliance with Berne.[234]

While the question of whether the US fair use doctrine is compliant with the international three-step test has long attracted academic attention, there has not been any challenge to the legality of fair use under the WTO.[235] Based on the guidance found in the WTO Panel decision, academics fail to agree on whether fair use complies with the obligations set out in Berne.[236] It seems that there is a case that fair use for the purposes of parody is non-compliant with the three-step test enshrined in Berne for failing to

227 *Bill Graham Archives v. Dorling Kindersley Ltd*, 448 F.3d 605 (2d Cir. 2006).

228 *Blanch v. Koons*, 467 F.3d 244 (2d Cir. 2006), 253.

229 *Cariou v. Prince*, 714 F.3d 694 (2d Cir. 2013), 707.

230 However, the expansive manner in which this US fair use doctrine is applied may tip the fair use doctrine towards non-compliance with the international test, as extending to third-party use which conflicts with the normal use of the protected work. This seems to be the position of Goldstein. P Goldstein, 'Berne in the USA' (2008) 39(2) *International Review of Intellectual Property and Competition Law* 220.

231 Section 43(a) Lanham Act, the general unfair competition provision, was expanded to protect the author's moral rights. Some state laws also recognized moral rights but their scope varied. See Chapter 6.

232 Pub. L. No. 101-650, tit. VI, 104 Stat. 5128, 8510–8515 (Dec. 1, 1990).

233 See Chapter 6, section 4.

234 Goldstein (n 230) 220.

235 R Okediji, 'Toward an international fair use standard' (2000) 39 *Columbia Journal of Transnational Law* 75, 161–2; J Bongiorno, 'Fair use of copyrighted images after Perfect 10 v. Amazon.com: diverging from constitutional principles & United States treaty obligations' (2009) 12 *Touro Int'l L. Rev.* 107, 153–4; R Tushnet, 'Content, purpose or both?' (2015) 90 *Wash. L. Rev*, 869; Jehoram (n 217) 359–64; D R Johnstone, 'Debunking fair use rights and copy duty under U.S. copyright law' (2005) 52 *J. Copyright Soc'y U.S.A.* 345, 398; P Samuelson, 'Possible futures of fair use' (2015) 90 *Wash. L. Rev.* 815, 852; J Hughes, 'Fair Use and its Politics--At Home and Abroad' in R Okediji (ed.), *Copyright Law in an Age of Exceptions and limitations* (Cambridge University Press, 2017) 22–4.

236 Positions can be summarized as follows: Hugues, Hugenholtz, Senftleben, Tushnet, Samuelson, and Ricketson argue that fair use is compliant while Goldstein, Cohen, Bronkamn, Geiger, Johnstone, Sun, Ginsburg, and Jehoram believe that the US fails to meet its international obligations in this regard. Ricketson (n 40); Goldstein (n 230) 220; J C Ginsburg, *Letter from the US: Exclusive Rights, Exceptions, and Uncertain Compliance with International Norms—Part II (Fair Use)* 3 (Columbia Law & Econ., Working Paper No. 503, 2014), available at http:// ssrn.com/abstract=2539178 (access date: 10 November 2018); Geiger et al (n 100) 612–16.

meet the third step. In other words, although the US may be compliant with the three-step test as enshrined in TRIPS, it may not be compliant with the same test contained in Berne owing to the lack of protection of moral rights.

5. Conclusion

It is undeniable that the three-step test continues to shape the scope and reach of copyright exceptions. Its influence is evident even in jurisdictions, such as the UK, which chose not to incorporate the test directly into national law. This political tool, intended initially to reconcile different legal traditions via international copyright law, seems to have transformed into a legal tool for the judiciary to use to determine appropriate application of copyright exceptions *in casu*.

This chapter has argued that the bespoke parody exceptions enshrined in the domestic law of the jurisdictions under consideration all have the potential to satisfy the international three-step test. By specifying the purposes for which the exception can be implemented and by framing the exception with the doctrines of fair dealing or the rules of the genre, and by retaining the option for the author to enforce moral rights, the parody exception in the UK, Canada, Australia, and France should meet the three steps required by international treaties. There is scope for conformity to be honed even further, because the boundaries of the exception are defined by the manner in which it is applied by the courts in specific cases.

Some reservations have emerged regarding the US's compliance with the three-step test. Indeed, as fair use solely relies on the factors set out in legislation, the courts carry more responsibility, by applying the factors to the facts before them, to ensure that the fair use doctrine is compliant with the test. While the current focus on the transformative nature of the use is flexible, and so adaptable to technological changes, there is a real risk that it becomes too broad in scope and reach to meet the first step of the test. It remains to be seen whether the restriction of the fair use doctrine for parody works to uses which directly comment or criticize the copyright-protected work parodied is sufficient to be confined to certain special cases. Furthermore, the abridged application of moral rights possibly impedes fair use to meet the third step of the test. Therefore, the compliance of a parody exception firmly hinges upon its judicial interpretation.[237]

As the influence of the three-step test has now extended to EU national judges, some (meagre) comfort may be found in *Deckmyn*. In this case, an enabling function of the three-step test emerges. This opens the door for national courts to hear arguments based on human rights in some cases, and directs them to strike a fair balance between the competing interests at stake. This appears to coincide with the Canadian approach since *CCH*. In *CCH*,[238] the Supreme Court promotes the role of the copyright exceptions as protection of *users' rights*. Hence, the interests protected by the exclusive rights of the copyright-holder must be balanced against those interests protected by any exception. Arguably, this requires Canadian courts to adopt a proportionality-based test between the competing interests, as suggested by the CJEU in *Deckmyn* to the courts in EU Member States.

Inevitably, as the bespoke parody exceptions under scrutiny use framework conceptions, such as fair use, fair dealing, or rules of the genre, it is necessary to delineate the

[237] This is also valid for Australia where compliance with the fair dealing defence for the purposes of parody will inherently depend on the factors adopted by judges in parody cases in the future.

[238] See n 210.

scope of the exception to ensure its compliance with international obligations. This is discussed in Chapter 4. But to preserve the legitimate interests of authors, it is also important to respect authors' moral rights, as dicussed in Chapter 6. Finally, as the parody exception and the moral rights require one party's interests be weighed up and balanced against competing interests, the analysis of fundamental rights values provided in Chapter 5 is inherent in satisfaction of the three-step test. Therefore, if this book adopts a linear approach for the reader's convenience, some overlaps may occur in practice. For example, as argued further in this work, the weight allocated to particular factors in the application of a parody exception is likely to depend on the human rights aspects involved which is of particular relevance where the parody is not clear-cut.

3

Consequences of the Nature of the Parody Exception

1. The 'Mechanics' Behind the Parody Exception

As a matter of procedure, the parody exception acts as a defence to a copyright infringement. It precludes enforcement of economic rights in circumstances which, bar the defence, would constitute an infringing activity.[1] We need to assess the relationship between the exception and the exclusive rights further, in order to understand the nature and function of the parody exception within the copyright paradigm. This relationship inherently influences the exception's scope and contributes to the satisfaction of the three-step test.[2]

In countries favouring a high level of protection for right-holders (e.g. France and the UK), the concept of fair dealing, or rules of the genre, remains largely linked to the personal property rights vested in copyright-protected works. Traditionally, the balance struck within common law jurisdictions is presented as putting exclusive rights equal with exceptions, whereas civil law jurisdictions support a hierarchy, which ranks the rights of authors over the interests of users.[3] The reality seems to be more nuanced as both traditions adopt a owner-centric approach.[4] Indeed, with the rapid legislative and judicial expansion of copyright in recent decades, the focus in both legal traditions has been on whether there was a need to strengthen copyright exceptions to provide a stronger counter mechanism to powerful right-holders attempting to control every use made of their works.[5] These attempts to rectify the balance between the competing interests at play has led developments in Canada, where the Supreme Court has adopted the notion of 'user rights', to bring exceptions on par with the personal property right of the copyright-owner.[6] While other juridictions may not have gone as far as Canada's user rights, they seem increasingly willing to accept that human rights have a role, serving as an external counter balance to copyright's expansive scope.[7]

[1] Hence, the work must be original, and copyright still in force; the use must be unauthorized. In common law countries, the use must reproduce a 'substantial part of the work'. In France, the exception may apply to any reproduction. P El Khoury, *Les exceptions au droit d'auteur* (thèse Montpellier, 2007) 377.

[2] See Chapter 2, section 4.

[3] A Lucas, *Droit d'auteur et numérique* (Litec, 1998) n°338; A Lucas and H J Lucas, *Traité de la propriété littéraire et artistique* (4th edn, Litec, 2012) n°342; *contra*: C Geiger, 'De la nature juridique des limites au droit d'auteur' (2004) 13 *Propriétés Intellectuelles* 882, 885; P-Y Gautier, *Propriété littéraire et artistique* (6th edn, PUF, 2007) n°334, 385 (arguing for a right of users).

[4] Already inferred in Chapter 2, section 1.

[5] It is noteworthy that the three-step test precludes uses which go beyond the 'normal' exploitation of the works. See Chapter 2, section 3.2.2.

[6] *CCH Canadian Ltd v. Law Society of Upper Canada* [2004] 1 SCR 339 (hereafter *CCH*).

[7] One could argue that the last requirement in *Deckmyn* to weigh the interests of right-holders with the users' right to freedom of expression constitutes an invitation for judges to place the parody exception face-to-face with the property right of the right-holder(s). C-201/13 *Johan Deckmyn and Vrijheidsfonds VZW v. Helena Vandersteen and Others* [2014] ECLI:EU:C:2014:2132 (hereafter *Deckmyn*), [34]. Additionally, some commentators have taken the same path by suggesting that exceptions with greater human rights values should weigh more heavily against the enforcement of

Often perceived as being close to the user's interests, the US fair use doctrine has equally suffered in recent decades. As further explained later in the chapter, fair use was initially conceived as a defence which placed copyright interests on an equal footing with users' and public interests. Originally, the onus fell on the right-holder to show that the unauthorized use was not 'fair' use, but over time, the shift was made towards what is described as 'affirmative defense',[8] i.e. the onus has been transferred from the claimant onto the defendant user.

Currently, fair use, fair dealing, and rules of the genre all require the defendant to demonstrate that the use for the purpose of parody is permissible. This chapter will therefore focus on the nature and function of the parody exception in copyright law to understand how these influence the interpretation of factors covered in Chapter 4.

2. The Nature of a Parody Exception in Copyright Law

The main feature of the parody exception is to allow a user to reproduce another's copyright-protected work without requiring the right-holder's authorization and without remunerating the right-holder for the use of the work. Whilst the particular legal nature of copyright exceptions remains nebulous, as we will see later, we should not underestimate its importance.[9] Not only is its impact felt when interpreting any particular exception, but it also determines the relationship between copyright legislation and contract law.[10]

2.1 A right or an interest?

Chapter 2 explained the careful balance between opposing interests which copyright legislators seek to maintain.[11] As currently understood, the balance sought requires a greater role for the public interest and fundamental rights whenever copyright exceptions are interpreted.[12] But does this imply that copyright exceptions, especially the parody exception, amount to *rights* or are more akin to *interests*?

As the role of the parody exception is firmly anchored in the recognition of freedom of expression,[13] it is reasonable to argue that in all the jurisdictions considered, the parody exception constitutes something more important than a mere interest, which judges ought to take into consideration as secondary to an infringement. As it affirms essential democratic values within copyright legislation, the better view is that the parody exception acts as a *right*.[14] Yet this conclusion begs the question: what *kind* of right does it grant parodists?

copyright. See P B Hugenholtz, 'Copyright and freedom of expression in Europe' in R C Dreyfuss, H First, and D L Zimmerman (eds), *Innovation Policy in an Information Age* (OUP, 2001); Wittem EU Copyright Code Project.

[8] Originally mentioned in *Harper & Row* 471 US 539 (1985), [561] and confirmed in *Campbell v. Acuff-Rose Music Inc* 510 US 569 (1994) (hereafter *Campbell*), [590]. For more on the historical development: L P Loren, 'Fair use: an affirmative defense' (2015) 90 *Washington Law Review* 685, 694. Loren argues that the qualification of affirmative was probably not intended as the House Report 1967 noted: 'The committee believes that any special statutory provision placing the burden of proving fair use on one side or the other would be unfair and undesirable.'

[9] Geiger (n 3) 882.

[10] See Chapter 1, section 5.1.

[11] See Chapter 2, section 3.2.

[12] See Chapter 1, section 5.1 and Chapter 2, section 4.

[13] See Chapter 1, section 5.1 and Chapter 5, section 2.

[14] *CCH* (n 6) [48]; In *Suntrust*, Judge Birch includes in a footnote: 'I believe that fair use should be considered an affirmative right under the 1976 Act, rather than merely an affirmative defence, as it is defined in the Act as a use that is not a violation of copyright. However, fair use is commonly

Does the parody exception grant authentic *subjective* rights to parodists? Traditionally, copyright law only grants legally enforceable rights to right-holders. A significant distinction is that a parodist cannot initiate legal enforcement of the exception,[15] in essence, an injunction against the right-holder which prevents them from exercising their rights. As a defence, judges may only refrain from enforcing exclusive rights against the parodist, if, as a defendant, the parody exception is successfully invoked. As such, the parody exception does not vest a right as we typically know them. It necessitates prior action from right-holders.[16] The parody exception further departs from the subjective rights insofar as anyone may benefit from the exceptions, while the exclusive rights only benefit the right-holder. Consequently, reliance upon the exception by one individual does not prevent another from benefiting from it too.[17]

There has been little discussion in most jurisdictions that a user wanting to rely on a parody exception bears the burden of proof, but this question has attracted more attention in the US,[18] because there, this has not always been the case. This fact led some commentators to conclude that the focus of the US fair use doctrine focus is on the public and users, rather than authors.[19] However, in *Campbell*, the US Supreme Court could not have been clearer: 'Since fair use is an affirmative defense, its proponent would have difficulty carrying the burden of demonstrating fair use without favourable evidence about relevant markets.'[20] Hence, the Supreme Court confirms that fair use for parody purposes qualifies as an affirmative defence, such that the defendant bears the burden of proving that it should apply.

According to Loren, the Supreme Court's qualifying of fair use as an affirmative defence in *Campbell* is contrary to the intent of US Congress. Consequently, she cautions against attaching too much importance to the Supreme Court's statement, since the *Campbell* case did not study the question in great depth.[21] However, once the plaintiff has established copyright infringement of a protected work (e.g. proof of ownership, substantial copying, and access to the earlier work), determining whether copying amounts to excessive copying for the purpose of copyright is determined through the fair use factors.[22]

These factors are tools for judges to appreciate the lawfulness of a particular activity, meaning that the amount copied allowed under fair use will vary from purpose to purpose and case to case. The underpinning ideology is that copyright does not aim

referred to as an affirmative defence, and, as we are bound by Supreme Court precedent, we will apply it as such. Nevertheless, the fact that the fair use right must be procedurally asserted as an affirmative defence does not detract from its constitutional significance as a guarantor to access and use for First Amendment purposes', *Suntrust Bank v. Houghton Mifflin Company*, 268 F.3d 1257 (11th Cir. 2001) [FN 3]; repeated recently in *Lenz v. Universal Music Corp.*, 815 F.3d 1145, 1153 (9th Cir. 2016); Geiger (n 3) 882; P Chapdeleine, *Copyright User Rights* (OUP, 2017) 33.

[15] Geiger (n 3) 886; *US: Perfect 10, Inc. v. Amazon.com, Inc.*, 508 F.3d 1146, 1158 (9th Cir. 2007); *Campbell* (n 8) [590], 114 S.Ct. 1164; *Dr Seuss Enters., L.P. v. Penguin Books, U.S.A., Inc.*, 109 F.3d 1394, 1403 (9th Cir. 1997) (hereafter *Dr Seuss II*).

[16] S Dusollier, *Droit d'auteur et protection des oeuvres dans l'univers numérique* (Larcier, 2007) chapitre 4 Titre 3; legitimizes the business practices in place: see Chapter 7, section 1.

[17] B Galopin, *Les exceptions à usage public en droit d'auteur* (IRPI, 2012) 351.

[18] Loren (n 8) 685; N Snow, 'The forgotten right of fair use' (2011) 62 *Case W. Res. L. Rev.* 135; W Patry, *The Fair Use Privilege in Copyright Law* (2nd edn, BNA Books, 1995).

[19] See recently J-M Bruguière, 'La réception du fair dealing britannique dans le système d'exception fermée français' (2018) *RIDA* (forthcoming) 5.

[20] *Campbell* (n 8) [590]. [21] Loren (n 8) 685.

[22] This negative effect is magnified in countries which do not have statutory factors as it renders the scope of the defence even more uncertain.

to provide right-holders with the means to control every single use of a work,[23] but a certain (often, economic) harm should be caused to the right-holder.[24] In US law, the difference between a defence and an affirmative defence is that a defence recognizes that the defendant's acts are non-infringing, whereas in an affirmative defence, the defendant's acts have violated the exclusive rights, but the facts and justification defeat the plaintiff's claim. The defendant, thus, must persuade the judge that they have good reasons to justify their infringing activity. There are several considerations which determine whether a defence should result in an *affirmative* defence (whereby the defendant must prove mitigating circumstances for a use which would otherwise be considered as infringing). These include understanding which party has better access to the relevant evidence, as well as policy and fundamental rights considerations which tip the balance in favour of indulgence. Although these considerations may represent just a question of degree, these can be decisive in deciding the outcome of particular cases.[25]

In the context of *Campbell*, the US Supreme Court went one step further. Having qualified fair use for parody purposes as an affirmative defence, it reversed presumptions of unfairness and market harm previously adopted by the Court of Appeal,[26] possibly based upon the defendant's commercial motivation. In these circumstances, the appreciation of the fourth factor (i.e. market harm) can shift the evidentiary burden onto the plaintiff, who has better access to the relevant evidence necessary to determine market harm.[27] And yet, as Snow illustrates with the *Dr Seuss* case, in later decisions courts appear reluctant to shift the onus.[28] Here, the defendant trying to prove the lack of any market harm could only speculate, since their parody had yet to be published. Sadly, such speculation was considered insufficient to rule out market harm, and this contributed to the fair use defence being rejected.[29] Nevertheless, it is noteworthy that even in cases where the burden of proof is shifted onto the plaintiff, ultimately, the defendant's powers of persuasion must still establish that the use was fair.

If legislative history casts some doubts over the conception of fair use as an affirmative defence, then statutory language also supports the position that fair use is a consideration when determining infringement. According to section 106 US Code, the enforcement of exclusive rights is *subject to* section 107 (i.e. the application of fair use). Section 107 itself begins: 'Notwithstanding the provisions of sections 106 and 106A' fair use does not constitute copyright infringement. Furthermore, section 108 even speaks of '*right* of fair use'.[30]

Albeit infringement should not be seen as an exemption from an infringement but should help in shaping the scope of protection,[31] backing a more holistic appreciation of copyright infringement.[32] This may be relevant for setting the alleged infringer on an equal footing with the right-holder to determine whether the use of the work made was

[23] As such would go against the promotion of Art and Science as intended within the US Constitution. U.S. CONST. art. I, § 8, cl. 8.

[24] C Bohannan, 'Copyright harm, foreseeability, and fair use' (2007) 85 *Wash. U. L. Rev*. 969, 973.

[25] As well as outside of court dispute resolution given the autonomy and greater power given to users.

[26] *Campbell* (n 8) [583]–[584], [591]. These paragraphs should be read alongside *Sony Corporation of America v. Universal City Studios, Inc.* (1984) 464 US 417 (hereafter *Sony*) which made the use presumptively unfair if a defendant had commercial intent. This case represents the first decision after the enactment of fair use and, interestingly, it never refers to affirmative defence or defence at all.

[27] This position was also endorsed in *Cambridge University Press v. Patton* (11th Cir. 2014) 769 F.3d 1232, 1279.

[28] Snow (n 18) 172.

[29] Ibid.

[30] Author's emphasis.

[31] *Sony* (n 26) [448]. Other decisions repeat this idea: *Eldred v. Ashcroft* 537 (2003) US 186.

[32] Ibid.

lawful. Loren notes that as trial judges are reluctant to accept arguments that freedom of expression serves as an external limit to copyright, understanding fair use as an exception to an infringement, rather than using it to determine the scope of copyright protection, weakens the internal balance struck between freedom of expression and property rights within the copyright system.[33] She further argues that comprehending fair use as excusing an infringement requires the defendant to establish afresh that they have a right to freedom of expression, thereby creating an 'unnecessary and inappropriate burden on free speech'.[34] This is especially true outside courtrooms since it creates a chilling effect for risk-averse users. In other words, despite appreciating that their activity may be covered by fair use, a parodist will still refrain from basing their expression on a copyright-protected work fearing that they may have to prove the legitimacy of this use a posteriori.

In Canada, there is a willingness to grant a higher status to users than a mere interest. Here, the reasoning of the Canadian Supreme Court in *CCH* is particularly significant.[35] In this decision, the Court clarified the relationship between fair dealing exceptions and copyright infringement in some detail. Without departing from the common stance that a fair dealing exception requires the defendant to demonstrate that their use was fair, [36] the Court adds:

> [T[he fair dealing exception is perhaps more properly understood as an integral part of the Copyright Act than simply a defence. Any act falling within the fair dealing exception will not be an infringement of copyright.[37]

By characterizing fair dealing as non-infringement, and thereby establishing these exceptions as 'user's rights', the Supreme Court pioneers a recalibration of exceptions within the copyright paradigm, adapting the owner-centric focus to take account of the current activities of users.[38]

Nevertheless, some still wonder whether the shift to recognize user rights results in a beneficial change, or one which falls short of its promise.[39] Currently, it is difficult to say whether the new approach has led to more flexibility and adaptability within the copyright system to users' habits.[40] Whilst acknowledging that user rights have the potential to promote the public interest in the copyright balance, Craig warns that they equally carry risks for the public interest, and wider societal values, unless these rights are carefully construed.[41] Especially as the copyright paradigm is underpinned

[33] Loren (n 8) 696. Similarly, Snow revisits the *Dr Seuss II* (n 15) case relating to the parody of *The Cat in the Hat* to comment on O.J. Simpson's trial. Here, the author points out the language of the court which refers to fair use as a means to 'excuse' an infringement. According to this author, as the use was inherently funny and protected by free speech, the court was wrong to reject fair use. Snow (n 18) 171.

[34] Loren (n 8) 709–10. [35] *CCH* (n 6). [36] Ibid, [48].

[37] Ibid. Simultaneously, the concept of abuse of rights (well-known in civil law countries such as France) made its way into Canadian law with *Kraft Canada v. Euro-Excellence* (2007) SCC 37. See P-Y Moyse, 'Kraft Canada c Euro-Excellence: l'insoutenable légèreté du droit' (2008) 53 *R.D. McGill*, 741.

[38] *CCH* was later reaffirmed in *Society of Composers, Authors and Music Publishers of Canada v. Bell Canada* [2012] 2 SCR 326, [11] (hereafter *Bell Canada*) and *Alberta v. Canadian Copyright Licensing Agency* [2012] 2 SCR 326, [22] (hereafter *Alberta*).

[39] C J Craig, 'Globalizing user rights-talk: on copyright limits and rhetorical risks' (2017) 33(1) *Am. U. Int'l L. Rev.* 1.

[40] As confirmed in *United Airlines* where the judge adopted a restrictive approach to the appreciation of the parody exception. *United Airlines, Inc. v. Jeremy Cooperstock* [2017] FC 616 (hereafter *United Airlines*).

[41] Ibid.

by an owner-centric approach which leads to high level of protection for right-holders and authors, the subject-matter, scope, and duration of protection.[42] As later reforms of copyright laws have jeopardized the careful copyright balance to grant greater protection to private interests over societal values, a downgrading of copyright defences to questionable and distrustful claims against the exclusive rights (becoming sacrosanct) of right-holders followed. This explains to some extent the following restrictive approach undertaken by courts towards the dealing purposes and assessment of fairness which appears to persist despite attempts to restore an equilibrium.[43]

Despite the existence of differences in legal approaches to exceptions, the preferred approach is to treat the parody exception as granting an *objective* right[44] to parodists;[45] i.e. whenever the exception's requirements are met, right-holders should be unable to enforce their exclusive rights.[46] In effect, by providing a specific copyright exception for parody, the legislator prioritizes an individual's right of freedom of expression over another's property right.[47] To do otherwise, it seems, would call into question the legitimacy of copyright laws in light of the fundamental freedoms.[48] Therefore, the parody exception should be interpreted in a manner which permits the right of freedom of expression to be realized. While this should result in a uniformity of approach, it does not follow that exactly the same parody uses will be deemed lawful according to each national copyright law. The extent of harmonization depends ultimately on the principle of interpretation adopted,[49] the interplay of the exception with contract law,[50] national factors attached to the exception,[51] and the balance struck by courts in the rare cases where fundamental freedoms are in direct conflict.[52]

2.2 Strict interpretation vs 'user rights' as rules of interpretation

The nature and procedural role of the parody exception within copyright law also influence the way that rules of interpretation will be applied. For example, in EU Member States, a high level of copyright protection prevails and exceptions are considered to excuse an infringement. Here, exceptions will be interpreted strictly and from a copyright-holder's perspective.[53] In contrast, in Canada, as fair dealing exceptions have been characterized as users' rights, courts are better positioned to give a 'large and liberal interpretation'[54] of fair dealing purposes and from the perspective of the user. It seems that in *CCH*, the Supreme Court of Canada not only clarified the role of fair dealing exceptions in Canadian copyright law, but it also established a new rule of interpretation requiring better consideration of users' interests. The following

[42] See Chapter 2, section 2. [43] See section 2.2.

[44] Meaning the judicial norms governing society and whose keeping is guaranteed by public authority. These are immediately applicable, compulsory, and susceptible to be executed by an external power.

[45] Dusollier (n 16); Geiger (n 3) 886; L Guibault, *Copyright and Contracts: An Analysis of the Contractual Overridability of Limitations on Copyright* (Kluwer, 2002) 95; D J Gervais, 'Quelques reflexions à propos de la distinction des "droits" et "intérêts"' in *Mélanges en l'honneur de Paul Roubier* (Dalloz, 1961) 243.

[46] Geiger (n 3) 886.

[47] And the freedom of expression exercised by the original author. Ibid, 887; M Buydens and S Dussollier, 'Les exceptions au droit d'auteur: évolutions dangereuses' (2001) 22 *CCE* 10.

[48] See Chapter 1, section 5.1. [49] See section 2.2. [50] See section 3.

[51] See Chapter 4. [52] See Chapter 5, section 5 and Chapter 7, section 2.

[53] This is also the case in Australia as further explained in section 2.2.1.

[54] *CCH* (n 6) [51]; *Bell Canada* (n 38) [15]; *Alberta* (n 38) [19].

section considers the impact which this choice has upon the rules of interpretation which are applied.

2.2.1 *Strict interpretation as a rule of interpretation*

2.2.1.1 Mixed guidance at EU level

So far, we have established that EU copyright law allows some latitude for Member States to tailor the non-mandatory exceptions to their own legal systems,[55] while also providing (mandatory) guidance on the interpretation of copyright exceptions. As a general principle, the InfoSoc Directive establishes a high level of protection for copyright works.[56] Traditionally, this led to an axiom of interpretation which favours right-holders by requiring exclusive rights to be interpreted broadly.[57] In keeping with this general principle, the CJEU has held that the exclusive right of reproduction must be construed consistently as an autonomous concept of EU law.[58] Indeed, wherever a term is not defined by the InfoSoc Directive itself, or by reference to a Member State's definition, it should be construed in light of the context of the provision and the objectives of the Directive.[59] As exceptions derogate from the general principle of providing a high level of protection, they should be interpreted strictly.[60]

The InfoSoc Directive sets out to provide a fair balance of rights and interests between the different categories of right-holders and users of protected subject-matter. It recognizes that existing copyright exceptions and limitations in place in the national law of Member States need reassessment in the light of the digital environment. Proper functioning of the EU single market also requires copyright exceptions to be defined more harmoniously, as any disparity between copyright-restricted acts has direct detrimental effects on efficient functioning of the single market for copyright-protected works. This is only likely to become more pronounced as trans-border exploitation of works and cross-border activities become more prevalent. The degree of harmonization needed should, thus, be determined by their impact on the functioning of the internal market.[61] Hence, even a 'strict' interpretation does not preclude a fair balance between the interests of right-holders and those intended to benefit from the exception.[62]

Recital 31 of the InfoSoc Directive requires exceptions to be effective in their stated aim, and this principle has been honed further by the EU case law. For example, in *Painer*,[63] the CJEU tempers the strict interpretation principle by noting

[55] See Chapter 2, section 3.

[56] Recitals 4 and 9 InfoSoc Directive.

[57] Recitals 21 and 23 InfoSoc Directive.

[58] C-5/08 *Infopaq International A/S v. Danske Dagblades Forening* [2009] ECLI:EU:C:2009:465 (hereafter *Infopaq I*) [56].

[59] Advocate-General's opinion in *Deckmyn* [2014] ECLI:EU:C:2014:458 (hereafter AGO in *Deckmyn*), [35].

[60] *Deckmyn* (n 7) [22]; AGO *Deckmyn* (n 59) [43]; C-360/13 *Public Relations Consultants Association Ltd v. Newspaper Licensing Agency Ltd and Others* [2014] ECLI:EU:C:2014:1195, [23] (hereafter *NLA*); Order in C-302/10 *Infopaq International A/S v. Danske Dagblades Forening* [2012] ECLI:EU:C:2012:16 (hereafter *Infopaq II*), [27]; C-145/10 *Eva-Maria Painer v. Standard Verlags GmbH and Others* [2011] ECLI:EU:C:2011:798 (hereafter *Painer*), [109]; *Infopaq I* (n 58) [56]–[57]; C-403/08 *Football Association Premier League Ltd and Others v. QC Leisure and Others* and C-429/08 *Karen Murphy v. Media Protection Services Ltd* [2011] ECLI:EU:C:2011:631 (hereafter *FAPL*), [162]; C-277/10 *Martin Luksan v. Petrus van der Let* [2012] ECLI:EU:C:2012:65, [101]; C-435/12 *ACI Adam BV and Others v. Stichting de Thuiskopie and Stichting Onderhandelingen Thuiskopie vergoeding* [2014] ECLI:EU:C:2014:254, [23]; C-36/05 *Commission of the European Communities v. Kingdom of Spain* [2006] ECLI:EU:C:2006:672, [31]; C-476/01 *Criminal proceedings against Felix Kapper* [2004] ECLI:EU:C:2004:261, [72].

[61] Recital 31 InfoSoc Directive.

[62] *FAPL* (n 60) [162]–[164].

[63] *Painer* (n 60).

that any exception's requirements must be interpreted in a way which enables the exception to fulfil its purpose. In this case, interpretation of the quotation exception[64] required the exclusive rights of the right-holder to be circumscribed to strike a fairer balance between those rights and freedom of expression.[65] Arguably, this same reasoning should extend to the parody exception, as both exceptions are justified by the same fundamental freedoms.[66] This approach militates against a literal interpretation of the exception in favour of a 'purposive' interpretation driven by the end to which it aspires. In essence, the requirements associated with an exception must be interpreted in a way which preserves its effectiveness and respects its purpose.[67] That said, it remains unclear whether the Court's reasoning in *Painer* represents a general principle that exceptions must be effective, or whether the Court, instead, intended to afford special treatment to those copyright exceptions founded upon respect of fundamental freedoms.[68]

As mentioned,[69] additional uncertainty remains because of apparent inconsistencies in CJEU guidance. The CJEU has noted that the three-step test of article 5(5) of the InfoSoc Directive should guide interpretation of copyright exceptions.[70] Yet, in subsequent cases relating to article 5(1) of the InfoSoc Directive, the Court also notes that where the requirements of the exception are met, the three-step test should be deemed satisfied.[71] Furthermore, the most recent jurisprudence of the Court suggests that the defendant's use must not only satisfy the requirements of an exception, but must also satisfy the three-step test.[72]

The CJEU may be seen as further honing these principles in *Deckmyn*. Having established that parody is an autonomous concept having a uniform meaning throughout the EU territory,[73] the Court repeats that the strict interpretation principle applies to the parody exception.[74] However, the Court goes on to counsel that the interpretation of the exception adopted must enable the exception to function effectively (requiring the purpose of the exception to be taken into consideration),[75] and that national courts should ensure that competing interests are balanced proportionately.[76]

According to one reading of *Deckmyn*, the CJEU may be imposing a tripartite assessment in which national courts consider: 1) the purpose of the use, 2) the application of fairness factors to the particular facts, and 3) the proportionality test between the fundamental rights in play. On balance, however, it seems that *Deckmyn* is better understood as proposing a more 'holistic' approach, which adopts a global appreciation of all relevant factors, the purpose of the use as well as the influence of fundamental rights. When assessing whether a use should be lawful, most weight should be given to those aspects which contribute to the realization of freedom of expression, and a correct understanding of the exception's purpose should guide which national factors are pertinent to the application of the parody exception.[77]

64 Article 5(3)(d) InfoSoc Directive.
65 *Painer* (n 60) [134]–[136].
66 See Chapter 5, section 2.
67 *FAPL* (n 60) [133].
68 De Wolf & Partners, *Study on the Application of Directive 2001/29/EC on Copyright and Related Rights in the Information Society* (2013) 489.
69 See Chapter 2, section 3.1.2.
70 *Infopaq I* (n 58) [58] in relation to article 5(1) InfoSoc Directive.
71 *Painer* (n 60) [104]–[108], [132]; *FAPL* (n 60) [181]; *Infopaq II* (n 60) [56]; C-275/06 *Productores de Música de España (Promusicae) v. Telefónica de España SAU* [2008] ECLI:EU:C:2008:54, [68].
72 *NLA* (n 60) [54]–[63]; see Chapter 4, section 3.3.
73 *Deckmyn* (n 7) [17].
74 Ibid, [22].
75 Ibid, [23].
76 Ibid, [34].
77 See Chapter 7, section 2.

2.2.1.2 National interpretations

In accordance with the civil law tradition in France, any derogation from legally entrenched exclusive rights, including copyright exceptions, must be interpreted strictly.[78] This well-established principle is not contained in any legislation, but derives from the legal axiom: *exceptio est strictissimae interpretationis* (exceptions must be strictly interpreted).[79] This principle may seem too limiting and inflexible, but such criticism may be based upon a misconception, since it is not advocating a 'restrictive' interpretation (based solely on the literal wording), as a 'strict' interpretation is not policy blind.

Properly understood, the principle of strict interpretation involves focusing both on the text of the provision *and* its justifications and objectives.[80] Adopting Galopin's position,[81] this suggests that whenever freedom of expression surfaces in copyright law in the form of a new exception, that exception is not merely an exception to the exclusive right, but rather a restatement of the underlying fundamental principle of freedom of expression, which must be taken into consideration by the judge.[82] Thus, an exception in copyright law in this instance is a balancing of fundamental freedoms, and not just a derogation from a legal right. Based upon this analysis, it is submitted that the French principle of strict interpretation is in harmony with the CJEU understanding of the same principle.

Given the CJEU guidance, there can be no doubt that UK courts should currently interpret copyright exceptions strictly, in light of the purpose and objective of the particular statutory provision.[83] Yet, Griffiths discerns bifurcated approaches to interpretation evidenced in UK fair dealing cases.[84] The first approach seeks to uphold the maximum possible protection for the right-holders (in line with the general principle of affording broad protection) by adopting the most restrictive interpretation of the copyright exception.[85] The second approach is more permissive and favours the realization of freedom of expression,[86] to the extent that a common law parody exception seemed to exist prior to the introduction of the statutory defence.

But which approach prevails today? Recent UK jurisprudence is increasingly and inevitably influenced by CJEU case law. Most recently, in *Meltwater*,[87] the court was required to determine whether businesses which made use of the services of an online news aggregator required permission from the right-holders in newspaper articles, given that the aggregator's use was already licensed. In response to keywords selected by business clients, the aggregator emailed back their report which repeated short snippets

[78] Lucas (n 3) 170 n° 335, 337.

[79] Author's translation. H Roland and L Boyer, *Adages du droit français* (4th edn, Litec, 1999).

[80] J-L Bergel, 'Méthodes et principes de coordination des règles juridiques' in *Méthodologie Juridique* (1st edn, PUF, 2001) 245.

[81] Galopin (n 17) 327. As well as Tulkens and Strowel as discussed in Chapter 1, section 5.1.

[82] This echoes the legal nature of the exception.

[83] *Newspaper Licensing Agency & Ors v. Meltwater BV & Ors* (2010) EWHC 3099 (Ch), [43]; Appeal: [2011] EWCA Civ 890; Supreme Court: [2013] UKSC 18; *Hawkes & Son (London) Ltd v. Paramount Film Service Ltd* [1934] 1 Ch 593, [604].

[84] J Griffiths, 'Preserving judicial freedom of movement—interpreting fair dealing in copyright law' (2000) 2 *IPQ* 164.

[85] *Ashdown v. Telegraph Group Ltd* [2001] EWCA Civ 1142; *Hyde Park Residence Ltd v. Yelland* [2000] 3 WLR 215, CA; *Distillers Co (Biochemicals) Ltd v. Times Newspapers* [1975] 1 All ER 41; *Beloff v. Pressdram Ltd* [1973] 1 All ER 241.

[86] *Pro Sieben Media AG v. Carlton UK Television* [1999] 1 WLR 605; *Time Warner v. Channel Four Television* [1994] EMLR 1; *BBC v. BSB* [1992] Ch 141, [1991] 3 WLR 174; *Williamson Music v. the Pearson Partnership Ltd* [1987] FSR 97; *Hubbard v. Vosper* [1972] 2 QB 84, CA (Civ Div), 90; *Johnston v. Bernard* [1938] 2 All ER 37.

[87] See n 83.

from newspapers which included those keywords, along with an electronic link to the associated article. The aggregator argued that their clients' use was permitted by the temporary copies exception (article 5(1) of the InfoSoc Directive), whereas the right-holders argued for a narrow interpretation of the exception, to best preserve their exclusive rights.

Clearly influenced by *Infopaq*,[88] *Infopaq II*,[89] and *FAPL*,[90] the UK Supreme Court directed that a restrictive approach should be set aside. Although concluding that reproduction of the snippets in the emails did infringe the reproduction right, the Court concluded that on-screen browsing and internet caching fell within the scope of the temporary copies exception. However, appreciating the significance of the decision for online browsing throughout the EU territory, the Court referred the matter to the CJEU, which confirmed the Supreme Court's interpretation of the exception.[91]

In conclusion, despite adopting alternative approaches in the past, UK courts now seem aware of the need to interpret copyright exceptions strictly (and not restrictively), taking in consideration the development of new technologies and the need to strike a fair balance between the rights and interests of rights-holders and of users of protected works. Given the *Meltwater*[92] precedent, it is reasonable to presume that UK courts will follow the same approach in parody cases.

In Australia, very little has been said about the principles of interpretation applied to fair dealing, and there is no statutory guidance. Furthermore, it is unclear what approach the court adopted in *TCN*, the leading fair dealing case. Indeed, the trial judge's reasoning sheds no light upon whether he was endorsing a liberal, strict, or restrictive interpretation.[93] According to Handler and Rolph, the full court 'provided only a superficial interpretation of the prescribed statutory purposes'.[94]

Given the paucity of scholarly or judicial comment on the matter, some indicators may be evident in policy documents. The Australian Law Review Committee appears to endorse the Canadian approach in the *CCH* decision, discussed earlier, which rejects a restrictive interpretation of exceptions, since the report emphasizes the need to maintain a fair balance between users' rights and the interest of right-holders.[95] This would encompass both a strict interpretation and a liberal interpretation.

Given their shared common law history, Australian courts are also influenced by UK copyright case law. This might suggest that Australian judges would apply a strict interpretation, as is now (arguably) adopted in UK fair dealing cases. The adoption of the new statutory fair dealing exception for parody might also point to a strict, rather than a liberal interpretation, since a liberal approach to copyright exceptions permits such wide interpretation to be tantamount to the introduction of new exceptions.

[88] *Infopaq I* (n 58). [89] *Infopaq II* (n 60). [90] *FAPL* (n 60).

[91] *NLA* (n 60). [92] See n 83.

[93] Conti J established interpretation principles based upon previous case law. While some appear more liberal (like the fair dealing purpose which should not be construed narrowly; *TCN Channel Nine v. Network Ten* [2001] FCA 108 (trial) (hereafter *TCN*), [66]), the overall appraisal of the principles remains conservative. Additionally, '[T]he full court did not examine the fair dealing arguments to the extent that the court at first instance did; in this way, an opportunity to set more authoritative and coherent precedent for the interpretation of fair dealing was arguably missed.' S Christou and A Maurushat, '"Waltzing Matilda" or "Advance Australia Fair"? User-generated content and fair dealing in Australian copyright law' (2009) 29 *UNSWLRS* 1, 29; M Handler and D Rolph, 'A real pea souper: the panel case and the development of the fair dealing defence' (2003) 27 *Melbourne University Law Review* 381, 382 and 390.

[94] Handler and Rolph, 'A real pea souper', 408.

[95] http://www.alrc.gov.au/publications/28-copyright-and-databases/alrc%E2%80%99s-views, [28.87].

Consequently, it is submitted that Australian courts are likely to cast both restrictive and liberal interpretation of fair dealing aside, in favour of a strict interpretation of the parody exception.[96]

Surprisingly, US courts appear to adopt a mix of liberal and restrictive interpretative approaches to fair use. Whilst the first factor is partly imprinted with a broad interpretation, as demonstrated by the new focus upon transformativeness, the other factors seem to be interpreted in a rather restrictive manner.[97] As most attention is placed upon economic considerations, and given reluctance to hear arguments based upon fundamental rights, some decisions appear at odds with the First Amendment which protects free speech. In the case of parodies, this has led to an artificial distinction between parodies and satires.[98] Although both seem equally rooted in the First Amendment,[99] one seems to be more priviledged than the other.

2.2.2 User's rights as a rule of interpretation

In contrast with the other jurisdictions considered, a liberal approach to interpretation is evident in Canada, evolving from its common law tradition. Here, copyright exceptions must be interpreted broadly and liberally since users' rights are considered to be an integral part of the Copyright Act.[100]

Simard,[101] writing on Canadian legislative interpretation in 1989, identifies that the traditional approach is to deduce the legislator's intent merely from the wording of the legislation. As in all the other countries studied here, the legislation enacted represents the legislator's particular social and political choices.[102] Adopting this approach, a literal interpretation of the Copyright Act which focuses upon the actual wording of the text best reflects the legislator's initial intent. Unlike in France and other civil law countries, where supremacy lies in the law as codified, in the common law tradition, legislation is used to perfect or codify case law. Against this backdrop, statutes are to be strictly interpreted by applying a literal approach enlightened by the legislator's intent. Consequently, civil and common law countries appear similar in their traditional approach to legislative interpretation.[103] In line with the traditional approach to interpretation, Canadian courts have adopted a narrow interpretation of fair dealing pursuant to the Copyright Act.[104]

[96] However, in the *Pokemon Company International, Inc. v. Redbubble Ltd* [2017] FCA 1541, Pagone J seems to have favoured a restrictive approach.

[97] See Chapter 4.

[98] Following the seminal *Campbell* (n 8) decision. See Chapter 1, section 5.3.

[99] See Chapter 1, section 5.1.

[100] See *CCH* (n 6) [48].

[101] J Simard, *L'interprétation législative au Canada: la théorie à l'épreuve pratique* (University of Montréal, 1998) 345.

[102] Echoing Jean-Jacques Rousseau's social contract.

[103] Simard (n 101) 16.

[104] Examples of a narrow interpretation of fair dealing: *Zamacois v. Douville* [1943] 3 Fox Pat. C. 44 (C. Échiquier); *The Queen v. James Lorimer* [1984] 1 FC 1065; *B.W. International v. Thomson Canada, Ltd* (1996) 137 DLR (4th) 398; *Hager v. ECW Press Ltd* (1999) 85 CPR (3d) 289; *Boudreau v. Lin* (1997) 150 DLR (4th) 324, [48] and most strikingly in *Compagnie Générale des Établissements Michelin-Michelin & Cie v. National Automobile, Aerospace, Transportation and General Workers Union of Canada* (1996) 71 CPR (3d) 348 (hereafter *Michelin*), in relation to parodic works. For more: M Tawfik, 'The supreme Court of Canada and the "fair dealing trilogy": elaborating a doctrine of user rights under Canadian copyright law' (2013) 51 *Alta. L. Rev.* 191, 195; C J Craig, *Copyright, Communication and Culture: Towards a Relational Theory of Copyright Law* (Edward Elgar, 2011) chapter 6; G D'Agostino, 'Healing fair dealing? A comparative copyright analysis of Canada's fair dealing to U.K. fair dealing and U.S. fair use' (2008) 53 *McGill Law Journal* 309, 324 and 329; El Khoury (n 1) 173; C J Craig, 'The changing face of fair dealing in Canadian Copyright Law: a

Therefore, prior to the codification of a parody exception, courts rejected parody as a defence owing to the restrictive interpretation given to the purposes of the dealings. In 1967, a parody of the lyrics of Woody Guthrie's song, *This Land is Your Land*,[105] was found infringing. Having recognized that the underlying work enjoyed copyright protection (without distinguishing between the musical and literary works contained therein),[106] the judge did not see fit to afford parody any special treatment, and granted an injunction to the copyright owner, because the parody had reproduced a substantial part of the original.[107] This same approach was adopted in *MCA Canada Ltd v. Gilberry & Hawke Advertising Agency Ltd*,[108] a case in which an advertising agency used a parody version of the song, *Downtown*, to promote a car dealership. Similarly, in *ATV Music Publishing of Canada Ltd v. Rogers Radio Broadcasting Ltd et al*,[109] the lyrics of The Beatles' track, *Revolution*, were parodied as *Constitution*. Again, the court afforded no latitude based upon its status as a parody, and granted an injunction preventing its use.

The supremacy of the substantiality doctrine (i.e. the right-holders' prerogatives) was also recognized in cases in which the defendant lacked any commercial motive. In *Rôtisseries St-Hubert Ltée c. Syndicat des Travailleurs(euses) de la Rôtisserie St-Hubert de Drummondville (C.S.N.)*,[110] the defendants used a parody of the plaintiff's logo to promote industrial action. Unsurprisingly, an argument that this use exercised a right based on freedom of expression was quickly brushed aside. The judge dismissed claims that this freedom had been stifled, because the defendant could still convey the same message, simply by using another means.[111] In other cases coming before the Canadian courts, the lack of a specific statutory exception resulted in the defendant arguing that the parodic use fell within the fair dealing exception for the purpose of criticism.[112] In *Compagnie Générale des Établissements Michelin-Michelin & Cie v. National Automobile, Aerospace, Transportation and General Workers Union of Canada*,[113] the trade union defendant had produced a leaflet which depicted the plaintiffs' well-known *Bibendum man* crushing a Michelin worker. The court did not consider the meaning of criticism could be stretched to encompass the union's parody.[114]

Yet, in the landmark case of *CCH*,[115] the Supreme Court made a paradigm shift to bring back some flexibility into the copyright regime.[116] The case itself considered whether the Law Society's provision of self-service photocopiers fell within a fair dealing exception. The shift had been initiated in an earlier case,[117] in which the Court of Appeal had noted the need to arrive at a fair balance between the public interest and

proposal for legislative reform' in M Geist (ed.), *In the Public Interest: The Future of Canadian Copyright Law* (Part II, Irwin Law, 2005) 452.

[105] *Ludlow Music Inc. v. Canin Music Corp.* [1967] 2 Ex CR 109, [51].

[106] Ibid, [34]–[36]. [107] Ibid, [58]. [108] (1976) 28 C.PRP (2d) 52 (FCTD).

[109] (1982) 35 OR (2d) 417 (HCJ). [110] [1987] RJQ 443, [93] appeal was waived.

[111] Similar approach was adopted in *Canwest Mediaworks Publications Inc v. Horizon Publications*, [2008] BCSC 1609, [15] (parody of the *Vancouver Sun* newspaper).

[112] A tactic adopted in *Williamson Music v. The Pearson Partnership*, n 86.

[113] (1996) 71 CPR (3d) 348.

[114] Ibid, Teitelbaum J. Some indulgence can be found in *Productions Avanti Ciné-Vidéo Inc. v. Favreau*. The case dealt with the creation of a pornographic film called *La Petite Vie* relying on a well-known television series. The judge did not reject the parody exceptions as a copyright defence. Nevertheless, as in this particular case the defendant was trying to ride on the popularity of the earlier work rather than making a parody, the judge did not accept the defence. (1999) 177 DLR (4th) 129 leave to appeal to SCC refused, 27527 (25 May 2000), [574]–[575].

[115] *CCH* (n 6).

[116] N Elkin-Koren, 'Copyright in a digital ecosystem: a user-rights approach' in R L Okediji (ed.), *Copyright in an Age of Limitations and Exceptions* (CUP, 2015) 132.

[117] *Théberge v. Galerie d'Art du Petit Champlain Inc.* [2002] SCC 34, [30]–[31].

that of right-holders, when interpreting fair dealing. The Supreme Court emphatically endorsed this users' rights doctrine in *CCH*.[118] Here, the Court held that fair dealing must be understood 'as an integral part of the Copyright Act' rather than as a derogation or encroachment upon the right-holders' exclusive rights.[119] As a consequence, fair dealing should not be interpreted restrictively, in order that a fair balance between users' and right-holders' interests may be struck.[120]

Since it is the role of the courts to maintain the proper balance between these competing interests, courts must temper the owner-oriented approach of the Copyright Act to confer greater weight to the public interest.[121] The Supreme Court identified that this required judges to interpret the purpose of any unauthorized use broadly,[122] by making an objective assessment of the motives underlying the use of the copyright work.[123] Yet, the Supreme Court also confirmed that the general rules of statutory interpretation must be respected:[124]

> [T]he words of an Act are to be read in their entire context and in their grammatical and ordinary sense harmoniously with the scheme of the Act, the object of the Act, and the intention of Parliament.[125]

Thus, a liberal interpretation does not give courts complete free rein. But also, *CCH* marks a change from a two-step assessment (dealing and fairness) to a one-step assessment where the dealing is relegated to the first fairness factor when determining the purpose of the use.[126]

This sentiment is echoed in subsequent Supreme Court case law. Firstly, in *ESAC v. SOCAN*,[127] the Court identified the need to focus on the wording of an exception and to construe this in light of the legislator's intent. Secondly, in *SOCAN v. Bell*[128] and *Alberta v. CCLA*,[129] the Supreme Court expressly rejected that in *CCH* they had endorsed an open-ended approach, akin to 'fair use'[130] in the US.[131] By the same token, the Court noted that while Canadian and UK copyright law share a legal history, the UK courts have adopted a more restrictive approach to defining the purpose of a use than in Canada. As a result, this trilogy of cases appears on a continuum with *CCH*, which clearly establishes a users' rights doctrine.[132]

In these recent decisions, the Supreme Court has determined where fair dealing lies in the copyright paradigm. The Court has moved away from an owner-centric approach, to one which takes account of the interests of subsequent authors too. In doing so, the interests of users and right-holders are given equal weighting: neither interest supersedes the other. To achieve this balance, the purpose of any fair dealing exception must be broadly construed and the factors appreciated from a user's perspective.

[118] *CCH* (n 6) [10] quotes *Théberge*.
[119] Ibid, [48].
[120] Ibid. Abraham Drassinower, 'Taking user rights seriously' in M Geist (ed.), *The Public Interest: The Future of Canadian Copyright Law* (Irwin Law, 2005) 467.
[121] Craig (n 104) chapter 6.
[122] *CCH* (n 6) [51]; Also in *UK: Pro Sieben* (n 86) [614].
[123] *CCH* (n 6) [54].
[124] Ibid, [9].
[125] Ibid; *Bell Express Vu Limited Partnership v. Rex* [2002] 2 SCR 559, [26].
[126] D'Agostino (n 104) 6; Australia could potentially follow the same path as demonstrated in *Pokemon* (n 96) [70].
[127] *Entertainment Software Association of Canada v. SOCAN* [2012] SCC 34 (hereafter *SOCAN*), [71].
[128] Ibid.
[129] *Alberta* (n 38) 345.
[130] Section 107 US Copyright Code.
[131] *SOCAN* (n 127) [25]–[26].
[132] Also confirmed in the first Canadian parody case after the introduction of a specific exception: *United Airlines* (n 40) [107].

However, is this semantic change sufficient to better protect the public interest and societal values? According to Craig, the shift to user rights might not lead to the desired results because of the international legal framework which still promotes a high protection of authors, and users' rights lack statutory entrenchment.[133] Whilst the label as a 'right' can be useful to acknowledge the role of the public interest within the copyright balance, it also places authors and users in a situation of conflict with opposing interests. What is favourable to one party is, by default, detrimental to the other.[134] This view is clearly over-simplistic since authors will, at times, also be users. Additionally, copyright rests on the belief that there is an equilibrium where the various interests meet in the name of creativity and dissemination of cultural works. Therefore, instead of a binary scale, we are faced with a dynamic and complex relationship between authors, right-holders, and users where roles reshuffle and interests can be complementary at times. As Craig explains,[135] the danger is that by rushing to embrace users' rights, we may disrupt the copyright balance by placing too much weight on the public interest. This would harm the maximization of social interests sought by granting individualized rights to all parties.

Although we are right to heed Craig's words of caution, it is worthwhile reviewing recent decisions to investigate whether the change in label has led in fact to a more liberal approach to copyright exceptions, or whether it merely camouflages the status quo. Having regard to the only parody case available to date,[136] it is difficult to discern that the user rights approach resulted in any noticeably broader interpretation.[137] In *United v. Cooperstock ('United Airlines')*, the Canadian Federal Court first endorsed the CJEU's parody characteristics[138]—i.e. humour and absence of confusion. The court found humour to be present and arguably broadened the second EU requirement (evocation of an existing work while exhibiting noticeable differences) as it merely required 'some differences'[139] between the two works. Having determined that the unauthorized use was 'for the purpose of parody', the court moved on to assess fairness of the dealing. Rather surprisingly, on consideration of the first fairness factor, the purpose of the dealing, the decision favoured the right-holder. Although the defendant spoof website employed a pop-up dialogue box to inform users that the website was not that of the claimant, and displayed a prominent disclaimer banner, the trial judge considered that the defendant's website might be confusing with that of the copyright owner. Additionally, the judge considered that the defendant's use went beyond the limits of humour and mockery, since the motivation was to defame or punish the claimant for its wrongdoing.[140]

The reasoning in this decision is problematic. Not only does it portray a restrictive interpretation of factors and does not follow the adjustment of the test as held in *CCH* (which preferred a one-step over a two-step assessment), but it represents an unjustified and unjustifiable limit upon freedom of expression. As will be further explained in Chapter 5, limitations to freedom of expression require a proportionality test which also influences the appreciation of fairness factors. As the defendant's use was neither defamatory nor an invasion of privacy, for example, it is hard to understand how the 'purpose' factor was found to point against permitting the use, which sought to use parody to highlight the claimant's poor complaint-handling procedure. The court failed to grasp the opportunity of the shift to user rights to shift the onus onto the claimant to demonstrate that the use caused actual or probable serious harm. Indeed,

[133] Craig (n 39) 41. [134] Ibid, 44. [135] Ibid, 48. [136] *United Airlines* (n 40).
[137] See Chapter 1, section 5.5. [138] *United Airlines* (n 40) [119]. [139] Ibid, [120].
[140] Ibid, [124]–[125].

the decision's reasoning in respect of the other fairness factors also seemed tainted by a restrictive interpretative approach, lacking recourse to the intended purpose of the exception to permit parodic uses. Therefore, factors such as the amount of the work copied in the dealing also weighed against the defendant, without seeming to consider the extent to which significant borrowing is inherent in the creative process behind parodies.

Thus, this first application of the newly introduced parody exception in Canadian copyright law raises doubt that the user rights approach has brought about a shift towards broader and better consideration of copyright exceptions within the copyright paradigm. If exceptions must be assessed head-to-head with the right-holders' exclusive rights, then perhaps there should be some onus upon the right-holder to demonstrate why their interest should prevail. Whilst the copyright paradigm is founded upon the idea that property right interests can outweigh freedom of expression, equally a shift from a position which ostensibly considers exceptions as a subset of infringement is evidence of the desire that the freedom of expression of the user should prevail in certain specific cases. Accordingly, not only should the dealing be interpreted broadly but the fairness factors should equally not be interpreted restrictively.[141] We consider this in more detail in Chapter 4.

As argued in the next chapter, such factors should be interpreted in light of the purpose and underlying justifications of the copyright exception. Such an interpretative approach would be more compliant with *CCH* where the Supreme Court assessed the copyright exceptions fairness factors in light of the purpose of the dealing and would restrict Canadian courts from a schizophrenic legal reasoning, providing more legal certainty for right-holders and users wishing to rely on the parody exception. Therefore, *CCH* knocked the evaluation of whether the use could be construed as a legitimate purpose under the Act to the second stage of fair dealing and, more specifically, the appreciation of the first factor. Bringing this closer to the US's approach to copyright exceptions, it can lead to a more liberal appreciation of fairness in two ways: 1) in terms of determining the scope of the purpose allowed under the exception, and 2) in providing ways to shift the onus onto the plaintiff where desirable.[142] However, the Court in *United Airlines* reverted to a stricter interpretation where the use needs to satisfy a purpose enumerated by the Act before turning to the appreciation of fairness. If subsequent courts adopt the same approach as *United Airlines*, it seems that there is a real risk that this will undermine the steps taken by the Canadian Supreme Court and jeopardize the recalibration intended between exclusive rights and exceptions.

2.2.3 *Conclusion*

It is apparent from the foregoing analysis that each jurisdiction under consideration has acknowledged that it has traditionally applied too restrictive an approach to copyright exceptions. During the last decade, there has been evidence of a desire to redress this balance. Although legislators in different jurisdictions have adopted different solutions to the problem, it remains to be seen whether, and to what extent, these different solutions will lead to different results.

[141] *CCH* (n 6) [56] notes that the amount factor, for example, should be evaluated in light of the purpose. However, in *United Airlines* (n 40), the judge appears to assess the amount copied without considering the purpose of the use, [128]–[130].

[142] E.g. encroachment on the right-holder's economic rights.

The EU Directive advocates that right-holders should enjoy a high level of protection, and this lent support to a restrictive interpretation of copyright exceptions. Yet its recitals also indicate that exceptions must be effective. Recent CJEU case law notes that, to be effective, the interpretation must balance the interests of users (representing the general public interest) and right-holders. As a result, a strict interpretation is appropriate which not only relies on the wording of the provision, but which should seek out the justification supporting that exception, to then arrive at a fair balance between the interests at stake. Given that the main justification for the parody exception is that of freedom of expression, the scope of the parody exception should be construed as broadly as needed to respect this fundamental freedom. Here, use for the purpose of parody requires a liberal interpretation, even though a strict interpretation of the requirements attached to the parody exception should prevail.[143] Similarly, factors which contribute to the realization of this fundamental right should count more in the overall assessment than factors which do not.[144] Thus, freedom of expression provides flexibility for courts to determine the lawfulness of the use of a copyright-protected work for the purpose of parody.

Despite lack of consistent Australian authorities, and awaiting judicial confirmation, Australian courts have adopted a restrictive approach in the past,[145] there is ongoing pressure to infuse flexibility into the application of copyright exceptions which courts may follow in future cases.[146] It is believed that Australian courts are, therefore, likely to shift towards a strict statutory interpretation.

In the US, fair use exceptions have lost some of their original flexibility. Initially perceiving fair use from the perspective of the user, courts required the plaintiff to demonstrate that the unauthorized use was unfair. The more recent characterization of fair use as an affirmative defence has brought about a shift to a stricter (and arguably restrictive) appreciation of fair use factors, with particular weight placed upon the potential for economic harm. Additionally, the strict interpretation in *Campbell* has created an artificial distinction between parody and satire. If this distinction appears to be slowly fading, it remains an important factor in the flexibility and the fair use doctrine's ability to adapt to new uses.

Canada appears to be in the vanguard, with its adoption of a users' right doctrine. This not only requires a broad interpretation of the purpose of the permitted use, but eschews an owner-centric approach by placing users' and right-holders' interests on a par with one another. While not rejecting the traditional approach to statutory interpretation altogether, courts should apply a purposive interpretation to the parody exception and identify the motives underlying the unauthorized use. This maintains a fair balance between the interests in play. Yet, despite the difference in emphasis which appears evident in Canada, the first application of the parody exception by Canadian courts illustrates that the users' rights doctrine may result in a narrower interpretation of the parody exception than the EU's strict interpretation principle.[147]

[143] See Chapter 2, section 2. [144] See Chapter 4.

[145] And again recently in *Pokemon* (n 96).

[146] The current restrictive approach prevailing arguably fuels the policy proposals on adopting fair use in Australia.

[147] *United Airlines* (n 40). Yet Craig suggests a strict interpretation departing from the restrictive approach in *Michelin* (n 104), which would align Canada more closely with the other countries under scrutiny. Craig (n 104) 168.

3. Can the Parody Exception be Waived by Contract?

The efficacy of the parody exception nevertheless relies on the autonomous powers of users over the copyright-protected works. We have mentioned that the nature and function of the exception in the courtroom spills over to affect the relationships between parties outside of court.

While the digital environment has made unauthorized copying more straightforward in many instances, the same environment has also made it more straightforward for right-holders to control other uses of their works. The internet has permitted new business models to emerge, whereby right-holders contract directly with end-users,[148] in place of the more traditional and cumbersome forms of distribution of cultural works needed in the analogue world. These new models result in an imbalance in bargaining power: often, right-holders are positioned to impose their terms on users.[149]

Contracts between right-holders and users may attempt to restrict the application of the parody exception. A contractual clause may attempt to restrict a user from performing an act which would be permitted by the parody exception. Given the care with which legislators and courts seek to appropriately balance the interests of relevant parties, the aims of the parody exception would be undermined if right-holders can effectively side-step the provision by 'contracting-out' of the exception.[150] We now consider the extent to which freedom of contract renders the parody exception optional in the countries of interest.

3.1 Principle: freedom of contract

Freedom to contract is a principle which prevails in the jurisdictions studied in this book. In effect, the parties to any contract are free to determine the terms which will bind their dealings, and the court will then enforce these contract terms, on the premise that the contract reflects the parties' intentions.[151]

Yet to what extent do circumstances surrounding many current digital contracts concerning copyright echo the principles underpinning freedom to contract? Guibault differentiates between two contract models. In the traditional, classic contract model, parties have equal bargaining power and negotiate contract terms in good faith.[152] Under this model, each party is reasonably deemed to be aware of its rights and

[148] We are currently seeing an increased amount of 'browse-wrap', 'click-wrap', 'click-through', 'mouse-click', and 'shrink-wrap' contracts in the online environment; Galopin (n 17) 337; C Geiger, *Droit d'auteur et droit du public à l'information* (IRPI, 2004) 202; Guibault (n 45) 325; Buydens and Dusollier (n 47) 13; P B Hugenholtz, 'Adapting copyright to the information superhighway' in *The Future of Copyright in a Digital Environment* (Kluwer Law International, 1996) 84.

[149] Geiger (n 3) 889; Buydens and Dusollier (n 47) 13.

[150] For a detailed study: M Kretschmer, E Derclaye, et al, *The Relationship between Copyright and Contract Law* (2010), IPO Research Paper No. 2010 (04), available at www.ssrn.com; Guibault (n 45).

[151] *Canada: Photo Production Ltd v. Securicor Transport Ltd* [1980] AC 827 (HL), [848] (Diplock LJ); For more: S Ben-Ishai and R D Percy, *Contracts: Cases and Commentaries* (8th edn, Carswell, 2014) chapter 1, sections 3–4; for a classic approach: P S Atiyah, *The Rise and Fall of Freedom of Contract* (Clarendon Press, 1979); *UK: Chappell & Co Ltd v. Nestle Co Ltd* [1960] AC 87 (Lord Somervell of Harrow); *France*: R Sacco, 'Liberté contractuelle, volonté contractuelle' (2007) 59(4) *RIDC* 743–60; O Bustin, 'La liberté contractuelle existe-t-elle en droit d'auteur' (2003) 205(10) *Legipresse* 117; *Australia*: Australian CLRC Report 2002, Chapter 1; *US: Lochner v. New York*, 198 US 45 (1905); *ProCD v. Ziedenberg* 86 F.3d 1447 (7th Cir. 1996); D P Weber, 'Restricting the freedom of contract: a fundamental prohibition' (2014) 16(1) *Yale Human Rights and Development Journal*, Article 2.

[152] Guibault (n 45) 198.

obligations under copyright law, such that, if a party agrees to waive exercise of any statutory exception, this is based upon an understanding of the implications.

As discussed further in Chapter 7,[153] in certain specific business models, the classic contract model has been largely superseded by the standard form of contract model. Here, one party sets out its 'standard terms', and is unwilling to deviate from these. Instead the other party must either accept or refuse the standard terms.[154] In many areas of business, where the parties are on an equal footing, and there is a wide choice of alternative suppliers, this approach may be unproblematic. In contrast, if the bargaining powers are unequal, and there is little choice between suppliers, the strongest party is able to unilaterally dictate the terms of contract.

3.2 Exceptions: mandatory character of the parody exception

The principle of freedom of contract is not without limits. The next part of this section enquires whether the parody exception's protection of higher values in a democratic society itself constitutes an exception to the principle of contractual freedom. But before considering the national level, some insight can be gained at a supra-national level.

Firstly, the jurisprudence of the European Court of Human Rights ('ECtHR') provides guidance as to the importance of the right to freedom of expression in specific circumstances.[155] These cases underline the importance of this fundamental freedom[156] which relates to the social value attributable to an enlightened public.[157] Any limitation to the exercise of fundamental rights must be proportionate to the legitimate aim pursued. Here, Guibault concludes that any contract term which, in order to protect a copyright interest, renders an individual impotent in exercising their right of freedom of expression is unlikely to be proportionate.[158]

Secondly, the InfoSoc Directive contains no guidance as to whether the copyright exceptions are mandatory. However, the earlier Computer Programs Directive[159] specifically mandates that any contractual provision between right-holders and end-users which aims to avoid its stated exceptions 'shall be null and void',[160] and the Database Directive includes a similar provision.[161] The fact that the EU legislator has elected to make the mandatory nature of exclusions explicit in these directives, and yet, is silence in the InfoSoc Directive leaves us to draw our own conclusions. Until the CJEU sheds any light on this matter, it falls to Member States to decide whether copyright exceptions derived from the InfoSoc Directive may be overridden by contract law or not.

The UK alone puts the position beyond doubt,[162] despite much lobbying to the contrary by those representing the right-holders' interest. The legislation is clear regarding the need to preserve the parody exception in contractual relationships. Section 30A(2) CDPA states:

[153] See Chapter 7, section 1.

[154] Guibault (n 45) 205.

[155] See Chapter 5, section 4.

[156] Decisions from the ECtHR will only be referred to by name. For full references, see Bibliography. *Handyside v. The United Kingdom* (1976) 1 EHRR 737, [49].

[157] *The Sunday Times v. The United Kingdom (No 1)* (1979) 2 EHRR 245, [65].

[158] Guibault (n 45) 268.

[159] Council Directive 91/250/EEC of 14 May 1991 on the legal protection of computer programs, OJ L122, 17 May 1991, 42–6.

[160] Ibid, art. 9(1).

[161] Directive 96/9/EC of 11 March 1996 on the legal protection of databases, OJ L77/20, 27 March 1996, art. 14.

[162] Section 30A(2) CDPA.

To the extent that a term of a contract purports to prevent or restrict the doing of any act which, by virtue of this section, would not infringe copyright, that term is unenforceable.

A contrario, the contract remains enforceable except those terms seeking to control lawful parodies.

In the other countries in the study, legislators have refrained from specifying in the legislation whether the exception is mandatory. In France, this aspect only gained significance with the copyright amendment in 2006, and currently remains unsettled.[163] There is nothing in the Canadian preparatory works which indicates whether the legislator intended the parody exception to be mandatory, or not.

The situation is also ambiguous in the US. Despite the supremacy of freedom of contract, courts have held that in some circumstances, copyright exceptions could not be waived.[164] Following Reichman and Franklin, both copyright and the First Amendment protect and promote critique as well as social commentary which would be jeopardized if fair use could easily be circumvented.[165]

Similarly, neither the Australian legislation, nor the preparatory works indicate the legal nature of the exception.[166] Yet earlier in 2001, the Copyright Law Review Committee ('CLRC') was instructed[167] to investigate the extent to which electronic agreements sought to modify or exclude copyright exceptions. The CLRC report, published in 2002,[168] acknowledges the role of the exceptions in encouraging creativity and disseminating knowledge by permitting subsequent authors space to create new works. Unsurprisingly, its consultation identified a division between right-holders arguing for stronger exclusive rights and user groups seeking reassurance that hard-fought-for exceptions are not overridden in terms of use. However, an interim CLRC discussion paper of 2001 reveals a finding that terms seeking, explicitly or implicitly, to modify copyright exceptions did feature in copyright licences. In its final report entitled 'Copyright and contract', fair dealing is seen as so 'fundamental to defining the copyright interests'[169] that contractual overriding would significantly disrupt the balance intended in the Copyright Act. It remains to be seen whether this approach will be followed. To date, there has been little judicial consideration of this point, which might clarify the position. Indeed, one commentator has gone as far as suggesting that courts appear to avoid embarking on a determination of the legal nature of the parody exception.[170]

In general, commentators support the UK legislator's approach that the parody exception should be mandatory.[171] This view is based upon the important justification

[163] It must be remembered that the codification of the parody exception attracted little attention as the exception resulted from well-established judicial practices. See Chapter 2, section 4.

[164] This was noted in a case involving first sales rights: *UMG v. Augusto* (2008) 558 F. Supp. 2d 1055.

[165] J H Reichman and J A Franklin, 'Privately legislated intellectual property rights: reconciling freedom of contract with public good uses of information' (1999) 147 *U. PA. L. Rev.* 875, 877.

[166] M De Zwart, 'Seriously entertaining: the panel and the future of fair dealing' (2003) 8 *MALR* 8.

[167] CLRC, Parliament of the Commonwealth of Australia, *Terms of reference* [23 April 2001].

[168] CLRC, Parliament of the Commonwealth of Australia, *Copyright and Contract* (2002).

[169] Ibid, [2.01] and [7.25].

[170] Galopin (n 17) 343.

[171] *France*: C Caron, 'Les exceptions au regard du fondement du droit d'auteur en droit français' in A Lucas, P Sirinelli, and A Bensamoun (eds), *Les exceptions au droit d'auteur: état des lieux et perspectives dans l'Union européenne* (Dalloz, 2012) 22; Galopin (n 17) 360; C Colin, 'La contractualisation des exceptions en droit d'auteur: oxymore ou pléonasme?' (2010) 2 *CCE*, étude n°3, 9; M Vivant and J-M Bruguière, *Droit d'auteur* (Dalloz, 2009) 388; A Guilbert, *La contractualisation des exceptions* (University Panthéon-Assas, 2009) 18; C Alleaume, 'La contractualisation des exceptions en France' in *Droit d'auteur et numérique, quelles réponses de la DADVSI?* (Colloque organized by l'IRPI and l'AFPIDA, 9 March 2007, Prop. Int. 2007, n. 25) 438; El Khoury (n 1) 35; S Joly, 'L'ordre public et le droit d'auteur' in J-M Bruguiere, N Mallet-Poujol, and A Robin (eds), *Propriété intellectuelle et droit commun* (PUAM, 2007) 343; Dusollier (n 16); C Rigamonti in R M Hilty and C Geiger (dir.),

underlying the exception,[172] and the argument raised in the CLRC report, that permitting right-holders to circumvent the parody exception via contract would disrupt the intended balance sought by legislators to meet international, EU, and domestic obligations.

In the situation of a classic contract model, the courts might find a clause preventing one party from relying upon the parody exception as null and void, having regard to factors including relative bargaining position, the fundamental rights involved (like freedom of expression), the purpose of the contract, the seriousness of the encroachment upon the freedom of expression, and proportionality. It is argued that the motives behind the right-holder's claim for breach are as pertinent. An assessment of these factors may lead courts to conclude that the term offends against the principle of good faith[173] or public policy.

Taking this a step further, it seems legitimate to question whether there should be uniform treatment of contractual restrictions to the application of an exception and technical restrictions, i.e. anti-circumvention methods, imposed by right-holders to prevent unauthorized access to works in the digital environment.[174] Although it is arguable that a parodist does not need to rely on the access to the medium of the original work if technical protective measures are in place, this however may make it more difficult to parody the work. None of the countries under scrutiny have sought to target this problem specifically, or study the extent to which technical measures are hindering efforts to create parody works. However, as further explained in Chapter 4, circumventing an encryption to access a work may weigh against the parodist.[175]

4. Conclusion

Throughout this chapter, the nature of the parody exception has been explored. Commencing with consideration of the legal nature of the exception, the analysis concluded that the parody exception is currently conceived as an objective right. Therefore, although parodists cannot initiate proceedings to determine whether their use is permitted by the parody exception, it has been argued that the exception as a defence must be interpreted in such a way as to allow exercise of the freedom of expression. Ultimately, this influences the principle of interpretation of the exception. It remains to be seen whether the different approaches adopted in different jurisdictions (strict interpretation or users' rights doctrine) greatly influence the outcome as to when the exception applies in particular cases.

Although there seems to be broad agreement that the parody exception, in particular, is founded in support of the fundamental right of free expression, its characterization as a defence requires the user to justify their use, rather than perceiving

La balance des intérêts en droit d'auteur (Conference Proceedings, 2004); S Dusollier in Hilty and Geiger, ibid; Bergel (n 80) 188; Planiol cited by P Malaurie, *L'ordre public et le contrat* (Paris, 1950) 263; *Canada*: D Gervais, 'Le droit d'auteur au Canada: le point après CCH' (2005) 203 *RIDA* 7–61; *Australia*: CLRC, Parliament of the Commonwealth of Australia, *Copyright and Contract* (2002), [2.01] and [7.25]; Zwart (n 166) 8; M De Zwart, 'Technological enclosure of copyright: the end of fair dealing?' (2007) 18 *AIPJ* 7; *US*: see n 165, *contra: France*: A Lucas, *Propriété littéraire et artistique* (4th edn, Dalloz. Coll. Connaissance du droit, 2010) 58; Y Gaubiac, 'France: rapport général', in L Baulch, M Green, and M Wyburn (eds), *Alai Study Days—The Boundaries of Copyright: Its Proper Limitations and Exceptions* (Australian Copyright Council: Sydney, 1999), 199.

[172] Colin (n 171) 9. [173] Guibault (n 45) 300. [174] Galopin (n 17) 364.

[175] See Chapter 4.2 and 4.3.

this kind of use as beyond the scope of infringement. This can hamper realization of its underlying objectives. Thus, despite its procedural label as a defence, this does not prevent judges from assessing fair use, fair dealing, or rules of the genre in light of the right to freedom of expression. It has been argued that 'fairness' factors which point in favour of freedom of expression should be given greater weight when assessing whether the parody exception applies, or not.

Based on the solid justification supporting the parody exception, right-holders should not be permitted to use contract law to allow their private interests to prevail over the public interests recognized by the exception. The parody exception is more than a mere exception to a legal right, but rather a statutory recognition of a fundamental freedom. This factor is significant not only in the interpretation of the exception, but in allocating appropriate weight when upholding contractual relationships; particularly if the nature of the contractual relationship is such that principles like freedom to contract appear tendentious.

4

Factors to Consider for the Application of the Parody Exception

By framing the parody exception as 'fair use', 'fair dealing', or the 'rules of the genre' legislators leave flexibility to shape the contours of assessing the parody exception.[1] The judicial interpretation will eventually define the boundaries of the exception, counterbalancing the flexibility initially introduced by legislators, to provide greater legal certainty.

The power vested in courts should not be underestimated. Indeed, the efficacy of the parody exception directly correlates with the ability of parodists to predict whether their use of a protected work falls within the parody exception. Predictability thwarts attempts by right-holders to take advantage of uncertainty, for example, by making unjustified claims of infringement, pressuring users to take unnecessary licences, or agree to stricter terms of use than the law would otherwise impose.[2] This chapter sketches out the range of different factors which are potentially pertinent to the application of the parody exception.

1. The Difficulty of Defining the Exception's Contours

The exact contours of the parody exception in Australia, Canada, and the UK will only be defined once there is a sufficient body of cases which considers its various aspects. As this is currently lacking, the content of this section is clearly speculative. However, although no statutory factors exist, it is legitimate to consider landmark decisions[3] covering related areas, as the principles enunciated therein often extend beyond the particular purposes of the case at hand.[4] In addition, as the parody exception operates

[1] See Chapter 2, section 4.

[2] See Chapter 7, section1 for examples in music parodies; M Handler and D Rolph, 'A real pea souper: the panel case and the development of the fair dealing defence' (2003) 27 *Melbourne University Law Review* 381, 407–8.

[3] *UK: Hubbard v. Vosper* [1972] 2 QB 84, CA (Civ Div) (hereafter *Hubbard*), 94; *Australia: TCN Channel Nine v. Network Ten* [2001] FCA 108 (trial) (hereafter *TCN*), (Conti J.). The Full Court missed the opportunity to make these authoritative by not examining them. Yet Hely J. notes them without endorsing or rejecting them [438]–[439]; and *Canada: CCH Canadian Ltd v. Law Society of Upper Canada* [2004] 1 S.C.R. 339 (hereafter *CCH*), [53].

[4] P Torremans, 'The perspective of the introduction of a European fair use clause' in *Codification of European Copyright Law: Challenges and Perspectives* (Kluwer, 2012) 319–37. Yet these factors should not be overly relied upon: during the amendment of the Australian Copyright Act, there were discussions as to the expansion of these factors to all fair dealing purposes. This has been expressly rejected by Parliament. However, many commentators extend the application of the factors. J McCutcheon, 'The new defense of parody or satire under Australian copyright law' (2008) 2 *IPQ* 163, 181; Copyright Law Review Committee, Parliament of Australia, *Report on the Simplification of the Copyright Act 1968: Part 1--Exceptions to the Exclusive Rights of Copyright Owners* (1998) [2.04] and [6.44]; [4.09] and [4.21]; CLRC, Parliament of Australia, *Copyright and Contract* (2002), [3.39] and [3.37]; Handler and Rolph (n 2) 15; Parliament of Australia, Explanatory Memorandum to the Copyright Amendment Bill 1986, [25].

under a shared legal concept of fair dealing in common with other copyright exceptions, it seems a reasonable hypothesis that these cases can help shed light on the assessment of fairness.[5]

It is also timely to recall a number of points identified in the earlier analysis of the exception, which applies to all jurisdictions of the study. Firstly, fair dealing and rules of the genre traditionally constitute a two-step assessment:[6] courts must assess whether the use of the work is 'for the purpose of parody'.[7] Although this traditional approach still prevails, some countries such as Canada and Australia may be paving the way towards a one step assessment.[8] If this provision is satisfied, the courts then determine whether the use is fair or abides by the rules of the parody genre through a meticulous examination of the works.[9] If either limb of the test is not satisfied, then the exception does not apply. In the case of fair use in the US, the assessment is formed of the four statutory factors and the purpose is considered within the first factor.[10]

Secondly, courts apply an objective standard, meaning they must ask themselves 'whether a fair minded and honest person would have dealt with the copyright work in the manner as the defendant did, for the relevant purpose'[11] or whether the copying work 'merely "supersede[s] the objects" of the original [...], or instead adds something new, with a further purpose or different character, altering the first with new expression, meaning, or message'.[12] This does not mean that there is no scope for the courts to introduce some degree of subjectivity. Indeed, judges determine the *weight* to be attributed to each factor, depending on the particular facts at hand, in arriving at

[5] J Boccara, *La fausse parodie* (Université Panthéon-Assas Paris II, 2007–2008) 25; *CCH* (n 3) [55].

[6] *UK: Hubbard* (n 3) 94; *Beloff v. Pressdram Ltd* [1973] 1 All ER 241 (hereafter *Beloff*), [59]; *Canada: United Airlines, Inc. v. Jeremy Cooperstock* [2017] FC 616 (hereafter *United Airlines*), [106]; *CCH* (n 3) [50]; *Compagnie Générale des Établissements Michelin-Michelin & Cie v. National Automobile, Aerospace, Transportation and General Workers Union of Canada* (1996) 71 C.P.R. (3d) 348 (hereafter *Michelin*), [59]; *Zamacois v. Douville* [1943] 3 Fox Pat. C. 44 (C. Échiquier) (hereafter *Zamacois*), 68–9; *Australia: TCN* (n 3) [49]; *US*: see first factor, the purpose and character of the use, before turning to the assessment of the three other factors.

[7] As the purpose has been dealt with in Chapter 1, it will not be covered again in this chapter. See Chapter 1, section 5.

[8] See Chapter 3, section 2.2.2 for Canada and the approach endorsed in *CCH* (n 3); see *Pokemon Company International, Inc. v. Redbubble Ltd* [2017] FCA 1541 (hereafter *Pokemon*), [70] for Australia.

[9] *France*: V C Colombet, *Précis Dalloz de propriété littéraire et artistique* (9th edn, Dalloz, 1999) n°389; Durrande, Rép. pén. Dalloz, v° Propriété littéraire et artistique, n°58.

[10] To a certain extent, it could be argued that the Canadian Supreme Court in *CCH* intended to relegate the assessment of purpose to the second step of the enquiry, when determining the first fairness factor. See G d'Agostino, *Healing Fair Dealing? A Comparative Copyright Analysis of Canadian Fair Dealing to UK Fair Dealing and US Fair Use* (2007) 3(4) CLPE Research Paper 28/2007, 6. However, this approach was not followed in *United Airlines* (n 6) where the Canadian Federal Court reverted to a strict traditional approach to fair dealing. See [106]–[140].

[11] *UK: Hyde Park Residence Ltd v. Yelland* [2000] 3 WLR 215 CA (hereafter *Hyde Park*), [38]; *Pro Sieben Media AG v. Carlton UK Television* [1999] 1 WLR 605 (hereafter *Pro Sieben*), [467]; *Banier v. News Group Newspapers Ltd* [1997] FSR 812 (hereafter *Banier*), [815]; *Beloff* (n 6) [61]; *Hubbard* (n 3) 94; *France*: the well-established concept of 'pater familias' surrounds the formula; B Galopin, *Les exceptions à usage public en droit d'auteur* (IRPI, 2012) 305, esp. 312; B Mouffe, *Le droit à l'humour* (Larcier, 2011) 317; C Castets-Renard, *Notions à contenu variable et droit d'auteur* (L'Harmattan, 2004); Trib. Corr. Paris, 6 février 1834. Gaz. Trib. 8 février 1834; *Australia: TCN Channel Nine Pty Ltd v. Network Ten Pty Limited* [2002] FCAFC 146, [96]; *TCN* (n 3) [53]; *Canada: CCH* (n 3) [52]; G D'Agostino, 'Healing fair dealing? A comparative copyright analysis of Canada's fair dealing to U.K. fair dealing and U.S. fair use' (2008) 53 *McGill Law Journal* 309, 327; N Tamaro, *Loi sur le droit d'auteur: Texte annoté* (4th edn, Toronto, Éditions Carswell, 1998) 8; *Michelin* (n 6) [70].

[12] *Campbell v. Acuff-Rose Music Inc.* 510 US 569 (1994) (hereafter *Campbell*), [579] citing *Folsom v. Marsh*, 9 F.Cas. 342 (hereafter *Folsom*), [348] (C.C.D. Mass. 1841).

their overall impression.[13] It constitutes an 'equitable rule of reason', requiring careful balancing on behalf of judges in light of copyright purposes.[14] As a consequence, uniform outcomes might not result, despite ostensibly similar facts.[15] Yet, the nature of a fairness-based exception requires the underlying protected work to have been communicated to the public already.[16] This is generally not an issue for genuine parodies, since these rely upon public recognition of the underlying work, at least for the target audience. Finally, the courts' interpretation of the parody exception is underpinned by the need to preserve the right of freedom of expression, generally colouring the factors in the assessment of the exception.[17]

In addition to these common factors, judicial freedom within the EU is required to conform to the CJEU guidance in *Deckmyn*. Here, the two mandatory requirements of humorous character and absence of confusion overarch the national court's appraisal of the unauthorized use. Additionally, as demonstrated in the Canadian decision in *United Airlines, Inc. v. Cooperstock*,[18] there is a certain permeability and influence of EU teachings in other territories outside the EU.[19] We shall see that there is a certain influence of the interpretation of US factors on other territories as well.

[13] *France*: Boccara (n 5) 25; *UK: Hubbard* (n 3) 94; restated by *Sillitoe v. McGraw-Hill* [1983] FSR 545 (hereafter *Sillitoe*), [563]; *BBC v. BSB* [1992] Ch 141 (hereafter *BSB*), [149]; *Banier* (n 11) 11; *Pro Sieben* (n 11) [613]; *Hyde Park* (n 11) [21]; *Canada: CCH* (n 3) [52]–[53]; *Entertainment Software Association of Canada v. SOCAN* [2012] S.C.C. 34 (hereafter *SOCAN*), [32]; *Alberta v. Canadian Copyright Licensing Agency* [2012] 2 S.C.R. 326, [22] (hereafter *Alberta*), [19]; *Australia: TCN* (n 3); *TCN Channel Nine v. Network Ten* [2002] 55 IPR 112 (hereafter *TCN appeal*), [110], (Sundberg J.), [2] and (Finkelstein J.), [16]; *De Garis v. Neville Jeffresse Pidler* (1990) 37 FCR 99 (hereafter *De Garis*), [94] and [109]–[110]; *University of New South Wales v. Moorhouse* (1975) 133 CLR 1, [12]; *US*: *Campbell* (n 12) [577]–[578].

[14] *US: Sony Corp. of Am. v. Universal City Studios, Inc.*, 464 U.S. 417, 448, 104 S. Ct. 774, 78 L. Ed. 2d 574 (1984) (hereafter *Sony*); *Campbell* (n 12) [578]; *Dr. Seuss Enters., L.P. v. Penguin Book USA, Inc.*, 924 F.Supp. 1559 (S.D. Cal. 1966) (hereafter *Seuss I*), 1399 (quoting *Iowa State Univ. Research Found., Inc. v. American Broadcasting Cos.*, 621 F.2d 57, 60 (2d Cir. 1980)); *Dr. Seuss Enters., L.P. v. Penguin Books USA, Inc.*, 109 F.3d 1394, [1399] (9th Cir. 1997) (hereafter *Seuss II*).

[15] This does not preclude judges from providing grounds for its decision. The judges must rely on underlying principles to justify their reasoning. Handler and Rolph (n 2) 418; *Australia: TCN* appeal (n 13) [110], (Sundberg J.), [2] and (Finkelstein J.), [16].

[16] *France*: L. 122-5 IPC 'divulguer'; TGI Paris 9 mars 2017, *Bauret v. Koons*, RG n°15/01086 (hereafter *Les Enfants*) (where the application of the parody exception was denied partly as the original work was not known by the French public); *UK*: H.M. Government, *Modernising Copyright: A Modern, Robust and Flexible Framework* (2012) 14; J Haynes, 'Critically reconceptualizing the United Kingdom's fair dealing exception to copyright infringement in light of the government's most recent proposals for reform and lessons learnt from civil law countries' (2012) 34(12) *EIPR* 811; A Sims, 'Strangling their creation: the courts' treatment of fair dealing in copyright law since 1911' (2010) 2 *IPQ* 192, 201; R Burrell, 'Reining in copyright law: is fair use the answer?' (2001) 4 *IPQ* 361; *Ashdown v. Telegraph Group Ltd* [2001] EWCA Civ 1142 (hereafter *Ashdown*), [194]; *Hyde Park* (n 11) [20]; *British Oxygen v. Liquid Air* [1925] 1 Ch 383 53, 393; *Hubbard* (n 3) 94–5; *Beloff* (n 6) [61]; *Canada*: D'Agostino (n 11) 323; *CCH* (n 3) [58]; it must be noted that several decisions weighed the use of unpublished works in favour of the application of fair dealing given that this contributes to the wider dissemination of cultural works (see section 4.3); *Australia*: M Sainsbury, 'Parody, satire and copyright infringement: the latest addition to Australian fair dealing law' (2007) 12 *MALR* 292, 313. It must be noted that sometimes the reproduction of an unpublished work will tilt the balance in favour of fairness if it is accompanied by an acknowledgment as it contributes to further dissemination of cultural works; *US: Campbell* (n 12) [586]; repeated in *Suntrust Bank v. Houghton Mifflin Co.*, 268 F.3d 1257 (11th Cir. 2001) (hereafter *Suntrust*); *Brownmark Films, LLC v. Comedy Partners*, 682 F.3d 687 (7th Cir. 2012) (hereafter *Brownmark*); *Northland Family Planning Clinic, Inc. v. Ctr. for Bio-Ethical Reform*, 868 F.Supp.2d 962 (C.D. Cal. 2012) (hereafter *Northland*); *TCA Television Corp. v. McCollum*, No 15 Civ. 4325 (S.D.N.Y. Dec. 17, 2015).

[17] See Chapter 7, section 2.

[18] *United Airlines* (n 6).

[19] See Chapter 1, section 5.5.

In what follows, the factors potentially relevant to the parody exception are considered in turn. As there is no hierarchy[20] or standard weighting of factors and none are mandatory (other than those identified for EU Member States), nothing should be inferred from the order in which the factors are considered.[21] For ease, we consider the factors which are likely to be examined in all the jurisdictions under scrutiny first, and then turn to factors adopted in only some. Finally, we conclude by identifying factors which ought to be rejected if the objectives of the parody exception are to be realized.

2. Factors Commonly Applied

In this category, we review the factors which the jurisdictions share in common. For the application of the parody exception, courts are required, or will consider, the intent of the parodist, the lack of confusion between the two works,[22] the amount copied, and the commercial objective as being relevant for assessing the application of the parody exception. As a comparative exercise, we shall assess any differences in how these factors are considered or applied in particular circumstances.

2.1 The intent of the parodist

The intent of the parodist refers to their plan to create a parody. For the purpose of parody, should the court take account of the effect of the putative parody, or the creator's intent? The former would seem to be imply a subjective assessment of the court, whereas the latter would be an objective test. We shall see that it is the latter approach which already seems to be accepted in the jurisdictions of interest.

As further explained in what follows,[23] French courts pay particular attention to the parodist's intent when considering whether the use should be permitted. The aim is to protect right-holders from malevolent behaviour. Accordingly, if the parodist intends their use to harm the work, the author, or the right-holder, this factor weighs against the parodist.[24]

UK courts are also familiar with this factor as an aspect of fair dealing.[25] Although an alleged infringer's intentions are likely to be irrelevant when determining whether the use is for the purpose of parody, intent does play a role in establishing fairness.[26] Adopting an objective standard, courts determine where the user's intent lies on a spectrum ranging from altruistic to malicious. In *Time Warner Entertainment Co Ltd v. Channel 4 Television Corporation Plc*,[27] a documentary reproduced brief extracts from the film, *A Clockwork Orange*. The Court characterizes fair dealing as referring to the true purpose of the use, meaning attention must be given to the genuineness of the user's intention. A fair dealing exception cannot be invoked to disguise an infringement.

[20] Although D'Agostino argues that *Ashdown* (n 16) may have introduced the following hierarchy from most important to least important: (1) market substitution; (2) nature of the work; (3) amount reproduced. See D'Agostino (n 10) 33.

[21] However, the weight of each factor can arguably be determined by its relationship with freedom of expression. See Chapter 5.

[22] Arguably these two first factors will increasingly gain importance in the application of this specific exception.

[23] See sections 2.1.1 and 2.1.2.

[24] Ibid.

[25] *Hyde Park* (n 11) [36]; *Pro Sieben* (n 11) [614]; *Time Warner v. Channel Four Television* [1994] EMLR 1 (hereafter *Time Warner*), [15]; *Beloff* (n 6) [61]; *Hubbard* (n 3) 94.

[26] *Pro Sieben* (n 11) [614].

[27] *Time Warner* (n 25) [468]–[469].

Given the interpretation of the exception in *Deckmyn* requiring parodic use to have a humorous character, it seems that courts are likely to (or should) allocate more weight to this factor in future parody cases.

Australian courts have also considered the user's intent to be a relevant factor in assessing fairness. Finkelstein J. in *TCN*,[28] having considered UK case law,[29] notes that a user's intent may be apparent based upon an examination of the context of the unauthorized use.[30] *In casu*, the fact that the popular TV show, *The Panel*, was known for discussing current events in a humorous way, tipped the balance in favour of fairness. Statements made by the Attorney-General in the lead-up to the introduction of the exception may also have some sway. His comment that an average Australian values parody particularly for its humorous character[31] caused leading commentators, including McCutcheon, to question whether the exception will favour comical parodies over those which are critical.[32]

Canada adopts the same approach, arriving at the same result, without reference to decisions from other common law jurisdictions. In a case relating to an unauthorized parody of the *Bibendum*, the *Michelin* man,[33] the court likewise stated its view that intent plays no role when determining the purpose of the use, but it conceded that it might be relevant when assessing its fairness.[34] This position was later confirmed in *Boudreau v. Lin*,[35] *Avanti v. Favreau*,[36] and *Alberta v. CCLA*.[37] Here, the courts noted the influence of the user's intent by denying the defence in circumstances where the defendant's intent was seen as free-riding on the popularity of the work it had reproduced.

Interestingly, in *CCH*,[38] despite confirming that the real purpose or motive is influential,[39] the court does not seem to have been influenced by the defendant's intent.[40] The fact that this influential decision is silent on the matter does not mean that this factor is no longer relevant. Rather, it highlights the nature of the fair dealing assessment, and the discretion given to each court to determine which of the possible factors are relevant to the case at hand. This is confirmed in *United Airlines*,[41] in which the Canadian Federal Court posits that determining the real purpose or motive of the dealing includes considering whether the defendant may have ulterior motives behind the dealing.[42] The parody under evaluation was a rework of the plaintiff's *UNITED* logo. The defendant altered this by reversing the order of the letters I and T (to form the word *UNTIED*), changing their colour from blue to red, and adding a red frowning face onto the globe design. Although the Federal Court noted that the use had a humoristic character by displaying mockery, the Federal Court was unconvinced that the

[28] See Chapter 1, section 5.4.

[29] *TCN* appeal (n 13) [97]: Hely J. citing *Hyde Park* (n 11) and *Pro Sieben* (n 11) [614].

[30] *TCN* appeal (n 13) [17].

[31] P Ruddock, 'Protecting precious parody', *Daily Telegraph*, 30 November 2006.

[32] McCutcheon (n 4) 173. To some extent, the parodist's intent was considered in the recent *Pokemon* case when determining the purpose of the use. Here Talbot J. noted that although some uses could be found humorous or satirical, nothing in the evidence demonstrated the defendant's intention to create these works for the purpose of parody. *Pokemon* (n 8) [70].

[33] *Michelin* (n 6).

[34] Ibid, [70].

[35] In the present case, a professor had reproduced a student's research at a symposium without any acknowledgement. The court could not hold in favour of the professor he had actively removed the name of the student from the paper to substitute with his own. This evidence of malicious intent could not support fair dealing. *Boudreau v. Lin* (1997) 150 D.L.R. (4th) 324, [68].

[36] See the facts in Chapter 2, section 2.6; *Productions Avanti Ciné-Vidéo Inc. v. Favreau* (1999) 177 D.L.R. (4th) 129 (hereafter *La Petite Vie*), [57]–[58].

[37] *Alberta* (n 13) [23].

[38] *CCH* (n 3).

[39] *CCH* (n 3) [54].

[40] *CCH* (n 3) [66].

[41] *United Airlines* (n 6).

[42] Ibid, [122].

dealing was the result of a humorous intent.[43] In the eyes of the court, the intent was one to shame and punish United Airlines for its failings, and this weighed against the findings of fair dealing. Essentially, and citing *Deckmyn*, the court held that parody requires a humorous intent or an element of mockery, but does not extend to include intent to harm.[44] Therefore, defamatory expressions appear to fall beyond the limits of humorous character.[45]

Since the *Campbell* decision,[46] US courts have shied away from any direct appreciation of the parodist's intent to focus on the transformative character of the use.[47] Therefore, intent is analyzed less in terms of humorous character,[48] and more from the perspective of the expressive purpose combined with the other fair use factors.[49] This is illustrated by the transformation of the song *I Love New York* into *I Love Sodom* as part of a *Saturday Night Live* spoof which passed comment on the failing public image of New York City in the late 1970s. Elsemere Music Inc., failing to see the humour in the sketch, sued the National Broadcasting Company's network for copyright infringement, which, in turn, sought reliance upon the fair use doctrine. Ultimately, the court decided in favour of the defendant. Although relegated to a footnote, the articulate opinion from Goettel J. notes that substantial copying may be fair if the parodist 'builds upon the original, [. . .] contributing something new for humorous effect and commentary.'[50]

On occasion, intent has been alluded to as a limiting principle when attempts at parody border upon obscene humour. For example, neither transposing Disney characters into adult-only scenarios[51] nor reworking The Andrews Sisters' *Boogie Woogie Bugle Boy* into a sexual and racy musical, *Let My People Come*,[52] was upheld as fair use. This line of reasoning has even led scholars, such as Schneider, to argue that the content of the expression should be introduced as a new factor,[53] such that any expression of a sexual or obscene nature should weigh against the finding of fair use.

While most common law jurisdictions accept intent as a factor relevant to fairness, its appreciation will vary upon the particular facts of the case. Equally, many common law judges will avoid a direct appreciation of the parodist's intent to focus on the other

[43] Ibid, [124]. [44] Ibid.

[45] Though it is somewhat surprising that the Canadian court first decides that the use is humoristic and then decides that it is not. This is somewhat confusing and could perhaps be avoided by adopting a more holistic approach whereby fairness factors help in deciding whether the use was for the purpose of parody.

[46] *Campbell* (n 12).

[47] Essentially, if the defendant intends to give a whole new meaning to the work, it is more likely to be fair use. *Galvin v. Ill. Republican Party*, 130 F.Supp.3d 1187 (N.D. Ill. Sept. 9, 2015) (hereafter *Galvin*).

[48] *Irving et al v. E.C. Publications, Inc.* 329 F.2d 541 (2d Cir. 1964) (hereafter *Irving*) noted: 'our individual tastes may prefer a more subtle brand of humor, this can hardly be dispositive here' referring to *Bleistein v. Donaldson Lithographing Co.*, 188 U.S. 239, 47 L.Ed. 460 (1903). Confirmed in *Campbell* (n 12) [582]–[583].

[49] Here, US courts adopt a liberal approach, which can be contrasted with their French counterparts. As recently held by the Tribunal of First Instance of Paris, the creation of a new expression does not suffice to trigger the application of the parody exception. *Les Enfants* (n 16). In contrast, fair use was found in a parody of an educational abortion campaign video for an anti-abortion campaign: *Northland* (n 13).

[50] *Elsmere Music, Inc. v. National Broadcasting Co.*, 623 F.2d 252, [253 n.I] (2d Cir. 1980) (hereafter *Elsmere*).

[51] *Walt Disney Prods. v. Air Pirates*, 581 F.2d 751 (9th Cir. 1978), cert. denied, 439 U.S. 1132 (1979) (hereafter *Air Pirates*).

[52] *MCA, Inc. v. Wilson*, 677 F.2d 180 (2d Cir. 1981) (hereafter *Wilson*).

[53] J N Schneider, 'Parody and the fair use defense: the best way to practice safe sex with all your favorite characters' (2016) 81 *Brook. L. Rev.* 1777.

more economic-oriented factors. A direct appreciation of intent is more developed in France where the condition can be neatly summarized as 'to entertain without causing harm'.[54] This approach will be considered next, since it may prove useful guidance for other jurisdictions. Firstly, we shall determine what kind of humorous intent is required before, secondly, establishing its contribution to defining the outer limits of the French parody exception.

2.1.1 Humorous intent

In France, it is well established that parodies should have a humorous character.[55] Sometimes the term is applied more strictly to allow comic expressions,[56] however, the current interpretation of the humorous intent expands to encompass expression of homage and criticism.[57]

As an illustration, the French court has accepted that a painting of the famous surrealist artist Magritte in *Playboy Magazine* did result in an expression of humour.[58] Here, the humorous character was perceived as deriving from the juxtaposition of Playboy's sexual elements with Magritte's artistic world. Humour can be even more biting. French courts have found the criterion satisfied in works which lack any comic element. For example, humour was considered present in a parody of the well-known *CAMEL* logo which depicted a dying camel (used in an anti-tobacco campaign);[59] a drawing of Yves Montand next to reworked lyrics of *Les Feuilles Mortes* paying tribute to the then recently deceased singer;[60] a rework of *Tintin*'s adventures in playful novels, in which characteristic elements of the protected work were unexpectedly distorted;[61] use of *Tarzan* as an anti-hero;[62] a light opera, *Couchés dans le foin*, parodying the Toreador tune from the opera *Carmen*;[63] and even a reworking

[54] TGI Paris, 13 février 2001, *SNC Prisma Presse & EURL Femme c/ Monsieur V*, N RG 00/16766; Galopin (n 11) 305.

[55] Confirmed in *Deckmyn and Vrijheidsfonds VZW v. Helena Vandersteen and Others* [2014] ECLI:EU:C:2014:2132 (hereafter *Deckmyn*), [20] including mockery.

[56] TGI Evry, 9 juillet 2009, RG n°09/02410 confirmed Paris, 18 février 2011, RG 09/19272, Propr. Int. 2011 n°39 p. 187 (hereafter *Saint-Tin*); Versailles, 17 septembre 2009, N°RG: 06/11732; TGI Nanterre, 1ère ch., 22/05/2008, n°06/11732; Paris, 4e ch. B, 13/10/2006, D.E.; TGI Paris, 7 octobre 1992, *affaire Faizant*, RIDA, janvier 1993, 222; TGI Clermont Ferrand, *Ets Michelin c/ CFDT*, 27 octobre 1993, n°848/01, inédit; P El Khoury, *Les exceptions au droit d'auteur* (thèse Montpellier, 2007) 358.

[57] The *Faizant* case was reversed on appeal, Paris, 11 mai 1993, RIDA, juillet 1993, 340; *Saint-Tin* (n 56); TGI Paris, 31 octobre 2007, *Coco Mademoiselle*; Cass., 4 février 2002, *La Bicyclette Bleue*; appeal of TGI Clermont Ferrand, *Ets Michelin c/ CFDT*, Riom, 15 septembre 1994; TGI Paris, 5 janvier 1978 speaking of 'grossissement burlesque' or 'imitation burlesque' (TGI Paris, 14 mai 1992; TGI Paris 9 janvier 1970) or 'travestissement comique' (Cass., 12 janvier 1988, RIDA, n°137, 98 (hereafter *Douces Transes*)).

[58] TGI Paris, 3e ch., 1 avril 1987, cah. Dr. d'auteur 1988, n°1, 16.

[59] Paris, 14e ch., 22 mai 2002, 2002/00949 confirmed by Cass., 2e ch. Civ., 19 octobre 2006, n°05-13489. Interestingly, this decision was decided under trade mark law where there is no parody exception to date. See S Jacques, 'A parody exception: why trade mark owners should get the joke' (2016) 38(8) *EIPR* 471, 477.

[60] *Faizant* (n 56) 222, which refused the application of the parody exception, overturned on appeal, Paris, 11 mai 1993, RIDA, juillet 1993, 340.

[61] The humorous intent stems from the comic allusions, word games, puns, and additional turn-over cues which enable the reader to recognize and enjoy the allusions (p. 18). *Saint-Tin* (n 56).

[62] TGI Paris, 3 janvier 1978, D. 1979, p. 99 obs. Desbois (hereafter *Tarzoon*).

[63] Trib. Comm Seine, 26 juin 1934, Gaz. Pal. 1934. 2. 594.

of a Mylène Farmer song in a movie, used to emphasize the sexual character of the scene.[64]

Yet, the broad interpretation of humorous intent adopted in France is not so broad as to extend to a mere reworking. For example, French courts have found humorous intent to be lacking where the only change is one of colour, such as replacing the red colour in the *DANONE* logo with black,[65] where song lyrics were used for a political campaign,[66] where minor amendments have been made to lyrics[67] or drawings,[68] and in an unauthorized sequel to the *Tintin* series of Hergé.[69] In the latter case, for example, the defendant had reproduced the original comic strips in his book, which had, in the court's view, created a new work borrowing from Hergé's world, rather than parodying the original.[70] Most recently, in *Naked*,[71] the court denied artist Jeff Koons' claim to a parody defence in respect of his transformation of a photograph taken by Jean-François Bauret into a sculpture, merely adding pop art elements such as flowers.

In light of these illustrative examples, it is reasonable to conclude, firstly, that appraising humorous character is inherently subjective[72] and sensitive to the practices, social customs, and norms at a point in time within a particular society. Therefore, courts must ensure that their reasoning upholds artistic neutrality and refrains from any qualitative judgement on the work's artistic merits.[73] It appears that judges find this easier to do where the object of the parody is the underlying work,[74] but it does not preclude the target of the comment being directed at an external object such as customs, a societal event, or the parodist himself.[75]

Secondly, preservation of the right of freedom of expression requires a broad interpretation of this criterion to ensure that all expressions of humour are covered.[76] Therefore, humorous character is a spectrum ranging from provoking laughter,[77] being

[64] TGI Paris, 3e ch., 29 novembre 2000: RIDA, mars 2001, p. 377.

[65] TGI Paris, 4 juillet 2001, *Société Compagnie Gervais Danone et Société Groupe Danone v. Olivier M., Réseau Voltaire et autres*, www.legalis.net, upheld on appeal, Paris, 30 avril 2003.

[66] Paris, 4e ch., 21 juin 1988: RIDA, avril 1988, p. 304 after referral from Cass. 1ère Civ., 27 mars 1990: JCP G. 1990, IV, p. 203.

[67] TGI Paris, 9 janvier 1970, RIDA, février 1970, p. 172.

[68] Paris, 17 octobre 1980 D. 1982, somm. 42.

[69] TGI Nanterre, 1ère ch., 22 mai 2008, n°06/11732, *Garcia c/ Sté Moulinsart* confirmed by Versailles 17 septembre 2009.

[70] Similar reasoning was already adopted in *La Bicyclette Bleue*, a parody of *Gone with the Wind*. While the court of first instance found that the defendant's act resulted in a mere transposition of action of the copyright-protected novel, the Supreme Court and Court of Appeal on referral from the Supreme Court eventually decided that no infringement was established as only the ideas had been copied rather than the expression of these ideas. Unfortunately, it seems that this decision of first instance has not been published. Cass., 4 février 1992, n°90-21630; Dalloz, 2 avril 1992, n°14, p. 182, note Gautier; Paris, 21 novembre 1990, in D. 1991, p. 85, obs. Gautier. *Le Monde*, 23 novembre 1990; analysis can be found in A Strowel, 'La parodie selon le droit d'auteur et la théorie littéraire' (1991) 26 *RIEJ* 44, 47 (discussing the court of first instance's decision). This example demonstrates that transformativeness can justify more uses than uses permissible under the parody exception.

[71] *Les Enfants* (n 16).

[72] Ibid; TGI in *Saint-Tin* (n 56); TGI Paris, 3e ch., 1 avril 1987, cah. Dr. d'auteur 1988, n°1, p. 16; Trib. Civ. Seine, 12 juin 1879, Ann. propr. ind. 1879, p. 239; Trib. Civ. Seine, 23 février 1872, Ann. propr. ind. 1873, p. 162.

[73] P Bloch, *Image et droit* (L'Harmattan, 2002) 129.

[74] See n 65; *Douces Transes* (n 57); P-Y Gautier, 'La bicyclette bleue n'est pas une contrefaçon d'autant en emporte le vent' (1991) *Recueil Dalloz* 85.

[75] *Tarzoon* (n 62).

[76] See Chapter 5, section 4.1.2.

[77] *Saint-Tin* (n 56); TGI Paris, 31 octobre 2007, *coco mademoiselle*; Paris, 13 septembre 2005; *Douces Transes* (n 57); A Françon, 'Questions de droit d'auteur relatives aux parodies et productions similaires' (1988) 6 *Droit d'auteur* 302, 304.

playful,[78] paying tribute,[79] to providing positive or negative criticism at the other extreme.[80]

Thirdly, determining whether a humorous character is realized requires judges to consider the *intent* of the parodist, and not the *effect* of the parody on the public. This is justified because a parody's impact relies heavily on external factors; not just the parodist's talent, but also on the audience—over which the parodist has no control.[81]

Finally, recent decisions demonstrate that intent serves more as a supporting factor, rather than being at the heart of the consideration. Rather than focusing on humour, judges tend to focus on the effect of the putative parody on the original work, and the likelihood that the expression will harm the original author or their work.[82] It remains to be seen whether courts will give more importance to humorous intent following *Deckmyn*.

In conclusion, it is hard to pin down the exact characteristics of an appraisal for humorous intent. If courts have adopted different positions in similar cases, they have done so based on a combination of factors surrounding the humorous requirement, such as parasitism or confusion created between the two works. Additionally, this requirement should not be analyzed in isolation without also assessing the presence or absence of harm.

2.1.2 Absence of harm

The absence of harm truly defines the outer limits of humour in French parody cases. This factor denies a parodist benefit from the exception if their intention is to harm the original author or his works through parody.[83]

Considering this factor first, courts determine whether the parodist reproduces the earlier work with the intent to harm the reputation or honour of the author.[84] As a corollary, if this is demonstrated, the author has a claim based upon moral rights,[85] and on other personality rights, such as defamation. In essence, courts seek to limit the degree of harm permitted by the exception. Harm under a veil of humour is allowed, provided that it does

[78] *Saint-Tin* (n 56); TGI Paris, 31 octobre 2007, *coco mademoiselle*; Cass, 4 février 2002, *La Bicyclette Bleue*; TGI Paris, 3e ch., 29 novembre 2000: RIDA, mars 2001, p. 377; Paris, 3e ch., 1 avril 1987, cah. Dr. d'auteur 1988, n°1, p. 16; *Tarzoon* (n 62).

[79] *Saint-Tin* (n 56); TGI Paris, 31 octobre 2007, *coco mademoiselle*; Paris, 11 mai 1993, RIDA, juillet 1993, p. 340 nevertheless negatively criticized by Françon, obs. sous Paris, 11 mai 1993, RTDcom., 1993, p. 507.

[80] *Saint-Tin* (n 56); TGI Paris, 31 octobre 2007, *coco mademoiselle*; TGI Paris, 23 mars 2001, *jeboycottedanone.com* CCE juillet–août 2001, Comm. n°70, note Huet; TGI Paris, 8 juillet 2002 *Esso c/ Greenpeace* (référé) CCE nov. 2002, Comm. n°140, obs. Caron et Linant de Bellefonds overturned in Paris 26 février 2003, *SA Société des participations du Commissariat à énergie atomique c/ Association Greenpeace France/Internet* FR CCE avril 2003, Comm. n°38, prop. Int. juillet 2003, n°8, p. 322, obs. Lucas, D. 2003, p. 1831, n. Edelman. Accepted in Riom, 15 septembre 1994, D. 1995, p. 429, note Edelman; Cass., 21 février 1995, *Reynolds Tobacco*; Versailles, 17 mars 1994, *Marlboro*, D. 1995; RIDA, février 1995, p. 350; *Tarzoon* (n 62).

[81] TGI Paris, 14 mai 1992, RIDA, octobre 1992, p. 174; Mouffe (n 11) 290 and 292; A Berenboom, 'La parodie' in E Cornu (ed.), *Bande dessinée et droit d'auteur* (Larcier, 2009) 115.

[82] Versailles, 17 mars 1994, *Marlboro*, D. 1995; E Delfour, *L'imitation créatrice* (University of Toulouse, 2000) 74; Paris 11 mai 1993, RIDA, juillet 1993, p. 340; TGI Paris, 17 octobre 1984, D. 1985, IR p. 324, obs. Lindon; Bercheron, art. 1382–1386 Civil Code, fasc. 133-1, n°66; Strowel (n 70) 48.

[83] Strowel (n 70) 48; Françon (n 77) 304.

[84] *Douces Transes* (n 57).

[85] Galopin (n 11) 307; Mouffe (n 11) 314; Berenboom (n 81) 116; X L de Bellefonds, *Droits d'auteur et droits voisins* (Dalloz, 2002) 217; M Isgour, 'La satire: réflexions sur le "droit à l'humour"' (2000) 1&2 *A&M* 59–68; Strowel (n 70) 48; Françon (n 77) 304.

not constitute an unlawful act according to some other area of law. If the primary intent is to defame, denigrate, or cause injury, the parodist is considered to have gone beyond the rules of the genre, and arguably beyond what a fair-minded and honest person would have done with the work. In contrast, if the primary intent is to entertain or criticize, then any harshness or maligning can be excused, because the rules of the genre are respected.

For example, the French Supreme Court has held that a music parody in which revised lyrics are sung to the original melody in a voice seeking to mock the original singer via imitation is a legitimate caricature, provided there is no confusion or obvious rudeness.[86] Courts rarely consider that a caricature will harm the personality of the author, provided it is not obviously outrageous.[87] This is justified because such mockery is at the heart of caricature, and consequently courts are willing to concede a degree of harm, so as to respect the nature of the genre.

Considering now the intent to denigrate the underlying work via parody,[88] the character Tintin provides another good example. In a parody which featured this famous fictional character in scenarios in which Tintin takes illicit drugs or performs sexual acts, i.e. the antithesis of the world created by Hergé, the court considered that such use denigrated the original work to such an extent that it should not benefit from the parody exception.[89] Yet, *in casu*, it is debatable whether this was the appropriate conclusion. While ostensibly refraining from judging the use based upon artistic merits, it appears that French courts are less lenient where a parody is based upon a work forming part of the cultural heritage, *even if* the rules of the genre appear to be respected. That said, as in the case of potential harm to the author, if a parody is considered to be too outrageous, it seems to fall beyond the limit of the harm allowed under the exception. Therefore, it remains to be seen whether parodies like the creations of Ole Ahlberg[90] which reproduce well-known works belonging to French, Belgian, or Italian cultural heritage to transpose them to a fantasy world far from the world in which the original evolves would be found non-harmful.[91]

In conclusion, this factor reminds parodists that freedom of expression is not absolute, meaning that not all expressions made under the cover of humour will benefit from the exception.[92] In addition, the factor enables courts to consider the other interests of authors, including moral rights, and to consider harm protected by other areas of law, as required by the three-step test.[93] Yet, this factor is inherently a question of degree.[94] While preserving freedom of expression requires a liberal interpretation of humour, it does not support an obviously outrageous or malevolent statement. These are rightly prohibited.[95]

[86] *Douces Transes* (n 57); TGI Paris, 9 janvier 1970, JCP, 1970, II, 16645.

[87] Cass., 2 mars 1997, JCP II jurispr. N°5, 28 janvier 1998, p. 185; Paris, 28 février 1995, légipresse, 1995, n°8125, I p. 92; TGI Paris 12 janvier 1993, légipresse n°108 II p. 11; TGI Paris 26 février 1992 légipresse n°96 1992 p. 127; Cass, 13 février 1992, légipresse, n°93, p. 87; *Douces Transes* (n 57); Paris 19 juin 1987, JCP 1988, II, n°20957; TGI Paris (ref) 24 février 1975, D. 1975, jurispr, p. 438, note Lindon.

[88] TGI Paris, *Société Moulinsart, Mme Fanny R. c/ Eric J.*, 11 juin 2004, available on www.legalis.net; Cass., *Exocom c/ Boomerang*, 2003; TGI Paris, *OneTelFuck*, 29 mai 2001 available at http://www.legalis.net/spip.php?page=jurisprudence-decision&id_article=319 (access date: 1 June 2018).

[89] *Société Moulinsart* (n 88).

[90] See http://www.artnet.com/artists/ole-ahlberg/ (access date: 1 June 2018).

[91] This example can be compared to *Air Pirates* (n 51) mentioned in section 3.1.

[92] See Chapter 5. [93] See Chapter 2.

[94] For example, in *Commissaire Crémèr*, the facts dealt with a cartoon parody of a famous comedian (Bruno Cremer) known for impersonating Commissaire Maigret in a TV series. The Supreme Court held that the parody exception was applicable despite the parody being 'particularly ridiculous and belittling'. Cass. 1ère ch. Civ., 10 septembre 2014, n°13-14.629 on appeal from Paris (Pole 5 ch. 2), 21 septembre 2012. This decision is criticized by Pollaud-Dulian, RTD Com. 2014, p. 815.

[95] Bloch (n 73) 131.

2.2 Absence of confusion

A related aspect to the concept of harm to the author or the work is a parody which causes confusion. Currently a consideration mainly in France,[96] this factor requires the court to assess whether the audience confuses the parody with the underlying work. When encountering the parody, the public should not believe that they are encountering the original, or assume that there is a link, whether creative or economic, between the two works. In essence, the parodic nature of the defendant's use must be immediately apparent. The original work is reproduced not because the parodist seeks to benefit from another's creative efforts, but because copying is essential to this particular creative endeavour.

In *Deckmyn*, the CJEU establishes this as a mandatory consideration for all EU Member States.[97] Thus, it is no longer only French courts that will have to devote attention to this factor. However, lack of confusion is already familiar in the common law countries of the study, as is illustrated in what follows.

Absence of confusion is not alien to the appreciation of the copyright exceptions in common law jurisdictions. In the very first fair dealing case to come before the UK courts,[98] the defendant had published a book of study materials which included the plaintiff's examination papers. The court refuted that this was 'fair dealing', but held that it was mere reproduction, as the defendant had done nothing to transform the original work.[99] The role that transformation plays in avoiding confusion is established in Australia too. Analysis of the court's reasoning in *De Garis v. Neville Jeffress Pidler Pty Ltd*[100] and the US case *Disney Productions v. Air Pirates*,[101] leads one commentator to conclude that the more the original work is distorted, the more likely it is that the use will fall within the parody exception.[102] Absence of confusion is also a factor in Canadian fair dealing cases, and these highlight a different form that confusion may take. In *CCH*[103] and *SOCAN*,[104] the court held there was no fair dealing in the case of plagiarism. Here, attempts to 'pass off' another's work as your own is not only unfair, but it may confuse.[105] Plagiarism is sometimes classed as an economic encroachment upon the use on the market of the original, instead of as a factor of confusion. Nevertheless, in *United Airlines, Inc. v. Jeremy Cooperstock*,[106] Phelan J. arguably misinterpreted the *Deckmyn* requirement of evocation of an existing work while exhibiting noticeable differences as an absence of confusion criterion. According to the judge, showing *some* difference (e.g. content and disclaimers) is sufficient to satisfy the EU requirement. This does not mean that confusion did not play a role in the federal court's reasoning. To the contrary, when determining the fairness of the dealing, the court questions whether a confusing parody use can ever be fair.[107] As parody relies on the public to recognize

[96] Though the Canadian decision in *United Airlines* (n 6) demonstrates the increasing importance of this criterion in Canada, [123] and [138].

[97] *Deckmyn* (n 55) [20].

[98] *University of London Press Ltd v. University Tutorial Press Ltd* [1916] 2 Ch 601.

[99] Ibid, [613]; confirmed in *Hubbard* (n 3) 94.

[100] See n 13.

[101] *Air Pirates* (n 51).

[102] Sainsbury (n 16) 311–12; M Sainsbury, 'Parody, satire, honour and reputation: the interplay between economic and moral rights' (2007) 18 *AIPJ* 149, 154.

[103] *CCH* (n 3) [54].

[104] *SOCAN* (n 13) [33].

[105] Therefore, the entire reproduction of the original work generally leads to the finding of confusion. See section 2.3.

[106] *United Airlines* (n 6).

[107] Ibid, [123].

the references made to the original work, this precludes confusing uses from being fair.[108]

How should the confusion factor be appraised? Arguably, it is the absence of confusion rather than the degree of modification which is key for parody works. As we have seen already,[109] a successful parody may result from the subtlest of changes to the original work, or it may even reproduce the totality of the earlier work. Hence, it is dangerous for courts to assess parodic use quantitatively, based upon the amount of the work reproduced relative to the new input from the parodist, as this is likely to result in subjective assessment of the resultant work's merit. Indeed, much of the creative effort on the part of the parodist generally takes place prior to the work's expression, for example, in the selection of the work(s) to parody and in the selection of the best elements to modify in order to communicate the desired message. It is this aspect of the parody which determines whether it is successful. Inherently, there is a fine line between the amount of copying needed for the purpose of parody and that which will lead to confusion. Unless a parodist is permitted to copy a sufficient amount of a protected work, the public will fail to recognize the allusions made to the original work(s). However, if the parodist copies too much, the parody will be lost, and the public will question whether the work(s) is just a variant, linked to the original.

Examples of how this careful balance should be struck are evident in French and US decisions. Generally, lack of confusion results from the distortion made by the parodist.[110] Here, courts tend to find that the more modification of the underlying copyright-protected work there is (e.g. France) or *transformativeness* (e.g. US), the less likely it is that the parody creates confusion. Therefore, in a song, reproduction of the entire musical work while changing its lyrics was held as sufficient to avoid confusion;[111] whereas the addition of a commentary to a song by a comedian in a sketch (adding quips such as 'I make songs like this every day' or 'if he could do this, then I may have a chance, too') were insufficient.[112] While the French courts acknowledged that mockery was intended, it held that parody requires an actual

[108] Arguably, this case implies that the threshold for absence of confusion for parody as established in *Deckmyn* is lower than the traditional appreciation of confusion in common law jurisdictions. *Deckmyn* (n 55).

[109] See Chapter 1, section 1.

[110] *France: Saint-Tin* (n 56); Paris, *Paul B c/ Moulinsart*, 13 septembre 2005 at www.legalis.net; référé 11 juin 2004; Paris (4e ch. sect. b) 17 janvier 2003, *Le monde d'Anne Sophie*, Prop. Int. 2003, n°7, p. 169, obs. Lucas; TGI Paris, *Agence France Presse (et autres) c/ M. Ivan Callot, Sarl Magnitude*, 13 février 2002; TGI Paris, *Femme*, 13 février 2001; TGI Paris, 29 novembre 2000, RIDA, juillet 2001, n°189 p. 377; TGI Paris 1 février 2001, Exp. July 2001, p.275, note Herest & chron. Kéréver, RIDA, 2001, n°190, p. 379; ass. plen. 12 juillet 2000, JCP 2000, II 10439; TGI Paris, 24 mars 2000, légipresse 2000, I p. 71 (hereafter *Calimero*); Paris 11 mai 1993, RIDA, 1993, n°157, p. 340, RTD com. 1993. 510, obs. Françon; TGI Paris, 16 février 1993, Dalloz 1994, somm., p. 195, obs. Bigot; TGI Paris, 7 octobre 1992, RIDA, 1993, n°155, p. 222, obs. Kéréver; TGI Paris, 9 janvier 1992, Dalloz 1994, somm., p. 195 obs. Bigot; TGI Paris, 3e ch., 30 octobre 1991, SPE c/CAP, RDPI 1992, n°45, p. 98; Cass. ch. Civ 1ère, 27 mars 1990, Bull. n°75; TGI Paris, 17 mars 1988, Gaz. Pal. 1988, 2 somm., p. 360; *Douces Transes* (n 57); Paris, 14 février 1980, D. 1981, somm. 86, obs. Colombet; *Tarzoon* (n 62); Paris 20 décembre 1977, TGI Paris, 19 janvier 1977, RIDA, 1977, n°92, pp. 167–9 (hereafter *Peanuts*); Trib. Comm. Seine, 26 août 1886, Ann. 1889, p. 352; Trib. Civ. Seine, 12 juin 1879, Ann. propr. ind. 1879, p. 239; *US: Campbell* (n 12).

[111] *Douces Transes* (n 57); repeated in TGI Paris, 29 novembre 2000, RIDA, juillet 2001, n°189 p. 377 (change of lyrics while keeping the tune for a movie scene).

[112] *Jean T. dit Jean Ferrat, Sarl Productions Alléluia, Gérard Meys, Sarl Teme / Sté I-France (venant aux droits de la SA Opsion Innovation) c/ association Music Contact*, Paris, 18 septembre 2002, Dalloz 2002 A.J., p. 3208.

modification of the underlying work.[113] The French court in a *Tintin* case[114] summarized it well:

[P]arody [is] the result of a work of distortion or subversion and thus, a detachment from the original work, in order for the public not to be mistaken on the impact of the words and on the author of the parody.[115]

Here, lack of confusion resulted from a change of genre from comic book to novel, new contemporaneous characters, word games only possible in novel literary form, distortion of the characters' names,[116] and the links created with the underlying work (i.e. *Tintin* appears as the father of the main character, *Saint-Tin*).

Yet, modifications of a copyright-protected work may be insufficient if, despite modification, the parodist work is perceived as a sequel to the original work. In another *Tintin* case,[117] the defendant's posters featured Tintin in new situations, such as reproducing the entire cover of the original *The Blue Lotus* book as if it were part of a film set.[118] The court noted that as Hergé's books had been adapted into films in the past, the public may assume that these posters had been authorized by the late author's estate. Here, the French court did not hesitate in examining the ways in which the right-holder had exercised their exclusive rights, and this was relevant in the court's conclusion that the use had not distanced itself far enough from the original to avoid confusion. An attempt at parody which results in artistic confusion is not covered by the parody exception.

In a further case, considering a reproduction of the famous Calimero cartoon chicken in a sadomasochist context, the court held that transposing an exact copy of the fictional character into a new context, albeit far removed from its natural environment, was insufficient to avoid confusion.[119] Therefore, it seems that although theoretically parody may result simply from a subversive change in context, it will be far easier to establish in practice when there is an actual distortion, because confusion is less likely.

A similar case arose in the US, which reached a similar conclusion. In *Walt Disney Productions v. Air Pirates*,[120] an appropriation of Disney cartoon characters (including Mickey Mouse, Minnie Mouse, and Donald Duck) in other comic books, *Air Pirates Funnies*, engaging in antithetical activities, was held as being an infringement for similar reasons to the French *Calimero* case.

US courts have developed an intrinsic test which seeks to establish whether the defendant's use captures the 'total concept and feel' of the original.[121] If the ordinary public would recognize the use *as* the original, then the subjective assessment should

[113] Similar reasoning was held in TGI Paris, *Agence France Presse (et autres) c/ M. Ivan Callot, Sarl Magnitude*, 13 février 2002 whereby the defendant reproduced the copyright-protected material accompanied by denigrating comments.

[114] *Saint-Tin* (n 56). [115] Ibid.

[116] For example, Tintin becomes 'Saint-Tin' and Milou becomes 'Lou'.

[117] Paris, *Paul B c/ Moulinsart*, 13 septembre 2005 at www.legalis.net.

[118] Hence, fan fiction works are unlikely to be covered by the exception unless these result in a clear parody.

[119] Confirmed in TGI Paris, 11 mai 1988, *Fanny Vlamynck c/ Wolf*, LPA 17 janvier 1989, n°7, p. 8, RIDA, 1989, n°142, p. 344; the literature nevertheless argues that the parody exception should apply where the defendant reproduces protected characters to put them in contexts where the original author would never have put them. Françon (n 77) 303; and as decided in *Peanuts* (n 110); *Tarzoon* (n 62).

[120] *Air Pirates* (n 51).

[121] *Litchfield v. Spielberg*, 736 F.2d 1352, 1357 (9th Cir. 1984), cert. denied, 470 U.S. 1052, 105 S. Ct. 1753, 84 L. Ed. 2d 817 (1985).

weigh against fair use as this may result in confusion.[122] In 1979, for example,[123] when a defendant reproduced almost every aspect of the trailers used for the 'official' Superman television series to advertise their business (merely replacing the Superman name with their own), the US court held in favour of the plaintiff. In doing so, the court concluded that the 'lay observer would instantly identify the defendant's commercial with the copyrighted material'.[124] The same year, the Court of Appeal for the Fifth Circuit refused to find fair use for parody in a case in which the defendant's posters reproduced the pose used in a number of Dallas Cowboys cheerleader posters.[125] The defendant's cheerleaders wore nearly identical uniforms too, but with the key difference that their blouses were unbuttoned to reveal their breasts. It is noteworthy that the cheerleaders in the defendant's poster were all former Dallas Cowboys cheerleaders, which was seen as increasing the likelihood of confusion.

Stemming from these US decisions, the transformative character of the use appears as essential to the appreciation of the first fair use factor, i.e. the purpose and character of the use.[126] This explains why in *Columbia Pictures Indus., Inc. v. Miramax Films Corp.*,[127] the district court held against fair use. The case concerned a poster and trailer promoting Michael Moore's documentary, *The Big One*, which bore a striking resemblance to those used to promote the *Men in Black* film. The main differences lay in the number of characters and use of a microphone in place of the weapons featured in the original (Figure 4.1). According to the court, the use did not create a transformative work, but merely reproduced elements from the original, i.e. both featured a similar strapline and similarly dressed protagonists adopting a similar stance while carrying a large 'weapon' against a backdrop of the New York skyline at night.[128] In short, instead of transforming the copyright-protected work to comment on or criticize the original, the defendant merely used the well-known elements of the *Men in Black* poster to attract the attention of potential viewers of the documentary.

As in France, a US court has recently held that a twenty-one-minute film, *Star Trek: Prelude to Axanar*, an unauthorized prequel to Paramount's original series, should not benefit from a fair use defence.[129] Here, the court was unable to discern any comment or criticism of the copyright-protected works in the copy. Rather, the defendant sought to remain as faithful to the original as possible, to appeal to existing *Star Trek* fans. Thus, borrowing from the *Campbell* decision, if the would-be parodist copies the 'heart' of the copyright-protected work with minimal transformation, then it is likely that the use will be characterized as merely a non-permissible superseding use, rather than a parody, since it may act as a market substitute of the original.[130]

If distortion is necessary to avoid confusion, then this goes hand-in-hand with the need for the public to be able to identify the new work as a parody. This identification[131]

[122] *Campbell* (n 12) [582]: 'The threshold question when fair use is raised in defense of parody is whether a parodic character may reasonably be perceived.'

[123] *DC Comics Inc. v. Crazy Eddie, Inc.*, No 79 Civ. 3786-PNL (S.D.N.Y. 1979) (hereafter *Crazy Eddie*).

[124] Ibid, per Leval J.

[125] *Dallas Cowboys Cheerleaders, Inc. v. Scoreboard Posters, Inc.*, 600 F.2d 1184 (5th Cir. 1979), [14].

[126] *Seuss II* (n 14) [1400]; *Mattel, Inc. v. Walking Mountain Prods.*, 353 F.3d 792, 800 (9th Cir. 2003) (hereafter *Mattel*).

[127] 11 F.Supp.2d 1179 (C.D. Cal. 1998) (hereafter *Miramax*).

[128] Ibid, [36].

[129] *Paramount Pictures Corp. v. Axanar Prods., Inc.*, No 2:15-cv-09938-RGK-E (C.D. Cal. 2017) (hereafter *Axanar*).

[130] *Campbell* (n 12) [588].

[131] Identification does not equate to express acknowledgement of the underlying copyright-protected work. The inadequacy of express acknowledgement is further detailed in Chapter 4 in relation to the paternity right and expressly rejected in *Deckmyn* (n 55) [21].

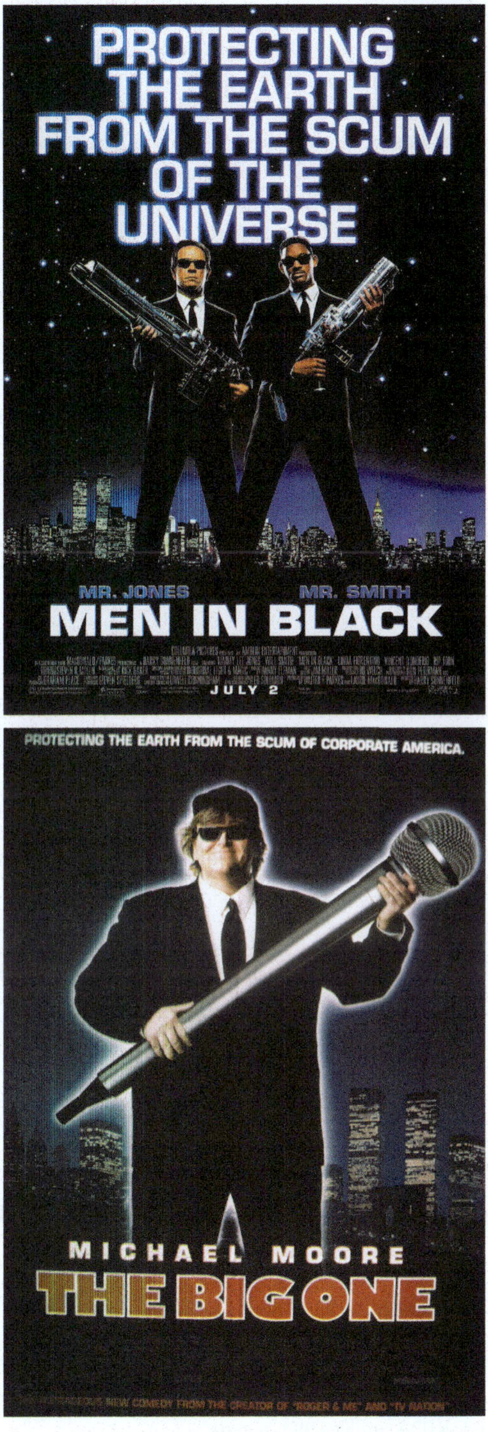

Figure 4.1 Michael Moore sought to promote his new documentary by reproducing the poster of the Men in Black movie. The differences lie in the main protagonist and the replacement of weapons with a microphone.

MEN IN BLACK, US poster, from left: Tommy Lee Jones, Will Smith, 1997. © Columbia/ Everett Collection, Inc. / Alamy Stock Photo.

THE BIG ONE, Michael Moore, 1997. © Miramax/ Everett Collection, Inc. / Alamy Stock Photo.

may be achieved in different ways. Firstly, parodists should only copy noticeable and distinctive elements of the earlier work.[132] Secondly, the more recognizable the underlying work,[133] the easier it is for the public to identify it, and simultaneously recognize that the work has been parodied.[134] This is not to say that only parodies of 'well-known' (in some absolute sense) works may benefit from the exception. As there is no recognized European or international legal standard of renown, this would lead to an over-restrictive application of the exception.[135] Nevertheless, the notoriety of the original work does serve as an indicator that the parodist has not created the copied material. Hence, the more well-known the copyright-protected work is, the less distortion the parodist needs to make, to avoid public confusion.

Likelihood of confusion will also be reduced if the parodist makes the parodic nature of their act explicit.[136] For example, French courts have applied the parody exception in a case where the parody itself included captions like 'After Prévert'[137] or 'Boycott Danone'.[138] In *Brel*,[139] the claimed parody rearranged selected lyrics from one of Brel's songs. However, it did so in such a way that it was impossible to tell that it was a juxtaposition of excerpts, rather than a copy of the original song. Since confusion was likely, the parody fell beyond the exception. As the Supreme Court noted in this case, the crux of the matter is that the public must be aware they are not being exposed to the original work.[140]

[132] TGI Paris, 3e ch., sect. 3, 5 mars 2008, RIDA, 2008, n°217, pp. 338–42; *Douces Transes* (n 57); Trib. Comm. Seine, 26 août 1886, Ann. 1889, p. 352; Trib. Civ. Seine, 12 juin 1879, Ann. propr. ind. 1879, p. 239.

[133] *Les Enfants* (n 16); *Saint-Tin* (n 56); TGI Paris, 3 mars 2008, *Fort Boyard*; TGI Paris, *Agence France Presse (et autres) c/ M. Ivan Callot, Sarl Magnitude*, 13 février 2002; *Calimero* (n 110); Paris, 11 mai 1993, RIDA, juillet 1993, p. 340; TGI Paris, 7 octobre 1992; TGI Paris, 14 mai 1992, RIDA, octobre 1992, p. 174; Cass., ch. Civ. 1ère, 27 mars 1990, Bull. N°75; Paris, 4e ch., 27 novembre 1990, *aff. Jacobs Suchard Franc c/ Antenne 2*, inédit (cited in Mouffe (n 11) 458); Paris, 21 juin 1988, RIDA, octobre 1988, p. 304; *Douces Transes* (n 57); *Tarzoon* (n 62); *Peanuts* (n 110).

[134] *Douces Transes* (n 57).

[135] Recent French decisions appear to elevate the well-known character of the earlier work as a requirement for the application of the parody exception. It is doubtful that this reasoning is doubtful post-*Deckmyn*. Yet, as mentioned, in certain cases, parodies can be covered by the UGC exception in Canada. In which case, section 29.21(b) Copyright Act 1985 requires 'the source—and, if given in the source, the name of the author, performer, maker or broadcaster—of the existing work or other subject-matter or copy of it are mentioned, if it is reasonable in the circumstances to do so'. Some parodies might qualify under the UGC exception subject to the respect of this condition. As opposed to the US where fair use was found in relation to parodies of little-known works (e.g. cookie stamp designs), implicitly recognizing that the object of a parody need not be well-known. *Rycraft, Incorporated v. Ribble Corporation*, No 97-1573-KI, 1999 WL 375610, [8]–[12], 1999 U.S. Dist. LEXIS 6052, [24]–[31] (D. Or. 1999) (hereafter *Rycraft*). This possibility was already noted in *Kane v. Comedy Partners,* 68 U.S.P.Q.2d (BNA) 1748, 2003 WL [975] 22383387, [1], 2003 U.S. Dist. LEXIS 18513, [1] (S.D.N.Y. 2003), aff'd, 98 Fed.Appx. 73 (2d Cir. 2004) and confirmed in *Northland* (n 13). Although in *Campbell*, the Supreme Court also held that parodies 'almost invariably copy publicly known, expressive works' *Campbell* (n 12) [586].

[136] Though this raises the question of whether the parody can still be successful if the public is forewarned of the parody nature of the use. This is the same as telling the punchline before the joke itself, thereby ruining it. See, for example, *Les Enfants* (n 16) 19, where the French court derived confusion from the lack of publicity as to where the parodist's inspiration was derived from.

[137] Paris, 11 mai 1993, RIDA, juillet 1993, p. 340.

[138] TGI Paris, ordonnance de référé du 23 avril 2001.

[139] Cass. Civ. I, 27 mars 1990, Bull., I n°75, *Madame Jacques Brel c/ Rpr* (hereafter *Brel*).

[140] See *Deckmyn* (n 55), where the defendant incorporated the caption 'Fré vrij naar Vandersteen' meaning 'Fré freely in the style of Vandersteen'. This caption is an additional evidence for the public to recognize that they are not being exposed to the original.

Ultimately, including a factor which requires a distortion or modification of the original work delineates between permitted use of a copyright-protected work and unlawful use.[141] Consequently, satisfaction of these two requirements is linked. For example, lack of confusion may result from the selected form of expression. The more comical or detached the parody is from the original, the less the audience will confuse it with the original. In the US, absence of confusion is linked to the amount reproduced and any encroachment upon the protected economic rights.[142] This interlinking of factors helps us to understand why the legal concepts of fair use, fair dealing, or the rules of the genre do not rely upon a checklist of linear reasoning, but comprise a global appreciation or constitute a matter of overall impression.

2.3 Amount reproduced

As we have established, parody, by its very nature, requires copying, but this inevitably begs the question: how much copying is permitted within the exception? While it is already clear that if a defendant is seeking to rely upon a fair dealing defence, their use must already constitute a substantial part of the an earlier protected work, would it be possible for a parodist to reproduce an entire work and yet still benefit from the exception?

Early UK fair dealing decisions did not seem to consider the quantity reproduced as decisive.[143] Yet, later case law appears to allocate more weight to this when assessing whether a dealing was fair.[144] Analysis of fair dealing decisions, especially those concerning use for the purposes of criticism, indicates that courts measure the amount borrowed against the weight of comment made,[145] so bringing a qualitative aspect into the appreciation.[146] It is not only the amount of the material which is reproduced which is seen as important, but also the nature of the material copied, meaning that the copied material represents the main features of the original work for which it was granted protection in the first place. Here, the more the defendant has copied from the most prominent features of the work, the less likely it is that the dealing will be considered fair.

Yet, in the landmark decision of *Hubbard v. Vosper*,[147] a case in which the defendant's book, *The Mind Benders*, reproduced materials copied from various Scientology documents in order to criticize the movement, the UK Court of Appeal conceded that copying an entire work may be fair dealing, provided the nature and the purpose of the unauthorized use fitted within the goal of the exception. This point was also raised in

141 This has been expressly noted in a French decision of 6 February 1834 (Trib. Corr. of Paris) where the judge adopted a very liberal approach by stating that as with criticism, parodies should not be considered as infringing copyright unless it amounts to unlawful use. Accordingly, the reproduction of copyright-protected elements should not result in riding on the coat-tails of somebody else's success. Court of Appeal in *Saint-Tin* (n 56).

142 Whilst in France, the amount will be considered with the presence of acknowledgement of the original to determine whether there is confusion.

143 *University of London Press Ltd v. University Tutorial Press Ltd* (n 98) [608]–[614].

144 *Hyde Park* (n 11) [23]; *Ashdown* (n 16) [153]; *Pro Sieben* (n 11) [613]; *Time Warner* (n 25) [12]–[16]; *Associated Newspapers Group Plc v. News Group Newspapers Ltd* [1986] RPC 515, p. 519; *Hubbard* (n 3) 94; *Ladbroke Ltd v. William Hill Ltd* [1964] 1 All ER 465, 469; *Johnstone v. Bernard* [1938] 2 All ER 37 (hereafter *Johnstone*); *BBC v. Wireless League Gazette Publishing Co* [1926] 1 Ch 433, [439] (hereafter *BBC*).

145 *Johnstone* (n 144).

146 *Hyde Park* (n 11) [28] and [32]; *Pro Sieben* (n 11) [613]–[614]; *BBC* (n 144).

147 *Hubbard* (n 3) [94] and [98].

a UK government report released in advance of the introduction of the parody exception.[148] Here, the report notes that while fair dealing will typically apply in respect of only partial reproductions of original works, wholesale reproduction is not excluded. Thus, in the UK, there appears room for parodies which copy the original entirely, provided sufficient distortion is achieved.

Canadian courts appear to adopt a more stringent approach than the UK. In two early cases it was established that an entire reproduction would not be a fair dealing, at least in respect of the exception for criticism.[149] Yet in *Allen v. Toronto Star Newspapers Ltd*,[150] the court adopted a more liberal approach when a newspaper report reproduced an entire magazine cover, since it was accepted that the photograph was reproduced for the purpose of reporting a current event. The court emphasized that 'the test of fair dealing is essentially purposive' and 'not simply a mechanical test of measurement of the extent of copying involved'.[151] Thus, we can assume any quantitative assessment would be accompanied by a qualitative assessment which takes the nature of the use into account. It remains to be seen how the judiciary will develop this factor in relation to parodies. However, based upon *CCH*,[152] amount is only one factor which determines fairness, rather than being decisive. Therefore, in Canada too it seems possible that a complete reproduction of a copyright-protected work might still be considered fair.[153]

The quantitative factor is also likely to be considered in Australia.[154] The *TCN* case suggests that this will be given significant weight.[155] Although the full court failed to establish definitively whether or not fair dealing would extend to use of an entire work, the first instance decision, which relies upon various UK precedents, provides some guidance. The trial court cited *Beloff v. Pressdram Ltd*,[156] to stress the importance of assessing fairness relative to the purpose of the use.[157] Similarly, the court relied on *Pro Sieben*[158] and *Hyde Park*[159] when noting that the amount copied is indicative, but not conclusive, of the fairness of the use. As the fairness is assessed on an objective fair-minded person standard, each case must be considered on its own merits, meaning that copying the same amount of the same work may be fair in one case, but not in another. The full court hinted that a defendant might feasibly copy entire earlier works.[160]

Australian scholarship rightly recognizes the potential inaptness of this factor in relation to the parody exception,[161] as a parody must reproduce enough of the earlier work for the parody to succeed. Indeed, it has been noted that unless certain parodists are able to reproduce an entire work, whole classes of parody, such as those in the visual arts, will fall beyond the exception. This is illustrated in Figure 4.2 which depicts the famous Mona Lisa portrait alongside Duchamp's parody. Duchamp has merely

[148] H.M. Government, *Modernising Copyright* 14.

[149] *Zamacois* (n 6); D'Agostino (n 11) 321.

[150] (1997) 26 O.R. (3d) 308, [211].

[151] Ibid.

[152] *CCH* (n 3) [56] citing *Hubbard* (n 3), also mentioned in *Michelin* (n 6) [65]; *SOCAN* (n 13) [41]; *Alberta* (n 13).

[153] Based on these decisions from the Supreme Court, the federal court was wrong to decide otherwise in *United Airlines* (n 6) [129]–[130]. For completeness, it is argued that the parodies which fall within the non-commercial UGC exception are not limited to a particular amount of borrowing. Indeed, section 29.21 CA 1985 does not enunciate this factor as a condition for the application of the exception.

[154] N Suzor, 'Where the bloody hell does parody fit in Australian copyright law?' (2008) 13 *MALR* 243.

[155] *TCN* appeal (n 13) [434]; *TCN* (n 3).

[156] *Beloff* (n 6).

[157] *TCN* (n 3) [49]–[50].

[158] *Pro Sieben* (n 11).

[159] *Hyde Park* (n 11) [38].

[160] *TCN* appeal (n 13) [276].

[161] McCutcheon (n 4) 185; Suzor (n 154) 243; Handler and Rolph (n 2) 403.

Figure 4.2 Da Vinci's Mona Lisa (1503–1505) Duchamp's L.H.O.O.Q. (1919)*

*This example borrows from a work where copyright protection has lapsed but the questions raised remain valid.

Leonardo da Vinci, *Mona Lisa*, 1503–1506, oil on canvas, 770 × 530 mm. Paris, Musée Du Louvre.

Marcel Duchamp (1887–1968), *L.H.O.O.Q. La Joconde*. Centre Georges Pompidou, Paris. © Association Marcel Duchamp / ADAGP, Paris and DACS, London 2018. Photo ©: Heritage Image Partnership Ltd / Alamy Stock Photo.

changed the colours of the original painting and added a beard and moustache.[162] A parody exception which precludes an entire reproduction a priori would reduce the scope of the exception unduly.

Since French and US copyright law both have long-standing parody exceptions, it is interesting to see how courts in these jurisdictions take the quantity reproduced into account.

Initially US courts articulated this factor within the 'conjure up' test developed under the third factor considering the amount and substantiality of the use in relation to the protected work taken as a whole. Consequently, US courts initially articulated this 'conjure up' test as 'the parodist is permitted a fair use of a copyrighted work if it takes no more than is necessary to "recall" or "conjure up" the object of his parody'.[163] Later, in *Campbell*, the Supreme Court recalled Story J.'s words in *Folsom v. Marsh*, which state that the amount and substantiality of the portion copied must be interpreted in terms of 'quantity and value of the materials used'.[164]

The 'conjure up' test bears an important role in determining fair use for the purposes of parody. Early US decisions merely referred the outer limits of the amount to the substantiality of the taking factor. Indeed, as noted in *Air Pirates*,[165] if substantial copying did not automatically preclude fair use, verbatim or almost-wholesale copying generally should not be allowed.[166] *In casu*, the court found that it would have been easy for the parodist to evoke, rather than reproduce, the copied Disney cartoon characters by drawing them as recognizable caricatures, a technique which would involve less copying.[167]

This interpretation of the conjure up test was restrictive, essentially asking whether the parodist had copied more than strictly necessary to enable the public to recall the original.[168] In *Elsmere Music, Inc. v. National Broadcasting Company*,[169] the Second Circuit sought to re-establish the enabling function of the test:

> The concept of 'conjuring up' an original came into the copyright law not as a limitation on how much of an original may be used, but as a recognition that a parody frequently needs to be more than a fleeting evocation of an original in order to make its humorous point. A parody is entitled at least to 'conjure up' the original.[170]

This was further honed in *Fisher v. Dees*.[171] In this dispute, the defendant appropriated the first six bars of a thirty-eight-bar song, *When Sunny Gets Blue*, to create a parody version, *When Sonny Sniffs Glue*. In weighing the fair use factors, Sneed J. noted that musical parodies might require exact or near-exact copying because of a 'special need for accuracy', which might be less important in relation to visual arts.[172] Therefore, reproducing the *heart* of a copyright-protected work would not automatically render the copying excessive.[173]

[162] The original work was created before copyright, but the reasoning remains valid for parodies of copyright-protected work.

[163] Ibid. [164] *Folsom* (n 12) [348]. [165] *Air Pirates* (n 51). [166] Ibid, [756].

[167] Ibid, [758].

[168] *Seuss II* (n 14) [1400]. We can appreciate how difficult it might be to apply this factor without imposing an artistic judgement on the user.

[169] *Elsmere* (n 50). [170] Ibid, [253, n 1]; also in *Mattel* (n 126) [804].

[171] 794 F.2d 432, 438 (9th Cir. 1986) (hereafter *Fisher*).

[172] As in France, there seems to be a possibility to rely on fair practices commonly agreed upon in a particular art field to determine whether a particular use is fair.

[173] *Fisher* (n 172) [439] repeated in *Northland* (n 13) [980].

In the *Sony* decision,[174] although not discussing parody, the US Supreme Court held that fair use might permit reproduction of an entire work. In the *Campbell* parody case,[175] the Supreme Court echoes this statement by confirming that the permitted amount requires a quantitative and qualitative assessment of the circumstances. The significance of the portion reproduced to the original should be taken into account, but without prohibiting verbatim copying. The Supreme Court also recognized that greater copying may be necessary for musical parodies than for other parody types, simply to enable the public to identify the original. Thus, the reasonableness of the percentage copied would depend upon the likelihood that the parody would serve as a market substitute for the original.[176] The Supreme Court goes further by stating that extensive copying may be justified in light of the transformation of the copyright-protected work by the parodist, thus reminding us that parodies are inherently context-based.

This leniency extended to musical parodists does not imply a free rein, however. In *Henley v. DeVore*,[177] the defendant's political advertisements featured songs, *The Hope of November* and *All She Wants to Do Is Tax* (referring to Barack Obama and Nancy Pelosi, respectively) which recorded modified lyrics over karaoke versions of Don Henley's *The Boys of Summer* and *All She Wants to Do Is Dance*. In determining whether the amount copied was justified, the court distinguished between the two uses. Having established that the use of *All She Wants to Do Is Dance* was a satire, the minimal amount of transformation was held insufficient to justify the borrowing.[178] However, the use of *The Boys* incorporated aspects of parody, which might justify the amount taken. Interestingly, the court reached its decision in this case by comparing the amount of copying which other courts had permitted, instead of dealing strictly with the case at hand. Concluding that the amount approached the limit where fair use had previously been denied, and having regard to the fact that parody only derived from the need to 'conjure up' with the original author rather than the work itself, the court held that the amount reproduced was excessive for fair use to apply.[179]

In sum, US courts authorize more, or less, copying depending upon the parody's medium, the popularity of the original, and the purpose of the parody.[180] If the parody involves a film,[181] speech, or music,[182] then more (even wholesale verbatim) copying

[174] *Sony* (n 14) [449]–[450]. This is not a parody case but is concerned with home videotaping of television programmes.

[175] *Campbell* (n 12) [587]–[588].

[176] *Campbell* (n 12) [589]. Therefore, the third factor also overlaps to some extent with the fourth fair use factor. *Campbell* (n 12) [587].

[177] 733 F.Supp.2d 1144 (C.D. Cal. 2010) (hereafter *Henley*).

[178] Ibid, [1160].

[179] Ibid, [1161]: 'Indeed, the Defendants' appropriation approaches or exceeds the amounts borrowed in many cases where courts rejected the fair use defense.' See e.g. *Seuss II* (n 14) [1402]–[1403] (defendants copied visual elements of main character and rhyme scheme but substantially changed language); *Wilson* (n 52) [185] (defendants merely substituted dirty lyrics into song); *Air Pirates* (n 51) (defendants copied visual elements of animated characters rather than evoking them); *Miramax* (n 127) [1185]–[1186] (defendants copied the 'total "look and feel"' of plaintiff's poster and merely substituted character).

[180] *Fisher* (n 172) [439]; repeated in *Northland* (n 13) [981].

[181] Although in *New Line Cinema Corp. v. Bertlesman Music Group., Inc.*, the court eventually decided that for the purposes of the use, the defendants had copied more than necessary. Here, the defendants' use consisted of a song and music video referring to the plaintiffs' movies by reproducing part of the plot and its protagonists. 693 F.Supp. 1517 (S.D.N.Y. 1988) (hereafter *Bertlesman*).

[182] *Irving* (n 48) where Metzner J. notes that 'the humorous effect achieved when a familiar line is interposed in a totally incongruous setting, traditionally a tool of parodists, scarcely amounts to a "substantial" taking, if that standard is not to be woodenly applied'.

may still be fair use. In contrast, it is considered that the visual arts, including comic books and photographs, provide the parodist with alternatives to call up the original without needing to resort to exact or near-exact copying.[183] Further, the more well-known the work is, the less of that work the parodist needs to copy to identify the original work to the public.[184] Finally, appreciation of the amount reproduced goes hand-in-hand with the underlying purpose of the parody.[185] This means that if the copying is for another purpose than creating a parody, then the reproduction of large portions is less likely to be permissible.

This explains why fair use was found in a case in which pro-life organizations used several elements of an earlier video campaign which sought to de-stigmatize abortion.[186] Given that the plaintiff's videos were not well-known, the defendants were permitted to copy large portions of the original videos. The court went further to note that the media of video or film, like speech and music, are hard to parody unless substantial amounts are copied.[187] Finally, given its directly opposing message, the defendants' use would not serve as a market substitute for the plaintiff's work. Here, the court decided that the true purpose of the defendants' use was to parody the original.[188]

In France, we shall see that although early French decisions appear to grant parodies certain latitude in terms of the amount copied,[189] later decisions tend to elide this factor with the risk of confusion, as discussed already.[190] French scholarship is divided between those who consider that complete reproduction should be permitted,[191] and those who consider that permitted use should extend to substantial copies only.[192]

The divergence appears to stem from different interpretations of the *El Gringo le Jaloux* decision.[193] This case involved a promotional advert which incorporated segments from a rival's earlier advert. The Court of Appeal held that the question of whether the parody exception would permit a reproduction depended upon whether the use created confusion. Furthermore—and this is the source of the divergence among scholars—the court noted that the parody exception should not allow entire, or almost complete, reproduction.[194] One camp equates the latter statement with a

[183] *Air Pirates* (n 51).

[184] *Fisher* (n 172) [439]; *Suntrust* (n 16); *Air Pirates* (n 51) [756] (near-verbatim copying of Disney characters impermissible) or *Axanar* (n 129) (each scene conjured up with *Star Trek*); *Rycraft* (n 135) [28] (near-verbatim copying of cookie stamp sheets permitted despite the original being little known).

[185] See n 173. [186] *Northland* (n 13).

[187] This case can be compared with the controversial decision in *Benny v. Loew's, Inc.*, 239 F.2d 532 (9th Cir. 1956), aff'd by an equally divided court, 356 U.S. 43, 78 S.Ct. 667, 2 L. Ed.2d 583 (1958) where the use was not permitted and *Columbia Pictures Corp. v. National Broadcasting Co.*, 137 F.Supp. 348 (S.D. Cal. 1955) where the parody exception was successfully invoked.

[188] *Northland* (n 13) [981].

[189] Paris, 1ère ch., 20 décembre 1977, Ann. propr. ind. 1979, p. 84.

[190] See section 2.2.

[191] A Lucas, *Fasc. 1248: Droits des auteurs.—Droits patrimoniaux.—Exceptions au droit exclusif* (2013) Jurisclasseur, [44]; Mouffe (n 11) 296; El Khoury (n 56) 69; Strowel (n 70) 48.

[192] A Bertrand, 'Exceptions à la protection en matière de droit d'auteur qui figurent au CPI' in *Droit d'auteur* (Dalloz, 2012) 350; Dalloz, *Exception au droit d'exploitation* (2006) 9; D Voorhoof, 'Freedom of expression, parody, copyright and trademarks', in X., Proceedings of the ALAI Congress, 13–17 June 2001 on Adjuncts and Alternatives to Copyright, Columbia University, New York, ALAI-USA, 2002, 636–49.; Dalloz, 'La parodie ne saurait justifier la reproduction intégrale ou quasi intégrale de l'oeuvre originale' (1991) *Recueil Dalloz* 35; Françon (n 77) 303.

[193] Paris, 4e ch., 27 novembre 1990, *Suchard c/ Antenne* 2, D. 1991, IR 35.

[194] See nn 192 and 193.

requirement before the parody exception will apply. The other camp considers that the statement is tempered by the Court's preceding comment which renders confusion paramount. The second interpretation seems more plausible, arguably, based upon the fact that the defendant had used excerpts from the earlier commercial to promote its own business either by causing confusion and/or to take advantage of the notoriety of the earlier work. This interpretation is also consistent with the earlier *Brel* decision,[195] discussed previously, in which the Supreme Court also refused to apply the parody exception where the defendant reproduced protected lyrics for a political campaign in such a way that confusion was likely whether the use was a parody or the original.

Indeed, the French Supreme Court has accepted a parody defence in a case where an entire earlier work had been copied.[196] In a dispute concerning a musical parody, new lyrics were sung to the original musical. The parody was permitted, despite the amount of the musical work copied, because there was no confusion. The public could easily distinguish the parody from the original. In this case, the court compared 'song' with 'song', rather than considering the underlying copyright works separately. The crucial point has been emphasized in a more recent decision in which the trial judge noted that the parody exception prevents partial or full reproduction of an earlier work *used as such*.[197] Hence, it is the illusion of being exposed to the original work which should be prohibited, irrespective of the amount copied.

Pursuant to the French regime, the amount reproduced in quantitative terms is not determinative, but rather *whether* the reproduction (in whatever amount) is presented to the public in such a manner that confusion is likely to result. Thus, it is reasonable to conclude that provided the public recognizes the work as a parody because an element of distortion has been introduced, then the parody may reproduce an earlier work in its entirety.

Assessing eligibility for the parody exception based upon the quantity of work borrowed, as US courts have sometimes required, seems tantamount to enquiring whether the end result might have been achieved by other means which reproduced less. This appears to require courts to make an artistic judgement, which should fall beyond the judicial role. Rather, courts should limit their enquiry to whether the reproduction of earlier work is necessary to the objective pursued, rather than being a thin disguise for, for example, forgery. Therefore, the French court's linkage of the amount copied to public confusion seems a more legitimate approach.[198]

On balance, it seems that whether the amount copied is substantial (assessed quantitatively or qualitatively) should not be decisive per se, but only ever used as one indicator for fairness.[199] As a parody exception has been introduced to enable parodies to be created, this aim will be stymied if parodists are not given free rein to copy significant amounts of protected works, and potentially entire reproduction of a copyright work in some instances.[200] Therefore, it appears illogical to invalidate a use based on the amount copied alone. Indeed, curtailing the amount which may be lawfully reproduced might actually increase the likelihood of confusion. Forcing a parody to make only a weak allusion to an earlier work may fail on its own terms. Eventually,

195 See section 2.2. Cass., ch. Civ. I, 27 mars 1990, Bull., I n°75, *Mme Jacques Brel c/ Rpr*.

196 *Douces Transes* (n 57).

197 TGI Paris, *Femme*, 13 février 2001, available at www.legalis.net.

198 See section 2.2.

199 Here, the author believes that the Canadian Federal Court rushed in its assessment of the amount copied in *United Airlines* (n 6) [128]–[130].

200 B Mee, 'Laughing matters: parody and satire in Australian copyright law' (2002) 20 *Journal of Law, Information and Science* 55, 82.

the effectiveness of a parody exception will depend upon whether and how strictly this factor is applied by national courts.

2.4 Motives of the parodist

The parodist's motivation is another sensitive issue. Is a parodist permitted to commercially exploit the creative endeavours of others under the cover of the parody exception? US and French case law on this aspect will provide some insights which might help us to predict the likely attitudes of the UK, Canadian, and Australian courts.

In the US, the commercial nature of the use is generally studied systematically under the first factor: the purpose and character of the use.[201] In a relatively early case, *Harper & Row v. Nation Enterprises*,[202] the Supreme Court held that the commercial/non-commercial distinction is not concerned with unpicking whether or not a parodist sought monetary gain from their efforts, but rather, whether they aimed to profit from the copying of copyright materials without fairly remunerating the right-holders.[203] Consequently, fair use presupposes good faith on behalf of the parodist.[204]

With this task in mind, a US court found fair use in the case of a song, *When Sonny Sniffs Glue*, a parody of *When Sunny Gets Blue*,[205] despite the commercial nature of the use, having been included on a comedy album. The court held that the parody did not harm the economic value of the original unfairly, as consumers fond of the plaintiff's song would not be satisfied by listening to its parody version instead. Similar logic was applied in respect of the parody novel, *The Wind Done Gone*, as no detrimental effect on the market for the original, *Gone With The Wind*, was established.[206] Rather, the circuit court acknowledged the significant transformative value of the parody, which supported a finding of fair use,[207] thereby reversing the earlier decision of the district court.

When considering commercial motives, US judges seem to pay particular attention to the potential market for derivative uses which a right-holder is likely to develop. In the *Mattel* case,[208] which considered use of a Barbie doll in photographs commenting on societal values, the court was willing to find in the defendant's favour, reasoning that the plaintiff was unlikely to enter this market or license creators likely to be critical of the protected work.[209] It is not in the public interest to grant right-holders complete control over derivative works which comment upon or criticize copyright-protected work, and so, this should be avoided.

The *Northland* decision[210] illustrates what may be included under the notion of profit. Here, the video aiming to de-stigmatize abortion was parodied in order to generate funds, albeit indirectly, for a not-for-profit anti-abortion organization. In this case, the court noted that the defendant's use generated internet traffic to its websites, and thereby benefited the organization by aiding dissemination of its message.[211] Ultimately, this 'commercial' exploitation of the parody did not prevent a finding of

[201] As a reminder, this factor has two limbs: (1) transformative use, (2) commerciality.

[202] 471 U.S. 539 (1985) (hereafter *Harper*).

[203] Ibid, [562]; repeated in *Blanch v. Koons*, 467 F.3d (hereafter *Blanch*), [253].

[204] Ibid, quoting *Time Inc. v. Bernard Geis Associates*, 293 F.Supp. 130, 146 (S.D.N.Y. 1968). See *Hill v. Whalen & Martell, Inc.*, 220 F.359 (S.D.N.Y. 1914) where the parody defence was invoked in bad faith and, therefore, rejected. Similarly, in *Wilen v. Alt. Media Net, Inc.*, bad faith derived from the attempt to justify the removal of the copyright notice from the copyright-protected work as parody use. No 03CIV2524 (RMB) (JCF) (S.D.N.Y. 2005).

[205] *Fisher* (n 172).

[206] *Suntrust* (n 16) [1274].

[207] Ibid, [1275]–[1277].

[208] *Mattel* (n 126).

[209] At [49]–[50]. See also section 3.1.

[210] *Northland* (n 13).

[211] Ibid, [979].

fair use since the defendant had transformed the plaintiff's work for the purposes of criticism, rather than to exploit 'its creative virtues'.[212] Furthermore, when examining when the parody might harm the market of the original, the court relied upon the teachings established in *Campbell.* Here, the Supreme Court conceded that a parody, by virtue of its message, might well kill off demand for the original work but harm of this kind was not protected within the realm of copyright law. Rather, what is relevant is whether the defendant's use constitutes a substitute for the original. In light of *Campbell*, even if a parody's message is, as in *Northland*, the antithesis of that of the original work, there is no cognizable market harm.[213]

In similar vein, advertising revenues derived from uploading a parody to a sharing platform, such as YouTube, may constitute a profit foreseeable under the US Copyright Act, but here,[214] a successful parody does not necessarily usurp the market for the original. Instead, it may increase advertising revenue for the original if the right-holder has applied 'match policies'[215] on the platform.[216]

The *3C* case illustrates that the commercial character of a use might stem from seeking primarily an artistic goal.[217] Applying the teachings from *Harper & Row*, the court was willing to find that creating a parody play from a television series might still constitute a commercial exploitation under the Act, even if there was no intent to seek a pecuniary profit. Nevertheless, the court permitted the use as fair, because its transformative nature promoted the arts.[218] As the play created a dark version of the original comedy, it was not serving as a sequel of the original, and left open the possibility that the right-holder could create their own stage adaptation of the copyright work in the future. Therefore, the parodic play was unlikely to threaten the market for the original.[219]

Prior to the seminal *Campbell* decision, the defendant in *New Line Cinema Corp. v. Bertlesman Music Group, Inc.*,[220] sought to use the characters and plot line from the movie, *A Nigtmare on Elm Street* and its sequels, to create a music video, *A Nightmare On My Street.* Considering the music video to be purely commercial, and that the unauthorized use merely served to promote the defendant's song, the court found in favour of the right-holder. This provides a clear indication that any use which attempts to exploit the creative endeavours embodied in a protected work for financial gain takes the use beyond fair use. Likewise, post-*Campbell*, a court rejected Honda's fair use arguments in relation to a commercial which copied elements from the *James Bond* series of films.[221] What tipped the balance against fair use here was that Honda sought to benefit from the success of the *Bond* films with the aim of selling more *Honda* cars, rather than to pass comment on the copyright-protected works.[222] Hence, if the

[212] Ibid. [213] Ibid, [982]. [214] *Brownmark* (n 16).

[215] S Jacques, C Garstka, M Hviid, and J Street, 'Automated anti-piracy systems as copyright enforcement mechanism: the need to consider cultural diversity' (2018) 40(4) *European Intellectual Property Review* 218–28.

[216] *Brownmark* (n 16) [694].

[217] *Adjmi v. DLT Entm't Ltd*, 97 F.Supp.3d 512 (S.D.N.Y. 2015) (hereafter *3C*).

[218] Ibid, 40.

[219] Ibid, 52. A similar outcome was reached in *Galvin* (n 47) in relation to a parodic use of a photograph used in a political campaign as the audience for the two works was different, see [1188]–[1189].

[220] *Bertlesman* (n 182).

[221] *Metro-Goldwyn-Mayer, Inc. v. Am. Honda Motor Co.*, 900 F.Supp. 1287 (C.D. Cal. 1995) (hereafter *MGM*).

[222] Similar outcomes in *Miramax* (n 127) (documentary commercial copying *Men in Black*); *Tin Pan Apple, Inc. v. Miller Brewing Co.*, 737 F.Supp. 826, 832 (S.D.N.Y. 1990) (beer commercial copying music video); *Original Appalachian Artworks v. Topps Chewing Gum*, 642 F.Supp. 1031 (N.D.Ga. 1986) (Garbage Pail Kid stickers distributed by a chewing gum manufacturer); *Crazy Eddie* (n 123) (commercial copying Superman).

motivation to copy is to attract the interest of the public in an attempt to free-ride on the original, the use should not be allowed because it results in an 'unjustifiable appropriation of copyrighted material for personal profit'.[223]

This last decision brings us to an important question as to the position of US courts on parodies in commercial advertising. While the advertising purpose of the parody will not automatically take the use outside the parody exception, nevertheless, it might erode the leniency generally exercised in favour of parodic expressions.[224] The marketing materials for the film *Naked Gun 33 1/3* included a parody of the famous nude photograph of then-pregnant actress, Demi Moore.[225] When the photographer, Annie Leibovitz, complained, the Second Circuit found in favour of the defendant because of the strong parodic nature of the use. The defendant's argument that the film poster should be seen as an extension of the film, and that the latter commented on pregnancy and parenthood, found favour with the court. It accepted that the advertisement went beyond a mere contrasting with the original photo to reinforce the comedic nature of the movie.[226] The strength of the parody tipped the analysis of the first factor in the defendant's favour despite its advertising context.

US courts have also had the opportunity to determine cases involving songs used for political campaigning,[227] and have given thought to whether political uses are commercial. After all, according to the *Harper & Row* standard, commercial use is understood more widely than direct financial gain.[228] In *Henley v. DeVore*,[229] for example, De Vore issued an advertisement featuring a copy of Henley's music which encouraged viewers to donate toward his campaign. The court held that DeVore had gained an advantage from the use without paying the customary licensing fees, and it found in favour of the plaintiff. However, the court noted that there were circumstances in which the political nature of the use in the campaign might neutralize the commercial nature.[230] This can lead to deadlock whereby the interpretation of the first fair use factor based upon the commercial nature leans against fair use while the transformative nature weighs in its favour. This arose in *Galvin v. Illinois Republican Party*.[231] In the absence of a conclusive balance, the dichotomy of the first factor is generally resolved in light of the fourth factor, which focuses on whether the new work supersedes the original.[232]

Therefore, in the US, the possibility to exploit a parody commercially inherently depends on the transformativeness of the original. If, traditionally, commercialization weighs against fair use findings,[233] a commercially exploited parody may become less critical depending on the extent of the transformative character of the use.[234] Equally, the commercial motive can be balanced by demonstrating to the court that the use does not unfairly harm the economic value of the copyright-protected work.[235] Therefore,

[223] *Crazy Eddie* (n 123) approved in *Warner Bros. v. American Broadcasting Companies* 654 F.2d 204 (2d Cir. 1981); *Warner Bros., Inc. v. ABC, Inc.*, 720 F.2d 231 (2d Cir. 1983).

[224] *Campbell* (n 12) [585].

[225] *Leibovitz v. Paramount Pictures Corp.*, 137 F.3d 109 (2d Cir. 1998) (hereafter *Leibovitz*).

[226] This case can be compared to *Steinberg v. Columbia Pictures Industries, Inc.*, where fair use was denied because the use did not result in a parody as it merely copied *The New Yorker*'s parody for advertising purposes of *The Moscow on the Hudson* movie. 663 F.Supp. 706 (S.D.N.Y. 1987).

[227] *MasterCard Int'l, Inc. v. Nader 2000 Primary Comm., Inc.*, No 00 CIV. 6068 (GBD) (S.D.N.Y. 2004) (copying of MasterCard's commercial advertisement in a presidential campaign);

[228] *Harper* (n 203) [562].

[229] *Henley* (n 178).

[230] Referring to *Kienitz v. Sconnie Nation LLC*, 766 F.3d 756, 759 (7th Cir. 2014), [1159].

[231] *Galvin* (n 47).

[232] Ibid. See section 3.1.

[233] *Harper & Row*, 105 S. Ct. 2231; *Sony* (n 14).

[234] *Campbell* (n 12) [579]–[580]; *Mattel* (n 126) [803]; *Blanch* (n 204) [254].

[235] *Fisher* (n 172), referring to *Milky Way Productions*, 215 U.S.P.Q., n. 9. *Fisher*'s presumption of unfairness of commercial motives was overturned in *Campbell* (n 12), see n 284.

commercial use is not presumptively unfair.[236] In the US, transformativeness and commercial exploitation of a parody are interrelated and 'profit' goes beyond the mere monetary gain to include reputation[237] or any other benefit.[238] Hence, courts tend to be more lenient on the question of commercialism where the use produces a value that benefits the broader public interest such as granting 'access to the arts and the humanities' which fosters 'wisdom and vision and makes citizens masters of their technology and not its unthinking servants'[239] or if exploited for 'its own sake'.[240]

In contrast, interrogating a parodist's motivation for producing a parody features erratically in French parody decisions. Although the French courts have considered whether it is legitimate for a commercially exploited parody to benefit from the parody exception,[241] the approach to commercial use seems highly fact-specific.

In a first scenario, French courts seem to apply the exception if any commercial exploitation results from an exercise of freedom of expression.[242] Hence, a political parody may be commercialized on small badges,[243] or disseminated via newspapers,[244] TV shows,[245] films,[246] or in plays[247]—all vehicles traditionally used for freedom of expression. Essentially, the parodist's main aim is to disseminate the expression to an audience, albeit it that this may generate some form of revenue.

In a second scenario, the parodist's motivation is primarily commercial. Here, French courts are careful to identify whether the parodist mainly intends to create a parody for commercial exploitation, or whether parody is merely to disguise the commercial exploitation of another's work. For example, a court is less likely to apply the exception if the defendant has borrowed another's protected work to promote their own products. Thus, French courts have found infringement when a parody has been used to promote underwear,[248] lighters,[249] branded clothes,[250] political campaign advertisement,[251] posters and postcards,[252] an operating system,[253] or card games.[254] French courts are equally reluctant to permit a user to benefit from the parody exception if

236 Campbell (n 12) [584]–[585].

237 *Time Inc. v. Bernard Geis Associates,* 293 F.Supp. 130, 146 (S.D.N.Y. 1968).

238 *Northland* (n 13) (where the parody generated traffic and encouraged discussion on the defendant's website).

239 *Blanch* (n 204) [254].

240 *Campbell* (n 12) [585].

241 TGI Paris, 3e ch. Civ., 1ère sect., 13 mai 2008, *Che Guevara*; Paris, 4e ch., 9 septembre 1998, *Société Seri Brode c/ Procter & Gamble France*; Cass. (1ere ch. Civ), 13 janvier 1998, D. 1999, somm. p. 167, obs. Bigot; Trib. Civ. Seine, 12 juin 1879, Ann. propr. ind. 1879, p. 239.

242 Cass., 13 janvier 1998 (n 242); TGI Paris, 3 mars 1993, légipresse 1994, n°108, II, p. 10; Paris, 8 juillet 1992, légipresse 1992, n°100, p. 40; Paris, 20 septembre 1993, légipresse 1994, n°108, p. 9; Cass., 7 décembre 1993, n°92-81091 (hereafter *Fluide Glacial*).

243 Cass., 13 janvier 1998 (n 242).

244 *Fluide Glacial* (n 243); Paris, 20 septembre 1993, *Agrif c/ Godefroy*, légipresse, n°108, II, p. 9; TGI Paris, 3 mars 1993, *Caroline Grimaldi c/ Société Kalachnikof*, légipresse, n°108, II, p. 10; Paris, 8 juillet 1992, légipresse 1992, n°100, p. 40.

245 Reims, 9 février 1999; Delfour (n 82) 58–9 with the exception of application of publicity rights such as illustrated by TGI Paris, 17 septembre 1984, D. 1985 IR 16, obs. Lindon confirmed in Paris, 22 novembre 1984, D. 1985 IR 164, obs. Lindon.

246 TGI Paris, 29 novembre 2000, RIDA, n°189, juillet 2001, p. 377, obs. Kéréver.

247 Trib. Civ. Seine, 12 juin 1879, Ann. propr. ind. 1879, p. 239.

248 TGI Paris, 24 janvier 1976, cited by Mouffe (n 11) 398.

249 TGI Paris, 2 octobre 1996, légipresse 1997, n°138, I, p. 4.

250 TGI Paris, 30 avril 1997, Gaz. Pal., 17–19 mai 1998.

251 Paris, 4e ch., 25 mars 2005, Gaz. Pal., 2005, jurispr., p. 4318.

252 Paris, *Paul B c/ Moulinsart,* 13 septembre 2005 at www.legalis.net.

253 TGI Paris, 13 février 2001, *SNC Prisma Presse et EURL Femme c/ Charles V. et association Apodeline.*

254 TGI Nancy (référence), 15 octobre 1976, JCP, 1977, n°18526, obs. Lindon.

they are in direct competition with the right-holder and have parodied their work in an attempt to win business.[255]

In a third scenario, French courts look unfavourably upon commercial parodies which capitalize upon their shock value, or cause offence. For example, a court refused to apply the exception when Korda distorted the famous photograph of *Che Guevara* into an image of a hostile monkey, even though it was arguably humorous and there was no public confusion.[256] Similarly, in a dispute which arose when a fashion house launched an advert which was a provocative distortion of a painting of *The Last Supper*, the court held that the parodied image was likely to offend those of the Christian faith, and so fell outside the exception use.[257] This decision was later quashed by the Supreme Court on the basis that the commercial expression aimed to shock rather than insult the Christian community.[258] Again, it is evident that limits to freedom of expression are shaping the outer limits of the parody exception.[259]

Thus, it is evident that French courts do apply the parody to commercial use in certain circumstances, but in respect of this factor in particular, similar facts may lead to different outcomes owing to the subtlety in the balancing. This makes it difficult to predict the likely outcome given any particular set of facts. However, it is believed that the *bonus pater familias* principle, i.e. the reasonable man, helps restore legal certainty. Indeed, in most of the cases where the parody exception was found not to apply, the outcome was also contingent upon other factors, because the parodist acted in bad faith, did not respect the rules of the genre (i.e. by creating confusion or harming the author), lacked a genuine intent to parody (intending instead to benefit from the success of the original works), or was offensive to part of society.

In terms of how US and French law might provide guidance on the likely approach in our other jurisdictions, as the common law tradition typically prioritizes protection of economic rights, it might be expected that commercial motivation would count against fair dealing in the case of a parody exception. However, it is necessary to explore whether this assumption is reflected in fair dealing case law, bearing in mind that US courts seem willing to treat at least some commercial parodies as fair use, despite the US's common law tradition.

In the UK, when a commercial exploitation is permitted as a fair dealing exception, the user must demonstrate that they do not have an ulterior motive.[260] This suggests that UK courts will consider a parodist's motivation.[261] If a user has *animus furandi*, i.e. a 'deliberate intention to steal', oblique motives,[262] or intends improper actions,[263] then this will go against the use being fair.

As with all of the other factors, commercial motivation alone should not be decisive in excluding fair dealing. It should be possible for a parodist to leverage a parody for commercial benefit, or for one competitor to parody another and still enjoy the exception's protection.[264] However, where one business uses a work created by a rival, it is reasonable to assume that this will weigh heavily against the dealing being fair. Essentially, all the other factors 'in the mix' would then need to point directly to the

[255] Paris, 4e ch. A, 27 novembre 1990.

[256] Paris, 4e ch., 13 octobre 2006, Gaz. Pal. 2007, jurispr., p. 2110.

[257] Paris, 8 avril 2005, Recueil Dalloz 2005/20, 1327, note Rolland; Voorhoof (n 193) 18.

[258] This is in line with the ECtHR stance as recently repeated in *Sekmadienis Ltd v. Lithuania*, App No 69317/14 (20 January 2018).

[259] See Chapter 7, sections 2 and 3.

[260] *BSB* (n 13) [144]; *Sillitoe* (n 13) [563]; *Johnstone* (n 144).

[261] *Hyde Park* (n 11) [37]; *Pro Sieben* (n 11) [614].

[262] Such as personal gain.

[263] Sims (n 16) 198.

[264] *Pro Sieben* (n 11) [616]–[617]; *BSB* (n 13) [157]–[158].

fairness of the use.[265] Thus, the court will need to be satisfied that the parody claim is not merely a trick to cover an infringement.[266] The more the use is a straightforward parody, the more likely it is that commercial exploitation will be lawful.[267] However, in borderline cases, for example, where confusion is arguable, a commercial motive may be the factor in the overall assessment which tips the balance against the finding of fair dealing.

This analysis of case law supports the position articulated in an official policy document issued prior to the introduction of the exception. This contemplates disputes arising between direct commercial competitors, and identifies the parties' relationship as a relevant factor. However, the mere fact that the parties are competitors was not seen as precluding a parody defence.[268]

The position in Australia is similar to that in the UK. Australian copyright law does not exclude commercial exploitation as a fair dealing use.[269] Hence, even though private or non-commercial use is more likely to be assessed as fair, users who do commercialize their work might still be eligible to benefit from the defence.[270] Given the scarcity of fair dealing cases which consider this aspect, the *TCN* dispute remains the main touchstone, as this case concerned use between two rival television stations.[271] At first instance, the court placed reliance upon UK case law,[272] and noted that the key aspect of fair dealing is whether the use is really made for the exempted purpose, such that hidden motives may render a use unfair.[273] Citing the UK *Pro Sieben* case,[274] the first instance court acknowledged that the commercial nature of any use would have an impact on its fairness, but without being decisive.

Despite this sentiment, much of the *TCN* court's analysis of the facts concentrated upon the relationship between the parties.[275] This seems likely to result in an incorrect balancing of factors, since the court's main focus should be on the manner in which the user deals with the protected material, rather than on the characteristics of the user.[276] McCutcheon skilfully articulates this point by distinguishing between two scenarios.[277] If a court determines that it is the parody itself which is being commercialized, then the parody should be permitted. It is reasonable that the creator of a parody, as with any other creative work, might wish to disseminate their work in a commercial manner. Alternatively, if a parody is merely being used as a vehicle to promote another product; either to undermine a competitor's product or to compete with it, the court should consider this a factor weighing against the application of the exception.[278] This is similar to the two first scenarios also taken into account in France.

The Canadian approach is consistent with McCutcheon's proposal. The few cases which have considered the commercial character of the use have concluded that it is

[265] *Newspaper Licensing Agency v. Marks & Spencer Plc* [1999] RPC 536, [546]–[547] (hereafter *NLA*).

[266] *Time Warner* (n 25) [469]; *Hubbard* (n 3) 94.

[267] It must be remembered that the ECHR protects commercial expressions. See Chapter 5, section 4.1.

[268] H.M. Government, *Modernising Copyright* 14.

[269] Sainsbury (n 102) 154.

[270] Sainsbury (n 16) 311.

[271] *TCN* (n 3).

[272] Ibid, [49] citing *Beloff* (n 6) and *BSB* (n 13) [514].

[273] *TCN* appeal (n 13) [97]: Hely J citing *Hyde Park* (n 11); *TCN* (n 3) [115] also citing *Time Warner* (n 25).

[274] *TCN* appeal (n 13) [104]; TCN (n 3) [52] citing *Pro Sieben* (n 11).

[275] Handler and Rolph (n 2) 404.

[276] Ibid, 405.

[277] McCutcheon (n 4) 182.

[278] She illustrates her theory with the *Telstra* decision assuming there had been substantial copying. In this case, she argues that the court should render the use unfair as the defendant has a competitive commercial purpose. *Telstra Corp Ltd v. Royal & Sun Alliance Australia Ltd* [2003] FCA 786 (Fed. Ct).

relevant in the fairness assessment. Any use of a work which seeks an unfair commercial advantage over the right-holder weighs against a fair dealing.[279] Indeed, in *CCH*, the Supreme Court affirmed this liberal approach, pointing out that the wording of the fair dealing exceptions in the legislation is not limited to non-commercial use.[280] Although *CCH* was concerned with fair dealing for the purposes of criticism, and as the new parody exception has been implemented within the same section of the Canadian Copyright Act, it seems reasonable to conclude that commercial exploitation of parody works should be possible in Canada as well.[281] This interpretation is further supported by the fact that the exception for user-generated content ('UGC'), discussed earlier in Chapter 2,[282] states explicitly that it only applies to non-commercial use.[283]

In light of this analysis of common law jurisdictions, it appears likely that a parodist's motivation will always be a relevant factor when assessing whether their dealing is fair. Although commercial exploitation does not automatically prevent the parody defence from applying, it presents a significant hurdle because it is indicative that the use might be unfair, particularly if the parodied work is that of a competitor. Similarly, it seems that there is consensus that a dealing will be seen as unfair when it is really the original work which is being exploited, rather than the parody itself. This is correct because a true parody is not seeking to camouflage infringement, and a true parodist is not looking to pass off the borrowings as their own or to gain financial benefit directly from the earlier work.[284]

In conclusion, it should be possible for a commercially exploited parody to benefit from the parody exception, but the parodist's motivation is relevant because this assists the court's understanding of the real object of commerce.[285] However, this consideration should not introduce the status of the user, in the sense of their relationship with the right-holder, as an additional factor or a determinative factor. Instead of presuming that a dealing with a rival's protected work is unfair, the court should assess the nature of the dealing, albeit that the parties' relationship may play a role in this consideration.

The main types of scenario, as illustrated in the table which follows (Figure 4.3) may be summarized, thus.

In a first scenario, a parodist is motivated initially by non-commercial concerns, but later identifies commercial avenues of exploitation. In such cases, it is suggested that a court should find the use lawful under the exception, provided the other requirements are satisfied. For example, a parody disseminated non-commercially via an online platform, such as YouTube, may, if it becomes popular enough, generate revenue through the platform's advertising system. This revenue should not prevent the parody from benefiting from the exception.[286]

In the second scenario, the parodist always intends to exploit their parody commercially. In such circumstances, the court should look favourably on exploitation via a commercial medium which is generally recognized as promoting free speech,

[279] *La Petite Vie* (n 36) [57]; *Michelin* (n 6) [56]; *Allen v. Toronto Star Newspapers Ltd* (1995), 26 O.R. (3d) 308, 129 D.L.R. (4th) 171 (Ct. J. (Gen. Div.)), [211]; *Zamacois* (n 6).

[280] *CCH* (n 3) [51].

[281] Interestingly, this factor was not considered in *United Airlines* (n 6). This either means that the commercial motives of the defendant are strictly defined to mean pecuniary gain (and not generating internet traffic) or that this factor is not that important when assessing the application of the parody exception.

[282] See Chapter 2, section 4.4.

[283] Section 29.21(1) CA 1985.

[284] See Chapter 1, section 1.

[285] A Tricoire, 'L'exception de parodie est-elle recevable en matière publicitaire?' (July/August 2005) 223 *Chroniques et opinion Légipresse* 77.

[286] See Chapter 7, section 1.5.

for example, a satirical publication or programme. Here, two situations can be distinguished. In some cases, there will be no market connection between the parodist and the right-holder. For example, a party may claim the defence when generating revenue from selling t-shirts which depict a parody of a protected work, or a film may include a parody song in one scene. In the second situation, the parties may be business rivals; one party creates an advert which parodies that of a competitor, or one TV show parodies another TV show, for example.

Irrespective of the difference in circumstances, both kinds of such users should be able to benefit from the parody exception, provided the parodist has respected the other fairness requirements. It seems unduly restricted to impose an additional barrier of non-commercial exploitation, as this serves only to deter the creation of parodies. The exception is justified based upon the social value which results from freedom of expression and information. Yet the risk is that this ultimate goal becomes overlooked if the debate turns to whether it should be lawful for one party to make money from copying something which someone else has created. If commercial motivation per se renders a use unlawful, this incorrectly and undesirably ignores the potential social value derived from parody, which is often unrelated to the motivation for its creation.

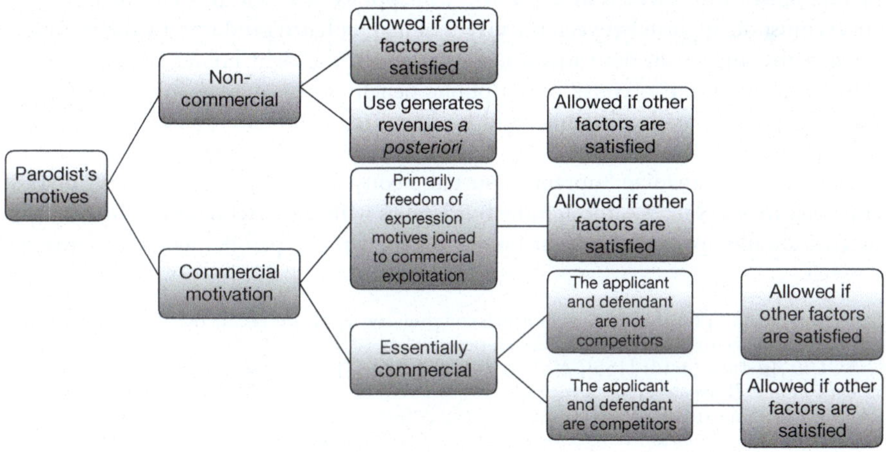

Figure 4.3 Chart summarizing the relationship between the motives of the parodist and the application of the parody exception.

3. Factors Relevant for Certain Jurisdictions Only

Having considered the factors which appear common to all of the jurisdictions of interest, we now consider those which appear relevant only in some. The following sections consider the encroachment upon economic rights, alternatives to the dealing, and the impact of a national three-step test.

3.1 Encroachment upon the right-holder's economic rights

Traditionally, the common law approach to fair dealing or fair use defences is to consider the extent to which an unauthorized use encroaches upon the economic rights of right-holders.[287] This factor is well established under UK and US law.[288] It is understood as the need to appraise to what degree a use competes with the exploitation of the copyright-protected work by its right-holder. If the judge finds that the use acts as a substitute for the original work or has an adverse impact on the market for the original, the balance should tilt in the plaintiffs' favour (certainly in older US cases and possibly in Canada following *CCH*).[289] Additionally, courts must consider the *potential* impact if the defendant's conduct existed on a larger scale.[290] While actual harm has to be demonstrated by the plaintiff, in this latter scenario, the onus falls on the defendant to demonstrate that the use will not harm potential markets.[291]

But when it comes to parody uses, should market harm even be of importance? For as much as parody may stifle the demand for the original, this is likely to be because of the message it conveys rather than because of direct substitution.[292] This suggests that if there are signs of encroachment, courts should look to determine the underlying reason. After all, as noted in *Irving Berlin v. E.C. Publications, Inc.*,[293] a parody tends to acknowledge the importance of the original work, indicating that parody might only rarely harm the marketability of the earlier work. Indeed, in the landmark *Campbell* decision, the US Supreme Court acknowledged that a parody use might legitimately quash consumer demand for the original. Therefore, courts must distinguish between the effectiveness of the parody's comment (which should be permitted)[294] and direct market substitution (which should not).[295] In appraising this fourth fair use factor, US courts must distinguish between the extent of market harm produced by the infringing use and the impact on derivatives, i.e. a use which the right-holder might license.[296] Equally, courts need to consider the public benefit which derives from allowing the use.[297] Therefore, market harm should be permitted if the parody use creates greater public benefit.[298]

In *CCH*, the Canadian Supreme Court also considered this factor and developed an approach to assess it.[299] Although the burden lies with the defendant to prove that the defence should apply, if the right-holder claims that the parodic use has encroached

[287] This factor is probably the way in which common law legislators ensure the compliance of copyright exceptions with the international three-step test.

[288] *UK: Ashdown* (n 16) [155]; *NLA* (n 266) [546]–[547]; *Hubbard* (n 3) 94–5; *Hawkes & Son (London) Ltd v. Paramount Film Service Ltd* [1934] 1 Ch 593, [598]; H.M. Government, *Modernising Copyright* 14; Sims (n 16) 192; *US: Irving* (n 48); *MGM* (n 223); *Seuss II* (n 14); *Miramax* (n 127); *Leibovitz* (n 226); *Suntrust* (n 16); *Mattel* (n 126); *Abilene Music, Inc. v. Sony Music Entertainment, Inc.*, 320 F.Supp.2d 84 (S.D.N.Y. 2003); *MasterCard Int'l, Inc. v. Nader 2000 Primary Comm., Inc.*, No 00 CIV. 3802 (HB) (S.D.N.Y. 2004); *Henley* (n 179); *CCA and B, LLC v. F + W Media, Inc.*, 819 F.Supp.2d 1310 (N.D. Ga. 2011); *Northland* (n 13); *Brownmark* (n 16); *3C* (n 218); *Galvin* (n 47); *Axanar* (n 129).

[289] This factor ultimately contributes to the realization of the second step of the three-step test.

[290] *Campbell* (n 12) [590].

[291] Interestingly, this led the court, in *Henley* (n 178), to note that this factor weighs against fair use where a parody song copies the musical composition in its entirety.

[292] '[T]here is no protectible derivative market for criticism. The market for potential derivative uses includes only those that creators of original works would in general develop or license others to develop.' *Campbell* (n 12) [592].

[293] *Irving* (n 48).

[294] e.g. *Northland* (n 13); *3C* (n 218); *Galvin* (n 47).

[295] *Campbell* (n 12) [591]–[593] confirmed in *Suntrust* (n 16); *Mattel* (n 126); *Henley* (n 178), *CCA and B, LLC v. F + W Media, Inc.*, 819 F.Supp.2d 1310 (N.D. Ga. 2011). This involves relying on the *Sony* test, 'when a commercial use amounts to mere duplication of the entirety of an original, it clearly "supersede[s] the objects,"' *Sony* (n 14), citing *Folsom* (n 12) [348]; and more recently applied in *Axanar* (n 129).

[296] *Seuss II* (n 14) [1403].

[297] *Wilson* (n 52) [183] confirmed in *Miramax* (n 127) [46]–[47].

[298] Ibid.

[299] *CCH* (n 3) [59].

upon their own market, then it is for the right-holder to satisfy the court that this is the case.[300] This is reasonable because only the right-holder has access to information concerning any loss in sales. This relieves the defendant from having to prove a negative. Even then, the approach is somewhat inadequate to decide whether the parody use is fair, as it omits an additional step which evaluates whether any loss of sales which the right-holder has suffered is attributable to a legitimate criticism of the copyright work.[301] Based upon the facts of this particular dispute, it is clear the encroachment factor alone was not decisive. Ultimately, the court found the dealing to be fair despite an adverse effect upon the original's market. Conversely, and as held in *Breen v. Hancock*,[302] Canadian courts should not find a dealing fair, simply because the right-holder is unable to demonstrate any financial detriment resulting from the unauthorized use. Fair dealing is not contingent upon lack of damage to the right-holder. Nevertheless, only evidence that a use has caused actual harm, not just the possibility of harm, should be required in order to tip the balance against the user and towards unfairness.[303]

As the first parody case since the new parody exception, *United Airlines*[304] provides an interesting development. In this dispute, the Canadian Federal Court considered it appropriate to reframe how market encroachment was considered. According to the court, 'it is not the effect on the market that ought to be considered, but rather the confusion caused by the similarity between Untied.com and the United Website.'[305] Referencing the US Supreme Court's *Campbell* decision, Phelan J. identified similarities between the parody exception and the copyright exception for criticism and review.[306] He noted that criticism, including when conveyed via parody, might affect the public opinion of the original leading to market consequences. Harm derived from criticism should not be taken as an indicator of unfairness. Only if a harmful encroachment is the result of the substantial copying should the balance tilt towards an unfair dealing. In the case in point, as UNTIED.com was established to host consumer criticism of United, the trial judge was less concerned about the potential impact which the site's negative comments might have on the plaintiff's business, but rather the real risk that consumers might believe that the website was that of the plaintiff because of the amount of material from the 'official' website which the defendant had copied (although the author disagrees with the decision of the court as confusion seems unlikely owing to the numerous disclaimers present on the defendant's website). Thus, it seems that the Canadian court rightly placed weight on consideration of public confusion, preferring to assess market encroachment indirectly via the presence or absence of confusion.[307]

In Australia, based upon analysis of the *TCN* case, the court also appears to ascribe secondary importance to market encroachment. Yet, some Australian scholars anticipate that this factor will rank more highly in fair dealing cases following the new parody exception.[308] Suzor considers that any potential markets for the original work are as relevant as its existing markets.[309] Contrary to the Canadian approach already

[300] Ibid, [72].

[301] The decision should be made upon proper economic evidence, and not upon court speculation as to the potential economic damage which might result.

[302] *Breen v. Hancock House Publisher Ltd*, 6 C.P.R. (3ed) 433 (1985).

[303] *Alberta* (n 13) [35]; *SOCAN v. CAIP*, 2004 S.C.C. 45. [304] *United Airlines* (n 6).

[305] Ibid, [138]. [306] Ibid, [139]–[140]; section 29.21 CA 1985.

[307] As discussed earlier, the problem is more in the court's appraisal of confusion.

[308] Suzor (n 154) 243; McCutcheon (n 4) 185; Sainsbury (n 102) 154; Sainsbury (n 16) 312–14; Handler and Rolph (n 2) 404.

[309] Suzor (n 154) 243.

described, (although writing before the recent *United Airlines* decision) he advocates that the relevant factor for the court to weigh up is whether the unauthorized parody use might adversely affect the markets of the original. Sainsbury suggests that this factor is best evaluated both in terms of loss of sales arising from substitution of the parody for the original, as well as potential loss of licensing revenue from the unauthorized use. She argues that market substitution should weigh against the dealing being fair, whereas loss of potential royalties generally should not. This acknowledges that a typical right-holder will refrain from granting permission for others to make parodic use of their works out of fear that they will be the target of the parody. However, she suggests that loss of revenue for satirical uses might be a legitimate concern, since satire generally reproduces a work to comment upon something else, and consequently she suggests that satirists may convey the same message without needing to copy another work.

We have seen already, however, that any distinction made between parody and satire is arguably artificial, because the same justification underpins both types of use.[310] It seems that right-holders are likely to be equally reticent to grant permission for use for the purpose of satire as they are for parody. In both cases, right-holders' refusal to license does not arise from economic considerations, but from concern to control any 'message' associated with their protected works.

Given the heavier influence of natural law upon civil law jurisdictions, it is often believed that French courts are unconcerned with economic considerations. This view is unfounded, as protection of economic rights features in the underpinnings of the French copyright system, as it does in other civil law jurisdictions.[311] In terms of the parody exception, French courts would typically consider how far a parody encroaches upon a right-holder's economic rights when considering aspects of the exception such as the absence of confusion[312] or intent to harm the author.[313] Hence, the economic impact is an indirect factor. The parody defence is unlikely to apply if the public treat the new use as an alternative to the original, because this is a strong indicator that the new use is not a true parody.[314]

Overall, it seems likely that the question of whether and how far the parodic use encroaches on the right-holder's economic rights will continue to be used by courts in all of the jurisdictions considered as a direct or indirect factor which will influence whether the parody exception will apply in particular cases. Provided that this is applied appropriately, it should weed out false parodies—those which seek to take advantage of the original work, rather than to use it as a vehicle for a new creation. In this way, the factor may contribute usefully to ensuring that a fair balance is struck between the exclusive rights of the right-holders and the public interest.

One almost inevitable drawback associated with determining the encroachment upon economic rights is that many courts consider that this requires extensive economic analysis, even though they are ill-equipped to interpret what results. Additionally, this might confuse encroachment with loss of appeal of the original in light of justified criticism by the parody. However, we have seen that few 'true' parodies will actually encroach upon a right-holder's ability to fully commercialize their works, or will result

[310] See Chapter 1, section 5.
[311] See Chapter 2, section 2.
[312] See Chapter 4, section 2.2.
[313] See Chapter 4, section 2.1.2.
[314] *Saint-Tin* (n 56); TGI Paris, 5 mars 2008, *Fort Boyard*, Prop. Int. 2008 n°28 p. 327, obs. Bruguiere, RIDA, n°217, juillet 2008, p. 338 and Sirinelli p. 233; Paris, 4e ch. sect. b), 17 janvier 2003, *Le monde d'Anne Sophie*, Prop. Int. 2003, n°7, p. 169, obs. Lucas; TGI Paris, 9 janvier 1970, JCP 1971.II. 16645.

in lost licensing revenue. As the French decisions and *United Airlines* in Canada demonstrate, it would seem far more straightforward to assess whether a parody has caused any market harm during the analysis of the likelihood of confusion between the parody and the protected work. This suggests that encroachment need only be taken into account once it has already been found that there is a risk of confusion in the minds of the public, in case confusion results from an intent to free-ride on another's efforts.

3.2 Alternatives to the dealing

Whenever a party elects to convey a message through parody, there is likely to be an alternative method which could have been adopted to impart the same information. In France, during the many years that a parody exception has been in place, it does not appear that this has *ever* been held to be a relevant consideration in a decided parody case. However, as some do raise this as being relevant, as foreshadowed in the preceding section, we shall consider what, if any, weight courts will and should place on necessity when considering the parody exception in the US, UK, Australia, and Canada.

In terms of other fair dealing exceptions, courts in the US,[315] UK,[316] and Canada[317] have all identified that it is essential to evaluate how far the unauthorized dealing was necessary to achieve the intended purpose. A use is much more likely to be unfair if the same result could have been achieved without infringing copyright, but equally, the case law recognizes that necessity involves an assessment of whether that alternative means would have been equally effective. Necessity has proved to be a significant factor in exceptions including fair dealing for research or private study (as per the Canadian *CCH* case) and the reporting of current events.

Arguably, if necessity is relevant to the parody exception too, then a court should give consideration to three possibilities. Could the parodist have achieved the same end result by parodying an alternative work in the public domain? Could the same message have been conveyed other than via parody? Was it open to the user to obtain the right-holder's permission to use the protected work, for example, by way of a licence.

With respect to the first two of these three sub-factors, it is important to recognize that by selecting a particular medium for their message, a parodist is making a creative choice. Furthermore, having elected to convey a message via parody, a parodist may have little choice as to which earlier work to select. We also need to bear in mind the teaching in the UK *Pro Sieben* case,[318] that fair dealing should respect copyright law's approach to artistic neutrality: courts should not arbitrate on matters of artistic merit. Arguably, this rule would be breached either by requiring a parodist to justify their choice of parody, or by requiring them to demonstrate that no other means of communication would have been as effective. Taking this all into account would lead us to conclude that, as in France, necessity should be afforded little weight in relation to the parody exception.

As for the possibility of securing permission, the Canadian Supreme Court, in *CCH*, considered this factor irrelevant to fair dealing, since it would render the defences redundant. A right-holder could simply circumvent an exception based upon the possibility that the user could have paid for the use. This would stretch the right-holder's

[315] This led to the distinction between parodies (target) and satires (weapon) as noted in the landmark case of *Campbell* (n 12) [581] and [597].

[316] *Hyde Park* (n 11) [154]–[155]; *Pro Sieben* (n 11) [613]–[614]; *Beloff* (n 6) [262]; *Hubbard* (n 3) 94.

[317] *CCH* (n 3) [57].

[318] *Pro Sieben* (n 11) [613]–[614]; also *Hyde Park* (n 11).

monopoly in a manner incompatible with the balance which copyright law aims to strike.[319] In any event, it has been seen that this requirement is equally inapt for the parody exception, as right-holders typically refuse to grant permission for parody uses, based on subjective justifications, such as a fear of criticism.[320]

In light of the above, necessity and possible alternatives to the dealing should play no role when considering the parody exception.[321] The very existence of a parody exception in the national copyright law is evidence that the legislator considers parody as a legitimate choice of expression. This policy choice would be undermined if the monopoly of right-holders interfered unnecessarily with the creative process underlying a parody.

3.3 The resurgence of the three-step test

As we saw in Chapter 2, in the US, Australia, and Canada the fairness factors are considered to be sufficient to ensure national compliance with the international three-step test of Berne and TRIPS. In contrast, the wording of EU legislation may require national courts in EU Member States, including the UK and France, to apply the three-step test[322] as an additional stage, when deciding whether, or not, the exception should apply, given the specific facts of the case. This requires us to consider what the impact of an additional three-step test might be for the parody exception in UK and France.

Following the implementation of the InfoSoc Directive in 2006, the French legislator introduced the second and third steps of the three-step test into the Intellectual Property Code, thereby making it mandatory for French judges to apply the test in every case.[323] At the time, this action faced severe criticism, based upon the lack of clarity of the test, unpredictability of the likely outcome, and the disruption of traditional competences between the legislator and the judiciary.[324] This French legislative choice may have profound consequences on the outcome of any dispute concerning the parody exception.[325] While UK legislation does not include the three-step test in its domestic legislation, as a result of EU influence, UK courts have applied the three-step test to particular disputes. As explained in Chapter 2, this gives rise to doubts as to the proper application of UK copyright exceptions, as it is unclear whether the UK judiciary considers that the three-step test contained within the InfoSoc Directive is addressed to them, or only to the CJEU.

The inclusion of the three-step test in domestic legislation undermines the legal certainty aimed at by the framework notions, such as rules of the genre, and other general principles.[326] Indeed, judges from different Member States who have applied the test to

[319] *CCH* (n 3) [70].

[320] See Chapter 2, section 2.

[321] While this is a factor in Australia: P Brundenall, 'Fair dealing in Australian copyright law' (1997) 20 *UNSW Law Journal* 449; it is criticized in relation to the parody exception. McCutcheon (n 4) 185.

[322] See Chapter 2, sections 3, and 4.

[323] Confirmed by the French Constitutional Council and the literature. Decision n°2006-540 DC, 27 juillet 2006, La loi relative au droit d'auteur et aux droits voisins dans la société de l'information, indent 35; Galopin (n 11) 387; C Caron, 'La loi du 1er août 2006 relative au droit d'auteur et aux droits voisins dans la société de l'information' (2006) *CCE* étude 22, 11; A Lucas, '3. Nouvelles exceptions et triple test', in A Lucas and P Sirinelli, 'La loi n°2006-961 du 1er aout 2006 relative au droit d'auteur et aux droits voisins dans la société de l'information: premières vues sur le texte promulgue a l'issue de la censure du Conseil Constitutionnel' (2006) 20(297) *Prop. Intell.* 315.

[324] A study of the debate and surrounding criticisms falls beyond the subject of this project and belongs to a past debate, but see Galopin (n 11) 386–91.

[325] Not even in the latest decision, *Les Enfants* (n 16).

[326] Galopin (n 11) 387.

the same facts have reached opposite results, which does nothing to further the unity of the internal market which the InfoSoc Directive seeks. Furthermore, the application of this test by the courts is likely to deter users from adopting parody, simply because they are unable to predict whether their use is likely to benefit from the exception, or not.

Not only does the application of the three-step test undermine legal certainty but it also has procedural consequences. Having considered the shortcomings in detail in Chapter 2, this will not be repeated here. In relation to parodies, this will rarely be possible as it is not a parody which is harmful to the normal exploitation of a work but the multiplication of parody uses.[327] But, in reality, it is nearly impossible for the right-holder to show evidence of the two requirements. Furthermore, it is suggested that the judge is inadequately equipped to apply the three-step test to particular disputes.

Yet in *Deckmyn*,[328] the CJEU did not interpret the InfoSoc Directive's three-step test, but rather the Court seemed to translate it into a requirement that national courts strike a fair balance between the competing fundamental interests at stake. This approach results in a refined proportionality test which attempts to reconcile the competing interests to maximize the realization of all the fundamental rights in play bringing EU Member States closer to Canada and their users' rights doctrine.[329]

If, by its decision in *Deckmyn*, the CJEU has relegated the addressee of the three-step test in the InfoSoc Directive to a past debate, the Court appears to have possibly clarified the role of the test within the EU context without explicitly interpreting it.

4. Irrelevant Factors for the Application of the Parody Exception

In *Deckmyn*,[330] the CJEU provided a clear mandate that the national courts of EU Member States should disregard certain factors as irrelevant to a parody defence, namely, the originality of the parody, the target of the parody, lack of acknow-ledgement of the author of the underlying work, and that the parody does not have to be 'attributable to a person other than the author of the original work itself'.[331]

This list cannot be assumed to be exhaustive, since the Court's guidance was limited to answering the specific question posed by the referring Belgian court. Nevertheless, the decision is enlightening, since it may be possible to extrapolate the reasoning adopted, in the eventuality that other potential factors are identified. While *Deckmyn* is clearly binding on UK and French courts, the Canadian court's reference to the case in *United Airlines* suggests that its influence might extend to other jurisdictions. We shall, therefore, consider each of the four excluded factors in turn.

4.1 Originality of the parody

This factor has mainly arisen in pre-*Deckmyn* parody cases before the French courts, which sought to tie the parody exception to the degree of creativity embodied in the

[327] P-Y Gautier, 'L'élargissement des exceptions aux droits exclusifs, contrebalancé par le "test des trois étapes"' (2006) 11 *CCE* 9, 12.

[328] *Deckmyn* (n 55).

[329] See Chapter 2, sections 3 and 4 and Chapter 5 for the balancing of competing fundamental freedoms.

[330] *Deckmyn* (n 55) [21].

[331] Ibid.

parodic expression. Thus, originality of the parody has been considered as part of the fairness assessment, i.e. whether originality is essential for a parody to comply with the rules of the genre.

If we accept the characterization of a parody as a distorted reproduction of an earlier work used to communicate a message, then the task for a court is to distinguish between an unlawful reproduction[332] and the right kind of distortion. Faced with the predicament of drawing the line between the two,[333] some French courts elected to make the outcome contingent upon the originality of the parody.[334] In other words, did the parody embody enough creativity to be eligible for copyright protection in its own right?

The best-known example is *Korda*, in which the defendant had parodied the famous portrait of Che Guevara as an angry monkey. The trial judge accepted that there was sufficient distortion that the two works would not be confused, and permitted the use under the parody exception. This decision was later overturned on appeal.[335] The appeal court viewed the parody as too similar to the original photograph. The parody defence was denied only because the parody lacked originality based upon the modest nature of the modifications made. This reduction in scope of the exception was seen as unjustified by many commentators.[336]

In *Deckmyn*, the CJEU rightly rejected originality as a requirement for the parody exception,[337] identifying that within the EU at least, the parody exception remains available not just to transformative, original works, but to all transformative uses which have a humorous character and are not confusable with the underlying work.

It seems likely that many parodies will be 'original', since originality, in whatever EU jurisdiction, amounts to the author's own intellectual creation. While relevant, if the parodist seeks to claim copyright in their own work,[338] it is inappropriate to the exception, as it is seems unrelated to the nature of the exception. Much of the creativity in parody lies in the selection of the underlying work, and the distortion applied. Hence, trying to measure a parody in terms of the quantitative changes made to the underlying work simply misses the objective of the exception.

In light of the foregoing, courts in jurisdictions outside the EU should follow *Deckmyn* and reject originality as a factor governing the parody exception.

[332] Paris, 17 juin 1987, JCP, 1988 II 20957, note Auvret; Paris, 17 octobre 1980, Dalloz 1982, IR, p. 42, obs. Colombet.

[333] El Khoury (n 56) 161; Bloch (n 73) 117; B Edelman, 'Le personnage et son double' (1990) 30 *Recueil Dalloz* 227.

[334] Paris, 4e ch., 13 octobre 2006, Gaz. Pal. 2007, jurispr., p. 2110; TGI Paris, *Femme*, 13 février 2001; TGI Paris, 14 avril 1999, CCE, octobre 1999, pp. 23–4; Versaillles 15 décembre 1993, *La Bicyclette Bleue*; Paris, 11 mai 1993, RIDA, 1993, n°157, p. 340, obs. Kéréver and Françon, Rev. trim. dr. comm., 1993, p. 510; TGI Paris, 30 avril 1987, Gaz. Pal., 3–4 juin 1987; TGI Paris, 17 septembre 1984, D. 1985, IR, p. 16; TGI Paris, 13 septembre 1984, D. 1985, IR, p. 16, obs. Lindon; Paris, 20 décembre 1977, ann. propr. ind. 1979, p. 84; TGI Paris (ref), 26 novembre 1977, JCP, ed. G, 1978, II, n °18924; *Peanuts* (n 110); TGI Nancy, 15 octobre 1976, JCP, 1977, II, n°18526 obs. Lindon.

[335] Paris, 4e ch., 13 octobre 2006, Gaz. Pal. 2007, jurispr., p. 2110.

[336] Mouffe (n 11) 289; Berenboom (n 81) 109; Bloch (n 73) 117; F Fletcher-Boulvard, 'La caricature: dualité ou unité' (1997) *RTD Civ.* 67; Françon (n 77) 304.

[337] *Deckmyn* (n 55) [21].

[338] Similar considerations are present in US cases as demonstrated in *Keeling v. Hars*, No 13-694 (2d Cir. 2015) where the Second Circuit held that if the defendant adds substantial original expression of ideas, then copyright protection may subsist in the parody.

4.2 Target of the parody

As discussed in Chapters 1 and 2, a parody has several possible targets. It may comment on the underlying work, comment on the author of that work, or comment on something completely external to the work reproduced, such as the parodist themselves or a current event. Mostly, when considering whether a use of a protected work is for the purpose of parody, the target is an aspect which is accepted as belonging to a past debate.

This requirement, nevertheless, did find some support in the US, especially in the aftermath of the *Campbell* case. We saw in Chapter 1, that this case relied upon the target to differentiate between (lawful) parody and (unlawful) satire during the appraisal of the first fair use factor. However, we also saw how this distinction between parody and satire is slowly fading in recognition of the need to preserve freedom of expression.

In *Deckmyn*, the CJEU explicitly rejected that the nature of the target should be relevant to the parody exception in copyright law in EU Member States,[339] presumably because both activities result from an exercise of freedom of expression particularly valuable in a democratic society. There seems little reason to doubt that the other jurisdictions under scrutiny will follow suit. For example, the choice of legislative wording used to frame the exception in Canada and Australia shies away from distinguishing between parody and satire based upon the target's identity.[340] This choice should not be seen as trivial, but rather demonstrative of a willingness to cover the full ambit of possible targets. This lends addition weight to the conclusion that target type should not play a role in determining whether a parody use should be deemed lawful or unlawful.

4.3 Acknowledgement of the original

The question of whether a lawful parody needs to acknowledge the underlying work is perhaps one of the most debated aspects of the parody exception. Indeed, failure to acknowledge the original is a major contributing factor which denies parodies a permitted use under other fair dealing exceptions. For example, acknowledgement is generally specified as necessary for the quotation exception to apply. Only recently have later EU case law developments relaxed the form of the acknowledgment necessary for this particular exception.[341] This has led leading UK copyright scholars Bently and Aplin[342] to suggest that such a broader understanding is not only more firmly compliant with the international copyright framework, but might render the parody exception redundant.

In *Deckmyn*, the CJEU rejected acknowledgement as a mandatory requirement,[343] since a parody which satisfies the two mandatory requirements (humorous intent and absence of confusion) should leave those exposed to the parody able to identify the original work automatically.[344] Arguably, emphasizing that the parody *is* a parody by flagging up its original basis and its author might simply 'spoil the joke', and

[339] *Deckmyn* (n 55) [21]. [340] See Chapter 2, sections 4.3 and 4.4.

[341] *Eva-Maria Painer v. Standard Verlags GmbH and Others* [2011] ECLI:EU:C:2011:798 (hereafter *Painer*), [149].

[342] L Bently and T Aplin, 'Whatever became of global mandatory fair use? A case study in dysfunctional pluralism.' Forthcoming in S Frankel (ed.), *Is Intellectual Property Pluralism Functional?* (Edward Elgar, 2018).

[343] *Deckmyn* (n 55) [21]. [344] See Chapter 1, section 5.

consequently, undermine the parody's effect. Equally, the explicit identification of the original author might actually nurture confusion, by giving the illusion that the parody is the original or that the original author endorses the parody or its message.

In certain contexts, however, explicit identification may help to avoid confusion between the original and its parody, or provide evidence for the public to recognize that they are not being exposed to the original work. For example, in *Deckmyn*, the defendant's parody had incorporated a caption stating 'Fré vrij naar Vandersteen', meaning 'Fré (the parodist) freely in the style of Vandersteen (the author of the original drawing)'. As set out in section 2 of this chapter, French decisions have tended to perceive acknowledgement of the original as establishing that a parody has built upon the earlier work, rather than merely intending to free-ride on another's creative efforts. More recently, in *Les Enfants*,[345] the French court equated (indirectly) lack of identification of the original with a lack of intent to parody. As the putative parody in question reproduced a work which would be largely unknown to the French public, the court concluded that the defendant should publicly acknowledge his inspiration and use some form of captioning to reveal the creative process behind the work. Here, given the relative obscurity of the original, the lack of any additional clues to enable the public to recognize that the work was a parody contributed to a finding that permitting the use would be unfair.

In Canada, the traditional appreciation of fairness led Canadian courts to authorize uses copying unpublished works if the borrowing was acknowledged by the defendant. This is justified by a wish to contribute to a greater dissemination of the original should be set aside for parody uses.[346]

As outlined at the start of this chapter, a parody which relies upon a work which is unpublished, or is otherwise confidential, precludes the audience from identifying the borrowing as such. This is contrary to the rules of the parody genre, as traced throughout its historical developments.[347] Any would-be parody which the public fails to appreciate as being a reference to an earlier work is not truly a parody.[348] Thus, it is not unreasonable that this kind of borrowing should fall beyond the scope of the parody exception. However, the specific means used to establish the required link should be a creative choice for the parodist to elect. On balance, the CJEU guidance in *Deckmyn* appears correct and arguably should be applicable beyond the EU jurisdiction.

4.4 Attribution of the identity of the parodist

Related to the question which we have just considered is whether courts should only permit parodies if the parodist is identified in the parody. Should courts require that parodists take responsibility for the expression they create? According to the CJEU, this should not be a condition for the parody exception to apply in copyright law.[349]

Since a parodist, via parody, is inevitably creating a new expression (whether original enough to surpass the protection threshold or not), potentially they will have an interest in being associated with their own expression. Indeed, we have seen that this may reinforce the parodic nature of their efforts by reducing the chance that the public

[345] *Les Enfants* (n 16). [346] *CCH* (n 3) [58]; *SOCAN* (n 13) [47].
[347] See Chapter 1, sections 2 and 3.
[348] Given the lack of engagement of the Canadian federal court with this factor in *United Airlines* (n 6), it could be posited that the factor is less relevant in parody cases.
[349] *Deckmyn* (n 55) [21].

will mistake the parody for the original work. If present, it may also contribute to the overall assessment of fairness. However, it seems that this should be another choice for the parodist to make, rather than being a mandatory requirement of law. After all, if copyright law protects works without requiring authors/right-holders to be identified with their work, it does not seem just to impose stricter conditions to control uses in which copyright might not even subsist. Thus, the CJEU was correct to reject this factor as being a mandatory condition for the parody exception in copyright law to apply. We shall return to consider this aspect in more detail in Chapter 6.[350]

5. Can Domestic Courts Adopt Additional Factors?

Previous sections analyzed the relevance of the 'traditional' fairness factors adopted in the judicial consideration of the parody exception, as well as evaluating the specific factors which have been established since a specific legislative parody exception has been introduced. However, both the arts and users' habits are prone to constant development, and the speed of this has been greatly facilitated by the advent of new technologies and increasing use of the internet. This final section considers whether national courts might introduce new factors and seek to adapt the parody exception to new kinds of uses.

In jurisdictions in which the fairness factors are developed in case law by the judiciary, such as the UK, Australia, and Canada, the system is sufficiently flexible that courts are open to the introduction of new aspects and considerations, generally pertaining to 'fairness', which will assist their determination of the lawfulness of the parody under review. This is already well established. Previously, for example, in *CCH*, the Canadian Supreme Court noted that it 'may be relevant to consider the custom or practice in a particular trade or industry to determine whether or not the character of the dealing is fair'.[351] In doing so, the Canadian Court relied on an earlier UK case, *Sillitoe v. McGraw-Hill Book Co. (U.K.)*,[352] in which the court reviewed customary practices to establish whether the use complained of was for the purpose of criticism. Thus, we may reasonably expect courts to look to new and evolving industry practices to understand whether any particular use is a fair dealing.

Bruguière argues that even in France, courts can rely on best and fair practices within a sector to establish fairness.[353] Consideration of best practices, he argues, leads to the establishment of new fairness factors as is necessary within the framework of copyright exceptions to ensure that it adapts to retain its legitimacy in the eyes of the public. As we have seen, there is a similar approach adopted in the US and Canada.

In the US, where the fairness factors have been cemented in the US Copyright Act, the possibility remains open to add new factors into the statute.[354] This possibility could gain popularity in future parody cases. Indeed, the parody exception should be applied in a way which fosters the realization of its objectives.[355] The overview of national disputes which have reached the courts illustrates why the content of the parodic expression often results in a copyright infringement claim. It is understandable why

[350] See Chapter 6, section 4.1. [351] *CCH* (n 3) [55]. [352] *Sillitoe* (n 13).

[353] J M Bruiguière, 'La réception du fair dealing britannique dans le système d'exception fermée français.' Forthcoming in (2018) *RIDA* 27, 28 and esp. 37; similarly in the UK, industry practices have played a role in the assessment of fairness; see early UK cases such as *Sillitoe* (n 13).

[354] Confirmed by Congressional intent: H.R. REP. No. 1476, 94th Cong., 2d Sess. 66 (1976); S. REK No. 473, 94th Cong., 1st Sess. 62 (1975).

[355] e.g. Painer (n 342); On compliance with the three-step test see Chapter 2, section 4.

right-holders and authors will try, for example, to prevent a parody which imports a sexual connotation into the original work or which is used in a political speech to convey a message which is contrary to their own beliefs or corporate brand message. We return to review the legitimacy of such concerns in the next chapter and again in Chapter 7.[356]

This is not to say that we should rely on human rights considerations in every parody dispute, in which case we might jeopardize the copyright balance intended by legislators. Instead of brandishing a freedom of expression argument in every scenario, a better understanding of the relationship between freedom of expression and copyright leads to recourse to the proportionality principle well-known in human rights law in these exceptional borderline parody cases.[357]

6. Conclusion

The core of this chapter focused upon the requirements attached to the parody exception in national law, including the 'fairness factors'—the kind of considerations which are used to establish whether the use is 'fair'.

In section 2, we saw that the most important factor in a parody defence is the absence of confusion between the use and the protected work. An immediately perceivable distinction between the altered reproduction and the original is intrinsic to what we understand parody to be. True parodists do not want their expression to create confusion or to appropriate the original work. Rather, the medium of parody requires them to reproduce the protected content and distort it to some extent, thereby distancing the parody from the original. The intent is to create a new expression which conveys a different message to the public than the original.

In terms of the requirement that a parody is humorous, it was argued that this requirement is best appraised based on the parodist's own intent at the time the parody was created. Additionally, rather than establishing positive characteristics which are indicative of 'humour', it was argued that a negative approach is preferable. In other words, rather than enquiring whether any particular form of humour should be permitted under the exception, a better approach is to ascertain whether the parody results from a specific intent to harm the right-holder or the original work.

All the other factors studied constitute different ways to interrogate the parodist's intent. Therefore, no single factor ought to be decisive, and each will weigh differently depending on the circumstances of the case. Elevating an absence of confusion as primary filter and humour as secondary filter enables the specific nature of a parody to be legally recognized because it is from the distortion needed to satisfy this criterion that the humorous character can be derived.

The jurisdictional comparison identified distinctions between the application of the parody exception in the countries considered. Nevertheless, based upon the global appreciation of factors which the national courts undertake, it does not seem that these differences will manifest to affect the scope of the exception to any significant extent. On the contrary, it appears that the different national provisions all aim to achieve the same result, albeit that in specific cases, different outcomes might arise because of the fact-intensive nature of the enquiry. The artificially linear analysis of the potentially

[356] See Chapter 5, section 4.1.5 and Chapter 7, sections 2 & 3.

[357] As previously argued by E Treppoz, 'Retour sur la denaturation contextuelle du dialogues des Carmelites' (2017) 352 *Légipresse* 441.

relevant factors in this chapter has only served to reinforce why it is inherent in the question of fair dealing, fair use, or compliance with the rules of the genre, that an overall, contextual assessment of the use is required.

While US, Canadian, and Australian courts may be drawn to consider the same economics-driven factors[358] developed for fair use/dealing under other copyright exceptions, in the UK and France (as in other EU Member States), courts must confine attention to the two mandatory requirements from *Deckmyn*: humorous intent and an absence of confusion. This is not to say that EU Member States must set aside the factors developed in accordance with their own legal tradition, but it does require courts to refrain from applying these factors beyond what is needed to determine whether these two requirements are satisfied. Therefore, considerations based on the parody's originality; the question of whether there are alternatives to the parodic dealing, requiring the creator of the parody and/or original to be acknowledged; or any competitive relationship between the parties should be set aside. The analysis of section 3 strongly suggests that none of these factors is pertinent to the *Deckmyn* requirements, and they are in fact more likely to hinder, rather than further, realization of the objective underlying this copyright exception.

Nevertheless, the variety of factors which are all potentially relevant in determining whether the parody exception should apply begs the question whether the InfoSoc Directive's harmonization objectives are achievable. With *Deckmyn*, the CJEU grants national courts significant discretion whether to apply the exception in particular cases. The two requirements set out in *Deckmyn* are questions of fact, which allow local factors to influence the outcome, for example, whether there is a humorous character. Therefore, despite mandating an autonomous definition of 'parody', a use may be found infringing in some Member States while being permitted as lawful in others.

Finally, the need for an objective appraisal when considering the exception to particular facts is influenced by the national concept of good faith or the notion of a fair-minded person. These concepts are already well-developed in the jurisdictions considered in this book.

[358] Especially relevant in the US once again as the fourth factor is generally decisive.

5

How Freedom of Expression Defines the Parody Exception

1. Introduction

Whilst initially, copyright policy was rooted in natural law and, more specifically, in the Lockean moral-desert theory,[1] today, copyright is more often justified based upon broadly utilitarian principles. This shift, explained by the mercantile approach to intellectual property endorsed since the eighties,[2] makes recourse to human rights principles, including the right to property, more difficult.[3] Largely unconcerned with trade-related matters, the human rights framework is nevertheless, a posteriori, a beneficial counterweight to the development of imperfect copyright policy. In an increasingly complex haystack of copyright rules, the human rights framework usefully reinjects values into the system. It counterbalances economic analysis by emphasizing the cultural values ingrained in creative endeavours. Revisiting the well-trodden debate on the interaction between intellectual property rights and fundamental rights is beyond the scope of this book.[4] Nevertheless, some references to it are unavoidable, and it is briefly summarized in what follows.

The parody exception exacerbates tensions between copyright and freedom of expression as well as providing avenues to delineate its scope. As Gervais has eloquently argued, 'intellectual property and human rights can live together' and must learn from each other.[5] Departing from the frequent depiction of two systems in conflict, it is more helpful to see fundamental rights as enabling means to *humanize* the copyright paradigm. Instead of merely regarding copyright as a tool to foster economic growth and enrich the big players of creative industries,[6] human rights considerations lend legitimacy to the scheme by appealing to the conscience of stakeholders and users. This

[1] J Locke, *Second Treatise of Civil Government* (1690) available at http://www.constitution.org/jl/2ndtreat.htm (access date: 10 November 2018); J Hughes, 'Copyright and incomplete historiographies: of piracy, propertization, and Thomas Jefferson' (2006) 79 *Southern California Law Review,* 1011–13.

[2] See the amendments made to section 301 of the US Trade Act 1974. This provision enables the imposition of sanctions on international treaty violations burdening or restricting US commerce. This has been increasingly used in the field of intellectual property. Furthermore, the change in forum from the WIPO-administered Berne Convention to the WTO which is trade specific inherently taints copyright policy.

[3] And to a certain extent this explains the reluctance of accepting human rights considerations when applying framework notions such as 'fair use', 'fair dealing', and 'rules of the genre'.

[4] For a more complete study, see e.g. C Geiger and E Izyumenko, *Intellectual Property before the European Court of Human Rights* (2018) Centre for International Intellectual Property Studies Research Paper No 2018-01, forthcoming in C Geiger, A Nard, and X Seuba (eds), *Intellectual Property and the Judiciary* (EIPIN series vol. 4, EE, 2018).

[5] D Gervais, 'How intellectual property and human rights can live together' in P Torremans (ed.), *Intellectual Property Law and Human Rights* (3rd edn, Kluwer, 2015) chapter 1.

[6] Here, the author makes a presumption that in the eyes of the wider public, copyright policy has lost legitimacy due to the perception that the current rules only benefit multinational companies at the expense of creators.

appeal to moral imperatives introduces a new, implicit sense of which uses should, or should not, be allowed. This is of particular relevance for the parody exception, which can be used as a vehicle for particularly acerbic comment. Therefore, right-holders may attempt to rely on the user's sympathy for an author, or his work, in the process of creating a parody.

Additionally, it is inevitable that the wording of any new copyright exception is the result of policy compromises. Consequently, the resulting legislation is imprinted with a certain degree of vagueness.[7] The parody defence is no exception. Here, the human rights framework can guide the courts in defining the scope. As further observed later, this role is particularly well established in France but also in the US, to a certain extent. However, there are avenues available for other jurisdictions to follow suit. For example, in European countries, ECtHR case law can assist in defining the outer boundaries of the parody exception.[8] However, some caution is needed, as human rights-based arguments are not a panacea for all ills. Whilst human rights considerations can guide the judge as to the relevant factors and appropriate weighting, direct recourse to human rights arguments should only be relied upon in particular equivocal cases.

Leaving the property-based rhetoric aside, this chapter focuses on the role freedom of expression may serve as a 'double gate-keeper', wrestling against the excessive expansion of exclusive rights, while also constraining the outer limits of the parody exception. Consequently, this chapter does not endeavour to provide a comprehensive study of freedom of expression either. It first outlines how human rights are intrinsically embodied in the parody exception (section 2), before establishing freedom of expression within the international and European legal order framework (section 3). These foundations enable us to review factors established in the ECtHR's rich jurisprudence which may legitimately restrict freedom of expression so as to protect the rights of others (section 4). The final step is to understand how national legislators and courts strike a balance between freedom of expression values and copyright values in the jurisdictions under scrutiny.

2. The Parody Exception Embodying Human Rights Aspects

The prevailing trend of only strengthening copyright displays a tendency to overlook that the granting of exclusive rights to right-holders has limited legitimacy.[9] Before legislation incorporated a specific parody exception, some courts sought to limit copyright law's expanding scope by imposing external limits, applying fundamental freedoms to balance the rights of authors and the interests of parodists.[10] We shall see

[7] See Chapters 2 and 4.

[8] Especially since the judicial reticence for the ECtHR to hear intellectual property cases has vanished. *Anheuser-Busch Inc. v. Portugal* (2007) 44 EHRR 42 (ECtHR, Grand Chamber) (hereafter *Anheuser-Busch*) [66]–[72]; *Smith Kline and French Laboratories Ltd v. the Netherlands* (1990) 66 DR 70 (ECommHR) (hereafter *Smith Kline*). For more, see Chapter 7, section 2.

[9] C Geiger, 'The constitutional dimension of intellectual property' in P L C Torremans (ed.), *Intellectual Property and Human Rights* (3rd edn, Kluwer, 2008) 121; C Geiger, 'Constitutionalising: intellectual property law? The influence of fundamental rights on intellectual property in the European Union' (2006) 37(4) *IIC* 371, 378; C Geiger, 'Fundamental rights, a safeguard for the coherence of intellectual property law?' (2004) 35(3) *IIC* 268, 271; P B Hugenholtz, 'Copyright and freedom of expression in Europe' in R C Dreyfuss, H First, and D L Zimmerman (eds), *Innovation Policy in an Information Age* (OUP, 2001) 346.

[10] Yet asking courts to balance freedom of expression and copyright is not desirable given that it might jeopardize the balance intended by the legislator between these rights. This resulted in

that the introduction of a parody exception into copyright legislation reinstates some legitimacy by correcting the internal balance, thereby maximizing the realization of all the fundamental rights at play.

Copyright's linkages with human rights could be described as integrated.[11] As a property right, copyright enjoys protection as part of the human right to property, which is enshrined in article 17 of the Universal Declaration of Human Rights ('UDHR').[12] Furthermore, article 27 UDHR recognizes a right to participate in cultural life,[13] a provision which does not merely focus on economic incentives but includes a right to protect both moral and material interests of the creator resulting from any scientific, literary, or artistic endeavour. Notably, this right is not limited to creators, but extends to users, who have the right to participate in cultural life and to enjoy the arts in a society. Consequently, copyright can be seen as an instrument to foster the realization of both human rights and policy goals. It can strike a balance between both article 27 UDHR objectives by enabling individuals to access and create works while

the rejection by courts of arguments based on freedom of expression to authorize a parody. C-337/95 *Evora v. Dior* [1997] ECLI:EU:C:1997:517; M Senftleben, 'Chapter 13: quotations, parody and fair use' in P B Hugenholtz, A Quaedvlieg, and D Visser (eds), *A Century of Dutch Copyright Law* (deLex, 2012) 372; A Lucas, 'Droit d'auteur, liberté d'expression et droit du public a l'information' (2005) 1 *A&M* 13, 21; P B Hugenholtz, 'Copyright and freedom of expression' in N Elkin-Koren and N W Netanel (eds), *The Commodification of Information* (Kluwer, 2002) 357. Yet, the argument of freedom of expression led to a recognition of parody uses in trade mark law in France: TGI Paris, ord. réf. 24 octobre 1991, inédit; upheld on appeal Paris, 28 janvier 1992; Cass. Comm. 21 février 1995, BC, IV, n°55; D. 1995, IR, p. 97 (hereafter *Marlboro case*); TGI Paris, 17 février 1990, J.-CL. Marques, fasc. 7140, n°15; Cass. (2e Civ.), 2 avril 1997; Cass. 12 juillet 2000, D. 2001, n°3, jur., 259, note Edelman (hereafter *Peugeot v. Canal+*); Versailles 17 mars 1994 (hereafter *Michelin*); TGI Paris 4/07/2001, *Société Compagnie Gervais Danone et Société Groupe Danone v. Olivier M., Réseau Voltaire et autres*, www.legalis.net upheld on appeal Paris, 30 avril 2003, *M. Olivier (jeboycottedanone.com) v. Société Compagnie Gervais Danone et Société Groupe Danone*, www.forum.internet.org; Ordonnance /07/2002 TGI Paris; TGI Paris 30 janvier 2004, *Esso v. Greenpeace*, Internet Fr., www.legalis.net; confirmed on appeal Paris, 16 novembre 2005; TGI Paris, ord. réf., 2 août 2002, Propr. ind. 2002, Comm. n°68, note Tréfigny; Paris, 26 février 2003, D. 2003. Jur. 1831, note B. Edelman; CCE 2003, Comm. n°38, note Caron; Propr. intell. 2003, p. 322, note Bénabou (hereafter *Areva*).

[11] But it must be noted that this is not unanimously accepted. See for example, Farida Shaheed, UN Special Rapporteur in the field of cultural rights, who spoke on 6 May 2015, and argued that intellectual property rights are not human rights, but only instrumental in permitting other human rights, e.g. freedom of expression to be realized. In this light, exceptions are vital to safeguard the balance the interests of right-holders and the interests of others to participate in cultural activities. Speech available at https://juliareda.eu/2015/05/intellectual-property-rights-are-not-human-rights/ (access date: 10 November 2018); more on this scepticism: J Griffiths and L McDonagh, 'Fundamental rights and European IP law: the case of Art 17(2) of the EU Charter' in C Geiger (ed.), *Constructing European Intellectual Property* (EIPIN, 2013) 75.

[12] See, for example, in European countries: Protocol 1 Article 1 of the ECHR, and explicitly in Article 17(2) of the EU Charter. The ECtHR recognized intellectual property to be protected under the fundamental right to property. C-479/04, *Laserdisken ApS v. Kulturministeriet* [2006] ECLI:EU:C:2006:549, [65]; C-275/06 *Productores de Música de España (Promusicae) v. Telefónica de España SAU* [2008] ECLI:EU:C:2008:54, [61]–[70]; ECtHR *Anheuser-Busch* (n 8) [66]–[72]; *Smith Kline* (n 8). For more on copyright as a property right and the scepticism attached thereto: Griffiths and McDonagh (n 11) 75; for the EU, C-277/10 *Martin Luksan v. Petrus van der Let* [2006] ECLI:EU:C:2006:549, [68]–[71]; J Griffiths, 'Constitutionalising or harmonising? The Court of Justice, the right to property and European Copyright law' (2013) 38(1) *E. L. Rev.* 65–78.

[13] This provision should be read alongside articles 15(1)(c) and 27 ICCPR. Further guidance can be found in Office of the High Commissioner for Human Rights, CCPR General Comment No 23, adopted on 8 April 1994 and available at http://www.refworld.org/docid/453883fc0.html (access date: 10 November 2018).

also ensuring that creators (who may be the same individuals) secure personal and economic interests vested in the works created.[14]

Traditionally, exercise of the freedom of expression, enshrined in article 19 UDHR, has two strands: the right to express ideas, and the right to receive information.[15] It is evident that both are pertinent to parody. By allowing the creation of new cultural works, the parody exception contributes to the realization of the first strand of freedom of expression.[16] Parodies can also raise concerns under the right to freedom of information when copyright owners enforce their rights in an attempt to stifle this form of social commentary, including when this is perceived as prejudicial to their honour or reputation.[17]

The parody exception impacts on the realization of the right to freedom of expression. A parodist may wish to borrow another author's (copyright-protected) expression in order to exercise their own right of free expression. The parody exception underlines that copyright law should provide some latitude for subsequent authors to use existing works to create new ones. However, applying it involves a delicate balancing exercise, distinguishing between instances in which a right-holder should retain control over their protected work and those when the public interest supersedes the enforcement of their exclusive rights.[18] If exclusive rights are construed too narrowly, authors might have inadequate incentive to create new works, which is potentially detrimental to cultural diversity. Conversely, if these rights are construed too broadly, right-holders might have an undesirable censorial control over critical and parody uses of their works.[19] Again, this is potentially detrimental to society as a whole. Exceptions to economic rights—such as the parody exception—should perhaps be seen as a way to preserve the freedom of expression of others at the expense of the copyright-owner's prerogatives.[20] Yet, the parody exception should not be absolute and might itself be restricted in specific circumstances to preserve the rights of others.[21]

[14] This is also valid in the US and facilitated by the constitutional embedding of copyright and freedom of expression. See *Harper & Row v. Nation Enterprises*, 471 U.S. 539 (1985) (hereafter *Harper*), [558]. See section 5.5.

[15] P El Khoury, *Les exceptions au droit d'auteur* (thèse Montpellier, 2007) 157.

[16] The realization of freedom of expression is the primary justification for the introduction of a parody exception. *RJR MacDonald Inc. v. Canada (Att. Gen.)* [1995] 3 S.C.R. 199 (hereafter *RJR*), [72]: 'both critical and non-critical parodies can be seen as promoting the fundamental values underlying the constitutionally protected right to freedom of expression, "including the search for political, artistic and scientific truth, the protection of individual autonomy and self-development, and the promotion of public participation in the democratic process."' See Chapter 5, section 5.1. Under the French legal tradition, parodies are close to sacred as they are seen as the exercise of the right of critique in an unconventional way. El Khoury (n 15) 161; A Lucas, *Fasc. 1248: Droits des auteurs.—Droits patrimoniaux.—Exceptions au droit exclusif* (2013) Jurisclasseur, [19].

[17] See Chapter 4, section 2.3.

[18] To borrow the words of Craig: 'Herein lies the explanation for the copyright system: copyright is an institution whose existence and maintenance encourage the kinds of communicative activity that lie at the heart of the rationale for freedom of expression, and so at the heart of a culture and society that furthers the capacities of the human self that we most value.' C J Craig, 'Putting the community in communication: dissolving the conflict between freedom of expression and copyright' (2006) 56 *U. Toronto L.J.* 75, 108.

[19] While limited copyright can serve as the 'engine of free expression', copyright laws that exceed their proper limits can serve as an effective engine for censorship and suppression. B Mouffe, *Le droit à l'humour* (Larcier, 2011) 35; N W Netanel, *Copyright's Paradox* (OUP, 2008) 3.

[20] As expressed by Geiger, where the exercise of exclusive rights does not contribute to the objective of copyright to encourage the creation of new works, the system must be corrected. Geiger (n 9) 121.

[21] See chapter 7, section 2.7.

Overall, copyright and freedom of expression share the same objectives:[22] both rights promote the creation of new expressions and mandate that ideas must remain free. The introduction of a parody exception may be conceptualized as constituting an internal copyright mechanism to balance the exclusive rights granted to authors with freedom of expression. Therefore, copyright grants individual rights because the making available of new works is beneficial for society at large, and a parody exception legitimately limits the exercise of those rights in those particular circumstances when it is socially valuable to do so. In this way, the perceived conflict between the two bodies of law is resolved. While this synopsis is reasonable at a macro level, the exact influence exerted by the human rights framework and constitutional values varies at a national level, including in the jurisdictions of interest in our study. Having first surveyed the scope of freedom of expression at a supra-national level, including limiting factors, we shall then review how differences in legal traditions emerge to shape the contours of the parody exception at national level.

3. Scope of Freedom of Expression at Supranational Levels

A brief overview of the right to freedom of expression may be useful at this point, to set the stage for this discussion. Freedom of expression is widely accepted as an essential component of promoting values of tolerance and pluralism in a democratic society.[23] Consequently, this fundamental right is protected in most international human rights treaties[24] and European instruments.[25]

3.1 International recognition of the right to freedom of expression

The UDHR is a non-binding instrument[26] which resulted from the historical events of the Second World War and the Holocaust.[27] Article 19 provides:

[22] Demonstrating the absence of conflict between IPRs and Human Rights: E Derclaye (2008), 'Intellectual property rights and human rights' in P Torremans (ed.), *Intellectual Property and Human Rights* (2nd edn, Kluwer, 2008) 133, esp. 154; D Gervais, 'Intellectual property and human rights: learning to live together' in P L C Torremans (ed.), *Intellectual Property and Human Rights* (3rd edn, Kluwer, 2008) 21; P Torremans, 'A clash between theory and practice? Introduction' in F Brison, S Dussollier, M-C Janssens, and H Vanhees (eds), *Moral Rights in the 21st Century* (Larcier, 2015) 224.

[23] Amongst others: C-288/89 *Stichting Collectieve Antennevoorziening Gouda and Others v. Commissariat voor de Media* [1991] ECLI:EU:C:1991:323; *Handyside v. The United Kingdom* (1976) 1 EHRR 737 (hereafter *Handyside*).

[24] Article 19 UDHR; article 19 ICCPR; article 5(d)(viii) of the International Convention on the Elimination of all Forms of Racial Discrimination ('CERD'); article 13 of the Convention on the Rights of the Child; article 6 of the Declaration on Human Rights Defenders—Declaration on the Right and Responsibility of Individuals, Groups and Organs of Society to Promote and Protect Universally Recognised Human Rights and Fundamental Freedoms; and article 6 of the Declaration on Human Rights Defenders—Declaration on the Right and Responsibility of Individuals, Groups and Organs of Society to Promote and Protect Universally Recognised Human Rights and Fundamental Freedoms.

[25] *EU*: Article 10 ECHR; article 11 of the EU Charter. *Other regional instruments*: article 13 of the American Convention on Human Rights; and article 9 of the African Charter on Human and Peoples' Rights.

[26] A Weber, *Manual on Hate Speech* (Council of Europe Publishing, 2009) 8.

[27] A Callamard, 'Expert Meeting on the Links between Articles 19 and 20 of the ICCPR: Freedom of Expression and Advocacy of Religious Hatred That Constitutes Incitement to Discrimination, Hostility or Violence', *Article XIX* (UNHCHR, 2-3/10/2008), 1; similarly, at European level with the ECHR. D Sugarman and M Butler, *A Handbook on European Discrimination Law* (European

Everyone has the right to freedom of opinion and expression; this right includes freedom to hold opinions without interference and to seek, receive and impart information and ideas through any media and regardless of frontiers.

The right is repeated and clarified in article 19(2) of the International Covenant on Civil and Political Rights ('ICCPR') which reads:

Everyone shall have the right to freedom of expression; this right shall include freedom to seek, receive and impart information and ideas of all kinds, regardless of frontiers, either orally, in writing or in print, in the form of art, or through any other media of his choice.

As these formulations indicate, the right to free expression is broad in scope. Not only is the right extended to every individual,[28] but its application is unrestricted as to the protected forms of expression. Consequently, it encompasses political, artistic,[29] and commercial[30] expressions disseminated through any media. The content of such expressions is equally unrestricted, such that the freedom potentially applies to all expressions including those which offend, shock, or disturb. Yet, in particular circumstances, certain types of expressions may be legitimately restricted by national legislation mainly in order to preserve the rights of others.[31]

3.2 European recognition of the right to freedom of expression

In Europe, two instruments are applicable. As Member States of the Council of Europe, the UK and France, being of interest in our study, are bound by the ECHR and its protocols. Article 10(1) ECHR is the most relevant provision for the protection of freedom of expression:

Everyone has the right to freedom of expression. This right shall include freedom to hold opinions and to receive and impart information and ideas without interference by public authority and regardless of frontiers.[32]

Article 10 is similarly worded to its international counterpart,[33] but there is an important distinction. Unlike the influential, but non-binding, UDHR and ICCPR, the

Union Agency for Fundamental Rights, 2011) 12, available at http://eprints.lancs.ac.uk/34017/ (access date: 10 November 2018).

[28] Therefore, there cannot be any distinctions 'of any kind, such as race, colour, sex, language, religion, political or other opinion, national or social origin, property, birth or other status' for the application of this right (article 2 ICCPR).

[29] *Hak-Chul Shin v. Republic of Korea* (926/2000), CCPR/C/80/D/926/2000 (2004); 11 IHRR 928 (2004), [7.2] and [8].

[30] *Ballantyne, Davidson, McIntyre v. Canada* (359/1989 and 385/1989), CCPR/C/47/D/359/1989 (1993); 1-1 IHRR 145 (1994), [11.3]. In this decision, the Committee notes that freedom of expression includes commercial speech though it holds a lower level of protection than political expressions. On the application of article 19 to political expressions see Human Rights Committee, General Comment No 10: Freedom of expression (article 19), 29/06/1983, HRI/GEN/1/Rev. 9 (Vol. I), [181]; 1–2 IHRR 9 (1994), [2]; *Zeljko Bodrožić v. Serbia and Montenegro* (1180/2003), CCPR/C/85/D/1180/2003 (2006); 13 IHRR 389 (2006) (hereafter *Bodrožić*), [7.2]; *Rakhim Mavlonov and Shansiy Sa'di v. Uzbekistan* (1334/2004), CCPR/C/95/D/1134/2004 (2009); 16 IHRR 650 (2009). This includes commercial advertising, Human Rights Committee, General Comment, General Comment No 34: Freedom of expression (article 19), 12 September 2011; CCPR/C/GC/34, [11]; E Barendt, 'Copyright and free speech theory' in J Griffiths and U Suthersanen (eds), *Copyright and Free Speech* (OUP, 2005) 25.

[31] See Section 4.1.5 and Chapter 7, section 3.

[32] The article further indicates that it does not prevent states from requiring broadcasting, television, or cinema enterprises to be licensed.

[33] Being media-neutral, freedom of expression is applicable to all types of communication. Weber (n 26) 20.

provisions of the ECHR may be invoked directly before the national courts of Member States, and the resulting decisions are subject to the review of the European Court of Human Rights ('ECtHR').[34] This provision is, therefore, very powerful because it imposes obligations[35] upon legislators and governments, as well as the judiciary, and even in respect of disputes between private individuals.[36]

Additionally, the European Union reaffirms the protection of fundamental freedoms through the Charter.[37] Article 11(1) of the Charter repeats the provision of Article 10(1) ECHR to preserve freedom of expression.

Although it is possible for the European Union to accede to the ECHR,[38] this step has not yet been taken.[39] The provisions of the Charter are almost identical to the ECHR, and the CJEU often relies on the application of the ECHR to interpret the provisions of the Charter.[40] Therefore awaiting further jurisprudence interpreting the Charter, the following sections will refer to the ECHR when analysing European jurisdictions.

4. Restrictions to Freedom of Expression to Respect the Rights of Others

As mentioned earlier, the right of freedom of expression is broad but not absolute. As certain restrictions have already been established at supra-national level, these will be reviewed next, as they will inform the legitimate limits of the parody exception at national level.

Under the supra-national human rights framework, any restriction to the exercise of the right of freedom of expression must satisfy a three-pronged test.[41] Applying

[34] Amongst others: *Karataş v. Turkey,* (1999) IHRL 2880 (hereafter *Karataş*); *Ceylan v. Turkey,* (2000) 30 EHRR 73 (hereafter *Ceylan*), [32]; repeated in *Ashby Donald and others v. France,* App No 36769/08 (hereafter *Ashby*), [38]. D Voorhoof, 'Is freedom of expression a legitimate argument for disrespecting copyright? The parody as a metaphor' (2000) 14, available at http://www.psw.ugent.be/Cms_global/uploads/publicaties/dv/05recente_publicaties/FOXandParody.actualised.sept2006.CPH.pdf (access date: 10 November 2018).

[35] *The Sunday Times v. The United Kingdom (No 1)* (1979) 2 EHRR 245 (hereafter *Sunday Times*) but also in *Handyside* (n 23).

[36] *Özgür Gündem v. Turkey* (2001) 31 EHRR 49, [43]; *Khurshid Mustafa and Tarzibachi v. Sweden,* App No 23883/06, [33].

[37] As stated by the Preamble of the Charter, the Charter aims to reaffirm rights resulting from international and constitutional traditions within the EU territory. For an analysis of the increasing reference to the Charter by the CJEU in copyright cases, see Griffiths (n 12).

[38] This possibility was provided by Protocol No 14 of the ECHR which entered into force on 1 June 2010. The EU Lisbon Treaty of 2009 enables the EU's accession to the ECHR.

[39] Accession is currently at a standstill following a negative opinion delivered by the CJEU in Opinion C-2/13 of the full Court, 18 December 2014, ECLI:EU:C:2014:2454.

[40] Articles 52(3) and 53 of the Charter provide that the meaning and scope of the right to freedom of expression are identical to those under the ECHR. EU Network of Independent Experts on Fundamental Rights, 'Commentary of the Charter of Fundamental Rights of the European Union' (June 2006) available at http://ec.europa.eu/justice/fundamental-rights/files/networkcommentaryfinal_en.pdf (access date: 10 November 2018); also the approach in Advocate General's Opinion in *Deckmyn* [2014] ECLI:EU:C:2014:458, [80].

[41] Article 19(3) ICCPR provides: 'The exercise of the rights provided for in paragraph 2 of this article carries with it special duties and responsibilities. It may therefore be subject to certain restrictions, but these shall only be such as are provided by law and are necessary: (a) for respect of the rights or reputation of others; (b) for the protection of national security or of public order (*ordre public*), or of public health or morals. This provision must be read alongside article 20 ICCPR prohibiting '[a]ny advocacy of national, racial or religious hatred that constitutes incitement to discrimination, hostility or violence shall be prohibited by law'. The combination of these two provisions enables the

this test, a restriction must be provided by law (principle of predictability), pursue a particular aim (principle of legitimacy), and be necessary (principles of necessity and proportionality).[42] The latter is interpreted as requiring the interference to be 'necessary in a democratic society'.[43]

Analysis of the decisions handed down by both the Human Rights Committee (the independent body monitoring the respect of the ICCPR) and the ECtHR reveals that a generally rigorous approach is adopted to ensure that freedom of expression is realized. While the approach adopted interprets restrictions strictly,[44] this does not mean that restrictions are impossible. The Special Rapporteur notes, [45] for example, that a restriction is desirable when permitting free expression would seriously encroach upon the fundamental rights of others, as might be the case for hate speech[46] or other discriminatory messages.[47] Yet, while restricting the expression of hatred or discrimination, care is required to preserve freedom of expression where possible and to avoid censorship.[48] Indeed, as expressions which might (merely) offend, shock, or disturb[49]

prohibition of any kind of discrimination. Under the ECHR, this three-pronged test is provided in article 10(2).

[42] Hence, national authorities must demonstrate that the restriction is 'relevant and sufficient'; see ECtHR, *Leroy v. France*, App No 36109/03 (hereafter *Leroy*), [46]; *Handyside* (n 23) [50]; *Sunday Times* (n 35) [62]; *Jersild v. Denmark* (1994) 19 EHRR 1 (hereafter *Jersild*), [31].

[43] This echoes the language of article 10(2) ECHR: *Bodrožić* (n 30) [7.2]; *Malcolm Ross v. Canada*, Communication No 736/1997, U.N. Doc. CCPR/C/70/D/736/1997 (2000), [11.6]; *Tae-Hoon Park v. Republic of Korea*, Communication No 628/1995, U.N. Doc. CCPR/C/64/D/628/1995 (3 November 1998), [10.3]; M O'Flaherty, 'Freedom of expression: article 19 of the International Covenant on Civil and Political Rights and the Human Rights Committee's General Comment No 34' (2012) 12 *EHRLR* 2, 13; A Callamard (Article 19 Executive Director), Expert Meeting on the Links Between Articles 19 and 20 of the ICCPR: Freedom of Expression and Advocacy of Religious Hatred that Constitutes Incitement to Discrimination, Hostility or Violence (UNHCHR, 2–3 October 2008, Geneva) 11, available at http://www.article19.org/pdfs/conferences/iccpr-links-between-articles-19-and-20.pdf (access date: 24 October 2015); ARTICLE 19 Submission to ICJ Panel of Eminent Jurists on Terrorism, Counter-Terrorism and Human Rights—ARTICLE 19, London, 2006—Index Number: LAW/2006/0424, p. 2.

[44] O'Flaherty (n 43) 2–28; ECtHR: amongst others *Peta Deutschland v. Germany*, App No 43481/09 (hereafter *Peta*), [46].

[45] Special Rapporteur on the promotion and protection of the right to freedom of opinion and expression, A/HRC/14/23 (20 April 2010), [79].

[46] Article 20 ICCPR; article 4(a) of the CERD.

[47] Article 14 ECHR; 'Any restriction or limitation must be consistent with other rights recognized in the Covenant and in other international human rights instruments, as well as with the fundamental principles of universality, interdependence, equality and non-discrimination as to race, colour, sex, language, religion, political or other belief, national or social origin, property, birth or any other status.. Special Rapporteur on the promotion and protection of the right to freedom of opinion and expression, A/HRC/14/23 (20 April 2010), [79].

[48] UN Secretary-General: 'In case of freedom of expression ... there are zones in which it is both very difficult and very dangerous to draw the line between legitimate and illegitimate exercise of liberty', cited by Partsch 1992, p. 26.

[49] *Sunday Times* (n 35) repeated in *Ashby* (n 34) [31]; *Peta* (n 44) [46]; *Aguilera Jeminez v. Spain*, App Nos 28389/06, 28955/06, 28957/06, 28959/06, 28961/06, 28964/06, 8 December 2009 (hereafter *Jeminez*), [22]; *Vereinigung Bildender Künstler v. Austria*, App No 68354/01 (hereafter *Vereinigung*), [26]; *Raichinov v. Bulgaria*, App No 47579/99, [47]; *Pedersen and Baadsgaard v. Denmark (No 2)* (2006) 42 EHRR 486, [79]; *Özgür Gündem v. Turkey*, [43]; *Castells v. Spain* (1992) 14 EHRR 445 (hereafter *Castells*), [42]; *Oberschlick v. Austria* (1995) 19 EHRR 389 (hereafter *Oberschlick*), [57]; *Handyside* (n 23) [49]; D Voorhoof, 'Freedom of expression under the human rights system from Sunday Times (n 1) v. U.K. (1979) to Hachette Filipacchi Associés ('ici Paris') v. France (2009)' (2009) 2 *Inter-Am. & Eur. Hum. Rts. J.* 3, 10; A Strowel and F Tulkens, 'Equilibrer la liberté d'expression et le droit d'auteur' in A Strowel and F Tulkens (eds), *Droit d'auteur et liberté d'expression: regards francophones, d'Europe et d'ailleurs* (Larcier, 2006) 12.

are considered to be an integral aspect of pluralism—a democratic society is required to demonstrate tolerance and broadmindedness.[50]

The final requirement of necessity 'in a democratic society' has been the focus of most attention and discussions.[51] It grants a certain margin of appreciation to national authorities to balance the interests at stake. Whilst it is reasonable to respect national values and sensitivities, this also represents a barrier in practice to the harmonization of copyright exception and uniform application between jurisdictions.

In point of fact, the ECHR affords Member States discretion to appreciate on a case-by-case analysis that the restriction satisfies the test. National courts are thus entitled to render a parody unlawful where the restriction is deemed necessary in a democratic society. Yet, as is explained in the following sections, the ECtHR does not confer the *same* margin of appreciation upon national authorities. In determining whether the restriction is necessary in a democratic society, this margin varies depending on diverse factors as examined in what follows.[52] The study of the application of these factors by the ECtHR provides the groundwork for understanding how courts should apply the parody exception in ambiguous cases where the lawfulness parody is *not so clear-cut.*

4.1 Relevant factors under the ECHR

A thorough study of the ECtHR's jurisprudence on the margin of appreciation not only goes beyond the scope of this book, but has already been undertaken by others.[53] Yet, it can be distilled from the Court's decisions that a restriction will be deemed necessary in a democratic society if it addresses a 'pressing social need'.[54] Social need itself turns upon several factors, including the nature, form, attitude, context, and content of the expression. We shall briefly review each of these in turn.

4.1.1 Nature of the expression

Generally, the ECHR protects all expressions, but ECtHR decisions indicate that some expressions (those which are political,[55] of public interest,[56] or artistic[57]) are more

[50] *Verein Gegen Tierfabriken Schweiz v. Switzerland (No 2),* App No 32772/02 (hereafter *Tierfabriken*), [107]; *Handyside* (n 23) [49]; *Observer & Guardian v. UK* (1991) 14 EHRR 229, [50]; *The Sunday Times v. The United Kingdom (No 2)* (1992) 14 EHRR 229, [40–[41], 64]; *Lingens v. Austria* (1986) 8 EHRR 407 (hereafter *Lingens*), [41]; *Oberschlick* (n 49) [57]; *Castells* (n 49) [42]; *Jersild* (n 42) [23]–[24]; *Jeminez* (n 49) [22]; *Vereinigung* (n 49) [26]; *Karataş* (n 34) [48]; *Ceylan* (n 34) [32]; A Mowbray, *Cases, Materials, and Commentary on the European Convention on Human Rights* (3rd edn, OUP, 2012) 637.

[51] *Handyside* (n 23) [45], repeated in *Sunday Times* (n 35) [59]–[66], *Lingens* (n 50) [47].

[52] As demonstrated, the national margin of appreciation is rather limited when dealing with political expressions or public matters and wider in relation to artistic or commercial expressions. *Ashby* (n 34); *Peta* (n 44) [46]; P B Hugenholtz, 'Copyright and freedom of expression in Europe' in Dreyfuss, First, and Zimmerman (eds), *Innovation Policy* 350.

[53] Mowbray (n 50); A Nicol QC, G Millar QC, and A Sharland, *Media Law & Human Rights* (2nd edn, OUP, 2009).

[54] Mowbray (n 50) 632; Voorhoof (n 49) 14.

[55] *Lingens* (n 50) [41]–[43]; *Oberschlick* (n 49) [57]–[61]; *Baka v. Hungary*, App No 20261/12 (hereafter *Baka*), [159]; *Satakunnan Markkinapörssi Oy and Satamedia Oy*, App No 931/13 (hereafter *Satamedia*), [167].

[56] *Sunday Times* (n 35) [65]; *Barfod v. Denmark,* App No 11508/85, [29]–[32]; *Baka* (n 55) [159]; *Satamedia* (n 55) [167]; *Thorgeir Thorgeirson v. Iceland* (1992) 14 EHRR 843, [63].

[57] *Alinak v. Turkey*, App No 40287/98, [41]–[42]; *Karataş* (n 34) [49]; *Müller and Others v. Switzerland*, App No 10737/84, [27].

deserving of protection than others (for example, purely commercial expressions[58]) because of their particular discursive role in a democratic society.[59] Over time, the ECtHR has been consistent in emphasizing that the need to preserve freedom of political expression and freedom of information arises from the great importance of political debate.[60] Hence, criticism of politicians[61] is generally justified because the nature of their occupation opens up their personal actions to closer scrutiny. The Court has extended the same approach to other public figures, including members of parliament, government, the judiciary, and other authorities. By accepting a public role, a person knowingly exposes themselves to public scrutiny, meaning public figures must show more tolerance than individuals who are not well-known. [62] Thus, expressions which criticize public figures, for example, should be given greater latitude than those targeting private individuals.[63]

Yet, the characteristic of many expressions (including parodies) is such that they blend artistic, political, and commercial expressions, meaning that they simultaneously span several categories. For example, in *Karataş v. Turkey*,[64] the Court considered a poem, authored by a Turkish citizen, which was directly critical of the Turkish authorities.[65] The Turkish government sought to censure its publication, characterizing the work as illegitimate propaganda which threatened the 'unity of the State'. Here, the nature of the individual's expression was deemed particularly pertinent, being both artistic and political. The Court acknowledged that the poem's message might incite hatred and violence (which is not permitted pursuant to the ECHR), but equally, the author's choice of medium—poetry—limited its reach to a minority of people.[66] Thus, a call to arms presented in this form would have far less impact than a political statement made in the mass media.[67] In addition, given the political character of the poem, the Turkish authorities enjoyed only a narrow margin of appreciation to limit freedom of expression,[68] leading the Court to conclude that by preventing publication of the poem, the Turkish government had violated article 10 ECHR.[69]

In contrast, where the nature of an expression is purely commercial, national authorities are afforded a wider margin of appreciation to restrict freedom of expression.[70] For example, the ECtHR reviewed an Austrian decision which sought to restrain publication of a newspaper advertisement[71] comparing one journal's subscription rates

[58] *Ashby* (n 34) [39]; *Markt Intern Verlag GmbH and Klaus Beermann v. Germany* (1990) 12 EHRR 161, [33]; *Hertel v. Switzerland*, App No 25181/94, [47]; *Mouvement Raëlien Suisse v. Switzerland* (2013) 56 EHRR 14, [61].

[59] Confirmed recently in *Sekmadienis v. Lithuania*, App No 69317/14 (hereafter *Sekmadienis*).

[60] Also in *Ceylan* (n 34) [33] (similar approach for public figures as for politicians).

[61] Mouffe (n 19) 47; Voorhoof (n 49) 19; *Vereinigung* (n 49) [34]; *Alves Da Silva v. Portugal*, App No 41665/07 (hereafter *Da Silva*), [28]; *Ukrainian Media Group v. Ukraine*, App No 72713/01, [65]–[70]; *Handyside* (n 23) [48]–[50]; *Lingens* (n 50) [42]; *Oberschlick* (n 49) [58]–[59]; *Castells* (n 49) [43].

[62] Voorhoof (n 49) 20.

[63] *Handyside* (n 23) [48]–[50]; *Lingens* (n 50) [42] where the Court dealt with the revision of an interference with one's freedom of expression because of defamation through the criticism of a politician during an interview. The Court said that the limits of criticism are wider for politicians as their position inherently implies close public scrutiny; *Oberschlick* (n 49) [58]–[59]; *Castells* (n 49) [42]–[46] where the Court operates an internal ranking between different types of political expression.

[64] *Karataş* (n 34). [65] Ibid, [49].

[66] It must be remembered that the right to freedom of expression not only protects the content but also the form of the expression. *De Haes and Gijsels v. Belgium* (1998) 25 EHRR 1, [48].

[67] *Karataş* (n 34) [52]; *Jersild* (n 42) [31].

[68] *Wingrove v. the United Kingdom* (1996) 24 EHRR (hereafter *Wingrove*), [58].

[69] Ibid, [54].

[70] *Krone Verlag GmbH & Co KG (No 3) v. Austria* (2003) 36 EHRR 57, [30]. [71] Ibid.

with those of a competitor. The Austrian authority had held that even though the advert contained accurate information, interference with this commercial expression was necessary to protect more generally against unfair competition via misleading advertising.[72] After undertaking its own balancing of the interests at stake, the Court disagreed, finding that the Austrian measure violated article 10 ECHR because it was a disproportionate sanction for the objective sought.

4.1.2 Form of the expression

The form of the expression also impacts the margin of appreciation granted to national authorities. Although the Court has yet to consider a case involving parody, the ECtHR has considered criticism made utilizing humour.[73]

Apocolypse,[74] for example, concerned display of the eponymous artwork at a contemporary art exhibition. 'Apocolypse' depicted numerous figures engaging in sexual acts.[75] Although the bodies in the picture were hand-drawn by the artist, the face of each figure was made from a cropped photo of a different Austrian politician or public figure. Overturning the Austrian courts' ban on the exhibition of the artwork, the ECtHR held that this was an illegitimate interference with the artist's freedom of expression. The Court noted that the eyes in the photos used had been blocked out, and the bodies depicted in an unrealistic and exaggerated manner. This made it clear that the work was one of satire, and not an attempt to depict reality, and so it should have been interpreted as such by the national courts.[76]

The ECtHR described satire as 'a form of artistic expression and social commentary and, by its inherent features of exaggeration and distortion of reality, naturally aims to provoke and agitate'.[77] Having regard to its function, the Court cautioned that national institutions must take particular care when restricting this form of expression. By permitting satires[78] to prevail over the private interests of others, the ECtHR shows a determination to grant greater protection to humorous expression compared to non-humorous forms.

4.1.3 Attitude of the speaker

The ECtHR identifies the attitude of the individual exercising their freedom of expression as a relevant consideration.[79] In *Oberschlik v. Austria (No 2)*,[80] a journalist was sued for defamation as a result of an article in which he was critical of the leader of a far-right party, labelling the politician an 'idiot' based upon a speech the leader had given. The Court held that personal attacks might be protected as a legitimate expression, provided that the speaker could provide an objectively reasonable explanation for the criticism.[81]

[72] Ibid, [31].

[73] *Leroy* (n 42); *Jeminez* (n 49); *Da Silva* (n 61); *Nikowitz and Verlagsgruppe News GmbH v. Austria*, [2007] EMLR 245; Mouffe (n 19) 173.

[74] *Vereinigung* (n 49). This case was not dealt with under copyright law but instead defamation law.

[75] Damaged by a visitor who threw red paint over the painting.

[76] *Vereinigung* (n 49) [33].

[77] Ibid, [33]; repeated in *Da Silva* (n 61) [27].

[78] As argued in Chapter 1, parody is a multivalent concept which encompasses multiple uses including satire.

[79] For example, good faith is interpreted in favour of the defendant. *Lingens* (n 50) [46].

[80] *Oberschlick* (n 49).

[81] Ibid, [33].

It would seem that the same consideration should be applied in the case of a parody, because it appropriately reflects the humoristic intent requirement for the application of the parody exception.[82] As argued in Chapter 4,[83] humoristic intent which has the aim of harming authors and/or their works, or where the parodist acts in bad faith to plagiarize the protected materials should not be covered by the exception. The Court's approach demonstrates that it is legitimate for an individual to make value judgements when expressing their opinion, and as such the statement made does not have to be objectively *true* to be protected speech. The same reasoning appears to be directly transferrable to parodies. As a manifestation of criticism, parodies may be accurate and true, but equally they may be neither.[84] Overall, if a parody meets the requirements of the parody exception under copyright law, this should be indicative that a parodist has not exceeded his right to freedom of expression.

4.1.4 Context in which the expression is made

The ECtHR has had cause to examine the significance that the context of an expression may have on several occasions.

The ECtHR considered the interplay between freedom of expression and governmental measures aimed at fighting discrimination in *Jersild*.[85] The case relates to a documentary made for a Danish current affairs television programme. The documentary interviewed a particular group of young people who had been identified as racist in the Danish press. In the course of filming, the interviewees made various abusive and derogatory remarks directed at immigrants and the ethnic groups present in Denmark. In light of these offensive comments, the Danish authorities sought to prevent the programme from being aired, which the film's producer argued violated his right to freedom of expression under article 10 ECHR. The Court affirmed 'the vital importance of combating racial discrimination in all its forms and manifestations',[86] since inter-racial tolerance and respect is fundamental in any democratic, pluralistic society. Therefore, the offensive statements made by the group during the interview did not warrant the protection of article 10 ECHR. However, the article 10 rights of the producer had been breached because of the important role of the press as a 'public watchdog'[87] to discuss matters of public interest.[88] Given that the interview was preceded in the final documentary by a public discussion of racism in Denmark, the context made clear that the producer's intent was to challenge, rather than to promote or proliferate, the racist views of the interviewees.[89]

The Court relied upon *Jersild* and confirmed the importance of context in *Soulas and Others v. France*.[90] These proceedings concerned an attempt to block publication of a book exploring the integration of Islamic immigrants into European society. The ECtHR was required to determine whether this interference by the French court was in violation of the publisher's and author's right to freedom of expression. Although the Court acknowledged that the book's subject matter constituted a topic of legitimate debate in Europe,[91] the Court concluded that this particular expression should not be

[82] Such as in C-201/13 *Johan Deckmyn and Vrijheidsfonds VZW v. Helena Vandersteen and Others* [2014] ECLI:EU:C:2014:2132 (hereafter *Deckmyn*).

[83] See Chapter 4, section 2.1.

[84] Parodies do express some kind of truth although the parody does not have to accurately reflect reality. Edelman, note under Cass., 12 juillet 2000, D., 2001, 260.

[85] *Jersild* (n 42) (expression of unlawful racist views). [86] Ibid, [30].

[87] Ibid, [31]. [88] Ibid, [35]. [89] Ibid, [33]. [90] Ibid. [91] Ibid, [11].

permitted under the Convention,[92] because it sought to encourage readers to reject immigrants, a message which undermined the ideals of a pluralistic society.[93]

These principles were further honed in *Leroy v. France*.[94] Here, the Court was required to adjudicate over a cartoon which focused on the 9/11 attacks on the World Trade Center. The cartoon featured the phrase 'We have all dreamt of it ... Hamas did it'—being a parody of Sony's slogan: 'We have all dreamt of it ... Sony did it'. The cartoonist argued that the cartoon was a legitimate political expression which aimed, through satire, to comment upon the decline of American imperialism. The ECtHR considered otherwise. Although the image related to an event which *was* a matter of public interest, the cartoon itself went beyond that necessary for legitimate criticism. Given the sensitivity surrounding the subject matter used as the vehicle for comment, the cartoon would be construed as indicating the cartoonist's support for the terrorist attacks, and could provoke a public reaction which could lead to new acts of violence. Consequently, the national court's interference to prevent publication was 'relevant and sufficient' to the legitimate aim of maintaining public order.

Most recently, in *Sekmadienis v. Lithuania*,[95] the ECtHR took the opportunity to explain that an expression which cannot be restricted based solely upon its content *could* be restrained for having an offensive impact in specific circumstances. In the case at hand, a clothing company was fined because of the use of religious references to promote its products in, arguably, a humoristic way. The adverts featured halo-ed models wearing the company's clothing, alongside captions such as 'Jesus, what trousers!' and 'Dear Mary, what a dress!'. The Court emphasized the national court's duty to ensure that there are sufficient reasons to limit the protected freedom of commercial expression.[96] Here, the ECtHR established that a restriction was not justified simply because the religious symbols had been used for a non-religious purpose.[97]

Context is, therefore, extremely important when it comes to assessing a parody. Parody, as we have seen, introduces a distance from the original work.[98] Humour (understood liberally) creates a separation between the reality of the original and the 'other' world in which parody expressions evolve. This distance may vest in the parody itself, but it may also arise from the context in which a parody expression is made.

4.1.5 Content of the expression

A parody is required to have humorous intent to benefit from the parody exception.[99] Furthermore, if the parody's message is of relevance to the public interest, then it should receive greater protection based on the additional support of article 10 ECHR.[100] The converse is also true. In this part we examine how far a parodist is permitted to go. A careful examination is needed to determine the distinction between an expression which may (only) 'offend, shock or disturb'[101] and one which falls outside the protection of article 10 ECHR, because it amounts to a serious incitement to extremism ('hate speech') or discrimination (article 14 ECHR).[102] A parody which crosses this line

[92] Referring to article 20 ICCPR (prohibition of discrimination) alongside article 4 CERD.

[93] Repeated in *Le Pen v. France*, App No 18788/09.

[94] *Leroy* (n 42).

[95] *Sekmadienis* (n 59).

[96] Citing *Tierfabriken* (n 50) [75]–[76].

[97] *Sekmadienis* (n 59) [79] as previously decided in *Giniewski v. France*, App No 64016/00 (hereafter *Giniewski*), [52]–[53] and *Terentyev v. Russia*, App No 25147/09, [22].

[98] See Chapter 1 section 2.

[99] See Chapter 4, section 2.1.

[100] *Ashby* (n 34) [39].

[101] *Handyside* (n 23) [49].

[102] Declaration of the Committee of Ministers on freedom of political debate in the media, adopted on 12 February 2004; Voorhoof (n 49) 34.

might arguably harm the author of the original work, or diminish the work itself. In this respect, the ECtHR has provided some helpful guidance.

4.1.5.1 Racially and ethnically discriminatory messages

Although the ECtHR approach makes it difficult to draw a clear line between the expressions which warrant protection pursuant to article 10 ECHR and those which violate the right to freedom of expression, statements which convey a message likely to incite discrimination or arouse hatred towards certain racial or ethnic groups are unlikely to be protected, because such statements stand in contradiction with the Convention's values of tolerance and pluralism.[103]

For example, in *Féret v. Belgium*,[104] the ECtHR considered that criminal sanctions imposed on the leader of a far-right political party were legitimate. The party had been distributing leaflets during an election campaign which included statements such as: 'Stand up against the Islamification of Belgium', 'Stop the sham integration policy', and 'Send non-European job-seekers home'. The ECtHR held these statements were an incitement to racial discrimination, meaning that sanctions did not violate the leader's right to freedom of expression.[105]

4.1.5.2 Offending personal religious convictions

Where personal religious beliefs are involved, national authorities benefit from a wider margin of appreciation. In *Wingrove v. UK*,[106] the ECtHR explained:

> [A]s in the field of morals, and perhaps to an even greater degree, there is no uniform European conception of the requirements of 'the protection of the rights of others' in relation to attacks on their religious convictions. What is likely to cause substantial offence to persons of a particular religious persuasion will vary significantly from time to time and from place to place, especially in an era characterised by an ever growing array of faiths and denominations. By reason of their direct and continuous contact with the vital forces of their countries, State authorities are in principle in a better position than the international judge to give an opinion on the exact content of these requirements with regard to the rights of others as well as on the 'necessity' of a 'restriction' intended to protect from such material those whose deepest feelings and convictions would be seriously offended. This does not of course exclude final European supervision. Such supervision is all the more necessary given the breadth and open-endedness of the notion of blasphemy and the risks of arbitrary or excessive interferences with freedom of expression under the guise of action taken against allegedly blasphemous material.

Whilst blasphemy laws have been abolished in all the jurisdictions under scrutiny, this case provides some guiding principles which might justify restricting a parodist's expression if it attacks another's religious beliefs. Therefore, with the wider margin of appreciation granted, the ECtHR recognizes the importance of respecting an individual's expectation to peacefully enjoy the rights guaranteed under article 9 ECHR, including a corresponding duty to avoid causing gratuitous offence to others by use of profanity.[107]

This might arise if the content of the expression directly targets those of a specific faith—for example by insulting use of religious symbols, if the message jeopardizes the right of individuals to express their faith, denigrates a religion, or incites hatred or violence towards those holding a particular belief.

[103] Voorhoof (n 49) 36. [104] *Féret v. Belgium*, App No 15615/07, [78].
[105] This could have been influential in *Deckmyn* (n 82). See Chapter 7, section 2.
[106] See n 68, [58]. [107] *Sekmadienis* (n 59) [74].

A good case in point concerned a poster produced by Norwood, a member of the far-right British National Party ('BNP') in the wake of the 9/11 attacks. This depicted the Twin Towers in flames alongside the Islamic crescent and star symbol represented as a prohibition sign, accompanied by the statement: 'Islam out of Britain—Protect the British People'.[108] Norwood argued his display of the poster was a permissible criticism of Islam, rather than representing an intention to attack those who followed Islamic beliefs, or an incitement for others to do so. The ECtHR disagreed. It considered the poster was a clear attack on Muslims living in the UK because it associated them all with the terrorist attacks.[109] Thus, displaying the poster constituted a prohibited act (pursuant to article 17 ECHR—abusive exercise of rights) meaning the applicant did not enjoy the protection of article 10 ECHR.[110]

Similarly in *I.A. v. Turkey*,[111] the ECtHR had to determine whether state interference with an author's statement that 'God Muhammed' did not condemn necrophilia or bestiality[112] was a legitimate restriction necessary in a democratic society. In this case, the Court determined the expression to be an abusive attack of the Prophet which did justify the Turkish court's interference.[113]

Although article 9 ECHR recognizes the right to freedom of religion, the ECtHR does not consider that this shields those individuals who exercise this freedom from all criticism.[114] Criticism should be permitted to a reasonable extent to allow others to exercise their own right to free expression. Legitimate criticism may take the form of denial, or dissemination of material which is hostile to a particular faith.[115]

4.1.5.3 Message contrary to morality

The ECtHR has also held that concerns of morality may provide justification to override an individual's right to freedom of expression.

In *Muller v. Switzerland*, [116] the Court refrained from revising a national decision to restrict the freedom of expression of the artist of a painting depicting 'vulgar images of sodomy, fellatio between males, bestiality, erect penises and masturbation'[117] based upon obscenity grounds. The Court, while recognizing art's vital role in a democratic society to promote cultural diversity,[118] confirmed that this did not preclude the public

[108] *Norwood v. UK* (2004) 40 EHRR SE 111. Repeated in *Pavel Ivanov v. Russia*, App No 35222/04 (hereafter *Ivanov*). The application was consequently declared inadmissible by the Court because it was incompatible *ratione materiae* with the provisions of the Convention.

[109] '[S]uch a general, vehement attack against a religious group, linking the group as a whole with a grave act of terrorism, is incompatible with the values proclaimed and guaranteed by the Convention, notably tolerance, social peace and non-discrimination', *Ivanov* (n 108) [53]. Non-discrimination is also protected through article 14 ECHR and Protocol no 12 to the ECHR.

[110] The Court also supported its reasoning under the admissibility criteria of article 35(3) and (4) ECHR.

[111] *I.A. v. Turkey*, App No 42571/98 (hereafter *I.A. v. Turkey*).

[112] Ibid, [29].

[113] Ibid, [30]; *Otto-Preminger-Institut v. Austria* (1994) 19 EHRR 34 (hereafter *Otto-Preminger-Institut*), [47]; recently repeated in *Sekmadienis* (n 59) [81].

[114] Weber (n 26) 49.

[115] Cases where the court decided against a violation of article 10: *Otto-Preminger-Institut* (n 113) [47]; *Wingrove* (n 68) [60]; *I.A. v. Turkey* (n 111) [29]; *Murphy v. Ireland* (2004) 38 EHRR 212 (hereafter *Murphy*), [82]; *contra: Giniewski* (n 97) [51]–[52]; *Aydın Tatlav v. Turkey*, App No 50692/99, [28]; *Klein v. Slovakia*, App No 72208/01, [52]; *Nur Radyo Ve Televizyon Yayıncılığı A.Ş. v. Turkey*, App No 6587/03, [30]; *Sekmadienis* (n 59) [84], *Giniewski v. France*, App No 64016/00, [56].

[116] *Müller and Others v. Switzerland*, App No 10737/84 (hereafter *Müller*).

[117] The words of the Cantonal Court in *Müller* (n 116) [14].

[118] Ibid, [33].

display of specific artistic expressions in cases of abuse.[119] In issues involving morality, national authorities benefit from a wider margin of appreciation because a uniform European conception of morality just does not exist.[120] In this case, the ECtHR found no reason to interfere with the Swiss court's findings, since they were best placed to determine whether the images depicted would offend 'the sense of sexual propriety of persons of ordinary sensitivity' in that Member State.[121] Therefore, the artist's right to free expression should not prevail.[122]

The Court reached similar conclusions regarding religious morals. In *Otto Preminger Institute v. Austria*, the conviction of a writer for blasphemy following the screening of his film was the subject of debate. Here, the Court noted that uniformity of religious morals might not exist even within a single country.[123] This afforded national authorities a wide margin of appreciation for deciding whether freedom of expression might be justifiably curtailed on religious morality grounds. Thus, the Austrian court's interference to prevent the film from being shown was a legitimate violation of the right to freedom of expression to protect the religious sensibilities of the local Catholic community,[124] even though the film was only accessible to paying viewers aged eighteen years and over.

Since there is no uniform European conception of 'morality', the ECtHR grants a wider margin of appreciation to national courts when dealing with works which are alleged to be obscene or blasphemous.[125]

4.1.5.4 Denialism

In the final scenario which we shall consider, the ECtHR has also identified that it may be appropriate to curtail expressions which seek to deny certain significant historical events. In *Lehideux*,[126] the Court considered a French newspaper's publication of pro-Nazi statements contained in a eulogy of Marshal Pétain. The ECtHR acknowledged that the act of praising a prominent Nazi collaborator went against the values underlying the Convention, and that pro-Nazi statements enjoyed no protection pursuant to the right to freedom of expression.[127] Thus, the Court was satisfied that the criminal conviction of the article's authors met the first two requirements of article 10(2) ECHR. Ultimately, the ECtHR held that the French court's interference was in violation of article 10 ECHR, nevertheless. This was based upon the fact that while reporting the pro-Nazi statements, the paper had stated expressly its disapproval of 'Nazi atrocities and persecutions'.[128] This satisfied the Court that the article's aim was to engender debate concerning the country's history, thereby promoting the broadminded, pluralist values essential in a democratic society. Thus, in this case, interference was not necessary, even though the publication might offend, shock, or disturb the newspaper's readers.[129]

119 Ibid, [34].
120 Ibid, [35]. 121 Ibid, [36]. 122 Ibid, [37]. 123 Ibid, [50].
124 Ibid, [56].
125 *Handyside* (n 23) [48]; *Müller* (n 116) [35]; *Otto-Preminger-Institut* (n 113) [50].
126 *Lehideux and Isorni v. France*, App No 24662/94 (hereafter *Lehideux*), [53–[58] repeated in *Garaudy v. France*, App No 65831/01.
127 This reinforces the teachings of *Jersild* (n 42) [35] by noting which expressions fall outside the scope of protection of article 10 ECHR.
128 *Lehideux* (n 126) [53]. 129 Ibid, [55].

4.2 Lessons from ECtHR jurisprudence

As is apparent from the preceding snapshot of ECtHR jurisprudence, the balancing exercise which national courts are required to undertake is far from straightforward. Although courts must interpret an individual's right to free expression broadly,[130] this right should not be preserved to such an extent that it extinguishes the competing rights of others. Rather, courts must take the particular facts of the case into consideration to ensure realization of all fundamental rights at stake.

Although the cases identified have not considered parody works, they provide an insight into the type of balancing which would be required. Arguably, where the balance tips in favour of exercise of free expression, then the parody should also enjoy the benefit of the parody exception, whereas those which would be legitimately curtailed as an abuse of the right to freedom of expression[131] should not be covered by the parody exception either. The lessons which national courts can draw from our analysis of key ECtHR decisions are summarized in what follows.

Firstly, courts should determine whether the purpose of the expression is to propagate a discriminatory message (hate speech), or to engender debate.[132] Only in the second scenario is the expression within the scope of article 10 ECHR.

Secondly, courts enjoy a varying margin of appreciation, which is determined by the form and content of the expression. For example, given that article 10 ECHR does not protect hate speech, Member States have only a narrow margin of appreciation for expressions inciting hatred. Similarly, because of the value attributed to truth in a democratic society, little margin of appreciation is granted for political speeches. Greater margin of appreciation is permitted where courts are dealing with messages relating to religion,[133] several reports demonstrating that the current legal framework is adequate to protect religious beliefs, such that freedom of expression should not be further restricted.[134]

Thirdly, the context in which the expression is made is relevant. Although freedom of expression is recognized for all types of expressions, some forms attract greater protection than others. For example, expression made in any form of media is considered as close to sacred by the ECtHR. National authorities also enjoy a broader margin of

[130] Voorhoof (n 49) 10. [131] Weber (n 26) 30–47.

[132] For example, in *Jersild* (n 42), the aim of the journalist was to expose problems of public concern, [33]; in *Lehideux* (n 126), the applicants did not deny or revise what they referred to as 'Nazi atrocities and persecution', [47]; in *Gündüz v. Turkey*, App No 35071/97 the Court held that the programme was made in a way to encourage the debate on a question of public interest, [44].

[133] A wider margin of appreciation for religious matters is justified by the absence of European consensus among the member states. *Wingrove* (n 68) [58]; *Otto-Preminger-Institut* (n 113) [50]; *Murphy* (n 115) [67], [81]–[82]; *TV Vest AS and Rogaland Pensjonistparti v. Norway*, App No 21132/05, [67].

[134] Report adopted by the Commission at its 70th plenary session (16–17 March 2007); Recommendation 1805(2007) on blasphemy, religious insults and 'hate speech' against persons on grounds of their religion, adopted on 29 June 2007 where the Council of Europe Parliamentary Assembly discussed the caricatures of Muhammad published by a Danish newspaper; *Ben El Mahi and Others v. Denmark*, App No 5853/06. The case was held inadmissible by the ECHR; Resolution 1510(2006) on freedom of expression and respect for religious beliefs, adopted on 28 June 2006; General Policy Recommendation No 7 on national legislation to combat racism and racial discrimination (2002). This last Recommendation by the European Commission against racism and intolerance (which was established by the Council of Europe) calls for criminal law provisions combating various racist expressions. Such expressions concern public incitement to violence, hatred, or discrimination; public insults and defamation; or threats against a person or a group of persons on the grounds of their race, colour, language, religion, nationality, or national or ethnic origin. Public expression, with a racist aim, of racist ideology or the public denial, with a racist aim, of crimes of genocide, or crimes against humanity or war crimes should also be penalized by law.

appreciation when dealing with commercial expression, as compared with political or artistic forms of expression.

Finally, while the limits to freedom of expression turn on the particular facts at issue, there is general agreement that expressions which are intentionally racist, glorify human rights violations, or are defamatory[135] are the most prone to restriction.

5. Striking a Balance at Domestic Level: the Importance of Constitutional Influences

However, in order for the factors discussed to be taken into consideration by judges, national authorities should be comfortable to hear arguments based on human rights considerations which is not always the case. The balancing of freedoms involves issues of 'necessity' and 'proportionality' to be taken into account, assessments which are highly fact-sensitive. Added to this is a varying margin of appreciation, based upon national values and sensitivities which vary over time and from place to place. As a result, the outcome of any balancing exercise is uncertain, and the same facts may result in divergent outcomes in different jurisdictions. If this flexibility can be appreciated to tailor restraints to national sensitivities and values, it also infuses uncertainty at national level as a consequence. Additionally, the supranational human rights law only provides an overarching framework for balancing freedom of expression, copyright, and other interests. National legislation and constitutional influences provide additional guidance, adding further levels of complexity.

This section considers the impact which national considerations may have on the outer boundaries of the parody exception at a macro level. As we have already reviewed the European regime, this section commences with a review of France and then the UK. The latter stands in for individual analysis of the Australian and Canadian regimes, in light of their shared influence of the common law tradition.[136] Attention then turns to the US, which is distinguishable from other common law jurisdictions by the significant constitutional influence upon copyright law.

5.1 France: a liberal interpretation of freedom of expression through a bifurcated system

In France, the supra-national human rights framework protecting freedom of expression is supplemented by the constitutional protection of article 11 of the Declaration of the Rights of Man and of the Citizen of 1789. As we have discussed previously, in France, parody is perceived as a continuation of the right to critique,[137] which the historical revolutionaries considered essential.

Additionally, the French legal system has adopted a bifurcated regime to protect freedom of expression based upon the context in which the expression is made. Where an expression (including a parody) is published in the media,[138] any restriction to

[135] Example: insulting the government is not permitted. *Castells* (n 49); *Lindon, Otchakovsky-Laurens and July v. France*, App Nos 21279/02 and 36448/02.

[136] Canada is actually a mixed regime featuring French and English influences.

[137] A Strowel, 'La parodie selon le droit d'auteur et la théorie littéraire' (1991) 26 *RIEJ* 23, 44; M Buteau, *Le droit de critique en matière littéraire, dramatique et artistique* (L. Larose et L. Tenin, 1909).

[138] This term is understood broadly as comprising print press but also magazines, TV, film, theatre, etc.

exercise this freedom of expression needs to be determined by the specific body of law governing the freedom of the press.[139] In these cases, French courts recognize the media's role as the public's watchdog in a democratic society, by applying a higher threshold before their freedom of expression is curtailed. In all other cases, any restriction to the exercise of freedom of expression is governed by the application of other general laws, such as criminal law, civil responsibility, and defamation law. These two regimes are mutually exclusive,[140] meaning that a claimant who is unsuccessful in establishing that there has been a violation of the Freedom of the Press Act cannot seek damages based on tort law, for example,[141] as an alternative cause of action.

Despite this demarcation, courts have on occasions blurred the line between the two regimes, as illustrated in *Scouts v. New Look*.[142] Although this decision does not relate to unauthorized reproduction of a copyright-protected work, it does demonstrate how conventional laws may be overridden by the Freedom of the Press Act in circumstances in which freedom of expression is in conflict with other fundamental rights. An issue of *New Look*, an adult magazine, included risqué photographs of young models wearing Scout uniforms captioned with phrases which parodied well-known scouting expressions. The Scouting Association sought an injunction from the court restraining circulation of the offending magazine. The Court of Appeal's analysis emphasized that freedom of expression could only be restricted in those cases of abuse proscribed by law. As the images complained of appeared in a magazine, the Freedom of the Press Act was determinative, thereby affording wide latitude to the magazine's rights of freedom of expression. Here, the Act limits the scope of tort actions to those situations where the use violates the fundamental rights of the claimant.[143] As no violation of fundamental rights could be established, the court found no reason to prevent publication of the pictures.

The Supreme Court quashed the decision, holding that nothing could be implied in the Freedom of the Press Act which could impose a limitation of tort law. In the court's view, the scope of a tort action, whether brought under the Freedom of the Press Act or under the general law (article 1382 Civil Code) was the same. However, the case was dismissed because fault (one of the three mandatory requirements for a tort action)[144] had not been established. Following the Court's approach, if the aim of the Freedom of the Press Act was to limit the faults giving rise to a tort action, the legislator would

[139] Loi du 29 juillet 1881 sur la liberté de la presse.

[140] Abuses of freedom of expression repressed by the Freedom of the Press Act cannot be pursued under ordinary law: Cass., 1ère Civ., 31 janvier 2008, *F et autres c/ Mme. M.*, n°07.12.643N, Gaz. Pal, recueil novembre–décembre 2008, p. 4165; Cass., 2e Civ., 20 novembre 2003, *Le Goff c/ Guyader—Le Ny*: Juris-data n°2003-021061; JCP n°3, 14 janvier 2004, somm., IV 1 064-1 072, p. 96; Cass, 2e Civ., 8 mars 2001, *Alliance générale contre le racisme et pour le respect de l'identité française et chrétienne c/ Godefroid*, n°98-17.574.

[141] Amongst others: Cass. (2e ch. Civ.), 8 mars 2001, Bull. Civ., II, nos 46–7; JCP, 2001, IV, nos 1799–1800; Cass. (ass. plén.), 12 juillet 2000, D., 2000, IR, p. 218; 2001, jurispr., p. 259, obs. Edelman; JCP, 2000, jurispr., II, n°10439; Bull., 2000, n°7, p. 10; Sem. Jur., 13 décembre 2000, p. 10, obs. Lepage.

[142] Cass., 2e Civ., 5 mai 1993, *Association Scouts unitaires de France c/ SA Editions des Savanes*, Recueil Dalloz Sirey, 1994, 25e cahier, sommaires commentés, pp. 193–4, obs. Massis. Cass., 19 novembre 1990 (1ère ch. A) légipresse, n°79, p. 16; D. 1991 IR 9.

[143] Based upon the principle *lex specialis derogat lex generalis.*

[144] Article 1382 French Civil Code: 'Any act of a person which causes damage to another makes him by whose fault the damage occurred liable to make reparation for the damage.' The success of this tort action relies on the ability to prove three elements: a fault, damage, and a causal link between the fault and the damage.

have specified it within the code. Given that the code does not characterize the fault required for tort, the general approach as in ordinary law is applicable.

General law is criticized for being inadequate given the uncertainties in the application of article 1382 Civil Code. The principal criticism levied is that the jurisprudence under article 1382 is insufficiently specific and predictable to satisfy the second requirement of article 10(2) ECHR.[145] Additionally, balancing freedom of expression and tort law is a perilous exercise because the establishment of a fault in this context requires a subjective appraisal from courts, resulting in somewhat arbitrary decisions. Massis criticizes this decision in *Scouts v. New Look*[146] for feeding the debate on the adequacy of the regime of ordinary law when conflicting with freedom of expression. Such reasoning is said to result in a negative impact on the realization of freedom of expression.[147] As Massis notes, this justifies the approach of the Court of Appeal which moderated the application of article 1382 Civil Code in the context of the press.[148]

Such criticisms appear legitimate, because the Supreme Court's approach seems to curtail the tolerance traditionally granted to parodists by law based upon justification founded in freedom of expression. Parodists did not enjoy absolute freedom under this traditional liberal approach, since two limits were applied to protect the rights of others. Firstly, the parodist needed to comply with the requirements of the parody exception. Freedom to parody is limited by an intent to harm; since this did not comply with the rules of the genre, for example, passing beyond the limits of humour tilts the balance back in favour of the other competing rights. Secondly, the freedom to parody is limited by the content of the parody in a scenario in which the parody violates the fundamental rights of others. As a result of the broad scope of the law on freedom of the press, few parodies of copyright works will fall within the ambit of the ordinary law, which might only apply to parodies made by private individuals, or in a strictly private context.

Guignols de l'info[149] serves as an illustration of how the conflict may be resolved. The case relates to a TV sketch which used puppets to parody Peugeot cars. This depicted the company's CEO as a dissatisfied Peugeot customer. Peugeot objected to the use of its registered trade mark, considering the sketch denigrated both the reputation of the company and that of its goods. Although Peugeot commenced an action under trade mark law, the court established that as the dispute related to press freedom,[150] rather than ordinary law, the dispute should be decided on this basis.[151] The court concluded

[145] i.e. a restriction to the exercise of freedom of expression needs to be provided by law.

[146] Cass., 2e Civ., 5 mai 1993, *Association Scouts unitaires de France c/ SA Editions des Savanes*, Recueil Dalloz Sirey, 1994, 25e cahier, sommaires commentés, 193–4, comm. Massis.

[147] This can be explained by, first, the right to freedom of expression having been interpreted by the ECtHR as being broad when in the context of the press (because of its public watchdog role) and second, the adoption of a specific law regulating conflicts in a press context.

[148] A mutually exclusive relationship between the Freedom of the Press Act and article 1382 Civil Code implies that if an applicant is not successful in a tort action under the Freedom of the Press Act, this does not prevent him/her from claiming damages under ordinary law as a subsidiary action if the three requirements are satisfied. Notably, these three requirements do not take into account the intent of the speaker. Therefore, a speaker might engage his civil responsibility even where there is no intent to harm. Inherently, this amounts to a paradoxical situation as the adoption of the Freedom of the Press Act aimed to raise the standard for restriction to the right of freedom of expression; Cass., 2e Civ., 2 avril 1997; *SA Automobiles Peugeot c/ Canal Plus;* JCP n°5, 28 janvier 1998, jurispr., II 10 010, p. 185.

[149] Cass., 12 juillet 2000, D., 2000, IR, p. 218, et 2001, jurispr., p. 259, obs. Edelman; JCP, 2000, jurispr., II, n°10439; Bull., 2000, n°7, p. 10; Sem. Jur., 13 décembre 2000, p. 10, obs. Lepage.

[150] Ibid.

[151] This decision is confirmed in several later decisions: Cass., 20 novembre 2003, *Le Goff c/ Guyader—Le Ny*: Juris-data n°2003-021061; JCP n°3, 14 janvier 2004, sommaires de jurisprudence,

that the parody had caused no real harm or negative impact[152] because it featured in a satirical news programme which was founded upon making provocative statements (rather than in a car magazine, for example). As such, the parodic nature of the sketch would be evident from its use of humour and over-exaggeration. Neyret concludes that this decision's reasoning, which links humour to the expression's context, has served to raise the threshold for establishing fault in a tort claim.[153]

The French courts considered the interplay between copyright and freedom of expression again in *Bauret v. Koons*.[154] The tribunal rejected that the parody exception applied to Koons' transformation of Bauret's photograph, *Les Enfants*, into a pop art sculpture, *Naked*,[155] but it went on to consider whether the used was nevertheless justified, based upon Koons' right of freedom of expression. As a preliminary step to this assessment, the tribunal noted that the right to property (specifically copyright), and the right to freedom of expression were of equal importance in a democratic society. In order to reconcile these two fundamental rights, the court's assessment focused upon proportionality. In essence, the court sought to reconcile whether upholding the right-holder's exclusive legal rights would be disproportionate having regard to the user's interests. In this case, the tribunal concluded that the restriction on Koons' use was proportionate to the legitimate aim which copyright protection pursued. There seemed to be no apparent need for Koons to copy Bauret's work to convey his own expression, not least because the photograph copied was largely unknown to the French public.

In other words, by placing both fundamental rights on an equal footing, the French tribunal required the later artist's expression to be justified by a pressing social need before he should be allowed to reproduce another's copyright-protected work which fell beyond the parody exception.[156] Here, the mere continuation of an artistic movement (e.g. *objets trouvés* or appropriation art) was insufficient as this in itself did not constitute exercise of the right to critique deriving from Revolutionary times.

5.2 The UK: perceptible tensions between freedom of expression and copyright

In the UK, the Human Rights Act 1998 ('HRA') incorporates the principles of the ECHR into the legal framework.[157] Perhaps given its relatively recent enactment, very little case law exists under the HRA which analyzes the tensions between freedom of expression[158] and copyright. Arguably, *Ashdown*[159] is most enlightening, not least because Lord Phillips specifically identifies the potential for copyright to clash with

IV 1 064-1 072, p. 96; Cass, 31 janvier 2008, *F et autres c/ Mme. M.*, n°07.12.643N, Gaz. Pal, recueil novembre-décembre 2008, 4165. The scope of the Freedom of the Press Act is broad given that the court established that this law was applicable in relation to expressions in blog posts. Cass. 6 octobre 2011, n°10-23606, non publié au bulletin.

[152] This decision led some scholars to wonder whether the court had implicitly recognized the existence of a parody exception in trade mark law through the interplay of freedom of expression. Note Edelman under Cass., 12 juillet 2000, D. 2001, n°3, jur., 259. This reasoning was repeated in TGI Paris, 1ère ch. 1ère section, 14 avril 1999, *Dion c/ Société Cogerev*, CCE, October 1999, pp. 23–4, comm. Desgorges. This case dealt with a caricature of Céline Dion in a satirical magazine.

[153] Neyret (2008) 2402.

[154] TGI Paris, 3e ch. 4e section, 9 mars 2017, *Bauret v. Koons*, N° RG: 15/01086.

[155] See Chapter 4, section 2.2.1.

[156] Repeated in Versailles, 16/03/2018, *Malka v. Klasen*, RG n° 15/06029, p. 13.

[157] This Bill has constitutional characteristics.

[158] Section 12 HRA.

[159] *Ashdown v. Telegraph Group Ltd* [2001] EWCA Civ 1142 (hereafter *Ashdown*).

freedom of expression.[160] The Court of Appeal, considering the publication of a copyright-protected transcript of a private discussion between two leading politicians, held that copyright law legitimately restricts freedom of expression, provided that the conditions of article 10(2) ECHR (i.e. be prescribed by law, pursue a legitimate objective, and be proportionate) are met.[161] As such, the court confirmed that the CDPA is self-contained, i.e. the legislator had achieved the appropriate balance between copyright law and freedom of expression via the framing of the various doctrines enshrined in the legislation, such as the idea/expression dichotomy, the substantiality doctrine, the fair dealing exceptions, and the public interest defence, concluding that UK courts ought to respect this internal balancing.[162]

Nevertheless, whenever two bodies of laws are directly in conflict, section 3 HRA requires courts to apply legislation in a manner which is compatible with the ECHR.[163] In this light, it is reasonable to require that, whenever a defendant invokes a fair dealing exception, and the court considers all the surrounding circumstances of the case, it should be able to attribute most weight to those factors which contribute to realization of the defendant's freedom of expression. Similarly, it is legitimate that expressions which, owing to their nature, are excluded from protection of freedom of expression are also denied the benefit of an exclusion in copyright law too, and/or may be restricted by other bodies of law, whether in criminal or civil proceedings.

Unsurprisingly, these restrictions must satisfy the requirements set out in article 10(2) ECHR.[164] Hence, whenever a court is confronted with conflicting fundamental rights, it must base its decision on the result which permits maximum realization of all the rights in play. Overall, whatever balance is achieved 'internally' by copyright law does not preclude further judicial review for compliance with the overarching requirements of the ECHR and the Charter.[165]

5.3 Canada: increased role of the Canadian Charter of Rights and Freedoms

Freedom of expression is protected at national level in section 1 and 2(b) of the Canadian Charter of Rights and Freedoms.[166] Section 1 establishes that the freedoms which the Canadian Charter guarantees may only be restricted by 'such reasonable limits prescribed by law as can be demonstrably justified in a free and democratic society' while section 2(b) establishes as a fundamental right, 'freedom of thought,

[160] Ibid, [30]: 'The Act gives the owner of the copyright the right to prevent others from doing that which the Act recognises the owner alone has a right to do. Thus copyright is antithetical to freedom of expression. It prevents all, save the owner of the copyright, from expressing information in the form of the literary work protected by the copyright.'

[161] Ibid, [38].

[162] The question remains whether the internal balance struck under copyright law necessarily preserves the exercise of freedom of expression. The interpretation of case law does not lead to the maximization of the realization of the freedom of expression. Barendt (n 30) 15; K Q Garnett, 'The impact of the Human Rights Act 1998 on UK copyright law' in Griffiths and Suthersanen (eds), *Copyright and Free Speech* 172.

[163] *Ashdown* (n 159) [45].

[164] See Chapter 5, section 4.

[165] C Angelopoulos, 'Freedom of expression and copyright: the double balancing act' (2008) 3 *IPQ* 328, 341 and 352; M D Birnhack, 'Acknowledging the conflict between copyright law and freedom of expression under the Human Rights Act' (2003) 14(2) *Ent. L. Rev.* 24–34.

[166] Part I of the Constitution Act, 1982, being schedule B to the Canada Act 1982 (UK), 1982, c.11 ('Canadian Charter').

belief, opinion and expression, including freedom of the press and other media of communication'.

Freedom of expression itself enjoys a liberal interpretation.[167] It protects all forms of expression including political speech, artistic expression, search for truth, and commercial expressions.[168] Freedom of expression does not extend to expressions which are particularly hostile to the values enshrined in the Canadian Charter because these are inconsistent with the values promoted in a democratic society.[169] Similarly, as in the other jurisdictions under scrutiny, Canadian courts take context into account when considering whether a restriction placed upon an expression is justifiable. Hence, courts are less likely to accept restrictions to political expressions than in respect to advertising expressions[170] or expressions with a more problematic content, such as pornography[171] or violence.[172] In practice, Canadian courts have limited freedom of expression where an expression is likely to harm the interests of others or concerns public order.[173]

Traditionally, it was believed that the Charter did not apply to the judiciary but simply to government acts.[174] This issue was considered by the Canadian Supreme Court in *Irwin Toy v. Quebec*.[175] Firstly, the Supreme Court interpreted freedom of expression so broadly that all copyright works are likely to be protected under section 2(b) of the Canadian Charter.[176] Secondly, once a court has established that an expression is protected under the Canadian Charter, it must consider whether the purpose or effect of the government's legislative action is to restrict this fundamental freedom. Only the effect of the legislation is susceptible to be infringing a Charter's right. Thirdly, the applicant must demonstrate that their protected expression complies with the principles enshrined in the Canadian Charter.[177] Finally, if the application of the law amounts to a restriction of freedom of expression, the onus shifts to the defendant to demonstrate that the restriction is justifiable pursuant to section 1 of the Canadian Charter.[178]

Hence, freedom of expression is not absolute and should be limited where this is 'prescribed by law' and a 'pressing and substantial objective' through 'reasonably and demonstrably justified' means.[179] This echoes the European system.[180] In short, the Canadian Charter strikes a balance between individual rights and freedoms on the one hand and the collective rights to cultural identity and equality on the other hand.[181]

[167] *R. v. Keegstra* [1990] 3 S.C.R. 697 (hereafter *Keegstra*), [729].

[168] *Irwin Toy Ltd v. Quebec (AG)* [1989] 1 S.C.R. 927 (hereafter *Irwin Toy*); *R. V. Edwards Books and Art Ltd* [1986] 2 S.C.R. 713.

[169] *Keegstra* (n 167), [733].

[170] R Moon, *The Constitutional Protection of Freedom of Expression* (University of Toronto Press, 2000) 76.

[171] *R. v. Butler* [1992] 1 SCR 452; *Irwin Toy* (n 168), [970]. On how obscenity legislation was set aside to censor pornographic content: Moon (n 170) 105.

[172] Moon (n 170) 35.

[173] Ibid, 36.

[174] D Fewer, 'Constitutionalizing copyright: freedom of expression and the limits of copyright in Canada' (1997) 55 *U.T.L.J.* 175, 217.

[175] *Irwin Toy* (n 168).

[176] Any activity that 'conveys or attempts to convey a meaning' Ibid, [968].

[177] This should be easily achieved given that the broad interpretation given in *Irwin Toy* (n 168) 'is expressive if it attempts to convey meaning'.

[178] *Irwin Toy* (n 168) [978]–[979].

[179] Section 1 Canadian Charter.

[180] S Beaulac, *Legal Interpretation in Canada: Opening up Legislative Language as a Means to Internationalisation* (2010) 5/2010 University of Edinburgh Working Papers Series 1, 24. See section 3.2.

[181] Section 15 Canadian Charter.

As in the UK courts, 'external' freedom of expression considerations have often been ignored[182] or rejected[183] by courts in copyright litigation in early cases. Fewer[184] criticizes this approach as now being inconsistent with the Supreme Court's decision in *Irwin Toy v. Quebec*,[185] since freedom of expression is protected at constitutional level by the Canadian Charter, and copyright is equally protected to the extent that it does not unjustifiably hinder freedom of expression.[186]

When the application of the Copyright Act is found to breach a Charter right, the test provided in *R. v. Oakes*[187] is applied. Here, the Supreme Court established four criteria which must be present for a restriction on freedom of expression to be lawful: the law must pursue a sufficiently important objective to justify the limitation; the restriction must be reasonably connected to this objective; the restriction must not impair the right more than necessary to meet the objective; and, finally, the effect of the restriction must not have an adversely disproportionate effect on the person it applies to.[188] This approach should be applied in copyright disputes in which the Canadian Charter is raised directly against the Copyright Act (e.g. the parody exception), being a government action going against freedom of expression.

Yet, even violent expressions constitute an expression in the sense of section 2(b) of the Canadian Charter, meaning that a restriction must still respect section 1 of the Canadian Charter.[189] Protection of freedom of expression and provisions against hate speech or discrimination must be interpreted in a manner consistent with Canada's multi-culturalism. Therefore, aspects such as context and content of the expression will be relevant to determine the validity of the restriction.[190] For example, an expression of hatred targeting a minority will be considered differently from hate speech towards the majority culture.

The *Michelin* decision in 1996[191] is the Canadian case which brings the tensions between copyright law and freedom of expression into sharpest relief. The case considered a parody of the Bibendum figure before a specific parody exception was introduced into Canadian copyright law. In this case, the court held that the parodist's right of freedom of expression did not justify the reproduction of the copyright-protected image.[192] Indeed, the court did not consider that the defendant's freedom of expression had been restricted unduly, since it was considered that the defendant could have conveyed the same message using different means.[193] In reaching this conclusion, the court found no reason to review the compliance of the copyright law's restriction with section 1 of the Canadian Charter, given that the parody in dispute was held to be outside the scope of section 2(b) of the Canadian Charter.[194] Referring to *Weisfeld v. Canada*,[195] the court found it insufficient to prove that the freedom of expression has

[182] Craig (n 18) 78; Fewer (n 174) 195.

[183] In relation to parody: *Compagnie Générale des Établissements Michelin-Michelin & Cie v. National Automobile, Aerospace, Transportation and General Workers Union of Canada* (1996) 71 C.P.R. (3d) 348 (hereafter *Michelin*), [70]; *The Queen v. James Lorimer* [1984] 1 FC 1065; *Source Perrier SA v. Fira-Less Marketing Co. Ltd* (1983) 70 C.P.R. (2d) 61 (FCTD). These decisions demonstrate the strength of the proprietary vision of intellectual property rights. For more: C Craig, *Copyright, Communication and Culture: Towards a Relational Theory of Copyright Law* (Edward Elgar, 2011) 208–22.

[184] Fewer (n 174) 193.

[185] See *Irwin Toy* (n 168).

[186] J Bailey, 'Deflating the Michelin Man' in M Geist (ed.), *In the Public Interest: The Future of Canadian Copyright Law* (Irwin Law, 2005) 141.

[187] [1986] 1 S.C.R. 103.

[188] Ibid, [138]–[139]; in *RJR* (n 16), the Supreme Court favoured freedom of expression over a federal law prohibiting the advertising of tobacco products for not being proportionate to the objective sought. There might have been a different outcome if the law limited the prohibition to advertising targeting children.

[189] See *Irwin Toy* (n 168).

[190] *Keegstra* (n 167), [734].

[191] *Michelin* (n 183).

[192] Ibid, [78]–[79].

[193] Ibid, [79] and [106].

[194] Ibid, [86]–[88].

[195] [1995] 1 C.F. 68 (CA), [85].

been compromised simply by demonstrating that the use amounts to a new expression. Noting that the fundamental rights are not absolute, the court construed section 2(b) not only as excluding expressions of violence but also expressions using another's property in the name of freedom of expression.[196]

The *Michelin* court further expounded that even had the defendants' expression been found to be protected by the Canadian Charter, the defendant would still have failed under the section 1 test, since it was 'demonstrably justified in a free and democratic society' to override freedom of expression in order to enforce copyright.[197] Here, the court characterized copyright law as reflecting a 'pressing and real' need to protect authors within a democratic society by ensuring them remuneration for use of their works. Ultimately, the court held that one right-holder's property interests should be prioritized over another's exercise of freedom of expression. However, by focusing on one specific copyright justification, it seems that this decision oversimplifies the true nature and purpose of copyright. Although remuneration of authors is one aspect, it overlooks the goal of promoting cultural diversity. This aspect recognizes the need for authors to be able to rely upon previous works in order to create new ones.[198]

As the court acknowledged, copyright-protected works are expressions falling within the ambit of section 2(b) of the Canadian Charter. Hence, the defendants' use arguably contributes to opening the dialogue within society and the diversification of ideas, concepts which are at the centre of both copyright protection and freedom of expression.[199] By rendering the parody use unlawful, the court applied copyright law in a restrictive manner, depriving copyright protection of its justification.[200] Despite the criticisms surrounding this decision, *Michelin* remains good authority in Canada,[201] pending any judicial review of the newly introduced parody exception.

In sum, the nature of freedom of expression in Canada is such that as soon as one party attempts to communicate, their expression is eligible for protection by section 2(b) of the Canadian Charter,[202] irrespective of the content of the message.[203] Once it is determined that an expression is protected by the Charter, a court must apply the criteria established in *R. v. Oakes* to determine whether any claimed restriction to the right of free expression is justified. Despite a generally liberal interpretation of freedom of expression in Canada[204] and the Supreme Court *Irwin Toy* ruling[205] which ostensibly places freedom of expression and copyright protection on equal footing, *Michelin* has curtailed this fundamental freedom in respect of expressions via parody, because of its reliance upon another's protected work to convey its message. It remains to be seen whether *Michelin* remains good law, in light of the new parody exception.

[196] Craig vigorously criticizes this reasoning of the court, reminding us that the recognition that copyright is intangible property is fundamental to understanding the copyright paradigm, but the reasoning of the court appears to be heavily focusing on the assumption that copyright should be considered as any other form of private property; for example, the act of buying a book does not give property over the expression exercised by the author of the book to the book's owner. By treating copyright as akin to tangible property, the court appears to grant a power to the right-holders to exercise a certain kind of censorship over the use of their forms of expression, as the 'property' granted by copyright is the expression in itself. Craig (n 183) 212–22; Craig (n 18) 93.

[197] *Michelin* (n 183) [109].

[198] Craig (n 18) 81.

[199] Ibid, 112.

[200] Also criticized Bailey (n 186) 125; J S T Kotler, 'Trade-mark parody, judicial confusion and the unlikelihood of fair use' (2000) 14 *IPQ* 219, 231.

[201] Referred to by the Supreme Court in *Théberge v. Galerie d'Art du Petit Champlain Inc.* [2002] SCC 34, [46] and [73], for example.

[202] *Irwin Toy* (n 168) [968].

[203] *Keegstra* (n 167) [729].

[204] Ibid.

[205] See *Irwin Toy* (n 168).

5.4 Australia: a patchwork of state laws

In Australia, and in contrast to the other countries under scrutiny, freedom of expression has no federal constitutional guarantee in Australia.[206] Australian courts only recognize a more limited constitutional right[207] to freedom of political and public expression which does not extend to other kinds of expressions.[208] Therefore, the protection of freedom of expression derives from direct application of international treaties, as exposed previously,[209] as the notion of freedom of expression is a well-established principle of common law.

Additionally, a patchwork of state laws[210] restricts freedom of expression in various ways through laws which regulate obscenity, blasphemy, and defamation, as well as anti-discrimination provisions.[211] These laws are justified based upon the need to protect public morality or the reputation of others, and to prevent hate speech.[212] Given that constitutional protection of freedom of expression only extends to political communications, Australian state laws have not faced challenge for unduly impairing freedom of expression. They have the potential, nevertheless, to restrict parodists' freedom of expression severely, unless their provisions are strictly construed.[213]

5.5 The US: a robust culture of promoting free speech

The US legal system is alone in the fact that copyright protection and freedom of expression both enjoy protection within the Constitution. Copyright law features in Article I, section 8, clause 8,[214] while freedom of expression is contained in the First

[206] Yet, political communications have been recognized by courts since 1992 as deriving from the Constitution. Additionally, two legislative Bills protect freedom of expression but these do not have constitutional value, they are ordinary legislation. The first one is s. 16 of the Human Rights Act 2004 and s. 15 of the Charter of Human Rights and Responsibilities Act 2006. This lack of constitutional protection led scholars to describe the protection of freedom of expression in Australia as 'delicate' and 'partial and unsatisfactory'. K Gelber, 'Hate speech and the Australian legal and political landscape' in K Gilbert, and A Stone, (eds), *Hate Speech and Freedom of Expression in Australia* (The Federation Press, 2007) 3.

[207] The courts reached this conclusion by relying on sections 7 and 24 of the Constitution inferring freedom of political communications. *Unions NSW v. New South Wales* [2013] HCA 58; *Nationwide News Pty Ltd v. Wills* (1992) 177 CLR 1 (political insults); *Australian Capital Television Pty Ltd v. the Commonwealth* (1992) 177 CLR 106 (political broadcast and advertising). For more on the interpretation of the freedom to political expressions: R Burrell and J Stellios, 'Copyright and freedom of political communication in Australia' in Griffiths and Suthersanen (eds), *Copyright and Free Speech* 257–86.

[208] *Langer v. The Commonwealth of Australia* 96/002 (High Court); *Theophanous v. The Herald Weekly Times Limited and Another* (1994) 182 CLR 104; *Stephens and Others v. West Australian Newspapers Limited* (1994) 182 CLR 211; *Cunliffe and Another v. The Commonwealth of* Australia (1994) 182 CLR 272; *Australian Capital Television Pty. Limited and Others v. The Commonwealth* (1992) 177 CLR 106.

[209] Mainly respecting articles 19 UDHR, 19 ICCPR, and 4 CERD.

[210] The State of Victoria enacted the Charter of Human Rights and Responsibilities Act 2006 (Vic). This includes a provision dealing with freedom of expression, section 15. However, as a State Act, it is limited in its application to Victorian laws, courts, and public authorities; section 16(2) Human Rights Act 2004 applicable in the Australian Capital Territory.

[211] Known as anti-vilification provisions.

[212] There appears to be a consensus that anti-vilification laws should not be overly protective, Gelber (n 206) 5.

[213] The author regrets having found very little on the relationship between copyright and freedom of expression in Australia.

[214] This provision grants the power to Congress to pass legislation which promotes 'the progress of science and useful arts by securing for limited times to authors and inventors the exclusive right in their respective writings and discoveries'.

Amendment of the US Constitution. Yet, remarkably few decided cases have ventured to discuss the potential conflict between these two constitutional rights in parody cases.[215]

As in the other jurisdictions under scrutiny, the US copyright regime has in-built freedom of expression safeguards. In addition, a study of the eighteenth-century framers' intentions suggests that the Copyright Clause was seen as a tool for promoting the First Amendment freedom of expression values.[216] Hence, freedom of expression affects the US copyright paradigm in several ways. Firstly (and as for other jurisdictions examined in this book), the idea/expression dichotomy is seen to define the balance between the two constitutional rights.[217] In addition to the ability to reuse unprotected ideas, the fair use doctrine enables users to reproduce copyright-protected expressions in the specified circumstances to preserve these constitutional values.[218] In other words, since the Constitution grants 'authors […] the exclusive right to their respective writings […] for limited times' for the purpose of promoting progress in the arts, the fair use doctrine promotes progress by allowing the public to build upon earlier protected works.[219]

The Constitutional mission statement impacts on the scope of protection of the US copyright regime and, consequently, fair use.[220] According to US scholarship, the fair use doctrine enables individuals to reuse parts of earlier copyright-protected works to promote freedom of expression values and engage in a socially-valuable commentary or criticism.[221] The underlying goal of this doctrine is to strike a balance between property rights that foster the creation of new cultural works and the ability of other creators to draw on previous works as raw material for new expressions. Here, freedom of expression justifications have been relied upon to define the scope of the parody exception by reminding that quality or bad taste should not weigh negatively in the court's assessment. In other words, freedom of expression goes beyond protecting successful parodies and protects uses which comment or criticize earlier works (to some degree at least).[222] In contrast, a use which merely reproduces an earlier copyright work for want of effort should weigh against the finding of fair use.[223] Here, the First Amendment both limits and broadens the scope of the fair use doctrine, firstly by requiring some form of commentary, and secondly, by refraining from defining parody based upon

[215] *Adjmi v. DLT Entm't, Ltd*, 97 F.Supp.3d 512 (S.D.N.Y. Mar. 31, 2015); *New York Times Co. v. United States*, 403 U.S. 713 (1971); *Dallas Cowboys Cheerleaders, Inc. v. Pussycat Cinema, Ltd*, 604 F.2d 200 (2d Cir. 1979); *Sid & Marty Krofft Television Prods. v. McDonald's Corp.*, 562 F.2d 1157 (9th Cir. 1977); *Rosemont Enters., Inc. v. Random House, Inc.*, 366 F.2d 303 (2d Cir. 1966); *Walt Disney Prods. v. Air Pirates*, 345 F.Supp. 108 (N.D. Cal. 1972); *Time, Inc. v. Bernard Geis Assoc.*, 293 F.Supp. 130 (S.D.N.Y. 1968). But see also *Harper* (n 14).

[216] *Harper* (n 14) [58].

[217] Ibid, [556]; *Feist Publications, Inc. v. Rural Telephone Service Co.* (1991) 499 U.S. 340 (hereafter *Feist*), [349]–[350].

[218] *Eldred v. Ashcroft* (2003) 537 U.S. 186 (hereafter *Eldred*), [219].

[219] *Campbell v. Acuff-Rose Music Inc.* 510 US 569 (1994) (hereafter *Campbell*), [575].

[220] Not only does the Constitution enable Congress to enact legislation but it simultaneously limits its powers, e.g. *Graham v. John Deere Co. of Kansas City* (1966) 383 U.S. 1, 5 (1966). *Feist* (n 217). This case notes that Congress has no constitutional power to protect unoriginal works under copyright law. See Chapter 4. Courts tend to have relied on this to avoid a direct discussion confronting free speech and copyright, i.e. if it is fair use, the courts do not see a reason to appreciate an argument based on the First Amendment.

[221] *Eldred* (n 218) [219].

[222] *Campbell* (n 219) [583].

[223] Recently recalled in *Kienitz v. Sconnie Nation LLC*, 766 F.3d 756, 758 (7th Cir. 2014) (hereafter *Kienitz*), [760].

some element of humour.[224] It follows that the first fair use factor—the *purpose* and *character* of the use—taints the appreciation of the remaining fair use factors (the nature of the protected work, the substantiality of the portion copied, and the market effect of the use) in particular cases.[225]

This is illustrated in early cases and is repeated in most recent decisions. For example, in the 1964 case of *Berlin v. E.C Publications, Inc.*,[226] the defendant released parodies of popular songs without copying either the original lyrics or the music. Rather, the magazine published parodic lyrics, written in the same metre as the originals, along with instructions that the reader should sing song X 'to the tune of' song Y. In determining whether this use was 'fair', the court took the opportunity to comment on the relationship between parody, copyright, and freedom of expression:

> [A]s a general proposition, we believe that parody and satire are deserving of substantial freedom—both as entertainment and as a form of social and literary criticism [. . .] At the very least, where, as here, it is clear that the parody has neither the intent or the effect of fulfilling the demand for the original, and where the parodist does not appropriate a greater amount of the original work than is necessary to 'recall or conjure up' the object of his satire, a finding of infringement would be improper.[227]

This reasoning gave rise to the often-referred-to 'conjure up test',[228] which seeks to establish whether the amount which the defendant has reproduced from the original is more than, or just the minimum amount, needed to ensure the public's ability to recall the earlier work. This test is seen as a free speech safety valve within copyright, but equally, it protects copyright interests too, as the right-holder is guaranteed the maximum protection of property rights which is compatible with the other constitutional values.[229] What is noteworthy is that the court recognized that parodies and satires were justified on the same basis. As a result, we should expect a similar regime irrespective of whether the third party use seeks to comment on the earlier protected work or something else. Despite this, the 'conjure up' approach led to the seminal parody decision, *Campbell*, and its progeny.

In the *Campbell* decision,[230] the Supreme Court's consideration of the Copyright Clause of the US Constitution led it to endorse that it is the transformative nature of a use which should weigh most heavily in favour of fairness because the creation of a new expression can be seen as promoting 'progress' in the arts. Thus, 'the more transformative the new work, the less will be the significance of other factors, like commercialism, that may weigh against a finding of fair use.'[231] This emphasis upon transformation has caused critics to argue for a return to a narrower understanding of the fair use doctrine, based upon a more even weighting on the remaining factor.

[224] This is most prominently evident from *Suntrust Bank v. Houghton Mifflin Co.*, 268 F.3d 1257 (hereafter *Suntrust*), 1276–7 (11th Cir. 2001); *Castle Rock Entm't, Inc. v. Carol Publ. Group, Inc.*, 150 F.3d, [142]; *Adjmi v. DLT Entm't, Ltd*, 97 F.Supp.3d 512 (S.D.N.Y. Mar. 31, 2015), [531].

[225] *Campbell* (n 219) [580]–[584]. For example, *Loew's Inc. Columbia Broadcasting System, Inc.* was heavily criticized for having put too much reliance on the financial motivation of the parodist and may limit the availability of raw material to create new art and valuable forms of expression. 131 F.Supp. 165 (S.D. Cal. 1955), aff'd sub nom. *Benny v. Loew's*, 239 F.2d 532 (9th Cir. 1956), aff'd sub nom. *Columbia Broadcasting Sys., Inc. v. Loew's, Inc.*, 356 U.S. 43 (1958). Criticized later by Judge Kaufman in *Berlin v. E.C Publications, Inc.* For more on criticisms of Loew's decision, see C Goetsch, 'Parody as free speech—the replacement of the fair use doctrine by First Amendment protection' (1980) 3 *W. New Eng. L. Rev.* 39, 51.

[226] 329 F.2d 541 (2d Cir.), cert. denied, 379 U.S. 822 (1964).

[227] Ibid, 545.

[228] See Chapter 1 section 5.3 and Chapter 4, section 2.3.

[229] *Blanch v. Koons*, 467 F.3d, [250].

[230] See Chapter 1, section 5.3.

[231] *Campbell* (n 219) [579].

In terms of parody, the court's endorsement of transformation may stretch the meaning of parody under US copyright law,[232] but *Campbell* is most notable for our study as a result of the distinction it drew between parody and satire (i.e. distinguishing 'parody of' from 'parody with'). Post-*Campbell*, courts have interpreted the decision as saying that parodies are de facto presumptively fair even though the Supreme Court expressly refrained from stating this to be so.[233] For example, in *Dr Seuss v. Penguin Books*, a satire of the protected work was held to infringe despite its transformative nature, and the low likelihood that it would supplant demand for the original.[234] However, slowly, this distinction seems to be fading.[235]

More recently, in *Blanch v. Koons*,[236] the Second Circuit concluded that a collage which Koons created by appropriating photographic images of pairs of feet and legs from various commercial adverts fell within *Campbell's* definition of transformative use.[237] By emphasizing the transformativeness of the use, the court considered that there was no need to dwell upon the parody/satire distinction which was held as being crucial in *Campbell*. Consequently, the arguably satirical use was deemed to be fair.[238] The Second Circuit adopted the same approach and expanded it further in the highly controversial *Cariou v. Prince* decision.[239] In another case involving appropriation art, Prince had taken photographs which appeared in Cariou's book concerning Rastafarianism to use as raw material for a collage painting. Although the district court took a firm stance against Prince, and upheld Cariou's copyright,[240] the Second Circuit was critical of the first instance court's narrow interpretation of transformativeness. Instead, the Second Circuit considered the use as transformative because Prince's painting was seen as manifestly different from the Cariou photographs. The latter sought to depict the natural beauty of subjects and landscapes in black and white while the former created a 'hectic and provocative' expression which played with colours and distorted scales (see Figure 5.1). The appeal court concluded that any reasonable observer would understand the two expressions to convey different messages and meanings.[241] In other words, if the unauthorized use creates a new expression, there is no further requirement as to the subject of the comment according to this interpretation of the fair use doctrine.[242]

In *Kienitz v. Sconnie Nation LLC*,[243] the Seventh Circuit expressed reservations about the Second Circuit's approach in *Cariou*. The first criticism was that the Second Circuit seemed to reduce fair use to a question of transformativeness. The Seventh Circuit considered that this focus was too extreme, and might jeopardize a right-holder's possibility to license works for derivative uses as envisaged by section 106(2) US Copyright Act.[244] In the case at hand, the court reviewed unauthorized use of a photograph of Soglin, the Major of Madison, Wisconsin, taken by Kienitz to create a protest t-shirt

[232] *Suntrust* (n 224) [1259]. [233] *Campbell* (n 219) [580].

[234] *Dr. Seuss Enters. v. Penguin Books, USA, Inc.*, 109 F.3d 1394 (9th Cir. 1997). See also *Rogers v. Koons*, 960 F.2d 301 (2d Cir. 1992).

[235] *Blanch v. Koons* (n 229); *Cariou v. Prince* 714 F. 3d 694 (2d Cir. 2013); *Bourne Co. v. Twentieth Century Fox Film Corp.*, 602 F. Supp. 2d 499, 507 (S.D.N.Y. 2009); *Burnett v. Twentieth Century Fox Film Corp.*, 491 F. Supp. 2d 962, 968–9 (C.D. Cal. 2007). However, the split was applied in *Henley v. DeVore*, 733 F.Supp. 2d 1144 (C.D. Cal. 2010) (hereafter *Henley*); *Dr. Seuss Enters., L.P. v. Penguin Books USA, Inc.* (hereafter *Seuss I*), 924 F.Supp. 1559, 1568 (S.D.Cal. 1996).

[236] 467 F.3d 244 (2d Cir. 2006). [237] Ibid, [253]. [238] Ibid, [254]–[255].

[239] See n 234. cert. denied 134 S. Ct. 618 (2013). [240] Ibid.

[241] *Cariou v. Prince* (n 234) [707].

[242] *Campbell* (n 219) 579; *Blanch* (n 229) [253]; *Castle Rock* (n 224) [142]. *Cariou v. Prince* was eventually settled out of court as the plaintiff failed to convince the Supreme Court to review the Second Circuit's decision, [699], cert. denied, 134 S. Ct. 618 (2013).

[243] *Kienitz* (n 223). [244] Ibid, [759].

Figure 5.1 Patrick Cariou, *Yes Rasta*, pp. 11, 59; Richard Prince, *James Brown Disco Ball*.
© 2002 powerHouse Books. **© Richard Prince. Courtesy Gagosian. Photo: Robert McKeever.**

which mocked Soglin for attempting to shut down a local annual event. The defendant had sold some of the shirts with a view to making a modest profit. While the Seventh Circuit noted that the form of the use as a political comment went in the defendant's favour because it was consistent with constitutional values,[245] the political nature of

[245] However, US commentators warn that one should refrain from elevating the fair use doctrine to having constitutional status. See R C Denicola, 'Copyright and free speech: constitutional limitations on the protection of expression' (1979) 67 *Cal. L. Rev.* 283, 299.

their new expression, per se, was insufficient to override the photographer's copyright claim. Although the First Amendment protected healthy democratic debate, copyright law grants exclusive rights to those political expressions which are fixed and original. The Seventh Circuit considered that the balancing of rights required courts to compare the two works to establish whether the (transformed) use sought to complement or supplant the market for the original work. Here, the court held that the parody did not replace the original, and might even lead to an increase in demand as it came to the attention of a wider audience. Therefore, the defendant's use was deemed to be fair, although the Seventh Circuit preferred to assess all four statutory factors, and place any emphasis on the fourth factor of market substitution.[246]

This was more recently reiterated in in *ADJMI v. DLT Entertainment Ltd*,[247] in which a district court in the southern district of New York noted in respect of a dark theatrical take on a famous TV sitcom that:

> Transformative use is neither a sufficient nor exclusive means to establish fair use, but '[s]uch works [. . .] lie at the heart of the fair use doctrine's guarantee of breathing space within the confines of copyright [. . .] and the more transformative the new work,' the greater the likelihood of a finding of fair use.[248]

Hence, the balance which needs to be struck within US copyright law is to promote *progress* in the arts and sciences by providing economic incentives (property rights) but not to such an extent that it prevents others building on previous works, as this might stifle creativity. With this in mind, it is clear that US courts have recognized that parody has a valid purpose. Once this worthy purpose has been established, the parody, like any other use, must be measured against the statutory fair use factors.[249] Whilst the transformative nature of the use tilts the balance in favour of the defendant, it does not preclude courts from offsetting this by the combined weight of the remaining factors.

The robust US First Amendment culture also explains why courts tend to refrain from finding infringement of publicity rights unless the use complained of constitutes defamation or a violation of privacy.[250] Even in such cases, courts seem to have raised the threshold by requiring evidence of 'actual malice' on the part of the defendant.[251] Although *Kienitz v. Sconnie* considered the rights of a politician,[252] the principle may be expanded to any public figure, such as a famous musician,[253] especially if the parody comments upon the target individual's opinions.[254]

[246] Repeated in *Quenton Galvin and Jacob Meister v. Illinois Republican Party, Illinois House Republican Organisation, Roderick Drobinski, Friends of Rod Drobinski, Jamestown Associates LLC, and Majority Strategies, Inc.* (2015) No 14 C 10490.

[247] 97 F.Supp.3d 512 (2015).

[248] Ibid, [531].

[249] *Campbell* (n 219) [579]–[580]; *ADJMI* (n 247) [531].

[250] *Quenton Galvin and Jacob Meister v. Illinois Republican Party, Illinois House Republican Organisation, Roderick Drobinski, Friends of Rod Drobinski, Jamestown Associates LLC, and Majority Strategies, Inc.* (2015) No 14 C 10490; *Dhillon v. Does* 1-10, No C 13-01465 SI, 2014 WL 722592 (N.D. Cal. Feb. 25, 2014), [5]; *Henley* (n 235); *Hustler Magazine v. Falwell*, 485 U.S. 46, 108 S. Ct. 876, 99 L. Ed. 2d 41 (1988); *N.Y. Times Co. v. Sullivan*,376 U.S. 254, 84 S. Ct. 710, 11 L. Ed. 2d 686 (1964) (hereafter *Sullivan*).

[251] *Blanch v. Koons* (n 236) [279]–[280].

[252] *Kienitz* (n 223).

[253] *Henley* (n 235).

[254] *Bourne Co. v. Twentieth Century Fox Films Corp.* (2009) 602 F.Supp.2d 499 (S.D.N.Y. 2009), [507]–[508], finding parody where the parody ridiculed Walt Disney for holding anti-Semitic views; *Burnett v. Twentieth Century Fox Film Corp.* (2007) 491 F.Supp.2d 962 (C.D. Cal. 2007), [968]–[969], finding parody where the work ridiculed Burnett's image. *Contra: Salinger v. Colting et al* (2009) 641 F.Supp.2d 250 (S.D.N.Y. 2009).

6. Conclusion

Copyright law aims to reward authors and right-holders to foster creative endeavours. The bundle of exclusive rights granted to right-holders is not absolute. Limits are necessary to enable future creators to draw upon earlier ideas. Whilst the idea/expression dichotomy ensures free access to abstract ideas, copyright exceptions go one step further and grant access to expressions as well, but only in particular circumstances. Both breathing spaces are essential to preserve and promote the values of freedom of expression. Although a parody exception might be perceived as a threat to the existing balance of rights and interests, it is required to ensure that this particular form of expression can be shielded from infringement. The provision of a specific exception focussed upon parody provides courts with the most appropriate tool to fine-tune the balance as appropriate for this form of social and artistic criticism.

However, the parody exception incorporates its own limits. Certain parodic uses will still be curtailed. Locating where the outer boundary lies is far from straightforward for parodists (seeking guidance whether their use is permitted), right-holders (assessing whether copyright infringement is likely to succeed), and judges (required to assess the defence on a case-by-case basis) alike. Whilst the underlying parodic purpose may serve as a presumption of fairness, the exception still requires delineation into workable factors which determine whether any particular use, given the surrounding circumstances, should be lawful. The individual factors bear national characteristics and so will vary according to legal tradition and judicial development in this area of law. Our evaluation of national jurisprudence reveals that differences are inter- and intra-jurisdictional, since there is a degree of inconsistency between decisions applying the exception within a single territory.[255] For example, although the exception is well-established in France and the US, similar facts have led to opposite outcomes, exacerbating legal uncertainty and jeopardizing the promotion of creative expression.

We have located the source of this uncertainty. Firstly, fair use or fair dealing relies on factors which are not parody-specific, but are common to a number of different copyright exceptions. Secondly, as case law evolves, courts attach varying priorities to the relevant factors,[256] which may lead to apparently irreconcilable outcomes between allowed and prohibited uses.[257] In contrast, in France, 'the rules of the genre' is a test which is specific to the parody exception, although, even then, courts enjoy some latitude when applying the factors to the use in question. Most importantly, although courts generally acknowledge that the parody exception is founded in the protection of the human rights, there is a marked reticence to resolve potential conflicts between copyright and freedom of expression head-on. Understandably, judges typically use the parody exception to resolve this conflict indirectly, although our overview of ECtHR case law suggests that there may be an alternative route which might provide stakeholders with more specific guidance for assessing the legality of a use.

The objective of a parody exception is to preserve a new critical comment made not by producing a journalistic or educational text, but by reproducing the whole or a substantial part of a prior protected work, to create a new creative expression. Hence, a parody is both complementary to the earlier work (since it conveys a different message

[255] See Chapters 4 and 7, section 2.

[256] *US*: first preference for the purpose (first factor) and now a combination of 2 and 4 (market substitution is prevalent).

[257] *US: Benny v. Loew's, Inc.* (1956) 239 F.2d 532 (9th Cir. 1956); decisions after *Campbell* (n 219).

to the original), as well as being creative (giving rise to a new work). Once the purpose of the use is established as being of the correct kind, the second stage is to verify the 'fairness' of the use, according to the variety of factors which have been established by the legislature and courts: fair dealing, fair use, or the rules of the genre. Although procedurally, the parody exception acts as a defence, this should not become a barrier which disengages it from its roots and function.[258] Currently, as there is no established hierarchy or single decisive factor, the overall fact-based assessment carried out by courts may appear rather perilous and subjective.

As the parody exception is so deeply rooted in the fundamental value of freedom of expression, this chapter has proposed that exception should include a balancing test based upon expressive values.[259] Such an approach would not only clarify the relationship between parody, copyright, and freedom of expression but it would bolster the safeguards in place for right-holders, by shielding them from uses which have minimal social value, while fostering parodies of the type which society values the most. As has been demonstrated throughout this chapter, the outer limits of the parody exception in each jurisdiction which has been studied are determined by the influence of freedom of expression on copyright, the margin of appreciation, and the proportionality test.

Since parody is a vehicle for freedom of expression to be realized by encouraging discursivity in democratic societies, national courts must respect the limits attached to this fundamental right. This means that a judicial weighing-up of all the relevant rights at stake, which may appear inevitable in ambiguous parody cases, becomes more straightforward, if based upon the guidance which has been evolved already under human rights law. The human rights framework would seem to inject the much-needed legal certainty required in this area of copyright law, as well as increasing the likelihood of greater harmonization of the parody exception, which is especially attractive in a borderless world.[260]

[258] See Chapter 3, section 1. [259] See also Chapter 7, section 2.
[260] See section 4.1 and Chapter 7, sections 2 and 3.

6

Parody and Moral Rights

1. Introduction

While the parody exception constitutes an exception to the economic rights of right-holders, a comprehensiveappreciation of the exception requires an evaluation of the interaction between parodies and an author's moral rights.[1] Not only does a consideration of moral rights enable a fuller understanding of a creator's relationship with their work, but it may also shed some light upon the boundaries of the parody exception.[2]

According to the traditional civil law approach, moral rights are distinct from economic rights. They seek to preserve the imprint of the author's personality on the work which they have created,[3] thereby recognizing and protecting their personal interest surrounding artistic reputation, honour, and dignity. 'Moral' rights, therefore, have acquired a somewhat incongruous label, since they are not concerned with 'morality' per se, but rather in safeguarding an author's non-pecuniary interests.[4]

Ever since their inception during the late eighteenth century, primarily in Western Europe, moral rights have developed in a fragmented and uneven fashion around the world, despite having received some level of international recognition in a revision to the Berne Convention in 1928.[5] Article 6bis Berne enshrines a minimum level of protection of the rights of paternity[6] and integrity, although the form that implementation takes[7] and further development is left to the signatory parties.[8] Pursuant to article 6bis(1):

[1] Also recognized recently in France in Versailles, 16 March 2018, *Alix Malka v. Peter Klasen*, n° RG 15/06029 (case remanded) 13.

[2] Some argue that moral rights are anchored in article 8 ECHR and the right to a private life and family life. See C Geiger and E Izyumenko, *Intellectual Property before the European Court of Human Rights* (2018) Centre for International Intellectual Property Studies Research Paper No 2018-01, 57, forthcoming in C Geiger, C A Nard, and X Seuba (eds), *Intellectual Property and the Judiciary* (EIPIN series Vol. 4, EE, 2018).

[3] R C Bird and L M Ponte, 'Protecting moral rights in the United States and the United Kingdom: challenges and opportunities under the U.K.'s New Performances Regulations' (2006) 24 *Boston University International Law Journal* 213, 217; *Desputeaux v. Editions Chouette (1987) Inc.* [2003] 1 S.C.R. 178 (hereafter *Desputeaux*), [57]; C Caron, *Abus de droit et droit d'auteur* (Litec, 1998) 121; M Goudreau, 'Le droit moral au Canada' (1994) 25 *R.G.D.* 403, 404; D Vaver, 'Authors' moral rights—reform proposals in Canada: charter or barter of rights for creators?' (1987) 25 *Osgoode Hall L.J.* 749, 752.

[4] G Davies and K Garnett QC, *Moral Rights* (Sweet & Maxwell, 2010) 3; A Dietz, 'The moral right of the author: moral rights and the civil law countries' (1994) 19 *Colum. VLA J.L. & Arts* 199, 207 and 211; Goudreau (n 3).

[5] Amended in 1948.

[6] 'Right to claim authorship' in article 6bis Berne Convention.

[7] Article 6bis(3) Berne Convention.

[8] Article 27(2) UDHR apparently provides a fundamental justification for author's right's moral interests; like article 15(1)(c) ICESCR, moral rights are also enshrined in article 1 WCT (referring to articles 1 to 21 Berne) and article 5 WPPT. Moral rights are expressly left out of the TRIPS Agreement (article 9(1) TRIPS). E Adeney, *The Moral Rights of Authors and Performers: An International and Comparative Analysis* (OUP, 2006) 150; W Grosheide, 'Transition from guild regulation to modern copyright law—a view from the low countries' in L Bently, U Suthersanen, and P L C Torremans (eds), *Global Copyright: Three Hundred Years since the Statute of Anne, from 1709 to Cyberspace* (Edward Elgar, 2010) 256; A Dietz, 'The artist's right of integrity under copyright law—a comparative approach'

Independently of the author's economic rights, and even after the transfer of the said rights, the author shall have the right to claim authorship of the work and to object to any distortion, mutilation or other modification of, or other derogatory action in relation to, the said work, which would be prejudicial to his honor or reputation.

Moral rights arguably provide protection beyond the author's personal interests. By preserving the integrity of artistic and cultural expressions, the public interest is protected too, insofar as this ensures that the public is exposed to a work in the form which the author intended.[9] By permitting an author to maintain some control over their own work, the public is reassured that a work receives its proper attribution, even if the associated economic rights are controlled by another. This might suggest that the public interest here is usually aligned with the personal interests of the author,[10] but such an inference is based upon too simplistic a model.

In the case of parody and satire, the public interest also often lies with those users who would adapt authorial works because, as we have seen, modifications made for these purposes stimulate public discourse.[11] As others have already undertaken a comprehensive study of moral rights,[12] this chapter focuses on the three moral rights most affected by parodies: the right of paternity[13] (i.e. the author's right to have their name associated with their own work), the integrity right (protecting the work against unauthorized distortion), and the right against false attribution (guarding against an erroneous representation that an individual is the author of a work).[14]

2. Why Parodies Sit Uncomfortably with Moral Rights

The idea underlying moral rights is to respect the author's own conception of how their expression should be embodied in a tangible good. It is, thus, easy to appreciate why moral rights might conflict with another's wish to create a parody based upon that expression. Firstly, as a parody is, by its very nature, a 'distortion' of another work, parodies have the potential to conflict with the integrity right. Similarly, a parody which criticizes or mocks has the potential to hurt the artistic sensibilities of the original author, as well as his honour and/or reputation. Secondly, the right of paternity may be problematic, given that a parody will reproduce a substantial enough part of an earlier expression to enable the public to recognize it *as* a parody of that the earlier work.

(1994) 25(2) *IIC* 177; G Dworkin, 'Moral rights in English law—the shape of rights to come basic features of the droit moral' (1986) 8(11) *EIPR* 329.

[9] Dworkin (n 8) 330.

[10] C Caron, 'Abus de droit et droit d'auteur: une illustration de la confrontation du droit spécial au droit commun en droit civil français' (1998) 176 *RIDA* 3, 56.

[11] See Chapter 2, section 2.

[12] For more on moral rights, see Davies and Garnett (n 4); P-Y Gautier, *Propriété littéraire et artistique* (6th edn, PUF, 2007) first part, second title; Adeney (n 8); E Bellini, 'Moral rights and droit moral: a matter of paradigms' (2005) 204 *RIDA* 3; M Sainsbury, *Moral Rights and their Application in Australia* (The Federation Press, 2003) 234; Goudreau (n 3); S Ricketson, 'Moral rights and the droit de suite: international conditions and Australian obligations' (1990) 1 *Ent. L. R.* 78; Dworkin (n 8) 329–36; P Sirinelli, *Le droit moral de l'auteur et le droit commun des contrats* (thesis, 1985); D Nimmer, *Nimmer on Copyright* (Matthew Bender, 1997) vol. III, § 8D.

[13] Also known as 'right of attribution'. The author will refer to 'paternity right'.

[14] Other moral rights include: right of divulgation (or right of first publication in the US) and right of withdrawal and the related *droit de suite* (or resale royalty right in the US). It is noteworthy that the right against false attribution is not actually a moral right but is usually associated with these. See *UK*: section 84 CDPA and *Australia*: section 195AC(1) CA 1968 combined with section 195AD(a)(i)–(ii) CA 1968.

Should an author's paternity right extend to parodies of their works? Thirdly, in those jurisdictions, including the US,[15] UK,[16] and Australia,[17] which recognize the right to object to any false attribution, there may be infringement if the original author's name is associated with an altered, parody version of their work which the original author has not authorized. In each of these scenarios, it is apparent why the original author might want to oppose such acts.

While it is open for a parodist to seek the author's permission to parody their work, this might prove to be an impossible quest, but additionally, it seems rather counter-productive to leave the ability to criticize, satirize, or ridicule to the gift of one party, who might be the target of that critique. Considering that authorization might be perceived as approval of the parody message conveyed, it is reasonable to imagine that authors and parodists alike might rather avoid this endorsement. Arguably, the uncertainty which results inherently has a chilling effect. Parodists wishing to utilize a copyright-protected work to create their new expression might elect to self-censor rather than risk liability arising from moral rights. The relationship between parody and moral rights seems to create tension between authors—the author of the original work on one side and the putative parodist on the other.

Evaluating whether moral rights are real, rather than merely theoretical concerns to parodists, requires us to consider the contours of moral rights protection in more detail. Since the difference between legal traditions in copyright law is most evident in the national treatment of moral rights, it is helpful to undertake a theoretical overview first, before drilling down to examine whether an author's moral rights will be preserved if their work is subject to parody.

3. The Implications of Monist and Dualist Theories for the Parody Exception

As we have touched upon already, the protection of moral rights contained in the Berne Convention has permitted diverse schemes at national level. However, divergence seems almost inevitable, since the Convention, an international compromise, merely reflects two established and competing theories[18] underlying the protection of authorial interests.[19]

The first—the 'monist' theory—conceptualizes authors' works as the embodiment of the author's personality.[20] Translating this theory into doctrinal law, moral and economic rights are so inextricably intertwined that infringement of one will automatically indicate infringement of the other, and the award of double damages is envisaged.[21] The second—the 'dualist' theory—identifies an author's personal and economic interests as being separable and distinct, thereby paving the way for aspects, such as duration and alienability, of economic and moral rights to differ. Hence, whilst monism begs for unity of treatment under copyright law, dualism would permit personal interests to be regulated by other bodies of law.

[15] Section 43(a) Lanham Act. [16] Section 84(6) CDPA.

[17] Section 195AC(1) CA 1968 combined with section 195AD(a)(i)–(ii) CA 1968.

[18] For more, see M T Sundara Rajan, *Moral Rights* (OUP, 2011).

[19] A Lucas-Schloetter, 'Rapport général: le droit moral dans les différents régimes du droit d'auteur' in F Brison, S Dussollier, M-C Janssens,.and H Vanhees (eds), *Moral Rights in the 21st Century* (Larcier, 2015) 50–2.

[20] This is the case for Germany. [21] See Sundara Rajan (n 18) 75–88.

Whilst the jurisdictions under scrutiny are founded on dualism, additional conceptual differences are evident.

3.1 France: *Le droit moral*

In France, moral rights (or '*le droit moral*'[22]) are almost sacred.[23] Founded in Kantian theory, an author has 'an inherent right in his own person, namely a right to prevent another making him address the public without his consent'.[24] Adopting a Kantian perspective, society should hold the author's personality supreme in order to promote creativity.[25] In this vein, the civil law tradition affords creative works legal protection, specifically to preserve the imprint of the author's personality in the works created.[26] This arguably romantic and old-fashioned conception of the author as 'creative genius' resulted in a form of subjective individual rights to protect non-economic authorial interests, meaning authors' rights comprise two integral components: exclusive rights (protecting economic interests)[27] and moral rights (protecting personality-based interests).[28]

3.2 Common law tradition and moral rights

In contrast, authors under the common law tradition have never enjoyed this 'romantic' conception. Based upon a utilitarian approach, moral rights are typically perceived as a 'necessary evil' and only instrumental in encouraging creativity and fostering exercise of the right of freedom of expression. Consequently, moral rights are protected only to the extent they are socially useful. Societal benefits accrue if the public is able to *identify* the originator of a work and have confidence that an identified work is *authentic*. Originally, these aspects were considered as separate to copyright protection,[29] with the result that any protection thereof arose under other areas of law, such as tort, contract, defamation, passing off, privacy etc.[30] Only later did moral rights become statutory

[22] *Le droit moral* in civil law jurisdictions acts as a single overarching principle. Alternatively, the concept of moral rights has a plural form in common law jurisdictions. For simplification, I refer to 'moral rights'. Nimmer (n 12), vol. III, § 8D.01[A], fn 4.

[23] J De Werra, 'Moral rights, a view from continental Europe' in Brison et al (eds), *Moral Rights* 69.

[24] Kant cited by Adeney (n 8) 26.

[25] Notably, moral rights provisions are placed before economic rights in the IPC (articles L. 113-1, L. 121-1 to L. 121-9). A Lucas and H J Lucas, *Traité de la propriété littéraire et artistique* (4th edn, Litec, 2001) n°503.

[26] Bird and Ponte (n 3) 217; *Desputeaux* (n 3) [57]; Sainsbury (n 12) 2; Caron (n 3) 121; Goudreau (n 3) 404; Vaver (n 3) 752.

[27] See Chapter 4 on the application of the exception.

[28] Davies and Garnett (n 4) 25; Dietz (n 8) 202–6; Caron (n 3) 120; influenced by Québec, moral rights in *Canada* are not conceived as separate to copyright as in other common law jurisdictions but are treated as a separate branch under the copyright umbrella. *Théberge v. Galerie d'Art du Petit Champlain Inc.* [2002] S.C.C. 34 (hereafter *Théberge*). The Supreme Court noted that the presence of the two sets of rights in different sections of the Act demonstrates the separation between economic and moral rights.

[29] Therefore, the ownership, duration of protection, and provisions for infringement and remedies are different for moral rights than for economic rights. *UK*: Adeney (n 8) 390; *Australia*: M Sainsbury, 'Parody, satire, honour and reputation: the interplay between economic and moral rights' (2007) 18 *AIPJ* 149, 152.

[30] Except in *Canada*, which under the influence of Québec, introduced specific moral rights legislation in 1931. For more on the history of moral rights in Canada: Adeney (n 8) 291; Davies and Garnett (n 4) 27, 36, and 677. For more on the protection of moral rights in other areas of law: Bird and Ponte (n 3) 213; M T Sundara Rajan, 'The "New Listener" and the virtual performer: the need for a new approach to performers' rights' in M Geist, *In the Public Interest: The Future of Canadian Copyright Law* (Irwin Law, 2005) 316; Ricketson (n 12) 82.

rights within the remit of copyright legislation (although the US still relies heavily on other areas of law).[31]

3.3 Moral rights and economic rights: unity or separation?

Having identifed how the different legal traditions led to different conceptualizations, we may consider how this difference has influenced the legal protection of moral rights. In terms of legislation, the almost-divine character of moral rights in France materializes into a statement of overarching principle,[32] rather than the more detailed rules which are characteristic of legislation in common law jurisdictions.[33] Although moral and economic rights embody different components of a unitary copyright paradigm, the two components receive separate treatment. Moral rights are perpetual, inalienable, and imprescriptible,[34] whilst economic rights are of fixed term, transferable, and susceptible of prescription. Consequently, any legal exceptions provided in copyright law for economic rights are not automatically applicable to moral rights.

Relevantly recent, and eventually bowing to international pressure, specific moral rights provisions were introduced into copyright law in the UK[35] and Australia[36] relatively recently.[37] In each case, the legislative provisions are prescriptive and specific, leaving little room for judicial discretion. What is interesting is that the UK and Australian legislators adopted different approaches. While the Australian provisions are concerned with delineating the scope of moral rights protection, the primary focus of the UK provisions is identifying those aspects which moral rights do not protect.[38] While both sets of legislation include a statutory list of exceptions, neither includes an exception for parody. Thus, despite the enactment of a parody exception in respect of copyright's economic rights, a permitted parody might still infringe moral rights in France, the UK, and Australia.

Although Canada is a common law jurisdiction, its legal tradition is founded in a combination of English and French law. Canada introduced moral rights provisions into copyright law as early as 1931,[39] and consideration of this early legislation reveals a monist theory influence. For example, the moral rights remain in force for the same duration as the corresponding economic rights last.[40] Furthermore, as in France, there seems to be a correlation between acts which infringe copyright and moral rights.[41]

[31] This recognition results from the international pressure following Berne. For more on the history of the introduction of moral rights in *Australian* copyright law: Davies and Garnett (n 4) 34; Adeney (n 8) 541; Sainsbury (n 12) 31. On the history of moral rights in the *UK*: Adeney (n 8) 365, 394–406.

[32] Resulting in a greater weight allocated to judicial interpretation. Grosheide (n 8) 256.

[33] This statement must be tempered for Canada which, in contrast to the UK or Australia, has less detailed moral rights provisions also resulting in a greater power of interpretation in the hands of judges.

[34] L. 121-1 at 4° IPC. For more: Lucas and Lucas (n 25) n° 504–11.

[35] Mainly chapter IV of the CDPA 1988 (sections 77–95).

[36] Part IX of Copyright Act 1968 (sections 189–195AZR).

[37] Yet, earlier recognition of moral consideration was present, see in the *UK: Donaldson v. Beckett* (1774) 98 ER 257.

[38] Adeney (n 8) 570.

[39] For more on the history of Canada and the introduction of moral rights, see Sundara Rajan (n 18) 122–7.

[40] This is the minimum set in Berne: fifty years after the author's death.

[41] More evidently than in France, different provisions deal with infringement of copyright and moral rights, respectively sections 27 and 28.1 CA. However, there are also overlaps, bringing the Canadian system closer to that of Germany (i.e. monist theory). See Sundara Rajan (n 18) 131.

Despite retaining the possibility for claimants to bring claims of infringement on both copyright and moral rights grounds, Canadian courts have tended to determine infringement of works based upon the economic component only.[42] There are recent signs this might change.[43] This may be explained by the reluctance of English-speaking judges so far to align economic with moral considerations, affirming a dualist approach to be preferred.[44] Nevertheless, French-speaking judges (probably under the influence of the French system) have had less of a struggle to do so.[45] Despite the paucity of case law on moral rights, Canadian courts seem to be moving away from a secondary role to one which achieves a closer balancing between moral and economic rights.[46] Yet, as in the other jurisdictions, as moral rights curently remain distinct from economic rights, fair dealing exceptions, including parody, remain applicable to economic rights alone.

3.4 European Union influence despite the lack of EU harmonization

When considering UK and French national legislation, we cannot ignore the influence of the partial EU harmonization of copyright law. Although the InfoSoc Directive has not harmonized moral rights[47]—these remain an exclusive competence of Member States—this does not mean that EU legal texts are silent on this matter. For example, Recital 19 of the InfoSoc Directive states:

> [M]oral rights of right holders should be exercised according to the legislation of the Member States and the provisions of the Berne Convention for the Protection of Literary and Artistic Works and of the WIPO Copyright Treaty and of the WIPO Performances and Phonograms Treaty.

Additionally, the EU General Court has identified that an essential function of copyright is to 'protect the moral rights in the work and ensure a reward for creative effort'.[48] Thus, when the CJEU noted subsequently, in *Deckmyn*, that in principle a right-holder may have a legitimate interest not to be associated with a comment made through a particularly parody[49] (e.g. when it is legitimate to restrict freedom of expression),[50] this seems most likely to have been a timely reminder that national courts should keep in mind the moral rights obligations of International law. An alternative interpretation preferred by Rosati (at least) is to infer that the CJEU is attempting de facto harmonization of moral rights within the EU. [51]

[42] *Théberge* (n 28) [11]–[12]; Goudreau (n 3) 404. [43] See Chapter 4.

[44] See *Théberge* (n 28). [45] *Desputeaux* (n 3) [57].

[46] One can speculate that the view expressed by the Supreme Court in *CCH* could amount to interpreting moral rights in harmony with the public interest, which comprises the interests of users in manipulating works to create new ones. *CCH Canadian Ltd v. Law Society of Upper Canada* [2004] 1 S.C.R. 339 (hereafter *CCH*).

[47] T-E Synodinou, *Codification of European Copyright Law: Challenges and Perspectives* (Kluwer, 2012) chapter 11.

[48] Decision in T-76/89 *Independent Television Publications Ltd v. Commission* (1991) ECLI:EU:T:1991:41, [56].

[49] *Deckmyn and Vrijheidsfonds VZW v. Helena Vandersteen and Others* [2014] ECLI:EU:C:2014:2132 (hereafter *Deckmyn*), [31].

[50] See Chapter 5, section 4.

[51] Argued by E Rosati, 'Just a matter of laugh? Why the CJEU decision in *Deckmyn* is broader than parody' (2015) 52 *CMLR* 511, 529.

3.5 The United States and the patchwork of protection

In the US, as for the other common law jurisdictions, the focus of copyright law is to provide property rights as a means to secure investment in creative endeavours rather than as a tool to protect personal interests.[52] However, having ratified the Berne Convention in 1989, the US was required to comply with the minimum level of moral rights protection which is defined therein. In the lead up to the US accession to Berne, a working group was tasked with identifying the existing level of compatibility with Berne. Despite the dissonance expressed by signatory parties at the time, the working group concluded that US statutory and common law was already Berne compliant,[53] such that new moral rights legislation was deemed superfluous. Only later, with the advent of new technologies, has the strengthening of the moral rights protection been considered.[54]

Thus, the current US moral rights protection framework for an author's paternity and integrity rights consists predominantly of a combination of state and federal law torts, including defamation, libel, misrepresentation, and unfair competition.[55] In addition, a call to strengthen moral rights relating to motion pictures was met by the National Film Preservation Act 1988. This authorized the Library of Congress to select twenty-five films annually to be added to a national register, based upon their social and cultural significance.[56] This instrument was shortly followed by the Visual Artists Rights Act 1990 ('VARA').[57] However, given the overall scepticism towards moral rights,[58] VARA recognizes paternity and integrity rights for a limited set of works, i.e. pictorial, graphic, and sculptural works.[59] Later, in order to join WCT and WPPT (which encompass moral rights-related concerns by incorporation of the relevant Berne provisions[60]), the Digital Millennium Copyright Act ('DMCA') was enacted in 1998. Once again, Congress did not consider that substantial changes were needed either to copyright law, or otherwise, to implement the WIPO treaties.[61] Yet, DMCA did add two provisions which affect moral rights: section 1201, addressing technological protection measures and section 1202, which protects rights management information.[62] The latter has been interpreted by courts as providing a right against false attribution.[63] Finally, trade mark legislation goes some way to protect personal interests

[52] This explains why there was basically no moral rights protection in the Copyright Act 1976.

[53] This was confirmed by the House and Senate hearings on the subject of moral rights. The moral rights provisions were therefore removed from the Berne Implementation Act 1988. See S. Rep. No 100–352, at 9–10 (1988); H.R. Rep. No 100–609, at 37–8 (1988); see also S. Exec. Rep. No. 100–17, at 55 (1988) (to accompany S. Treaty Doc. No. 99–27 (1986)).

[54] The United States Copyright Office is undertaking a public study to assess the current state of US law recognizing and protecting moral rights for authors, specifically the rights of attribution and integrity (23 January 2017). See https://www.federalregister.gov/documents/2017/01/23/2017-01294/study-on-the-moral-rights-of-attribution-and-integrity (access date: 1 June 2018).

[55] Privacy and contract law are also used to protect the authors' personal interests. G J Yonover, 'Artistic parody: the precarious balance: moral rights, parody, and fair use' (1996) 14 *Cardozo Arts & Ent. L.J.* 79, 94.

[56] See the National Film Preservation Act 1988. This legislation expired in 1991. The 1992 Act no longer focused on moral rights. Nimmer (n 12) vol. III, § 8D.02[D][3].

[57] Visual Artists Rights Act of 1990, Pub. L. No. 101-650, 104 Stat. 5128, 17 U.S.C. § 106A ('VARA').

[58] There was a general fear from creative industries of the litigation, which the introduction of moral rights in US law would attract.

[59] These rights could nevertheless be waived in particular circumstances (17 U.S.C. 106A(e)). Interestingly, this statute includes a right to prevent destruction of the work (17 U.S.C. 106A(3)(b)).

[60] It must be remembered that TRIPS includes no equivalent of article 6bis Berne.

[61] H.R. Rep. No. 105-551, pt. 1, [9] (1998).

[62] 17 U.S.C. §§ 1201–1202.

[63] *Williams* v. *Cavalli S.p.A.*, No CV 14–06659–AB (JEMx), 2015 WL 1247065, [3] (C.D. Cal. Feb. 12, 2015); *Leveyfilm, Inc. v. Fox Sports Interactive Media, LLC,* 999 F.Supp.2d 1098, 1101–2

with section 43(a) Lanham Act providing protection against false designation of origin and preventing the nature or quality of a protected work from being misrepresented.[64] Hence, this provision contains three rudimentary types of protection against false attribution, preservation of authorship, and integrity.[65]

Contract law also plays a certain role in preserving the author's moral rights in the US as it does in other jurisdictions under scrutiny (although its effectiveness is yet to be proven). Whether in the form of guild agreements or other personal contracts, these allow authors to negotiate the protection of their paternity and integrity rights. Here, the Creative Commons and its various licences are usually brandished as a successful example in which private ordering protects authors' moral interests.[66]

In this disparate landscape of under-developed protection, the author's personal interests are protected in various ways, which are all external to copyright law. As a result, the fair use parody defence does not apply to moral rights as protected under US law. Thus, as in the other jurisdictions, we must consider the rights in more detail and evaluate whether moral rights are likely to buttress creators against attempts to rely upon the parody exception, potentially erecting an additional barrier for parodists in their creative endeavours.

3.6 Conclusion

Our study has identified a wide jurisdictional variation in the nature and scope of protection afforded to moral rights.[67] This is attributable to different attitudes engrained in the civil and common law traditions, which remain evident to this day.[68] The scattered protection of personal interests according to the Anglo-American tradition may create difficulties for an author wishing to bring a claim to protect these interests.

One common thread is that the parody exception in 'copyright' law does not extend to moral rights.[69] Insofar as moral rights actions remain distinct and separate from

(N.D. Ill. 2014); *Compare Murphy v. Millennium Radio Grp. LLC*, 650 F.3d 295, 305 (3d Cir. 2011); *Fox v. Hildebrand*, No CV 09–2085 DSF (VBKx), 2009 WL 1977996, [3] (C.D. Cal. July 1, 2009). Though some courts limited this possibility to the digital sphere: *Textile Secrets Int'l Inc. v. Ya-Ya Brand Inc.*, 524 F.Supp.2d 1184, 1201 (C.D. Cal. 2007); *IQ Grp., Ltd v. Wiesner Publ'g, LLC*, 409 F.Supp.2d 587, 597 (D.N.J. 2006).

[64] Lanham Act, 15 U.S.C. §§ 1051–1129 (2000).

[65] It is noteworthy to mention that some states have strengthened the protection given to authors' personal interests by adopting a type of moral rights legislation. For example, the states of New York and California (see, respectively, New York Arts & Cult. Aff. Law § 14.03 and Cal. Civ. Code § 987). Other states include California, Connecticut, Louisiana, Maine, Massachusetts, Nevada, New Jersey, New Mexico, Pennsylvania, and Rhode Island. However, as specified by §301 17 U.S.C., preemption be might applied. For discussion on states besides California and New York, see generally Nimmer (n 12) § 8D. 09; § 8D. 07[C]; Yonover (n 55) 95–6.

[66] The default licence option now includes attribution. *Creative Commons Project*, Cover Pages (22 August 2008), available at http://xml.coverpages.org/creativeCommons.html (access date 10 November 2018).

[67] Traditionally, France is seen as providing a high level of protection of moral rights whereas common law jurisdictions (especially the UK and Australia) are criticized for providing a minimum level of protection deriving from article 6bis Berne (for example, common law jurisdictions do not protect against divulgation or provide for withdrawal rights). L Bently and B Sherman, *Intellectual Property Law* (4th edn, OUP, 2014) 276 and 283–4.

[68] For a comprehensive study of the paternity right in the US, UK, Australia, and Canada, see Ginsburg (n 130) 263.

[69] *UK*: section 79(4)(a) CDPA does not include parody as an exception to the paternity right; UK Government, *Impact Assessment: Copyright Exception for Parody* (20 December 2012); H.M. Government, *Modernising Copyright: A Modern, Robust and Flexible Framework* (UK, 2012) 4; P Groves, 'Pistache?—A consultation paper' (2008) 19 *Ent. L. R.* 89, 92; Adeney (n 8) 417; E Baden-Powell, 'Whose line is it anyway?—new exceptions for parody and private copying' (2013) 24(4) *Ent.*

copyright infringement, it remains to be determined whether, and in what circumstances, the author of a copyright work could enjoin a parodist from reproducing their work based upon a protected personal interest.

4. Does the Parody Exception Clash with the Personal Interests of the Author?

As we have seen, the purpose of moral rights is to protect an author from harm arising as a consequence of a distortion of their work or an inadequate/inaccurate attribution. To what extent will the paternity and integrity rights come to the rescue if an author wishes to object to a parodic use of their work?

4.1 The paternity right

The right of paternity requires acknowledgement of an author's claim to authorship each time their work is exploited. This requirement serves as a public mark of a work's authenticity[70] and facilitates an author in establishing a reputation.[71] Neither national nor international legislation defines the form which this recognition should take.[72] Although identification is traditionally achieved by affixing the author's signature to the work, customary practices in different authorial fields prescribe other forms of attribution.[73]

4.1.1 Countries with dedicated authorship provisions in their copyright law

In order to respect article 6bis(1) Berne, the national legislation provides:

France: 'An author shall enjoy the right to respect for his name, his authorship and his work.'[74]

Canada: 'The author of a work has, […], the right, where reasonable in the circumstances, to be associated with the work as its author by name or under a pseudonym and the right to remain anonymous.'[75]

L. R. 130, 131; E Baden-Powell and J Woodhead, 'Big leeks will inspire you, but who gets the credit?' (2012) 23(3) *Ent. L. R.* 59; Sir Robin Jacob, 'Parody and IP claims: a defence?—a right to parody?' in R C Dreyfuss and J C Ginsburg (eds), *Intellectual Property at the Edge: The Contested Contours of IP* (CIPIL, 2014) 436; B Spitz, 'Droit d'auteur, copyright et parodie ou le mythe de l'usage loyal' (2005) 2 *RIDA* 55; S Bate, 'Moral rights: parody and caricature' (1989) 7 *International Media Law* 81–2; *Australia*: Government, *Parodies, Satires & Jokes. —Information Sheet* (Australian Copyright Council G083v03, 2008) 1–6; Nevertheless, the Commonwealth Attorney-General did not fail to mention that the introduction of the integrity right is not intended to stifle parody or satires; Commonwealth, Parliamentary Debates, House of Representatives, 18 June 1997, 5547–8 (Hon Daryl Williams QC); J McCutcheon, 'Property in literary characters—protection under Australian copyright law' (2007) 29(4) *EIPR* 140, 148–9; *Canada*: M Geist, *The Copyright Pentalogy: How the Supreme Court of Canada Shook the Foundations of Canadian Copyright Law* (University of Ottawa Press, 2013) 443; E A C Mohammed, 'Parody as fair dealing in Canada: a guide for lawyers and judges' (2009) 4 *JIPLP* 468, 471; *France*: Lucas-Schloetter (n 19) 62. This is also the position in the Wittem European Copyright Code: see article 5.6(2) which requires parody to respect the right of attribution.

[70] Davies and Garnett (n 4) 5; Adeney (n 8) 179; Dworkin (n 8) 329.

[71] Davies and Garnett (n 4) 6; Dworkin (n 8) 331.

[72] The Australian provision requires the identification to be clear and prominent. Section 195AA CA 1968; B Galopin, *Les exceptions à usage public en droit d'auteur* (IRPI, 2012) 265; Sainsbury (n 12) 47; Ricketson (n 12) 81.

[73] E Gairal, *Les oeuvres d'art et le droit* (University of Lyon, 1900) 261.

[74] L. 121-1 IPC.

[75] Section 14.1(1) CA 1985.

UK: 'The author of a copyright literary, dramatic, musical or artistic work, and the director of a copyright film, has the right to be identified as the author or director of the work in the circumstances mentioned in this section; but the right is not infringed unless it has been asserted in accordance with section 78.'[76]

Australia: 'The author of a work has a right of attribution of authorship in respect of the work. The author's right is the right to be identified in accordance with this Division as the author of the work if any of the acts (the attributable acts) mentioned in section 194 are done in respect of the work.'[77]

The UK provision clearly departs from the other jurisdictions by making protection contingent upon prior assertion of the right by the author.[78] Hence, unless the paternity right has been asserted, a parodist, for example, will not infringe this moral right, even if they have failed to attribute authorship of the original.[79] Australia distinguishes itself by establishing an exhaustive list of those acts which are attributable.[80] It also provides a 'reasonableness' defence,[81] meaning that the the failure adequately to attribute a work to its author will not constitute a paternity right violation if it was reasonable in the circumstances.[82] The French and Canadian provisions are characterized by their brevity. This can be explained by the fact that the codification of the paternity right is simply 'formal' recognition of an uncontroversial and well-established legal principle.[83] However, the reasonableness criterion in Canadian legislation enables courts to recognize an implied waiver of this right, weakening the author's claim to identification.

4.1.2 *The US: the odd one out*

In contrast to the other common law jurisdictions which have introduced specific provisions to protect the paternity right, we have seen that the US patchwork relies on a feeble recognition of the right in VARA, indirect application via section 43(a) of the Lanham Act, a somewhat dubious route through the DMCA[84] and a mandate to protect copyright management information ('CMI').[85] Unsurprisingly, therefore, the weak, indirect protection has been widely criticized as disserving creators and breaching the US international obligations under Berne.[86] It also explains why, in practice, the paternity right is frequently preserved by contract law, providing some redress for uncredited uses.

Firstly, the limited scope of VARA prevents a wider application of the paternity right. This legislation only applies to works of visual art which are embodied in a

[76] Section 77(1) CDPA. [77] Section 193(1)–(2) CA 1968.

[78] In contrast to France and Canada, the CDPA determines the circumstances in which the right arises. Section 77(2)–(6) CDPA. Section 77(3) CDPA also mentions the need to respect the right of attribution where there is an adaptation made but, as explained in Chapter 1, parody is not considered as infringing the adaptation right.

[79] Section 78 CDPA; Davies and Garnett (n 4) 137. [80] Section 194 CA 1968.

[81] E.g. sections 195, 195AA, and 195AB CA 1968.

[82] This defence is also available for a violation of the integrity right but not the right against false attribution.

[83] Trib. Civ. Seine 26 juin 1832 cited by P Sirinelli, *Le droit moral de l'auteur et le droit commun des contrats* (Paris II, 1985) 6; Paris, 8 août 1837 cited in R Sarraute, 'Current theory on the moral right of authors and artists under French law' (1968) 16 *Am. J. Comp. L.* 465, 478.

[84] For example, article 10(3) Berne makes attribution a condition to the quotation right.

[85] Furthermore, the name of the author is required for registering copyright. See 17 U.S.C. §409(2).

[86] J Ginsburg, 'The most moral of rights: the right to be recognized as the author of one's work' (2016) 8(1) *Geo. Mason J. Int'l Com. L.* 44. However, as acknowledged by Ginsburg, what represents a violation of US international obligations is less the lack of protection of US authors than the failure to protect foreign authors (see article 5 Berne). Ibid, 49.

limited number of originals (up to 200 reproductions of a painting, print, drawing, or sculpture). Photographs are only protected if these have to be produced for exhibition purposes only, thereby preventing many commercial artists from relying on this provision. Yet, a waiver will only be enforceable if it has been agreed in writing, designating the works specifically and signed by the author.[87]

Secondly, section 1202 US Copyright Act, which is concerned with the integrity of CMI (and implements article 12 WCT), offers a cause of action against any usurpation of rights management information which might facilitate infringement of an economic right. This establishes a higher threshold for protection as compared with the right enshrined in article 12 WCT.[88] It undermines a claimant's position, since they must establish that the defendant has actual or constructive knowledge that the removal or alteration of the CMI would induce copyright infringement.[89] Moreover, section 1202(c), which provides a definition of CMI, requires details of the author, the right-holder, and the title of the work to be included. In some circumstances, the writer, performer, and director of a work also need to be mentioned.

Thirdly, section 43(a) of the Lanham Act bestows a private federal cause of action on 'any person who believes that he is or is likely to be damaged' by a 'false designation, description or representation in a commercial context'.[90] Therefore, the Lanham Act makes a misleading or erroneous indication of origin actionable, but apparently only if inaccurate authorship claims are made. Arguably, it does not extend to situations where no credit is given. For example, in *Batiste v. Isaac Bolden, Inc.*,[91] the Ninth Circuit considered the defendant's sampling from the Batiste brothers' track, *Funky Soul*. Originally, *Funky Soul* had been recorded with the help of Isaac Bolden, a local music publisher and record label. To this end, the eldest Batiste brother (and group manager) signed a contract to transfer all the economic rights associated with the recording to Bolden. This agreement asserted that Batiste senior was the sole right-holder. In fact, the track was authored by both brothers. Subsequently, Bolden granted a licence to the Cordes brothers to permit them to sample *Funky Soul* in their track, *So On*. The liner notes accompanying the release of *So On* only credited the eldest Batiste brother. When Bastiste junior commenced proceedings on the basis of section 43(a), the court found for the defendant because of the lack of confusion between the original and the sampled version. While the liner notes did not credit each of the Batiste brothers, it referred to the band's name and the eldest brother which was held sufficient.

What is even more worrisome is that the Supreme Court's ruling in *Dastar Corp. v. Twentieth Century Fox Film Corp*[92] has been seen to suggest that attribution claims are only protectable within the limits of VARA.[93] Against this backdrop, the general assumption seems to be that an author has no right to guarantee their association with their own work, particularly if that right has been waived or if ownership of the work has been transferred without an express requirement that authorship is to be credited in subsequent uses.[94] This suggests that the fact that a parodist has not acknowledged the author of the copyright-protected work will not be actionable unless it is brought under the remit of the right against false attribution as it is more likely to create confusion between the two works.[95]

[87] In this respect, the US is closer to its Australian counterpart.

[88] Section1202 is nevertheless broader than article 12 WCT insofar as it is not limited to electronic communications. Ginsburg (n 86) 62.

[89] E.g. *McClatchey v. Associated Press*, 2007 U.S. Dist. LEXIS 17768, [1] (W.D. Pa. March 9, 2007).

[90] Also known as 'reversed passing off'.

[91] 179 F.3d 217 (5th Cir. 1999).

[92] 539 U.S. 23 (2003) (hereafter *Dastar*).

[93] See section 4.2.2.

[94] Nimmer (n 12), vol. III, § 8D.03[A][2][a].

[95] See section 4.2.

4.1.3 Reconciling parody with the paternity right

The relationship between the copyright exceptions and moral rights remains largely unexplored. As is now familiar to us, a parody only 'succeeds' if the public identifies the underlying parodied work(s). A parodist is not aiming to *confuse* the public as to authorship, but seeks to build upon the common reference point provided by the earlier work to convey a new expression. Arguably, requiring a parody to identify the author of the parodied work explicitly would severely compromise it as a parody. In effect, it would carry a warning label that would potentially 'spoil the joke'. Alternatively, the presence of the original author's name on the parody might confuse the public, causing them to wonder whether the altered work is a parody, or the original author's own work. Indeed, requiring parodists to identify original authors might preclude them from being able to identify themselves as authors of the parody. In any event, it is questionable whether the original author would want their name linked explicitly with a parody, since they may prefer to avoid any direct association with the message which the parody of their work conveys.[96]

The legislative guidance which has been provided indicates that a party which benefits from a copyright exception must still respect the paternity right.[97] In France, while the legislation is explicit in respect of the exceptions enshrined in L.122-5, 3° Intellectual Property Code (IPC), the parody exception, in L.122-5, 4° IPC, is silent in this regard. This strongly suggests that those reliant upon the parody exception do not need to have regard to the paternity right. Similarly in Canada, although all other fair dealing exceptions are contingent upon acknowledgment of authorship,[98] in the case of fair dealing for the purpose of parody, the requirement is absent.[99] There has been only one Canadian case which has considered moral rights directly.[100] Here, the Court of Appeal recognized the potential for the same use to infringe both the moral and economic rights in a work; the decision itself offered no further indication as to how the paternity right should be respected in the event that an exception rendered the use lawful in respect of the economic rights. However, it appears that the manner in which the paternity right is recognized should not completely circumscribe use which is permitted because of an exception applying to the associated economic rights only.

But is it possible for the paternity right to be reconciled with a parody in practice? Since the statutory requirements concerning the parody exception are open-ended, then it seems possible that the intrinsic label left by the parodist which permits the public to identify the original work is sufficient attribution. Indeed, the French Supreme Court thought so in *Douces Transes*.[101] In considering a musical parody with altered lyrics, the court considered that the vocal imitation and the reproduction of the entire musical

[96] Davies and Garnett (n 4) 116; Groves (n 69) 92.

[97] The relationship between economic rights and moral rights is hard to define. Lucas and Lucas (n 25) n° 502-3.

[98] Section 29.21 CA 1985. This right has to be reasonably executed. It is possible that in applying the teachings from *CCH* (n 46), courts will rebalance moral rights and users' rights to protect the public interest. This is likely to result in even allowing parody works argued under the user-generated content exception to still be held as non-infringing by courts despite the lack of the presence of the name of the author of the parts reproduced.

[99] Section 29 CA 1985. This approach should not be extendable to the UK and Australia because they consider moral rights as separate to copyright. Nevertheless, a study of the exceptions suggests such extension is possible. Certain exceptions (such as the English exception for research and private study or criticism, review, and news reporting—sections 29 and 30 CDPA) must be accompanied by a 'sufficient acknowledgement'. A similar indication exists in Australia. See sections 41–42 CA 1968.

[100] *Desputeaux* (n 3) [57].

[101] Cass., 12 janvier 1988, RIDA, n°137, 98 (hereafter *Douces Transes*).

work was sufficient for the public to recognize the original song, and thus satisfy the paternity right of the original author. Furthermore, the new lyrics ensured that the two works were not confused, since it was customary in musical parodies for one performer to impersonate another, by (over-)exaggerating the distinctive characteristics of their voice. As an accepted form of mockery, the court determined that the parody should not be an actionable treatment under moral rights provisions.

The UK courts have adopted a similar approach, albeit not in a parody case. In *Preston v. Raphael Tuck & Sons*,[102] the High Court considered whether attribution needed to be explicit. Here, the defendant had altered the shape of a painting by trimming its borders to an oval shape, changed the background colour to black, and omitted any reference to the original artist. The court identified that mere recognition, or a more general association with the 'original' work, was insufficient, but that the appropriate test was whether a reasonable person seeing the altered work would recognize it and associate its authorship with the original author.[103] Provided the test was satisfied, however, there was no need for the author's name to appear on the work. This suggests that in the case of a parody, the original author's attribution does not need to be explicit, since sufficient attribution is made implicitly.[104]

Infringement of the right of attribution is heavily fact dependent, turning upon the nature of the work and the circumstances surrounding the use.[105] In the case of a parodic use, if the parodist does seek to rely upon implicit attribution, much will depend upon whether the parodist has selected a well-enough known work to parody, and their skill in execution. A true parody, i.e. one which avoids infringement of the economic rights because the parody exception applies, would seem to automatically respect the paternity right in that original work too. As such, the paternity right will not jeopardize the aims of the parody exception. Conversely, if a parodist's efforts are unsuccessful, and the public is unsure whether they are exposed to an original or to a parody, then not only is the altered work unlikely to fall within the parody exception, but it is reasonable to assume that the work does not respect the author's paternity right either. Infringement of both rights may be measured by the same yardstick.

The reasonable person test, proposed by the UK court, seems a sensible approach.[106] The nature and prominence of the 'signage' needed to identify the underlying work in the parody is proportional to the renown of the earlier work. The more famous the underlying work, the more subtle the signposting can be, and still respect the paternity right.[107] If a parodist elects to parody a lesser known work, then they may need to be more explicit to ensure proper identification by the public.[108] If the work selected is too obscure, then the parodist may need to expressly mention the original author's name to meet the requirements of the paternity right. This in turn may lead to public confusion in which case the parody 'fails' on both counts.

Essentially, even though authors receive a lower level of protection in some jurisdictions in terms of the right of attribution, this does not mean that the authors' interests are not protected in another way. When it comes to parody, for example, these interests

[102] [1926] 1 Ch 667. [103] Echoing defamation law principles.

[104] Based on this argument, it could be suggested that under Canadian law, the paternity right can be deemed as waived in parody cases under the reasonableness criterion. See also *Eva-Maria Painer v. Standard Verlags GmbH and Others* [2011] ECLI:EU:C:2011:798.

[105] Adeney (n 8) 686.

[106] S McCausland, 'New room to lampoon: the new fair dealing exception for parody or satire' (2007) 1 *Art+Law* 3, 4.

[107] Groves (n 69) 92. Also rejected in *Deckmyn* (n 49) in relation to economic rights, [21].

[108] TGI Paris, 9 mars 2017, *Bauret v. Koons*, RG n°15/01086 (hereafter *Les Enfants*).

are taken into account when assessing the application of the exception. By compelling the parodist to avoid confusion between the original work and its parody use, the law requires the public to be able to identify the original and its author. Therefore, if the acknowledgement of the earlier author is not made explicit, it is nevertheless present in another form.

Finally, although appropriate authorship of any altered work is always potentially problematic, it is opined that parodists should always be able to be recognized as the author of their parodies.[109] It is the parodist who, by altering an existing work, has created a new work, and so it is fitting that they are identified by the public as its author.

4.2 The right against false attribution

A reasonable corollary to an author's right to be identified with their work is that the original author should not be identified as the author of a work which they have not created. This premise is the basis of a moral right which permits an author to object to a false attribution of authorship, and use of their name on the work of another.[110]

4.2.1 Objecting to a parody based on false attribution

In France, this right is integral to, or the obverse of, the right of paternity,[111] whereas the UK,[112] Australia,[113] and the US[114] perceive this as a separate right[115] Canada adopts something of a hybrid approach, and although Canada does not have a specific right, it might adopt the same approach as in France.[116] As with the paternity right, the right against false attribution applies to the exploitation of the copyright-protected work, including adaptations thereof.[117] While in Australia, the duration of protection is aligned on the duration of the right of paternity,[118] in the UK, this right expires twenty years after the death of the author who is falsely attributed.[119] The rationale here is that after this time, little damage is caused to any residual reputation.[120] Australia is likely to adopt a similar approach to the UK owing to the influence of UK jurisprudence on the development of the law there.

As discussed in the preceding section, as parody is a reworking of earlier works,[121] at first blush, it seems reasonable that the original author might have a basis to object

[109] See n 70. [110] For more: Davies and Garnett (n 4) 209.

[111] Recognized by judges in Paris, 1ère ch., 17 décembre 1986, *Utrillo*: RIDA 2/1987, p. 66; Lucas and Lucas (n 25) n°502-3.

[112] *UK*: section 84 CDPA.

[113] *Australia*: section 195AC(1) CA 1968 combined with section 195AD(a)(i)–(ii) CA 1968.

[114] *US*: section 43(a) Lanham Act (deriving from unfair competition); *Dastar* (n 92).

[115] Analytically distinct from moral rights which traditionally assert authorship instead of disclaiming authorship.

[116] *Canada* does not have a separate right to object to false attribution. Adeney (n 8) 328. Nevertheless, Adeney argues that the absence of the right against false attribution is compensated by the right of anonymity. This right of anonymity only exists for an author in relation to his work, leading to unclear situations related to altered works. Indeed, courts need to determine whether the altered work can be considered as a work of the original author in the first place.

[117] *UK*: section 84(2)-(8) CDPA; *Australia*: sections 195AD–AH CA 1968.

[118] *Australia*: section 195AM CA 1968. [119] *UK*: section 86(2) CDPA.

[120] Since the heavily criticized *Dastar* (n 92), actions under section 43(a) Lanham Act are limited to the duration of copyright.

[121] Though probably not 'adaptation' as intended under copyright law. See the Conclusion in Chapter 1.

to a parody as a false attribution of their work. In this part, we examine whether this position stands up to further scrutiny.

4.2.2 The right against false attribution in the US

In the US, it was traditionally possible to bring an action for a 'false designation of origin'[122] by relying upon trade mark law. Authors could bring an action pursuant to section 43(a) of the Lanham Act. For example, the Monty Python team brought an action against broadcaster, ABC,[123] in order to disassociate themselves from an unauthorized abridged version of their work. The Lanham Act has also been applied in parody cases, as exemplified by *Waits v. Frito-Lay, Inc.*[124] Singer-songwriter Waits had always expressed a strong belief that an artist's musical integrity was compromised by permitting their works to feature in commercial advertising. Unsurprisingly, therefore, he took no exception to a Frito-Lay parody of one of his songs, which also mimicked his distinctive gravelly voice to promote a new line of *Doritos* corn chips. The Ninth Circuit affirmed the jury's finding that the advert might lead to consumer confusion. By imitating his song and his voice, the defendant was making a false representation that Waits had endorsed the promoted product line.[125]

However, in 2003, the US Supreme Court reviewed the legitimacy of this approach in *Dastar*.[126] In 1995, to mark the fiftieth anniversary of World War II, Dastar produced a video of edited clips from a 1948 television series, *Crusade in Europe*. The series was based on a book of the same name by Dwight Eisenhower. Although the Dastar video reproduced about half of the original TV series, neither the book nor the original programme nor its producers received any credit. Fox had acquired the rights to the original book, and although the TV series had entered the public domain in 1977, the company had licensed others to distribute *Crusade in Europe* on video. Fox launched proceedings against Dastar under the Lanham Act for inadequate attribution of the film clips used.[127] Essentially, Fox argued that Dastar were 'passing off' others' work as their own.

Although the district and appeal courts found for Fox, the Supreme Court disagreed. The court held that the Lanham Act claim was concerned with the commercial origin of the tangible goods, meaning the Dastar videos were correctly attributed. As the rights to the intellectual property embodied in those goods protecting the creative efforts of the original authors had expired, the Lanham Act did not oblige Dastar to give any credit for the excerpts which it had copied.[128] The court was concerned that claims about authorship might be used to circumvent the time limit placed upon copyright law's exclusive rights. The ruling proved to be controversial. On one hand, adopting a broad interpretation, the decision seems to accept that authorship should be properly attributed, albeit that attribution claims should be based upon the US Copyright Act.

[122] For older decisions, see *Smith v. Montoro*, 648 F.2d 602 (9th Cir. 1981); *Geisel v. Poynter Products Inc.*, 283 F.Supp. 261 (S.D.N.Y. 1968); *Rich v. RCA Corp.*, 390 F.Supp. 530 (S.D.N.Y. 1952).

[123] *Gilliam v. American Broadcasting Companies (ABC), Inc.*, 538 F.2d 14, 24, 192 USPQ 1, [24] (CA, 2d Cir. 1976).

[124] 978 F.2d 1093 (CA, 9th Cir. 1992).

[125] Ibid, [1106]–[1111].

[126] *Dastar* (n 92).

[127] For a detailed report of this case, see T Ochoa, 'Introduction: rights of attribution, section 43(a) of the Lanham Act, and the copyright public domain' (2003) 24 *Whittier L. Rev.* 911.

[128] *Dastar* (n 92) [33]. Hence, the idea of misattribution and non-attribution in the US is linked to consumer deception.

However, a narrower interpretation limits its teachings to circumstances, as in *Dastar*, where copyright in the work has expired.[129]

Beyond the controversy surrounding *Dastar*,[130] section 1202(a) US Copyright Act requires consideration. This provision, implementing article 12 WCT, protects against false copyright management information, which may include identification information concerning a work's authorship. Yet, as we have seen already,[131] this provision is of limited scope, since removal of authorship information will only be a violation if it is reasonably foreseeable that removal amounts to, or facilitates, infringement of economic rights.[132]

Given that the right of attribution receives such a low level of protection,[133] one may wonder whether there is any interplay between a parody of a copyright-protected work and a false attribution claim in US law. If it is accepted that authors do have a moral claim to be recognized as the author of their own creation, and equally, be able to object to being associated with a work which they have not (solely) created, then it needs to be recognized that this might not always further the public interest. As the US right to false attribution is closely linked to protecting consumers, it seems fair to assess where the consumer interest lies in relation to parody works. Whilst requiring accurate authorship attribution information to be affixed on the work would inform most consumers as to the work's originator,[134] it might also devalue the consumer experience in two ways. Firstly, additional attribution might spoil the visual appeal of the work, especially in the case of a visual works. Secondly, attribution might ruin the message which the parody is conveying, in terms of the criticism or comment being made via parody.[135] Here, it might actually be in the consumer's best interest *not* to be told who the author is, so that they work this out for themselves.[136]

With a parody, the public will be exposed to the work of at least two creators: the author of the earlier work and the creator of the parody. In the absence of a statutory attribution requirement in establishing lawful use, contextual attribution may serve the same purpose as an explicit disclaimer.[137] As mentioned, the more popular the earlier work, the more likely it is that a parodic treatment of that work will be recognized as such. If fair use obliged a parodist to credit the author of the original, the amusement provoked by the realization of the reference made would be lost. Equally, some members of the public might feel intellectually offended. Furthermore, it may

[129] And the Supreme Court's commitment to preserve the public domain.

[130] Reviewing the influence of *Dastar* (n 92), see J C Ginsburg, 'Moral rights in the US: still in need of a guardian ad litem' (2012) *Cardozo Arts & Ent. L.J.* 73, 81–2; J C Ginsburg, 'The right to claim authorship in US copyright and trademarks law' (2004) 41 *Houston Law Review* 268.

[131] See section 4.1.2.

[132] Interestingly, US courts have noted that uploading works online without attribution does not amount to false CMI as posting generally does not amount to asserting ownership over works. See *Tomelleri v. Zazzle, Inc.*, No 13-2576, 2015 U.S. Dist. LEXIS 165007 (D. Kan. Dec. 9, 2015), [36]–[37]; *Pers. Keepsakes, Inc. v. Personalizationmall.com, Inc.*, 975 F.Supp. 2d 920, 929 (N.D. Ill. 2013).

[133] For more: Ginsburg (n 130).

[134] Though this may lead to impracticalities based on the nature of the work involved which explains why other jurisdictions such as Canada and the EU have limited the right to attribution to situations where it is reasonable and feasible to do so. Additionally, this requirement may lead to confusion for the rushed consumer exposed to thousands of works on a daily basis. This latter position is argued by R Tushnet, 'Naming rights: attribution and law' (2007) 3 *Utah L. Rev.* 781, 803.

[135] Ibid.

[136] Therefore, an alternative theory supports reliance on defamation and invasion of one's privacy. Defamation, as accepted in cases where the work falsely attributed is of an inferior quality compared to the original. See Nimmer (n 12) vol. III, § 8D.03[B][1].

[137] This is already recognized in US trade mark parodies: see *Cliffs Notes, Inc. v. Bantam Doubleday Dell Publ'g. Group, Inc.*, 886 F.2d 490, 496 (2d Cir. 1989) cited by R Tushnet (n 134) 816.

be argued that US courts already consider attribution implicitly as part of the fair use assessment.[138] Consequently, although US law seems to lack a specific right of false attribution (pending clarification of *Dastar*'s reach), a flexible approach to the right against false attribution seems appropriate in fair use cases.

4.2.3 Parody and the tolerance of temporary confusion

Firstly, an author who wishes to rely upon the right against false attribution must demonstrate a misrepresentation of the copyright-protected work which creates confusion concerning authorship. In terms of whether a parody creates such confusion, it seems that a parodist's intention is exactly the opposite. The parodist, by reproducing an earlier work which is familiar to the target public, is certainly alluding to this earlier work, but this is only one step in the parody process. The next step is that the public identify the work as a parody. The parodist does not intend the author of the original work to receive the credit for the comment conveyed by the parody itself. Thus, providing the parody is recognized as such (i.e. the requirements for the parody exception are met), it is reasonable to presume that parody is not attributed to the author of the original work.[139]

This position finds support in UK case law[140] which has had to specifically reconcile a parody with the right against false attribution. In *Clark v. Newspapers Ltd*,[141] the High Court had to determine whether the publication of a parody diary ostensibly written by Alan Clark (a then prominent politician) resulted in false attribution. The parody series, published in *The Evening Standard*, featured a photograph of Mr Clark accompanied by banner titles including: 'Alan Clark's Secret Election Diary' and 'Alan Clark's Secret Political Diary'. The likelihood of confusion arose because, although the entries in the parody diary were fairly outlandish and comical, the politician was known for his outspoken views and unorthodox private life, which he had documented in his own published diaries. Therefore, it was conceivable that some readers would believe that *The Evening Standard* was actually publishing the politician's own work. The Court held that false attribution can only 'be neutralised by an express contradiction, [which] has to be as bold, precise and compelling as the false statement'.[142] In the present case, although the real author's details were mentioned in the standfirst, it was simply too discrete, and Mr Clark's rights had been infringed.

Although this case was determined long before the UK's parody exception was introduced, it provides some insight, since it notes the need to consider the parody as a whole, to ensure that the parody signals are sufficient that the public are not deceived. In this light, transitory confusion may be excused, but more prolonged, or even permanent, confusion should be excluded. This seems consistent with the parody exception. Although it has been argued that the right against false attribution adds an additional requirement to the parody exception 'in the sense that the notional

[138] *Rogers v. Koons*, 960 F.2d 301, 310 (2d Cir. 1992), [310]. The public needs to be aware of the original for adequate attribution to be given. The court goes further and adds that the audience also needs to recognize another expression attributable to another person.

[139] Otherwise, these parodies create confusion in the public and would not be exempted under the exception.

[140] A similar position is likely to be held in Australia too. Given the paucity of case law, scholars refer to the UK *Clark v. Newspapers Ltd* decision. Sainsbury (n 29) 165.

[141] [1998] 1 All ER 959, Ch D.

[142] Ibid, 971.

[audience] should not be confused'[143] about the true authorship of the parody, this appears already implicit in the main requirement of absence of confusion.

Additionally in *Deckmyn*,[144] the CJEU expressly rejected that the parody exception should only apply if the parody 'could reasonably be attributed to a person other than the author of the original work itself'. This seems to suggest that, pursuant to EU law at least, there is probably no conflict between this right and the parody exception. Any parody which creates confusion—either with respect to its authorship, or the work itself—is arguably not a parody, or at least not one which would be considered as a fair dealing, or abiding by the rules of the genre.[145] Therefore, economic rights and moral rights seem to be reconciled on this issue too.

4.3 The integrity right

The integrity right is probably both the most important moral right for authors and the most challenging to reconcile with parody works. The integrity right protects authors against distortion, mutilation, or other modifications of their works.

4.3.1 Respect of the work in the way intended by its author

According to article 6bis(1) of the Berne Convention, an author has 'the right ... to object to any distortion, mutilation or other modification of, or other derogatory action in relation to, the said work, which would be prejudicial to his honor or reputation'. Despite its importance, its implementation into national law varies greatly, leading to various degrees of protection.

4.3.1.1 Protecting the integrity of works through copyright legislation

The national legislation provides:

France:[146] 'An author shall enjoy the right to respect [...] his work.'

Canada:[147] 'The author of a work has, [...], the right to the integrity of the work ...' to which section 28.2(1) CA 1985 adds: '(1) The author's or performer's right to the integrity of a work or performer's performance is infringed only if the work or the performance is, to the prejudice of its author's or performer's honour or reputation, (a) distorted, mutilated or otherwise modified; or (b) used in association with a product, service, cause or institution.'

UK:[148] 'The author [...] has the right [...] not to have his work subjected to derogatory treatment.

(2) For the purposes of this section—

(a) 'treatment' of a work means any addition to, deletion from or alteration to or adaptation of the work, [...]; and
(b) the treatment of a work is derogatory if it amounts to distortion or mutilation of the work or is otherwise prejudicial to the honour or reputation of the author or director ...'

Australia:[149] 'A person infringes an author's right of integrity of authorship in respect of a work if the person subjects the work, or authorises the work to be subjected, to derogatory treatment.'

[143] P Torremans, 'A clash between theory and practice? Introduction' in Brison et al (eds), *Moral Rights* 48.
[144] *Deckmyn* (n 49) [21].
[145] Also admitted by Torremans (n 143) 48.
[146] L. 121-1 IPC.
[147] Section 14.1 CA 1985.
[148] Section 80(1)–(2) CDPA.
[149] Section 195AQ(2) CA 1968.

Derogatory treatment is defined as: '(a) the doing, in relation to the work, of anything that results in a material distortion of, the mutilation of, or a material alteration to, the work that is prejudicial to the author's honour or reputation; or (b) the doing of anything else in relation to the work that is prejudicial to the author's honour or reputation.'[150]

The first major difference is the fact that in France no legislative standard is set: an author's work must be respected.[151] In the UK, Canada, and Australia,[152] the author's right to object to a treatment of their work applies the Berne criterion. The integrity right is violated only if it can be established that the treatment is prejudicial to the author's honour or reputation. It is accepted that article 6bis(1) Berne refers to the 'honour or reputation' of the author as an author, rather than extending to any personal convictions.[153] If an author feels under personal attack, there are alternative legal remedies.[154] However, the Berne wording remains open to an objective or subjective approach.

In the UK[155] and Australia,[156] an objective approach is preferred.[157] Accordingly, the impact of any distortion of a work is measured against the notional standard of a 'right-thinking person'. This ensures that personal feeling or justified criticisms do not violate the integrity right.[158] Also, as the integrity right attaches to a particular work, general statements or criticisms fall outside the scope of this right.[159]

In France, although ostensibly any 'treatment' of a work may infringe an author's right of integrity,[160] the 'detriment to honour or reputation' standard is still relevant[161] as French courts had already developed this as being integral to the right prior to its codification within defamation law.[162] It is apparent from any review of the cases

[150] Section 195AJ CA 1968.

[151] A Waisman, 'Rethinking the moral right to integrity' (2008) 3 *IPQ* 268, 274.

[152] It is noteworthy that the terminology differs insofar as Canada refused to adopt the expression 'derogatory treatment' in its legislation. Also, the UK in section 80(2)(a) CDPA provides a detailed definition of what is supposed to be understood as derogatory treatment. Like the UK, Australia reproduces the concept of 'derogatory treatment' but specifies what is understood under the concept for each category of work.

[153] Dietz (n 8) 181; Ricketson (n 12) 82.

[154] Particularly defamation law and privacy laws.

[155] On the integrity right in the *UK*: K Q Garnett, J R James, and G Davies, *Copinger and Skone James on Copyright* (16th edn, Sweet & Maxwell, 2011) [11-41]–[11-48].

[156] Given the absence of case law, the subjective approach cannot be ruled out completely: see <<<REFO:JART>>>E Adeney, 'The moral right of integrity: the past and future of "honour"' (2005) 2 *IPQ* 111<<<REFC>>>, 129.

[157] Echoing defamation law tests. *Confetti Records v. Warner Music UK Ltd* [2003] EMLR 790, [149]–[150]; *Pasterfield v. Denham* [1999] FSR 168, [182]; *Delves-Broughton v. House of Harlot* [2012] PCC 29, [24]; *Tidy v. Trustees of the National History Museum* [1995] 39 IPR 501 per Rattee J. The latter two cases nevertheless refer to the subjective approach taken by the Canadian courts in *Snow v. Eaton* but refuse to follow it. S Teilmann 'Framing the law: the right of integrity in Britain' (2005) 1 EIPR 19, 22. Doubts concerning the interpretation of this objective test are expressed by Griffiths. J Griffiths, 'Not such a "timid thing": the UK's integrity right and freedom of expression' in J Griffiths and U Suthersanen (eds), *Copyright and Free Speech* (OUP, 2005) 235, 239.

[158] This is the aim of defamation law or injurious falsehood. *UK*: M Spence, 'Intellectual property and the problem of parody' (1998) 114 LQR 594, 613; *Australia*: Australian Copyright Council, *Moral Rights* (Information Sheet G043v13, 2012) 1–8; Sainsbury (n 29) 149–66, 154; Sainsbury (n 12) 234.

[159] See Chapter 6, section 2.2.2 for an overview of moral rights in music; for analysis of the integrity right in the *UK*: Griffiths (n 157) 211–44.

[160] This leads to a subjective approach as the author can object to any unauthorized treatment. Lucas-Schloetter (n 19) 56.

[161] S Grégoire, 'Fasc. 1213: Propriété littéraire et artistique.—exercice des droits des auteurs.—droit moral. droit au respect (CPI, Art. L. 121-1)' (2013) *Jurisclasseur* 1, 4.

[162] Adeney 2005, p. 113.

concerning defamation and the integrity right, in conjunction with the legal literature, that the 'honour and reputation' standard is applied.[163] Yet, the integrity right is broader than that recognized in either the common law jurisdictions or in international treaties, because the French interpretation adopts a subjective approach. Thus, authors enjoy an absolute, discretionary right to object to any alteration of their work, irrespective of its form or amount.[164]

Canada sits midway between Australia and the UK on one side, and France on the other. In *Snow v. The Eaton Centre*,[165] a sculpture in a shopping centre was altered by the temporary affixing of Christmas garlands. The Ontario High Court found the integrity right had been infringed because the sculptor considered that the alteration was detrimental to their honour or reputation, and the court considered that these concerns were reasonable. This finding illustrates how powerful moral rights can be.

In light of the *Snow* decision, Adeney defines 'honour' under Canadian law as 'moral dignity which is enjoyed when one has the feeling of meriting respect and of maintaining self-esteem' whilst 'reputation' is 'a matter of being honourably regarded from a moral point of view'.[166] Therefore, the appraisal of the prejudice to the honour or reputation also carries an objective element as well as a subjective aspect.[167] Although Canadian law sets out a subjective approach, this is only actionable if an objection is reasonably exercised.[168] However, in the case of paintings, sculptures, or engravings *any* distortion is *deemed* prejudicial to the author's honour or reputation.[169] Additionally, the Canadian Copyright Act provides authors with a kind of association right,[170] permitting them to prevent the use of their work in association with products which would be preducial to their honour or reputation.[171]

A second difference between national laws is the type of acts which amount to an actionable 'treatment'. While in France, there is no requirement relating to the form or amount of an actionable alteration,[172] in the remaining jurisdictions which have adopted tailored versions of the Berne provision wording,[173] the different forms adopted have influenced the resulting scope of the integrity right. There is consensus that the right to object arises in the case of a material distortion,[174] meaning the

[163] Grégoire (n 161) 6; Gairal (n 73) 264; Adeney 2005, p. 114.

[164] Grégoire (n 161) 11; Davies and Garnett (n 4) 373; *French Supreme Court in TF1 v. Sony*, Cass., ch. Civ., 24 février 1998 [1998] 177 RIDA 212.

[165] [1982] 70 C.P.R. (2d) 105.

[166] Adeney (n 8) 337; L Carrière, 'Droit d'auteur et droit moral: quelques réflexions préliminaires' in Barreau du Québec (ed.), *Développements récents en droit de la propriété intellectuelle* (Les Editions Yvon Blais Inc., 1991) 270.

[167] As confirmed in *Prise de Parole Inc. v. Guerin* (1996) 66 C.R.P. (3d) 257.

[168] *Prise de Parole Inc. et al v. Guérin, éditeur Ltée* [1995] 66 C.P.R. (3d) 257 (C.F.), p. 264, esp pp. 267–8; confirmed 73 C.P.R. (3d) 557 (C.A.F.); Davies and Garnett (n 4) 691; JS McKeown, *Canadian Intellectual Property Law and Strategy* (OUP, 2010) 214; Adeney (n 8) 334; Adeney 2005, p. 128; Goudreau (n 3) 420.

[169] Section 28.2(2) CA 1985.

[170] Section 28.2(2)(1)(b) CA 1985.

[171] For more, see Sundara Rajan (n 18) 127.

[172] *Barbelivien et autres c/ SA Universal music publishing anciennement dénommée Polygram éditions* 7+ Cass., 5 décembre 2006; Grégoire (n 161) 11; Davies and Garnett (n 4) 373; *TF1 c/ Sony* in Cass., ch. Civ., 24 février 1998 (1998) 177 RIDA 212.

[173] Canada refused to implement 'other derogatory treatment' but included contextual treatment. The UK in section 80(2)(a), (3), (4) CDPA provides a detailed definition of what is supposed to be understood as derogatory treatment. Like the UK, Australia reproduces the concept of 'derogatory treatment' but specifies what is understood under the concept for each category of work.

[174] *France*: Lucas and Lucas (n 25) n°545; Gautier (n 12) 235; *UK*: section 80(2)(a) CDPA; R Burrell and A Coleman, *Copyright Exceptions: The Digital Impact* (CUP, 2005) 77; *Canada*: section 28.2(1)(a) CA 1985; *Australia*: Adeney (n 8) 581 and 588; E Adeney, 'Defining the shape of Australia's moral rights: a review of the new laws' (2001) 4 IPQ 291, 299.

addition or deletion of elements of the work, mutilation, or other modification of the work.[175] However, the subjective nature of the tests in Canada[176] and France[177] recognizes the need to respect the 'spirit' of the work. This enables the author to object to any use which denatures[178] the meaning or ambit[179] of the work which might not be deemed a 'treatment' in the UK or Australia. This includes a change of context,[180] or unauthorized use of the work in commercial advertising.

4.3.1.2 The US reluctance to recognize an integrity right for distortion or mutilation

Some early decisions have granted authors the right to object to unauthorized pornographic distortion of works[181] and subsequent displays of works in a context which they do not approve of.[182] However, difficulties arise as to the standard to be applied. Can it be good taste? Artistic worth? Religious beliefs? Political ideology? Or something else? This inherently constitutes a practical difficulty for courts in their application of the moral rights doctrine.

Although fair practices have filled in the US legislative gaps in relation to the paternity right, the integrity right continues to face continued hostility.[183] Nevertheless, the right is protected to some extent by VARA and other areas of law—mainly contract, defamation, and trade mark laws, which afford an author some degree of protection against an unauthorized treatment of their work.

The first avenue is via the civil tort of defamation,[184] which arises from common law and statutory law. Some have argued that the US protection against libel[185] or slander[186] is broader than the minimum requirements of article 6bis Berne, since the derogatory treatment does not have to relate to a specific protected work.[187] However, the safeguard of free speech protected by the First Amendment to the US Constitution provides strong ammunition for anyone wishing to engage with a work even if this might be deemed derogatory to its author, unless the author is able to prove that the statement made is false. In this respect, defamation laws are more restrictive than

[175] Echoing the wording of Berne (article 6bis(1)).

[176] Section 28.2(1)(b) CA 1985. Davies and Garnett (n 4) 691; Adeney (n 8) 333.

[177] Lucas and Lucas (n 25) n°546.

[178] The author has the right to ensure that the work in form and in spirit remains the way it has been thought by its creator. Grégoire (n 161) 6; Adeney (n 8) 182; Sirinelli (n 12) 10.

[179] Like discriminatory content or hate speech. See Chapter 5, section 4.1.5.

[180] This is not the case in the UK, where a change of context does not alter the character of the work and therefore there is no violation of the integrity right. Garnett (n 155) [11-48]; *contra*: Porsdam interprets 'distortion' and 'otherwise prejudicial' as including contextual uses. E Porsdam, *Copyright and Other Fairy Tales: Hans Christian Andersen The Commodification of Creativity* (Edward Elgar, 2007) 62.

[181] Citing *Benson v. Paul Winley Sales Corp.*, 452 F.Supp. 516 (S.D.N.Y. 1978).

[182] Citing *Shostakovich v. Twentieth Century-Fox Film Corp.*, 196 Misc. 67, 80 N.Y.S.2d 575 (Sup. Ct. N.Y. County 1948), aff'd, 275 A.D. 692, 87 N.Y.S.2d 430 (1st Dep't 1949).

[183] This can be partly explained from the strong protection granted to free speech (e.g. criticism and comment) in the US under the First Amendment to the Constitution which influenced the shaping of the US copyright regime. Recognizing an integrity right would add a limitation to free speech by restricting the individual's use of prior creative works. For more, see R Kwall, *The Soul of Creativity* (Stanford University Press, 2010) 53–68.

[184] Similar to the situation prior to the introduction of specific integrity right provisions in the other jurisdictions analysed. See section 4.3.

[185] For published written statements. [186] For published spoken words.

[187] A Adler, 'The US perspective' (2016) 8(1) *Geo. Mason J. Int'L Com. L.* 26, 28. See *Shostakovich v. Twentieth Century-Fox Film Corp.*, 196 Misc. 67 (1948) where the Supreme Court noted that the use of music in a film was insufficient to demonstrate the composer's approval and endorsement even if the association is unsympathetic to their political ideology.

the Berne Convention, since article 6bis does not impose a veracity requirement.[188] Consequently, defamation laws offer different protection to the integrity right contained in the Berne Convention.

Section 43(a) of the Lanham Act provides the second avenue available to authors. In addition to protecting against any 'false designation of origin', the provision also extends to shielding against any misrepresentation of the nature, characteristics, and qualities of goods. In *Gilliam v. ABC*,[189] the Monty Python team had transferred the right to broadcast their TV performances to the British Broadcasting Company ('BBC'), while retaining artistic control over the programme content. BBC licensed the rights to ABC in the US, in accordance with the terms of the agreement, but ABC then edited the show to shorten its length by over 25 per cent. Gilliam, a member of the Monty Python team, sued ABC for violating the agreement, claiming the alterations fell within the scope of the authors' artistic control. The Second Circuit agreed that the editing was an unauthorized treatment which was no longer faithful to the original work, and found in favour of the British comedians. However, in light of the subsequent *Dastar* decision of the Supreme Court,[190] some argue that VARA is now the only avenue to protect an author's integrity right.[191]

As we have seen, VARA, contained in 17 U.S.C. section 106A,[192] only provides protection to the authors of paintings, drawings, prints, sculptures, and certain still photographic images.[193] However, these authors enjoy the right to object to 'any intentional distortion, mutilation, or other modification' of the work 'which would be prejudicial to his or her honor or reputation'.[194] While being faithful to article 6bis Berne, this right comes with certain limitations attached. For example, some potential harmful modifications which are attributable to 'the passage of time or the inherent nature of the materials' will not be actionable.[195] Additionally, an author can only object to a modification required to preserve or display the work in public if this results from gross negligence.[196] Furthermore, the 'reproduction, depiction, portrayal, or other use of a work' will not amount to modification as intended under the Act.[197]

The limited scope of protection is revealed by a dispute between the artist, Frederick Hart, and Warner Brothers concerning a reproduction of Hart's famous sculpture, *Ex Nihilo*, in the film, *The Devil's Advocate*. Hart commenced proceedings claiming the unauthorized mutilation of his work. While the original sculpture, on public display in the National Cathedral in Washington resulted from his personal quest for Catholic faith, the Warner Brothers' film featured a similar-looking sculpture decorating the apartment of a character who is later revealed to be the Devil. In the film's closing scene, the human forms featured in the sculpture come to life and engage in sexual acts. Hart claimed that the film served to demonize his work which depicted his own spiritual journey. Had the dispute not been settled,[198] it seems that Hart would have

[188] This differentiates the US defamation regime from the English one where truthfulness is only considered in terms of defences to the allegation made. Another limitation related to the standing of the speaker which will be further considered in Chapter 7, section 2.1.

[189] *Gilliam v. American Broadcasting Companies (ABC), Inc.*, 538 F.2d 14, 24, 192 USPQ 1, (CA, 2d Cir. 1976).

[190] Nimmer (n 12), § 8D. 04[A][2].

[191] See subsection 4.3.1.2.

[192] 17 U.S.C. § 106A(a)–(b). See *Cort v. St. Paul Ins.*, 311 F.3d 979, 985 (9th Cir. 2002).

[193] The limitations linked to this instrument were covered earlier. See subsection 3.5.

[194] 17 U.S.C. §106A(a)(2).

[195] 17 U.S.C. §106A(c)(1).

[196] 17 U.S.C. §106A(c)(2).

[197] 17 U.S.C. §106A(c)(3).

[198] For more, see P K Yu, *Intellectual Property and Information Wealth* (vol. 1, Greenwood Publishing Group, 2007) 100.

faced difficulty in relying upon VARA, as 'reproduction, depiction, portrayal, or other use of a work' is not a modification which is covered under the Act.[199] However, very recently, graffiti writers have successfully brought a claim under VARA for the destruction of their art by real estate developers in the *5Pointz* litigation.[200]

The most significant limitation, however, is that both rights of attribution and integrity are subject to a fair use defence.[201] Yonover cautions that it is unclear whether Congress intended to create a presumption such that any parody which benefits from the parody fair use exception in respect of the copyright work will also enjoy a fair use parody defence in respect of moral rights.[202]

Finally, authors may resort to contract law to protect their interests. As Nimmer explains, just as a contractual obligation may require a party to attribute the work to its author,[203] the agreement might also include an obligation not to distort the work.

4.3.2 Reconciling parody with the integrity right

We have established that the integrity right may be enforced to protect a work from distortion. This might suggest that a parodic use permitted by the parody exception applied to the economic rights might then be thwarted based upon exercise of the author's integrity right, since parody mandates some element of distortion of the underlying original work. This apparent clash requires us to enquire whether parodic works can accommodate the interests of both authors and the public.[204]

The French courts have considered the balancing of the public's interest in permitting parodies and the right of authors to preserve the integrity of their works on several occasions. In *Peanuts*,[205] for example, concerning a pornographic parody of the *Snoopy* cartoon character, the court considered that neither the economic rights nor the author's integrity right were infringed. Although conceding the parody arguably altered the spirit of the original work, the parody's transposition of the children's cartoon character into an adult context satisfied the rules of the genre. Thus, the parodist's right of criticism should prevail over the original author's moral interests. Similarly, in *Tarzoon*,[206] which morphed the heroic Tarzan character into an X-rated cartoon, 'The Shame of the Jungle', the court held that because there was no confusion between the parody and the original work, the author's integrity right was not infringed.[207]

Thus, French courts attempt to reconcile the public's interest in the creation of parodies and the right of authors to preserve the integrity of their works, by directly equating the parody standard[208] with respect for the author's moral rights.[209]

[199] 17 U.S.C. §106A(c)(3). A similar exception exists in relation to the reproduction of works by libraries and archives (17 U.S.C. §108) and the performance and display of visual works in an educational context (17 U.S.C. §110(1)).

[200] *Cohen and Others v. G&M Realty LP and Others* (unreported, E.D.N.Y. 2018).

[201] 17 U.S.C. § 107. [202] Yonover (n 55) 110.

[203] Nimmer (n 12) vol. III, § 8D.06[D].

[204] J De Werra, 'The moral right of integrity' in E Derclaye (ed.), *Research Handbook on the Future of EU Copyright* (Edward Elgar, 2009) 269.

[205] See Chapter 1, section 5.2.1.1, for the facts.

[206] TGI Paris, 3 janvier 1978, D., 19790, p. 99 obs. Desbois.

[207] Yet the opposing outcome was reached in *Calimero*, TGI Paris, 24 mars 2000, légipresse 2000 I, p. 71.

[208] See Chapter 4, section 2.1.

[209] Galopin (n 72) 266; Davies and Garnett (n 4) 380; Adeney (n 8) 188–9; P Vivant, 'Courte citation et parodie: des exceptions au droit moral?' (2006) 2 *RLDI* 59, 60.

Accordingly, provided a parody complies with the rules of the genre, the right of integrity in the underlying work is deemed to have been respected.[210]

But the parody exception does not grant parodists a *carte blanche* exemption from moral rights concerns. The fact that a use falls within the parody exception of economic rights does not absolve courts of their responsibility to consider whether the parodist's use is an abuse of that legal defence.[211] This would occur if the permitted use fails to abide by the exception's rationale.[212] Here, courts pay particular attention to the impact of the parody's message,[213] as well as the impact of the alterations made to the original work on the public. Consequently, if the public perceives the parody as resulting in an abuse, moral rights resurface, as a regulative instrument to counterweigh these possible abuses of the application of the parody exception.[214] In effect, a parody which infringes the integrity of the original work fails to satisfy the rules of the genre.

Traditionally, using a non-commercial work in a commercial context changes the spirit of a work. A copyright-protected work created for non-commercial purposes, if reproduced in commercial advertising without permission, is therefore likely to infringe the integrity right of the author in France.[215] As a result, it is often seen as unnecessary to resort to contract law to regulate commercial uses,[216] since authors generally retain control over whether commercial use of their work is permitted, or not.[217]

Overall, although the French integrity right is seen as an absolute right exercised at the author's discretion, in practice its scope is subject to the parody exception. For this specific purpose, the French copyright doctrine establishes a direct correlation between the economic rights exception and the limit of moral rights. Ergo, use permitted by the parody exception will not then be curtailed by exercise of integrity right. Given that this is the position in the jurisdiction seen as most protective of the integrity right, it might be presumed that the less protective common law jurisdictions would reach the same conclusion. Yet the situation is actually more complex, as the following paragraphs will explain.

In Canada, moral rights provisions have yet to be considered in relation to the new parody exception. However, the following may be reasonably deduced. While Canada will not necessarily adopt the same correlation as in France,[218] the Canadian Supreme Court's shift in approach in *CCH*[219] seems to provide lower courts with an avenue to reconcile the public interest with the moral rights of the original author. In *CCH*, the court characterized copyright as a unified system which necessitates a balance between the rights of authors and the rights of users. As Canada, like France, conceives moral rights as an integral part of copyright, if the court's directions in *CCH* are extended

[210] This is easily conceivable as economic rights and moral rights are conceived as parts of the author's rights.

[211] For more, see Chapter 4, section 3.1.

[212] Therefore, if there is a breach of moral rights, the parody is said to go beyond what is prescribed by the rules of the genre. There is thus infringement of the author's right. Cass., *Cremer et le maillon faible*, 10 septembre 2014.

[213] See Chapter 5, section 4.1.5 and Chapter 7, section 2.7.

[214] TGI Paris, 15 janvier 2015, *Aigle Noir*.

[215] Cass. 1ère Civ., 2 avril 2009, n°08-10194; *TF1 c/ Sony;* Cass. 1ère Civ., 24 février 1998: Bull. Civ. I, n°75; JCP E 1998, panor. p. 636: reproduction of music snippets to enrich the advertisement; Paris 7 avril 1994: D. 1995, Somm. 56, obs. Colombet. The musical work was added to an advertisement 1) for a voice mailbox and 2) for an erotic TV show.

[216] Moral rights are of public order. Cass. 1ère Civ., 2 avril 2009, n°08-10194.

[217] Ibid.

[218] *Prise de Parole Inc. v. Guerin* (1996) 66 C.P.R. (3d) 257 whereby the court found a use to be non-infringing of economic rights but, nevertheless, infringing of moral rights.

[219] See n 46.

from economic rights to moral rights, then it appears that an author's moral rights must be counterbalanced, likewise, by those of users, including subsequent authors.[220] Hence, the proposed unified system will simply fail to function, if a reproduction permitted by a fair dealing exception is then precluded by the integrity right.

Similarly, the UK courts have yet to consider the integrity right's interaction with the new parody exception. It seems clear that general comments or criticisms of an author's style, as may occur in some works of pastiche or satire, already fall beyond the scope of the UK integrity right,[221] because a parody is a 'treatment' as defined in the CDPA,[222] which distorts a protected work. Hence, it is conceivable that this kind of use might infringe the author's integrity right, if owing to its nature, it harms the author's honour or reputation.

The question of whether or not a treatment is 'derogatory' is an objective assessment according to UK law. It seems unlikely that most parodies, even those which are 'near the knuckle', will undermine the standing of the underlying work, or the original author, because any reasonable observer is aware of how parody operates.[223] There is no presumption, for example, that the author of that work has endorsed the parody or countenanced its message. This suggests that an author's integrity right will be considered intact, because objectively, neither their honour nor reputation has been prejudiced.[224] In rare cases, however, it does seem possible that a parody might be prejudicial to the original author's integrity, and yet still fall within the parody exception. While this might be seen to jeopardize the intended legislative balance between the interests of right-holders and authors, it might serve to protect a more fundamental balance.

Although freedom of expression is taken into account for the economic rights through the fair dealing defences, the motivation behind the distortion of a protected work appears unaccounted for in the case of moral rights, a seeming case of 'legislative failure'.[225] Nevertheless, as Chapter 5 explained, although article 10 ECHR requires a balancing between the rights of an author and the right of freedom of expression of others, locating the balance point is not always clear-cut in parody cases. Here, we face a conflict between the right of freedom of expression of the original author and the same right exercised by the parodist. While the UK integrity right is usually described as a 'timid thing',[226] in fact, its potency may lie in an occasional case where a parodic use conflicts with the original author's right to freedom of expression.[227] Here, the parody should be upheld as an infringement of the author's integrity right.

In this regard, *Deckmyn* brings vital insight. In that case, the parody in dispute implied that the Mayor of Ghent prioritized city spending upon immigrants and refugees over the local population. Given this arguably discriminatory message, the CJEU seems to remind national courts of the need to have regard to the interests of the author of the underlying work.[228] This interpretation does not the CJEU to have harmonized moral rights,[229] but rather it recognizes that EU jurisprudence must have regard to

[220] Geist (n 69). [221] Davies and Garnett (n 4) 236.
[222] Section 80(2)(a): '[A]ddition to, deletion from or alteration to or adaptation of the work.'
[223] The parody evolves in a fantasy world separate from the original.
[224] *Clark* (n 141); Garnett (n 155) [11-46]; J Griffiths, 'Not such a "timid thing": the UK's integrity right and freedom of expression' in J Griffiths and U Suthersanen (eds), *Copyright and Free Speech* (OUP, 2005) 239.
[225] Ibid, 223.
[226] As for the other common law jurisdictions, there is very little case law interpreting moral rights. See section 5.
[227] Griffiths (n 224) 212. [228] *Deckmyn* (n 49) [29]–[30].
[229] As proposed by Rosati (n 51) 512.

moral rights which are recognized by international and EU law, although provided for in the national legislation of the EU Member States.[230]

Had *Deckmyn* to be decided pursuant to UK (rather than Belgian) law, then requiring an author's work to be associated with a racially intolerant message which they did not endorse might be seen as an objectively derogatory treatment which would infringe the integrity right.[231] If not, the explicit CJEU reference to the need to consider other competing fundamental rights might solve the issue.[232] Accordingly, it is possible to envisage that a parody which violates an author's moral rights might nevertheless be permitted because the harm resulting from this violation is outweighed by the public interest in permitting the parodist to exercise their right of freedom of expression, and vice versa.[233]

In Australia, the interaction between the integrity right and parody was considered before the Australian moral rights legislation was introduced. Here, the legislative intent was plainly expressed that permitted parody or satire should not be stifled by the exercise of moral rights.[234] Thus, a discussion paper, for example,[235] proposes that a parody or satire of a film would not be considered a derogatory treatment under the Act, because of its value as a vehicle for the exercise of freedom of expression within a democratic society. The discussion paper, nevertheless, acknowledges that there may be borderline cases (without defining these further) in which a permitted parody will infringe the author's integrity right.[236]

Yet to be applied by Australian courts, it is feasible that at least some works of parody or satire will be considered to harm the 'honour or reputation' of the original author.[237] We may find a good (hypothetical) example in threatened legal proceedings concerning parodic use of the Tintin cartoon character. Tintin, an intrepid young reporter, relies upon Snowy, the faithful dog companion who accompanies Tintin into dangerous adventures and always ends up saving the day. Bill Leak, an Australian cartoonist, often used an aged Tintin-*esque* character to depict politician Kevin Rudd, former Prime Minister of Australia, serving from 2007 to 2010 and again in 2013. In the threatened proceedings, Leak used the Rudd/Tintin analogy to depict the criticism levied at the then-Prime Minister's budget in 2007 and general lack of a real economic plan for the country .[238]

It is easy to imagine that Hergé's estate might argue that Leak's distortion of Tintin's facial features to portray the middle-aged politician betrays that fundamental part of work which embodies eternal youthfulness.[239] Alternatively, the estate might object to the politicizing of their character or the association with specific (and potentially

[230] See Chapter 4, section 1.

[231] Therefore, parodies also raise concerns under the right to freedom of information, see Chapter 5.

[232] See detailed analysis of the balancing exercise in Chapter 5.

[233] See Chapter 7, section 2.

[234] Commonwealth, Parliamentary Debates, House of Representatives, 18 June 1997, 5547–8 (Hon Daryl Williams QC).

[235] Discussion Paper, Proposed Moral Rights Legislation for Copyright Creators, Commonwealth of Australia (ACT, 1994) 46–9.

[236] A Spies, 'Revering irreverence: a fair dealing exception for both weapon and target parodies' (2011) 34 *UNSW Law Journal* 1122, 1141.

[237] M Weir, 'Making sense of copyright law relating to parody: a moral rights perspective' (1992) 18 *Monash University Law Review* 194, 196.

[238] http://www.abc.net.au/news/2007-05-11/costello-attacks-rudd-budget-cliches/2545144 (access date: 10 November 2018).

[239] After threatening Leak with infringement, the right-holder agreed to refrain from legal action, provided the parody was not commercialized; see https://www.pressreader.com/australia/the-australian/20070601/282119222117475 (access date: 10 November 2018).

objectionable) political viewpoints which betrays the essence of the original.[240] In either case, the parody could be argued to prejudice the honour and reputation of the author.

To succeed in an integrity rights claim in Australia, Sainsbury identifies that an author must demonstrate that any treatment satisfies two requirements. Firstly, they must identify some form of prejudice to their honour or reputation which they attribute to the parody; and secondly, they need to demonstrate the reasonableness of this belief.[241]

This resembles the UK position, as there is an objective assessment whether the parodic treatment is likely to harm the author's honour or reputation. As long as the public understands the parody as being a separate work from the original,[242] it will be difficult for the author to demonstrate damage to their integrity,[243] unless the parodic context includes an undesirable aspect, such as pornography or discrimination. Then, the original author might be able to establish that the parody has caused harm, for example, because the original work will always be tainted by recollection of the offensive parody.

In sum, although the parody exception relates only to economic rights and so does not apply to the integrity right of the original author, the nature of parody is such that a parodic use which is permitted by the parody exception is also likely to respect this moral right too, provided that the parody exception is interpreted correctly. However, at the margins, it is possible to envisage cases where the parody exception and integrity right are not completely aligned. In such cases, courts need to balance the interests of the original author against the parodist's right to freedom of expression. Here, the integrity right of the author is protecting their right of freedom of expression, so one party's right of free expression is being balanced against the same right of another. The nature of the parody's message seems to provide the means to determine whose right of expression should prevail.

The law in the US contrasts with those in the other jurisdictions under consideration, since US copyright legislation has its main emphasis on the economic rights, leaving the safeguarding of an author's interests and compliance with the Berne Convention to other areas of law. As these alternative avenues are available to authors in other jurisdictions too, this suggests that US law offers inadequate and ineffective redress when compared to other countries which have elected to incorporate moral rights as an integral part of copyright law. Despite modest legislative changes to incorporate VARA, the general resistance to embrace moral rights persists, which is most apparent in relation to the integrity right. This stems from concerns that integrity right might interfere with the constitutional protection afforded to free speech. Thus, from a moral rights perspective, parodists are least likely to face legal barriers in the US.

Given the feeble protection of moral rights in the US, could copyright claims be used to censor a distasteful parody? The jurisprudence indicates no.[244] In the words of

[240] This is based on the French dispute over a sequel of *Les Misérables* whereby the Supreme Court upheld that, irrespective of the high reputation of the original, the plaintiffs need to establish that the use jeopardizes the essence of the work. Yet the inclusion of contextual uses under Australian law remains unclear. Cass, 30 janvier 2007, n°04-15.543; V L Benabou and S Dussollier, 'Draw me a public domain' in P Torremans (ed.), *Copyright Law. A Handbook of Contemporary Research* (Edward Elgar, 2007) 180.

[241] Sainsbury (n 29) 158.

[242] Therefore, no confusion is created in the public.

[243] N Suzor, 'Where the bloody hell does parody fit in Australian copyright law?' (2008) 13 *MALR* 218, 246.

[244] See *Hustler Magazine v. Falwell*, 485 U.S. 46 (1988) (finding of parody where a commercial advertisement for Campari liqueur depicted Reverend J Falwell having sexual intercourse with his mother); *MCA, Inc. v. Wilson* 677 F.2d 180, 191 (2d Cir. 1981): here, parody was nevertheless rejected because it did not target the song itself. The use was found to be infringing but the song was

Judge Mansfield dissenting in *MCA, Inc. v. Wilson*:[245] '[P]ermissible parody, whether or not in good taste, is the price an artist pays for success, just as a public figure must tolerate more personal attack than the average private citizen.'[246] Suffice it to say here that if a parodist goes too far, there will be possible causes of action, but outside the scope of copyright law.[247] Therefore, if the parody is legitimate, commercial depreciation of the original resulting from the commentary is not a purpose of copyright law unless it amounts to market substitution.[248]

5. Conclusion

Although the parody exception does not extend explicitly to constitute an exception to moral rights, in this chapter we have seen that the copyright paradigm demands a unified understanding of the economic *and* moral rights. Otherwise, the system risks becoming perceived by the public as a seemingly incoherent web of rights of questionable legitimacy.[249] Consequently, as copyright[250] protects the object of expression, it is a somewhat inappropriate tool either to appraise the message conveyed or to protect the personal sensibilities of the expressor.[251] Thus, although moral rights exist in recognition of the creative process, they should not be used as a barrier to another's creativity without due cause. This is necessary to reflect inter-generational fairness. Over-broad exercise of moral rights, while benefiting current authors, would limit later authors, including parodists and satirists, to build upon existing protected works to create and exploit new works.

While the copyright parody exception introduces a policy-led free space which applies in the case of economic rights, legislators appear to have overlooked the need to consider moral rights, too. However, it has been posited that once a court is satisfied that the unauthorized use has been for the purpose of parody, infringement of attribution rights could be tested based upon the likelihood of confusion. The court should enquire whether the public exposed to the parody is likely to confuse the parody with the original work, or is left unsure whether the parody has been created by the author of the original work. There is an inverse proportionality relationship in play. If the public is no more than transiently confused regarding the authorship of the parody, then the special link between an author and their work is not affected. In most parody cases, there will be no confusion as it is in the nature of a parodic work that the public recognizes that a borrowing has been made. The second requirement of humour enables courts to delineate what types of message, or kinds of alteration, will prejudice the author or their work (i.e. the respect of the integrity right).

sung and played as background music while an actress and three actors engaged in a variety of sexual activities; *Walt Disney Prods. v. Air Pirates*, 345 F.Supp. 108 (N.D. Cal. 1972); *Adjmi v. DLT Entm't Ltd*, 97 F.Supp.3d 512 (S.D.N.Y. Mar. 31, 2015), [531]–[532].

[245] 677 F.2d 180, 191 (2d Cir.1981) citing *New York Times Co. v. Sullivan*, 376 U.S. 254, 84 S. Ct. 710, 11 L. Ed.2d 686 (1964).

[246] Repeated in *Kienitz v. Sconnie Nation LLC*, 766 F.3d 756, 759 (7th Cir. 2014), [759].

[247] This may be an additional difference between intellectual property and traditional property where a land owner has grounds to exclude unwanted individuals from their lands.

[248] *Campbell v. Acuff-Rose Music Inc.*, 510 U.S. 569 (1994), [592].

[249] A Ramalho, 'Parody in trademarks and copyright' (2009) 5 *CSLR* 59, 72.

[250] Understood here as including economic and moral rights.

[251] Also supported by the goals of the Berne Convention; B Mee, 'Laughing matters: parody and satire in Australian copyright law' (2002) 20 *Journal of Law, Information and Science* 55, 85; Adeney (n 8) 126.

Therefore, in the case of parodies, we have observed an overlap between the regime applied to the economic and moral rights,[252] based upon a reasonable exercise of moral rights based upon a purposive interpretation. This does not suggest that a parodist is unrestrained, since an author feeling under attack retains means of redress beyond copyright law. Any interpretation of moral rights which fails to permit all parodic uses of a work satisfying the parody exception diminishes their legitimacy, since its effect is to permit one generation of authors to wield a right of artistic censorship over the next, while simultaneously shielding their own works from critical comment.

In all the jurisdictions studied, moral rights legislation includes the flexibility essential to balance the different interests involved. By relying on legal concepts, such as a 'right-thinking person', 'reasonableness', or 'good faith', and the two main parody requirements, courts are equipped to balance a parodist's right to comment and communicate in their chosen medium (even if these may offend the feelings or artistic sensibilities of original authors to a reasonable degree) and the need for later authors to show due respect to the author whose work they have reproduced.

If parodies are able to respect moral rights, then the international three-step test (and more specifically its third step) is easier to satisfy.[253] Yet any author's exercise of their moral rights in relation to parodies of their work must also take account of the public interest which parody represents. This may require some jurisdictions, such as France, to relax the protection afforded to moral rights. Arguably, in the US, a wider range of authors require the kind of protection which VARA affords.

While moral rights are sometimes perceived in the UK as the 'last hope' for cases having little chance of succeeding based upon economic rights, it appears that, for parody at least, this final glimmer has been extinguished. A parody which benefits from the copyright exception should not falter under moral rights either. But our consideration suggests that evaluation of the fundamental interests in play in the integrity right might assist a court to determine whether the copyright protection *should* apply.

[252] See Chapter 4. [253] See Chapter 2, section 4.

7

The Music Industry and the Future of the Parody Exception in Copyright Law

This book represents an attempt to define the scope of the parody exception in copyright law using a comparative methodology. Although it would be unproductive for legislators to continually attempt to re-draw the line between legitimate and illegitimate parodies as the arts and users' habits develop, certain factors can help to preserve some degree of legal certainty for right-holders and users alike. However, this is far from a simple task. Not only is parody difficult to define within specific art fields,[1] making it difficult to devise a legal definition, which is not overly broad, or too narrow, but judicial application of any copyright exception has been seen to vary over time as well as being dependent upon jurisdiction and context.[2]

Yet, it is clear that parody is something distinct from a mere re-working or altered copy. A parody communicates a new and distinctive message from the earlier work it reproduces, and typically results in the creation of a new expression which may be eligible for copyright protection in its own right. Indeed, the essence of a true parody is that, despite relatively modest degrees of modification, a parody retains an independent relationship with the earlier work which is simple for the public to grasp. Hence, the public has a specific role to play in any parody. A parody will only succeed if the target public recognizes the underlying parodied work. Arguably, this constitutes basis for a more holistic assessment of the parody exception as proposed in this book. Thus, the most appropriate way to define parody is, purposively, by reference to its two main characteristics, a humorous intent (beyond merely synonymous with 'comic') and absence of confusion, as a yardstick. This parodic purpose should not only influence the exception's scope, but locates parody appropriately within the broader legal system.

National legislators have sought to ensure that parodic uses do not conflict with the normal exploitation of the original work, which would unduly prejudice the legitimate interests of right-holders and authors, by framing the parody exception within their own legal traditions as 'fair dealing', 'fair use', or subject to 'the rules of the genre'. Whilst these framework notions ought to confine the exception's reach while enabling courts to realize the exception's goals, the analysis of the French and US case law reveals a different picture in practice.[3] Instead, the outcome of a specific case is often very difficult to predict. However, some degree of legal certainty is still evident, as the recognizable form of the exception combined with established characteristics of a parody provides parties with basic guidelines. It is argued that lack of harm to the right-holder (measured by an objective standard) might serve as a practical first proxy for the requirement for 'humorous intent'. This enables national courts to take every facet of humour into account, while also establishing limits on the use falling within the exception. Similarly, the requirement of absence of confusion ensures that only true

[1] See Chapter 1, section 2. [2] See Chapter 1, section 5 and Chapter 4.

[3] The other jurisdictions under scrutiny are omitted since, at the current time, a well-established body of case law is still lacking.

parodic uses are permitted. Here, the comparative analysis has identified a range of factors which courts might adopt, according to the particular principles of interpretation applied in each jurisdiction.[4]

In this final chapter, we venture modest predictions as to what the future might hold in this area of copyright law, based upon an evaluation of existing business practices. It then outlines some additional avenues which might promote legal certainty while furthering the goals sought by the enactment of a specific parody exception.

1. The Role of Business Practices in the Realization of the Goals Underpinning the Parody Exception

Overall, the parody exception adds more credibility to the copyright paradigm because it recognizes that the nature of creativity involves borrowing and taking inspiration from others. Nevertheless, it requires that all levels (policy, legal, and industry) accept the consequences of this provision and adapt their practices. This may require the judiciary to reframe how questions, such as infringement, are assessed. Similarly, it is uncontroversial that intellectual property is important for creative industries, in terms of production, distribution, and consumption, but current industry practices sometimes focus almost exclusively on distribution concerns. A rounded policy perspective must acknowledge the need for a fair balance between *all* actors if creativity is to be maximized. At this early stage, the jury is still out on whether the parody exception will meet its objectives. Yet, an optimum outcome will only be achieved if business models cease equating parody with plagiarism or a denigrating use.

In this section, we adopt the UK music industry as our example.

1.1 The music business

Every wave of new technology has brought new challenges for copyright law. The same is true of the music industry which has needed to continually reinvent itself in light of technological changes. Initially designed to control public performances of musical works,[5] current business models adopted in the music industry seek to capture all revenue streams generated by performing, communicating, and reproducing music. These result in new layers of complexity to the functioning of the industry itself.[6]

The copyright regime and the recent CJEU *Deckmyn*[7] ruling seem to indicate that the concept of parody is fairly simple to grasp. Any parody meeting the two requirements could be lawful. Considering parodies as instantly recognizable, such an

[4] See Chapter 4.

[5] See the story on the birth of the French collecting rights society ('SACEM'). M Kretschmer, G M Klimis, and R Wallis, 'The changing location of intellectual property rights in music: a study of music publishers, collecting societies and media conglomerates' (1999) 17 *Prometheus: Critical Studies in Innovation* 267, 269.

[6] Pallas revisits the complexity of music licensing through the lens of dual competing narratives in music copyright. 'The first narrative explains the varying treatment of music businesses as being aimed at maintaining fair remuneration for copyright owners in light of changing technologies. The second narrative sees the varying treatment as being aimed at protecting incumbent entities from the competition brought about through changing business models made possible by technological advances.' L Pallas-Loren, 'The dual narratives in the landscape of music copyright' (2014) 52 *Houston Law Review* 537.

[7] C-201/13 *Johan Deckmyn and Vrijheidsfonds VZW v. Helena Vandersteen and Others* [2014] ECLI:EU:C:2014:2132 (hereafter *Deckmyn*).

interpretation should imply that actors within the music industry adjust their business practices. Simultaneously, the CJEU indicated that the parody exception has limits, but it refrained from clearly revealing what these limits are. Given the uncertainty revolving around the exception, actors in the music industry see parody as a threat to the exploitation of copyright-protected works.[8]

1.2 The actors

Copyright aims to foster creation and dissemination of works by granting rightholders a financial reward. Translated into the music recording industry, this economic incentive benefits both content creators and intermediaries. Copyright law grants composers and songwriters[9] exclusive rights in their authorial works, which they can license or assign to intermediaries (usually record labels or publishers[10]) who, in turn, administer these rights on the author's behalf in return for a percentage of revenue.[11] Predominantly, licences are made available for public performances[12] and reproduction.[13] Additionally, producers obtain distinct rights in the sound recordings of particular performance. Again, these rights can be assigned or licensed to intermediaries (record labels) in exchange for management and financial support for the promotion and distribution of the recordings. These sound recordings consist intrinsically of multiple works: the sound recording itself and the underlying authorial work(s) (Figure 7.1).[14]

Thus, the music industry is uniquely characterized by its multiple layers of distinct rights and multiple copyright-owners and licensees, with copyright at the centre of this complex web of rights.[15] In this ecosystem, the public are consumers who provide the money to sustain the industry by paying for recorded or printed music. Additionally, the wider public has a general interest in accessing knowledge and culture, of which music is a part.

The new digital environment has altered this traditional model. In economic terms, prior to the advent of online music distribution, the market structure has often been depicted as an oligonomy.[16] In other words, many artists were ready to sell their works to intermediaries (the oligopsony role) while at the same time, many consumers were ready to buy end products (the oligopoly role). It is evident that copyright legislation

[8] This is reinforced by the fact that the parodies reproduce already well-known works and, therefore, commercially successful works.

[9] Creators of music and lyrics are members of the British Academy for Songwriters, Composers and Authors ('BASCA'), defending their interests.

[10] Who themselves are members of the Music Publishers Association ('MPA').

[11] Here, only economic rights are considered. Moral rights stay with the author (creator) unless they have not been asserted or they have been waived in writing. Publishers often require authors to partially waive their integrity rights to authorize them to make an adaptation of the work, for a movie for example.

[12] This licence is essential to lawfully perform a protected work publicly (either live performances or radio broadcasts). This licence is usually granted by PRS for Music ('PRS').

[13] A mechanical licence, traditionally granted by MCPS (part of PRS), refers to the authorization for the reproduction or distribution of works, such as through vinyl records, CDs, or digital products.

[14] This latter might include two authorial works depending on whether lyrics have been attached to the tune.

[15] See also Gammons' metaphor between copyright in music and Ying Yang. H Gammons, *The Art of Music Publishing* (Focal Press, 2011) 21.

[16] i.e. 'companies act as an oligopoly to one group and an oligopsony to another'; A Solo, 'The role of copyright in an age of online music distribution' (2014) 19 *MALR* 169, 171; F MacMillan, 'Commodification and cultural ownership' in J Griffiths and U Suthersanen (eds), *Copyright and Free Speech* (OUP, 2005) 48.

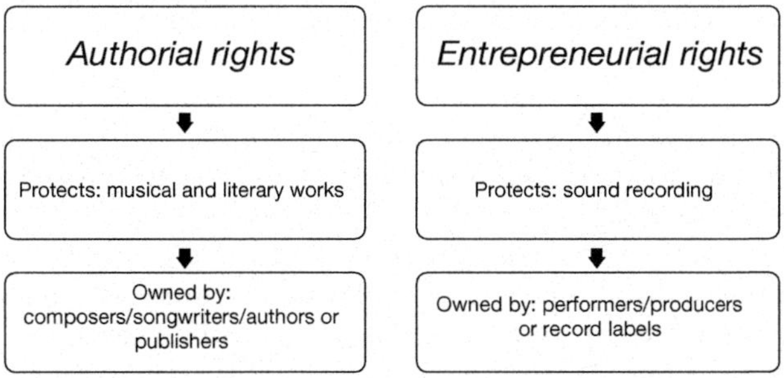

Figure 7.1 Traditional model of the multi-layering of rights involved in the music industry.

is key for market players, because it is this which determines the extent of their control of distribution. This has now changed. Intermediaries (especially publishers) were once essential, because content creators required their financial support upfront before they could create[17] or to disseminate their works. The rise of online music distribution has restricted the role of record labels because the upfront costs are now greatly reduced (although it will be argued that their role is still fundamental in ensuring remuneration). In the new digital environment, artists can record their tracks at home using inexpensive software, and then market their music themselves on an online platform.[18]

Collecting rights societies still have a crucial role in this new environment, in licensing the works and collecting the royalties on the right-holders' behalf. Right-holders are not obliged to register their works with a collecting right society, such as PRS for Music, and may retain control over the distribution and licensing of their works. Passing this responsibility for the management of songs over to PRS significantly reduces the otherwise high transaction costs.[19] In both analogue and digital worlds, if any business wants to play music (whether in the form of a live performance or simply playing a radio broadcast), they require a licence from PRS. Equally, before any online platform, such as Apple Music, Deezer, or Spotify, is only able to provide a worthwhile service if they have access to an extensive catalogue of music. Costs would be exorbitant if each of these platforms had to negotiate a licence with every individual right-holder, and such a catalogue would be impossible to manage, since each individual licensor might demand different terms. Therefore, PRS reduces the transaction costs, since PRS is able to grant blanket licences for its repertoire, and then remunerate the right-holders from the royalties it receives. Traditionally, two revenue streams flow

[17] See the endless inexpensive new processes to rework music such as digital sampling and mash-up etc.

[18] Solo (n 16) 169. Yet, it is not implied that the role of record labels and publishers has been lessened but rather that the focus has changed. In the digital world, these intermediaries are fundamental for at least five reasons: they provide high quality music; effectively enforce intellectual property rights; ensure fair remuneration to songwriters through the interplay of royalties, facilitating the relations between lyricists and composers but also deciding which composition is better for which artist; tour revenues are not enough to provide fair remuneration to composers and songwriters; and, finally, while fan fundraising seems to increase, the amounts raised are not enough for emerging artists. M F Schultz, 'Live performance, copyright, and the future of the music business' (2009) 43 *University of Richmond Law Review* 685–755; B R Day, 'In defense of copyright: creativity, record labels, and the future of music' (2011) 21 *Seton Hall J. Sports & Ent. L.* 61–103.

[19] Pallas-Loren (n 6) 539.

back to right-holders:[20] one stream to the composers and songwriters,[21] and one stream to the performers featured on the recording.[22]

In this setting, the music industry is based on 'control over publishing rights, marketing and promotional power and control of distribution'.[23] But does this system foster creativity including the creation of parodies? Or, does this central control morph into a censorship power?

Based upon the current configuration of contractual rights arising out of copyright, it can be appreciated that the interests of creators and performers are not always aligned with those of publishers, labels, broadcasters, and other businesses involved in music-making and distribution.[24] And this is reflected in the contractual relationships between the various actors involved.

1.3 Publishing and recording contracts

Before the parody exception was enacted, parodists either ran the risk of being sued or had to secure a licence or other permission for the use. Generally, requests to use resulted in an outright refusal from the right-holders (rarely the original authors themselves), who saw the use as detrimental to the value of the protected works.

In order to release an album on the music market, songwriters often require the help of intermediaries: publishers and record labels.[25] Although no two publishing or recording contracts are identical,[26] there are common provisions which we shall now evaluate so that we may assess their likely impact on original authors, right-holders, and parodists.

1.3.1 Rights

The author of an original musical work, or the producer of the sound recording, is the first right-holder of the exclusive rights granted by copyright in a musical composition,[27]

[20] L Bently, 'Authorship of popular music in UK copyright law' (2009) 12 *Information, Communication & Society* 179, 189.

[21] These are called *mechanical royalties,* paid by MCPS for the reproduction of copies of the work. When the work is played in public or communicated to the public, the royalties are paid by PRS to the composer and songwriter.

[22] These are paid by the record label and by PPL for the revenues deriving from communication to the public.

[23] P Tschmuck, 'Copyright, contracts and music production' (2009) 12 *Information, Communication & Society* 251, 254.

[24] Pietilä argues, in relation to the South African music industry but it can legitimately be extended to the global music industry, for a better control of copyright of composers, songwriters, and musicians against the interests of publishers and labels. Additionally, she advocates a re-modelling of the financial incentive system in place to prevent the concentration of ownership in the hands of a few dictating the market. T Pietilä, 'Whose works and what kinds of rewards' (2009) 12 *Information, Communication & Society* 229–50.

[25] This section only focuses on major labels (as opposed to indie labels, for example). UK major labels are: EMI Group, Sony Music Entertainment, Warner Music Group, and Universal Music Group. Traditionally, this meant that these labels had manufacturing and distribution facilities in main territories. The advent of online music distribution (i.e. download-based models like iTunes and streaming based models like YouTube) impacted their essential role in distribution. Today, their main feature is to have important offices and qualified staff in different territories and to ensure high quality music.

[26] A Thompson, 'Recording contracts' in N Riches (ed.), *The Music Management Bible* (SMT, 2012) 37.

[27] Here, musical composition is understood in the legal sense as copyright subsisting in the music and in the lyrics, and copyright in the sound recording.

but these rights can be assigned or licensed.[28] In order to create the relationships described in the preceding section, a typical publishing contract[29] requires a songwriter to assign[30] their rights in their songs to a music publisher. In return, the publisher promotes and exploits the work,[31] and provides the songwriter with financial support in the form of advances and royalties (typically a percentage of sales).[32] A publisher's main competence is onward licensing of the works to record labels, so the music is available to end-consumers. In the case of a typical record contract for a sound recording,[33] the producer of the sound recording assigns their copyright to a record label.[34] In return, the record label provides upfront capital for the production, promotion, and distribution of the recording, as well as paying royalties based upon record sales. Record companies and music publishers use the royalties they receive to recoup the initial financial advances, but more significantly, these contracts allow intermediaries to control the uses made of these works and creations.[35]

1.3.2 Creativity control and moral rights

Songwriters and performers, like authors, are entitled to a bundle of moral rights associated with their copyright works.[36] The first of the moral rights is the right to be identified as the author or performer of the work each time a performance is broadcast, or otherwise communicated to the public.[37] Before moral rights take effect, the

[28] Section 9(1) CDPA.

[29] The different forms of publishing contract include (1) the *administration deal* where no advances are made and the songwriter retains ownership. The administrator is responsible for registering the works with the collecting rights societies, licenses others to use the works, collects the licensing fees, and prepares the accounts; (2) the *sub-publishing deal* which is a mix between the administration deal and the exclusive deal. Only some rights are licensed to the publisher and the deal might come with some capital advance; (3) the *exclusive deal* is generally a demonstration of publishers' trust in the talent. This deal comes with important capital advances and an assignment of exclusive rights from the songwriter. A Harrison, *Music: The Business* (6th edn, Random House, 2014) 128–45.

[30] Assignment implies a transfer of ownership to the co-contractor while licensing does not infer transfer of ownership to the co-contractor. Licensing generally occurs in B2B relationships, such as a deal between publishers of two territories in an administration contract. Yet, licensing can occasionally happen between a songwriter and a producer bearing the advantage of eschewing creative control from the publisher's side but the inconvenience of not having any capital advance. Gammons (n 15) 82.

[31] From offering *mechanical licences* for the reproduction of a song on a sound recording (in the UK, this is usually done by MCPS but MCPS can only license for straight covers, not derivative works, which requires permission from writers and publishers); *synchronization* licences for combining a song with visual images (film, advert etc.); *performing rights* covering the right to publicly reproduce a song but this is not limited to live performances and includes broadcast and internet making available to the public (this is generally achieved through PRS); print licences; and grand rights for theatrical productions and musicals. Harrison (n 29) 119–27.

[32] Tschmuck (n 23) 259.

[33] These can take different forms: licence, exclusive long-term recording contract, development deal, production deal, and the most recent 360° model. Harrison (n 29) 73–89; Kretschmer et al (n 5) 178.

[34] In standard contracts, musicians exclusively license all exploitation of rights throughout the world during copyright protection to a label to ensure that all present and future performances can be recorded.

[35] S Greenfield and G Osborn, 'Copyright and power in the music industry' in S Firth and L Marshall (eds), *Music and Copyright* (2nd edn, Edinburgh University Press, 2009) 96.

[36] As a reminder, moral rights only concern authorial works and therefore, not sound recordings. Moral rights were extended to performers in 2006 with the enactment of the Performances (Moral Rights, etc) Regulations 2006. See Chapter 6.

[37] In relation to performers, there are exceptions when it is not reasonably practicable to do so: section 205C CDPA.

rights must be asserted pursuant to UK copyright law. For a songwriter or performer, these rights are most easily achieved by having a credit clause within the contract.[38] The second moral right is the moral right not to have their work subjected to any derogatory treatment,[39] enabling creators to retain a certain creativity control over their works. Finally, songwriters have the right to be protected against false attribution whether in writing, orally, or even implied.[40]

In the UK, copyright mainly focuses upon economic rights. Therefore, it is not surprising that moral rights can be waived via contract.[41] This waiver can apply to specific works or works in general and can be done for existing or future works or creations. This has resulted in the standard music industry contracts including a moral rights waiver in the widest possible terms.[42]

Even if moral rights have been waived, publishers will generally agree to impose contract terms in ongoing transactions, which require songwriters to be given appropriate credit and restrict certain uses of the licensed work. For example, publishers generally state that any adaptations or re-arrangements of the work require the songwriters' consent. Typically, and prior to the introduction of the new parody exception, publishing contracts would classify parody in the same way, a type of work which would only be licensed with the songwriters' permission. While such a clause might be justifiable under the old law, the task of the parodist should be facilitated by the mandatory nature of the exception, since any contractual terms seeking to override the exclusion will be unenforceable. Previously, parodists wanting to obtain permission to alter the words or music to a song were required to seek a 'mechanical'[43] licence from the publisher, which would be subject to the songwriter also granting permission. The introduction of the parody exception suggests that a parodist who is confident that their parody satisfies the exception's requirements no longer need to seek permission, thereby rendering a mechanical licence superfluous. Yet, the exception only acts as a defence.[44]

While licensing a work for commercial use (termed a 'synchronization licence') can be a significant source of revenue, some songwriters are categorically opposed to any such commercial use, or at least require that their prior authorization is sought, so that they may vet which commercial ventures are associated with their work. Given that musical parodies for commercial adverts are unlikely to fall within the scope of the fair dealing exception,[45] companies interested in using a musical work to promote their particular products should still seek mechanical and synchronization licences, and might also require the songwriter's permission, depending upon the nature of the particular publishing contract in place.

1.3.3 Denigrating content

But what if the parodist is a party to a publishing contract? Can the publisher take action against the parody songwriter, for example, if its content is defamatory (and therefore not a true parody)? A publishing contract typically includes an indemnity clause,

[38] Sections 78 and 205D CDPA. Exceptions: sections 79 and 205E CDPA. See Chapter 3, section 3.

[39] Sections 80 and 205F CDPA. See Chapter 6, section 5.

[40] Section 84 CDPA. See Chapter 6, section 4.

[41] Section 87 CDPA. Moral rights can be waived in Canada as well but not in France or Australia. In these latter countries, moral rights will be enforceable irrespective of contractual terms.

[42] Harrison (n 29) 145.

[43] See n 13.

[44] See Chapter 3, section 1.

[45] See Chapter 4, section 2.4 and Chapter 6, section 4.

in which the artist agrees to indemnify the publisher against any third-party proceedings which might arise as a result of their work.[46] Hence, if a parody songwriter's work goes beyond what is permitted under the exception,[47] the parodist will be financially liable and the publisher will be protected to a degree.[48]

The preceding analysis is based on the presumption that the parodist also alters the musical composition to create the new work. But many popular musical parodies reproduce at least one of the works making up the musical composition (e.g. the original tune is retained) using, for example, a sampling technique. If a parodist wants to sample a sound recording legally, they need a licence from the record label[49] which owns the rights in the sound recording, as well as a licence from the right-holders of the underlying composition.[50] However, a parody involving sampling which falls within the scope of the new fair dealing exception could be created without requiring any licence.

It must be kept in mind that because the parody exception is merely a defence, it always carries with it a degree of unpredictability. 'Weird Al' Yankovic, a well-known parodist in the US, is often cited by music industry representatives as the appropriate role model which parodists should follow. Despite the US fair use defence available for parody works, Weird Al always secures appropriate permissions in advance for any parodic use because of the certainty it provides. Because of his approach, the relevant right-holders are now more willing to countenance his use, and so he has secured greater bargaining power. In practice, even well-established artists are reluctant to embark on litigation to determine whether their use will ultimately be deemed fair. More successful artists might be a more attractive target for legal proceedings. Therefore, for some, advance clearance, although perhaps unnecessary, is just a simpler option.[51]

1.3.4 Conclusion

The artificial fragmentation of songs into multiple copyright works, and the sheer number of right-holders involved demonstrate why the mandatory character of the exception is crucial to the realization of the objectives of the exception. Yet, as the parody exception is a defence, cautious parodists may continue to seek an arguably unnecessary licence for their use. In contrast with the old regime, any licence should only be subject to the authors' permission, when the use is for advertising a commercial product, rather than an artistic pursuit. In the case of an advertisement, for example, use is solely driven by commercial motives, so it seems appropriate that right-holders and/or songwriters would need to give permission as it could lead to the belief that the original creator is in some way linked to the product advertised.

Therefore, the parody exception should render the copyright regime more in line with music making, since it acknowledges that certain borrowings are permissible.

[46] This clause is also found in most recording deals.

[47] See, for example, the songs of neo-Nazi music groups like No-Remorse, Skrewdriver, RaHoWa, or Skullhead.

[48] The publisher is therefore protected financially—to the extent to which the parodist has sufficient resources, against uses which do not fall within the exception as determined in Chapters 4, 5, and 6. The user remains liable under the new law.

[49] Or, rather, from PPL given that major labels are members of PPL.

[50] Which most likely will be from the publisher because of the transfer of copyright ownership through the publishing contract.

[51] K McLeod and P Dicola, *Creative License: The Law and Culture of Digital Sampling* (Duke University Press, 2011) 239.

However, as a practical matter, its potential is restricted, since the copyright objectives might be overridden by contractual terms. Even if the contractual terms are legally unenforceable, this outcome would only result from a formal determination at the end of legal proceedings, and only a small proportion of relevant cases ever reach this stage. In the meantime, restrictive contract terms serve as a deterrent to the creation of parodies.

1.4 Collecting rights societies

As most musical works likely to be parodied are registered with collecting rights societies, we need to explore the extent to which the practices of these organizations are likely to impact the creation of musical parodies.

We have seen how the fragmentation of ownership of rights creates barriers for those who need to license works and those owners trying to monitor how their works are used. Collective rights management organizations have been established to administer rights on behalf of right-holders.[52] Essentially, they provide a practical and efficient mechanism to administer and enforce copyright.[53]

The advent of the internet has not altered their role, but arguably requires an expansion of territorial activity from administering rights within a single national territory to, for example, Pan-European licensing.[54]

1.4.1 Modus operandi

As we have touched upon already, one of the main roles of a collecting society, such as PRS, is to grant blanket licences to users. A society has the ability to license its entire repertoire, which may comprise many thousands of works to an interested party, for a particular period and at a fixed rate.[55] This provision of a 'one-stop' service enables businesses, such as radio stations, to secure licences for sound recordings expediently to meet their business needs. Additionally, Phonographic Performance Limited ('PPL'[56]) has a wider reach, and collects income internationally in respect of use of the neighbouring rights granted to performers.[57] In this way, collecting societies, such as PRS and PPL, manage copyright for the authors, songwriters, and performers of musical compositions. Their activities extend beyond granting licences to third parties on the owner's behalf, to monitoring that use of the works is in compliance with the agreed licence terms, and collecting the royalties due. Royalties generated from exploitation of the works managed are distributed to their members and the operation of the societies is funded by charging each member an administration fee, which is usually a percentage of the gross income collected.

[52] Section 116(2) CDPA defines 'licensing body'.

[53] Harrison (n 29) 365.

[54] This is ongoing as the European Commission approved the joint venture (ICE) between PRS, STIM (Sweden), and GEMA (Germany) for cross-border licensing of online music. See press releases from PRS on the launch of the Hub on 20 July 2015 available at https://www.prsformusic.com/aboutus/press/latestpressreleases/Pages/prs-for-music-stim-and-gema-establish-the-worlds-first-integrated-licensing-and-processing-hub.aspx (access date: 10 November 2018) and from the European Commission, Mergers: Commission approves joint venture for cross-border licensing of online music between PRSfM, STIM, and GEMA, subject to commitments (Brussels, 16 June 2015) available at http://europa.eu/rapid/press-release_IP-15-5204_en.htm (access date: 10 November 2018).

[55] The latter can take the form of a flat fee or a percentage of earnings.

[56] PPL is the record industry's licensing body. It licenses public performances and negotiates collective agreements with broadcasters but does not include an anti-piracy unit.

[57] In their attempt to provide a one-stop service, PRS and PPL sometimes provide joint licences to clear both the master and the publishing rights. While these joint licences are rather limited at the moment (small workplaces, community buildings, and amateur sports clubs), improvements are in the pipeline. Harrison (n 29) 372.

On becoming a member, some of the right-holder's exclusive rights are either assigned or licensed to the collecting society. Whilst PRS manages performing rights, MCPS administers the right to reproduce the work.[58] Aside from efficiencies gained in administration and enforcement of their rights, members also gain a significant advantage in terms of being able to leverage greater collective bargaining power to better serve their interests. This is even more important in the digital age, with the emergence of various online music platforms which base their business model upon exploitation of unlicensed music. With their collective muscle, the societies are better placed than any individual right-holder to police unauthorized uses and negotiate royalty rates.[59]

1.4.2 Licensing for the purpose of parody

One might imagine that a parodist seeking a licence to reproduce an earlier work would simply approach MCPS. Yet, MCPS does not have authority to license the reproduction or adaptation of a work for parody.[60] This means that parodists have been required to negotiate with authors and creators directly.[61] If a parodist was successful in tracking down the relevant parties and securing permission (or decided, instead, to 'run the risk' and proceed without consent) and then wished to commercialize their work, they might elect to register their parody with PRS.[62] The current PRS registration form requires any parody to identify itself as such, and to detail the previous works on which it is based. In effect, the parody work is then treated as a jointly-owned work, as between the parodist and the original work's right-holder. As the collecting societies are privately owned, it is the membership which sets the remuneration formula to be applied to particular types of works. PRS, thus, determines how to allocate any licensing revenue generated by the registered parody between the parodist and the right-holders of the original work, irrespective of any direct agreement reached between the parodist and the right-holders.

1.4.3 Exploiting a parody commercially

Prior to the introduction of the UK parody exception, the royalty formula for any PRS-registered parody allocates all the income generated from exploitation under the PRS scheme to the right-holders of the original works, and none to the right-holder of the parody. Under the new regime, this practice has the appearance of an impermissible contract which seeks to override the exception. Furthermore, lack of remuneration does little to incentivize parodists to create such works,[63] thus undermining one of the stated policy goals of the new legislation.[64]

[58] MCPS is itself owned by PRS, but remains autonomous in its decision-making, although PRS manages its royalty processing services.

[59] On the benefits of joining PRS, see Gammons (n 15) 39.

[60] See clause 4.5(a) of the PRS Limited Online Music Licences available at http://www.prsformusic.com/SiteCollectionDocuments/Online%20and%20Mobile/loml-terms-and-conditions.pdf (access date: 10 November 2018).

[61] Section 1.3 demonstrates that licensing for parody purposes often remains outside the rights transferred or licensed to publishers and labels, requiring parodists to negotiate with every author, songwriter, composer, and artist involved.

[62] Which only happens in rare cases.

[63] P Tafforeau, *Pratique de la propriété littéraire et artistique: contrats et gestion collective, droit d'auteur et droits voisins* (LexisNexis, 2013) 238.

[64] Currently, policy makers seem to dress up any change in the law in terms of economic growth—whereas the more general point is probably just one of fairness. Yet one of the strongest rationales for permitting parodies is justified on a more rounded view of what adds value to society.

In France, with its established parody exception, SACEM,[65] the equivalent of PRS in France, operates a similar regime for musical parodies, but in this case 12.5 per cent of the gross income of the revenue generated from the reproduction right is allocated to the parodist, while the remaining 87.5 per cent is allocated to the right-holders of the original authorial works. Similarly, in terms of revenue generated from the performing right, one-sixth is allocated to the performer of the parody, while five-sixths is allocated to the performance right-holder of the original.[66]

One argument which might be advanced to justify the collecting societies' approach is that there is no right to parody.[67] Rather, the parody exception is merely a (limited) defence (in certain cases). As such, why should private commercial entities revise their practices to accommodate what might be the exceptional case, rather than the norm as if the exception was a right?[68] Is a parodist even entitled to remuneration for their parody?

The answers to these questions depend upon the breadth of cultural diversity which society is seeking. After all, diversity is what the copyright system is also meant to promote. Because the revised law recognizes parody as a legitimate art form, and because it is reasonable to assume that an independent copyright could subsist in the parody,[69] its creators should be entitled to exploit their work in the same way as any other creator.

But this is not tantamount to saying that parodists should be able to 'free-ride' on the successful works of others. The exception comes with safeguards through the mandatory requirements which are attached. Also, given the difficulty of predicting the outcome of legal proceedings, commercially-motivated parodists using sampling techniques or creating parodies for advertising purposes will still seek licences for their use, and, as such, collecting societies gain from facilitating further licensing of such works.

In this regard, it is worthwhile considering whether there may be a role for the Copyright Hub. Launched in September 2013 to provide a common platform for online transactions for use by the creative industries, and established in response to a proposal of the Hargreaves Review,[70] the Hub still enjoys wide support from industry actors, including PRS and PPL. Its goal is to facilitate content licensing, as well as providing information about copyright law to those wishing to create. It is based on the simple idea of creating a single destination where individuals in particular may find out how to secure permission to use any particular work. This initiative is still at an experimental stage, currently operating in relation to photographs and images only.[71]

While the project is warmly welcomed, and while it may prove more practically effective than any statutory or judicial approach, it seems that it has limited impact for parodies. However, it may be beneficial for those right-holders who are willing to

[65] It is noteworthy that while PRS and MCPS are separate bodies under the same brand, SACEM manages both performing and reproduction rights for its members.

[66] Remuneration keys come from an interview between Saceml and SACEM:available at http://saceml.deepsound.net/reponses_sacem.html.

[67] See section 5. [68] See Chapter 3, section 2.

[69] Although the CJEU did not include originality as one of the requirements for the application of the exception, given the low originality threshold of *Infopaq*, it seems that originality will be met if the 'distancing' requirement is met. *Deckmyn* (n 7) [21].

[70] I Hargreaves, *Digital Opportunity. A Review of Intellectual Property and Growth* (Independent Report, 2011) 33.

[71] A beta version of this private initiative can be accessed at www.copyrighthub.co.uk.

consider licensing their works for such uses, since they would be able to use this interface to set licence terms for users. The Copyright Hub has the further advantage that content providers have flexibility to decide whether or not to license on a case-by-case basis, as well as the level of fees and the period of the licence. Besides, the Hub will only be valuable if it is reliable and, as is particularly pertinent in the case of musical works, if it properly identifies all the relevant right-holders which need to agree to the work. Only then may users be assured that they have all necessary permissions in place to avoid legal proceedings.[72]

Given the current limitations of the Hub, how might the current system be improved to encourage the creation of musical parodies? One way might be via compulsory licences, as these are already well-established in the music business. In the US, for example, statutory compulsory mechanical licences exist between record labels and publishers, so obviating the need for parties to negotiate with each other for this use.[73] While an equivalent compulsory licence scheme does not exist in the UK, the idea is attractive. Parodists doubting the legality of the work would always be able to secure a licence. Yet, such a scheme is not without its hurdles;[74] to be both fair and effective, the licence fee should take account of the amount borrowed, for example.[75]

The issue of whether music industry business practices foster or hinder music parodies is further exemplified by the agreements which collecting societies have reached with online sharing platforms, as well as the operation of the platforms themselves. The next section considers these issues further.

1.5 Online sharing platforms

The launch of YouTube in 2005 (owned by Google since 2006) marked the start of a new battle for collecting societies: controlling unauthorized use of music by private individuals. Online video distribution platforms, such as YouTube, not only simplify the way users access content, but also facilitate the uploading and distribution of content. The site combines both amateur and professional content on a single website. By inviting individuals to *Broadcast Yourself*, YouTube quickly became the most popular online sharing website, with global reach, and it hosts countless parody works in all their forms. In addition to simplifying the sharing of home movies, YouTube also simplified online piracy and infringement. So, copyright-owners started a never-ending game of notice-and-take-down procedures against YouTube users.

1.5.1 Content ID

In 2007, YouTube introduced a content recognition system, called Content ID. This uses a complex algorithm to cross-check all newly-uploaded content against an

[72] Otherwise we might end up in a situation like the Verve saga where the band had sought licence clearance for sampling the Rolling Stones but had missed one publisher which led the Verve to have to give up 100 per cent of the royalties on the album opener *Bittersweet Symphony*. This saga led some scholars to argue for the establishment of a single right-holder for downstream users to license from. L Pallas-Loren, 'Untangling the web of music copyrights' (2002) 53 *Case W. Res. L. Rev.* 677.

[73] J Toynbee, 'Musicians' in S Frith and L Marshall (eds), *Music and Copyright* (2nd edn, Edinburgh University Press, 2009) 135.

[74] Including further legislative changes, or somewhat of an about-turn from the industry to establish a voluntary scheme.

[75] This would also be a solution for the sampling music and other parodies which are not clear-cut cases under the law.

established database of works from the collecting societies' repertoires to identify potential copyright infringement. The algorithm detects complete and partial matches. Right-holders receive an automated notification each time any new content is uploaded which finds a 'match'. Right-holders are offered five possibilities: (1) do nothing, (2) block the content, (3) mute any audio, (4) add an advertisement and collect the revenue, or (5) monitor its viewing statistics.

Revisiting the UK's case for change and the parody of *Empire State of Mind*, now famous *Newport State of Mind* parody fared in 2010: once the parody was uploaded onto YouTube, the representatives for artist Jay-Z, the author of the original musical work used in the parody track, received a standard form notice from YouTube alerting of a potential copyright infringement. Not wishing his work to be parodied, the decision was taken to block the work. Faced with the additional threat of legal proceedings, the parody's creator, Delaney, sought a licence for the use, but this was refused.

YouTube has not revised its procedure since the UK parody exception was introduced in October 2014,[76] meaning any parody uploaded to the site will still be identified as a potential copyright infringement. The YouTube procedure fails to take proper account of the fact that, in the vast majority of cases, the parties do not have the same bargaining power, so it has an incentive to favour the right-holder's position to preserve its safe harbour provided under the E-Commerce Directive.[77] Although the uploader has some limited opportunity for dialogue with the right-holders to try to persuade them that their parody is lawful given the exception, there is no independent arbitration. The decision to block lies with copyright-owners.[78] As a result, right-holders have de facto power to censor parodies on YouTube (although they may prefer to simply re-direct the advertising revenue towards their account), and to deprive parodists of the recognition of their work, as well as remuneration. Whilst this procedure is not limited to parodies but to any content reproducing earlier works, it ultimately renders the dissemination of parodies more difficult.

[76] And applies fair use, expanding the reach of fair use beyond the US territory.

[77] Article 14 E-Commerce Directive provides the intermediary with a shield against liability for the uploading of infringing content by third parties as long as the intermediary was not aware of the presence of the infringing content on its platform. Upon notification, the intermediary must act expeditiously to remove access to the infringing content. Directive 2000/31/EC of the European Parliament and of the Council of 8 June 2000 on certain legal aspects of information society services, in particular electronic commerce, in the Internal Market (17 July 2000) OJ L 178, 1–16. This safe harbour is threatened by the current copyright reform and leans towards the introduction of automated anti-piracy systems with complaints and redress mechanisms operated by private actors, namely platforms and right-holders. See text proposed by the EU Commission Proposal for a Directive of the European Parliament and of the Council on copyright in the Digital Single Market—COM (2016) 593. For more, see S Jacques, C Garstka, M Hviid, and J Street, 'Automated anti-piracy systems as copyright enforcement mechanism: the need to consider cultural diversity' (2018) 40(4) *European Intellectual Property Review* 218.

[78] This is explained by the safe harbour provisions which dictate that online intermediaries should not be aware of the infringing content to avoid liability. This led intermediaries to prefer blocking content rather than investigating whether the content is indeed legitimate. Additionally, agreements exist between PRS and YouTube to automatically take down content. Yet, in the US, Google announced on 19 November 2015 that they will start to proactively defend uses under the cover of fair use even in court if necessary. Parody and critique are cited as examples. Press release available at http://googlepublicpolicy.blogspot.nl/2015/11/a-step-toward-protecting-fair-use-on.html?m=1 (access date: 1 June 2018).

1.5.2 Licensing online sharing platforms

It might be fair to say that the original online notice-and-take-down procedure has slowly transformed into 'notice-and-share-the-revenue' systems. Collecting rights societies, such as PRS, have grasped an opportunity to generate revenue from online platforms. PRS and YouTube have agreed licence terms, such that a proportion of revenue generated from use of protected works on YouTube is passed on to PRS members. These joint online licences are not limited only to transformative uses, but cover all works included in the collecting right societies' repertoire. One notable characteristic of the dealings between PRS and YouTube is that the terms agreed are kept confidential.[79] However, based upon what little information is available, the agreement does not seem to take account of works which are lawful because of the copyright exceptions. For example, the PRS website previously stated:

> If PRS for Music becomes aware that a member's work fits the definition of derogatory use, PRS for Music can notify YouTube on that member's behalf and work with YouTube to remove that content. Under the Joint Online Licence, a derogatory use is defined as a parodied work, or one that is insulting or detrimental to the composer of the commercially released sound recording.[80]

Whether such a clause remained in a more recent agreement reached in 2016is unclear, but there is nothing to indicate that any changes were made to reflect the new parody exception. In these circumstances, contract law is being exploited to permit these powerful actors to dictate what content is created and disseminated, regardless of the objectives of copyright law.[81]

Given that, on one side, Google is seeking to monetize data and collecting bodies, on the other side, seeks to maximize the revenue generated for right-holders, the careful balance crafted by legislators in copyright law is simply lost. One solution may be the implementation of an alternative dispute resolution ('ADR') scheme, such as mediation or arbitration,[82] which would provide parties with a framework when negotiating a licence for (parody) use.[83] It seems feasible that the Copyright Tribunal[84] could oversee such proceedings.[85] Referral to an independent third party is appealing because it would enable parodists and other creators of transformative content to overturn decisions of YouTube's internal dispute resolution system.[86] Nevertheless, it may stretch

[79] So confidential that even the members of PRS are kept in the dark which has led to BASCA being asked to swap this secrecy for more transparency.

[80] Available at http://www.prsformusic.com/creators/helpcentre/pages/youtubedealhelp.aspx (access date: 21 July 2015).

[81] See the study carried out by Kretschmer et al, which describes the uneven bargaining powers which result in outcomes favourable to right-holders who continue to dictate the terms of the licence, which often conflicts with copyright statutory exceptions. M Kretschmer, E Derclaye, M Favale, and R Watt, *The Relationship between Copyright and Contract Law: A Review commissioned by the UK Strategic Advisory Board for Intellectual Property Policy* (SABIP), 2010. Available at SSRN: http://ssrn.com/abstract=2624945.

[82] Thompson provides a summary on the arbitration system within the music industry in the UK. Thompson (n 26) 239.

[83] This solution is also shared by Benabou: V-L Benabou, *Rapport de La Mission du CSPLA sur les 'Oeuvres Transformatives'* (2014) 72.

[84] Sections 149 and 205B and schedule 6 CDPA.

[85] Yet, currently, the copyright tribunal only deals with commercial uses and would have to be extended to non-commercial uses too.

[86] Note, that to benefit from safe harbour provisions, YouTube must not be aware of the content uploaded to its website. Therefore, the organization often prefers to consider alleged infringing content as infringing, rather than analysing whether, based upon the specific fact, the use is covered by a copyright exception. In any event, it seems inappropriate for a private body to determine such cases.

the abilities of at least some ADR schemes to set an appropriate licence rate, having regard to all the various factors of this creative industry. A further option is to establish a 'licence of right' system, as currently established in CDPA in respect of design law.[87]

1.6 Reflecting on UK practices

There is more to the parody exception than a desire to foster economic growth. The primary aim of the change in UK legislation sought added the social and cultural value which this particular kind of work provides. Yet, the way in which business actors rely on copyright undermines these goals. Shielding behind arguments that the exception is vague and unpredictable, business practices have established a system which fortifies established copyright works by considering all unauthorized reproduction as unlawful irrespective of whether the parody exception applies. Ultimately, in this scenario, a parodist's position is no better position than before the parody exception was introduced.

How far parodists should be tolerated is a difficult question to answer, and one which is further complicated by the fragmentation of copyright's exclusive rights between different actors in the music industry, each having different, and potentially conflicting, interests. All too often, the net result is a strengthening of the right-holders' established position at the parodist's expense. While the introduction of a specific parody exception under copyright law may (ultimately) go some way to redress the balance, legislation alone, is insufficient to break down the barriers parodists face which derive from established practices implemented by the key commercial actors in this creative sector.

The mandatory nature of the exception provides a parodist with some ammunition when their lawful parody clashes with an unyielding contractual clause. Yet, the position still remains uncertain whether the parody exception is such that a parodist is entitled to exploit any lawful parody commercially on the same footing as any other original copyright work. Certainly, by failing to revise their practices in light of the legislative changes, the major music industry actors have taken the stance that, whatever the legal reality, musical parodies undermine the interests of original right-holders, such that parodists should not be able to generate revenue from their work.

Right-holders should be protected against those infringers who attempt to label a substantial reproduction as a 'parody', but the current attitude of blanket denial is likely to thwart the parody exception, and impinge upon the proper functioning of the internal market. Given Brexit, the UK legislature could take action at a national level to mitigate the current status quo, whether through the adoption of ADR schemes (which are known to operate well to resolve disputes concerning registration of domain names, and as implemented in consumer law to settle disputes between consumers and traders),[88] or through the introduction of copyright licences of right (used in design

[87] Section 237(2) CDPA. Any design protected by UK unregistered design right is subject to a compulsory licence for the final five years of protection. Anybody, including an infringer, must be granted a licence. If the parties cannot reach an agreement on the terms of use, then an application can be made for the licence terms to be determined by the Comptroller.

[88] The Alternative Dispute Resolution for Consumer Disputes Regulations 2015, SI 2015/542; Directive 2013/11/EU of the European Parliament and of the Council of 21 May 2013 on alternative dispute resolution for consumer disputes and amending Regulation (EC) No 2006/2004 and Directive 2009/22/EC OJ L 165, 18 June 2013, pp. 63–79 and Regulation 524/2013 of the European Parliament and of the Council of 21/05/2013 on online dispute resolution for consumer disputes and amending Regulation (EC) No 2006/2004 and Directive 2009/22/EC OJ L 165, 18 June 2013, pp. 1–12.

law). Both aim at, firstly, rebalancing the unequal bargaining positions of the parties to any dispute by encouraging negotiation; secondly, providing access to an independent third party to bring an objective view of the relative strength of the case; and, finally, concluding a legally binding agreement as to future uses.

Finally, a solution closer to home lies in the interpretation of the exception. It is beneficial to identify business practices which hinder the ultimate goal of creativity, but good business practices can only be adopted where the law is clear and predictable. Current actors within the music industry perceive uncertainty around the application of the exception, justifying the barriers exposed throughout this section. Yet, further factors can be derived from the ECtHR case law to deal with parody cases which are not so clear-cut.

2. Shaping the Parody Exception Using the Human Rights Framework

One of the difficulties which courts face when determining whether the parody exception should apply to a specific use is the potential conflict between copyright and freedom of expression.[89] Although this can be reasonably explained by the devolution of powers within a jurisdiction, it can create apparently inconsistent outcomes (between or even within jurisdictions). Certainly, the form of the exception, i.e. fair use, fair dealing etc., goes some way to provide the flexibility needed to enable a court to weigh up the human rights values in issue, but this can be further developed in two ways. Firstly, human rights values colour the appraisal of the traditional fair use, fair dealing, or rules of the genre factors. If the use enables a realization of freedom of expression, it is more likely that the use should be lawful (e.g. the intent, the form, the medium, and the type of the expression). Secondly, judges are invited to consider other parameters which traditionally fall outside the scope of copyright such as the standing of the speaker, the context, and the content of an expression. As we have established that parody is deeply embedded as a tool for promoting this human right, this section considers whether national courts should take guidance, when applying the parody exception, from human rights cases.[90] Although traditionally, copyright law adopts a somewhat 'content neutral' approach, in *Deckmyn*, the CJEU, [91] has suggested that evaluation of content may enable the fundamental rights in tension in any particular case to be resolved.

2.1 The standing of the speaker

The standing of the speaker, i.e. the parodist, is a relevant consideration, since this has an impact on the way in which the message conveyed will be construed and, therefore, whether the parodic nature of a work would be evident to the public. For example, a parody communicated by an established comedian seems more likely to satisfy the parody exception's requirements than the same message conveyed by a newsreader. Recipients of the comedian's message are aware that they must not take the content too seriously, or that a serious message being delivered under the cover of comedy may include exaggeration. Either offset the potential harm created. Conversely, the more

[89] See Chapter 1, section 5.1 and Chapter 5.
[90] Building on the factors established, see Chapter 5, section 4.2.
[91] *Deckmyn* (n 7).

authoritative the speaker's position, the more likely it is that their message will be taken at face value, therefore requiring more cues for the public to decipher the parodic nature of the use. For example, Chapter 5 identifed the vital role of the press within a democratic society.[92] This suggest that 'speakers', such as journalists and other social commentators, owe a special duty to society to ensure that their message is unlikely to be misconstrued.[93] As a result, a politician seeking to use parody to convey a political message might need to provide more and/or less subtle cues to ensure that the public understand that they are communicating via parody.

2.2 The intent of the speaker

It has been seen that the parodist's intent is a significant factor, but this requires courts to differentiate between legitimate criticism conveyed by acerbic or caustic humour and illegimate claims of parody to shield otherwise malicious or insulting comments.[94]

As explained earlier, this is not to say that parodists should enjoy more legal protection than other speakers;[95] but, it is the role of the parody exception to ensure that they do not end up enjoying less. Even if a parody is lawful according to copyright law, defamation law might still apply to the parody if it is an unjustified attack upon a person's work or reputation. We saw that in *Douces Transes*,[96] the French Supreme Court recognized that a song which complied with the rules of the genre for the parody exception in copyright law did not create a freedom to parody which overrode defamation law.[97] A parodist might then still defeat a defamation claim by demonstrating that their statement is true, and given that parody typically involves some degree of exaggeration, the comment made might not need to be completely accurate to be justified[98] under defamation law either.[99]

This further reinforces the idea that parodies exist in a separate reality to the original work. Provided the public is able to recognize the parody genre, this mitigates the harm to the original, because the detachment ensures that it is still likely to be able to convey its own, independent message.[100]

[92] See Chapter 5, section 4.1.3.

[93] TGI Paris, 17e ch. Corr., 9 janvier 1992, *Le Front National c/ Bedos*, Gaz pal. 1992.1.182, note Bilger; TGI Paris, 17e ch. Corr., 17 février 1993, *Sabatier c/ Du Roy et autres*, Recueil Dalloz Sirey, 1994, 25e cahier, sommaires commentes, pp. 195–6; note Bigot.

[94] B Mouffe, *Le droit à l'humour* (Larcier, 2011) 485.

[95] Yet the study of the national case law demonstrates that French courts adopt a liberal approach to determining the intent of parodists.

[96] Cass., 12 janvier 1988, RIDA, n°137, 98.

[97] Repeated in, amongst others, Cass. 14 novembre 2006, *Marithe v. Association Croyances et libertés* Bull. 2006, I, n° 485, p. 417; Versailles ch. 01 Sect. 01 28 septembre 2006 n°05/04741.

[98] *Jersild v. Denmark* (1994) 19 EHRR 1.

[99] D Türk and L Joinet, 'The right to freedom of opinion and expression: current problems of its realization and measures necessary for its strengthening and promotion' in K Boyle and F D'Souza (eds), *Striking a Balance: Hate Speech, Freedom of Expression and Non-Discrimination* (Article XIX, London and Human Rights Centre, University of Essex, 1992) 52.

[100] This is also the case in the US as seen in Chapter 5, section 5.5. *Quenton Galvin and Jacob Meister v. Illinois Republican Party, Illinois House Republican Organisation, Roderick Drobinski, Friends of Rod Drobinski, Jamestown Associates LLC, and Majority Strategies, Inc.* (2015) No. 14 C 10490; *Dhillon v. Does* 1-10, No. C 13-01465 SI, 2014 WL 722592, [5] (N.D. Cal. Feb. 25, 2014); *Henley v. DeVore*, 733 F.Supp.2d 1144 (C.D. Cal. 2010); *Hustler Magazine v. Falwell*, 485 U.S. 46, 108 S. Ct. 876, 99 L.Ed.2d 41 (1988); *N.Y. Times Co. v. Sullivan*,376 U.S. 254, 84 S. Ct. 710, 11 L.Ed.2d 686 (1964).

2.3 The form of the expression

The form of the expression is probably the most obvious element which must sidered. A parody warrants special treatment from other kinds of 'borrowed' wo adaptations because it results in the dissemination of a separate expression. T comfortably 'borrowed' works fit within the limits determined by the parody the more likely it is that a fair balance will favour the copyright-holder.[101]

This point is illustrated in the French *Glam & Shine* decision.[102] An artist produ collage which reproduced three fashion photographs without the permission of the right-holder. The photos were slightly altered, by cropping and changing the skin to the models to blue (Figure 7.2). The artist claimed his reproduction was a parody w invited the public to reflect upon the tastes and priorities of current society, and thus a legitimate exercise of his right to freedom of expression.

Figure 7.2 Example of Peter Klasen's use of Alix Malka's photograph.
Peter Klasen, *Blue face red machine high voltage*, 2008, inkjet print and acrylic, 130 x 97 cm. © ADAGP, Paris and DACS, London 2018. Photo ©TAJAN.

[101] Paris, 14e ch. B, 28 novembre 2008, Recueil Dalloz, 2009 n°9, p. 610, note Edelman; Cass. (1ère ch. Civ.), 13 janvier 1998, D., 1999, somm. p. 167 (in relation to the right of privacy).

[102] TGI Paris, 31 janvier 2012, *Alix Malka v. Peter Klasen*, n° RG 10/02 (First instance); Paris, 18 septembre 2013, *Alix Malka v. Peter Klasen*, N° RG 12/02480 (appeal); Cass., 1ère Civ., *Alix Malka v. Peter Klasen*, 15 mai 2015, n° 13-27.391 (Supreme Court); Versailles, 16 mars 2018, *Alix Malka v. Peter Klasen*, n° RG 15/06029 (case remanded).

Here, the claim to the parody defence failed because none of the courts accepted the work was more than a mere appropriation of another's work.[103] The parody was unsuccessful because the artist had failed to distance his work enough from conventional fashion images. Any message which the artist intended the artwork to convey was so subtle that it had been lost. In reaching its conclusion, the court of appeal underlined the need to ensure that freedom of expression did not overwhelm the exclusive rights afforded by copyright. When the case was remanded to the court of appeal of Versailles, the court further considered the parody exception as well as its interaction with freedom of expression. On the application of the parody exception, the court held that humorous character was lacking and there was not material alteration of the original works beyond cropping and the blue tint applied to the photographs. Therefore, the parody was not obvious to the public exposed to the defendant's use. The court then moved on to consider whether denying the use as a parody which fell exception had the effect of violating the defendant's right of freedom of expression. The court paid particular attention to the commercial nature of the use and noted that the use did not contribute to a debate of public interest. If the parodist claims that his freedom of expression has been unduly restricted, he bears the burden of proof. In any case, the parody exception is not a means to justify any kind of borrowing. Additionally, the court noted the artist's motive was primarily commercial. Finally, the fact that his freedom of expression had not been violated unjustifiably was underlined as the defendant had himself conceded that use of the copyright-protected photographs was not essential to convey his message.

The distance between the parody and the original required to avoid confusion is also present in the US through the transformativeness approach. However, as we have seen, not all transformation amounts to fair use, and not all transformations are parodies. When, in *Cariou v. Prince*, the district court in the Second Circuit found in favour of appropriation artist Richard Prince, it is implicit that the court's determination turned upon whether it resulted in a new artistic expression.[104] Concluding that his use did result in a new expression, the court found in favour of the parodist. Although criticized,[105] this decision demonstrates the importance of freedom of expression in the US appreciation of the parody exception which can lead to a result which would be difficult to reach in other jurisdictions scrutinized in this book.[106]

2.4 The type of the expression

The right of freedom of expression protects expression of all types. However, there is a hierarchy in place, which affords national courts more margin of appreciation in respect of some types than others. Social-political[107] and cultural expressions,[108] are held in highest esteem, but even commercial expressions are protected.[109]

[103] While the Supreme Court did not criticize the final conclusion, it did criticize the decision for not fully explaining how the balance between competing interests had been struck; Cass., 15 mai 2015, 13-27.391, Publié au bulletin.

[104] However, perhaps the Second Circuit misapplied or failed to consider other factors such as market substitution.

[105] See Chapter 5, section 5.5.

[106] And this despite the *Ashby* ruling (*Ashby Donald and Others v. France*, App No 36769/08, 10 January 2013) as demonstrated in *Malka* (n 102).

[107] *Vereinigung Bildender Künstler v. Austria*, App No 68354/01.

[108] *Akda v. Turkey*, App No 41056/04, 16 February 2010.

[109] *Krone Verlag GmbH & Co KG (No 3) v. Austria* (2003) 36 EHRR 57.

Parodies similarly serve different functions in the public forum, ranging from light entertainment to matters of serious public concern. To quote Nobel Peace Prize winner, Kofi Annan:

> Cartoons make us laugh. Without them, our lives would be much sadder. But they are no laughing matter: They have the power to inform, and also to offend.[110]

Thus, the parody exception in copyright law should reflect the same spectrum of protection afforded to freedom of expression based upon its social value.[111]Political parodies, typically political cartoons, should enjoy greater latitude under copyright law compared with those which are merely artistic or commercial expressions. Given this, the mere fact a parody might cause offence should not be taken to imply that it should not benefit from the exception, but rather the level of offence to be tolerated should be proportionate to the gravity of the parody's message.

This point is nicely illustrated by the efforts[112] of Hergé's estate to restrain publication of the cartoon depicting politician Kevin Rudd, as a Tintin parody, which we considered previously in Chapter 6.[113] Clearly, cartoons of this type are capable of engaging a wider/different audience than a conventional political commentary,[114] thereby providing a valuable resource which informs and invites public debate of current events.[115] The example also demonstrates the importance of satire as a form of artistic expression within a democratic society. Satire inherently requires reality to be exaggerated and distorted, as its very aim is to engender a public reaction of shock, surprise, or offence. The same logic should be applied to parodies at large. Indeed, since satire represents one facet of parody, there seems no reason to distinguish between these forms of expression.[116] For example, a parody which has an obviously humorous character creates a separation between the reality of the original work and the altered reality in which the parody is located. An adequate separation means that the public will not take the parody's message at face value but will seek out a secondary meaning to the message: the rules of the parody genre are respected.

Owing to the important role of political comment in the public arena, any interference with a political parodist's freedom of expression requires careful analysis. However, purely commercial expressions do not carry the same significance. Consequently, it is legitimate that national courts might place more restriction upon free expression and more weight upon the exclusive rights of the right-holder in respect of an unauthorized parody of a copyright work for a parody used in an advertising context.

[110] Kofi Annan, Nobel Peace Prize at the symposium 'Unlearning Intolerance', New York, 16 October 2006 at http://www.cartooningforpeace.org/en/presentation/ (access date: 1 June 2018).

[111] See Chapter 5, section 2.

[112] The dispute arose prior the introduction of a parody exception in Australian copyright law, and was eventually settled between the parties.

[113] See Chapter 6, section 4.3.2.

[114] For more on the power of political cartoons, see R Phiddian, *Censorship and the Political Cartoonist*, refereed paper presented to the Australasian Political Studies Association Conference (University of Adelaide, 29 September–1 October 2004).

[115] J McCutcheon, 'The new defense of parody or satire under Australian copyright law' (2008) 2 *IPQ* 163, 172.

[116] As demonstrated in the previous chapter, the parody/satire distinction seems to be fading in the US. This is welcomed especially in a country with such a robust protection for the First Amendment.

2.5 The medium used

The medium used to disseminate a parody may also influence a national court to decide whether the use should be permitted, or not. ECtHR jurisprudence has established that the medium may influence the impact of an expression. For example, print media tend to have less impact than a broadcast because the latter has a wider reach.[117] Similarly, the ECtHR has also held an expression communicated via a book of poetry to have less impact because the need to purchase the work inevitably reduced the number of people having access to the potentially harmful expression.[118]

In terms of parody, we have seen that in France and in the US, the fact that a parody has been reproduced on goods which do not aim to commercially exploit the parodic expression (e.g. lighters, pins, t-shirts) is likely to go against the parodist. Commercialization in this form is seen as indicative that the parodist may intend to do more than simply seeking remuneration for their creative efforts, by potentially free-riding on the creative efforts of the right-holder. Finally, in the digital world, a freely available online parody is likely to have more impact than one behind a paywall.

If humorous character is established negatively by establishing lack of harm, then this would be connected to the medium used to disseminate the parody.

2.6 The context of the expression

Context, i.e. the manner in which a parody is communicated, should also influence whether the use is permitted or restricted. The ECtHR has emphasized that this is significant in terms of the right to freedom of expression.

For example, in *Karataş v. Turkey*,[119] discussed earlier,[120] the Court took account of the fact that the commentator had selected poetry to express concern about the state of political unrest in Turkey and published it in a poetry book. The Court considered that this context of expression was likely to have limited public appeal,[121] such that the publication was likely to have a negligible impact on public order. However, had a context of work having mass appeal been selected to convey the same comment, then the conclusion was likely to have been different.

In light of the important role of a free press as a safeguard of democracy, any restriction to an expression made in the press, which raises awareness or opens a valuable debate, should be reserved for exceptional circumstances, for example, where the speaker uses the wide dissemination to call for social disorder.[122] In contrast, parodies used in a purely commercial context might have less social value, and this change in context might be sufficient to tip the balance in favour of upholding the property rights of a copyright-holder.[123]

Considerations of context also need to take account of historical and social factors, since different sectors of society and different nationalities have different sensitivities. For example, parodies which use protected works to comment on events such as the Holocaust will be dealt with differently in Germany and France, where the state has specific duties to their Jewish population, than in other countries, such as the UK, Australia, or Canada.[124]

[117] Jersild (n 98).

[118] Therefore, the expression was unlikely to incite hatred and violence, despite its content. *Karataş v. Turkey* (1999) IHRL 2880.

[119] Ibid. [120] See Chapter 5, section 4.1.1. [121] *Karataş* (n 118) [52].

[122] *Jersild* (n 98). [123] *Ashby Donald and Others v. France*, App No 36769/08.

[124] *Peta Deutschland v. Germany*, App No 43481/09; *Leroy v. France*, App No 36109/03.

Context provides the unwritten cipher which indicates whether a message should be taken literally (which could adversely affect the rights of others) or as a parody. Only when the parodic context is misconstrued (such that its humour and the message are taken at face value) is there the potential for conflict with the fundamental rights of others. Depending upon the particular facts, this might lead to the conclusion that the parody constitutes an abuse such that the rights of others should prevail. The fact that the parody is used for commercial purposes is not sufficient in itself to tip the balance against the parodist.

In conclusion, assessing whether a parody amounts to an abuse of freedom of expression cannot be achieved by analysing the parody in isolation. National courts should have regard to the context in which the parody arises, in terms of the context of its publication, as well as the particular sensitivities of its likely audience.

2.7 The content of the expression

The message conveyed by a parody is another significant factor which national courts should take into account. While an individual's right to free expression is unlikely to require restriction when it manifests itself in a light-hearted parody, the same cannot be assumed where a parody conflicts with the very values underpinning that fundamental right or offends against the accepted moral norms of a particular society.

The first distinction to be made is to identify whether the reproduction of the protected work for parody is intended to criticize the work itself, including the values which it encapsulates (i.e. a 'parody of') or whether it comments on something external and unrelated to the work copied (i.e. 'parody with'). In either case, the right-holder may not endorse the parody's message. Where the message is uncontentious, courts should award greater weight to preservation of freedom of expression than to preservation of the right-holder's property rights. Conversely, where the message itself is on the boundary of acceptability, courts should enjoy a greater margin of appreciation to strike a balance between the rights of the right-holders, the interests of the author of the derivative work, and the interests of society at large.

These issues were explored in *Deckmyn*.[125] In this case, Vlaams Belang, a right-wing and Flemish nationalist political party, distributed a leaflet featuring a parody of the well-known *Spike and Suzy* comic book cover entitled 'De Wilde Weldoener'—The Compulsive Benefactor (Figure 7.3). The copyright-protected image had been altered to promote the party's political message. The main figure was replaced with an image of Ghent's mayor, M. Termont, sporting a belt coloured like the Belgian flag. Instead of throwing coins to adults and children, as in the original image, the Mayor is depicted handing out money to people from different ethnic backgrounds. The parody clearly intended to convey the message that M. Termont had prioritized public spending on immigrants rather than on other causes.

In cases such as this where the parody is not strikingly evident, a national court must determine whether the parody before them remains within the acceptable limits of freedom of expression. If the parody fails to respect another fundamental right (such as the right to religion) or promotes values which are contrary to principles overarching fundamental rights (e.g. racial hatred, discrimination, or glorification of terrorism), then, as the ultimate balance struck by the court must realize *all* fundamental rights in

[125] *Deckmyn* (n 7).

Figure 7.3 The Compulsive Benefactor cover of one of the comic albums of Spike and Suzy and its parody.

issue, this might justify restricting the parodist's freedom of expression in favour of the fundamental rights of others.

This does not imply that *any* message contrary to what is accepted by a society at large has to be censored. Democratic societies encourage pluralism, including messages that shock, disturb, or offend. However, human rights law recognizes that freedom of expression does have a limit. In *Deckmyn*,[126] it was argued that the Vlaams Belang message which incited violence, hatred, or discrimination fell beyond this limit. Also, there is a general consensus that it is unacceptable to circulate images which depict paedophilia, necrophilia, or bestiality. If the content of the parody goes against the morals of a particular society, the national court has a greater margin to interfere with the parodist's freedom of expression, particularly when exercise of this right potentially compromises the property rights of others. But morals do evolve over time and vary from place to place,[127] and account should be taken of this to avoid unnecessary censorship.[128]

3. Preventing Abuses

The previous section considered the influence of freedom of expression on the appreciation of the requirements attached to the parody exception. When the parodist's right to free expression is in conflict with the exercise of another's fundamental right, including exercise of copyright law's exclusive rights, a court should consider whether exercise of the right of freedom of expression amounts to an abuse of that right. If so, limiting freedom of expression is justified to preserve the rights of others. In this section, we shall consider examples where exercise of the right to freedom of expression has been curtailed in order to protect abuse of other fundamental rights. The focus is on French parody cases, because of the relative wealth of relevant case law available. However, these are not limited to copyright cases. This section therefore serves two purposes: (1) demonstrating that the parody exception may extend its reach beyond copyright law, and (2) providing insight as to how the balance between copyright and freedom of expression may be struck.

3.1 Freedom of expression v. personality rights

Personality rights[129] is collective term used in France to refer to the basic human rights deemed necessary to protect an individual's essential interests.[130] Traditionally, these recognize a right to life, right to human dignity, right to respect for private life, and image rights. In a balancing of fundamental rights, all of these rights must be balanced against freedom of expression.

[126] Ibid.

[127] Hence, it seems dubious to assume that a 'European' sense of morality exists, even though the EU Intellectual Property Office and designated EU trade mark and design courts are meant to assess designs and trade marks as if it did. Yet this is implied by the AGO in *Deckmyn* (n 7) [83]: 'most deeply rooted beliefs in European society'.

[128] As discussed previously in relation to the French Supreme Court in ch. Crim., 12 septembre 2007, 06-86763, Non publié au bulletin. Child pornography is not morally acceptable and constitutes a criminal offence. Therefore, a cartoon hero resembling a child engaging in sexual relationships with adults has been restricted. Yet, if the cartoon had depicted a non-human juvenile hero, such as a Smurf, in similar situations it would not call for a restriction. See section 3.3.

[129] Mostly referred to as publicity rights such as tort and passing off in common law jurisdictions.

[130] Author's own translation from Cornu (ed.), see 'Personnalité', in *Vocabulaire juridique*.

Thus, for example, French courts consider that freedom of expression must be balanced against invasion of privacy. In a dispute relating to publication of a cartoon in a satirical newspaper, Jean-Marie Le Pen, then leader of the French National Front, objected to an image evidently depicting himself and his wife semi-clad with the captions: 'Recent developments in the Le Pen case' and 'Buttock to buttock of the infernal couple'.[131] While the court recognized that the genre of satirical caricature permits exaggeration, distortion, and irony, the court did not consider that it extended to an image which was tantamount to an invasion of privacy. In Auvret's opinion,[132] the court should have characterized the nature of the expression attacking the ex-leader as being an invasion of privacy or not, given that the difficulty in this case arose from a separation between Le Pen's public political role and his personal life.

Freedom of expression, even in a press context, does not shield the speaker from potential criminal conviction. Harm to another's reputation by making an expression which is proved to be false can give rise to a defamation claim,[133] while particularly outrageous comments may give rise to criminal liability.[134] The line between the exaggeration allowed under satire and that precluded as an outrageous comment is unclear. This opens the door to courts making ostensibly subjective appraisals.

If sued for defamation, a speaker may still protect their right to freedom of expression by showing the statement made is either true or was made in good faith. For the truth defence to apply, the defendant must demonstrate the veracity of his statement, although this defence is not available for defamatory allegation regarding one's right to privacy or racial defamation.[135] For a good faith defence to be successful, the defendant must satisfy four requirements which have been established by courts:[136] legitimacy of the goal sought, absence of malicious intent, particular care in the expression and quality of the speaker.[137]

French courts have established that parodies which remain true to the rules of the genre for the purposes of copyright law also lack the intent required for a tort action, such as breach of privacy or defamation, to succeed. Thus, when a satirical newspaper published a pastiche of another article to criticize Scientology, the trial judge held that the pastiche was not defamatory.[138] In this case, the pastiche genre permitted a message which was harsh and provocative, and because the article satisfied the rules of the genre, the use lacked the intent required to defame.

[131] TGI Paris, ref., 17 juin 1987, *Le Pen c/ le Canard Enchainé;* Paris, 1ère ch., sect. B, 19 juin 1987; JCP 1988.II.20957, note Auvret.

[132] See n 131.

[133] Article 29 of the Freedom of the Press Act of 29 July 1881.

[134] R621-1 and 621-2 Penal Code.

[135] Sylvie Menotti, *La preuve de la vérité du fait diffamatoire* (courdecassation.fr 2004) available at https://www.courdecassation.fr/publications_cour_26/rapport_annuel_36/rapport_2004_173/deuxieme_partie_tudes_documents_176/tudes_theme_verite_178/fait_diffamatoire_6395.html (access date: 10 June 2015).

[136] TGI Paris, 17e ch. Corr., 9 janvier 1992, *Le Front National c/ Bedos*, Gaz pal. 1992.1.182, note Bilger; TGI Paris, 17e ch. Corr., 17 février 1993, *Sabatier c/ Du Roy and Others*, Recueil Dalloz Sirey, 1994, 25e cahier, sommaires commentés, pp. 195–6; note Bigot.

[137] The weight attributed to each factor varies depending on the facts of the case. TGI Paris, 17e ch. Corr., 9 janvier 1992, *Le Front National c/ Bedos*, Gaz pal. 1992.1.182, note Bilger (an allegation made by Bedos (comedian, journalist, and historian) about the National Front political party receiving money from the Iraqi regime, enemy in time of war, is likely to amount with treason and harm to national defence or impairment to morality); TGI Paris, 17e ch. Corr., 17 février 1993, *Sabatier c/ Du Roy and Others*, Recueil Dalloz Sirey, 1994, 25e cahier, sommaires commentes, pp. 195–6; note Bigot.

[138] Based on Articles 23, 29(2), and 33(2) Freedom of the Press Act. Corr. Paris, 17e ch., 25 avril 2003, *Gonnet v. Gounord et Dupuis*.

The context of the expression is also important. In *Gigliotti v. Bern*,[139] a radio commentator's song which described the claimant (the brother of a famous French singer) as a thug, a bastard, and a sadist was held not to be defamatory either. The court conceded that certain phrases, taken in isolation, could be seen as offensive, but overall, the song was evidently humorously outrageous in character. The fact that the public would not take the song seriously prevented it from being defamatory.

Similarly, in *Dion v. Cogerev*,[140] Céline Dion, the Canadian singer, sued the publisher of a photomontage for defamation. The image appeared to depict Dion naked and covered with faeces. As the picture featured in a satirical magazine, and the singer was well-known for taking particular care of her appearance, the court held that the magazine's readership, viewing the image in context, would not take the montage to be real. Thus, the lack of confusion between the published caricature and the image of the singer led the tribunal to conclude that Dion's reputation had not been harmed.[141]

In *G. v. Canal Plus*,[142] the court was required to consider a sketch in a satirical TV puppet show, which depicted the claimant, a prince, as lazy, work-shy, and gay.[143] The court held that the parody would only defame, i.e. harm the personality rights of its target, if the defendant displayed a malicious intent towards the target. Only then would it be legitimate to limit freedom of expression.

It is evident from this jurisprudence that the presence or absence of humour is the measure which determines whether the balancing of rights favours protection of freedom of expression in the parody use or points to upholding the personality rights of the parody's target.[144] The parody's context is an essential component when striking a fair balance.

It is apparent that in the case of a clash of fundamental rights involving parody, the rules of the genre guide French courts in their determination of whether the balance favours protection of freedom of expression or the personality rights of the claimant. Thus, the 'parody exception' in French law extends beyond the confines of copyright law. While freedom of expression calls for a liberal interpretation of the parody exception, it is not absolute. When freedom of expression conflicts with image rights or the right to privacy, humoristic character influences the court's balancing of rights. Firstly, the humorous character, appraised through the intent of the speaker, informs the court on the legitimacy of the criticism or comment made. Malicious intent tips the balance towards the protection of the rights of the person targeted, while harsh criticism made non-maliciously via humour tips the balance in favour of protecting freedom of expression.[145] Secondly, humour enables the public to detect the parody,

[139] TGI Paris, 17e ch. Civ., 3 avril 2006, *Bruno Gigliotti c/ Stephane Bern et autres*, légipresse n°238 (janvier/février 2007), I-Actualite, p. 11.

[140] TGI Paris, 1ère ch. 1ère sect., 14 avril 1999, *Dion c/ Ste Cogerev*; Juris-data n°040882; CCE, octobre 1999 p. 23.

[141] This was already the result in 1982 in a similar case. Paris, 4e ch. B., 28 janvier 1982, *Dame Goya c/ S.A.R.L. Editions du Square*, IR, p. 165, appeal from TPI Paris, 1ère ch., 18 juin 1981.

[142] Paris, 1ère ch. A, 11 mars 1991, *G. c/ Canal Plus*, légipresse n°91-I, Informations d'actualite, p. 49.

[143] The court made the parodist's interests prevail over the personality rights of the targeted person.

[144] Similar reasoning in Paris, *Le Pen v. Laurent Gerra*, 23 janvier 2013 n°11/11023.

[145] Malicious intent can be shown through any factual elements. In a case dealing with the sale of a voodoo doll caricaturing French ex-President Sarkozy along with a satirical leaflet as a complement to a newspaper, the court decided that the requirement of humour was not satisfied; the fact that the doll is sold with pins that the public can stick into it mirrors the intent to hurt which goes beyond the rules of the genre of parody. Nevertheless, the interdiction of the voodoo doll is not a proportionate means in relation to the harm caused. Therefore, the judges compelled the editor to sell the dolls with a disclaimer ('it has been decided that the incitement of readers to pin needles in the doll joined to the booklet implies the idea of physical harm, even symbolically, which amounts to an attack to the

meaning they do not take the message of the expression literally, but as a second degree joke. This eliminates confusion between reality and the use made. Provided the public is not confused, the rights of the parody's target are not harmed,[146] yet if the court notes a manifestly illicit character within the expression, then freedom of expression of the parodist must be set aside.

3.2 Freedom of expression v. non-discrimination

In France, protection against discrimination, hate, and racial violence typically prevails over the right to freedom of expression. Therefore, those wishing to exercise their right to freedom of expression to pass comment on these sensitive topics are required to take extra care.

In *Bruel v. Sebastien*,[147] a French comedian sought to comment upon the views of the National Front. He did this by dressing up as its then leader, Jean-Marie Le Pen, and performing a song—*Casser du noir* ('Crush the black'[148]), a parody of *Casser la voix*. Although the court recognized from the song's lyrics that it was intended to be a parody, the court considered that the parodist had placed insufficient distance between the anti-racist ideals behind the original song and the racist views of the National Front. There were insufficient signals for the public to seek a double meaning to the lyrics.[149] Given the context of the use, which featured as part of a political debate concerning immigration, there was a risk that the altered lyrics would appear to incite, rather than criticize, discrimination, hate, and racial violence. On balance, the work went beyond legitimate free speech.[150]

The importance of establishing this distance between the parody and its target in the public mind has been confirmed by later French decisions, although its application is not straightforward. In *La Grosse Bertha*,[151] a satirical magazine published a drawing, captioned: 'I suck was his name by Robert Obscene'.[152] This depicted an image of a moribund Christ, looking on as the Pope engages in sexual acts with a Brazilian transvestite, a priest drowns a child in baptismal font, and a naked woman is ripped open by a crucifix. The General Alliance against Racism and for the respect of the French and Catholic Identity ('AGRIF') sued for incitement to discrimination, hatred, and violence against Catholics. The trial judge noted the obvious satirical and humoristic character of the magazine, and held in favour of freedom of expression, a decision later confirmed on appeal. Here, the court considered it relevant that the images were not on public display, but only available to those who decided to purchase the magazine.

dignity of Mr Sarkozy' and underneath 'Court injunction'). Paris, 14e ch. B, 28 novembre 2008, Recueil Dalloz, 2009 n°9, p. 610, note Edelman.

146 Caen, ch. Civ. n°1, 4 décembre 2007, *Le Roi Pétaud et Sa Cour c/ Crédit Agricole*, n°06-2537; TGI Paris, 1ère ch. 1ère sect., 14 avril 1999, *Dion c/ Ste Cogerev*; Juris-data n°040882; CCE, October 1999, p. 23.

147 Cass., ch. Crim., 4 novembre 1997, *Patrick Bruel v. Patrick Sebastien and TF1*, n°96-84338.

148 Author's own translation.

149 This could be criticized as dressing up may not be enough to enable the recognition by the public. In addition, the programme was pre-recorded, such that the defendant would have been aware how the message would come across. This precluded a 'good faith' defence.

150 This decision was upheld by the Supreme Court. The Court confirmed that, taken literally, the song lyrics constituted an incitement to hatred, violence and discrimination which is not allowed under either the law of the press: Article 24(6) of the law on the freedom of the press.

151 Versailles, 18 mars 1998, n°1996-2195, *'La Grosse Bertha'* (on referral from Cass., 28 février 1996).

152 Author's own translation.

Yet the appeal decision was quashed by the Supreme Court and referred back to the Court of Appeal. Given their outrageous character, the Supreme Court considered that publication of the drawing might still result in an abuse of free expression. Ultimately, the Court of Appeal decided that, while the drawings clearly ridiculed the Catholic church, beliefs, and religious symbols, given the context of the parody within a magazine known by its readers for its provocative nature, there was no intent to incite general public hatred or violence.[153] The court concluded that in the particular circumstances, there was no abuse of freedom of expression.[154] This same reasoning was adopted in relation to the publication of caricatures of the Prophet Muhammed in the satirical magazine *Charlie Hebdo*.[155]

Although the line of reasoning might appear to be clear, these cases can be contrasted with the outcome in others which appear similar. One case concerned a caricature depicting the Pope[156] being both guillotined and targeted by a swinging wrecking ball. In this case the Court of Appeal acknowledged the acerbic nature of the cartoon, but considered that the image was an impermissible incitement to violence. Much seems to have hinged upon the timing of the drawing's publication, since there was a particular sensitivity surrounding the subject matter, as the Pope had just been the victim of a violent attack.[157]

Finally, the fact that a parody has a commercial character does not automatically tip the balance against freedom of expression. This is exemplified by the *Last Supper* decision,[158] in which a commercial clothing company parodied the famous Leonardo Da Vinci painting of that name to promote the launch of their new collection. The male subjects in the original painting were replaced by women wearing the company's clothing, while the only man featured was only partially clothed. Copyright in the painting was not in issue, but the French association protecting beliefs and individual freedoms failed to see any humour in the image, and sued the company. It considered that use of such a sacred scene for advertising purposes was a gross insult to the Catholic community.[159] The Supreme Court found in favour of freedom of expression, and held the commercial nature of the use was not determinative as to whether the expression was lawful. Ultimately, it was satisfied that the image aimed to shock, rather than to insult, the Catholic community and its symbols.[160]

[153] Therefore, there was no infringement of article 1382 of the Civil Code or article 24 of the Law on the Freedom of the Press.

[154] This case went back to the Supreme Court which dismissed the appeal. Cass, 2e Civ., 8 mars 2001, *Alliance générale contre le racisme et pour le respect de l'identité française et chrétienne c/ Godefroid*, n°98-17.574. A similar case went all the way up to the Supreme Court whereby the facts dealt with the publication of drawings which are allegedly an incitement to hatred, violence, and discrimination towards Catholics. As an example, one of the six drawings depicts Michael Jackson carrying out an act of paedophilia on baby Jesus. Baby Jesus is represented with characteristic features of Hitler. Therefore, literally, these drawings incite to violence, hatred, and discrimination. Yet the Court deemed the action barred.

[155] This issue reproduced amongst others the caricatures published in the Danish Newspaper *Jylland-Posten*. Paris, 11e ch., 12 mars 2008.

[156] Paris, 11e ch. B, 13 novembre 1997, *X*. . . , D. 1998, IR, pp. 21–2.

[157] This was repeated in another case dealing with religious caricatures in a case where an armed hand was firing at the head of baby Jesus to which the statement 'they want money, let's give them lead' was affixed. Cass., 28 janvier 1999, n°96-16992, JCP G, 23 juin 1999, p. 1183, note Viney.

[158] Cass. 14 novembre 2006, *Marithe c/ Association Croyances et libertés* Bull. 2006, I, n°485, p. 417.

[159] Under articles 29(2) and 33 of the Law of the Press.

[160] The Supreme Court quashed the decisions at first instance and on appeal, which both held that the commercial character joined to the suggestion made through the depiction of the half-naked man tilted the balance in favour of the association for a finding of insult to Catholics. These courts concluded thus after studying the jurisprudence of the ECtHR and especially the *Otto-Preminger-Institut v. Austria* (1994) 19 EHRR 34, [47].

3.3 Freedom of expression v. morals

Religious hate or discrimination is not the only target under the scrutiny of French courts. Child pornography is another area which the courts have ruled as going beyond the limits acceptable for the exercise of freedom of expression. The Supreme Court applied the penal law which makes child pornography a criminal offence to prevent publication of a cartoon featuring a juvenile hero, *Tintin*, engaging in pornography.[161] Interestingly, the court commented that, had a juvenile Smurf been depicted in a similar context, the outcome might have been different. Here, the significance turns upon Tintin's human resemblance, whereas Smurfs lack such obvious human features.

4. A Desirable Harmonization

If a court's consideration of the parody exception necessarily involves a balancing of fundamental rights (section 3), against a complex factual matrix (section 2), does this mean that international or even EU-wide harmonization within copyright law is inevitably ill-fated? The short answer is: no, not necessarily, although the two 'universal' requirements attached to the parody exception might leave right-holders and creators with a bitter taste because they will inevitably need to relinquish some control over their protected work.

The additional guidance suggested in section 2 of this chapter contributes to the ultimate goal of harmonization. As the guidance is based upon international human rights law principles, it provides an attractive, if not definitive, solution because it is applicable to all the jurisdictions considered within this book. Nevertheless, it is unrealistic to expect that national courts would reach the same decision in the same or closely similar cases. This is not a failure of harmonization, but recognition that harmonization does not demand uniformity, because it is necessary to take national cultural and social sensitivities into account.

Taking account of national cultures fosters the integration of cultural diversity within the EU and international legal frameworks. Cultural diversity is used in a broad sense to cover the 'manifold ways in which the cultures of groups and societies find expression'.[162] It is often brandished as a policy goal which should be reflected in the application of substantive provisions, including the parody exception, within the internal single market.[163] In its goal of harmonization, the EU legislator must consider two legal traditions: common law and civil law countries. Whilst we have seen that the boundaries between the two can sometimes be blurred, differences subsist. Copyright exceptions and limitations represent an example where harmonization is more difficult to achieve. As Member States have introduced exceptions and limitations in their national law according to their legal culture and traditions, these tend to vary greatly. Therefore, harmonization does require a compromise to be reached. By endorsing the French requirements for the parody exception, the CJEU seems to have gathered inspiration from this national tradition. As we have seen, in civil law jurisdictions including France, the terms 'parody, pastiche and caricature', if not true synonyms, exist along an overlapping spectrum of genres, whereas the common law tradition is more likely to interpret the three terms as distinct and distinguishable. If this is maintained, then

[161] Cass. Crim., 12 septembre 2007, n°06-86763, non publié au bulletin.
[162] Article 4(1) UNESCO Convention on Cultural Diversity of 20 October 2005.
[163] At least ever since the Treaty of Maastricht in 1992.

the harmonization goal will be jeopardized, given that the net result is that the exception will be deemed to apply to different types of uses. Consequently, the autonomous understanding of parody, as defined by the CJEU in *Deckmyn*,[164] should be seen as a trade-off between the copyright and *droit d'auteur* legal traditions. National cultures and traditions may then resurface when it comes to shaping the exception to specific factual scenarios. As EU law leaves Member States unrestrained when it comes to implementation of copyright exceptions, common law and civil traditions may elect fair dealing or the rules of the genre to fine-tune the parody exception to their own legal tradition.

The CJEU's direction to pay more attention to human rights values when applying the parody exception can also be seen as an indication of respecting national specificities while achieving broad harmonization. In this chapter,[165] we have identified that the human rights framework has two functions in relation to the parody exception. First, an understanding of freedom of expression, as explained in ECtHR jurisprudence, offers guidance to national courts when assessing, for example, fair dealing or rules of the genre as to the factors which must be considered to ensure freedom of expression is promoted and preserved. Second, the human rights framework provides guidance regarding the balancing of fundamental rights, while allowing enough flexibility for national cultural differences to be preserved. Although the copyright paradigm remains largely content neutral, the proportionality requirement added by the CJEU in *Deckmyn*[166] reminds national authorities of their international obligations to give some effect to all the human rights at stake. This requires national courts to take the content of an expression into account, which might indicate that, despite the exception's requirements being met, the use results in an abuse and should not be allowed as it endangers human rights values.

In Chapter 4, we saw that the protection afforded to moral rights is linked to a jurisdiction's legal traditions with arguably less market impact than the associated economic rights. Nevertheless, the lack of harmonization between economic and moral rights in terms of a common parody exception could curtail the effectiveness of the parody exception. Within the EU, moral rights have not been harmonized, and the divergent protection afforded between Member States was shown to have a potential indirect effect on the scope of the parody exception in copyright law. As we have seen, civil law jurisdictions, such as France, operate a direct relation between the lawfulness of a use under the parody exception and the lawfulness of a use under a moral rights claim, whereas common law jurisdictions, such as the UK, were more likely to treat the same use differently. Thus, use permitted by the parody exception in copyright law might be precluded as a derogatory treatment, for example. Divergent outcomes could hinder the objectives of a harmonized parody exception. Yet, we also saw that as a result of the narrow scope of moral rights in common law jurisdictions, as well as the adoption of objective standards, it appears that moral rights would seldom preclude a use permitted by copyright law. Indeed, the advocated approach to interpretation of the parody exception would tend to exclude uses which would harm the moral rights of authors.

The ultimate aim of copyright law should be to offer a workable framework which enables the creative process to flourish and be adequately rewarded. This is achieved by striking a balance between the rights granted to right-holders—especially the reproduction right—and subsequent uses built upon earlier copyright-protected expressions. After all, even if this is not consistently stated throughout the EU copyright

[164] *Deckmyn* (n 7). [165] See sections 2 and 3. [166] *Deckmyn* (n 7) [27] and [31].

instruments, the policy goal has always been to protect end-users, as evidenced by the existence of copyright exceptions and limitations in EU copyright law. Nevertheless, the very fact that the interest of end-users is protected through exceptions, such as the parody exception, makes these interests appear secondary to those of the right-holders.

5. Conclusion: Towards a *Right* to Parody?

Whether deliberately, or not, the framing of the parody exception as a defence—thereby placing the burden of proof on the parodist—both stymies freedom of expression in copyright cases and reinforces the music business practices outlined earlier. Ultimately, as the parody exception is rooted in the human rights framework and the protection of freedom of expression, one may wonder whether protecting parodies through a defence is the best way to realize its underpinning goals.

We have seen that copyright protection, including at an international level, favours the interests of right-holders and places the user's interests in a secondary position. However, this approach is perhaps unsustainable given the expansion of the scope of exclusive rights through legal instruments and jurisprudence. There have been several calls to balance exclusive rights with stronger copyright exceptions which better protect users' interests. Notably, Canada is at the vanguard. Through its establishment of the user's rights doctrine, the Canadian Supreme Court requires equal weighting between exclusive rights and defences. While it remains to be seen whether this will lead to a broader interpretation of the parody exception, it marks a shift in the balancing of interests within copyright law. This contrasts with the situation in the EU, where the InfoSoc Directive requires that right-holders receive a high level of protection, which has resulted in exceptions being narrowly construed.[167] This has prompted commentators to seek alternative routes. Hugenholtz, for one, has argued that those copyright exceptions which are in place to protect human rights require enhanced protection compared to others. Largely adopting Hugenholtz's reasoning, this book has proposed ways for courts to take proper account of fundamental rights when assessing whether a parody falls within the scope of exception, irrespective of whether this is undertaken via a fair dealing, fair use, rules of the genre enquiry, or otherwise.

Procedurally, the inadequacy of protecting parodies through a defence has been noted by the judiciary. In the US, Judge Birch of the Eleventh Circuit has noted on two occasions that the parody defence would be better recast as a right, but even as currently provided, the defence should be applied to guarantee higher fundamental values.[168] Fair use should be seen as a 'breathing space within the confines of

[167] Recitals 9, 31, and 32 InfoSoc Directive.

[168] See *Suntrust Bank v. Houghton Mifflin Co.*, 268 F.3d 1257, n. 3 (11th Cir. 2001) (Birch J.): 'I believe that fair use should be considered an affirmative *right* under the 1976 Act, rather than merely an affirmative defense, as it is defined in the Act as a use that is not a violation of copyright [. . .] Nevertheless, the fact that the fair use right must be procedurally asserted as an affirmative defense does not detract from its constitutional significance as a guarantor to access and use for First Amendment purposes'; echoing *Bateman v. Mnemonics, Inc.*, 79 F.3d 1532, 1542 n.22 (11th Cir. 1996) (Birch J.): 'Although the traditional approach is to view "fair use" as an affirmative defense, this writer, speaking only for himself, is of the opinion that it is better viewed as a right granted by the Copyright Act of 1976. Originally, as a judicial doctrine without any statutory basis, fair use was an infringement that was excused—this is presumably why it was treated as a defense. As a statutory doctrine, however, fair use is not an infringement. Thus, since the passage of the 1976 Act, fair use should no longer be considered an infringement to be excused; instead, it is logical to view fair use as a right. Regardless of how fair use is viewed, it is clear that the burden of proving fair use is always on the putative infringer.'

copyright'[169] to guarantee the First Amendment in order to foster the creation of cultural works. The legal history of this doctrine demonstrates that wherever there is a public interest in a particular use, right-holders should not be in a position to impede it.[170]

Additionally, the fact that the defendant bears the burden of demonstrating that their parodic use is lawful creates the impression that the enquiry is concerned with 'excusing' infringing (wrongful) conduct whereas the enquiry should be devoting attention to promoting the right of freedom of expression and creativity. In other words, the fundamental roots of this copyright exception are generally absent in the courts' reasoning, altering the intended balance between property rights and freedom of expression values to favour the copyright-holder.[171] But why should the right-holder's expression prevail, since other expressions, including parody, also enjoy protection under the right to freedom of expression?

In the overview provided in Chapter 4, the range of judicially-developed 'fairness factors' applied to assess whether an unauthorized use of a copyright expression should be permitted were considered.[172] This leads to a flexible tool which is adaptable to various circumstances. A court's assessment of these factors might seem unpredictable, owing to the need to determine fairness on a case-by-case basis, which renders some of the factors inapplicable in certain cases. Although this flexibility in necessary and intentional, the legal uncertainty which may result can be divisive for the defendant. As the current state of play favours right-holders, any doubt in the fairness appreciation tips the balance in favour of upholding the claimant's rights.

In Chapter 5, we reviewed how a fair balance could be reached between copyright's property rights and competing freedom of expression values. If circumstances suggest that a parodist's right to freedom of expression prevails over copyright, then perhaps it should be the right-holder's role to prove that the use is unfair?[173] This debate seems to be moot in the current climate which requires those seeking to rely upon a copyright exception to 'justify' their use.

The mandatory character of the parody exception, as recognized in France and the UK, goes some way to redress the balance. By removing the ability for copyright-owners to 'contract out' of the parody exception, this suggests there is some will to

More notably, despite the reluctance of the US Congress to settle the debate as to the burden of proof of fair use at the time of its inception, section 108 US Copyright Code refers specifically to the 'right of fair use as provided under section 107'. Section 108(f)(4) of the US Copyright Act.

[169] *Campbell v. Acuff-Rose Music Inc.* 510 US 569 (1994), [579].

[170] See *Harper & Row, Publishers, Inc. v. Nation Enterprises*, 105 S. Ct. 2218, 2230 (1985); going even further, the First Amendment would grant authors a right not to speak in agreement with William F. Patry, 'Fair use after Sony and Harper & (and) Row' (1986) 8 *Comm. & L.* 21, 30.

[171] According to Snow, this shift leads to deeper consequences: 'free speech once defined the scope of copyright; today, copyright defines the scope of free speech.' Ned Snow, 'The forgotten right of fair use' (2011) 62 *Case W. Res. L. Rev.* 135, 137.

[172] Although the US has chosen to codify the fair use factors, it must be reminded that these were initially developed by courts and that the list remains non-exhaustive. For example, *Campbell* (n 169) [585] n 18 (considering defendant's intent and explaining that permission is not necessary if use is fair); *Harper* (n 170) [562] (stating fair use presumes good faith and fairness); *Fisher v. Dees*, 794 F.2d 432, 437 (9th Cir. 1986) ('courts may weigh "the propriety of the defendant's conduct" in the equitable balance of a fair use determination' (citation omitted)).

[173] Early English cases which contemplated introducing the fair use doctrine described this mechanism as a way to define the scope of the rights granted under copyright, delineating the scope of infringement. Hence, the burden of proof was on the right-holder to show that the use was unfair also in early English case law. W Patry, *The Fair Use Privilege in Copyright Law* (2nd edn, BNA Books, 1995) 3–26.

remove right-holders' control over the exception. This book goes one step further, by arguing that courts should respect the proportionality test, prescribed at an international level, in order to protect and promote freedom of expression. The current expansive scope of protection which copyright-protected works enjoy may be enforced to undermine protection of freedom of expression. In parody cases, in recognition of the value attached to this form of social comment in a democratic society, the human rights framework should provide guidance in the application of the 'fairness factors', which might rescue the defendant's use, as well as offering greater clarity.[174]

Furthermore, jurisprudence which has interpreted the right of freedom of expression suggests a hierarchy of priorities, which may assist in determining whether permitting use is objectively fair, including in circumstances in which the parody's content is seen as sensitive or controversial. Despite the fact that, typically, copyright assessments aim to be content neutral, this arrangement seems to offer an avenue for copyright-holders to enforce their exclusive rights in order to censor the message conveyed. Yet, most concede that expressions which may offend, shock, or disturb should be allowed in a democratic society. This is particularly relevant in parody cases. Although many parodies are comic and light-hearted, others use a protected work to convey a message concerning a distasteful topic or to express a view which the original author might not endorse,[175] but which are an essential part of a healthy political discourse. As parody is an effective communication tool, it increases citizen participation in the democratic process. Parodies should only be unlawful, then, in situations of abuse. In the absence of an established legal right to parody, factors such as the standing of the speaker, the intent of the parodist, the form of the expression, its context, the medium used, the content of the message, and the type of expression transposed from the well-established human rights context enable the parody exception in copyright law to refocus on the realization of freedom of expression.

Overall, this book argues for a more holistic approach in the appraisal of the parody exception in copyright law, determining the legality of the use by reference to the human rights framework. It certainly does not exhaust this area of the law but, hopefully, it provides ideas as to how one might construe the parody exception to foster cultural diversity and strike a fair balance between the interests of right-holders, parodists, and society at large.

[174] See section 2.

[175] This is particularly the case in satire cases.

Bibliography

BOOKS

Adeney, E (2006), *The Moral Rights of Authors and Performers: An International and Comparative Analysis* (OUP, 2006)

Andrew, N Q C, Millar, G Q C, and Sharland, A (2009), *Media Law & Human Rights* (2nd edn, OUP, 2009)

Atiyah, P S (1979), *The Rise and Fall of Freedom of Contract* (Clarendon Press, 1979)

Baasch Andersen, C (2011), 'Applied uniformity of a uniform commercial law' in M Andenas and C Baasch Andersen (eds), *Theory and Practice of Harmonisation* (Edward Elgar, 2011)

Bailey, J (2005), 'Deflating the Michelin Man' in M Geist (ed.), *In the Public Interest: The Future of Canadian Copyright Law* (Irwin Law, 2005)

Bakhtin, M (1981), *The Dialogic Imagination* (University of Texas Press, 1981)

Barendt, E (2005), 'Copyright and free speech theory' in J Griffiths and U Suthersanen (eds), *Copyright and Free Speech* (OUP, 2005)

Bellefonds, X L de (2002), *Droits d'auteur et droits voisins* (Dalloz, 2002)

Benabou, V L and Dussollier, S (2007), 'Draw me a public domain' in P Torremans (ed.), *Copyright Law. A Handbook of Contemporary Research* (Edward Elgar, 2007)

Ben-Ishai, S and Percy, R D (2014), *Contracts: Cases and Commentaries* (8th edn, Carswell, 2014)

Bently, L (2010), 'Introduction to Part I: the history of copyright' in L Bently, U Suthersanen, and P L C Torremans (eds), *Global Copyright: Three Hundred Years since the Statute of Anne, from 1709 to Cyberspace* (Edward Elgar, 2010)

Bently, L and Aplin, T (2018), 'Whatever became of global mandatory fair use? A case study in dysfunctional pluralism' Forthcoming in S Frankel (ed.), *Is Intellectual Property Pluralism Functional?* (Edward Elgar, 2018)

Bently, L and Sherman, B (2014), *Intellectual Property Law* (4th edn, OUP, 2014)

Berenboom, A (2009), 'La parodie' in E Cornu (ed.), *Bande dessinée et droit d'auteur* (Larcier, 2009)

Bergel, J-L (2001), 'Méthodes et principes de coordination des règles juridiques' in *Méthodologie Juridique* (1st edn, PUF, 2001)

Bertrand, A R (2012), 'Exceptions à la protection en matière de droit d'auteur qui figurent au CPI' in *Droit d'auteur* (Dalloz, 2012)

Blackmur, R P (1964), 'Parody and critique: Mann's Doctor Faustus' in *Eleven Essays in the European Novel* (Harcourt, Brace & World, 1964)

Bloch, P (2002), *Image et droit* (L'Harmattan, 2002)

Booth, W C (1961), *The Rhetoric of Fiction* (Chicago: University of Chicago Press, vol. III, 1961)

Burrell, R and Coleman, A (2005), *Copyright Exceptions: The Digital Impact* (Cambridge University Press, 2005)

Burrell, R and Stellios, J (2005), 'Copyright and freedom of political communication in Australia' in J Griffiths and U Suthersanen (eds), *Copyright and Free Speech* (OUP, 2005)

Buteau, M (1909), *Le droit de critique en matière littéraire, dramatique et artistique* (L. Larose et L. Tenin, 1909)

Butler, H E (1953), *The Institutio Oratoria of Quintilian* (4 vols II, Loeb Classical Library, 1953)

Caron, C (1998a), *Abus de droit et droit d'auteur* (Litec, 1998)

Caron, C (2012), 'Les exceptions au regard du fondement du droit d'auteur en droit français' in A Lucas, P Sirinelli, and A Bensamoun (eds), *Les exceptions au droit d'auteur: état des lieux et perspectives dans l'Union européenne* (Dalloz, 2012)

Carre, S (2013), 'Le rôle de la Cour de Justice dans la construction du droit d'auteur de l'Union' in C Geiger (ed.), *La contribution de la jurisprudence à la construction de la propriété intellectuelle en Europe* (Collection du CEIPI, LexisNexis, 2013)

Carrière, L (1991), 'Droit d'auteur et droit moral: quelques réflexions préliminaires' in Barreau du Québec (ed.), *Développements récents en droit de la propriété intellectuelle* (Les Editions Yvon Blais Inc., 1991)

Castets-Renard, C (2004), *Notions à contenu variable et droit d'auteur* (L'Harmattan, 2004)

Chapdeleine, P (2017), *Copyright User Rights* (OUP, 2017)

Cohen, D (2005), 'La liberté de créer' in *Libertés et droits fondamentaux* (9th edn, Montchrestien, 2011)

Colombet, V C (1999), *Précis Dalloz de propriété littéraire et artistique* (9th edn, Dalloz, 1999)

Copinger, W and Skone James, F (2010), *On Copyright* (16th edn, Sweet & Maxwell, 2010)

Cornish, W (2010), 'The Statute of Anne 1709: its historical setting' in L Bently, U Suthersanen, and P L C Torremans (eds), *Global Copyright: Three Hundred Years since the Statute of Anne, from 1709 to Cyberspace* (Edward Elgar, 2010)

Couto, A (2008), 'Copyright and freedom of expression: a philosophical map' in A Gosseries, A Marciano, and A Strowel (eds), *Intellectual Property and Theories of Justice* (Palgrave Macmillan, 2008)

Covash, J (2005), 'Form in rock music' in D Stein (ed.), *Engaging Music* (OUP, 2005)

Crabbe, V C R A C (1994), *Legislative Drafting* (The Glass House, 1994)

Craig, C and Laroche, G (2014), 'Out of tune: why copyright law needs music lessons' in B C Doagoo and others (eds), *Intellectual Property in the 21st Century: Interdisciplinary Approaches* (Irwin Publishing, 2014)

Craig, C J (2005), 'The changing face of fair dealing in Canadian copyright law: a proposal for legislative reform' in M Geist (eds), *In the Public Interest: The Future of Canadian Copyright Law* (Part II, Irwin Law, 2005) available at https://www.irwinlaw.com/content_commons/in_the_public_interest (access date: 10 November 2018)

Craig, C J (2011), *Copyright, Communication and Culture: Towards a Relational Theory of Copyright Law* (Edward Elgar, 2011)

Davies, G (1994), *Copyright and the Public Interest* (Thomson, 1994)

Davies, G and Garnett, K QC (2010), *Moral Rights* (Sweet & Maxwell, 2010)

De Werra, J (2009), 'The moral right of integrity' in E Derclaye (ed.), *Research Handbook on the Future of EU Copyright* (Edward Elgar, 2009)

De Werra, J (2015), 'Moral rights, a view from continental Europe' d'auteur' in F Brison, S Dussollier, M-C Janssens, and H Vanhees (eds), *Moral Rights in the 21st Century* (Larcier, 2015)

Deazley, R (2006), *Rethinking Copyright* (Edward Elgar, 2006)

Dentith, S (2000), *Parody* (Routledge, 2000)

Derclaye, E (2008), 'Intellectual property rights and human rights' in P Torremans (ed.), *Intellectual Property and Human Rights* (2nd edn, Kluwer, 2008)

Desbois, H (1978), *Le droit d'auteur en France* (3rd edn, Dalloz, 1978)

Dinwoodie, G B (2008), 'Copyright and free expression: engine or obstacle' in *Copyright and Freedom of Expression* (Huygens Editorial, 2008)

Durrande, S (1995), 'La parodie, le pastiche et la caricature' in *Mélanges en l'honneur de André Françon* (Dalloz, 1995)

Dusollier, S (2007), *Droit d'auteur et protection des œuvres dans l'univers numérique* (Larcier, 2007)

Dyer, R (2007), *Pastiche* (Routledge, 2007)

Feinberg, L (1963), *The Satirist: His Temperament, Motivation and Influence* (Iowa State University Press, 1963)

Ficsor, M (2002), *The Law of Copyright and the Internet—The 1996 WIPO Treaties, Their Interpretation and Implementation* (OUP, 2002)

Galopin, B (2012), *Les exceptions à usage public en droit d'auteur* (IRPI, 2012)
Gammons, H (2011), *The Art of Music Publishing* (Focal Press, 2011)
Garnett, K Q (2005), 'The impact of the Human Rights Act 1998 on UK copyright law' in J Griffiths and U Suthersanen (eds), *Copyright and Free Speech* (OUP, 2005)
Garnett, K Q, James, J R, and Davies, G (2011), *Copinger and Skone James on Copyright* (16th edn, Sweet & Maxwell, 2011)
Gautier, P-Y (2007), *Propriété littéraire et artistique* (6th edn, PUF, 2007)
Gautier, P-Y (2012), 'Les exceptions au regard du droit d'auteur de l'Union Européenne' in A Lucas, P Sirinelli, and A Bensamoun (eds), *Les exceptions au droit d'auteur: état des lieux et perspectives dans l'Union Européenne* (Dalloz, 2012)
Geiger, C (2004), *Droit d'auteur et droit du public à l'information* (IRPI, 2004)
Geiger, C (2010), 'The influence (past and present) of the Statute of Anne in France' in L Bently, U Suthersanen, and P L C Torremans (eds), *Global Copyright: Three Hundred Years Since the Statute of Anne, from 1709 to Cyberspace* (Edward Elgar, 2010)
Geiger, C (2015), 'The constitutional dimension of intellectual property' in P L C Torremans (eds), *Intellectual Property and Human Rights* (3rd edn, Kluwer, 2008)
Geiger, C and Izyumenko, E (2018), *Intellectual Property before the European Court of Human Rights* (2018) Centre for International Intellectual Property Studies Research Paper No 2018-01, forthcoming in C Geiger, C A Nard, and X Seuba (eds), *Intellectual Property and the Judiciary* (EIPIN series Vol. 4, EE, 2018)
Geiger, C, Gervais, D, and Senftleben, M (2015), 'Understanding the "three-step test"' in D Gervais (ed.), *International Intellectual Property* (Edward Elgar, 2015)
Geist, M (2013), *The Copyright Pentalogy: How the Supreme Court of Canada Shook the Foundations of Canadian Copyright Law* (University of Ottawa Press, 2013)
Gelber, K (2007), 'Hate speech and the Australian legal and political landscape' in K Gilbert and A Stone (eds), *Hate Speech and Freedom of Expression in Australia* (The Federation Press, 2007)
Gendreau, Y (1999), 'Synthèse possible ou impossible du droit civil et de la common law—l'exemple du Canada' in *La mise en œuvre des droits d'auteur. Le rôle de la législation nationale en droit d'auteur* (ALAI, 1999)
Gendreau, Y (2015), 'Copyright and freedom of expression in Canada' in P L C Torremans (ed.), *Intellectual Property and Human Rights* (3rd edn, Kluwer, 2008)
Genette, G (1982), *Palimpsestes* (Le Seuil, 1982)
Gervais, D (2015), 'Intellectual property and human rights: learning to live together' in P L C Torremans (ed.), *Intellectual Property and Human Rights* (3rd edn, Kluwer, 2008)
Gervais, D J (1961), 'Quelques réflexions à propos de la distinction des "droits" et "intérêts"' in *Mélanges en l'honneur de Paul Roubier* (Dalloz, 1961)
Gervais, D J (2009), 'A Canadian copyright narrative' in P L C Torremans (ed.), *Copyright Law: A Handbook of Contemporary Research* (Edward Elgar, 2009)
Goldstein, P (2003), *Copyright's Highway: From Gutenberg to the Celestial Jukebox* (Stanford Law and Politics, 2003)
Greenfield, S and Osborn, G (2009), 'Copyright and power in the music industry' in S Frith and L Marshall (eds), *Music and Copyright* (2nd edn, Edinburgh University Press, 2009)
Griffiths, J (2005), 'Not such a "timid thing": the UK's integrity right and freedom of expression' in J Griffiths and U Suthersanen (eds), *Copyright and Free Speech* (OUP, 2005)
Griffiths, J and McDonagh, L (2013), 'Fundamental rights and European IP law: the case of Art 17(2) of the EU Charter' in C Geiger (ed.), *Constructing European Intellectual Property* (EIPIN, 2013)
Grosheide, W (2010), 'Transition from guild regulation to modern copyright law —a view from the Low Countries', L Bently, U Suthersanen, and P L C Torremans (eds), *Global Copyright: Three Hundred Years since the Statute of Anne, from 1709 to Cyberspace* (Edward Elgar, 2010)

Guibault, L (2002), *Copyright and Contracts: An Analysis of the Contractual Overridability of Limitations on Copyright* (Kluwer, 2002)

Habermas, J (1962), *The Structural Transformation of the Public Sphere. An Inquiry into a Category of Bourgeois Society*, translated by Thomas Burger with the assistance of Frederick Lawrence (MIT, 1962)

Harrison, A (2014), *Music: The Business* (6th edn, Random House, 2014)

Hofman, J (2009), *Introducing Copyright. A Plain Language Guide to Copyright in the 21st Century* (Commonwealth of Learning, 2009)

Hugenholtz, P B (1996), 'Adapting copyright to the information superhighway' in *The Future of Copyright in a Digital Environment* (Kluwer, 1996)

Hugenholtz, P B (2001), 'Copyright and freedom of expression in Europe' in R C Dreyfuss, H First, and D L Zimmerman (eds), *Innovation Policy in an Information Age* (OUP, 2001)

Hugenholtz, P B (2002), 'Copyright and freedom of expression' in N Elkin-Koren and N W Netanel (eds), *The Commodification of Information* (Kluwer, 2002)

Hugenholtz, P B and Okediji, R L (2008), *Conceiving an International Instrument on Limitations and Exceptions to Copyright* (IVIR, 2008)

Hughes, J (2017), 'Fair use and its politics—at home and abroad' in R Okediji (ed.), *Copyright Law in an Age of Exceptions and Limitations* (CUP, 2017)

Hutcheon, L (1985), *A Theory of Parody: The Teachings of Twentieth-Century Art Forms* (University of Illinois Press, 1985)

Jacob, Sir Robin (2014), 'Parody and IP claims: a defence? A right to parody?' in R C Dreyfuss and J C Ginsburg (eds), *Intellectual Property at the Edge: The Contested Contours of IP* (CIPIL, 2014)

Jameson, F (1986), 'Postmodernism and consumer society' in E Hal Foster, *The Anti-Aesthetic* (Bay Press, 1986)

Janssens, M C (2009), 'The issue of exceptions: reshaping the keys to the gates in the territory of literary, musical and artistic creation' in E Derclaye (ed.), *Research Handbook on the Future of EU Copyright* (Edward Elgar, 2009)

Joly, S (2007), 'L'ordre public et le droit d'auteur' in J-M Bruguière, N Mallet-Poujol, and A Robin (eds), *Propriété intellectuelle et droit commun* (PUAM, 2007)

Kwall, R R (2010), *The Soul of Creativity* (Stanford University Press, 2010)

Liddell, H G, Scott, R, Crane, G, Jones, H S, McKenzie, R, and Barber, E A (2002), *A Greek-English Lexicon* (Oxford, UK: Clarendon, 2002)

Locke, J (1690), *Second Treatise of Civil Government* (1690) available at http://www.constitution.org/jl/2ndtreat.htm (access date: 10 November 2018)

Lucas, A (1998), *Droit d'auteur et numérique* (Litec, 1998)

Lucas, A (2010b), *Propriété littéraire et artistique* (4th edn, Dalloz. Coll. Connaissance du droit, 2010)

Lucas, A and Lucas, H J (2001), *Traité de la propriété littéraire et artistique* (4th edn, Litec, 2001)

Lucas-Schloetter, A (2015), 'Rapport général: le droit moral dans les différents régimes du droit d'auteur' in F Brison, S Dussollier, M-C Janssens, and H Vanhees (eds), *Moral Rights in the 21st Century* (Larcier, 2015)

McDonagh, L (2018), 'UK patent law and copyright law after Brexit: potential consequences' in O Fitzgerald and E Lein (eds), *Complexity's Embrace: The International Law Implications of Brexit* (MQUP, 2018)

MacDonald, D (1960), *Parodies: An Anthology from Chaucer to Beerbohm and After* (Random House, 1960)

Mack, R L (2007), *The Genius of Parody Imitation and Originality in Seventeenth-Century English Literature* (Palgrave Macmillan, 2007)

McKeown, J S (2010), *Canadian Intellectual Property Law and Strategy* (OUP, 2010)

McLeod, K (2005), *Freedom of Expression (R): Overzealous Copyright Bozos and Other Enemies of Creativity* (Doubleday, 2005)

McLeod, K and Dicola, P (2011), *Creative License: The Law and Culture of Digital Sampling* (Duke University Press, 2011)

MacMillan, F (2005), 'Commodification and cultural ownership' in J Griffiths and U Suthersanen (eds), *Copyright and Free Speech* (OUP, 2005)

Malaurie, P (1965), 'La jurisprudence combattue par la loi' in *Mélanges offerts à René Savatier* (Dalloz, 1965)

Mazziotti, G (2008), *EU Digital Copyright and the End-user* (Springer, 2008)

Meyer, L B (1956), *Emotion and Meaning in Music* (University of Chicago Press, 1956)

Moon, R (2000), *The Constitutional Protection of Freedom of Expression* (University of Toronto Press, 2000)

Mouffe, B (2011), *Le droit à l'humour* (Larcier, 2011)

Mowbray, A (2012), *Cases, Materials, and Commentary on the European Convention on Human Rights* (3rd edn, OUP, 2012)

Murray, L J (2005), 'Copyright talk: patterns and pitfalls in Canadian Policy discourses' in M Geist (ed.), *In The Public Interest: The Future of Canadian Copyright Law* (Irwin Law, 2005)

Netanel, N W (2008), *Copyright's Paradox* (OUP, 2008)

Partsch, K J (1992), 'Racial speech and human rights: article 4 of the Convention on the elimination of all forms of racial discrimination' in K Boyle and F D'Souza (eds), *Striking a Balance: Hate Speech, Freedom of Expression and Non-Discrimination* (Article XIX, London and Human Rights Centre, University of Essex, 1992)

Patry, W (1995), *The Fair Use Privilege in Copyright Law* (2nd edn, BNA Books, 1995)

Patterson, L R (1968), *Copyright in Historical Perspective* (Vanderbilt University Press, 1968)

Paull, H M (1928), *Literary Ethics* (London: Butterworth, 1928)

Paulson, R (1967), *The Fictions of Satire* (Baltimore, MD: Johns Hopkins University Press, 1967)

Paulson, R (2007), 'Pictorial satire: from emblem to expression' in R Quintero (ed.), *A Companion to Satire: Ancient and Modern* (Malden, Oxford, Victoria: Blackwell Publishing, 2007)

Petri, G (2010), 'Transition from guild regulation to modern copyright law (Sweden)' in L Bently, U Suthersanen, and P L C Torremans (eds), *Global Copyright: Three Hundred Years since the Statute of Anne, from 1709 to Cyberspace* (Edward Elgar, 2010)

Porsdam, E (2007), *Copyright and Other Fairy Tales: Hans Christian Andersen The Commodification of Creativity* (Edward Elgar, 2007)

Reinbothe, J and Lewinski, S v. (2002), *The WIPO Treaties 1996 —The WIPO Copyright Treaty and the WIPO Performances and Phonograms Treaty—Commentary and legal analysis* (Butterworths, 2002)

Ribon (1965), *Parodies bachiques sur les airs et symphonies des Opera* (Paris, 1695)

Ricketson, S and Cresswell, C (2001), *The Law of Intellectual Property: Copyright, Designs and Confidential Information* (Sweet & Maxwell, 2001)

Ricketson, S and Ginsburg, J (2005), *International Copyright and Neighbouring Rights* (OUP, 2005)

Roland, H and Boyer, L (1999), *Adages du droit français* (4th edn, Litec, 1999)

Rose, M (1993a), *Parody: Ancient, Modern and Post-Modern* (Cambridge University Press, 1993)

Rose, M (1993b), *Authors and Owners: The Invention of Copyright* (Harvard University Press, 1993)

Rosen, R S (2008), *Music and Copyright* (OUP, 2008)

Sainsbury, M. (2003), *Moral Rights and their Application in Australia* (The Federation Press, 2003)

Sangsue, D (1994), *La parodie* (Hachette Supérieur, 1994)

Schiek, D (2011), 'Comparative law and European harmonization—a match made in heaven or uneasy bedfellows?' in M Andenas and C Baasch Andersen (eds), *Theory and Practice of Harmonisation* (Edward Elgar, 2011)

Schuermans, H (1861), *Code de La Presse* (Larcier, 1861)

Senftleben, M (2004), *Copyright, Limitations and the Three-Step Test: An Analysis of the Three-Step Test in International and EC Copyright Law* (Kluwer, 2004)

Senftleben, M (2011), 'Overprotection and protection overlaps in intellectual property law—the need for horizontal fair use defences' in A Kur and V Mizaras (eds), *The Structure of Intellectual Property Law* (Edward Elgar, 2011)

Senftleben, M (2012), 'Chapter 13: quotations, parody and fair use' in P B Hugenholtz, A Quaedvlieg, and D Visser (eds), *A Century of Dutch Copyright Law* (deLex, 2012)

Sherman, B and Bently, L (1999), *The Making of Modern IP Law* (Cambridge University Press, 1999)

Sirinelli, P (2008), 'Le droit d'auteur à l'âge du numérique' in X Greffe and N Sonnac (eds), *Culture Web. Création, contenus, économie numérique* (Dalloz, 2008)

Sisman, E R (1993), *Haydn and the Classical Variation* (Harvard University Press, 1993)

Smith, A (1904), *An Inquiry into the Nature and Causes of the Wealth of Nations* (5th edn, Methuen & Co., 1904)

Stamatoudi, I A (2001), *Copyright and Multimedia Products* (Cambridge University Press, 2001)

Stone, C (1914), *Parody* (London: Martin Secker, 1914)

Strowel, A (1993), *Droit d'auteur et copyright: divergences et convergences* (Bruylant and L.G.D.J., 1993)

Strowel, A and Tulkens, F (2006), 'Equilibrer la liberté d'expression et le droit d'auteur' in A Strowel and F Tulkens (eds), *droit d'auteur et liberté d'expression: regards francophones, d'Europe et d'ailleurs* (Larcier, 2006)

Sugarman, D and Butler, M (2011), *A Handbook on European Discrimination Law* (2011) available at http://eprints.lancs.ac.uk/34017/ (access date: 10 November 2018)

Sundara Rajan, M T (2005), 'The "New Listener" and the virtual performer: the need for a new approach to performers' rights' in M Geist (ed.), *In the Public Interest: The Future of Canadian Copyright Law* (2005) available at http://www.irwinlaw.com/pages/in-the-public-interest--the-future-of-canadian-copyright-law (access date: 10 November 2018)

Sundara Rajan, M T (2006), *Copyright and Creative Freedom—a Study of Post-Socialist Law Reform* (Routledge Studies in International Law, 2006)

Synodinou, T-E (2012), *Codification of European Copyright Law: Challenges and Perspectives* (Kluwer, 2012)

Tafforeau, P. (2013), *Pratique de la propriété littéraire et artistique: contrats et gestion collective, droit d'auteur et droits voisins* (LexisNexis, 2013)

Tamaro, N (1998), *Loi sur le droit d'auteur: Texte annoté* (4th edn, Toronto, Éditions Carswell, 1998)

Thompson, A (2012), 'Recording contracts' in N Riches (ed.), *The Music Management Bible* (SMT, 2012)

Torremans, P (2015), 'A clash between theory and practice? Introduction' in F Brison, S Dussollier, M-C Janssens, and H Vanhees (ed.), *Moral Rights in the 21st Century* (Larcier, 2015)

Torremans, P L C (2012), *The Perspective of the Introduction of a European Fair Use Clause. In Codification of European Copyright Law: Challenges and Perspectives* (Kluwer, 2012)

Torremans, P L C (2015), 'Copyright (and other intellectual property rights) as a human right' in P L C Torremans (ed.), *Intellectual Property and Human Rights* (3rd edn, Kluwer, 2008)

Toynbee, J (2009), 'Musicians' in S Frith and L Marshall (eds), *Music and Copyright* (2nd edn, Edinburgh University Press, 2009)

Tréfigny, P (2000), 'Les conditions de licéité de l'imitation en droit d'auteur' in *L'imitation: contribution à l'étude juridique des comportements référentiels* (P.U.S., 2000)
Türk, D and Joinet, L (1992), 'The right to freedom of opinion and expression: current problems of its realization and measures necessary for its strengthening and promotion' in K Boyle and F D'Souza (eds), *Striking a Balance: Hate Speech, Freedom of Expression and Non-Discrimination* (Article XIX, London and Human Rights Centre, University of Essex, 1992)
Vaidhyanathan, S (2001), *Copyrights and Copywrongs: The Rise of Intellectual Property and how it Threatens Creativity* (New York University Press, 2001)
Vivant, M and Bruguière, J-M (2009), *Droit d'auteur* (Dalloz, 2009)
Voorhoof, D (2006), 'La Liberté d'expression est-elle un argument légitime en faveur du non-respect du droit d'auteur?' in A Strowel and F Tulkens (eds), *Droit d'auteur et liberté d'expression: regards francophones, d'Europe et d'ailleurs* (Larcier, 2006)
Weber, A (2009), *Manual on Hate Speech* (Council of Europe Publishing, 2009)
Wright, T (1985), *A History of Caricature and Grotesque in Literature and Art* (Chatto & Windus, 1985)
Yu, O K (2007), *Intellectual Property and Information Wealth* (Vol. 1, Greenwood Publishing Group, 2007)

ARTICLES

Abramson, E M (1988), 'How much copying under copyright? contradictions, paradoxes, inconsistences' (1988) 61 Temple Law Review 133
Adams, K (2015), 'What did Danger Mouse do? The Grey Album and musical composition in configurable culture' (2015) 37(1) Music Theory Spectrum 7
Adeney, E (2001), 'Defining the shape of Australia's moral rights: a review of the new laws' (2001) 4 IPQ 291
Adler, A (2016), 'The US perspective' (2016) 8(1) Geo. Mason J. Int'l Com. L. 26
Adeney, E (2005), 'The moral right of integrity: the past and future of "honour"' (2005) 2 IPQ 111
Althoff, J (2014), 'Case comment the parody exception: seeing the funny side of it' (2014) 25(7) Ent. L.R. 265
Angelopoulos, C J (2008), 'Freedom of expression and copyright: the double balancing act' (2008) 3 IPQ 328
Arewa, O B (2006), 'From J.C Bach to Hip Hop: musical borrowing, copyright and cultural context' (2006) 84 Case Research Paper Series in Legal Studies Working Paper 04
Arnold, R and Rosati, E (2015), 'Are national courts the addressees of the InfoSoc three-step test?' (2015) JIPLP 741
Arnold, R, Bently, L, Derclaye, E, and Dinwoodie, G B (2017), 'The legal consequences of Brexit through the lens of IP law' (2017) Oxford Legal Studies Research Paper No 15/2017
Baden-Powell, E (2013), 'Whose line is it anyway?—new exceptions for parody and private copying' (2013) 24(4) Ent. L.R. 130
Baden-Powell, E and Woodhead, J (2012), 'Big leeks will inspire you, but who gets the credit?' (2012) 23 Entertainment Law Review 59
Bate, S (1989), 'Moral rights: parody and caricature' (1989) 7 International Media Law 81
Beaulac, S (2010), 'Legal interpretation in Canada: opening up legislative language as a means to internationalisation' (2010) 5/2010 University of Edinburgh Working Papers series 1–36
Bellini, E (2005), 'Moral rights and droit moral: a matter of paradigms' (2005) 204 RIDA 3
Bently, L (2009), 'Authorship of Popular Music in UK Copyright Law' (2009) 12 Information, Communication & Society 179
Biles, Z (2001), 'Intertextual biography in the rivalry of Cratinus and Aristophanes' (2002) 123(2) The American Journal of Philology 169

Bird, R C and Ponte, L M (2006), 'Protecting moral rights in the United States and the United Kingdom: challenges and opportunities under the U.K.'s New Performances Regulations' (2006) 24 Boston University International Law Journal 213 available at https://www.bu.edu/law/central/jd/organizations/journals/international/volume24n2/documents/213-282.pdf (access date: 10 November 2018)

Birnhack, M D (2003), 'Acknowledging the conflict between copyright law and freedom of expression under the Human Rights Act' (2003) 14(2) Ent. L.R. 24

Bohannan, C (2007), 'Copyright harm, foreseeability, and fair use' (2007) 85 Wash. U. L. Rev. 969

Bond, C, Paramaguru, A, and Greenleaf, G (2007), 'Advance Australia Fair? The copyright reform process' (2007) 10(3/4) The Journal of World Intellectual Property 284

Bongiorno, J (2009), 'Fair use of copyrighted images after Perfect 10 v. Amazon.com: diverging from constitutional principles & United States treaty obligations' (2009) 12 Touro Int'l L. Rev. 107

Bruguière, J-M (2018), 'La réception du fair dealing britannique dans le système d'exception fermée français' forthcoming in RIDA

Brundenall, P (1997), 'Fair dealing in Australian copyright law' (1997) 20 UNSW Law Journal 449

Burrell, R (2001), 'Reining in copyright law: is fair use the answer?' (2001) 4 IPQ 361

Bustin, O (2003), 'La liberté contractuelle existe-t-elle en droit d'auteur?' (2003) 205(10) Légipresse 117

Buydens, M and Dussollier, S (2001), 'Les exceptions au droit d'auteur: évolutions dangereuses' (2001) 22 CCE 10

Camachan, R (1999), 'Sampling and the music industry: a discussion of the implications of copyright law' (1999) 8 AULR 1033

Caron, C (1998b), 'Abus de droit et droit d'auteur: une illustration de la confrontation du droit spécial au droit commun en droit civil français' (1998) 176 RIDA 3

Caron, C (2002), 'Les exceptions: l'impact sur le droit français' (2002) 2 Propriétés Intellectuelles 25

Caron, C (2006), 'La loi du 1er août 2006 relative au droit d'auteur et aux droits voisins dans la société de l'information' (2006) CCE étude 22

Carroll, M (2004), 'Whose music is it anyway?: how we came to view musical expression as a form of property' (2004) 72 U.Cin.L.Rev. 1405

Carroll, M (2005), 'Struggle for music copyright' (2005) 57 Fla.L.Rev. 907

Chatman, S (2001), 'Parody and style: rhetoric and film' (2001) 22(1) Poetics Today 25

Christie, A F and Wright, R (2014), 'International review of intellectual property and competition law: a comparative analysis of the three-step tests in international treaties' (2014) 45(4) IIC 409

Christou, S and Maurushat, A (2009), '"Waltzing Matilda" or "Advance Australia Fair"? User-generated content and fair dealing in Australian copyright law' (2009) 29 UNSWLRS 1

Colin, C (2010), 'La contractualisation des exceptions en droit d'auteur: oxymore ou pléonasme?' (2010) 2 CCE, étude n°3

Condren, C, Davis, J M, McCausland, S, and Phiddian, R A (2008a), 'Defining parody and satire: Australian copyright law and its new exception (Part 1)' (2008) 13(3) MALR 273

Condren, C, Davis, J M, McCausland, S, and Phiddian, R A (2008b), 'Defining parody and satire: Australian copyright law and its new exception (Part 2)' (2008) 13 MALR 401

Craig, C J (2006), 'Putting the community in communication: dissolving the conflict between freedom of expression and copyright' (2006) 56 U. Toronto L.J. 75.

Craig, C J (2017), 'Globalizing user rights-talk: on copyright limits and rhetorical risks' (2017) 33(1) Am. U. Int'l L. Rev. 1

D'Agostino, G (2008), 'Healing fair dealing? A comparative copyright analysis of Canada's fair dealing to U.K. fair dealing and U.S. fair use' (2008) 53 McGill Law Journal 309

Davies, G (1995), 'The convergence of copyright and authors' rights—reality or chimera?' (1995) 26(6) IIC 964

Day, B R (2011), 'In defense of copyright: creativity, record labels, and the future of music' (2011) 21 Seton Hall J. Sports & Ent.L. 61

De Zwart, M (2003), 'Seriously entertaining: the panel and the future of fair dealing' (2003) 8 MALR 1

De Zwart, M (2004), 'Copyright in television broadcasts: Network Ten v. TCN Channel Nine—"A Case Which Can Excite Emotions"' (2004) 9 MALR 277

De Zwart, M (2007a), 'A historical analysis of the birth of fair dealing and fair use: lessons for the digital age' (2007) 1 IPQ 60

De Zwart, M (2007b), 'Technological enclosure of copyright: The end of fair dealing?' (2007) 18 AIPJ 7

Deazley, R (2010), 'Copyright and parody: taking backward the Gowers review?' (2010) 73 MLR 794

Dietz, A (1994), 'The artist's right of integrity under copyright law—a comparative approach' (1994) 25(2) IIC 177

Dietz, A (1994a), 'The moral right of the author: moral rights and the civil law countries' (1994) 19 Colum. VLA J.L. & Arts 199

Dusollier, S (2005), 'L'encadrement des exceptions au droit d'auteur par le test des trois étapes' (2005) 2 I.R.D.I. 213

Dworkin, G (1986), 'Moral rights in English law—the shape of rights to come basic features of the droit moral' (1986) 8 (11) EIPR 329

Edelman, B (1990), 'Le personnage et son double' (1990) 30 Recueil Dalloz 227

Elkin-Koren, N (1997), 'Copyright policy and the limits of freedom of contract' (1997) 12 Berkeley Tech. L.J. 93

Evans, T M (2011), 'Sampling, Looping, and Mashing ... Oh My!: How Hip Hop music is scratching more than the surface of copyright law' (2011) 21 Fordham IPLJ 843

Falck, R (1979), 'Parody and contrafactum: a terminological clarification' (1979) 65 The Musical Quarterly 1

Fewer, D (1997), 'Constitutionalizing copyright: freedom of expression and the limits of copyright in Canada' (1997) 55 U.T.L.J. 175

Ficsor, M (2010), 'Comments on the UGC provisions in the Canadian Bill C-32' (2010) available at www.copyrightseesaw.net

Fletcher-Boulvard, F (1997), 'La caricature: dualité ou unité' (1997) RTD Civ. 67

Françon, A (1988), 'Questions de droit d'auteur relatives aux parodies et productions similaires' (1988) June Droit d'auteur 302

Gaudrat, P (2001), 'Les démêlés intemporels d'un couple à succès: le créateur et l'investisseur' (2001) 190 RIDA 70.

Gautier, P-Y (1991), 'La bicyclette bleue n'est pas une contrefaçon d'autant en emporte le vent' (1991) Recueil Dalloz 85

Gautier, P-Y (2001), 'De la transposition des exceptions: à propos de la directive "droit d'auteur dans la société de l'information"' (2001) 25(19) CCE 10

Gautier, P-Y (2006), 'L'élargissement des exceptions aux droits exclusifs, contrebalance par le 'test des trois étapes' (2006) 11 CCE 9

Geiger, C (2004a), 'De la nature juridique des limites au droit d'auteur' (2004) 13 Propriétés Intellectuelles 882

Geiger, C (2004b), 'Fundamental rights, a safeguard for the coherence of intellectual property law?' (2004) 35(3) IIC 268

Geiger, C (2006), 'Constitutionalising: intellectual property law? the influence of fundamental rights on intellectual property in the European Union' (2006) 37(4) IIC 371

Geiger, C (2007), 'The role of the three-step test in the adaptation of the information society' (2007) January–March UNESCO e-copyright bulletin 1

Geiger, C, Gervais, D J, and Senftleben, M (2014), 'The three-step test revisited: how to use the test's flexibility in national copyright law' (2014) 29(3) Am U Int'l L Rev 581
Geiger, C, Griffiths, J, and Hilty, R M (2008), 'Declaration on a balanced interpretation of the "three-step test" in copyright law' (2008) 39(6) IIC 707
Gervais, D (2005a), 'Le droit d'auteur au Canada: Le point après CCH' (2005) 203 RIDA 7
Gervais, D J (2005b), 'Towards a new core international copyright norm: the reverse three-step test' (2005) 9 Marq.Intell.Prop.L.Rev. 1
Gervais, D J (2008), 'Making copyright whole: a principled approach to copyright exceptions and limitations' (2008) UOLTJ 1 available at www.uoltj.ca
Giles, K (2005), 'Mind the gap: parody and moral rights' (2005) 18(5) AIPLB 69
Ginsburg, J C (2001), 'Toward supranational copyright law? the WTO Panel decision and the "three-step test" for copyright exceptions' (2001) The Centre for Law and Economics Studies, Columbia University, Working Paper No 181, 1
Ginsburg, J C (2004), 'The right to claim authorship in US copyright and trademarks law' (2004) 41 Houston Law Review 263
Ginsburg, J C (2012), 'Moral rights in the US: still in need of a guardian ad litem' (2012) Cardozo Arts & Ent. L.J. 73
Ginsburg, J C (2016), 'The most moral of rights: the right to be recognized as the author of one's work' (2016) 8(1) Geo. Mason J. Int'l Com. L.
Goetsch, C C (1980), 'Parody as free speech—the replacement of the fair use doctrine by First Amendment protection' (1980) 3 W. New Eng. L. Rev. 39.
Goldstein, P (2008), 'Berne in the USA' (2008) 39(2) International Review of Intellectual Property and Competition Law 220.
Gordon, W J (1982), 'Fair use as market failure: a structural and economic analysis of the Betamax case and its predecessors' (1982) 82 Columbia Law Review 1600
Gordon, W J (2003), 'Excuse and justification in the law of fair use: transaction costs have always been part of the story' (2003) 50 J. Copyright Soc'y U.S.A 149
Goudreau, M (1994), 'Le droit moral au Canada' (1994) 25 R.G.D. 403
Grégoire, S (2013), 'Fasc. 1213: Propriété littéraire et artistique.—exercice des droits des auteurs.—droit moral. droit au respect (CPI, Art. L. 121-1)' (2013) Jurisclasseur 1
Griffiths, J (2000), 'Preserving judicial freedom of movement— interpreting fair dealing in copyright law' (2000) 2 IPQ 164
Griffiths, J (2009), 'The "three-step test" in European copyright law—problems and solutions' (2009) 4 IPQ 428
Griffiths, J (2013), 'Constitutionalising or harmonising? The Court of Justice, the right to property and European copyright law' (2013) 38(1) E. L. Rev. 65–78
Grinvalsky, P (1992), 'Idea-expression in musical analysis and the role of the intended audience in music copyright infringement' (1992) 28 Cal. W. L. Rev. 395
Grout, D J (1941), 'Seventeenth-century parodies of French opera—Part I' (1941) 27(2) The Music Quarterly 211
Groves, P (2008), 'Pistache?—A consultation paper' (2008) 19 Ent. L. R. 89
Guibault, L (1998), 'Pre-emption issues in the digital environment: can copyright limitations be overriden by contractual agreements under European Law?' (1998) available at http://www.ivir.nl/publicaties/download/337 (access date: 10 November 2018)
Handler, M (2003), 'The Panel case and television broadcast copyright' (2003) 25 Sydney Law Review 391
Handler, M and Rolph, D (2003), 'A real pea souper: the panel case and the development of the fair dealing defence' (2003) 27 Melbourne University Law Review, 381
Hart, M and Holmes, S (2004), 'Implementation of the Copyright Directive in the United Kingdom' (2004) 26(6) EIPR 254

Haynes, J (2012), 'Critically reconceptualizing the United Kingdom's fair dealing exception to copyright infringement in light of the government's most recent proposals for reform and lessons learnt from civil law countries' (2012) 34(12) EIPR 811

Hilbert, M and López, P (2011), 'The world's technological capacity to store, communicate, and compute information' (2011) 332(6025) Science (journal) 60; available at http://www.martinhilbert.net/WorldInfoCapacity.html./ (access date: 10 November 2018)

Hudson, E (2017), 'The pastiche exception in copyright law: a case of mashed-up drafting?' (2017) 4 IPQ 346

Hughes, J (2006), 'Copyright and incomplete historiographies: of piracy, propertization, and Thomas Jefferson' (2006) 79 Southern California Law Review 1011

Isgour, M (2000), 'La satire: réflexions sur le droit à l'humour.' (2000) 1&2 A&M 59

Jacques, S (2015), 'Are the new fair dealing exceptions an improvement on the old law?' (2015) 10(9) JIPLP 699

Jacques, S (2016), 'A parody exception: why trade mark owners should get the joke' (2016) 38(8) EIPR 471

Jacques, S (2017),'First application of the Canadian parody exception' (2017) 12(11) JIPLP 895

Jacques, S, Garstka, C, Hviid, M, and Street, J (2018), 'Automated anti-piracy systems as copyright enforcement mechanism: the need to consider cultural diversity' (2018) 40(4) European Intellectual Property Review 218

Jehoram, H C (2005), 'Restrictions on copyright and their abuse' (2005) 27(10) European Intellectual Property Review 359

Jewell, P and Louise, J (2012), 'It's just a joke: defining and defending (musical) parody' (2012) 10(2) Australian Review of Public Affairs 1

Johnstone, D R (2005), 'Debunking fair use rights and copy duty under U.S. copyright law' (2005) 52 J. Copyright Soc'y U.S.A. 345

Kairalla, R (2012), 'Works as weapon, author as target: why parodies that target authors (not just their works) should be fair uses' (2012) 2 NYU J. Intell. Prop. & Ent. L., 234.

Keller, B P and Tushnet, R (2004), 'Even more parodic than the real thing: parody lawsuits revisited' (2004) 94 TMR 979

Kerbrat-Orecchioni, C (1980), 'L'ironie comme trope' (1980) 41 *Poétique* 108–27

Keyes, J M (2003), 'Musical musings: the case for rethinking music copyright protection' (2003) 10 Mich. Telecom. & Tech. L. Rev. 407

Kiremidjian, G D (1969), 'The aesthetics of parody' (1969) 28(2) The Journal of Aesthetics and Art Criticism 231

Klang, M and Nolin, J (2012), 'Tolerance is law: remixing homage, parodying plagiarism' (2012) 9 Scripted 154

Koelman, K J (2006), 'Fixing the three-step test' (2006) 8 European Intellectual Property Review 407

Kotler, J S T (2000), 'Trade-mark parody, judicial confusion and the unlikelihood of fair use' (2000) 14 IPQ 219

Kretschmer, M and Pratt, A C (2009), 'Legal form and cultural symbol: music, copyright and information studies' (2009) 12 Information, Communication & Society 165

Kretschmer, M, Klimis, G M, and Wallis, R (1999), 'The changing location of intellectual property rights in music: a study of music publishers, collecting societies and media conglomerates' (1999) 17 Prometheus: Critical Studies in Innovation 267

Kur, A (2008), 'Of oceans, islands, and inland water—how much room for exceptions and limitations under the three step-test?' (2008) Max Planck Institute for Intellectual Property, Competition & Tax Law Research Paper Series No 08-04, 1

Lai, A (2015), 'Copyright law and its parody defense: multiple legal perspectives' (2015) 4 NYU J. Intell. Prop. & Ent. L. 311.

Lepage, A (2003), 'Vue générale sur les exceptions et les limitations au droit d'auteur dans l'environnement numérique' (2003) January–March e.Bulletin du droit d'auteur 1

Liebesman, Y J (2007), 'Using innovative technologies to analyze for similarity between musical works in copyright infringement disputes' (2007) 35 AIPLA Q.J. 331

Liu, D (2014), 'Test of infringement: what is it now?' (2014) 36(9) EIPR 588

Livingston, M and Urbinato, J (2013), 'Copyright infringement of music: determining whether what sounds alike is alike' (2013) 15 Vanderbilt J. of Ent. and Tech. Law 227

Loren, L P (2015), 'Fair use: an affirmative defense' (2015) 90 Washington Law Review 685

Loughlan, P (2006), 'Parody, copyright and the new four-step test' (2006) December IPSANZ 46

Lucas, A (2004), 'fasc. 1248' (2004) Juris-Classeur Propriété littéraire et artistique

Lucas, A (2005), 'Droit d'auteur, liberté d'expression et droit du public a l'information' (2005) 1 A&M 13

Lucas, A (2010a), 'For a reasonable interpretation of the three-step test' (2010) 32(6) EIPR 277

Lund, J (2011), 'An empirical examination of the lay listener test in music composition copyright infringement (2011) 11(1) Va. Sports & Ent. L.J. 137

McCausland, S (2007a), 'Protecting "a fine tradition of satire": the new fair dealing exception for parody or satire in the Australian Copyright Act' [2007] 29(7) EIPR 287.

McCausland, S (2007b), 'New room to lampoon: the new fair dealing exception for parody or satire' (2007) 1 Art+Law 3 available at http://search.informit.com.au/documentSummary;dn=200705452;res=IELAPA (access date: 10 November 2018)

McCrann, M (2009), 'A modest proposal: granting presumptive fair use protection for musical parodies' (2009) 14 Roger Williams U. L. Rev. 96

McCrudden, C (2006), 'Legal research and the social sciences' (2006) 122 LQR 632

McCutcheon, J (2007), 'Property in literary characters—protection under Australian copyright law' (2007) 29(4) EIPR 140

McCutcheon, J (2008), 'The new defense of parody or satire under Australian copyright law' (2008) 2 IPQ 163

McDonagh, L T (2012), 'Is the creative use of musical works without a licence acceptable under copyright law?' (2012) 43 IIC 401

Mee, B (2009), 'Laughing matters: parody and satire in Australian copyright law' (2002) 20 Journal of Law, Information and Science 55

Mera, M (2002), 'Is funny music funny? contexts and case studies of film music humor' (2002) 14 Journal of Popular Music Studies 91

Milne, E (2013), 'Parody affective registers, amateur aesthetics and intellectual property' (2013) 19 Cultural Studies Review 193

Mohammed, E A C (2009), 'Parody as fair dealing in Canada: a guide for lawyers and judges' (2009) 4 JIPLP 468

Netanel, N (1996), 'Copyright and democratic civil society' (1996) 106 Yale Law Journal 283

Neyret, L (2008), 'La responsabilité civile arbitre du conflit entre droit des marques et liberté d'expression' (2008) Recueil Dalloz 2402

O'Connor, W v. (1964), 'Parody as criticism' (1964) 25(4) College English 241

O'Flaherty, M (2012), 'Freedom of expression: Article 19 of the International Covenant on Civil and Political Rights and the Human Rights Committee's General Comment No 34' (2012) 12 E.H.R.L.R. 2

Ochoa, T T (2003), 'Introduction: rights of attribution, section 43(A) of the Lanham Act, and the copyright public domain', (2003) 24 Whittier L. Rev., 911

Okediji, R (2000), 'Toward an international fair use standard' (2000) 39 Columbia Journal of Transnational Law 75

Pallas-Loren, L (2002), 'Untangling the web of music copyrights' (2002) 53 Case W. Res. L. Rev. 673

Pallas-Loren, L (2014), 'The dual narratives in the landscape of music copyright' (2014) 52 Houston Law Review 537
Parmar, S (2009), 'The challenge of "defamation of religions" to freedom of expression and the international human rights' (2009) 3 E.H.R.L.R. 353
Patry, W (1986), 'Fair use after Sony and Harper & (and) Row' (1986) 8 Comm. & L. 21
Pevernage, A and Hoekstra, G R (1979), 'An eight-voice parody of Lassus: André Pevernage's "Bonjour Mon Coeur"' (1979) 7 Early Music 367
Pietilä, T (2009), 'Whose works and what kinds of rewards' (2009) 12 Information, Communication & Society 229
Plante, S (1998), 'Les nouvelles exceptions en droit canadien: un faux débat' (1998) 11 Cah. prop. intell. available at http://cpi.robic.ca/Cahiers/11-1/08Plante.html (access date: 10 November 2018)
Pollaud-Dulian, F (2007), Propriété littéraire et artistique (2007) April/June RTD.com
Posner, R A (1992), 'When is parody fair use' (1992) 21 J. Legal Stud. 67
Ramalho, A (2009), 'Parody in trademarks and copyright' (2009) 5 Cambridge Student Law Review 59
Reichman, J H and Franklin, J A (1999), 'Privately legislated intellectual property rights: reconciling freedom of contract with public good uses of information' (1999) 147 U. PA. L. Rev. 875
Reitz, J (1998), 'How to do comparative law' (1998) 46 ASCL 617
Ricketson, S (1990), 'Moral rights and the droit de suite: international conditions and Australian obligations sources of Australia's international obligations' (1990) 1 Ent. L. R. 78
Ricketson, S (2003), 'SCCR/9/7: WIPO Study on Limitations and Exceptions of Copyright and Related Rights in the Digital Environment (related)' (2003) WIPO Study Committee on Copyright and related rights 1
Riewald, J G (1966), 'Parody as criticism' (1966) 50 Neophilologus 125
Rogers, M, Tomalin, J, and Corrigan, R, 'The economic impact of consumer copyright exceptions: A literature review' (2009) Consumer Focus 1
Rosati, E (2015), 'Just a matter of laugh? Why the CJEU decision in Deckmyn is broader than parody' (2015) 52 CMLR 511
Rutz, C (2004), 'Parody: a missed opportunity?' (2004) 3 IPQ 284
Sacco, R (2007), 'Liberté contractuelle, volonté contractuelle' (2007) 59(4) RIDC 743
Sainsbury, M (2007a), 'Parody, satire and copyright infringement: the latest addition to Australian fair dealing law' (2007) 12 MALR 292
Sainsbury, M (2007b), 'Parody, satire, honour and reputation: the interplay between economic and moral rights' (2007) 18 AIPJ 149
Samuelson, P (2015), 'Possible futures of fair use' (2015) 90 Wash. L. Rev. 815
Sarraute, R (1968), 'Current theory on the moral right of authors and artists under French law' (1968) 16 Am. J. Comp. L. 465
Savatier, R (1957), 'Loi du 11 mars 1957 sur la propriété littéraire et artistique' (1957) 42(2) JCP 677
Scherer, F M (2008), 'The emergence of musical copyright in Europe from 1709 to 1850' (2008) 5(2) RERCI 3
Schultz, M F (2009), 'Live performance, copyright, and the future of the music business' (2009) 43 University of Richmond Law Review 685
Serazio, M (2008), 'The apolitical irony of generation mash-up: a cultural case study in popular music' (2008) 31 Popular Music and Society 79
Silva, P D and Garcia, J L (2012), 'YouTubers as satirists: humour and remix in online video' (2012) 4 JeDEM 89
Simon, William G, (1990), 'Bakhtin: parody' (1990) 12(1–2) Quarterly Review of Film & Video 23

Sims, A, (2010), 'Strangling their creation: the courts' treatment of fair dealing in copyright law since 1911' (2010) 2 IPQ 192
Schneider, J S (2016), 'Parody and the fair use defense: the best way to practice safe sex with all your favorite characters' (2016) 81 Brook. L. Rev. 1777
Smithies, T and Papanikitas, G (2002), 'TCN Channel Nine Pty Ltd v. Network Ten Pty Ltd' (2002) 7 MALR 249
Snow, N (2011), 'The forgotten right of fair use' (2011) 62 Case W. Res. L. Rev. 135
Solo, A (2014), 'The role of copyright in an age of online music distribution' (2014) 19 MALR 169
Spence, M (1998), 'Intellectual property and the problem of parody' (1998) 114 LQR 594
Spies, A (2011), 'Revering irreverence: a fair dealing exception for both weapon and target parodies' (2011) 34 UNSW Law Journal 1122 available at http://heinonline.org/HOL/Page?handle=hein.journals/swales34&div=56&g_sent=1&collection=journals (access date: 10 November 2018)
Spitz, B (2005), 'Droit d'auteur, copyright et parodie ou le mythe de l'usage loyal' (2005) 2 RIDA 55
Strowel, A (1991), 'La parodie selon le droit d'auteur et la théorie littéraire' (1991) 26 RIEJ 23
Sun, H (2007), 'Overcoming the Achilles heel of copyright law' (2007) 5(2) NJTIP 264
Suzor, N (2008), 'Where the bloody hell does parody fit in Australian copyright law?' (2008) 13 MALR 218
Tawfik, M (2013),'The Supreme Court of Canada and the "fair dealing trilogy": elaborating a doctrine of user rights under Canadian copyright law' (2013) 51 Alta. L. Rev. 191
Teilmann, S (2005), 'Framing the law: the right of integrity in Britain' (2005) 1 EIPR 19
Torremans, P (2002), 'La lettre d'Angleterre : évolutions récentes en droit d'auteur' (2002) 3 Propriétés Intellectuelles 1
Tran-Gervat, Y-M (2006), 'Pour une définition opérationnelle de la parodie littéraire: parcours critique et enjeux d'un corpus spécifique' (2006) 13 Cahiers de Narratologie 1
Tricoire, A (2005), 'L'exception de parodie est-elle recevable en matière publicitaire?' (July/August 2005) 223 Chroniques et opinion Légipresse 77
Tschmuck, P (2009), 'Copyright, contracts and music production' (2009) 12 Information, Communication & Society 251
Tunç, A (2002), 'Pushing the limits of tolerance: functions of political cartoonists in the democratization process: the case of Turkey' (2002) 64(1) International Communication Gazette 48
Tushnet, R (2007), 'Naming rights: attribution and law' (2007) 3 Utah L. Rev. 781
Tushnet, R (2015), 'Content, purpose or both?' (2015) 90 Wash. L. Rev, 869
Tuve, R (1969), 'Sacred "parody" of love poetry, and Herbert' (1969) 8 Studies in Renaissance 249
Van Gestel, R and Micklitz, H (2011), 'Revitalizing doctrinal legal research in Europe European' University Institute Working Paper 2011/05 available at http://cadmus.eui.eu/bitstream/handle/1814/16825/LAW_2011_05.pdf (access date: 10 November 2018)
Van O'Connor, W, 'Parody as criticism' (1964) 25(4) College English, 248
Vaver, D (1987), 'Authors' moral rights—reform proposals in Canada: charter or barter of rights for creators?' (1987) 25 Osgoode Hall L.J. 749
Vivant, P (2006), 'Courte citation et parodie: des exceptions au droit moral?' (2006) 2 RLDI 59
Voorhoof, D (2000), 'Is freedom of expression a legitimate argument for disrespecting copyright? The parody as a metaphor' (2000) available at http://www.psw.ugent.be/Cms_global/uploads/publicaties/dv/05recente_publicaties/FOXandParody.actualised.sept2006.CPH.pdf (access date: 10 November 2018)

Voorhoof, D (2009), 'Freedom of expression under the human rights system from Sunday Times (n 1) v. U.K. (1979) to Hachette Filipacchi Associés ('ici Paris') v. France (2009)' (2009) 2 Inter-Am. & Eur. Hum. Rts. J. 3

Waisman, A (2008), 'Rethinking the moral right to integrity' (2008) 3 IPQ 268

Walsh, A (2010), 'Parody of intellectual property: prospects for a fair use/dealing defence in the United Kingdom' (2010) 21 (11) I.C.C.L.R 388

Ward, J (1952), 'The use of borrowed material in 16th-century instrumental music' (1952) 5(2) Journal of the American Musicology Society 88

Weber, D P (2014), 'Restricting the freedom of contract: a fundamental prohibition' (2014) 16(1) Yale Human Rights and Development Journal, Article 2

Weir, M (1992), 'Making sense of copyright law relating to parody: a moral rights perspective' (1992) 18 Monash University Law Review 194

Wong, M W S (2009), '"Transformative" user-generated content in copyright law: infringing derivative works or fair use?' (2009) 11 Vanderbilt J. of Ent. and Tech. Law 1075

Yonover, G J (1996), 'Artistic parody: the precarious balance: moral rights, parody, and fair use' (1996) 14 Cardozo Arts & Ent. L.J. 79

Yurkowski, R A (2001), 'Is Hyde Park hiding the truth? an analysis of the public interest defence to copyright infringement' (2001) 32 Victoria University of Wellington Law Review 1

DOCUMENTS AND CONFERENCE PAPERS

Attorney-General's Department, *Submission No 69A to the Senate Standing Committees on Legal and Constitutional Affairs*, Inquiry into the Provisions of the Copyright Amendment Bill 2006, 8 November 2006

Australian CLRC Report (2002)

Australian Copyright Council, *Moral Rights* (2012)

Australian Government, *New Australia Copyright Laws, Parody and Satire* (factsheet 2006)

Australian Government Discussion Paper, 60. *Proposed Moral Rights for Copyright Creators* (Commonwealth of Australia, Canberra, 1993)

Australian Government Discussion Paper, *Proposed Moral Rights Protection for Copyright Creators* (Australian Government Printer, June 1994)

Australian Government, *New Australian Copyright Laws – Parody and Satire* (Attorney General's Department, 2006)

Australian Government, *Parodies, Satires & Jokes* (Information sheet, Australian Copyright Council, 2008)

Australian Government, *Parodies, Satires & Jokes* (Information sheet, Australian Copyright Council, 2012)

Berne, 'Report on the Work of Main Committee I (Substantive Provisions of the Berne Convention: Articles 1 to 20)', (1967) *Records of the Intellectual Property Conference of Stockholm* (June 11 to July 14, 1967 Volume II, 1145)

Bill C-60: An Act to amend the Copyright Act, 38th Parl., 1st Sess., 53-54 Eliz. II (2004); see preamble of the copyright modernization Act, SC 2012, c20, available at http://laws-lois.justice.gc.ca/eng/AnnualStatutes/2012_20/FullText.html (access date: 16 May 2013)

Bill C-61: An Act to amend the Copyright Act, 39th Parl., 2d Sess., 56-57 Eliz. II (2008) available at http://www.parl.gc.ca/LegisInfo/BillDetails.aspx?Language=E&Mode=1&billId=3188787 (access date: 10 November 2018)

Callamard, A., *Expert Meeting on the Links between Articles 19 and 20 of the ICCPR: Freedom of Expression and Advocacy of Religious Hatred That Constitutes Incitement to Discrimination, Hostility or Violence*, Article XIX (UN HCHR, 2–3 October 2008)

CLRC, Parliament of Australia, *Copyright and Contract* (2002)

CLRC, Parliament of Australia, *Report on the Simplification of the Copyright Act 1968: Part 1—Exceptions to the Exclusive Rights of Copyright Owners* (1998)

CLRC, Parliament of the Commonwealth of Australia, *Terms of reference* (23 April 2001)

Commerce and Economic Development Bureau, Bills Committee on the Copyright (Amendment) *Bill 2011—Copyright Exception for Parody* (Intellectual Property Department, 2011)

Commonwealth of Australia, Parliamentary Debates, 29 November 2006

Commonwealth of Australia, Parliamentary Debates, House of Representatives, 19 October 2006, (Philip Ruddock, Attorney-General)

Commonwealth, Parliamentary Debates, House of Representatives, 18 June 1997, pp 5547–8 (Hon Daryl Williams QC)

De Wolf & Partners, *Study on the application of Directive 2001/29/EC on Copyright and Related Rights in the Information Society* (2013) available at https://publications.europa.eu/en/publication-detail/-/publication/9ebb5084-ea89-4b3e-bda2-33816f11425b (access date: 10 November 2018)

Erickson K, Evaluating the Impact of Parody on the Exploitation of Copyright Works: An Empirical Study of Music Video Content on YouTube (2013)

Erickson, K, Kretschmer, M, and Mendis, D, *Copyright and the Economic Effects of Parody: An Empirical Study of Music Videos on the YouTube Platform and an Assessment of the Regulatory Options* (IPO, 2013)

EU Network of Independent Experts on Fundamental Rights, *Commentary of the Charter of Fundamental Rights of the European Union* (June 2006) available at http://ec.europa.eu/justice/fundamental-rights/files/networkcommentaryfinal_en.pdf (access date: 10 November 2018)

Gaubiac, Y, 'France: rapport general' in L Baulch, M Green, and M Wyburn (eds), *Alai Study Days—The Boundaries of Copyright: Its Proper Limitations and Exceptions* (Australian Copyright Council Sydney, 1999)

Gowers, A, *Gowers Review of Intellectual Property* (London: HM Treasury, November 2006)

Hargreaves, I, *Digital Opportunity. A Review of Intellectual Property and Growth* (2011), available at https://www.gov.uk/government/uploads/system/uploads/attachment_data/file/32563/ipreview-finalreport.pdf (access date: 10 November 2018)

HM Government, *Modernising Copyright: A Modern, Robust and Flexible Framework* (2012)

H.R. REP. No 1476, 94th Cong., 2d Sess. 66 (1976); S. REK No 473, 94th Cong., Ist Sess. 62 (1975)

Initial proposal from the Commission COM (1997) 628 and finally, the 1999 amended proposal COM (1999) 250

Kretschmer, M, Derclaye, E, Favale, M, and Watt, R, *The Relationship Between Copyright and Contract Law* (2010) April report available at http://eprints.bournemouth.ac.uk/16091/1/_contractlaw-report.pdf (access date: 10 November 2018)

Kretschmer, M, Derclaye, E, Favale, M, and Watt R, *The Relationship between Copyright and Contract Law: A Review Commissioned by the UK Strategic Advisory Board for Intellectual Property Policy (SABIP)*, (2010) available at SSRN: http://ssrn.com/abstract=2624945

Lauzière, L, *L'interprétation des lois* (2012) https://www.redactionjuridique.chaire.ulaval.ca/sites/redactionjuridique.chaire.ulaval.ca/files/lauziere-interpretation_des_lois_2012.pdf (access date: 8 September 2015)

Organisation for Economic Co-operation and Development, *Participative Web: User-Generated Content DSTI/ICCP/IE(2006)7/FINAL Unclassified Working Party on the Information Economy* (2007)

Parliament of Australia, *Explanatory Memorandum to the Copyright Amendment Bill* (1986)

Reda, J (2015), *Report on the implementation of Directive 2001/29/EC of the European Parliament and of the Council of 22 May 2001 on the harmonisation of certain aspects of copyright and related rights in the information society* (2014/2256(INI)) (24 June 2015) available at https://juliareda.eu/copyright-evaluation-report/ (access date: 10 November 2018)

Ricketson, S, 'SCCR/9/7: WIPO Study on Limitations and Exceptions of Copyright and Related Rights in the Digital Environment (related)' [2003] *Standing Committee on copyright and related rights*

Rigamonti, C in R M Hilty and C Geiger (dir), *La balance des intérêts en droit d'auteur*, Conference 2004

Ruddock, P, 'Protecting precious parody', *Daily Telegraph*, 30 November 2006

Ruddock, P, *Issues Paper Fair Use and Other Copyright Exceptions: An examination of fair use, fair dealing and other exceptions in the Digital Age* (2005) available at http://infojustice.org/download/copyright-flexibilities/articles/K%20Weatherall%20Copyright%20exceptions.pdf (access date: 10 November 2018)

Senate Inquiry, Parliament of Australia, Senate Legal and Constitutional Affairs Committee, *Inquiry into the Provisions of the Copyright Amendment Bill 2006* (available at www.aph.gov.au), Report dated 13 November 2006

S. Rep. No. 100–352, at 9–10 (1988); H.R. Rep. No. 100–609, at 37–38 (1988)

S. Exec. Rep. No. 100–17, at 55 (1988) (to accompany S. Treaty Doc. No. 99–27 (1986))

The Wittem Project (2010) https://www.ivir.nl/copyrightcode/european-copyright-code/ (access date: 10 November 2018)

UK-IPO, *Exceptions to Copyright: Guidance for Creators and Copyright Owners* (2014) available at https://www.gov.uk/government/uploads/system/uploads/attachment_data/file/448274/Exceptions_to_copyright_-_Guidance_for_creators_and_copyright_owners.pdf (access date: 10 November 2018)

UK-IPO, *Impact Assessment BIS1057 on a copyright exception for parody* (2012), available at http://webarchive.nationalarchives.gov.uk/20140603093549/http://www.ipo.gov.uk/ia-exception-parody.pdf (access date: 10 November 2018)

UK-IPO, *Taking Forward the Gowers Review of Intellectual Property: Changes to Copyright Exceptions* (Newport: UK-IPO, 2008)

UK-IPO, *Taking Forward the Gowers Review of Intellectual Property: Second Stage Consultation on Copyright Exceptions* (Newport: UK-IPO 2009) (Second Consultation Paper)

Weatherall's Law (available at http://weatherall.blogspot. com (access date: 10 November 2018)), post dated 5 July 2006

WIPO, *Agreed Statements Concerning the WIPO Copyright Treaty, Statement Concerning Article 10*, WIPO Diplomatic Conference, WIPO Doc. No CRNR/DC/96 (1996)

WTO Document WT/DS160/R available at https://www.wto.org/english/tratop_e/dispu_e/1234db.pdf (access date: 10 November 2018)

WTO Documents WT/DS114/R available at https://www.wto.org/english/tratop_e/dispu_e/cases_e/ds114_e.htm (access date: 10 November 2018)

THESES

Boccara, J, *La fausse parodie* (University Panthéon-Assas Paris II, 2007–2008)

Delfour, E, *L'imitation créatrice* (University of Toulouse, 2000)

El Khoury P, *Les exceptions au droit d'auteur, étude de droit comparé* (University of Montpellier, 2007)

Gairal, E, *Les oeuvres d'art et le droit* (University of Lyon, 1900)

Guilbert, A, *La contractualisation des exceptions* (University Panthéon-Assas, 2009)

Korkut, N, *Kinds of Parody from Medieval to Postmodern* (Middle East Technical University, 2005)

Malaurie, P, *L'ordre public et le contrat* (Paris, 1950)

Simard, J, *L'interprétation législative au Canada: la théorie à l'épreuve pratique* (University of Montréal, 1998)

Sirinelli, P, *Le droit moral de l'auteur et le droit commun des contrats* (Paris II, 1985)

DICTIONARIES

American Heritage Dictionary
Collins Dictionary of the English Language
Cornu, G., *Vocabulaire juridique* (PUF)
Macquarie Dictionary
Oxford English Dictionary
Oxford Music Dictionary

Index

The manufacturer's authorised representative in the EU for product safety is Oxford University Press España S.A. of El Parque Empresarial San Fernando de Henares, Avenida de Castilla, 2 - 28830 Madrid (www.oup.es/en or product.safety@oup.com). OUP España S.A. also acts as importer into Spain of products made by the manufacturer.
Printed and bound by CPI Group (UK) Ltd, Croydon, CR0 4YY
14/09/2026
02216284-0007

THE STORY OF THE MAMMALS IN 25 DISCOVERIES

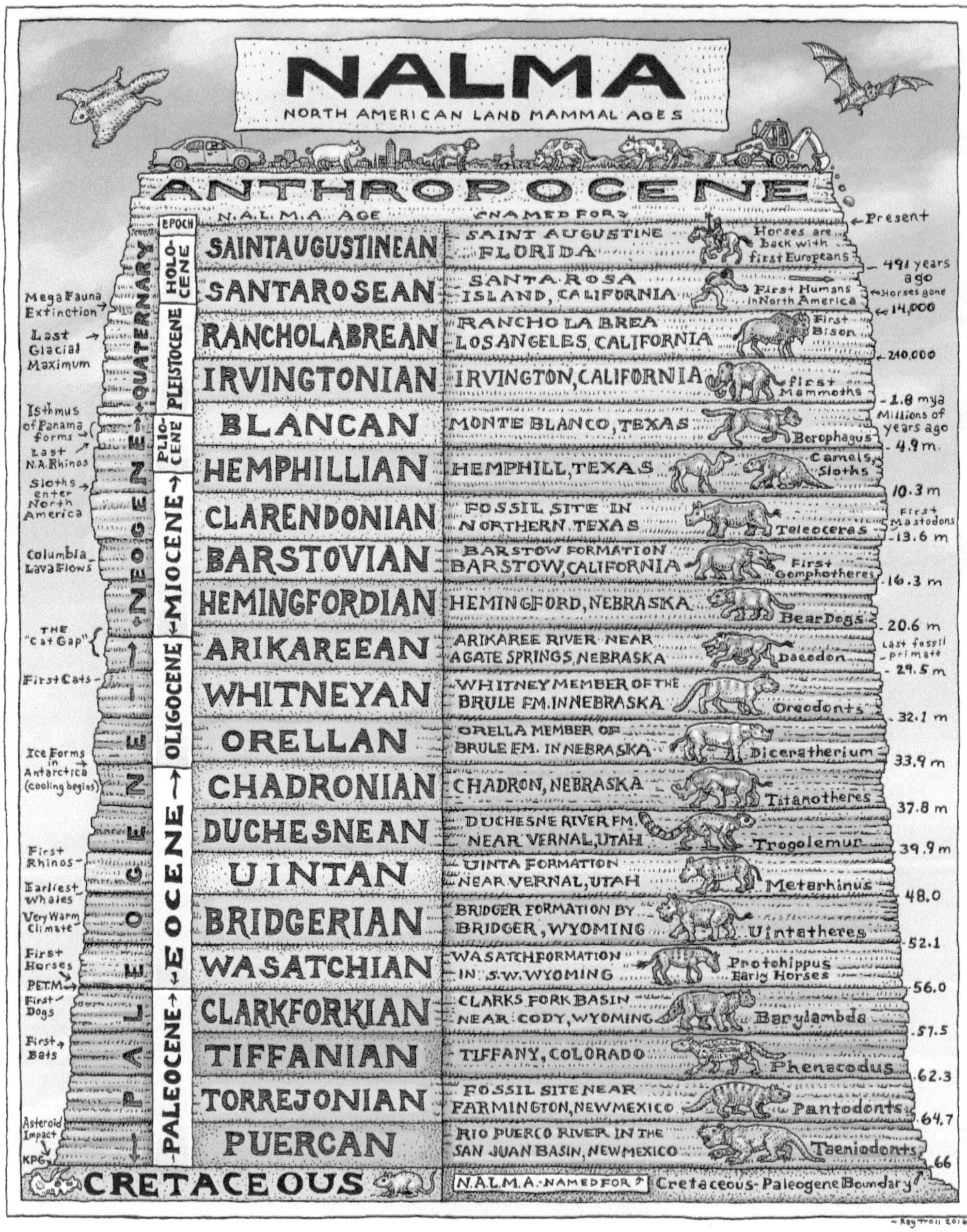
NALMA
NORTH AMERICAN LAND MAMMAL AGES
ANTHROPOCENE
N.A.L.M.A. AGE
NAMED FOR
EPOCH
Present
QUATERNARY
NEOGENE
PALEOGENE
HOLOCENE
PLEISTOCENE
PLIOCENE
MIOCENE
OLIGOCENE
EOCENE
PALEOCENE
SAINTAUGUSTINEAN
SAINT AUGUSTINE FLORIDA
Horses are back with first Europeans
491 years ago
SANTAROSEAN
SANTA ROSA ISLAND, CALIFORNIA
First Humans in North America
Horses gone
14,000
Mega Fauna Extinction
RANCHOLABREAN
RANCHO LA BREA LOS ANGELES, CALIFORNIA
First Bison
Last Glacial Maximum
240,000
IRVINGTONIAN
IRVINGTON, CALIFORNIA
First Mammoths
1.8 mya Millions of years ago
Isthmus of Panama forms
BLANCAN
MONTE BLANCO, TEXAS
Borophagus
4.9 m.
Last N.A. Rhinos
HEMPHILLIAN
HEMPHILL, TEXAS
Camels, Sloths
Sloths enter North America
10.3 m
CLARENDONIAN
FOSSIL SITE IN NORTHERN TEXAS
Teleoceras
First Mastodons
13.6 m
Columbia Lava Flows
BARSTOVIAN
BARSTOW FORMATION BARSTOW, CALIFORNIA
First Gomphotheres
16.3 m
HEMINGFORDIAN
HEMINGFORD, NEBRASKA
Bear Dogs
20.6 m
THE "Cat Gap"
ARIKAREEAN
ARIKAREE RIVER NEAR AGATE SPRINGS, NEBRASKA
Daeodon
Last fossil primate
29.5 m
First Cats
WHITNEYAN
WHITNEY MEMBER OF THE BRULE FM. IN NEBRASKA
Oreodonts
32.1 m
ORELLAN
ORELLA MEMBER OF BRULE FM. IN NEBRASKA
Diceratherium
33.9 m
Ice Forms in Antarctica (cooling begins)
CHADRONIAN
CHADRON, NEBRASKA
Titanotheres
37.8 m
DUCHESNEAN
DUCHESNE RIVER FM. NEAR VERNAL, UTAH
Trogolemur
39.9 m
First Rhinos
UINTAN
UINTA FORMATION NEAR VERNAL, UTAH
Metarhinus
48.0
Earliest Whales
Very Warm Climate
BRIDGERIAN
BRIDGER FORMATION BY BRIDGER, WYOMING
Uintatheres
52.1
First Horses
PETM
WASATCHIAN
WASATCH FORMATION IN S.W. WYOMING
Protohippus Early Horses
56.0
First Dogs
CLARKFORKIAN
CLARKS FORK BASIN NEAR CODY, WYOMING
Barylambda
57.5
First Bats
TIFFANIAN
TIFFANY, COLORADO
Phenacodus
62.3
TORREJONIAN
FOSSIL SITE NEAR FARMINGTON, NEW MEXICO
Pantodonts
64.7
Asteroid Impact
KPG
PUERCAN
RIO PUERCO RIVER IN THE SAN JUAN BASIN, NEW MEXICO
Taeniodonts
66
CRETACEOUS
N.A.L.M.A. NAMED FOR
Cretaceous-Paleogene Boundary
Ray Troll 2016

THE STORY OF THE MAMMALS in 25 DISCOVERIES

AMAZING FOSSILS AND THE PEOPLE WHO FOUND THEM

DONALD R. PROTHERO

COLUMBIA UNIVERSITY PRESS NEW YORK

COLUMBIA UNIVERSITY PRESS
Publishers Since 1893
New York   Chichester, West Sussex
cup.columbia.edu

Library of Congress Cataloging-in-Publication Data

Names: Prothero, Donald R. author
Title: The Story of the mammals in 25 discoveries : amazing fossils and the people who found them / Donald R Prothero.
Description: New York : Columbia University Press, 2026. | Includes bibliographical references and index.
Identifiers: LCCN 2026000036 | ISBN 9780231218306 hardback | ISBN 9780231562171 ebook | ISBN 9780231567091 PDF
Subjects: LCSH: Mammals | Paleontology—History | Paleontologists | LCGFT: Indexes
Classification: LCC QL706 .P86 2026 | DDC 599—dc23/eng/20260326
LC record available at https://lccn.loc.gov/2026000036

Cover image and design: Henry Sene Yee
Frontispiece: Ray Troll

GPSR Authorized Representative: Easy Access System Europe, Mustamäe tee 50, 10621 Tallinn, Estonia, gpsr.requests@easproject.com

CONTENTS

PREFACE

The history of mammals is one of the most amazing and well-documented examples of evolution in the fossil record, but it has been long overshadowed by the popularity of dinosaurs. Yet stories about saber-toothed cats and giant mammoths and ground sloths often get a lot of attention, and they are not even the most amazing and peculiar mammals that ever lived. Having already written a series of books organized in this format (*The Story of Life in 25 Fossils, The Story of the Earth in 25 Rocks, The Story of Dinosaurs in 25 Discoveries*, and *The Story of Evolution in 25 Discoveries*), I thought it was appropriate to finally write a book about the topic I know best, fossil mammals.

Like those previous books in the series (especially *The Story of Dinosaurs in 25 Discoveries*), each chapter focuses on an individual fossil genus or group of fossils and the story it tells. In addition, this book discusses a particular example or line of evidence for the evolution of a particular group of mammals. I have tried to frame the science in terms of the fascinating stories of the people who made the discoveries, and the importance of the discovery in the context of the science. Each chapter focuses on some interesting tidbit about mammalian evolution, usually illustrating a simple point, such as "How did horses evolve?" or "What were the biggest mammals that ever lived?" or "How did whales evolve from land mammals?" Typically, I take the discovery of a particular genus of mammal as the main theme and weave in the biographical details of the important paleontologists who worked on these animals as well. There is an undeniable "cool" factor with each bizarre or interesting anecdote that illustrates some of the amazing and incredible examples of how different kinds of mammals evolved, from horses to rhinos to camels to elephants to the great whales—and the surprising and amazing things we have learned about them, especially in the past thirty years as their fossil record became much better known and new evidence emerged from fields such as molecular biology.

As a mammalian paleontologist by training, I have studied personally and published my own research on many of these examples, or I know the fossils from firsthand study. I have published two previous books related to this topic (*Princeton Field Guide to Prehistoric Mammals*, 2016; *Horns, Tusks, and Flippers: The Evolution of Hoofed Mammals*, 2002), but the format and approach of this book is totally different. It does not attempt to cover all mammalian groups (that was done in *Princeton Field Guide to Prehistoric Mammals*) but just those that lend themselves to a treatment that focuses on the people or events that led to their discovery, as well as the groups that capture public interest. Because this book is focused on the human-interest aspect of most of these discoveries, the topics will not be grouped systematically, as I did in *Princeton Field Guide to Prehistoric Mammals*. Instead of comprehensive coverage, I will focus on twenty-five of the most interesting and popular examples. The topics will start out with the historically oldest recognized examples of prehistoric mammals (mammoths, mastodonts, and ground sloths), then will be grouped by their history of discovery and common themes (for example, three chapters on the three groups of mammals that returned to the sea) in sequence.

ACKNOWLEDGMENTS

I thank the many paleontologists who have taught me all about fossil mammals, especially my undergraduate professor Michael Woodburne, and my graduate mentors Malcolm McKenna and Richard Tedford. I benefited from studying the best collection of fossil mammals in the world in the American Museum of Natural History in New York, and from my friends and colleagues who have studied and deciphered it and taught me in the process. These include Earl Manning, Henry Galiano, John Flynn, Rich Cifelli, George Engelmann, John Wahlert, Matt Mihlbachler, Brian Lee Beatty, Christine Janis, Jim Honey, Bruce MacFadden, Dave Webb, and many others. I am eternally grateful for the legendary paleontologists who have collected and studied these fossils in the past, especially William Diller Matthew, Chester Stock, and Morris Skinner, without whom such an understanding of the mammalian fossil record would not be possible.

I thank my editor at Columbia University Press, Miranda Martin, for supporting this book idea, and Kathryn Jorge at CUP for overseeing the project, Ben Kolstad at KGL for project management, and Kay Mikel for copyediting the manuscript.

Finally, I thank the loving support of my boys, Erik, Zachary, and Gabriel Prothero, and my loving wife, Dr. Teresa LeVelle. They have been so patient while I vanished for months in my office to write this book.

THE STORY OF THE MAMMALS IN 25 DISCOVERIES

01 THE "GREAT *INCOGNITUM*"—MASTODONS AND THEIR RELATIVES

MAMMUT

There were giants in the earth in those days.

—GENESIS 6:4

GIANTS IN THE EARTH

Many cultures around the world have a mythology that includes legends about gigantic races of humans that lived on Earth in the dark mysterious past. They may have fought against the gods, or they may have been destroyed by floods. These stories were reinforced by the discovery of gigantic bones, much larger than those of any living human, all over the Mediterranean and Europe. The Greek philosopher Empedocles (492–432 BCE) reported gigantic bones from Sicily, supposedly remnants of a race of giants. The Roman historian Pliny the Elder (23–79 CE) mentioned fossil ivory in the ground, and according to the Roman historian Suetonius (69–122 CE), Emperor Augustus owned a collection of large bones that had been found on the island of Capri, near Pompeii. The skulls of elephants, with their huge central opening in front (for the trunk), were thought to be the skulls of the one-eyed cyclops (figure 1.1).

In the Middle Ages, these huge bones were again attributed to gigantic humans or other monsters (Genesis 6:4) that were drowned in Noah's flood. Giant tusks from Siberia were thought to be the horns of the mythical unicorn or the tusks of dragons. In some places gigantic teeth or vertebrae

Figure 1.1 ▲
Comparison of the skull of a pygmy elephant, with the large nasal opening in the front that reminds most people of an eye socket, with a sculpture of the one-eyed cyclops. (Courtesy of Wikimedia Commons)

of mammoths were revered as relicts of saints. Nearly every possibility was suggested except that they were the bones of extinct elephants.

In the early seventeenth century, some giant bones dug up in a sand pit near Langon in southeastern France were exhibited around France as the remains of the giant Teutons, Germanic tribes that once roamed Gaul and were defeated by the Romans in 101 BCE. But in 1613 the famous anatomist Riolan attacked the prevailing interpretation, suggesting that they were the bones of an elephant. This generated a raging controversy between physicians and anatomists and the barber-surgeons who called them gigantic human bones. Others thought they were hoaxes or generated by mysterious "plastic forces" (*vis plastica* in Latin) that percolated through Earth. Still others attacked the anatomists for questioning the biblical account of giants on Earth. The controversies died down without being resolved, and for the next two centuries most people continued to interpret new finds as gigantic humans.

The giant bones that kept turning up in the New World were also a source of much mystery and consternation. The Native American tribes usually attributed them to giant monsters fought by their ancestors and incorporated them into their folklore. When these bones were first seen by European settlers, they were thought to be the bones of gigantic humans that roamed the earth in biblical times. Others thought that the giant tasks so revered by the Native Americans were the works of Satan, placed there to tempt the believer. In 1519, the Spanish explorer and conquistador Hernan Cortez received a bone of a "giant," a gift from the friendly Tlascalan tribe of Mexico during the conquest of the Aztecs. He sent it back to the King of Spain as proof that giants at once lived in the New World. In 1706, the Reverend Cotton Mather of the Massachusetts Bay Colony pronounced them to be "the remains of godless giants drowned in Noah's Flood." He sent some bones to the Royal Society in London to have them certified as evidence of this "wicked giant" because biblical scholars were calculating Adam's height at 123 ft. 9 in. The Royal Society never pronounced an opinion on these bones, although by that time many members were becoming skeptical of the literal interpretations of Genesis.

The stifling effect of religious dogma about giants and Noah's flood was complicated by another idea: the notion of Divine Providence. An omnipotent, benevolent God would never allow any of his creatures to become extinct. As the poet Alexander Pope wrote in *An Essay on Man* (1734), "who sees with equal eye, as God of all, a hero perish, or a sparrow fall." The prevailing concept was that of a "great chain of being" that linked the animals to man to the angels to God. Breaking any link in that chain implied the destruction of the whole chain. In the same poem, Pope also wrote:

> Where, one step broken, the great scale's destroy'd;
> From Nature's chain whatever link you strike,
> Ten or ten thousandth, breaks the chain alike.

By the late 1700s, however, it was becoming more and more apparent that many of the recently discovered fossils had no living counterparts. Remote corners of the world were being explored, and although many new and surprising beasts were discovered, clearly the gigantic beasts were not hiding in South America or Africa or the East Indies. Many strange fossils, such as the bones of hippopotami in Paris and London, were clearly related to tropical animals, but it was assumed that these bones had been washed from the tropics during the Great Flood. The notion of extinction was still blasphemous.

The New World soon provided unequivocal evidence that these large bones were not simply gigantic humans. In 1739, Charles le Moyne, the second Baron de Longueil, left Montreal with French and Indian troops to fight the Chickasaw Indians along the Ohio River. Somewhere along the Ohio he found the remains of what appeared to be three elephants. When the war ended in 1740, le Moyne collected the bones and shipped them to New Orleans and ultimately to Paris, where they came to the attention of French naturalists. In the 1740s and 1750s, English settlers in the region sent more of these bones from Big Bone Lick, Kentucky, off to England and also to Benjamin Franklin in America. Most of the bones (especially the tusks) were clearly like those of elephants and mammoths, but the teeth were puzzling (figure 1.2). They were clearly unlike any living elephant, yet they were part of an animal of elephantine size. (We now know that these were specimens of the American mastodon, *Mammut americanum*.) Franklin speculated that the teeth were reminiscent of a carnivorous animal, although he and others later decided it was a vegetarian. In 1769, the famous British anatomist William Hunter took the carnivory suggestion seriously and suggested this was not a true elephant but a "pseudelephant" or "American *incognitum*" (Latin for "unknown") that had independently developed ivory tusks:

> This monster, with the agility and ferocity of a tiger . . . cruel as the bloody panther, swift as the descending eagle, terrible as the angel of night. . . . And if this animal was indeed carnivorous, which I believe cannot be doubted, though we may as philosophers regret it, as men we cannot but thank Heaven that its whole generation is probably extinct.

This very precocious suggestion was still not accepted by naturalists of the time. Nevertheless, remains of the "*incognitum*" and also of the Siberian mammoth (including frozen carcasses with hair and skin—see chapter 2) were turning up again and again. Georges Louis Leclerc, the Comte de Buffon (1707–1788), concluded in his *Théorie de la terre* in 1749 that although most of the supposedly extinct animals were hiding somewhere in an unknown region, it was likely that the large terrestrial mammals such as the mammoth and "*incognitum*" had actually perished. By 1778, Buffon was relating their disappearance to his ideas of violent cataclysms in Earth's

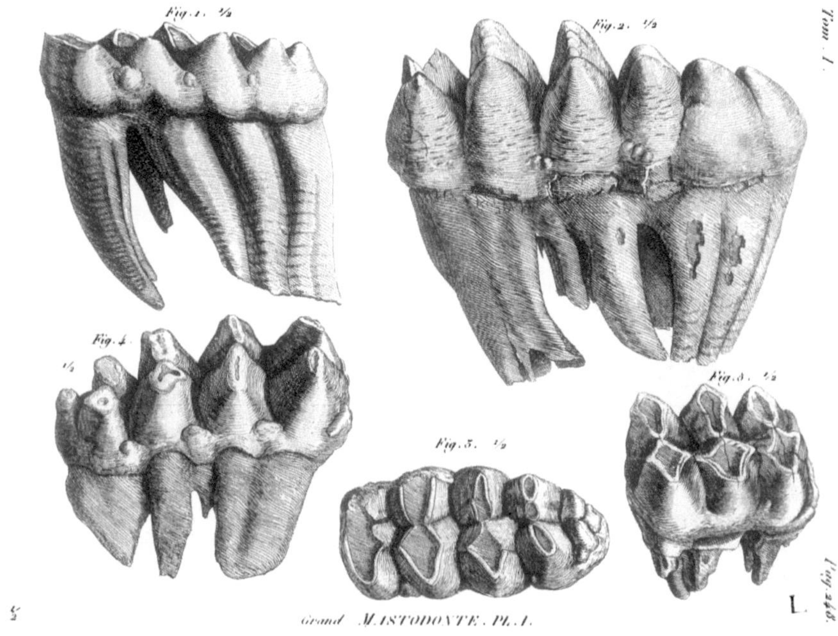

Figure 1.2 ▲
Cuvier's original plate showing some of the teeth of the "American *incognitum*." (Courtesy of Wikimedia Commons)

early history. During this time the climate was warmer and polar regions had once been tropical, so "elephants" (meaning mammoths) could live in Siberia. This implied a nonbiblical Earth of much greater antiquity. Buffon suggested it was as much as 75,000 to 3,000,000 years old, rather than the 6,000 years demanded by most literalist biblical scholars. Naturally, such revolutionary ideas were not popular with the theologians in the Sorbonne. Buffon was protected by the king, however, so he was not persecuted for his heresy, although his ideas were not widely accepted either.

The fact of extinction was finally proved by one of the greatest scientists of all time, the Baron Georges Cuvier (1769–1832). Jean Leopold Frederic Georges Cuvier was an impressive man (figure 1.3). Tall of stature, he had a "massive" head crowned by a large mane of hair. One admirer wrote that his head "gave to his entire person an undeniable cachet of majesty and to his face an expression of profound meditation." After his death, scientists weighed his brain and found that it was a massive 1830 grams, more than

Figure 1.3 ◄
A portrait of Baron Georges Cuvier. (Courtesy of Wikimedia Commons)

400 grams above average, and 200 grams heavier than any brain ever measured at that time.

More important, he was one of the most brilliant men of his time, with a command of many subjects, some of which he invented all by himself. Before Cuvier, natural history was a field that resembled stamp collecting, with many amateur naturalists compiling long lists and descriptions of new species without analyzing the similarities in their anatomy. Cuvier almost single-handedly revolutionized natural history by dissecting many different animals and discovering their underlying similarities and differences. This became the foundation of comparative anatomy, a subject that has been fundamental to biology ever since. Naturalists and explorers sent him their fossil bones, and he was the first to correctly describe many types of extinct animals. Cuvier solved the mystery of the puzzling fossil teeth called the "*Great Incognitum*" and recognized them as the teeth of the elephant-like mastodons. He also correctly deciphered the huge marine lizards we now know as mosasaurs. For this reason, he is also considered to be the founder of vertebrate paleontology.

Cuvier is most famous for his "law of correlation of parts," wherein he discovered that certain types of anatomical features tend to be associated. If you are a flesh eater, you will have sharp teeth and claws; if you are a plant eater, you will have flat grinding teeth and hooves; and so on. Using this law, paleontologists have been able to reconstruct whole animals from just a few key bones because the other parts of the anatomy are so predictable.

Cuvier was not only a scientific genius but also a politically astute person. He was born of humble bourgeois origins in the Jura Mountains of southwest France, but he was brilliant in school. He easily mastered all his subjects at a young age, including history, geography, mathematics, law, chemistry, mineralogy, zoology, botany, mining, police work, diplomacy, commerce, finance, economics, geometry, and Latin and Greek. Then he studied in Germany and quickly became fluent in German as well. During the horrors of the French Revolution, he was a tutor for a noble family up in Normandy and thus avoided the dangers in Paris.

In 1795, the great French naturalist Etienne Geoffroy Saint-Hilaire invited the 26-year-old genius to come to Paris and work at the newly established Musée National d'Histoire Naturelle. It had originally been the king's *Jardin du Roi* ("royal garden") but lost its royal title when the king lost his head. Cuvier quickly rose through the ranks and kept his position (or improved it) when the Revolutionary government was overthrown by Napoleon. Napoleon appointed him Inspector-General of public education and also State Councillor. When the Little Emperor was exiled and the Bourbon monarchy was restored, Cuvier kept his status under three successive kings of France—a remarkable feat considering that many educated scholars of the time (such as Antoine Lavoisier, the great chemist) had lost their heads to the guillotine.

In 1796, Cuvier read a paper before the French Institute on living and fossil elephants. He was the first scientist to recognize the difference between the Asian and African elephant. Then he showed that the mammoth and the American *incognitum*, although related to elephants, were clearly not the same as living elephants and did not require Earth to be much warmer in the past. Since they were different animals, it was possible that they lived in cold climates, unlike modern elephants. He pointed to the Siberian woolly rhinoceroses, the giant cave bear, the strange marine reptile from Maastricht (now known as a mosasaur, a giant marine monitor lizard from the Cretaceous), or the giant ground sloth from Patagonia (chapter 3) he had just described. Where could such great animals be hiding today if they were still alive? They "prove the existence of a world before ours, and destroyed by some catastrophe." Cuvier went on to develop his ideas of great catastrophes that had preceded our world and were not mentioned in Genesis. This was the "antediluvian" world before the flood, a time of darkness, great monsters, and cataclysmic changes. Over his long career, Cuvier described many other important fossils, such as the tapir-like palaeotheres from the Eocene gypsum deposits of the Paris Basin and the first pterodactyls. Although his notion of catastrophist geology was gradually replaced by the uniformitarian ideas of James Hutton and Charles Lyell in the 1830s and 1840s, his proof of extinction was never challenged. Indeed, more and more bizarre beasts, including the first dinosaurs, were described in the 1840s, driving home the reality of extinction beyond any doubt.

THE "GREAT MISSOURIUM"

The American mastodon was the first extinct animal collected and described from the New World. Since it had the bones and tusks, but not the teeth, of living elephants, it was a great mystery. As we discussed earlier in the chapter, many prominent Americans, including Benjamin Franklin and Thomas Jefferson, puzzled over the "American *incognitum.*" Since it apparently lived in a marshy habitat and was abundantly preserved in ancient bog deposits, eighteenth-century Americans occasionally discovered its bones when draining the swamp or excavating for peat. The Big Bone Lick, near the Ohio River in eastern Kentucky, was a common source for these mysterious bones. Apparently, mastodons were concentrated there by a natural salt lick that attracted them as well as other wild animals.

The most famous find, however, was made in the Hudson Valley, near Wallkill, New York. In 1782, the Reverend Robert Annan found some gigantic teeth and bones while digging an irrigation ditch. He sent them to General Washington, who at the time was preoccupied with fighting the Revolutionary War. They eventually reach the hands of Charles Willson Peale, the famous American artist, who was asked to draw them. These bones, along with numerous paintings, stuffed animals, and wax figures, became part of the first natural history museum in the United States: Peale's Museum of Natural Curiosities in Philadelphia. When the fossils were sold to a Dutch professor in 1787, Peale needed something to replace them.

He got his chance in 1801 when another farmer in the Walkill area found giant bones in a peat bogs about four miles from Reverend Annan's farm. The farmer and his helpers had broken up the ribs badly as they dug, but the huge thighbones were intact. Peale and sons rushed to the scene and purchased the rights for "$100 in silver or gold." They excavated from July to September, rigging up a water wheel to keep pumping out the copious ground water (figure 1.4). After all that digging, there were plenty of leg, backbone, and rib pieces, but no skull or jaws. They tried several other places, and just as they were about to give up they found an excellent skull and two sets of jaws. (Today the site is covered by Walkill River). Wrapped in canvas, the bones were carted to Philadelphia where the Peales put together one of the first skeletal mounts of an extinct animal in history. It was a huge success, pronounce by the press to be the "ninth wonder of the world."

However, the level of anatomical understanding in this country was still abysmally low, and few in America had ever seen an elephant. In fact, enslaved Africans were adept at recognizing mammoth teeth because they closely resemble the elephant teeth that they had seen before their

Figure 1.4 ▲

Charles Willson Peale's 1806 painting, *Exhumation of the Mastodon* (Courtesy of the American Museum Digital Library)

enslavement. Most people interpreted the strange bone remains as being from a gigantic carnivorous beast.

After the Peale Museum success, other places begin to collect and exhibit mastodon skeletons as well. Some reconstructions were so poor, however, that they seem laughable today. In 1841, a mastodon found in Gasconade County, Missouri, was exhibited as "the great Missourium" or the "Leviathan Missourium." Reconstructed by the showman Albert Koch, it was supposedly large enough that (according to the *London Times*) "a mammoth would have strutted with ease between his legs. . . . The animal supposed to be aquatic in its nature. This we should have inferred from the anatomical structures of its neck." The Philadelphia editor James Pedder was convinced that Koch's reconstruction was wrong, but his idea was even more fantastic (figure 1.5):

> I have been led to conclude that the animal was a monster of the tortoise tribe 32 feet long and corresponding width with the power [of] withdrawing his head within the shell; the tusks then forming a mail of defense around the edge to ward off obstruction . . . [the tusks were] carried near the Earth, and resting upon it, at the wheel of the animal.

Despite this confusion, the mysteries of the mastodon had been resolved long before 1841. Cuvier correctly realized that these animals were related

Figure 1.5 ▲
Pedder's construction of the mastodon as a giant turtle with fangs. (Courtesy of Wikimedia Commons)

to elephants. After seeing Peale's drawings of *Mammut americanum*, he decided it was different from the frozen furry animal of Siberia. That beast had long been called "Mammot" ("earth burrower" in Tartar) by medieval eastern European farmers who found huge bones in their fields and thought they belonged to a giant burrowing beast. Since the American beast had conical cusps on its molars that resembled a woman's breasts, Cuvier called it *le mastodonte* or "breast tooth." Eventually, the name "mastodon" stuck and only the woolly Siberian animals were called "mammoths." However, according to the rules of naming animals, the first scientific name applied to an animal must take priority, even if it's inappropriate or forgotten in favor of a more popular name. Thus zoologists and paleontologists must use the name *Mammut* for the mastodon because it was first applied to that animal 18 years before Cuvier renamed it *le mastodonte*. The true mammoth is now known by the genus *Mammuthus*, an unfortunate confusion because mastodons and mammoths are not very similar or even closely related.

Since Cuvier's time, much more has been learned about the American mastodon and its family, the Mammutidae. This family diverged from the rest of the Proboscidea long before the rest of the elephants. The earliest known mastodon, *Zygolophodon*, first migrated from Africa to North America around 18 Ma, and the entire family remained very conservative throughout their long history. Although generally elephant-like in build, *Mammut* was only about 10 feet (3 meters) tall at the shoulders and had no great forehead or shoulder hump like true elephants (figure 1.6). It also had a longer skull, flatter brow, deeper chest, broader pelvis, longer back, and shorter legs. Tusks were present in both sexes, although those of males were larger, extending up to 10 feet (3 meters) from their skull. These tusks projected forward from the skull, then curved outward and finally inward. The males also had smaller vestigial lower tusks that were lost in maturity. One tusk is usually shorter than the other, indicating that these animals were typically either right-tusked or left-tusked. Their tusks were probably used to pry up bark and branches and break them up into pieces, along with sparring with rivals in their herd, establishing dominance, and fighting off predators.

During the Ice Ages, mastodons apparently preferred open spruce woodlands and spruce forests, where they browsed on leaves and vegetation. Although they were most common in the northeastern United States, they were also found in the forested valley lowlands and bogs in

Figure 1.6 ▲

(*A*) Mounted skeleton of the Pacific mastodon adult and juvenile at La Brea tar pits. (*B*) Reconstruction of the American mastodon. ([*A*] Photo by the author; [*B*] art by Z. Burian, courtesy of Wikimedia Commons)

Florida, Texas, and the Great Plains. They are also found in a handful of localities in the western United States, including the Snowmastodon site near Snowmass, Colorado, the Diamond Valley Lake sites near Hemet, California, and the La Brea tar pits in Los Angeles. Recently, these western specimens have been distinguished from the eastern and midwestern species *Mammut americanum* and interpreted to be a different species, *Mammut pacificum*. Mastodon molars have even been found by fisherman on the Atlantic continental shelf over 250 miles (400 kilometers) from the present shoreline in water more than 200 feet (70 meters) deep. Apparently, they lived on conifer-covered shelf areas exposed during the glacial low in sea level twenty thousand years ago, and these fossils remained even as the sea level rose and drowned the continental shelf. Stomach contents found in their rib cages included twigs and cones of conifers, leaves, coarse grasses, swamp plants, and mosses. Mastodons had coarse, brownish outer hairs around 3 centimeters long and a fine woolly undercoat, much like other aquatic and semiaquatic mammals. Given their preference for bog habitats, it is likely that they were as fond of water as the Ice Age moose.

Mammut was one of the most conservative and long lived of all known fossil mammal genera. It spread all over Europe, South and North America, and persisted without change for at least four million years. Surviving past the end of the last Ice Age, the best dates for the extinction may be as young as six thousand years ago. Native American legends describe a beast like the mastodon, so some scientists speculate that it survived until historic times. It is clear that Paleoindians hunted the mastodon. Possibly the oldest known dated evidence of humans in North America with mastodon bones apparently killed by Paleoindians and butchered is the Cerutti mastodon site in San Diego. It may date to about 130,000 years ago, although this is controversial. The best-known kill site is Kimmswick, about twenty miles south of St. Louis and close to the Mississippi River. Two mastodons were killed at different times, and Clovis projectile points were found among the bones. It may be that Paleoindians were responsible for the extinction of mastodons from overhunting them, although their survival until six thousand years ago contradicts this idea. Like the extinction of other large Ice Age mammals discussed elsewhere in this book, climate and humans are probably both responsible for the extinction of Ice Age megafauna.

EARLY TUSKERS

Although mammoths and mastodons were clearly related to elephants, they did little to show from whence elephants came. They are so late in the evolution of the Proboscidea that they are virtually modern in the development of tusks or trunk or size (figure 1.7). The first fossils that show the origin of the Proboscidea were discovered by the English paleontologist Charles W. Andrews, when he collected fossils in the Fayûm Basin of Egypt around 1900. Among the peculiar Fayûm mammals was the boar-sized beast Andrews called *Moeritherium*. (Lake Moeris was the old Greek name for a dry lake basin in the Fayûm depression.) About a meter high at the shoulder, *Moeritherium* had a very pig-like appearance (figure 1.8). It had a large head with ears located high on the side of the skull, a long body, and very short slender limbs. It probably weighed around 500 pounds (225 kilograms). Although *Moeritherium* probably did not have a full-fledged trunk, its nasal bones are far back on the skull, suggesting that it had a short fleshy proboscis. However, the upper and lower jaws both have prominent short tusks.

Indeed, in most features *Moeritherium* is similar to the living pygmy hippopotamus, and it may have lived in ancient marshes and riverbanks, feeding on vegetation. It is almost always found in deposits from major river deltas, consistent with an amphibious life. But the rest of its anatomy, especially the skull bones, clearly show that it's related to Proboscidea, and it is not a pig or a hippo.

Moeritherium comes from Fayûm rocks in Egypt that are about 34–37 Ma (million years before present). But we find specimens of older fossils in other parts of North Africa (figure 1.6). Since the early 1990s, French paleontologists have discovered numerous more primitive Proboscidea in the rocks of Morocco and other parts of North Africa. They are much less complete than *Moeritherium*, but they show the characteristic molars found in primitive proboscideans as well as other features of the skull.

In 1984 a partial skeleton of a primtive proboscidean found in the earliest Eocene (55 Ma) of Algeria provides an even more primitive species. Later found in Mali and Libya as well, it was named *Numidotherium* in 1986. Although the specimens are not complete, they already had a very tall high forehead like many proboscideans and unlike *Moeritherium*. The nasal opening is further back on the skull, suggesting the beginnings of a trunk

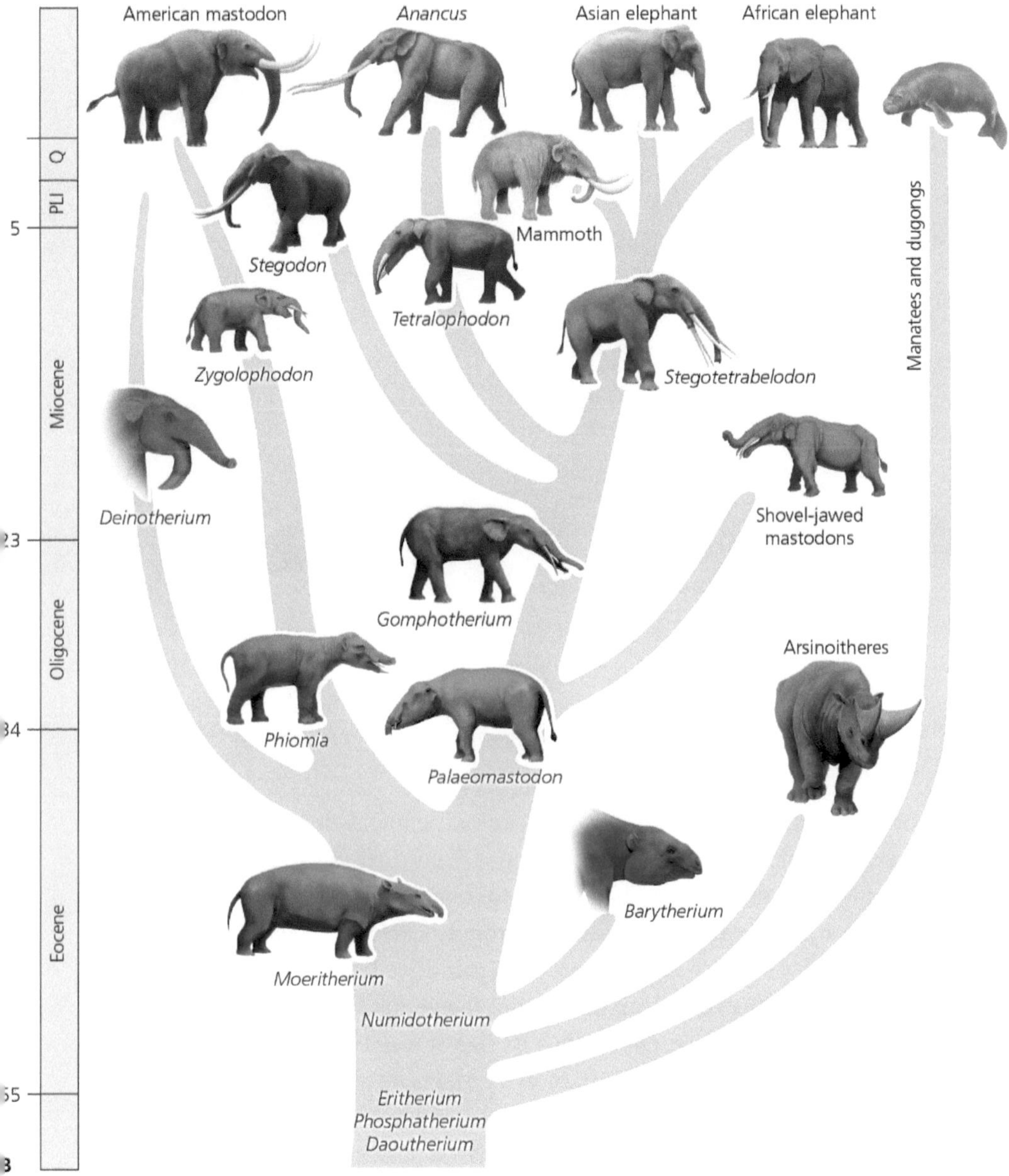

Figure 1.7 ▲

A phylogenetic tree illustrating the evolution of elephants and their relatives (Proboscidea) over geological time, from the Eocene to the present. (Redrawn from an original by C. R. Prothero)

Figure 1.8 ▲
Reconstruction of *Moeritherium*. (Photo by the author)

or proboscis. The upper tusks were beginning to develop, but like *Moeritherium* it did not lose the rest of the upper front teeth. Even more important, the lower front teeth are beginning to develop into a broad scoop that is common among all the primitive mastodonts. (Note: "Mastodont" is a general term for lots of different unrelated primitive Proboscidea. "Mastodon" refers only to the American mastodon, the genus *Mammut*.) The most surprising feature of *Numidotherium* is its size. It was only about 1 meter (3 feet) tall at the shoulder, smaller than even *Moeritherium*. Its limb bones were fully developed for bearing great weight with limb segments showing the proportions of later proboscideans. It was a perfect intermediate between *Moeritherium* and later proboscideans.

But what about specimens even older and more primitive than *Moeritherium* or *Numidotherium*? In 1996, Emmanuel Gheerbrant and others described *Phosphatherium* from upper Paleocene (57–55 Ma) rocks in Morocco, then in 2002 described *Daouitherium*, and then in 2009, these same scientists reported *Eritherium* and *Khamsaconus* from the same rocks. Although most of these species are known only from fragmentary skulls and jaws, but without tusks (they are not complete enough to determine if they had a proboscis), they already show many key characteristics of the Proboscidea, especially in the teeth and the cheekbones. They all show that the primitive Proboscidea were already established 57 Ma and had begun to diverge from their common ancestry with the sirenians (sea cows and manatees) and others related to the Tethytheria at that time.

The elephant family tree has numerous primitive species from the late Paleocene, *Numidotherium* from the early and middle Eocene, and *Moeritherium* from the late Eocene. The next side branch is the tapir-like *Barytherium* ("heavy beast") from the late Eocene of the Fayûm, which was a zoological mystery for over a century after Andrews discovered it. Recent specimens from Libya have shown that the skull is very mastodont-like, with a high forehead and the beginnings of a trunk. The skull is almost a meter long, and the limb bones are heavy enough that it was approaching the size and proportions of typical mastodonts. Like *Moeritherium* and *Numidotherium*, but unlike later proboscideans, it still had two incisors in the upper and lower jaws. *Barytherium* was not yet down to a single pair of upper tusks only. The upper tusks were still short and pointed downward, wearing against the forward-pointing lower tusks (much like a modern hippopotamus).

"TERRIBLE BEASTS"

In the late 1600s, a French surgeon named Matsorier found some huge bones and tusks in an area known as "the field of giants" near Lyon, France. He exhibited those bones around France and Germany as the supposed bones of a French king, but eventually he was exposed and the bones ended up in the natural history museum in Paris. By 1775, some scholars realized that the bones were "similar to a mammoth." But in the early 1800s, the great Cuvier, who had correctly related mammoths and mastodons to elephants, thought the bones belonged to a large tapir with upward-curving tusks he called *Tapir gigantesque*. Its molars had very well-developed cross-crests, like the teeth of tapirs, which fooled him (but they are very much like the molars of *Barytherium*). Others thought the bones belonged to a sirenian that used the tusks to anchor itself to the seafloor while sleeping.

The great British geologist Sir William Buckland reconstructed the bones something like a walrus.

In 1829 a complete skull and jaws were found in the Miocene bone beds of Eppelsheim in Germany, and it was named *Deinotherium giganteum* by the pioneering paleontologist Johann Jakob von Kaup. At first they thought it was the evolutionary link between sloths and mammoths. The mystery was not solved until the skeleton was found in 1853 after the collapse of an embankment of the Paris-Brunn railway. From the rest of the skull and the skeleton it was clear that the strange beast was closely related to proboscideans.

The skull looks very peculiar, with huge downward-curved tusks in the lower jaw and a broad scoop-like nasal region on the upper snout with no upper incisors or canines, but apparently room for attachment of the muscles of a long trunk (figure 1.9). No one is sure how these tusks were used. Some suggested that they used them for digging, or even for swinging down from branches by their tusks! John Harris studied them in detail and found that the tusks have normal wear at the tips, indicating that they were rubbed or abraded during feeding. Harris speculated that they were used (as are normal elephant tusks) as a point of leverage for the trunk. They may have also aided in stripping off bark and vegetation with the downward movement of their head. There's no evidence from their wear or abrasion that deinotheres used their tusks for digging.

Unlike the rest of the primitive Proboscidea we have discussed, deinotheres did not stay in Africa. The earliest form, *Prodeinotherium*, from the early Miocene of Libya, was about the size of a cow. Its skull does not yet show the extreme shortening and retraction of the nasal opening, indicating that it had a much flatter head and a shorter trunk than a typical elephant. Its lower tusks pointed downward but not backward. By the middle of the Miocene, *Prodeinotherium* was widespread all over northern and eastern Africa and also spread to Eurasia. There it was replaced by the best-known genus, *Deinotherium*, which reached true elephantine size toward the end of its evolution. It was a widespread inhabitant of the Miocene and Pliocene forests of Europe, Russia, the Middle East, and Pakistan, but unlike true mastodonts it never reached eastern Asia or North America. It was most abundant in the early Pliocene and then rapidly disappeared from Eurasia. These last deinotheres were enormous, larger than any living elephant or most mammoths, reaching 3.6 meters (12 feet) at the shoulder

Figure 1.9 ▲
Reconstruction of *Deinotherium giganteum* in life. (Courtesy of Wikimedia Commons)

and weighing almost 10 tons. Most species were extinct by the Pliocene, but the last *Deinotherium* managed to hold on until the early Pleistocene in East Africa where it undoubtedly interacted with our early hominid ancestors. It is found in many of the classic localities, such as Olduvai Gorge and Lake Turkana, where the best hominin fossils also occur. By the middle of the Ice Ages it was extinct, along with many of the large mammals of Africa. Certainly, the rapid climatic changes to wetter and drier climates had much to do with their extinction, although it is possible that when our ancestors first became hunters, they pushed deinotheres even faster to the brink of oblivion.

The moeritheres, barytheres, and deinotheres were all early experiments in proboscidean evolution that no longer survive (although our hominin ancestors knew deinotheres well). By the early Oligocene, however, the ancestors of the major groups of mastodons and mammoths are known from the Fayûm. These include animals such as *Palaeomastodon beadnelli* and *Phiomia serridens*, which had much larger tusks and a significant trunk (figure 1.10). *Palaeomastodon* stood about 2 meters (6 feet) high at the shoulder, and probably weighed as much as a small rhinoceros. Its upper and lower tusks were oval in cross section, and the cusps on the molars were already arranged in pairs so they formed V-shaped cross-crests about 1.3 meters (4.3 feet) at the shoulder. It also had short upper tusks with oval cross sections like *Palaeomastodon*, but the lower tusks were flattened into a spatula-like shape. The cusps on its molars were not arranged in pairs but staggered in two rows. As the main cusps and their small side cusps wore down, they formed a looping three-leaf-clover pattern. Both of these animals were well-suited to browsing leaves in the dense forests of North Africa around 33 Ma.

Palaeomastodon and *Phiomia* are classic intermediate fossils between *Numidotherium* and more advanced proboscideans. They had moderate (but not long) trunks, short upper tusks (but still retain lower tusks), and were intermediate in body size between the pig-sized *Moeritherium* and typical elephants. By the early Oligocene, the Proboscidea had split into two major groups: the true mastodons (family Mammutidae) and the group including gomphotheres, the shovel-tusked mastodonts, the mammoths, and the elephants.

In the early Miocene about 22 Ma, both of these groups made their escape from Africa along with hyraxes and our early primate ancestors. The reason for this has now become clear. Africa and India were once part of the southern supercontinent, Gondwana, which had persisted for more than 600 million years. It began to break up around 100 Ma, and both Africa and India moved northward on a collision course with Eurasia. The great Tethys seaway that once separated these continents was crushed between

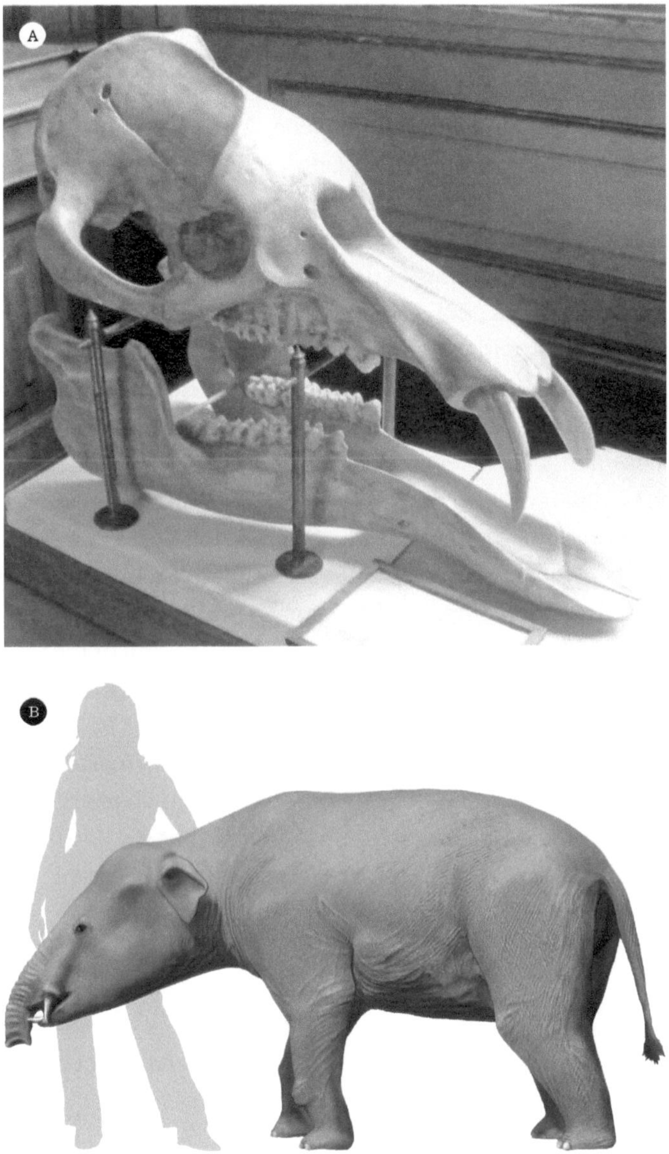

Figure 1.10 ▲

(*A*) Skull of *Palaeomastodon*. (*B*) Reconstruction of *Palaeomastodon*. ([*A*] Courtesy of Wikimedia Commons; [*B*] courtesy of N. Tamura)

the colliding continents. This collision also pushed up great mountain ranges such as the Alps, the Caucasus, the Zagros Mountains of Iran, and the Himalayas into gigantic folds like a wrinkled rug.

Before this collision, during the Eocene, Africa and India were close to Eurasia, but still remained isolated. Consequently, the Tethys seaway was still dominant. So we find many kinds of animals were widespread across its shores, from Africa to East Asia. Africa had still not docked with Asia during the Oligocene, so most of these mammals were unique inhabitants: proboscideans, hyraxes, the weird two-horned arsinoitheres, and anthropoid primates, along with endemic African rodents and artiodactyls. By the end of the Oligocene, however, Africa was so close to Eurasia that mammals could hop across the island chains or walk across dry land between the two continents in this region that is now the Middle East. The Tethys seaway was apparently closed off in the middle, and its western half was about to become the Mediterranean. Africa's isolation as an island continent, with its own peculiar mammals, had ended. From now on its native species would have to compete with Eurasian immigrants.

The proboscideans were probably the most successful of the immigrants from Africa. We find their fossils in the Middle East and Pakistan around 22 Ma, in western Europe and China around 19 Ma, and in North America around 18 Ma. From the middle Miocene on, both the mastodons and the other elephantoids (gomphotheres, mammoths, and elephants) wandered among the continents, reaching South America (but not Australia) by the end of the Pliocene. In chapter 2, we will review the long complex history of the elephantoids.

FOR FURTHER READING

Agusti, J., and M. Anton. *Mammoths, Sabertooths, and Hominids: 65 Million Years of Mammalian Evolution in Europe*. Columbia University Press, 2002.

Dooley, A. C., Jr., E. Scott, J. Green, K. B. Springer, B. S. Dooley, and G. J. Smith. "*Mammut pacificus* sp. nov., a Newly Recognized Species of Mastodon from the Pleistocene of Western North America." *PeerJ* 7 (2019), https://doi.org/10.7717/peerj.6614.

Kurtén, B. *Before the Indians*. Columbia University Press, 1988.

——. *Pleistocene Mammals of Europe*. Columbia University Press, 1968.

Kurtén, B., and E. Anderson. *Pleistocene Mammals of North America*. Columbia University Press, 1980.

Lambert, W. D., and J. Shoshani. "Proboscidea." In *Evolution of Tertiary Mammals of North America: Volume 1, Terrestrial Carnivores, Ungulates, and Ungulate-like Mammals*, ed. C. M. Janis, K. M. Scott, and L. L. Jacobs, 606–621. Cambridge University Press, 1998.

Larramendi, A., and M. Ferretti. *Elephants and Their Fossil Relatives: A 60 Million Year Journey*. Princeton University Press, 2026.

Pardi, M. I., and. L. R. G. DeSantis. "Interpreting Spatially Explicit Variation in Dietary Proxies Through Species Distribution Modeling Reveals Foraging Preferences of Mammoth (*Mammuthus*) and American Mastodon (*Mammut americanum*)." *Frontiers in Ecology and Evolution* 10 (2022), https://doi.org/10.3389/fevo.2022.1064299.

Prothero, D. R. *After the Dinosaurs: The Age of Mammals*. Indiana University Press, 2006.

——. *The Princeton Field Guide to Prehistoric Mammals*. Princeton University Press, 2016.

——. *Vertebrate Evolution: From Origins to Dinosaurs and Beyond*. Taylor & Francis/CRC Press, 2022.

Sanders, W. J. *Evolution and Fossil Record of African Proboscidea*. CRC Press, 2023.

Savage, R. J. G., and M. R. Long. *Mammal Evolution: An Illustrated Guide*. Facts-on-File, 1986.

Semonin, P. *American Monster: How the Nation's First Prehistoric Creature Became a Symbol of National Identity*. NYU Press, 2000.

Shoshani, J., and P. Tassy, eds. *The Proboscidea: Evolution and Palaeoecology of Elephants and Their Relatives*. Oxford University Press, 1996.

Turner, A., and M. Anton. *National Geographic Prehistoric Mammals*. National Geographic Society, 2004.

02 | MAMMOTHS—MONSTERS OF THE ICE AGES

MAMMUTHUS

Faced with a new mutation in an organism, or a fundamental change in his living conditions, the biologist is frequently in no position whatever to predict its future prospects. He has to wait and see. . . . For instance, the hairy mammoth seems to have been an admirable animal, intelligent and well-accoutered. Now that it is extinct, we try to understand why it failed. I doubt that any biologist thinks he could have predicted that failure. Fitness and survival are by nature estimates of past performance.

—GEORGE WALD, "INNOVATION IN BIOLOGY"

WOOLLY WANDERERS

Schumachoff the fisherman had a hard life. He fished for sturgeon in the icy Lena River in northern Siberia, but usually he had a little luck. Then he salvaged his fishing expeditions by collecting the mysterious chunks of ivory that showed up on the banks of the Lena River. During a particular trip in 1799, he proceeded a little further up the river than ever before. As he rounded the bend in the river, he said they came face-to-face with a huge hairy monster standing upright, embedded in pure ice on the cliff face (figure 2.1). It appeared to have just stepped right out of the cliff and frozen in place. Schumachoff was so astonished and awed that he did not approach too closely, and he made several more trips over the years to stare at it and wonder. Finally, he summed up the courage to approach and touch it, but the monster made no signs of eating him up. His superstition and awe overcame by greed, he broke the barrier of ice and chopped out the

Figure 2.1 ▲
Artist's impression of the discovery of the mammoth frozen in the cliff on the banks of the Lena River in Siberia in 1799. The beast was encased in ice but appears to have just stepped out from behind the cliff, startling the fisherman who found it. (From B. A. Tikhomirov, "An Expedition That Never Was: Benkendorf's Expedition to the River Indigirka," *Geographical Journal* 128, no. 4 [1962]: 443–46)

tusks. Soon the wolves and bears had eaten the flesh. Two years later a Russian scientist heard about the wonderful discovery and made a voyage to see it. Although most of it was reduced to a skeleton, the eyes and brain were still in the skull.

As discussed in chapter 1, tusks and bones of the strange beast known as the *mammot* had been discovered all over northern Europe and Siberia since the Middle Ages. Enough bones and frozen hides with hair had been discovered by 1799 that Cuvier and others could distinguish the *mammot* from the "American *incognitum*" (the mastodon). But this frozen mammoth was the first case of any long-extinct beast found intact after thousands of years of burial.

Many people did not believe the accounts, and when the first scientists arrived on the scene, too little was left to prove them. In 1846, the scientific world was stunned again with an even more spectacular find. A young Russian engineer name Benkendorf was surveying the coast at the mouth of the Lena and Indigirka rivers. As he sailed up to Indigirka in a small boat, he discovered a truly remarkable sight. As he wrote to a friend later:

> In 1846 there was uncommon warm weather in the north of Siberia. Already in May unusual rains poured over the moors and bogs, storms shook the Earth, and the streams carried out not only ice to the sea but also large tracts of land, thawed by the masses of warm water fed by the southern rains . . . we steamed on the first favorable day up the Indigirka; there were no thoughts of land. We saw around us only a sea of a brown water, and knew the river by the rushing and roaring of the stream. While we were all quiet, we suddenly heard under our feet a sudden gurgling and stirring, which betrayed the working of the disturbed water. Suddenly our hunter, ever on the lookout, call loudly, and pointed to a singular and shapely object, which rose and sank through the disturbed waters. I had already marked it, but not given it my attention, considering it only driftwood. Now we all hastened to the spot on the bank, had the boats drawn near, and waited until the mysterious thing should again show itself. Our patience was tried but at last a black, horrible, giant-like mass was thrust out of the water and we beheld a colossal elephants head, armed with mighty tusks, with its long truck moving in the water, in an unearthly manner, as though seeking for something lost therein. Breathless with astonishment, I beheld the monster hardly 12 feet from me, with its half-open eyes yet showing the whites. It was still in good preservation.
>
> "Mammoth! A mammoth!" broke out the Tschermomori, and I shouted, "Here, quickly! Chains and ropes. . . ."
>
> We therefore fastened a rope around his neck, threw a chain around his tusks, that were 8 feet long, drove a stake into the ground about 20 feet from the shore, and made chain and rope fast to it . . . the position of the animal was interesting to me; it was standing in the Earth, not lying on its side or back as a dead animal naturally would, indicating this by the manner of his destruction. The soft peat or marshland on which it had stepped thousands of years ago gave way by the weight of the giant, and he sank as he stood on it,

feet foremost, incapable of saving himself, and a severe frost came and turned him into ice, as well as the moor which had buried him; the latter however grew and flourished, every summer renewing itself; possibly the neighboring stream had heaped plants and sand over the dead body. God only knows what causes had worked for the preservation; now however, the stream at once more brought it to the light of day, and I, an ephemera of life compared to this primeval giant, was sent here by heaven just at the right time to welcome him.

You can imagine how I jumped for joy. . . . Picture to yourself an elephant with a body covered with thick fur, around 13 feet in height, and 15 feet in length, with tusks 8 feet long, thick and curvy outward at their end, a stout trunk of 6 feet in length, colossal limbs of 1 foot and a half in thickness, and a tail naked up to the end, which was covered with thick, tufty hair. The animal was fat and well grown; death had overtaken them in the fullness of his powers. His parchment-like, large naked ears lay fearfully turned up over his head; about the shoulders and back he had stiff hair, about a foot in length, like a mane. The long outer hair was deep brown and coarsely rooted. The top of the head looked so wild, it was so penetrated with pitch, that it resembled the rind of an old oak tree. On the side it was cleaner, and under the outer hair there appeared everywhere a wool, very soft, warm, and thick, and of a yellow-brown color. The giant was well protected against the cold. The whole appearance of the animal was fearfully wild and strange. It had not the shape of our present elephants. As compared to our Indian elephants, its head was rough, the braincase low and narrow, but the trunk and mouth are much larger. The teeth were very powerful. Our elephant is an awkward animal, but compared with this mammoth it is an Arabian steed to a coarse ugly dray-horse.

I could not divest myself of a feeling of fear as I approached the head; the broken, widely opened eyes gave the animal appearance of life, as though it might move in a moment and destroy us with a roar. . . . The bad smell the body warned us that it was time to save of it that what we could, and the swelling flood, bade us to hasten. First of all, we cut off the tusks, and sent them to the cutter. Then the people tried to hew the head off, but, notwithstanding their good will, this was slow work. As the belly of the animals was cut open, the intestines rolled out, and then the smell was so dreadful that I could not overcome my nauseousness and was obliged to turn away. But I had the stomach separated and brought on one side. It was well filled, and the contents instructive and well preserved. The principal were of young shoots of the fir and pine; a quantity of young fir cones also, in a chewed state, were mixed with the mass.

Additional frozen mammoths were found in the next century, but the best studied was a Berezovka mammoth (figure 2.2). In the winter of 1900, a Cossack dealer of mammoth ivory bought some tusks from a Lamut tribesman who had chopped them out of a complete frozen animal. It took some time for word to reach scientists, so an expedition to study this find did not depart St. Petersburg until May 1901. By the time they reached it in September, much of the head had been eaten by carnivores during its two years of exposure. Nevertheless, most of the skin, tongue, and internal tissues were well preserved. Although some of the braver scientists tasted the ancient meat, most of it was fed to the sled dogs who suffered no ill effects. The Berezovka mammoth had woolly fur described by Benkendorf and a short tail with hair 10 inches (25 centimeters) long. Apparently it had fallen into some sort of hole or crevasse in the ice, because its death must have been almost instantaneous. It had broken its ribs, shoulder blade, and pelvis, and its viscera were wrenched to one side and filled with clotted blood. Then it was freeze-dried by the permafrost conditions in Siberia. There was still

Figure 2.2 ▲

The Berezovka mammoth found in Siberia in 1901 and now mounted on display in St. Petersburg, Russia. (Courtesy of Wikimedia Commons)

food between his teeth, including buttercups, and its stomach held grasses, but no pinecones or larch needles. It was apparently in good health at the end of the summer feeding season, because it had 3.5 inches (90 millimeters) of fat on his torso. The scientists collected it and brought it back to St. Petersburg, where it has been on display for years.

Other partial mammoth mummies were found over the years, but the most significant find was in 1977. Placer gold miners, strip-mining the thawed soil from the frozen ground in Magadan in eastern Siberia, uncovered the frozen mummy of a baby mammoth. Nicknamed "Dima," it is by far the best-preserved mammoth mummy ever unearthed (figure 2.3). The body had been frozen rapidly with a little decomposition, and it was found and collected rapidly before scavenging and decay could take place. Although most of his hair had fallen off, the preservation of the internal soft tissues is nearly perfect. Dima was truly a baby mammoth, only about a meter high at the shoulder, and based on the stage of tooth eruption, it was

Figure 2.3 ▲
Dima, the baby mammoth mummy found in Siberia in 1977. (Courtesy of Wikimedia Commons)

about four to eight months old. It was emaciated, starving, and completely lacking in body fat when it died, and it suffering from parasites. Except for the colon, the digestive tract was nearly empty. The few plants preserved were mostly detritus of tundra grasses, and dirt was evidently inhaled and ingested as the trapped animal struggled. Dima must have sunken into quicksand during the late summer thaw, struggling for days as it began sinking deeper and starved to death. Because of its small body mass, empty stomach contents, and low body fat, it froze rapidly once it died, resulting in excellent preservation.

The fact that there have been a number of well-preserved freeze-dried mammoths found in Siberia has encouraged scientists to try to extract their DNA and other biomolecules and maybe even clone them. The idea would be to replace the nucleus of an Asian elephant sex cell with that of a mammoth. This clone would then be implanted into a living female Asian elephant, who could give birth to an animal that has been extinct for more than nine thousand years! So far, these efforts have not succeeded because DNA degrades very fast as soon as the animal dies. Its half-life is only about eight hundred years, so even a specimen that is nine thousand years old has very little original DNA left in it. Nonetheless, the possibilities are intriguing and raise ethical questions about whether it is appropriate to bring an extinct animal back to life, and try to give it a good life, since its original habitat has long since vanished. Other efforts with mammoth molecules have been more successful. A number of labs have sequenced the DNA and other molecules of mummified mammoth tissues, including blood cells, tissue proteins, and reactions to blood serum. All of these studies show that woolly mammoths were closely related to the Asian elephant, as was long suggested by the fossil record. Mastodon tissues are much less similar to the living elephant they are to mammoths, as would be expected because mastodons are only distantly related.

A number of other less complete mammoth mummies have been found in Alaska and Siberia. Along with cave paintings by prehistoric humans, they give us the most complete picture possible for any long-extinct species. Most fossil mammals must be reconstructed from just their bones; their hair and skin color are based on complete guesswork. Not so for these mummified Ice Age animals. The woolly mammoth, for instance, was a smaller species and the most specialized of all the mammoths. It was only about 9 feet (2.8 meters) at the shoulder, covered long black hair with a woolly undercoat. Underneath that was an insulating layer of fat around 3 inches (80 millimeters) thick in a well-fed animal. Woolly mammoths had a high domed head, a strongly humped shoulder, a sloping back, and a short tail with very long hairs. The ears are small and round to reduce heat loss, and contrast with African elephant ears, which are unusually large to aid heat loss. The trunk was short with two "fingers" at the tip for grasping bunches of grass and had broad flaring flanges of flesh on the side for scooping up snow to drink. The long tusks curved backward into a semicircle, and the lower edges of the tusks show evidence of scraping. Apparently, their tusks were used to scrape away snow to find vegetation as many modern tundra animals still do today (figure 2.4).

Analysis of the stomach contents show that the woolly mammoth was an opportunistic steppe grazer. During the summer it ate a large percentage of grasses and tundra legumes (including buttercups). In the winter most of its diet was leaves, twigs, and bark. For this highly abrasive diet, the woolly mammoth has the largest and most complex molars of any proboscidean, with many more enamel ridges and the highest crown height of all mammoth molars.

Figure 2.4 ▲

Reconstruction of the woolly mammoth using its tusks to scrape away snow to find food in the winter. (Art by Z. Burian, courtesy of Wikimedia Commons)

Although the woolly mammoth (*Mammuthus primigenius*) is most familiar to us because of the many specimens and familiar drawings of them, it was not typical of mammoths. As far as we know, most mammoth species did not have the long hair of the woolly mammoth; they were thinly furred or bare-skinned, more like living elephants. Whether woolly or not, all mammoths can be distinguished from other elephants by the high, foreshortened skull and concave forehead and highly complex, narrow molars. Most mammoth tusks curved backward and inward in adults. Some had a spiral twist, and their points may even have crossed in front of the head.

The genus *Mammuthus*, like most extinct Proboscidea, was once a mess of confusing names and invalid species. In Henry Fairfield Osborn's 1936 Proboscidea monograph, for example, the early mammoths were called *Archidiskodon*, the intermediate mammoths *Parelephas*, and only the late mammoths were *Mammuthus*. Vince Maglio's 1973 classification had reduced 16 invalid species in three genera down to just one genus with five species. *Mammuthus* first arose in Africa in the early Pliocene, along with the ancestors of living African and Asian elephants. From there, it spread to North Africa and Europe in the late Pliocene, becoming a common species: *Mammuthus meridionalis*, the "southern mammoth." In the middle Pleistocene, this ancestor evolved into two different lineages: the woolly mammoth, which dominated Siberia and eventually invaded North America, and the descendants of the earlier invasion of North America, the Columbian mammoth.

About 1.6 Ma in the early Pleistocene, the southern mammoth migrated across the Bering land bridge into North America. Here it was able to spread out over the temperate and subtropical grasslands without competition from elephants, as it had faced in the Old World. (Mastodons were already here, but they were woodland browsers and did not compete much with mammoths.) By the middle Pleistocene, the southern mammoth had evolved into the Columbian mammoth (also known as the Imperial mammoth or Jefferson's mammoth). It was the largest of all the mammoths, reaching 13 feet (4 meters) at the shoulder. It was widespread all over North America in the middle of the Pleistocene, south of the ice-margin areas that supported woolly mammoths. The Columbian mammoth is very well known from La Brea tar pits in Los Angeles. In the late Pleistocene, the Columbian mammoth became slightly smaller with more complex teeth. This animal was a highly specialized plains grazer, with molars suitable to abrasive grasses. The late Pleistocene also saw the migration of woolly mammoths from their Siberian homeland into Canada and Alaska, and eventually down to the ice-margin areas in the northern United States.

Because they are large and spectacular, mammoth bones have been found in Ice Age deposits all over North America. Some of the most impressive and well-known Pleistocene sites are dominated by mammoths. There are river deposits in Alaska with the bones of hundreds of individual mammoths, and river deposits and ancient springs and ponds all over the west with dozens of individuals. One of the most spectacular of the sites was found near Hot Springs, South Dakota, in 1975. A bulldozer excavating for housing development on the south edge of town struck mammoth bones, and soon the importance of the site became apparent. More than 61 mammoths (the count increasing each year) were discovered in a small area less than 60 meters across (figure 2.5). The locality turned out to be

Figure 2.5 ▲

A portion of the many skeletons of Columbian mammoths at the Mammoth Site of Hot Springs, South Dakota. (Photo by the author)

an ancient pond deposit, or possibly a sinkhole, caused by the collapse of an underground cavern. Mammoths waded in to drink but could not climb out of the steep muddy banks and eventually starved and drowned. Most bones are found within 20 feet (6 meters) of the sinkhole bank, where they had been trying to climb out across the bank of slippery red shale. Many were nearly completely articulated when they were found, including their very thin, fragile bones of the throat (the hyoids) that are rarely found in fossil organisms. Other individuals were disarticulated by the trampling of the other trapped mammoths, or by the circulating water in the natural hot spring.

All of the individuals were Columbian mammoths, dated around 26,000 years ago, or near the peak of the last glacial maximum. Most are young adult or fully mature males, and there were almost no juveniles. The mammoth fossils are found in many different layers of the deposit. This indicates that most were trapped as isolated individuals, wandering in and dying one at the time, over a long period of time, rather than a single herd being killed catastrophically. This site is so amazing that it has been excavated every summer since 1975, and the proud residents of Hot Springs raised the money for a huge building to house continued excavation. It is now a very popular tourist attraction as visually striking and paleontologically significant as a famous wall of dinosaur bones at Dinosaur National Monument.

PYGMY GIANTS

We think of mammoths as the giants of the Ice Ages, but Pleistocene proboscideans also underwent multiple instances of dwarfing. When mammals reach isolated islands where the ecology is entirely different, they often evolve into new species with unique adaptations. It is common for large mammals such as elephants and hippos to become dwarfed. On the Channel Islands just south of Santa Barbara, California, there were mammoths only 8 feet (4.4 meters) high as a shoulder (figure 2.6A). In Malta, Crete, and Sicily, cave deposits yield bones of elephants that became progressively more dwarfed until they're only 3 feet (1 meter) high at the shoulder (figure 2.6B). There were also dwarfed elephants on some of the islands of Southeast Asia. This is a common trend since some Mediterranean islands and Madagascar also had dwarf hippopotamuses, and during the Miocene, there were dwarfed rhinoceroses in North America. In contrast,

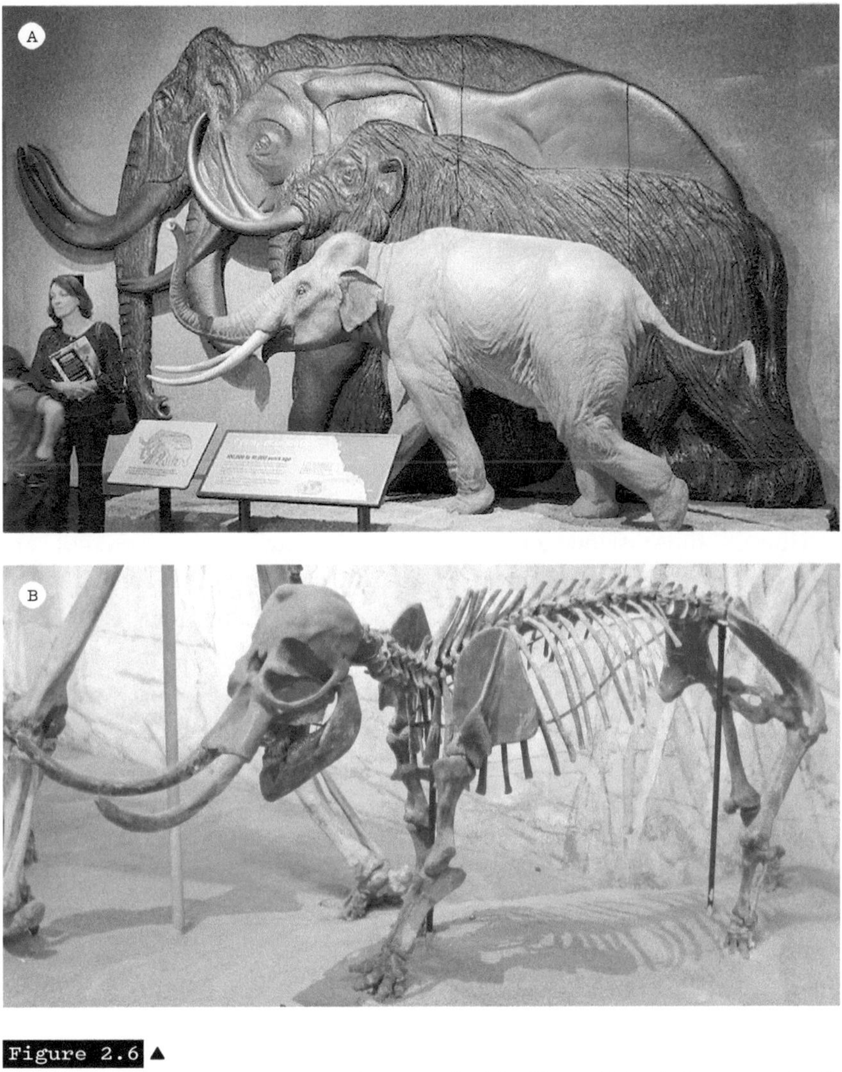

Figure 2.6 ▲
(*A*) Comparison of the size of the dwarf mammoth of the Channel Islands (*foreground*) with extinct Columbian mammoths and modern elephants (*background*). (*B*) The skeleton of the pygmy elephant of Crete, *Palaeoloxodon falconeri* is only 1 meter tall at the shoulder. ([*A*] Photo by the author; [*B*] courtesy of Wikimedia Commons)

small mammals on islands tend to get larger. There is an extinct island hedgehog that is almost 3 feet (1 meter) long.

Why do animals change body size when they reach islands? Several reasons have been suggested. For big grazing animals such as elephants, a large area of open grassland is necessary. Most islands are much smaller and have a limited area for grasslands, with a greater mixture of plants. Island dwarfs all seem to have reduced their needs for large amounts of coarse, poor-quality grass and shifted to browsing smaller amounts of high-quality leaves. We see something similar happening today, with the forest-browsing subspecies of African elephant, *Loxodonta africana cyclotis*, which is much smaller than its grazing plains elephant counterpart. The pygmy hippo is also a forest browser, rather than a grazer, like the common hippo. In addition, most islands do not have many large predators such as those found on the mainland, so there is no need for the protection of large body size. Large body size is costly in terms of energy needs and time for growth. By speeding up growth and reaching reproductive maturity at a smaller body size, dwarf elephants and mammoths reached a size suitable for their habitat and diet without excess energy devoted to growth.

How did those island elephants get there? Certainly, they were not carried in canoes. Although some of these islands had direct land connections to the mainland when the sea level was much lower during the peak glacial stages of the Ice Ages, some did not. However, it turns out the elephants are excellent swimmers. Elephants have frequently been seen swimming very wide rivers, and in 1856 one elephant swam to safety from a sinking boat 30 miles offshore. During lowstands of sea level, the distance between the California mainland and the Channel Islands was only 4 miles (6.5 kilometers) at the narrowest point on the continental shelf. Water-loving elephants could smell the vegetation and see the dark shape of the island on the horizon and did not find the trip particularly difficult, although they probably didn't do it very often. Similar scenarios could apply to the elephants of Malta and Sicily, although the distances are greater.

THE MYSTERY OF THE MISSING MAMMOTHS

During the peak of the last glaciation, 20,000–18,000 years ago, mammoths roamed all over the Northern Hemisphere. Columbian mammoths dominated the temperate regions of North America south of the ice sheets, and the ice-free regions of Siberia, Alaska, and northwestern Canada were a habitat that paleontologist Dale Guthrie called the "mammoth steppe." It was a relatively dry, cold, windy region, as much of the steppes of high Central Asian plateaus are today. Nevertheless, it was very fertile, with an enormous variety of grasses during the long growing season when the summer sun never sets. Consequently, there was a rich fauna of woolly mammoth, large steppe bison, steppe horses, wild asses, woolly rhinos, saiga envelopes, ibex, reindeer, camels, muskoxen, giant deer, elk, reindeer, lions, giant bears, sabertoothed cats, hyaenas, wolves, and cheetahs.

Likewise, the La Brea tar pits in Los Angeles show that forty thousand years ago the region was temperate and rich in wildlife. These included Columbian mammoths, mastodons, horses, camels, bison, pronghorns, three kinds of ground sloths, and many other herbivores. These were killed or scavenged by sabertoothed cats, dire wolves, giant lions, short-faced bear, and a variety of predatory and scavenging birds. Simpler abundant faunas of large mammals, or "megafauna," comparable to those seen in the East African savanna today are found in many other localities throughout the world at the end of the last glacial episode. Nearly all this megafauna disappeared between thirteen thousand and nine thousand years ago. Today, only a pitiful remnant of a few survivors, such bison and moose and elk in North America, remain of the community of large herbivores that once roamed the Americas and Eurasia and Africa.

So what caused this great mass extinction of the megafauna (mammals weighing at least 100 pounds or about 40 kilograms) at the end of the last Ice Age? Scientists have come up with a number of possible explanations, but there's not a single simple explanation yet that is universally accepted by scientists. Some explanations have included a pandemic of extremely virulent diseases infecting all the large mammals—but no such disease exists that would infect so many different groups of animals, and only those of large body sizes. In addition, there is no way to test this "hyperdisease" hypothesis because there would be no evidence in the bones or anywhere else. Another explanation is the claim of an extraterrestrial impact in the Carolina Bays region of the United States. However, nearly all the supposed "evidence" of this alleged impact has been debunked since 2011. Even if such an impact occurred, it would not explain the extinctions in South America or Australia.

The two main explanations still are taken seriously by paleontologists are the possible effects of climate at the end of the Pleistocene or overhunting by humans as they invaded the Americas and Australia. This second hypothesis is often called the "overkill" model because it is assumed that when sophisticated human hunters first arrived in the New World, none of their prey had defensive adaptations to avoid them and survive. We do know for a fact that the arrival of humans (and their pests, such as rats, plus their domesticated dogs, cats, sheep, pigs, and goats) has caused major extinctions of native species whenever they invade small islands, so there is some basis for this idea.

The main advocate of the "overkill" model was the late Paul Martin of the University of Arizona. From the late 1960s through the 1990s, he argued that not only were humans responsible for all the places with a megafaunal extinction event, but that they did so in a "blitzkrieg" as they swept across a continent after their first arrival. Martin published papers suggesting that as soon as humans arrived in North America, animals would go extinct in a wave from north to south as humans spread southward from ice-free corridor between the ice sheets that covered Alaska and Canada, around thirteen thousand years ago. At that time, there were almost no good radiocarbon dates for the last appearance of most megafaunal species, and those that were known seemed to coincide with the arrival of people with Clovis points, which were produced by sophisticated hunters.

Mammoths are particularly well known as prey of these early hunters. A number of sites have been found all over North America, many with Clovis projectile points embedded between their bones, and butchering marks on the bones. At Lehner Ranch, near Hereford, Arizona, are the remains of at least eight mammoths killed near an ancient watering hole. Thirteen projectile points were found among the bones, and a butchering site was found at a nearby ancient sandbar. Lebec Lake, near Lubbock, Texas, has a mammoth kill site with Clovis points dated around 12,650 years ago and a bison kill site at a higher level which is dated 9,883 years ago. Clearly, Paleoindians hunted mammoths, and there's clear evidence they hunted mastodons as well (the Kimmswick site mentioned in chapter 1), as well as horses, camel, and bison.

However, there are lots of problems with the overkill model, especially the idea that it was a blitzkrieg in a few thousand years. For example, 32 other extinct species of large mammals, including ground sloths, have never been found with evidence of human hunting. If a human blitzkrieg occurred, we should have more evidence of hunting among the rest of the megafauna. In addition, animals that clearly were hunted, especially bison, elk, and deer, survived despite the alleged blitzkrieg of Paleoindians.

The most fatal blow to the blitzkrieg version of the "overkill" model has been the wave of new dates on the earliest evidence of human occupation and the last appearance of megafauna. For the blitzkrieg model to be viable, these events should occur at virtually the same time, or no more than about a thousand years apart. But the last appearance of many of the megafauna keeps getting pushed later and later as new dates are analyzed. More fatal to the blitzkrieg model, the evidence of human habitation keeps getting pushed earlier and earlier. For a long time, there were sites in North America, such as the Meadowcroft Rock Shelter in Pennsylvania, dated to nineteen thousand years ago, and the Monte Verde site in southern Chile was even older, at least eighteen thousand years old, and possibly thirty thousand years old! Contrary to Martin's "wave of humans" model going from north to south, it appears that humans reached the southern tip of South America very early, probably using canoes to follow the coast, so they were not marching in a "human wave" across the middle of the continent when the ice-free corridor in Alberta opened.

Year after year, the evidence mounts for even earlier appearance of humans. In 2022, human footprints fossilized in lakebeds near White Sands, New Mexico, were found alongside footprints of mammoths and ground sloths that were dated at twenty-three thousand years ago. In 2023, the Hartley mammoth butchery site with stone tools on the border between Colorado and New Mexico was dated at thirty-seven thousand years ago. A number of sites in South America are also dated over thirty thousand years ago. So if humans were responsible for the extinction of the megafauna, it was certainly no blitzkrieg because the arrival of humans in the Americas was at least twenty-five thousand years before most of the megafaunal extinctions.

Many other critics of the overkill hypothesis favorite climate change as the primary cause of extinction. They point out that at the beginning of the current interglacial, around thirteen thousand to ten thousand years ago, there was an extreme climatic and vegetational change, so naturally large herbivores and their predators were the most severely affected. There is abundant evidence from the pollen record for this dramatic vegetational change and it corresponds quite well with some of the megafaunal extinctions. Critics, however, point out that throughout the Ice Ages there were many interglacial periods before the present one, and they did not result in mass extinctions; only the recent interglacial associated with human immigration coincided with extinctions.

In answer to this, many of the advocates of climate-induced extinction point out that the climate events of the last glacial-interglacial transition are different from any previous glacial-interglacial transition. In particular, there was an interval between 12,900 years ago and 11,700 years ago called the Younger Dryas. This event began with a rapid cooling and glaciation 12,900 years ago, with a return to a full glacial in just a decade. Such an extremely rapid beginning of a full glacial episode is not seen in any previous interval, suggesting that this is an unusual climate event.

Other evidence also suggests that the current interglacial of the last eleven thousand years was unlike any other that had preceded it. Climate data show that it was much colder and dryer than had ever occurred before, with a great expansion of deserts. The pollen and animal record showed that plants and animals that now live apart once lived together. Climate advocates suggest that prior to twelve thousand years ago there was a greater mosaic of habitats with a wide variety of animals overlapping in ranges. In contrast, today we have a few monotonous habits that extend over long distances. Many animals living today have been driven out of certain areas and are now restricted to narrow niches, so they no longer overlap with other animals that once shared their habitat.

This is particularly true of the "mammoth steppe" discussed previously. Although these Arctic grasslands were cold and relatively dry, they still managed to support a great variety of edible grasses. From examining food particles embedded in the crevices of their teeth, we know that each large herbivore had a slightly different diet. In contrast, today's tundra has only a small variety of plants, and many of these new plant arrivals are full of toxins that make them inedible. Thus it can support only a few muskoxen and caribou, not the great variety of megaherbivores once found on the "mammoth steppe."

If the problem is with the quality of vegetation, we would expect that only the most efficient herbivores would survive. And, indeed, this seems to be true. The main survivors of the mass extinction event were cud-chewing ruminants including bison, pronghorns, deer, and elk. In contrast, herbivores with relatively inefficient hindgut fermentation, such as mammoths, horses, rhinos, and sloths, were the main victims of the extinction.

However, there is the fact that human hunters are closely associated with extinction in many parts of the Americas. They clearly did not come as a blitzkrieg wave overwhelming naïve animals unfamiliar to hunters, as Martin envisioned. Instead, it appears that humans might have been contributors to the extinction, putting hunting pressure on faunas already stressed by climate and vegetational change. In short, the media and some scientists like to give a simplistic answer such as "humans did it, end of story." But like most problems in science, the answer is not simple or neat or reducible to a single sound bite. Instead, it is much better summarized as "it's complicated."

FOR FURTHER READING

Agusti, J., and M. Anton. *Mammoths, Sabertooths, and Hominids: 65 Million Years of Mammalian Evolution in Europe*. Columbia University Press, 2002.

Cohen, C. *The Fate of the Mammoth: Fossils, Myth, and History*. University of Chicago Press, 2002.

Kurtén, B. *Before the Indians*. Columbia University Press, 1988.

——. *Pleistocene Mammals of Europe*. Columbia University Press, 1968.

Kurtén, B., and E. Anderson. *Pleistocene Mammals of North America*. Columbia University Press, 1980.

Lambert, W. D., and J. Shoshani. "Proboscidea." In *Evolution of Tertiary Mammals of North America: Volume 1, Terrestrial Carnivores, Ungulates, and Ungulate-like Mammals*, ed. C. M. Janis, K. M. Scott, and L. L. Jacobs. Cambridge University Press, 1998.

Lange, I. M. *Ice Age Mammals of North America: A Guide to the Big, the Hairy, and the Bizarre*. Mountain Press, 2017.

Larramendi, A., and M. Ferretti. *Elephants and Their Fossil Relatives: A 60 Million Year Journey*. Princeton University Press, 2026.

Lister, A., and P. Bahn. *Mammoths*. Macmillan, 1994.

Pardi, M. I., and L. R. G. DeSantis. "Interpreting Spatially Explicit Variation in Dietary Proxies Through Species Distribution Modeling Reveals Foraging Preferences of Mammoth (*Mammuthus*) and American Mastodon (*Mammut americanum*)." *Frontiers in Ecology and Evolution* 10 (2022). https://doi.org/10.3389/fevo.2022.1064299.

Prothero, D. R. *The Princeton Field Guide to Prehistoric Mammals*. Princeton University Press, 2016.

——. *Vertebrate Evolution: From Origins to Dinosaurs and Beyond*. Taylor & Francis/CRC Press, 2022.

Sanders, W. J. *Evolution and Fossil Record of African Proboscidea*. CRC Press, 2023.

Savage, R. J. G., and M. R. Long. *Mammal Evolution: An Illustrated Guide*. Facts-on-File, 1986.

Shoshani, J., and P. Tassy, eds. *The Proboscidea: Evolution and Palaeoecology of Elephants and Their Relatives*. Oxford University Press, 1996.

Tikhomirov, B. A. "An Expedition That Never Was: Benkendorf's Expedition to the River Indigirka," *Geographical Journal* 128, no. 4 (1962): 443–46.

Turner, A., and M. Anton. *National Geographic Prehistoric Mammals*. National Geographic Society, 2004.

03 | JEFFERSON'S "LION"—GIANT GROUND SLOTHS

MEGATHERIUM

My absolute favourite piece of information is the fact that young sloths are so inept that they frequently grab their own arms and legs instead of tree limbs, and fall out of trees.

—DOUGLAS ADAMS, *THE SALMON OF DOUBT* (2002)

THE "GREAT AMERICAN BEAST"

As discussed in chapters 1 and 2, teeth and bones of mammoths reached scholars in western Europe during the Middle Ages, and when mastodon bones and teeth were brought over from North America in the 1740s, they caused a sensation with the different learned men trying to figure out what they were. In both cases, it wasn't until 1799 that Baron Georges Cuvier correctly recognized that they were proboscideans: related to elephants but of a different kind that was now extinct.

A third very early discovery came from South America. In 1787, enormous fossil bones were found in the banks of the Lujan River in Argentina by Manuel de Torres, a Dominican friar. Torres described the bones as a "wonder and providence of the Lord." On the orders of the then Viceroy of la Plata, Nicholas Cristobal de Campo, the specimen was moved to Buenos Aires, the provincial capital. There the skeleton was drawn for the first time by José Custodio Sáa y Faria in a sway-backed quadrupedal posture (figure 3.1A), although what kind of animal the skeleton came from was unknown. Campo asked the local Native tribal leaders to ask if they had heard of the animal.

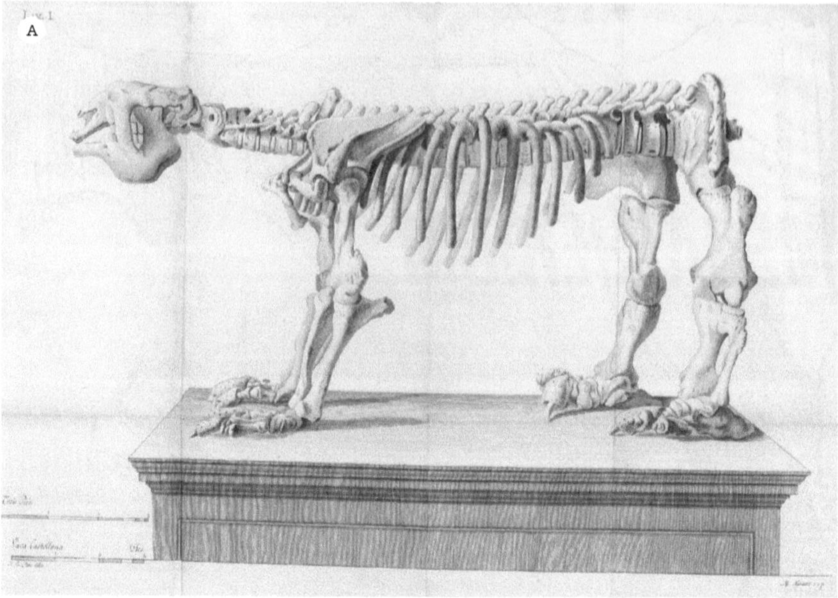

Figure 3.1 ▲ ▶

(*A*) Cuvier's original illustration of *Megatherium*, based on drawings by Bru.

The skeleton was then shipped by Campo to the Royal Cabinet of Natural History of Madrid, which had been founded a decade prior. It arrived in seven crates, which had been unpacked by late 1788. The cabinet's main taxidermist Juan Bautista Bru had the specimen mounted for public exhibition, and it remains today at the National Museum of Natural Sciences in Madrid in its original sway-backed mount (figure 3.1B). In 1796 Bru and engineer Joseph Garriga published a scientific description of the skeleton, with engravings by Manuel Navarro. It was still in press in 1795, when preliminary prints of the paper were obtained by French diplomat Philippe-Rose Roume (who was in Madrid at the time). He sent them to the Musée National d'histoire Naturelle in Paris, France, where they finally reached Cuvier.

Cuvier never traveled to Madrid to see the specimen, but instead relied entirely on Navarro's engravings to describe and analyze the specimen. Using his brilliant talents as a comparative anatomist, he could see from the skull, the peculiar teeth made of pegs of dentin with no enamel coating, and from the shoulder bones that it was a gigantic sloth, even though the limbs and claws were more like those of digging animals such as anteaters and armadillos. In any case it was clearly related to all of them in what Linnaeus had called

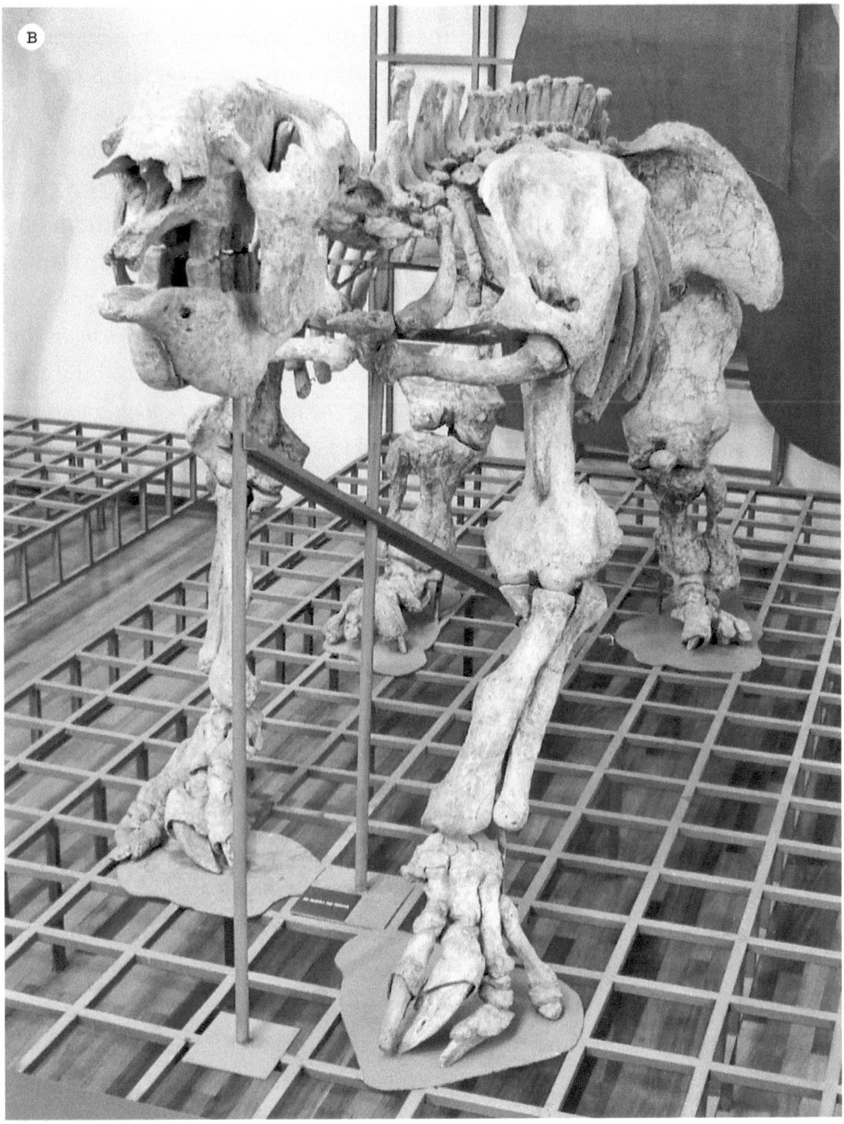

Figure 3.1 ▲

(*continued*) (*B*) The original skeleton is still on display in Madrid with the original incorrectly mounted posture. (Courtesy of Wikimedia Commons)

the "Edentata" or edentates (Greek for "toothless," although only anteaters are toothless among the edentates), a group that is today called the Xenarthra (because Linnaeus included pangolins in his order Edentata; we now realize pangolins are not related to sloths or anteaters or armadillos at all). Scooping the Spaniards in 1796 before they could finish full publication of their work, Cuvier published a paper naming the species *Megatherium americanum* (literally "Great American beast"). This was the first fossil mammal to be given both a genus and species name, because the mastodon and mammoth had not been formally named yet. Cuvier's name has been a bit controversial because he didn't fully describe it in 1796, but he did so in a later paper in 1804, and then redescribed it in his 1812 book *Recherches sur les ossemens fossiles de quadrupèdes.* Based on the limb proportions, Cuvier pointed out that *Megatherium* certainly didn't crawl like living sloths, and obviously it was too large to hang from trees. Instead, he pointed to the shoulder girdle and claws and suggested that it could rear up on its hind legs and tail to reach branches—all essentially ideas consistent with our modern view of how it moved.

Since the days of Cuvier, a lot more has been learned about *Megatherium.* Multiple species have been named in South America. Along with *Eremotherium*, which also reached North America, *Megatherium* was the largest of the ground sloths, weighing about 4 long tons (4 metric tonnes), as much as an Asian elephant. Its body was 20 feet (6 meters) long, so it could easily reach high into the tree branches for leaves. It had a prehensile upper lip for grasping and stripping leaves, and a long retractile tongue for grasping branches as well. The front of the lower jaw has a toothless "drool spout," where the tongue could slide in and out. Its simple peg-like teeth were composed only of prisms of soft dentin with no enamel coating them, forming a crude interlocking mechanism that allowed them to grind these enamel prisms into cross-crests, which were self-sharpening with wear. The roots of these teeth never closed up (what are known as hypselodont teeth), so they were ever-growing and never ran out of more tooth as they wore down.

In contrast to the sway-backed posture of the first mount, large ground sloths had a strong stable posture in both the quadrupedal and bipedal positions (figure 3.2). The Madrid reconstruction had their hand and foot claws pointed forward and down, which would have been awkward to walk with and would wear down the points of the claws. Instead, we now know that they knuckle-walked with their claws folded in on their hands, while their ankles permanently rolled to the side so the soles of their feet point inward, and the claws lie sideways on the ground.

Figure 3.2 ▲

Mounted skeleton of *Megatherium* in the Natural History Museum in London. (Photo by the author)

JEFFERSON'S "GREAT CLAW"

Many Americans know that Thomas Jefferson was the primary author of the Declaration of Independence and a major contributor to the Constitution, our first Secretary of State, then Vice President, and finally our third President. They may know of his travels to the court of Louis XVI to secure French support for the American Revolution, or of his role in the Louisiana Purchase that doubled the size of the United States, or sending Lewis and Clark to explore that country, or of his founding of the University of Virginia.

What most Americans do not know was that Thomas Jefferson was also our first American paleontologist. He was a true Renaissance man who dabbled in science and natural history and invented numerous small devices. While he was still vice president under President John Adams in 1796, Jefferson received some fossilized bones from a cave in what is now West Virginia. They were mostly foot bones, but they had enormous claws on them (figure 3.3). Naturally, Jefferson thought such huge claws belonged

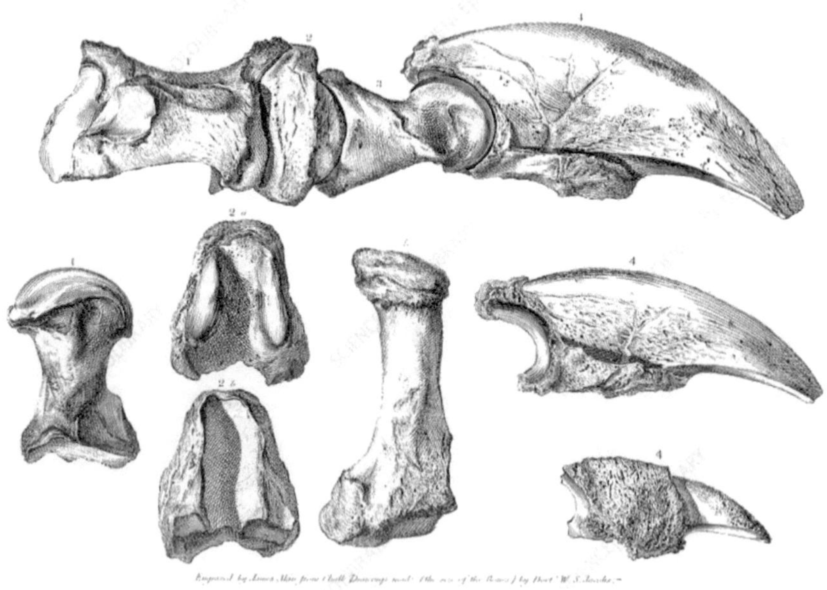

Figure 3.3 ▲
Jefferson's fossil foot bones and claws of *Megalonyx*. (Courtesy of Wikimedia Commons)

to a large predator. In a presentation in front of the American Philosophical Society, he named the creature *Megalonyx* ("giant claw") and argued that it belonged to a giant lion. In addition, most scholars at the time did not believe that God would allow any of his creations to go extinct. As Jefferson wrote in 1797,

> The bones exist: therefore the animal has existed. The movements of nature are in a never-ending circle. The animal species which has once been put into a train of motion, is probably still moving in that train. For if one link in nature's chain might be lost, another and another might be lost, till this whole system of things should vanish by piece-meal. . . . If this animal had once existed, it is probable on this general view of the movement of nature that it still exists.[1]

He was convinced that these strange animals were still living out in the unexplored Northwest. As he wrote in 1797,

> It may be asked why I [list] the mammoth as if it still existed? I ask in return, why should I omit it, as if it did not exist? Such is the economy of nature, that no instance can be produced of her having permitted any one race of her animals to become extinct; of her having formed any link in her great work so weak as to be broken. To add to this, the traditional testimony of the Indians that this animal still exists in the northern and western parts of America, would be adding the light of a taper to that of the meridian sun.[2]

When delays prevented Lewis and Clark from leaving on their expedition to the great Northwest until 1804, President Jefferson instructed them to go to Big Bone Lick (see chapter 1), a famous bone bed in Kentucky full of Ice Age mammals, and collect some more of the mysterious beast. He instructed Lewis and Clark to be on the lookout for a gigantic lion in the American West. They turned out to be claws of the extinct ground sloth now known as *Megalonyx jeffersoni*, not those of a lion.

Thus, by the time Darwin's fossils from the *Beagle* voyage were identified by Richard Owen in 1836 and later years, *Megalonyx* was the name given to any medium-sized ground sloths smaller than *Megatherium*. A large *Megalonyx* weighed about (2,200 pounds (1,000 kilograms), and was about 8–10 feet (2.5–3 meters) in length (figure 3.4), about half as big as *Megatherium*

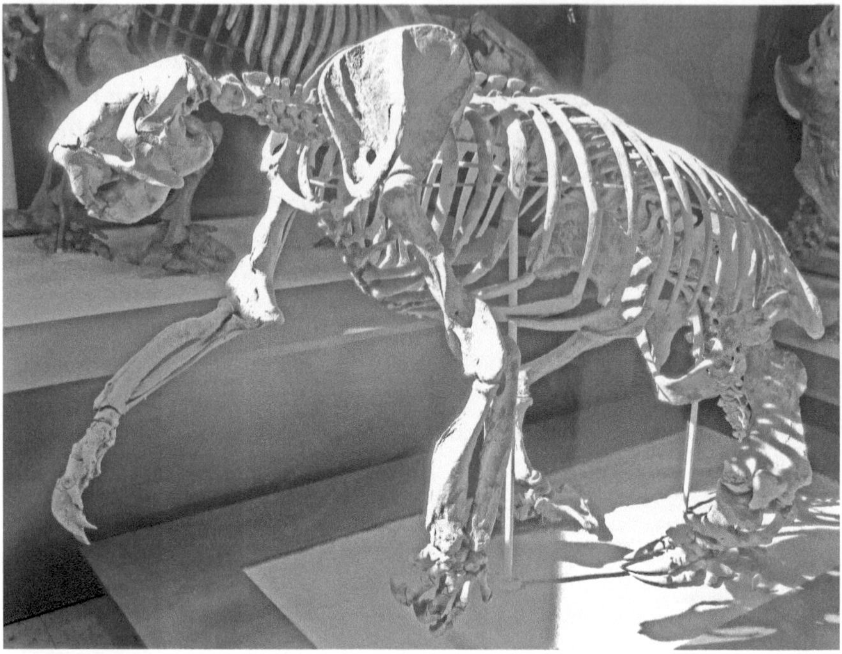

Figure 3.4 ▲
The complete skeleton of *Megalonyx jeffersoni*, on display at the American Museum of Natural History in New York. (Photo by the author)

(but still towering over a human). Since Jefferson's discovery, *Megalonyx* has been found in many Ice Age sites all over North America, including many caves in the eastern United States. For that reason, *Megalonyx* is the official state fossil of West Virginia. It is also common in the western United States in localities such as the La Brea Tar Pits in Los Angeles, and found in localities ranging from Alaska to Central America. However, it turns out that *Megalonyx* was not actually known from South America. Later scientists determined that Owen's identification of *Megalonyx* in Darwin's collections belonged to a similar-sized sloth, *Mylodon*.

DARWIN'S DISCOVERIES

Charles Darwin was a medical school dropout with no real direction in his life until he learned from Cambridge mentor Professor Henslow that there was an opening for a "gentleman companion" on the Royal Navy survey ship H.M.S. *Beagle*, setting sail for South America in the winter of 1831. After much resistance from his father, the twenty-two--year-old Darwin boarded the vessel in Portsmouth, and by early 1832 he was in Argentina and Brazil. The *Beagle's* mission was to generate nautical charts of the Argentinian and Brazilian coast for the Royal Navy, so Charles often went ashore and collected numerous fossils while the ship sailed back and forth, focused on its main mission. On August 24, 1832, Darwin found a locality on the Rio de la Plata called Punta Alta that was rich in the bones of Ice Age fossils. He listed the following among his discoveries (with their names given by Richard Owen who described them for Darwin when he returned):

> First, parts of three heads and other bones of the *megatherium*, the huge dimensions of which are expressed by its name. Secondly, the megalonyx, a great allied animal. Thirdly, the scelidotherium, also an allied animal, of which I obtained a nearly perfect skeleton. It must have been as large as a rhinoceros: in the structure of its head it comes nearest to the Cape anteater, but in some other respects it approaches to the armadillos. Fourthly, the Mylodon Darwinii, a closely related genus of little inferior size. Fifthly, another gigantic edental [mammals that include sloths, armadillos, and anteaters] quadruped. . . .[3]

As Darwin wrote in *The Voyage of the Beagle*:

> The great size of the bones of the *Megatheroid* animals, including the Megatherium, Megalonyx, Scelidotherium, and Mylodon, is truly wonderful. The habits of life of these animals were a complete puzzle to naturalists, until Professor Owen solved the problem with remarkable ingenuity. The teeth indicate, by their simple structure, that these *Megatheroid* animals lived on vegetable food, and probably on the leaves and small twigs of trees; their ponderous forms and great strong curved claws seem so little adapted for locomotion, that some eminent naturalists have actually believed that, like the sloths, to which they are intimately related, they subsisted by climbing back downwards on trees, and feeding on the leaves. It was a bold, not to say preposterous, idea to conceive even antediluvian trees, with branches strong enough to bear animals as large as elephants. Professor Owen, with far more probability, believes that, instead of climbing on the trees, they pulled the

> branches down to them, and tore up the smaller ones by the roots, and so fed on the leaves. The colossal breadth and weight of their hinder quarters, which can hardly be imagined without having been seen, become, on this view, of obvious service, instead of being an encumbrance: their apparent clumsiness disappears. With their great tails and their huge heels firmly fixed like a tripod on the ground, they could freely exert the full force of their most powerful arms and great claws. Strongly rooted, indeed, must that tree have been, which could have resisted such force! The *Mylodon*, moreover, was furnished with a long extensile tongue like that of the giraffe, which, by one of those beautiful provisions of nature, thus reaches with the aid of its long neck its leafy food. I may remark, that in Abyssinia the elephant, according to Bruce, when it cannot reach with its proboscis the branches, deeply scores with its tusks the trunk of the tree, up and down and all round, till it is sufficiently weakened to be broken down.[4]

The immense size of *Megatherium* made it a popular creature in the imagination of Europeans in the early 1800s, as one of the first of the great prehistoric creatures to be discovered (long before dinosaurs or giant marine reptiles were known). In fact, several museums displayed these incredible skeletons to draw big crowds. By the 1830s and 1840s, however, the discovery of dinosaurs and giant marine reptiles captured the imagination of the public because they were not only huge but also fearsome reptiles, and *Megatherium* tended to be pushed aside in the public eye.

A BRAZILIAN DANISH

Another key figure in sloth paleontology was the Danish naturalist Peter Wilhelm Lund, often known as "the father of Brazilian paleontology." Born in 1801, Lund came from a wealthy family in Copenhagen, and originally (like Darwin) was supposed to pursue a career in medicine. The death of his father changed those plans, so he ended up studying natural history at the University of Copenhagen, where he wrote two prize-winning dissertations (one of which was published in German and won him international recognition).

However, he was suffering from a mild case of tuberculosis, so to avoid the smoky dank cold air of Denmark he emigrated to tropical climates of Brazil in the 1825, where he became an accomplished collector of all the exotic plants, birds, and insects around Rio de Janeiro. In 1829, Lund returned to Europe, earning his doctorate at the University of Kiel, and then traveled widely in Italy and France, eventually spending time in Paris learning from Cuvier himself.

By 1832, he was back in Brazil, where he spent the rest of his life. He and some associates started a program of collecting fossil bones from many different local caves, especially near the town of Lagoa Santa (in the Minas Gerais province, north of the modern city of Belo Horizonte) where they found huge deposits of fossil bones (more than twenty thousand specimens combined from several caves). Lund spent the rest of his life working in these caves and describing and publishing the bones he found. These included numerous bones of the ground sloths *Nothrotherium, Catonyx* and others. Lund first began publishing these finds in 1832, just as Darwin was sailing off the coast of Argentina. Lund was also the first to discover and describe the saber-toothed cat *Smilodon*, long before it was discovered in North America. By 1845 and 1846, Lund retired from active field work because he no longer had the resources to finance major excavations. Due to his fragile health, he stayed in Lagoa Santa and never returned to Europe. He spent the next thirty-five years in retirement, corresponding with other scientists around the world (including Charles Darwin); he died in 1880 at age seventy-eight. The most important specimens in his collections were shipped back to Denmark, where they remain (and not in Brazil, where the rest of the fossils, and the scientists who study them, are located).

SLOTHS DIVERSIFY

Along with armadillos and anteaters, the sloths are the third great branch of the xenarthrans (figure 3.5). Today there are three species of the three-toed sloth *Bradypus*, and two of the two-toed sloth *Choloepus*. These small animals are legendary for hanging upside down from trees their entire lives, moving very slowly, and feeding on and digesting leaves slowly between long naps. Although they can fight with their long foreclaws, their main defense is their stillness and concealment. They even harbor symbiotic algae in their fur that make them invisible in the tree canopy. But they must crawl down to the ground to defecate in the same latrine, about once a week, and at this time they are vulnerable to predation by jaguars. Sloths are also decent swimmers when they need to cross bodies of water for food or shelter.

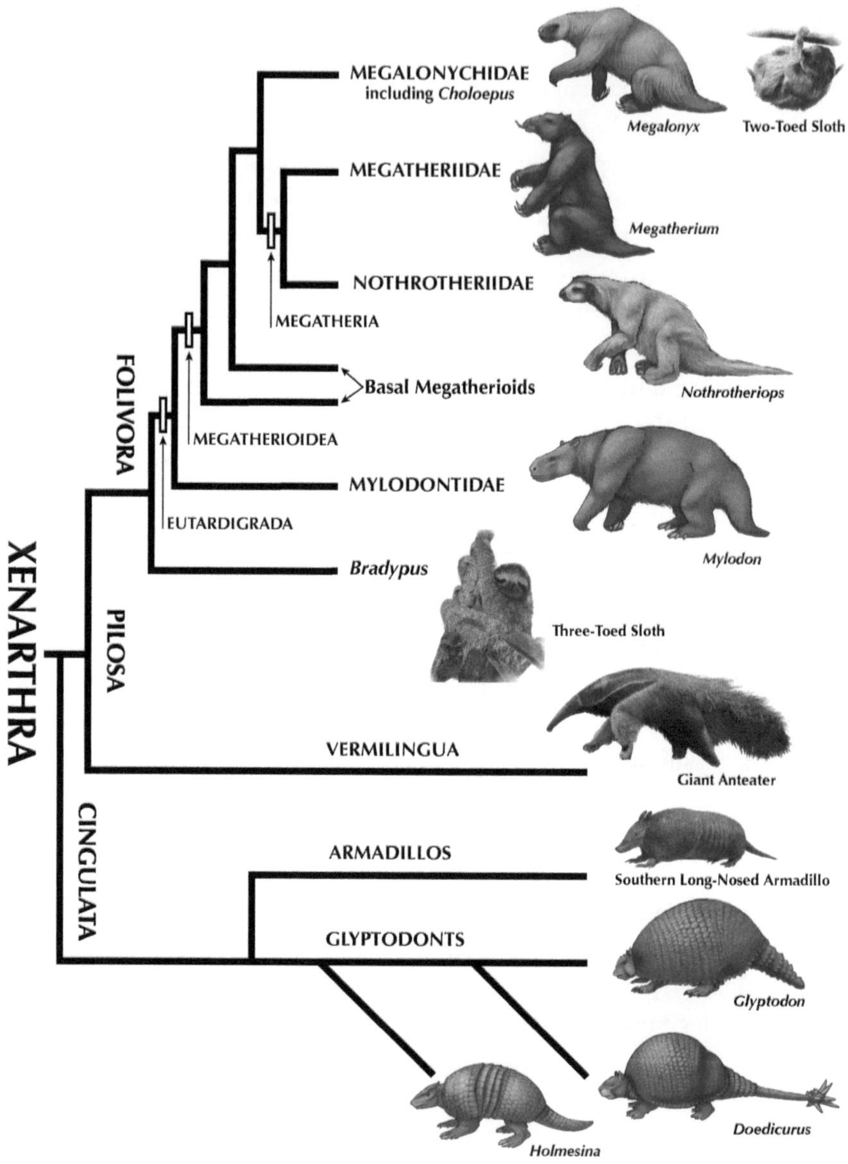

Figure 3.5 ▲

Family tree of the Xenarthra. (Drawing by Mary Persis Williams)

Sloths have large complex stomachs with several chambers, so they are almost as effective in bacterial digestion of plants as the ruminant hoofed mammals are. They eat nothing but leaves, which are low on nutrition but high in water content, so they must eat slowly and allow a long time for digestion (especially with their slow metabolism). Their long tongues reach as far as 12 inches from their mouth, so they can gather food farther than they can reach. Leaves are not a very nutritious food, but sloths compensate by having a very slow metabolism and low body temperature, so they don't need much energy or nutrition.

But these small living species are tiny remnants of a once huge evolutionary radiation of ground sloths). Big ground sloths were the norm, with dozens of species in 86 genera among four extinct families. The tiny living ones hanging from trees are pathetic remnants of the great evolutionary radiation of sloths dating back to the early Eocene. The two living sloth species actually diverged about 40 Ma, and are not that closely related, so that many of their similarities are due to convergent evolution. Two-toed sloths are related to the mylodontid sloths, and the three-toed sloths are related to the megalonychids. Their similarities thus are due to convergent evolution from different giant ground sloth ancestors and represent a secondary dwarfing of these ancient giants.

Ground sloths were truly remarkable creatures. Their skulls looked like something out of a science fiction movie, with a few simple peg-like teeth made of soft dentin, huge bony protuberances from their cheek bones, and a toothless "drool spout" on the front of the lower jaw where their long flexible tongue slid back and forth, gathering leaves. They had strangely shaped shoulder blades, powerful forelimbs, and long foreclaws that curved inward when they knuckle-walked. The front claws were probably used to haul down limbs so their long tongues could strip the branches of leaves. Studies of the claws showed they were not for digging, but they may have been some help in defense. They had long hindlimbs with such long claws they could not walk in a normal way, but walked on the side of their strangely deformed-looking ankles with the hind claws curved inward. Their strong tails helped balance them in a tripod stance when they reared up on their hind legs to reach high branches. Although they had no armor plating like the armadillos and their kin, sloths had thousands of pea-sized nodules of bone (osteoderms) embedded in their thick hides. These may have made their hides even more difficult for a predator to pierce when its canines struck these bony pellets.

Four families of ground sloths are represented in the fossil record (Fig. 3.5). The Mylodontidae are small to medium-sized ground sloths, with dozens of species in about 28 genera distributed among several subfamilies. They are the ancestral group of the living three-toed sloth. Most were restricted to South America, but *Thinobadistes* managed to island-hop across Central America and reach North America about 8 Ma, long before the Panama land bridge formed about 3.5 Ma. *Paramylodon*, the biggest sloth at La Brea Tar Pits (figure 3.6), was about 10 feet (3.8 meters) tall on its hind legs, and weighed about 1,000 kilograms.

The Megalonychidae includes 28 genera of medium-sized sloths in several subfamilies and are the ancestral group of the living two-toed sloth. Most were South American, but *Pliometanastes* was the first sloth to island-hop through Central America about 9 Ma, even earlier than did the

Figure 3.6 ▲

Harlan's ground sloth, *Paramylodon harlani*, a typical mylodont sloth, on display at the San Diego Natural History Museum. (Photo by the author)

Figure 3.7 ▲

The Shasta ground sloth, *Nothrotheriops shastense*, a typical nothrothere, on display at the La Brea Tar Pits Museum. (Photo by the author)

mylodontid *Thinobadistes*. As mentioned previously, President Thomas Jefferson himself described *Megalonyx* ("giant claw" in Greek) in 1796 from claw fossils brought to him by Col. John Stuart.

The Nothrotheriidae were a small-bodied group of sloths, with about 10 genera in two subfamilies. They date back to about 11.5 Ma, and were not able to spread from their South American base to North America until about 2.6 Ma. Several specimens of *Nothrotheriops* (figure 3.7) are known from mummified specimens with skin and hair found in dry caves in Mexico, New Mexico, and Arizona. Many of these caves yield sloth dung that has been dried and preserved for more than ten thousand years.

The most incredible of the nothrotheriids was *Thalassocnus*, a late Miocene genus from Peru and Chile that returned to the sea (figure 3.8). The oldest species from the late Miocene were apparently semiaquatic, and four successive species show the gradual transition in the skeleton from terrestrial to fully marine modes of life. The bones of each successive species show increasing density necessary for ballast in a marine mammal, and their limbs gradually change shape as they became more committed swimmers who used their long claws to cling to rocks in the surf (as do modern

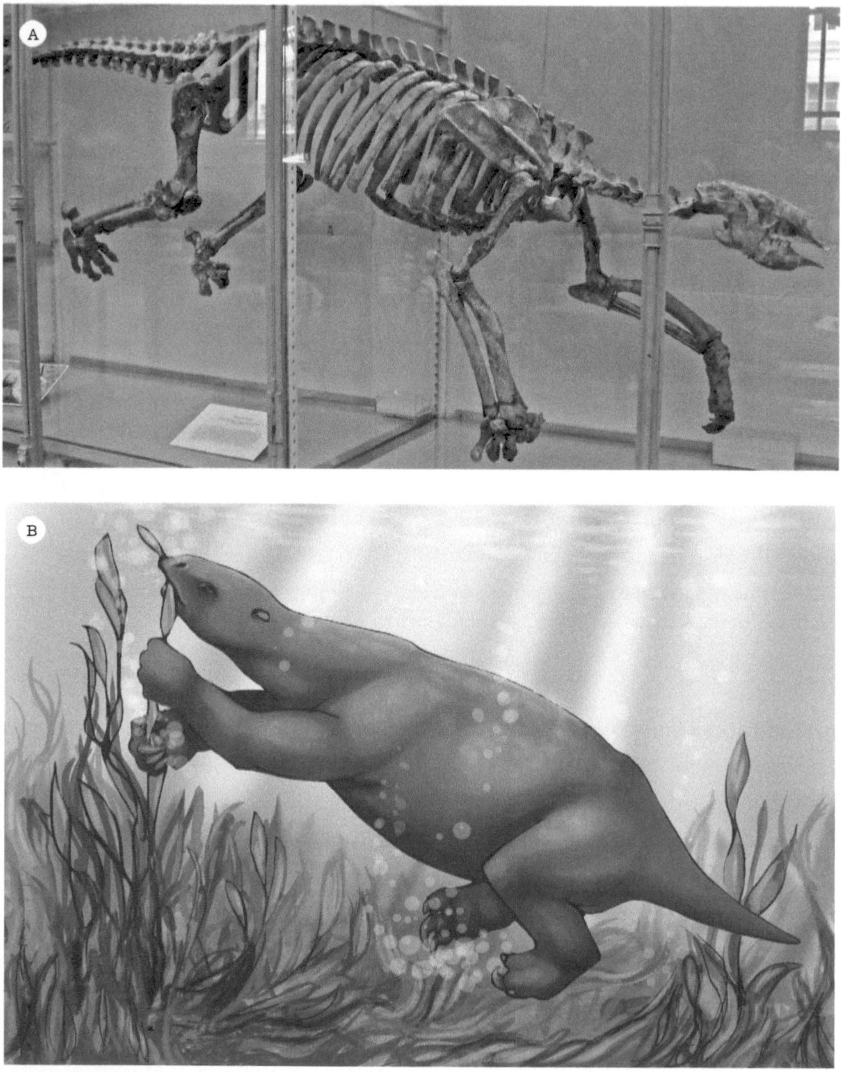

Figure 3.8 ▲

The marine sloth, *Thalassocnus*. (*A*) Skeleton on display. (*B*) Reconstruction of the sloth swimming and feeding on seaweed. ([*A*] Courtesy of Wikimedia Commons; [*B*] drawing by Mary Persis Williams)

marine iguanas). The teeth show the wear and chemistry of eating vegetation mixed with sand from the nearshore beaches and sea bottom, but later forms show no such wear, and instead are adapted for eating sea grasses and algae.

The most spectacular of the ground sloths, however, are the Megatheriidae, with 20 genera in three subfamilies. As we discussed at the beginning of the chapter, *Megatherium* was first found in South America in 1787, and then described by the pioneering French anatomist and paleontologist Georges Cuvier in 1796. *Megatherium* and another giant, *Eremotherium*, reached truly elephantine proportions, weighing up to 4 tonnes and stretching 20 feet (6 meters) from head to tail figure 3.10). This is about the size of the modern Indian elephant, and only certain mammoths and the gigantic rhino *Paraceratherium* were larger. Nearly all the megatheres remained in South America, except for *Eremotherium*, which managed to migrate up Central America and reach Florida and Georgia about 2 Ma.

During the late Pleistocene, there were three species of megatheres recognized in South America, including *Eremotherium* in both South America and in southern North America, such as Florida and Texas. There were two species of nothrotheres in South America, and one of which was also found in North America. Four species of megalonychids were found in South America, with *Megalonyx* in North America. There were four species of scelidotheres, all in South America, and four species of mylodontids, one of which (*Paramylodon harlani*) was common in North America. That makes 21 species of ground sloths in the late Pleistocene, and they all vanished during the late Pleistocene megafaunal extinctions, leaving only the two genera of tree sloths to survive until today (see discussion in chapter 2).

The exception was the primitive group of sloths known as the Megalocnidae, which include six extinct genera (figure 3.5). Most are smaller than the giants of the mainland, which is consistent with the fact that big animals become smaller or even dwarfed when they move to islands. The most striking example was *Megalocnus rodens* from Cuba (figure 3.10), which was built like a giant rodent the size of a black bear, with rodent-like chisel-shaped incisors in front (most sloths lack incisors). Indeed, it was first misidentified as giant rodent based on the fossils of its lower jaw. Its limbs had relatively short claws, possibly suited for digging rather than rearing up and hauling down big branches. Megalocnids persisted in Cuba, Hispaniola, Puerto Rico, and other Caribbean islands until only 4,700 years ago (about 2700 BCE, overlapping with much of the ancient history of Eurasia and Africa). Since humans arrived in Cuba about 5,900 years ago, they definitely overlapped with megalocnid sloths in time. Whether humans were responsible for their extinction, however, is controversial.

A
B

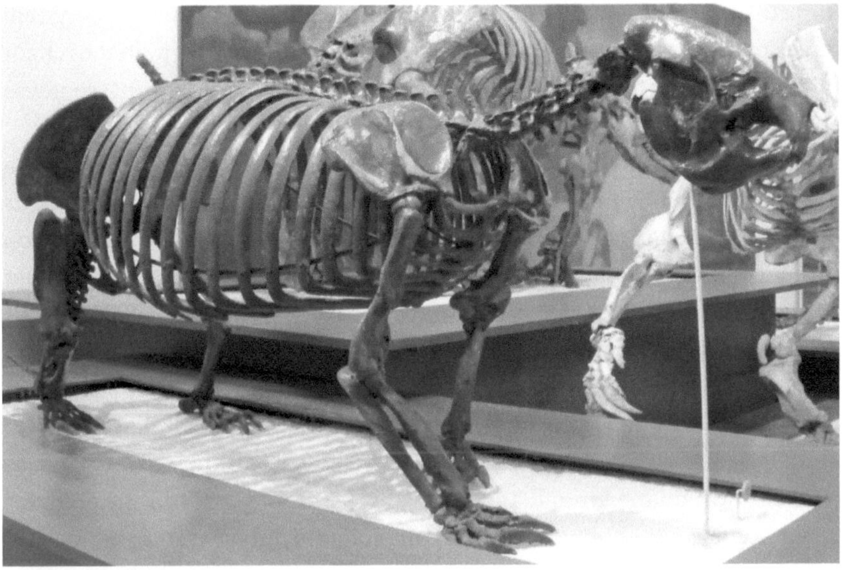

Figure 3.10 ▲
The "rodent-sloth" of Cuba, ***Megalocnus rodens***, with its chisel-shaped front incisors, on display at the American Museum of Natural History in New York. (Photo by the author)

ARMADILLO TANKS

Among the fossils that Darwin brought back to Owen was fragments of "a large animal, with an osseous coat in compartments, very like that of an armadillo."[5] All that Darwin found were tile-shaped pieces of armor from the shell, or "osseous coat," of an armadillo-like creature, and a few isolated bones and teeth. Owen gave the name "*Glyptodon*" ("carved tooth") to the fragments he had available but could only tell that it resembled a huge armadillo. Later specimens gave us a much better concept of glyptodonts.

From complete fossils, we now know that some glyptodonts were the size of a Volkswagen Beetle (figure 3.11A). They were over 10 feet (3.3 meters) in length and weighed about 2 tonnes. Their most striking feature was the

Figure 3.9 ◀
The gigantic megathere sloth *Eremotherium*. (*A*) Skeleton. (*B*) Reconstruction. (Courtesy of Wikimedia Commons)

domed bony shell, made out of more than one thousand small polygonal plates that were over an inch thick. Their head could not be pulled back for protection inside their shell (as a turtle can) but stuck out in front, so it was covered by another bony armor plate on the top of the skull.

The long tapering tail was also wrapped in rings of armor, so it was flexible but completely protected. *Glyptodon* had nothing extra on the tip of its tail but other glyptodonts such as *Doedicurus* had a bony spike "mace" on the end of its tail (figure 3.11B), and *Panochthus* and *Hoplophorus* (also found by Darwin) had a bony club on the end of its tail.

Most of time these monsters probably had no reason to fear predators, especially once they were fully grown. With their short stumpy legs and body completely wrapped in armor down to the belly and along the tail, there was almost no place for a predator to attack. All they had to do was hunker down on the ground and swing their armored tail, and the predator could not harm them. Nevertheless, glyptodonts did have some predators, because the fossilized skullcap of one young glyptodont shows the twin holes made by a bite with the canines of a saber-toothed cat.

The skulls of glyptodonts are truly strange (figure 3.11A). They are very short and very deep, with large areas of attachment for very strong jaw muscles. Even though their teeth were just simple pegs, they must have chewed enormous amounts of coarse fibrous vegetation based on the wear on their teeth. In addition, the nasal region is very short and has many muscular attachment sites around it. This has led to more than one paleontologist suggesting that glyptodonts might have had a short trunk or proboscis.

Despite their short stumpy legs, glyptodonts were surprisingly widespread, mobile, and successful. We find pieces of their distinctive mosaic armor in Ice Age localities throughout the Americas. Most of them remained in South America, but *Glyptodon* reached as far north as Guatemala, and the similar *Glyptotherium* reached the United States about 2.5 Ma. However, it apparently preferred the warm subtropical and tropical regions during the Ice Ages, because it was restricted to Florida, South Carolina, and across the desert southwest states from Texas to Arizona (but not at the La Brea Tar Pits).

All the large armored glyptodonts vanished from both North and South America at the end of the last Ice Age. Today, only much smaller armadillos are left. There are about 20 species alive today, from the living giant armadillo that is 60 inches (1.5 meters) long and weighs up to 120 pounds (54 kilograms), down to the pink fairy armadillo, which is only 5 inches

Figure 3.11 ▲

Glyptodonts. (*A*) The skeleton of a large glyptodont on display at the American Museum of Natural History in New York. (*B*) Reconstruction of the spike-tailed *Doedicurus* and a pampathere without spikes. ([*A*] Photo by the author; [*B*] drawing by Bruce Horsfall, courtesy of Wikimedia Commons)

(13 centimeters) long. Most are restricted to South America, but the nine-banded armadillo is common in the southwestern United States and is expanding its range northward as the climate warms up. Their armor is protection against most predators, although they also use it to plunge into thorny undergrowth where predators with sensitive skin cannot follow. Some dig down quickly to protect themselves, leaving only their armored backs exposed to predators. The nine-banded armadillos have a habit of jumping straight up when startled, which often means they get killed by the bumpers or undercarriage of cars when they collide.

Armadillos are not only excellent diggers but have very poor eyesight and rely on hearing and smell to detect predators and prey. They dig down quickly to catch insects, grubs, and other invertebrates in their burrows. A few of the armadillos are specialized for breaking down termite nests, just as anteaters and aardvarks do. Because of their heavy armor, armadillos will sink when they are in water. Yet they overcome this by taking a huge gulp of air to fill their lungs and stomach and make them buoyant, and by this means they can swim across most rivers or other water barriers.

Armadillos have some very unusual biological characteristics. The young are born with a soft leathery skin on their back that hardens into a shell after a few weeks. Armadillos always give birth to four genetically identical quadruplets because the original fertilized egg in the female splits into four parts that each become a different youngster. This has made them popular in medical and biological research studies when a set of genetically identical offspring are tested for differences that are not due to genetics. In addition, due to their low body temperature, armadillos are the only animals other than humans that can be infected with leprosy. Thus they have been very useful to medical research labs that need to culture the leprosy bacterium, and researchers cannot risk trying it in humans. However, since leprosy is contagious, humans have to be careful when handling infected armadillos; humans can also get it by eating armadillo meat. Armadillos also can carry Chagas disease, a wasting disease caused by a pathogen carried by the bite of assassin bugs.

WORMTONGUE

Sloths and armadillos and their kin are the two most familiar families of the Xenarthra. The third are the anteaters, which are placed in the group "Vermilingua," which means "worm tongue" in Latin. (No connection to the villain Grima Wormtongue in J. R. R. Tolkien's *Lord of the Rings*). There are only four living species of anteaters alive in Latin America today, although there were many more in the South American fossil record.

As their name implies, anteaters have a long wormlike tongue because they are specialists in eating ants and termites. They use their powerful front claws to rip open the anthill or termite nest, and then lap up hundreds of insects with their two-foot-long sticky tongues covered with sticky saliva. The long "nose" of the anteater is actually their entire snout and jaw forming a long tube through which their tongue flicks in and out. Since tiny insects are easy to swallow, anteaters are completely toothless and do not chew; their jaws just form the support for their tubular mouth, so they crush their prey with their palate before swallowing. However, they have a muscular stomach that grinds up the insects and powerful digestive juices to break down all the hard cuticle in their prey. They may eat as many as thirty thousand ants or termites in a day! But they will also eat ripe fruit if they find it on the ground.

There are four living species of anteater, including the tree-climbing tamanduas and the silky anteater, whose long silky fur gives it its name. The most impressive of all, however, is the giant anteater. It is the largest of its kind, reaching 7 feet (2.2 meters) in length and weighing up to 100 pounds (45 kilograms). Its long coarse fur with the distinctive gray, black, and white markings serve not only to keep the animal warm but also prevents attacking ants and termites from biting it. The bushy coat and broad broom-like tail make it look bigger than it really is, which discourages predators. Its huge front claws are great for digging up anthills and termite mounds, but it must knuckle-walk with its claws curled under because the claws would be in the way if they were stretched forward. Its scientific name is *Myrmecophaga tridactyla*, "three-toed anteater," which is a good description of it. Although they have no defensive armor like armadillos, they will rear up on their hind legs and slash with their claws against predators such as jaguars and pumas, and they have been known to kill jaguars in a fight. They will do the same to humans if threatened or cornered, and several hunters have been mauled or killed by cornered anteaters.

Anteaters are revered by many of the tribes in South America that live in their range. When Spaniards conquered the New World, they sent anteaters back to Spain. There the Europeans got the strange notion that all anteaters were female and that they mated with their noses. The surrealist artist Salvador Dali wrote a tall tale about an anteater that "reaches sizes bigger than the horse, possesses enormous ferocity, has exceptional muscle power, is a terrifying animal,"[6] and he depicted it in his painting "The Great Masturbator." The writer André Breton compared the temptations that man experiences in life to what "the tongue of the anteater must offer to the ant."[7] Anteaters have appeared in many comic books and movies, and in the comic strip *B.C.*, which inspired the University of California at Irvine to adopt the anteater as its mascot.

NOTES

1. Thomas Jefferson, *Memoir on the Megalonyx* (1797), 12.
2. Thomas Jefferson, *Notes on the State of Virginia VI* (1797), 13.
3. Charles Darwin, *The Voyage of the Beagle* (1836), 63.
4. Darwin, *The Voyage of the Beagle*, 88.
5. Richard Owen, *Description of the Skeleton of the Extinct Gigantic Sloth* Mylodon Robustus, (1842), 11.
6. Salvador Dali, *The Horseman of Death* (1935), 33.
7. André Breton, *Le Temps Passé* (1933), 3.

FOR FURTHER READING

Agusti, J., and M. Anton. *Mammoths, Sabertooths, and Hominids: 65 Million Years of Mammalian Evolution in Europe*. Columbia University Press, 2002.

Argot, C. "Changing Views in Paleontology: The Story of a Giant (Megatherium, Xenarthra)." In *Mammalian Evolutionary Morphology*, ed. E. Sargis and M. Dagosto, M. (eds.), 37–50 Springer-Verlag, 2008.

Kurtén, B. *Before the Indians*. Columbia University Press, 1988.

——. *Pleistocene Mammals of Europe*. Columbia University Press, 1968.

Kurtén, B., and E. Anderson. *Pleistocene Mammals of North America*. Columbia University Press, 1980.

Lange, I. M. *Ice Age Mammals of North America: A Guide to the Big, the Hairy, and the Bizarre*. Mountain Press, 2017.

Prothero, D. R., *The Princeton Field Guide to Prehistoric Mammals*. Princeton University Press, 2016.

——. *Vertebrate Evolution: From Origins to Dinosaurs and Beyond*. Taylor & Francis/ CRC Press, 2022.

Turner, A., and M. Anton *National Geographic Prehistoric Mammals*. National Geographic Society, 2004.

04 | MAMMALS FROM THE AGE OF DINOSAURS

AMPHITHERIUM

Amphitherium is not less extraordinary than *Megalosaurus*.

—WILLIAM BUCKLAND, 1824

THE ZOOPHAGE

William Buckland was one of the most amazing and colorful figures in the history of science (figure 4.1). Born in 1784 in Axminster in Devon in southwestern England, he would accompany his father (the local church rector) on fossil-collecting walks on the coastline at Lyme Regis (later famous for the marine reptiles found by Mary Anning), so he developed an early interest in natural history. After attending several schools, he ended up studying mineralogy and chemistry at Corpus Christi College in Oxford, where he would spend most of the rest of his life. By 1813, he succeeded his mentor John Kidd as a reader in mineralogy at Oxford, and he soon became famous for his popular and engaging style of lecturing. Buckland was known for his dramatic delivery and gestures during his lectures, sometimes acting out the behavior of the animals he was describing. He even gave lectures on horseback. He wore his heavy academic robes at every lecture, even when he was scrambling around outcrops on a field excursion.

His eccentricities extended to his household, which was loaded with specimens of fossils, minerals, and animals he had collected. John Ruskin marveled at the Buckland house "Aladdin's Cave" ambience: "not a chair fit to

Figure 4.1 ◀
A portrait of William Buckland. (Courtesy of Wikimedia Commons)

sit down upon—all covered with dust . . . frogs cut out of serpentine—broken models of fallen temples, torn papers—old manuscripts—stuffed reptiles."[1] Buckland's wife, Mary Morland (a talented naturalist and illustrator in her own right), and her husband would debate which species of fly was buzzing around the table, a common phenomenon in the early 1800s when both men and women were obsessed with natural history. They even had a pet bear, which his sons would dress in academic robes for garden parties. The entire family (nine children, five of whom survived into adulthood) was recruited for collecting natural history specimens. Buckland was so enthusiastic about experiencing animals directly that he claimed he had eaten his way through the animal kingdom. The Bucklands tried to make a meal from almost every animal they could obtain, a practice known as zoophagy. Apparently, mole and bluebottle fly were the most disgusting, but his guests also recorded him eating panther, crocodile, and mouse. According to Augustus Hare, "Talk of strange relics led to mention of the heart of a French King [possibly Louis XIV] preserved at Nuneham in a silver casket. Dr. Buckland, whilst looking at it, exclaimed, 'I have eaten many strange things, but have never eaten the heart of a king before,' and, before anyone could hinder him, he had gobbled it up, and the precious relic was lost forever."[2]

Buckland had been looking at the huge bones in the Oxford museum collections from the Stonesfield Slate quarries, to the north of Oxford. These bones had been collected by quarrymen over the years, and then sent to the Ashmolean Museum in Oxford, where Buckland had a position. Buckland was struck by the fact that these fragmentary bones looked like the remains of a gigantic lizard, which Buckland named *Megalosaurus* (Greek for "huge lizard") in 1824. This was the first dinosaur to receive an official name in science.

But the same Stonesfield Slate quarries that yielded *Megalosaurus* also produced tiny inch-long jaws that didn't fit the prevailing notions of the fossil record of the time. They were sometimes called lizard jaws, but to others they looked like opossums or shrews. Whatever they were, they definitely appeared to be tiny mammals because their teeth had two or three roots (reptiles have only a single root) and multiple cusps. These Oxford rocks were thought to be from the old "Secondary" period in the archaic geologic timescale used in those days, supposedly deposits from Noah's flood. They were known for producing extinct fossils such as ammonites and eventually marine reptiles (discovered by Mary Anning in Lyme Regis on the Devonshire coast of England) and now *Megalosaurus*, but it had always been assumed that fossil mammals were only found in "Tertiary" beds that were deposited above the Secondary. Buckland acquired one of these jaws from a student in 1812.

In 1818 (after the end of the Napoleonic Wars), the legendary anatomist and paleontologist Baron Georges Cuvier came to visit Oxford and see the remarkable huge fossils that Buckland had talked about. Cuvier looked at them closely (especially the giant jaw with its reptilian teeth, many of which were just erupting) and confirmed that they were indeed reptilian. Buckland also showed him a tiny Stonesfield jaw, and Cuvier identified it as an opossum. The identification is not surprising—the jaw looks like a miniature of a modern opossum. But it must have been a shock to Cuvier, coming as it did from the same rocks that had produced giant saurians. Its implications for his clear-cut scheme of Secondary saurians and Tertiary mammals were disturbing. A Secondary occurrence of marsupials, which seem more primitive than placentals because they give birth to fetal young instead of gestating them, would have hinted at transmutation and progress. This was an anathema to Cuvier and his peers after people such as Lamarck were advocating the idea that the fossil record showed change and progress through time, a clear violation of biblical literalism, or of Cuvier's tenuous compromise between geology and Genesis.

Cuvier made no mention of the Secondary "opossums" in most of his later works, but he passed the problem over to a junior associate, Constant Prévost, who wrote a paper insisting that the Stonesfield Slate must be Tertiary rocks, like the Paris gypsum, because they contained mammals (even though *Megalosaurus* came from the same quarries). In his only other mention of the specimen, Cuvier called the Stonesfield jaws *Didelphis prevosti*, putting them in the genus of the living opossum and with a species name honoring Prévost.

Finally, in 1838, Cuvier's successor at the Paris museum, an anatomist named Henri de Blainville, published two papers maintaining that the jaws really were reptilian and changed their identification from the genus of the living opossum *Didelphis* to *Amphitherium*, "beast on both sides" (figure 4.2).

Figure 4.2 ▲

Illustration of *Amphitherium*. (From G. Cuvier, *Recherches sur les ossements fossiles*, [Paris: A. Belin, 1822])

Blainville acknowledged that the teeth, including incisors, canines, and molars, were more complex than those of most reptiles. But this distinction was muddied by the misidentification of some giant Eocene whale jaws from Alabama as reptile jaws; these were given the name *Basilosaurus* ("emperor lizard" in Greek). The teeth of *Basilosaurus* were also double rooted and had cusps like those of mammals but were thought to be reptilian, so the peculiarities of the Stonesfield jaws might not be so important after all. Later, Richard Owen corrected this mistake and confirmed that *Basilosaurus* was a large whale, not a reptile. He tried to have its name changed to "*Zeuglodon*" ("yoked tooth" in Greek), but the rules of zoological nomenclature are very clear that *Basilosaurus* was the first name given and thus has priority, even if it inappropriately suggested that this whale was a reptile.

Blainville wrote about the jaws without ever seeing them, so Buckland went on a tour of Europe and brought the tiny specimens with him to show the leading European anatomists of the time. He also had casts made that could be left in their collections. A zoologist named Achille Valenciennes decided that the jaws belonged to marsupials after all, although he changed the genus from *Didelphis* to *Thylacotherium*, "pouched beast," because they seemed more like those of the South American mouse opossum than a Virginia opossum. Even the famous zoologist Etienne Geoffroy Saint-Hilaire acknowledged that the jaws were those of a marsupial, although, as with monotremes, he put marsupials in a transitional class. But de Blainville and the Edinburgh zoologist Robert Grant were not convinced, so Buckland recruited the rising star of British zoology, Richard Owen. With the zoological treasures of the British Empire flowing into his museum collections, Owen was able to compare them to a variety of mammals, especially the recently described numbat, an ant-eating marsupial from Australia, whose long, narrow jaw contains nine cheek teeth, the same as in Buckland's original Stonesfield jaw. In an 1838 paper, Owen said that this similarity definitely put the Stonesfield jaws in the marsupials.

Still, there was some resistance to these jaws belonging to mammals from the Secondary rocks. Charles Lyell, whose work brought geology into the modern age through his book *Principles of Geology* (published in three volumes from 1831–1833), was famously reluctant to accept the idea that the fossil record showed change through time. In his early works, he embraced an extreme form of uniformitarianism that viewed the story of earth and life as proceeding in cycles rather than changing progressively through time. In this concept, organisms never vanished from the planet completely but would come back at some later time. Lyell's colleagues found this view hard to accept because the unidirectional change in life's history had long been clear from William Smith's discovery of faunal succession. In one famous cartoon by the British geologist Henry de la Beche, Lyell's idea is ridiculed as a "Professor Ichthyosaurus," holding a human skull, lectures his students about a strange beast from the previous creation (figure 4.3). De La Beche embraced the Stonesfield jaws as showing that mammals and dinosaurs had always lived together, and there was no progressive change through time from a world ruled by dinosaurs to a world ruled by mammals. Eventually, even Lyell was forced to admit that the fossil record did show change through time, and that there was no reason to believe that extinct species would ever return.

The controversy over the Stonesfield jaws eventually died down as more and more of them were found, and there were more different types than

Figure 4.3 ▲

Henry de la Beche's satirical cartoon, poking fun at Lyell's notion that life was not directional but cyclical. Here, Prof. Ichthyosaurus points to a skull of a creature from a previous creation. (Courtesy of Wikimedia Commons)

just *Amphitherium*. In 1838, Owen described *Phascolotherium*, which had a totally different configuration of teeth, with three cusps in a row, typical of a group called triconodonts. In 1871, Owen described *Amphilestes*, which had a different configuration of triconodont teeth. By this point, there was no longer any question that the fossil record did not demonstrate a simplistic notion of progressive change through time, and that mammals occurred through much of the Age of Dinosaurs.

BONE BONANZA

In March 1877, the Union Pacific railroad worker William Harlow Reed was hunting pronghorns in the flats east of Medicine Bow, Wyoming, to feed railway workers in his group. He shot one and hiked up a ridge to retrieve his kill. On the way back down the ridge, he noticed huge bones lying all over the ground and sticking out of the rocks.

Reed had heard the news about some Eastern scientist paying good money for such huge bones. He talked to his friend, stationmaster William Edwards Carlin, about the exciting find. They both agreed that such a find might pay very well, especially since they were living on bare subsistence wages in the desolate sagebrush flats of Wyoming. So they wrote a letter to Marsh. It read:

> I write to announce to you the discovery not far from this place, of a large number of fossils, supposed to be those of the *Megatherium*, although there is no one here sufficient of a geologist to state for certainty. We have excavated one (1) partly, and know where there is several others that we have not, as yet, done any work upon. The formation in which they are found is that of the Tertiary Period. We are desirous of disposing of what fossils we have, and also the secret of the others. We are working men and are not able to present them as a gift, and if we can sell the secret of the fossil bed and procure work in excavating others we would like to do so. We have said nothing to any-one as yet. We measured one shoulder-blade and found it to measure four feet eight inches 4 Ft. 8 in. in length. As proof of our sincerity and trust, we will send you a few fossils, at which they cost us in time and money in unearthing. We would be pleased to hear from you, as you are well-known as an enthusiastic geologist, and a man of means, both of which we are desirous of fining—more especially the latter. Hoping to hear from you very soon, before the snows of winter set in . . .

They signed the letter "Harlow" and "Edwards" and also hinted darkly that someone else had people in the area looking for bones.

The mysterious letter and specimens reached Professor Othniel Charles Marsh at Yale University (discussed in chapter 7), and he immediately got excited because his other collectors were having little luck out in Colorado. He sent one of them, Samuel Wendell Williston, to take the next train to Wyoming. When he arrived at Como Station (which consisted of a couple of shacks on the railroad siding), he was told that the mysterious Harlow and Edwards lived at a ranch out by the bluff. There were crates of bones on the floor of the station, so he knew he was in the right place. Eventually they met, and Williston gave them Marsh's check made out to "Harlow" and "Edwards." But they could not cash their checks because they had used their middle names as aliases to hide their identities.

Nonetheless, Williston was elated when Carlin and Reed took him up to the bluffs. On November 14, he wrote to Marsh that the bones "extend for seven miles & are by the ton. . . . The bones are very thick, well preserved, and easy to get out." In his next letter on November 16, he told Marsh, "Cañon City & Morrison [Colorado localities that Marsh's men had worked earlier] are simply nowhere in comparison to this locality—both as regards perfection, accessibility, and quantity." Williston urged Marsh to pay Carlin and Reed $75 each (a princely sum in those days), and to get their claim established because they feared Marsh's rival Edward Drinker Cope might be looking for a chance to poach the locality (as indeed he was).

Marsh sent Carlin and Reed a contract, paying them $90 a month (he was paying poor hard-working Williston only $40 a month), with instructions to keep out all rival collectors. Soon they had opened Quarry 1, started crating up huge bones and sent them along on the railway. Marsh's collectors kept this up for ten years, sending a ton of bones east almost every week.

Reed was the only constant figure at the quarries as other workers came and went, even though his pay was unpredictable and so were his supplies. Reed found most of the new quarries and the most important discoveries. Once he almost drowned in an icy creek rafting across it. Most of the time he had no wagons or pack animals, so he had to carry the bones down from the hill, often 5 miles (8 kilometers) to the station. He once dragged a 400 pound (186 kilogram) leg bone over half a mile (0.8 kilometers) down to the tracks. By 1886, after six years of hard work with no appreciation from Marsh or his crew, he resigned to take up sheep farming and guiding hunting parties. Nevertheless, the haul from Como Bluff and its 13 quarries was amazing. Many tons of bones in excellent state of preservation yielded 26 new species of dinosaurs, as well as complete or nearly complete skeletons of others previously named.

Como Bluff yielded not only dinosaurs but many other animals, including crocodiles, turtles, lizards, frogs, and salamanders, and pterosaurs. In addition, the first-ever Mesozoic mammals from North America were discovered at Como Bluff. These little animals were no bigger than shrews and had jaws with teeth the size of pinheads. They were nearly all found in Quarry 9, and most were overlooked by the original collectors, who were rushing to crate up as many big dinosaur bones as they could in a hurry. The tiny jaws were spotted when Marsh's preparators began to clean matrix away from the dinosaur bones that had been found in that quarry. In 1878 and 1879, Marsh reported this astonishing discovery in a series of papers describing these tiny jaws and touting their importance. They shed a whole new light on the tiny amount of information then known about Mesozoic mammals because many were more complete than the Oxford specimens and they were from the Upper Jurassic Morrison Formation, while the British fossils were from the Middle Jurassic.

But Marsh's descriptions were typically very short and not very diagnostic, and usually his papers were not even illustrated. Marsh died in 1899 without finishing the work on them or having them all completely cleaned and prepared out of the matrix. The next person to examine them closely was the brilliant George Gaylord Simpson, who made them the subject of his PhD thesis at Yale University during the mid-1920s. In 1928 and 1929, he published two full-scale monographs on all the Mesozoic mammals known at the time, with the first decent illustrations of the Morrison mammals from Marsh's Yale collection. He also visited Britain and redescribed and re-illustrated all the British specimens as well.

I also have a personal connection to these fossils. Thanks to renewed excavations at Quarry 9, the main mammal quarry, by a joint expedition of the American Museum of Natural History and Yale University in 1968–1970, many new mammal fossils were recovered. In 1977, when I was a graduate student at the American Museum, I had the great fortune of studying these new specimens, as well as Marsh's original Jurassic mammals in the Yale collections (figure 4.4). One of them was a new species I named *Comotherium richi*. The genus was named after Como Bluffs (plus *-therium*, Greek

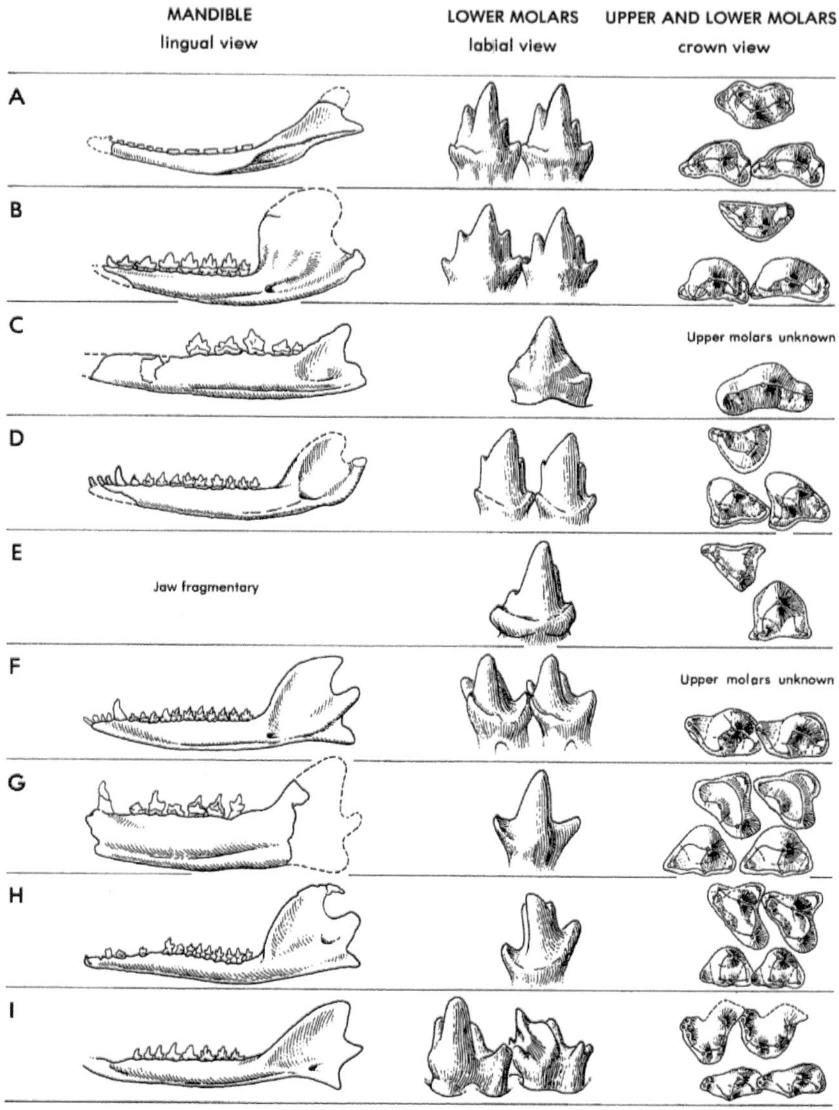

Figure 4.4 ▲

The jaws and teeth of some Jurassic mammals from Como Bluff and elsewhere. (Drawing by C. R. Prothero; from D. R. Prothero, "New Jurassic Mammals from Como Bluff, Wyoming, and the Interrelationships of Non-Tribosphenic Theria," *Bulletin of the American Museum of Natural History* 167, no. 5 (1981).

for "beast"), and the species name honors Dr. Thomas Rich, who led the 1968–1970 American Museum-Yale party that found it. Between 1977 and 1981 I was immersed in studying and publishing Mesozoic mammals, but I also identified and published some fossil lizards from Como Bluff (appearing in the journal *Science* in 1980) and several other miscellaneous mammal fossils from the Jurassic of the Rocky Mountains. These became part of my master's thesis (published in the *Bulletin of the American Museum of Natural History* in 1981), but after these projects were completed, Mesozoic mammals appeared a dead end for further research at that time. No additional new specimens were available for study, and we still only had small numbers of jaws and teeth, with only a few (undescribed) Jurassic mammals known from partial skeletons found in Portugal. I moved on to different research projects, so I switched to studying American rhinos (which didn't require a microscope, which was important for someone with eyesight as bad as mine). I also began my PhD dissertation project doing magnetic stratigraphy and biostratigraphy of the rocks of the Big Badlands of South Dakota and correlative rocks. I could not have continued to work on Mesozoic mammals, but luckily more specimens would be found after I left that field behind. I'm pleased to have been part of a research legacy that started with Marsh, then moved to Simpson, and finally became part of my career.

GEORGE GAYLORD SIMPSON, GIANT AND GENIUS

Before we continue talking about Mesozoic mammals I want to say a bit about George Gaylord Simpson and his legacy for paleontology and evolutionary biology (figure 4.5). Born in Chicago in 1902, he grew up in Denver, Colorado, when it was still a "rough and ready" frontier town. He first attended the University of Colorado, then transferred and went east to Yale University, where he earned his BA and finally his PhD in 1926, working on Jurassic mammals. While he was still a grad student at Yale in 1924, he was recruited by William Diller Matthew as a summer field assistant to help with excavating Plio-Pleistocene horses in the Blanco beds of the Texas Panhandle where he had his first experience with serious field paleontology. Growing as a frontier kid, he soon proved adept at it. After a year in England to work on their Mesozoic mammals, in 1927 Simpson received an offer to become an Assistant Curator at the American Museum of Natural History. There Simpson spent the next 32 years, the prime of his career, working first

Figure 4.5 ▲

George Gaylord Simpson shown at his American Museum desk, holding his 1953 book *The Major Features of Evolution.* (Courtesy of Wikimedia Commons)

on early Cenozoic mammals from localities in Montana and Wyoming and New Mexico, doing his own field work and making large collections.

From the beginning Simpson proved that his two early scientific monographs were no fluke, publishing at a such remarkable rate that he soon establishing himself as the leading expert on early Cenozoic mammals. In the 1930s, he raised funds from donors to mount several American Museum expeditions to Patagonia, where he made large collections, and began his long-term quest to clean up the mess of South American mammal taxonomy left by Florentino Ameghino, an Argentinian paleontologist who pioneered the study of South American mammals in the late 1800s and early 1900s.

Meanwhile, in the 1920s and 1930s the American Museum of Natural History and Columbia University were in the center of the research effort to reconcile the newest breakthroughs in genetics (pioneered by Thomas Hunt Morgan and his experiments on fruit flies at Columbia, then by his successor Theodosius Dobzhansky), and systematics (led by Ernst Mayr, then an ornithologist at the American Museum) with Darwin's ideas about the importance of natural selection. The idea that selection could explain evolution had fallen out of favor in the 1880s, but thanks to the mathematical modeling of population genetics, and the better understanding of animal and plant genetics, the evidence now supported the importance of natural selection. By the late 1930s, several scientists wrote books that brought all these ideas together. In 1937, Dobzhansky published *Genetics and the Origin of Species*, which synthesized all that was known of genetics at the time and showed that it was consistent with Darwinian natural selection. In 1942, Mayr published *Systematics and the Origin of Species*, which addressed the problem of natural selection in wild populations and laid the groundwork for his allopatric speciation model. And in 1944 (written in the late 1930s but delayed by World War II), Simpson published *Tempo and Mode in Evolution*, which attempted to reconcile the fossil record with Darwinian natural selection. After the war, in the late 1940s and 1950s, many other scientists joined this emerging consensus, so that Julian Huxley described their ideas as the "the modern synthesis," or as others labeled it, Neo-Darwinism. By the time of the centennial celebration of *On the Origin of Species* in 1959, the Neo-Darwinian synthesis dominated evolutionary biology, and most evolutionists thought that all the major problems had been solved. Most current evolution textbooks still reflect a strict Neo-Darwinian approach.

In the early twentieth century, paleontologists were uncertain about their role in the community of evolutionary biologists. Originally, they actively opposed Darwinian natural selection (Owen) or were Lamarckians (like Cope and ammonite expert Alpheus Hyatt), or proposed their own idiosyncratic ideas (Osborn), or were agnostic about the mechanism of evolution (for example, William Berryman Scott), even as they found more and more evidence that evolution had occurred. Gould (1983) describes this as the period of "irrelevance," when paleontologists contributed very little to evolutionary theory.

This situation changed completely in 1944 with the publication of George Gaylord Simpson's *Tempo and Mode in Evolution*. As a part of the scientific community in New York City (American Museum of Natural History and Columbia University) in the 1930s, Simpson was in contact with Dobzhansky (Columbia) and Mayr (American Museum) and was aware of the new developments in genetics and evolution. With *Tempo and Mode in Evolution*, Simpson set out to undo all the confusion about the nature of the fossil record caused by the unfounded speculations of Cope and Osborn. Using his vast firsthand knowledge of fossils, Simpson tried to show that nothing in paleontology was inconsistent with the concepts of Neo-Darwinism as they were just emerging. In some respects, he was too successful. Simpson gave the evolutionary biology community no reason to believe that the fossil record contained anything new or unusual that they could not see better with their lab rats or fruit flies.

Ironically, just as Simpson reached the apex of his scientific productivity and influence, he was drafted into the U.S. Army during World War II, serving from 1942 to 1944. Given his education and command of at least 18 languages, he was soon commissioned into Army intelligence because he could interrogate prisoners in German, French, Italian, or Berber. He served first in North Africa, then in Sicily, and then in the Italian campaign. Famously, he wore a small goatee most of his life, and General George Patton was furious that he was not clean-shaven like all other troops under his command. Simpson outmaneuvered Patton by pointing out (with reporters present) that he had permission to keep a neat beard from Gen. Eisenhower himself, and it made the news back home. Patton could do nothing but send MPs to shadow and harass him until they finally gave up. (Simpson's autobiography recounts his hatred of Patton, and Simpson was actually in the same hospital tent in Sicily where he witnessed the famous incident of the enraged Patton cursing and slapping a soldier with PTSD, which nearly got Patton fired).

When Simpson returned from the war, he finally got to see *Tempo and Mode of Evolution* published (expanded and revised as *The Major Features of Evolution* in 1953), and then he embarked on an even broader mission. In 1945, his long-term project on classification of mammals was published, a landmark that my own advisor, Malcolm McKenna (Simpson's successor), matched in 1997. Simpson spent the later 1940s and 1950s working on South American mammals, expanding the Neo-Darwinian synthesis, and in a famous American Museum symposium in 1949 he opposed the idea of continental drift with his own groundbreaking studies on mammalian biogeography. (Simpson lived long enough to see plate tectonics come along in the 1960s and 1970s, which completely invalidated his own resistance to the idea of the movement of continents.)

He also collaborated with his second wife Anne Roe Simpson, a psychologist and expert at statistics, and pioneered the effort to introduce population biology thinking and biostatistics to paleontology, which began with their 1939 book *Quantitative Zoology*. In this, he was far ahead of his time. While most paleontologists of his generation were still giving a name to every slightly different fossil that came out of the ground, Simpson was the first to think of them as samples of biological populations with natural variability, which had to be analyzed statistically. Today this is the standard approach of nearly all paleontologists, but few in Simpson's lifetime adopted it. They kept on publishing outdated thinking as late as the 1960s.

In August 1954 Simpson was on an expedition to the headwaters of the Amazon when one of the local workers carelessly chopped down a tree and it accidentally fell on Simpson, crushing him and breaking numerous bones in his body. Simpson would have died on the spot if not for the American Museum preparator George Whittaker (whom I knew quite well), who wrapped him in splints and paddled him downriver fast enough that eventually he was bundled onto a plane and flown back to the United States, where his life was spared. But Simpson spent almost five years slowly recuperating from all the broken bones and damage to internal organs. He was still the Chair of the Department of Vertebrate Paleontology, but he was seldom in the museum due to being in hospitals and care facilities. Eventually, the hatred between the American Museum Director and Simpson grew so intense that in 1959, Simpson resigned and accepted an offer at Harvard's Museum of Comparative Zoology, where he stayed until his retirement in 1982. He then moved to Tucson, Arizona, and became affiliated with the paleontologists at the University of Arizona, before he passed away on October 6, 1984.

Simpson left behind an enormous legacy to which every person who studies fossil mammals is forever indebted. Not only did he do incredible work on the fossil mammals he studied, but he brought paleontology into the Neo-Darwinian synthesis, introduced statistics and population thinking to vertebrate paleontology, created a classification of mammals that was influential for over 50 years, and left behind an incredible record of publications unmatched by anyone. He was (along with Alfred Romer of Harvard) one of the cofounders of the Society of Vertebrate Paleontology, and today its highest award for lifetime achievement is called the Romer-Simpson Prize.

CHINA ROCKS THE PALEO WORLD

During the Chinese "Cultural Revolution" from 1966 to 1976, scholars and educated people were purged from most institutions, and many were killed or forced to work in labor camps and undergo indoctrination for not being good communists. Chinese scientists at the Institute for Vertebrate Paleontology and Paleoanthropology (IVPP) were also under scrutiny, so most of them tried to lay low and hoped that the authorities would not arrest them. Even if their lives were not threatened, they had no contact with the outside world. Almost all research ceased, and they had no access to the scientific publications of the rest of the world, nor could they leave China to see other fossils and make comparisons with their own specimens. Finally, in the late 1970s and early 1980s, the political winds in China changed when Mao Zedong died in 1976 and the "Gang of the Four" were overthrown, and a more open and practical regime under Zhou Enlai took over. Gradually more and more Chinese scientists were allowed to travel and publish, and Western scientists were allowed into China for the first time since before World War II.

Some of the most important Chinese localities are the famous Lower Cretaceous lake shales of the Yixian Formation in Liaoning Province of northeastern China. These shales were deposited at the bottom of a stagnant lake with no oxygen at the bottom, so when animals died, they sank down and did not decay until they were covered with many more fine layers of silt and mud. The lack of oxygen allowed even soft tissues to be preserved. As a result, the Jehol biota from these shales includes many incredible specimens, including thousands of leaves, insects, and small animals. More famous are the birds and non-avian dinosaurs with their original feathery coating (even some with the original pigment cells preserved) and stomach contents, plus some of the earliest complete fossils (including fur and body outline) of marsupial and placental mammals and other more archaic groups.

There was very limited collecting in Liaoning Province in the early twentieth century, but after China was closed to most Western scientists the specimens kept accumulating in the collections. They were studied but not published. This remained true during the dark days of the "Cultural Revolution" and well into the early 1980s. But in the late 1980s and 1990s, the floodgates burst, as more and more scientists found and studied the amazing specimens. In addition, a few Chinese scientists were finally allowed to travel abroad, study fossils in other museums, attend professional meetings and present their work, and describe their fossils in international journals so everyone could see their incredible discoveries.

The Liaoning fossils included hundreds of exquisitely preserved Early Cretaceous birds, some of which were published but many of which are still being studied. (My former student, Dr. Jingmai O'Connor, is now a curator at the Field Museum in Chicago, working on enantornithine birds and publishing many papers each year.) Each fall at the annual Society of Vertebrate Paleontology (SVP) meeting during the 1980s and 1990s, paleontologists were stunned by presentations showing these incredible fossils. Some were seen by the scientific world for the first time in 50 years,

But equally impressive were the beautifully preserved (but flattened) specimens of mammals, which still had their hair and soft tissues fossilized. Although some were described by scientists in China, most were the focus of the research of Dr. Luo Zhexi. He was part of the younger generation of brilliant young minds that were born in China during and after the dark days of the Cultural Revolution, received training in the United States, and then used their connections to do amazing research on Chinese fossils that were published in all the top journals. Luo got his undergrad training at Nanjing University, then earned his PhD at the University of California, Berkeley, did a post-doc at Harvard, and then held a position at the Carnegie Museum in Pittsburgh. He escaped staff and budget cuts at the Carnegie Museum and landed on his feet, and he is now a star professor at the University of Chicago.

Luo and colleagues have described a number of important specimens, including the earliest known marsupial, *Sinodelphys szalayi*, as well as the early placental, *Eomaia scansoria*, both from the Lower Cretaceous beds in Liaoning, China. He also described the oldest placental mammal fossil, the Late Jurassic *Juramaia sinensis*, which was much more advanced than its contemporaries, the archaic Late Jurassic mammals I had studied from Como Bluff, Wyoming.

More important, these Chinese localities gave us the first complete skeletons of mammal groups that had long been poorly understood and only known from isolated teeth and jaws. One of the biggest puzzles were the docodonts. *Docodon* itself had first been described by O. C. Marsh from the Como Bluff beds, but no one knew what they were related to. For a century, jaws and teeth with strangely squared crowns with a saddle-shaped ridge between the cusps at each end (rather than the typical three-cusped pattern of triconodonts) were common from the same Upper Jurassic beds that produced other Mesozoic mammals as well as huge sauropod dinosaurs. Docodonts had teeth suggesting they were slightly more omnivorous and not as insectivorous as were most Mesozoic mammals. Nothing was known about the skeleton of these animals until the last decade or so, when more complete skeletons were found of fossils such as *Haldanodon* and *Castorocauda*.

Haldanodon, from the Upper Jurassic Guimarota coal beds of Portugal, was about 15 inches (38 centimeters) long and had a mole-like body with powerful forelimbs with short curved fingers and claws for digging. The snout bones had a roughened area for some sort of shield or nail-like hardening on the nose, consistent with the digging idea. Its jaws were very robust, with features showing that they had relatively powerful bite forces.

Even more surprising is *Castorocauda*, known from a remarkable complete skeleton from the Middle Jurassic (164 Ma) Daohugou lake beds of Inner Mongolia (figure 4.6 and figure 4.7). Described by Luo and colleagues, the specimen is so beautifully preserved that even the hair and soft tissues are visible. Its body was about 17 inches (43 centimeters) long and it weighed almost 2 pounds (about 800 grams), making it one of the largest mammals of its time. It was built a bit like that of an otter or a platypus, with a broad swimming tail covered with scales like that of a beaver. This is how it got its name *Castorocauda lutrasimilis* ("beaver tail like an otter"). Its vertebrae were flattened like those of an otter or a beaver, a feature associated with undulating its body as it swims, and it even had webbed feet. Its forelimbs are very robust for digging or strong swimming and look like those of the living platypus, which both digs and swims. Its docodont teeth have been highly modified for fish catching, so they resemble the teeth of seals and other fish eaters.

Several Chinese Jurassic docodonts were announced in 2015, based on beautiful complete articulated skeletons with hair impressions from the Ganggou site in Hebei Province, China. One of them, *Agilodocodon*, was built much like a squirrel, and spent its live in trees. Another one from the same beds is known as *Docofossor*. It had skeletal features suggesting that it burrowed like a mole. Thus docodonts were very different from most of the shrew-like insectivorous Mesozoic mammals in that they had distinctively different teeth for an omnivorous diet, and some skeletons show they were built more like moles, or squirrels, or otters.

Among the other discoveries published by Luo and colleagues were complete skeletons of the triconodonts, mammals that had first been found in

Figure 4.6 ▲

A scene from the middle Jurassic of China, showing *Agiliocastor* (in the ginkgo trees) and *Docofossor* (emerging from burrow) and *Castorcauda* (shown swimming). (Illustration by April I. Neander, University of Chicago; courtesy of Luo Z.-X.)

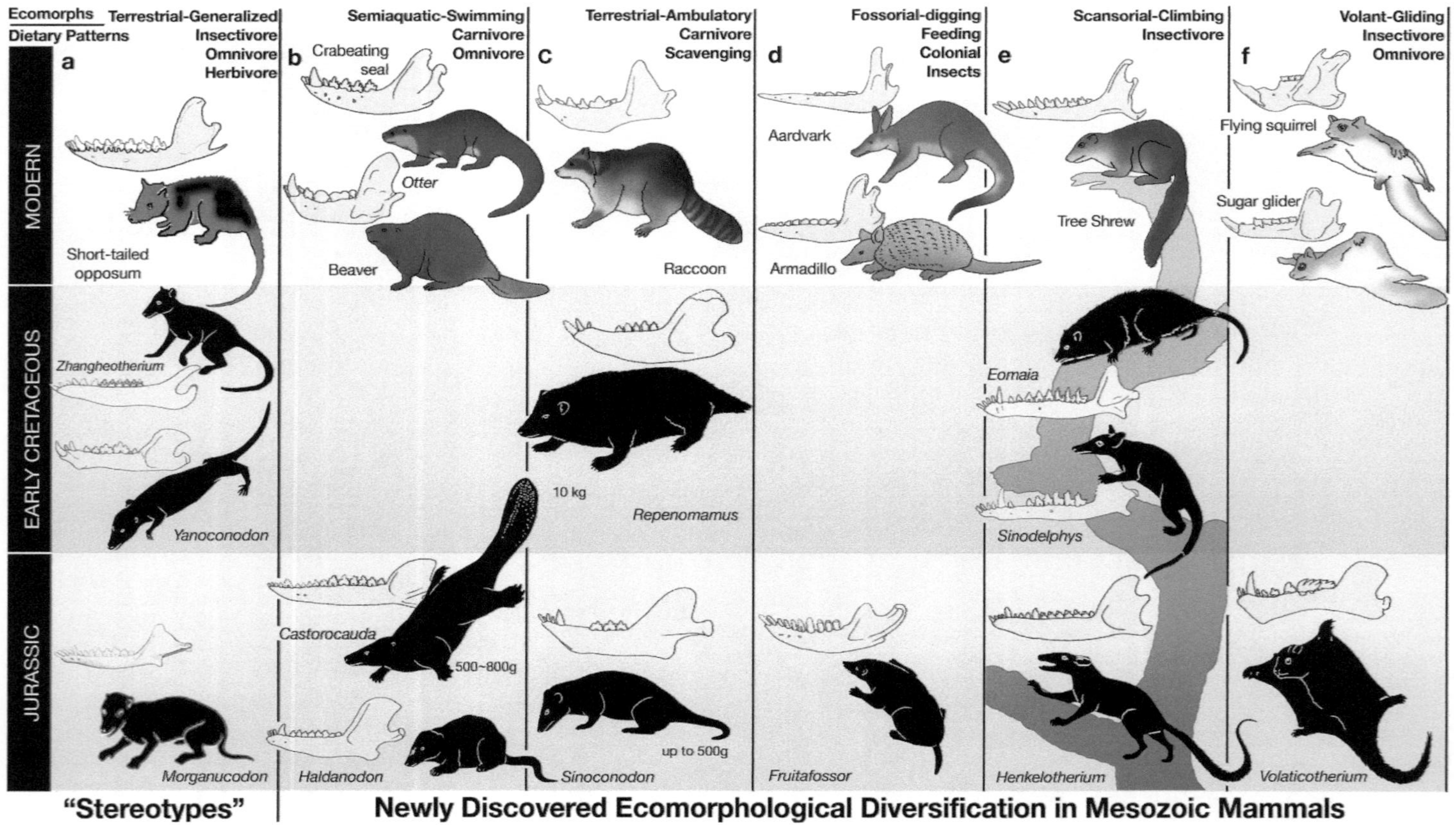

Figure 4.7 ▲

Ecological niches of Mesozoic mammals. (Courtesy of Luo Z.-X.)

the Stonesfield Slate and also in the Morrison Formation, but only known from their jaws and distinctive cheek teeth with three conical cusps aligned in a row (hence their name). When complete skeletons of specimens such as *Yanoconodon* and *Jeholodens* were found, they were small insectivorous creatures much like shrews, as previous specimens had suggested. But a big shock was the discovery *Repenomamus*, a bulldog-sized tricondont that had baby dinosaurs in its stomach—a reverse of the usual scenario of dinosaurs eating tiny mammals. Then there was the discovery of *Volaticotherium* from the Jurassic of Mongolia. It was a nearly complete skeleton that showed very long delicate limbs and body and the dark carbon film of a membrane between the limbs, called a patagium, suggesting that it had a gliding membrane like that of a flying squirrel. Just like docodonts, the triconodonts seemed to come in variety of shapes and ecological niches, all convergent on body forms that placentals would rediscover many millions of years later.

We have come a long way from the scraps of jaws and teeth I studied in the late 1970s. In 1979, when I was working on them, only 116 fossil mammal genera were known from the Mesozoic, and these were mostly from the uppermost Cretaceous beds that produced *Tyrannosaurus* and *Triceratops*. Since then, however, the number of specimens (especially good complete skeletons) has exploded and over 310 genera were known in 2007 and that list continues to grow. More important, we now realize that many of these groups that never survived the Mesozoic and have no direct descendants had a huge diversity and a variety of body shapes, and they were not all insectivorous creatures like shrews. They occupied many different ecological niches in the Jurassic and Cretaceous, such as the flying squirrel niche, the beaver niche, the mole niche, and many other ectomorphs that would be re-occupied by more advanced mammals many millions of years later.

NOTES

1. John Ruskin, *Praeterita and Dilecta* (1839), 22.
2. Augustus Hare, *Story of My Life*, vol. 5 (1882), 358.

FOR FURTHER READING

Celik, M. A., and M. J. Phillips. “Conflict Resolution for Mesozoic Mammals: Reconciling Phylogenetic Incongruence Among Anatomical Regions.” *Frontiers in Genetics* 11 (2020): 0651.

Chen, M., and G. P. Wilson. "A Multivariate Approach to Infer Locomotor Modes in Mesozoic Mammals." *Paleobiology* 41, no. 2 (2015): 280–312.

Gould, S. J. "Irrelevance, Submission, and Partnership: The Changing Role of Paleontology in Darwin's Three Centennials, and a Modest Proposal for Macroevolution." In *Evolution from Molecules to Men*, ed. D. S. Bendall, 347–366. Cambridge University Press, 1983.

Hopson, J. A. "Synapsid Evolution and the Radiation of Non-Eutherian Mammals." In *Major Features of Vertebrate Evolution*, ed. D. R. Prothero and R. M. Schoch, 190–219. Paleontological Society Short Course 7, 1994.

Kempt, T. S. *The Origin and Evolution of Mammals*. Oxford University Press, 2005.

Kielan-Jaworowska, Z. *In Pursuit of Early Mammals*. Indiana University Press, 2021.

Laporte, L. F. *George Gaylord Simpson: Paleontologist and Evolutionist*. Columbia University Press, 2000.

Lillegraven, J. A., Z. Kielan-Jaworowska, and W. A. Clemens, eds. *Mesozoic Mammals: The First Two-Thirds of Mammalian History*. University of California Press, 1979.

McKenna, M. C. "Toward a Phylogenetic Classification of the Mammalia." In *Phylogeny of the Primates*, ed. W. P. Luckett and F. S. Szalay, 21–46. Plenum Press, 1975.

Prothero, D. R. "New Jurassic Mammals from Como Bluff, Wyoming, and the Interrelationships of the Non-Tribosphenic Theria." *Bulletin of the American Museum of Natural History* 167 (1981): 277–326.

——. *The Princeton Field Guide to Prehistoric Mammals*. Princeton University Press, 2016.

——. *Vertebrate Evolution: From Origins to Dinosaurs and Beyond*. Taylor & Francis/ CRC Press, 2022.

Rougier, G. W., J. R. Wible, and J. A. Hopson. "Basicranial Anatomy of *Priacodon fruitaensi* (Triconodontidae, Mammalia) from the Late Jurassic of Colorado, and a Reappraisal of Mammaliaform Interrelationships." *American Museum Novitates*, no. 3183 (1996).

Savage, R. J. G., and M. R. Long. *Mammal Evolution: An Illustrated Guide*. Facts-on-File, 1986.

Simpson, G. G. *Concession to the Improbable: An Unconventional Autobiography*. Yale University Press, 1978.

——. *Major Features of Evolution*. Columbia University Press, 1953.

——. *Tempo and Mode in Evolution*. Columbia University Press, 1944.

Simpson, G. G., and A. Roe. *Quantitative Zoology*. Harcourt Brace, 1939.

Springer, M. S., R. W. Meredith, J. E. Janecka, and W. J. Murphy. "A Historical Biogeography of Mammalia." *Proceedings of the Royal Society B* 366, no. 1577 (2011): 2478–2502.

Szalay, F. S., M. J. Novacek, and M. C. McKenna, eds. *Mammal Phylogeny*. Springer-Verlag, 1993.

Turner, A., and M. Anton. *National Geographic Prehistoric Mammals*. National Geographic Society, 2004.

05 | PLATYPUS, GIANT KANGAROOS, AND WOMBATS—AUSTRALIA'S CURIOUS MAMMALS

DIPROTODON

I like the duck-billed platypus
Because it is anomalous.
I like the way it raises its family,
Partly birdly, partly mammaly.
—OGDEN NASH, "THE PLATYPUS" (1953)

"THE BRITISH CUVIER"

Born in Lancaster in 1804, Richard Owen (figure 5.1) was the son of a West Indian merchant; his mother had Huguenot ancestry. He attended schools in Lancaster, then (like Gideon Mantell, the discoverer of dinosaurs such as *Iguanodon*) he was apprenticed to a local apothecary and surgeon to begin learning the medical trade. In 1824, he spent a year at the University of Edinburgh medical school (where he preceded Charles Darwin by one year). Dissatisfied by the situation at Edinburgh, he finished his medical education at St. Bartholomew's Hospital in London, mentored by the surgeon John Abernethy.

After earning his medical degree, Owen realized that he was not cut out for the life of a country doctor, and instead he focused on anatomy. Abernethy recommended him for a post at the museum of the Royal College of Surgeons, where he soon organized and catalogued all of their

Figure 5.1 ◄
Sir Richard Owen as a young man, holding a moa leg bone. (Courtesy of Wikimedia Commons)

collections, including the recently acquired Hunterian collection of some fourteen thousand specimens, with some three thousand animals, many already dissected. In the process, he taught himself zoology and comparative anatomy by studying all the specimens in his charge, and he soon had an encyclopedic knowledge of anatomy second to none. Indeed, later in life he was nicknamed "the British Cuvier" because his talent and discoveries led people to compare him to the great Baron Georges Cuvier, the founder of comparative anatomy and vertebrate paleontology.

In 1836 he was appointed the Hunterian Professor of the Royal College of Surgeons, and in 1849 he was the curator of that collection. Then, in 1856, he was appointed curator of the natural history collections of the British Museum. There he spent decades working hard for a new building to house the natural history collections separate from the original British Museum in the Bloomsbury section of London (which focuses on art and archaeology). Finally, in 1881 his great "cathedral to science" was dedicated in the South Kensington section of London, and it became the British Museum (Natural History), now just called the Natural History Museum. It is still one of the world's greatest museums, with collections unrivaled by almost any other museum in the world.

Despite his accomplishments, his standing in the scientific community was marred by his personal behavior and peculiar theoretical ideas. By all accounts, he was a very ambitious, driven man who was determined to succeed and reach the top (which he did more than once at the Hunterian Museum and then at the British Museum). He was especially jealous of people who disagreed with him, and he used all sorts of malicious and underhanded methods to battle his rivals or undermine their scientific position. According to one biographer, he was described as a malicious, dishonest, and hateful individual. Another biographer called him a "social experimenter with a penchant for sadism. Addicted to controversy and driven by arrogance and jealousy."[1] The biographical passages written by Deborah Cadbury described Owen as possessed by an "almost fanatical egoism with a callous delight in savaging his critics."[2] One of Owen's Oxford colleagues called him as "a damned liar. He lied for God and for malice." Gideon Mantell claimed it was "a pity a man so talented should be so dastardly and envious."[3] Richard Brooke Freeman put it this way: "Owen: the most distinguished vertebrate zoologist and palaeontologist . . . but a most deceitful and odious man."[4] In an 1860 letter to Asa Gray, Charles Darwin described him thus: "No one fact tells so strongly against Owen . . . as that he has never reared one pupil or follower."[5]

Owen did everything he could to steal credit from Gideon Mantell and his dinosaur discoveries. He claimed that he and Cuvier discovered *Iguanodon*, completely ignoring the man who first found and described the actual fossils. He used his influence in the Royal Society to prevent some of Mantell's papers from being published. Eventually the Royal Society threw him out of their Zoological Council for plagiarizing Mantell's work. When Mantell was crippled and near death and unable to write or publish much, Owen had the audacity to rename some of Mantell's dinosaurs and claim that he had found them. After Mantell's death, Owen wrote a scathing and demeaning obituary that dismissed Mantell as a mediocre amateur naturalist and doctor with discoveries of no consequence. Even though it was published anonymously, everyone knew it came from Owen. Eventually, Owen was denied the presidency of the Geological Society of London for his petty and nasty treatment of Mantell.

When Darwin's ideas about evolution came out in 1859, Owen was insanely jealous because his own weird ideas about nature had never gotten any traction. He did everything he could to battle against Darwin's ideas in scientific circles, and especially with his powerful friends in high places. Darwin wrote of him: "Spiteful, extremely malignant, clever; the Londoners say he is mad with envy because my book is so talked about. . . . It is painful to be hated in the intense degree with which Owen hates me."[6] Owen's nastiest attack was an anonymous book review that distorted and savaged Darwin's book while praising his own work in the third person.

Owen's enmity soon extended to all of Darwin's friends and supporters, including the zoologist Thomas Henry Huxley, the botanist Joseph Hooker, and many others. They eventually became the powerful elite of British science, with Owen and his ideas becoming increasingly irrelevant. When Huxley debated the Archbishop "Soapy Sam" Wilberforce at Oxford in 1860, Owen coached Wilberforce on what to say because the archbishop knew no science—and Huxley could see the fingerprints of Owen's coaching of Wilberforce right away.

When Huxley confidently showed the connection between humans and other great apes, Owen claimed that only human brains had a region called the hippocampus, which set humans apart from all other animals. Huxley did his own dissections and showed that both apes and humans had a hippocampus, and Owen never forgave him. When Owen, as the official paleontologist of the British Museum, first described *Archaeopteryx* in 1861, he did everything possible to minimize what a good example of a transitional form it was between birds and dinosaurs. Huxley corrected that in print as well. Owen also did everything he could to end government funding for Kew Gardens, Hooker's botanical marvel, and have it absorbed into the British Museum.

Despite Owen's constant attacks, the importance of the revolutionary ideas of Darwin, Huxley, Hooker, and their allies made them the masters of British natural history in the second half of the 1800s. Huxley, in particular, reached one of the top positions of power in British science. He used his clout and worked hard not only to support evolution but to modernize British science education and promote a new generation of scientific labs and permanent research programs. Meanwhile, Owen and his peculiar ideas were seen as more and more of a quaint, outdated notion that no one took seriously. Owen's reputation and his ability to hurt other scientists also declined. Owen died in 1892 at age 88, having outlived his wife and children, an embittered man whose scientific descriptions were first-rate but whose theoretical ideas have not held up well.

AN EGG-LAYING MAMMAL? OR A HOAX?

Because of his standing at the top of British zoology, Owen had the right of first refusal on any recently dead animal in the London Zoo. One time his wife got home and found the carcass of a recently deceased rhinoceros in their hallway. He had access to all sorts of exotic animals that had never been dissected before, so Owen published the first descriptions of the anatomy of many new animals from all over the world. In addition, as the foremost anatomist and paleontologist in Britain, almost every important new zoological specimen or fossil found in the British Empire around the world found its way back to London and to Owen. As a result, Owen's work on zoology and paleontology was amazing for his time, and he is responsible for many important discoveries, from the first descriptions of the chambered nautilus, the African lungfish, the dodo, the great auk, the giant elephant birds (*Aepyornis*) of Madagascar, and huge moas (*Dinornis*) of New Zealand, to the first description of the skeleton of *Archaeopteryx*. As discussed in chapter 6, Owen described and published the South American fossil mammals that Darwin brought back from the *Beagle* voyage in 1836. He also recognized and formally named the major groups of even-toed (Artiodactyla) and odd-toed (Perissodactyla) hoofed mammals. Although most of his theoretical ideas have not stood the test of time, his basic talent for descriptive anatomy and comparison with other animals was unparalleled. He published over a dozen books and scientific monographs and more than a hundred scientific papers. For this he received many honors in his lifetime. He was the first to recognize that the "fearfully great lizards" of the Mesozoic were a distinct group, which he named the "Dinosauria" in 1841.

One of the more important parts of Britain's colonial empire was Australia, which was inhabited almost exclusively by zoological oddities. For example, the extraordinary duck-billed platypus was only a legend until European settlers in Australia observed them in the wild and collected them in 1797. The first specimens shipped back to Europe were thought to be hoaxes, some kind of furry mammal like a mole with a duck's bill sewn on

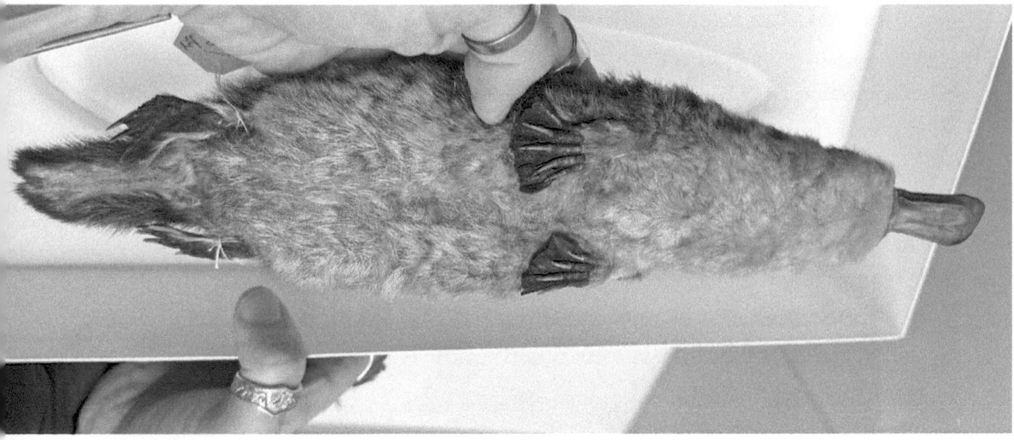

Figure 5.2 ▲
The first specimen of a platypus to be formally described in science (the "type specimen") by George Shaw in 1799, now in the collections of the Natural History Museum in London. (Photo by author)

the front. (Such taxidermized hoaxes were not unusual in those days, and were usually exhibited in sensationalistic fashion as freaks of nature, such as the "Feejee Mermaid," a composite of the torso of a monkey sewn onto the back half of a fish and exhibited in P. T. Barnum's famous "museum"). Finally, a complete specimen (figure 5.2) was described in 1799 by George Shaw, Keeper of Natural History in the British Museum (Owen's predecessor), and this dispelled all doubt as to the reality of the platypus, although there were still debates as late as 1823 about it. For example, Robert Knox, the Edinburgh anatomist (whose name is now associated with grave robbing and possibly even murder to obtain cadavers for dissection), wrote in 1823:

> It is well known that the specimens of this extraordinary animal first brought to Europe were considered by many as impostures. They reached England by vessels which had navigated the Indian seas, a circumstance in itself sufficient to rouse the suspicions of the scientific naturalist, aware of the monstrous impostures which the artful Chinese had so frequently practised on European adventurers; in short, the scientific felt inclined to class this rare production of nature with eastern mermaids and other works of art; but these conjectures were immediately dispelled by an appeal to anatomy.[7]

In 1802, the anatomist Sir Everard Home reported that the platypus had a common opening for both the excretory and reproductive systems, or a cloaca, a feature found in reptiles but not in mammals. Other studies showed that the platypus had a surprisingly primitive skeleton, with reptilian bones that were not found in any group of living mammals. In 1832, Lauderdale Maule reported that the platypus mother had mammary glands that produced milk but did not have nipples on these glands.

But the key distinction hinged on whether the platypus gave live birth, like a mammal, or laid eggs, like a reptile. The Aborigines knew that platypuses laid eggs, but this was not taken seriously by European naturalists. As reported by B. K. Hall:

> In the debate over the anatomy and systematic position of the platypus, national pride and supremacy were at stake. Then as now, much kudos accrued to the nation whose citizens led the scientific world. Britain was pitched against France, Englishman against Frenchman, typologist against evolutionist. Although they agreed that the duckbill was a mammal, England's representatives—Richard Owen and Home—maintained that the eggs remained within the body as in mammals, even though, at up to 17 mm in diameter, the eggs were much larger than normal mammalian eggs. Across the English Channel, France's representatives—Geoffroy and Blumenbach—insisted that the eggs were laid, as in birds and reptiles, but that platypuses represented a separate group. Meckel, Cuvier, and other Europeans maintained that platypuses were true mammals that produced live young. All saw that the key to understanding the paradoxical platypus lay in its eggs. For a time after the discovery of mammary glands and milk production, whether platypuses laid eggs was irrelevant to the debate. The belief that all milk-producing animals give birth to live young was so strongly entrenched that reports of egg laying by platypuses were not taken seriously.[8]

Owen, with his access to the specimens sent from Australia, was keen to solve this zoological mystery once and for all. His close friend, George Bennett, was the first curator of the Australian Museum, and Bennett sent Owen many specimens that had recently been collected in Australia. Owen named and described more living Australian mammals than anyone has ever done and published 25 papers alone on the anatomy of marsupials and monotremes (the group that includes the platypus and the "spiny anteater," or echidna). Two of those papers, on the kangaroo uterus and on an impregnated platypus, led to Owen's election to the Royal Society in 1834. Owen asked Bennett to shoot female platypuses when they were about to give birth, so they could be dissected, and it could be determined whether they were carrying eggs or live young. By 1860, however, Bennett was reluctant to do so because he could see signs that unrestrained hunting had begun to decimate the populations of Australia's native mammals, which were already showing evidence of population decline.

Finally, in 1884, the Scottish zoologist William Hay Caldwell spent many weeks in the creeks of Burnett River in Queensland, Australia, with Aboriginal hunters, where they collected whatever they could find, including specimens of the Australian lungfish and other exotic animals. They found echidnas with both eggs in their uterus and also in a groove on the mother's belly, and finally a platypus mother with a freshly laid egg glued to her belly, and another egg in the oviduct, about to be laid. Caldwell was so excited that he sent a telegram (in the usual minimal wording to save cost) to his mentor, Professor Archibald Liversidge at Sydney University, reading "Monotremes oviparous, ovum meroblastic." This message was then sent around the world.

An eighty-five-year-old controversy had finally been solved—and it was clear that the platypus and echidna were intermediate between reptiles and mammals in many features, from their fur to their bones, to their mode of reproduction, which had reptilian eggs but mammalian milk glands. Bennett had spent fifty years trying to solve the mystery without killing too many animals, but Caldwell recruited an army of Aborigines and slaughtered some 70 platypuses and more than 1,400 echidnas to finally answer the question. Bennett and Owen had been scooped—but at a steep price. Owen was eighty years old when the news finally reached him, and it is hard to know what he thought.

WONDERS DOWN UNDER

Owen not only received specimens of Australia's living mammals to dissect and publish, but he also received some amazing fossils from Australia's prehistoric past, giving him the opportunity to be the first person to unlock the secrets of the prehistory of the island continent. He developed close contacts with Major Sir Thomas Mitchell, one of the great early explorers in Australia, and the first Surveyor General of Australia from

1828–1855. In 1830, the local explorer George Ranken found the famous Wellington Caves, near Wellington, New South Wales. A few years later, Ranken led one of Mitchell's expeditions to these caves, where they excavated enormous bones of a mysterious animal. Based on their size, these pioneers thought they might belong to elephants, rhinos, hippos, or dugongs. On a trip back to England in 1837, Mitchell brought some of these bones to Owen, including a right lower jaw with an incisor. In 1838, Owen named the new genus *Diprotodon* ("two protruding teeth" in Greek), but based on such incomplete material, he could not decide if it was related to a wombat or to a weird kind of mastodon or hippo. The molars had simple cross-crests like those of a mastodon, and unlike any Australian mammal known at the time.

In 1843, lots of fossil bones were found in Darling Downs, in southern Queensland, and Major Mitchell had some of them shipped to Owen in London. The features of the thighbones, front incisors, and molars led Owen to decide *Diprotodon* was related to the mastodon or to *Deinotherium* (see chapter 1), and he ended up renaming it *Deinotherium australis*. But in 1844, the German naturalist Ludwig Leichhardt pointed out that its incisors were clearly those of a marsupial, and Owen changed his mind about it (although he still thought the isolated molars belonged to a *Deinotherium*). Finally, complete skull and skeletons were recovered from Darling Downs in 1847 and sent to Owen. One of the massive skeletons (figure 5.3) was put on display in Sydney and attracted huge crowds. Leichhardt still thought it might be an aquatic animal and suggested that it might still be alive and roaming the great unexplored wastes of northern Australia. Eventually, Owen and others realized that *Diprotodon* was a wombat relative that reached the size of a rhino, and they came around to the modern interpretation that it was one of many giant Ice Age marsupials that used to roam Australia. Later expeditions by the South Australian Museum to Lake Callabonna by the Australian geologist Henry Hurst in 1893 produced up to 360 skeletons of *Diprotodon* in a few acres of a dry lakebed, so it is now one of the best known of all of Australia's Ice Age megafauna.

Figure 5.3 ▶

Diprotodon, the rhino-sized wombat, first named and described by Owen. (*A*) Skeletal mount, now in the Museé National d'Histoire Naturelle in Paris. (*B*) Reconstruction of *Diprotodon* in life. (Courtesy of Wikimedia Commons)

B

Other specimens sent to Owen were much easier to identify. During the Ice Ages, a number of giant kangaroos roamed Australia. One of these was *Protemnodon anak*, described by Owen in 1874, which was built like a wallaby but weighed up to 170 kilograms. Even more distinctive were the giant short-faced kangaroos. The best known of these was *Procoptodon goliah*, which was the largest kangaroo that ever lived (figure 5.4), standing about 8.8 feet (2.7 meters) tall and weighing up to 530 pounds (240 kilograms). Its toes are fused together to form a single 'hoof"-like structure, and it was so large that most paleontologists thought it could not hop without breaking tendons in its feet. Instead, it probably walked as a biped, much like humans do, but balanced with its tail dragging behind it. Another giant short-faced kangaroo was *Sthenurus*, described by Owen in 1873. Although not as tall as *Procoptodon*, it also weighed about 240 kilograms, so it was too large to hop and probably walked instead. It too had fused its claws into a hoof-like nail on its foot and had a relatively short tail compared to living kangaroos or *Procoptodon*. Yet it had relatively long arms and fingers to compared to any

Figure 5.4 ▲

Procoptodon goliah, one of the gigantic extinct short-faced kangaroos from the Pleistocene of Australia, all first described and named by Owen. (Courtesy of N. Tamura)

other modern or extinct kangaroo. As many as three different-sized species of *Sthenurus* have been found in the Lake Callabonna beds, along with the hundreds of *Diprotodon*.

Even weirder than gigantic kangaroos and wombats the size of rhinos were the strange beasts known as *Palorchestes*. The first specimens were described by Owen in 1873 and were fragmentary specimens of jaws and a few other parts, which Owen decided were some kind of kangaroo. He coined the name *Palorchestes* from the Greek words for "ancient leaper." However, as the skeleton became better known, it became clear that it was not a kangaroo but a weird kind of diprotodontid, like a cross between a ground sloth and a tapir (figure 5.5). *Palorchestes* had a massive long body, reaching 8.2 feet (2.5 meters) in length, with thick powerful limbs, and it might have weighed up to 1,000 kilograms (1 long tonne). The front legs were long and powerful, and the hands were armed with long claws, like those of a ground sloth or a koala, which presumably were used to grab branches and pull down limbs and leaves or to strip bark from trees. However, they had a limited range of motion, suggesting that they had a sprawling gait. Their skulls were even weirder, with the nasals retracted far back on the face (like the condition in tapirs), suggesting that they had a tapir-like trunk or proboscis, or at least a very large prehensile upper lip. Their

Figure 5.5 ▲

Palorchestes, the marsupial with a tapir-like snout and with arms and claws like a ground sloth. It was named and first described by Owen. (Courtesy of N. Tamura)

eye sockets were extremely small, so they had very limited vision, and they must have used the sense of smell in their large complex noses to detect threats or food.

But by far the weirdest of all the Australian animals that Owen received was the "marsupial lion," *Thylacoleo carnifex* (figure 5.6). Described by Owen in 1859, it was about the size and build of a regular lion, reaching about 287 pounds (130 kilograms) in weight. The first skulls were collected by the sheepherder William Adeney in 1843 near Lake Colongulac in Victoria and sent to London for Owen to study. When Owen looked at it, he thought it might be related to modern carnivorous marsupials such as the quoll and Tasmanian devil, because it seemed so obviously specialized as a predator. But in 1868, the anatomist William Henry Flower disagreed and pointed out that the detailed skull anatomy was laid out more like a koala or a wombat, so it was another kind of diprotodontid, and thus an herbivore like the rat kangaroo. Owen eventually conceded that it was a diprotodontid, not a quoll, but pointed to its sharp teeth and lack of any kind of grinding teeth and insisted that it had to be predator, not a herbivore, even if it was descended from herbivorous diprotodontids. The debate was still going in the late 1800s when the South African paleontologist Robert Broom argued for a predatory lifestyle in 1898, while the American paleontologist Henry Fairfield Osborn was still convinced it was a herbivore. Other suggestions were that it was a hyena-like scavenger, or a specialist on crocodile eggs, or even a melon-eater.

The skulls were truly odd-looking (figure 5.6A). They were short and rounded and resembled the skull of a turtle in many ways. However, it had large stabbing incisors in front, rather than enlarged canines such as dogs and cats use to kill prey. Its true canines were stubby and vestigial. Even weirder, instead of a series of many pointed triangular, and blade-like cheek teeth, as found in dogs and cats and other placental carnivores, *Thylacoleo* had one gigantic slicing blade shaped like a cleaver, made of an enlarged third premolar, in its upper and lower jaws. This feature makes it look even more like a turtle, whose short, rounded skull lack teeth but

Figure 5.6 ▶

The "marsupial lion," *Thylacoleo carnifex*, first named and described by Owen. (*A*) The bizarre turtle-like skull. (*B*) Reconstruction of *Thylacoleo* in life. (Courtesy of Wikimedia Commons)

A

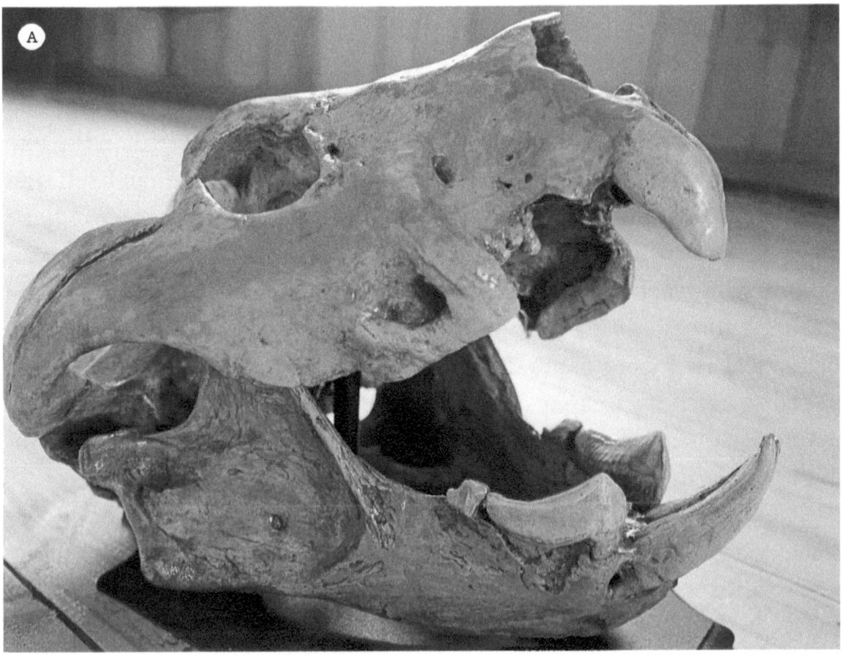

B

develop a blade-like sheath of horny keratin on the front and sides of the jaws instead. Studies have shown that pound-for-pound *Thylacoleo* had the strongest bite of any mammalian species, even stronger than the bite of a lion, so it could kill and slice up animals much larger than itself. But computer modeling of the skull shows that it did not crush the windpipe of its prey to suffocate them, as modern cats do, but instead its powerful bite with stabbing canines and the huge slicing third premolar would slash the throat of a prey animal, causing it to bleed out very quickly. In fact, it was such a big-game specialist that its jaws and teeth were not very suited to catching smaller prey, so that may have made it vulnerable to extinction during the late Ice Ages when the other Australian megamammals vanished.

The debate over whether *Thylacoleo* was a predator or herbivore remained in doubt when looking only at its odd skull, but when the skeleton was finally found in the early 1900s, there was no question of its predatory capabilities. It had long flexible arms with retractile claws like those of a cat, but it had semi-opposable thumbs so it could grab a prey animal even better than the paws of cats are able to do. In this respect, its skeleton (especially its arms) is much better suited for grabbing and subduing prey than those of any living cat or other placental carnivore. Its long limbs were not very suited to running, but it was probably a good climber, so it most likely ambushed prey from a short distance or jumped down from trees, and like a leopard it might have dragged its kill up onto a tree branch to feed without being driven off by other predators. The biggest problem in understanding its ecology is that there is no living analogue to it among predatory mammals or any other group of animals.

These were just a few of the exotic and strange extinct mammals that Owen revealed to the world. He also received fossils of the gigantic flightless birds of Australia, known as the dromornithids, describing the genus *Dromornis* in 1872. It was Owen who received the first specimens of the gigantic flightless birds known as moas from New Zealand, describing *Dinornis* in 1843. These birds were only recently extinct; they were wiped out by the Polynesian peoples who became the Maoris of New Zealand between 1300 and 1445 CE. In short, it was Richard Owen, more than any other person, who brought to light the bizarre extinct creatures of the island continent.

NOTES

1. Deborah Cadbury, *Terrible Lizard: The First Dinosaur Hunters and the Birth of a New Science* (Holt, 2000), 33.
2. Cadbury *Terrible Lizard*, 40.
3. https://www.strangescience.net/owen.htm
4. Richard Brooke Freeman, *Charles Darwin: A Companion* (2007), Darwin Online.
5. Charles Darwin, *More Letters of Charles Darwin* (Library of Alexandria, 2001), 153.
6. Darwin, *More Letters of Charles Darwin*, 166.
7. Robert Knox, "Observations on the Anatomy of the Duckbilled Animal of New South Wales, the *Omithorhynchus paradoxus* of Naturalists," *Memoirs of the Wernerian Natural History Society* 5 (1823): 26–41.
8. B. K. Hall, "The Paradoxical Platypus," *BioScience* 49, no. 3 (March 1999): 211–218. https://academic.oup.com/bioscience/article/49/3/211/242550.

FOR FURTHER READING

Beck, R. M. D., H. Godthelp, V. Weisbecker, M. Archer, and S. J. Hand. "Australia's Oldest Marsupial Fossils and Their Biogeographical Implications." *PLOS ONE* 3, no. 3 (2008): e1858.

Lillegraven, J. A. "Biological Considerations of the Marsupial-Placental Dichotomy." *Evolution* 29 (1974): 707–722.

Long, J., M. Archer, T. Flannery, and S. Hand. *Prehistoric Mammals of Australia and New Guinea: One Hundred Million Years of Evolution*. Johns Hopkins University Press, 2002.

Moyal, A. M. *Platypus: The Extraordinary Story of How a Curious Creature Baffled the World*. Johns Hopkins University Press, 2004.

Nilsson, M. A., G. Churakov, M. Sommer, N. Van Tran, A. Zemann, J. Brosius, and J. Schmitz. "Tracking Marsupial Evolution Using Archaic Genomic Retroposon Insertions." *PLOS Biology* 8, no. 7 (2010): e1000436.

Prothero, D. R. *The Princeton Field Guide to Prehistoric Mammals*. Princeton University Press, 2016.

——. *Vertebrate Evolution: From Origins to Dinosaurs and Beyond*. Taylor & Francis/ CRC Press, 2022.

Savage, D. E., and D. E. Russell. *Mammalian Paleofaunas of the World*. Addison Wesley, 1983.

Savage, R. J. G., and M. R. Long. *Mammal Evolution: An Illustrated Guide*. Facts-on-File, 1986.

Sánchez-Villagra, M. "Why Are There Fewer Marsupials Than Placentals? On the Relevance of Geography and Physiology to Evolutionary Patterns of Mammalian Diversity and Disparity." *Journal of Mammalian Evolution* 20, no. 4 (2012): 279–290.

Szalay, F. S., M. J. Novacek, and M. C. McKenna, eds. *Mammal Phylogeny*. Springer-Verlag, 1993.

Szalay, F. "A New Appraisal of Marsupial Phylogeny and Classification." In *Carnivorous Marsupials*, vol. 2, ed. M. Archer, 621–640. Royal Zoological Society of New South Wales, 1982.

Turner, A., and M. Anton. *National Geographic Prehistoric Mammals*. National Geographic Society, 2004.

van Rheede, T., T. Bastiaans, D. Boone, S. Hedges, W. De Jong, and O. Madsen. "The Platypus Is in Its Place: Nuclear Genes and Indels Confirm the Sister Group Relation of Monotremes and Therians." *Molecular Biology and Evolution* 23, no. 3 (2006): 587–597.

06 | DARWIN'S MYSTERIOUS MAMMAL

TOXODON

Lastly, the *Toxodon*, perhaps one of the strangest animals ever discovered: in size it equaled an elephant or megatherium, but the structure of its teeth, as Mr. Owen states, proves indisputably that it was intimately related to the Gnawers, the order which, at the present day, includes most of the smallest quadrupeds: in many details it is allied to the Pachydermata: judging from the position of its eyes, ears, and nostrils, it was probably aquatic, like the Dugong and Manatee, to which it is also allied. How wonderfully are the different Orders, at the present time so well separated, blended together in different points of the structure of the *Toxodon*!

—CHARLES DARWIN, *THE VOYAGE OF THE BEAGLE* (1836)

DARWIN THE DROPOUT

Charles Darwin was a dropout.

His family held high hopes for him, their younger son. After all, he came from a distinguished family. His grandfather, Erasmus, had once been the king's own personal doctor, and a distinguished naturalist and poet as well. His father, Robert, was also a successful and wealthy doctor. Thus Charles was expected to follow in his grandfather's and father's footsteps and take up a career in medicine as well.

In 1825, when he was sixteen years old, his father sent him to the medical school at the University of Edinburgh in Scotland, then one of the best in the world. But young Charles could not stomach dissecting stinking rotting corpses that had been robbed from graves. He could not stand to watch as doctors conduct surgery without anesthetics, so the patients screamed in agony as their limbs were sawn off. He spent more time collecting insects, shooting birds to make stuffed mounts with his taxidermy skills, and collecting marine life from the local tide pools. Within two years, he dropped out.

Exasperated, his father then sent him to Cambridge University in 1828, hoping that he might earn a degree and become a local country parson. In that role, he could still be useful to society while indulging his love of collecting natural history objects. Once again he paid little attention to what he was supposed to be studying, and instead he hung out with some of the prominent natural historians at Cambridge. Professor John Stevens Henslow introduced him to collecting plants; a cousin got him hooked on collecting beetles. Darwin went in the field with Professor Adam Sedgwick, the first person ever to bear the title Professor of Geology. From him Darwin learned just about all there was to know about geology at that time. By 1831 he had gotten a degree from Cambridge, but he was no closer to settling on a career—and he was clearly not interested in his father's plan to make him a country parson (figure 6.1).

Figure 6.1 ▲

Charles Darwin, as a child (*left*) and as a 27-year-old man (*right*) shortly after returning from the *Beagle* voyage. (Courtesy of Wikimedia Commons)

His father had just about given up on him when an extraordinary opportunity came his way. Henslow sent Darwin a letter telling him about an opportunity on board the HMS *Beagle* (figure 6.2). It was a British naval ship that was getting ready to make a voyage to South America to do surveys up and down the coast of Brazil and Argentina and produce navigational charts for the Royal Navy. The ship's captain, Robert FitzRoy, was a gentleman and aristocrat, and he needed a self-financing passenger on board of the same social class just to talk to during dinners on the long voyage. In the British Navy, the captains were not allowed to socialize with any of the crew they commanded; they only spoke to the crew when they gave orders. It was not uncommon for sea captains to go crazy from the loneliness and isolation without being able to talk to a peer. Indeed, the *Beagle*'s previous captain had shot himself, and FitzRoy's own uncle had slit his throat. Later in life, FitzRoy himself would go crazy too. After pleading and getting support from Henslow and his uncle Josiah Wedgwood (of Wedgwood pottery fame), Darwin's father relented.

Figure 6.2 ▲
The HMS *Beagle* as it passed through Tierra del Fuego in the southern part of South America. (Courtesy of Wikimedia Commons)

Two days after Christmas in 1831, the *Beagle* sailed from Portsmouth harbor with twenty-two-year-old Charles on board. Initially, all he had to do was have dinner with the captain, but he also collected specimens and made notes every time he got the chance (although he spent much of the first few months seasick in his hammock). By the second stop, the official ship's naturalist and surgeon, Robert McCormick, left the expedition, and Charles took over the role of naturalist. As a civilian with no shipboard duties, Charles could spend a lot more time collecting specimens than could the official ship's surgeon, who had to tend to the crew. McCormick eventually joined Captain James Clark Ross (whose name was given to the huge Ross Ice Shelf) on the famous 1839 voyage of the HMS *Erebus* to Antarctica. McCormick's work on that ship was again overshadowed by another promising young naturalist, Joseph Hooker, who went on to become one of Britain's greatest botanists (and Darwin's closest friend).

Meanwhile, young Charles Darwin was making amazing discoveries every time the *Beagle* let him disembark to do exploring and collecting. He saw the tropical rain forests of Brazil, which amazed him, and the horrors of slavery on the plantations in Brazil, which sickened him. The voyage continued down the coast of Argentina, and on September 22, 1832, the *Beagle* reached Punta Alta in Argentina, about 450 miles southwest of Buenos Aires. Darwin, Fitzroy, and a crew of rowers visited the rocky outcrops just above the water level. Despite the name, Punta Alta ("high point") is not that high; it is only about 20 feet above sea level. But the outcrops were full of large bones. Darwin and a crewman worked hard on the soft sandstone and excavated skulls, jaws, and many large limb bones. By the time they finished collecting, they had the fossils of nine huge mammals that were previously unknown to science.

Darwin made brief notes on these specimens, but the specimens were quickly packed into crates and loaded onto the *Beagle* for future study by qualified specialists. When Darwin returned to London in 1836, he invited the leading paleontologist in Britain at that time, Sir Richard Owen of the Natural History Museum (see chapter 5), to study and publish his fossils.

THE "BOW TOOTH"

Richard Owen studied Darwin's fossils of the giant ground sloth and was able to relate them to modern tree sloths and the glyptodonts to armadillos (see chapter 3). But some creatures were complete puzzles to him. In 1833, Darwin had found a number of "large cutting teeth" in several localities along the Argentine coast. On November 26, 1833, he purchased a large, nearly complete skull (figure 6.3) from a farmer in what is now Uruguay. As Darwin wrote,

> I set out on my return in a direct line for Monte Video. Having heard of some giant's bones at a neighbouring farmhouse on the Sarandis, a small stream entering the Rio Negro, I rode there accompanied by my host, and purchased for the value of eighteen pence the head of an animal equaling in size that of the hippopotamus. Mr. Owen, in a paper read before the Geological Society, has called this very extraordinary animal *Toxodon*, from the curvature of its teeth.[1]

When Richard Owen looked at the specimens a few years later, he was equally confused. Again, Darwin described the quandary in *The Voyage of the Beagle*:

> Lastly, the *Toxodon*, perhaps one of the strangest animals ever discovered: in size it equaled an elephant or megatherium, but the structure of its teeth, as Mr. Owen states, proves indisputably that it was intimately related to the Gnawers, the order which, at the present day, includes most of the smallest quadrupeds: in many details it is allied to the Pachydermata: judging from the position of its eyes, ears, and nostrils, it was probably aquatic, like the Dugong and Manatee, to which it is also allied. How wonderfully are the different Orders, at the present time so well separated, blended together in different points of the structure of the *Toxodon*![2]

Here, Owen was justifiably confused, because he was looking at the very first specimen ever found of one of South America's unique radiation of hoofed mammals. The notoungulates were South American hoofed mammals that evolved to look like mammals from other continents. Some looked like rabbits, others like pigs or sheep, others like rhinos.

Toxodon was particularly puzzling (figure 6.3A and figure 6.3B). In its body shape, it looked vaguely like a hippo or a hornless rhinoceros. It was about 8–10 feet (2.7–3.0 meters) long, and weighed about 3,300 pounds (1,500 kilograms), with a high hump over its shoulder about 5 feet (1.5

Figure 6.3 ▲

(*A*) The skeleton of the hippo-like Ice Age notoungulate *Toxodon*, one of the last of its lineage. (*B*) Reconstruction of *Toxodon* by R. Bruce Horsfall. (Courtesy of Wikimedia Commons)

meters) above the ground. The skeleton was heavy and massive like that of a hippo or rhino, with robust stumpy legs and short stubby toes for bearing the great weight.

Owen coined the name *Toxodon*, which means "bow tooth," because the broad molars have crests shaped like a bow. The molars are massive for eating huge amounts of gritty vegetation. However, it was odd for a hoofed mammal in that it had a pair of chisel-like teeth in the front, similar to the gnawing teeth in rodents. This completely confused Owen, as the quote above demonstrates. The chisel-like front teeth fooled Owen into thinking that this hippo-like creature was a rodent! Instead, *Toxodon* was performing the role of large rhino-like or hippo-like herbivore in South America, a region that never had native rhinos or hippos. Although early paleontologists thought it might have lived the lifestyle of a hippo, its body posture and the wear on its teeth argue against that. In addition, it is not found in river or stream sediments, but in the dry land pampas deposits along with most of the other animals Darwin found. Thus its analogue is more likely to be a rhino than a hippo.

THE BROTHERS AMEGHINO

Darwin was an early pioneer in South American paleontology, collecting just a few specimens during his brief land excursions from the *Beagle*. In addition, specimens of giant ground sloths collected from South America from the late 1700s were sent to Europe, where pioneering anatomists and paleontologists such as Georges Cuvier figured them out (see chapter 3).

Europeans had studied and described nearly all of the early South American fossils when the bones were brought back from South America. There were almost no South American naturalists who could study the fossils of the "Lost World." The first such paleontologists were two brothers named Carlos and Florentino Ameghino (figure 6.4). Children of Italian immigrants, both were born in Luján, about 60 miles west of Buenos Aires, Argentina (Florentino in 1854, and Carlos in 1865). This is the place where the first South American fossil mammals were found (the ground sloths discussed in chapter 3). Darwin had recovered many of his specimens from the Luján Formation as well. Today the Lujanian South American land mammal age ranges from 800,000–11,000 years in age and represents the late Pleistocene.

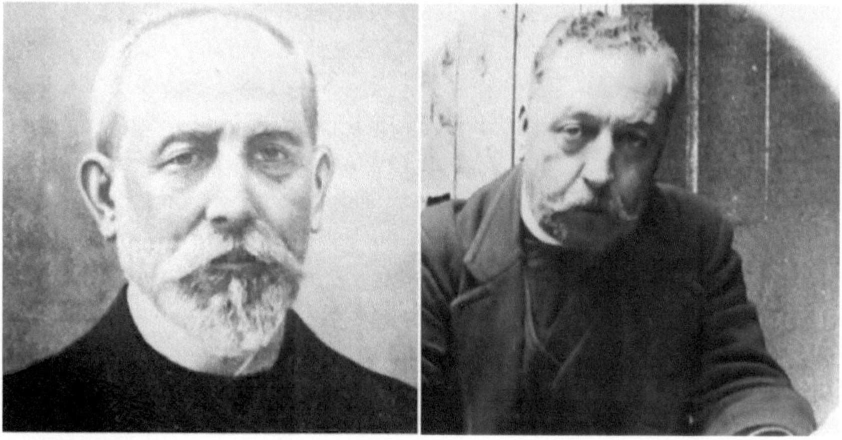

Figure 6.4 ▲
Florentino Ameghino (*left*) and Carlos Ameghino (*right*). (Courtesy of Wikimedia Commons)

Both of the Ameghino brothers were self-taught because there were few universities in Argentina at that time, and none had instruction in paleontology. They began to collect spectacular mammal fossils eroding from the dry desolate badlands of the Patagonian pampas and soon had built up a huge collection. Carlos eventually focused on doing the fossil collecting, spending sixteen long lonely years under harsh, primitive conditions, while Florentino stayed back in Buenos Aires, working in the family business, and writing up descriptions of them for the scientific literature. Their brother Juan didn't have the fossil bug, so instead he maintained the family bookstore (helped by Florentino), which supported their work on fossils until Florentino earned a museum job.

By the time the explorer and anthropologist Francisco Moreno established the Museo de la Plata in 1888, thirty-five-year-old Florentino was well known in the region. Moreno hired him as deputy director, secretary, and also head of the paleontology department of the new museum. The Ameghinos transferred their collections to the new museum, and their efforts became better supported and more professional. A year later, Florentino's huge 1,028-page volume, *Mammalian Fossils in the Argentine Republic*, appeared in the *Proceedings of the National Academy of Science* and won the bronze medal at the 1889 Exposition Universelle in Paris. It brought all their amazing discoveries to the attention of scientists worldwide. The Ameghinos were now the world's experts on South American fossil mammals and became the first important home-grown paleontologists in South America.

While Carlos kept on finding new localities and new fossils, Florentino was a research dynamo, publishing more than 24 volumes of 700–800 pages describing more than nine thousand species of extinct animals before he died at age fifty-six in 1911. He and Carlos not only described fossils but worked out the sequence of fossils in Argentina and described the patterns of evolution in mammals through the entire Age of Mammals. Carlos lived on for another twenty-five years after Florentino, dying at age seventy-one in 1936. Today they are considered the founding founders of paleontology in South America.

Unfortunately, Florentino's work was hampered by his geographic and intellectual isolation from paleontologists in Europe and North America, and also from the lack of specimens from other continents that he could use to compare his finds. He had no real way to establish the age of Argentinian fossils with respect to those from elsewhere. Consequently, he often thought they were older than they really were and argued that South American fossils were the ancestors of groups found elsewhere in the world. He was also continually fooled by the amazing examples of evolutionary and ecological convergence in South American mammals. Thus he often mistook his fossils for relatives of mammals found in the northern continents when in fact they were members of groups that were unique to South America. Some of this was also motivated by a bit of nationalist pride. South America was still a scientific backwater, but Florentino wanted to put it on the map and make it the homeland of every group of mammals found elsewhere. Later paleontologists, such as John Bell Hatcher, William Berryman Scott, and George Gaylord Simpson (see chapter 4), spent much of the twentieth century correcting these mistakes, but in the process they established just how amazing these creatures were in their own right.

The Greek and Latin roots of many of Florentino's scientific names for these fossils suggest that they are horses, hyraxes, primates, or other animals, when in fact they were not closely related to any of these creatures. Eventually, Florentino had described so many new fossils that he was running out of ideas for new names. He began naming his new specimens after famous scientists from around the world, so there are genera such as *Carolodarwinia* (after Charles Darwin), *Thomashuxleya* (after Thomas

Henry Huxley), *Ricardowenia* (for Richard Owen), *Asmithwoodwardia* (after the British paleontologist A. Smith Woodward), *Oldfieldthomasia* (after the British anatomist Oldfield Thomas), *Ricardolydekkeria* (after the British mammalogist Richard Lydekker), *Guilielmofloweria* (after the British anatomist William Flower), plus *Henricosbornia, Gulielmoscottia, Edvardocopeia, Josepholeidya*, and *Othnielmarshia* (after the pioneers of American paleontology, Henry Fairfield Osborn, William Berryman Scott, Edward Drinker Cope, Joseph Leidy, and Othniel C. Marsh). There were names based on six French and three German paleontologists as well; at least 20 were published. He even named *Carloameghinia* in honor of his brother, and *Leontinia* in honor of his wife Leontine Ameghino. Not many later paleontologists have followed this peculiar practice. However, there is a fossil named *Florentinoameghinia*. It was an Eocene manatee relative found Patagonia, which George Gaylord Simpson named in 1932 as a tribute to Florentino.

PSEUDO-HIPPOS, PSEUDO-RHINOS, AND PSEUDO-BUNNIES: THE NOTOUNGULATES

So if *Toxodon* wasn't related to rhinos or hippos or rodents as Owen or Ameghino thought, what was it? *Toxodon* is just one of the most extreme examples of the largest group of native South American hoofed mammals, the notoungulates (which means "southern hoofed mammals" in Greek and Latin). They were extremely diverse, with at least 14 families, dozens of genera, and several hundred species over the past sixty-five million years in South America (figure 6.5). Not only was *Toxodon* a good rhino mimic, but there was also an even better pseudo-rhino known as *Trigodon*, a toxodont that had a short bony horn on its forehead, as did the sheep-sized *Adinotherium*. Another peculiar mammal, *Homalodotherium*, was built like the extinct chalicotheres, a group of clawed horse-like hoofed mammals from the Northern Hemisphere. Like chalicotheres and ground sloths, *Homalodotherium* probably used its long arms and hooked claws to drag down branches so it could feed on leaves. Another was a pseudo-horse called *Rhynchippus*, which Florentino Ameghino thought was a real horse ("hippus" is the Greek word for "horse"). *Rhynchippus* closely resembled some of the primitive three-toed horses found in North America in the Miocene, except that the teeth and other details show it's a

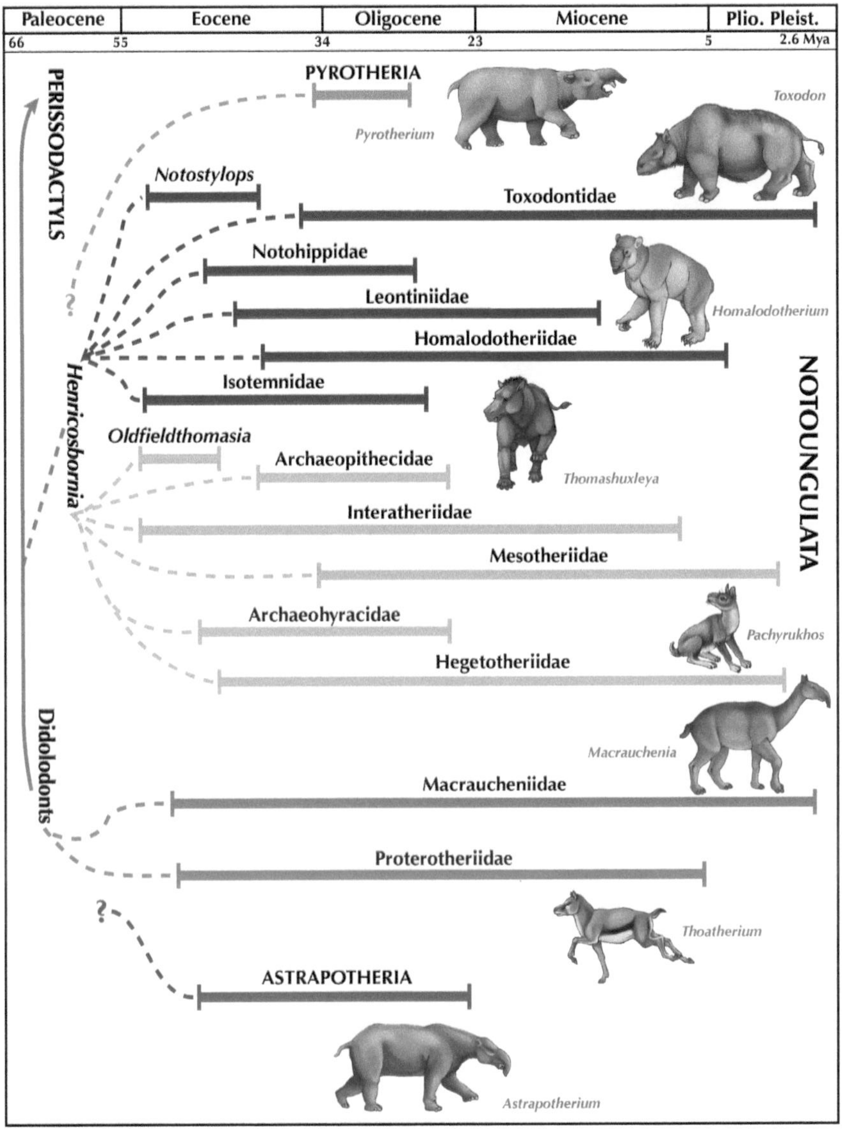

Figure 6.5 ▲

The evolutionary history of South American native hoofed mammals. Most of the lineages are notoungulates, subdivided into the toxodonts and the typotheres. The second largest group is the litopterns subdivided into the camel-like macraucheniids and the horse-like proterotheriids. Both of these groups appear to be closely related, based on their protein sequences. The relationships of the mastodon-like pyrotheres and the tapir-like astrapotheres are less well established. (Drawing by M. P. Williams)

Figure 6.6 ▲
An array of unusual South American hoofed mammals. In the lower left is the tiny pony-like litoptern *Thoatherium*. In the left background is the large litoptern *Macrauchenia*, with the long proboscis. The large beast between them with the tusks and proboscis is *Astrapotherium*. On the right middle is another beast with a trunk, *Pyrotherium*. The rest of the creatures are notoungulates. The tiny rabbit-like creature on the lower right is *Pachyrukhos*. The animal behind it is *Thomashuxleya*. The large creature to the right of the human is *Homalodotherium*. The horned toxodont to the left is *Trigodon*, and the big hippo-like animal in the background is *Toxodon*. (Drawing by M. P. Williams)

notoungulate, not a real horse. Yet another fossil, *Thomashuxleya*, was an ecological equivalent of a warthog, except it had teeth nothing like those of a pig (figure 6.6).

All of these animals belong in the same group of notoungulates, known as the toxodonts (named after *Toxodon*, of course). Yet another group of notoungulates was the typotheres (figure 6.5), which were just as clever as the toxodonts in mimicking the body forms of mammals found elsewhere. There were the strange, sheep-like interatheres. The mesotheres had chisel-like front teeth like those of a rodent. The archaeohyracids, as their name suggests, vaguely resembled the hyraxes of Africa and the Middle East. The hegetotheres were remarkably convergent on rodents and rabbits. One of them, *Propachyrukhos*, even had large ears, long legs for hopping, large eyes for nocturnal vision, and chisel-like front teeth (figure 6.7).

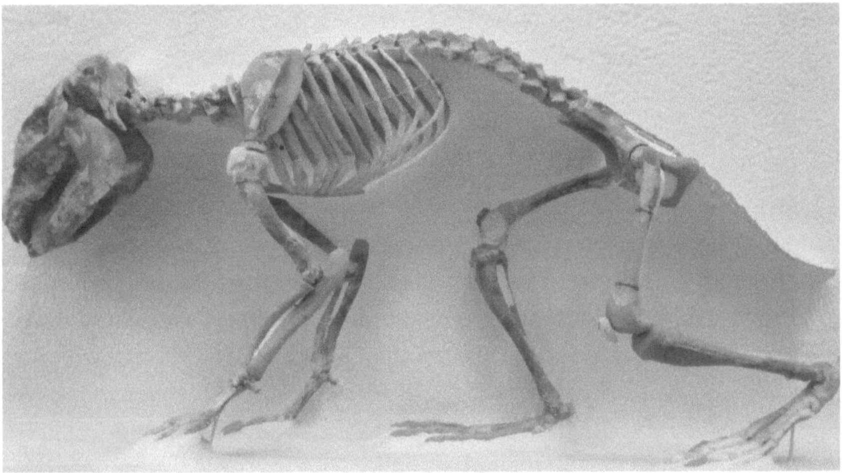

Figure 6.7 ▲
The rabbit-like notoungulate known as *Pachyrukhos*. (Courtesy of Wikimedia Commons)

PSEUDO-CAMELS AND PSEUDO-HORSES: THE LITOPTERNS

Let us return to the voyage of the *Beagle*. On February 9, 1834, at Port Julian further south on the coast of southern Patagonia, Darwin found the bones of yet another creature that reminded him of a camel. Even though South America does have camel relatives (the llama, alpaca, vicuña, and guanaco), this creature would prove to be a case of extraordinary convergent evolution. Indeed, the name that Owen gave it was *Macrauchenia* ("big llama" in Greek). As Darwin wrote:

> . . . . a tooth of a Pachydermatous animal, probably the same with the Macrauchenia, a huge beast with a long neck like a camel, which I shall also refer to again.[3]

The only fossils that Owen had to work with were several neck bones, plus leg bones, some teeth, and other bone fragments. The neck bones look much like camel neck vertebrae, so it was no wonder that Owen was confused. Once most of the skeleton was found, it was apparent that *Macrauchenia* was not related to any group of mammals from any other continent (camel or otherwise). Instead, it was a member of a uniquely South

American group, the litopterns (LITT-top-terns) (figures 6.5, 6.8). It was a classic case of convergent evolution by an unrelated South American hoofed mammal trying to *look* like a camel.

This is apparent once you look at the entire animal, not just the neck bones. It was a big animal, about 10 feet (3 meters) long and weighing about 1,000 kilograms (1 metric tonne), more the size of a giraffe than a camel. Its head was large with a prominent snout, and the fact that its nostrils are high on the top of its skull suggests that it had a snout or proboscis, much like that of a tapir or mastodont (figure 6.8A and figure 6.8B). Even though its neck was long and slender, it had a massive body with feet more like those of a rhinoceros, not the delicate two-toed feet seen in modern camels like llamas and guanacos. Yet research into its feet and ankles suggest that it had unusually high mobility, and was able to change directions quickly, much like certain living antelopes do to avoid predators. It had a full set of 44 teeth with a crown pattern unique to litopterns, and not found in any group of non-South American mammals, including camels, antelope, giraffes, rhinos or tapirs. Analysis of the wear on its teeth, and the carbon chemistry in them, suggest that it fed on a mixture of grasses and leaves, and was not a specialist in either. In short, *Macrauchenia* is a bizarre composite of a camel, a tapir, a rhino, and an antelope or giraffe—a creature designed by a committee.

Macrauchenia was just the tip of the iceberg. It is just one extreme example of a litoptern (figure 6.5). Just like notoungulates, litopterns were very diverse over the past sixty-five million years, with at least five families and dozens of species. Many were sheep-sized hoofed mammals with a variety of adaptations for different kinds of diets.

One of the most distinctive types of litopterns was the proterotheres, including the three-toed *Diadaphorus*, which resembled three-toed horses of North America, and the one-toed *Thoatherium*. In body form, *Thoatherium* closely resembled the late Miocene horses that lived in North America, but it was an even more specialized runner than any true horse. While even living horses still have tiny splints of their reduced side toes alongside their main toe, *Thoatherium* had only one central toe on each foot, with no trace of side toes. Once again, South American hoofed mammals demonstrate amazing convergence on unrelated mammals from other continents (figure 6.9). In this case, *Thoatherium* has reduced its side toes even more than has the living horse, so it was a better one-toed horse than any living horse!

Figure 6.8 ▲

(*A*) The skeleton of *Macrauchenia*, the Ice Age litoptern with the elephant-like proboscis, but built like a camel. In the left foreground is the archaic North American ungulate *Phenacodus*. (*B*) Reconstruction of *Macrauchenia* by R. Bruce Horsfall. (Courtesy of Wikimedia Commons)

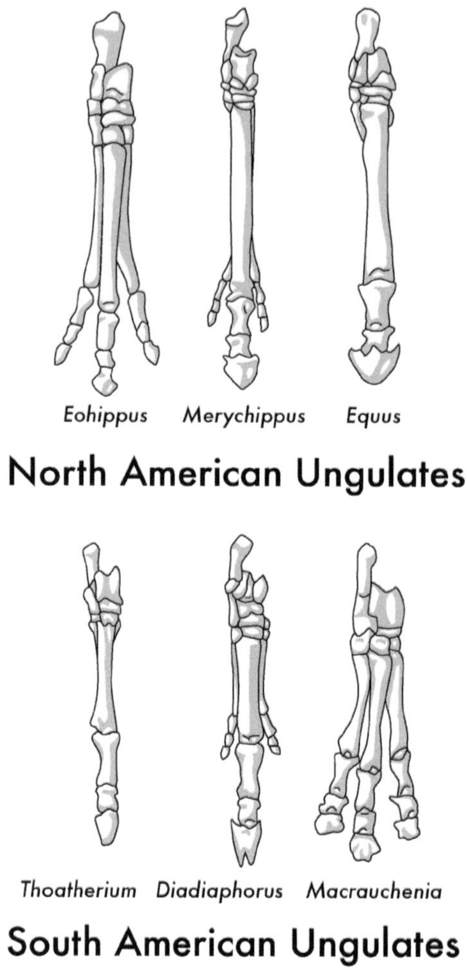

Figure 6.9 ▲

Comparison of the feet of three-toed and one-toed horses (*top row*) that show evolutionary convergence with the feet of some litopterns (*bottom row*). *Macrauchenia* retains the robust three-toed foot seen in the earliest horses like *Eohippus*, but *Diadaphorus* resembles the three-toed horses like *Merychippus* or *Mesohippus*, and *Thoatherium* was completely one-toed, losing even more of its side toes than did the living horse *Equus*. This is a remarkable example of evolutionary convergence because in the rest of the skeleton (especially the details of the teeth and skulls) litopterns looked nothing like a horse. (Redrawn from several sources)

LIGHTNING AND FIRE

Notoungulates and litopterns make up most of the diversity of South America's native hoofed mammals. But there are two other peculiar groups of creatures that are placed in their own lineages, and whose relationships to other mammals are controversial. In many ways, they appear to be South American imitations of the mastodonts, or maybe tapirs, found on the rest of the continents, but in detail they are clearly not related to any other kind of mammal.

The first of these were the pyrotheres, whose name means "fire beasts." Pyrotheres were about the size and build of a rhinoceros or mastodont, with short slender legs, a long barrel-shaped body, and a skull with short upper and lower tusks (figure 6.10). The nasal bones on the tip of the snout are shifted backward, suggesting that it also had a short trunk like that of a tapir or mastodont as well. Pyrothere molars have well-developed cross-crests

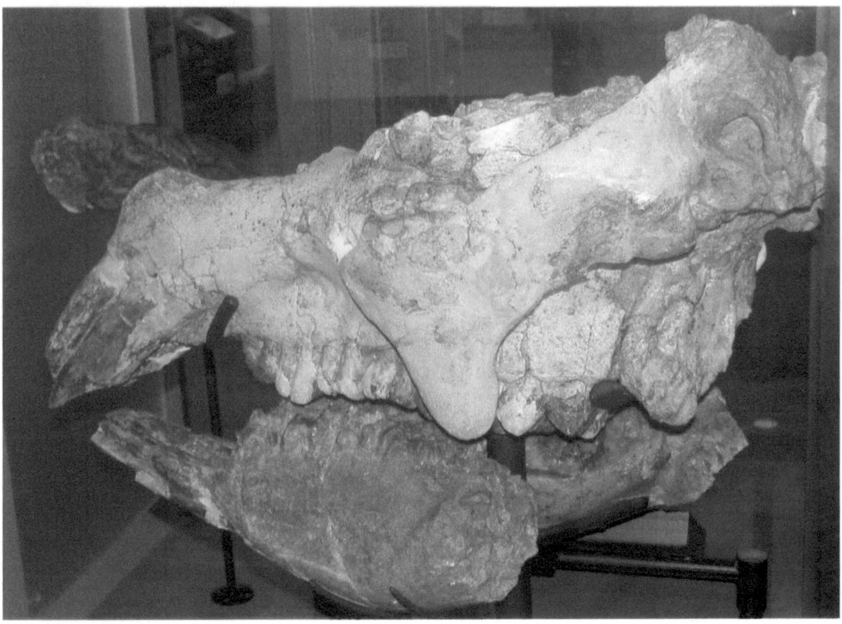

Figure 6.10 ▲
The skull of *Pyrotherium*, on display at the Beneski Museum of Natural History in Amherst College, which had prominent upper and lower tusks, and a big opening in the nasal region for the attachment of a trunk or proboscis. (Photo by author)

like those of tapirs and some mastodonts, suggesting a leaf-browsing diet. Only six genera of pyrotheres are known, scattered from the Paleocene to the Oligocene, and their relationships are controversial. Despite the tusks and proboscis that fooled Ameghino and other early scientists, they are clearly not related to mastodonts. They have anatomical features that resemble a wide range of extinct mammals from other continents, although some paleontologists consider them to be close relatives of the notoungulates. Unfortunately, there are not enough good anatomical characters in the fossils to answer this question yet.

Even more peculiar than the pyrotheres were the astrapotheres, or "lightning beasts." About thirteen genera of astrapotheres are known. The strangest of all of them was *Astrapotherium* itself, which was the size of a rhino or mastodont (about 10 feet or 3 meters long), with a very long trunk and spindly legs, features that suggest it was amphibious. Its skull is truly amazing, with large hippo-like or mastodont-like curved upper and lower tusks protruding from its mouth, and large openings in the snout region around the nostrils, suggesting a longer proboscis or trunk (figure 6.11).

Figure 6.11 ▲

The skull of the bizarre beast known as *Astrapotherium*. It had peculiar upper and lower tusks unlike that seen in any other mammal, and the nasal notch retracted far back on the skull, suggesting a large proboscis or trunk. Yet in the teeth and every other detail of the skull it looks nothing like an elephant or mastodont, so this is an amazing example of evolutionary convergence. (Courtesy of Wikimedia Commons)

Once again, we have an example of a South American hoofed mammal mimicking tapirs or mastodonts, complete with the trunk and tusks.

JURASSIC PARK REDUX

So what are all these peculiar creatures related to? Because they are all extinct, scientists have done their best with their bones and teeth to figure out what they might be related to among more familiar mammals, but with limited success. Then in 2015, a startling piece of science was published that seemed to finally solve at least part of the puzzle. It smacks of "Jurassic Park," but this is an example of molecular paleontology that gives long-sought answers, not monsters out to get you.

Scientists have been trying to sequence the genomes of extinct animals for a long time, mostly to see if they could recognize and decipher their genes and see how they differ from living animals. However, contrary to "Jurassic Park," DNA is fragile and decays rapidly once an animal dies. There is no possibility that the DNA of dinosaurs sixty-five million years old or older could survive intact, so "Jurassic Park" and all its sequels are pure fiction. Instead, scientists have focused on very young specimens, less than 100,000 years old from the last Ice Age, which have the best chance that their DNA is still intact.

Even with this limited goal, the problem was much harder than anyone expected. Nearly all the early announcements of the genomes of mammoths, saber-toothed cats, dire wolves, and early humans turned out to be false alarms because there are so many ways that modern DNA (even from the dust in a normal lab) can contaminate the specimens. While the fossils lie in the permafrost, or the tar pits, or in the soil, or in museum drawers, not only does the original DNA break down and disappear but the DNA from bacteria and many other contaminants gets into the sample, and this is what confounded all the early studies.

Now research procedures and protocols are extremely strict, and checked and rechecked many times, so most of these false alarms can be ruled out, and the truly ancient genetic sequences determined. In the past decade, certain labs have successfully determined not only the genomes of mammoths but also of several kinds of extinct humans, such as Neanderthals, and possibly a previously unrecognized species of humans known as Denisovans that lived in Siberia during the last Ice Age.

But the South American hoofed mammals have been extinct for a long time, so getting their DNA is unlikely. However, there are a few well-preserved specimens of *Toxodon* and *Macrauchenia* that date from the end of the last Ice Age, and their preservation is as good as any notoungulate or litoptern we have. Instead of DNA, a group of scientists looked at the sequences of the proteins in these fossils and compared them to the proteins of living hoofed mammals. Protein sequences are much more stable and do not degrade as fast as DNA does. From this method, they found that at least one notoungulate (*Toxodon*) and one litoptern (*Macrauchenia*) both seem to be distantly related to the perissodactyls, the group of odd-toed hoofed mammals that includes horses, rhinos, and tapirs. It would be nice to have data from more specimens of other notoungulates and litopterns, but for the moment, these are the only choices because these two species were the last survivors of their lineages and vanished at the end of the Ice Ages.

This doesn't definitively prove that *all* South American hoofed mammals are very distantly related to horses and rhinos, but it's a start. So far, there are no fossils of astrapotheres or pyrotheres that are young enough (both groups were gone by the end of the Miocene), so protein analyses are unlikely to solve that mystery. The result is consistent, however, with the strong similarity of an early Paleocene South American fossil group, the didolodonts, which are considered primitive litopterns but also resemble some types of extinct Paleocene hoofed mammals from North America known as mioclaenids. Indeed, there are some mioclaenids in the Paleocene rocks of South America, showing that they were able to walk from North America on the remnants of the land bridge that brought duckbilled dinosaurs and ankylosaurs down in the latest Cretaceous, and was apparently still connected in the Paleocene.

As scientists since Ameghino have shown, the details of their teeth and skull bones show that these are uniquely South American groups only distantly related to any groups of hoofed mammals from other continents. Like the rest of the endemic groups of South America, such as carnivorous marsupials and the xenarthrans, they got to the island continent early before it was isolated (probably during the late Cretaceous or Paleocene, based on the earliest fossils) and never had genetic links with other groups of mammals afterward. Once they were established, they had no competition from the more familiar mammals that evolved on the northern continents or

Africa because South America was completely isolated. Without any true mastodonts or horses or rhinos or hippos or rabbits around, South America's native hoofed mammals evolved to fill the same ecological niches these creatures occupied in other places—just as the opossums evolved to fill the niches of wolves, hyaenas, and saber-tooths. This is one of the most extraordinary examples of evolutionary convergence ever demonstrated, and it's all due to the isolation of South America and the power of evolution and ecology.

NOTES

1. Charles Darwin, *The Zoology of the Voyage of the H.M.S.* Beagle, Geological Introduction, Part I: Fossil Mammalia (1839), 4.
2. Charles Darwin, *The Voyage of the Beagle* (1836), 85.
3. Darwin, *The Zoology of the Voyage of the H.M.S.* Beagle, 4.

FOR FURTHER READING

Billet, G. "Phylogeny of the Notoungulata (Mammalia) Based on Cranial and Dental Characters." *Journal of Systematic Palaeontology* 9, no. 4 (2011): 481–497.

Buckley, M. "Ancient Collagen Reveals Evolutionary History of the Endemic South American 'Ungulates.'" *Proceedings of the Royal Society B: Biological Sciences* 282, no. 1806 (2015): 20142671.

Cifelli, R. L. "The Phylogeny of the Native South American Ungulates." In *Mammal Phylogeny: Placentals*, vol. 2, ed. F. S. Szalay and M. J. Novacek, 195–216. Springer-Verlag, 1993.

Croft, D. A., J. N. Gelfo, and G. M. López. "Splendid Innovation: The Extinct South American Native Ungulates." *Annual Review of Earth and Planetary Sciences* 48, no. 1 (2020): 259–290.

Desmond, A., and J. Moore. *Darwin: The Life of a Tormented Evolutionist*. Warner, 1991.

Lister, A. *Darwin's Fossils: The Collections That Shaped the Theory of Evolution*. Smithsonian Books, 2018.

McKenna, M. C. "Toward a Phylogenetic Classification of the Mammalia." In *Phylogeny of the Primates: A Multidisciplinary Approach* (Proceedings of WennerGren Symposium, no. 61, Austria, July 6–14, 1974), ed. W. P. Luckett and F. S. Szalay, 21–46. Plenum, 1975.

Prothero, D. R. *Giants of the Lost World*. Smithsonian Books, 2016.

——. *The Princeton Field Guide to Prehistoric Mammals*. Princeton University Press, 2016.

——. *Vertebrate Evolution: From Origins to Dinosaurs and Beyond*. Taylor & Francis/CRC Press, 2022.

Savage, D. E., and D. E. Russell. *Mammalian Paleofaunas of the World*. Addison Wesley, 1983.

Savage, R. J. G., and M. R. Long. *Mammal Evolution: An Illustrated Guide*. Facts-on-File, 1986.

Welker, F., M. J. Collins, J. A. Thomas, M. Wadsley, S. Brace, E. Cappellini, et al. "Ancient Proteins Resolve the Evolutionary History of Darwin's South American Ungulates." *Nature* 522, no. 7554 (2015): 81–84.

Westbury, M., S. Baleka, A. Barlow, S. Hartmann, J. L. A. Paijmans, A. Kramarz, et al. "A Mitogenomic Timetree for Darwin's Enigmatic South American Mammal." *Macrauchenia patachonica*." *Nature Communications* 8 (2017): 15951.

07 | SIX-HORNED SABER-TOOTHS AND THE "BONE WARS"

UINTATHERIUM

King of living things at that dawn of tertiary time, I named him *Eobasileus*, and the species from its peculiar horns, *Eosbasileus pressicornus*.

—EDWARD DRINKER COPE, "THE MONSTER OF MAMMOTH BUTTES" (1873).

COPE VS. MARSH

Most of the early discoveries of American fossil mammals were made by the two most important American vertebrate paleontologists of the late 1800s: Edward Drinker Cope and Othniel Charles Marsh (figure 7.1). They were similar in many ways: strong-willed, brilliant, egotistical, driven, self-centered, quarrelsome, jealous, mistrustful, and never satisfied. Cope was a scientific prodigy with a talent for anatomy, but he was also pugnacious, short-tempered, and inclined to irritate and alienate everyone who could help him. Marsh was much slower and more methodical, and more introverted—but even more jealous and paranoid than Cope. As one author wrote, "The patrician Edward may have considered Marsh not quite a gentleman. The academic Othniel probably regarded Cope as not quite a professional."[1]

They came from very different circumstances. Cope was from a wealthy and influential Philadelphia Quaker family, which helped him land positions at the Academy of Natural Sciences and a teaching post at Haverford College. He showed his genius for anatomy and natural history at age six, drawing incredibly detailed sketches of specimens and learning all their

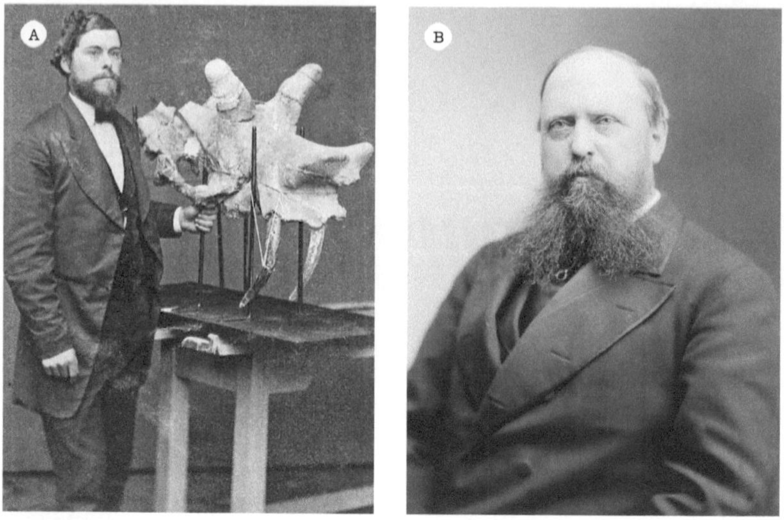

Figure 7.1 ▲

(*A*) Edward Drinker Cope, standing next to the skull of one of his uintatheres. (*B*) Othniel Charles Marsh. (Courtesy of Wikimedia Commons)

names. The founder of vertebrate paleontology in America, Joseph Leidy himself, had taught Cope in comparative anatomy, so in a very a real sense, Cope was the successor to the beginning of vertebrate paleontology in America. Cope used his personal wealth and influence to secure a position on the famous Hayden Survey out west, where he began his career collecting important fossils from the Rocky Mountain region.

In comparison, O. C. Marsh was eight years older than Cope and came from a poor family from Lockport, New York. He started out being forced to work the family farm, but he was an avid fossil collector in his spare time. He never thought of making fossils his career until a local collector and retired Army officer, Col. Ezekiel Jewett, encouraged him in his studies. Eventually, he was a star student at Phillips Andover Academy prep school, and then at Yale. Because he started late, he was much older than his classmates, who called him "Daddy" or "Captain." This expensive schooling was only possible because his rich uncle George Peabody decided to support his education, then gave Yale the funds to set up the Peabody Museum of Natural History with a position for Marsh as head of the museum and curator of paleontology. Marsh was extremely hard-working and industrious, making the best of the incredible opportunity to build the museum and collect fossils from out west that would make it one of the world's best natural history museums.

The two men first met in Europe during the Civil War years, when both were urged to go abroad to avoid getting drafted into the war. Marsh had bad eyesight and would never have been accepted in the Army, and Cope was a Quaker pacifist and could not bear arms for religious reasons. Both men were getting the equivalent of a PhD degree by attending lectures from the best European (especially German) scholars and studying the major museum collections. (No universities in the United States offered a PhD in anything relevant to paleontology at that time.) In Berlin, they got along famously and actually spent several days together visiting museums. They even named some of their first newly described species after each other.

They met again in 1868 when Marsh visited Cope in the Haddonfield, New Jersey, marl pits, where William Parker Foulke had found and given to Leidy the first specimens of American dinosaurs, *Hadrosaurus*. After Cope left, Marsh secretly bribed the pit operators to send him all future fossils, a pattern that would continue for the rest of their careers. Their relationship deteriorated further when Cope published a reconstruction of his long-necked plesiosaur from Kansas, *Elasmosaurus*, and Marsh pointed out that Cope had put the skull on the end of the tail, not the neck—and Leidy agreed. Cope was humiliated, and their grudges began to grow as each attacked the other in print again and again. These feuds exploded into the all-out "bone wars" as both men went out West to get spectacular fossils and outdo each other. In this process, they collected an incredible number of species and named hundreds of new species—but at the price of nearly destroying each other and paleontology as well.

Marsh was the first to go out to the West. In 1870, he arranged a field trip with a number of rich Yale students paying their way to help him in his excavations and prospecting. The photos of these Yale trips, with the rich young dandies dressed up as tough western gunslingers, are unintentionally hilarious (figure 7.2). Through his connections, he had the U.S. Cavalry guarding them all the way, even as the Native peoples were becoming restless. Marsh mounted several expeditions like these, then he gave up traveling to the West altogether and left the collecting to his paid assistants. Nonetheless, he made big collections and studied the local geology of the bone beds, so

Figure 7.2 ▲

O. C. Marsh and his Yale field party, 1871. Even though they are a bunch of rich Yale preppies, they posed with guns and Western gear to look tough for the frontier photographer. Marsh is in the center of the back row. (Courtesy of Wikimedia Commons)

he was aware of the age of his fossils. He also cultivated good relations with the tribes who were not hostile, especially the Lakota chief Red Cloud, who counseled the tribes not to go on the warpath. In 1880, when Red Cloud complained of the poor food and conditions on the reservations to Marsh, he used his influence to bring Red Cloud to Washington and visit the White House, and then lobbied for better conditions on the reservations.

Cope had collectors sending him fossils from the chalk beds of western Kansas (such as his *Elasmosaurus* with the skull mounted incorrectly on the tail) as early as 1867. But in 1872, Cope embarked on his first expedition out to the West, attached to the Hayden Survey (but receiving no money from them). Once out there, he roamed freely without paying much heed to Hayden or his crew, and collected wherever the fossils were rich. During the summer of 1872, all three men—Leidy, Cope, and Marsh—were in the field and often collecting in overlapping areas. Their competition drove Leidy out of field collecting altogether, which ended his supply of new fossils that Hayden had originally given to him.

Marsh's last Yale trip was in 1873, while Cope continued to collect most summers for several years attached to the Army Corps of Engineers. When Cope was out in the Judith River Badlands of Montana collecting in the summer of 1876, Custer and his men were being slaughtered at the Battle of Little Bighorn. The Army warned him to get out of the territory before hostile tribes found him. Cope refused because he was having too much good luck collecting. He had often defused the tension when dealing with Native Americans by taking out his set of false teeth and then replacing them, which amazed them.

SIX HORNS AND SABER TEETH

One of the strangest of all fossil mammals are the bizarre beasts known as uintatheres ("beasts of the Uinta Basin" in Greek), or the order Dinocerata (the name Dinocerata means "terrible horns," based on Marsh's genus *Dinoceras*). Reaching the size of the elephant, with three rows of knob-like horns protruding from its nose, forehead, and back of the head, and long saber-like upper tusks that were protected by a bony flange on the lower jaw, they seem to be more the stuff of fantasy and science fiction than they are of paleontology (figure 7.3). They were by far the largest mammals of the middle Eocene (40–49 Ma), so they are an iconic animal used by illustrators who wanted to show the Eocene of North America. Yet despite their huge body size, all uintatheres had remarkably simple, small cheek teeth, with crown patterns that resemble a giant version of the teeth of the earliest relatives of rabbits (which also appeared in Mongolia and China at the same time as the earliest uintatheres). Several scientists have noted that their cheek teeth seemed much too small to grind the amount of vegetation needed to sustain such huge bodies.

When the first uintatheres were discovered, their large bizarre skulls were important trophies in the "bone wars" between Leidy, Cope, and Marsh. In the summer of 1872, all three men and their crews were working in the middle Eocene beds of the Bridger and Washakie basins of Wyoming. They found skull after skull of these large and impressive uintatheres, but they were in a remote part of the wilderness with no opportunity to publish their finds and get their name in print first. Nonetheless, that didn't stop them from trying. All three men would go to the nearest railway depot not only to ship out their specimens but also to send telegrams east

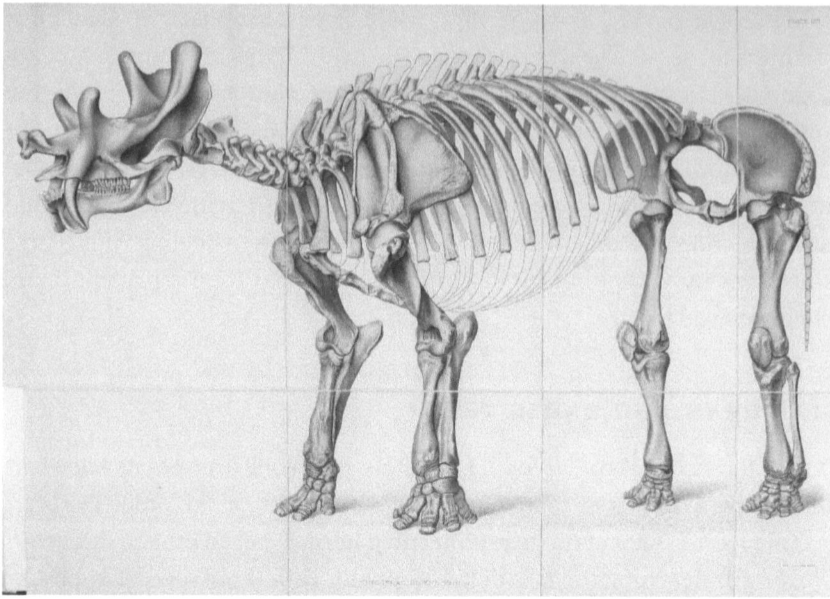

Figure 7.3 ▲
Marsh's plate of *Uintatherium* from the *Dinocerata* monograph. (Courtesy of Wikimedia Commons)

to have their scientific name and description published in their local journal to get credit. Today such slapdash methods are frowned upon, but it was common practice in those days.

Although he was not normally one to rush to publish, Leidy got there first by describing *Uintatherium robustum* on August 1, 1872. On August 17, Cope's telegram from Black Buttes in the Washakie Basin of Wyoming arrived badly garbled, so his intended name "*Loxolophodon*" ended up printed "*Lephalophodon.*" The next day, another notice arrived in Philadelphia that had actually been sent earlier and named Cope's new species *Eobasileus cornutus*. Although they didn't know it at the time, *Eobasileus* was a valid name for the last and biggest of the uintatheres (figure 7.4A and figure 7.4B). On August 22, Cope corrected the garbled telegram with another that restored the spelling "*Loxolophodon*," although that name was invalid because Cope had already recklessly used it on a different animal. Meanwhile, on August 20, Marsh sent a telegram naming his new specimens *Dinoceras* and *Tinoceras* (these names are now considered the same

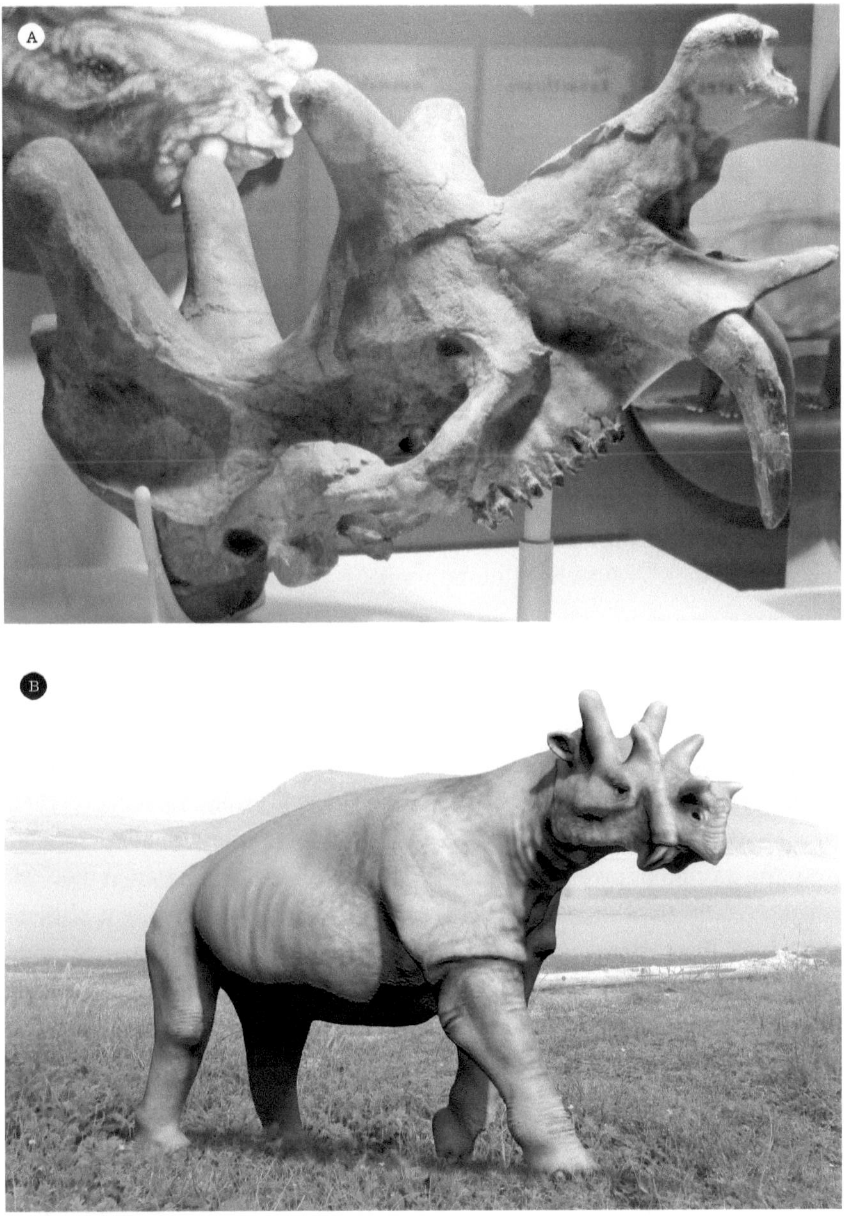

Figure 7.4 ▲

Eobasileus. (*A*) Skull, showing the extremely long horns. (*B*) Reconstruction of the Eobasileus in life. (Courtesy of N. Tamura)

thing as Leidy's *Uintatherium.*) All three were aware of the others working nearby, and disputed their rivals' right to work in "their" fossil field.

When all three scientists came back east that fall, they discovered the mess they had created, but each insisted that their names were valid. This dispute eventually drove Leidy, the founder of vertebrate paleontology in the United States, out of the field altogether. Meanwhile, Cope and Marsh fought it out in the journals, publishing 16 more articles on uintatheres between August 1872 and June 1873, ignoring their rival's names and also Leidy's work. The taxonomy of uintatheres reached a state of chaos, with dozens of invalid names for what are now recognized as just a handful of genera and species. Eventually the "uintathere wars" segued into battles over other fossils. By 1884 Marsh had enough fossils to publish a huge 237-page volume entitled *Dinocerata: A Monograph of an Extinct Order of Gigantic Mammals*, with giant folio pages and lavish illustrations. Not until almost a century later in 1961 did Walter Wheeler unravel the mess and establish the valid names for American uintatheres.

THE "BONE WARS" BOIL OVER

Meanwhile, the Bone Wars that had peaked in the late 1870s began to enter a new phase in the 1880s. Originally, Cope and Marsh had resorted to spying on each other and bribing people to switch sides or reveal the location their rival's fossil sites. Both men routinely destroyed fossils they could not remove from the ground or take with them, and they took great pains when they finished a quarry to fill it in with rocks and dirt to hide it and make it difficult to reopen. In one instance, the rival crews even threw rocks at each other. Luckily they didn't resort to gunplay as was common in the Wild West back then. But by the 1880s, Marsh was flush with tons of bones arriving at Yale every week, whereas Cope had only limited field crews working for him, but he already had so many bones in his house that there was no place for more.

Cope's fortunes took a turn for the worse as he burned through his inheritance by buying the journal *American Naturalist* (still a famous journal today). He also had a hard time landing a paying position at a college or a museum, possibly because of Marsh's influence and also because of his legendary temper and grouchy attitude. Cope undertook several field seasons alone by himself, which damaged his health, especially after a bout of malaria. In desperation, Cope risked the remainder of his inheritance in various speculative gold and silver mining investments, only to lose it all when they turned out to be worthless.

Meanwhile, Marsh had established powerful contacts in Washington and eventually became the official paleontologist of the newly created U.S. Geological Survey, headed by his friend John Wesley Powell. A one-armed Civil War veteran, Powell is now famous as the leader of the first expedition that floated down the Colorado River and all the way through the Grand Canyon. Yet most of Marsh's assistants hated working for him because Marsh never gave them any credit in the publications, and paid them very little, or forgot to pay them entirely.

In 1884, the bad situation between Cope and Marsh reached a critical point. Powell told Cope that all his specimens obtained during the Hayden Survey and other government surveys belonged to the US government, and he had to give them up. Cope disagreed, of course, because he had not taken government money while in the field but financed his work with the Hayden Survey out of his own pocket. Cope's hatred of Marsh boiled over, and he decided it was time to get revenge. As Congress was investigating the US Geological Survey, Cope sent them a long list of mistakes made by Marsh, accusations of plagiarism and theft of government specimens, and charges that Marsh had misappropriated government funds. The congressional inquiry didn't get very far, so Cope then gave the damaging charges and evidence to a reporter from New York, William Hosea Ballou. He wrote a series of shocking articles in the *New York Herald* that raised the issue to the level of a national scandal. The scientific community had known about the battle between the two men for years, but now their dirty laundry was causing public disdain of science. As Elizabeth N. Shor wrote about it:

> Most scientists of the day recoiled to find that Cope's feud with Marsh had become front-page news. Those closest to the scientific fields under discussion, geology and vertebrate paleontology, certainly winced, particularly as they found themselves quoted, mentioned, or misspelled. The feud was not news to them, for it had lurked at their scientific meetings for two decades. Most of them had already taken sides.[2]

The papers filled with more of Cope's charges, then rebuttals by Marsh and Powell accusing Cope of similar misdeeds. Cope called Marsh and Powell "partners in incompetence, ignorance, and plagiarism," and called the Survey a "gigantic politico-scientific monopoly next in importance to Tammany Hall."[3] The controversy played out for a few more months, then died as public interest moved to other topics, with both sides severely wounded but their status unchanged. But in 1892, drought conditions and water problems out West caused Congress to launch another investigation of the Survey, which led to close scrutiny of how Marsh had spent government funds. Many were upset about his support of Darwinian evolution and his description of creatures not in the Bible. Typical of these was a giant scientific monograph Marsh wrote on the "Odontornithes," or the early toothed birds *Hesperornis* and *Ichthyornis* from the chalk beds of Kansas. The inquiry led to such incredible scenes as fundamentalist Alabama Congressman Hilary Herbert saying on the floor of Congress, "Birds with teeth! That's where your hard-earned money goes, folks—on some professor's silly birds with teeth."[4] The appropriation for the US Geological Survey was severely slashed, and Powell was forced to fire Marsh.

Meanwhile Cope obtained a professorship at the University of Pennsylvania, then support from the Texas Geological Survey, and succeeded Marsh as head of the American Association for the Advancement of Science when Marsh stepped down. Marsh, however, received the Cuvier Medal, one of the highest awards in paleontology at the time.

The rivalry did not die until Cope himself died in 1897 at the relatively young age of fifty-six, all alone in his house crowded with unstudied fossils. As his health began to decline, Cope was befriended by a young paleontologist who started at Princeton and was now teaching there, Henry Fairfield Osborn. Soon to become the head of the burgeoning American Museum of Natural History, Osborn championed Cope's work after his death. Desperate for money, Cope sold most of his collection to Osborn, which became the core of the future American Museum collection, eventually the largest in the world. Many of Cope's specimens were still in their crates when he died, so (for example) the famous *Allosaurus* skeleton now on display in the American Museum was untouched in field wrappings until the American Museum worked on it.

Marsh lived two years longer than his nemesis, but he died in 1899 at age sixty-seven. In the end he was also broke and asked Yale for a salary. He never lived to see much of his collection removed from crates, let alone published. And most of the people who chafed under his supervision and mistreatment did not mourn him much.

With the death of both men as the century ended, the field was soon taken over by the next generation: Osborn and many others at the American Museum, William Berryman Scott of Princeton, William J. Holland and others of the Carnegie Museum, plus Elmer Riggs at the Field Museum in Chicago, the Samuel H. Knight and Marsh's old Como Bluff collector William Reed at the University of Wyoming, and other rising museums. They soon developed their own competition for dinosaur bones to fill their halls, but it was a civil, friendly rivalry, not the bitter death-struggle of Cope and Marsh.

Even though the Bone Wars were unseemly and unprofessional, the consequences were mostly beneficial. Paleontology was just a tiny hobby science before the Bone Wars, with only Joseph Leidy publishing obscure articles for specialists. By the time Cope and Marsh died, paleontology was a major science, with a huge public profile, especially as giant dinosaur mounts came to the museums and captivated the public. Dinosaurs entered the public consciousness for good, and many of the poorly understood and incomplete specimens from Europe finally could be reconstructed accurately. This would not have happened so quickly without Cope and Marsh.

Both men wrote and published papers at an astounding rate. Cope published over 1,400 scientific articles in his lifetime, describing more than 1,300 new species. These included papers not only about fossils but also about living amphibians and reptiles. As a result, he became one of the pioneers of herpetology, and their primary journal, *Copeia*, is named after him. Marsh wasn't quite as prolific, but he still published dozens of short articles without illustrations each year, naming and staking claim to every fossil that had just emerged from one of his crates. Before the Bone Wars, only nine dinosaurs had been named from North America (based on isolated teeth named by Leidy, most of which are invalid now). By the time the Bone Wars were over, more than 150 dinosaurs had been named, including most of the famous ones that every kid learns. We will look at some of these in later chapters.

SO WHAT WERE UINTATHERES?

There has been much discussion of the paleoecology of uintatheres. Cope thought they were related to elephants and had small trunks

Figure 7.5 ▲
Cope's 1871 reconstruction of *Uintatherium* with elephantine trunks. (Courtesy of Wikimedia Commons)

(figure 7.5). More recently, Bill Turnbull pointed out that uintatheres have a very deep broad rib cage and huge hip region, suggesting that they had a large gut fermentation chamber to digest plants (which could not have been highly chewed up with such small molars). Uintatheres do have slightly retracted nasal bones, possibly indicating a prehensile lip, and a large spout-like front end of the lower jaw for a long prehensile tongue. A number of authors suggested that their best analogue might have been hippos because they are recovered from river-channel deposits in ancient jungles of the middle Eocene and have the stature of a semi-aquatic plant eater.

Uintatheres were so large that they would have had almost no real predators except when they were young. They lived between 40 Ma and 49 Ma, when the largest predators were wolf-sized, which were no threat to them. So the spectacular horns and upper canine tusks were probably not for fighting off predators but for display and combat with members of their own species. The fact that there seems to be a distinction between males and females (sexual dimorphism), with the presumed male skulls being

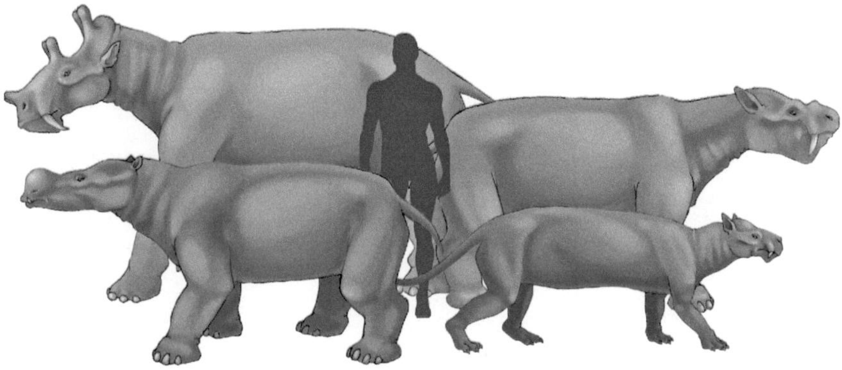

Figure 7.6 ▲
Reconstruction of four uintatheres. Left, front to back: *Gobiatherium*, *Eobasileus*. Right, front to back: *Prodinoceras*, *Bathyopsis*. (Illustration by Mary Persis Williams)

larger in size with longer horns, supports the idea that the horns were for intraspecific competition.

Uintatheres came in lots of shapes and sizes and went through a striking evolutionary history, spread out between North America and Asia (figure 7.6). The most primitive species from beds about 57 Ma in Mongolia is *Prodinoceras* (also known as *Mongolotherium*) (figure 7.7). It was about pig sized, with a long trunk and short legs and wicked canine tusks.

About 52 Ma *Prodinoceras* evolved into *Bathyopsis*, which was found in the early middle Eocene of the Bridger Basin of Wyoming. It was about the size of a sheep, with no horns on the top of its head, but it did have huge saber-toothed canines with sheaths on the lower jaw to protect them when the mouth was closed. About 49 Ma *Bathyopsis* eventually evolved into rhino-sized *Uintatherium* itself, which occurred not only in Utah and Wyoming but also in China. The largest and most spectacular species was Cope's elephant-sized *Eobasileus*, with its extra-long horns on the top of its head. Another of the last American uintatheres was *Tetheopsis*, which most authors regard as the same thing as *Uintatherium* but with slightly longer rear horns and tiny front horns.

Although they vanished from North America around 40 Ma, uintatheres were also evolving in Asia as well. Perhaps the strangest looking of all was *Gobiatherium*, a rhino-sized beast found in the beds about 47 Ma of the

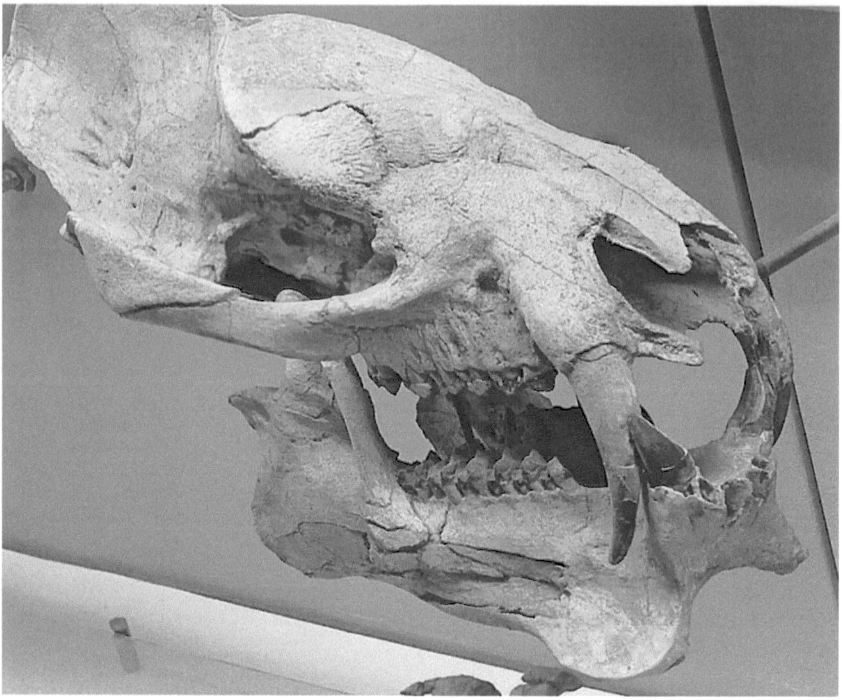

Figure 7.7 ▲
Skull of *Prodinoceras*. (Courtesy of Wikimedia Commons)

Gobi Desert of Mongolia. Instead of the many knobs on the top of the skull or huge canine teeth, it sported a huge bulbous nose supported by bone, with broad flaring cheekbones (figure 7.8). What this huge bulbous nose was needed for is anyone's guess, although lots of paleontologists have speculated about its function.

The relationships of uintatheres are still unresolved. Although their large body size tends to produce features that resemble those of other large hoofed mammals (an opinion that Earl Manning and I published in 1988), they have no definitive unique specializations of the true ungulates. In the 1980s Spencer Lucas and others suggested that their teeth most resemble the Mongolian rabbit relative *Pseudictops*, only much larger. In their view, uintatheres are giant horned bunnies. Given the lack of strong evidence for any relationship, most scientists regard the relationships of the Dinocerata with any other order of mammals as inconclusive.

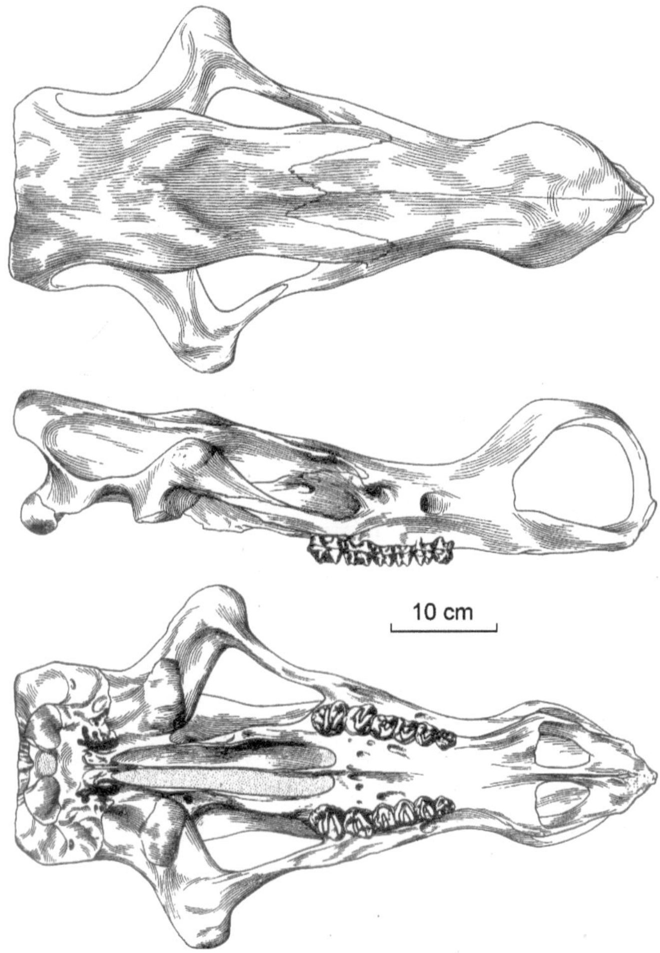

Figure 7.8 ▲
Skull of *Gobiatherium*, showing the bones that supported a bulbous nose. (Courtesy of Wikimedia Commons)

NOTES

1. Patrick Limerick, and Claudia Puska, "Making the Most of Science in the American West: An Experiment" (Center of the American West, 2003), https://web.archive.org/web/20080910045053/http://www.centerwest.org/publications/pdf/science.pdf.

2. Elizabeth N Shor, "The Fossil Feud Between E. D. Cope and O. C. Marsh" (Exposition Press, 1974), 99).
3. David Rains Wallace, *The Bonehunters' Revenge: Dinosaurs, Greed, and the Greatest Scientific Feud of the Gilded Age* (Houghton Mifflin, 1999), 257.
4. Wallace, *The Bonehunters' Revenge*, 260.

FOR FURTHER READING

Lucas, S. G. "*Gobiatherium* (Mammalia: Dinocerata) from the Middle Eocene of Asia: Taxonomy and Biochronological Significance." Paläontologische Zeitschrift 74, no. 4 (2001): 591–606.

Lucas, S. G., and R. M. Schoch. "Dinocerata." In *Evolution of Tertiary Mammals of North America*, ed. C. M. Janis, K. M. Scott, and L. L. Jacobs, 284–291. Cambridge University Press, 1998.

Prothero, D. R. *The Princeton Field Guide to Prehistoric Mammals*. Princeton University Press, 2016.

Prothero, D. R., and R. M. Schoch. *Horns, Tusks, and Flippers: The Evolution of Hoofed Mammals*. Johns Hopkins University Press, 2002.

Savage, R. J. G., and M. R. Long. *Mammal Evolution: An Illustrated Guide*. Facts-on-File, 1986.

Turnbull, W. D. "The Mammalian Faunas of the Washakie Formation, Eocene Age, of Southern Wyoming. Part IV. The Uintatheres." *Fieldiana Geology* 47, no. 1519 (2002).

Turner, A., and M. Anton. *National Geographic Prehistoric Mammals*. National Geographic Society, 2004.

Wheeler, W. H. "Revision of the Uintatheres." *Bulletin of the Peabody Museum of Natural History*, Bulletin 14 (1961): 5.

08 | THE "HYRAX BEAST"—THE EVOLUTION OF HORSES

HYRACOTHERIUM

The geologic record of the ancestry of the horse is one of the classic examples of evolution.

—WILLIAM DILLER MATTHEW, 1926

EXEMPLARS OF EVOLUTION

In 1859 Charles Darwin published *On the Origin of Species by Means of Natural Selection* and turned all of biology upside down. As the debates in scientific circles became more and more bitter, critics pointed to the shortage of good examples of sequences of fossils that led to living animals. There were spectacular examples of transitional forms such as the half-bird half-reptile *Archaeopteryx* (first discovered in 1861), but the record of fossil mammal evolution was incomplete in Europe. Nevertheless, some patterns were beginning to emerge. In 1872 Darwin's chief defender, Thomas Henry Huxley, pointed out that three fossil mammals, placed in order by their age, seemed to form a sequence leading to modern horse, *Equus*. These were the strange middle Eocene fossil *Palaeotherium*, described by Cuvier from the gypsum beds of Montmartre in northern Paris, the early Miocene browsing horse *Anchitherium*, and the late Miocene three-toed grazing horse *Hipparion*. In 1873 the Russian paleontologist Vladimir Kovalevsky, who had studied these same fossils, was even more certain that they represented the evolution of the horse. Both Huxley and Kovalevsky realized the sequence was very patchy and incomplete with just four fossil genera and with big gaps in between. Nevertheless, they correctly concluded that horses evolved from tapir-like animals with three toes and very low-crowned teeth.

European naturalists did not know that their sequence was not representative of the main line of horse evolution because that story occurred elsewhere. Those European mammals were immigrant side branches from North America, where most of the history of the horse took place. Horse fossils from the Big Badlands of South Dakota were first described by Joseph Leidy in 1850. He first referred those fossils to *Palaeotherium* from Europe, and then to the horse *Anchitherium*, not realizing that they were a new form unknown in Europe; today it is called *Mesohippus*. By 1869, Leidy had described quite a few fossil horses found all over western North America.

It was the Yale paleontologist Othniel Charles Marsh (see chapter 7) who took the next step. From 1871 through 1875, he and his crews began to find Eocene, Oligocene, and Miocene horses in the Rocky Mountains. He also found other horses that filled in some of the gaps and began to work out the changes of in their teeth, limbs, and feet from his more complete fossil skeletons, which neither Leidy nor any European paleontologist had seen. By 1874, Marsh boasted that "the line of descent appears to be direct, and the remains now known supply every important form" (figure 8.1). In 1873 his bitter rival Cope described specimens he had received from the lower Eocene beds of Wyoming as *Eohippus*, or "dawn horse." A few years later Cope realized that it was the American equivalent of *Hyracotherium*, and he placed *Eohippus* at the base of horse evolution.

During the American centennial year of 1876, Huxley sailed to the United States to give lectures on topics in natural history. He planned to give a learned discourse on the evolution of the horse in Europe, based on the work that he and Kovalevsky had done independently. But then he spent two days with Marsh in the collections at Yale, where he found that Marsh's evidence was convincing. As his son and biographer Leonard Huxley wrote, "at each inquiry, whether he had a specimen to illustrate such and such a point or to exemplify transition from earlier and less specialized forms to later and more specialized ones, Professor Marsh simply turned to his assistant and bid him fetch box number so-and-so, until Huxley turn upon him and said, 'I believe you are a magician; whatever I want, you just conjured it up.'"[1]

According to Marsh, [Huxley] "then informed me that this was new to him, and that my facts demonstrated the evolution of the horse beyond question, and for the first time indicated the direct line of an existing animal. With the generosity of true greatness, he gave up his own opinions

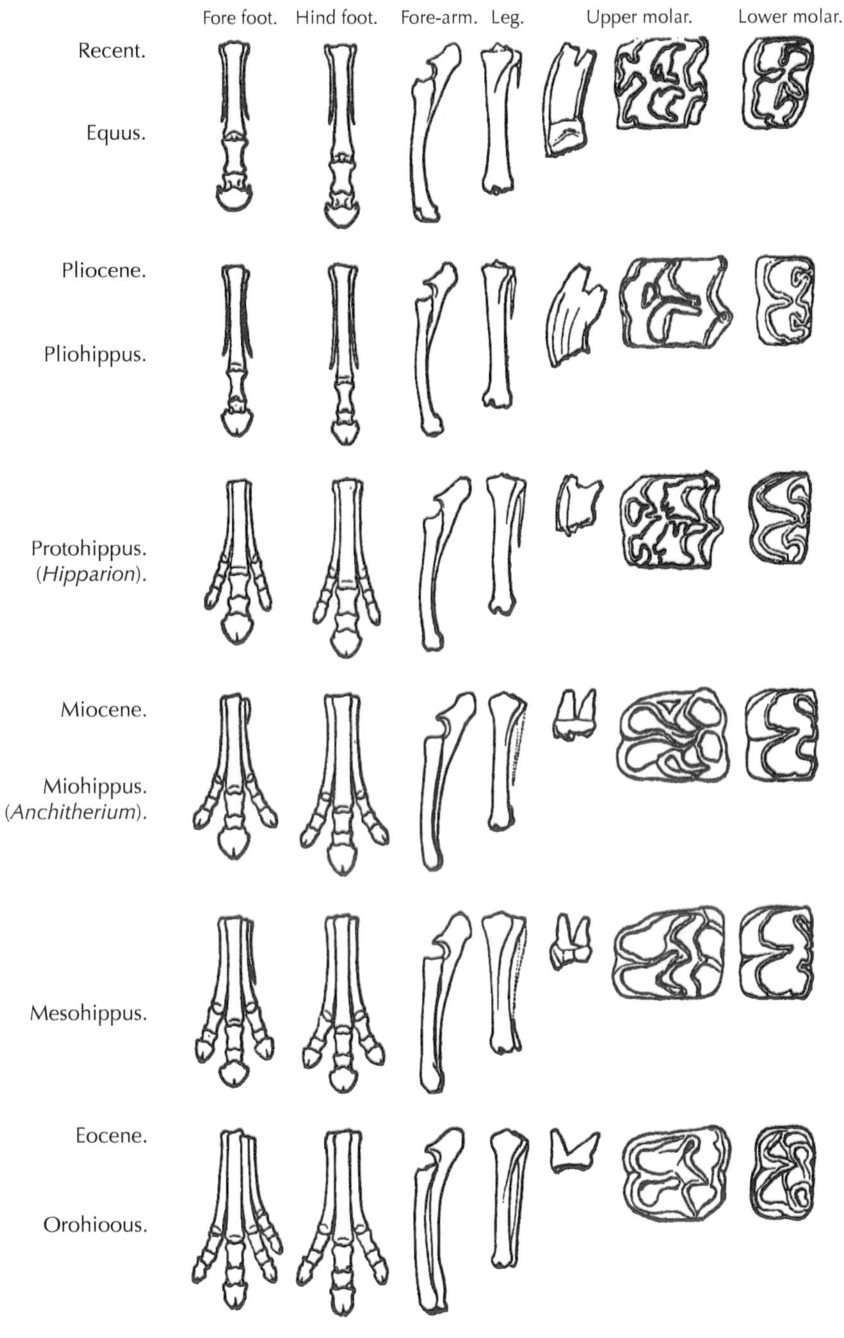

Figure 8.1 ▲

Marsh's sequence of horse teeth and limbs. (From O. C. Marsh, "Notice of New Tertiary Mammals, IV, *American Journal of Science*, series 3, 9, no. 51 [1875]:239–250)

in the face of new truth and took my conclusions."[2] Huxley later wrote to Marsh, "The more I think of it, the more clear it is that your great work is settlement of the pedigree of the horse."[3] Huxley then rewrote his lecture, using diagrams supplied by Marsh to retract his old ideas and present the new evidence. Horses had evolved in America, and his European fossils were occasional immigrants from the New World. Huxley was overjoyed with Marsh's evidence, for it showed not only the changes in teeth but also in the skull, limbs, and even the toes. It became one of his favorite examples of an evolutionary series, and it has been used almost exclusively in nearly every book written on evolution or fossils since that time. A famous sketch that Huxley drew while visiting Marsh shows little *Eohippus* being ridden by *Eohomo* (figure 8.2), illustrating the connection between the ideas of the evolution of horses and humans.

Figure 8.2 ▲
Huxley's famous sketch of "*Eohippus* riding Eohomo." (Courtesy of Wikimedia Commons)

THE "HYRAX BEAST"

But what about the earliest horses? In England in the early 1800s, people were obsessed with collecting natural history object: butterflies, seashells, plants, fish, and even fossils. As Lynn Barber describes in *The Heyday of Natural History*, collecting natural objects was a hobby suitable for both gentlemen and ladies. It had the morally uplifting purpose of revealing God by studying His handiwork. Thousands of upper-class and middle-class British with leisure time on their hands, particularly parsons and women, were running around the countryside collecting flowers and butterflies, wading in tidepools to collect marine life, or wandering in quarries to collect fossils. Their interest and enthusiasm were so great that it was not unusual for people to spot a fly at dinner and argue about its correct scientific name.

Among these enthusiasts was a gentleman named William Richardson, Esq., who had a Masters of Arts and was a Fellow of the Geological Society. Collecting on the coast of Kent in 1839, he was concentrating on the Eocene beds of the famous London Clay, looking around with "strong expectation for some form of animal life, whether a beast or bird, destined to be sustained by so rich a provision."[4] This time he was lucky, and he found the front half of a tiny skull as well as the bones of a bird.

This little skull was given to Richard Owen of the British Museum (see chapter 6). The skull, with large eyes and short snout (figure 8.3), looked

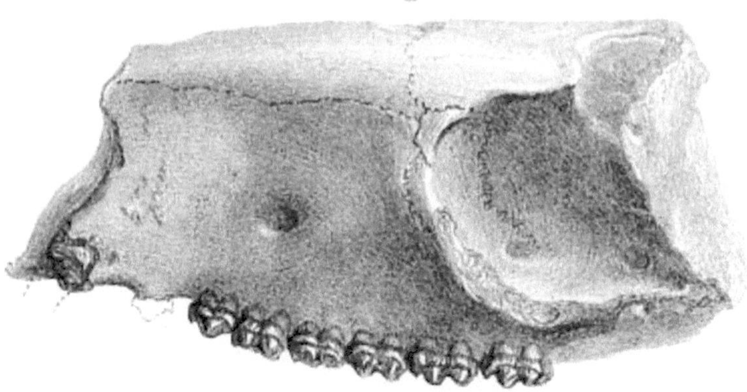

Figure 8.3 ▲
Owen's illustration of the most complete skull of *Hyracotherium leporinum*. (Courtesy of Wikimedia Commons)

more like "that of a Hare or other timid Rodentia."[5] However, the low, rectangular cheek teeth with small cusps were clearly those of a primitive hoofed mammal, most resembling the extinct *Choeropotamus*, a primitive artiodactyl from the same beds. Owen realized that the peculiar arrangement of cusps and ridges was more similar to living hyrax, so he called the animal *Hyracotherium leporinum*, or "rabbit-like hyrax beast."[6] The little *Hyracotherium* skull was one of the most primitive first perissodactyl fossils ever known, but it was not recognized as such until the 1870s.

LINEAR OR BRANCHING?

However, there were problems with straight-line evolution diagrams of horses. In the 1870s and even as late as the 1920s, the European sequence *Hyracotherium-Anchitherium-Hipparion-Equus*, or the American sequence *Eohippus-Orohippus-Mesohippus-Miohippus-Pliohippus-Equus* were decent first approximations of horse evolution based on very incomplete samples. They fit the prevailing linear notion of evolution, with one simple lineage marching through time from *Eohippus* to *Equus* (figure 8.4). As a simple way to convey the trends in the teeth, skull, limbs, and toes through time, this example is fine.

But in the past century of collecting, we have found dozens of additional species of fossil horses, represented by tens of thousands of fossils, which show that the evolution of the horse is not a simple line from *Eohippus* to *Equus*. Rather it is a complex bushy family tree, with many different lineages living at the same time (figure 8.5). This same pattern of a bushy, branching family tree is true of all known lineages that have a good fossil record: rhinos, camels, giraffes, elephants, and many others, including even humans. But the simplistic, outdated linear view of horse evolution persists, even in textbooks and online media, no matter how much paleontologists try to correct it. It seems to be partially the fact that a simple linear diagram is easier to understand and remember, but also it fit the old pre-Darwinian notion of the "chain of being" or "ladder of evolution."

Stephen Jay Gould pointed out another reason this simple linear model persists for horses, as it does for humans: today, there is just one surviving genus of horses or humans, so it is simple to represent it as a sequence of genera leading from one ancestor through intermediates to the one genus today. No one tries to put together a linear sequence of the history

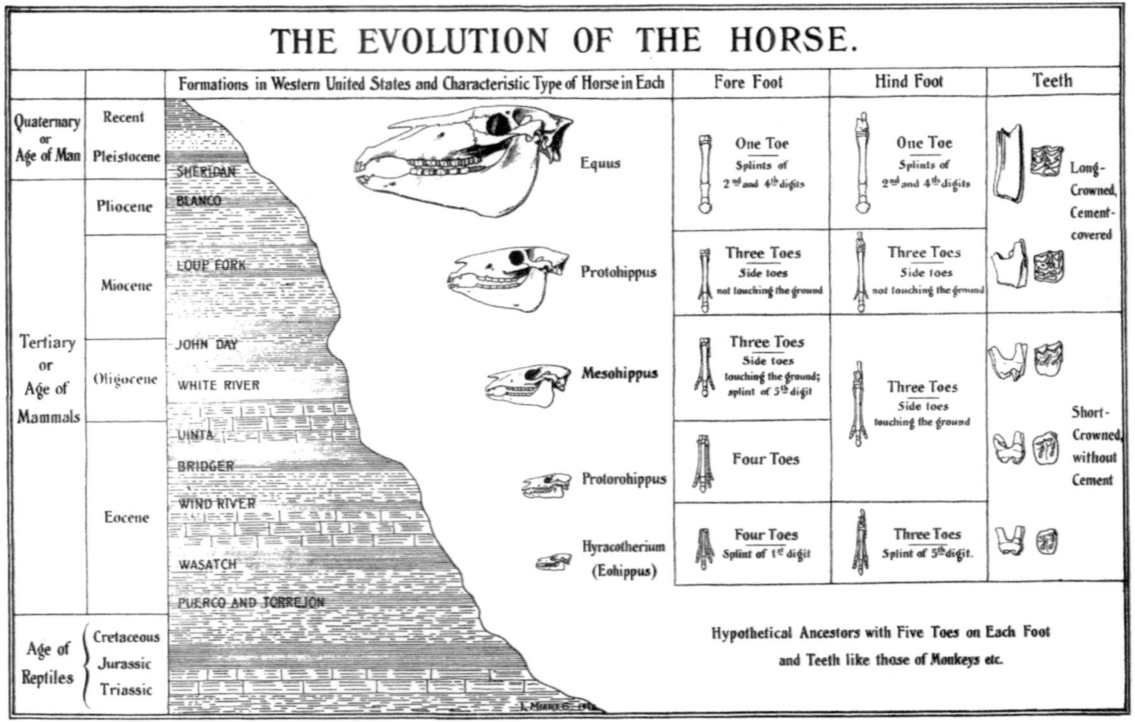

Figure 8.4 ▲

The classic diagram showing horse evolution as a linear sequence through time. (From W. D. Matthew, "The Evolution of the Horse: A Record and Its Interpretation," *Quarterly Review of Biology* 1 [1926]: 139–185)

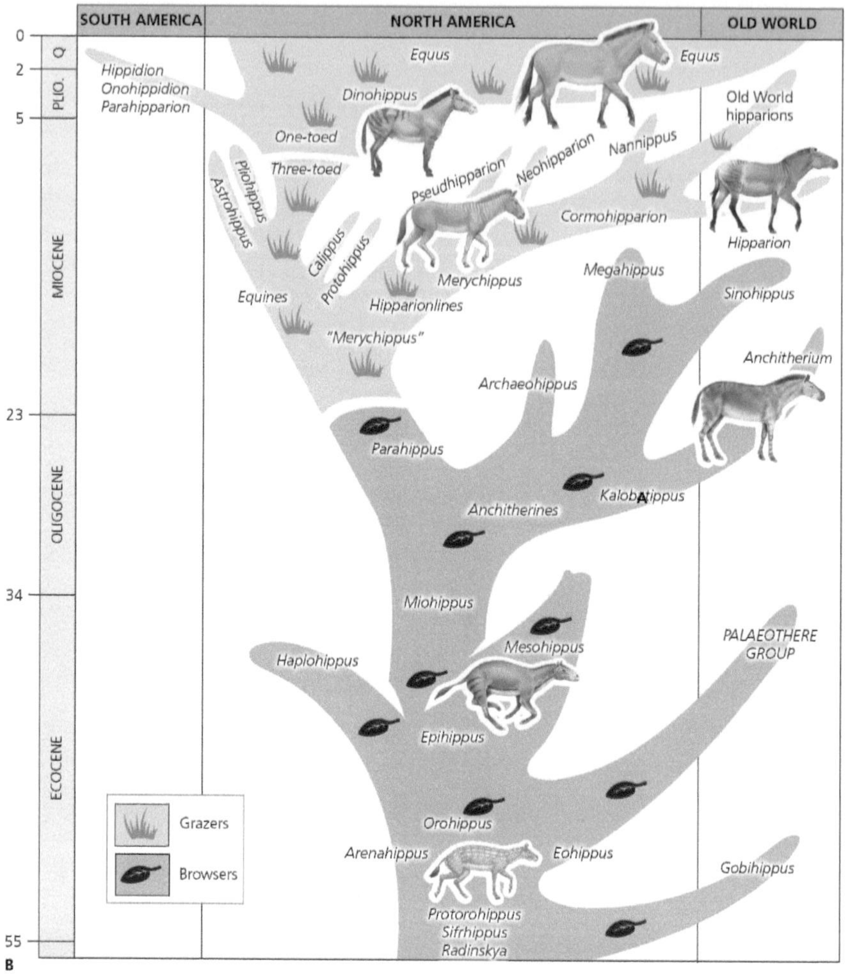

Figure 8.5 ▲

A modern view of horse evolution, which is bushy and branching with many more species. (Redrawn from several sources)

of elephants, because there are two different kinds today, or of rhinos, because there are five species still surviving. The linear "march through time" diagram only makes sense if there is only one ancestral fossil genus, one living genus, and just a few "links" in the "chain" in between.

A lot has been learned about the earliest Eocene horses since the 1920s. First of all, when horses first emerged, they were so similar to their close

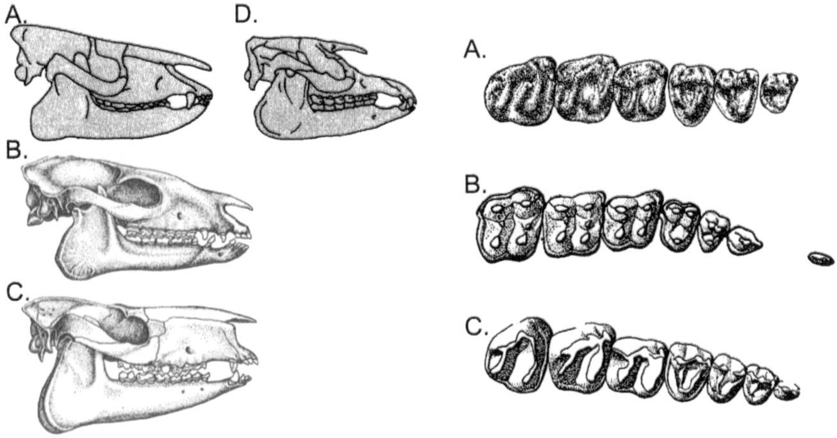

Figure 8.6 ▲

Comparison of the skulls and teeth of the earliest horses, rhinos, and tapirs, showing the great similarity of the skulls on the left and the crown view of the upper right cheek tooth rows on the right. (*A*) The earliest tapiroid *Homogalax*, showing the well-developed cross-crests of the molars, typical of tapiroids. (*B*) The earliest horse *Protorohippus*. (*C*) The earliest rhinocerotoid *Hyrachyus*, showing the characteristic "pi" (π) pattern of the crests of the upper molars. (*D*) Skull of a modern tapir for comparison. (Compiled from several sources)

relatives, the tapirs and the rhinos, that only a skilled eye could tell them apart (figure 8.6).

I vividly remember my final project in my undergraduate vertebrate paleontology class at the University of California Riverside in 1975. My professor, Mike Woodburne, gave everyone in the class a random sample of jaws and teeth from the lower Eocene beds in the Bighorn Basin near Emblem, Wyoming, to simulate what we might have collected if we had taken a trip there. I discovered that one of the most difficult tasks was telling the teeth of the earliest horses from the earliest tapir-rhino relative, *Homogalax*. It's just as hard to do if you have one of the rare skulls or jaws of these animals. Today any kid can tell a horse from a rhinoceros (and possibly recognize a tapir in a zoo), but if we went back 56 Ma, they would have looked nearly identical to our eyes. That's how much the three closely related groups have diverged through time, as each adapted to different niches. The same could be said of the other early perissodactyl groups, such as the brontotheres. The last members of their lineage were elephantine beasts with huge paired bony blunt horns on their noses, but the earliest forms (like *Lambdotherium*) were dog-sized creatures that can barely be distinguished from a horse, a tapir, or a rhino. All of these early Eocene perissodactyls can now be traced back to the Paleocene of Mongolia, where they seem to have a common ancestor in a fossil known as *Radinskya* (named after the late Leonard Radinsky of the University of Chicago, who did a lot of pioneering work in early perissodactyls and tapirs). From there, perissodactyls and *Radinskya* appear be closely related to a group of archaic hoofed mammals called phenacodonts—and these can be traced back to the earliest hoofed mammals in the early Paleocene.

HORSE OR PALAEOTHERE?

Going in the other direction from the roots back up the family tree, we come to the confused situation with the early Eocene fossils such as *Hyracotherium* and *Eohippus*. These two names and animals were considered different for a long time, until in 1932 the British paleontologist Sir Clive Forster Cooper decided that they were the same animal. Since *Hyracotherium* was named first, its name was applied to all the early Eocene horses in North America as well as in England, and most paleontologists learned it that way for decades. (A few American paleontologists still use that name even now.) But in 1989, the British Museum paleontologist Jerry Hooker was restudying all of the British *Hyracotherium* fossils accumulated since Owen's original report. He concluded that *Hyracotherium* was not a true horse at all, but related to a horse-like group called palaeotheres that are well known from the early and middle Eocene of Europe. In fact *Palaeotherium*, from the Eocene gypsum deposits of Montmartre in Paris, was one of the first extinct animals Cuvier ever described.

True horses only occurred in North America through most of their history until beasts such as *Anchitherium* and *Hipparion* escaped to Eurasia in the Miocene. Then in 2002, David Froehlich published a detailed analysis of all the species of early Eocene American horses and concluded that only one or two of the species could be referred to Cope's old genus *Eohippus*, which had fallen out of use since 1932. However, the rest of the early Eocene horses belonged to a variety of genera, including old names like *Protorohippus* and some new genera as well. Thus it is complicated when you want to refer to the earliest Eocene horses. You can't call them *Hyracotherium*, nor are most of them *Eohippus*, because there are actually multiple genera. Most people hate the complexity and prefer simple solutions, so they fall back on the old invalid names, usually because they just copy old outdated diagrams or just don't know any better.

HALFWAY HORSES

During the fifteen million years of the early and middle Eocene, horses such as *Protorohippus* and *Orohippus* were small, primitive mammals barely distinct for primitive rhinos, tapirs, and brontotheres. By the late Eocene and early Oligocene, horses became recognizably horse-like. First of these middle horses was the genus *Mesohippus*, whose name literally means "middle horse." *Mesohippus* was about 2 feet (60 centimeters) tall at the shoulder or about the size of a sheep (figure 8.7A and figure 8.7B). Its head was much more horse-like than that of *Orohippus*, with a longer snout, eyes slightly further back on the face, and a larger brain. Its teeth were better adapted for eating coarser vegetation, with well-developed ridges and crests, but they

Figure 8.7 ▲

A reconstruction of *Mesohippus*. (Reconstruction by R. Bruce Horsfall, courtesy of Wikimedia Commons)

were still not high-crowned, as seen in later horses. The body was longer, with an arched back that was more flexible than that of a modern horse, but not as primitive as early horses. Its most striking feature, however, was its longer legs with the upper arm and thigh segments much longer, and longer toes as well. Most *Mesohippus* fossils had three toes, with a strong central toe and reduce side toes. Some specimens of *Mesohippus* still have a fully functioning fifth finger (metacarpal 5), equivalent to our pinky, so not all specimens are three-toed. All later horses have lost the pinky, so these specimens show the transition from the four-toed hands of early Eocene horses to the three-toed foot and hand of later horses.

These side toes never completely vanish. Every once in a while, a modern horse is born with side toes somewhat like those of the *Mesohippus* (figure 8.8A and figure 8.8B). They are not a tremendous burden on the

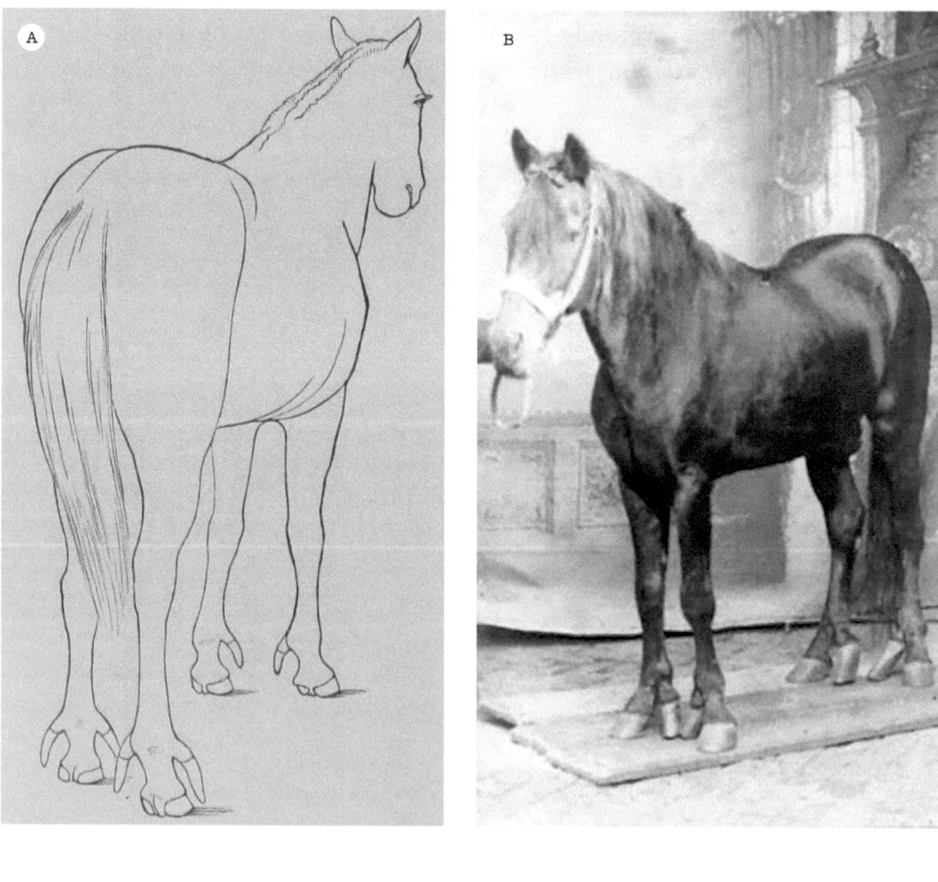

horse and don't seem to affect their running speed, but they do look odd. They have been nicknamed "horned horses," and their strangeness has often garnered attention. Julius Caesar is said to have ridden on a "horned horse" into battle as a way of looking more regal and almost mythological. This kind of development, or evolutionary throwback, is known as an atavism. It shows that all living horses still have the genes for side toes, but normally their gene regulation shuts off the instructions for making side toes so we never see them expressed—until the regulation fails and we get a three-toed horse. Modern horses also have tiny splints of their side toes running alongside their robust central toe. These splints serve no real function and are useless leftovers not quite removed by evolution yet—but if a racehorse breaks one of these side toes, it can be crippled for life. This produces a strong selective pressure against the genes for tiny side toes.

Mesohippus fossils are particularly common in the upper Eocene-lower Oligocene beds of the Big Badlands of South Dakota and related deposits in Nebraska, Wyoming, Montana, Colorado, and North Dakota. When we were both students in the American Museum of Natural History, Neil Shubin (of the University of Chicago) and I spent a lot of time looking at hundreds of these fossil horses. We found that the old simplistic picture of linear evolution from *Mesohippus* to *Miohippus*, with a single unbranched "trunk" of *Mesohippus* gradually transforming into *Miohippus*, was wrong. Instead, there were at least five different species of *Mesohippus* and four of *Miohippus*. At one level in the rocks near Lusk, Wyoming, we found three species of *Mesohippus* and two species of *Miohippus* coexisting in the same place and time. Once again, horse evolution looked simple and linear when just a few fossils were known, but with large collections and detailed analysis, we discover that the species form a branching, bushy family tree, with multiple lineages overlapping in time. *Mesohippus* was about the size of sheep, and *Miohippus* were about the size of a Great Dane, with a longer snout than *Orohippus*, eyes slightly bigger and further

Figure 8.8 ◂

(*A*) Marsh's sketch of a "horned horse" with two side toes that were developed and not suppressed. (*B*) A photograph of a horned horse with three toes. (Courtesy of Wikimedia Commons)

back on the face, and a larger brain. In *Mesohippus*, the molar teeth were already more advanced, with well-developed cross-crests for chopping up leaves. Both horses had much longer, more slender legs than earlier ancestors, with only three toes on each hand and foot, and the side toes were much smaller than the weight-bearing middle toe. This middle finger becomes so broad that by the time you reach *Miohippus*, its upper end touches the wrist bone known as the cuboid, a landmark that distinguishes the two genera. Multiple species of *Miohippus* persisted through much of the Oligocene, to be replaced by several genera including *Parahippus* and *Kalobatippus*.

BROWSING ANCHITHERINES

In the early and middle Miocene, there was an explosive radiation of horses (figure 8.5). One lineage was the subfamily Anchitherinae, which migrated to Europe and were part of the original sequence recognized by Huxley and Kovalevsky. Anchitherines retained the low-crowned cheek teeth of their ancestors, presumably because they lived in the dense forests and subsisted on soft leaves and other browse. *Anchitherium* was very successful inhabiting the forests of the early Miocene across all of Eurasia where they are fairly common. In fact, *Anchitherium* is so common in France that it was one of the first fossil mammals ever found there, described by Cuvier in 1822. *Anchitherium* persisted until the late Miocene in Turkey, spanning almost fifteen million years with little change. This is one of the longest records for any fossil mammal and even more remarkable for such a conservative primitive horse.

Even though their teeth remained primitive, the radiation of anchitherines such as *Anchitherium, Archaeohippus, Megahippus*, and *Hypohippus* evolved into a diverse range of body sizes, dividing up the niches of forest leaf browsers by reaching different parts of the leafy understory. *Archaeohippus* was a dwarfed form, about the size of its ancestor *Mesohippus*, that some paleontologists have nicknamed the "doll pony". But there were also giant anchitherines. The largest of these, such *Megahippus mckennai* (figure 8.9) and *Hypohippus*, reached the up to 900 pounds (400 kilograms), the size of a modern horse, but their huge teeth still retained the low-crowned cusps of the earliest horses.

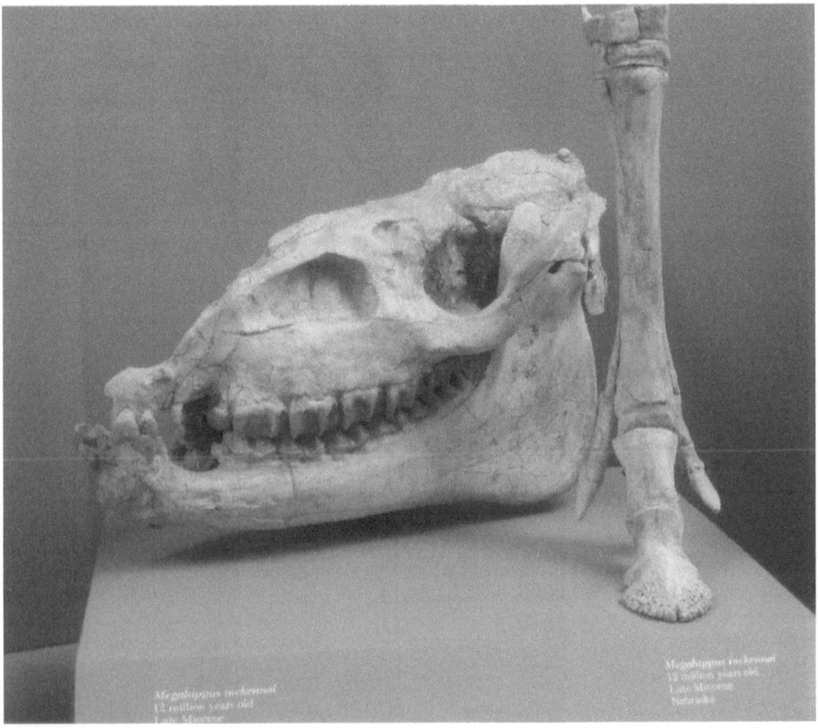

Figure 8.9 ▲
The skull of the giant anchitheriine horse *Megahippus mckennai*. (Courtesy of Wikimedia Commons)

GRAZING EQUINES

The main radiation of horses, the subfamily Equinae, went in the other direction, developing cheek teeth with deep roots so that as they wore their teeth down they would never run out of grinding surface (figure 8.5). Their teeth are ever-growing, such that a new tooth surface constantly replaces the one that was worn away. This means that the tooth is essentially one long prism, with no distinction between the root and the crown. The root can even be open at the base and filled with growing pulp cavity, so the new tooth is continually adding to the bottom as a top of erupts and wears away. In living horses, for example, the roots of the teeth penetrate almost to the bottom of the jaw and well up into the facial region (figure 8.10).

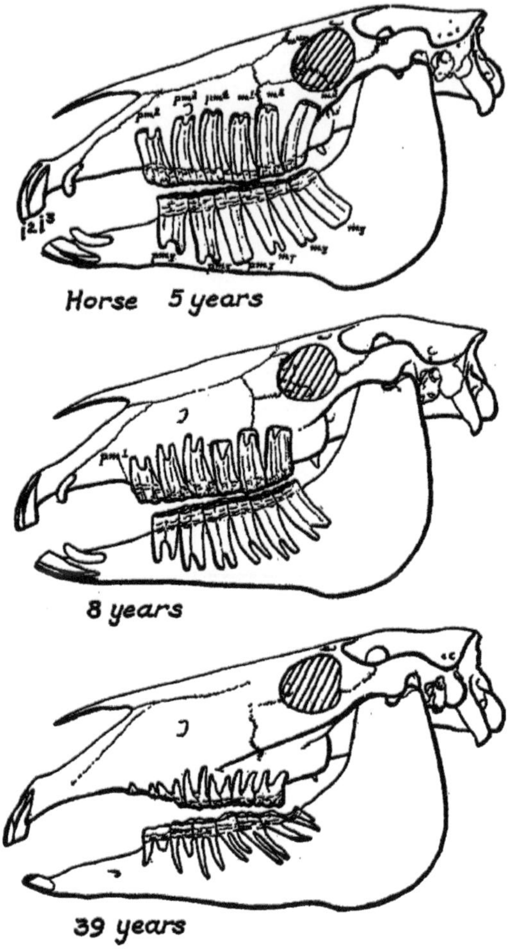

Figure 8.10 ▲

Sketch of the side views of the teeth in a modern horse, showing the extremely high crowns and deep roots that wear down over the life of the horse. (From William King Gregory, *Evolution Emerging* [Arno, 1951])

The reason for this heavy tooth wear has always been assumed to have been a diet of grasses because grass contains tiny gritty pieces of silica, called phytoliths, that wears down teeth quickly. In recent years that story has been modified, because it appears that high-crowned teeth appear about 17 Ma and earlier, while huge areas of modern temperate-tropical grassland did not appear until much later in the Miocene, around 7 Ma. However, another source of tooth wear is gritty sand and silt that sticks to the grass stalks, so that could explain why horses (and camels and rhinos and many other Miocene groups) evolved high-crowned teeth before the expansion of modern grasslands. As long as the conditions were dry enough that there was lots of dust and grit in the environment, the diet of grasses was very abrasive and high-crowned teeth were required to eat it.

There were multiple lineages of horses (figure 8.5) overlapping at the same time in the Miocene. They included the radiation of different horses that used to be lumped into the wastebasket genus "*Merychippus*" (now split into many genera); the huge radiation of the hipparionine horses, which spread to Eurasia and became very successful; plus the dwarf horses *Calippus* and *Nannippus*; and many more. In the Railway Quarry A in the Valentine Formation of north-central Nebraska, twelve different species of horse were found from the same hole in the ground, so many species lived in the same place and same time (one anchitherine, several hipparionines, and many others). Most of these horses were still three-toed, although the side toes were tiny and normally did not touch the ground, and the middle toe was robust and carried most of the weight. Their limbs were also much longer and slenderer, and their skulls look much like that of a modern horse, except not as big. And their lower arm bones (radius and ulna) are fused into a single bone, so they are stronger—but they can no longer move their arms or wrist side-to-side, but only in the front-to-back plane, meaning they had a total commitment to fast running and no other kind of locomotion.

The classification of these Miocene horses was long a mess because most species were based on isolated teeth and jaws, with no skulls or skeletons associated with these teeth. This dilemma was finally solved with the addition of huge new collections of fossils in North America. In the 1920s, Childs Frick, the son of the railroad and steel baron Henry Clay Frick (Andrew Carnegie's partner), decided to spend some of his enormous inheritance accumulating a collection of fossils of the ancestors of the big-game animals he had once hunted. He built a laboratory in New York, and he kept crews of professional collectors working continuously in the High Plains and Rocky Mountains from the mid-1920s to the 1960s. By the time he died in 1965, Frick had amassed the best collection of Oligocene through Pleistocene North American mammals the world had ever seen, with more than two hundred thousand specimens (figure 8.11). It surpassed all previous collections not only in quantity but also in quality. Where older collections had at best a few teeth or jaws from a given locality, the Frick Collection had dozens of skulls and skeletons. This collection became part of the American Museum of Natural History after Frick died in 1965. It was eventually housed in a new building that it was erected especially for it. It is so immense that the fossil proboscideans require a whole floor, the horses another, the camels a third, the rhinos a fourth, and so on through seven floors. The collection was moved to its new building and prepared for studying the early 1970s. It is so gigantic and requires so much time working in New York City to describe all the new fossils and solve all the taxonomic puzzles that many parts of the fossil collection are still unpublished and virtually unstudied by scientists for more than fifty years.

One of Frick's best collectors was a young farm boy from Ainsworth, Nebraska, named Morris Skinner (seen in figure 8.11). He started out by collecting mastodonts and rhinos for the University of Nebraska in 1926, but eventually he became a full-time employee of the Frick Laboratory. He worked many fossil fields, particularly in north-central and western Nebraska, and is responsible for much the best part of the Frick Collection, with more than forty-six thousand specimens to his credit. As he collected, he developed a fascination for fossil horses. Frick was primarily interested in camels, ruminants, and carnivores, but Skinner set aside the fossil horses as they came out of crates, fresh from the field. Frick's horse collection was superior to anything that preceded it in many ways. In particular, there are many complete skulls and skeletons of horses that had distinctive hipparion-like teeth. From the skulls, however, Skinner could see that horses with similar teeth had many other anatomical differences in the skull and the rest of anatomy. Clearly, there was more than one kind of horse with hipparion-like teeth. After Frick died in 1965, his collection was no longer private and closed to other scientists, and by 1975, it was possible for other paleontologists to join Skinner in documenting the details of horse skull evolution, and straightening out the mess with hipparions. During the 1980s and 1990s, most of this work was published, and now the systematics and evolution of middle and late Miocene horses is well understood.

Finally, in the late Miocene, nearly all of these three-toed horse lineages had vanished, and only the one-toed lineage from *Dinohippus* (not *Pliohippus*, as in the old diagrams) to *Equus* remained in the Pliocene. During the

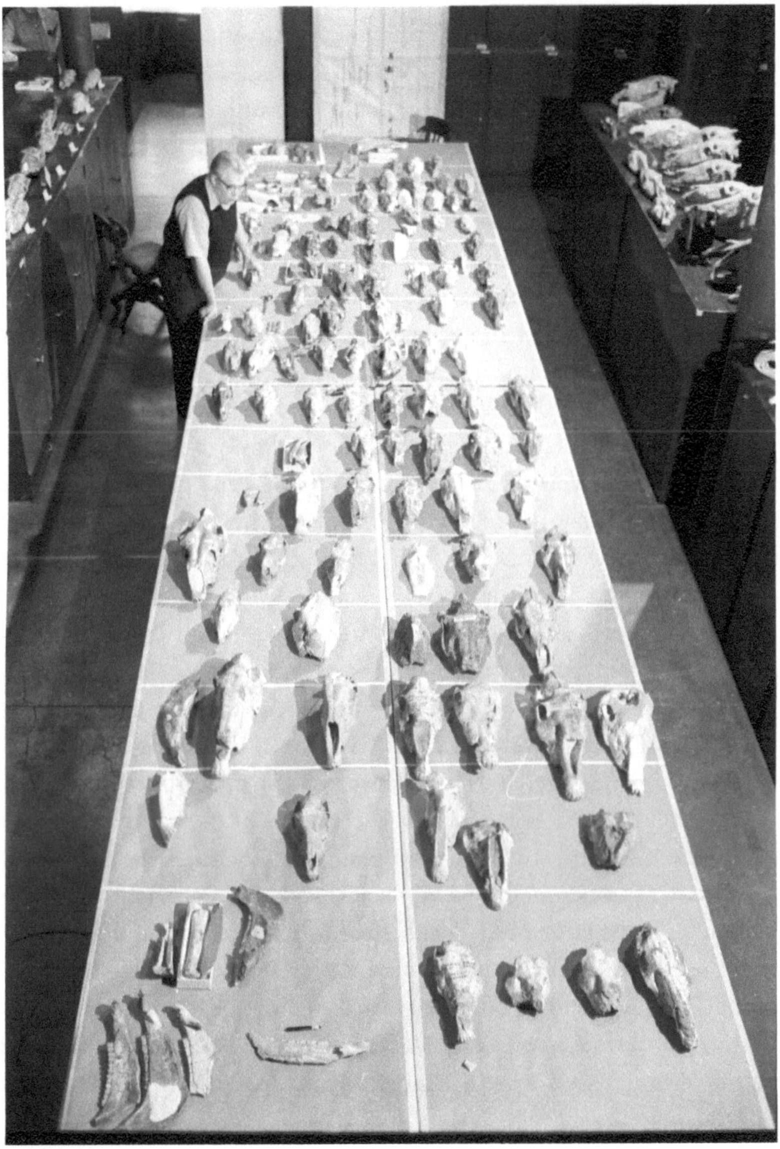

Figure 8.11 ▲

Morris Skinner stands at a table covered with fossil horse skulls arranged by their age sequence, from the Frick Collection of the American Museum of Natural History. (Courtesy of the American Museum Digital Library)

Ice Ages, the genus *Equus* underwent yet another huge radiation, but until recently the Ice Age horses (especially in North America) were split into dozens of different species, mostly based on small differences in the teeth and proportions of the skulls and limbs. The classification of Ice Age American horses was in chaos, with some people recognizing lots of species, and others lumping the variation into just a few species.

In 2005 and subsequent years, molecular biology jumped into the fray. There are enough of the youngest Ice Age horse fossils with excellent preservation that they were able to recover both nuclear DNA and mitochondrial DNA from a number of extinct species. For many living species, the answer confirmed what had already been suggested by their anatomy and behavior. The asses and onagers and kiangs of Eurasia and Africa turned out to be all closely related, as did the four species of zebra (one of which, the quagga, was driven to extinction in South Africa just over a century ago). This showed that the molecular data could be relied upon because it exactly matched the evolutionary history that had already been worked out based on fossils and living animals.

But for the North American horses the answer stunned and surprised everyone. The genetic evidence supported only a few species of North American Ice Age horse, not the dozens that had been named previously. Not only that, but they were all close relatives of the lineage of the living horse, *Equus caballus*. Genetic evidence also confirmed what zoologists had long expected: modern horses were descendants of the living Przewalski's horse, which still roams the steppes of Asia and Siberia. The one exception to this discovery concerned the extinct stilt-legged horses, which have very long slender limbs compared to caballine horses, zebras, and asses. Even though they were separated into several different species based on fossils, the genetic evidence showed they were a distinct genus and species that split from the main horse lineage about 5 Ma. The scientists renamed this horse *Haringtonohippus*, after the famous Canadian paleontologist Richard Harington, who first recognized its uniqueness. Today we have about nine species of living wild horses in the genus *Equus*, including three species of zebra (plus the quagga), three or four species of asses and onagers, plus Przewalski's horse.

During the Ice Ages, horses not only spread from their North American homeland to Eurasia to form the great radiation of living horses and asses but also spread to Africa, where they evolved into zebras. They even spread to South America, where a bizarre group of horses, the hippidions, apparently evolved a short proboscis like that of a tapir. Then at the end of the last Ice Age, about ten thousand years ago, horses vanished from the Americas, along with most of the other large mammals such as mammoths, mastodonts, ground sloths, saber-toothed cats, and many others. As discussed in chapter 2, the causes were complex and probably involved both climate change and possibly some human hunting, but for whatever reason, horses were gone from their ancestral North American homeland until 1473, when Columbus brought them from Spain on his second voyage. Today we see wild mustangs and all the domestic breeds of horses, or we see Plains Indians using horses as the basis for their nomadic culture, but these were relatively recent developments.

NOTES

1. Leonard Huxley, *Life and Letters of Thomas Henry Huxley* (Macmillan, 1900) vol. 2, chap. 8.
2. Robert Plate, *The Dinosaur Hunters: Othniel C. Marsh and Edward D. Cope*. (David McKay, 1964), 88.
3. Huxley, *Life and Letters of Thomas Henry Huxley*, vol. 2, chapter 8.
4. William Richardson, "Observations on the Locality of *Hyracotherium*," *Transactions of the Geological Society of London* 22 (1839): 211.
5. Richard Owen, "Description of the Fossil Remains of a Mammal (*Hyracotherium leporinum*) and of a Bird (*Lithornis vulturinus*) from the London Clay," *Transactions of the Geological Society of London* Series 2, no. 6 (1841): 203–208
6. Owen, "Description of the Fossil Remains of a Mammal (*Hyracotherium leporinum*) and of a Bird (*Lithornis vulturinus*) from the London Clay."

FOR FURTHER READING

Franzen, J. L. *The Rise of Horses: 55 Million Years of Evolution*. Johns Hopkins University Press, 2010.

Froehlich, D. J. "Quo vadis eohippus? The Systematics and Taxonomy of the Early Eocene Equids (Perissodactyla)." *Zoological Journal of the Linnean Society* 134, no. 2 (2002): 141–256.

Hooker, J. J. "The Beginning of the Equoid Radiation." *Zoological Journal of the Linnean Society* 112, nos. 1–2 (1994): 29–63.

MacFadden, B. J. *Fossil Horses*. Cambridge University Press, 1992.

—. "Fossil Horses: Evidence for Evolution." *Science* 307, no. 5716 (2005): 1728–1730.

Prothero, D. R. *The Princeton Field Guide to Prehistoric Mammals*. Princeton University Press, 2016.

—. *Vertebrate Evolution: From Origins to Dinosaurs and Beyond*. Taylor & Francis/CRC Press, 2022.

Prothero, D. R., and R. M. Schoch, eds. *The Evolution of Perissodactyls*. Oxford University Press, 1989.

—. *Horns, Tusks, and Flippers: The Evolution of Hoofed Mammals*. Johns Hopkins University Press, 2002.

Rose, K. D., and J. D. Archibald, eds. *The Rise of Placental Mammals*. Johns Hopkins University Press, 2005.

Savage, R. J. G., and M. R. Long. *Mammal Evolution: An Illustrated Guide*. Facts-on-File, 1986.

Turner, A., and M. Anton. *National Geographic Prehistoric Mammals*. National Geographic Society, 2004.

09 | "THUNDER BEASTS"—THE BRONTOTHERES

MEGACEROPS

Every now and then I like taking a break from the latest technical papers and conference volumes to read some vintage scientific work. Oftentimes this is an enjoyable experience, I love the history of science, but the evolutionary work of H. F. Osborn is frustratingly opaque. While Osborn certainly was one of the most prominent figures in early 20th century paleontology, he cultivated some very odd ideas which he made all the more confusing through his attempts to bring paleontology, genetics, chemistry, and physics together within evolutionary theory.

—RILEY BLACK, 2009.

THE THUNDER BEASTS

Some of the largest and most spectacular fossils from the Big Badlands of South Dakota are the bones of the huge animals known as brontotheres, or "thunder beasts." Native peoples such as the Lakota and Cheyenne had seen these enormous bones and told stories of enormous beasts that produced thunderstorms as they ran across the sky, and they called them "thunder horses." The Big Badlands, with their eerie stark rocky pinnacles and crags, were the place of many Native legends (figure 9.1).

In the 1840s, the first government surveys reached the region and began to collect some of these enormous bones. In 1846, Hiram Prout received a specimen from a fur trader and described this fragment of a lower jaw as a giant "*Palaeotherium*" (figure 9.2), a name originally given by Georges

Figure 9.1 ▲

Engraving of the Big Badlands from the reports of the Evans Survey, 1846. (Courtesy of Wikimedia Commons)

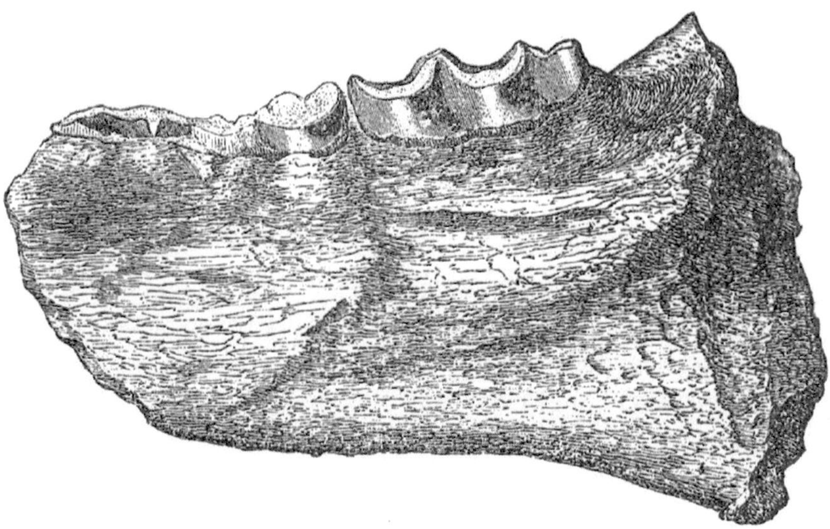

Figure 9.2 ▲

Prout's 1846 illustration of the first known Badlands fossil, a jaw of the "gigantic *Palaeotherium*." (From H. A. Prout, "Gigantic *Palaeotherium*," *American Journal of Science*, 2nd series, vol. 2 [1846]: 288–289)

Cuvier to an extinct relative of the horses found in the Eocene rocks of the Paris Basin. This was the first described and named specimen of a fossil animal from west of the Mississippi River, one of thousands to come from the Big Badlands in the next century. In 1849, the French geologist and paleontologist Auguste Pomel looked at Prout's illustrations and decided it was not *Paleotherium* but a new creature, and he gave it the name *Menodus giganteus*. In 1852, America's first vertebrate paleontologist, Joseph Leidy, wrote that it was "the first of the many mammalian remains which have been brought to the notice of the scientific world from the vast Eocene cemetery of Nebraska."[1] This is the first hint to scientists that "the region of Nebraska Territory of the United States appears to be as rich in the remains of Mammalia and Chelonia of the Eocene period as the deposits of the same age of the Paris Basin."[2]

In the ensuing decades, most of America's early paleontologists collected extensively in the Big Badlands, especially focusing on the enormous brontotheres. In November 1874, General Ord allowed the Yale paleontologist O. C. Marsh and his crews to collect in the Badlands, where they found may spectacular specimens. Marsh got the permission of the Lakota when he visited the Red Cloud reservation south of the Badlands, and he was appalled at the horrible conditions of the Natives. That winter he invited Red Cloud east to Washington, D.C., and lobbied President Grant's office and other government officials about how corrupt government agents were stealing from the money allotted to the reservations.

JOHN BELL HATCHER, KING OF THE COLLECTORS

But the biggest collections were made by the legendary paleontologist John Bell Hatcher (figure 9.3). In 1886, Marsh sent him to the Big Badlands, and in the span of two years Hatcher collected dozens of brontotheres skulls from beds about 34–37 Ma, which now reside in the Yale Peabody Museum. The enormous quantity of fossils found by Hatcher was fairly typical of his prowess as a collector and as a paleontologist. As Brinkman writes:

> Determined, confident, hard-working and often very temperamental, John Bell Hatcher was the most talented and respected field paleontologist of his generation, but he struggled mightily to find his own level in the hierarchical world of America vertebrate paleontology.[3]

Figure 9.3
John Bell Hatcher (Courtesy of Wikimedia Commons)

Hatcher was born a few months after the start of the Civil War, in October 1861, in Cooperstown, Illinois. When he was very young, his family moved to Cooper, Iowa. There he became fascinated by the fossils found all around him, lying on the ground. He started his higher education in 1880 at Grinnell College in central Iowa. To earn money, he worked in the local coal mines, where he became intrigued with the beautifully preserved fossil plants he found. After just one term he transferred to Yale's Sheffield Scientific School, where he graduated in 1884. Just before graduating he showed his fossil collection to the school's mineralogist, George Jarvis Brush. Impressed with the young man's enthusiasm, Brush introduced the twenty-three-year-old college graduate to Marsh.

Marsh needed a new young eager field assistant, so he sent Hatcher to Kansas to be trained by the legendary commercial collector Charles H. Sternberg. Cope was now broke and could not pay him, so Sternberg was now working for Marsh. Sternberg wasn't exactly excited to be training the young greenhorn, but he tried to be positive. He wrote that he "gave promise of a future even then by his perfect understanding of the work in hand and the thoughtful care which he devoted to it."[4]

The college-educated Hatcher, however, looked down on Sternberg, and especially his slapdash methods of getting the fossils out of ground. Already trained in geology, Hatcher was a perfectionist, and he was interested in the details of the sedimentary rocks in which the fossils were found as a clue to their ancient environments and how the fossil had died and become buried and fossilized (something most commercial collectors ignored, even today). About one of his finds, Hatcher wrote: "On one side of a bone, the matrix will be made up entirely of sand, while on the opposite side the stem and leaves of plants have been dropped. . . . This . . . shows the direction of the current to have been from that side containing only sand, and towards the side containing the plants. So shallow were the waters, the bone itself became an obstacle sufficient to produce an eddy on the lower side, in which the leaves and other vegetable materials accumulated and sank to the bottom."[5]

Sternberg helped Hatcher begin his training by collecting the hippo-like Miocene rhinoceros *Teleoceras* from Long Island Rhino Quarry in northern Kansas in 1885. Soon Hatcher was independent of Sternberg and reporting to Marsh directly. He roamed over much of the Rocky Mountain region, collecting fossil mammals he sent to Yale. In 1887 he married the sister of the paleontologist Olof A. Peterson of the Carnegie Museum and settled in Nebraska. That summer he revisited some of Cope's localities in Montana, sending a ton of bones back to Marsh.

Meanwhile, in 1889 Hatcher made the first-ever discovery of the teeth of Cretaceous mammals, which Marsh found extremely exciting. Hatcher stumbled on a technique used by many paleontologists since then—look at the anthills. In strata where there is nothing but muds and silts and fine sands and no gravel, the harvester ants will collect tiny hard gravel-sized objects like fossil teeth, creating an armored layer over the anthill to prevent it from blowing away. For more than a century, paleontologists have been abusing poor harvester ants by picking over the tops of their anthills or scooping them away and running them through fine screen mesh to retrieve all the precious fossil teeth the ants have collected.

By this time Hatcher was fed up with Marsh and his abusive ways. Not only did Marsh pay his collectors poorly, he paid them infrequently as well. He insisted that Hatcher labor through the blizzards of the hard western winters, rather than spend his winters in the museum on his finds of the previous year. More important, Marsh hogged all the credit for doing the work. He would not even give his assistants co-authorship on papers that they had written, putting his name over their writing. This had already driven Williston (who had started with Marsh in 1874) to leave in 1890 and start over in Kansas, becoming a professor at the University of Kansas.

Hatcher finally resigned in 1893 while he was still in the field. Before he left, Henry Fairfield Osborn was aware of the discontent that Marsh has fostered in his staff and tried to recruit Hatcher for the American Museum paleontology program he was trying to build. However, Hatcher backed out when he realized that Osborn himself didn't have his own job secured yet. Then, through the invitation of Osborn's friend William Berryman Scott, Hatcher got a job as a collector at Scott's and Osborn's alma mater, Princeton University, in 1893. Osborn forgave Hatcher and helped him get established and even arranged for him to receive an honorary degree from Princeton.

By this time the thirty-two-year-old Hatcher was suffering from rheumatism and assorted injuries caused by years of rough field work and could barely get on his horse. Nevertheless, he conceived of the idea of leading an expedition to Patagonia to collect fossil mammals where Darwin had once been. By this time, the self-taught Argentinian paleontologists, the brothers Florentino and Carlos Ameghino, were now making amazing and puzzling discoveries of weird mammals that completely challenged what people thought about mammal evolution (see chapter 6). Despite his infirmities, Hatcher planned an audacious trip to South America. and he got funding from millionaire J. Pierpont Morgan to fund the first Princeton University Expeditions to Patagonia in 1896.

Hatcher was a first-rate card sharp and gambler. During the month-long voyage down to South America in March 1896, he used the long boring periods at sea to play poker with all the other passengers, and he cleaned them out. He continued to do so any chance he got while in Argentina, and by this means he raised enough money to keep funding his Patagonian expeditions for three more years (1896–1899). In the first two years, the Princeton group was just Hatcher and his brother-in-law, Olof A. Peterson. The final season in 1899 included Barnum Brown of the American Museum, who had just been hired and was given only a few hours' notice by Osborn to join the expedition.

When Hatcher returned from the 1899 expedition, he was upset by the way Princeton was treating him. Despite the concerns of Osborn and Scott, he was ready to jump ship again. Meanwhile, W. J. Holland was trying to get the Carnegie Museum paleontology program back on track after his bad treatment of Jacob Wortman forced his resignation. To make up for the loss, Holland hired Olof Peterson and then Hatcher to replenish their staff of paleontologists.

By the spring of 1904, Hatcher was done with his work on the Morrison dinosaurs and ready to return to Lance Creek, Wyoming, where he had collected many *Triceratops*. He sent his brother-in-law Peterson to collect more fossil mammals in Nebraska. However, Marsh's death in 1899 had left a huge project behind: finishing the monograph on all the *Triceratops* that Hatcher had once collected for Yale. Osborn had succeeded Marsh as the official paleontologist of the US Geological Survey, and he was legally in charge of all the specimens at the Smithsonian that Marsh had accumulated. Osborn felt that Hatcher would be the best person to complete the task. In addition to his job at the Carnegie Museum, Hatcher had to make frequent trips to see all the *Triceratops* specimens at Yale and at the Smithsonian, so he was overworked.

In late June 1904, Hatcher was feeling "somewhat run down, having exerted himself rather strenuously."[6] Holland urged Hatcher to go home and get some rest, but the workaholic Hatcher refused. Instead, he returned to his office, locked the door, and worked late into the night, despite a high fever. "He joked about his illness and ignored his doctor's orders."[7] Holland had to order him out and had him put in an ambulance to the hospital, where he was diagnosed with typhoid fever. Given Hatcher's legendary stamina in the field, the doctors thought he would be over it in a week. Instead, Hatcher got sicker and died suddenly on July 3, 1904, at the young age of forty-two.

Holland sent Peterson a letter in the field in Agate Springs, Nebraska, notifying him of the news of his brother-in-law's death. However, he demanded that Peterson stay and continue the work because Hatcher would already be buried by the time the letter reached him. Osborn, on the other hand, sent a much more sensitive letter to the grieving Peterson and his sister, Hatcher's widow:

> I hasten to write you of my deep sorrow and sympathy in learning of the death of Hatcher. . . . I was greatly shocked, for when I saw him last he was looking very well and was full of bright plans for the future. This is a great personal loss for I greatly admired Hatcher's scientific ability and enthusiasm, and always felt a fresh inspiration from talking to him. It is a hard blow to American paleontology, to which Mr. Hatcher was making such splendid contributions following his many years of magnificent work in the field—he was certainly our greatest collector. It is especially sad to think of his dying at the

> beginning of what promise to be the brightest and most satisfactory period of his life—when people could see his work and recognize his ability. . . . I return early in September to take up my work and I shall always miss Hatcher.[8]

The entire paleontological world mourned Hatcher and praised his enormous contributions over such a short life. Sadly, his death meant that the large monograph project on *Triceratops*, which he had just begun to write up, but had all the illustrations complete, had outlived both Marsh (who started it) and Hatcher. Marsh's successor at Yale, Richard Swann Lull, took over the task, and it was finally published in 1907 with Hatcher as first author and Marsh as second author. Lull put himself last, even though he ended up writing nearly all of it.

HENRY FAIRFIELD OSBORN— PALEONTOLOGICAL ARISTOCRAT

But the king of brontothere research was Henry Fairfield Osborn, an interesting and pivotal figure in the history of paleontology (figure 9.4). He did more to bring the image of dinosaurs to the public eye than any other person, especially in commissioning huge skeletal mounts and paintings and models of dinosaurs that created the first real wave of public awareness and "dinomania" in the early 1900s. Modern paleontologists, however, are not

Figure 9.4
Henry Fairfield Osborn around 1910, in the middle part of his career. (Courtesy of Wikimedia Commons)

impressed with much of his scientific work, which was tinged with racism and eugenics and odd notions about evolution. They are particularly bothered by his habit of creating too many new species based on meaningless tiny differences between specimens, or his habit of taking credit for other people's work. He was a study in contrasts, but paleontology would not be nearly so popular without him, nor would there be nearly as many wonderful specimens in museums.

Osborn was born in 1857 to the prominent railroad tycoon William Henry Osborn, and for his entire life he lived and behaved and thought like an American aristocrat. The late 1800s, also known as the Gilded Age, was a time when the explosion of industrial might in the United States created a number of tycoons and "robber barons" who acted and thought they were like royalty. Osborn carried this haughty, aristocratic attitude throughout his life, which often chafed the people who worked under him.

Stories about Osborn's condescending, pompous, egotistical behavior are legendary. His biographer Ronald Rainger describes him as a powerful well-connected American aristocrat, running the department and the museum as a strict hierarchy, where he provided the administration and financial means. His subordinates (many of whom were much more competent paleontologists than Osborn) did all the grunt jobs (field work, preparation, curation, illustration, writing, and description), for which Osborn took complete or at least partial credit. He had a retinue of secretaries and assistants who attended to his every beck and call, and they even had separate quarters outside his mansion in Garrison, New York, where they did his bidding when he was at home. At social events, only his top scientific assistants and fellow curators could dine with at the table with Osborn and his family; the "lesser staff" were consigned to a different room. George Gaylord Simpson, the legendary mammalian paleontologist who overlapped at the American Museum with Osborn's later career (see chapter 4), describes an incident when he once tried to apply an ink blotter to Osborn's autograph from a flowing fountain pen. Osborn stopped him and said, "Never blot the signature of a great man."[9] Although his arrogance and aristocratic ideas may have made his workers angry, it served him well because he could mingle effortlessly with the rich tycoons of New York and get them to donate money to the cause of science.

Like the children of many rich Eastern families, Osborn grew up in a mansion with servants in Fairfield, Connecticut. Then he was sent to

Princeton from 1873 to 1877 to get his college education alongside other sons of rich men. However, at Princeton he heard of the amazing finds of Marsh and Cope during the Bone Wars and got hooked on the lure of finding amazing fossils on his own. In an act that only a rich overconfident child of wealth could imagine, he organized his own field trip out west in 1877 with his classmates Francis Speier Jr. and William Berryman Scott (figure 9.5). (Scott later went on to become a famous paleontologist in his own right and founded the Princeton Geology Department, where he spent his career.) Osborn and his friends didn't want Yale to have a monopoly on the rich bone beds out west, so they set up their own expedition. The three rich young greenhorns managed to survive the harsh conditions out west, avoid being killed by hostile warriors on the warpath, and did it again with a larger party in 1878. They came back more determined than ever to become

Figure 9.5 ▲

A young Osborn (*left*), Francis Speir (*center*), and William Berryman Scott (*right*) on the audacious student fossil-hunting expedition to the Rockies. (Courtesy of Wikimedia Commons)

important paleontologists. Osborn met with both Leidy and Cope during his college years, and Cope became his mentor—thus making Marsh his enemy. Osborn supported Cope during his battles with Marsh, and as the sickly Cope reached desperate financial conditions before he died, Osborn generously bought his entire collection for his American Museum.

Neither Osborn nor Scott could earn a PhD in the United States (such programs did not yet exist here), so they traveled to Europe to experience the cutting edge of scientific research in 1879–1880, taking courses from the biologist Thomas Henry Huxley and the embryologist Francis Balfour in England (and meeting Charles Darwin) and learning from the leading German paleontologists as well. In 1883, Princeton awarded Osborn its own doctorate and offered him a post teaching biology and comparative anatomy.

By 1891, Osborn's research in both paleontology and embryology and his powerful connections landed him a job at the young American Museum of Natural History in New York as curator and head of the newly formed Department of Vertebrate Paleontology (DVP). He was also appointed to a professorship at Columbia University in New York. This established the Columbia/American Museum paleontology doctoral program that continued for more than a century. It was where I was trained. It has recently become the Richard Gilder graduate program, and the American Museum now offers its own doctorates independent of Columbia.

Osborn quickly worked hard to make the American Museum DVP the best in the world. Not only did he purchase all of Cope's fossils as the core of their collections, but he used his connections among tycoons to get funding to send field crews out to the Rockies to find many more specimens. By the time Osborn died in 1935, the DVP collections were the largest and most important in the world, especially in dinosaurs and fossil mammals.

All this activity drew many of the most talented people to the DVP. These included not only important collectors such as Jacob Wortman, Olof Peterson, and Barnum Brown but the talented anatomists and paleontologists William King Gregory and William Diller Matthew. Osborn kept a preparators' lab staffed with numerous skilled men who cleaned and prepared the many crates of bones sent from the field and then invented new techniques for creating large mounts in lifelike poses while hiding most of the supporting structures. Marsh had done this to some extent, but Osborn had a different vision for paleontology: make these huge skeletons of extinct creatures famous in popular culture and draw big crowds to his American Museum (of which he was director from 1908 to 1933). For this purpose, he hired the first great paleoartist, Charles R. Knight, to create dynamic reconstructions of extinct animals in paintings, murals, and sculptures. Osborn also knew how to get great publicity from spectacular accounts of extinct monsters, which were ready-made for reporters to wow the public. A particularly fortunate stroke of luck was promoting a young daredevil named Roy Chapman Andrews, who spearheaded Osborn's legendary Central Asiatic Expeditions in the 1920s to find dinosaurs and mammals (and early humans, which they never found). Many people think Andrews was one of the models for hero/explorer/archeologist characters like Indiana Jones and Allan Quartermain.

Unfortunately, Osborn may have been wealthy and powerful, but his ideas about science were outdated and somewhat quirky, such as postulating that brontotheres had evolved from separate origins in parallel many times, with 11 separate subfamilies, or "seeing" tiny horns on the skull that were not actually there, or that brontothere evolution was a simple linear trend toward larger size and horns figure 9.6 and figure 9.7). All of these ideas were published in a huge monograph on brontotheres, which was released in 1929 in two big volumes of more than a thousand pages. Like many paleontologists of his time, he gave new species names to nearly every specimen that was slightly different from the others known at the time. He did not consider the possibility that the differences between skulls of brontotheres might be normal variation within a biological population, or possibly due to distortion after the specimen had been buried and crushed. The best parts of this work were produced by his subordinates: the illustrations (done by Osborn's staff) and the analyses by American Museum paleontologist William King Gregory, but most later authors regarded Osborn's own work as useless.

The unfortunate legacy of Osborn's huge volumes full of incompetent paleontology was that for the next sixty years no one really wanted to work with brontotheres because the gigantic mess that Osborn had created would be a monumental task to clean up and redo. Finally, in 2008, almost eighty years after Osborn's work, the complete updating of brontothere evolution and classification was published by Matt Mihlbachler, then a student at the American Museum and now at the New York Institute of Technology. Today we have a sound modern understanding of brontothere evolution, and we can begin to see how they really evolved.

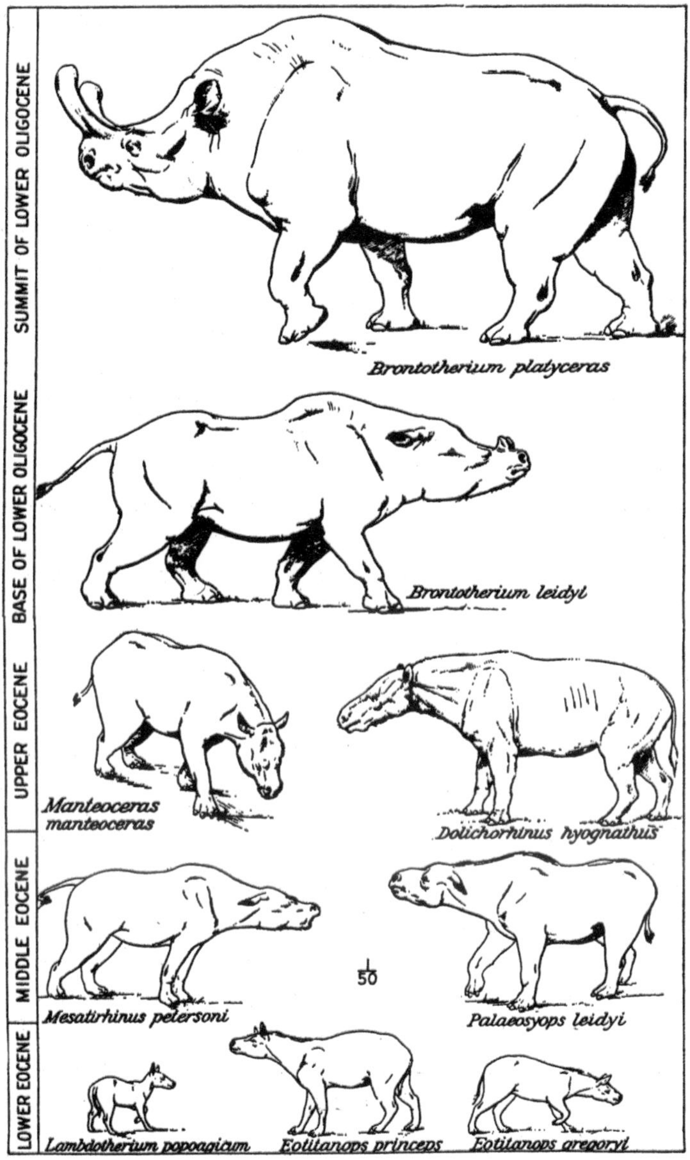

Figure 9.6 ▲

Osborn's highly outdated diagram showing his straight-line concept of brontothere evolution. (From H. F. Osborn, *The Titanotheres of Ancient Wyoming, Dakota, and Nebraska*, United States Geological Survey Monographs 55 [1929]: 1–701)

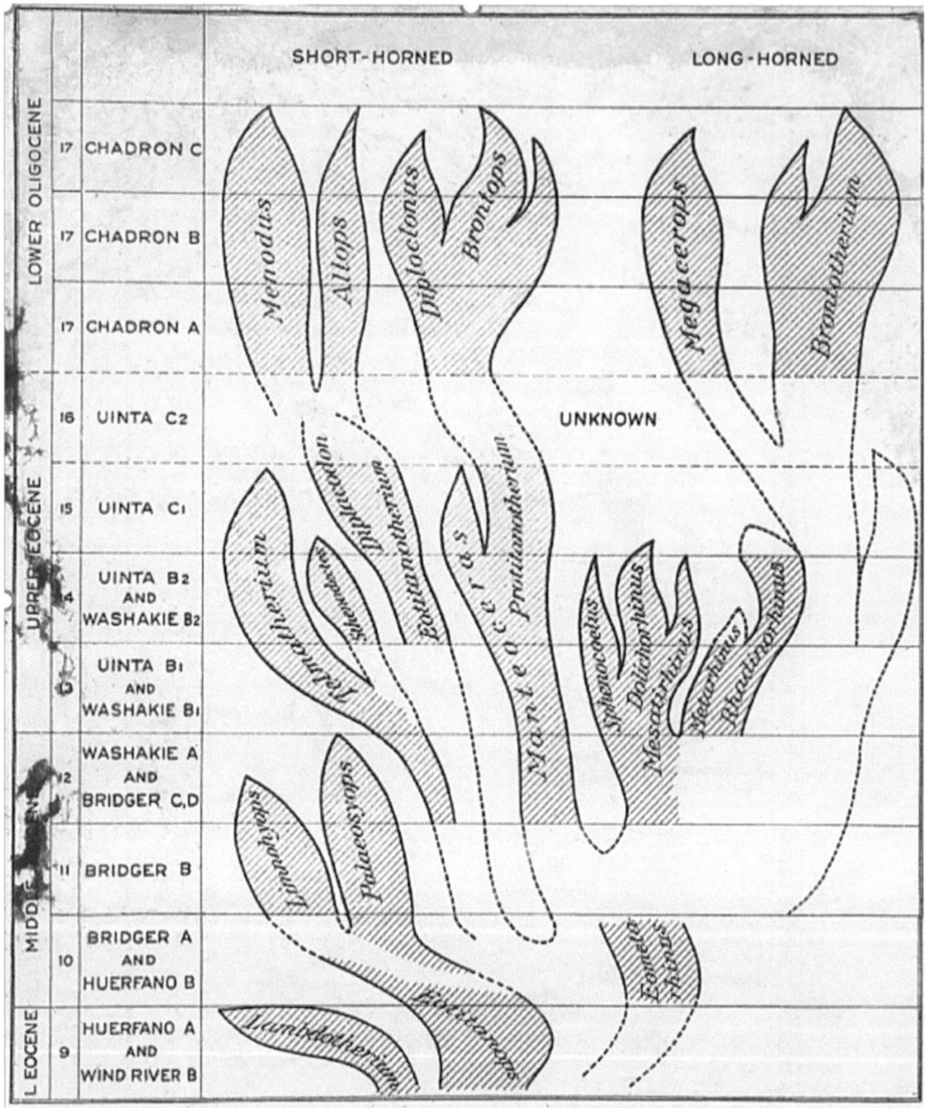

Figure 9.7 ▲

Osborn's discredited idea that there were many different lineages of brontotheres, all evolving in parallel (From H. F. Osborn, *The Titanotheres of Ancient Wyoming, Dakota, and Nebraska*, United States Geological Survey Monographs 55 [1929]: 1–701)

EVOLUTION OF THUNDER BEASTS

Brontotheres are members of the group of odd-toed hoofed mammals, the perissodactyls, because they have three digits on their hands and feet. Some have placed brontotheres closer to horses, others to the tapir-rhino branch of perissodactyls, but there is no clear consensus either way. Their evolution started almost 54 Ma, with beagle-sized creatures known as *Lambdotherium*, which were similar in overall shape and size to their closest relatives, the earliest horses and rhinos. Early on, brontothere upper molars develop a characteristic pattern, with the outer crest shaped like a W, and two large conical cusps on the inside of the upper molar crown. These primitive low-crowned teeth were suitable for eating leaves and soft vegetation but would never be good for eating gritty grasses. About 52 Ma, we find fossils in Wyoming of a slightly larger genus, *Eotitanops*, which was about the size of a sheep, about 1.5 feet high at the shoulder. About 47 Ma, the cow-sized *Palaeosyops* appeared, particularly in the Bridger Basin of Wyoming, as well as Pakistan. None of these early brontotheres had any signs of horns on their skulls; these would evolve later.

Around 45 Ma, in rocks of the Uinta Basin of Utah, we find the first larger brontotheres, such as the bull-sized narrow-snouted *Dolichorhinus* and *Sthenodectes*, and the broader-headed *Metarhinus, Mesatirhinus*, with their deep nasal notches, and *Telmatherium* and *Metatelmatherium*, with their shorter nasal notches and arched nasal bones. The first paired horns occur in genera like *Manteoceras, Diplacodon* (both from the Uinta Basin of Utah), *Protitanotherium* from Texas, and *Rhinotitan* from Mongolia. About 40 Ma, *Protitanops* from Death Valley appeared, along with *Duchesneodus* from the Duchesne River Formation of the Uinta Basin of Utah, which also had small paired horns on their noses.

Finally, we get to the huge horned brontotheres from upper Eocene beds about 34–37 Ma, at the base of the Big Badlands section. Cope, Marsh, and especially Osborn split these horned brontotheres into many genera, including *Menodus, Brontops, Brontotherium, Titanotherium, Allops, Menops, Ateleodon*, and *Oreinotherium*, with dozens of different species names. In 1989, Bryn Mader published a paper that reduced them to *Brontops, Allops*, and *Menops*. But in a 2004 paper and in his 2008 monograph, Matt Mihlbachler argued that most of the variation in the skulls referred to these different genera can be attributed to normal variation within a population, plus possibly differences between males and females, and a lot of distortion of the fossil after it was buried. He showed there were no longer any strong objective reasons for recognizing all these genera and species, so he reduced them all to the oldest valid name of a horned brontothere based on diagnostic material: *Megacerops coloradensis*, named by Leidy in 1870. Mihlbachler supported this argument by showing that large quarry samples of brontothere skulls were highly variable, and even though they represent a single population, they had been attributed to different genera and species. As an analogy, Mihlbachler and colleagues pointed to the population of modern giraffes. Within a single population sample, giraffes can have highly variable combinations of horns as well as bony bumps on their foreheads. Based on this, Mihlbachler and others concluded in 2004 that nearly all the late Eocene brontotheres were one species. There is one other valid species of brontothere between 34 and 37 Ma in North America besides *Megacerops coloradensis*. That is *Megacerops kuwagatirhinus*, which has small forks at the tips of each of its horns.

At the same time that huge horned *Megacerops* ruled North America, some truly bizarre brontotheres were found in Mongolia and China. First discovered by the American Museum expeditions in the 1920s, the huge embolotheres had fused the paired nasal horns into a single big horn (figure 9.8). Now there are a whole range of brontotheres known from Mongolia, China, and other parts of Asia from 34–37 Ma.

Brontotheres are often shown as using their horns for head-to-head ramming, like a bighorn sheep. However, this is impossible. For one thing, bighorn sheep have special shock-absorbing adaptations in their skulls to mitigate the effects of impact. Brontothere skulls, on the other hand, have only spongy tissue in the skull at the base of the horn, so the horns would break off if they slammed into each other head on. Instead, they probably used their horns to wrestle and spar with rivals, as we see today in rhinos, deer, and most horned ruminants. They may have slammed their horns sideways during this sparring but would never have collided head-to-head. Indeed, the mounted skeleton of a brontothere on display at the American Museum of Natural History in New York has a broken rib on its right side,

Figure 9.8 ▶

The "battering-ram" Mongolian brontothere *Embolotherium*. (*A*) Front view, and (*B*) side view. (Photos by the author)

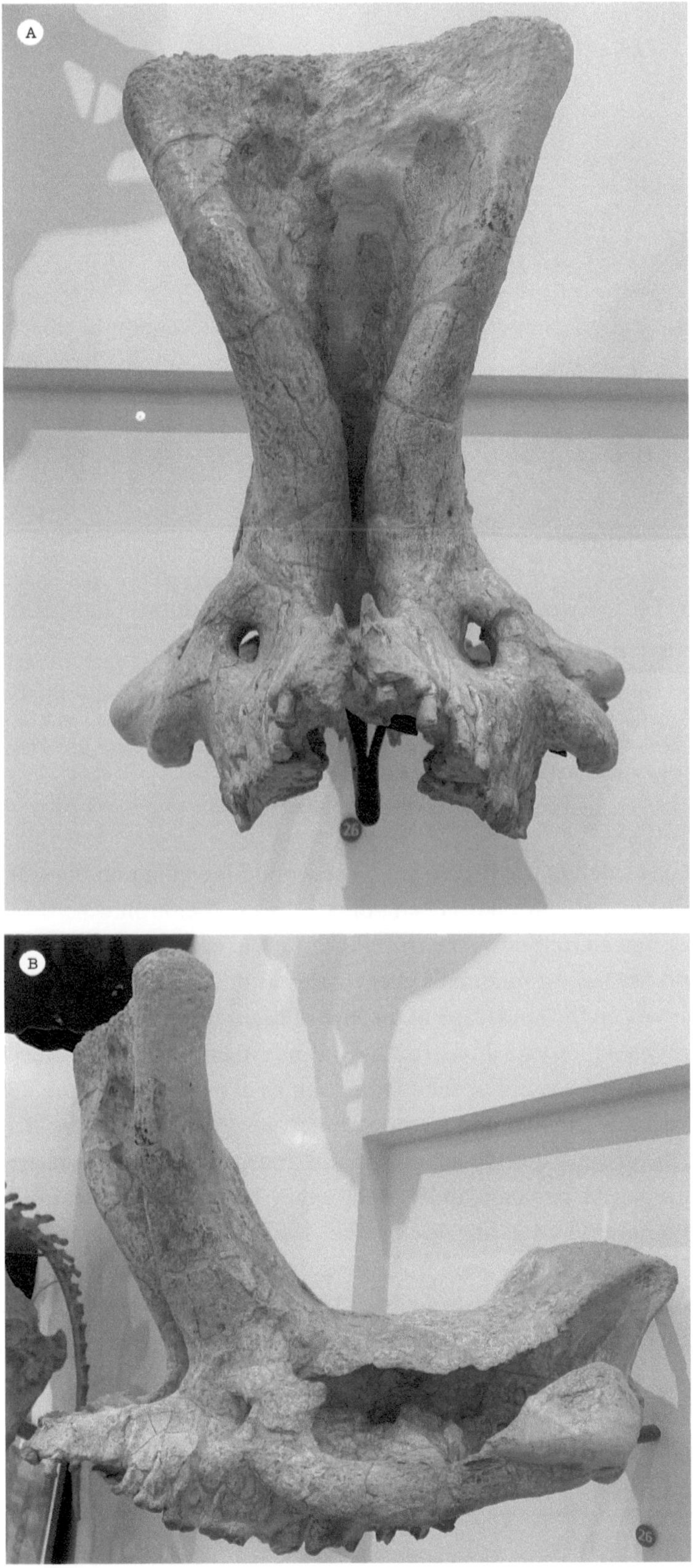
A
26
B
26

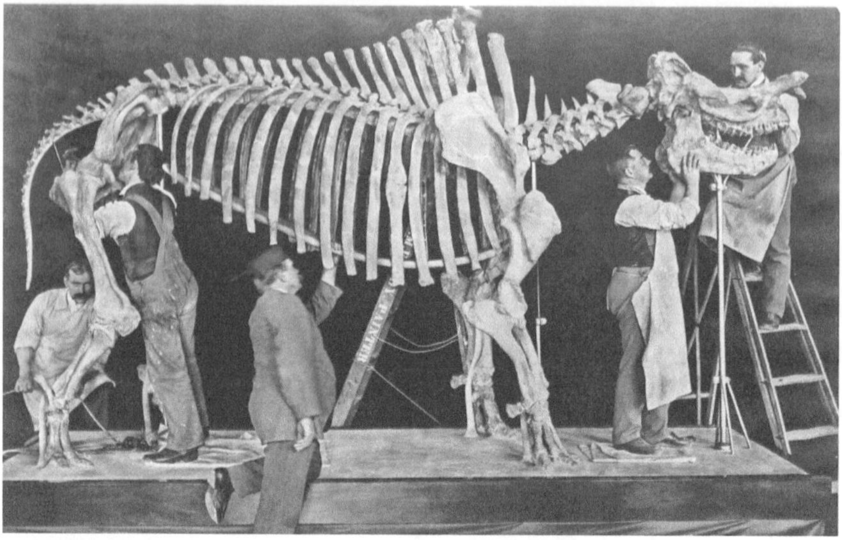

Figure 9.9 ▲

Mounted skeleton of the late Eocene brontothere *Megacerops coloradensis* on display at the American Museum of Natural History in New York. This specimen has a broken rib that healed while it was alive, suggesting it was hit by another brontothere. (Courtesy of the Library Service, American Museum of Natural History)

which re-healed in life (figure 9.9). The wound is so high on the side of its body that it could only have been inflicted by another brontothere.

Over just 20 million years, from 54 to 34 Ma, brontotheres evolved rapidly into the largest mammals ever to appear on land, and by far the largest animals on the landscape at the end of their history (figure 9.10). Then around 33 Ma they vanished in both Asia and North America. No one knows for sure what the cause of their extinction was, but it did happen during a major climate change, the Eocene-Oligocene transition. In the Big Badlands, the climate quickly got cooler and drier, and the forests nearly vanished, replaced by scrublands. Many other large archaic mammals who were committed to eating leaves also vanished at this time. The teeth of brontotheres clearly were not suited to eating anything but the softest leaves and could not tolerate a diet of gritty shrubs or grasses that appeared after the climate change. When they vanished, there were a few large rhinos around, but nothing reached the size of brontotheres until the mastodonts evolved about 18 Ma.

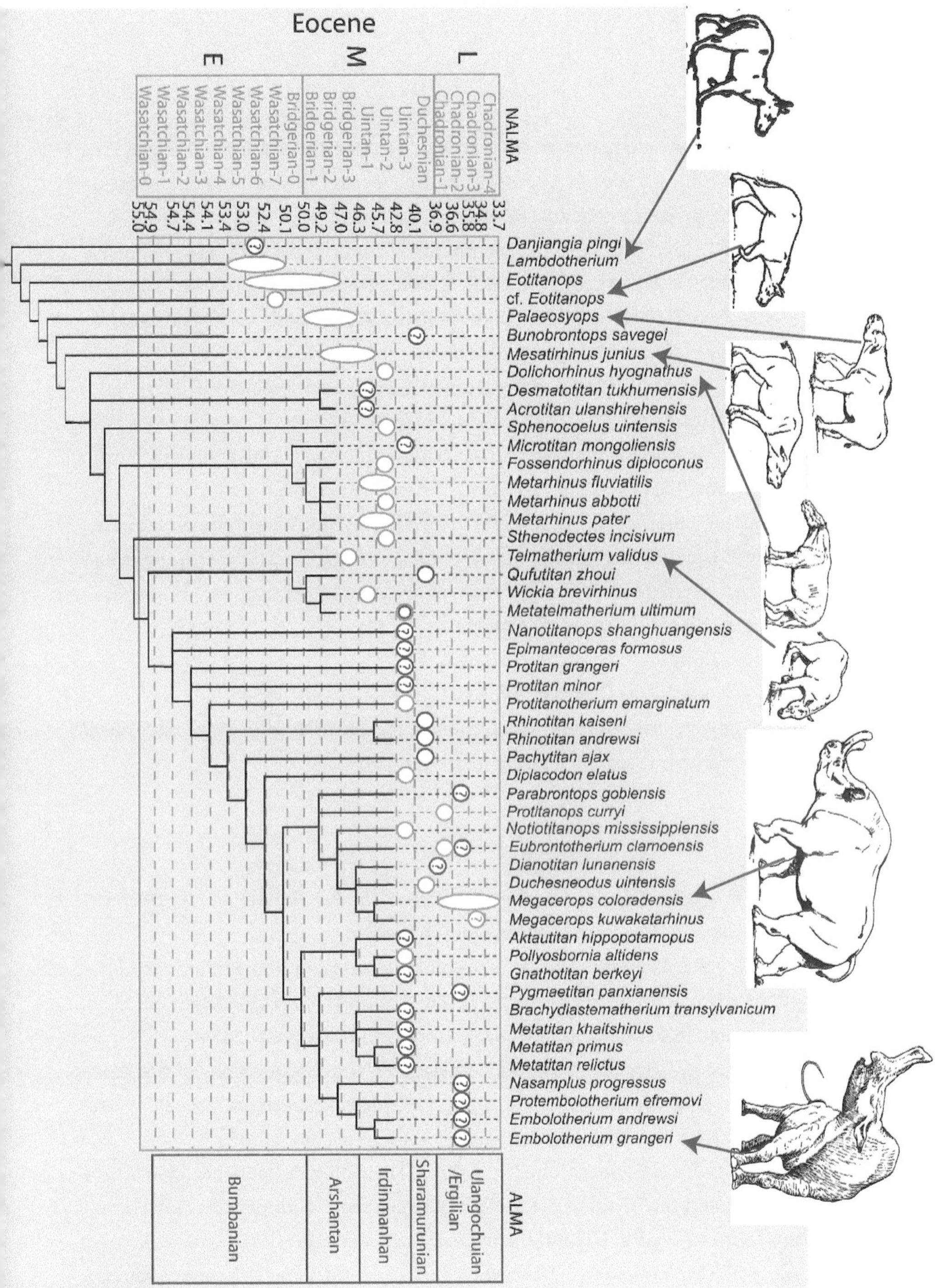

Figure 9.10 ▲

Phylogeny of brontotheres according to M. C. Mihlbachler, "Species Taxonomy, Phylogeny, and Biogeography of the Brontotheriidae (Mammalia: Perissodactyla)," *Bulletin of the American Museum of Natural History* 311 (2008): 1–475 (2008). (Courtesy of M. Mihlbachler)

NOTES

The epigraph is taken from Riley Black, "No One Gives Me a Headache Like H. F. Osborn," *Wired*, August 17, 2009, https://www.wired.com/2009/08/no-one-gives-me-a-headache-like-h-f-osborn/.

1. Joseph Leidy, "The Extinct Mammalian Fauna of Dakota and Nebraska, Including an Account of Some Allied Forms from Other Localities, Together with a Synopsis of the Mammalian Remains of North America," *Journal of the Academy of Natural Sciences, Philadelphia* 2 (1869), 72.
2. Leidy, "The Extinct Mammalian Fauna of Dakota and Nebraska," 17.
3. Paul D. Brinkman, P.D. *The Second Jurassic Dinosaur Rush: Museums and Paleontology in America at the Turn of the Twentieth Century* (University of Chicago Press, 2010) 123.
4. Charles H. Sternberg, *The Life of a Fossil Hunter* (Henry Holt, 1909), 120.
5. Lowell Dingus, *King of the Dinosaur Hunters: The life of John Bell Hatcher and the Discoveries That Shaped Paleontology* (Pegasus, 2018), 22.
6. Dingus, *King of the Dinosaur Hunters*, 122.
7. Dingus, *King of the Dinosaur Hunters*, 122.
8. Dingus, *King of the Dinosaur Hunters*, 144.
9. George Gaylord Simpson, *Concession to the Improbable: An Unconventional Autobiography* (Yale University Press, 1978), 99.

FOR FURTHER READING

Dingus, L., *King of the Dinosaur Hunters: The Life of John Bell Hatcher and the Discoveries that Shaped Paleontology*. Pegasus Books, 2018.

Mader, B. J. "The Brontotheriidae: A Systematic Revision and Preliminary Phylogeny of North American Genera." In *The Evolution of Perissodactyls*, ed. D. R. Prothero and R. M. Schoch, 458–484. Oxford University Press, 1989.

Mihlbachler, M. C. "Species Taxonomy, Phylogeny, and Biogeography of the Brontotheriidae (Mammalia: Perissodactyla)." *Bulletin of the American Museum of Natural History* 311 (2008): 1–475.

Mihlbachler, M. C., S. G. Lucas, and R. J. Emry. "The Holotype Specimen of *Menodus Giganteus*, and the 'Insoluble' Problem of Chadronian Brontothere Taxonomy." *New Mexico Museum of Natural History and Science* 26 (2004): 129–136.

Osborn, H. F. *The Titanotheres of Ancient Wyoming, Dakota, and Nebraska*. 2 vols. US Geological Survey, 1929.

Prothero, D. R. *The Princeton Field Guide to Prehistoric Mammals*. Princeton University Press, 2016.

——. *Vertebrate Evolution: From Origins to Dinosaurs and Beyond*. Taylor & Francis/CRC Press, 2022.

Prothero, D. R., and R. M. Schoch, eds. *The Evolution of Perissodactyls*. Oxford University Press, 1989.

——. *Horns, Tusks, and Flippers: The Evolution of Hoofed Mammals*. Johns Hopkins University Press, 2002.

Rainger, R. *An Agenda for Antiquity: Henry Fairfield Osborn and Vertebrate Paleontology at the American Museum of Natural History, 1890–1935*. University of Alabama Press, 1991.

Savage, R. J. G., and M. R. Long. *Mammal Evolution: An Illustrated Guide*. Facts-on-File, 1986.

Turner, A., and M. Anton. *National Geographic Prehistoric Mammals*. National Geographic Society, 2004.

CHALICOTHERIUM AND *MEGATAPIRUS*

No one had ever found the feet of *Chalicotherium*, or the skull, or teeth of *Ancylotherium*, yet they always occur together in the same beds; where you get one, you get the other.

—CHARLES FORSYTH MAJOR

CONTRADICTING CUVIER?

Baron Georges Cuvier was famous for many things, one being his "law of correlation of parts" (chapter 1). As a comparative anatomist, he noticed that predators usually had long sharp claws on their paws, and also had sharp knife-like and dagger-like teeth for stabbing and ripping up their prey. In contrast, herbivores usually had cheek teeth that were grinding mills for chewing up their food, and most of them had hooves as well. A famous (but probably false) legend about Cuvier claims that a prankster broke into his bedchamber one night, dressed as the Devil, and threatened to eat Cuvier. Allegedly Cuvier calmly replied, "You have hooves and horns, so you only eat plants."[1]

The idea of "correlation of parts" has been greatly expanded and modified since the days of Cuvier, but this is why paleontologists often can reconstruct whole skeletons from just a few bones. If we have certain key bones, and we know what the skeletons of close relatives look like, then we can fill in the missing parts of most other animals.

Of course, there are exceptions that prove the rule, even though it works in 99 percent of the cases. The most famous contradiction are the strange beasts known as chalicotheres. In 1833, the German paleontologist Johann Jacob von Kaup described some strange cheek teeth of a mammal with "W"-shaped crests on the upper molars from the late Miocene "bone beds of Eppelsheim" (also called the "*Dinotherion-sande*," in reference to the spectacular *Deinotherium* that Kaup found and described from there) in the German Rhineland (chapter 1). Kaup named it *Chalicotherium goldfussi*, "Goldfuss's pebble beast," possibly because of the pebble-like appearance of some of the teeth, or possibly because they came from pebbly beds. Also found in the same beds were some peculiar foot claws with cleft tips that didn't seem to match any of the skulls or teeth found there (figure 10.1). When Cuvier saw them, he thought they might come for a huge ant-eating pangolin ("*un Pangolin gigantesque*"), a group of living mammals that have a long snout and tongue for eating ants, sharp digging claws for tearing up termite mounds, but are covered in scales like a pine cone. Yet there was no way to know for sure what teeth belonged with which feet because the bones were all jumbled and disassociated and lots of different species were mixed together.

In 1837, the French paleontologist Edouard Lartet was describing fossils from the famous Miocene fossil beds near Sansan, in the department of Gers in southwestern France. This locality is famous for producing the Miocene ape *Propliopithecus* and dozens of other mammal species, such as the sabertooth *Sansanosmilus*. It also yielded numerous strange claws with cleft tips, which Lartet named *Macrotherium grande*. In 1863, the French paleontologist Albert Gaudry described yet another strange set of claws from the famous late Miocene Pikermi fauna in Greece, which he called *Ancylotherium*. Several people noticed that strange teeth like those of *Chalicotherium* were always found in localities with the odd clawed feet with clefts, but thanks to Cuvier's law of correlation of parts, it was unthinkable that they belonged together. As the British paleontologist Charles Forsyth Major wrote:

> No one had ever found the feet of Chalicotherium, or the skull, or teeth of Ancylotherium, yet they always occur together in the same beds; where you get one, you get the other.[2]

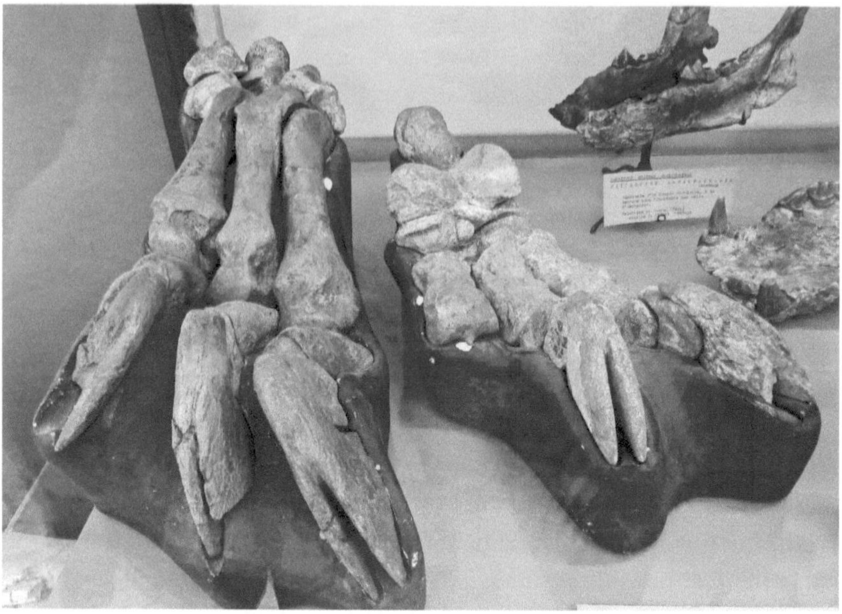

Figure 10.1 ▲
The peculiar cleft-tipped claws of chalicotheres, here showing the foot of *Anisodon*. (Courtesy of Wikimedia Commons)

Finally, in 1879, forty-two years after it was first described by Kaup, new discoveries by the French paleontologist Henri Filhol led him to realize that the headless limbs with cleft-tipped claws described as *Macrotherium* and *Ancylotherium* must have belonged to the teeth and skulls with no postcranial skeletons known as *Chalicotherium*. This was a truly bizarre combination! The teeth closely resembled those found in other odd-toed hoofed mammals, such as primitive tapirs and brontotheres, but the skull was more like that of a horse. Yet even though it was a hoofed mammal, it had huge powerful limbs with claws. And as *Chalicotherium* got to be better known, it was clear that they had long front limbs and short hind limbs and must have knuckle-walked like a gorilla or a ground sloth (figure 10.2).

Meanwhile, similar fossils were being discovered in the western United States. In 1877, Yale paleontologist Othniel Charles Marsh published a short note with no illustrations of a fossil he called *Moropus distans*, sent to him

Figure 10.2 ▲
Reconstruction of *Chalicotherium goldfussi*, with its gorilla-like long front limbs and short back limbs. (Courtesy of Wikimedia Commons)

by his collectors from the John Day beds of Oregon. In the same paper, he also described *Moropus elatus*, based on specimens from western Nebraska that had been given to him. All of these specimens were just isolated foot bones, so Marsh compared them to *Ancylotherium* from Europe, which at that time were thought to be the claws of a giant ground sloth or maybe a huge aardvark. *Moropus* means "foolish foot" in Greek, in reference to its strange claws.

But nothing more was found in the United States until almost thirty years later, when Captain James Cook of the Agate Springs Ranch in northwestern Nebraska allowed fossil collectors from the Carnegie Museum in Pittsburgh, the University of Nebraska Museum in Lincoln, and eventually the American Museum of Natural History in New York

Figure 10.3 ▲
Reconstruction of *Moropus*, the common chalicothere from Agate Fossil Beds National Monument. (Courtesy of N. Tamura)

to collect a huge bone bed on his ranch, now known as the Agate Fossil Beds National Monument. The two small hills that expose the bone bed are known as Carnegie Hill and University Hill because these two institutions were the first to collect there. In the end the fossils were so abundant that they ended up in many museums and are commonly found on display all over the country. Most of the logjam of bones belong to the little pair-horned rhinoceros *Menoceras arikarense*. But one of the other common mammals was Marsh's *Moropus elatus*, which was represented by dozens of skeletons (figure 10.3). When they were formally published by the Carnegie Museum paleontologist Olof Peterson in 1914, they turned out to be another strange mixture. The head was definitely horse-like and the limb proportions were also more horse-like and less like gorilla proportions of *Chalicotherium*. But *Moropus elatus* still had the distinctive claws on the feet, also with the cleft that divides each clawed toe into two branches, like other chalicotheres. The first illustrations of *Moropus* made it look even more horse-like, but more recent reconstructions downplay the horsey features. Whatever it actually looked like, it was definitely not a pangolin or a ground sloth or an aardvark, as Cuvier and Marsh and others had thought.

The Agate fossil beds yield a rich fauna of mammals that dates from about 22–19 Ma, including not only *Moropus* and little pair-horned rhinos *Menoceras*, but gigantic hippo-sized entelodonts, *Daeodon*, which looked vaguely hoglike, camels with long necks and legs, and other camels shaped like gazelles, three-toed horses, plus oreodonts, which have no close living relative or analogue, and the amphicyonid "bear-dog" *Daphoenocyon*,

So where do chalicotheres fit in the family tree of perissodactyls, or odd-toed hoofed mammals, such as horses, tapirs, and rhinos? In the past, they have been placed closer to horses, but recent work suggests that they are within the giant grouping that leads to tapirs and rhinos, called the Moropomorpha by my friend and frequent coauthor Robert Schoch. If you go back to beds around 55 Ma, the differences between the earliest rhinos, tapirs, horses, and chalicotheres are extremely slight and they are very difficult to tell apart (figure 10.4).

CHALICOTHERES IN TIME AND SPACE

The oldest chalicothere is *Protomoropus*, from beds around 55 Ma in Mongolia, but when it was first described by Russian paleontologists, it was assigned to *Hyracotherium*, which is a genus closely related to horses—that's how subtle the differences are (see chapter 8). From *Protomoropus*, the next youngest species are *Litolophus* and *Eomoropus*, from beds about 50 Ma in China and Mongolia. *Eomoropus* migrated from Asia to North America, where it is found in beds about 45 Ma in age in Wyoming and Utah.

Next comes the big split between the subfamily Schizotheriinae, such as the horse-like *Moropus*, and the subfamily Chalicotheriinae, such as the gorilla-like *Chalicotherium*. The schizotheres start with *Schizotherium* itself, from bed about 25 Ma in Europe, and *Borissiakia* from beds of that age in Kazakhstan. Other schizotheres include not only *Moropus*, previously discussed, but the bizarre dome-headed chalicotheres known as *Tylocephalonyx*. Two complete skulls of this weird animal have been found

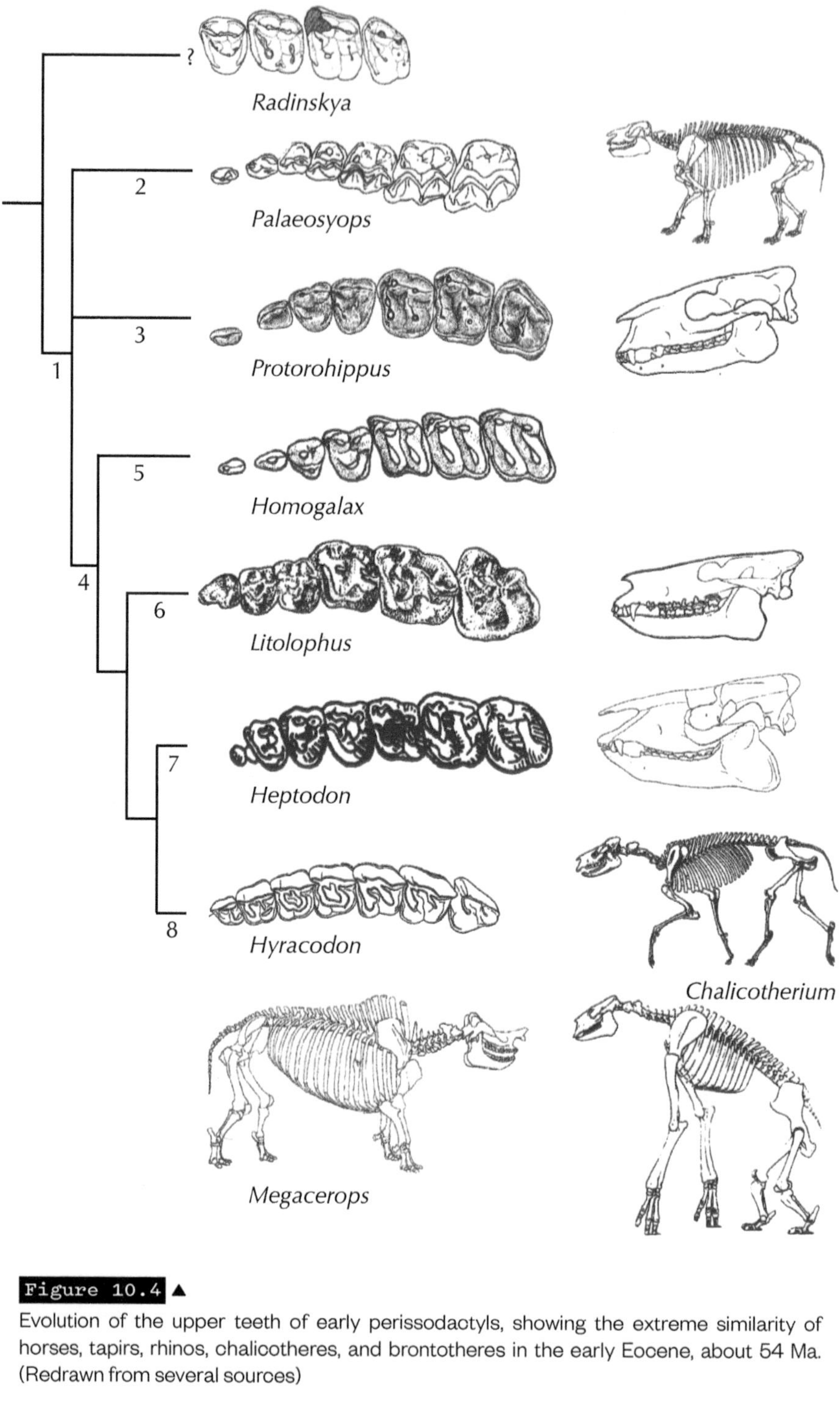

Figure 10.4 ▲

Evolution of the upper teeth of early perissodactyls, showing the extreme similarity of horses, tapirs, rhinos, chalicotheres, and brontotheres in the early Eocene, about 54 Ma. (Redrawn from several sources)

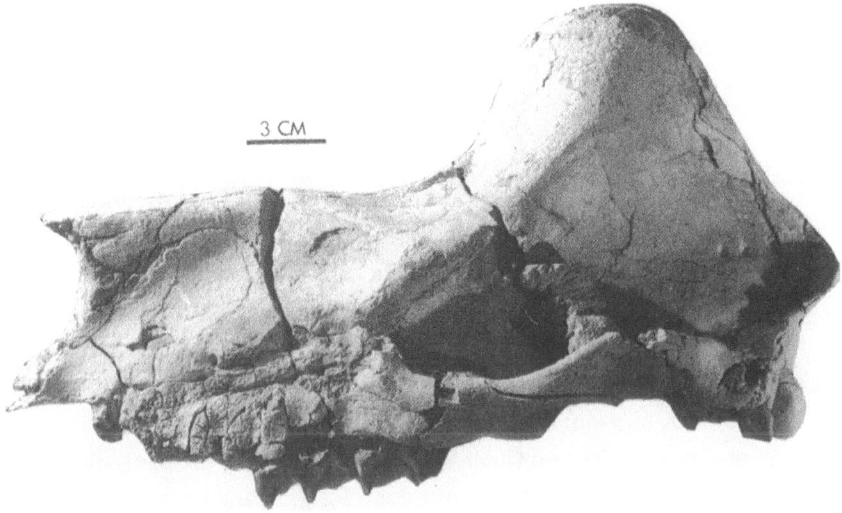

Figure 10.5 ▲
The domed skull of the chalicothere *Tylocephalonyx*. (Courtesy of M. C. Coombs)

(figure 10.5). One is from the Split Rock Formation of Wyoming, about 17 Ma, and the other is found in the marine Astoria Formation of Oregon, apparently washed out to sea, but then fossilized and discovered by the legendary collector Doug Emlong. Nearly complete skeletons of *Tylocephalonyx* have been found in the Sheep Creek Formation of western Nebraska, so it is very well known. The function of the dome on its head is controversial, but it was definitely not for head-to-head ramming because it is hollow inside with thin bony walls. Instead, Margery Coombs, who has spent her career working on chalicotheres, points out that it more likely was used in head and neck wrestling among males, where the force of the impact was not as great, and probably also served to display dominance among males, as do most cranial appendages. Skulls and other specimens of *Tylocephalonyx* are very rare, so it is difficult to decide if there are skulls of both males and females, and how they might differ.

The subfamily Chalicotheriinae were specialized in a different way. They include the gorilla-like *Chalicotherium* and *Anisodon*, which were found in beds from about 7 to 3 Ma in Eurasia and Africa. The last of chalicotheres included *Nestoritherium* from China and Myanmar until about

780,000 years ago. *Ancylotherium henningi* persisted in Africa until the end of the last Ice Age.

GORILLA-LIKE HORSES?

So what were their strange claws used for, and how did chalicotheres live and feed? Older literature suggested that the claws were for digging up roots and tubers, or possibly for fighting off large predators. But studies done by Helmut Zapfe and Margery Coombs showed that their claws were not well adapted for that purpose. Instead, Coombs pointed out that they were probably good for hauling down branches to bring them within range of their mouths, as ground sloths and gorillas feed. Indeed, the gorilla-like proportions of *Anisodon* and *Chalicotherium* (figure 10.2) are consistent with that idea. Not only are their forelimbs good for grasping branches, but they have callosities on their hip bones that show they spent a long time sitting back on their haunches in a feeding position. Detailed studies of the wear on their teeth confirm that their diet was mostly leaves, fruit, and seeds, and they didn't eat anything tough or gritty such as roots and tubers.

Originating about 55 Ma, and showing up in Eurasia, North America, and Africa off and on for the past 50 Ma, chalicotheres hung on until a few thousand years ago in Africa and eastern Asia, and then vanished. Why they went extinct is still a mystery, although it may have to do with the great megafauna extinctions at the end of the last Ice Age (see chapter 1). Certainly, our hominin ancestors in Africa knew of them for millions of years and may have hunted them, although they were large and powerful and could use their claws as effective weapons.

NANDI BEARS?

Or did they? Many East African cultures have legends of a beast called the Nandi bear. Descriptions of the Nandi bear portray a ferocious, powerfully built carnivore with high front shoulders (more than 4 feet tall) and a sloping back. Stories of the Nandi bear state that it is fierce, nocturnal, stands on its hind legs, and can kill animals. In 1902, Charles W. Andrews, the famous British paleontologist who discovered the Fayûm beds in Egypt, suggested that the Nandi bear might have been the extinct chalicotheres that had vanished only ten thousand years ago. In the 1930s, Louis

Leakey also suggested that Nandi bears were chalicotheres. But chalicotheres were never carnivorous, and they probably didn't kill other animals unless cornered. In 2000, the paleontologist Louis Jacobs commented that "if chalicotheres existed now, they would have been found out just like the giant forest hog was."[3] He concluded that "if there is anything to the Nandi-bear story besides imagination, I suspect it may be the word-of-mouth description of gorillas passed across the continent from areas where they live to areas where they do not." The zoologist Reginald Peacock claimed that reports of the Nandi bear were misidentified hyenas, specifically the spotted hyena. In 1932, Reginald I. Pocock of the British Natural History Museum stated that many reports of the Nandi Bear have "proved to have been nothing more than a spotted hyena."[4] Similarly, the paleontologist George Gaylord Simpson commented that the Nandi bear "turned out to be in most if not all cases a ratel [honey-badger], an animal which had been known to scientific zoologists since 1776."[5]

Whatever chalicotheres looked like and whether they were part of the Nandi bear legend, these weird animals that look like a cross between a horse and gorilla but with claws are now extinct. They show us that nature can still surprise us—like putting claws on an animal that is related to hoofed mammals like horses, tapirs and rhinos.

DRAGON BONES

For centuries, the remains of the tin-schu, subterranean dragon, have been highly valued among the Chinese for their strong medicinal properties. The Chinese dragon is considered beneficial, signifying wisdom (in contrast to the mythology of European dragons, which are often depicted as creatures of terror). Even today, one can find fung-lung-tschih (big white dragon teeth), tsing-lung-tschih (small black dragon teeth), and lung-ku (dragon bones) from shops in pharmacies in China and those serving Chinese communities elsewhere.

In the nineteenth century, western scientists first acquired some of these dragon teeth and dragon bones for analysis. What were these dragons? None other than fossil mammal remains! But for European scientists, this is both an exhilarating and saddening discovery. Certainly these fossils might have shed much light and history of life—but only if paleontologists could get to specimens before they were ground up and ingested. For centuries, the Chinese had been mining and destroying tons of fossils. And where were the actual localities from which the fossils came? Chinese merchants, traders, and pharmacists were not about to tell. Dragon bones sold for high prices and such information was top secret!

One could buy dragon's teeth on the open market, so at least western scientists could acquire specimens in this manner—as long as their money held out. Thus a few specimens purchased in Shanghai came into the hands of Richard Owen of the British Museum. In 1870, Owen described his specimens, which included a rhinoceros, a tapir, a chalicothere, and an extinct mastodont, *Stegodon*. The appetite of the scientists for more of these dragon teeth was whetted.

During the period from 1899 to 1902, a German scientist and physician, Dr. K. A. Haberer, acquired a large collection of dragon teeth and jaws through the Chinese drug vendors. He turned these over to his friend, Dr. Max Schlosser, a vertebrate paleontologist working in Munich. Based on Haberer's collections, Schlosser was able to identify approximately 60 different species of Pleistocene mammals from China. Among the specimens was a tooth that Schlosser identified as a fossilized human molar. Scientists soon began to search for ancient humans in China; their search culminated a quarter of a century later with the discovery of "Peking man."

In 1921, Walter Granger (figure 10.6) of the American Museum of Natural History in New York, a leading paleontologist and the main scientist on that museum's Central Asiatic Expeditions, went to the Sichuan province of China in search of dragon teeth. He was in China making connections and scouting for possibilities to get access to Mongolia. Granger was the lead paleontologist on all the expeditions during the 1920s, and there could not have been a more competent person assigned to the task. Born in Vermont in 1872, he was one of five children of the Civil War veteran and insurance agent Charles H. Granger. Like Roy Chapman Andrews, the expedition's official leader, Granger developed an early talent for taxidermy, and in 1890 when he was only seventeen he got a job doing taxidermy at the American Museum. Within a few years, he went on field expeditions to the American West searching for vertebrate fossils with American Museum paleontologists. After two field seasons (1894 and 1895), his fossil-hunting talents were better appreciated, and he was transferred to the Department of Vertebrate Paleontology in 1896. Granger discovered the legendary Bone Cabin Quarry near Laramie, Wyoming, in 1897, which he worked for the

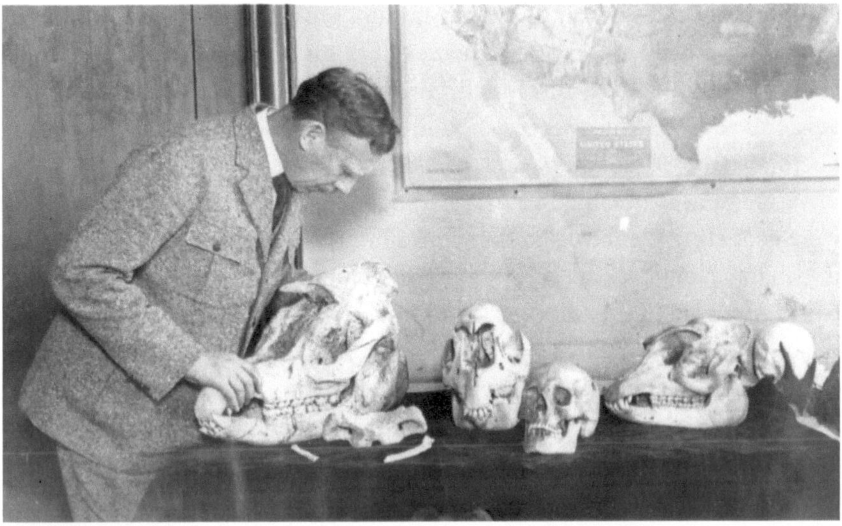

Figure 10.6 ▲
Walter Granger holding the skull of *Megatapirus* and comparing it to those of modern tapirs. (Courtesy of the American Museum Digital Library)

next eight field seasons. The site yielded thousands of bones representing 64 species of dinosaur, including the mounted skeletons of the big *Apatosaurus* ("*Brontosaurus*") and *Stegosaurus* currently on display at the museum today.

After working at Bone Cabin Quarry from 1897 to 1906, Granger accompanied Osborn on an expedition to the Eocene-Oligocene Fayûm beds of Egypt in 1907. This was one the first American Museum fossil trips outside North America. They made many important discoveries that complemented what had been discovered by the British Museum paleontologist Charles W. Andrews just a few years earlier. By this point, Granger was promoted to Assistant Curator, and he had a flexible schedule that allowed him at least five months in the field every year to find more fossils, while he continued to write two or three scientific papers each year as well.

In 1921, Granger began explorations in China, which eventually led to the discovery of the Zhoukoudian (formerly Choukoutien) caves near Beijing (formerly Peking). This work in China laid the foundation for the negotiations to go through China to Mongolia that allowed the 1922 American Museum expedition to succeed. When Granger finished the expeditions, he was promoted to Curator of Fossil Mammals, allowing him to continue to work on his many amazing discoveries until his death at age sixty-eight of heart failure in 1941. Entirely self-taught, Granger never earned a formal academic degree; this was rectified in 1932 when he received an honorary doctorate from Middlebury College.

While he was in China in 1921, Granger realized that the local farmers were collecting the fossils in the winter months and later sold them to the merchants, who in turn passed them on to retail vendors and pharmacists. Granger got rid of the middlemen by intercepting and purchasing the best bones from the local farmers. They could also tell them exactly where they came from. Soon he had an outstanding collection of dragon teeth. When it came time to study the specimens at home, among the specimens was a tapir skull (figure 10.7) and lots of teeth. Although it looked much like a modern tapir in many respects, its skull was 1.5 feet (half a meter) long, and it's estimated that the living animal may have weighed 1,700 pounds (800 kilograms), two to three times the weight of a living tapir, and similar to the size of large cow. Appropriately, in 1923 William Diller Matthew and Walter

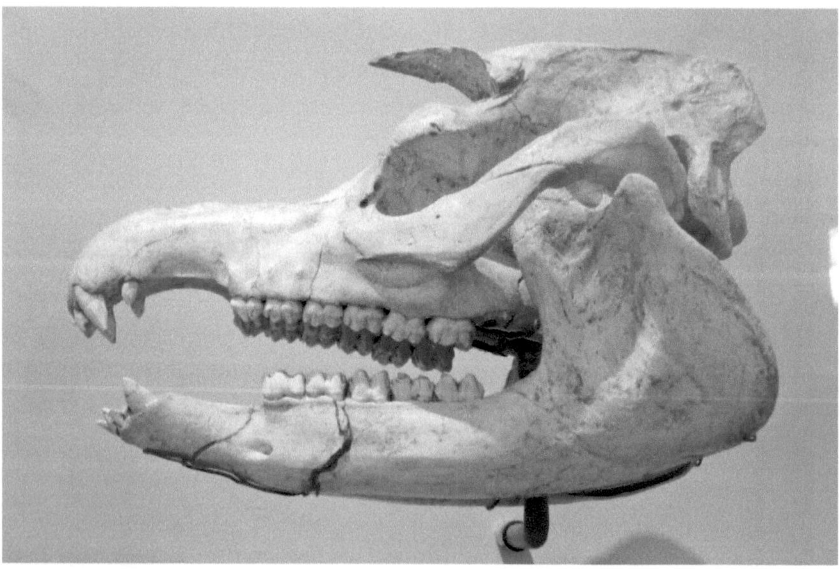

Figure 10.7 ▲
Close up of the skull of *Megatapirus*, on display at the American Museum of Natural History in New York. (Photo by the author)

Granger gave this tapir a new name, *Megatapirus augustus*. Since then, it's been placed as a species of *Tapirus*, but that doesn't diminish its distinctiveness or its huge size.

LIVING FOSSILS

Most people have never heard of tapirs, let alone seen one. To the average person, they look prehistoric. In the movie *2001: A Space Odyssey*, Stanley Kubrick used them as the prehistoric-looking animals in the opening scene, feeding peacefully beside the primitive hominins, before the latter discovered tools and weapons with which to kill animals. Tapirs look a bit like a cross between a pig and an elephant, with their short flexible snout or proboscis (figure 10.8), but they are related to neither. Their closest living relatives are rhinoceroses. Today they are a rare but important group of hoofed mammals in the jungles of Latin America and southeast Asia. At one time, about 45 Ma, they were one of the dominant groups of animals on the planet.

Today only four species of tapirs survive. Three live in Central and South America: Baird's tapir, *Tapirus bairdii*; the Brazilian tapir, *Tapirus terrestris*; and the mountain tapir, *Tapirus pinchaq*ue (figure 10.9A. figure 10.9B, and figure 10.9C. These three species have brown coats with some variation in color pattern. The fourth species, *Tapirus indicus*, is found in the jungles of southeast Asia. It is striking in its stark pattern of a black body with a broad white band around its midsection (figure 10.9D). Like all tapirs, it is equally at home in the water as it is on land.

Tapirs don't swim much, but when they are in shallow water, they dive and then walk along the bottom of the river, often hiding from predators as they do so, using their proboscis as a snorkel. They have few other defenses against their predators, such as jaguars in Latin America and tigers in Southeast Asia. All they can do is dive underwater, or plunge into the thick jungle with their tough hides protecting them. Tapirs feed exclusively on soft leaves and foliage, and their cheek teeth have simple cross-crests for chopping up this vegetation. They have low-crowned teeth, so tapirs cannot eat gritty grasses.

You might wonder why we say that the closest relatives of tapirs are the rhinoceroses. We can trace their ancestors back past 55 Ma, when tapirs and rhinos first split. In fact, the earliest tapir, *Homogalax*, have skulls

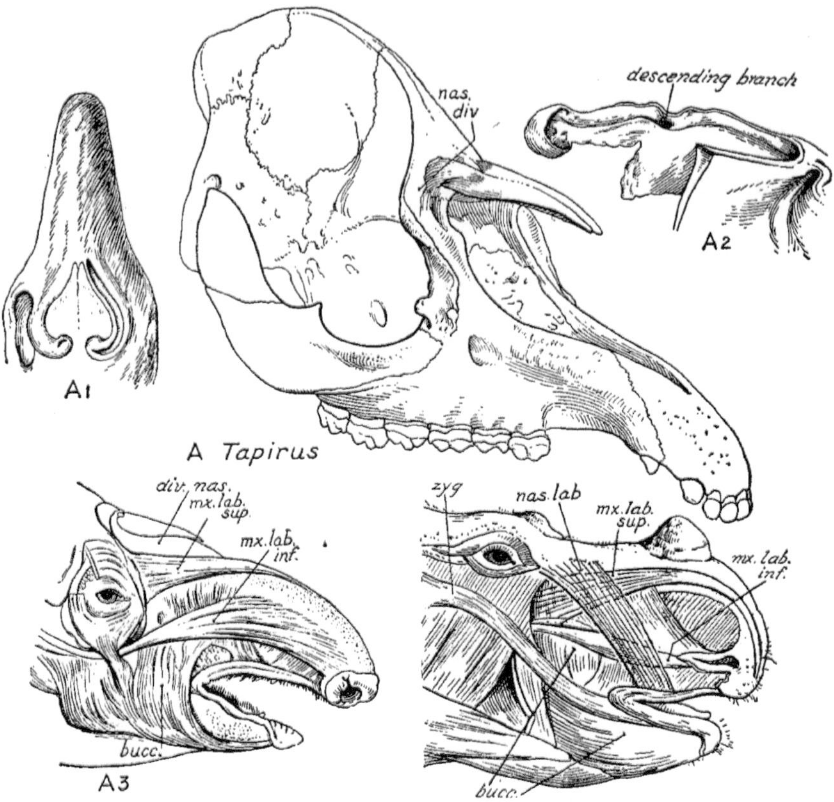

Figure 10.8 ▲

The retracted nasal bones and wide nasal incision of the tapir skull allow for the attachment of numerous muscles that control their long flexible proboscis. A diagram of the snout region of a living tapirs compared to the rhinoceros (*lower right*), showing how the proboscis muscles fit. (After William King Gregory, *Evolution Emerging* [Arno, 1951])

and teeth that are almost indistinguishable from those of their earliest rhino relative, *Hyrachyus*, and even the earliest horses, yet today even a child can tell a horse from a rhino from a tapir (figure 10.4). All three are members of the odd-toed hoofed mammals or perissodactyls, which have only one or three toes on their hands and feet. To support their long flexible snout or proboscis, the nasal bones on the tip of the snout are highly reduced, and retracted way back on the skull. This gives the muscles of the snout increased attachment points for all its complex muscles that control it (figure 10.8).

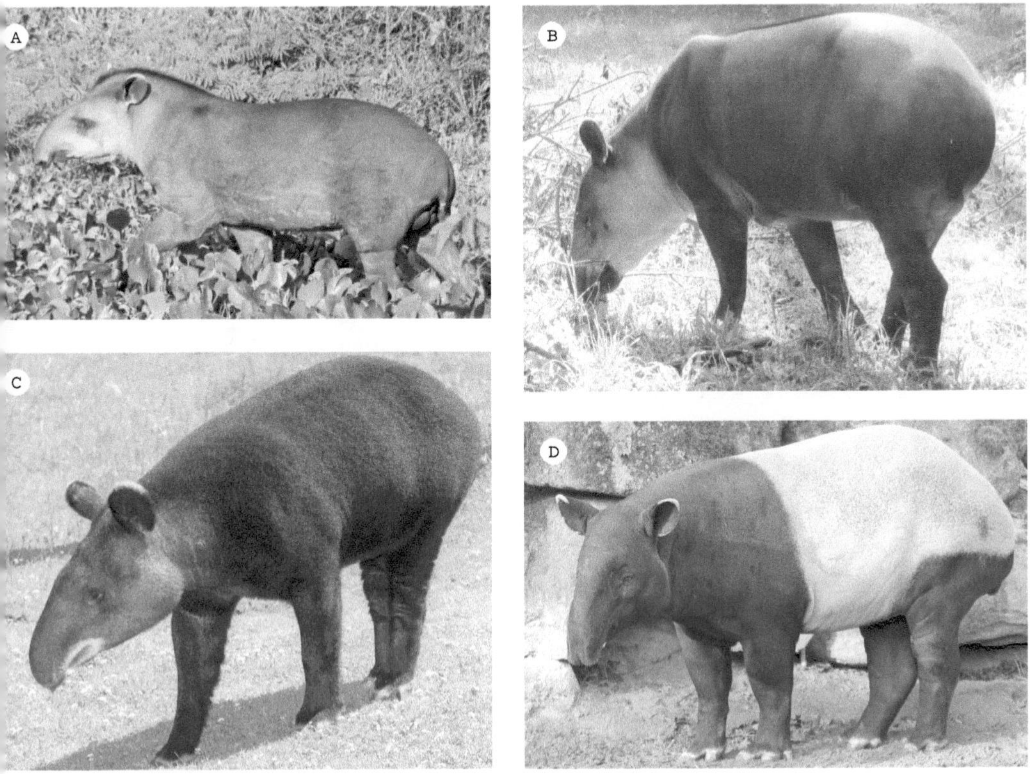

Figure 10.9 ▲

The four living species of tapirs. (*A*) *Tapirus terrestris*, the South American lowland tapir, in the Pantanal wetlands of Brazil, Bolivia, and Uruguay. (*B*) *Tapirus bairdii*, Baird's tapir. (*C*) *Tapirus pinchaque*, the mountain tapir. (*D*) *Tapirus indicus*, the Malayan tapir. (Courtesy of Wikimedia Commons)

Homogalax is known from fairly complete skulls and partial skeletons. They show the stereotyped pattern of their cheek teeth, with simple crests on the upper molars, and only two cross-crests found on their lower molars. This pattern is typical of specialized leaf eaters and is found in all later tapirs. From the earliest tapir relative 55 Ma, *Homogalax*, there was a great radiation of tapiroids in the Eocene between 55 and 37 Ma, with such primitive forms as *Isectolophus, Helaletes*, and *Lophioletes* in Asia and North America, and *Lophiodon* in Europe. From beds around 42 Ma in Wyoming, we find *Helaletes*, the oldest known tapiroid with a preserved skeleton. It too has the stereotyped cheek tooth crest pattern and does not show the retracted

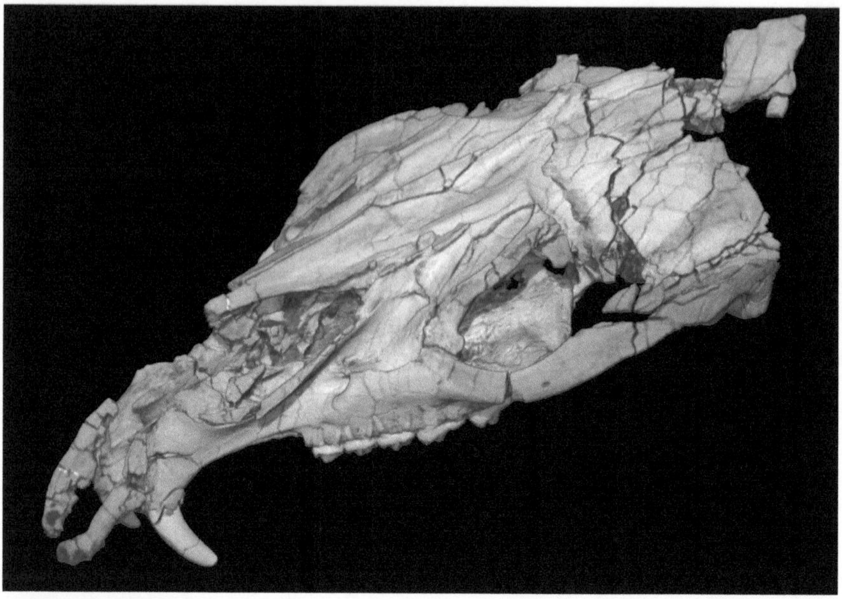

Figure 10.10 ▲

Digital image of the Eocene tapiroid *Hesperaletes* from San Diego County, California. (Courtesy of M. Colbert).

nasal bones indicating a proboscis yet. From beds in San Diego about 43 Ma comes *Hesperaletes*, the oldest tapiroid in the main line of tapir evolution to show the retraction of the nasal bones and the enlarged notch beneath the nasal bones, suggesting that the flexible snout of tapirs appeared quite early (figure 10.10).

From beds about 37–29 Ma in the Big Badlands of South Dakota, the next well-known tapir is *Colodon* (fig. 10.11), which is represented by complete skulls, jaws, and skeletons. Even though it was an extinct side branch of tapir evolution, it also shows the characteristic nasal notch suggesting it had a proboscis. Another Badlands tapir was *Protapirus*, which is on the main line of tapir evolution and had an even more retracted nasal notch.

From early-middle Miocene beds dating from about 20 Ma to about 11 Ma, the only tapir known in North America was *Miotapirus* (figure 10.11). It was a rare animal and found mostly in Nebraska, Oregon, and even in

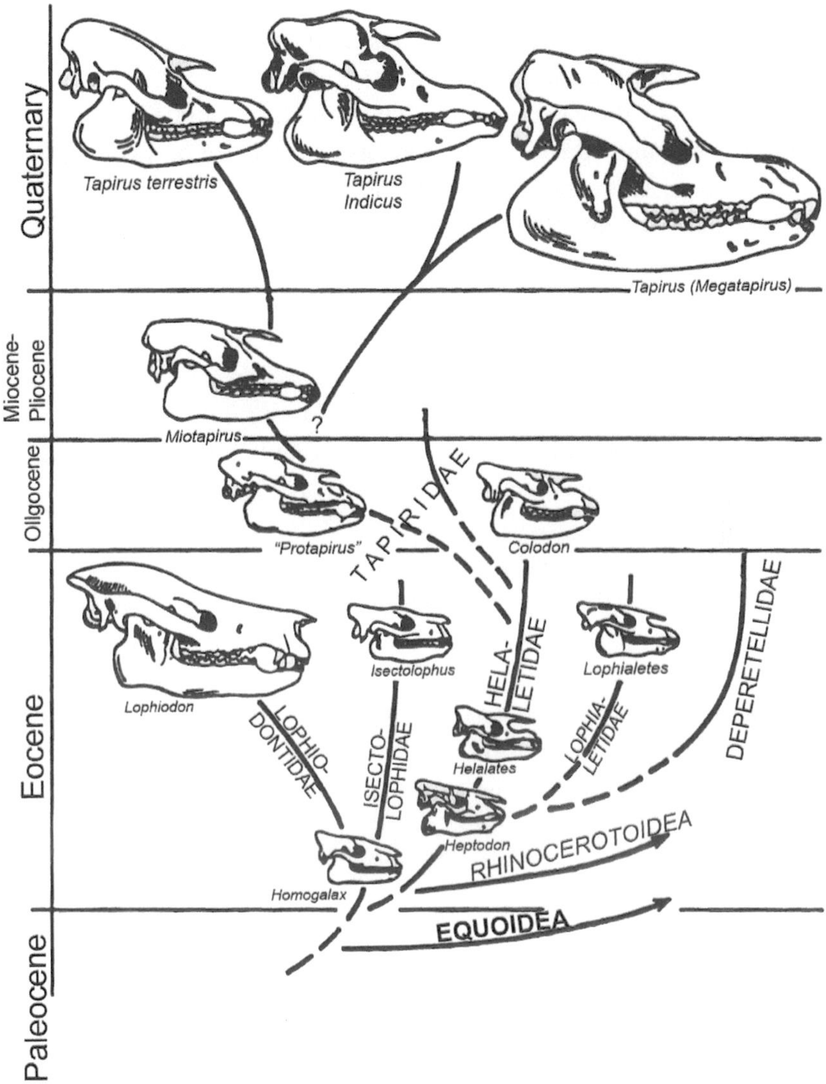

Figure 10.11 ▲

Evolution of the tapir skull, showing the increased enlargement of the nasal notch and retreat of the nasal bones as tapirs grew larger. (Modified from D. R. Prothero and R. M. Schoch, *Horns, Tusks, and Flippers: The Evolution of Hoofed Mammals* [Johns Hopkins University Press, 2002]) marine beds such as Sharktooth Hill in California. By the early Pliocene, about 4.7 Ma, we find complete skeletons of *Tapirus polkensis* at Gray Fossil Site in Tennessee, and also in the Gulf Coast of Florida.

Around 3.5 Ma, the Panama land bridge formed, and tapirs escaped from North America and spread to the previously isolated island continent of South America, where they gave rise to the three species now found in Latin America today. Many different species of *Tapirus* are found throughout the Ice Ages across North America, from the La Brea Tar Pits to the Anza-Borrego Desert in California to the swamps of Florida.

Today tapirs are living fossils, a tiny remnant of a once global history in every northern continent plus South America. Now restricted to the tropical jungles of the New World and Old World, during the Ice Ages they ranged across North America and Asia, and that broad distribution goes all the way back to their earliest fossils from 55 Ma, when they first split from rhinos.

Sadly, three out of the four living species of tapirs are endangered, and only the lowland tapir is listed as vulnerable rather than endangered. Tapirs are large animals that need a lot of territory to survive, and too much deforestation of their tropical homeland has reduced their habitat to remnants that are too small to support them. It would be truly tragic if these relicts that once dominated the world of the Eocene were to go extinct in our lifetimes due to the destruction of the rain forests of the world.

NOTES

1. Aldemaro Romero, "The Evolution of Cave Life," *American Scientist* 99, no. 2 (2011): 144, https://www.americanscientist.org/article/the-evolution-of-cave-life.
2. In Henry F. Osborn, *The Age of Mammals in Europe, Asia, and North America*, Macmillan: New York, 1910, p. 270.
3. Louis L. Jacobs, *Quest for the African Dinosaurs: Ancient Roots of the Modern World* (Johns Hopkins University Press, 2000), 250.
4. Reginald I. Pocock, "The Story of the Nandi Bear," *Natural History Magazine* 2 (1930): 162–169.
5. George Gaylord Simpson, "Mammals and Cryptozoology," *Proceedings of the American Philosophical Society* 128, no. 1 (1984): 1–19.

FOR FURTHER READING

Anquetin, J., P.-O. Antoine, and P. Tassy. "Middle Miocene Chalicotheriinae (Mammalia, Perissodactyla) from France, with a Discussion on Chalicotheriine Phylogeny." *Zoological Journal of the Linnean Society* 151, no. 3 (2007): 577–608.

Colbert, E. H. "Distributional and Phylogenetic Studies on Indian Fossil Mammals. III—A Classification of the Chalicotherioidea." *American Museum Novitates*, no. 798 (1935).

Coombs, M. C. "Interrelationships and Diversity in the Chalicotheriidae." In *The Evolution of Perissodactyls*, ed. D. R. Prothero and R. M. Schoch, 438–457. Oxford University Press, 1989.

——. "Large Mammalian Clawed Herbivores: A Comparative Study." *Transactions of the American Philosophical Society* 73, no. 7 (1983): 1–96.

——. "*Tylocephalonyx*, a New Genus of North American Dome-Skulled Chalicotheres (Mammalia, Perissodactyla)." *Bulletin of the American Museum of Natural History* 164 (1979): 1–64.

Coombs, M. C., R. M. Hunt Jr., E. Stepleton, L. B. Albright III, and T. J. Fremd. "Stratigraphy, Chronology, Biogeography, and Taxonomy of Early Miocene Small Chalicotheres in North America." *Journal of Vertebrate Paleontology* 21, no. 3 (2001): 607–620.

Holland, W. J., and O. A. Peterson. "The Osteology of the Chalicotheroidea with Special Reference to a Mounted Skeleton of *Moropus elatus* Marsh, Now Installed in the Carnegie Museum." *Memoirs of the Carnegie Museum* 3, no. 2 (1914): 203–205.

Hooker, J. J., and D. Dashzeveg. "The Origin of Chalicotheres (Perissodactyla, Mammalia)." *Palaeontology* 47, no. 6 (2004): 1363–1386.

Munthe, J., and M. C. Coombs. "Miocene Dome-Skulled Chalicotheres (Mammalia, Perissodactyla) from the Western United States: A Preliminary Discussion of a Bizarre Structure." *Journal of Paleontology* 53, no. 1 (1979): 77–91.

Prothero, D. R. *The Princeton Field Guide to Prehistoric Mammals*. Princeton University Press, 2016.

——. *Vertebrate Evolution: From Origins to Dinosaurs and Beyond*. Taylor & Francis/CRC Press, 2022.

Prothero, D. R., and R. M. Schoch, eds. *The Evolution of Perissodactyls*. Oxford University Press, 1989.

——. *Horns, Tusks, and Flippers: The Evolution of Hoofed Mammals*. Johns Hopkins University Press, 2002.

Radinsky, L. B. "Origin and Early Evolution of North American Tapiroidea." *Peabody Museum of Natural History Bulletin* 17 (1963): 1–118

Savage, R. J. G., and M. R. Long. *Mammal Evolution: An Illustrated Guide*. Facts-on-File, 1986.

Semprebon, G. M., P. J. Sise, and M. C. Coombs. "Potential Bark and Fruit Browsing as Revealed by Stereomicrowear Analysis of the Peculiar Clawed Herbivores Known as Chalicotheres (Perissodactyla, Chalicotherioidea)." *Journal of Mammalian Evolution* 18, no. 1 (2011): 33–55.

Turner, A., and M. Anton. *National Geographic Prehistoric Mammals*. National Geographic Society, 2004.

11 | WOOLLY RHINOS—AND RHINOS WITHOUT HORNS

COELODONTA

Rhinos are just fat unicorns. If we give them the time and attention they deserve, as well as a diet, they'd reveal the majestic ways.

—ASHLEY PURDY

RHINO MUMMIES

Before the rise of modern comparative anatomy and paleontology, the giant bones found in the earth were a great source of wonder, mystery, and eventually legends. In chapters 1 and 2, we saw how many of these "giants in the Earth" were interpreted as gigantic humans, although they were actually the remains of mammoths or mastodons. The remains of fossil rhinoceroses were likewise misinterpreted. The Siberians thought the horns of the woolly rhinoceros were the claws of a gigantic predatory bird, and they have been responsible for the myth of the griffin.

Fossil rhinoceroses have been found in many parts of Europe. A rhinoceros skull was found in Klagenfurt, Austria, in 1335, and was believed to be that of a dragon. In 1590, it was used as the basis for the head on a statue of a *lindwurm*, the mythical worm-like creature of Germanic legend. In 1663, the skull and some bones of a woolly rhino were combined with a faked "horn" to make the Magdeburg Unicorn, one of the most bizarre reconstructions of an extinct animal ever (figure 11.1).

The German naturalist Peter Simon Pallas was invited to work for the Saint Petersburg Academy of Sciences in 1767 by Russian Empress Catherine

Figure 11.1 ▲

The "Magdeburg Unicorn," a bizarre composite of woolly rhino skull, spine, and arm bones combined with a fake "horn." (Courtesy of Wikimedia Commons)

the Great. As a result, he was part of a long scientific expedition to Siberia between 1768 and 1774. When he published his results in 1777 and 1779, he described fossilized mummified remains of "large animals of India," which included elephants, rhinoceroses, and buffaloes. These are now recognized as extinct Ice Age woolly rhinos, mammoths, and bison. His most spectacular find was the mummy of a woolly rhinoceros, found with the skin intact in the frozen ground on the banks of the Viloui (= Vilyuy) River (figure 11.2A). To Pallas, this was "convincing proof that it must be a most violent and most rapid flood which once carried these carcasses toward our glacial climates, before corruption had time to destroy their soft parts."[1]

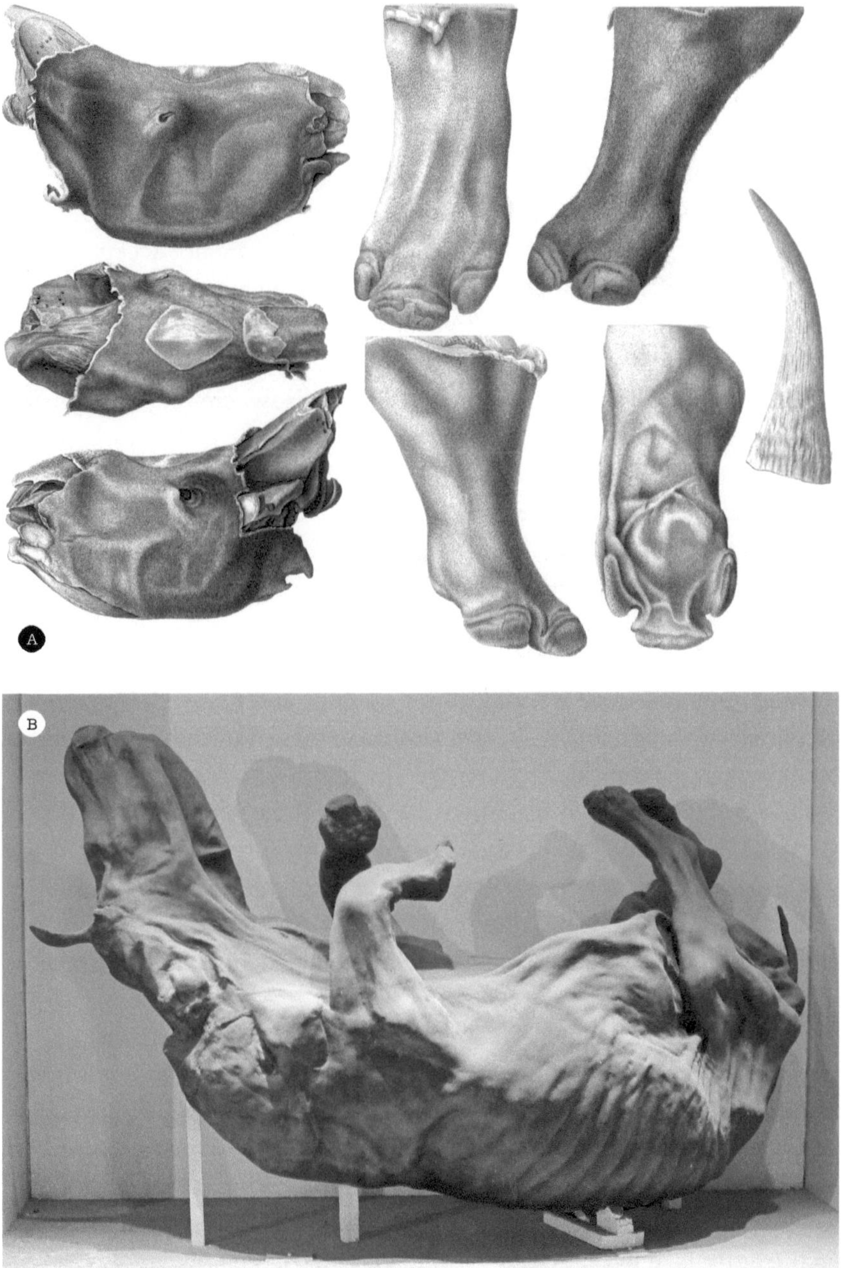

Figure 11.2 ▲

(*A*) Pallas's original plates of the partial woolly rhino carcass. (*B*) The Staurnia rhino mummy. (Courtesy of Wikimedia Commons)

Pallas's insistence on the Indian origin the Siberian mummies was a reaction to the non-biblical ideas proposed by Buffon in 1751. Buffon argued that the presence of these "Indian animals" in Siberia, and similar animals in North America, was proof that Earth's climate had changed and elephants and rhinos had migrated in response. This implied Earth was much older than orthodoxy was willing to admit, and that some of these beasts might be extinct. As we have seen, these heresies were not accepted until the early part of the nineteenth century, and most eighteenth-century naturalists try to find biblical explanations for these mysteries. Pallas, like most of his peers, thought that the great flood of Noah had moved these "Indian" animals to the perpetually cold regions of Siberia, where they could never have actually lived.

This freeze-dried woolly rhino was just the first of many discoveries. Additional specimens, some of them nearly complete and some so fresh that wild animals could eat them, were found off and on in Siberia. There were discoveries of complete or partial rhino carcasses in 1972, 1976, 2007, 2008, 2014, and 2020, just to list some of the more spectacular discoveries. But in 1907 miners in the town of Starunia, Ukraine (then part of the Russian Empire), were working in an oil field and excavating ozerite, a petroleum by-product that is most similar to paraffin, when they found a mammoth carcass pickled in this tar-like substance. A month later, they found a complete pickled specimen of a woolly rhino, also saturated in paraffin, that was about15 feet (5 meters) beneath it figure 11.2B). Although the hair and horn did not preserve, every other part of the carcass was complete and well preserved, and it shows the rhino in its death pose as it was trapped in ozerite. In 1929, a Polish expedition returned to Starunia and found three more rhino carcasses.

From all these specimens, along with cave paintings of what our ancestors saw, we have an excellent understanding of the woolly rhino. It was about 11.8 feet (3.6 meters) long and weighed up to 2 tonnes (2.2 short tons), so it was the size of the largest living rhino, the white rhino. As their name implies, they were covered in a thick reddish-brown fur coat, with a fine woolly undercoat and a layer of longer guard hairs covering it. The hair on the limbs is much shorter, so it wouldn't pick up too much snow. It had small ears and a smaller tail, minimizing heat loss through these structures. There was a big hump over the shoulder, not only for the muscles that held the head up but also acting as a fat reserve to allow the beast to survive the scarce food in the winter. And its horn (which, like all rhino horns, is made of fibers of keratin, like hair, glued together) was not conical in shape, like some rhino horns, but narrow and bladelike like a saber. There are usually scratches on its leading edge that show it was used for scraping away snow to find plant food beneath the snow in the winter. (Woolly mammoths are thought to have done the same with their tusks, and modern reindeer and musk oxen also scrape away snow with their antlers and horns to find food.)

The oldest fossils of the genus *Coelodonta* is *C. thibetana*, from the Pliocene of Tibet, dated around 3.7 Ma. These fossils show that woolly rhinos originated in the cold mountain climates of Tibet first, then spread across Siberia when the Ice Ages began and that region was covered by snow and ice. In the early Pleistocene, two other species, *C. nihowanensis* and *C. tologoijensis*, were found in Siberia and China. The familiar woolly rhino is the original type species, *C. antiquitatis*, from the late Pleistocene. As woolly rhinos evolved, the angle of the occiput (back of the skull) changed, so that the later species have a head that is naturally tilted down, the better to feed on grasses and sedges on the ground. Pollen analysis of the materials found in the mummified specimens showed that they ate conifers, alders, and willows, flowers, forbs, and mosses. They grazed on grasses and sedges during the summer months in the mammoth steppe but subsisted on shrubs, bark, and tree branches during the cold bitter winters. Their genomes (especially mitochondrial DNA) are known from several specimens, thanks to their excellent preservation, so we can confirm that they are most closely related to the living Sumatran rhino of Indonesia, which is the hairiest of the five modern species of rhino.

Finally, woolly rhinos vanished around fourteen thousand years ago, during the Bølling-Allerød warming event, which disrupted their habitat, so they were not wiped out by human hunters (as the overkill model suggests—see chapter 2). However, there is DNA in the frozen tundra dating to only 9,800 years ago that suggests they may have survived well into the warmer periods of the Holocene before going extinct.

THE LAST UNICORN?

The woolly rhino was not the only common rhino in Eurasia during the Ice Ages. An even larger extinct rhino was the giant one-horned rhino, *Elasmotherium* (figure 11.3A and figure 11.3B). The first specimens of this

Figure 11.3 ▲

(*A*) Mounted skeleton of the giant *Elasmotherium*. (*B*) Life-sized reconstruction of *Elasmotherium*. (Courtesy of Wikimedia Commons)

amazing beast were described by Gotthelf Fischer von Waldheim in 1809, based on a lower jaw with a few molars. Their molars have incredibly convoluted crests on them, with lots of folds of enamel within the dentin, and their name refers to that feature (*elasmo* means "laminated," and *therion* is "beast" in Greek). These were the largest members of the family Rhinocerotidae that ever lived, reaching 15 feet (4.5 meters) in length, 8 feet (2.8 meters) at the shoulder, and weighing about 5 tonnes (5.5 short tons). That is twice the weight of the living white rhinoceros, the largest living rhino, and about the size and weight of the woolly mammoth.

But their most amazing feature is their horn. Unlike modern rhinos, which might have a single horn at the tip of their nose, or (like African rhinos or the woolly rhino) tandem horns on the nose and forehead, *Elasmotherium* had a huge rounded horn boss a meter in circumference supporting a huge horn on their forehead, but they had no horn on their nose. Like all rhino horns that are made of keratin fibers, there are no fossils of this horn, but it must have been enormous! There was a large muscular hump on the back, where the long muscles that helped hold up the huge head and horn were anchored.

The huge skull of *Elasmotherium* had a very sharp angle at the back surface (occiput), showing that the head was held downward, with the snout always near the ground, so it mainly ate grasses and low-growing shrubs. Its teeth are extremely high crowned with no closure of the roots, so they were ever-growing, another adaptation to eating very gritty vegetation. As an animal the size of an elephant, they could move very fast—they might have managed 12 mph (20 km/h). However, an animal its size doesn't need to run from predators, and the only threats they faced would be combat with another member of the same species.

The giant horn on their forehead has led to speculation that elasmotheres were the source of the legend of the unicorn, but this seems unlikely. After all, the actual horn doesn't fossilize and its size is unknown, so there's no way they would be the source of such a legend when no horns are ever preserved. Most scholars think the unicorn legend might be derived from the Indian one-horned rhinoceros, although its horn tends to be short and stumpy. Others think it might be from one of the long straight-horned antelopes, like the oryx, looking in side view (so only one horn is visible). Still other scholars point out that Viking traders sold narwhal tusks on the European market, which are long and straight and pointed, and might be associated with a horse-like animal rather than a strange Arctic whale.

RHINOS WITHOUT HORNS

When we hear the word rhinoceros we think of huge lumbering thick-skinned animals with wicked horns on their faces. We think of animals that are prone to charging and attacking anything that gets in their way, and are not afraid even of elephants, let alone smaller animals. Yet most fossil rhinoceroses had no horns at all, and they were hugely diverse with body forms ranging from small dog-sized animals to the largest mammals that ever lived (figure 11.4). Only a handful of lineages ever developed horns and they were in a variety of combinations, from horns that are paired on their noses to horns that are tandem one in front of the other (like the woolly rhino and the two African species) to single horns on the

Figure 11.4 ▲

A stampede of rhinocerotoids. In the right foreground is the small ancestral *Hyrachyus*. On the extreme left is the running hyracodont rhino *Hyracodon*. Its relatives included the hyracodont *Juxia* from China (*middle rhino on the extreme right*) and the immense *Paraceratherium* from Asia, the largest land mammal known (*background*). To the left of the human silhouette is the hippo-like amynodont rhino known as *Metamynodon*. The remaining images are members of the true rhinos, Family Rhinocerotidae. In the middle left is the two-horned rhino *Menoceras*, the earliest rhino to develop horns. The hairy rhino in the right foreground is the woolly rhino *Coelodonta*, and the huge one-horned rhino in the center background is *Elasmotherium*. The hippo-like rhino in front of it is *Teleoceras*, and the small rhino charging the human is *Meninatherium*. (Drawing by M. P. Williams)

forehead (such as elasmotheres) to single horn on the nose (like the living Asian rhinos).

How do we know this? As I have already pointed out, rhino horns are not made of bone like the horns of many other large mammals. Instead, they're made of fibers of keratin glued together, the same substance that makes up your hair or fingernails. This material does not fossilize easily (except in the case of some woolly rhino mummies), so the only way to know if a rhino skull had a horn is to look for a spongy roughened area on the top of the skull from which the horn grew and attached.

For this reason, paleontologists cannot use horns to define what makes a rhino. Instead, there are a variety of anatomical features unique to rhinos. One of the most distinctive are the upper molars that are shaped like the Greek letter "pi" (π). This is a dead giveaway that you have a rhino fossil.

The earliest rhino relatives show this π-shaped pattern on the upper molars (figure 10.4), but they are almost indistinguishable from the earliest fossil horses and the earliest fossil tapirs around 55 million years ago. This is strong evidence of how closely related these three perissodactyl groups are.

The earliest fossil rhinos are typified by an animal known as *Hyrachyus*, from around 50 Ma, which was about the size of a sheep (figure 11.5A and figure 11.5B). It was relatively unspecialized, yet it still had the rhino-like upper molars (see figure 10.4). From this ancestor, rhinos diversified into three main groups (figure 11.6). The first group were the amynodonts, rhinos that seem to have specialized for a more aquatic lifestyle. The most extreme example of this is *Metamynodon*, from the beds around 32 Ma in the Big Badlands of South Dakota (figure 11.7). Its skull resembled that of a living hippo. Another amynodont, known as *Amynodontopsis*, comes from beds around 42 million years old in the western U.S. and China. It had nasal bones that were retracted far back on its face, which suggests that it had a small proboscis. An even larger proboscis appeared in the amynodont from rocks about 27 Ma in Pakistan, known as *Cadurcodon*. It was the last of the amynodonts.

The second group of rhinos were the hyracodonts (figure 11.8A and figure 11.8B). They started out as small, goat-sized animals and developed long running legs, so *Hyracodon* from the Big Badlands of South Dakota was one of the fastest animals on the landscape. But one hyracodont lineage became truly monstrous.

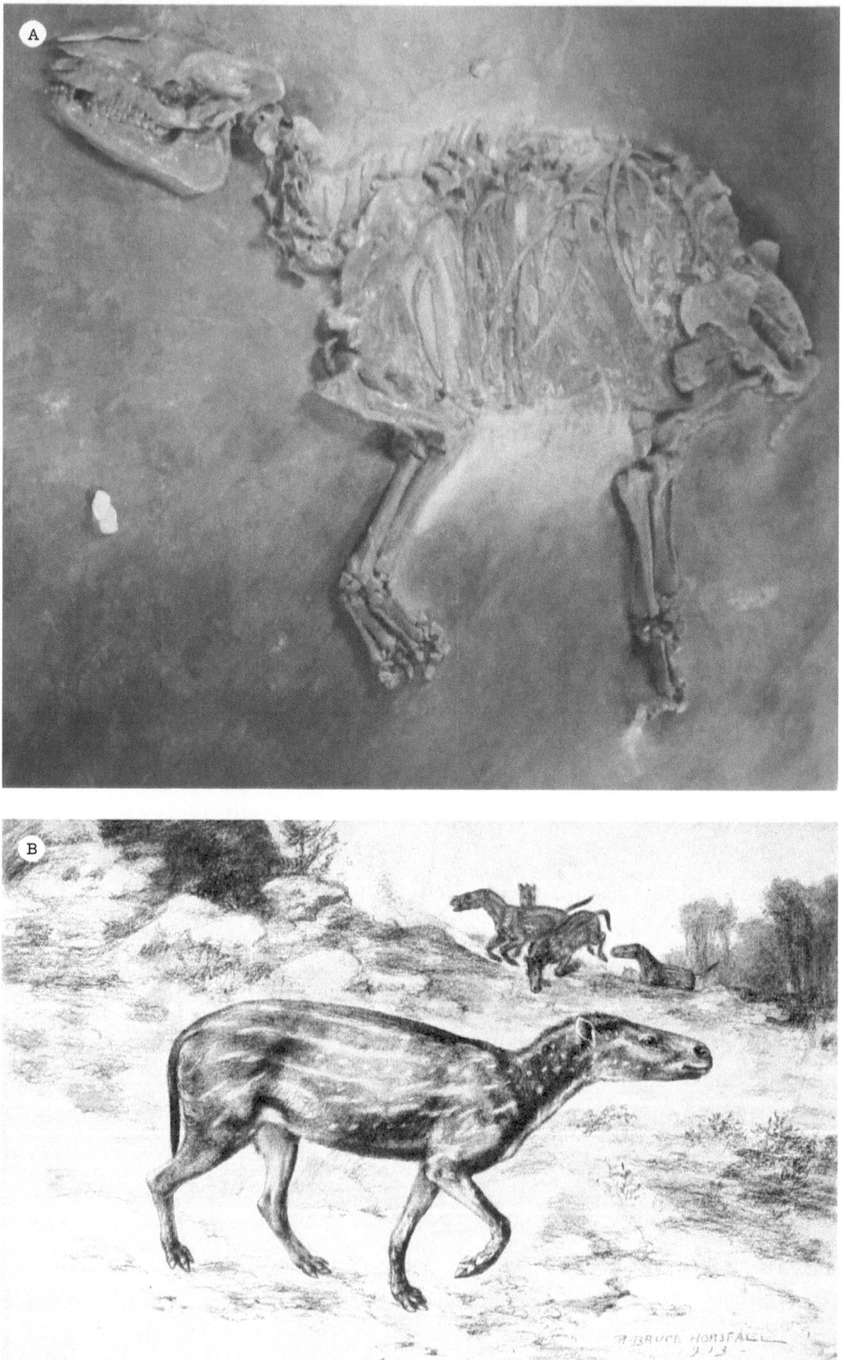

Figure 11.5 ▲

The primitive rhinocerotoid *Hyrachyus*. (*A*) Articulated skeleton from the middle Eocene Messel lake beds of Germany. (*B*) Reconstruction of the animal in life. ([*A*] Courtesy of Wikimedia Commons;]*B*] drawing by R. Bruce Horsfall, courtesy of Wikimedia Commons)

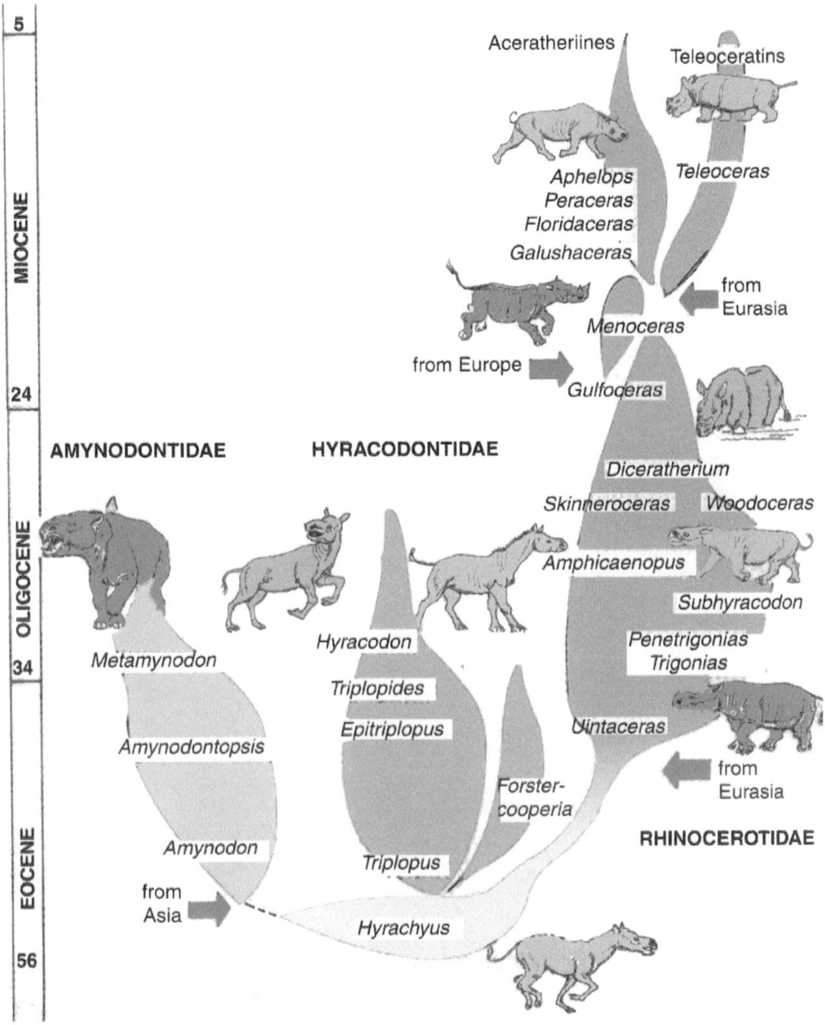

Figure 11.6 ▲

Three major families of rhinocerotoids, represented by dozens of genera and species that evolved in North America. These include the hippo-like amynodonts (*left*), the long-legged running hyracodonts (*center*), and the true rhinoceroses, Family Rhinocerotidae (*right*). The first two died out by the late Oligocene around the world, but the Rhinocerotidae survives today. (Drawing by C. R. Prothero; updated by E. T. Prothero)

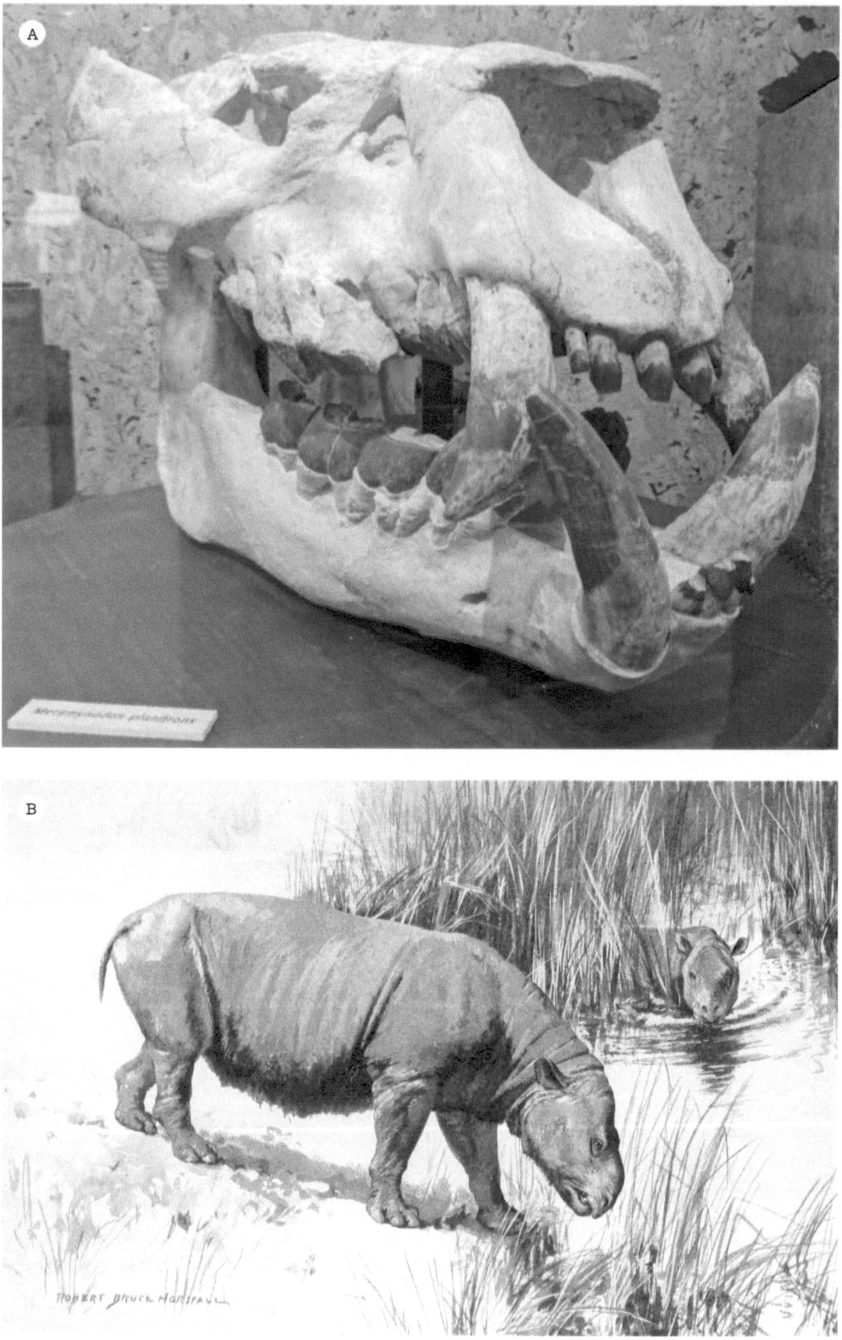

Figure 11.7 ▲

Metamynodon was a rhinocerotoid with very hippo-like features. (*A*) The skull, with its huge hippo-like tusks. (*B*) Reconstruction by R. Bruce Horsfall of *Metamynodon* in life. ([*A*, *B*] Courtesy of Wikimedia Commons)

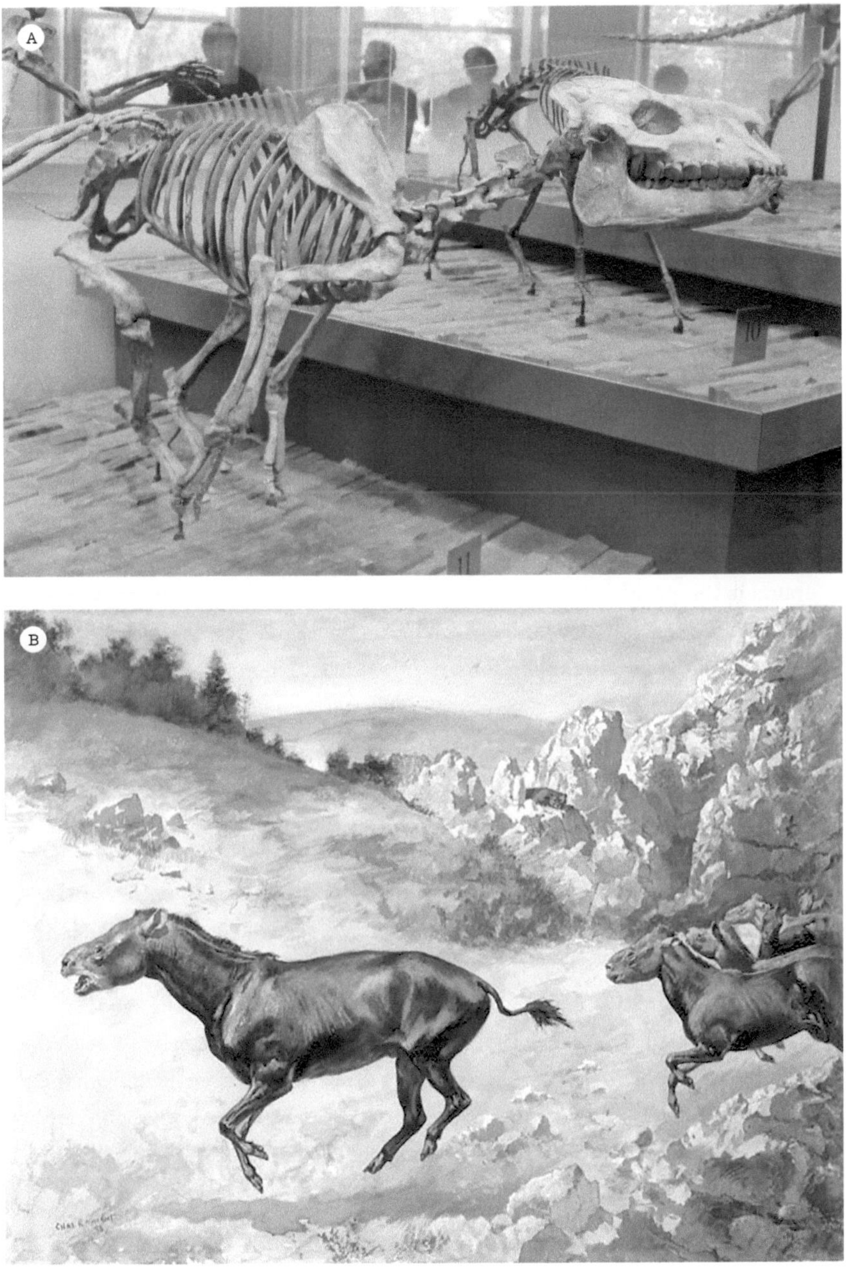

Figure 11.8 ▲

Hyracodon was a sheep-sized running rhinocerotoid with long legs and toes. (*A*) Mounted skeleton in the Natural History Museum of Los Angeles County. (*B*) Reconstruction by Charles R. Knight. ([*A*] Photo by the author; [*B*] courtesy of Wikimedia Commons)

RHINOCEROS GIANTS

One of the most incredible finds of the American Museum expeditions to Mongolia occurred in the 1925 field season. Expedition leader Roy Chapman Andrews provided a colorful and detailed account of all the expeditions in his massive volume with a very un-PC imperialist title, *The New Conquest of Central Asia* (1932): 279–280. As described by Andrews:

> The credit for the most interesting discovery at Loh belongs to one of our Chinese collectors, Liu Hsi-ku. His sharp eyes caught the glint of a white bone in the red sediment of the steep hillside. He dug a little and then reported to Granger who completed the excavation. He was amazed to find the foot and lower leg of a Baluchitherium STANDING UPRIGHT, just as if the animal had carelessly left it behind when he took another stride. Fossils are so seldom found in this position that Granger sat down to think out the why and wherefore. There was only one possible solution. Quicksand! It was the right hind limb that Liu had found; therefore, the right front leg must be farther down the slope. He took the direction of the foot, measured off about nine feet, and began to dig. Sure enough, there it was, a huge bone, like the trunk of a fossil tree, also standing erect. It was not difficult to find the two limbs of the other side, for what had happened was obvious. When all four legs were excavated, each one in a separate pit, the effect was extraordinary [figure 11.9]. I went up with Granger and sat down upon a hilltop to drift in fancy back to those far days when the tragedy had been enacted. To one who could read the language, the story was plainly told by the great stumps. Probably the beast had come to drink from a pool of water covering the treacherous quicksand. Suddenly it began to sink. The position of the leg bones showed that it had settled slightly back upon its haunches, struggling desperately to free itself from the gripping sands. It must have sunk rapidly, struggling to the end, dying only when the choking sediment filled its nose and throat. If it had been partly buried and died of starvation, the body would have fallen on its side. If we could have found the entire skeleton standing erect, there in its tomb, it would have been a specimen for all the world to marvel at.
>
> I said to Granger, "Walter, what do you mean by finding only the legs? Why don't you produce the rest?" "Don't blame me," he answered, "it is all your fault. If you had brought us here thirty-five thousand years earlier, before that hill weathered away, I would have the whole skeleton for you!" True enough,

Figure 11.9 ▲

The famous discovery of the four limbs of an indricothere buried in vertical position as if the animal had died in quicksand. (Courtesy of the American Museum Digital Library)

> we had missed our opportunity by just about that margin. As the entombing sediment was eroded away, the bones were worn off bit by bit and now lay scatted on the valley floor in a thousand useless fragments. There must have been great numbers of baluchitheres in Mongolia during Oligocene times, for we were finding bones and fragments wherever there were fossiliferous strata of that age.[2]

Although Andrews' storytelling skills are vivid, his account of the quicksand is a bit too much like the Hollywood movie version, rather than one based on reality. Fake quicksand in movies sucks the victim down in minutes until they are completely submerged. Real quicksand is a slurry of sand and water that remains fairly firm and solid until you disturb it. Then the water between the sand grains is mobilized and it becomes what is known as a fluidized sedimentary flow. The disturbed water from the pores between the sand grains pushes the sand grains apart so they flow freely, and you can sink down into the slurry. When you stop moving and disturbing the grains, the water stops moving and the entire mixture solidifies like concrete—unless you thrash around again and liquefy the mixture. Because a mixture of sand and water is actually denser than water alone, any body (human or animal) will float until it reaches its point of neutral buoyancy. Thus it is impossible to sink into quicksand above your head. Even if you thrash around in a panic and keep it liquefied so you sink as low as possible, you will still float at a level even higher than you would float in water alone.

In the case of this trapped indricothere rhino, it probably was mired down to its legs (as they found it), but the rest of the body did not sink in much deeper. Contrary to what Andrews wrote, it would not have toppled sideways if it were half-buried because the quicksand was thick and stiff enough to trap its legs in an upright pose without allowing the body to lean sideways, let alone move out of it. Instead, with the legs trapped the creature was helpless to move further, the indricothere died either of dehydration and starvation or by being eaten or scavenged by predators taking advantage of a helpless creature. Once it became trapped and could no longer struggle to liquefy the sand, its exposed upper body was easy pickings for scavengers, which is why none of its other bones were there. Only its entombed leg bones remained.

The indricothere rhinos were truly remarkable. They started with the cow-sized form *Forstercooperia*, found in the middle Eocene beds of both China and Utah. They continued to evolve in Asia, with the elephant-sized *Urtinotherium*. They culminated in the early Oligocene with the biggest of them all, *Paraceratherium*, probably the largest land mammal that has ever lived (figure 11.10A, 11.10B, and 11.10C). Formerly called *Baluchitherium* or *Indricotherium*, they reached (18 feet (6 meters) at the shoulder, were 25 feet (7.4 meters) long, and weighed about 44,000 pounds (20 tonnes). It is possible that a few mammoth species reached sizes close to this, but all of the specimens are too incomplete to know for sure.

Paraceratherium was so huge that it probably fed on leaves from the tops of trees most of the time. Its simple low-crowned teeth with distinctive wear patterns were only suitable for browsing leaves and softer vegetation, so it was like the rhino equivalent of a giraffe. In the Oligocene of Mongolia, China, and elsewhere in Asia where indricotheres are found, the climate was relatively dry and the vegetation sparse, so there was no dense ground cover of shrubs for medium-sized herbivores to feed on. The mammal

Figure 11.10 ▲ ▶

The gigantic indricothere *Paraceratherium*. (*A*) Mounted skeleton in Moscow. (*B*) Photo of the skull with American Museum preparator Otto Falkenbach. (*C*) Reconstruction in the University of Nebraska State Museum, next to an elephant, and its small ancestor *Hyracodon*. ([*A and C*]: Courtesy of Wikimedia Commons; [*B*] courtesy of the American Museum Digital Library)

assemblages from these Oligocene beds of Asia are remarkably unbalanced in that they have gigantic indricotheres feeding on the tree tops, then a dramatic drop to the next largest herbivores, which included *Chalicotherium*, pig-like entelodonts, and a few small ruminants—but the vast majority of fossils from these beds were rodents and rabbits, which could live in burrows and survive on the sparse fodder of the region. Given those conditions, indricotheres would have lived in small family groupings, moving from one stand of trees to another with their enormous legs covering long distances between strides, just to support their relatively small populations. These small populations are the reason most paleontologists accept only a few species of *Paraceratherium* in the region at one time, and not many different genera and species that were named over the last century—or the multiple genera and species that some Chinese authors insist on, ignoring the reality of biological populations.

Yet despite its huge size, its finger bones and toe bones were relatively long, just as in its hyracodont ancestors, even though indricotheres were clearly too big to run. This contrasts with other giant land animals, such as proboscideans and larger dinosaurs, whose finger and toe bones are short and stumpy in response to bearing great weight. In this case, the blueprint of its running rhino ancestors was not changed by the huge increase in body mass.

Another consequence of large body size is that indricotheres have the same problem as elephants: their surface area for dumping heat is relatively small compared to their large volume, so they are always in danger of heat exhaustion. Elephants use remarkable mechanisms to dump their body heat, such as filling their large ears with blood and fanning them to cool themselves, and most of them spend their day immersed in water or mud, or hiding in the shade, and feed mainly at night. Indricotheres would have had the same problem, only more so because they were up to three times as large as an elephant. They certainly must have spent most of the daytime in the shade or in the water, as elephants do, and fed mostly in the evening or at night or in the morning. In addition, most reconstructions show indricotheres with fairly normal, relatively small ears like other rhinos. There is no bony structure to determine the size of ears in extinct animals, but surely indricotheres must have had much larger, almost elephant-like ears, or at least some kind of fan-like structure on their body to help with dumping body heat. The bony tubes at the base of the ear opening in indricotheres is very strong and reinforced, consistent with the idea that muscles and cartilage support large fan-like ears that may have been attached there.

Indricotheres roamed Asia from Romania and Turkey to central Russia to China and Mongolia through the entire Oligocene (33–23 Ma), then vanished. The reason for their extinction is unknown, but in the early Miocene there were several invading large groups of animals, including the first mastodonts and deinotheres, which might have been competition for them. Proboscideans like modern African elephants are also important in that they break down trees and thin the forest, and otherwise change the vegetational landscape, which might have had an impact on indricotheres. In addition, during the Oligocene the only predators in much of Asia were the archaic hyaenodonts, which were wolf-sized and no threat to indricotheres. But in the Miocene, there were some huge predators that might have threatened them, such as enormous amphicyonids (misleadingly called "beardogs" although they are neither bears nor dogs). Whatever the reason, by the early Miocene indricotheres had vanished, and no other land mammal ever got quite this huge again.

TRUE RHINOS

One day early in December 1850, Joseph Leidy received a surprising package at his Philadelphia study. Since 1847, Leidy had been receiving many shipments of fossils from the Indian Territories of Dakota and Nebraska out West, and his description of these fossils made him the foremost paleontologist in the country. Some of these fossils were of typically American beasts, such as dogs, cats, rabbits, peccaries, and deer, although they were such archaic types they could barely be recognized as having modern descendants. Other parcels held remains of animals, such as brontotheres, with no living descendants. Still other packages held the remains of animals never previously known in North America. He had already discovered that camels and horses have been all-American natives, but on this particular day he realized he was looking at the first evidence of American rhinoceroses. A few days later Leidy described the specimen at a meeting in Philadelphia Academy of Natural Sciences. He christened it *Rhinoceros occidentalis* or "western rhinoceros" (it is now known as *Subhyracodon occidentalis*). In the remaining twenty years of his career, he described many more rhinos from the Dakotas, Oregon, California, Nebraska, Texas, and even Florida. Cope and Marsh also began describing rhinos from their collections out West. By the beginning of the twentieth century, it was clear that rhinoceroses not only lived in North America, but they were among the most common large herbivores in the continent for most of the last fifty million years.

Both the hyracodonts and the amynodonts had died out around 23 Ma (figure 11.6). The only group to survive was the living family Rhinocerotidae. Their earliest fossils include *Teletaceras*, from beds about 42 Ma in Oregon. By about 36 Ma, they had diversified into several different forms, including *Trigonias*, the last rhinoceros to still have four toes on its front foot. It was also the last rhino to still have more than one pair of incisors in its upper and lower jaws. Later rhinos evolved a combination of a bladelike upper incisor that occludes against a tusk-like lower second incisor. About 35 Ma, the common rhino was *Subhyracodon* (Leidy's discovery), which was about the size of a cow but still lacked horns. These evolved into *Diceratherium*, which had a pair of ridges along the tips of its nasals.

Then, about 23 Ma, the genus *Menoceras* arrived in North America from Eurasia. It had paired knob-like horn bosses with their noses, but it was only the size of a pony, with long slender limbs. It is often mistakenly called *Diceratherium* because of the paired nasal horns, but they are entirely different not only in the details of their horns but also in the rest of their anatomy. *Menoceras* shows strong sexual dimorphism, with male skulls having horns and females lacking them. *Menoceras* is the most common animal in the famous Agate Fossil Beds National Monument in western Nebraska. Hundreds of individuals that died in huge herds were fossilized there.

Menoceras lasted until about 17 Ma when it was replaced by two new immigrant groups from Eurasia (figure 11.6). One group was the hornless aceratherine rhinos. The most common of these in North America was *Aphelops*, which lasted until almost 5 Ma, becoming larger through its long evolutionary history. Another aceratherine was *Peraceras*, which was a much larger, more heavily built rhino, although it also had dwarf species in the Texas Gulf coastal plain.

Immigrating in from Eurasia alongside the aceratherines about 17 Ma was another lineage, *Teleoceras*. This rhino had short, stumpy legs, a barrel-shaped body, and eventually developed high-crowned teeth for eating grittier vegetation. Grasses were even found in the throats of some specimens. Its lifestyle has been compared to that of a hippo, although there are problems with that analogy. *Teleoceras* was the last rhinoceros in North America, dying out about 4 Ma during the great extinction of many groups of mammals that ended the North American Miocene savanna ecosystem. The last known individuals of *Teleoceras* came from early Pliocene pond deposits at the Gray Fossil Site in eastern Tennessee, which was still a densely forested swampy region at the time. *Teleoceras* had already vanished from the Great Plains.

Meanwhile, in Eurasia there were aceratherines and teleoceratines dominating the world of the Miocene from 20 Ma until 5 Ma. During the Ice Ages, new rhinos arose. These included the elephant-sized elasmotheres mentioned previously.

Out of this rich and diverse prehistory, only five species of rhino survive on the planet. The black rhino and white rhino of Africa, and the Indian, Sumatran, and Javan rhinos of Asia. All are threatened by decades of ferocious killing by poachers for their valuable horns, which are worth more per gram than gold or cocaine. Some of the horn goes to making fancy daggers for rich Arab sheikhs, but most of it goes to the market for traditional Asian medicine in China and Vietnam. Rhino horn is no more a medicine than your fingernail clippings or your hair, but in these cultures it is so valuable that the increased wealth in China and Vietnam has driven relentless poaching.

Today all five living species of rhino are on their last legs. Three are critically endangered and likely to vanish in the wild in the lifetimes of the people reading this book. The mysterious Javan rhino is thought to have fewer than 74 individuals left in the wild, in Java and in Vietnam. The hairy Sumatran rhino, a relative of the woolly rhino, has fewer than 80 living in Sumatra, most kept in captivity for their own protection. Even more shocking, the once common African black rhino has been decimated by poaching, so 96 percent of their population in 1970 is now gone. Of the several hundred thousand that used to roam all of eastern and southern Africa, or even the seventy thousand in the late 1960s, fewer than 4,800 remain, most in such small populations that their breeding success is uncertain, so they too are critically endangered. The western Black Rhino subspecies found in Chad, Mali, Niger, and Nigeria is now extinct. The African white rhino is "near threatened," with fewer than eighteen thousand left in the wild. Many of their smaller populations must have armed guards protecting them 24/7 (figure 11.11).

The Northern White Rhino subspecies is now extinct in the wild, and only the Southern White Rhino remains. Finally, the Indian rhino population has dropped down to fewer than 3,600 individuals, but those that are within game reserves on the south slopes of the Himalayas in India seem to be protected, so they are merely listed as "vulnerable." Rhinos were a

Figure 11.11 ▲
Some rhinos are so threatened by poaching that they must have twenty-four-hour armed guards to protect them in the wild. This is one of the last few Northern White Rhinos in the wild. (Courtesy of Wikimedia Commons)

success story for more than fifty million years, surviving mass extinctions and radiating into lots of habitats, from the gigantic indricotheres to the hippo-like amynodonts and teleoceratines. Yet in a few decades human greed and the demand for worthless folk "medicines" has just about wiped them off the face of the Earth.

NOTES

1. Peter Simon Pallas, *Observations sur la formation des montagnes* (1779), 22.
2. Roy Chapman Andrews, *The New Conquest of Central Asia* (American Museum of Natural History, 1932), 279–280.

FOR FURTHER READING

Bai, B., J. Meng, C. Zhang, Y.-X. Gong, and Y.-Q. Wang. "The Origin of Rhinocerotoidea and Phylogeny of Ceratomorpha (Mammalia, Perissodactyla)." *Communications Biology* 3, no. 1 (2020): 509.

Cerdeño, E. "Cladistic Analysis of the Family Rhinocerotidae (Perissodactyla)." *American Museum Novitates*, no. 3143 (1995).

Heissig, K. "Rhinocerotidae." In *The Evolution of Perissodactyls*, ed. D. R. Prothero and R. M. Schoch, 399–417. Oxford University Press, 1989.

Pandolfi, L. "Evolutionary History of Rhinocerotina (Mammalia, Perissodactyla)." *Fossilia* (2018): 26–32.

Prothero, D. R. *The Evolution of North American Rhinoceroses*. Cambridge University Press, 2005.

——. *The Princeton Field Guide to Prehistoric Mammals*. Princeton University Press, 2016.

——. *Rhinoceros Giants: The Paleobiology of Indricotheres*. Indiana University Press, 2013.

——. *Vertebrate Evolution: From Origins to Dinosaurs and Beyond*. Taylor & Francis/CRC Press, 2022.

Prothero, D. R., C. Guérin, and E. Manning. "The History of the Rhinocerotoidea." In *The Evolution of Perissodactyls*, ed. D. R. Prothero and R. M. Schoch, 322–340. Oxford University Press, 1989.

Prothero, D. R., E. Manning, and C. B. Hanson. "The Phylogeny of the Rhinocerotoidea (Mammalia, Perissodactyla)." *Zoological Journal of the Linnean Society of London* 87 (1986): 341–366.

Prothero, D. R., and R. M. Schoch, eds. *The Evolution of Perissodactyls*. Oxford University Press, 1989.

——. *Horns, Tusks, and Flippers: The Evolution of Hoofed Mammals*. Johns Hopkins University Press, 2002.

Radinsky, L. B. "The Families of the Rhinocerotoidea (Mammalia, Perissodactyla)." *Journal of Mammalogy* 47 (1966): 631–639.

——. "A Review of the Rhinocerotoid Family Hyracodontidae (Perissodactyla)." *Bulletin of the American Museum of Natural History* 136, no. 1 (1967): 1–46.

Savage, R. J. G., and M. R. Long. *Mammal Evolution: An Illustrated Guide*. Facts-on-File, 1986.

Wall, W. P. "The Phylogenetic History and Adaptive Radiation of the Amynodontidae." In *The Evolution of Perissodactyls*, ed. D. R. Prothero and R. M. Schoch. Oxford University Press, 1989.

Turner, A., and M. Anton. *National Geographic Prehistoric Mammals*. National Geographic Society, 2004.

DAEODON

Researchers have identified "meat caches" in Wyoming, attributed to hell pigs based on bite marks consistent with their jaw measurements. The evidence suggests that these creatures would behead their prey. They would then delve into the meatier, articulated rear halves of their prey. They would then stockpile "articulated thoracic leftovers" in these cashes for later. So not only are these hell pigs big and scary with gaping wide mouths–but they were also quite strategic, from the sounds of it. I don't know about you, but I'm glad there's no chance of encountering one of these meat-eating, jaw-crushing creatures on a casual hike, that's for sure.

—ERIC RALLS

THE LAST MAN WHO KNEW EVERYTHING

As the study of fossil mammals was emerging in Europe in the 1830s through 1850s, there was not yet any comparable discovery of mammals across The Pond. American engineering and science were still in their infancy, focused mainly on practical topics such as agriculture and canal building. Fossils of the first mastodonts had been found in the mid-1700s and puzzled scholars from America to France (see chapter 1). So had the giant claws studied by Thomas Jefferson, who thought they belonged to a giant lion and instructed Lewis and Clark to look for such a lion on their trip across the continent. (The claws came from a giant ground sloth, now named *Megalonyx jeffersoni* in his honor—see chapter 3.) But aside from these rare Ice Age mammals, few fossil bones had yet been found in North America. There were no paleontologists yet, but simply doctors and other scholars who had some biological training and who occasionally had a fossil bone sent to them for identification. Most naturalists, like John James Audubon and many others, were focused on discovering, collecting, and describing the living species of North American animals for the first time—not looking for fossils.

Into this void stepped America's first great naturalist, Joseph Leidy (figure 12.1). His work spanned many different fields of natural science, from paleontology to geology to parasitology to embryology to forensic medicine. At a commemorative meeting in his memory, Henry Fairfield Osborn wrote:

> Among zoologists he was the last to treat of the whole animal world from the protozoa to man, rendering in every branch contributions of permanent value. From his researches among the minerals, plants, infusorians, entozoa, and mollusks, he ranged into comparative anatomy as well as into his greatest field of research, vertebrate palaeontology. In the year 1852 we find him writing upon fossils from the West, the geology of the Badlands, the life history of bees, their anatomy and the physiology of their reproductive organs, as well as entering the discussion of some new fungi with an English microscopist, the specific determination of various parasites, as well as numerous plants, the investigation of some new points in comparative anatomy, the observation of the movements of some new Rhizopods. His encyclopaedic knowledge,

Figure 12.1 ◀
Portrait of Joseph Leidy, the founder of vertebrate paleontology in the United States. (Courtesy of Wikimedia Commons)

> broad grasp of the whole field of natural history, precision and originality of observation in every field, present a combination of endowments which will never reappear in a single individual.[1]

No wonder Leonard Warren's excellent 1998 biography of Leidy is subtitled, "The Last Man Who Knew Everything." By the time Leidy died in 1891, science had exploded in the amount of information it had accumulated (to which Leidy was a key contributor), so no subsequent natural historian could claim equal expertise in so many fields. From then on, all scientists were specialists in one field only, with limited knowledge of other fields of science, due to the very nature of the huge amount of information that science has accumulated.

Born September 9, 1823, in Philadelphia, Joseph Mellick Leidy's father Philip Leidy was a hatmaker of German ancestry. His mother, Catharine Mellick Leidy, died young while giving birth to his younger brother Thomas, and his father soon remarried, choosing his wife's first cousin Christiana Mellick to help him raise the young boys. His father wanted him to become a sign painter, but his stepmother supported him in more ambitious career goals, so he went to the University of Pennsylvania to study medicine. He was trained by the noted anatomist Dr. James McClintock, and the pioneering microscopist Paul B. Goddard. Once he earned his medical degree in 1844 at age twenty-one, his father expected him to set up a lucrative medical practice and earn his keep. Instead, he stayed around Penn medical school, helping the others teach medicine and microscopy, and beginning a research career. In 1845, he was commissioned to do dissections and illustrations for Amos Binney's book on American snails. The publication of this book brought Leidy many accolades, so he was soon elected to the scholarly societies of Philadelphia and Boston. By the end of his life, he was a member of more than 50 scientific societies. He finally received a permanent post in 1846 when he became a curator at Philadelphia's Academy of Natural Sciences.

Leidy rose quickly through the scholarly ranks as he began his research career, publishing more than 553 scientific papers in his lifetime. Leidy's skill in dissection and microscopy and brilliance in anatomy elevated him to a post in the University of Pennsylvania medical school by 1853, where he taught anatomy. Later he was offered posts at Swarthmore College and Wagner Free Institute, where he taught many subjects. His textbook on medical anatomy became the standard that were used by almost all American medical students for more than forty years. During the Civil War, Leidy served as an Army surgeon, where he pioneered many innovative practices that improved the outcomes of surgery.

Long before Sherlock Holmes or real forensic detective work existed, Leidy's skills as a microscopist made him one of the first scientists involved in solving crimes. In 1846, the police brought him a case where a man was accused of murdering a Philadelphia farmer. The suspect claimed that the blood on his clothes and hatchet was chicken blood that had spattered on him when he had killed some birds earlier. Leidy used his microscope to determine that the red blood cells had no nuclei, a feature of human blood. He further ruled out chickens by leaving samples of their blood out to dry, and they never lost their nuclei. This evidence forced the suspect to confess.

In addition to being the founder of American vertebrate paleontology, Leidy was also one of the founders of parasitology and protozoology. His 1879 monograph on protozoans was the beginning of that field of research. Using his microscope, he was able to identify many of the human parasites for the first time. His most famous discovery was the worm that infects pork and causes trichinosis in people who eat undercooked pork.

As one of the few people at that time with any knowledge of comparative vertebrate anatomy, most fossils found out West were sent to Leidy. Stuck with his many responsibilities in Philadelphia, these were mostly fragmentary fossils picked up and dumped into saddlebags by the early explorers of the American West. Starting in 1847, Leidy received a steady flow of fossils from what is now Badlands National Park in South Dakota, including the first American camel *Poebrotherium*, the first American rhinoceros *Subhyracodon*, and the first horse found in North America, *Mesohippus*, plus many other extinct archaic mammals like oreodonts and brontotheres that have no living relatives. He also was sent Ice Age horse teeth, which confirmed that horses had evolved in North America and then vanished long before Columbus reintroduced them in 1493. Leidy received numerous other Ice Age fossils, so he was the first to name and describe the dire wolf, the giant American lion, the short-faced bear, the American sabertoothed cat, the Ice Age camels, bison, and horse, and many others. For many American paleontologists today, a trip to the Academy of Natural Sciences is essential because it is necessary to see Leidy's original fossils to understand whether a particular genus or species name is valid or not.

In the 1860s and 1870s, Leidy managed to embark on a few collecting trips to the Rocky Mountains to obtain his own fossils. However, by 1871, vertebrate paleontology became a crowded and contentious field as the warfare between Edward Drinker Cope and O. C. Marsh soon escalated to outright stealing of fossils, bribery, and fraud. Leidy was too much of a gentleman to get into the midst of this nasty feud, so he gave up field work and most of his research in fossil vertebrates rather than get between Cope and Marsh and their self-destructive war on each other. He did publish on some fossils from Florida (including the hippo-like rhino *Teleoceras*) later in life, but he did not try to compete with Cope or Marsh, who had much more free time and more resources to corner the market on all the good specimens from the emerging fossil beds out West.

In the fall of 1850, Leidy was studying a puzzling specimen that had been brought to him from the Big Badlands. A portion of the front of the skull was preserved, and the cheek teeth had large blunt squared-shaped molars with four low rounded cusps, although both the cheek teeth and even the canines were extremely worn in old individuals, suggesting a very abrasive diet with lots of hard materials. The squared molars with low rounded cusps were very much like the teeth of pigs and peccaries, but these were much larger and more robust. Based on this incomplete specimen, Leidy thought it might be related to an extinct group of Eocene artiodactyls called anoplotheres. Uncertain about what they were related to, he gave this beast a new name, *Archaeotherium mortoni* ("Morton's ancient beast"), in honor of his friend Samuel George Morton, the president of the Philadelphia Academy of Natural Sciences. By 1853, Leidy had better material of this animal, and it was apparent to him that it was similar to a beast from the Oligocene of Ronzon in France that Auguste Aymard had named *Entelodon* in 1847. (*Entelodon* means "complete tooth," because the jaws have the primitive full complement of incisors, canine, premolars, and molars, with no loss of any teeth due to specialization.) In 1853, Leidy transferred *Archaeotherium* to *Entelodon*, although later authors showed that the two were distinct and Leidy's original name was valid.

As more and more complete specimens of *Archaeotherium* were recovered from the Big Badlands, the animal became more and more puzzling (figure 12.2). It was the size of a large hog, with many other pig-like features, including four trotters on its hands and feet. The blunt teeth with rounded cusps were like those of primitive pigs or peccaries, but its huge

Figure 12.2 ▲

Archaeotherium mortoni. (*A*) Mounted skeleton at the American Museum of Natural History. (*B*) Reconstruction. (Courtesy of Wikimedia Commons)

canines were not self-sharpening blades like those of pigs or peccaries, but robust conical teeth that usually were worn down on the tips. This showed that these canines were used to crush dense objects, rather than stabbing or slicing with them. But even more surprising was the grotesque skull and jaws. The head was huge compared to the spindly-legged body, with large bony ridges sticking out of the cheekbones below the eyes, and large bony bumps on the bottom of the lower jaws. These were features also found in European *Entelodon*, although not as extreme nor as well preserved as in the Badlands fossils.

At least 40 species in eight genera have been named for these Badlands entelodonts, including *Scaptohyus, Megachoerus, Choerodon, Pelonax, Ammodon*, and even the European synonym for *Entelodon, Elotherium*, based on the wide range of variations of their cheekbones and ridges and knobs on their faces. Today all of these old names are considered population variation within a single species, and they are all considered junior synonyms of *Archaeotherium mortoni*.

"HELL PIGS"

The next big find of entelodonts was in the famous Agate Fossil beds in western Nebraska, which yielded skeletons of the chalicothere *Moropus*, the rhino *Menoceras*, and the bear-dog *Daphoenocyon*, as well as small camels. But the most remarkable discovery was several complete skeletons of the huge entelodont that Olof Peterson, the lead paleontologist at Agate, who in 1905 named it *Dinohyus hollandi* ("Holland's terrible hog"), in honor of W. J. Holland of the Carnegie Museum, who supported and supervised the excavations at Agate. As head of the department, Holland was notorious for putting his name as the first author on everything the Carnegie Museum paleontologists published, whether or not he'd actually worked on them. Peterson may have gotten his revenge when a Pittsburgh newspaper announced the discovery with the front-page headline, "Dinohyus Hollandi: The World's Biggest Hog!"

Dinohyus was truly a terrifying creature, as big as a bison, with a frightening skull over a meter long, with wicked-looking broad flaring cheekbones (figure 12.3). It was almost 6.6 feet (2 meters) tall at the shoulders and weighed up to 2,000 pounds (900 kilograms), or almost a ton, even though it had relatively spindly legs compared to its massive head and body. These

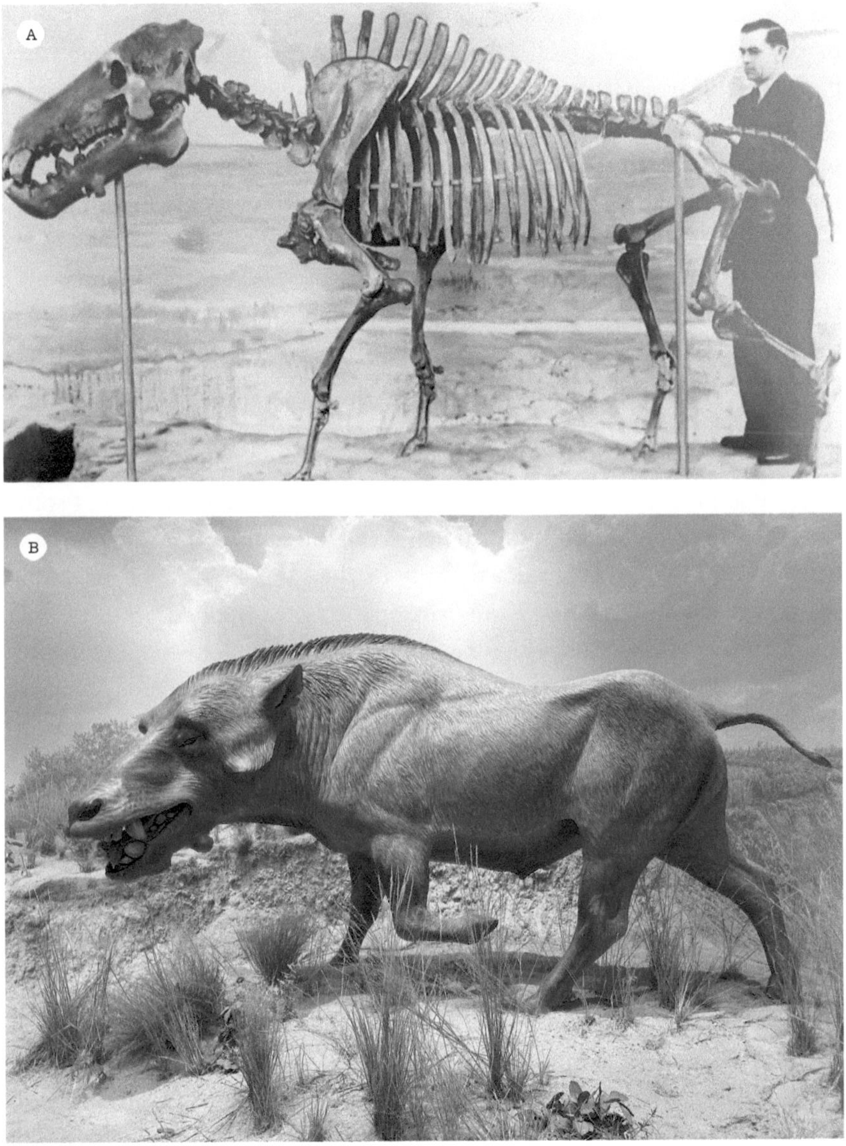

Figure 12.3 ▲

Daeodon shoshoniensis from Agate Fossil Beds National Monuments (formerly *Dinohyus hollandi*). (*A*) Mounted skeleton at the University of Nebraska State Museum. (*B*) Reconstruction at the Denver Museum of Nature and Science. (Courtesy of Wikimedia Commons)

are the animals that some science documentaries have come to call "hell pigs" or "terminator pigs." These and other vivid nicknames have been given to a bizarre entelodonts. They get a lot of publicity and a lot of exaggeration and speculations peddled as facts, because of their bizarre anatomy and huge size is so fascinating. They've even been described as one of the largest predators of their time, although there is much doubt that they were true predators.

Because of the famous images of the complete skeletal mounts and reconstructions of the living animal, which were copied over and over again, the name *Dinohyus* became iconic for this monster. But recent research has shown that before Peterson named *Dinohyus* in 1905, an earlier specimen of this beast from the John Day beds in Oregon had been described by Edward Drinker Cope in 1878 and named *Daeodon shoshoniensis*. It is not a very complete or diagnostic fossil, only the tip of the lower jaw of some kind of giant entelodont. But it matches the lower jaws from Agate Fossil beds, so most experts consider them to be the same beast. By the rules of priority in scientific names, *Daeodon* Cope 1878 was named first, so *Dinohyus* Peterson, 1905 is just a junior synonym and no longer valid. But it takes a long time for people and books and other sources to stop using *Dinohyus* and replace it with *Daeodon*, so you will still see Peterson's name floating around despite it being out of date.

EVOLUTION OF "HELL PIGS"

The oldest fossil entelodonts come from middle Eocene beds around 42–45 Ma in China and Mongolia and are known as *Eoentelodon* and *Proentelodon*. These specimens are not very complete, just a few fragmentary skulls and jaws. The teeth show the diagnostic features of entelodonts, but they were only the size of a small pig.

Around 37 Ma, entelodonts migrated across the Bering land bridge to North America, where they show up in upper Eocene deposits between 37 and 35 Ma in Canada and the western U.S. Known as *Brachyhyops* (figure 12.4), they were much larger than *Eoentelodon*, and clearly showed the diagnostic features of entelodonts, especially the development of large flaring cheekbones, and robust rounded canines and cheek teeth. In beds around 35–33 Ma in Saskatchewan and in the Great Plains and Rocky Mountains, we find a slightly larger and more advanced entelodont, *Cypretherium* (named after the Cypress Hills of Saskatchewan, where it was first found).

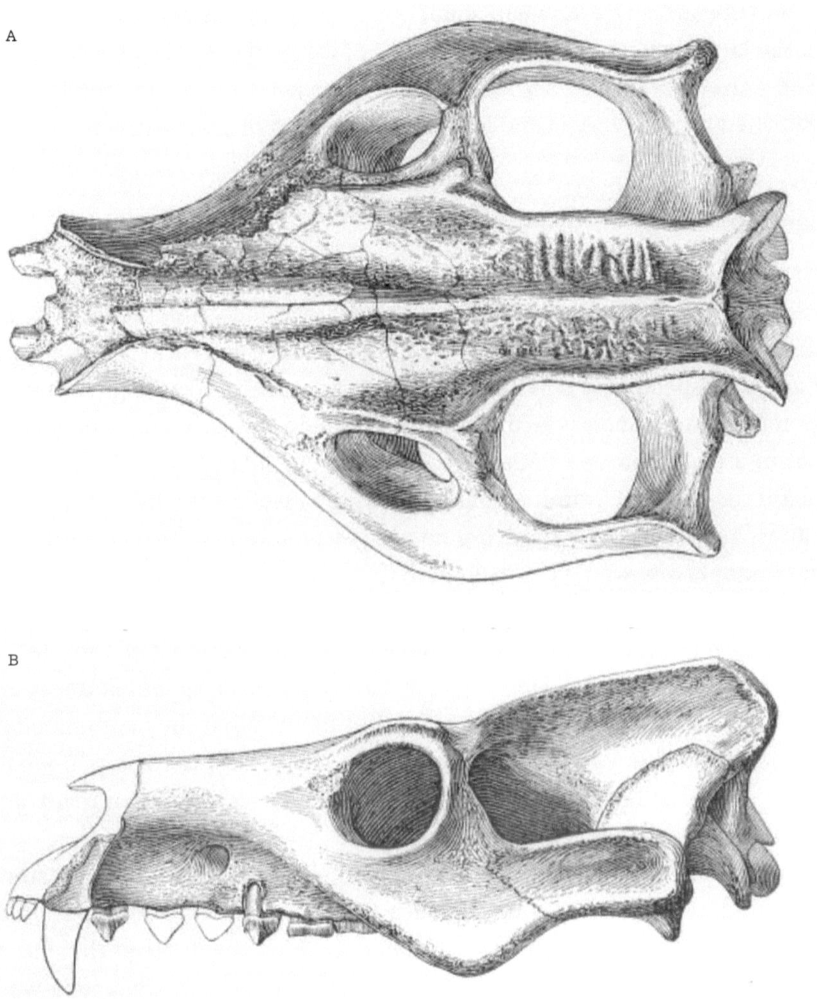

Figure 12.4 ▲
The original type skull of *Brachyhyops wyomingensis* from the middle Eocene beds of Beaver Divide in central Wyoming. (*A*) Top view; (*B*) side view. (After E. H. Colbert, "*Brachyhyops*, a New Bunodont Artiodactyls from Beaver Divide, Wyoming," *Annals of the Carnegie Museum* 27 (1938): 87–108)

Formerly called *Archaeotherium coarctatum*, it was the first entelodont with the huge flaring cheekbones and may other advanced features. In beds about 33–30 Ma (early Oligocene), we find *Archaeotherium mortoni*, previously discussed. And in beds about 23–21 Ma, we finally get the largest of the entelodonts, *Daeodon*, and the last species in North America.

Finally, after *Daeodon* vanished, one more giant entelodont was found in the late Oligocene of China from 21–25 Ma. Named *Paraentelodon*, it was rhino-sized, even bigger than *Daeodon*. However, by 21 Ma, entelodonts vanished from both Asia and North America, and became extinct.

THE LIFE OF A "HELL PIG"

So what were entelodonts related to? What were they like? What did they eat? The first question has been debated for a long time. Since the initial descriptions of *Archaeotherium* and *Entelodon* in North America and Europe, respectively, entelodonts have been compared to pigs in having simple squared molars with four low rounded cusps. Usually they were put in a bigger group of "Suioidea" or "Suina," which was a wastebasket taxon for all of the primitive pig-like fossils as well as the living pigs, peccaries, and hippos. But there are no unique evolutionary specializations in entelodonts that would connect them to pigs or peccaries or any group, living or extinct. All of the features they share with pigs are primitive features of all the pig-like artiodactyls, and not evidence of relationship. Despite the popular nicknames of "Hell Pigs" or "Terminator Pigs," entelodonts are not pigs, and not even distantly related to them. What they are related to is a mystery, although some analyses place them close to the hippo-whale clade—but that is also based on their large blunt teeth and not really any features that are distinctive and unique.

The popular media, especially the documentary "Prehistoric Predators: Entelodon," keep promoting the idea that entelodonts were huge predators. I was even involved when I filmed in short segments at the end of that video, although I never saw the script and realized what they were pitching. The video does not provide any concrete evidence for predatory entelodonts. Their only supposed evidence for this idea is a bone deposit near Douglas, Wyoming, with a cache of partial carcasses of juvenile *Poebrotherium* camels that have been broken up and have tooth marks that match *Archaeotherium*. But all this proves is that entelodonts scavenged these carcasses, which might have died of other causes—there is no evidence that entelodonts killed them or even dragged the carcasses to one place as a meat cache.

Weighing strongly against the idea that entelodonts were predators is their basic anatomy. All true mammalian predators, from dogs to cats to bears to weasels, rely on being able to tackle and pin down their prey with their front legs. They must be able to rotate their front paws inward to grab their prey and hold it. Entelodont legs had hooves for running and could only move in the front-to-back plane, and could not rotate to hold anything, so they would have to do everything with their enormous heads. It's possible to imagine them snapping up some smaller animal in an ambush, but it's unlikely they could have done this often because once the prey animal begins to escape, the entelodont has no way to pounce on it or restrain it.

All true mammalian predators have at least some of their teeth shaped like sharp blades for slashing prey and killing it, then slicing up the flesh so that they could swallow it in bite-sized chunks. Entelodont teeth are rounded and blunt and could never cut anything, only crush it. In fact, instead of sharp front canines that mammalian predators use to stab and hold their prey, entelodont canines are blunt and the tips are often worn off, so they could not stab anything. Instead they appeared to be using their teeth for crushing hard objects such as bone. Detailed studies of the wear on the teeth show evidence of bone breaking and the stripping of roots or other plant fibers, but this behavior is nothing like that of an omnivorous true predator such as bears. Entelodont diet was probably more like that of wild boars and other omnivorous pigs, which is mostly plant matter, but they often scavenge carcasses when the opportunity arises.

In short, it's very unlikely that entelodonts were active predators. Instead they were omnivores who focused mainly on scavenging carcasses and crushing bone, and they also ate roots and tubers and other plant material. It's possible they might be able to bite down and crush a much smaller animal that was crippled or not able to move very fast, but entelodonts didn't possess the anatomy to be active hunters who chase down prey, drag it down, and then slash its neck or belly, as all true carnivorous mammals do.

Speculation about diet is one thing, but there is good evidence of another kind of behavior: entelodonts were nasty and short-tempered. Many of their skulls have scars and bite marks on their snouts that match entelodont teeth, probably acquired during fights with other members of their species. This might also explain the large flaring cheekbones and flanges of bone around the eyes and face. Many of the bite marks are on these cheekbones, suggesting a similar function with warthogs, which also have flaring bony cheekbones that protect their eyes during fights with other warthogs. Also like warthogs, the cheekbones get larger as they mature, so the size of their cheekbones would advertise their mature status in their social groups.

So why did entelodonts vanish after more than twenty million years of being one of the largest animals in their world? We can never know for sure, but it is striking that when they start to disappear around 22–19 Ma, so did the archaic carnivorous mammals known as the hyaenodont creodonts. At the same time, there was an invasion of two new groups of more specialized predators. One of these were the so-called "bear-dogs," or amphicyonids, which are neither bears nor dogs but a group unto themselves. The largest ones, such as *Amphicyon ingens*, were polar bear-sized with huge robust teeth, and they could fight entelodonts to a draw and scavenge carcasses as well. The other arrival was the tribe of bone-crushing dogs known as borophagines, which had robust skulls with heavy-duty teeth for crushing bones and scavenging carcasses. Both of these true predators were not only better built for scavenging and preying on large animals, but they also had much large brains than did entelodonts, so they were smarter and probably had complex social behaviors, like pack hunting, that made them more successful. Whatever the reason, by 19 Ma, entelodonts were extinct, and never again would there be a scavenger so large—and so ugly!

NOTES

The epigraph is taken from Eric Ralls, "The Terrifying Biology of Hellpigs," Earth.com, https://www.earth.com/earthpedia-articles/the-terrifying-biology-of-hell-pigs/.

1. Henry Fairfield Osborn, "Joseph Leidy: Founder of Vertebrate Paleontology in North America," *Proceedings of the Academy of Natural Sciences of Philadelphia* 75 (1923): 54–61.

FOR FURTHER READING

Colbert, E. H. "*Brachyhyops*, a New Bunodont Artiodactyls from Beaver Divide, Wyoming." *Annals of the Carnegie Museum* 27 (1938): 87–108

Effinger, J. A. "Entelodontidae." In *Evolution of Tertiary Mammals of North America*, vol. 1, *Terrestrial Carnivores, Ungulates, and Ungulatelike Mammals*, ed. C. M. Janis, K. M. Scott, and L. L. Jacobs, 375–380. Cambridge University Press, 1998.

Foss, Scott E. "Family Entelodontidae." In *The Evolution of Artiodactyls*, ed. D. R. Prothero and S. E. Foss, 120–129. Johns Hopkins University Press, 2007.

Joeckel, R. M. "A Functional Interpretation of the Masticatory System and Paleoecology of Entelodonts." *Paleobiology* 16, no. 4 (1990): 459–482.

Lucas, S. G., and R. J. Emry. "The Entelodont *Brachyhyops* (Mammalia, Artiodactyla) from the Upper Eocene of Flagstaff Rim, Wyoming." *New Mexico Museum of Natural History and Science Bulletin* 26 (2004): 97–100.

Lucas, S. G., R. J. Emry, and S. E. Foss. "Taxonomy and Distribution of *Daeodon*, An Oligocene-Miocene Entelodont (Mammalia: Artiodactyla) from North America." *Proceedings of the Biological Society of Washington* 111, no. 2 (1998): 425–435.

Peterson, O. A. "A Revision of Entelodontidae." *Memoirs of the Carnegie Museum*, 9 (1909):41–158.

Prothero, D. R. *The Princeton Field Guide to Prehistoric Mammals*. Princeton University Press, 2016.

——. *Vertebrate Evolution: From Origins to Dinosaurs and Beyond*. Taylor & Francis/CRC Press, 2022.

Prothero, D. R., and R. M. Schoch. *Horns, Tusks, and Flippers: The Evolution of Hoofed Mammals*. Johns Hopkins University Press, 2002.

Rivals, F., R. I. Belyaev, V. B. Basova, and N. E. Prilepskaya. "Hogs, Hippos, or Bears? Paleodiet of European Oligocene Anthracotheres and Entelodonts." *Palaeogeography, Palaeoclimatology, Palaeoecology* 611 (2023): 111363.

Russell, L. S. "Tertiary Mammals of Saskatchewan. Part V. The Oligocene Entelodonts." *Life Sciences Contributions of the Royal Ontario Museum* (1980): 122.

Spaulding, M., M. A. O'Leary, and J. Gatesy. "Relationships of Cetacea (Artiodactyla) Among Mammals: Increased Taxon Sampling Alters Interpretations of Key Fossils and Character Evolution." *PLOS ONE* 4, no. 9 (2009): e7062.

Tsubamoto, T., M. Saneyoshi, M. Watabe, K. Tsogtbaatar, and B. Mainbayar. "The Entelodontid Artiodactyl Fauna from the Eocene Ergilin Dzo Formation of Mongolia with Comments on *Brachyhyops* and the Khoer Dzan Locality." *Paleontological Research* 15, no. 4 (2011): 258–268.

Yu, Y., H. Gao, Q. Li, and X. Ni. "A New Entelodont (Artiodactyla, Mammalia) from the Late Eocene of China and Its Phylogenetic Implications." *Journal of Systematic Palaeontology* 21, no. 1 (2023): 2189436.

13 CAMELS WITHOUT HUMPS

POEBROTHERIUM

The discovery of this specimen introduces to science one of the most interesting instances of convergence yet observed. The effect of extreme height, in order to enable the animal to feed upon the inaccessible foliage of high and thorny shrubs, is obtained in this species, as in the giraffe, by the elongation of the neck vertebrae and the legs. But the giraffe is derived from the early antelopes and this animal is from early camels and the difference of origin has caused the attainment of the desired result in a somewhat different manner.

—WILLIAM DILLER MATTHEW, 1901

THE MASTER OF FOSSIL MAMMALS

The names of famous paleontologists such as Leidy, Cope, Marsh, Osborn, and others are known to many amateur fossil buffs as well as to professional paleontologists. But fewer people know of the life or legacy of William Diller Matthew, who was probably the best paleontologist of his generation and published work that has stood the test of time for over a century (figure 13.1). He emerged just as the American Museum Department of Vertebrate Paleontology (DVP) was getting started, and he soon became the most accomplished and prolific scientist in the American Museum—but he was overshadowed by the pompous and powerful (but scientifically incompetent) Henry Fairfield Osborn, his boss (see chapter 9). In addition, he published relatively few works for public consumption, and most importantly, he never worked on dinosaurs, so he is undeservedly obscure among prominent early paleontologists.

Figure 13.1 ◂
Portrait of William Diller Matthew in the early 1920s. (Courtesy of the American Museum Digital Library)

Matthew was a Canadian by birth, although he spent most of his career in the United States. Born on February 19, 1871, in St. John, New Brunswick, he returned every year to keep his Canadian citizenship. His father, Dr. G. F. Matthew, was a distinguished amateur geologist who influenced his son to pursue a career in geology. William earned his bachelor's degree at the University of Halifax, Nova Scotia, then went to Columbia University to study geology, mineralogy, and metallurgy. But he also took classes from Osborn, and when he finished his degree in 1895, he came to work as a scientific assistant for Osborn in the Department of Vertebrate Paleontology, where he would spend the next thirty-two years, rising to Curator-in-Chief.

His early training was primarily in geology, so he spent considerable time visiting the important Cenozoic fossil beds of the western United States and examining their collections. At the beginning of his career, he published seven papers on geology and mineralogy, one on trilobites, and one in botany. In 1898, he published his "Provisional classification of the freshwater Tertiary of the west," which Osborn added his name to, although it was almost entirely Matthew's work. Building on the early work of Cope, Marsh, Hatcher, and the rest, Matthew established the stratigraphic relations of the major Cenozoic bone-bearing beds of the western United States, and also summarized their key index fossils and other diagnostic features. This summary was the first such wide-ranging analysis of the sequence of fossil beds of the western United States and was the foundation of what eventually became the "North American Land Mammal Ages." These were established in 1941 by a committee led by Horace E. Wood II, and became the foundation for all later work in mammalian biostratigraphy in the United States. Matthew also disputed the claim that the fossil beds in the Big Badlands, the Bridger Basin, the San Juan Basin, and elsewhere were "freshwater lake deposits" and showed convincingly that they were the deposits of river floodplains.

However, once he was hired by the American Museum, his first task was to go to Philadelphia and supervise the packing of Cope's collection, which Cope had donated to the American Museum upon his death. In this way, Matthew had access to Cope's large unstudied collections of Paleocene mammals, which had barely been examined. From this collection, he conducted the first analysis of the earliest Cenozoic mammals from the western United States, especially those collected in the San Juan Basin by David Baldwin for Cope in the 1880s. He carefully analyzed these early mammals, the survivors of the great Cretaceous extinction, and deciphered their origins and relationships as best he could, based on such fragmentary tooth and jaw fossils of such strange beasts with no living descendants. This work laid the foundation for all later work on Paleocene mammals in the United States.

From there he worked on just about any project that came his way, running frequent field expeditions in the summers to enhance the American Museum collections. He returned to the Bridger Basin of Wyoming, site of the Cope-Marsh-Leidy fights over uintatheres some thirty years earlier, and wrote a masterly review of the carnivorous mammals, a monograph that is still used today, even with much more and better fossils. In 1900, he led an expedition to the middle Miocene beds of the Pawnee Creek area in northeastern Colorado, where he made many important discoveries. He spent a lot of time collecting in the crucially important Sheep Creek-Snake Creek beds in western Nebraska, aided by Harold Cook, the son of Captain James Cook, who owned the Agate fossil beds. Matthew published four separate papers summarizing all of the mammals from this area, which are the foundation of almost all later work on Miocene camels, horses, rhinos, ruminants, dogs, and many other groups of mammals.

Matthew transferred a lot of his skills to his eventual successor, the young George Gaylord Simpson, who spent a field summer helping Matthew collect fossils in the Blanco beds of Texas, focusing on fossil horses. By the end of his career, Matthew had worked on fossils from the Paleocene to the Pleistocene, and on every order of mammals except whales, sirenians, and monotremes. Nobody ever published more on more groups of fossil mammals than he did, nor was anyone ever as competent in so many groups of animals as he was. Altogether, he published 248 papers on vertebrate paleontology, more than anyone except Leidy, Cope, or Marsh, whose "publications" mostly consisted of slapdash short notes with only a few paragraphs to lay claim to naming a fossil, and with no analysis.

Matthew's thinking about how and why to justify naming a new fossil species was well ahead of his time. Osborn and most of his peers typically gave a new species name to every new specimen that was collected, resulting in taxonomic chaos. Matthew, on the other hand, saw the variability of single quarry samples of horses from the Snake Creek beds of Nebraska, and wrote in 1924:

> This represents many thousands of individuals, no two of them exactly alike in the complex details of tooth construction. If the standards of species distinction that have been accepted by most American students of fossil Equidae were applied conscientiously to this great collection, the result would be to place upon record scores if not hundreds of "new species" from this one locality. But the thousands of isolated teeth or other fragmentary specimens would clearly show that there are no really constant and uniformly associated distinctions between such "species." They are mainly individual differences . . . I believe, however, that the hard and fast lines of distinction that it is customary among palaeontologists (and zoologists) to draw between "species" are not justified by the evidence; that when one deals with very extensive series of specimens from many closely succeeding stages and many localities, the amount and character of intergrading and mixture of their species characteristics is only explicable as the result of continual admixture of numerous interbreeding strains, so that the "species" is merely a more or less arbitrary selection of material representing approximations to a strain locally and temporarily dominant. It is to be pointed out in this connection that interbreeding does not produce exact intergradation in the characters of a series of specimens but various admixtures of more or less distinct and definite characters. . . . From this viewpoint the more detailed affinities of the later Equidae are matters of degree of relationship or dominance of

> one or another ancestral stock in a complexity of intercrossing strain which only slowly and gradually take on that complete infertility between progressively diverging groups which brings about definite and permanent distinctness. . . . *Equus* shows an admixture, somewhat varying in its different species, of progressive characters, some of which are assumed earlier by typical Pliohippi, some by typical Hipparions; there is nothing in the generic characters of either genus to exclude it from the ancestry of *Equus* but all the better-known species of each are off the direct line, although some are perhaps not excluded from participation in some degree in the ancestry of the modern horses.[1]

This kind of thinking was remarkably advanced for 1924, when most paleontologists of that time were still using the old "splitting" philosophy that every new fossil with a slight difference got a new name. This was true not only of Osborn but also of Childs Frick (who coined lots of invalid names in his 1937 horned ruminant monographs), and the authors of the oreodont monographs, C. Bertrand Schultz and Charles H. Falkenbach, as well as the foremost rhino expert, Horace E. Wood II, and many others trained before the 1940s. It was not until the 1940s and 1950s that Matthew's protégé, George Gaylord Simpson, followed similar lines in his own research. Simpson pushed for paleontologists to consider the variability of natural populations and sexual dimorphism of males and females in a population, as well as using statistical methods to sort out how many valid species names could be applied. Yet vestiges of this archaic thinking were still being published as late as 1968, with the last of Schultz and Falkenbach oreodont monographs.

Today, most paleontologists who don't work on North American fossil mammals have never heard of Matthew, mostly because he didn't work on dinosaurs (unlike Leidy, Cope, Marsh, Osborn, Barnum Brown, and many others). If there is any idea that is associated with him, it's the ideas in his classic 1915 paper, "Climate and Evolution," which summarized what was then known of Cenozoic climate and mammalian biogeography and postulated that (with some exceptions) most mammalian groups had originated in Holarctica (North America or Eurasia) and then spread southward from their "centers of origin." This idea wasn't too popular in the 1970s when biogeography went through a rethinking, but for the mammals and time periods that Matthew knew best, it still works pretty well.

In his obituary for the Royal Society of London, David M. S. Watson wrote:

> Dr. Matthew possessed a wider acquaintance with fossil mammals than any other man has had; his knowledge of them was encyclopaedic, covering European forms with which he had comparatively little first-hand knowledge, as well as those from all other parts of the world which he knew most intimately from the vast materials under his care in New York. He possessed in the highest degree a power of remembering and recalling the intricate pattern of a mammalian molar tooth, and had an equally clear memory of the structure of a skull or foot. This immense mass of accurate detailed knowledge was the basis of all his work. In everything he did Matthew was cautious; a man full of ideas, he checked them, never proceeding to a wide generalization unless his evidence was very wide, based on an abundant material. He was rightly critical of theories which outran their factual foundations, and especially of such as failed to take due account of possible alternative hypotheses.[2]

By 1927, Matthew was finally fed up with Osborn's treatment of him after thirty-two years. Osborn stole other people's work and hogged all the credit, even as Matthew and others could see that Osborn's work was incompetent. Then Matthew received an offer to teach at the University of California at Berkeley, where a distinguished Museum of Paleontology had been founded by John C. Merriam, who had left Berkeley for the Carnegie Institute in Washington, D.C. Matthew threw himself into his new post, training the next generation of young paleontologists, while continuing his own research. Sadly, he died on September 24, 1930, after only three years at Berkeley, at age fifty-nine, still energetic and productive, with several more papers that were published after he died, and some of his unpublished work being resurrected and published by others (with due credit to Matthew).

Matthew was outstanding in every group of mammals he worked on, but in this chapter we'll look at his contributions to understanding North American camels.

AMERICAN CAMELS

Most people are shocked to hear that camels once lived in North America, and even more so when they hear that most of camel evolution occurred primarily in this continent over 45 million years, with only one lineage escaping to Eurasia about 8 Ma (where they gave rise to the familiar dromedary and Bactrian camels) and another lineage escaping to South America when the Panama land bridge opened about 3.5 Ma (where they gave rise to vicuñas and guanacos, and their domesticated descendants, alpacas and llamas). Camels were a common element of almost every North American faunal assemblage, especially in the Oligocene beds of the Big Badlands, and the Miocene beds all over the western United States and Florida. They survived here until about ten thousand years ago at the end of the last Ice Age, when *Camelops*, the last North American camel, vanished during the Pleistocene megafaunal extinctions (see chapter 2).

That's not to say that camels wouldn't survive in the American deserts today. In 1857, the US Army experimented with the idea of introducing camels to their western forts as pack animals, and set up the US Camel Corps. They hired a Greek-Syrian camel driver (a citizen of the Ottoman Empire) named Hadji Ali (known as "Hi Jolly" to the American troops) to handle the 33 camels that were shipped overseas, then driven from Indianola, Texas, to California. The camels did fine in the long trek from the Texas coast. The biggest problem was that American mules and horses were not used to the smell and behavior of camels, and they often panicked in their presence. (Horses in Africa and Asia grew up with camels and had no such problem.) US cavalry troops were also not comfortable learning how to ride and take care of these strange creatures who would spit on you or bite you if you irritated them. Then, three years after the experiment started, the US Army shifted its focus to the Civil War, and funding and interest in the US Camel Corps ended. By 1864, the camels were auctioned off, and Hadji Ali had to find other work, running a freight service for mines in Arizona. However, he released some of his camels into the Arizona desert, and some say that there may be descendants of these camels still roaming the western deserts even today.

The first American camel fossil ever described was the very first new genus of mammal fossil to be reported from west of the Mississippi River. In November 1847, Joseph Leidy described a strange new skull of an extinct animal, *Poebrotherium wilsoni*, the very first fossil to reach him from the Big Badlands. He thought it was some sort of ruminant and compared it to deer and sheep, but he noted that it was different and much more primitive than any fossil ruminant described so far. In fact, it was so primitive that it did not even have the characteristic features of camels, and it wasn't until much later, with much more complete skulls and skeletons, that scientists realized *Poebrotherium* was an Eocene-Oligocene camel.

In 1854, Leidy received the front end of a skull from a gravel pit in Kansas. This specimen came from the Pleistocene and had the characteristic front teeth found in llamas and camels, so Leidy had no doubt that it was a camel relative. He called it *Camelops* ("camel face") *kansanus*, and this was his first realization that camels had once been native to North America.

CAMELS WITHOUT HUMPS

When we hear the word "camel," we think of them as the pack animals with humps: "ships of the desert" that wander across barren landscapes of Africa and Asia. But camels have not always been this way. Four of the six living species of camels do not have humps. In the Old World, there are two species: the dromedary camel with a single hump and the Bactrian camel that has two humps. They are part of the tribe Camelini. There are four other species of camels in South America, that have no humps at all: the domesticated llama, and alpaca, and their ancestors, the wild guanaco of the Pampas and the vicuña of the Andes. They are members of the tribe Lamini. All of these camels are descended from the original radiation of camels in North America and not until later did they spread to South America and Eurasia and Africa.

The hump of a camel is its most famous feature. It is formed by fleshy deposits of fat and connective tissue and has no bony support, so it's impossible to know whether most fossil camel skeletons have humps or not. However, the fact that humps only occur in the lineage of camels from the deserts of Eurasia and Africa (tribe Camelini), and not in the four species lamines from South America, suggests that most camels did not have humps.

The family Camelidae are members of the order Artiodactyla, or even-toed hoofed mammals, which have either two or four toes on their hands and feet. Molecular evidence shows that the camel branch split off early from the rest of the artiodactyls, even before pigs and hippos diverged from ruminants. Thus many of the features of camels, such as their ability to ruminate ("chew cud") and their cheek teeth with crescent-shaped crests (selenodont teeth), must have evolved independently from ruminants.

Like horses, camels started as small animals with low-crowned teeth, and through their evolution they developed higher-crowned teeth, larger body size, and especially longer limbs. The example of camel evolution is nowhere near as famous as that of the horse, even though it is just as powerful a demonstration of an evolving lineage through time. This is partially because the evolution of the horse has been portrayed as a simple linear trend through time (even though this is an oversimplification). Camel evolution is complex and branching (figure 13.2) with many different evolutionary pathways and cannot be easily simplified. The other problem is that until very recently camel evolution was poorly documented or understood, because huge collections of fossil camels in the Frick Collection of the American Museum of Natural History had not yet been fully studied or published—and some parts are *still* not studied.

Camels originated in North America in the middle Eocene about 45 Ma and had a huge evolutionary radiation on that continent. They came in every shape and size, from the tiny to the gigantic. Late in their evolution history some of them spread to Africa and Asia about eight million years ago, while the lamine lineage spread to South America around 3.5 million years ago (figure 13.2).

The earliest known camel fossil is *Poebrodon*, from middle Eocene beds in Utah and California that were about forty-five million years old. It was a tiny creature about the size of a housecat. No skeletons of it are known, but the skull and teeth are distinctive—and it already had the highest-crowned teeth of any mammal of its time.

In the late Eocene-early Oligocene about 33 Ma, the common camel from the Badlands was *Poebrotherium*, which was discussed previously. It was about the size of a goat. It had longer limbs, a larger skull and higher-crowned teeth (figure 13.3A and figure 13.3B). In the late Oligocene, it was followed by *Paratylopus* from beds around 30 Ma at the top level of the Badlands (figure 13.3C). In addition, there were several other camels at this time that were once highly confused, including *Pseudolabis* and *Miotylopus*. *Pseudolabis* was first named and recognized by Matthew himself. Another camel studied by Matthew but named by Richard Swann Lull in 1921 was *Paralabis*, but unfortunately that genus name was already given to a genus of earwig insect. In 2011, I published a replacement name, *Matthewlabis*, in honor of Matthew's many contributions to understanding camels. In 1982 (published in 1996), I had the opportunity to sort all of these camels out

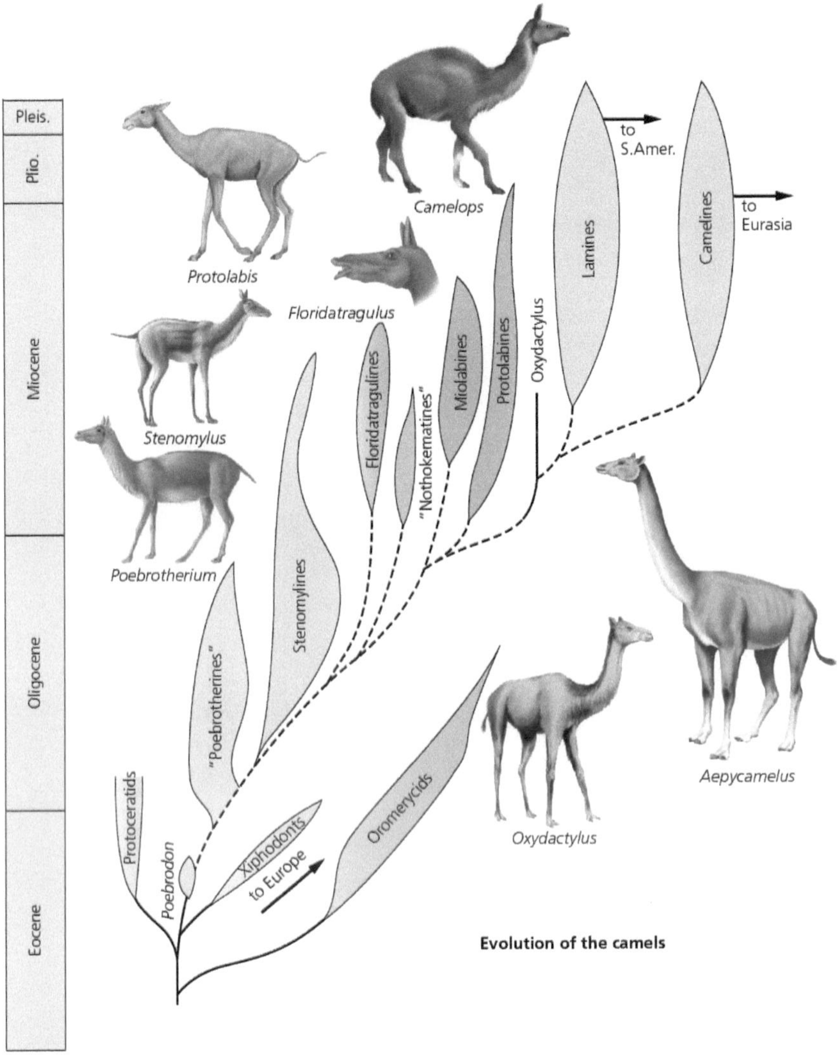

Figure 13.2 ▲
Family tree of camels. (Diagram by the author)

with lots of new specimens from the Frick Collection, so they are no longer a taxonomic mess.

By the late Oligocene, about 29 Ma, a lineage of camels known as the stenomylines split off from the main line of camel evolution (figure 13.2). They included the primitive genera *Pseudolabis* and *Miotylopus*, as well as

Figure 13.3 ▲

(*A*) Skeleton of *Poebrotherium* on display at the Natural History Museum of Los Angeles County. (Photo by the author). (*B*) Reconstruction of *Poebrotherium* by Jay Matternes (Courtesy of Wikimedia Commons). (*C*) Reconstruction of *Paratylopus* by R. Bruce Horsfall (Courtesy of Wikimedia Commons)

the more advanced genera, *Stenomylus, Rakomylus*, and *Blickomylus*. These camels were a taxonomic nightmare until my student Kristin Watmore and I published a complete update of all the valid species. Advanced stenomylines had a delicate gazelle-like body structure, with very long slender limbs (figure 13.4A and figure 13.4B). There were huge herds of specimens found in the *Stenomylus* Quarry, not far from Agate fossil beds in western Nebraska. The most distinctive feature of the tribe Stenomylini is their incredibly narrow, long, high-crowned last molars (upper and lower third molars), with roots that reached deep in their skulls and jaws (figure 13.4C). These teeth were almost as high-crowned as the cheek teeth of modern horses, but these stenomyline camels developed these teeth about 23 Ma, long before horses evolved high crowned teeth, and before grasslands evolved. Why they did so is still a mystery.

Another side branch of camel evolution were the floridatragulines (figure 13.5A and figure 13.5B). They had extremely long narrow snouts, shaped almost like that of a crocodile or gavial, but their low-crowned cheek teeth show they were primitive camels that ate soft vegetation. They are known only from the swampy coastal regions of Florida, Texas, Mexico, and Panama and are seldom found in the drier regions of the High Plains.

The main line of camel evolution (figure 13.2) continued with *Oxydactylus*, from lower Miocene beds deposited about 19–23 Ma. It is the first lineage of camels with relatively long necks and long legs (figure 13.6A and figure 13.6B). At one time, *Oxydactylus* had become a giant taxonomic wastebasket for almost all early Miocene camels, but my former student Daniella Balassa and I revised the group, and now only one species, *Oxydactylus longipes*, is considered valid. Matthew had named two other species of *Oxydactylus*, which were unpublished at the time of his death, so J. Reid Macdonald had them published under both of their names. Unfortunately, modern analysis using the bigger sample from the Frick Collection shows that neither of these species is valid.

The next side branch is the miolabine camels, including *Miolabis, Paramiolabis, Nothotylopus*, and *Cuyamacamelus*, which are distinctive for their relatively short limbs compared to other camels, with no fusion of the elongated wrist and ankle bones, or metapodials, into a "cannon bone," as is found in all the advanced camels and all ruminants as well. Miolabines also have distinctive "cupped" crowns of their lower incisors, which radiate in a circular arc on the front of the lower jaw. These camels were particularly

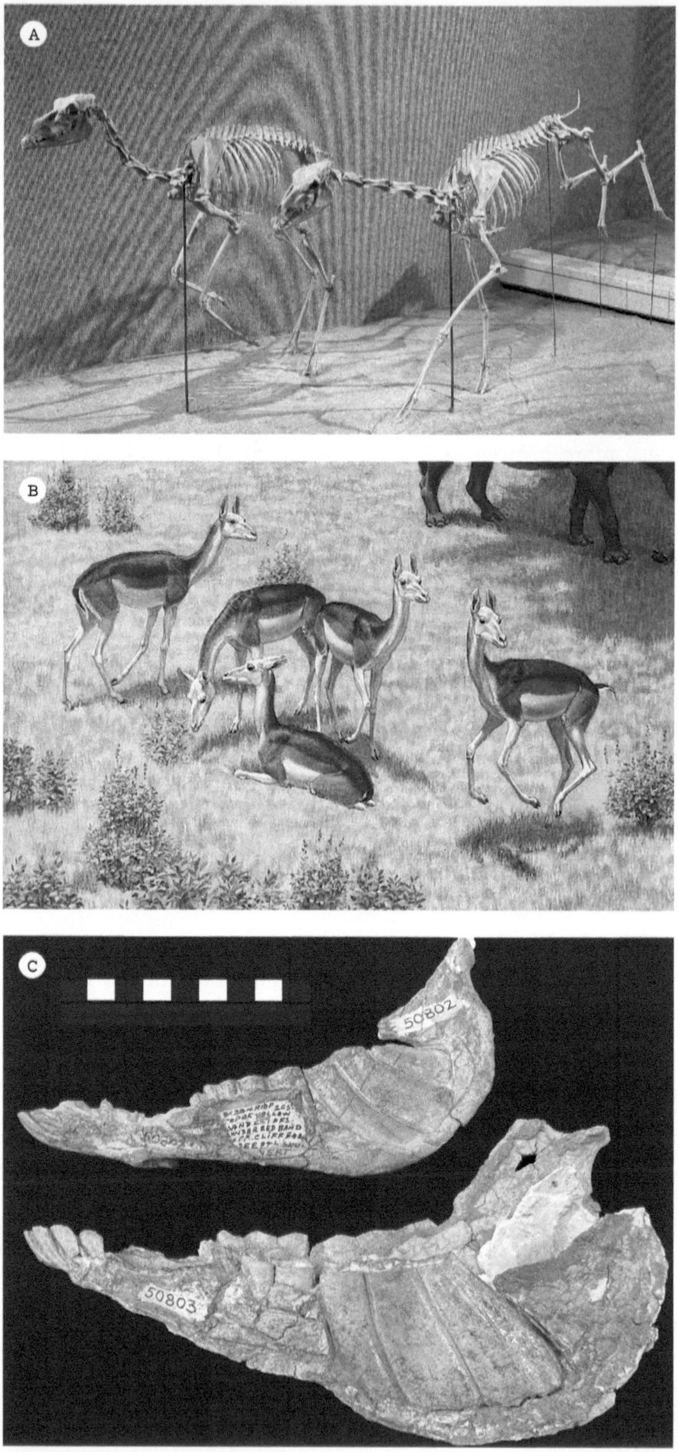

Figure 13.4 ▲

Stenomylines. (*A*) Skeletons of *Stenomylus* on display at the Denver Museum of Nature and Science. (*B*) Reconstruction of *Stenomylus* by Jay Matternes. (*C*) Jaws of the stenomyline *Blickomylus*, showing the extraordinarily long and deep last molars. ([*A*] Photo by the author; [*B*] courtesy of Wikimedia Commons; [*C*] photo by the author)

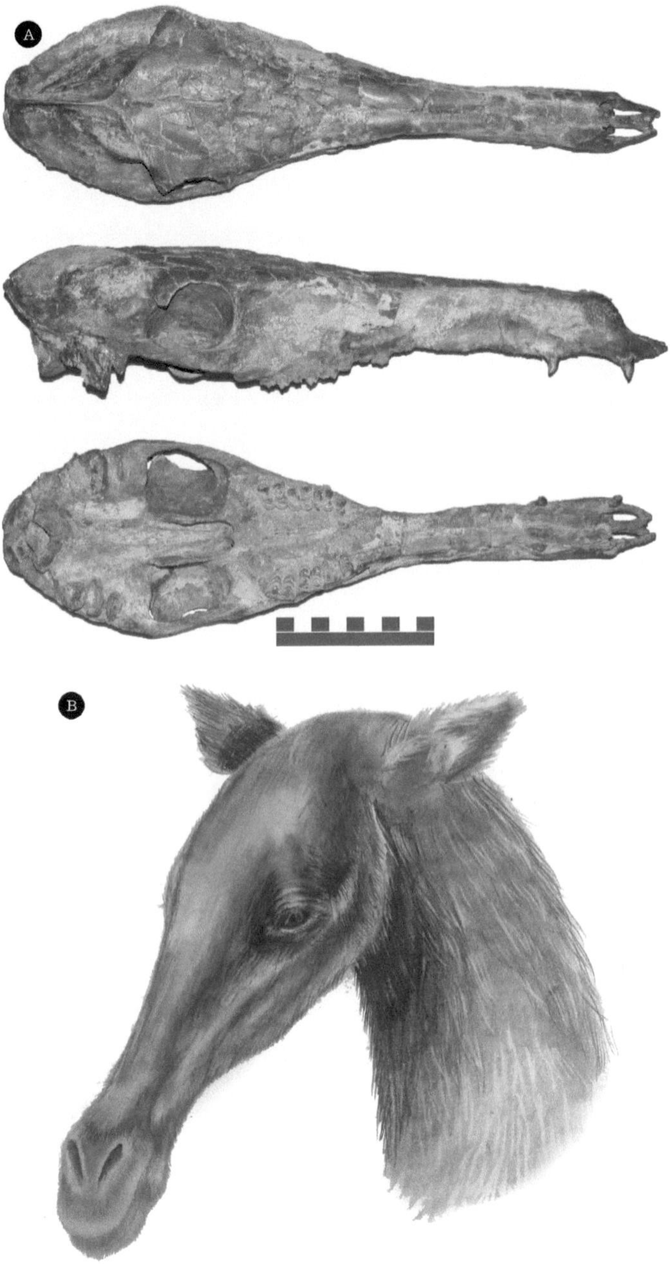

Figure 13.5 ▲

The long-snouted camel *Floridatragulus*. (*A*) Three views of type skull. (*B*) Reconstruction by K. Marriott. ([*A*] Photo by the author; [*B*] courtesy of K. Marriott).

Figure 13.6 ▲

The long-necked early Miocene camel *Oxydactylus*. (*A*) Skeleton of type specimen in the Carnegie Museum of Natural History. (Photo by the author). (*B*) Reconstruction of *Oxydactylus.* by R. Bruce Horsfall ([*A*] Photo by the author; [*B*] courtesy of Wikimedia Commons).

abundant in the middle Miocene, often found in the same beds with other more advanced camels. One miolabine genus is named *Capricamelus*, the "goat camel." It was found in upper Pliocene beds about 3 Ma in the Tecopa Dry Lake beds near Death Valley. Its limbs were very short and stumpy, like those of goats and other rock climbers, so apparently it was a camel convergently evolving to imitate a mountain goat.

Yet another tribe is the protolabines, including the genera *Protolabis, Tanymykter*, and *Michenia*, which were common from about 19 Ma until almost the beginning of the Pleistocene. They are distinctive in their highly pinched snouts and their unusual front teeth. They were very abundant in the early through late Miocene, with their earliest occurrence in the early Miocene Agate fossil beds, *Michenia agatensis*. They are frequently found in many Miocene localities, along with miolabines, as well as more advanced camels.

The lineage that leads to llamas (figure 13.2) begins with the giraffe-like camel *Aepycamelus* (figure 13.7). It was originally discovered by Matthew in 1899 from the Pawnee Creek beds of northeastern Colorado and called *Alticamelus*, in reference to its long neck and legs. As Matthew wrote in 1901:

> The discovery of this specimen introduces to science one of the most interesting instances of convergence yet observed. The effect of extreme height, in order to enable the animal to feed upon the inaccessible foliage of high and thorny shrubs, is obtained in this species, as in the giraffe, by the elongation of the neck vertebrae and the legs. But the giraffe is derived from the early antelopes and this animal is from early camels and the difference of origin has caused the attainment of the desired result in a somewhat different manner.[3]

Unfortunately, Matthew tied the genus name *Alticamelus altus* to some nondiagnostic ankle bones named *Procamelus altus* by Marsh, so it was not a valid name, which is why J. Reid Macdonald had to rename the genus *Aepycamelus*. The giraffe-camel is found from the early middle through late Miocene, from beds about 18–7 Ma. *Aepycamelus* had the longest necks and legs of any camel and probably performed the roles of giraffes on the North American savanna because giraffes themselves were never native to the Americas.

After *Aepycamelus*, the rest of the North American lamine camels including the Pleistocene species *Palaeolama mirifica*, plus *Pleiolama vera*, which originated in South America and then migrated back to North America. Some analyses suggest that Leidy's *Camelops* (figure 13.8), including the

Figure 13.7 ▲
Reconstruction of the long-necked giraffe-like camel *Aepycamelus* by R. Bruce Horsfall (Courtesy of Wikimedia Commons)

common species from La Brea Tar Pits, *Camelops hesternus*, also belongs in the tribe Lamini. *Camelops* is frequently reconstructed with a hump, although if it is a lamine camel, it would not have had a hump. *Camelops* lasted until the end of the Ice Ages, about eleven thousand years ago, when it vanished along with most of the rest of the North American megafauna. About 3.5 Ma, the lamine camels crossed the newly formed Panamanian land bridge and reached South America, where they evolved into the vicuñas of the Andes and the guanacos of the Pampas, and their domesticated descendants, alpacas and llamas.

Figure 13.8 ▲
Mounted skeleton of *Camelops hesternus* from La Brea Tar Pits. (Photo by the author)

Meanwhile, the tribe Camelini began with *Procamelus*, a camel whose fossils are often mistaken for *Aepycamelus* except that *Procamelus* was not a giraffe-camel and has relatively short neck and legs and higher-crowned cheek teeth (among other differences). The tribe Camelini then evolved a series of huge camels, including *Megatylopus*, *Megacamelus*, *Gigantocamelus*, and *Titanotylopus*, which were almost as tall as elephants. *Gigantocamelus* had distinctive broad spatulate lower incisors (figure 13.9A and figure 13.9B).

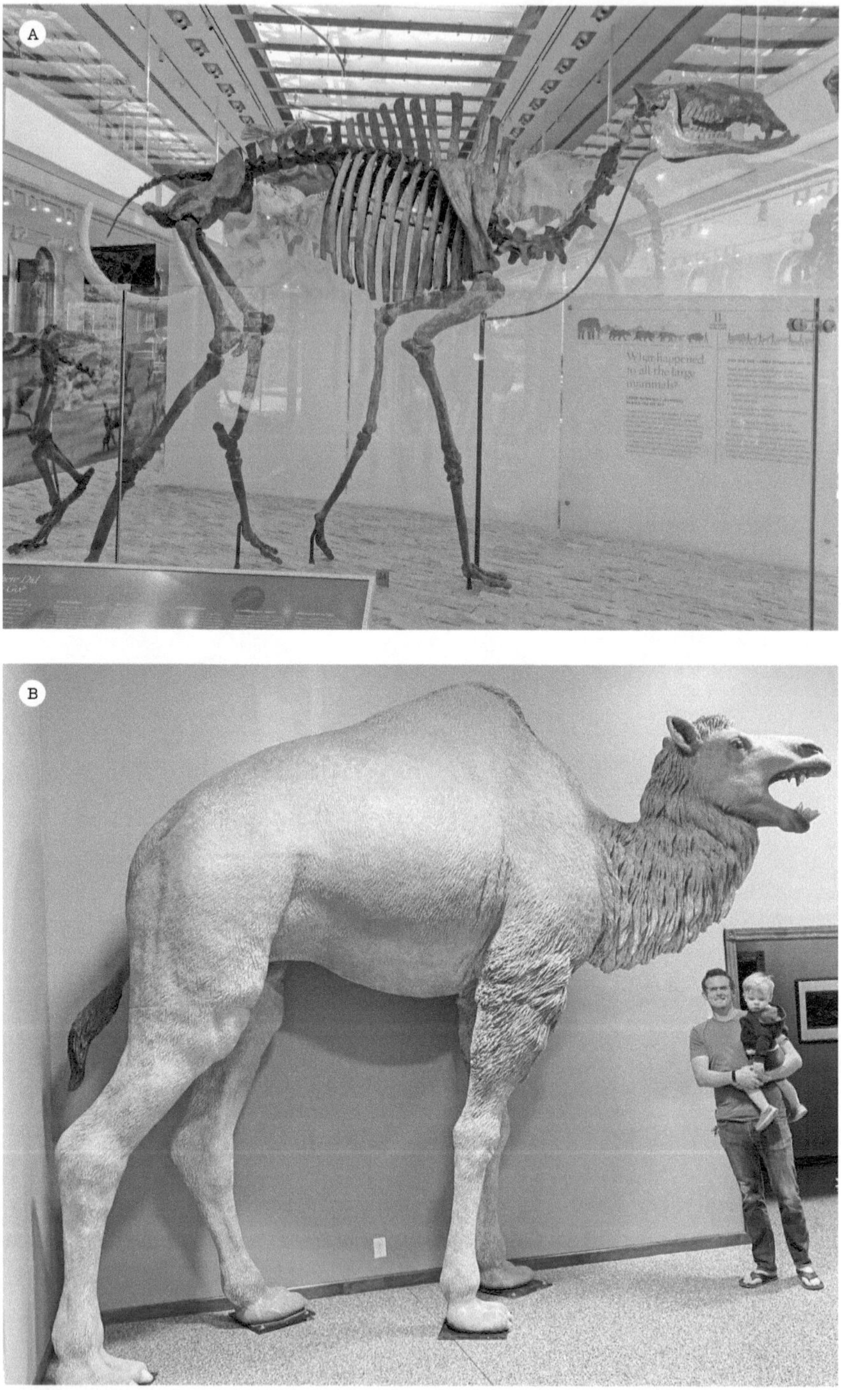

Figure 13.9 ▲ ▶

Giant camels. (*A*) Mounted skeleton of *Gigantocamelus*, on display at the Natural History Museum of Los Angeles County. (*B*) Reconstruction of *Gigantocamelus*. (*C*) Author holding the meter-long skull of *Megacamelus*. (Photos by the author)

Figure 13.9 ▲
(continued)

It was found in the late Miocene through early Pleistocene beds from California to Nebraska, one of the last camelids to vanish from North America until the extinction of *Camelops*. Its shoulder height reached 12 feet (3.5 meters), and it weight about 5,500 pounds (2,500 kilograms). *Titanotylopus* was of a similar size and build, but with slight differences in the lower jaw and in the limb bones. *Megatylopus*, originally described by Matthew from the Snake Creek beds of western Nebraska, ranged from the late Miocene to the Pliocene and was about 11 feet (3.4 meters) in shoulder height. Finally, *Megacamelus* was the biggest camel ever known. It was found in late Miocene and Pliocene beds from California to Florida, and reached 14 feet (4.2 meters) at the shoulder, with a skull over a meter long (figure 13.9C).

The tribe Camelini were restricted to North America until about 8 Ma, when *Paracamelus* migrated to Eurasia and eventually evolved into the modern dromedary and Bactrian camels.

Camels had an incredibly rich evolutionary history (figure 13.2), mostly in North America, and came in lots of different shapes and sizes compared to the few species alive today. Although the wild Bactrian camels are now critically endangered in the wild, the rest of the species are not. In addition, there will always be a huge population of the species that we have turned into domesticated animals.

NOTES

1. W. D. Matthew, "Third Contribution to the Snake Creek Fauna," *American Museum of Natural History Bulletin* 50 (1924): 59–210.
2. David M. S. Watson, *Obituary Notices of the Royal Society of London*, vol.1 (1932): 72–74.
3. W. D. Matthew, *Fossil Mammals of the Tertiary of Northeastern Colorado*, American Museum Collection of 1898: American Museum of Natural History Memoirs, vol. 1 (1901): 353–447.

FOR FURTHER READING

Colbert, E. H., *William Diller Matthew, Paleontologist*. Columbia University Press, 1993.

Harrison, J. A., "Giant Camels from the Cenozoic of North America." *Smithsonian Contributions to Paleobiology* 57 (1985): 1–29.

Harrison, J. A. "Revision of the Camelinae (Artiodactyla, Tylopoda) and Description of the New Genus *Alforjas*." *University of Kansas Paleontological Contributions* 95, no. 4 (1979): 1–28.

Honey, J., J. A. Harrison, D. R. Prothero, and M. S. Stevens. "Camelidae." In *Evolution of Tertiary Mammals of North America*, ed. C. Janis, K. M. Scott, and L. Jacobs, 439–462. Cambridge University Press, 1998.

Janis, C., J. Theodor, and B. Boisvert. "Locomotor Evolution in Camels Revisited: A Quantitative Analysis of Pedal Anatomy and the Evolution of the Pacing Gait." *Journal of Vertebrate Paleontology* 22, no. 1 (2002): 110–121.

Prothero, D. R. "Camelidae." In *The Terrestrial Eocene-Oligocene Transition in North America*, ed. D. R. Prothero and R. J. Emry, 591–633. Cambridge University Press, 1996.

——. *The Princeton Field Guide to Prehistoric Mammals.* Princeton University Press, 2016.

——. *Vertebrate Evolution: From Origins to Dinosaurs and Beyond.* Taylor & Francis/CRC Press, 2022.

Prothero, D. R., B. L. Beatty, and K. Marriott. "Systematics of the Long-Nosed Floridatraguline Camels (Mammalia: Artiodactyla: Camelidae)." *New Mexico Museum of Natural History Bulletin* 94 (2023): 533–545.

Prothero, D. R., and R. M. Schoch. *Horns, Tusks, and Flippers: The Evolution of Hoofed Mammals.* Johns Hopkins University Press, 2002.

Prothero, D. R., and others (eds.). "The Evolution of North American Camels." *New Mexico Natural History Museum Bulletin*, 2026.

Semprebon, G. M., and F. Rivals, "Trends in the paleodietary habits of fossil camels from the Tertiary and Quaternary of North America." *Palaeogeography, Palaeoclimatology, Palaeoecology*, v. 295, p.131-145, 2010.

Spaulding, M., M. A. O'Leary, and J. Gatesy. "Relationships of Cetacea (Artiodactyla) Among Mammals: Increased Taxon Sampling Alters Interpretations of Key Fossils and Character Evolution." *PLoS ONE* 4, no. 9 (2009): e7062.

Ursing, B. M., K. E. Slack, and U. Arnason. "Subordinal Artiodactyl Relationships in the Light of Phylogenetic Analysis of 12 Mitochondrial Protein-Coding Genes." *Zoologica Scripta* 29, no. 2 (2000): 83–88.

Watmore, K. I., and D. R. Prothero. "Dietary Modifications of the Teeth in the Early Miocene Stenomyline Camels (Artiodactyla: Camelidae)." *New Mexico Museum of Natural History Bulletin* 94 (2023):699–702.

Webb, S. D. "The Osteology of *Camelops*." *Los Angeles County Museum of Natural History Bulletin, Science*, no. 1 (1965): 1–53.

Whistler, D. P., and S. D. Webb. "New Goatlike Camelid from the Late Pliocene of Tecopa Lake Basin, California." *Contributions in Science* 503 (2005): 1–40.

14 GIRAFFES WITH SHORT NECKS

SAMOTHERIUM

The giraffe, by its lofty stature, much elongated neck, fore-legs, head and tongue, has its whole frame beautifully adapted for browsing on the higher branches of trees. It can thus obtain food beyond the reach of the other Ungulata or hoofed animals inhabiting the same country; and this must be a great advantage to it during dearths. . . . So under nature with the nascent giraffe the individuals which were the highest browsers, and were able during dearth to reach even an inch or two above the others, will often have been preserved; for they will have roamed over the whole country in search of food. . . . Those individuals which had some one part or several parts of their bodies rather more elongated than usual, would generally have survived. These will have intercrossed and left offspring, either inheriting the same bodily peculiarities, or with a tendency to vary again in the same manner; whilst the individuals, less favoured in the same respects will have been the most liable to perish. . . . By this process long-continued, which exactly corresponds with what I have called unconscious selection by man, combined no doubt in a most important manner with the inherited effects of the increased use of parts, it seems to me almost certain that an ordinary hoofed quadruped might be converted into a giraffe.

—**CHARLES DARWIN, *ON THE ORIGIN OF SPECIES***

THE SIWALIK HILLS

The story of the discovery of the evolution of giraffes begins with a colorful pioneering Scottish paleontologist, Hugh Falconer (figure 14.1). Born on Leap Year's Day in 1808, in Forres, near Elgin, Scotland, he was just four years older than his friend and colleague, Charles Darwin. He graduated from the University of Aberdeen in 1826, where he studied natural history,

Figure 14.1

A portrait of the pioneering Scottish paleontologist Hugh Falconer. (Courtesy of Wikimedia Commons)

then attended medical school at the University of Edinburgh, getting his MD in 1829. This was a few years after Charles Darwin attended medical classes in Edinburgh in 1825, so they just missed overlapping at medical school. At the University of Edinburgh, Falconer also learned botany from Robert Graham and studied geology under Robert Jameson, one of the last scholars to follow Abraham Gottlob Werner's "Neptunist" school of geology, which claimed that all layered rocks were laid down in water, including lava flows.

In 1830, Falconer became the assistant surgeon in the Bengal Establishment of the British East India Company. He immediately examined some bones from Burma and described and published them, building his scientific reputation in India. Falconer was then stationed with the British army at Meerut in northwestern India, and this was followed by becoming Superintendent of the Saharanpur Botanical Garden, where he remained from 1832 to 1842. Meanwhile, beginning in 1831, Falconer and his colleagues ventured into the Siwalik Hills of western British India (what is now Pakistan) and brought back tons of fossils. These included everything from crocodiles and gigantic tortoises to mastodonts, antelopes, rhinos, pigs, hippos, plus one of the first fossil apes ever found (*Sivapithecus*), and many other strange beasts from Asia that were unknown to science.

One of these fossils was a skull he named *Sivatherium* (figure 14.2), a huge powerful beast with a short thick neck and giant ossicones (the horn-like cranial appendages found in giraffids) that somewhat resembled moose antlers. It was about 7.2 feet (2.2 meters) tall at the shoulder, 10 feet (3 meters) in total height, and weighed up to 3,000 pounds (1,360 kilograms). As Falconer and Cautley first described it in 1836:

> The form of the head is so singular and grotesque, that the first glance at it strikes one with surprise. The prominent features are—Ist, the great size, approaching that of the elephant: 2d, the immense development and width of the cranium behind the orbits: 3d, the two divergent osseous cores for horns starting out from the brow between the orbits: 4th, the form and direction of the nasal bones, rising with great prominence out of the chaffron, and overhanging the external nostrils in a pointed arch: 5th, the great massiveness, width and shortness of the face forward from the orbits: 6th, the great angle at which the grinding plane of the molars deviates upwards from that of the base of the skull. Viewed in lateral profile, the form and direction of the horns, and the rise and sweep in the bones of the nose, give a character to the head widely differing from that of any other animal. The nose looks something like that of the rhinoceros; but the resemblance is deceptive, and only owing to the muzzle being truncated. Seen from in front, the head is somewhat wedge-shaped, the greatest width being at the vertex and thence gradually compressed towards the muzzle; with contraction only at two points behind the orbits and under the molars.[1]

Falconer could not tell what kind of ruminant *Sivatherium* was from a single skull, although he was inclined to think it was a bovid related to antelopes and cattle, or possibly a link between ruminants and "pachyderms" (elephants, rhinos, horses, and tapirs) because of the huge size and robust limbs.

In 1845, Falconer described another huge giraffid from the Siwalik Hills. Keeping to the theme of naming fossils after Hindu deities, he called it *Bramatherium*. It was built much like *Sivatherium* but had a set of four radiating ossicones, rather than the ossicones shaped like moose antlers seen in *Sivatherium*. By 1845, Falconer suspected that both *Sivatherium* and *Bramatherium* might be related to giraffes, although the evidence was not yet clear. It wasn't until 1882 that Richard Lydekker of the British Museum confirmed

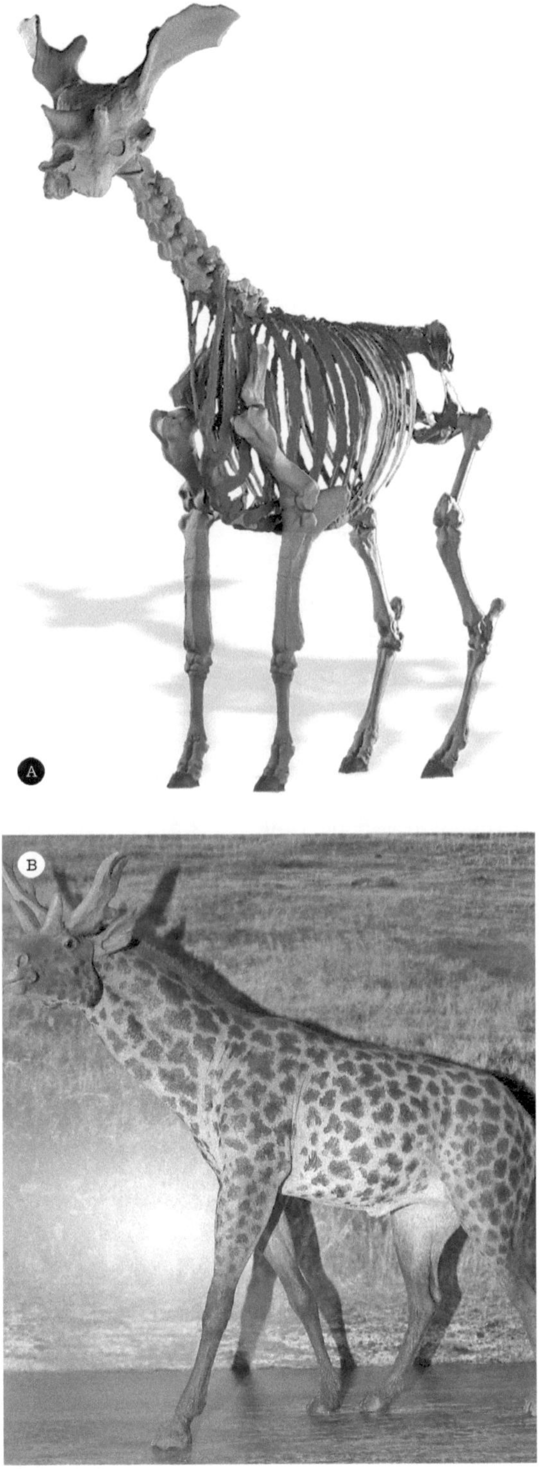

Figure 14.2 ▲

Sivatherium. (*A*) A skeletal reconstruction of the extinct giraffid *Sivatherium*. (*B*) Reconstruction. (Courtesy of Wikimedia Commons)

that Falconer's *Sivatherium* and *Bramatherium* were giraffids, along with *Vishnutherium* and *Hydaspitherium* from the Siwaliks, which Lydekker himself had described.

In 1842, Falconer had to come home to Britain because of bad health and brought with him 70 large chests of dried plants and 48 cases of fossils to study. But in 1847 he returned to India after being appointed the superintendent of the Calcutta Botanical Gardens, where he stayed until 1855, finally returning to England again because of ill health. Once back in England, he focused on fossils he brought back from India, along with many other fossils that came his way. Working on fossil bones brought from Pleistocene caves in Sicily, Malta, and Gibraltar, Falconer was one of the first to recognize the principles of island dwarfing (see chapter 2) with his studies of the dwarf elephants on Sicily and Malta (one of the dwarfs is now named *Palaeoloxodon falconeri* in his honor).

Falconer had been raised as a creationist, but he had enormous experience with the fossil record of mammals. Charles Darwin thought that Falconer, an experienced paleontologist with a good reputation, might be receptive to his views. In November 1859, Darwin sent a copy of his newly published *On the Origin of Species* to Falconer, with a note reading, "I am fully convinced that you will become, year after year, less fixed in your belief in the immutability of species." Falconer replied with a thank-you letter in June 1861, and soon began to reassess his views based on his extensive knowledge of the fossil record. In 1862 he sent Darwin a note pointing out that in his studies most fossil organisms showed little obvious change over time, even in the face of climate change. His evidence was strongest with his research on fossil proboscideans, and in 1863 he wrote:

> If we cast a glance back on the long vista of physical changes which our planet has undergone since the Neozoic Epoch, we can nowhere detect signs of a revolution more sudden and pronounced, and more important in its results, than the intercalation and subsequent disappearance of the Glacial period. Yet the mammoth lived before it, and passed through the ordeal of all the hard extremities which it involved, bearing his organs of locomotion and digestion all but unchanged[2]

Later scientists pointed out that Falconer made the first cogent argument for stasis despite climate changes in the fossil record, and how it anticipated aspects of the theory of punctuated equilibria, published by Niles Eldredge and Stephen Jay Gould in 1972.

Falconer died suddenly on January 31, 1865, of rheumatic disease in his heart and lungs; he was only fifty-six years old. He was a pioneer in many areas of paleontology as well as botany, and he died in the prime of his life. Who knows how many more discoveries he might have made had he lived to finish his work?

BARNUM'S CIRCUS

Barnum Brown was one of the greatest fossil collectors who ever lived, and he probably found more important fossils than anyone in his time or before (figure 14.3). A short list of the famous dinosaurs he discovered includes theropods *Tyrannosaurus rex, Albertosaurus, Struthiomimus, Dromaeosaurus*, and the ankylosaurs *Ankylosaurus, Euoplocephalus*, and *Edmontonia*, the duckbills *Corythosaurus, Kritosaurus, Hypacrosaurus, Saurolophus, Prosaurolophus*, and *Parasaurolophus*, and many ceratopsians including *Chasmosaurus, Leptoceratops, Centrosaurus*, and of course *Triceratops*, as well as many Morrison sauropods. Even though most people haven't heard of him

Figure 14.3

Portrait of the legendary fossil collector Barnum Brown in about 1920. (Courtesy of the American Museum Digital Library)

today, he is considered to be a giant in the field. As his biographers Lowell Dingus and Mark Norell wrote:

> Among paleontologists, Barnum Brown is almost universally recognized as the greatest fossil collector of all time, and although his name is no longer widely recognized among the general public, the name of the most famous dinosaur he ever discovered—*Tyrannosaurus rex*—most certainly is. The fossils he unearthed across continents from the Americas to Asia vastly expanded our knowledge not only of the evolution of dinosaurs but also of most major groups of reptiles and mammals. Crucial to his success was a penchant for eccentricity and risk, both professionally and personally. His expeditions, many of which he undertook with little or no backup, even from his trusted companions, led him to several of our planet's most remote and dangerous regions. As if that weren't risky enough, Brown often used his guise as a bone digger to cover a second, clandestine role as an American intelligence agent, gathering strategic geologic and geographic data that would aid both the country's exploration for oil and the government's war efforts.[3]

Brown's career started modestly. Born in Carbondale, Kansas, on the 64th anniversary of Abraham Lincoln's and Charles Darwin's birthday (February 12, 1873), he was named after the famous showman and circus founder, P. T. Barnum. However, no one could foresee the amazing show that Brown's fossil discoveries would eventually become. As Gil Troy wrote:

> The parental impasse over what to name the young lad ended after a few days when P. T. Barnum's dazzling circus visited. "There must be something in a name," Brown, who had his own genius for self-promotion would say "for I have always been in the business of running a fossil menagerie."[4]

His family lived on top of the Carboniferous coal beds of eastern Kansas. His father not only maintained a ranch but spent much of the Civil War running supplies in a wagon from the railheads in Kansas to remote outposts all over the Plains. He also had a small-scale strip-mining operation for coal on his land, which was much cheaper to collect locally than to ship via rail and wagons from remote coal mines. As the workers stripped away the rock from over the coal seams, they found incredibly fossiliferous limestones, as well as beautiful fossil ferns and other plants in the coal itself.

Barnum's love of fossils then led him to enroll at the University of Kansas where he studied paleontology under Samuel Wendell Williston (one of Marsh's early collectors), as well as learning the geology of his state and of coal and other fossil fuels such as oil. Williston wrote that he was "the best man in the field that I ever had. He is very energetic, has great powers of endurance, walking thirty miles a day without fatigue, is very methodical in all his habits, and thoroughly honest." During summer breaks in the mid-1890s, he went on university trips to the Big Badlands of South Dakota and the plains of Wyoming, where he discovered his aptitude for strenuous fieldwork and fossil collecting. In 1896, he was hired as part of a field crew for the American Museum collecting Eocene mammals in the San Juan Basin of New Mexico and the Bighorn Basin of Wyoming. He was such a talented collector that he was hired right away, even though he had not yet graduated from the University of Kansas. (He finally got his degree ten years later.) In 1897, he was an apprentice collector in the American Museum crew in Medicine Bow, Wyoming, where they found Morrison dinosaurs in abundance. Soon he was sent anywhere the American Museum needed a hardy, sharp-eyed, self-sufficient field collector. Dingus and Norell described it this way:

> On a December morning in 1898, a 25-year-old paleontologist named Barnum Brown trudged through the snow-choked streets of New York City for what he thought would be a routine day at the American Museum of Natural History. But before he could remove his hat, his supervisor, Henry Fairfield Osborn, anxiously summoned him. "Brown," he said, "I want you to go to Patagonia today with the Princeton expedition . . . to represent the American Museum. The boat leaves at 11; will you go?" "This is short notice," Brown replied. "But I'll be on that boat if . . . I [can] go home to pack my personal belongings and arrange for my absence." Although he had never been out of the country before, Brown did not return for almost a year and a half. In Patagonia he prospected for fossils largely on his own. On one excursion, he was shipwrecked off the Patagonian coast when a large wave slammed his small cutter; despite not knowing how to swim, Brown floated safely to shore grasping a barrel. By befriending the locals, he got his project back on track and eventually shipped 4.5 tons of fossil mammal bones back to the museum. Brown's gamble—to strike out by himself to search for fossils in a foreign land—established a precedent for his expeditions and launched his legendary career.[5]

After his Patagonia trip, Brown then spent nearly every field season for the next decade in the Hell Creek beds of Montana, where he found the first *T. rex, Ankylosaurus*, and many other dinosaurs. Between 1910 and 1915, he worked in the Red Deer River badlands of Alberta, where he discovered Late Cretaceous dinosaur fossils from 70–75 Ma, older than the latest Cretaceous Hell Creek fossils which are about 66–70 Ma. In Canada, he competed with the Sternberg family, who were commercial collectors hired by the Canadian government through the Royal Ontario Museum to find their native fossils—but Brown brought back amazing specimens that are now on display or in storage at the American Museum. He finished working in Canada in 1916, then went to Cuba in 1918, and back to the Rockies in 1918 and 1919.

After the First World War travel restrictions ended, he again went abroad and added to the American Museum's collections from many regions, including fossils from Ethiopia and Egypt in 1920–1921, Miocene mammals from the Siwalik Hills of India (what is now Pakistan) and Burma (now Myanmar) from 1922–1923, and Miocene mammals form the Greek island of Samos in 1923 and 1924.

Brown was legendary for his fieldwork and collecting prowess, but his personal life was a bit more complicated. He was a real ladies' man, famous for his affairs with rancher's daughters while he was in the field, and for seducing foreign ladies during his travels abroad. I vividly remember my first summer in the field with my graduate advisor Malcolm McKenna of the American Museum in 1977, who had known Brown in his old age. In the 1960s, Malcolm had also visited many of Brown's old localities, and more than once heard the stories of Brown's romantic exploits from the local ranch ladies, who would tell him how they still remembered Barnum Brown—and not for his paleontology. As Dingus and Norell document in their biography of Brown, he often stayed abroad for many months during periods when his New York lawyer was settling lawsuits of jilted lovers, and he had to hastily exit some foreign countries for the same reason.

As Gil Troy wrote:

> Someone that obsessed, who charmed New York's elite, effete Upper West Siders when he returned from his remote, sun-baked dry beds yielding ancient mysteries under layers of rock and dirt, was bound to be complicated. His first wife died of scarlet fever shortly after childbirth. The distraught Brown left

> their daughter to be raised by her grandparents. Brown remarried but, even in those more discrete times, was known as a cad. His second wife Lilian Brown got the last laugh, with a passive-aggressive, neglected-wife-of-a-workaholic memoir: *I Married a Dinosaur*.[6]

His later career was documented by Lowell Dingus and Mark Norell in their excellent biography of him, and by his second wife Lilian McLaughlin Brown (nicknamed "Pixie" by Barnum Brown), who wrote amusing books documenting their travails and triumphs. Her first book was *I Married a Dinosaur* in 1950, about their fieldwork in the Siwalik Hills of Pakistan and side trips to Burma. Her other books included *Cleopatra Slept Here* in 1951, with amusing stories about their escapades in Greece and about Barnum's collecting on the island of Samos, and *Bring 'Em Back Petrified* in 1956, about their field work in Guatemala excavating Ice Age mammals from the bottoms of rivers.

Brown's work in the Siwalik Hills in 1921–1923 was significant. Most of the collections from this region had gone to British museums (mainly the British Museum in London), and few other institutions had specimens. Brown collected crate after crate of Siwalik mammals, some of which have still not been opened. But some of the specimens included excellent skulls of *Sivatherium* and *Bramatherium*, which were on display at the American Museum for a long time were moved back to storage when the mammal exhibits were revamped in the early 1990s. From the older beds, Brown recovered a skull of the very primitive giraffid, *Giraffokeryx*, which was originally described by Guy Pilgrim in 1910, just based on teeth and jaws. Brown's specimen had a pair of pointed horns flaring from its snout, and a pair of sharply pointed ossicones on the back of its head (figure 14.4). Brown himself did not have time to do much research or publish his enormous Siwalik collections. They ended up being studied by the young Edwin H. Colbert, who had originally been hired by the Museum to be Osborn's assistant, then worked on writing up and publishing most of Brown's mammal collections. When Brown retired, Colbert became his successor as Curator of Fossil Reptiles and shifted his focus to dinosaurs, for which he is much better known.

Brown's collections from Samos in 1923 and 1924 were even more significant. The island of Samos had many ancient myths and legends associated with it. As Solounias and Mayor (2005) described, an ancient Greek

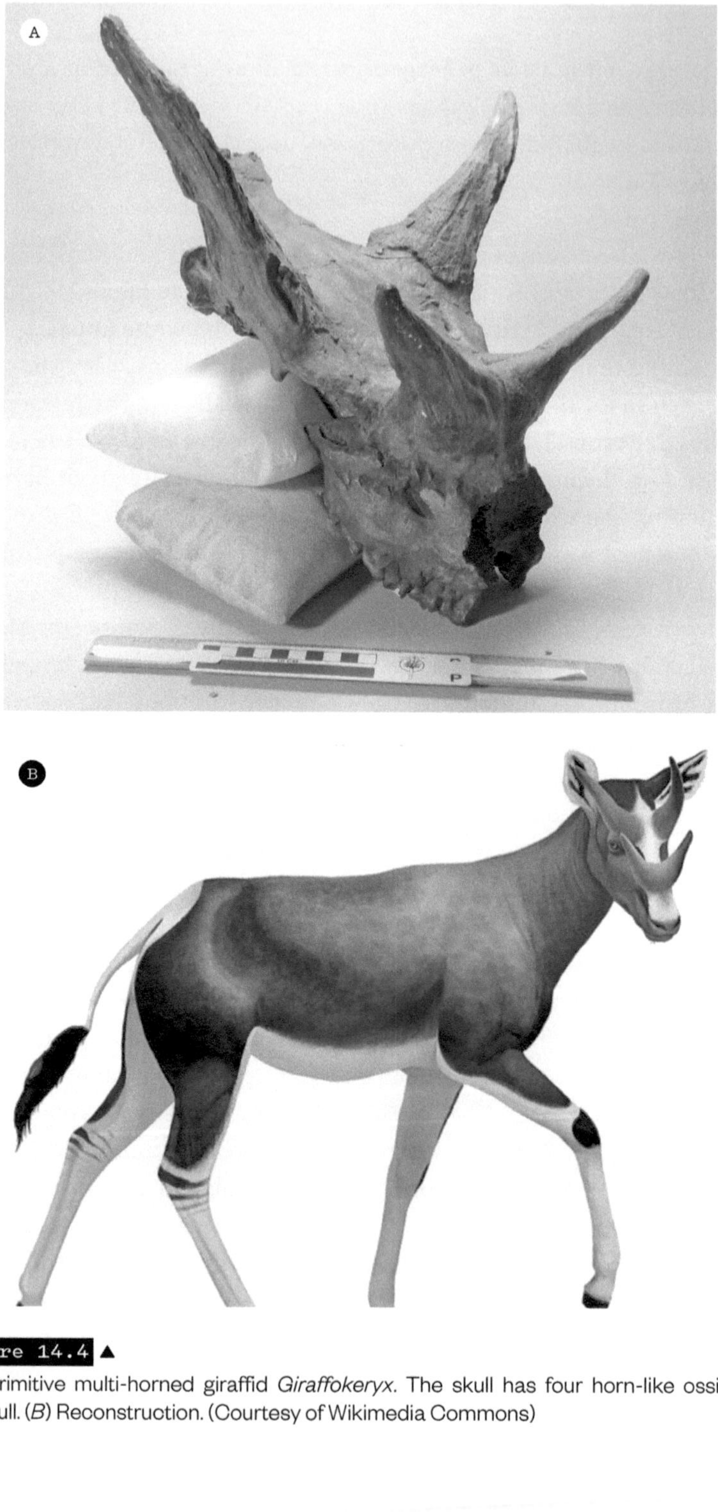

Figure 14.4 ▲

The primitive multi-horned giraffid *Giraffokeryx*. The skull has four horn-like ossicones (*A*) Skull. (*B*) Reconstruction. (Courtesy of Wikimedia Commons)

geographer named Euphorion wrote about monsters on Samos called the Neades around 200 BCE. The original work is lost, but the Roman natural historian Aelian wrote around 300 CE, "Euphorion says in his memoirs that during the very very old times, Samos became deserted; deserted due to very large and fierce beasts which appeared on it [on Samos], they caused sufferings and were called Neades, and their mere roar could fracture the earth; thus there is a proverb on Samos 'to scream louder than the Neades'." The bones of these monsters were on display, and the red soil at some important fossil localities led to a legend of a gigantic ancient bloodbath taking place on Samos, in a battle between Dionysus and the Amazons. The Samos fossils include fossil horse skulls of hipparions, which might have led to legends of the warriors riding horses in that place. In particular, at a spot called Phloios on Samos, the red soils were associated with elephant bones, and sure enough, there are bones there: Brown's quarry Q1.

The fossils of Samos had originally been collected by the Scottish doctor Charles Immanuel Forsyth Major, who was born in Glasgow but studied at universities in Switzerland and Germany and got his MD in Basel in 1868. By 1886, he stopped his medical practice and focused on collecting fossils in the Greek Islands. In 1887, he discovered bones on Samos and began extensive excavations, which he published in 1889, 1891, and 1894. Among his discoveries was a giraffid he named *Samotherium*, which has two long pointed ossicones (similar to that of the modern giraffe, but narrower and longer) (figure 14.5). As discussed below, recent work by Nikos Solounias and colleagues has shown that *Samotherium major* has a neck intermediate in length between a modern giraffe and the shorter-necked giraffids such as the okapi.

Brown's work opened numerous additional quarries not found by Forsyth Major. Although he did a lot of collecting on Samos by himself, Brown took advantage of the low costs of labor (thanks to the refugees of the Turkish war with Greece) to hire a team of 18 men and 6 women to haul dirt in baskets for "the attractive sum of 35 drachmas (70 cents) per day for men and 20 drachmas per day for the girls." When the work was done, he had 56 cases of beautiful bones, "representing three species of three-toed horses, rhinoceroses . . . many species of antelope and gazelle . . . birds, and a variety of carnivorous mammals", and the short-necked giraffe *Samotherium*.[7]

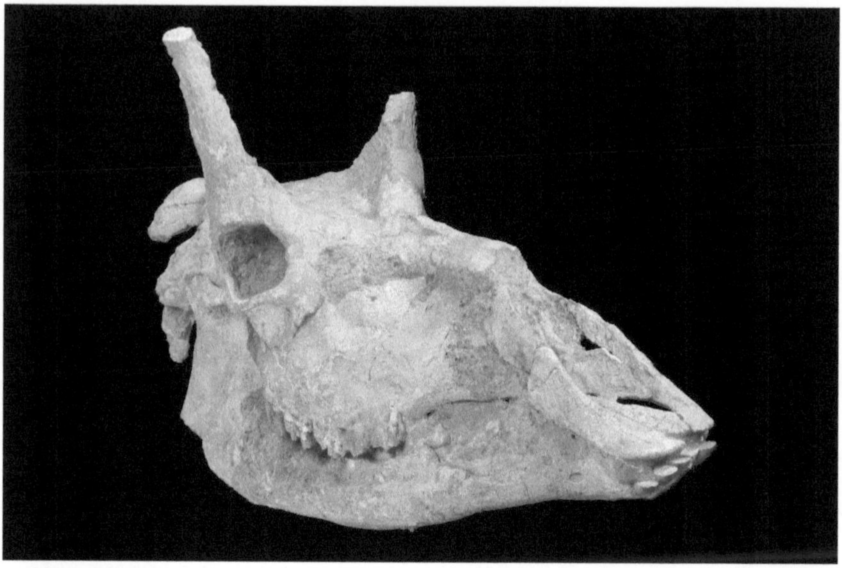

Figure 14.5 ▲
The skull of *Samotherium* has two short, horn-like ossicones on its head. (Courtesy of Wikimedia Commons)

Lilian Brown recounts the crucial moment when Barnum finally found the *Samotherium* specimen he had been seeking after months of work. In her words:

> Niko gulped for breath. "Dr. Brown . . . Dr. Brown wants you at the quarry quick."
>
> "Barnum isn't *hurt?*"
>
> Niko laughed, "Right now he's the happiest man in the world. He's. . . ."
>
> "I know! I know! I shouted. "He's found the *Samotherium*!"
>
> "Is it not wonderful! I was standing right by him when it happened. He was digging a test trench into the right bank and all of a sudden . . ."
>
> I raced to the quarry. A cloud of dust rose from one corner. It was coming from Barnum's pick. He was digging furiously, around him the crew. Pushing through, I touched his arm. He was trembling. Before him, where the clay had been dug away, lay a small skull with sharp pointed horns. Into the bank was a line of long neck bones.

It was several minutes before he spoke. When he did, his voice is shaking with excitement. “This is it! This is what we’ve been waiting for, Pixie! I believe the entire beast is in here—a *Samotherium*! Do you know what this means? The expedition is a success!”

With a whack of the pick, he cut still further into the bank, exposing another vertebrae. “I can see them back at the Museum when they get my wire,” he chortled. “President Osborn will be shouting hallelujahs all over the place”[8]

Once Brown had finished his fieldwork at Samos, he ran into problems shipping his specimens back home to America. Greek authorities pointed to their antiquities laws, which prevented ancient artifacts from leaving Greek soil. However, Brown eventually prevailed because these were fossils, not artifacts. He was helped by an American, Maria Tsipouras, who was married to a high-ranking Greek army officer, and through their combined efforts the specimens were eventually shipped to the American Museum in New York.

As Dingus and Norell wrote:

The peripatetic Brown collected so many specimens on his travels that even today dozens of large boxes of his fossils have yet to be opened. Crates labeled “mammals from Samos” and “ornithomimid from Hell Creek” rest on sanitized racks in the storerooms of the American Museum of Natural History simply because there are not enough staff workers to unpack them, remove the plaster, and prepare them all. As Brown neared his 90th birthday in 1963, his successor at the museum, Edwin Colbert, marveled at how much of the museum was Brown’s single-handed work: “There are, in our Tyrannosaur Hall, 36 North American dinosaurs on display. . . . You collected 27, an unsurpassed achievement.” For all of Brown’s success as a collector, his direct impact as a scientist was strangely modest, compromised by his time abroad and by his laxity in publishing his discoveries. The CV that he compiled for his memoirs—which he never finished—shows that there were only five years between 1897 and his retirement in 1942 in which he did not participate in a major expedition. Yet he penned few scientific papers, and those that he did publish are mostly short notes. On the other hand, his longer publications, like his monograph on *Protoceratops*, a Mongolian relative of the great horned

> dinosaurs, are classics, both for the freshness of the presentation and the quality of the analysis.[9]

Barnum Brown died in 1963 at the ripe old age of eighty-nine. As Dingus and Norell wrote, "First and foremost he was the greatest dinosaur collector the world has ever known. Through Brown's efforts, dinosaurs gained a strong foothold in the psyche of both the scientific community and the general public."[10] As Colbert had noted, Brown collected 24 of the 37 dinosaurs that were once in the Cretaceous Hall in the American Museum (57 of his specimens are currently on display in all the American Museum halls), so his finds were the public face of dinosaur paleontology for almost a century. He was as public a celebrity as any paleontologist was in those days, with weekly radio broadcasts, articles in newspapers, and many public appearances. Brown was also the main consultant on Walt Disney's pioneering movie *Fantasia*, where the dinosaurs and their world were animated to Stravinsky's "The Rite of Spring." This animation of dinosaurs was inspiring and iconic for many generations of future paleontologists (including me). As Dingus and Norell wrote: "Brown's real legacy lies with his discoveries themselves, which still serve as a foundation for numerous geologic and biological research projects in paleontology."

GIRAFFES WITH SHORT NECKS

The neck of the giraffe has long inspired wonder among naturalists who attempt to explain why it is so long and how it got to be that way. Darwin wrote all about it in *On the Origin of Species* (see the epigraph at the beginning of the chapter), attributing it to natural selection for longer and longer necks when hard times killed off the giraffes with shorter necks who could not reach the leaves from the tallest trees. However, in 1809 Jean-Baptiste de Monet, chevalier de Lamarck, used the neck of the giraffe as one of his examples of how creatures change through time:

> It is interesting to observe the result of habit in the peculiar shape and size of the giraffe: this animal, the tallest of the mammals, is known to live in the interior of Africa in places where the soil is nearly always arid and barren, so that it is obliged to browse on the leaves of trees and to make constant efforts to reach them. From this habit long maintained in all its race, it has resulted

> that the animal's forelegs have become longer than its hind-legs, and that its neck is lengthened to such a degree that the giraffe, without standing up on its hind-legs, attains a height of six meters.[11]

This short passage from Lamarck is often used to epitomize his entire complex theory of how life evolves, constantly cited in biology textbooks as well. Like most naturalists of his time, Lamarck thought that changes occurring in our adult bodies could be passed on directly to our descendants (known as the "inheritance of acquired characters"). According to his commonly held idea, the strong muscles of a blacksmith would be passed on to his sons, and the stretching for the highest leaves in a tree by ancestral short-necked giraffes would be passed on to their descendants. In Lamarck's words:

> variations in the environment induce changes in the needs, habits and modes of life of living beings . . . these changes give rise to modifications or developments in their organs and the shape of their parts.[12]

Sadly, this is often the only part of Lamarck's complex notions about evolution that are still remembered today, largely because Lamarck's rival, Baron Georges Cuvier, did his best to destroy and distort Lamarck's legacy after the great man died. In fact, before the discovery of the mechanism of Mendelian inheritance and early genetics in the late 1800s and early 1900s, most naturalists believed in inheritance of acquired characters—including Charles Darwin.

Yet today Lamarck is mocked as the "guy who got evolution wrong," when so many of his ideas were groundbreaking and on the right track. In addition, it was Lamarck who recognized the unity of zoology and botany and even coined the word "biology." Lamarck survived the French Revolution and the Reign of Terror but was forced to switch from botany to take the undesirable post of curator of "Insects and Worms" at the Natural History Museum in Paris. In the process, he ended up revolutionizing and essentially creating our modern field of invertebrate zoology. Unfortunately, the ideas of "Lamarckism" or "Lamarckian inheritance" have been reduced to just one wrong idea that was a minor part of his thinking and held by every naturalist for many decades to come.

This story about giraffe necks is very appealing and seems self-evident—but research on living giraffe behavior shows it is seldom true. In fact, most of the time giraffes feed with their necks held horizontally, and they also feed a lot on ground vegetation with their head down reaching to their feet. This allows them to create a large "feeding envelope," the area their mouths can reach without expending energy to move their feet. Only rarely are they seen reaching for the highest parts of the trees because most parts of the trees are too high for any other browser to reach. In 2010, a study showed that the longest necked individuals died more often than shorter individuals in drought conditions because a longer neck required more nutrients, which are scarce during a drought.

Instead, giraffe biologists have found that longer necks mostly convey reproductive advantage for the males, who tend to be significantly taller than the females. They compete for mates with other rival males, often with violent battles that involve a lot of pushing and shoving and slamming their necks against their rivals ("necking"), and sometimes injuring them. So overall size and long necks give a bigger male giraffe a mating advantage over rival smaller males. However, a 2024 study found that although males have thicker necks females actually have proportionally longer ones, which is probably because of their greater need to find more food to sustain themselves and their dependent young.

As we have seen already, the fossil record shows that most giraffes had short necks, just like the modern okapi, the only other living genus of giraffid. Starting in the early Miocene, there was an enormous evolutionary radiation of giraffids in the Old World, especially in Asia, and eventually in Africa as well (figure 14.6). We have already discussed how they were common in the Siwalik beds of Pakistan, and the Miocene beds of Samos, but there are many other places that produce them, such as China. Some of them, like *Prolibytherium*, had moose-like horns in the males. Others had horns like deer or antelopes. We have already discussed the huge *Sivatherium* from the Siwaliks, which was over 3 m (10 feet) tall with thick forked horns, and weighed half a ton, and the giant *Bramatherium* was almost as tall as a modern giraffe but with a short thick neck and enormous horns on its head. All of them have relatively short necks.

Recently, my friend Nikos Solounias, who has worked on the Samos fossils and especially giraffe fossils all his career, described new specimens of *Samotherium major* from Samos, which had long been collected by Forsyth Major and by Brown. This one had a complete neck—and it was intermediate in length between that of an okapi and the modern giraffe (figure 14.7).

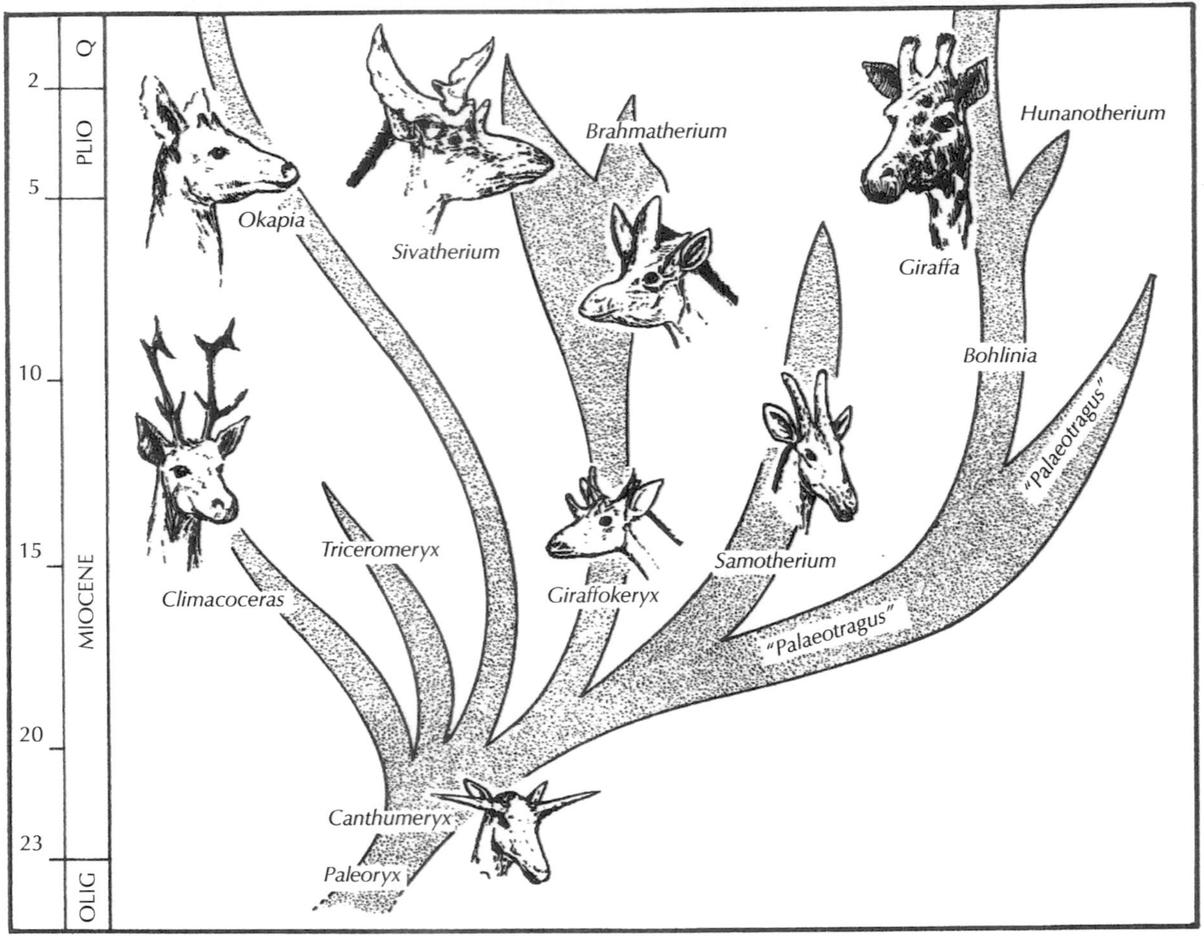

Figure 14.6 ▲

Evolution of the giraffes. (Diagram drawn by C. R. Prothero)

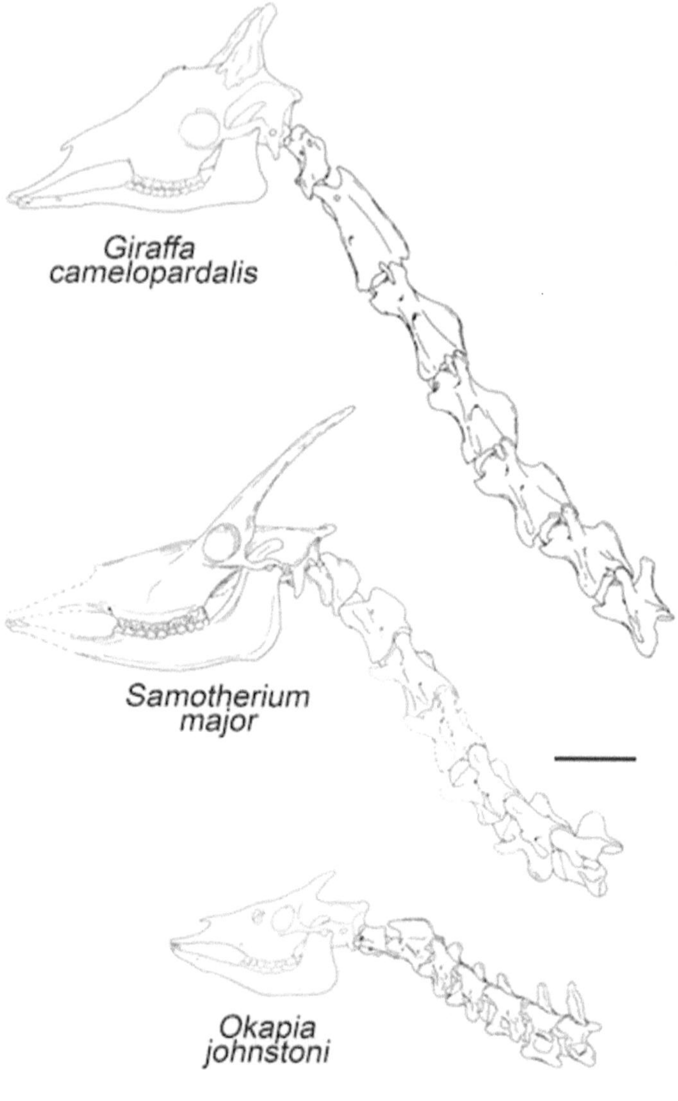

Figure 14.7 ▲

Evolution of long-necked giraffes (*Giraffa camelopardalis* on top) from short-necked forms (*Okapia johnstoni* on the bottom) via *Samotherium major* in the middle. (Courtesy of N. Solounias)

The fossil record has finally produced an intermediate form that is a perfect transition between short-necked giraffids and *Giraffa*. Evolution caught in the act!

NOTES

1. H. Falconer and P. T. Cautley, "Note on the Fossil Camel of the Sivalik Hills," *Asiatic Researches* 19, no. 1 (1836): 115–134.
2. H. Falconer, "Mammalian Remains from Grays Thurrock," *Geologist* 6, no. 12 (1863): 457.
3. Lowell Dingus and Mark Norell, *Barnum Brown: The Man Who Discovered* Tyrannosaurus rex (University of California Press, 2010).
4. Gil Troy, "The Man Who Brought Us T-Rex," Daily Beast, January 16, 2016, https://www.thedailybeast.com/the-man-who-brought-us-t-rex/.
5. Dingus and Norell, *Barnum Brown.*
6. Troy, "The Man Who Brought Us T-Rex."
7. Lilian MacLaughlin Brown, *Cleopatra Slept Here* (Dodd Mead, 1951), 202–203.
8. Brown, *Cleopatra Slept Here*, 202–203.
9. Dingus and Norell, *Barnum Brown.*
10. Dingus and Norell, *Barnum Brown.*
11. Jean-Baptiste de Monet, chevalier de Lamarck (1809), *Philosophie Zoologique.* Quoted in Stephen J. Gould, *The Structure of Evolutionary Theory* (Belknap, 2002), 188.
12. Lamarck, *Philosophie Zoologique*, 189.

FOR FURTHER READING

Brown, Lilian. *Bring 'Em Back Petrified*. Dodd, Mead, 1956.

——. *Cleopatra Slept Here*. Dodd, Mead, 1941.

——. *I Married a Dinosaur*. Dodd, Mead, 1940.

Danowitz, M., A. Vasilyev, V. Kortlandt, and V. Solounias. "Fossil Evidence and Stages of Elongation of the *Giraffa camelopardalis* Neck." *Royal Society Open Science* 2, no. 10 (2015): 150393.

Dingus, Lowell, and Mark Norell. *Barnum Brown: The Man Who Discovered* Tyrannosaurus rex. University of California Press, 2010.

Falconer, H. "Description of Some Fossil Remains of *Deinotherium*, Giraffe, and Other Mammalia, from Perim Island, Gulf of Cambay, Western Coast of India." *Journal of the Geological Society*, 1 (1845): 356–372.

Hamilton, H. R. "Fossil Giraffes from the Miocene of Africa and a Revision of the Phylogeny of the Giraffoidea." *Philosophical Transactions of the Royal Society of London.* Series B, *Biological Sciences* 283, no. 996 (1978): 165–229.

Kostopoulos, D. S. "The Late Miocene Mammal Faunas of the Mytilinii Basin, Samos Island, Greece: New Collection: 13. Giraffidae." *Beitrage für Paläontologie* 31 (2009): 299–343.

Laskos, K., and D. S. Kostopoulos. "On the Last European Giraffe, *Palaeotragus inexspectatus* (Mammalia: Giraffidae); New Remains from the Early Pleistocene of Greece and a Review of the Species." *Zoological Journal of the Linnean Society* (2024), https://doi.org/10.1093/zoolinnean/zlae056.

Lydekker, R. "On the Fossil Mammalia of Maragha, in North-western Persia." *Quarterly Journal of the Geological Society* 42, nos. 1–4 (1886): 173–176.

Mitchell, G., and J. D. Skinner. "On the Origin, Evolution, and Phylogeny of Giraffes *Giraffa camelopardalis.*" *Transactions of the Royal Society of South Africa* 58, no. 1 (2003): 51–73.

Prothero, D. R. *The Princeton Field Guide to Prehistoric Mammals.* Princeton University Press, 2017.

——. *Vertebrate Evolution: From Origins to Dinosaurs and Beyond.* Taylor & Francis/CRC Press, 2022.

Prothero, D. R., and R. M. Schoch. *Horns, Tusks, and Flippers: The Evolution of Hoofed Mammals.* Johns Hopkins University Press, 2003.

Ríos, M., I. M. Sánchez, and J. Morales. "A new giraffid (Mammalia, Ruminantia, Pecora) from the Late Miocene of Spain, and the Evolution of the Sivathere-Samothere Lineage." *PLOS ONE* 12, no. 11 (2017): e0185378.

Solounias, N. "Family Giraffidae." In *The Evolution of Artiodactyls*, ed. D. R. Prothero and S. E. Foss, 257–277. Johns Hopkins University Press, 2007.

Solounias, N., and A. Mayor. "Ancient References to Fossils from the Land of Pythagoras." *Earth Sciences History* 23, no. 2 (2004): 283–296.

15 | WHERE THE BUFFALO ROAM

BISON LATIFRONS

The buffalo gave us everything we needed. Without it we were nothing. Our tipis were made of his skin. His hide was our bed, our blanket, our winter coat. It was our drum, throbbing through the night, alive, holy. Out of his skin we made our water bags. His flesh strengthened us, became flesh of our flesh. Not the smallest part of it was wasted. His stomach, a red-hot stone dropped into it, became our soup kettle. His horns were our spoons, the bones our knives, our women's awls and needles. Out of his sinews we made our bowstrings and thread. His ribs were fashioned into sleds for our children, his hoofs became rattles. His mighty skull, with the pipe leaning against it, was our sacred altar. The name of the greatest of all Sioux was Tatanka Iyotake–Sitting Bull. When you killed off the buffalo you also killed the Indian–the real, natural, "wild" Indian.

—JOHN FIRE LAME DEER, *LAME DEER, SEEKER OF VISIONS* (1994)

OH, GIVE ME A HOME, WHERE THE BUFFALO ROAM . . .

One of the symbols of the Old West, and indeed, a symbol of America, is the bison. It is colloquially called a "buffalo," although it is not closely related to the true buffaloes, such as the Asian water buffalo and African Cape buffalo. Still, American and Canadian culture is replete with symbols of this animal, such as the buffalo nickel, and the official seal of the US Department of the Interior, and the bison is the official National Mammal of the United States, as well as of the states of Kansas, Nebraska, and Wyoming. Bison also appear on the seal and flag of Manitoba, the seal of the state of Indiana and Wyoming and many others, and the coat of arms of the Royal Canadian Mounted Police. There is also the city of Buffalo, New York, and the Buffalo Bills NFL team and Buffalo Bisons minor league baseball team, along with numerous college teams that adopted the bison or buffalo as a mascot (North Dakota State University, Marshall University, University of Manitoba, Howard University, Harding University, Bucknell University, and Lipscomb University, University of Colorado, West Texas A&M, and others). And of course, there are many historical figures associated with bison, especially "Buffalo Bill" William Cody, who gained fame first as a hunter and scout for the US Army, then traded on his fame in later life to create his own live circus show.

There are two living subspecies of *Bison bison* in North America today (figure 15.1A). The more numerous plains bison (*Bison bison bison*) lived mainly east of the Sierra Nevadas, and once inhabited most of what is now the United States, except for the Great Lakes area, New England, and part of the southeast. The plains bison also extended north into Manitoba, Saskatchewan, and southern Alberta. The woodland, wood, or mountain bison, *Bison bison athabascae*, inhabited the Rocky Mountain region of Alberta and even further north in the Yukon and Alaska (figure 15.1B). The wood bison is larger and heavier than the plains bison, weighing about 2,600 pounds (1,200 kilograms), making it the heaviest mammal in North America and Siberia. Its hump rises in front of the forelegs, rather than right over the forelegs, as in the plains bison. They also have larger horns, and darker and woolier hair on their forelegs.

Bison first crossed the Bering land bridge to America in the middle Pleistocene around 195,000 years ago. The North American radiation started from the Siberian steppe bison (*Bison priscus*), which then spread across Alaska and northern Canada. The steppe bison (figure 15.2) is anatomically very similar to its presumed ancestor, the European wisent, *Bison bonasus*, but they are genetically distinct so they are valid species. Steppe bison were about 6.5 feet (2 meters) at the shoulder, and weighed about 2,000 pounds (900 kilograms), much larger than later North American species. The tips of their horns were over a meter apart, and each horn was half a meter long. Even though they moved south from Alaska and evolved into other species, some steppe bison remained on the mammoth steppe until 5,400 years ago in Alaska, and recently as 4,400 years ago in Siberia.

The most famous fossil of a steppe bison is "Blue Babe," a 36,000-year-old mummy of a male steppe bison that was discovered north of Fairbanks in Alaska in July 1979 (figure 15.3). The mummy was noticed by a gold

Figure 15.1 ▲

(*A*) Photo of the plains bison. (*B*) Photo of the wood bison. (Courtesy of Wikimedia Commons)

Figure 15.2 ▲
Reconstruction of the steppe bison. (Courtesy of Wikimedia Commons)

miner who named it "Blue Babe." ("Babe" was Paul Bunyan's mythical giant ox, who was permanently turned blue when he was buried to the horns in a blizzard.) In the case of Blue Babe, the mummy's bluish cast was caused by a coating of vivianite, a blue iron phosphate covering much of the specimen. Blue Babe is also frequently referenced when talking about scientists eating their own specimens: the research team that was preparing it for permanent display in the University of Alaska Museum removed a portion of the mummy's neck, stewed it, and dined on it to celebrate the accomplishment. Several additional freeze-dried mummies of steppe bison have been found in Eurasia over the years, so the species known from a lot of fossils.

Steppe bison fossils are not rare in collections from Alaska, Canada, and Siberia, but in the American Museum of Natural History of New York, there is an incredible collection of over 178 skulls and 1,766 jaws of steppe bison

Figure 15.3 ▲
Babe, the blue bison. (Courtesy of Wikimedia Commons)

gathered by the Frick collectors from the mining operations near Fairbanks, Alaska. Gold miners in the region use hydraulic mining, in which they blast old river sands and gravels with huge fire hoses to wash the entire sedimentary deposit down into the sluice boxes and other gold-trapping devices. These miners ended up exposing a huge number of bison fossils that fortunately were collected rather than destroyed, and they were preserved in the Frick Collection in many rows of shelves (figure 15.4). The overall collection was first documented by Skinner and Kaisen (1947), although the taxonomic concepts in that paper are dated and do not hold up to scrutiny today. Research on these specimens is still ongoing, but my colleagues and I have noticed that these specimens have a high degree of pathological horn cores (and Skinner and Kaisen, 1947, documented numerous pathologies in the jaws and teeth). Such does not occur in most bison populations, including the modern ones my coauthors and I have examined, or in the huge

Figure 15.4 ▲
Rows and rows of shelves of bison skulls from Alaska in the American Museum of Natural History. (Photo by the author)

sample of *Bison antiquus* from the La Brea Tar Pits, which had no examples of pathological horn cores or teeth. Why these steppe bison had such a high frequency of pathologies is not known, although in the harsh environment of the mammoth steppe, there are often extreme conditions of hardship and starvation, especially in winter, that might have affected the growth of horns in juveniles. Bison from more temperate latitudes do not face similar problems, especially in the relatively stable mild climate of southern California around the La Brea Tar Pits.

The steppe bison was ancestral to several different species of bison found south of the Pleistocene glaciers. The most spectacular is the long-horned bison, *Bison latifrons* (figure 15.5). It was the largest bovid that ever lived, reaching 15.5 feet (4.75 meters) in length,.5 feet (2.3 meters) at the shoulder, and weighing about 4,400 pounds, or two tons (2,000 kilograms). In fact, it was one of the largest ruminants ever known, comparable in weight to the giraffe and the huge prehistoric long-horned buffalo from Africa, *Pelorovis*. The name *latifrons* ("broad front" in Latin) refers to its spectacular horns,

Figure 15.5 ▲
Mounted skeleton of *Bison latifrons*. (Courtesy of Wikimedia Commons)

which were up to 7 feet 4 inches (2.2 meters) from tip to tip, compared to 25 inches (90 centimeters) in modern bison.

Once *B. latifrons* began differentiating from *B. priscus* in the Arctic, it spread south, where the oldest specimens are found at the Snowmastodon site near Snowmass, Colorado, and date to about 120,000 years ago. Although its fossils are not common, *B. latifrons* is found everywhere from southern Mexico to southern Canada, as far west as California, all over the American Midwest, and east to Florida and Georgia. Due to the localities from which they are recovered, and their small numbers, it is thought that they didn't roam in huge herds like plains bison but were solitary or lived in small family groups, like modern moose. They are thought to have fed more on small trees and shrubs, although the chemistry of their teeth showed that they were mixed feeders, with significant grass in their diet whenever they lived in grassy habitats. In 2022, a specimen from South Texas was recovered that dated to only 13,000 years ago, so they overlapped in time and space with their close relatives, the smaller *Bison antiquus*.

Meanwhile, the main line of bison evolution in North America continued with *Bison antiquus*, or the "antique bison" (figure 15.6). Specimens of this bison were first found at Big Bone Lick, Kentucky (see chapter 1), and reached Joseph Leidy in 1852, who named it and described it. *B. antiquus* was taller, had larger bones and horns, and was 15 to 25 percent larger overall than modern bison. It was up to 7.4 feet (2.27 meters) tall, 15 feet (4.6 meters) long, and weighed 3,501 pounds (1,588 kilograms). The horns were on average 2.85 feet (87 centimeters) across tip to tip, but could reach as much as 3.50 feet (106.7 centimeters) across. The oldest known specimens date to about sixty thousand years ago, and it is known from thousands of specimens at the La Brea Tar Pits, which range from forty thousand to nine thousand years ago. Numerous studies have shown that there is a gradual size reduction over the past 120,000 years from *B. priscus* to *B. antiquus* to *B. occidentalis* to the modern *Bison bison*, which are its descendants, although research by my student Kristina Raymond Smith and I showed that there is

Figure 15.6 ▲

Bison antiquus from Rancho La Brea. (Photo by the author.)

no significant difference in size of the limbs through the samples at the La Brea Tar Pits from thirty-seven thousand to nine thousand years ago.

The latest Pleistocene-early Holocene (spanning 11,700 to 5,000 years ago) specimens of bison have been named *Bison occidentalis*, although there are complex taxonomic problems with that name. If it is a valid taxon, it is intermediate in size, smaller than *B. antiquus*, but larger than modern *Bison bison*.

BUFFALOES OF THE OLD WORLD

As previously mentioned, bison are not true buffalo. Instead, true buffalo are another, distantly related side branch of the tribe Bovini. Today the true buffalo consists only of the familiar water buffalo of Asia, *Bubalus bubalis*, as well as dwarf water buffaloes, the lowland anoa (*Bubalus depressicornis*) of the coastal swamps of northern Celebes in Indonesia, and the mountain anoa (*Bubalus quarlesi*) from the mountains of Celebes in Indonesia. There is also the Philippine pygmy buffalo (*Bubalus mindorensis*), a small but aggressive nocturnal buffalo found only in the bamboo forests and marshes of the island of Mindoro in the Philippines. All three of these dwarf buffaloes are endangered in the wild.

The other living genus of buffalo is the famous Cape buffalo of Africa, *Syncerus caffer*. It is distinguished by its broad horns, which form a boss over his head and span more than 3 feet. This beast is infamous among hunters for fighting back more fiercely than any other wild animal of Africa, including lions and leopards. Legends and stories recount the anger of a wounded Cape buffalo, goring and trampling hunters, sneaking up on them for revenge, or even attacking unprovoked.

Although the deadliness of the Cape buffalo has certainly been exaggerated, they kill more humans in Africa than any other wild animal, surpassing even the lion. However, in the protection of game reserves, Cape buffalo spend their daylight hours grazing in the savanna, and blissfully wallowing in waterholes. Even when their excellent senses pick up humans, they ignore them. Only after repeated persecution by hunters do they become wary and aggressive, fighting for their lives. Most the time, however, they hide from humans, and if a hunter misses, they usually retreat.

An extinct Pleistocene relative of the Cape buffalo is *Syncerus antiquus*, the African giant buffalo (figure 15.7A). At almost 4,400 pounds (2,000

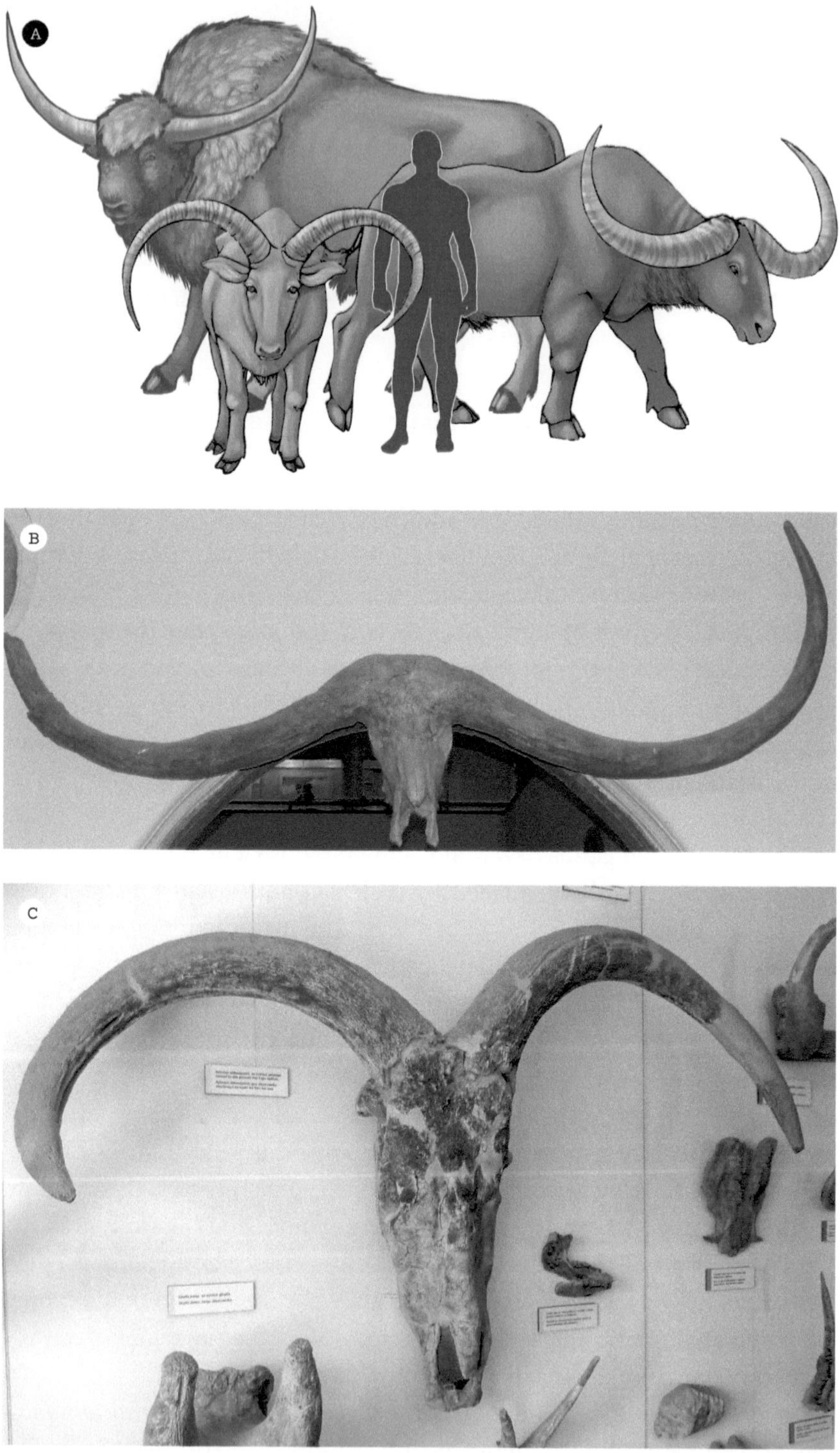

Figure 15.7 ▲

(*A*) Comparison of *Bison latifrons* (background), *Syncerus antiquus*, and *Pelorovis oldowayensis*. (*B*) Horns of *Syncerus antiquus*. (*C*) Skull of *Pelorovis oldowayensis*. ([*A*] Art by M. P. Williams; [*B and C*] courtesy of Wikimedia Commons)

kilograms), it was the largest bovid found in Africa (figure 15.7B). It reached 10 feet (3 meters) in length, was 6.1 feet (1.85 meters) at the withers, and its enormous upward-curved horns spanned almost 10 feet (3 meters). These horns had the same curvature as those of the water buffalo, although they were much larger, compared to the short horns of *Syncerus caffer*.

Syncerus antiquus used to be assigned to another extinct genus, *Pelorovis*, from the Pleistocene of Africa. The genus *Pelorovis* is best known from fossils of *P. oldowayensis* (figure 15.7C) from the late Pleistocene of Olduvai Gorge in Tanzania, the site of the famous hominin discoveries by Louis and Mary Leakey. It was another huge buffalo, bigger than any living species, and it may have weighed up to 4,400 pounds (2,000 kilograms). The horn cores were each about 3.3 feet (1 meter) long, and may have been twice that length when covered by keratin. These horns pointed outward from the head, and then downward, unlike the upward-curving horns of *Syncerus antiquus*.

AUROCHS AND WISENT

Before recorded history, two ferocious animals commonly known as the aurochs (plural, aurochsen) or urus (*Bos primigenius*, the ancestor of common domestic cattle) (figure 15.8A), and the wisent, or European bison (*Bison bonasus*), lived in Europe north of the Alps (figure 15.8B). Both of these species survived into historical times, but the former is now extinct and the latter has only just been saved from extermination by the intervention of concerned zoologists, just like the near extinction of American bison.

Julius Caesar wrote in his *Commentaries* on his wars in Gaul (mid-first-century BCE) that the aurochs resembled a bull, but it was nearly as big as an elephant, extremely strong, and swift. These animals were said to be hunted by the Native peoples via the use of pits in which they could be trapped and then slain. The slain animals were eaten, and the thick hides were used for various purposes such as the covering of shields, but the horns were highly valued. Caesar reported that hollow aurochs horns were edged with silver along their bases and used as drinking vessels at feasts.

During the late Pleistocene and into the early Holocene, the aurochs was in fact a very common species throughout Eurasia. The wild aurochsen tended to look similar to their descendants, modern domesticated cattle, but were larger (males reached 6.5 feet [2 meters] at the shoulder), and were

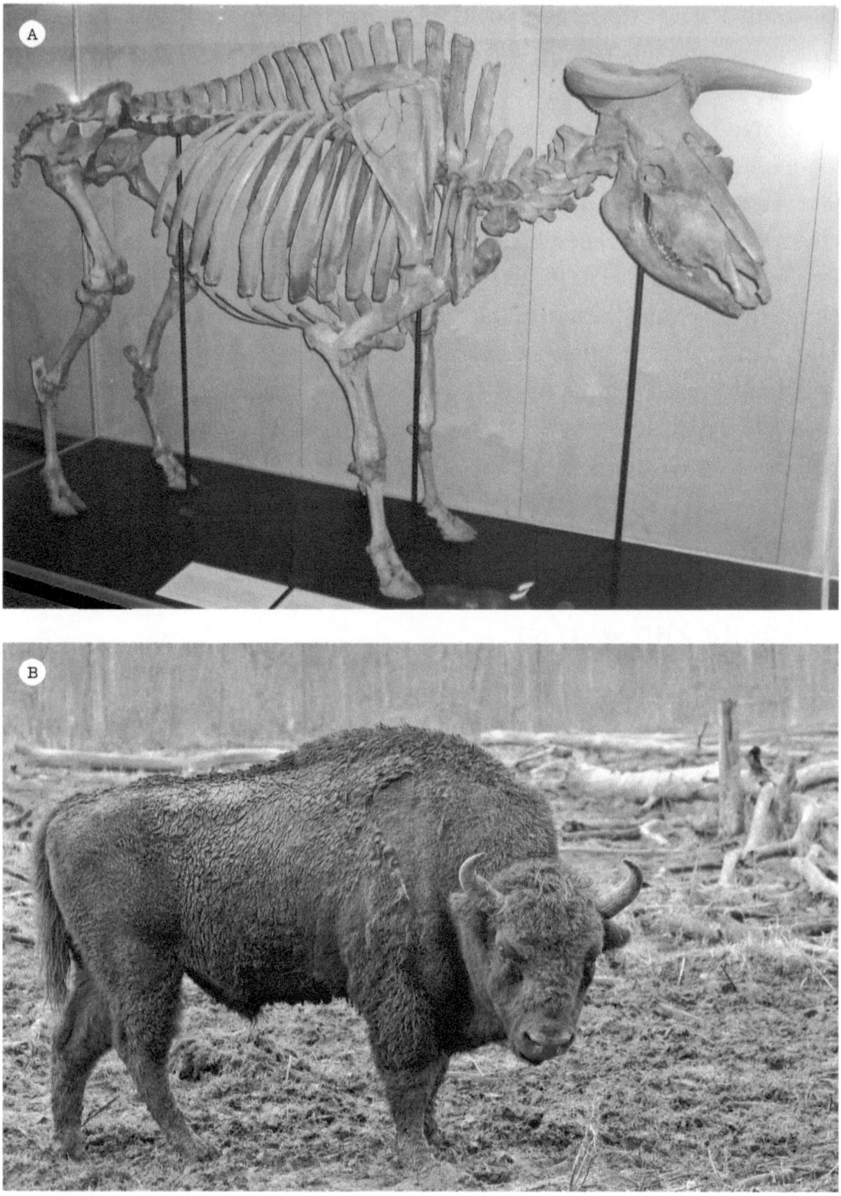

Figure 15.8 ▲

(*A*) Mounted skeleton of the extinct aurochs. (*B*) Photograph of the living wisent, or European bison. (Courtesy of Wikimedia Commons)

presumably fierce, temperamental beasts. The coats were often black or brownish red, with a lighter line down the back, and sometimes a large saddle of lighter hair on their back.

Aurochsen were hunted during the Stone Age and right up into historical times. As human populations increased and civilization spread, the size of aurochsen populations steadily decreased and became more and more restricted in range. During the Middle Ages, the aurochsen were rapidly being driven to extinction, especially by the destruction of the dense forests in which they had taken refuge. Their populations were progressively restricted. In sixth-century France they were already extremely rare, and by the fourteenth and fifteenth centuries they were confined to a few protected forests in Central Europe. Successive monarchs (such as the princes of Masovia in Poland) prohibited the general hunting of aurochsen, which were reserved for royalty.

By the sixteenth century, living aurochsen were restricted to the forest of Jaktorovka in Masovia, near Warsaw, Poland. There they lived in a protected reservation and were provided with hay in the winter by the local villagers. Royal officers took periodic censuses of the aurochsen, and these numbers record the sad decline and eventual extinction of this magnificent species in grim detail. In 1557 there were approximately 50 aurochsen, in 1562 the number had declined to 38, and by 1599 there were only 24 aurochsen known to be alive, despite the numerous decrees issued in an attempt to save the species. Two years later, in 1601, a plague killed 20 of the aurochsen, so that only 4 remained (three bulls and one cow). In 1630 the officer in charge of the preserve could find no living aurochsen, and he was told that the last individual (a female) had died three years earlier. The year 1627 marks the extinction of the aurochsen.

Even before the aurochs was actually extinct, it had become a beast of legend and a source of confusion. This was in large part because another large wild bovine, the wisent or European bison, also inhabited Europe. From early times some travelers, writers, and reporters confused the two types of beasts. In 1837 the Polish paleontologist Georg Gottlieb Pusch even tried to prove that the aurochsen, or the urus, had never existed. The core of his proof was that the Polish name for the aurochs, *tur*, and the Polish word for the wisent, *zubr*, were etymologically derived from the same source—thus there was only one animal (the European wisent), which had engendered legends of the mythical aurochsen. It is clear now, however, that the aurochs and the wisent were two distinct animals.

The European wisent is a shaggy-furred relative of the American bison. The two types of beasts not only look remarkably similar but in fact are very closely related. Indeed, the wisent and the American bison will readily interbreed, producing fully fertile offspring, and for this reason some zoologists consider them to simply be different subspecies of a single species. In fact, many of the species, and even genera, of the tribe Bovini are very closely related and can interbreed to a greater or lesser extent. In some cases, hybrids can be produced between parents of different species, but these hybrid offspring may be sterile. Just as the European and American bisons can interbreed fully, so can common European domestic cattle, *Bos taurus*, and Indian humped cattle or zebu, *Bos indicus*, and some zoologists accordingly classify these two species as one. The American buffalo has been crossed with domestic cattle, producing the so-called "catalo" or "beefalo."

Like the aurochs, the wisent was once abundant in the forests of Europe. Caesar also wrote of the wisent in his *Commentaries*. From physical appearance, the wisent seemed wilder and more ferocious than the aurochs, although in fact the opposite was true. After all, the aurochs looked like an overgrown domestic cow whereas the wisent was nothing like any beast seen before. During the height of the Roman Empire, wisents were used in gladiatorial combats.

As civilization advanced and forest area diminished, wild wisents were confined to ever more restricted areas. In the seventeenth century they were still fairly numerous, but by the next century their numbers were greatly reduced. The last pockets of wild wisents were in Prussia, Hungary, along the Polish-Russian border (in the forest of Bialowiecza, or Byelovyeh), and in the Caucasus. By 1755 wisents were extinct in Prussia, and by 1800 there were no more left in Hungary.

In the early nineteenth century, the Bialowiecza Forest was under Russian control, protected from tree felling and hunting by anyone other than the czars themselves and their privileged family and friends. In 1830 there were close to eight hundred wisents in the forest, and by midcentury about fifteen hundred, but by the beginning of World War I the number had dropped again to approximately 750. The primary reason for the decline in the wisent population, despite its protected status, was that other game animals were introduced into the forest and competed with the wisents. An overabundance of red deer, which the czar and his associates hunted, was apparently destroying the forest vegetation upon which the wisents depended.

With the outbreak of World War I in August 1914, the wisents of Bialowiecza were immediately put in danger. The next year the battlefront moved through the forest, and in September 1915, it was captured by the Germans after heavy fighting and severe losses on both sides. Of the 770 wisents that were recorded in the park on the eve of the battle, 650 were killed. German zoologists were as concerned about protecting the wisents as had been the Russian czar, and they immediately pressured the German High Command to take actions to protect the wisents. The population of wisents increased during the next few years under German protection, until they numbered 185 when the Germans withdrew in November 1918. Unprotected, the wisents were killed by desperate starving peasants and soldiers, both for their hides and their meat. The new Polish government issued orders protecting the wisents, but still they continued to be poached until the last survivor was shot by a former Russian forester, one Bartmoleus Szpakowicz, on February 19, 1921.

The other herd of wild wisents that survived into the twentieth century was located in the Caucasus Mountains. This herd was virtually unknown to western scientists before the middle of the nineteenth century, although in fact it had first been discovered during a scientific expedition to the Caucasus from 1768–1773. After one of the many Polish insurrections of the middle 1800s against their Russian overlords, a Caucasian lieutenant fighting alongside the Russian soldiers visited the museum in Lublin (Poland) and saw a specimen of a wisent from the forest of Bialowiecza. He mentioned to museum officials that he was familiar with similar beasts from his native land, and the reports from the previous century were confirmed. A herd of perhaps a thousand wisents lived in the Caucasus region.

Unfortunately, the Caucasian herd fared no better than the Polish herd. Most of the beasts were wiped out by military machine-gun hunts during the period 1918–19, and the last known wild Caucasian wisent was reported to have been killed in 1926. By the 1920s, all known wild wisents had been exterminated.

But were all wisents exterminated? There were a few small captive herds at the beginning of the century, notably at Tachina (Tashina) Park near

St. Petersburg, as well as one at Minsk, and a small herd on the Crimea. But all of these Russian animals were killed during the Russian Civil War, most either by Cossacks or the Red Army. At Mezerzitz, on properties split between Poland and Germany, the Prince of Pless had a herd of some 55 or 56 wisents that had originated from four animals donated by Czar Alexander II in 1869. But this herd also largely succumbed to the political turmoil of the times. When it was all over, only three animals survived, all with machine gun bullets in their bodies.

Fortunately, a few dozen wisents still survived in captivity in various zoological parks and preserves, such as England, in the Budapest Zoo and Forest Park, and in Swedish preserves. Planned breeding was carried out, and by 1939 there were about 94 purebred European wisents (along with some animals that had mixed wisent/American bison blood). Then World War II broke out and their numbers again suffered. In the next couple of decades, however, the breeding programs rapidly progressed and the wisent numbers multiplied. Herds have now been reintroduced into the Bialowiecza Forest, the Caucasus, and other parts of the former Soviet Union. After a very close call, it seems that we can optimistically say that the European wisent has been saved from extinction.

AMERICAN BUFFALO

Bison were an essential part of the Native cultures of the Great Plains since prehistoric times. We are all familiar with the traditional way of hunting them down on horseback, but before horses were brought to the Americas after 1493, Native peoples would drive bison off a cliff to their deaths (figure 15.9A). In his journals of the Lewis and Clark expedition, Meriwether Lewis described it this way:

> . . . one of the most active and fleet young men is selected and disguised in a robe of buffalo skin . . . he places himself at a distance between a herd of buffalo and a precipice proper for the purpose; the other Indians now surround the herd on the back and flanks and at a signal agreed on all show themselves at the same time moving forward towards the buffalo; the disguised Indian or decoy has taken care to place himself sufficiently near the buffalo to be noticed by them when they take to flight and running before them they follow him in full speed to the precipice; the Indian (decoy) in the mean time

Figure 15.9 ▲

(*A*) A painting depicting Native American hunters on horseback driving a large herd of bison over a cliff, a hunting method known as a buffalo jump. (*B*) The Hudson-Meng Bison Bonebed kill site. (Courtesy of Wikimedia Commons)

> has taken care to secure himself in some cranny in the cliff . . . the part of the decoy I am informed is extremely dangerous.[1]

There are numerous kill sites where prehistoric peoples hunted bison. At Jake Bluff in northern Oklahoma, Clovis points are associated with numerous butchered bones of the extinct bison species *Bison antiquus*, which represented a bison herd of at least 22 individuals, which dates to around 12,838 years ago. They were apparently herded into a steep-sided arroyo where they were trapped, and then killed. The Olsen-Chubbuck bison kill site southeast of Kit Carson, on the border between Colorado and Kansas, contains the remains of two hundred bison that were killed and butchered about 10,000–8,500 years ago, mostly of the extinct early Holocene species *Bison occidentalis*. Near Great Falls, Montana, is the famous cliff known as Buffalo Jump, where the Blackfoot tribes drove bison off a steep cliff to kill them.

The most famous mass bison kill sites is the Hudson-Meng site (figure 15.9B), on the north side of the Pine Ridge north of Crawford, Nebraska. Discovered in 1954 by local ranchers Bill Hudson and Albert Meng while digging for a pond, the site eventually covered four hundred square meters and yielded the bones of about six hundred bison. It is dated to about ten thousand years ago, so it is earliest Holocene, and the specimens found there are intermediate between modern *Bison bison* and the late Pleistocene species *Bison antiquus*. Although the original excavation by the late Dr. Larry Agenbroad in the 1970s concluded it was a mass kill site, subsequent research teams are not so sure because there are not many signs of butchery.

The Great Plains tribes used nearly every part of the bison for more than 150 different uses, as described by John Fire Lame Deer in the epigraph at the beginning of the chapter.

THE BISON MASSACRE

In North America bison were relentlessly hunted as soon as the European colonists arrived. The first major impact was along the East Coast, and by 1800, the bison was extinct east of the Mississippi River. But as late as the 1860s, bison were extremely abundant elsewhere in North America. On the Great Plains, dense herds of bison were described as being on the order of

25 miles (40 kilometers) wide and some 50 miles (80 kilometers) long, and the animals were so closely spaced that "the whole country is covered with what appeared to be a monstrous moving brown blanket" (letter from Col. C. Goodnight to Marin S. Garretson, describing a herd in the early 1860s). In 1871, Col. R. I. Dodge watched the herds pass through the valley of the Arkansas River. It took several days to pass, and it may have included four million animals. Yet in less than twenty years—from 1865 to 1884—more than sixty million bison were wiped out.

The introduction of the railroad to the West provided an easy means of transportation for professional hunters to reach the herds, and a method to ship bison products back east (figure 15.10). In the late 1860s, the first transcontinental railway divided the Plains bison into two major herds: a southern herd and a northern herd. It is reported in 1871 that five thousand professional buffalo hunters left from Kansas City to begin the slaughter of the bison in earnest. The professional hunters were joined by perhaps an equal number of amateur hunters. Hundreds of thousands, then millions of bison, felt to the hunters. Carcasses were left to rot on the plains, and settlers

Figure 15.10 ▲
An old lithograph of bison being hunted from a moving train. (Courtesy of Wikimedia Commons)

complained of the stench (figure 15.11A and figure 15.11B). By 1875, only a few percent of the original bison population in the southern herd were left. Both Kansas and Colorado passed laws attempting to protect the remaining bison. Still, one hundred thousand more bison, almost all that remained of the southern herd, were killed during the winter of 1877–78, and at most a few hundred animals remained. These few surviving animals made their way to Texas, but by 1889 they too had been shot, and so ended the southern herd.

An article written in 1889 described it this way:

> Thirty years ago millions of the great unwieldy animals existed on this continent. Innumerable droves roamed, comparatively undisturbed and unmolested. . . . Many thousands have been ruthlessly and shamefully slain every season for [the] past twenty years or more by white hunters and tourists merely for their robes, and in sheer wanton sport, and their huge carcasses left to fester and rot, and their bleached skeletons to strew the deserts and lonely plains.[2]

Between 1881 and 1883, there was a massive attack on the less numerous northern herd. Soldiers and Native Americans fought each other, but both hunted the bison. Many bison were slaughtered in the area of Yellowstone National Park. Even Sitting Bull and his people did their part to reduce the bison population. By 1884, the northern herd in the United States was virtually wiped out. Conditions were no better in Canada. By 1885, the wood or forest bison of Canada was almost extinct in the wild.

Why were the bison hunted so relentlessly? In most cases, much of the bison carcass was wasted and left to rot. Yet virtually all of the animal could be put to useful purposes, as the Native peoples knew. Some hunters went after the meat only, for which there was a considerable market. A meat hunter often took the tongue, and choice cuts at the hindquarters and the hump ribs. The rest was left to rot. Others went after hides, which could be shipped back and made into good leather that might go to numerous products, from machinery belts to shoes, saddles, or holsters. Then there were the fur traders who sought "buffalo robes" to be used for overcoats and wraps. Buffalo fat could be used in the manufacture of soap and candles, and buffalo horns were used in the hat racks.

Many bison were killed for pure sport, which was supposedly highly addictive. Chasing and shooting bison from horseback was considered great fun by some people. Expeditions were arranged for the interested parties in

Figure 15.11 ▲

(*A*) A photograph of a massive, towering pile of bison skulls with two men standing on and next to it, showing the immense scale of the pile. (*B*) Piles of bison hides near a railroad spur. (Courtesy of Wikimedia Commons)

a contest of shooting skills and to have a bit of adventure by slaughtering wild bison from a railway car. In addition, many people considered it to be in the best interest of the United States to destroy the herds of bison and to devastate the Native American populations. Native peoples depended on the bison for their livelihood but were the enemy of white settlers and the US government at that time. In 1869, General Phil Sheridan declared "every buffalo dead as an Indian gone." And in 1875 he said, "those buffalo hunters have done more in a few months to bring about peace with the Indians than the whole Army could do in thirty years."

Mark Twain described one such buffalo hunt in his epic tales of Western travel, *Roughing It:*

> Then the bull made a pass at him and uttered a bellow that sounded perfectly frightful, it was so close to me, and that seemed to literally prostrate my horse's reason, and make a raving distracted maniac of him, and I wish I may die if he didn't stand on his head for a quarter of a minute and shed tears. He was absolutely out of his mind—he was, as sure as truth itself, and he really didn't know what he was doing. Then the bull came charging at us, and my horse dropped down on all fours and took a fresh start—and then for the next ten minutes he would actually throw one hand-spring after another so fast that the bull began to get unsettled, too, and didn't know where to start in—and so he stood there sneezing, and shovelling dust over his back, and bellowing every now and then, and thinking he had got a fifteen-hundred dollar circus horse for breakfast, certain. Well, I was first out on his neck—the horse's, not the bull's—and then underneath, and next on his rump, and sometimes head up, and sometimes heels—but I tell you it seemed solemn and awful to be ripping and tearing and carrying on so in the presence of death, as you might say. Pretty soon the bull made a snatch for us and brought away some of my horse's tail (I suppose, but do not know, being pretty busy at the time), but something made him hungry for solitude and suggested to him to get up and hunt for it. And then you ought to have seen that spider legged old skeleton go! and you ought to have seen the bull cut out after him, too—head down, tongue out, tail up, bellowing like everything, and actually mowing down the weeds, and tearing up the earth, and boosting up the sand like a whirlwind! By George, it was a hot race! I and the saddle were back on the rump, and I had the bridle in my teeth and holding on to the pommel with both hands. First we left the dogs behind; then we passed a jackass rabbit;

> then we overtook a coyote, and were gaining on an antelope when the rotten girth let go and threw me about thirty yards off to the left, and as the saddle went down over the horse's rump he gave it a lift with his heels that sent it more than four hundred yards up in the air, I wish I may die in a minute if he didn't. I fell at the foot of the only solitary tree there was in nine counties adjacent (as any creature could see with the naked eye), and the next second I had hold of the bark with four sets of nails and my teeth, and the next second after that I was astraddle of the main limb and blaspheming my luck in a way that made my breath smell of brimstone.[3]

Even after most of the bison were gone, they still made a direct impact on the homesteaders of the prairies. In many areas, the ground was literally covered with scattered bison bones. The bones were collected to burn as fuel, and they were also shipped back East by the trainload. These bones could be ground up and used as fertilizer. In addition, they were used in sugar refining to neutralize the acids produced during the final processing. Their hooves and horns were used in the manufacture of glue. Well into the twentieth century, bison bones were being shipped to the East for commercial use. According to an estimate, more than 170 million bison skeletons may be commercially processed—several times the estimated number that ever roamed the continent at any one time. How could this be possible? The dry air of the Plains could preserve bison skeletons for decades, so it's feasible that this many skeletons accumulated on the ground long before the bone hunters came in earnest.

The demise of the North American bison occurred in a flash, and only after the fact did the Canadian and US governments intercede to try to put a halt to the destruction. Canada passed legislation protecting bison in 1885, but the United States did not move to protect them until as late as 1899. By the 1890s, there were only two groups of bison remaining in North America: a mixture of plains bison and wood bison in Canada, and a small herd of plains bison in Yellowstone National Park. At the close of the nineteenth century, William T. Hornaday, director of the New York Zoological Park (now the Bronx Zoo), made a census of all the living North American bison. He found that there just under 1,100 bison alive, scattered among the wild herds in Canada and Yellowstone, those captive in zoos, and a few maintained on private ranches. In 1905, Hornaday founded the American Bison Society, and the primary goal was to save the American bison from extinction.

The American Bison Society, with support in some people in high places, such as President Theodore Roosevelt, quickly acted to increase bison numbers. Reservations were established for the bison, and they provided a shelter and fodder. Results were achieved quickly because, under favorable natural conditions, a typical bison cow can birth a new calf each year. In 1910, there were more than 2,100 bison in North America, and by the 1930s there were more than twenty thousand. Today ranchers keep domestic herds throughout the continental United States, from Florida to New York to Texas to Wyoming to California, and there are sizable wild herds in government reservation such as Yellowstone National Park and Wood Buffalo Park in Alberta, Canada. Buffalo meat is actually quite popular in some parts of the West, and bison are much easier to ranch because they are hardier than domestic cattle. In many eateries in the Great Plains and Rocky Mountains, "buffalo burgers" and other popular food products are a fixture on the menus.

NOTES

1. Meriwether Lewis, *Journals of Lewis and Clark*, May 29, 1805.
2. "In the Prime of the Buffalo." *Overland Monthly and Out West Magazine*, 14, no. 83 (November 1889): 515.
3. Mark Twain, *Roughing It*, 1872, chapter 7.

FOR FURTHER READING

Boeskorov, G. G., O. R. Potapova, A. V. Protopopov, V. V. Plotnikov, L. D. Agenbroad, K. S. Kirikov, et al. "The Yukagir Bison: The Exterior Morphology of a Complete Frozen Mummy of the Extinct Steppe Bison, *Bison Priscus* from the Early Holocene of Northern Yakutia, Russia." *Quaternary International* 406 (2016): 94–110.

Froese, D., M. Stiller, P. D. Heintzman, A. V. Reyes, G. D. Zazula, A. E. Soares, et al. "Fossil and Genomic Evidence Constrains the Timing of Bison Arrival in North America." *Proceedings of the National Academy of Sciences* 114, no. 13 (2017): 3457–3462.

Galvez, S., D. R. Prothero, and V. J. P. Syverson. "How Did Bison Calves Grow Up? Postnatal Limb Allometry in *Bison antiquus* from La Brea Tar Pits." *New Mexico Museum of Natural History Bulletin* 79 (2018): 213–217.

Grange, T., J.-P. Brugal, L. Flori, M. Gautier, A. Uzunidis, and E.-M. Geigl. "The Evolution and Population Diversity of Bison in Pleistocene and Holocene Eurasia: Sex Matters." *Diversity* 10, no. 3 (2018): 65.

Guthrie, R. D. *Frozen Fauna of the Mammoth Steppe: The Story of Blue Babe*. University of Chicago Press, 1989.

Hardy, F. C., and S. M. Rowland. "Stable Isotopic Analysis of Fossil Bison Tooth Enamel Indicates Flexible Dietary Ecology Across Pleistocene North America." *Quaternary Science Reviews* 334 (2024): 108741.

Hofman-Kamińska, E., G. Merceron, H. Bocherens, G. G. Boeskorov, O. O. Krotova, A. V. Protopopov, A. V. Shpansky, and R. Kowalczyk. "Was the Steppe Bison a Grazing Beast in Pleistocene Landscapes?" *Royal Society Open Science* 11, no. 8 (2024).

Lewis, M. Entry for Wednesday May 29, 1805. *The Journals of the Lewis and Clark Expedition*. Vol. 4, ed. Gary E. Moulton.

Martin, J. M., J. I. Mead, and P. S. Barboza. "Bison Body Size and Climate Change." *Ecology and Evolution* 8 (2018): 4564–4574.

McDonald, J. N. *North American Bison: Their Classification and Evolution*. University of California Press, 1981.

Prothero, D. R. *The Princeton Field Guide to Prehistoric Mammals*. Princeton University Press, 2016.

——. *Vertebrate Evolution: From Origins to Dinosaurs and Beyond*. Taylor & Francis/CRC Press, 2022.

Prothero, D. R., and R. M. Schoch. *Horns, Tusks, and Flippers: The Evolution of Hoofed Mammals*. Johns Hopkins University Press, 2002.

Punke, Michael. *Last Stand: George Bird Grinnell, the Battle to Save the Buffalo, and the Birth of the New West*. University of Nebraska Press, 2009.

Raymond, K. R., and D. R. Prothero. "Did Climate Change Affect Size in Late Pleistocene Bison?" *New Mexico Museum of Natural History Bulletin* 53 (2011): 636–640.

Skinner, M. F., and O. C. Kaisen. "The Fossil Bison of Alaska and a Preliminary Revision of the Genus." *Bulletin of the American Museum of Natural History* 89, no. 3 (1947): 127–266.

Wilson, G. A., and C. Strobeck. "Genetic Variation Within and Relatedness Among Wood and Plains Bison Populations." *Genome* 42, no. 3 (1999): 483–496.

Zver, L., B. Toškan, and E. Bužan. "Phylogeny of Late Pleistocene and Holocene Bison Species in Europe and North America." *Quaternary International* 595 (2021): 30–38.

16 | WHERE THE DEER AND THE ANTELOPE PLAY

MEGALOCEROS

Nature herself seems by the vast magnitude and stately horns, she has given this creature, to singled it out as it were, and showed it such regard, with a design to distinguish it remarkably from the common herd of all other smaller quadrupeds.

—THOMAS MOLYNEUX, 1697

NEITHER IRISH NOR AN ELK

In 1695, a pair of huge antlers found near Dardistown in Ireland were officially described by the Irish physician Thomas Molyneux. He identified the antlers as coming from what the British call an "elk," or what North Americans call the moose, *Alces alces*, because its antlers had the broad flat palmate structure of moose antlers, only much larger. "Moose" or "British elk" used to roam all over northern Eurasia, but were exterminated from the British Isles about four thousand years ago (figure 16.1A and figure 16.1B). What North Americans call an "elk" is a completely different kind of deer, *Cervus canadensis*. Gigantic antlers like these had turned up in Irish peat bogs for centuries, but this was the first official published notice and description of them. The Molyneux (1695) article begins:

> That no real species of living creatures is so utterly extinct, as to be lost entirely out of the World, since it was first created, is the opinion of many naturalists, and 'tis grounded on so good a principle of Providence taking care in general of all of its animal productions, that it deserves our ascent.[1]

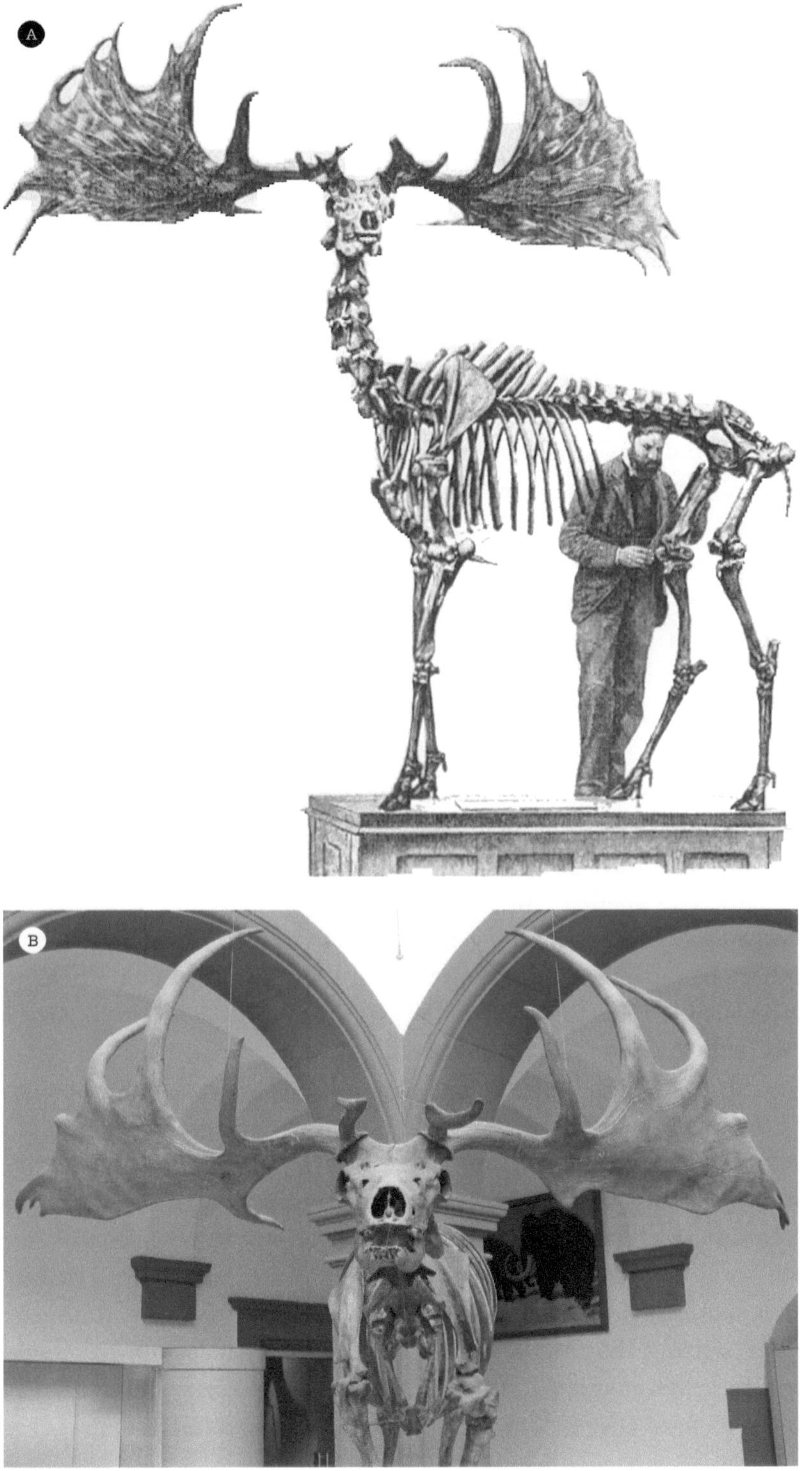

Figure 16.1 ▲

The "Irish elk" or giant deer, *Megaloceros giganteus*. (*A*) Antique image of the skeleton. (*B*) Head-on view of the antlers. (Courtesy of Wikimedia Commons)

Keep in mind that this is still 150 years before the reality of extinction was proven by Cuvier (see chapter 1), and the notion of Divine Providence and the "fullness of nature" did not allow for the possibility of extinction. Molyneux could not accept that this creature was extinct and seized on reports of the American moose as proof it must still live there.

However, this mysterious deer was not given a formal name until Friedrich Blumenbach described it as *Alce gigantea* in 1799, putting it in the same genus as the moose but using a different variant of its spelling. Blumenbach remarked that the distance between the summits of its giant antlers may attain about 14 feet (4.4 meters). In 1828, Joshua Brooke gave a listing of his zoological collection and replaced the name "*Alce*" with *Megalocerus* ("big horn" in Greek). As he wrote in 1827, "Amongst other Fossil Bones, there [are] . . . two uncommonly fine Crania of the *Megalocerus antiquorum* (Mihi)(Irish), with unusually fine horns, (in part restored)."[2] After this initial publication, Brookes and others abandoned the spelling "*Megalocerus*" and consistently spelled it *Megaloceros*, and that has been the official spelling (and the proper Greek spelling) ever since. The official type specimen is displayed in Barmeath Castle in Ireland, where Thomas Wright first saw and described it. In 1844, Richard Owen renamed it *Cervus (Megaceros) hibernicus*, making it a subgenus of the common European deer *Cervus*. During most of the nineteenth and early twentieth century, the name was spelled "*Megaceros*," ignoring the original spelling, until George Gaylord Simpson revised that name in his 1945 mammal classification. Not until 1989 did the International Commission on Zoological Nomenclature officially confirm the priority of *Megaloceros* over "*Megalocerus*" and "*Megaceros*."

By 1812, Georges Cuvier agreed that the huge antlers did not belong to any living animal, and he published a minute detailed description of it. He declared it to be extinct, and that it was "*le plus célèbre de tous les ruminans fossiles*" [the most famous of all fossil ruminants].[3] It was indeed celebrated among the famous extinct animals known to early paleontologists, such as the mammoth and the giant ground sloth, plus Cuvier's *Palaeotherium* and *Anoplotherium* from the Eocene of the Paris Basin. A life-sized model of it was featured in the famous Crystal Palace reconstructions of prehistoric life, created in 1851 by Waterhouse Hawkins under the supervision of Richard Owen. Some of these reconstructions are famous in their sprawling quadrupedal lizard-like versions of the first known dinosaurs, such as *Megalosaurus, Iguanodon, Hylaeosaurus*, plus ichthyosaurs and plesiosaurs in the water. They are still on display in a park in the Sydenham suburb of south London, even though the original Crystal Palace has long since burned down.

Giant deer remains were so abundant in the peat bogs in Ireland that for much of the nineteenth century there was a thriving trade in them to supply museums and collectors. Skulls of large bucks with their antlers still attached were particularly prized as decoration for castles and aristocratic homes. In 1865, full skeletons might fetch £30, while particularly good heads with antlers could cost £15, with £15 being more than thirty weeks' wages for a low-skilled worker at the time. Indeed, the Leeds Philosophical and Literary Society bought a full skeleton in 1847, from Glennon's in Dublin, for £38. Discovered at Lough Gur, near Limerick, Ireland, it is still on display at the Leeds City Museum.

Thanks to its long history of study, much has been written about *Megaloceros*. As Stephen Jay Gould wrote in his 1973 essay, "The Misnamed, Mistreated, and Misunderstood Irish Elk," *Megaloceros* was not an "elk," in the sense we understand it in North America, or what the Shawnee and Cree peoples called the "wapiti," or what scientists call *Cervus canadensis*. As briefly mentioned already, the confusion arises because in the British Isles the moose (*Alces alces*) had long been exterminated, so English-speaking peoples used the work "elk" for any "large deer," not having any memory of the European moose. When the first American colonists saw the wapiti, they incorrectly called this deer an "elk" and the name stuck. Scientists officially call it the "giant deer," although the media and the public refuse to stop using the misnomer "Irish elk."

Nor was the "Irish elk" exclusively Irish, but it is found all across northern Eurasia all the way to China, and as far south as northern Africa. The majority of the good specimens of *Megaloceros giganteus*, the last of the four named species in that genus, come from Ireland and are the vast majority of all the complete specimens with good antlers.

The most common topic of discussion about *Megaloceros* is the enormous size of its antlers (figures 16.1B, 16.2). The largest reached over 12 feet (4 meters) from tip to tip and weighed 88 pounds (40 kilograms)! What's even more amazing, bucks had to grow 40 kilograms of bone in a single growing

Figure 16.2 ▲

Reconstruction of the giant deer with human for scale. (Art courtesy of N.? Tamura)

season to have large antlers in time for the fall breeding season—then shed 40 kilograms of bone all at once, like all male deer do on an annual basis. This led to rampant speculation about the adaptive significance of growing such huge antlers every year. In the late nineteenth and early twentieth century, several scientists (such as Henry Fairfield Osborn) argued that these "bizarre" structures must have been maladaptive, examples of evolution moving in a straight line (orthogenesis) until it is out of control of natural selection, and they were actually detrimental to the animal. Some argued that its huge antlers made them more likely to be snagged in tree branches and led to their extinction. In 1925, the great Yale paleontologist Richard Swann Lull wrote: "natural selection will not account for overspecialization, for it is a manifest that, while an organ can be brought to the point of perfection by selection, it would never be carried to a condition where it is an actual menace to survival . . . [as in] the great branching antlers of the extinct Irish deer."[4]

This absurd notion was first debunked by Julian Huxley in the 1930s, who suggested that these antlers were not completely oversized—*Megaloceros* was just a huge deer, reaching 6.6 feet (2 meters) at the shoulder, and weighing about 1,540 pounds (700 kilograms) or more, so its antlers are the right size. Huxley argued that across all deer, the antlers do not increase in the same proportion to body size, but increase faster, a phenomenon known as allometric growth. The antlers of larger deer are not just absolutely larger than those of smaller deer but relatively larger as well. This was formally measured and established in a paper by Stephen Jay Gould in 1973, where he showed that the size of the antlers follows a standard allometric growth curve and are the right size for a deer this huge. Instead, as numerous authors pointed out by comparing it to other deer, it is clear that larger and larger antlers are required for bucks to show their relative strength to ward off rivals and impress the does, and, if necessary, to drive off predators. This explains why they are so broad in head-on view, and why they have such elaborate tines, making them very ornate and impressive. It is a classic case of sexual selection and allometric scaling, not evolution run amok.

So if it's not a true elk (genus *Cervus*, such as the red deer, sika deer, and American wapiti or "elk"), what is the giant deer related to? Based on mitochondrial DNA, it turns out that *Megaloceros* is most closely related to the Eurasian fallow deer, *Dama dama* (figure 16.3), whose bucks also sport broad palmate antlers, although nowhere near as large as those of *Megaloceros*. Fallow deer were originally spread all over Europe during the last interglacial and glacial maximum, but then their range collapsed due to the climatic changes, and they only survived in the Balkans, some Greek Islands, Turkey. and the Middle East. Later, they were spread across Central Europe and Britain by the Romans, so they used to roam across much of Europe. Now there are populations in game reserves and zoos all around the world.

Figure 16.3 ▲

Male fallow deer, the closest living relative of the giant deer, showing its broad palmate antlers. (Courtesy of Wikimedia Commons)

DEER TO US ALL

From the prehistoric cave paintings that Cro-Magnon people used to help their hunting, to Santa's reindeer, Bambi, and Bullwinkle the Moose, deer have long been a part of human culture. Cave paintings from ten thousand to twenty thousand years ago clearly depict various species of deer. Red deer remains have been found in more than 95 percent of all European Paleolithic and Mesolithic archaeological sites. Deer were so important in the Middle Ages that Norman kings planted special forests in southern England as their exclusive game reserves. Besides hunting deer for meat, hides, sinew, and bone, Pleistocene and early Holocene humans also apparently gathered shed deer antlers in large quantities. Antlers could be carved into variety of tools, such as picks and other digging implements, needles, fish hooks, atlatls (spear throwers), and spear straighteners. The strong but easily carved nature of antlers made them ideal for use as handles on stone knives and axes.

True deer, family Cervidae, are unique among ungulates in bearing antlers. These are structures growing from the head of the animals, somewhat analogous to horns, which are only found in the family Bovidae. But unlike true horns, which consist of a permanent bone horn core covered with a sheet of keratin or skin and remain on the animal for life, antlers consist of deciduous bone. The outer layer is composed of compact bone surrounded by spongy core. Once fully grown and in place, antlers lack a covering sheath of any kind, and each year they are shed, leaving only a short protuberance known as pedicel at the base, surrounded by a ring of bone known as the burr, and the next year they are regrown. Antlers are found only in males, or bucks, except in the case of reindeer, where both sexes have antlers.

Antlers are thought to be one of the fastest-growing animal tissues known. In the common European red deer (*Cervus elaphus*), the antlers are cast or shed in late fall or winter, and by early spring new antlers begin to grow. As they are growing, the antler is covered with velvet, or fur-covered skin, and the growing bone is well supplied with blood vessels. By late summer, the antlers are fully grown and the velvet dries up and begins to peel off in long strips of dead skin. The animal may rub its antlers against trees to wear off and remove the velvet. The male deer or bucks are now ready for the rut (mating season), prepared with their new antlers as weapons to fight with each other and for impressing the females.

Of the living artiodactyls, the deer are the second most diverse family alive, and one of the most familiar. There are at least 20 genera and 90 species alive today, and hundreds more known from fossils. Deer first appeared in the fossil record with *Amphitragulus* from the late Oligocene of Europe. A number of fossil deer, such as *Dicrocerus, Euprox*, and *Heteroprox*, evolved during the Miocene in Eurasia and North Africa (figure 16.4). *Dicrocerus* had single-forked antlers, and *Stephanocemas* had more complex, diffuse antlers, but most Miocene deer lacked the fully developed antlers found in the living cervids. Some middle Miocene cervids resemble the primitive deer with tiny antlers such as the muntjacs, or forms with no antlers but large canine tusks, such as the Chinese water deer, *Hydropotes*. By the late Miocene, Eurasian deer had diversified into dozens of species in a number of genera, some with small antlers, and other with large complex antlers.

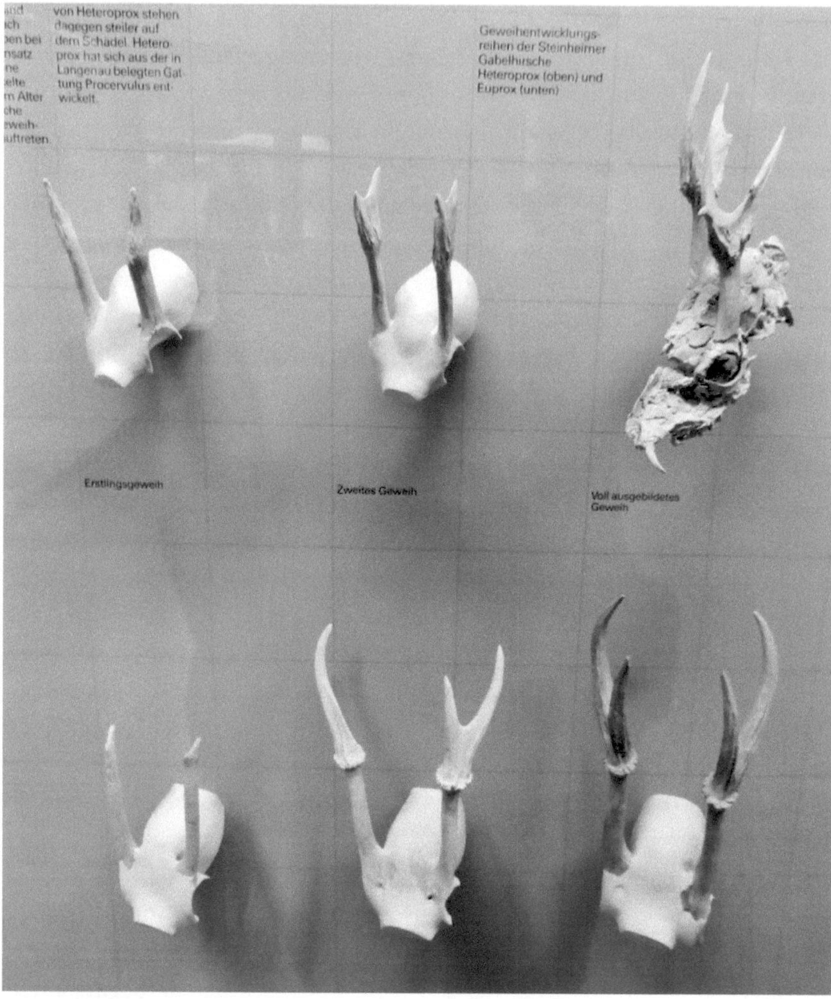

Figure 16.4 ▲

Museum display showing the range of variation of the primitive European deer *Euprox, Heteroprox*, and *Procervulus*. (Courtesy of Wikimedia Commons).

One of the strangest of these was *Hoplitomeryx*, a bizarre form with permanent bony horns rather than antlers (but still regarded as a deer relative, not a bovid). It has a long horn on its nose, and a pair of pronged horns over its eyes (somewhat like the dinosaur *Triceratops*), a horn on the center of its skull like a unicorn horn, plus long protruding canine tusks (figure 16.5). It

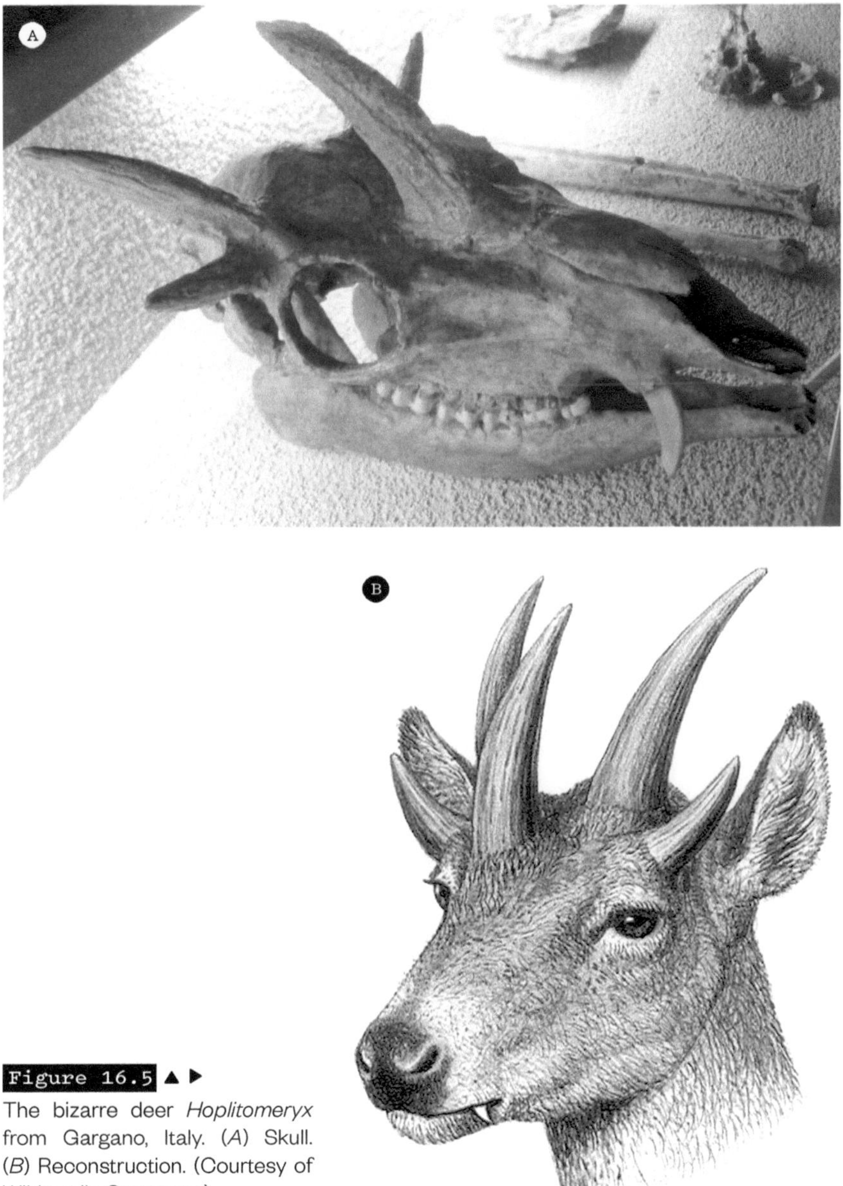

Figure 16.5 ▲ ▶

The bizarre deer *Hoplitomeryx* from Gargano, Italy. (*A*) Skull. (*B*) Reconstruction. (Courtesy of Wikimedia Commons)

is known only from cave deposits of late Miocene and early Pliocene age on the island of Gargano off the southern tip of Italy. It is certainly one of the strangest horned creatures ever found.

By the end of the Miocene, cervids immigrated from Eurasia to North America. During the Pliocene and Pleistocene, North America featured such extinct deer as *Bretzia* (figure 16.6), with palmate moose-like antlers, and the genus of the living white-tailed and mule deer, *Odocoileus*. Sometime before or during the formation of the Panama land bridge around 3.5 Ma, deer migrated to South America along with the other invading mammals from the North American fauna. Once established, an evolutionary radiation of uniquely South American deer occurred, leading to a modern diversity of six uniquely South American genera and dozens of species, including the brocket deer, pudus, huemuls, marsh deer, and pampas deer.

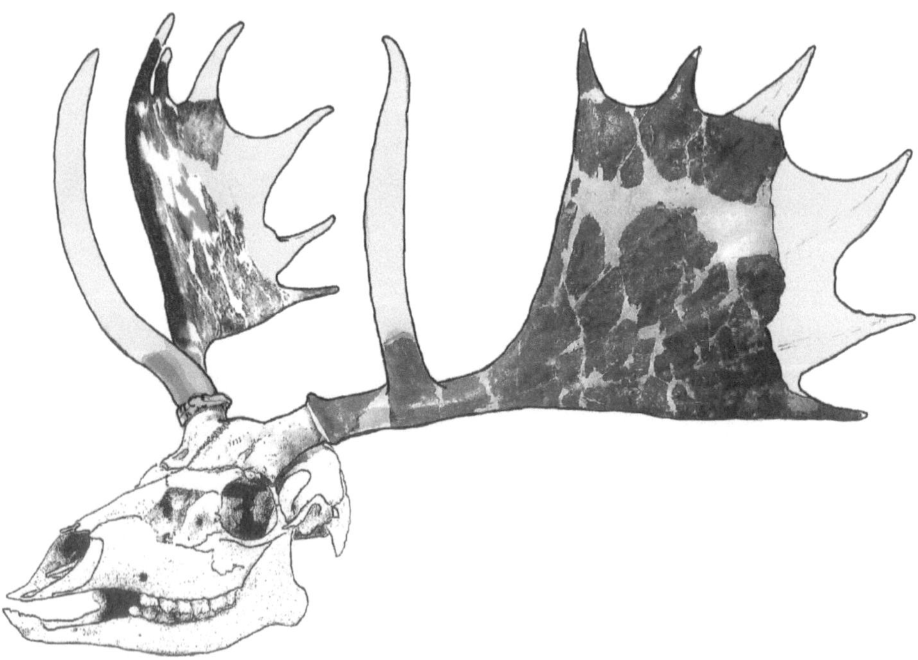

Figure 16.6 ▲
The primitive American deer *Bretzia* from the latest Miocene of Washington. (Courtesy of Wikimedia Commons)

Meanwhile, the Eurasian continent featured some truly spectacular fossil deer during the Pleistocene, such as the giant deer. Another one of these, *Eucladoceras*, was the size of a moose, and some species had huge antlers with more than a dozen tines on each side, making for extremely complex bushy antlers were over 5.6 feet (1.7 meters) wide (figure 16.7).

PSEUDO-DEER

In the early Miocene, another Eurasian family, known as the Palaeomerycidae, first appeared. Originally mistaken for true deer (Cervidae) or for pronghorns (Antilocapridae), they have since been recognized as a distinct

Figure 16.7 ▲
Reconstruction of the deer with multiple tined antlers, *Eucladoceros*. (Art by N. Tamura)

family. In many features, they look quite deer-like in their overall build, although they tend to have more primitive and lower-crowned teeth than cervids, and probably only browsed on soft vegetation. But unlike deer, they did not have antlers, which are shed each fall in males and grown back in the spring. Instead, the palaeomerycids had permanent bony horns that were never shed, apparently with a layer of skin around the bony horn core (like the ossicones in giraffes and okapis). For this reason, palaeomerycids have been a source of scientific debate: are they closer to giraffes, or are they closer to true deer? The anatomical evidence from the fossils suggests they are related to giraffes and not deer. Unfortunately, they are now extinct, so we have no molecular evidence on the question.

Palaeomerycids first appear in the early Miocene with European fossils like *Triceromeryx*, which has just two ossicones over its eye socket that were short and straight, like the living giraffe. *Palaeomeryx*, from the middle Miocene of Spain, appeared to be hornless. *Ampelomeryx* from the early Miocene of Spain had paired ossicones over the eye sockets which formed flat, wide eyeshades, and another forked Y-shaped ossicone on the back of its head. *Xenokeryx* was even stranger, with not only a pair of simple upward-pointing ossicones over its eyes, but a T-shaped appendage on the back of its head (figure 16.8A).

Another group of pseudo-deer are the North American dromomerycids. Until recently, they were thought to be related to palaeomerycids, but the latest work now separates them into a different family, whose relationships to other ruminants is still controversial. They first migrated from Eurasia to North America about 18.5 million years ago in three separate waves, which each became the basis for a great evolutionary radiation of different dromomerycids with a wide variety of cranial appendages (figure 16.9). Many had broad snouts and relatively short limbs with broadly flaring hooves, so they were probably browsers who lived in forests, like deer and especially moose, and not specialized for grazing or running as were camels, pronghorns, horses, and many other denizens of the Miocene North American savannas.

One of these subfamilies, the Aletomerycinae, were a small group that included the short-horned but fast-running *Aletomeryx* (known from large quarry samples in western Nebraska), and the peculiar *Sinclairomeryx*, with long cylindrical horns that curved upward, back, and then pointed forward (figure 16.9. The second subfamily, the Dromomerycinae, included

Figure 16.8 ▲ ▶

Palaeomerycoids and dromomerycids. (*A*) Reconstruction of the Miocene European palaeomerycoid *Xenokeryx*. (*B*) Reconstruction of the North American *Dromomeryx*. (*C*) The author holding the skull of the dromomerycid *Procranioceras skinneri*. ([*A*] Courtesy of Wikimedia Commons; [*B*] art by R. Bruce Horsfall, courtesy of Wikimedia Commons; [*C*] photo by the author).

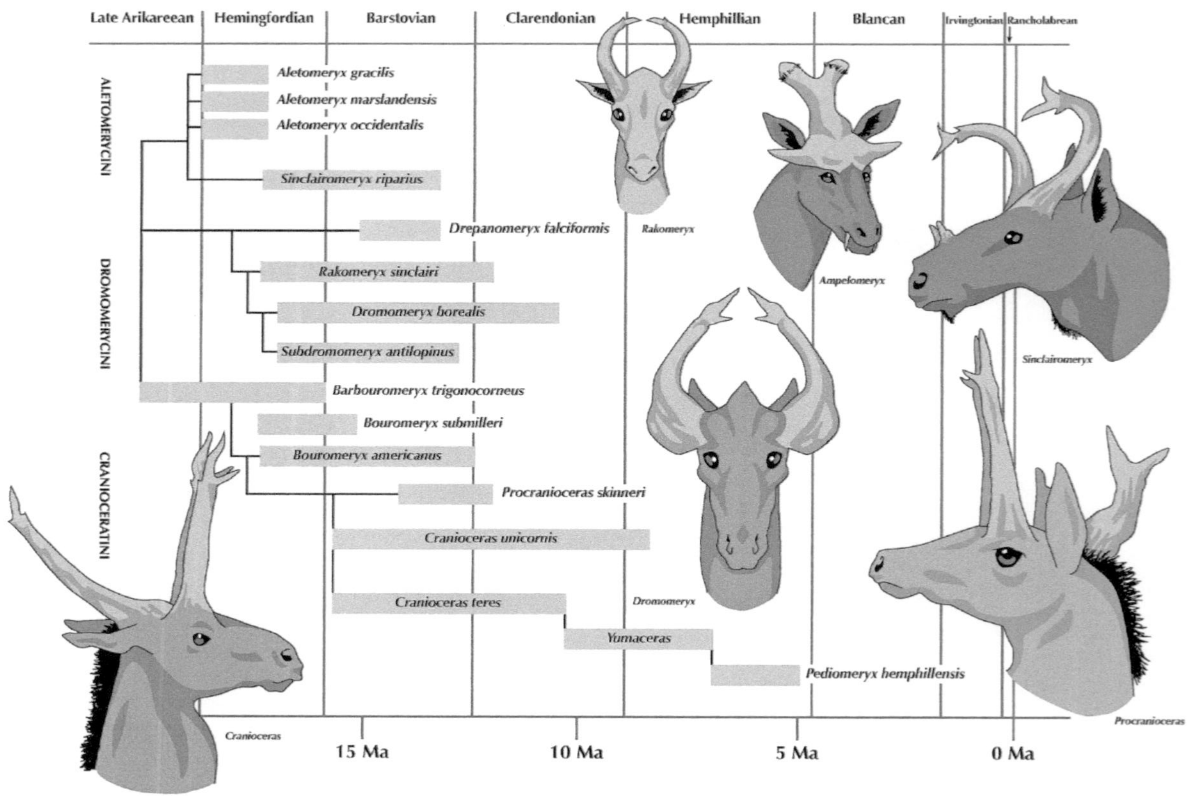

Figure 16.9 ▲

Phylogeny of the North American dromomerycids, showing the time ranges and relationships of the genera. (Art by M. P. Williams)

the straight-horned *Dromomeryx* (figure 16.8B), the banana-horned Rakomeryx, and the palmate horned *Drepanomeryx*. The third subfamily, the Cranioceratinae, was the most diverse of the group. Beginning with the stubby horned *Barbouromeryx*, they developed not only a straight upward-pointing horn over each eyebrow but a progressively longer horn that protruded upward and backward from the back of the skull, culminating with fossils like *Procranioceras* (figure 16.8C), *Cranioceras*, and *Pediomeryx* (figure 16.9).

All of these North American dromomerycids reached a peak in diversity in the middle Miocene, then declined rapidly, so only *Pediomeryx* survived to the end of the Miocene, when the group went extinct in both Eurasia and North America. As with the terminal Miocene extinction of North American rhinos, musk deer, protoceratids, and many other groups, they may have required more dense brush and wetter climates and could not survive in the Pliocene world of cool dry grasslands.

PRONGHORNS ARE NOT ANTELOPES!

If you travel across the plains and grasslands of western North America, you might see pronghorns racing across the landscape at up to 55 mph, the second fastest land animal on the planet after the African cheetah. No cougar or bear or wolf can catch them, so their only threat is from humans with guns. In fact, they are so common that hunting licenses for them are cheap in many states.

The American pronghorn is known to scientists by the name *Antilocapra americana*. It is found in the grasslands and prairies of the western half of North America, from southern Canada to northern Mexico. Native American cultures hunted them, and there are 330 different names of them recorded from 219 different languages. Pedro de Castañeda, who journaled Coronado's expedition in 1540, described them as flocks of goats that were "so fast that they disappeared very quickly." In 1776 Gabriel Maraga noted that they were called *berrendos*, a Spanish word meaning "two-colored," the same name they have today in Mexico. In 1804 Lewis and Clark saw them somewhere along the Niobrara River and called them "goat-like antelopes."

Although pronghorns are mentioned in a number of European bestiaries based on the Spanish accounts, they were not illustrated in European literature until a 1775 illustration in a volume by Johann Schreber. They were first formally described in 1815 by the American zoologist George Ord, who first called it the *Antelope americana*, but in 1818, he changed the name to "*Antilocapra*," which means "goat-antelope," their correct genus today.

The first common myth is that pronghorns are antelopes. Nearly everyone but scientists calls them "antelopes" or "pronghorn antelopes," but true antelopes live only in Africa and Asia and are members of the family Bovidae, along with cattle, sheep, and goats. Pronghorns do resemble some African antelopes, but this is a classic example of convergent evolution. They occupy the same ecological niche of antelopes in North America because true antelopes have never been native to this continent. Both their anatomy, and especially their DNA, show they are not related to true antelopes at all but are actually closest to giraffes among living mammal groups.

Pronghorns are a strictly North American family that has never dispersed to any other continent once they first arrived here from Asia about 21 Ma. They were very diverse on this continent, with more than a dozen genera known (figure 16.10), sporting many different kinds of horns, and as many as four different genera even at the end of the last Ice Age.

Pronghorns have a different kind of headgear from the horns you find in bovine, or the antlers in deer. All of these cranial appendages have a bony core, most of which are covered by a sheath of keratin, the same protein that makes up hair and nails and hooves. Bovines have true horns, where the sheath is attached to the bony horn core permanently. Deer have antlers, which are made of a bony core covered by skin or "velvet" when they are growing. In the fall, the velvet is shed, and eventually bucks shed their antlers as well, and then regrow them again the next spring. Giraffes have ossicones, made of bony core surrounded by skin.

But pronghorns have something else: a bony core with a keratinous sheath that is shed every year. For fossil pronghorns, only the bony core is preserved, so we do not know what kind of sheath they might have had. And the earliest pronghorns, the merycodonts, apparently grew a kind of velvet on their horns, because their horns often have burrs at the base, but never shed them like deer antlers are shed, because we never find merycodonts with pedicels and no horn. The bony horn core is usually the most distinctive feature of most fossil pronghorns and is what we use to recognize the genera and species because their teeth and other anatomy are highly stereotyped and don't change much.

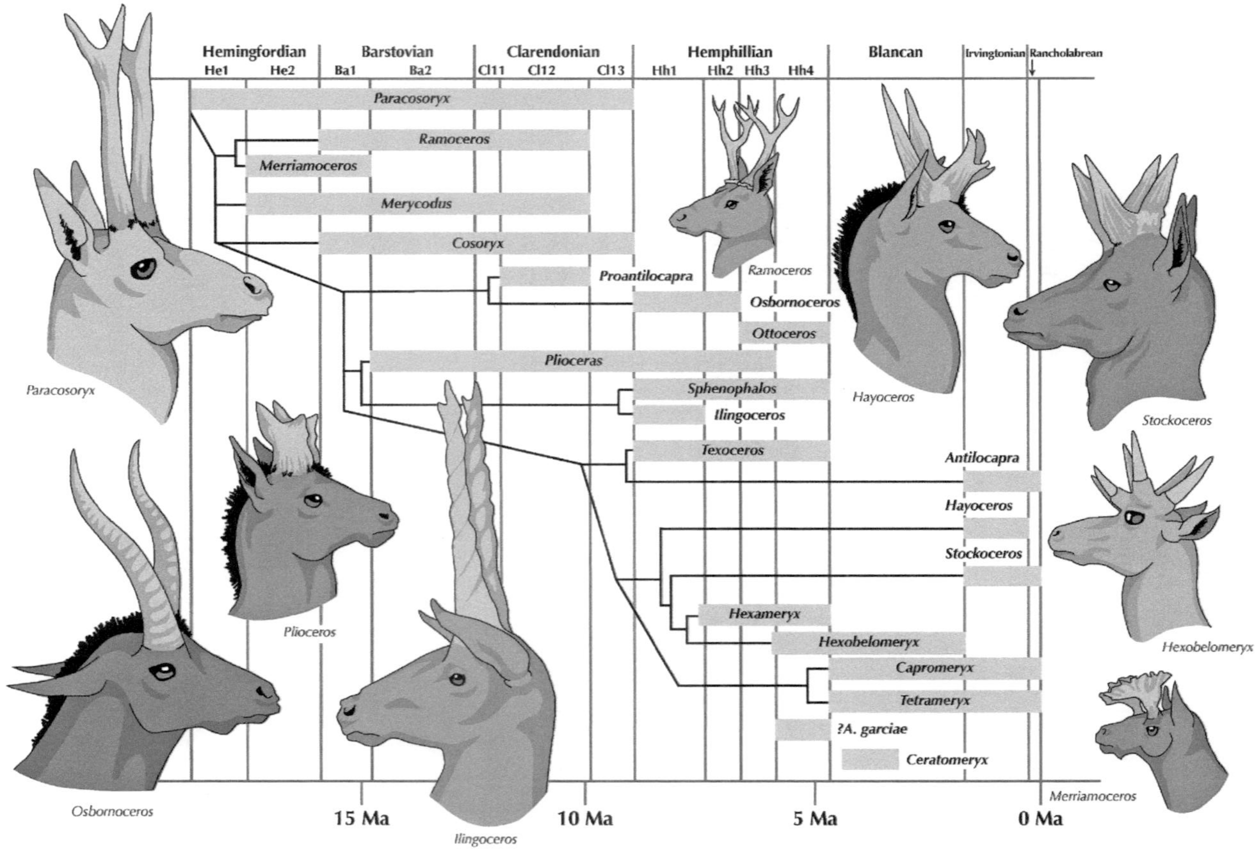

Figure 16.10 ▲

Phylogeny of the pronghorns, showing the time ranges and relationships of the genera. (Art by M. P. Williams)

The first great radiation of pronghorns, from about 21 Ma until about 10 Ma, were the merycodont pronghorns, which were often the most common fossils in many localities about 15–12 Ma (figure 16.2). The merycodonts include four and possibly five genera, with dozens of invalid genera and species that were in the literature until recently. These included the most primitive pronghorn, *Paracosoryx*, with long shafts on backward-pointing Y-shaped horns; the highly distinctive *Merriamoceros* (figure 16.11A), with palmate horns a bit like a tiny moose antler; *Ramoceros*, with multi-tined deer-like horns that were asymmetrical (figure 16.11B); and *Merycodus* and *Cosoryx*, which may not be distinct genera because the length of the shaft of the horns (used to tell the genera apart) varies continuously within populations.

Merycodonts vanished around 12 Ma, but in their place began a radiation of genera of the antilocaprine pronghorns, ancestors of the living species (figure 16.10). These began with *Proantilocapra* with short, hooked horns; *Osbornoceros*, with long curves horns like those of gazelles; *Sphenophalos*, with flat pointed horns; and *Plioceros*. One of the most distinctive was *Ilingoceros*, with long straight corkscrew horns. *Hayoceros* had short front horns and long back horns, while *Stockoceros* was a common Pleistocene genus with equal-length pairs of horns on both sides. Even more bizarre is *Hexameryx*, with six horns, and *Hexobelomeryx*, with a different configuration of six horns. The final lineage is *Tetrameryx*, with long back horns and tiny front horns, and the dwarf pronghorn, *Capromeryx*. It was the smallest of four genera of Ice Age pronghorns, including *Tetrameryx, Stockoceros*, and the living genus *Antilocapra*. *Capromeryx* is particularly common at La Brea Tar Pits, where hundreds of specimens are known (figure 16.11C and figure 16.11D).

As we mentioned already, the pronghorn is the second fastest land animal on Earth, with no predators in North America today that could catch them. Why do they need to be so fast? It turns out that there was a predator in the Ice Ages, the American cheetah *Miracinonyx*, which probably hunted them and forced them to become extremely fast. That predator has vanished, but the speedy pronghorn lives on, an evolutionary anachronism.

Pronghorns are a truly American original, so much so that they are the official symbol of the American Society of Mammalogists. Only one species now remains of what was once a huge radiation of pronghorns, with as many as four genera roaming North America only twelve thousand years ago.

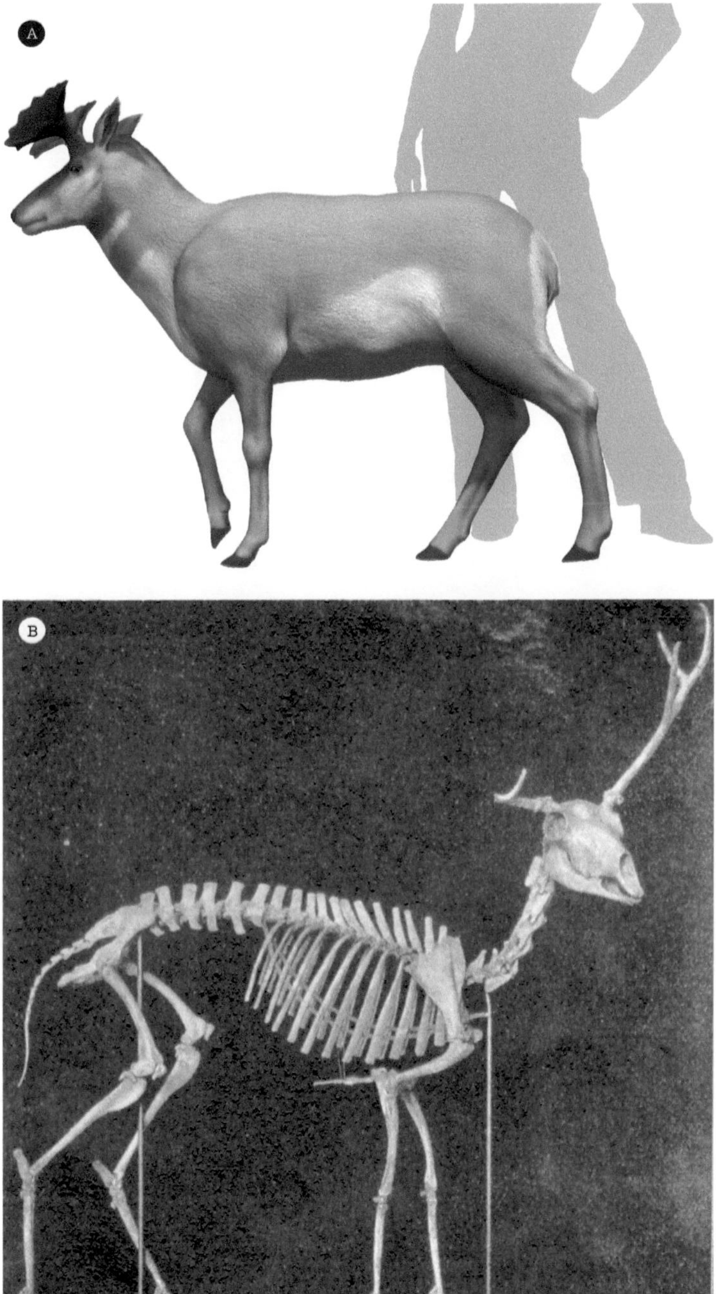

Figure 16.11 ▲ ▶

Some fossil pronghorns. (*A*) Reconstruction of *Merriamoceras*. (*B*) Mounted skeleton of *Ramoceros*, showing the horn asymmetry. (*C*) Mounted skeleton of the La Brea dwarf pronghorn, *Capromeryx minor*. (*D*) Life-sized model of *Capromeryx minor* in the display case at the La Brea Tar Pits Museum, with Collections Manager Aisling Farrell. ([*A*] Art by N. Tamura; [*B*] courtesy of Wikimedia Commons; [*C and D*] photos by the author).

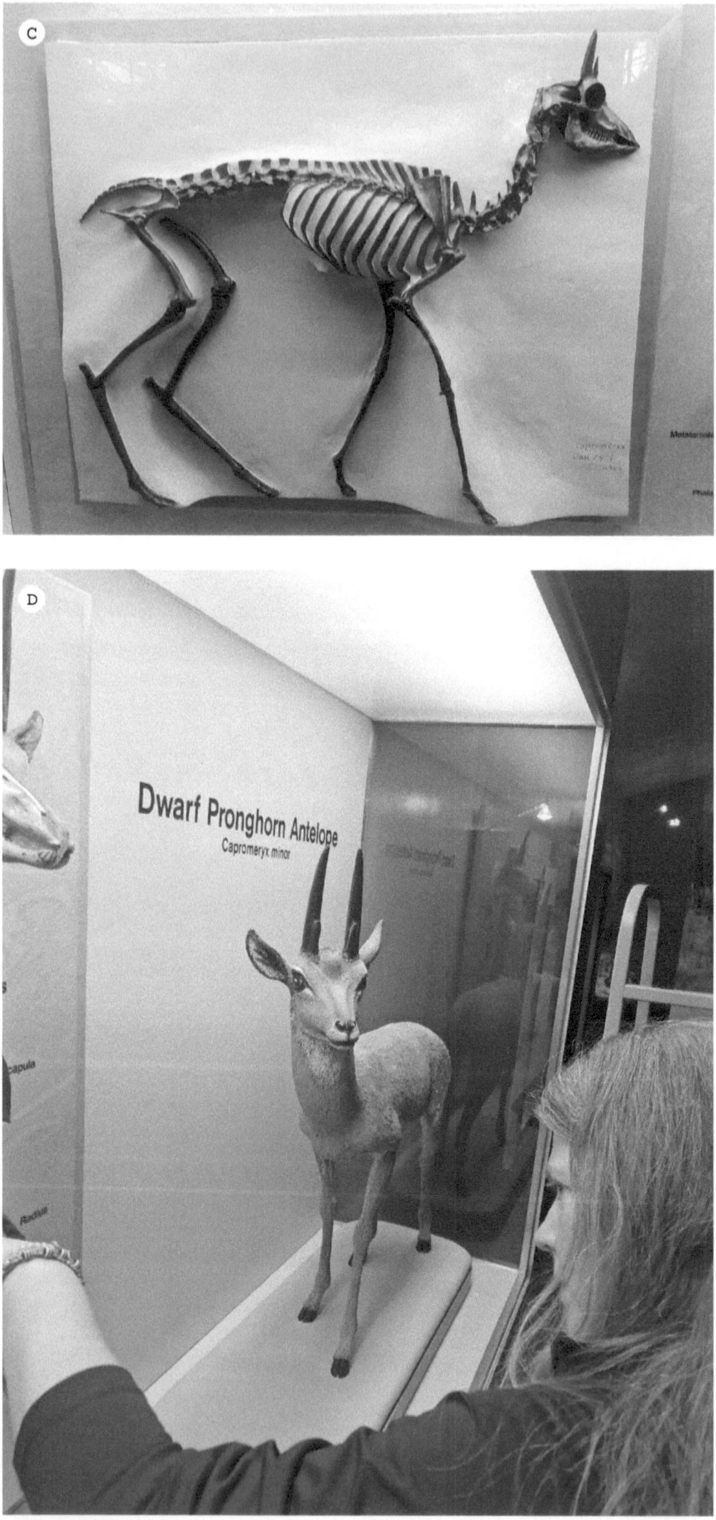

Figure 16.11 ▲
(*continued*)

NOTES

1. Thomas Molyneux, "A Discourse Concerning the Large Horns Frequently Found under Ground in Ireland, Concluding from Them That the Great American Deer, Call'd a Moose, Was Formerly Common in That Island: With Remarks on Some Other Things Natural to That Country," *Philosophical Transactions of the Royal Society* 19, no. 227 (1695): 489–512.
2. Joshua Brookes, *Brookesian Museum. The Museum of Joshua Brookes, Esq. Anatomical and Zoological Preparations* (Gold and Walton, 1827), 20.
3. Georges Cuvier, cited in Stephen Jay Gould, "The Origin and Function of 'Bizarre' Structures: Antler Size and Skull Size in the 'Irish Elk,' *Megaloceros giganteus*," *Evolution* 28, no. 2 (1974): 191–220.
4. Richard Swann Lull, cited in Gould, "The Origin and Function of 'Bizarre' Structures."

FOR FURTHER READING

Agustí, J., and M. Anton. *Mammoths, Sabertooths, and Hominids: 65 Million Years of Mammalian Evolution in Europe*. Columbia University Press, 2005.

Barnosky, A. D. *Taphonomy and Herd Structure of the Extinct Irish Elk, Megaloceros giganteus. Science* 228, no. 4697 (1985): 340–344.

Blumenbach, J. *Handbuch der Naturgeschichte*. 6th ed. 16 (1799): 697.

Byers, J. A. *American Pronghorn: Social Adaptations and the Ghosts of Predators Past*. Chicago University Press, 1997.

Croitor, R. "Taxonomy, Systematics and Evolution of Giant Deer *Megaloceros giganteus* (Blumenbach, 1799) (Cervidae, Mammalia) from the Pleistocene of Eurasia." *Quaternary* 4, no. 4 (2021): 36.

Di Stefano, G., and C. Petronio. "Systematics and Evolution of the Eurasian Plio-Pleistocene Tribe Cervini (Artiodactyla, Mammalia)." *Geologica Romana* 36 (2002): 311–334.

Emlen, D. J. "The Evolution of Animal Weapons." *Annual Review of Ecology, Evolution, and Systematics* 39 (2008): 387–413.

Geist, V. *Deer of the World: Their Evolution, Behaviour, and Ecology*. Stackpole, 1998.

Gentry, A. W., and G. Rössner. "The Miocene Differentiation of Old World Pecora (Mammalia)." *Historical Biology* 7, no. 2 (1994): 115–158.

Gilbert, C., A. Ropiquet, and A. Hassanin. "Mitochondrial and Nuclear Phylogenies of Cervidae (Mammalia, Ruminantia): Systematics, Morphology, and Biogeography." *Molecular Phylogenetics and Evolution* 40, no. 1 (2006): 101–117.

Gonzalez, S., A. Kitchener, and A. Lister. "Survival of the Irish Elk Into the Holocene." *Nature* 405, no. 6788 (2000): 753–754.

Gould, S. J. "The Misnamed, Mistreated, and Misunderstood Irish Elk." In *Ever Since Darwin*, 79–90. Norton, 1977.

——. "The Origin and Function of 'Bizarre' Structures: Antler Size and Skull Size in the 'Irish Elk,' *Megaloceros giganteus*." *Evolution* 28, no. 2 (1974): 191–220.

Groves, C. "Family Cervidae." In *The Evolution of Artiodactyls*, ed. D. R. Prothero and S. E. Foss, 249–256. Johns Hopkins University Press, 2007.

Higgins, P., J. Meachen, and D. Lovelace. "Were Pronghorns *(Antilocapra)* Primary Prey for North American Cheetahs (*Miracinonyx*)?" *Quaternary International* 647–648 (2023): 81–87.

Hughes, S., T. J. Hayden, C. J. Douady, C. Tougard, M. Germonpré, A. Stuart, et al. "Molecular Phylogeny of the Extinct Giant Deer, *Megaloceros giganteus*." *Molecular Phylogenetics and Evolution* 40, no. 1 (2006): 285–291.

Janis, C. M., and E. Manning. "Dromomerycidae." In *Evolution of Tertiary Mammals of North America*, ed. C. M. Janis, K. M. Scott, and L. L. Jacobs, 477–490. Cambridge University Press, 1998.

Klinkhamer, A. J., N. Woodley, J. M. Neenan, W. C. H. Parr, P. Clausen, R. Sánchez-Villagra, et al. "Head to Head: The Case for Fighting Behaviour in *Megaloceros giganteus* Using Finite-Element Analysis." *Proceedings of the Royal Society B: Biological Sciences* 286, no. 1912 (2019): 20191873.

Kolb, C., T. M. Scheyer, A. M. Lister, C. Azorit, J. de Vos, A. J. Schlingemann, et al. "Growth in Fossil and Extant Deer and Implications for Body Size and Life History Evolution." *BMC Evolutionary Biology* 15, no. 1 (2015): 19.

Lister, A. M. "The Evolution of the Giant Deer. *Megaloceros giganteus* (Blumenbach)." *Zoological Journal of the Linnean Society* 112, nos. 1–2 (1994): 65–100.

Lister, A. M., C. J. Edwards, D. A. W. Nock, M. Bunce, I. A. van Pijlen, D. G. Bradley, M. G. Thomas, and I. Barnes. "The Phylogenetic Position of the Giant Deer *Megaloceros giganteus*." *Nature* 438, no. 7069 (2005): 850–853.

Lister, A. M., and A. J. Stuart. "The Extinction of the Giant Deer *Megaloceros giganteus* (Blumenbach): New Radiocarbon Evidence." *Quaternary International* 500 (2019): 185–203.

Mennecart, B., D. DeMiguel, F. Bibi, G. E. Rössner, G. Métais, J. M. Neenan, et al. "Bony Labyrinth Morphology Clarifies the Origin and Evolution of Deer." *Scientific Reports* 7, no. 1 (2017): 13176.

Moen, R. A., J. Pastor, and Y. Cohen. "Antler Growth and Extinction of Irish Elk." *Evolutionary Ecology Research* 1, no. 2 (1999): 235–249.

Molyneux, T. "A Discourse Concerning the Large Horns Frequently Found under Ground in Ireland, Concluding from Them That the Great American Deer, Call'd a Moose, Was Formerly Common in That Island: With Remarks on Some Other Things Natural to That Country." *Philosophical Transactions of the Royal Society* 19, no. 227 (1695): 489–512.

Pitra, C., J. Fickel, E. Meijaard, and C. Groves. "Evolution and Phylogeny of Old World Deer." *Molecular Phylogenetics and Evolution* 33, no. 3 (2004): 880–895.

Prothero, D. R. *The Princeton Field Guide to Prehistoric Mammals*. Princeton University Press, 2016.

——. *Vertebrate Evolution: From Origins to Dinosaurs and Beyond*. Taylor & Francis/CRC Press, 2022.

Prothero, D. R., and M. R. Liter. "Family Palaeomerycidae." In *The Evolution of Artiodactyls*, ed. D. R. Prothero and S. Foss, 241–248. Johns Hopkins University Press, 2007.

——. "Systematics of the Dromomerycines and Aletomerycines (Artiodactyla: Palaeomerycidae) from the Miocene and Pliocene of North America." *New Mexico Museum of Natural History and Science Bulletin* 44 (2008): 273–298.

Prothero, D. R., and R. M. Schoch. *Horns, Tusks, and Flippers: The Evolution of Hoofed Mammals*. Johns Hopkins University Press, 2002.

Sánchez, I. M., J. L. Cantalapiedra, M. Ríos, and V. Quiralte. "Systematics and Evolution of the Miocene Three-Horned Palaeomerycid Ruminants (Mammalia, Cetartiodactyla)." *PLOS ONE* 10, no. 12 (2015). https://doi.org/10.1371/journal.pone.0143034.

Semprebon, G., C. Janis, and N. Solounias. "The Diets of the Dromomerycidae (Mammalia: Artiodactyla) and Their Response to Miocene Vegetational Change." *Journal of Vertebrate Paleontology* 24, no. 2 (2004): 427–444.

Stuart, A. J., P. A. Kosintsev, T. F. G. Higham, and A. M. Lister. "Pleistocene to Holocene Extinction Dynamics in Giant Deer and Woolly Mammoth." *Nature* 431, no. 7009 (2004): 684–689.

Tsuboi, M., B. T. Kopperud, M. Matschiner, M. Grabowski, C. Syrowatka, C. Pélabon, and T. F. Hansen. "Antler Allometry, the Irish Elk, and Gould Revisited." *Evolutionary Biology* 51, no. 1 (2024): 149–165.

Vislobokova, I. A. "Morphology, Taxonomy, and Phylogeny of Megacerines (Megacerini, Cervidae, Artiodactyla)." *Paleontological Journal* 47, no. 8 (2013): 833–950.

Webb, S. D. "Evolutionary History of New World Cervidae." In *Antelopes, Deer, and Relatives: Fossil Record, Behavioral Ecology, Systematics, and Conservation*, ed. E. S. Vrba and G. B. Schaller, 38–64. Yale University Press, 2000.

17 FROM LAND TO WATER I—THE EVOLUTION OF WHALES

BASILOSAURUS

In North America the black bear was seen by Hearne swimming for hours with widely open mouth, thus catching, like a whale, insects in the water. Even in so extreme a case as this, if the supply of insects were constant, and if better adapted competitors did not already exist in the country, I can see no difficulty in a race of bears being rendered, by natural selection, more and more aquatic in their structure and habits, with larger and larger mouths, till a creature was produced as monstrous as a whale.

—CHARLES DARWIN, *ON THE ORIGIN OF SPECIES* (1859)

KOCH'S "SEA SERPENT"

As long as human civilization has existed, there have been unscrupulous people who take advantage of others. Con men are not a recent invention, but there are just a few who try swindles on such a large scale that their con has become legendary. For example, most of the first good whale fossils were discovered in the early 1800s, but sadly they were misused by hucksters, not studied by qualified naturalists. The most famous of these promoters and con men was "Dr." Albert Koch. A famous swindler just a few degrees less honest than P. T. Barnum, Koch was always trying to make a buck from outlandish claims about natural history specimens. His prize was a huge skeleton he called "Hydrarchos" or the "Great Sea Serpent" (figure 17.1). In 1845, it was on display in Philadelphia, where it was the talk of the town. It stretched 114 feet (35 meters) through three rooms, with huge flippers up front. Its skull bore a long snout with huge triangular bladed teeth. It drew throngs of people anxious to gawk at it.

Figure 17.1 ▲
Contemporary illustration of Koch's fraudulent "Hydrarchos, the Great Sea Serpent," which was a composite of several prehistoric whale skeletons (Courtesy of Wikimedia Commons)

However good a promoter Koch was, he was no scientist. From a bunch of farmers, he had bought the vertebrae of the backbones of several specimens of a group of primitive whales known as archaeocetes, which are found in the middle Eocene (50–37 Ma) beds of Alabama, Mississippi, and Arkansas. These bones were so abundant that in some places in Alabama the farmers built stone fences from archaeocete bones. Koch then cobbled together a composite specimen made of at least three different whales to exaggerate its length and size. (This was a favorite strategy of Koch. Before this incident, he had exaggerated the size of a mastodon skeleton he owned by combining bones from different specimens and calling it "the Great Missourium"—see chapter 1.)

Koch then took his "sea serpent" on a tour of Europe, where it traveled from one city to the next, drawing huge crowds to see the "behemoth of the Bible." When scientists and naturalists in London and Berlin started warning the press that the specimen was a hoax, Koch took his specimen to Dresden, Breslau, Prague, and Vienna. King Frederick William IV of Prussia was so impressed that in 1847 he gave Koch an annual pension of 1,000 imperial thalers. Even though the king's own scientists denounced the specimen as a fraud, the aging monarch could not be convinced. In London, Gideon

Mantell (who found *Iguanodon*, the second named dinosaur) denounced the specimen and warned people about the damnable swindler. In New York, the anatomist Jeffrey Wyman exposed the fact that the specimen was not a reptile, nor was it from a single individual animal. Finally, Koch was reduced to taking it into rural backwaters, where the words of scientific experts had not yet reached. Eventually, he sold his monstrosity to the Wood Museum in Chicago. There it remained until it was destroyed by the Great Chicago Fire of 1871 allegedly started by Mrs. O'Leary's cow.

Despite Koch's fraudulent specimens, other Eocene whale fossils from Alabama had already reached the hands of legitimate naturalists. In 1834 the anatomist Richard Harlan named the huge bones *Basilosaurus*, or "emperor lizard." Harlan thought they were yet another kind of giant reptile we now call a dinosaur, some of which had just been discovered and named for the first time. However, in 1839 the great British anatomist Sir Richard Owen (the man who coined the word "Dinosauria" in 1841 and described some of the first dinosaur fossils ever found) looked at the distinctly mammalian double-rooted teeth of *Basilosaurus* and realized they were not reptiles at all, but huge whales. He tried to rename the creature "*Zeuglodon*" ("yoked tooth") to replace the misleading name "emperor lizard," but he was too late. By the rules of naming animals, the first name given is the accepted name, no matter how misleading it might be. This means that the correct name for this whale remains *Basilosaurus*, even though the "emperor lizard" is a mammal, not a lizard.

FISH OR MAMMAL?

One of our most amazing examples of evolution was the origin of whales from land mammals over the past fifty million years. Even though they have fish-like bodies, whales are not fish but mammals. They are warm blooded, breathe air with lungs, and some actually have hair in a few parts of their bodies. They are fully committed to life in the ocean, with amazing swimming and diving abilities. They no longer can live out of the water for very long and must give birth to live young in the water. Their nostrils have shifted from the tip of their snouts to the top of their heads, making a blowhole. Despite being fully aquatic, there are many signs that whales had to evolved from land mammals, and in the past thirty years, numerous fossils have been discovered that show how this incredible transition took place.

Even though humans had long classified whales as fish, it was the French naturalist Mathurin Jacques Brisson in 1756, who pointed out that whales were warm blooded and had lungs, not gills. The founder of modern classification, Carolus Linnaeus, picked this up from Brisson, and put whales in the Mammalia in his 1756 edition of the classification of animals. As he pointed out, whales breathed air through lungs, not gills, and were warm-blooded, and had many other anatomical differences that distinguished them from fish. "This order of *Cete* [which includes whales and dolphins] ought . . . to have been arranged with the class of Fishes; but . . . employing the circumstance of suckling their young as a characteristic mark for a number of animals, [I have included] these [as mammals]."[1]

Even though most people still treated whales as fish, by the 1800s Linnaeus's view was widely accepted by natural historians. As Oliver Goldsmith wrote in *A History of the Earth and Animated Nature* (1825, p. 137):

> As on land there are some orders of animals that seem formed to command the rest, with greater powers and more various instincts, so in the ocean there are fishes which seem formed upon a nobler plan than others, and that, to their fishy form, join the appetites and the conformation of quadrupeds. These are all of the cetaceous kind; and so much raised above their fellows of the deep, in their appetites and instincts, that almost all our modern naturalists have fairly excluded them from the finny tribes, and will have them called, not fishes, but great beasts of the ocean. With them it would be as improper to say men go to Greenland fishing for a whale, as it would be to say that a sportsman goes to Blackwall a fowling for mackerel.[2]

Still, how whales evolved was a mystery. In the 1859 first edition of *On the Origin of Species*, Darwin wrote, "In North America the black bear was seen by Hearne swimming for hours with widely open mouth, thus catching, like a whale, insects in the water. Even in so extreme a case as this, if the supply of insects were constant, and if better adapted competitors did not already exist in the country, I can see no difficulty in a race of bears being rendered, by natural selection, more and more aquatic in their structure and habits, with larger and larger mouths, till a creature was produced as monstrous as a whale."[3] Darwin was widely misunderstood as saying whales evolved from bears, but this was *not* what he said—he merely suggested a mechanism where a land animal could adapt to feeding on abundant small aquatic prey. By the 1880s, William Henry Flower of the British Museum had first suggested that whales had features in common with hoofed mammals, but that idea was way ahead of its time.

WHENCE THE WHALES?

Cut to the 1960s. A group of predatory hoofed mammals called mesonychids were becoming better and better known, and the paleontologist Leigh Van Valen noticed the similarity to their double-rooted triangular blade-like teeth and those of the earliest whale fossils. For the next thirty years, whales were thought to have originated from mesonychids.

Then in the late 1990s two astonishing discoveries were made. First, the molecular biologists looked at protein sequences and eventually DNA sequences, and over and over again, these data showed that the closest living relative of whales was the hippopotamus. Then in 2001, two independent paleontological research groups both reported discovering that two different fossil whales from Pakistan both had the distinctive double-pulley astragalus bone in their ankle, a feature only found in the even-toed hoofed mammals, or artiodactyls, which include the hippos. Two independent lines of evidence converged to confirm that whales were artiodactyls and descended from a common ancestor with hippos. That group of common ancestors is a peculiar extinct group of tapir-like artiodactyls known as anthracotheres, the direct ancestors of hippos, and very similar to the earliest whale fossils.

Anthracotheres were a group of pig-like creatures (figure 17.2) whose name literally means "coal beasts" (the first specimens of *Anthracotherium* came from a French coal mine). Some had relatively primitive pig-like skeletons, yet unlike other suoid artiodactyls (which usually have blunt rounded cusps), their upper cheek teeth have a strange mix of sharp W-shaped crests and small rounded cusps. Their teeth were suited to eating soft vegetation, and possibly roots and aquatic plants. Most anthracotheres were the size of a large pig or small hippo, but unlike a hippo most of them had a long narrow head and snout, making them unlike any other mammal that ever lived. They are usually thought to have been semi-aquatic animals like the pygmy hippo, and their fossils are usually found in ancient river and pond deposits, as well as in the coal swamps that gave them their name.

Figure 17.2 ▲
Reconstructions of the anthracotheres *Aepinacodon americanum* and *Elomeryx armatum*. (Drawings by K. Marriott)

Anthracotheres first appeared in the late middle Eocene, about 40 Ma, with small genera such as *Siamotherium* and *Anthracohyus* in Burma and Thailand. Shortly thereafter, the fossils of *Anthracotherium* appear across Eurasia, and *Heptacodon* fossils appeared in the middle Eocene beds of North America. From the late Eocene onward, anthracotheres are a ubiquitous element in Eurasian faunas, migrating all over the world from their

Eurasian base. There were additional immigration events to North America in the late Eocene (*Bothriodon, Aepinacodon*), and again in the late Oligocene (*Arretotherium*). Anthracotheres were among the first Eurasian groups to spread to Africa in the late Eocene, when it was still the domain of natives such as proboscideans and hyraxes. They went through another big evolutionary radiation in Eurasia in the early Miocene, but by the late Miocene only one genus, *Merycopotamus*, remained. When it vanished at the end of the Miocene, this entire family became extinct—except for those that gave rise to hippos.

The earliest known hippopotamus fossils appear in Africa in the early Miocene with *Morotochoerus* and *Kulutherium*, and then in the middle Miocene with *Kenyapotamus, Archaeopotamus*, and their relatives (figure 17.3). These early hippo skulls are extremely similar to the last of the anthracotheres such as *Merycopotamus*. Following a Miocene evolution of kenyapotamines, in the early Pliocene they were replaced by the modern subfamily Hippopotaminae. Most of these groups evolved in Africa, although one extinct genus *Hexaprotodon* occurred in southern Asia as well. Most of these

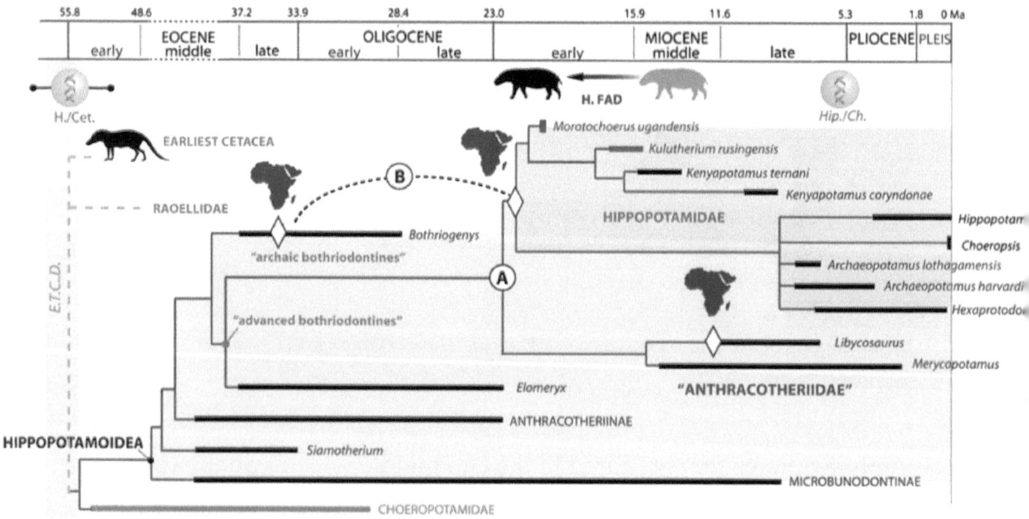

Figure 17.3 ▲

A phylogenetic tree showing the evolutionary relationships of hippos (Hippopotamidae) and their extinct relatives, the Anthracotheriidae, over geological time. (Redrawn from several sources)

fossil hippos were smaller primitive forms, more like the living pygmy hippo than the huge aquatic hippos.

A WHALE OF A TALE

Since the early 1990s, a remarkable series of ancestral whale fossils have been found that fill in all the gaps between the earliest anthracotheres and early whales (figures 17.3, 17.4). The oldest transitional whale fossil very similar to the early anthracotheres is *Indohyus*, a nearly complete skeleton from the early Eocene of Kashmir. Even though it was barely larger than a rabbit, with long hind legs for leaping and the body of a small deer, it had distinctive anatomical features that make it the link between whales and other artiodactyls. Its ear region shows many features that are found only in the whales. It also has limbs made of very dense bone (just like whales, hippos, and many other aquatic groups), which provides ballast and helps it wade or dive under water without floating out of control. Chemical analysis of the bones showed they were aquatic, but the chemistry of their teeth proves they ate land plants.

In 1978, Philip Gingerich and his colleagues found a fossil they called *Pakicetus*, named for Pakistan, the country where it was found (figure 17.4). It was a mostly terrestrial animal, with a wolf-like skeleton with four walking legs, but its skull was like that of an archaeocete whale, and there were features of the ear region that might have helped with underwater hearing. It came from river sediments that dated to about 50 Ma, older than any archaeocete. Even though its limbs were wolf-like for running, they were made of very dense bone that provide ballast, a feature that is common in aquatic animals, suggesting it spent a lot of time swimming and wading in the water.

From slightly younger beds in the same formation comes *Ambulocetus natans*, whose name literally translates to "walking swimming whale." It was from the Kuldana Formation, which is composed not only of nearshore marine beds but also of lake and river deposits. *Ambulocetus natans* is known from a nearly complete skeleton, it was about 10 feet (3 meters) long, had a long whale-like snout and triangular teeth, but still had four fully functional limbs with long fingers and toes that suggests it had webbed feet (figure 17.4). It was clearly not a fast swimmer. Instead, it was built more like a crocodile, with its long snout and body and large feet with webbed toes.

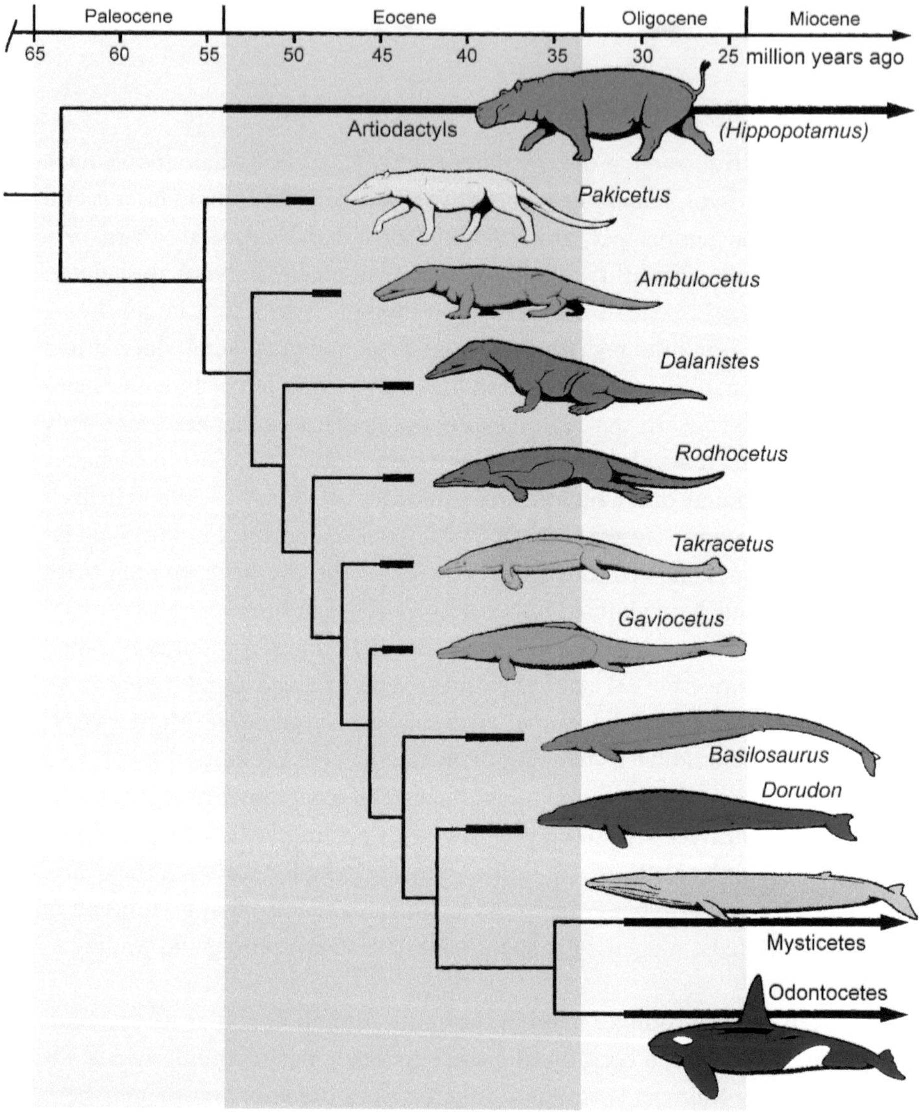

Figure 17.4 ▲

A diagram showing the evolution of whales from a land-dwelling artiodactyl ancestor related to the hippopotamus. The diagram traces a series of transitional species to modern whales, which are divided into mysticetes and odontocetes. (From D. R. Prothero, *Princeton Field Guide to Prehistoric Mammals* [Princeton Univerity Press, 2016].)

This suggests that it was an ambush predator, lurking semi-submerged in the shallow water and lunging out of the water to grab prey that came to drink. Chemical analysis of the bones showed it was primarily aquatic but lived in both fresh and saltwater.

The sequence of fossils continues with a smooth transition from specimens with four fully functional land legs to smaller and smaller hind limbs (figure 17.4). The same year that *Ambulocetus* was found in one part of Pakistan, Gingerich and colleagues discovered and reported another fossil they named *Rodhocetus* from different beds in the Balochistan region of Pakistan. Its skull is even longer and more whale-like than *Ambulocetus*, and the body is quite dolphin-like with a streamlined shape and no neck to separate the body from the head. More to the point, its limbs were very short and small with webbed feet, not very effective to drag its body across land, so it was primarily aquatic. But it did have hip bones and hip vertebrae fused together, so it was capable of limited land locomotion. The structure of the limbs and tail, however, suggested that it used mostly strokes of its hind feet to propel it with the tail acting as a rudder, so it did not yet have flukes or tail propulsion like modern whales.

The year after *Ambulocetus* and *Rodhocetus* were found, scientists in Pakistan found *Dalanistes* (figure 17.4). It is even more whale-like than *Ambulocetus*, with smaller but functional front and hind legs, but a much larger snout, more like that of an archaeocete whale. This made it a perfect intermediate between *Ambulocetus* and *Rodhocetus*. And *Rodhocetus*, in turn, is a beautiful transitional fossil linking more primitive whales with archaeocetes.

In the years since these discoveries of the 1990s, more and more transitional whale fossils have been found. *Takracetus* and *Gaviocetus* have even more reduced hands and feet, developing into whale-like flippers (figure 17.4). Their bodies are also more dolphin-like, with further development of tail propulsion (as in living whales), meaning they also probably had horizontal tail flukes as well. Today there are so many transitional whale fossils that it's impossible to decide where terrestrial animals end and aquatic whales begin. From a complete mystery with no good transitional fossils in 1980, today the origin of whales from land animals is one of the best evolutionary transitions documented in the fossils record.

As discussed at the beginning of the chapter, the big archaeocete whales were about 80 feet (24 meters) in length and weighed about 12,000 pounds (5,400 kilograms) (figure 17.5A). They resembled some modern whales in having a long pointed snout with triangular teeth for snagging fish, but they

A
Flippers and Fins in the Footlights
B

Figure 17.5 ▲
(*continued*)

are much more primitive than any living whale. For one thing, they do not have a blowhole near the top of their head (like all modern whales), but nostrils on the tip of the snout (as most other mammals do). Archaeocete ears are also very primitive, with no specialized ear bones like those found in modern whales adapted for echolocation in water.

Archaeocete hands and arms were modified into paddles, but no hind legs were found on the incomplete specimens dug up in the United States.

Figure 17.5 ◀ ▲
Basilosaurus, the largest and best-known archaeocete. (*A*) Skeleton formerly on display at the Smithsonian. (*B*) Complete articulated skeletons found in the Egyptian desert west of Cairo. (*C*) Reconstruction of *Basilosaurus* showing the vestigial hind limbs. (Courtesy of Wikimedia Commons)

Then in 1990, complete articulated archaeocete whale skeletons were found in Egypt, with their hind limbs still in place (figure 17.5B). These hind limbs were only about the size of a human arm on a whale over 80 feet long, so they were no longer functional as hind limbs (although they still anchor the muscles in the back of the body). Since whales no longer use them for walking, they are vestiges of the days when whales still walked on four legs (figure 17.5C). If you see a skeleton of a modern whale on display in a museum, look in the hip region just below the backbone and behind the end of the ribcage (figure 17.6). If the specimen is complete and mounted correctly, you will see the tiny nonfunctional remnants of their hip bones and thigh bones, buried deep in their bodies, doing absolutely nothing except proving that whales were descended from four-legged land animals. And once in a while a genetic mistake occurs, and whales are born with a tiny

Figure 17.6 ▲

Mounted skeleton of a blue whale, showing the vestigial hip bones just below the spine and behind the rib cage, held in place by a triangular armature of metal rods. (Photo by the author)

external hind limb that has no function, showing that whales still carry the genes for hind limbs.

RISE OF MODERN WHALES

The archaeocetes vanished about 33 Ma, but not before giving rise to the two great radiations of living whales: the baleen whales, or mysticetes, which filter-feed plankton from the ocean, and the toothed whales, or odontocetes (figure 17.7). Today these include not only the huge predatory sperm whales (of *Moby Dick* fame) but also the beaked whales, dolphins, porpoises, orcas, narwhals, belugas, beaked whales, and many others. Toothed whales use their conical teeth to catch active swimming prey, mostly fish, squid, seals, and other fast-moving aquatic life. Odontocetes have a number of unique specializations, including a single blowhole on their head (mysticete whales

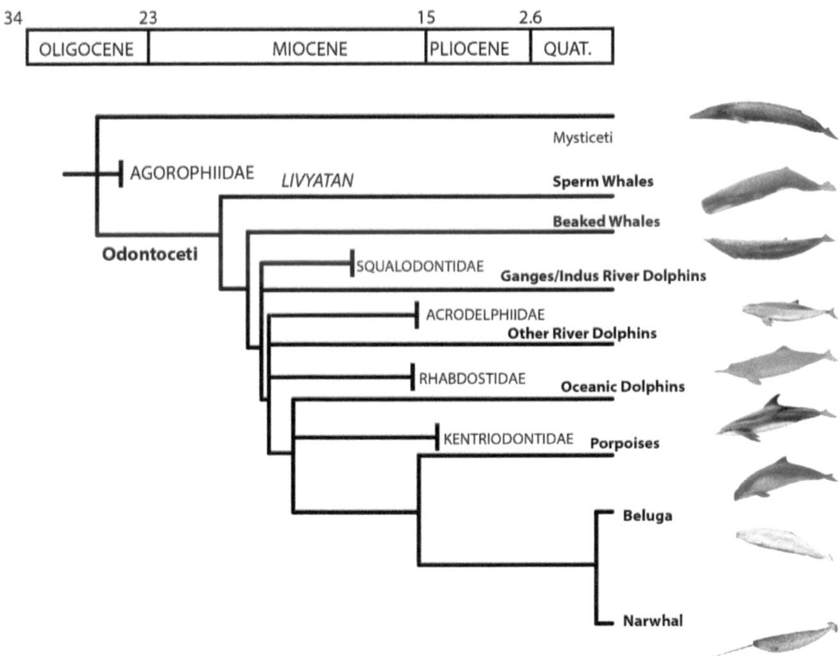

Figure 17.7 ▲

Evolutionary history of the toothed whales or odontocetes. (From D. R. Prothero, *Princeton Field Guide to Prehistoric Mammals* [Princeton Univerity Press, 2016].)

have a pair of blowholes), an asymmetric head, specialized hearing and sound production to improve their echolocation abilities, and a fatty organ over the snout called the melon, which is used like a sound lens to focus the echoes toward their ears. According to some classifications, there are at least 10 different families of odontocetes containing 46 genera and 70 species.

The oldest well-known fossil odontocete was *Squalodon*, the "shark-toothed whale," from the late Oligocene to middle Miocene (33–14 Ma). It was a medium-sized whale (10 feet or about 3 meters long) distributed from Eurasia to North America to Argentina and to New Zealand. Even though it still had the primitive serrated triangular blade-like teeth of archaeocetes, it had the nasal bones almost completely on the top of the head, and a much shorter neck than found in any Eocene whale.

By the middle Miocene, most of these fossil families were established, although with much more primitive representatives than their modern-day descendants. These families include the sperm whales, with fossils such as *Ferecetotherium* from the Oligocene of Azerbaijan, and a dozen genera by the middle Miocene. The most impressive of these is the late Miocene sperm whale *Livyatan melvillei* (figure 17.8). It was truly gigantic (60 feet or 19 meters long), the largest mammalian predator ever to swim the oceans. Its generic name is a homonym of the biblical sea monster "Leviathan" and the species honors Herman Melville, the author of *Moby Dick*.

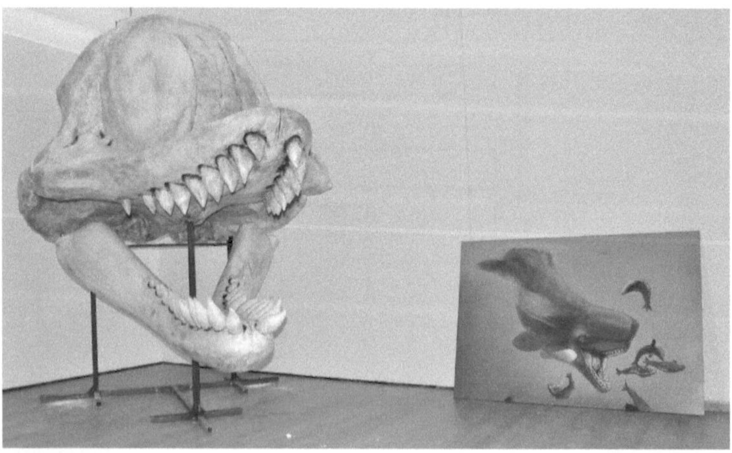

Figure 17.8 ▲

Reconstructed skull of the macropredatory sperm whale *Livyatan melvillei*. (Courtesy of Wikimedia Commons)

There are nine other additional families of odontocetes, most of which have an excellent fossil record. These include four families of river dolphins, plus the Phocoenidae, or true porpoises; the Ziphiidae, or beaked whales; the Delphinidae, or typical dolphins, plus orcas and related forms; the Monodontidae, or narwhals and belugas; and the Kogiidae, or the pygmy sperm whales. Most of these groups have fossil representatives by at least as early as the middle Miocene.

Baleen whales are the other main group of living whales. They the largest animals that have ever lived, yet they live on tiniest prey in the ocean, mostly the dense masses of crustaceans known as krill. They have a filtering device called baleen hanging down from their toothless upper jaws, which is made of keratin, the same substance that makes up your hair or fingernails (figure 17.9). They feed by gulping down a dense mass of krill in the ocean, then closing their mouth and forcing the water out through

Figure 17.9 ▲
Baleen hanging down from the upper jaws of a mysticete whale, with legendary explorer Roy Chapman Andrews in the foreground. (Courtesy of the American Museum Digital Library)

the sieve of baleen using their enormous tongues, all while squeezing down their throat pouch, and trapping their food in the baleen. Once the water is all expelled, they swallow many tons of krill in a single gulp.

Baleen whales are truly amazing creatures, but it is hard to imagine them evolving from toothed archaeocetes. But transitional fossils linking mysticetes to odontocetes have been found as well. *Llanocetus*, from the late Eocene of Antarctica, has both the ancestral triangular archaeocete teeth as well as baleen in the mouth. By the late Oligocene, there were even more advanced toothed mysticetes such as *Janjucetus* and *Mammalodon* from Australia (figure 17.10), which had both teeth and baleen in their mouth at the same time. In the early Oligocene, an archaic family of toothed mysticetes, the aetiocetids, appeared in Australia, but they soon became common whales in the North Pacific region (Japan and North America) during the late Oligocene to Pleistocene. Meanwhile, the first fossils of toothless mysticetes (*Eomysticetus*) appeared in the late Oligocene in South Carolina. That's why even today baleen whales develop tiny teeth during their early embryology, but then lose them when they become fully adult. This is yet another example of a vestigial organ in whales, to go along with the tiny vestigial hind limbs and hips.

Figure 17.10 ▲
The skull of *Janjucetus*, a primitive baleen whale that had both baleen and teeth in its jaws. (Courtesy of R. E. Fordyce)

By the middle Miocene, all four living families of mysticetes were well established, with numerous fossils known from every ocean and continent (figure 17.11). These include the Balaenidae (right whales and bowhead whales); the Neobalaenidae (pygmy right whales, plus the extinct cetotheres); the Eschrichtiidae (gray whales); and also the mighty rorquals (family

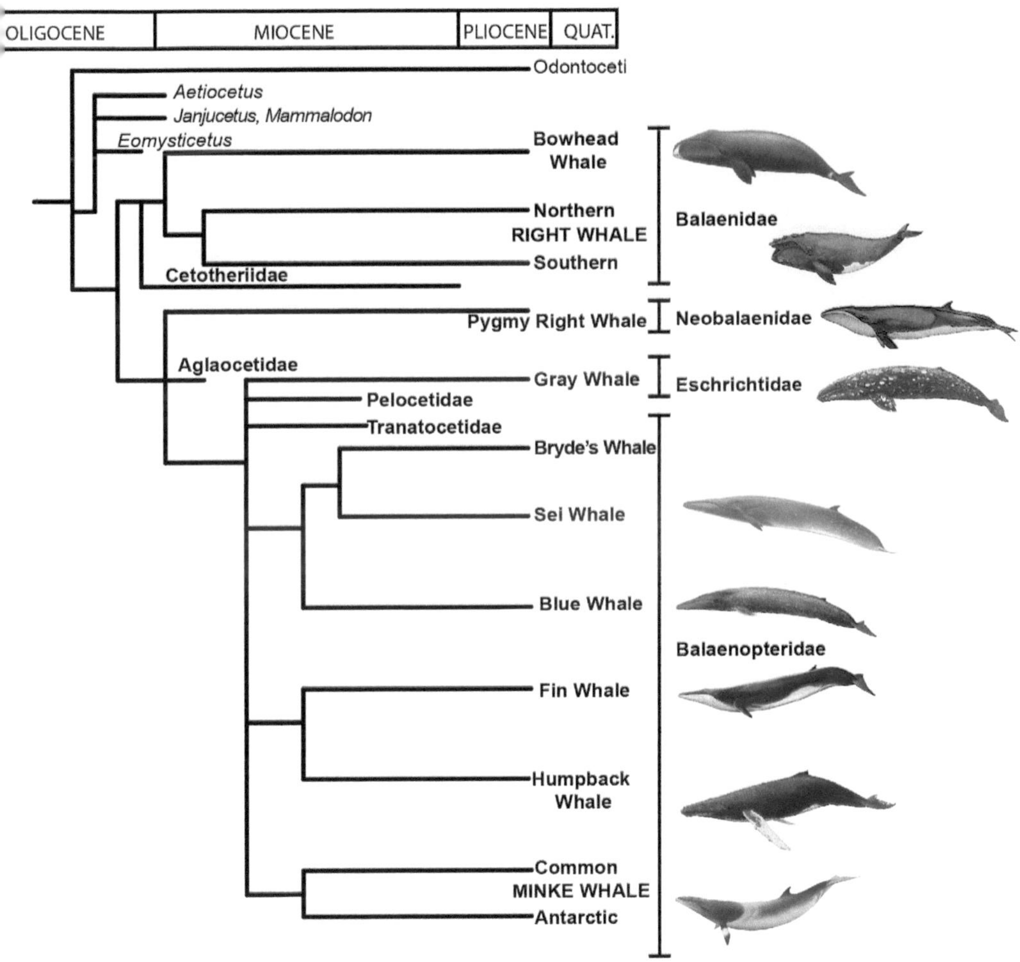

Figure 17.11 ▲

Evolutionary history of the baleen whales, or mysticetes. (From D. R. Prothero, *Princeton Field Guide to Prehistoric Mammals* [Princeton Univerity Press, 2016].)

Figure 17.12 ▲
Life-sized model of the blue whale. (Photo by the author)

Balaenopteridae), including the humpback whale, fin whale, minke whale, sei whale, and the mighty blue whale (figure 17.12). At 100 feet (30 meters) in length and 210 tons (190 metric tonnes) in weight, it is the largest animal alive—and larger than any animal that has ever existed, including the biggest dinosaurs and the most monstrous of all the marine reptiles.

The tale of the whales is truly remarkable, from their ancestry among anthracotheres and their close relationship to hippos, to the amazing transitional fossils that have been found to document every step of their evolution from land to water, to their amazing diversity today—and all the vestigial organs and embryological quirks that prove they were once four-legged land animals.

NOTES

1. Carolus Linnaeus, *Systema naturæ*, 9th ed (1756).
2. Oliver Goldsmith *A History of the Earth and Animated Nature* (1825), 137.
3. Charles Darwin, *On the Origin of Species*, (John Murray, 1859).

FOR FURTHER READING

Bajpai, S., J. G. Thewissen, and A. Sahni. "The Origin and Early Evolution of Whales: Macroevolution Documented on the Indian Subcontinent." *Journal of Biosciences:* 34, no. 5 (2009): 673–686.

Berta, A. *Marine Mammals: Evolutionary Biology*, 3rd ed. Academic Press, 2015.

——. *The Rise of Marine Mammals: 50 Million Years of Evolution.* Johns Hopkins University Press, 2017.

Boisserie, J.-R. "The Phylogeny and Taxonomy of Hippopotamidae (Mammalia: Artiodactyla): A Review Based on Morphology and Cladistic Analysis." *Zoological Journal of the Linnean Society* 143 (2005): 1–26.

Boisserie, J.-R., F. Lihoreau, and M. Brunet. "Origins of Hippopotamidae (Mammalia, Cetartiodactyla): Towards Resolution." *Zoologica Scripta* 34, no. 2 (2005): 119–143.

——. "The Position of Hippopotamidae within Cetartiodactyla." *Proceedings of the National Academy of Sciences* 102, no. 5 (2005): 1537–1541.

Déméré, T. A., M. R. McGowen, A. Berta, and J. Gatesy. "Morphological and Molecular Evidence for a Stepwise Evolutionary Transition from Teeth to Baleen in Mysticete Whales." *Systematic Biology* 57, no. 1 (2008): 15–37.

Fordyce, R. E., and L. G. Barnes. "The Evolutionary History of Whales and Dolphins." *Annual Review of Earth and Planetary Sciences* 22, no. 1 (1994): 419–455.

Gatesy, J. "More DNA Support for a Cetacea/Hippopotamidae Clade: The Blood-Clotting Protein Gene Gamma-Fibrinogen." *Molecular Biology and Evolution* 14, no. 5 (1997): 537–543.

Gingerich, P. D. "Land-to-Sea Transition in Early Whales: Evolution of Eocene Archaeoceti (Cetacea) in Relation to Skeletal Proportions and Locomotion of Living Semiaquatic Mammals." *Paleobiology* 29, no. 3 (2003): 429–454.

Gingerich, P. D., and D. E. Russell. "*Pakicetus inachus*, A New Archaeocete (Mammalia, Cetacea) from the Early-Middle Eocene Kuldana Formation of Kohat (Pakistan)." *Contributions from the Museum of Paleontology, the Museum of Michigan* 25, no. 11 (1981): 235–246.

Goldsmith, O. *A History of the Earth and Animated Nature.* Kinnersley, 1825.

Kron, D. G. B., and E. Manning. "Anthracotheriidae." In *Evolution of Tertiary Mammals of North America*, ed. C. M. Janis, K. M. Scott, and L. L. Jacobs, 381–388. Cambridge University Press, 1998.

Lihoreau, F., J.-R. Boisserie, F. K. Manthi, and S. Ducrocq. "Hippos Stem from the Longest Sequence of Terrestrial Cetartiodactyl Evolution in Africa." *Nature Communications* 6 (2015): 6264.

Prothero, D. R. *The Princeton Field Guide to Prehistoric Mammals*. Princeton University Press, 2016.

——. *Vertebrate Evolution: From Origins to Dinosaurs and Beyond*. Taylor & Francis/CRC Press, 2022.

Prothero, D. R., and S. Foss, eds. *The Evolution of Artiodactyls*. Johns Hopkins University Press, 2007.

Prothero, D. R., K. Marriott, and E. Welsh. "Review of the American Anthracotheres (Mammalia: Artiodactyla)." *Bulletin of the New Mexico Museum of Natural History* 90 (2022): 339–354.

Prothero, D. R., and R. M. Schoch, 2002. *Horns, Tusks, and Flippers: The Evolution of Hoofed Mammals*. Johns Hopkins University Press, 2002.

Pyenson, N. D. *Spying on Whales: The Past, Present, and Future of the World's Most Awesome Creatures*. Viking, 2018.

Savage, R. J. G., and M. R. Long. *Mammal Evolution: An Illustrated Guide*. Facts-on-File, 1986.

Spaulding, M., M. A. O'Leary, and J. Gatesy. "Relationships of Cetacea (Artiodactyla) Among Mammals: Increased Taxon Sampling Alters Interpretations of Key Fossils and Character Evolution." *PLOS ONE* 4, no. 9 (2009): e7062.

Thewissen, J. G. M., ed. *The Emergence of Whales: Evolutionary Patterns in the Origin of Cetacea*. Plenum Press, 1998.

——. *The Walking Whales: From Land to Water in 8 Million* Years. University of California Press, 2014.

Thewissen, J. G. M., L. N. Cooper, M. T. Clementz, S. Bajpai, and B. N. Tiwari. "Whales Originated from Aquatic Artiodactyls in the Eocene Epoch of India." *Nature* 450, no. 7173 (2007): 1190–1194.

Thewissen, J. G. M., L. N. Cooper, J. C. George, and S. Bajpai. "From Land to Water: The Origin of Whales, Dolphins, and Porpoises." *Evolution: Education and Outreach* 2, no. 2 (2009): 272–288.

Thewissen, J. G. M., S. I. Madar, and S. T. Hussain. "*Ambulocetus natans*, an Eocene Cetacean (Mammalia) from Pakistan." *Courier Forschungsinstitut Senckenberg* 191 (1996): 1–86.

Thewissen, J. G. M., and E. M. Williams. "The Early Radiations of Cetacea (Mammalia): Evolutionary Pattern and Developmental Correlations." *Annual Review of Ecology and Systematics* 33 (2002): 73–90.

Thewissen, J. G. M., E. M. Williams, L. J. Roe, and S. T. Hussain. "Skeletons of Terrestrial Cetaceans and the Relationship of Whales to Artiodactyls." *Nature* 413, no. 6853 (2001): 277–281.

Uhen, M. D. "The Origin(s) of Whales." *Annual Review of Earth and Planetary Sciences* 38, no. 1 (2010): 189–219.

Ursing, B. M., and U. Arnason. "Analyses of Mitochondrial Genomes Strongly Support a Hippopotamus-Whale Clade." *Proceedings of the Royal Society* 265, no. 1412 (1998): 2251–2255.

Zimmer, C. *At the Water's Edge: Macroevolution and the Transformation of Life*. Free Press, 1998.

18 FROM LAND TO WATER II—THE EVOLUTION OF SIRENIANS

PEZOSIREN

Down to the waist it resembled a man, but below this it was like a fish with a broad, crescent-shaped tail. Its face was round and full, the nose thick and flat; black hair flecked with grey fell over its shoulders and covered its belly. When it rose out of the water it swept the hair out of its face with its hands; and when it dived again, it snuffled like a poodle. One of us threw a fishhook to see if it would bite. Thereupon it dived and disappeared for good.

—HERBERT WENDT, *OUT OF NOAH'S ARK* (1959), DESCRIBING A FRENCH ENCOUNTER WITH A MANATEE/MERMAID NEAR MARTINIQUE IN 1671

MERMAIDS AND SIRENS

On January 9, 1493, Christopher Columbus was sailing near what is now the Dominican Republic. He reported seeing three "mermaids" and describes them as "not half as beautiful as they are painted" (figure 18.1). The famous English pirate Blackbeard (Edward Teach) claimed to have seen mermaids in the Caribbean and stayed away from waters where they were reported. Both sailors and pirates believed that mermaids would enchant them out of their gold, then drag them to the bottom of the sea. Two Frenchman sailing off Martinique made one of the most famous early reports (quoted in the epigraph).

The legends of the mermaids go back centuries in the lore of the sea and are found in many cultures all over the world. The oldest known legend comes from the Assyrian culture from about 2300 BCE, in which the goddess Atargatis transformed herself into a mermaid in shame for accidentally killing her human lover, a mortal shepherd.

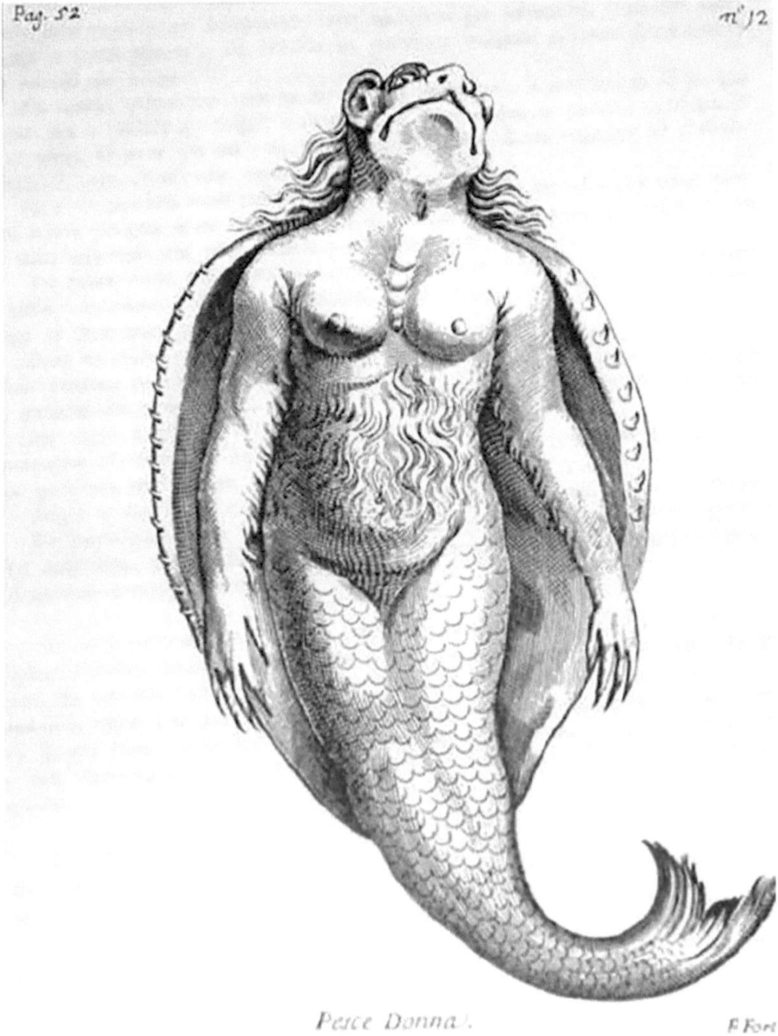

Figure 18.1 ▲

An old engraving of a mythological creature known as a "Pesce Donna" or "Fish Woman." The creature is depicted with a human-like torso, arms, and a scaly fish tail from the waist down. This is one early depiction of a mermaid. (Courtesy of Wikimedia Commons)

Sometimes mermaids were also called "sirens," the name of the beautiful creatures whose songs lured sailors onto the rocks and shipwreck. In Homer's *Odyssey*, Odysseus plugs the sailors' ears with beeswax so they will row past the sirens without hearing them, and he is tied to the mast so

Figure 18.2 ▲
A detail from an ancient Greek red-figure vase painting depicts a scene from Homer's *Odyssey*. The hero Odysseus is shown tied to the mast of his ship, with his crew rowing while their ears are plugged with beeswax so they are not seduced by the song of the sirens around them. The Sirens, depicted as large birds with the heads of women, are shown on rocky outcrops on either side of the ship, one flying down toward the vessel. (Courtesy of Wikimedia Commons)

he can hear their songs without being able to reach them (figure 18.2). This legend of the sirens is the source of the name of the group of manatees and dugongs—the order Sirenia.

Mermaids and mermen stories were widespread among nearly all of the Western European cultures over the past two thousand years. These legends were standardized by such popular stories as Hans Christian Andersen's *The Little Mermaid* (1836), which became a hit Disney movie in 1989. The hit 1984 movie *Splash*, which featured Daryl Hannah as a mermaid, also spread the legend to newer generations. As recently as 2012 and 2013, there were two faked "documentaries" on the Animal Planet network that claimed mermaids were real and had been found, causing a huge number of people to believe this hoaxed "evidence." These pseudo-documentaries were so influential that the scientists at the National Oceanographic and Atmospheric Administration (NOAA) had to twice waste their precious time posting statements on their website stating the fact that the broadcast was fiction, and there were no such things as mermaids.

THE SCIENCE OF SIRENIANS

But could there be any real basis for all of these legends? A number of zoologists have pointed to the manatees (mostly found in the shallow tropical waters of the New World) and dugongs (another group, found mostly in the Indian Ocean) and their relatives, an order of marine mammals known as the "sea cows," or Sirenia. Both the dugong and the manatee are known to float vertically with their heads above water when they want to observe a ship or some other object at the surface. All sirenians have a single pair of breasts on their chests, which might suggest the configuration of human breasts, and nurse their young in a posture that reminds us of human females. But how could something so plug-ugly be mistaken for a beautiful woman? If they had strands of seaweed across their foreheads that resembled hair and were sighted from far enough away (especially in the glare and bad lighting in the open ocean), it's not so hard to imagine them being mistaken for women floating out at sea—especially if the sailors had been away from land and women too long. Just a few such "sightings" by Columbus and other early explorers would shape the widespread myth that had been found in nearly every culture for more than four thousand years.

When manatees and dugongs were captured and brought to the attention of early naturalists, there was tremendous confusion. First of all, close examination showed that they were nothing like the mermaids of legend. The first naturalists to look at their anatomy classified them as whales because they were completely aquatic, like whales, and had fully developed flippers for hands, a tail fluke, and no hind legs. But Linnaeus spotted many anatomical specializations that allied them with elephants, and he was the first to classify them with the Proboscidea, the order that includes elephants, mammoths, and mastodonts. In 1816, the zoologist Henri De Blainville followed Linnaeus's interpretation, although most natural historians were still calling manatees and dugongs "whales."

But as more anatomical similarities were found, the connection between sirenians and proboscideans became stronger. Both groups have a range of unique specializations, especially in the details of the skull bones. Eventually, zoologists began to give up on the "whale" idea. The idea that Sirenia and Proboscidea were closely related finally reached a critical stage, when in 1975 my graduate advisor, Malcolm McKenna, proposed the idea that sirenians and proboscideans were closely related in a group he named "Tethytheria." They were so named because the fossils show that both groups originated around the ancient Tethys Seaway that ran from the Mediterranean through the Middle East, and past India to Australia. Since then, the idea of the Tethytheria has been supported by numerous molecular phylogenies that show the close relationships of sirenians with elephants, confirming the many anatomical similarities spotted by Linnaeus.

Today it is difficult to imagine these rotund docile creatures as mermaids or sirens, now that we can see them up close and know so much more about them. But even more amazing is how they evolved from land animals in Africa, then spread across the tropics, with fossils that document their evolution from creatures with legs to creatures with flippers.

The living Sirenia consist of three species of manatees (genus *Trichechus*) that live in the West Indies, Africa, and the Amazon, and one species of dugong (*Dugong dugon*) that live in the Indian Ocean and around Australia and Indonesia. They do not have a thick layer of blubber, like most whales and seals, so they are restricted to the warm waters of the tropics and subtropics. They are completely herbivorous, eating mostly sea grasses, kelp, and algae with their long flexible snouts and simple grinding teeth. Manatees have rounded flukes on their tails, whereas dugongs have tails with pointed flukes.

STELLER'S MONSTER

In the early 1700s, Czar Peter the Great was attempting to expand the Russian Empire and enlarge his influence over the world. He tried to modernize and civilize the backward politics and social habits of Russia. In particular, he wanted to emulate European customs and encourage the growth of science and scholarship that was happening in all the advanced nations such as France, England, the Netherlands, and Germany. He sent naval expeditions to the far reaches of his empire in Siberia, and especially to the Pacific Coast where remote regions like Kamchatka had long been neglected.

In his navy was a Danish sea captain named Vitus Bering, who had joined in 1704. By 1725, he was exploring the areas north of Kamchatka, which were virtually unknown. When his expedition returned in 1728, he thought there might be a sea between Asia and North America, but he never traveled far enough to explore it. For many years, he sought support and equipment and men to lead a bigger expedition and find out what was north and east of Kamchatka. Finally, in 1741 he led several ships with a large crew up to the northeast, where they visited many of the Aleutian Islands and reached Kodiak Island and the mainland part of Alaska—the first time Europeans had ever seen these regions. But the weather was harsh and stormy, and separated his ships several times, and one vessel was shipwrecked. In addition, the crew got sick and was dying from scurvy. They were eating nothing but meat and fish from the ocean and had no fruits with vitamin C. By August 1742 the remnant of his crew from one vessel (rebuilt after being wrecked) limped back to Russia. Bering himself died along the way and was buried on Bering Island. Today the Bering Strait and Bering Sea are named after him.

On the voyage was a German naturalist, Georg Steller. He was recruited for the 1741 voyage as the official scientist on board, and luckily for posterity he recorded the existence of the wildlife in the North Pacific when the Russians first arrived. He convinced Bering to let him roam and collect on Alaskan land, making him one of the first Europeans to set foot in Alaska. Steller discovered many new species of mammals and birds, many of which are named after him. These include the familiar Steller's jay (a cold-climate jay found in the mountains of western North America, with its distinctive black head and crest), plus many endangered species including the huge Steller's sea lion, Steller's eider duck, and Steller's sea eagle. Two others are now extinct: the spectacled cormorant, and Steller's sea cow.

When the hunters in the crew could no longer find otters for food, they turned to the gentle Steller's sea cow to eat. It was an immense creature, the largest living marine mammal at the time other than whales (figure 18.3). It grew to a length of 26–30 feet (8–9 meters) and weighed about 8–10 tons. Steller's sea cows were completely docile and unafraid of humans because no Europeans had ever hunted them. However, the Native peoples of the region had already reduced their populations to just a few thousand in a few remnants. As Steller wrote in his report:

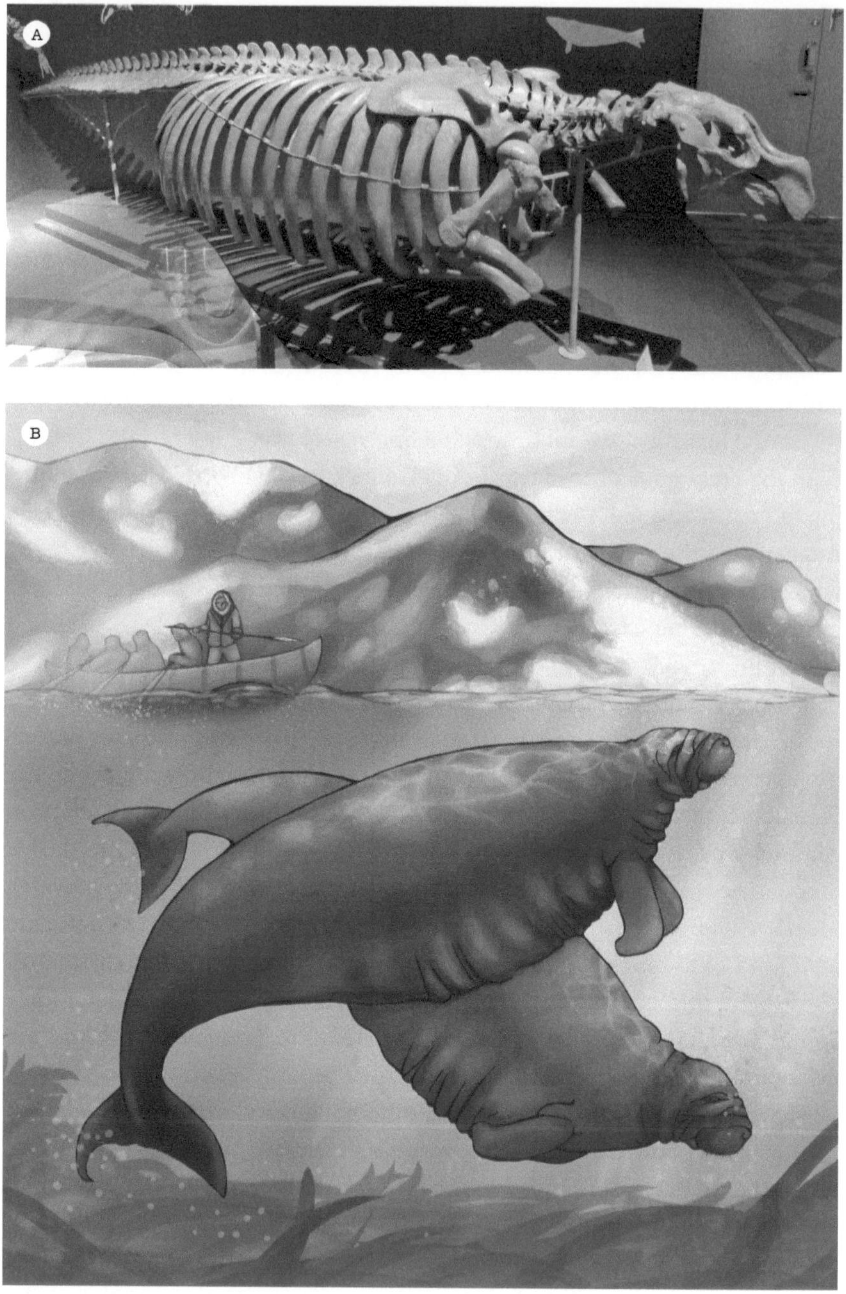

Figure 18.3 ▲

The extinct Steller's sea cow. (*A*) Mounted skeleton. (Courtesy of Wikimedia Commons) (*B*) Reconstruction of Steller's sea cow, being hunted by Arctic peoples. ([*A*] Courtesy of Wikimedia Commons; [*B*] art by M. P. Williams)

Along the whole shore of the island, especially where steams flow into the sea and all kinds of seaweed are most abundant, the sea cow . . . occurs at all seasons of the year in great numbers and in herds. . . . The largest are four to five fathoms long [~ 7 to 9 meters or 24 to 30 feet] and three and a half fathoms thick about the region of the navel where they are the thickest [~ 2.25 meters or 8 feet diameter]. Down to the navel it is comparable to the land animal; from there to the tail, a fish. The head of the skeleton is not the least distinguishable from the head of a horse, but when it is still covered with skin and flesh, it somewhat resembles the buffalo's head, especially as concerns the lips. The eyes of this animal, without eyelids, are no larger than a sheep's eyes. . . . The belly is plump and very expanded, and at all times so completely stuffed that at the slightest wound the entrails at once protrude with much hissing. Proportionately, it is like the belly of a frog. . . . Like cattle on land, these animals live in herds together in the sea, males and females usually going with one another, pushing the offspring before them all around the shore. These animals are busy with nothing but their food. The back and half of the belly are constantly seen outside the water, and they munch along just like land animals with a slow, steady movement forward. With their feet they scrape seaweed from the rocks, and they masticate incessantly. . . . When the tide recedes, they go from the shore into the sea, but with the rising tide they go back again to the beach, often so close we could reach and hit them with poles. . . . They are not the least bit afraid of human beings. When they want to rest on the water, they lie on their back in a quiet spot near a cove and let themselves float slowly hear and there. I could not observe indications of an admirable intellect. . . . but they have indeed an extraordinary love for one another, which extends so far that when one of them was cut into, all the others were intent on rescuing it and keeping it from being pulled ashore by closing a circle around it. Others tried to overturn the yawl. Some placed themselves on the rope or tried to draw the harpoon out of its body, which indeed they were successful several times. We also observed that a male two days in a row came to its dead female on the shore and enquired about it's condition. Nevertheless, they remained constantly in one spot, no matter how many of them were wounded or killed. The fat of this animal is not oily or flabby but rather hard and glandular, snow-white, and, when its been lying in the several days in the sun, as pleasantly yellow as the best Dutch butter. The boiled fat itself excels in sweetness and taste the best beef fat, is in colour and fluidity like fresh olive oil, in taste like sweet almond oil, and of exceptionally

> good smell and nourishment. We drank it by the cupful without feeling the slightest nausea. . . . The meat of the old animals is indistinguishable from beef and differs from the meat of all land and sea animals in the remarkable characteristic that even in the hottest summer months it keeps in the open air without becoming rancid for two whole weeks and even longer, despite its being defiled by blowflies that it is covered with worms everywhere.[1]

As soon as word reached Russia of Steller's and Bering's discoveries, Russian hunters and fur traders followed his route up from Kamchatka, across the Bering Sea and the Aleutian Islands, killing and eating almost any animal they could catch. They were primarily hunting sea otters for their valuable pelts, but they killed seals, sea lions, walruses, whales, and anything else they found. The limited population of a few thousand Steller's sea cows was easily slaughtered for meat, or just for sport. By 1768, only twenty-seven years after Steller had first seen them, the largest of all sirenians was extinct.

FROM LAND TO WATER

The anatomical and molecular evidence is overwhelming that sirenians split from the proboscidean ancestral root about 50 Ma. What does the fossil record show? The earliest fossil sirenian to be described was also among the most primitive. In 1855, the legendary British anatomist Sir Richard Owen described a strange skull that had come to London from a locality called "Freeman's Hall" in the Chapelton Formation on the island of Jamaica (now known to date from about 47–50 Ma). Although the fossil consisted only of an extremely primitive skull with parts broken away and teeth worn down to the roots (figure 18.4), Owen correctly realized that it had the slightly downturned snout, the nasal opening high on the skull, and many other features of the sirenians. The skeletal parts of the animal were mere fragments, but they suggested a sheep-sized animal that could walk with four legs. The skull and skeletal fragments of *Prorastomus* were found with pieces of ribs that were thick and very dense, a diagnostic feature of all sirenians. These dense ribs provide ballast against floating too high in the water, and the extremely dense bone of even a single rib fragment is sufficient to recognize any sea cow. Owen named the fossil skull *Prorastomus sirenoides*. *Prorastomus* means "broad front jaws" and *sirenoides* means "sirenian-like," so Owen clearly realized it was a very primitive form related

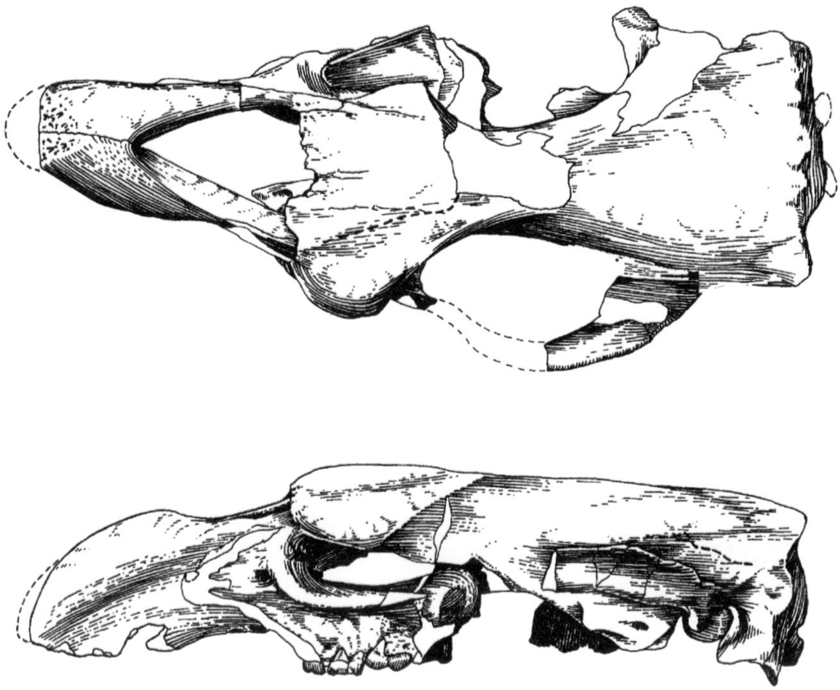

Figure 18.4 ▲

Skull of *Prorastomus sirenoides* from the middle Eocene of Jamaica, one of the first fossil sirenians discovered. The top drawing is a dorsal view, and the bottom drawing is a lateral view of the skull, (Courtesy of Wikimedia Commons)

to modern sea cows. Although Owen was one of the last real zoologists to deny evolution by natural selection, nonetheless he could not deny the affinities of the fossil with the modern Sirenia.

As the years went by, more and more fossils of sea cows were discovered in the Atlantic, the Pacific, and many other areas where marine waters once flooded the landscape. In 1904, the Austrian paleontologist Othenio Abel described a skull of a more advanced sirenian, *Protosiren fraasi*, from the middle Eocene (47 Ma) lower Building Stone Member of the Gebel Mokattam Formation in Egypt (figure 18.5). This is the same limestone that furnished the blocks for the pyramids of Egypt. The skull was much more like those of modern sirenians, with a more strongly downturned snout, the specialized nasal opening further back on the skull, and other more advanced features.

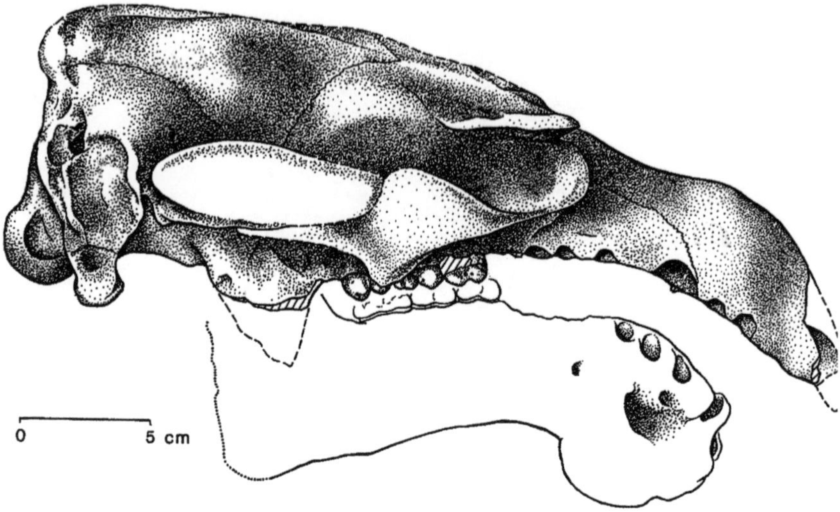

Figure 18.5 ▲

Skull of *Protosiren*, a slightly more advanced sirenian from the middle Eocene of Egypt. The image shows a side view of the skull and jawbone, with a scale bar in the bottom left corner indicating 5 centimeters. (Courtesy of Wikimedia Commons)

Later specimens were found in many different places, from North Carolina to Hungary and France, to Pakistan and India, so *Protosiren* had an almost worldwide distribution in warm tropical and subtropical waters. When the skeletal remains were found, it turned out that *Protosiren* had tiny hind limbs. In addition, its hips were not strongly attached to its lower backbone, so it was almost completely aquatic and could not walk on land. Most of the sirenian fossils younger than *Protosiren* have shrunken hind limbs and could no longer walk, so they were completely aquatic like all the living sea cows. The living manatee and dugong still have tiny bony remnants of their hips and thigh buried in the muscles around their lower back, which no longer have any function except to prove that they once evolved from four-legged land animals.

So our oldest fossil sirenian (*Prorastomus*) shows the beginning of sea cow skull features, and the thick dense ribs, but its limbs are poorly preserved. The next youngest, *Protosiren*, had already shortened its hind limbs and weakened their connection to the spine, so it was mostly aquatic. What was needed most was a fossil that clearly had a sirenian skull and ribs, but four walking legs, final proof that sea cows had evolved from land animals—and was older than *Protosiren* and even older and more primitive than *Prorastomus*.

Such a fossil finally did turn up—back in Jamaica. About 15 kilometers south of the resort town of Montego Bay are some remarkable bone beds in an area known as Seven Rivers, in the parish of St. James. For years, Roger Portell and other paleontologists had been collecting in the early middle Eocene (50 Ma) Chapelton Formation, the same unit that also yielded Owen's original skull of *Prorastomus*. The mollusc fossils that Roger Portell sought included the gigantic marine snail *Campanile* and many other extinct snails and clams. The bones in these beds were all fragmentary because they had been washed into an ancient lagoon or delta and buried alongside these marine molluscs. Over the years, however, they included bones of an iguana, a primitive rhinoceros, and possibly a lemur-like primate.

By the mid-1990s, however, the collections were growing and captured the attention of Dr. Daryl Domning of Howard University in Washington, D.C., the world's expert on fossil sea cows. They promised to yield more specimens of something like *Prorastomus* that had been collected over 150 years ago, so they were worth the effort. Several major seasons of collecting in Jamaica yielded hundreds of bones. But instead of more specimens of *Prorastomus*, Domning recognized an entirely new genus and species of primitive sea cow—and even better, its skeleton was nearly complete!

In 2001, Domning and his colleagues published his scientific description of the specimen in the world's most prominent scientific journal, *Nature*. He named the creature *Pezosiren portelli*, "Portell's walking siren" (figure 18.6). *Pezosiren* was about the size of a large hog (about 6.5 feet or 2.1 meters long), with a skull much like that of *Prorastomus*. In some ways (having a crest along the top of the skull) it was more primitive than *Prorastomus*, but in most features (ear region, and the downward deflection of the tip of the lower jaw) *Pezosiren* was more advanced. It also had the classic thick dense rib bones of all sirenians, which were part of a long barrel-shaped trunk, and a short tail. Most important, *Pezosiren* had nearly complete front and hind limbs and hip bones—these limbs were short, but perfectly normal hands and feet for walking on land, with no obvious specializations for swimming. Based on the details of the limbs and spine, *Pezosiren* swam by paddling with its feet and propelling itself along the bottom in shallow water (as hippos do today) rather than by swimming with up and down motions of its tail like all modern sirenians and whales and seals and sea lions and otters do.

In 2013, an important new specimen was found in the early Eocene rocks about 50 Ma near Chambi in Tunisia. It consisted only of some ear bones, but the details of the structure of the inner and middle ears showed

Figure 18.6 ▲

Pezosiren portelli, the walking sirenian from the Eocene of Jamaica. (*A*) Mounted skeleton with Daryl Domning, who described it. (*B*) Reconstruction. ([*A*] Courtesy of Wikimedia Commons; [*B*] courtesy of N. Tamura)

it belonged to a primitive sirenian. This specimen is still too incomplete to give it a formal name, but the Chambi sirenian not only pushes the origin of the order back to the early Eocene but confirms that sirenian origins began in the Tethys Seaway that once flooded northern Africa, alongside the earliest fossils of proboscideans (see chapter 1) and other tethytheres (as McKenna had predicted back in 1975).

In 2018, the slightly more advanced fossil *Sobrarbesiren* was described from beds about 47 Ma in Spain (figure 18.7). Its hind limbs were highly reduced but still functional. It had a mixture of primitive sirenian features like those of *Prorastomus*, with more advanced features. However, many of its specializations are those of the dugongid family, so it is considered the most primitive fossil dugong.

After *Sobrarbesiren*, there were many different fossil sirenians through their 50-million-year history (figure 18.8). During most of the last 30 million years, a primitive group of sirenians known as halitheres achieved a

Figure 18.7 ▲

Sobrarbesiren, a slightly more advanced walking sirenian from the Eocene of Spain. (Courtesy of Wikimedia Commons)

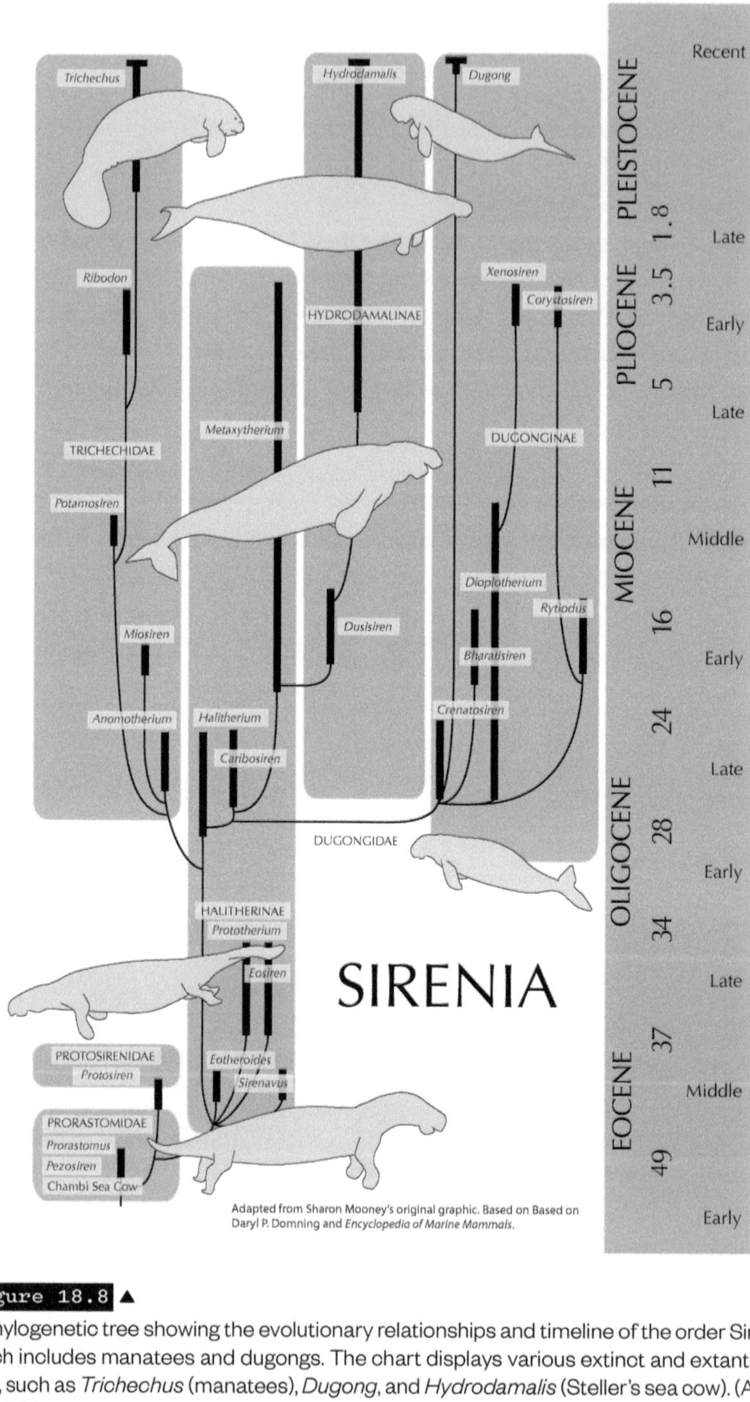

Figure 18.8 ▲

A phylogenetic tree showing the evolutionary relationships and timeline of the order Sirenia, which includes manatees and dugongs. The chart displays various extinct and extant species, such as *Trichechus* (manatees), *Dugong*, and *Hydrodamalis* (Steller's sea cow). (Art by M. P. Williams)

worldwide tropical distribution. By 20 Ma, there were primitive members of both the manatee and dugong family. Most of the time, sirenian evolution can be tied to their need to live on large areas of marine seagrasses. Today just the manatee and the dugong survive. This is the amazing story of the real mermaids, the legendary sirens that are no longer mythological.

NOTE

1. Georg Wilhelm Steller, "De Bestiis Marinis," *Novi Commentarii Academiae Scientiarum Imperialis Petropolitanae* (in Latin) 2 (1751): 289–398.

FOR FURTHER READING

Berta, A., J. L. Sumich, and C. Buell. *Return to the Sea: The Life and Evolutionary Times of Marine Mammals*. University of California Press, 2012.

Berta, A., J. L. Sumich, and K. Kovacs. *Marine Mammals: Evolutionary Biology*. Academic Press, 2005.

Díaz-Berenguer, E., A. Badiola, M. Moreno-Azanza, and J. Ignacio Canudo. "First Adequately-Known Quadrupedal Sirenian from Eurasia (Eocene, Bay of Biscay, Huesca, Northeastern Spain)." *Scientific Reports* 8, no. 1 (2018): 5127.

Domning, D. "Sirenia." In *Evolution of Tertiary Mammals of North America. Vol II: Small Mammals, Xenarthrans, and Marine Mammals*, ed. C. Janis, G. F. Gunnell, and M. D. Uhen, 629–638. Cambridge University Press, 1998.

Domning, D. P. "The Earliest Known Fully Quadrupedal Sirenian." *Nature* 413, no. 6856 (2001): 625–627.

——. "The Readaptation of Eocene Sirenians to Life in Water." *Historical Biology* 14, nos. 1–2 (2000): 115–119.

——. "Sirenian Evolution." In *Encyclopedia of Marine Mammals*, ed. W. F. Perrin, B. Würsig, and J. G. Thewissen, 1083–1086. Academic Press, 2002.

Prothero, D. R. *The Princeton Field Guide to Prehistoric Mammals*. Princeton University Press, 2016.

——. *Vertebrate Evolution: From Origins to Dinosaurs and Beyond*. Taylor & Francis/CRC Press, 2022.

Prothero, D. R., and R. M. Schoch. *Horns, Tusks, and Flippers: The Evolution of Hoofed Mammals and Their Relatives*. Johns Hopkins University Press, 2002.

Velez-Juarbe, J., D. P. Domning, and N. D. Pyenson. "Iterative Evolution of Sympatric Seacow (Dugongidae, Sirenia) Assemblages During the Past ~26 Million Years." *PLOS ONE* 7, no. 2 (2012): e31294.

19 | FROM LAND TO WATER III—THE EVOLUTION OF PINNIPEDS

ENALIARCTOS

Knowledge accumulates no faster than critical specimens of good quality come to light. A corollary of the principle that collecting is the mother progress is that discovery of spectacular new materials and/or intense dedication and great productivity in collecting seem more often than not to come from the ranks of unusually gifted and motivated amateurs (amateurs in the sense that they collect for love of the doing not by training or vocation).

—**CLAYTON RAY, 1976**

DIVING IN ANCIENT OCEANS

Fossils of marine mammals are often challenging to collect. They can only be found in sediments that were formed under the ocean. These rocks are not found in the middle of the continent, but typically are found along the coast. In some old Cenozoic marine beds, such as the Eocene beds in Alabama that produced archaeocete whales, marine fossils are found further inland because the coastline has retreated since the Eocene. But there are relatively few places to collect Cenozoic marine mammal fossils because they are not found in the midcontinent.

Occasionally they are found in places that were once under water but are now some distance from the modern ocean. Such a place is Sharktooth Hill, just northwest of Bakersfield, California, where scores of important fossils been collected for more than a century. It got its name from the huge number and diversity of shark teeth that have been collected there over the years, especially the huge teeth of the giant shark *Otodus megalodon*. (Known as "Megalodon" or "Meg" in the popular media, the genus *Megalodon* is actually a big extinct clam, so using the name "megalodon" does not mean the giant shark unless it's attached to the genus *Otodus*). These enormous and impressive teeth are popular with the collectors and fetch a good price on the commercial market if they are large and unbroken.

The bone bed is made of solid bone fragments and teeth (more than two hundred specimens per cubic meter of rock) and an occasional whale skull or skeleton, all surrounded by a loose sandy matrix that is relatively easy to brush away. No hard chisels or chipping away with a rock hammer required! Each scoop or probe loosens more small shark teeth. Gloves are helpful because the edges and points of the shark teeth are still sharp, and you can get a cut from them if you carelessly probe through the sand with your fingers. At Sharktooth Hill, the sharks may be long extinct but they still bite!

The teeth are overwhelmingly from different types of Mako sharks in the genus *Isurus*, although some 30 other species of shark teeth are known. You find lots of loose unidentifiable bone fragments, along with badly worn vertebrae of whales, which no one saves because they are not identifiable or diagnostic. Often you get the heavily calcified inner ear bones of whales (very distinctive to species), and more rarely parts of other marine mammals, which are definitely worth saving. The bone bed yields a wide range of marine mammals, from dozens of types of whales and dolphins, to sirenians, to various types of early seals and sea lions, to even stranger beasts such as the hippo-like extinct mammals known as desmostylians, as well as extinct relatives of manatees in abundance.

In contrast to Sharktooth Hill, other marine mammal localities are much closer to the modern ocean and require different collection strategies. Some of the best collecting occurs in bedrock exposures and cliffs on coastlines only exposed at very low tides, such as on the rocky coasts from California to Oregon to Washington. In these cases, you must plan your collecting trips differently. During the late 1980s and 1990s, I undertook a long-term project with students and colleagues, using the paleomagnetic dating technique on the Cenozoic marine rocks of the Pacific Coast (finally published in 2001). To work in the intertidal zone, you need a really low tide, called a spring tide, caused when the sun and moon are aligned and their combined gravity makes the tidal bulge more extreme (extremely high tides, followed by extremely low tides, as the Earth spins beneath the tidal bulge lined up with the axis of the sun and the moon). There are several excellent tide table websites online that give dates and times and sizes of all the predicted tides for any coast in the world.

You must plan your field work to catch three or four consecutive days of extreme spring tides (which typically happen at the crack of dawn), then you have to stop work when these favorable conditions end, or work on other localities that are not in the tidal zone before these excellent tides return in two weeks. You also have to time it perfectly to hike into the tidal area from the nearest place you can park your vehicle just as the tide is retreating, then work as quickly as you can during the few good hours of low tide, and make sure you can hike out before the tide comes back in. Otherwise, you might be trapped on some rocks for hours waiting for the next low tide. I did this kind of field work mostly in the summertime when I was not teaching, but the rocks are often overgrown with algae and it's a challenge to see the fossils in the rock. Amateur collectors who live close to these coasts and can collect at any time of year typically find that the best conditions occur in winter, when the cold dark weather suppresses algal growth, and the rocks are much cleaner and better exposed.

The rewards can be immense! If you look closely at the wave-cut bedrock beneath your feet in these coastlines, or in the walls of the sea cliffs, you might see not only shark teeth or other marine fossils such as scallops and clams and marine snails but on rare occasions a cross-section of vertebrate bone. If you are lucky, you can break the specimen out of the rock and retrieve it before the next tide comes in. It might be a partial whale skull or skeleton, or a seal or some other kind of marine mammal. From discoveries like these we reconstruct the early evolution of marine mammals.

I have had the great privilege of working with some of the best of these hard-core amateur collectors, especially Jim Goedert and Casey Burns, who live in the Puget Sound area and have made many important discoveries. When I did summer field research in the State of Washington in the late 1990s, they took time to guide me and my crew to the important marine sections they knew, so our paleomagnetic samples were precisely located and matched a measured stratigraphic section.

Figure 19.1 ◀
Doug Emlong with one of his discoveries. (Courtesy of Wikimedia Commons)

But the greatest of all collectors in the Pacific Northwest was the late Doug Emlong (figure 19.1). He was an amateur collector in the very best sense of the word. He could never hold down a steady job, or manage his money, so he was perpetually broke, but he always made time during the best tides to hike along the coast and look for fossils. He found a wide range of important specimens, including at least 15 new genera and species, as well as some of the best specimens of whales and other marine mammals ever found that had been previously named. These included several new and important whale fossils, plus the most primitive member of the Desmostylia, *Behemotops*, plus important fossil marine mammals such as the "beach bear" *Kolponomos* (discussed in this chapter), and one of the earliest seal relatives, *Enaliarctos*, also discussed in this chapter. In 1969, he found the best specimen of *Kolponomos* near Newport, Oregon, but it was cemented into a concretion that he could only partly remove. He kept going back, year after year, until his luck struck again and he found the rest of the specimen in 1977. Cleaning up the specimen took the Smithsonian preparators almost twenty years because the concretion had hardened and was also brittle due to tectonic stresses. According to Clayton Ray, it was one of "the most difficult materials ever encountered by our laboratory."[1] In some cases, his searching turned up surprising things, including terrestrial fossils, such as the second known skull of the dome-headed chalicothere *Tylocephalonyx*, which somehow floated out into deep waters and was preserved in the marine Miocene Astoria Formation in Oregon (see chapter 10).

Born in 1942, Doug Emlong started out obsessed with collecting fossils along the Oregon coast at age eight and made important discoveries by the time he was fourteen. He reportedly had an IQ of 138 and got top grades in high school, but he was psychologically troubled and only attended a few months at Lewis and Clark College. He greatly preferred his solo hikes along the beach cliffs all up and down the Oregon and Washington coasts, tirelessly collecting any time there were good low tides. At age twenty-two, he befriended the Smithsonian curator Clayton Ray (now retired), an expert on marine mammals, who tried to mentor him. Ray's advice and support eventually convinced Emlong to sell his collection to the Smithsonian for $30,000, in installments of $6,000 a year to keep collecting. (Ray knew that Emlong could not manage money and made sure he wouldn't squander it too fast.) The collection contained 580 specimens and weighed forty thousand pounds. It eventually grew to more than one thousand specimens, encompassing most major West Coast organisms of the past fifty million years. It takes up considerable space in the Smithsonian Paleobiology Department, and in outlying warehouses. The "Emlong collection" has been studied by scientists for decades and has transformed our understanding of the evolution of marine mammals. In July 1974, the Smithsonian made Emlong a Research Associate, and brought him to Washington, D.C., so that he could study his specimens and learn about paleontology. However, Emlong was strong-willed and opinionated and often argued with professionals with many more years of training and experience—and often he was right. Clayton Ray wrote that his brilliance was "matched by an impatience with technique and a refusal (or inability) to conform to society's standards for discipline. . . . He never learned to make a satisfactory plaster jacket, keep a proper field notebook, or follow instructions. It wasn't that he would not, rather that he could not."[2] Emlong stayed in Washington, D.C., only two weeks and then left, stressed out by all the noise and hustle and bustle compared to his quiet life in his tiny hometown in Lincoln City, Oregon.

According to his obituary, "Emlong was troubled, disturbed and broke most his life and spent all of his monies and energy on his beloved digging, his associates said. He found it hard to relate to people—was afraid of people—and never married, his mother and associates said."[3] Emlong had struggled with acute depression, and in early 1980 he committed suicide. He went to one of his favorite spots, Otter Rock in the central Oregon coast, chugged vodka and gin with an unknown number of pills, then plunged off the five-hundred-foot cliff onto the crashing surf. He was only thirty-eight.

As eulogized by Domning, Ray, and McKenna, "Douglas Emlong's Promethean prowess in discovery of unprecedented vertebrate fossils, alike in beds where many, few, or no collectors preceded him, is well known to specialists having personal knowledge of his activities. . . . his fossils were unprecedented in numbers, quality, variety, and novelty. . . . what well-trained methodical professional geologists and paleontologists had not be able to do in the 140 years since the discovery by the Wilkes Expedition of fish and whale remains at Astoria. . . . Emlong never forgot a specimen or a seemingly inconsequential fragment if the vagaries of storms, tides, and shifting sands exposed an additional piece years later. . . . He comprehended complex geology, obscure morphology, and abstruse relationships, apparently by divination. . . . Emlong's instant intuition of affinities, although based on unprepared specimens, virtually no literature or comparative material, and almost no formal training, proved in this case as in so many others to be uncannily perceptive, and to overshadow our own belabored conclusions. . . . Tragically, the flow from the wellspring of these riches ended abruptly on 8 June 1980 with Emlong's death but already his towering reputation as a fossil finder will be progressively and justifiably widened with every added publication as a result of studies in progress on the 'Emlong collection.' "[4]

Doug Emlong's story is indeed tragic, but professional paleontologists at universities and museums are indebted to dedicated amateur collectors like Emlong, Goedert, Burns, and so many others who do the long hours in difficult locations to find the fossils. Most professional paleontologists are tied down by teaching and other responsibilities, and our opportunities to spend time in the field collecting are severely limited.

SEAL OF APPROVAL

Seals, sea lions, and walruses: these three groups of marine mammals are familiar to all of us (figure 19.2). They are known as the Pinnipedia (Latin

Figure 19.2 ▲

Clockwise from top left: Steller sea lion (*Eumetopias jubatus*), southern elephant seal (*Mirounga leonina*), New Zealand fur seal (*Arctocephalus forsteri*), walrus (*Odobenus rosmarus*), and gray seal (*Halichoerus grypus*). (Courtesy of Wikimedia Commons)

pinna for "fin" and *pedes* meaning "foot") because their hands and feet have been modified into flippers. Fully adapted to an aquatic existence with streamlined bodies and many specializations for swimming and diving, they look so different from all other groups of land mammals—and yet they *are* mammals and must have come from land-dwelling creatures with legs, not flippers. Today they are quite a diverse group, with three families consisting of 22 genera and 34 species, but there are at least an additional extinct 50 genera known, and they have an excellent fossil record going back at least to 30 Ma.

The three families include the seals (family Phocidae), also called "earless seals" because they have no visible external ears. Phocids cannot rotate their hind limbs around into the forward position to walk with them, so they must drag their bodies or wriggle across the ground. They swim using mostly their hind flippers.

The sea lions (family Otariidae) are also known as "eared seals" because they have distinctive external ears. They can rotate their hind flippers into the forward direction to walk on land. They swim primarily with their front flippers. These animals are familiar in zoos and aquaria, barking on command and performing tricks for animal trainers.

Finally, the walruses (family Odobenidae) are famous for their huge blubbery bodies, giant paired tusks, and are restricted to the icy Arctic. They also lack external ears but can walk with their hind flippers rotated forward. Like seals, they swim using their hind flippers. There is only one species of walrus alive today, *Odobenus rosmarus*, but they have an excellent fossil record with many extinct species.

So what are pinnipeds related to? For the longest time, many scientists thought they were not a natural group but convergently evolved from two different lineages. The seal or phocids were thought to be related to the weasel and otters (family Mustelidae), and the sea lions and walruses were related to bears (family Ursidae). However, in the 1990s opinions changed, and it became a consensus that they were a natural monophyletic group, and probably most closely related to the bear lineage because of the number of anatomical similarities they all share, and not all of these similarities could be convergence due to their aquatic way of life.

As early as 1999, analyses of their molecules also suggested that pinnipeds were a natural monophyletic group but were related to mustelids. Then in 2021 mitochondrial DNA confirmed that pinnipeds were indeed monophyletic and more closely related to the mustelids than they were to bears. This is not a big surprise. The earliest fossils related to pinnipeds, such as amphicynodontids (figure 19.3), have variously been considered ancestral to bears, or to mustelids. Molecular evidence places the bears and the mustelids very close to each other, so the differences were slight when the pinnipeds first emerged about 33 Ma. All three groups are arctoid carnivorans (*arctos* is the Greek word for "bear"), so these form a group including bears and their closest relatives, with mustelids just slightly closer to pinnipeds than are bears.

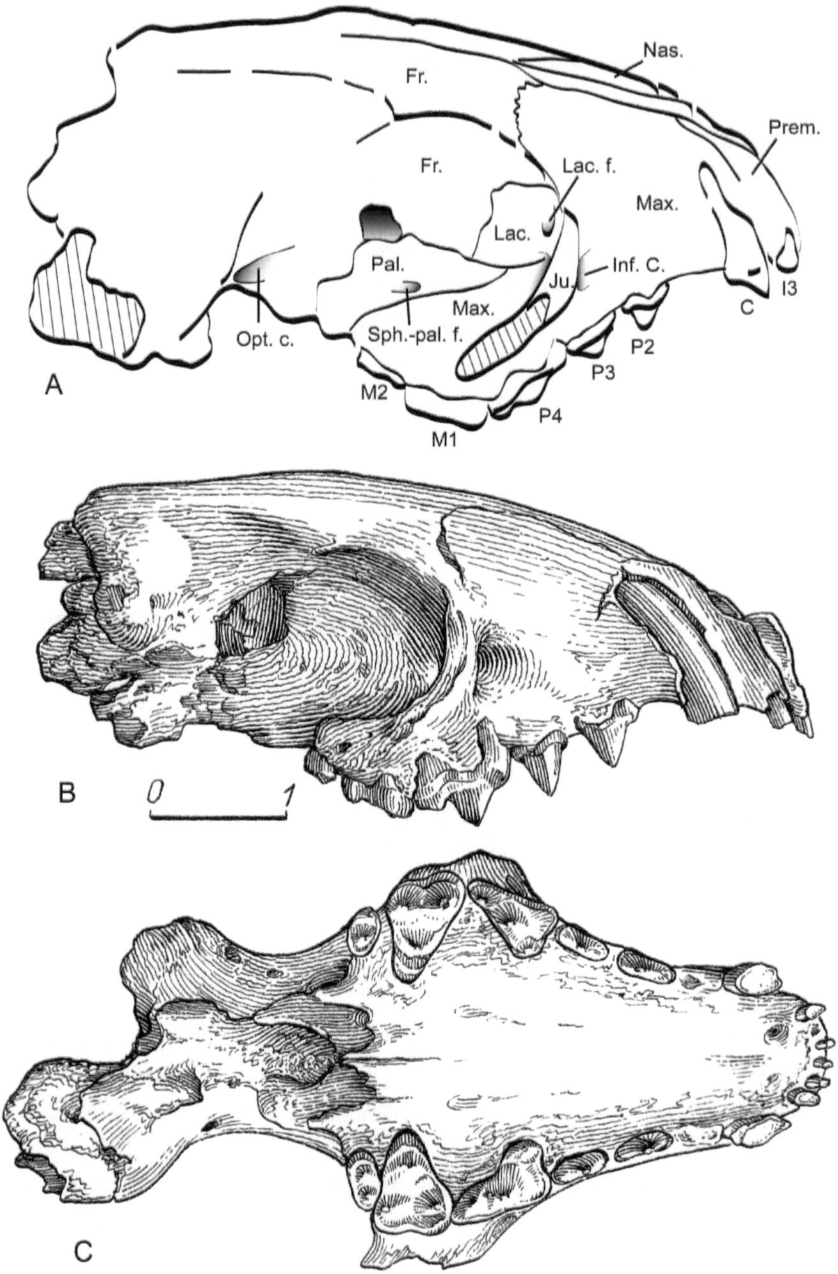

Figure 19.3 ▲

Line drawing of the skull of the primitive European Miocene relative of bears and pinnipeds and mustelids, *Amphicynodon*, in (*A*) a lateral view, (*B*) a detailed lateral view, and (*C*) a ventral view. (Courtesy of Wikimedia Commons)

THE FIRST PINNIPEDS

What does the fossil record tell us about the origin of pinnipeds? As mentioned previously, the oldest possible relatives are a group of small carnivorans known as amphicynodontids. They were about the size and shape of otters but much more primitive. Traditionally, they were thought to be among the most primitive members of the bear lineage, but now they are considered very primitive relatives of mustelids—or possibly the most primitive members of the pinnipeds. It is difficult to say much more than that because their fossils consist mostly of jaws and partial skulls. *Amphicynodon* specimens were found in beds dating back to 33 Ma in France, China, and Mongolia, along with other related genera such as *Allocyon* from the John Day beds of Oregon, *Drassonax* from northeast Colorado, *Pachycynodon* from France, *Amphicticeps* from Mongolia, and *Wangictis* from China.

One of the strangest of these extinct pinniped relatives is *Kolponomos clallamensis*, nicknamed the "beach bear" (figure 19.4). First discovered and described by Ruben Stirton in 1960, it was originally based on a partial skull found in marine beds of the Clallam Formation, about 20 Ma, from the Olympic Peninsula of Washington. When it was first found, it was compared to primitive bear fossils and assigned to the bear group. But it had a strange downturned snout, and even stranger broad flat molars that suggest it crushed molluscs for its food. Its powerful jaws resembled those of a saber-toothed cat in their mechanics for a powerful bite, but they ate molluscs, not meat. Jack Tseng and coauthors did a functional analysis of digital models of it and found that the front of the jaws worked like the jaws of saber-toothed predators in that they had a lot of leverage in the bite for prying off prey items from rocks. This makes it even more of a specialized mollusc eater, probably haunting tidepools where many invertebrates attach to the rocky surface. Others have compared its feeding morphology to the giant otter *Siamogale* from the late Miocene of China and Thailand. So it was more like a sea otter than a "beach bear," and closer to the roots of otters and pinnipeds than to bears.

Next on the family tree is *Pujila darwini*, based on a complete skeleton found in lake beds inside the Haughton impact crater in Arctic Canada in 2007 (figure 19.5). *Pujila* is the Inuktitut word for "young sea mammal" or "seal," and this name honors the people and languages of Arctic Canada

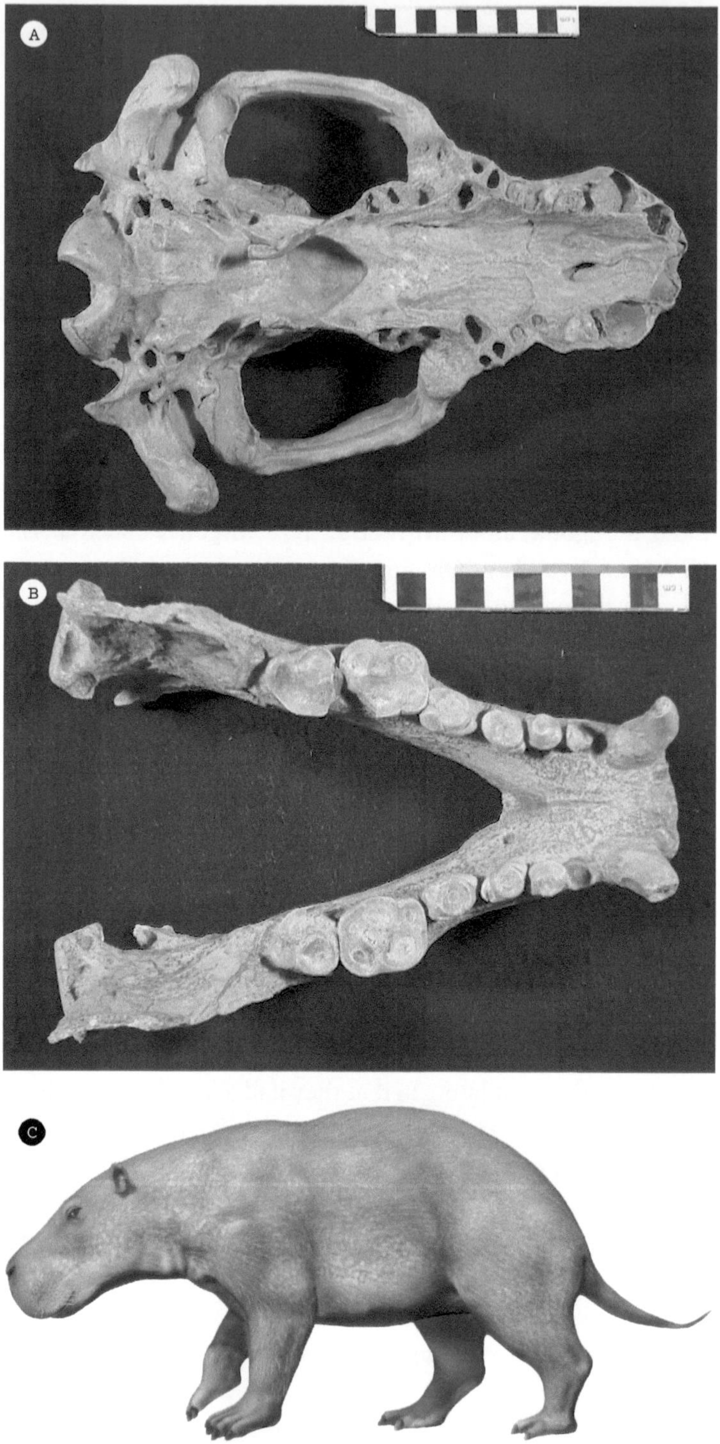

Figure 19.4 ▲

The "beach bear" *Kolponomos*. (*A*) Skull, showing the flattened molar crowns, adapted for crushing shells. (*B*) Lower jaw, showing the lower molars adapted for crushing. (*C*) Reconstruction. (Courtesy of Wikimedia Commons)

Figure 19.5 ▲

The primitive pinnipediamorph *Pujila darwini*. (*A*) Skeleton. (*B*) Reconstruction by N. Tamura. (Courtesy of Wikimedia Commons)

in Nunavut, where it was found. Pronounced "Pe-oh-YEE-lah," it dates back to 22 Ma. It is not an amphicynodontid but is one of the most primitive pinnipediamorphs (extinct relatives of pinnipeds) ever found. Its long slender body and long tail also resembled that of an otter, and it probably had webbed feet rather than flippers. But its skull has many features in common with seals, such as a large hole on each side of the snout for the sensitive nerves in their noses that seals use to find food underwater. Other pinnipediamorph fossils are less complete that *Pujila*, but very similar, such as *Potamotherium* from the early Miocene of central France, and *Semantor* from the Miocene of Kazakhstan.

From *Pujila*, the next step is *Enaliarctos mealsi*, originally found in the late Oligocene Pyramid Hill locality just north of Sharktooth Hill, and northeast of Bakersfield, California (figure 19.6). An even more complete specimen, *Enaliarctos emlongi*, was later found by Doug Emlong in the upper Oligocene Nye Formation in Oregon and named in 1991 in memory of Emlong by Annalisa Berta. *Enaliarctos* is now known from several species going all the way back to beds dated about 30 Ma to 22 Ma, each of which is named after paleontologists who were influential in the study of these fossils: *E. tedfordi* after the late Richard Tedford of the American Museum of Natural History in New York, a pioneer in the study of carnivorans, especially pinnipeds; *E. mitchelli*, after the late Edward Mitchell, a research associate at the Natural History Museum of Los Angeles County, another giant in the study of fossil marine mammals; and *E. barnesi*, after Larry Barnes, now retired from the Natural History Museum of Los Angeles County, for decades the expert on marine mammals, especially from the Pacific Coast.

Enaliarctos had has a seal-like body and webbed feet, but the feet are not as fully developed as flippers as you would see in modern seals. It had large eyes, sensitive ears, and specialized inner ear bones for hearing underwater. And yet its teeth still looked like those of bears and otters, with slicing cheek teeth, so it could not just grab and gulp down fish with many simple cone-shaped teeth, as seals do. Although it looks superficially like a seal, its teeth and some other features are very primitive and more like those of otters.

Another slightly more advanced pinnipediamorph is *Pinnarctidion*, from the early Miocene beds, such as the Jewett Sand near Sharktooth Hill in California, the Nye Formation in Oregon, and the Pysht Formation on the northern Olympic Peninsula of Washington. One of the species, *P. rayi*,

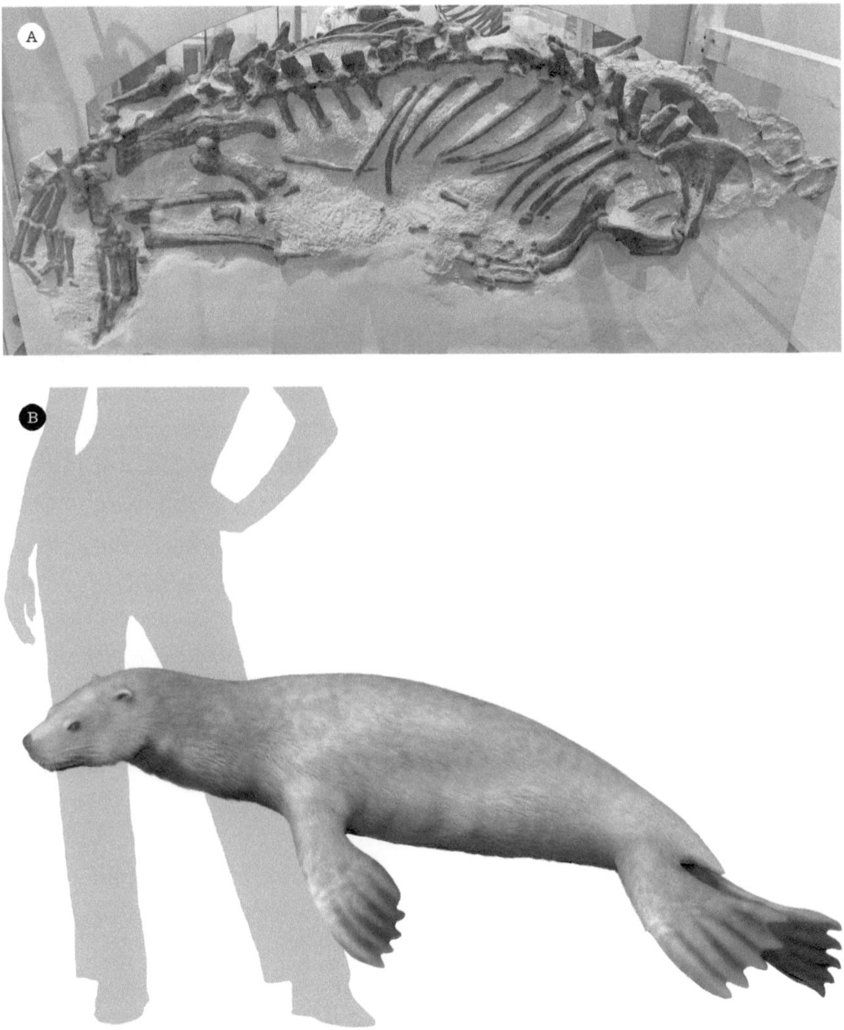

Figure 19.6 ▲

The extinct pinnipedimorph *Enaliarctos*. (*A*) A partial skeleton, with the bones of the rib cage, spine, and some limbs, on display at the American Museum of Natural History. (*B*) Reconstruction. ([*A*] Photo by the author; [*B*] courtesy of N. Tamura.)

from the Nye Formation of Oregon, was also collected by Doug Emlong, and is named after Clayton Ray, the fossil marine mammal expert of the Smithsonian previously mentioned. First thought to be a primitive phocid, it is now regarded as a more primitive pinnipediamorph outside the three main families. It looked very similar to *Enaliarctos* except its eyes were further forward on the skull.

A slightly more advanced pinnipediamorph is *Pteronarctos*. First described as an enaliarctine by Larry Barnes in 1989 and 1990, it consists of the type species *P. piersoni*, from the lower Miocene portion of the Astoria Formation near Schooner Point in Oregon, and a second species, *P. goedertae*, found by my friend Jim Goedert's wife Gail and named after her, from the middle Miocene part of the Astoria Formation near Jumpoff Joe in Oregon. However, with the discovery of better specimens, it turns out that it is not an enaliarctine. *Pteronarctos* is much more advanced in the snout region, where the maxilla (upper jawbone) contributes to the eye region, and the lacrimal bone (connected to the tear ducts) are highly modified, so it no longer can produce tears (a feature of true pinnipeds, which live in water and don't require tear ducts). Its teeth are much more simplified than those of *Enaliarctos*, with the beginning of the trend of reducing every tooth to simple conical pegs.

Yet another of the extinct side branches of pinnipeds are the desmatophocids, which were common between 22 and 12 Ma. The early Miocene *Desmatophoca* from the Astoria Formation of Oregon was discovered and described by the pioneering Oregon geologist Thomas Condon in 1906 and was pivotal in proving that pinnipeds evolved from carnivorous land mammals. *Desmatophoca* was smaller than modern seals but had a much more powerful bite force and large eye sockets, both indicators of a predator specializing in fish in shallow, well-lit waters.

The desmatophocid *Allodesmus* is particularly well known from places like Sharktooth Hill northeast of Bakersfield, where it reached 8 feet long and weighed 800 pounds (figure 19.7) There are currently eight recognized species of *Allodesmus*, some of which come from California, Oregon, and Washington, and Baja California, Mexico, and others from Japan, so they spread around the North Pacific rim in the early and middle Miocene. Like many pinnipeds, there was a big difference in size and canine tusks between males and females, suggesting that they had the common pinniped habit of a single bull guarding a breeding beach with a harem of females and their pups.

Figure 19.7 ▲
Mounted skeleton of the extinct pinniped *Allodesmus*. (Courtesy of Wikimedia Commons)

PHOCIDS

There are more than a dozen extinct and nineteen living species of phocids, or true seals. They first appeared about 19–14 Ma with *Afrophoca* from marine beds in Libya, *Devinophoca* from beds about 15–16 Ma in Slovakia, and *Noriphoca* from about 22 Ma in Italy. Other phocids include the long necked "swan seal" *Acrophoca longirostris*, plus *Piscophoca* from the marine Pisco Formation of Peru, *Pliophoca* from beds about 4 Ma in Italy, and many other species. They break down into two well-established subfamilies with multiple tribes, all with living representatives. These are the monk seals (tribe Monachini), the Lobodontini (*Lobodon*, the crab-eater seal, with its strange multi-cusped cheek teeth that are hooked backward, similar to the teeth of archaeocete whales), and the Miroungini, the amazing elephant seals (figure 19.8A). The males weigh up to 11,000 pounds, about three times the size of females. Elephant seal bulls are legendary for their flexible proboscis or trunk, which gives them their name. They often spend much of their time on preferred beaches in huge colonies, where they rest after long sessions of feeding at sea, and where they mate, and where the females have their pups and nurse them. The difference in size between males and females is especially obvious in their skulls (figure 19.8B), with male skulls

Figure 19.8 ▲

Elephant seals. (*A*) Male and female Northern elephant seal, showing the huge difference in size and the prominent snout on the males. (*B*) Contrast between male and female skulls, with the larger male skull showing the wide nasal opening that supports its proboscis. (Courtesy of Wikimedia Commons)

being three times the size of female skulls. Male skulls have a huge open area in their nasal region that supports the muscles of their proboscis.

OTARIIDS

Meanwhile, the eared seals, or sea lions or otariids go back to fossils about 17 Ma from the Topanga Formation in California with a primitive otariid known as *Eotaria crypta*. Even though it is known only from partial jaws and teeth, it is already showing the characteristic simplification of its cheek teeth down to pointed conical pegs that is typical of otariids. *Eotaria* was followed by *Pithanotaria starri* from the upper Miocene Monterey Formation and Santa Margarita Sandstone (10–7 Ma) in coastal California. An even better-known fossil is *Thalassaleon* from beds about 5 Ma in Japan and southern California and Mexico. It was as large as some of the largest sea lions, weighing about 800 pounds. Sea lions have been confined to the North Pacific region during most of their history, except for those species of fur seals and sea lions that reached the Southern Hemisphere. But otariids they never lived in the Central or North Atlantic.

Today there are 7 genera and 16 species of otariids, especially the fur seals of the genus *Arctocephalus*, the California and Galapagos sea lions of the genus *Zalophus*, and the Steller's sea lion of the genus *Eumetopias*, whose huge males are 10 feet (3 meters) long and weigh 2,500 pounds (1,130 kilograms). That's larger than a grizzly bear!

I AM THE WALRUS!

The most amazing story of all, however, is the evolution of walruses. The most primitive walruses, such as *Proneotherium* and *Neotherium* occur in beds about 12–15 Ma (figure 19.9A). They are barely different from *Enaliarctos*, except that they are larger and more robust, and already begin to show the size and canine tusk differences between males and females that is so characteristic of walruses and not of enaliarctines. A few million years later, we find *Imagotaria*, which was about the size of the living walrus, with ear bones already suited to underwater hearing. *Imagotaria* was beginning to develop the tusk-like canine and simplified peg-like molars and premolars in its cheek teeth that all walruses have. By the late Miocene and early Pliocene, there were at least eight different kinds of walruses along the

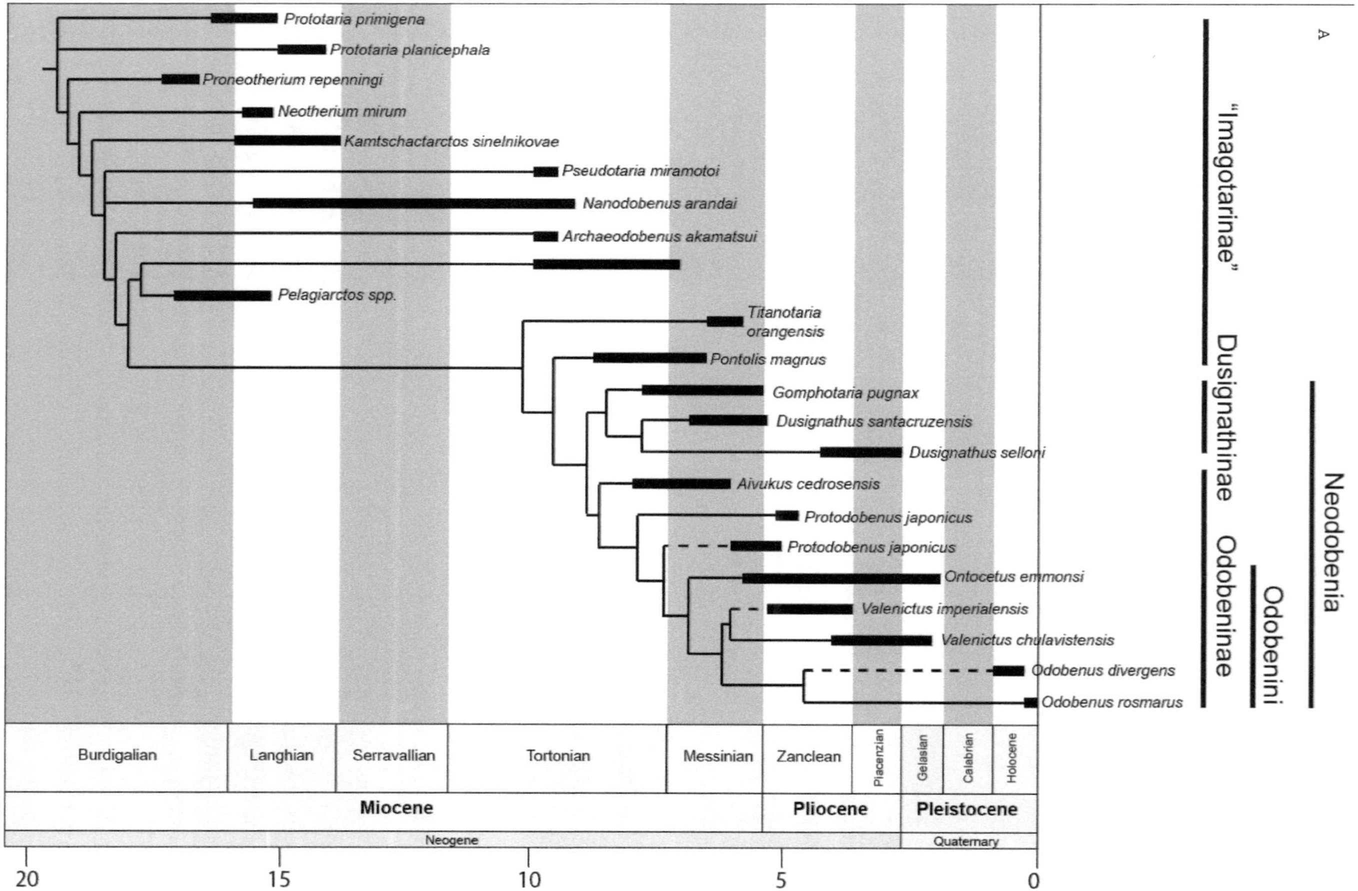

Figure 19.9 ▲▼

(*A*) A phylogenetic tree of walruses, which traces the evolution of the Family Odobenidae. (*B*) Skull of the four-tusked walrus *Gomphotaria*. (*C*) Skulls of the short-tusked walrus *Valenictus* (*front right*) compared to that of *Dusignathus* (*left*) and of the modern walrus *Odobenus rosmarus* (*left rear*), on display at the San Diego Natural History Museum. ([*A*] Redrawn from several sources; [*B*] courtesy of L. Barnes; [*C*] photo by the author).

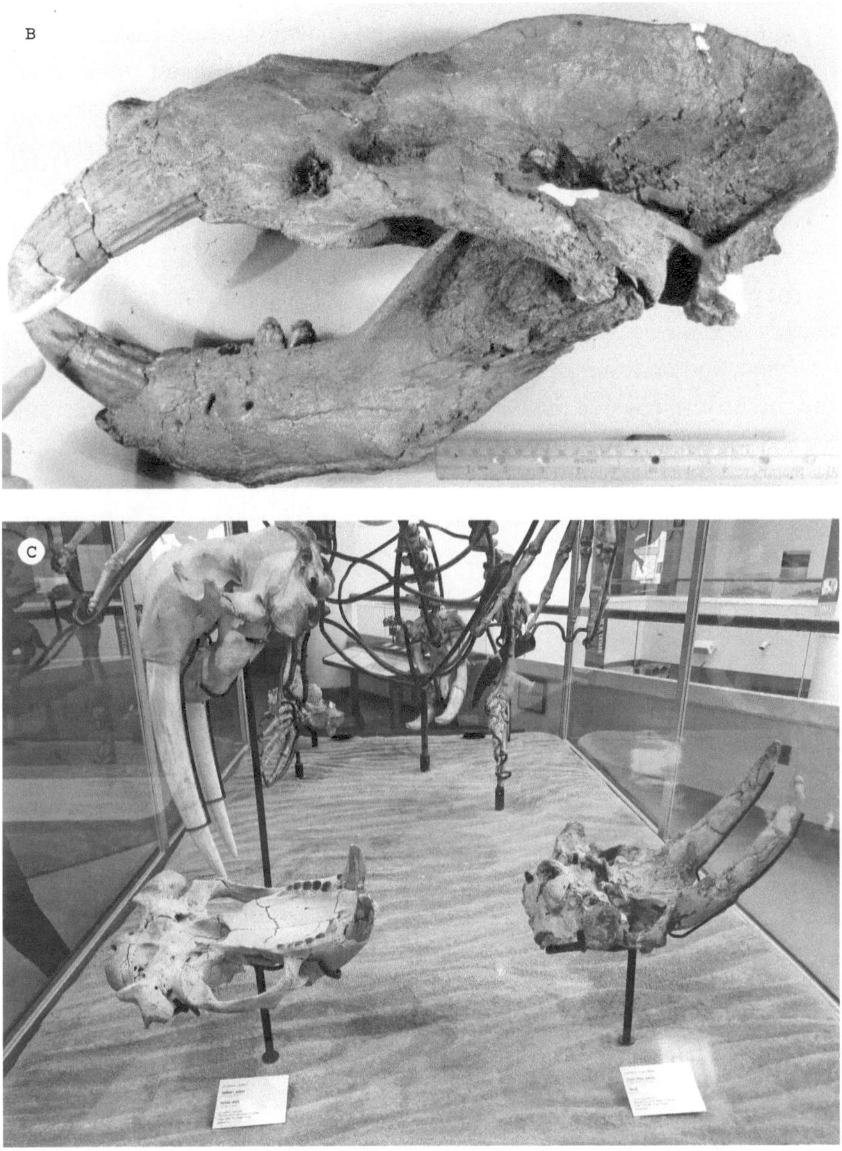

Figure 19.9 ▲
(continued)

Pacific Rim, most of which looked like unusually large sea lions with short to medium-sized tusks. They included the enormous short-tusked walrus *Pontolis*, plus the four-tusked *Gomphotaria* (figure 19.9B) and *Dusignathus*, with completely peg-like simplified cheek teeth, large lower tusks, and small upper canine tusk, and *Aivukus*, with slightly larger upper tusks, broad cheek teeth, and a deep lower jaw with a small canine. *Aivukus* apparently lived in shallow water as a bottom-feeder and crushed its molluscan food like modern walruses do.

Then about 6-4 Ma, the walruses spread through the Central American seaway (there was no Panamanian land bridge until 3.5 Ma), up the Atlantic Coast, and on to Europe and the Mediterranean. About 4 Ma in Europe and the African coast of the Mediterranean, we find fossils of *Alachtherium*, which looked slightly more like a modern walrus, with large tusks, reduced peg-like molars, a deep lower jaw with no canine, and only a few other cheek teeth. In almost every respect, it is an ideal intermediate between the primitive walruses and the modern groups.

Finally, beds 6-4 Ma also yield an even better transitional form, *Valenictus*, which has long upper tusks (but still considerably shorter than the tusks of the living walrus, *Odobenus*) and almost no teeth in the lower jaw (figure 19.9C). These walruses also had the characteristic arching of the palate that we see in living walruses. This arched palate, combined with the action of the tongue, allows living walruses to suck their prey (mostly molluscs) into their mouths, where they then crush the shells and suck out the contents.

This is the amazing story of the evolution of pinnipeds. It is one of the best examples of evolution in action, documented with an excellent fossil record.

NOTES

1. Clayton E. Ray, "Fossil Marine Mammals of Oregon," *Systematic Zoology* 25, no. 4 (1976): 420–436.
2. Ray, "Fossil Marine Mammals of Oregon."
3. Anne Sullivan, "Marine Fossils Great Passion in Life of Coastal Plunge Victim," *The Oregonian*, June 10, 1980.
4. Daryl P Domning, Clayton E. Ray, and Malcolm C. McKenna, 1986. "Two New Oligocene Desmostylians and a Discussion of Tethytherian Systematics," *Smithsonian Contributions to Paleobiology* 59 (1986).

FOR FURTHER READING

Barnes, L. G. "Otaroidea." In *Evolution of Tertiary Mammals of North America. Vol II: Small Mammals, Xenarthrans, and Marine Mammals*, ed. C. Janis, G. F. Gunnell, and M. D. Uhen, 523–541. Cambridge University Press, 2008.

Berta, A. "New *Enaliarctos* (Pinnipedimorpha) from the Oligocene and Miocene of Oregon and the Role of 'Enaliarctids.'" *Smithsonian Contributions to Paieobiology* 69 (1991): 1–28.

——. *The Rise of Marine Mammals*. Johns Hopkins University Press, 2017.

Berta, A., M. Churchill, and R. W. Boessenecker. "The Origin and Evolutionary Biology of Pinnipeds: Seals, Sea Lions, and Walruses." *Annual Review of Earth and Planetary Sciences* 46, no. 1 (2018): 203–228.

Berta, A., C. E. Ray, and A. R. Wyss. "Skeleton of the Oldest Known Pinniped, *Enaliarctos mealsi*." *Science* 244, no. 4900 (1989): 60–62.

Boessenecker, R. W., and M. Churchill. "The Last of the Desmatophocid Seals: A New Species of *Allodesmus* from the Upper Miocene of Washington, USA, and a Revision of the Taxonomy of Desmatophocidae." *Zoological Journal of the Linnean Society* 184, no. 1 (2018): 211–235.

Deméré, T. A., A. Berta, and P. J. Adam. "Pinnipedimorph Evolutionary Biogeography." *Bulletin of the American Museum of Natural History* 279 (2003): 32–76.

Domning, D. P., C. E. Ray, and M. C. McKenna. "Two New Oligocene Desmostylians and a Discussion of Tethytherian Systematics." *Smithsonian Contributions to Paleobiology* 5 (1986): 1–56.

Hunt, R. M., Jr., and L. G. Barnes. "Basicranial Evidence for Ursid Affinity of the Oldest Pinnipeds." *Proceedings of the San Diego Society of Natural History* 29 (1994): 57–67.

Koretsky, I., and L.G. Barnes. "Phocidae." In *Evolution of Tertiary Mammals of North America, Vol II: Small Mammals, Xenarthrans, and Marine Mammals*, ed. C. Janis, G. F. Gunnell, and M. D. Uhen, 542–556. Cambridge University Press.

Prothero, D. R. *The Princeton Field Guide to Prehistoric Mammals*. Princeton University Press, 2016.

——. *Vertebrate Evolution: From Origins to Dinosaurs and Beyond*. Taylor & Francis/CRC Press, 2022.

Ray, C. E. "Fossil Marine Mammals of Oregon." *Systematic Zoology* 25, no. 4 (1976): 420–436.

Rybczynski, N., M. R. Dawson, and R. H. Tedford. "A Semi-Aquatic Arctic Mammalian Carnivore from the Miocene Epoch and Origin of Pinnipedia." *Nature* 458, no. 7241 (2009): 1021–1024.

Scheffer, Victor B. *Seals, Sea Lions, and Walruses: A Review of the Pinnipedia*. Stanford University Press, 1958.

Stirton, R. A. "A Marine Carnivore from the Clallam Miocene Formation, Washington: Its Correlation with Nonmarine Faunas." *University of California Publications in Geological Sciences* 36, no. 7 (1960).

Tedford, R. H., L. G. Barnes, and C. E. Ray. "The Early Miocene Littoral Ursoid Carnivoran *Kolponomos*: Systematics and Mode of Life." *Proceedings of the San Diego Society of Natural History* 29 (1994): 11–32.

Tseng, Z. J., C. Grohé, and J. J. Flynn. "A Unique Feeding Strategy of the Extinct Marine Mammal *Kolponomos*: Convergence on Sabretooths and Sea Otters." *Proceedings of the Royal Society B: Biological Sciences* 283, no. 1826 (2016): 20160044.

Wallace, D. R. *Neptune's Ark: From Ichthyosaurs to Orcas*. University of California Press, 2007.

20 CLAN OF THE CAVE BEAR

URSUS SPELAEUS

Bears with their great size and strength, remind us of how weak and ineffectual we are as organisms: a bear, even a small one, could abolish a human fairly easily.

—CHARLES FERGUS

Most animals show themselves sparingly. The grizzly bear is six to eight hundred pounds of smugness. It has no need to hide. If it were a person, it would laugh loudly in quiet restaurants, boastfully wear the wrong clothes for special occasions, and probably play hockey.

—CRAIG CHILDS

CAVE OF BONES

The gruesome, terror-inspiring, immeasurable cavern, the lightless grotto, O Muse, bring back to my mind, and those death-like realms! We begin our walk, armed with walking sticks, ladders, and torches. Stopping at the crest of the wood, we look for the lightless cave. . . . At long last it opens wide before our eyes, a cleft in the woods, in a desolate distant area. . . . I feel my limbs quaking as I step into the wide hall through the fissures in the rock. With silent steps, I tread my way, and the cave widens and winding galleries lose themselves in deepest darkness, and in hundreds of corners and fissures. With torches I investigate the passages, and I see a thousand forms, which Nature has skillfully called forth, better than any human hand, from the living rock. Soon, as I look down, I see a greater number of horrendous human bones;

> teeth, too, I recognize; I could see bodies turned to stone, and skeletons left lying on the floor.[1]

This vivid account, *Descriptio antri subterranei prope Galgenreuth*, was written in 1748 by Thomas Grebner, a professor of theology and philosophy at the University of Würzburg, when he visited the famous Zoolith Cave of Gailenreuth in southern Germany. Of several caves near the town of Muggendorf, Zoolith Cave is the most famous one of all. This same cave yielded the first skull that was correctly identified as a cave bear (figure 20.1), although Grebner mistook the bones for human bones. Others thought the bones were from apes, cats, dogs, or even dragons or unicorns. In 1774, F. J. Esper in his publication *Newly Discovered Zoolites of Unknown Four-Footed Animals*, correctly identified most of these "human bones" as the bones of the cave bear, and he also found actual human remains in the cave as well. Finally, in 1794, Johann Christian Rosenmüller of the University of Leipzig formally named it *Ursus spelaeus* ("cave bear" in Latin).

Cave bear bones are so numerous in certain caves that most people had little regard for them. During the First World War, the demand for phosphates to make explosives and the scarcity of phosphate-rich dung led the Germans to mine the earth from the caves where bear bones occurred. When the "dragon caves" in the Styria region of Austria were exploited for phosphates, only the skulls and leg bones were kept. In Central Europe, many caves yield skeletons of cave bears, such as the *Heinrichshöhle* in Hemer, and the *Dechenhöhle* in Iserlohn, both in Germany. In 1966, a complete skeleton, five complete skulls, and 18 other bones were found Kletno Bear Cave in Poland. In 1983, a cave called Bears' Cave in Romania yielded 140 cave bear skeletons.

The reason for the abundance of so many bones is hotly debated, but several factors might explain it. Cave bears apparently lived in caves most of the year (compared to most bears, which only use them to hibernate). In addition, many of the skeletons that were found showed signs of disease, sickness, bone pathologies, and most are either very young or very old.

Figure 20.1 ▶

The cave bear. (*A*) Skeleton as it was found in one of the many European caves. (Courtesy of Wikimedia Commons) (*B*) Mounted skeleton on display at the American Museum of Natural History. ([*A*] Courtesy of Wikimedia Commons; [*B*] photo by the author).

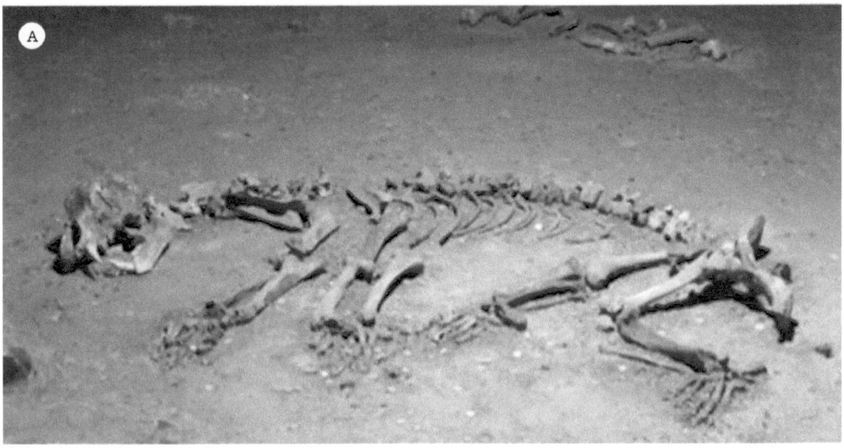
A

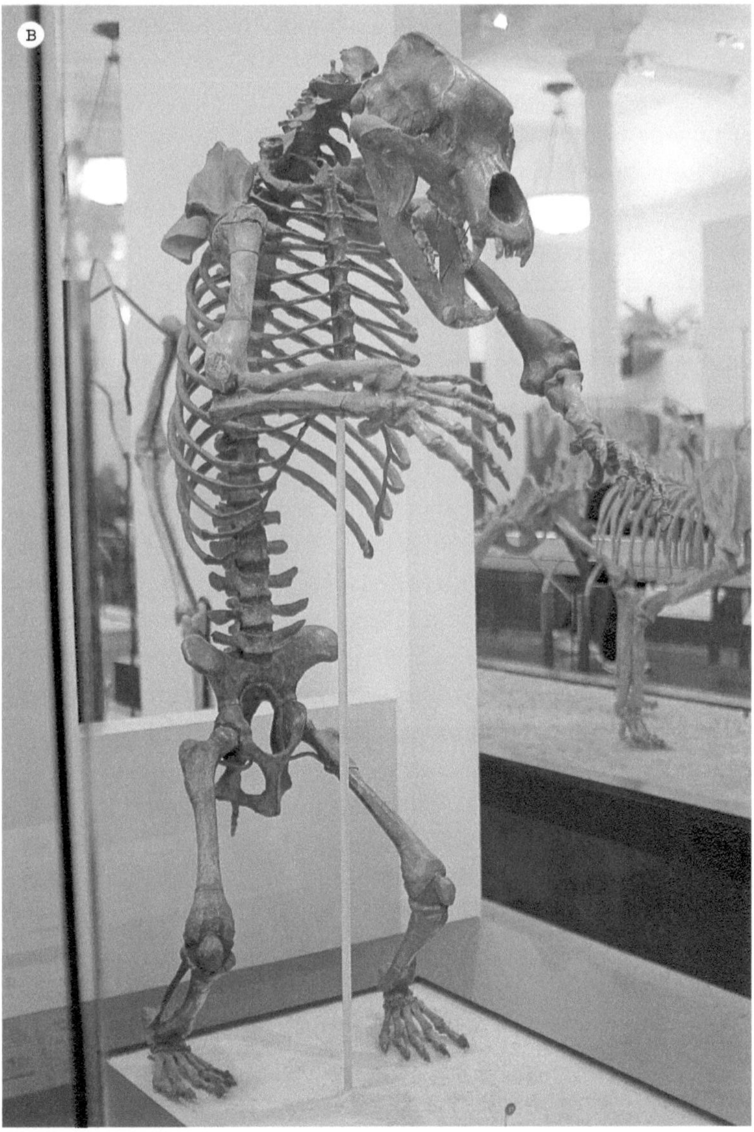
B

This points to the possibility that they died over their winter hibernation, not having obtained enough food to build up their body fat to survive the winter. However, some of these cave bear bone accumulations spanned one hundred thousand years, so only two or three bears needed to die in an average decade to result is so many skeletons; there is no need to invoke a catastrophic mass death assemblage. Finally, skeletons of cave lions and cave hyenas are also found in these same caves, suggesting that they may have come in and killed and eaten weak or vulnerable bears, or even those that could not wake up from hibernation. Some specimens show clear evidence of being eaten or scavenged by lions or hyenas.

Compared to most living bears (including their closest relatives, the brown bear, which diverged from them about 1.2–1.4 Ma), cave bears were less omnivorous and much more herbivorous. Thus they were not as likely to kill humans as the cave lion or other large predators, but there is plenty of evidence that humans and cave bears came into conflict nonetheless. The Drachenloch cave in Switzerland was excavated in 1917 and 1923 by Emil Bächler, who uncovered more than thirty thousand cave bear skeletons. It also uncovered a stone chest consisting of a low wall built from limestone slabs near a cave wall with a number of bear skulls inside it. A cave bear skull was also found with a femur bone from another bear stuck inside it. This is thought to be proof that prehistoric humans had religious rites involving the cave bear, or that the Drachenloch cave bears were hunted as part of a ritual, or that the skulls were kept as trophies. In another cave near Regourdou in southern France, a rectangular pit contained the remains of at least twenty bears, covered by a massive stone slab. A Neanderthal skeleton lay nearby in another stone pit, with various objects, including a bear arm bone, a scraper, a core, and some flakes; these were interpreted as grave offerings. We have some evidence of humans killing cave bears and vice versa, as well as numerous funerary objects and even cave paintings showing the cave bears were a big part of human lifestyle during the Paleolithic. It has even been argued that as human populations increased and their hunting technology improved in the late Pleistocene, they began pushing cave bears out of the caves to make their own homes. In a study of Spanish cave bear mitochondrial DNA, each cave used by bears was found to contain almost exclusively a unique lineage of closely related haplotypes, indicating a homing behavior for birthing and hibernation. The conclusion of this study is cave bears could not easily colonize new sites when in competition with humans for homes. Cave bears became scarce around thirty-five thousand years ago, and the last ones are dated at twenty-four thousand years ago, so they were not among the animals that vanished during the end-Pleistocene megafaunal extinction around eleven thousand years ago (see chapter 1).

THE "BEAR MAN"

Cave bears may have been known since the late 1700s, but research on them was outdated and scattershot until the legendary paleontologist Björn Kurtén started working on them. Born in Vasa, Finland, on November 19, 1924, of Swedish parents, Kurtén's native language was Swedish, but he spoke German very well, taught himself English and Finnish, and knew several other languages. Kurtén was enrolled at the University of Helsinki, and in 1943 he was called to duty to help fight the Soviet invasion of Finland. After the war and the completion of his military service, he resumed his studies in 1945 and took a wide range of courses in geology, chemistry, and zoology to train in paleontology. The war soured him on politics and ideology and many other things that most people want to fight about (and die for), so in his own words, he favored paleontology because he was determined never to engage in "anything useful" (and thus potentially tied to politics or business or something else that leads to strife). According to Fortelius and Werdelin (2024), "the least useful thing he could imagine was the study of fossils."[2]

Since there were almost no important paleontological collections in Helsinki to study at that time, he went to the University of Uppsala in Sweden to earn his doctoral degree, working under the pioneering Swedish paleontologist Birger Bohlin. This set a pattern for the rest of his life, and he traveled to museums all over the world to study their collections for his own research. According to Fortelius and Werdelin (2024), Kurten wrote that "only the paleontologist who doesn't have a collection of his own get to see the big picture. . . . People who have big fossil collections of their own end up fossilized themselves."[3]

In the 1920s, Bohlin had amassed a huge collection of the Miocene *Hipparion* faunas from China, which became the topic of Kurtén's master's thesis, *The Chinese Hipparion Fauna*, published in 1952. His doctoral dissertation, entitled "On the Variation and Population Dynamics of Fossil and Recent Mammal Populations," was published in 1953. It was his first foray into combining the latest ideas in population biology with the fossil record, which had never been done before. Kurtén then returned to Helsinki, where he was hired and held a faculty post until his death in 1988 at age sixty-four.

As described by Elaine Anderson, bears were his favorite subject, and he wrote at least 15 papers and a book, *The Cave Bear Story*, about ursids.[4] Indeed, his first name Björn means "bear" in Swedish. His first study was on the hundreds of isolated teeth and limb bones in the Helsinki collection, and eventually he visited and measured virtually every cave bear collection in every museum in Europe.

As he wrote in *The Cave Bear Story*,

> no one escapes his fate. It might be said that my affair with the cave bear started half a century ago when it was decided to give the child a name that happen to be Swedish for "bear." They were early difficulties in living up to it, but in time it led to the distinction of a mention in the "Authors and Subjects" section of the *Journal of Insignificant Research*. Still, the real thing began in the early 1950s. Eager to apply the newfangled population ideas to fossil mammals, I was casting about for a statistically respectable sample of some fossil mammal—*any* fossil mammal. The one that happened to be at hand had been collected over hundreds of years and had been lying around more or less forgotten for many decades in the cupboards of the geology department of the University of Helsinki. It was the cave bear: hundreds and hundreds of teeth and bones. I spent happy hours playing around with them, and with the ensuing statistics. But, of course, there came the time when I had to go and find out if other cave bears, elsewhere, behaved the same way. Well, some did and some did not, and this made it necessary to look at other species of bears and see how *they* behaved. And there you are—there is no end to it.

Kurtén's career continued to expand as he visited more and more museums, not only in Europe, but especially in North America, where he became an expert on North American Pleistocene mammals. He eventually wrote semipopular books on *Pleistocene Mammals of Europe* (1968), *The Ice Age* (1969), *The Age of Mammals* (1973), and *Pleistocene Mammals of North America* (with his former student Elaine Anderson, 1980). He then branched out into writing semipopular books for the general audience, such as *How to Deep-Freeze a Mammoth* (1986) and *Before the Indians* (1988), popularizing paleontology. He even ventured into the field of speculative fiction, writing novels imagining the world of the Pleistocene and how Paleolithic humans coped with giant mammoths and cave bears as well as glaciers and Ice Ages. Starting with *Dance of the Tiger* (1980), he launched an entire genre that has sprouted into numerous movies about Paleolithic peoples coping with the hard realities of life in the Stone Age. This was copied in the best-selling series of eleven novels by Jean Auel, starting with *Clan of the Cave Bear*, which have sold forty-five million copies. Kurtén created this popular genre, which he called "paleofiction."

But Kurtén's greatest claim to fame among paleontologists was his pioneering work on statistics and population biology applied to fossil mammals. During the 1940s, George Gaylord Simpson may have been the original pioneer of thinking of fossils as part of a biological population sample and applying statistical approaches to them, at a time when everyone else was naming each slightly different new fossil they found without thinking of the natural variations of biological populations. But Kurtén pioneered many other techniques, going back to his original 1953 thesis. He was the first to look at allometric size changes in fossils, the first to study selection by differential survival, the first to apply the half-life concept to the duration of fossil species, the first to do research on dental correlation fields, the first to apply survivorship methods from population biology, and to develop population statistics and age-mortality curves, and so many more innovations (many of his classic papers are collected in the volume *Evolution and Fossil Mammals*, published in 1988). If someone over in biology came up with a bright idea, Kurtén was quick to snap it up and apply it to some large sample of Pleistocene mammal fossils.

In the early 1950s, Kurtén and Simpson were among the most respected mammalian paleontologists in the world, because of their innovative thinking and openness to new methods, and their interdisciplinary approaches that brought paleontology into the modern era. Both of them were powerful advocates for the development of the Neo-Darwinian synthesis starting in the late 1940s. Kurtén was constantly invited to give thought-provoking presentations at university seminars and at professional meetings, or to organize and chair symposia on paleozoology, evolution of mammals, continental drift, the Ice Ages, or early humans. In 1974, he was at the First International Theriological Congress in Moscow and was asked to give the keynote address on just a few hours' notice (since Simpson had been forced to cancel)—he gave a legendary talk on rates of evolution of fossil mammals with almost no preparation.

According to Fortelius and Werdelin (2024), Kurtén was extremely skeptical of authority. He "was no admirer of received wisdom and often ready to tentatively embrace new ideas in science even when others felt there wasn't yet enough information for a decision. . . . He liked to see himself as an *enfant terrible* and he clearly enjoyed shocking conservative colleagues with his liberal ways."[5] Fortelius remembers Björn as complementing him after an international seminar in France in 1979 on contradicting his peers in public. "A picture [of] how we cooperate in Finland," he said.[6]

This is not to say that every idea Kurtén came up with or published was right—no scientist can claim that. Some of his early work has been rethought in the past fifty years, but most of it has held up remarkably well given that it was pioneering work breaking new ground and bound to be corrected as better data emerged. Famously, he held rather odd ideas that humans originated from the Miocene fossil ape *Propliopithecus*, through *Ramapithecus*, and then the South African australopithecines, rather than from many of the late Miocene ape relatives of hominins. He promoted these ideas in his book *Not From the Apes* (1971), which was written when the only primitive hominin fossils known were the few specimens from South African caves (which could not be dated), and the first few discoveries at Olduvai Gorge by Louis and Mary Leakey. Most paleoanthropologists of his time considered this notion to be an embarrassment, and it is now dismissed thanks to the enormous number of hominin fossils that have been found since 1971. (And it turned out that *Ramapithecus* was a primitive relative of the orangutans, not a hominin—see chapter 24.)

I vividly remember meeting Kurtén several times at paleontology meetings. He was a small man with a distinctive gray mustache and goatee (figure 20.2). I really got to know him when he attended the special research conference on horse evolution, held in the fossil horse storage floor of the Frick Collection of the American Museum of Natural History in 1981. Sitting in my grad student office in the storage floor above, I could hear the vigorous debate over how to classify fossil horses going on below me, with clashing schools of thought between the Europeans who attended (Kurtén, French paleontologist Vera Eisenmann, Spanish paleontologist Maria Theresa Alberdi, Finnish paleontologist Ann Forstén, and others) and the new school of horse research precipitated by all the beautiful skulls collected by Morris Skinner for the Frick Collection, and promoted by American

Figure 20.2 ▲
Photo of Björn Kurtén. (Courtesy of M. Fortelius)

paleontologists such as Skinner, Mike Woodburne, Bruce MacFadden, and Ray Bernor. They focused on features of the skull not usually preserved in more fragmentary European fossils. It was interesting to see the clash of philosophies, as well as established scientists having to rethink their long held conclusions in the light of all the new fossils in the Frick Collection.

Sometimes Kurtén was right for the wrong reasons. One of my students and I did research on a thick-legged Pleistocene deer that Kurtén named *Navahoceros* in 1975, based on specimens from San Josecito Cave in Nuevo Leon, Mexico. Kurtén called it the "mountain deer" and compared it to other mountain dwellers, like the South American "mountain deer" *Hippocamelus antisensis*, plus mountain goats and takins, which have stumpy limbs adapted for "low-gear locomotion" during rock climbing. Other scientists dismissed *Navahoceros* as just another bunch of fossils of mule deer. In our research, we can clearly show that *Navahoceros fricki* is a distinct and valid genus and species and is not closely related to mule deer but to reindeer. However, his comparisons of it to mountain-dwelling ruminants is way off base because its limbs are nowhere near as specialized for mountain climbing as those found in takins, ibex, chamois, or mountain goats.

Such is the complicated legacy of Björn Kurtén. He was ahead of his time in most of his research and inspired many other people to follow in his footsteps, but like any scientist (especially one so daring and groundbreaking) he made his share of mistakes. When he started, there was no paleontology in Finland, and he worked in virtual isolation for years, training most of the vertebrate paleontologists working in Finland today. The Paleontological Society of Finland, which now has many members, was an outgrowth of the Björn Kurtén Club, an informal group of paleontologists at the University of Helsinki that has been going since 1997; almost all its original members were his students, or students of his students.

THREE BEARS (AND MORE)

Bears are one of the most flexible and adaptable groups of terrestrial carnivorans, spreading to every continent except Australia and Antarctica. Unlike most members of the order Carnivora, like dogs and cats and seals, most bears are omnivores, capable of consuming almost 90 percent of their diet as plant material with minimal meat when the hunting is poor, or focusing on fish, carrion, and wild game when the hunting is good. Yet there are extremes. Polar bears feed almost exclusively on marine mammals (primarily seals), and pandas are the only members of the order Carnivora that eat nothing but plants, primarily bamboo.

Bears have been familiar animals to North American and European cultures over many centuries. They are found in many of our legends and media, from Goldilocks and the Three Bears, Pooh Bear, Paddington Bear, Yogi Bear, to Fozzie Bear, the Berenstain Bears, and Smokey the Bear. Sports teams are named the Bears, the Bad News Bears, the Golden Bears, the Bruins, and for centuries the international symbol for Russia has long been the Russian bear. When California declared its independence from Mexico, they called it the Bear Flag Republic because at one time grizzly bears roamed the entire state as top predators.

Today only eight species of bears are left on the planet (figure 20.3). They are found across Eurasia and North America, as well as the spectacled bear of South America, and the sun bear of southeast Asia. They range in size from the enormous polar bear, which weighs up to 1,500 pounds (700 kilograms), to the small sun bear of southeast Asia which weighs only about 145 pounds (65 kilograms).

Figure 20.3 ▲
A diagram of the eight species of living bears. (Courtesy of Wikimedia Commons)

At one time there were bears in Africa as well. But bears have a long evolutionary history going back at least forty million years with dozens of genera and species of extinct bears, which came in every shape and size from tiny weasel-shaped creatures to the biggest land carnivorans that ever lived.

Let's look at some of the unique anatomical features of bears. Most bears have massive robust skulls with huge canines, capable of biting with tremendous force and killing almost any animal. Their wicked teeth are adapted to do a lot of things because most bears are omnivores. In particular, bears are different from other members of the order Carnivora, such as cats and dogs, in that they have transformed the blade-like shearing cheek teeth typical of flesh eaters to broad low molars with crushing cusps, and only limited shearing function, capable of grinding food and eating plants as well as meat (figure 20.4). This transformation occurs in most omnivores, so we also see it in pigs, peccaries, and some primates, including humans, which are also

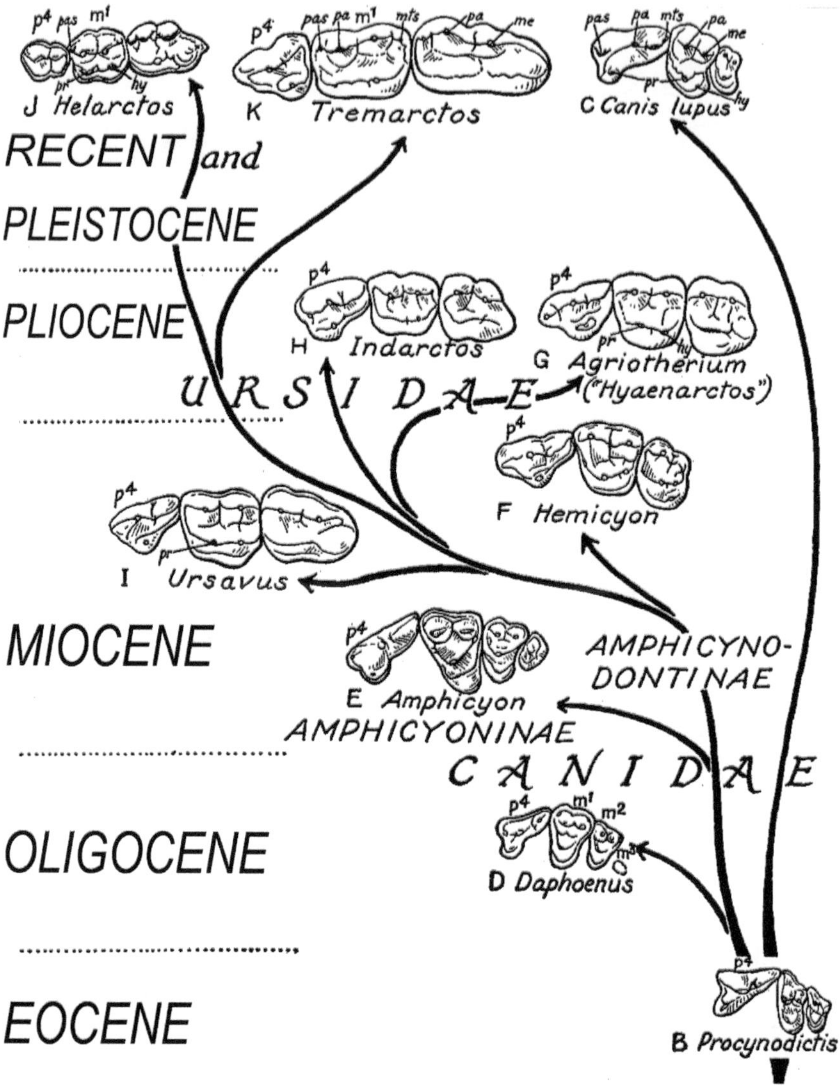

Figure 20.4 ▲

The molar teeth of bears are relatively low crowned with lots of rounded cusps, suitable for their omnivorous diet. (From William King Gregory, *Evolution Emerging* [Arno, 1951])

omnivorous. And yet, if we go back to 50 Ma to the earliest members of the order Canivora, their teeth are still highly adapted to shearing and slicing, so the bear lineage is the first to give up that function and become omninvorous. Bears are also unusual in that they are plantigrade, walking on the palms of their forepaws and the soles of their hind feet, like we do, rather than digitigrade, walking on the tips of their toes, like most carnivorans.

The family Ursidae is part of the subgroup of order Carnivora known as the Caniformia, or the dog-bear-weasel branch of carnivorans, rather than the Feliformia, which includes cats, hyenas, and mongoose. Among Caniformia, they are most closely related to the weasel lineage, as well as the pinnipeds or seals, sea lions, and walruses.

The oldest know bear relative, or ursoid, is the raccoon-like *Parictis* (figure 20.5), from beds around 37 Ma in the Big Badlands of South Dakota.

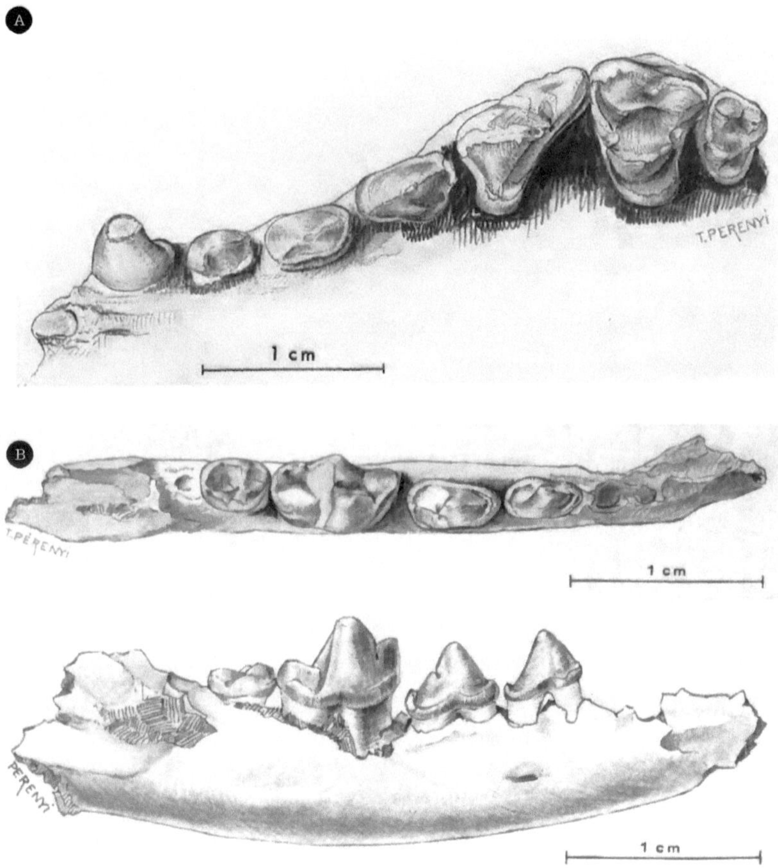

Figure 20.5 ▲

The teeth of the earliest known ursoid, *Parictis*. (*A*) Upper teeth. (*B*) Lower teeth. (Courtesy of Wikimedia Commons)

Although it was raccoon-sized as well, it had key features in its teeth that show us it was an ursoid, or bear relative. Another primitive ursoid was *Eoarctos vorax* (figure 20.6), recently described from beds around 33 Ma in North Dakota.

After these primtive bear relatives, the first great evolutonary radiation of bears were the Hemicyonines, or "dog bears," and their name means "half dog" because most of them were built more like dogs with longer legs and they were much more committed to carnivory rather than omnivory.

Figure 20.6 ▲
Reconstruction of the primitive Oligocene ursoid *Eoarctos vorax*. (Art by M. Hallett, courtesy of X. Wang.)

They evolved from *Parictis*-like ancestors to larger more advanced forms like *Cephalogale* from 28–20 Ma in North America and Europe, and *Phoberogale*, from 20–22 Ma, in France, Pakistan, and California. From beds around 16–12 Ma in Eurasia and North America, we get the much bigger hemicyonine *Plithocyon* (figure 20.7A), and espeically the beast that gave the group its name, *Hemicyon*, which was about 5 feet (1.6 meters) long with long legs and toes. Unlike most bears, it was digitigrade, or it walked on the tips of its toes, rather than on the palms and soles of its feet like modern bears do (figure 20.7B).

The next subfamily of bears is the Agriotheriinae, or agriotheres (figure 20.8). They can be traced back to *Ursavus*, which was a small dog-sized animal with a slender build, short legs, and a long torso (figure 20.9). It originated in North America about 18 Ma, then spread to Eurasia, and persisted until about 8 Ma. Some paleontologists consider *Ursavus* to be the ancestor of all the advanced non-hemicyonine bears, not just the agriotheres. A more advanced agriothere is *Indarctos*, known from beds around 11–7 Ma in Arizona, Oregon, Texas, then spreading to China, Turkey, and Spain about 9 Ma. Finally, *Agriotherium* itself dates back to 11 Ma and persisted until the beginning of the Ice Ages around 2.5 Ma. It was about 7 feet (2 meters) long and weighed 1,600 pounds (750 kilograms), and was the only bear to be found not only in North America and Eurasia but even in Africa during the beginning of the Ice Ages, where it competed with saber-toothed cats, lions, and other huge predators.

All of these subfamilies are now extinct with no living relatives or descendants. But the short-faced bears, or Tremarctinae, do have a living relative, the spectacled bear of South America, which gets its name from the white markings on its face that somewhat resemble glasses (figures 20.3, 20.8). There is even a fossil species of spectacled bear, *Tremarctos floridanus*, that comes from Ice Age deposits in Florida. In South America, there was the enormous tremarctine *Arctotherium*, that rivals some other bears for the largest land carnivoran that ever lived (figure 20.10). It stood as high as 11 feet (4.3 meters) tall and weighed up to 3,500 pounds (1,750 kilograms), although these bears varied enormously in size, both within and between species, and show strong sexual dimorphism, with males 30 percent larger than femaless. *Arctotherium* migrated from North America across the Panama Land bridge about 3 Ma, then took over the large predator niche on South America until the end of the Ice Ages.

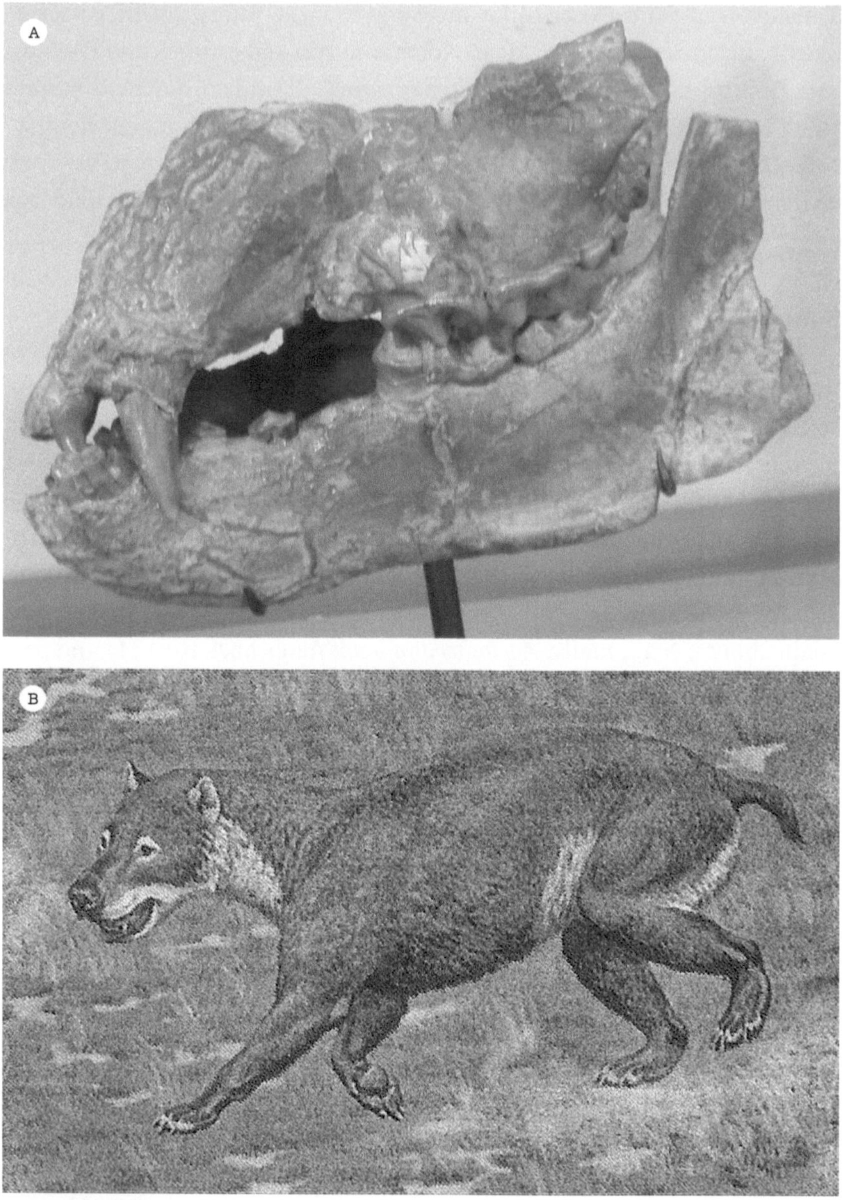

Figure 20.7 ▲

Hemicyonines were dog-like bears with long running legs. (*A*) Jaws of *Plithocyon*. (*B*) Reconstruction of *Hemicyon* by Jay Matternes. (Courtesy of Wikimedia Commons)

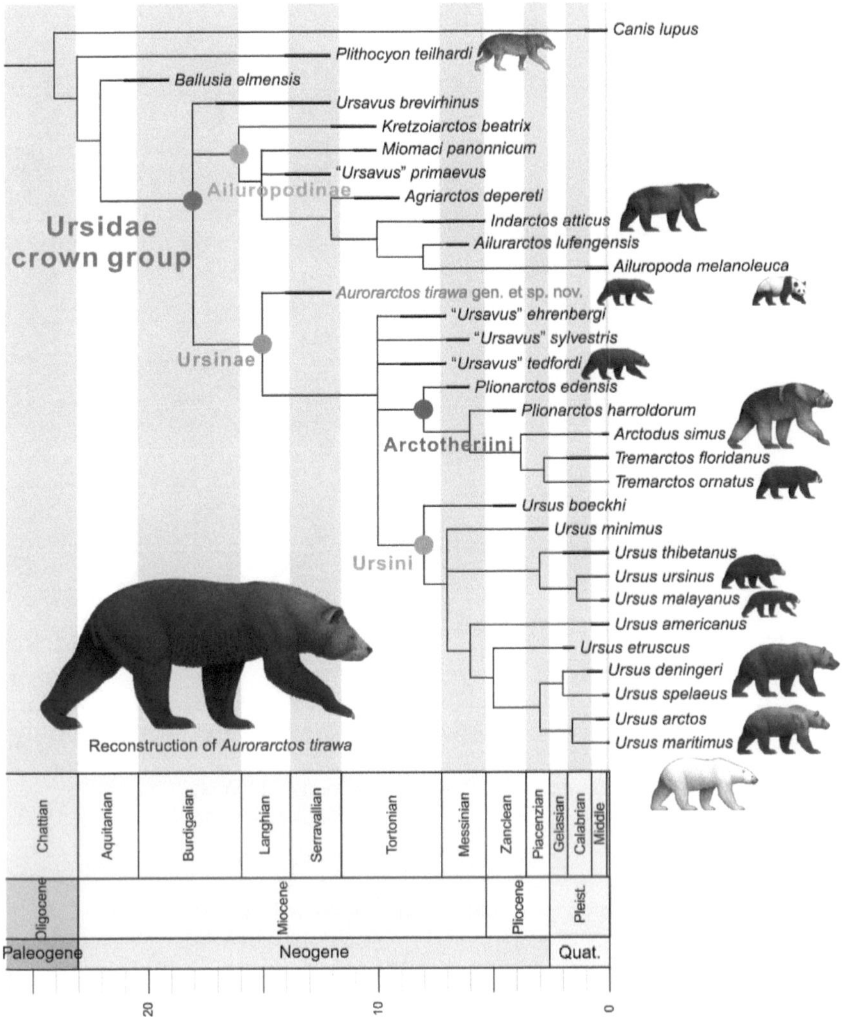

Figure 20.8 ▲
Family tree of ursoids. (Courtesy of Wikimedia Commons)

But North America was ruled by its own genus and species of giant short-faced bear, *Arctodus simus*, which stood more than 6 feet (3 meters) at the shoulder and weighed over a ton. When it reared up on its hind legs, it stood over 12 feet (4.5 meters) above the ground (figure 20.11). It is known from Ice Age beds all over North America, from Florida, the La Brea Tar Pits, and

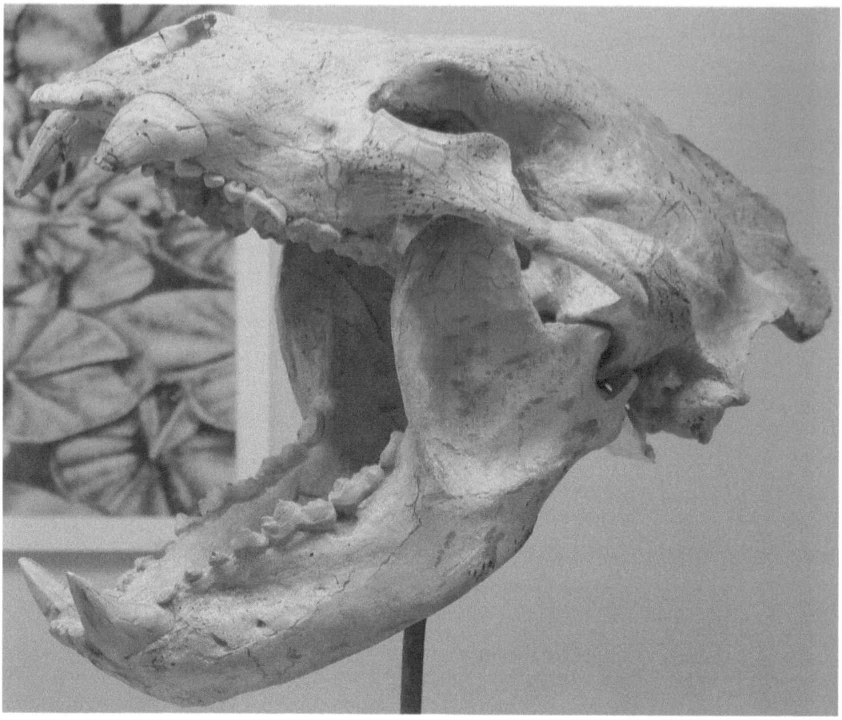

Figure 20.9 ▲
Skull of the primitive ursoid *Ursavus*. (Courtesy of Wikimedia Commons)

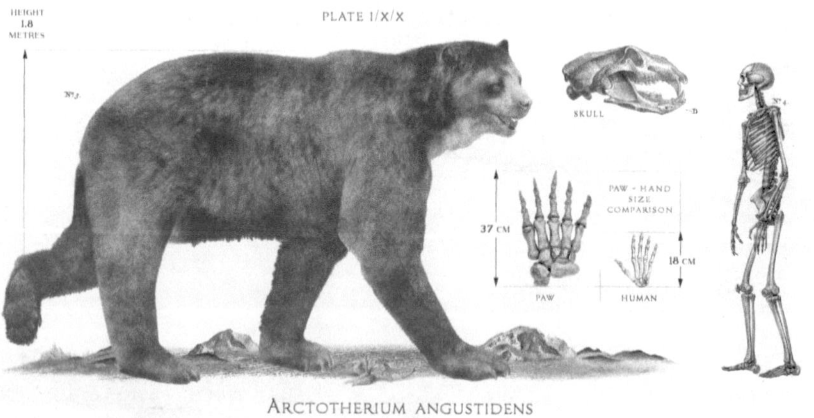

Figure 20.10 ▲
Reconstruction of the gigantic South American bear *Arctotherium*. (Courtesy of G. Ugueto)

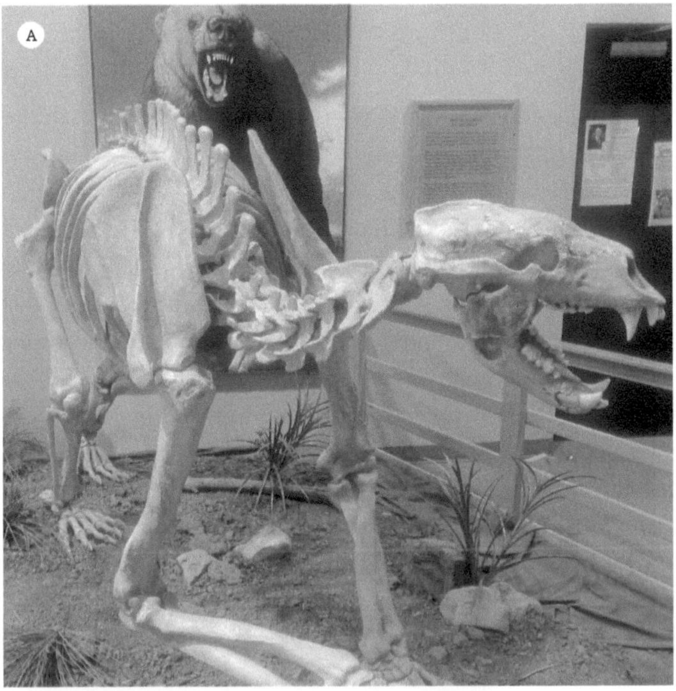

Figure 20.11 ◀ ▲
The enormous short-faced bear, *Arctodus simus*. (*A*) Mounted skeleton on display at the Mammoth Site of Hot Springs, South Dakota (Courtesy of Wikimedia Commons) (*B*) Life-sized model on display at the La Brea Tar Pits Museum. ([*A*] Courtesy of Wikimedia Commons; [*B*] photo by the author)

central Mexico, to Alaska and Alberta. It was considerably larger than the saber-toothed cat or the giant Ice Age lion, *Panthera atrox*, so it had no real competition as the top predator.

Finally, we come to the subfamiy Ursinae, which includes all living bears except the spectaacled bear and the pandas (figures 20.3, 20.8). Most of them are species of the genus *Ursus*. The evolution of the many extinct and living species of ursines is quite complex, so we will only discuss the major taxa. These include the black bear, *Ursus americanus*, a smaller bear that can be black but also brown. However, the brown phase of the black bear should not be confused with the taxon that is officially known as the brown bear, *Ursus arctos*, which includes several subspecies, such as grizzly bears (*Ursus arctos horribilis)*, the giant Kodiak bears of Alaska (*Ursus arctos middendorffi)*, and several subspecies of Eurasian bear, such as the Himalayan brown bear (*Ursus arctos isabellinus*). The Indian sloth bear, *Melursus*, was the model for Baloo in the jungle book. *Helarctos*, the sun bear of southeast Asia, is the smallest living bear, and the polar bear, *Ursus maritimus*, is by far the largest (figure 20.3).

THE PANDA'S THUMB

Finally, let's talk about pandas. The giant panda, *Ailuropoda melanoleuca*, a crowd favorite of the few zoos that have them, is clearly a member of the bear family, but the first group to branch off from the rest of the living bear lineages (figure 20.6). Famously, it's one of the few members of the order Carnivora that's a strict herbivore, eating nothing but bamboo. As scientists have pointed out, it has a strange arrangement in its front paws (figure 20.12A). The true thumb is closely aligned with the rest of the fingers, the same as the dew claw in cats and dogs, so its true thumb cannot grasp anything. To compensate, the panda has enlarged a wrist bone, called the radial sesamoid, to serve as a "sixth finger," a patchwork "thumb" that serves just well enough to strip leaves from bamboo stalks. It's nowhere near as flexible and strong and useful as the opposable thumb that we primates have, but it doesn't have to be—it just needs to create a device for stripping leaves. The key to nature is not its perfection but how its temporary solutions and jury-rigged contrivances show that organisms do not need to be perfectly engineered—they just need to work well enough to survive and leave offspring. As Stephen Jay Gould pointed out in his book, *The*

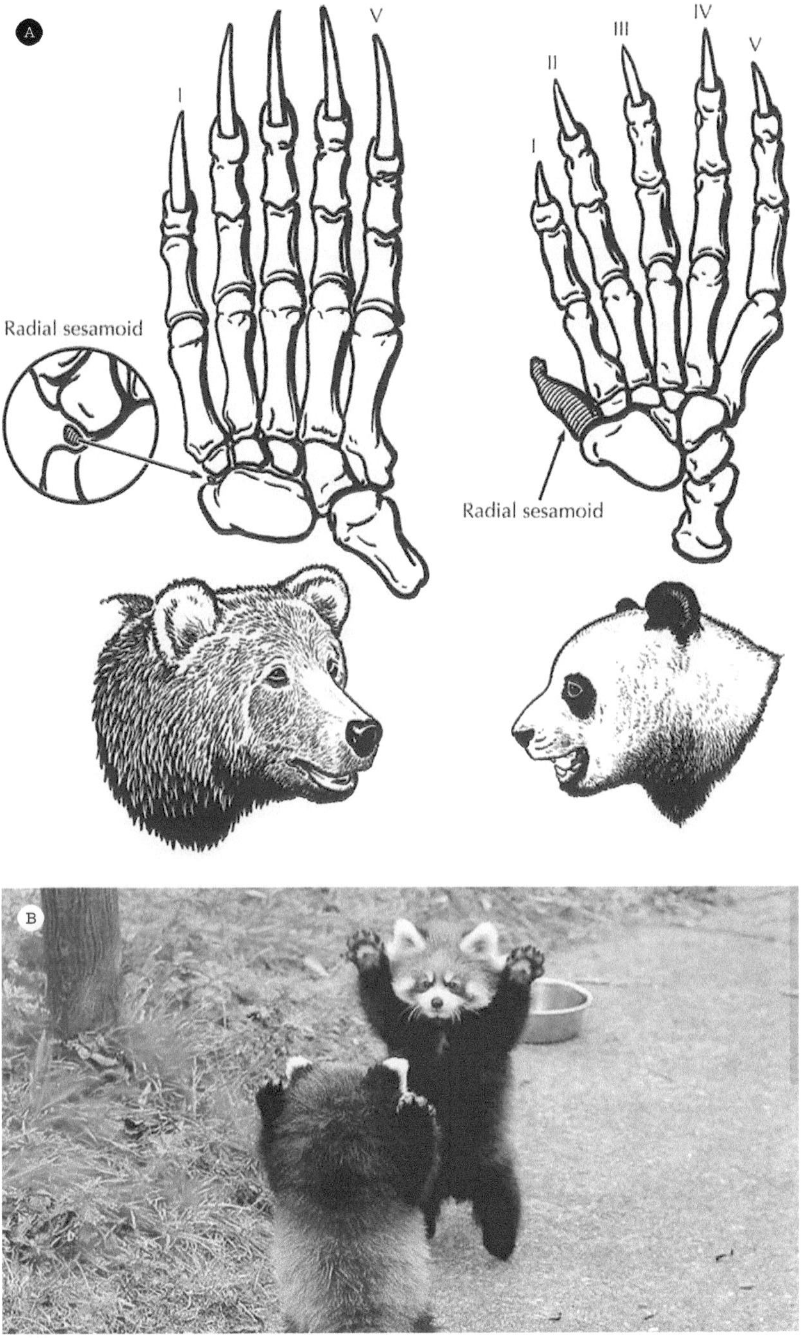

Figure 20.12 ▲

(*A*) The panda, like all Carnivora, has all five fingers forming a paw, but unlike other Carnivora, it eats bamboo. Consequently, it has modified a wrist bone, the radial sesamoid, into a crude "thumb" that enables it to strip the leaves off bamboo. It works just well enough to feed a panda; it is not beautifully designed, but crude, clumsy, and jury-rigged. (*B*) The lesser or "red" panda, showing their six fingers including a false thumb. ([*A*] Drawing by C. Buell, from D. R. Prothero, *Evolution: What the Fossils Say, and Why It Matters*, [Columbia University Press, 2007], figure 2.3; [*B*] courtesy of Wikimedia Commons)

Pandas Thumb, it's not a great design, and it works just well enough to allow the panda to survive, but it is evidence of crummy jury-rigged adaptations in nature.

As Gould wrote in his 1978 essay, "The Panda's Thumb," about what the anatomist D. Dwight Davis found when he studied the giant panda:

> As with the radial sesamoid, these muscles did not arise *de novo*; like the parts of Darwin's orchids, they are familiar bits of anatomy remodeled for a new function. The abductor of the radial sesamoid (the muscle that pulls it away from the true digits) bears the formidable name abductor pollicis longus ("the long abductor of the thumb"—*pollicis* is the genitive of pollex, Latin for "thumb"). Its name is a giveaway. In other carnivores, this muscle attaches to the first digit, or true thumb. Does the anatomy of other carnivores give us any clue to the origin of this odd arrangement in pandas? Davis points out that ordinary bears and raccoons, the closest relatives of giant pandas, far surpass all other carnivores in using their forelegs for manipulating objects in feeding. Pardon the backward metaphor, but pandas, thanks to their ancestry, began with a leg up for evolving greater dexterity in feeding. Moreover, ordinary bears already have a slightly enlarged radial sesamoid. In most carnivores, the same muscles that move the radial sesamoid in pandas attach exclusively to the base of the pollex, or true thumb. But in ordinary bears, the long abductor muscle ends in two tendons: one inserts into the base of the thumb as in most carnivores, but the other attaches to the radial sesamoid. Two shorter muscles also attach, in part, to the radial sesamoid in bears. "Thus," Davis concludes, "the musculature for operating this remarkable new mechanism—functionally a new digit—required no intrinsic change from conditions already present in the panda's closest relatives, the bears. Furthermore, it appears that the whole sequence of events in the musculature follows automatically from simple hypertrophy of the sesamoid bone."[7]

Now we have fossils from 6 Ma in China called *Ailurarctos*, which show how the panda's thumb evolved as a compromise between the ability to walk effciently and needing the ability to strip bamboo. The curvature of the false thumb allows the panda to walk without tripping, but it is still straight enough and long enough to serve as a device for gripping bamboo stalks.

Even more amazing is the story of the red panda, or lesser panda, *Ailurus fulgens* (figure 20.12B). It is a reddish-brown color and is about the size and shape of a cat with a bushy tail and red and white stripes on its tail and body. Its face has a mask of black stripes and a white muzzle, and its ears are black and white as well. It also lives in the highest mountains in China and Tibet and Nepal, coping with snowy winters and eating other kinds of small prey when bamboo is scarce.

For a long time, it was associated with the giant panda because it too eats mostly bamboo, and it too has the bizarre jury-rigged thumb made from a wrist bone. But all of the detailed evidence from molecular biology shows that the red panda is *not* a true panda after all, and not even a bear! Its closest relatives are raccoons, weasels, and skunks, so the complex apparatus of its false thumb evolved convergently. This is consistent with lots of earlier research in their karyology, serology, behavior, anatomy, and reproduction, and especially their fossil record, which allies them more closely with raccoons and weasels, not bears and pandas. Not only that but genetic analysis has shown that both animals have evolved the genes for tastng and digesting bamboo as well.

The overwhelming evidence suggests that the weird jury-rigged "panda's thumb" has evolved twice independently in two unrelated groups of carnivorans. In earlier days, scientists might regard such a specialized paw structure like the "panda's thumb" as a truly unique feature and could not imagine that it could evolve in parallel. But the fossil, molecular, and behavioral data cannot be denied, so we are forced to admit that it is. Keep in mind, however, that both animals came from common ancestors (like bears and raccoons) that already had highly flexible grasping forepaws with a small radial sesamoid partially developed. And they both needed a solution to stripping leaves from bamboo stalks and have the same basic tool kit of a paw with a tiny "dew claw" thumb that cannot be made opposable. So they are both starting with the same basic anatomy and modifying it for a similar function, which leads to a similar solution. Thus the carnivoran paw is so constrained by evolution that if they are going to develop a new thumb for grasping bamboo, they have to use the same bones of the wrist to do so.

This has been confirmed by the discovery of a ten-million-year-old fossil of the ancestor of the red panda, *Simocyon battaleri*. It already had the enlarged radial sesamoid, even though it lived in Spain where there was no bamboo. Paleontologists have suggested that this bone had another function: it may have used its false thumb to grasp at branches because both it and the modern red panda are very arboreal species.

Thus bears and their kin have evolved some amazing features over the last forty million years. Sadly, almost all wild bear species are now endangered and threatened, not just due to habitat loss but also to poaching because bear gall bladders are highly prized in Chinese medicine. Even worse, climate change is melting the Arctic so fast that polar bears will soon be endangered. In fact, it has gotten so warm in the polar regions that they are interbreeding with grizzlies to form hybrids known as pizzlies. The world of the bears is under threat from humans, both directly and indirectly.

NOTES

1. Thomas Grebner, "Descriptio antri subterranei prope Galgenreuth aus dem Jahre 1748," *Geologische Blätter für Nordost-Bayern und angrenzende Gebiete* 6 (1748): 32–40.
2. Mikael Fortelius and Lars Werdelin, "Double Exposure: Recollections of Björn Kurtén," *Annales Zoologiques Fennici* 61, no. 1 (2024): 47–55.
3. Fortelius and Werdelin, "Double Exposure."
4. Elaine Anderson, "Björn Kurtén, an Eminent Paleotheriologist," *Annales Zoologiques Fennici* 28 (1998): 123–126.
5. Fortelius and Werdelin, "Double Exposure."
6. Fortelius and Werdelin, "Double Exposure."
7. Stephen Jay Gould, *The Panda's Thumb* (Norton, 1980), 19–25.

FOR FURTHER READING

Anderson, E. "Björn Kurtén, an Eminent Palaeotheriologist." *Annales Zoologici Fennici* 28 (1992): 123–126.

Davis, D. Dwight. *The Giant Panda: A Morphological Study of an Evolutionary Mechanism.* Chicago Natural History Museum, 1964.

Flynn, J. J., M. A. Nedbal, J. W. Dragoo, and R. L. Honeycutt. "Whence the Red Panda?" *Molecular Phylogenetics and Evolution* 17, no. 2 (2000): 190–199.

Fortelius, M., and L. Werdelin. "Double Exposure: Recollections of Björn Kurtén." *Annales Zoologici Fennici* 61 (2024): 1–15.

Gould, S. J. *The Panda's Thumb.* Norton, 1980.

Glatston, A. R. *Red Panda: Biology and Conservation of the First Panda.* William Andrew, 2010.

Hunt, R. M., Jr. "Ursidae." *Evolution of Tertiary Mammals of North America, Vol. 1: Terrestrial Carnivores, Ungulates, and Ungulatelike Mammals*, ed. C. M. Janis, K. M. Scott, and L. L. Jacobs, 174–195. Cambridge University Press, 1998.

Krause, J., T. Unger, A. Noçon, A. Malaspinas, S. Kolokotronis, M. Stiller, et al. "Mitochondrial Genomes Reveal an Explosive Radiation of Extinct and Extant Bears Near the Miocene-Pliocene Boundary." *BMC Evolutionary Biology* 8, no. 220 (2008): 220.

Kumar, V., F. Lammers, T. Bidon, M. Pfenninger, L. Kolter, M. A. Nilsson, and A. Janke. "The Evolutionary History of Bears Is Characterized by Gene Flow Across Species." *Scientific Reports* 7 (2017): 46487.

Kurtén, B. *Before the Indians*. Columbia University Press, 1988.

——. *The Cave Bear Story*. Columbia University Press, 1976.

——. *Dance of the Tiger*. University of California Press, 1978.

——. *Istiden* (The Ice Age). Forum, 1969.

——. *Not from the Apes*. Pantheon, 1971.

——. *On Evolution and Fossil Mammals*. Columbia University Press, 1988.

——. *Pleistocene Mammals of Europe*. Columbia University Press, 1968.

Kurtén, B., and E. Anderson. *Pleistocene Mammals of North America*. Columbia University Press, 1980.

McLellan, B., and D. C. Reiner. "A Review of Bear Evolution." *International Association for Bear Research and Management* 9, no. 1 (1992): 85–96.

Pàges, M. "Combined Analysis of Fourteen Nuclear Genes Refines the Ursidae Phylogeny." *Molecular Phylogenetics and Evolution* 47, no. 1 (2008): 73–83.

Prothero, D. R. *The Princeton Field Guide to Prehistoric Mammals*. Princeton University Press, 2016.

——. *Vertebrate Evolution: From Origins to Dinosaurs and Beyond*. Taylor & Francis/CRC Press, 2022.

Slattery, J. P., and S. J. O'Brien. "Molecular Phylogeny of the Red Panda (*Ailurus fulgens*)." *Journal of Heredity* 86, no. 6 (1995): 413–422.

Soibelzon, L. H., and B. W. Schubert. "The Largest Known Bear, *Arctotherium angustidens*, from the Early Pleistocene Pampean Region of Argentina: With a Discussion of Size and Diet Trends in Bears." *Journal of Paleontology* 85, no. 1 (2011): 69–75.

Soibelzon, L. H., E. P. Tonni, and M. Bond. "The Fossil Record of South American Short-Faced Bears (Ursidae, Tremarctinae)." *Journal of South American Earth Sciences* 20, nos. 1–2 (2005): 105–113.

Waits, L. "Rapid Radiation Events in the Family Ursidae Indicated by Likelihood Phylogenetic Estimation from Multiple Fragments of Mtdna." *Molecular Phylogenetics and Evolution* 13, no. 1 (1999): 82–92.

Wang, B., and Z. Qiu. "Notes on Early Oligocene Ursids (Carnivora, Mammalia) from Saint Jacques, Nei Mongol, China." *Bulletin of the American Museum of Natural History* 279, (2005): 116–124.

Wang, X., M. C. McKenna, and D. Dashzeveg. "*Amphicticeps* and *Amphicynodon* (Arctoidea, Carnivora) from Hsanda Gol Formation, Central Mongolia and Phylogeny of Basal Arctoids with Comments on Zoogeography." *American Museum Novitates*, no. 3483 (2005): 1–58.

Ward, P., and S. Kynaston. *Wild Bears of the World*. Facts on File, 1995.

Wesley-Hunt, G. D., and J. J. Flynn. "Phylogeny of the Carnivora: Basal Relationships Among the Carnivoramorphans, and Assessment of the Position of 'Miacoidea' Relative to Carnivora." *Journal of Systematic Palaeontology* 3, no. 1 (2005): 1–28.

21 THE DIREST WOLF

AENOCYON DIRUS

CHORONZON: I am a dire wolf, prey-stalking, lethal prowler.

—**NEIL GAIMAN, *PRELUDES & NOCTURNES* (1991)**

TREASURES OF LA BREA

The La Brea Tar Pits are some the most famous fossil deposits in the world, representing the last fifty thousand years, including the end of the last Ice Age—yet they are located right in the middle of metropolitan Los Angeles. More than three million fossils have been recovered, including 139 species of birds and 59 species of mammals (both living and extinct), as well as reptiles, amphibians, fish, and numerous plant remains. A huge amount of research has been conducted here over the past century, and much of what we know about late Ice Age mammals and birds comes from La Brea (figure 21.1). More than one hundred separate excavation pits have been found in the area, although only a few have yielded lots of bones.

Initially, it was part of a Spanish land grant, Rancho La Brea, where the asphalt was frequently mined to lubricate axles on wooden carts, to waterproof boats, or later to form a seal for tar roofs. *La Brea* is the Spanish word for "tar" or "asphalt," so saying the phrase "The La Brea Tar Pits" is equivalent to saying "the the tar tar pits." Rancho La Brea was then part of the huge Sixth Street Oil Field, which is still active beneath Los Angeles today, with many wells in rich parts of the town like Beverly Hills. Early

Figure 21.1 ▲
Reconstruction of La Brea Tar Pits during the Pleistocene. (Courtesy of Wikimedia Commons)

landowners thought the bones recovered from the tar were from lost cattle or pronghorns, but in 1901 the oil geologist W. W. Orcutt recognized that the bones were from extinct animals like saber-toothed cats, and the bone rush was on.

The first collections were made by the University of California Berkeley, from 1905–1912, and they are still up at Berkeley, mostly stored in their famous Campanile, or bell tower, for lack of any other space to keep them. Other groups, such as local high schools and colleges and the Southern California Academy of Sciences, also began excavations, and it was chaos with different groups excavating without authorization. In 1913 the landowner, G. Allan Hancock, gave the exclusive rights of excavation to the fledgling Los Angeles County Museum. Eventually Hancock deeded all the land to the County of Los Angeles, where it is now Hancock Park.

Most of the specimens were recovered by the Natural History Museum between 1913 and 1915, and then were stored in the downtown museum building. There was nothing to see in the park itself but a small bone deposit in what is now called the Observation Pit on the west side of the park, which has a spiral ramp surrounding a mass of bones still left in the asphalt the way they were discovered. The only other things on the site were life-sized concrete sculptures of the giant short-faced bear and the largest ground sloth, so there was almost nothing to see at the actual site of discovery when I was a kid growing up in Los Angeles in the 1950s and 1960s. Finally, in 1977, the Page Museum of La Brea Discoveries (now "The La Brea Tar Pits Museum") was opened in Hancock Park, and it houses most of the La Brea collections on site. There is also Pit 91, which was one of the early abandoned pits that has now been slowly and steadily excavated with careful grid reading of the position and orientation of every bone; this project started in 1969, and is still going today, fifty-seven years later. I got my first experience in paleontology as a young high school volunteer there in the summer of 1970. I did not drive yet, so I had to ride the buses from my Glendale home, transferring to the Wilshire bus on Skid Row, and then back each day, for about four hours of working time, sorting the washed matrix to find tiny rodent bones, bird bones, beetle wing covers (still iridescent after thirty thousand years), and other microfossils.

Of the many mammal species at La Brea, the most common is the dire wolf, *Aenocyon dirus*, followed by the saber-toothed cat, *Smilodon fatalis*. There are literally thousands of bones of both of these animals in the La Brea collections. Predators, like the dire wolf, saber-toothed cat, plus the giant lion *Panthera atrox*, and the short-faced bear *Arctodus simus*, dominate the assemblage, whereas herbivores like horses, bison, camels, and ground sloths are much less common. Likewise, all the common birds at La Brea are either predators of scavengers, including eagles, hawks, owls, vultures, condors, and many more. Normally, predators are much less numerous than prey because a predator population needs about ten times as many prey animals to support their energy demands, so this is clearly not a natural predator/prey ratio. La Brea probably was a predator/scavenger "death trap"—one stuck prey animal, panicking and making terrified noises, attracted multiple predators and scavengers who thought they were getting an easy meal.

WEST COAST PALEONTOLOGY

Since the initial collections from La Brea were made by the University of California at Berkeley, most of the original research on those fossils was conducted there as well. In 1894, the University of California hired John C. Merriam (figure 21.2). He had been a Berkeley undergrad studying under Joseph Le Conte, the founder of the geology department, then did graduate work in Germany before returning to California. Merriam then established the first significant paleontology program west of the Mississippi, leading expeditions and field crews to important fossil beds in California, Oregon, Nevada, and elsewhere to build up their collections and make their mark on paleontology research. In 1912, he became chair of the first (and only) Department of Paleontology in any university in the United States, several years after they began their regular trips down to the La Brea Tar Pits in 1905. Merriam left Berkeley to become head of the Carnegie Institute

Figure 21.2 ▲

University of California, Berkeley, showing the faculty and instructors of the Department of Paleontology about 1915. *Top row, left to right*: E. L. Packard, W. S. W. Kew, J. O. Nomland. Bottom row, left to right: John P. Buwalda, John C. Merriam, Chester Stock, and Bruce L. Clark. (Courtesy of the University of California Museum of Paleontology?)

of Washington in 1921, effectively ending his research career for a job in administration.

Of all the many distinguished Merriam students in the Department of Paleontology, probably the most famous was Chester Stock. Born in 1892 in San Francisco, his family home was burned to the ground in the 1906 San Francisco earthquake and fire. He went to UC Berkeley in 1910, where he got hooked on paleontology after taking a course from Merriam. Stock began undergraduate research on La Brea specimens before his graduation in 1910, then worked on the Pleistocene bones of Hawker Cave for his dissertation and finished in 1918. Berkeley then hired him to be an instructor, and he took over most of the teaching when Merriam left in 1921.

In 1926, the Nobel Prize–winning physicist Robert Millikan was building up the faculty and research programs at the newly founded and rapidly expanding California Institute of Technology in Pasadena. He hired Stock and Berkeley geologist John P. Buwalda to establish the geology program there; it is now one of the top programs in earth and planetary sciences in the entire world. Stock, Buwalda, and his associates collected fossils all over southern California, discovering the majority of important vertebrate fossil localities in that state from 1926 onward, and amassing a huge collection of fossils from California, as well as Oregon, Nevada, Arizona, and even further afield. Almost all significant paleontology in the southern half of California was started by Stock and Caltech, and their collection was second to none. Then Stock died suddenly in 1950 at the age of fifty-eight, and the Caltech vertebrate paleontology program came to an end. Over the years, Caltech ended up focusing on other things, like its world-famous seismology lab, and its connection to the Jet Propulsion Lab and planetary geology, but paleontology was allowed to languish. Stock was never replaced, and after the retirement of their only invertebrate paleontologist, Heinz Lowenstam, paleontology vanished entirely—even though the Caltech geology program was originally founded by paleontologists. Caltech didn't want to store Stock's priceless collection, so now it resides in the Natural History Museum of Los Angeles County, on a "permanent loan." The only fossils still on the Caltech campus is a skeleton of a La Brea *Smilodon* on display in a glass case in the lobby.

I have a personal connection to this story. My graduate advisor, Malcolm McKenna, was admitted to Caltech as Stock's student—then had to transfer to Berkeley after Stock died suddenly. And I have taught paleontology at

Caltech numerous times because they still have not hired a full-time paleontologist in decades.

FROM *CANIS* TO *AENOCYON*

Of all the research that Merriam and Stock did, perhaps their most influential is their work on La Brea fossils. Merriam published descriptions of the dire wolves in 1912 and 1918, the horses in 1913, and began work on the cats before leaving for the Carnegie Institution. Stock published a huge landmark monograph on the ground sloths in 1925, and then finally published the La Brea cats (including *Smilodon*) in 1932, late in Merriam's career.

Dire wolf fossils are so abundant at La Brea that there are literally thousands of them in the collections, a huge sample of the variability of a single fossil species. This point is driven home by the displays at the La Brea Tar Pits Museum, especially a wall with 404 dire wolf skulls backlit by a huge yellow lighted panel on the wall behind them (figure 21.3A). (There are hundreds more skulls and skeletons in the collections, hidden underneath the slopes of the east side of the museum). The dire wolf collection is so large that only the skulls and jaws are kept in the main collection; the limb bones are in another room elsewhere in the building behind an unmarked door that the tourists don't notice. A lot of interesting research is possible with such huge collections, some of which has been done by my former students, who have published studies on the change in size of their limbs through the last thirty-seven thousand years, or how their limb proportions changed from puppies to adults.

From all these specimens, we know that dire wolves (figure 21.3B) were on average just slightly larger in overall body size than the living gray wolf, weighing about 150 pounds (68 kilograms). They had a larger, more powerful, more robust skull with teeth that exerted a bite force stronger than any living canid. The isotopes in their teeth and bones show that they were the main predators of the common herbivores at La Brea, especially horses (their preferred prey), bison, camels, and ground sloths. The La Brea wolves showed a much higher incidence of tooth breakage than do modern wolves, suggesting that they fed close to the bone and may have tried to crack bone more than living wolves do. Dire wolves show no strong evidence of sexual dimorphism, or differences in size and proportions, between presumed males and females; indeed, such dimorphism is rare in all living canids

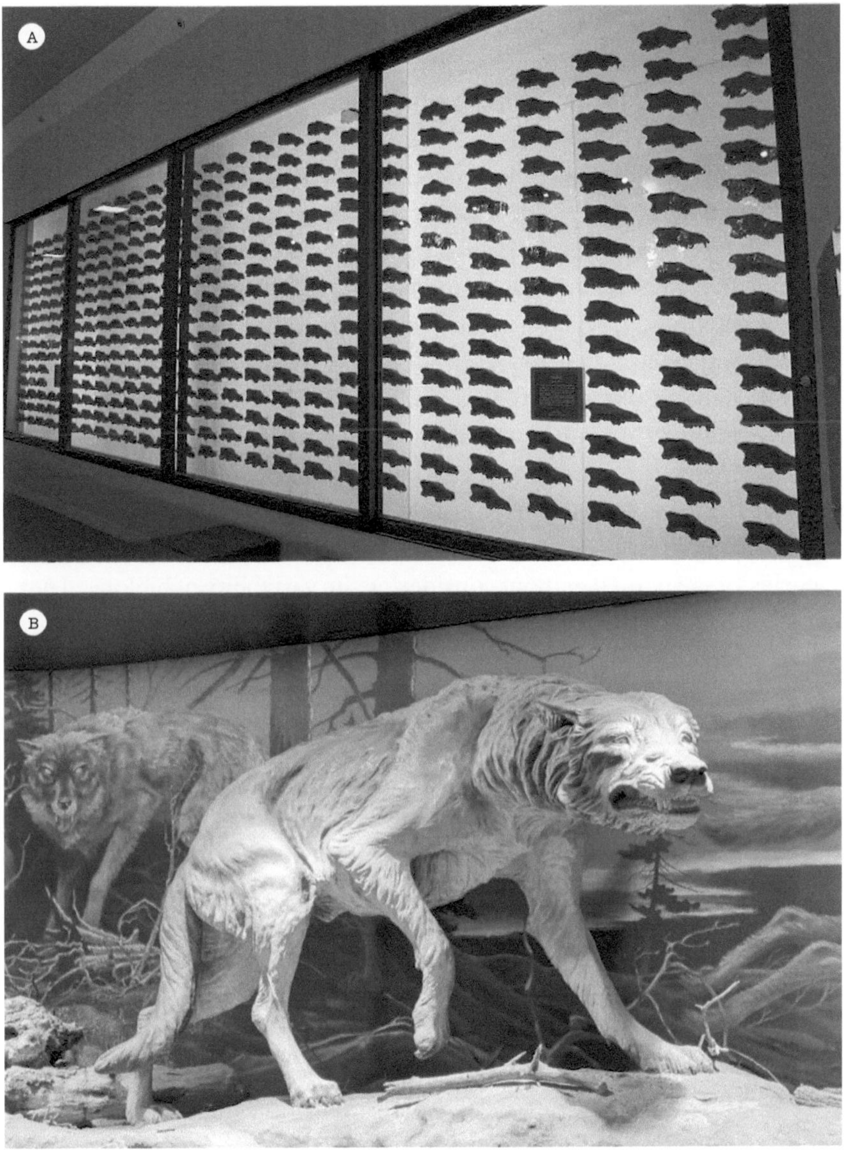

Figure 21.3 ▲

(*A*) The wall of 440 dire wolf skulls at the La Brea Tar Pits Museum. (*B*) Reconstruction of the dire wolf displayed at the La Brea Tar Pits Museum. (Photos by the author)

as well. There has been some evidence of the dire wolves changing their skull size and proportions at La Brea in response to climate over the last glacial-interglacial cycle. However, my students and I found no statistically significant changes in limb size or proportions over the course of the last thirty-seven thousand years at La Brea.

Although the largest sample comes from La Brea, dire wolves are known from just about every American state, including Arizona, California, Florida, Idaho, Indiana, Kansas, Kentucky, Missouri, Nebraska, New Mexico, Oregon, Pennsylvania, South Carolina, South Dakota, Texas, Utah, Virginia, West Virginia, Wyoming, and Nevada, as well as Canada and Mexico. They also reached South America, where they were reported from Venezuela, Ecuador, Bolivia, Peru, and Chile. In fact, the first specimens to be formally named *Canis dirus* by Joseph Leidy in 1858 were from Evansville, Indiana. He named another specimen *Canis primaevus* in 1854, only to find out that name was already used for the Asian dhole dogs, so he renamed it *C. indianensis* in 1869. Typical of the practice at that time, many more "species" were named without considering the variability of biological populations, including *C. mississsippiensis, C. nehringi, C. ayersi*, and *C. dirus nebrascensis*, and it was not until 1972 that Ernie Lundelius of the University of Texas and then Ronald Nowak in 1979, showed that these names all pertained to the same wolf.

In 1984, the Finnish paleontologist Björn Kurtén studied the dire wolves all over North America (see chapter 20). He split them into two subspecies, *Canis dirus guildayi* for smaller specimens found in the western states with shorter limbs and longer teeth, and *C. dirus dirus* for specimens east of the Continental Divide with longer limbs and shorter teeth. And *Canis dirus* is what everyone has been calling this species since Leidy's time, until a 2021 study was done on dire wolf DNA. It turns out that not only is their DNA very different from any modern *Canis*, but they branched off before many of the living canid genera, including *Cuon* (Asian dholes), *Lycaon* (African wild dogs), and *Lupulella* (African jackals). Since they could not be in the genus *Canis*, a different genus name was required. Back in 1918, John C. Merriam had studied the La Brea dire wolves and decided they were distinct from the genus *Canis* and proposed a new genus name for them, *Aenocyon* (Greek *ainos*, "terrible," and *cyon* "dog"). The name was not widely accepted by others at that time, and mostly forgotten, until the DNA evidence showed that dire wolves belong to a genus other than *Canis*, and

Aenocyon became the oldest name available. Now thousands of books and museum exhibits and other permanent labels are out of date, but most of these will not be updated for a very long time. (I've learned from experience that once a museum exhibit is finished, no amount of begging or shaming the curators and exhibit designers will make the museum update its labels, and they will remain outdated for decades until the museum executives tell the curators and exhibit designers to completely remodel the entire exhibit hall. Science may move fast and change every year, but museum exhibits don't change over decades).

A DOG'S LIFE

The howl of the wolf. The sly fox. The wily coyote. Man's best friend. The dogs, or family Canidae, are not only a big part of nature but also have a huge influence on human culture, from the first domesticated dogs that gave early humans an advantage at hunting and defense to the most popular pets on the planet. Dogs are highly social pack animals, so they bond to humans better than any other domesticated animal.

Today the family Canidae has 37 species in about 13 genera, but there are dozens of extinct canid species going back to 47 Ma. Their systematics were a mess for over a century until Xiaoming Wang of the Natural History Museum of Los Angeles County, working with the late Richard Tedford and Beryl Taylor of the American Museum of Natural History in New York, published a series of three huge monographs based on the amazing specimens in the Frick Collection in the American Museum, which sorted them all out. The Canidae is part of the Caniformia branch of carnivores, along with bears, pinnipeds, mustelids, and raccoons. They fall into three distinct subfamilies: the early primitive canids, known as the Hesperocyoninae; the bone-crushing dogs, or Borophaginae; and the branch that leads to living dogs, or the Caninae.

Like almost all members of the order Carnivora, canids have a pair of robust shearing teeth near the back of their mouth known as the carnassials, which are made of the fourth upper premolar and the first lower molar (figure. 21.4). Carnassials are the main crushing and breaking teeth in carnivorans, which are strong enough to cut and break tough sinews and meat, and in some species, even crack bones. If you ever watch a dog chew on a bone, you will see it move the bone to the side of its mouth,

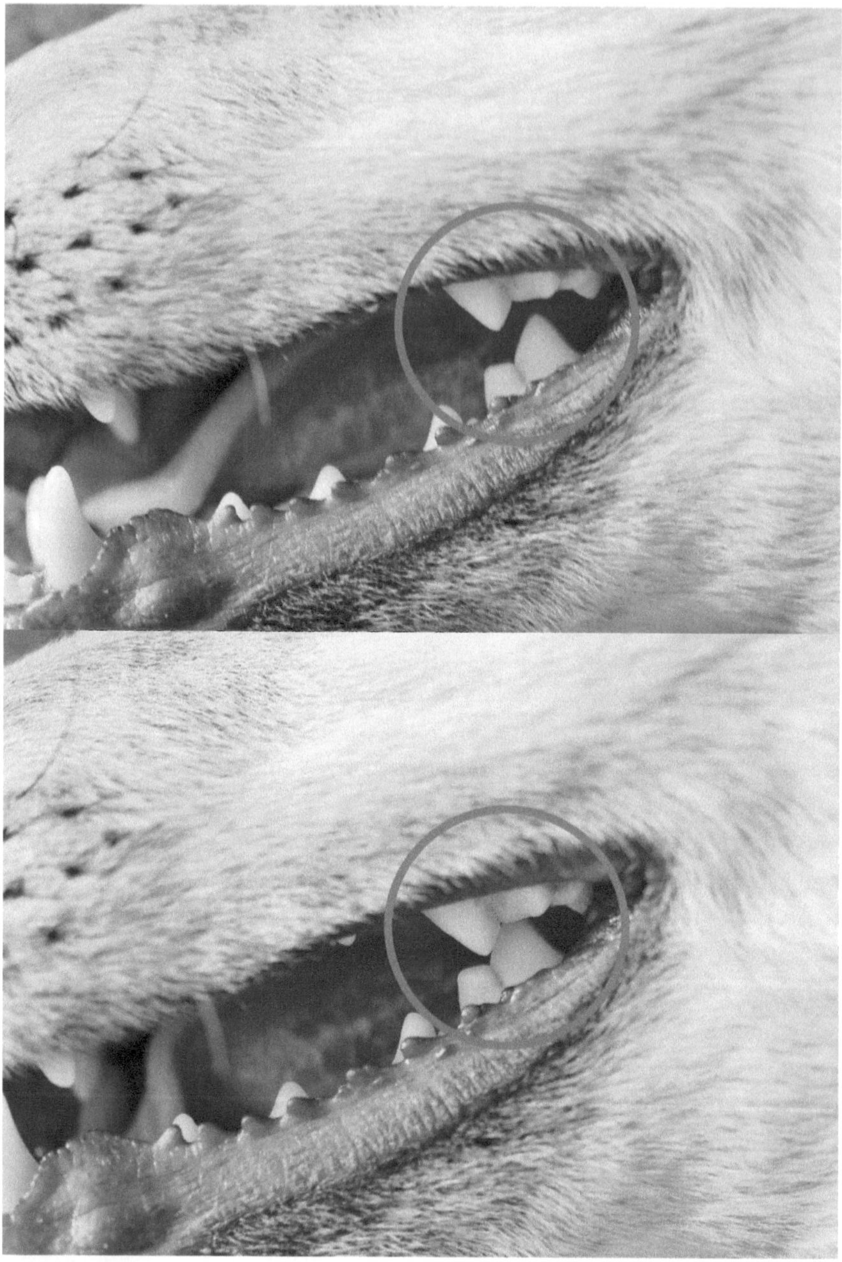

Figure 21.4 ▲

Close up of the carnassial teeth in a dog's mouth, showing the enlarged upper fourth premolar and the lower first molar. (Courtesy of Wikimedia Commons)

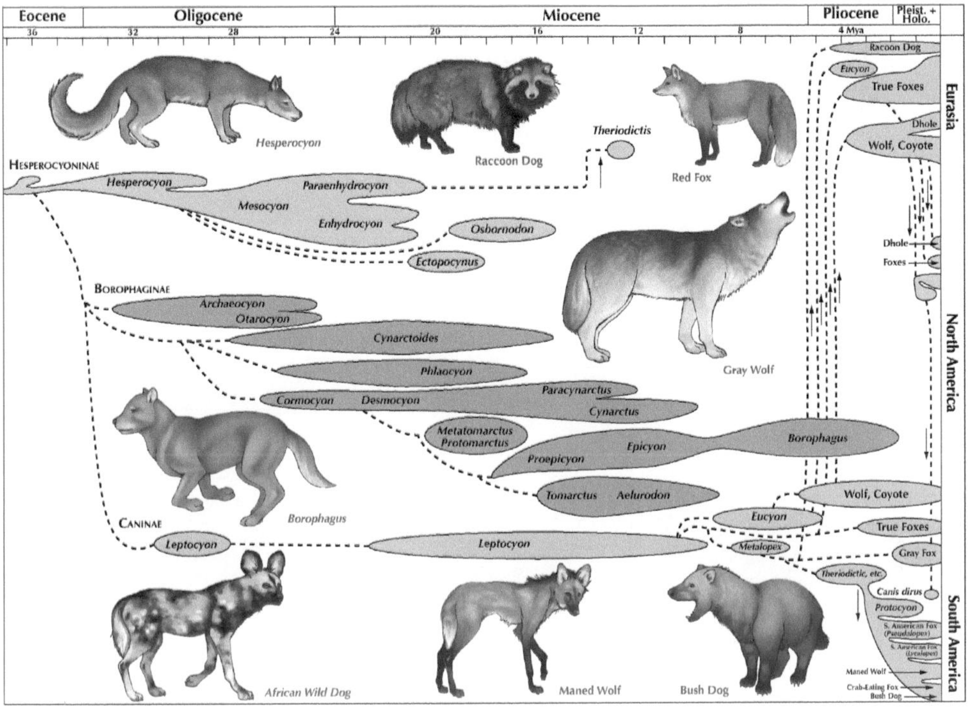

Figure 21.5 ▲

Evolutionary history of the Canidae. (From D. R. Prothero, *Princeton Field Guide to Prehistoric Mammals* [Princeton Univerity Press, 2016].)

where these powerful carnassials can be brought to bear. In both the upper P4 carnassial, and the lower m1 carnassial, there are V-shaped notches between the sharp crests of the teeth. When these upper and lower crests shear together during the bite, they form a diamond-shaped gap called an akis, which is capable of cutting even the toughest muscles and cartilage and even tendons.

The Canidae can be traced back to about 47 Ma, with a number of primitive carnivorans that are close relatives, known as miacids (figure 21.5). The first known dog is *Prohesperocyon*, from about 47 Ma in Texas, a transitional fossil that has features of the ancestral miacids, but in other ways is a very primitive dog. It was followed by *Hesperocyon*, from about 42 Ma until about 31 Ma (figure 21.6A and figure 21.6B). *Hesperocyon* was the size of a weasel or a small fox, but had long delicate limbs and very long tail, with a small

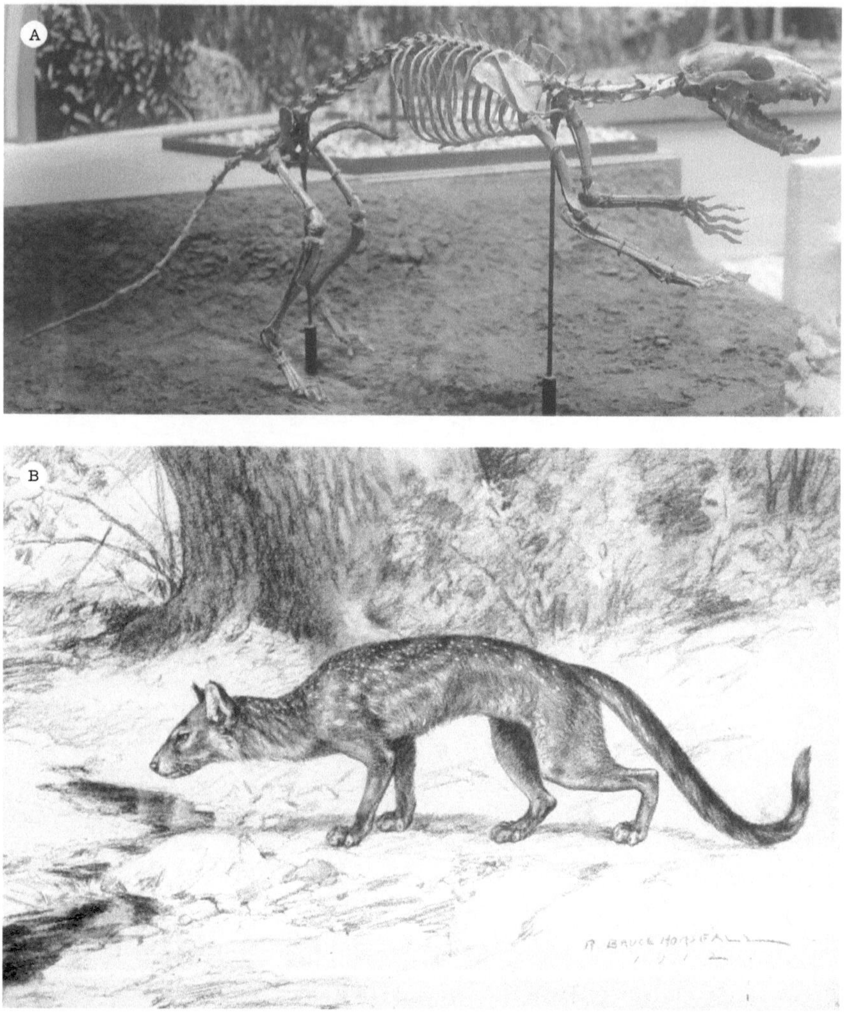

Figure 21.6 ▲

Hesperocyon, one of the earliest canids, from the late Eocene-Oligocene of North America. (*A*) Mounted skeleton. (*B*) Reconstruction by R. Bruce Horsfall. (Courtesy of Wikimedia Commons)

unspecialized head, so it was built differently from any canid living today. It also had cat-like retractable claws, a feature that dogs later lost, so *Hesperocyon* was probably a good tree climber. Other hesperocyonines include *Mesocyon, Enhydrocyon, Ectopocyon, Osbornodon*, and the coyote-sized *Cynodesmus*.

The second branch of the Canidae (figure 21.5) is the bone-crushing borophagine dogs. They started out small with *Archaeocyon*, but about 20 Ma they diversified, while the hesperocyonines were vanishing. Primitive borophagines include the fox-sized *Tomarctus*, and the wolf-sized hypercarnivorous *Aelurodon*. But about 15 Ma the most specialized borophagines evolved, including the huge bear-sized *Epicyon*, the largest dog that ever lived, twice the size of any living dog (figure 21.7A). Other later borophagines were *Osteoborus* and *Borophagus*, the last of which vanished only 2 Ma (figure 21.7B). All of these dogs had enlarged robust carnassial teeth, just like hyaenas do, presumably for crushing bones and killing big prey. Their skulls are also robust, with a high domed forehead and short snout, for bringing more force to bear on a smaller surface area in order to break bones. As they got larger in size, not only the teeth but especially their jaws got more robust and developed large powerful carnassials (figure 21.7C). They were stout-legged ambush predators that probably preyed on a wide array of hoofed mammals of the time, such as horses, camels, and many other extinct groups. The reason they declined is not known, but it started when the first true cats, who are also ambush predators, arrived in North America, and possibly outcompeted them for this niche.

The third branch of the Canidae is the subfamily Caninae, which can be traced back to the small canid *Leptocyon*, which first appeared 34 Ma when hesperocyonines were in their heyday (figure 21.8). But the Caninae really came to dominate about 6 Ma, just as the last borophagines were dying out. The Caninae include all the living species of dogs, wolves, foxes, and other wild species. Unlike borophagines, the Caninae have lost one of their side toes and are built for long-distance running, so they hunt in packs that run down their prey to exhaustion, therefore they probably did not directly compete with the ambush predators such as borophagines and cats.

One branch of the Caninae is the radiation of dogs that occurred when an ancestral member of the Caninae crossed the Panama Land Bridge about 3.5 Ma and invaded South America. There they evolved to a radiation of uniquely South American canids, including the maned wolf, the bush dog, the short-eared dog, and a variety of different foxes unique to South America. Today the family Canidae break down into several distinct groupings based on molecular evidence. The gray fox (genus *Urocyon*) is in its own subgroup, separate from the rest of the foxes of genus *Vulpes*. The South American canids form their own group, and the remaining wolves,

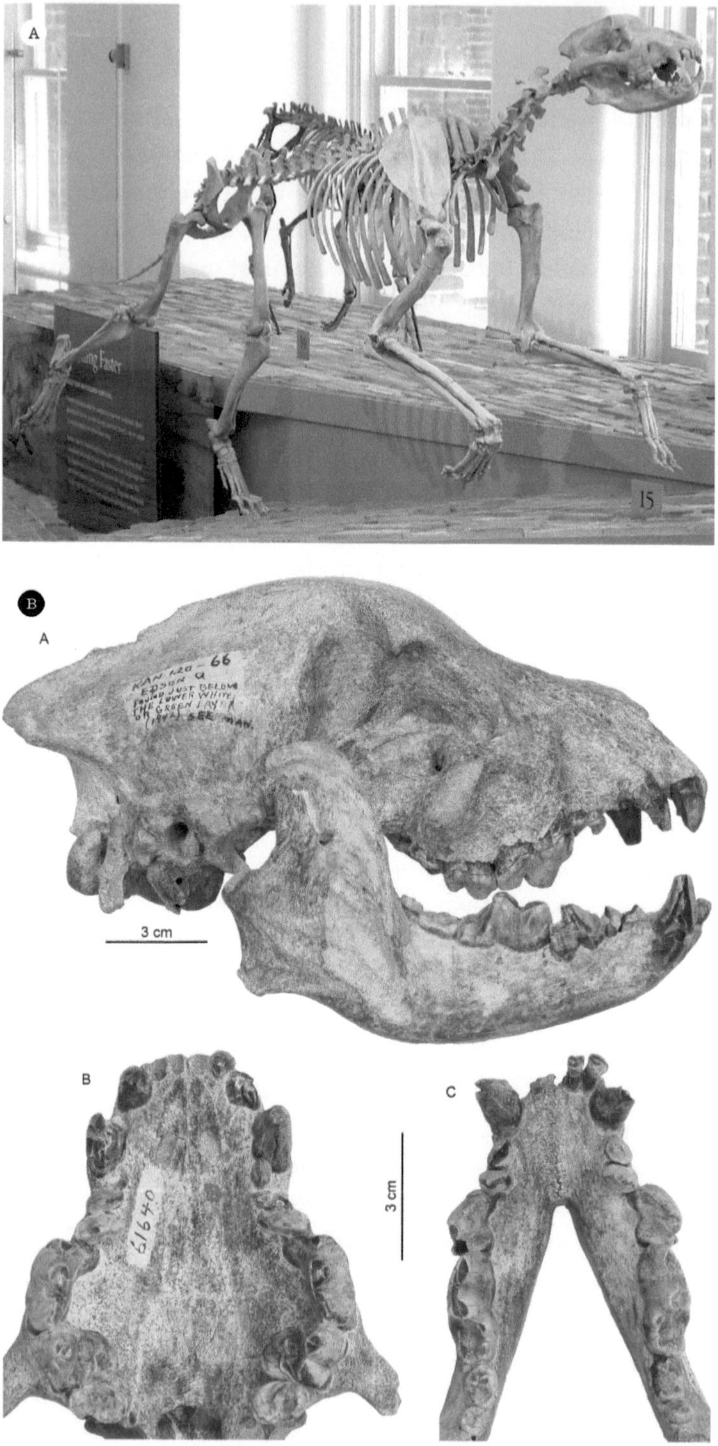

Figure 21.7 ▲ ▶

Borophagines were huge running dogs with powerful skulls and enlarged teeth for bone-crushing, like hyaenas. (*A*) Mounted skeleton of *Epicyon haydeni* in the Natural History Museum of Los Angeles County. (*B*) Skull and jaws of *Borophagus secundus*

Figure 21.7 ▲

(*continued*) (*C*) Reconstruction of *Epicyon* by Jay Matternes. ([*A*] Photo by the author; [*C*] courtesy of Wikimedia Commons)

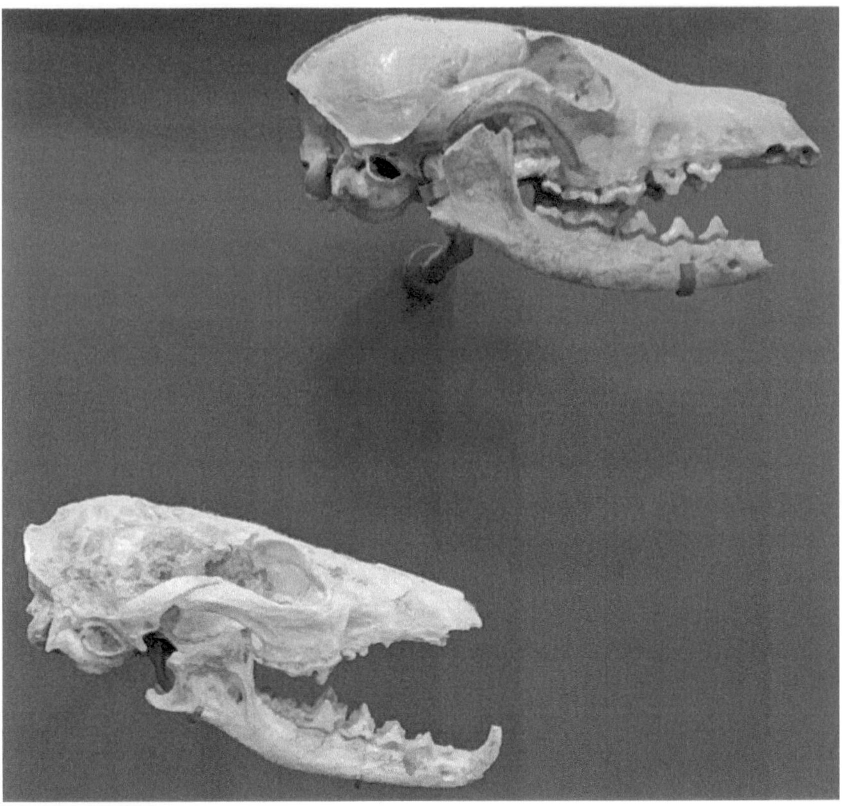

Figure 21.8 ▲

Skull of *Leptocyon* (*bottom*) compared to a living red fox (*top*). (Courtesy of Wikimedia Commons)

coyotes, dholes, jackals, dingoes, and African wild dogs are all closely related to each other.

The family Canidae is a remarkable group, with a history going back 47 Ma with highly successful predators that have exploited many different niches, including those now occupied by hyenas and others. Most wild canids carry on their lives doing nothing more to humans than stealing a few chickens, but humans tried to hunt out almost all the wolves in the United States, leading to ecological disaster, and still ruthlessly hunt coyotes and foxes when they can. Sadly, eleven wild species, including the Mexican wolf, the African wild dog, the Arctic fox, and most of the rarer canids of South America such as the maned wolf, raccoon dog, and their unique foxes, are now endangered or threatened with extinction as we destroy their habitat and introduce other exotic predators (like invasive dogs and foxes) that push them out of their last refuges.

FOR FURTHER READING

Agusti, J., and M. Anton. *Mammoths, Sabertooths, and Hominids: 65 Million Years of Mammalian Evolution in Europe*. Columbia University Press, 2002.

Berta, A. "Quaternary Evolution and Biogeography of the Large South American Canidae (Mammalia: Carnivora)." *University of California Publications in Geological Sciences* 132 (1988).

Dundas, R. G. "Quaternary Records of the Dire Wolf, *Canis dirus*, in North and South America." *Boreas* 28, no. 3 (1999): 375–385.

Ewer, R. F. *The Carnivores*. Cornell University Press, 1973.

Flynn; J. J., J. A. Finarelli, and M. Spaulding. "Phylogeny of the Carnivora and Carnivoramorpha, and the Use of the Fossil Record to Enhance Understanding of Evolutionary Transformations." In *Carnivoran Evolution: New Views on Phylogeny, Form, and Function*, ed. A. Goswami and A. Friscia, 25–63. Cambridge University Press, 2010.

Flynn, J. J., J. A. Finarelli, S. Zehr, J. Hsu, and M. A. Nedbal. "Molecular Phylogeny of the Carnivora (Mammalia): Assessing the Impact of Increased Sampling on Resolving Enigmatic Relationships." *Systematic Biology* 54, no. 2 (2005): 317–337.

Flynn, J. J., N. A. Neff, and R. H. Tedford. "Phylogeny of the Carnivora." In *The Phylogeny and Classification of the Tetrapods, Vol. 2: Mammals*, ed. M. J. Benton, 73–116. Clarendon Press, 1988.

Janis, C., K. M. Scott, and L. L. Jacobs, eds. *Evolution of Tertiary Mammals of North America, Vol. I: Terrestrial Carnivores, Ungulates, and Ungulate-like Mammals.* Cambridge University Press, 1998.

Kurtén, B. *Before the Indians.* Columbia University Press, 1988.

Kurtén, B., and E. Anderson. *Pleistocene Mammals of North America.* Columbia University Press, 1980.

Martín-Serra, A., B. Figueirido, and P. Palmqvist. "In the Pursuit of the Predatory Behavior of Borophagines (Mammalia, Carnivora, Canidae): Inferences from Forelimb Morphology." *Journal of Mammalian Evolution* 23, no. 3 (2016): 237–249.

Merriam, J. C. "Note on the Systematic Position of the Wolves of the *Canis dirus* Group." *Bulletin of the Department of Geology of the University of California* 10 (1918): 533.

Miklosi, A. *Dog Behaviour, Evolution, and Cognition.* 2nd ed. Oxford University Press, 2015.

Nowak, Ronald M. *North American Quaternary Canis. 6. Monograph of the Museum of Natural History.* University of Kansas, 1979.

Perri, A. R., K. J. Mitchell, A. Mouton, S. Álvarez-Carretero, A. Hulme-Beaman, J. Haile, et al. "Dire Wolves Were the Last of an Ancient New World Canid Lineage." *Nature* 591, no. 7848 (2021): 87–91.

Prothero, D. R. *The Princeton Field Guide to Prehistoric Mammals.* Princeton University Press, 2016.

——. *Vertebrate Evolution: From Origins to Dinosaurs and Beyond.* Taylor & Francis/ CRC Press, 2022.

Savage, D. E., and D. E. Russell. *Mammalian Paleofaunas of the World.* Addison Wesley, 1983.

Savage, R. J. G., and M. R. Long. *Mammal Evolution: An Illustrated Guide.* Facts-on-File, 1986.

Stock, C., and J. Harris. *Rancho La Brea: A Record of Pleistocene Life in California.* Natural History Museum of Los Angeles County, 1992.

Tchaicka, L., T. R. O. de Freitas, A. Bager, S. L. Vidal, M. Lucherini, A. Iriarte, et al. "Molecular Assessment of the Phylogeny and Biogeography of a Recently Diversified Endemic Group of South American Canids (Mammalia: Carnivora: Canidae)." *Genetics and Molecular Biology* 39, no. 3 (2016): 442–451.

Tedford, R., X. Wang, and B. E. Taylor. "Phylogenetic systematics of the North American Fossil Caninae (Carnivora: Canidae)." *Bulletin of the American Museum of Natural History* 325 (2009): 1–218.

Turner, A., and M. Anton. *National Geographic Prehistoric Mammals.* National Geographic Society, 2004.

Van Valkenburgh, B. "Iterative Evolution of Hypercarnivory in Canids (Mammalia: Carnivora): Evolutionary Interactions Among Sympatric Predators." *Paleobiology* 17, no. 4 (1991): 340–362.

Van Valkenburgh, B., and F. Hertel. "Tough Times at La Brea: Tooth Breakage in Large Carnivores of the Late Pleistocene." *Science* 261, no. 5120 (1993): 456–459.

Van Valkenburgh, B., and T. Sacco. "Sexual dimorphism, Social Behavior, and Intrasexual Competition in Large Pleistocene Carnivorans." *Journal of Vertebrate Paleontology* 22, no. 1 (2002): 164–169.

Wang, X. "How Dogs Came to Run the World." *Natural History Magazine*, July/August 2008.

——. "Phylogenetic Systematics of the Hesperocyoninae (Carnivora, Canidae)." *Bulletin of the American Museum of Natural History* 221 (1994): 1–207.

Wang, X., and R. H. Tedford. *Dogs: Their Fossil Relatives and Evolutionary History.* Columbia University Press, 2008.

Wang, X., R. Tedford, and B. Taylor. "Phylogenetic Systematics of the Borophaginae (Carnivora, Canidae)." *Bulletin of the American Museum of Natural History* 243 (1999).

Wayne, R. K. "Molecular Evolution of the Dog Family." *Trends in Genetics* 9, no. 6 (1993): 218–224.

22 SABER-TOOTHED KILLERS

SMILODON

Tho' Nature, red in tooth and claw
With ravine, shriek'd against his creed.

—ALFRED LORD TENNYSON, *IN MEMORIAM A.H.H.* (1850)

NOTHING SMILES LIKE *SMILODON*

Saber-tooth! The very name conjures up images of the most terrifying predator of the Ice Ages, a giant muscle-bound cat with wicked dagger-like teeth, like a mouth equipped with steak knives. Many people are fascinated with saber-toothed cats (*not* tigers—they are not related to tigers), and lots of research has been done on them. It is even more surprising that saber-like teeth evolved at least four times independently, and possibly even five times, within the mammals alone—and there are saber-toothed salmon and other animals with wicked large stabbing teeth (figurr 22.1).

Although the first saber-toothed cats of the genus *Smilodon* were discovered and named by the Danish naturalist Peter Wilhelm Lund in Brazil in 1842 (see chapter 3), the most famous species is *Smilodon fatalis*, found all over North America during the Pleistocene, especially at the La Brea Tar Pits (figure 22.2). At one time, the La Brea specimens were assigned to their own species, *Smilodon californicus*. Partly as a result of this, *Smilodon* was made the Official State Fossil of California. Some people protested and suggested it be the Cambrian trilobite *Olenellus* instead because those are

Figure 22.1 ▲

The evolution of saber-toothed vertebrates occurred multiple times during the Phanerozoic. (*Top left*) *Inostrancevia alexandri*, a saber-toothed synapsid "protomammal" from the Permian of Russia. (*Top right*) *Hoplophoneus primaevus*, a saber-toothed nimravid, from the Oligocene of the Big Badlands, South Dakota. (*Middle left*) *Barbourofelis loveorum*, another saber-toothed predator from the late Miocene, which might be a nimravid, or possibly an independent evolution of saber-toothed anatomy. (*Middle right*) *Smilodon populator*, the largest species of saber-toothed cat from South America. (*Lower left*) *Machaeroides eothen*, a saber-toothed creodont. (*Lower right*) *Thylacosmilus atrox*, a saber-toothed marsupial from the late Miocene of South America. (Courtesy of Wikimedia Commons)

easy to collect in several localities in the Mojave Desert, so anyone can own one. However, the saber-toothed cat is clearly more charismatic, even if it's nearly impossible to legally own one, so this consideration swayed the committee that decided on California's Official State Fossil.

Figure 22.2 ▲
Smilodon fatalis from the La Brea Tar Pits. (Courtesy of Wikimedia Commons)

Smilodon was a very powerful cat with robust limb bones, which enabled it to tackle and drag down most prey species. The manner of how they used their sabers has been a topic of hot debate. In the early twentieth century, it was argued that the long sabers were examples of evolution going out of control, and no longer subject to natural selection. It was even proposed that the saber-toothed predators were inferior to modern cats, as the ever-growing canines were thought to inhibit their owners from feeding properly. But the enormous success of saber-toothed predators around the world, and the independent evolution of saber teeth four separate times within the mammals alone, discredits that notion.

Instead, the debates revolved around how they killed their prey. Early on, it was clear that they could not attack the prey animal just anywhere, because if they bit into a hard bony part of the body such as the skull or spine, they risked breaking a saber tip. Most modern large cats, such as lions or tigers, kill by gripping the throat of the prey animal in their jaws, then clamping down until the prey suffocates. But the long sabers suggest something else. Perhaps they slashed the throats, or the soft underbellies of their prey, then held on until it bled out and died. Likewise, their long canines meant that they could only feast on the soft tissues in a carcass and needed to avoid the bony parts, leaving those for scavengers. And in contrast to modern lions and tigers, which have a powerful bite necessary to hold prey by the throat until dead, the bite of a saber-tooth was only about one-third as strong. This is consistent with the idea that they slashed the throat or belly quickly and did not clamp their jaws on the prey animal for very long. *Smilodon* not only attacked prey species but many specimens showed scars from fights with their own species, including puncture wounds to the top of the head made by saber-like teeth.

It was long thought that *Smilodon* preyed mostly on the common La Brea herbivores such as bison, horses, and camels, but more recent chemical analyses of their teeth suggest they fed largely on forest-dwelling mammals such as llamas, deer, tapirs, and peccaries, while the dire wolves, the short-faced bear, and the giant "lion" *Panthera atrox* hunted the big herbivores of the open habitats. However, chemical analysis of *Smilodon* bones and teeth from Argentina suggests that they hunted nearly all the potential prey in their habitat, most of whom were grazers, so saber-toothed cats were versatile.

The large samples of *Smilodon* at La Brea allow scientists to undertake many different kinds of studies. My former student Katherine Long and I looked at how *Smilodon* kittens grew up, by looking at the proportions of the long bones in juveniles and adults. Did they start out with normal cat proportions, and then develop more robust limbs for their powerful muscles as they grew? We found that in fact the kittens were muscle-bound from the start, with limbs that were already robust for their size, and that they maintained those proportions as they grew to adults. Another study showed that *Smilodon* had a very fast growth rate compared to living lions and tigers, but their growth was also prolonged so the kittens were dependent on adults for a long time (like modern lions). Even more striking, saber-toothed kittens had a milk dentition (deciduous teeth or "baby teeth") that included not only the incisors and premolars but also deciduous saber-like canines, all of which had to be shed when the adult teeth erupted. The deciduous sabers erupted between 12 and 19 months of age, after they were weaned, and then they were shed when they reached 22–30 months of age. Meanwhile, their adult sabers began to erupt side-by-side with the deciduous sabers that had not yet been shed, and these grew about 7 mm/year. During this time, these retained deciduous teeth reinforced the emerging adult sabers, so they were "double-fanged" on each side of their mouth. Finally, at about three years in age, the permanent sabers were fully grown and the juveniles were completely independent of adults for feeding themselves.

Several species of *Smilodon* are recognized. The first to be discovered and named was *Smilodon populator* from Brazil, the largest species of the genus, named by Lund in 1842. In 1869, the larger North American species, *Smilodon fatalis*, was named by Joseph Leidy, and this is the species found at the La Brea Tar Pits. Finally, there is a smaller species, *Smilodon gracilis*, best known from the Ice Age beds of the East Coast.

The family Felidae contains all the true cats, which are split into two main groups (figure 22.3). One is the Felinae, to which all living cats belong. Felids evolved from *Proailurus* in Eurasia about 25 Ma. The first American cat, *Pseudaelurus*, arrived here from Eurasia about 18.5 Ma. *Smilodon* is a member of the other branch (subfamily Machairodontinae), the big late Cenozoic radiation of felids that evolved a saber-toothed dentition. The Machairodontinae includes all the different kinds of saber-toothed felids. These include not only *Smilodon* but also *Megantereon*, a long-legged saber-tooth from North America, Eurasia, and Africa, that lived from about 4.5 Ma until about 2.5 Ma, and *Machairodus* from beds about 7–4 Ma in Eurasia, Africa, and North America, plus *Xenosmilus*, *Homotherium*, and *Dinofelis*.

Smilodon was one of the many megamammals that vanished during the late Pleistocene (see chapter 2). Typically, it is asserted that they died out because they were specialized in killing large prey animals, most of whom vanished during this extinction (although the bison, tapirs, deer, and peccaries did not). The latest dating shows that *Smilodon fatalis* vanished from La Brea around 13,025 years ago, well before the wave of mass extinctions in North America, and well before the Younger Dryas climate event that is tied to most of the extinctions. There are claims that *Smilodon populator* was still around in southern Chile around ten thousand years ago in the Holocene, although there are some doubts about this radiocarbon date.

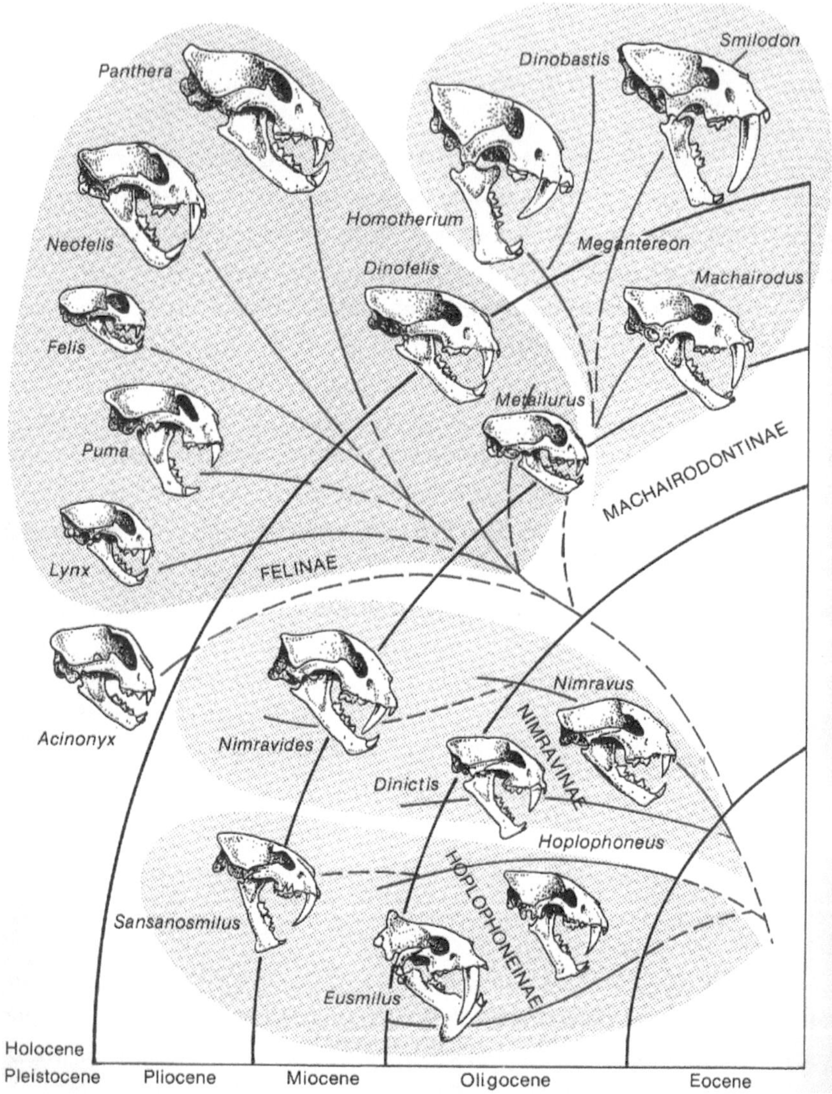

Figure 22.3 ▲

Evolution of the cat-like nimravids in the Eocene and Oligocene, followed by the evolution of true cats, the Felinae (modern cats and their relatives) and the Machairodontinae (saber-toothed cats). (Courtesy of Wikimedia Commons)

Either way, these are the last of the great radiation of machairodontine cats that flourished during the late Cenozoic all over the globe.

COPYCATTING

Apparently having huge saber-like canines was an advantageous feature, and it evolved over and over again during the history of vertebrates. The first instance of saber-like canines evolving was in the protomammals (formerly but incorrectly called "mammal-like reptiles"). About 270 Ma *Tiarajudens* lived in what is now Brazil, and they sported the first pair of huge fangs (figure 22.4). Even though it had huge protruding canine teeth, the rest of the teeth indicated it was herbivorous—one of the few examples of saber-toothed animals that were *not* predators. *Tiarajudens* didn't kill prey with its sabers, so the teeth must have been used for display or fighting off rivals or possibly fighting off their own predators.

Another instance was the protomammal *Inostrancevia* from the Late Permian of Russia and South Africa, in beds about 255 Ma. It was a member of the "gorgon beasts," or Gorgonopsia, an 11 foot (3.3 meter) long bear-sized predator, and the largest predator of its time, capable of killing and eating almost every other animals on the landscape. Another gorgonopsian from the same beds, *Smilesaurus*, had the longest canine teeth of any

Figure 22.4 ▲
Tiarajudens from the Permian of Brazil, a sabertoothed synapsid or "protomammal." (Reconstruction by N. Tamura)

saber-toothed predator ever. These lineages all became extinct, but some of their close relatives evolved into mammals about 200 Ma.

Let's look at the multiple times saber-teeth appeared in at least four unrelated groups of mammals. One of these was *Thylacosmilus*, a pouched marsupial from South America that lived about 3 Ma (figure 22.1). If you can imagine a huge opossum with fangs, that's *Thylacosmilus*. It vaguely resembled saber-toothed cats with its large canines, but the lower jaws had very differently shaped flanges on them to protect the sabers when the mouth was closed. For the mouth to open wide enough to clear their enormous sabers, *all* saber-tooths had lower jaws that could swing open to form an angle of more than 90°—truly jaw-dropping! However, *Thylacosmilus* also had features that other saber-tooths lacked, such as no upper incisors, and blunt cheek teeth, suggesting it could not slice up tough tissues but ate a softer diet restricted to meat. Its sabers were triangular in cross section rather than narrow blades, so its canines were not as fragile as those of saber-toothed cats. Some researchers suggest it had a weaker bite force than saber-toothed cats and may have specialized on slashing the soft underbelly of its prey and eating the entrails. So in important ways *Thylacosmilus* was very different from cats, and the saber teeth are an example of extreme convergent evolution. It vanished from South America during the Pliocene, possibly due to competition from immigrant saber-toothed cats that crossed the Panama land bridge from North America.

The next evolution of saber-toothed mammals occurred in an extinct group of flesh-eating mammals known as creodonts. These animals were distantly related to true carnivorans but occupied the predatory niche about 63 Ma and remained the top predator until the evolution of cats and dogs about 30 Ma. Among these creodonts were *Machaeroides* and *Apataelurus*, from about 50 Ma in Utah and Wyoming, and *Diegoaelurus* from about 42 Ma near San Diego, California (figure 22.1). All of these had well-developed saber-like canines. Their lower jaws also had relatively small flanges on them that protected the sabers when the mouth was closed. By 39 Ma, the saber-toothed creodonts had vanished.

CATTING AROUND

True cats are members of the Feliformia branch of the carnivorans. About 40 Ma, before cats evolved, there was a group of "false-cats" or "pseudo-cats," or more properly, the family Nimravidae. Nimravids were originally mistaken for cats because their teeth and skull shape are extremely similar (figure 22.1). But the details of the braincase and middle ear region show that they are not cats at all, but very primitive carnivorans; some think they are even closer to the dog-bear-weasel branch of carnivorans, the Caniformia. Nimravid skulls and teeth are another example of the extraordinary evolutionary convergence brought on by a specialized meat-eating diet—and the development of sabers an additional further convergence on saber-toothed cats. Yet they were fundamentally different from cats in many ways. They walked flat-footed on the palms on their hands and soles of their feet, and not on the tips of their toes like cats and all other carnivorans do. The earliest known genus, *Pangurban*, comes from beds about 40 Ma in San Diego. In the Big Badlands of South Dakota, beds about 37–31 Ma yield *Dinictis*, the "dirk-toothed" nimravid, which had shorter, thicker, straighter fangs, and *Hoplophoneus*, which has the classic long narrow scimitar-shaped canines. Later nimravids include *Nimravus* from beds about 30–23 Ma in the John Day region of Oregon, along with *Pogonodon* from the same beds.

In North America, nimravids appeared to vanish about 25 Ma, and there were no catlike mammals on this continent until about 18.5 Ma, when true cats (*Pseudailurus*) first arrived. This interval of 6.5 million years in duration has been called the "cat gap." Its causes are disputed, but there was definitely global cooling and drying that might have changed vegetation from forests to grasslands and provided less cover for ambush predators such as nimravids. It is also possible that the huge hypercarnivorous amphicyonids, or "bear-dogs," that arrived at this time might have driven nimravids to local extinction, as well as hypercarnivorous bone-crushing dogs, or borophagines (see chapter 21), that might have performed the cat-like role.

Yet another group of saber-toothed carnivorans were the barbourofelids (figure 22.1). These had huge robust skulls with large ridges for strong muscles, and large flanges on the lower jaw to sheath their sabers. Some paleontologists think these are the second wave of nimravids, others considered them to be closer to true cats, and others consider them to be another independent instance of developing a saber-toothed feliform mammal that was not a cat. They first appeared in Africa about 20 Ma and flourished in Eurasia, and Africa from 17 to 9 Ma, with genera such as *Sansanosmilus, Vampyrictis, Cyrtosmilus*, and *Ginsburgsmilus* from Eurasia, *Afrosmilus* from Africa,

Oriensmilus from China, and others. *Barbourofelis* itself reached North America about 8 Ma.

So the saber-toothed adaptation has occurred many times in mammals, from the marsupial *Thylacosmilus*, to the creodont *Machaeroides*, to the nimravid *Hoplophoneus*, to *Barbourofelis*, and finally to true felids such as *Smilodon* and other machairodontines. Clearly being a saber-toothed predator was a successful way to live, because it evolved at least four or five times just in the mammals. So why are there no saber-tooths today? We don't really know, but the last of them died out at the end of the last Ice Age, along with most of their large mammal prey. Whatever the reason, there are no saber-tooths alive now to stalk us, very different from the times when our ancestors in Africa had to worry about being stalked. The big cats are reduced to lions, tigers, cheetahs, leopards, cougars, jaguars, and smaller species, and humans rarely have to fear them anymore. If saber-toothed cats still lived, they would be the stuff of our nightmares.

FOR FURTHER READING

Agusti, J., and M. Anton. *Mammoths, Sabertooths, and Hominids: 65 Million Years of Mammalian Evolution in Europe*. Columbia University Press, 2002.

Anton, M. *Sabertooth*. Indiana University Press, 2013.

Anton, M., and M. Turner. *The Big Cats and Their Fossil Relatives*. Columbia University Press, 2000.

Barycka, E. "Evolution and Systematics of the Feliform Carnivora." *Mammalian Biology* 72, no. 5 (2007): 257–282.

Berta, A. "The Status of *Smilodon* in North and South America." *Contributions in Science, Natural History Museum of Los Angeles County* 370 (1985): 1–15.

Bocherens, H., M. Cotte, R. Bonini, D. Scian, P. Straccia, L. Soibelzon, and F. J. Prevosti. "Paleobiology of Sabretooth Cat *Smilodon Population* in the Pampean Region (Buenos Aires Province, Argentina) Around the Last Glacial Maximum: Insights from Carbon and Nitrogen Stable Isotopes in Bone Collagen." *Palaeogeography, Palaeoclimatology, Palaeoecology* 449 (2016): 463–474.

Christiansen, P. "Evolution of Skull and Mandible Shape in Cats (Carnivora: Felidae)." *PLOS ONE* 3, no. 7 (2008): e2807.

Domínguez-Rodrigo, M., C. P. Egeland, L. Cobo-Sánchez, E. Baquedano, and R. C. Hulbert. "Sabertooth Carcass Consumption Behavior and the Dynamics of Pleistocene Large Carnivoran Guilds." *Scientific Reports* 12, no. 1 (2022): 6045.

Ewer, R. F. *The Carnivores*. Cornell University Press, 1973.

Feranec, R. S. "Growth Rate and Duration of Growth in the Adult Canine of *S. gracilis* and Inferences on Diet Through Stable Isotope Analysis." *Bulletin of the Florida Museum of Natural History* 45, no. 4 (2005): 369–377.

Flynn; J. J., J. A. Finarelli, and M. Spaulding. "Phylogeny of the Carnivora and Carnivoramorpha, and the Use of the Fossil Record to Enhance Understanding of Evolutionary Transformations." In *Carnivoran Evolution. New Views on Phylogeny, Form, and Function*, ed. A. Goswami and A. Friscia, 25–63. Cambridge University Press, 2010.

Flynn, J. J., J. A. Finarelli, S. Zehr, J. Hsu, and M. A. Nedbal. "Molecular Phylogeny of the Carnivora (Mammalia): Assessing the Impact of Increased Sampling on Resolving Enigmatic Relationships." *Systematic Biology* 54, no. 2 (2005): 317–337.

Flynn, J. J., N. A. Neff, and R. H. Tedford, "Phylogeny of the Carnivora." In *The Phylogeny and Classification of the Tetrapods, Vol. 2: Mammals*, ed. M. J. Benton, 73–116. Clarendon Press, 1988.

Kurtén, B. *Before the Indians*. Columbia University Press, 1988.

——. *Pleistocene Mammals of Europe*. Columbia University Press, 1968.

Kurtén, B., and E. Anderson. *Pleistocene Mammals of North America*. Columbia University Press, 1980.

Kurtén, B., and L. Werdelin. "Relationships Between North and South American *Smilodon*." *Journal of Vertebrate Paleontology* 10, no. 2 (1990): 158–169.

Long, K., D. R. Prothero, M. Madan, V. J. P. Syverson, and T. Smith. "Did Saber-Tooth Kittens Grow Up Musclebound? A Study of Postnatal Limb Bone Allometry in Felids from the Pleistocene of Rancho La Brea." *PLOS ONE* 12, no. 9 (2017): e0183175.

Meachen, J. A., F. R. O'Keefe, and R. W. Sadleir. "Evolution in the Sabre-Tooth Cat, *Smilodon fatalis*, in Response to Pleistocene Climate Change." *Journal of Evolutionary Biology* 27, no. 4 (2014): 714–723.

Meachen-Samuels, J., and W. Binder. "Sexual Dimorphism and Ontogenetic Growth in the American Lion and Sabertoothed Cat from Rancho La Brea." *Journal of Zoology* 280, no. 3 (2010): 271–279.

Meloro, C., S. Elton, J. Louys, L. C. Bishop, and P. Ditchfield. "Cats in the Forest: Predicting Habitat Adaptations from Humerus Morphometry in Extant and Fossil Felidae (Carnivora)." *Paleobiology* 39, no. 3 (2013): 323–344.

Mihlbachler, M. C., M. A. Wysocki, R. S. Feranec, Z. J. Tseng, and C. S. Bjornsson. "Using a Novel Absolute Ontogenetic Age Determination Technique to Calculate the Timing of Tooth Eruption in the Saber-Toothed Cat *Smilodon fatalis*." *PLOS ONE* 10, no. 7 (2015): e0129847.

O'Keefe, F. R., R. E. Dunn, E. M. Weitzel, M. R. Waters, L. N. Martinez, W. J. Binder, et al. "Pre-Younger Dryas Megafaunal Extirpation at Rancho La Brea Linked to Fire-Driven State Shift." *Science* 381, no. 6659 (2023): eabo3594.

Prothero, D. R. *The Princeton Field Guide to Prehistoric Mammals*. Princeton University Press, 2016.

——. *Vertebrate Evolution: From Origins to Dinosaurs and Beyond*. Taylor & Francis/CRC Press, 2022.

Savage, R. J. G., and M. R. Long. *Mammal Evolution: An Illustrated Guide*. Facts-on-File, 1986.

Shaw, C. A., H. G. McDonald, and L. Werdelin, eds. *Smilodon: The Iconic Sabertooth*. Johns Hopkins University Press, 2018.

Slater, G. J., and B. V. Valkenburgh. "Long in the Tooth: Evolution of Sabertooth Cat Cranial Shape." *Paleobiology* 34, no. 3 (2008): 403–419.

Turner, A., and M. Anton. *National Geographic Prehistoric Mammals*. National Geographic Society, 2004.

Tseng, Z. J. "Bending Performance Changes During Prolonged Canine Eruption in Saber-Toothed Carnivores: A Case Study of *Smilodon fatalis*." *The Anatomical Record* 307, no. 5 (2024), https://doi.org/10.1002/ar.2544.

Turner, A., and M. Antón. *The Big Cats and Their Fossil Relatives: An Illustrated Guide to Their Evolution and Natural History*. Columbia University Press, 1997.

Van Valkenburgh, B., and F. Hertel. "Tough Times at La Brea: Tooth Breakage in Large Carnivores of the Late Pleistocene." *Science* 261, no. 5120 (1993): 456–459.

Van Valkenburgh, B., and T. Sacco. "Sexual Dimorphism, Social Behavior, and Intrasexual Competition in Large Pleistocene Carnivorans." *Journal of Vertebrate Paleontology* 22, no. 1 (2002): 164–169.

Werdelin, L., and W. L. Sanders, eds. *Cenozoic Mammals of Africa*. University of California Press, 2010.

Werdelin, L., N. Yamaguchi, W. E. Johnson, and S. J. O'Brien. "Phylogeny and Evolution of Cats (Felidae)." In *Biology and Conservation of Wild Felids*, ed. D. W. Macdonald and A. J. Loveridge, 59–82. Oxford University Press. 2010.

Wroe, S., C. McHenry, and J. Thomason. "Bite Club: Comparative Bite Force in Big Biting Mammals and the Prediction of Predatory Behaviour in Fossil Taxa." *Proceedings of the Royal Society* 272, no. 1563 (2004): 619–625.

23 RODENTS OF UNUSUAL SIZE

CASTOROIDES

Buttercup: *Westley, what about the R.O.U.S.'s?*

Westley: *Rodents of Unusual Size? I don't think they exist.*

—WILLIAM GOLDMAN, *THE PRINCESS BRIDE*, 1973

THE BEAR-SIZED BEAVER

In the classic movie *The Princess Bride*, the hero Westley (played by Cary Elwes) and the heroine Princess Buttercup (played by Robin Wright) are fleeing the villains when they stumble and roll down a long hill and find themselves in the "fire swamp." There they deal with the "three terrors of the fire swamp." They encounter "flame spurts" from the ground that singe them, and "lightning sands" (a fictional Hollywood version of quicksand), which they barely escape. The third terror was the "Rodents of Unusual Size." Westley replies to Buttercup's question about "R.O.U.S.'s" by claiming they don't exist—and then as soon as he finishes saying it, one of them attacks him. If you look closely in the film, you realize that Westley has already seen the Rodents of Unusual Size, but he's telling Buttercup a white lie to comfort her.

In movie, the Rodents of Unusual Size are actually very small actors wearing costumes that are vaguely rat-like. They don't look very realistic or terrifying but are suitable for a fantasy movie that is supposed to be family friendly. And both the writer, William Goldman (who won Oscars for writing the movie *Butch Cassidy and the Sundance Kid* and for the adapted screenplay of *All the President's Men*) and the moviemakers (director Carl Reiner and others) treat such huge rodents as fantasy as well. But unknown to them, there are numerous examples of gigantic rodents in the fossil record, although they are all herbivorous and none of them looked like the vicious giant rats in the movie.

One of the first of these to be described was the gigantic Ice Age beaver *Castoroides* (figure 23.1A and figure 23.1C), whose Greek name means "like a beaver" (beavers are in the genus *Castor*). Fossils of this beast were first found in an Ohio peat bog in 1837, so American geologist and naturalist John Wells Foster named the species *Castoroides ohioensis*. Its fossils were soon found in many other Pleistocene localities, such as Sheriden Cave in Ohio, where it was found with Paleoindian artifacts, as well as remains of the flat-headed peccary, giant short-faced bear, and the stag moose. Over the past two centuries, *Castoroides* have been found over most of the northern midwestern states around the Great Lakes, particularly Illinois, Indiana, and Ohio, but they range from Alaska to Florida. In Canada, they are found in the Old Crow Basin in the Yukon Territory, as well as in the Toronto area, and on Indian Island in New Brunswick. The specimens from the southeastern United States (especially Florida) are now placed in their own species, *Castoroides dilophidus*, and are found in more than fifty localities in Florida ranging from the late Pliocene (late Blancan land mammal age) to the late Pleistocene (Rancholabrean land mammal age). However, they do not occur in the mountainous western part of the United States.

Castoroides was truly huge by rodent standards. They reached 7.2 feet (2.2 meters) in length and weighed up to 276 pounds (125 kilograms). This is the largest known rodent ever to live in North America, and the largest member of the beaver family, or Castoridae. *Castoroides* had much larger hind feet but relatively shorter legs than those of the modern beaver, and its feet were probably webbed, like those of living beavers. They had relatively long tails, but there is no evidence that it was paddle-shaped, like the living species. The skull of *Castoroides* is enormous (figure 23.1B)

Figure 23.1 ▶

The gigantic Pleistocene beaver *Castoroides ohioensis*. (*A*) Mounted skeleton. (*B*) Comparison of the skull with a modern beaver. (*C*) Reconstruction by Charles R. Knight. ([*A and C*] Courtesy of Wikimedia Commons; [*B*] photo by the author)

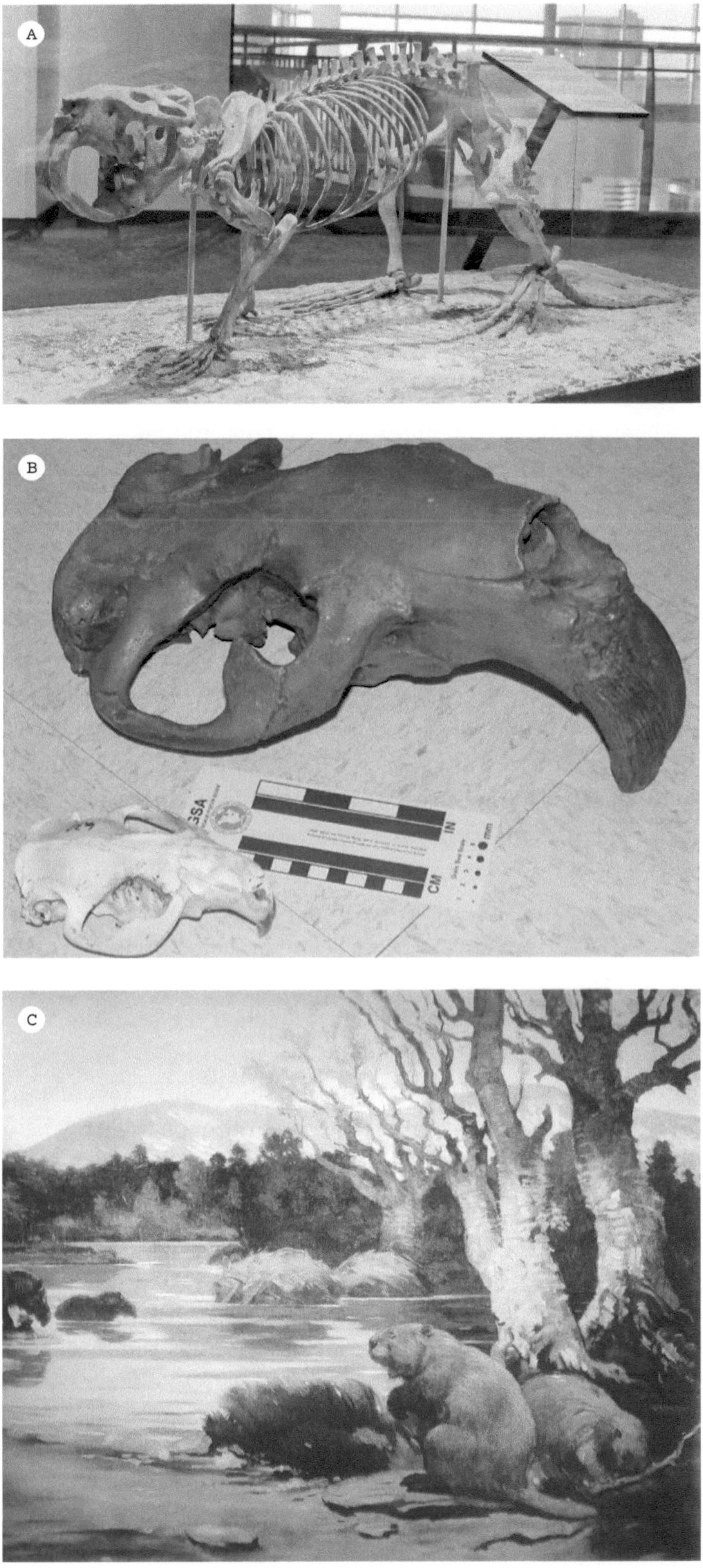
A
B
GSA
IN
CM
mm
C

compared to their modern counterpart. There is evidence that they could hold their breath underwater for a long time. The front incisors of *Castoroides* had striated textured enamel on the front surface, and the hard enamel provides a self-sharpening edge to the chisel-like tooth found in most rodents. Their incisors were also huge, reaching up to 6 inches (15 centimeters) in length.

Geochemical evidence from their teeth and bones indicates that they ate mostly submerged water plants, and almost none of the woody diet of saplings preferred by modern beavers. The shape of their incisors would not have been as effective at cutting down trees, and there is no evidence that they ever built dams. Instead, they lived in wetlands where there was abundant vegetation they liked, rather than traveling upstream in drier and even mountainous country to live on the bark of young trees, as modern beavers do. This might also explain why they are not found in the rugged mountainous western United States, but only in the lowlands around lakes and rivers.

Although there are fossils of *Castoroides* found in caves with Paleoindian artifacts (like Sheriden Cave, mentioned previously), it is not clear whether humans hunted them or whether they drove the giant beaver to extinction. Native Americans such as the Innu and Missisauga have a giant beaver in their traditional mythology, which some members of these tribes believe is evidence of human interaction with *Castoroides.* An Anishinaabe story describes "giant beavers" who walked upright and stood as tall as the tallest man. There is an Algonquin myth in which a gargantuan beaver created a dam so high on the St. John River that it caused the lake behind it to rise until it almost reached the sea. The Wabanaki hero Glooscap chopped it down with his axe, creating the Reversing Falls. Glooscap chased the monster beaver upstream, creating several islands in the river while attempting to strike the beaver through the ice. The beaver constructed another dam that created the Great Lakes and fled through these to the land beyond.

Giant beavers were not confined to North America. There was also a giant beaver in Eurasia during the Pliocene and Pleistocene called *Trogontherium* (figure 23.2). It was first described by Gotthelf Fischer von Waldheim in 1809, based on fossils given to him by the Russian aristocrat Alexander Stroganov, who received them from collectors near the

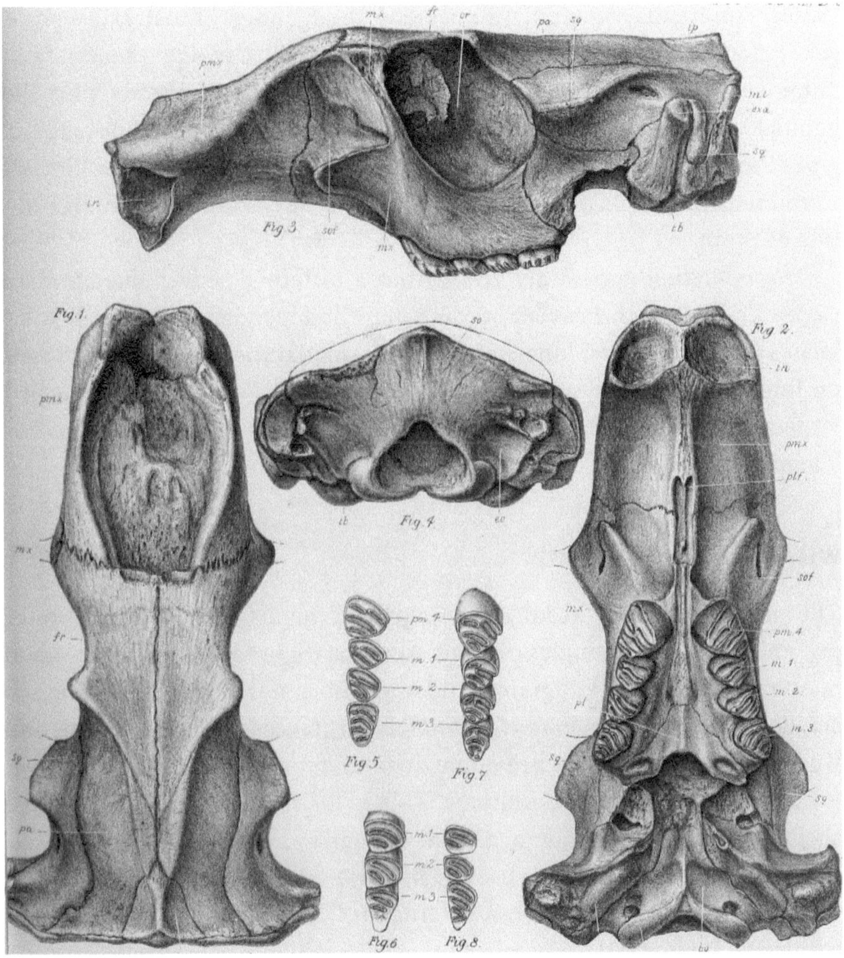

Figure 23.2 ▲
Von Waldheim's original illustrations of the giant European beaver *Trogontherium*. (Courtesy of Wikimedia Commons)

Sea of Azov. Von Waldheim was a prominent Saxon naturalist, trained by Cuvier, who focused mainly on plants and invertebrates, although he did dabble in vertebrate fossils. He is responsible for the formal creation of many taxonomic names in zoology, including the families Canidae, Felidae, Leporidae (rabbits), Cricetidae (New World rats and mice), Caviidae

(South American rodents), Erinaceidae (hedgehogs), Mustelidae (weasels), Sciuridae (squirrels), Soricidae (shrews), Ursidae (bears), and Talpidae (moles), and many other mammalian family names, plus the genus *Rattus*, as well as the first description of the Old World porcupine, giant Pleistocene rhino *Elasmotherium*. In 1824, the great Cuvier himself examined the fossils of *Trogontherium* and rendered his own interpretation of them.

Trogontherium apparently arose from a different beaver lineage than *Castoroides*, so both beavers became giant independently. Its skull is 8.3 inches (21 centimeters) long, considerably smaller than *Castoroides*. Based on limited fossils and scaling up from the skull, *Trogontherium* reached 7.2 feet (2.2 meters) in length and weighed about 200–265 pounds (90–125 kilograms).

WHAT ARE RODENTS?

The largest rodent alive today is the capybara (genus *Hydrochoerus*, "water pig" in Greek) of the jungles of South America (figure 23.3). They can weigh up to 200 pounds (91 kilograms), although most of the time they are much smaller than that. Capybaras feed mainly on grasses and water plants, and fruit and tree bark. They are adept swimmers, able to remain underwater on one breath for five minutes. This helps them flee some predators such as the jaguar and puma, as well as eagles, caimans, and anacondas, although they do not always escape all these voracious attackers. But first we must define what we mean by "rodent." And where do capybaras fit within the Rodentia?

The rodents are by far the most numerous and diverse mammals on the planet, with some animals (rats and mice) with populations in the millions around the world. The latest classification schemes recognize 33 families, 481 genera, and 2,277 species of living rodents. They make up about 40 percent of the living mammal species, and there are least five times that number of extinct genera and species. They range from the small rats, mice, hamsters, voles, gophers, chinchillas, Guinea pigs, and chipmunks, to medium-sized creatures such as squirrels and porcupines, to the largest rodents, such as beavers, muskrats, porcupines, and capybaras. The classification of rodents is still a contentious issue, and many different classification

Figure 23.3 ▲
The capybara, largest rodent alive today. (Courtesy of Wikimedia Commons)

schemes and family trees have come and gone over the years (figure 23.4). Even the recent efforts at molecular phylogeny have not resolved some of the questions and problems, so there is still a lot of work to do. Some general things about rodents can be pointed out, but there is no room in a short chapter to discuss every living species or family of living rodent, let alone the thousands of fossils species, most of which are known only from small differences in their teeth.

Like all the members of the order, the most striking feature of the rodents is their chisel-like pair of gnawing front incisors in both upper and lower jaws (figure 23.5). Rodents use them not only to gnaw on their food but also to gnaw on wood to create holes or cut down trees, and some even dig burrows with them. These incisors are rootless and constantly growing, and they curve deeply back into the skull and lower jaw. They are continuously worn down by use as they gnaw, and the incisors must grow continuously to compensate for this wear. The incisors are made of

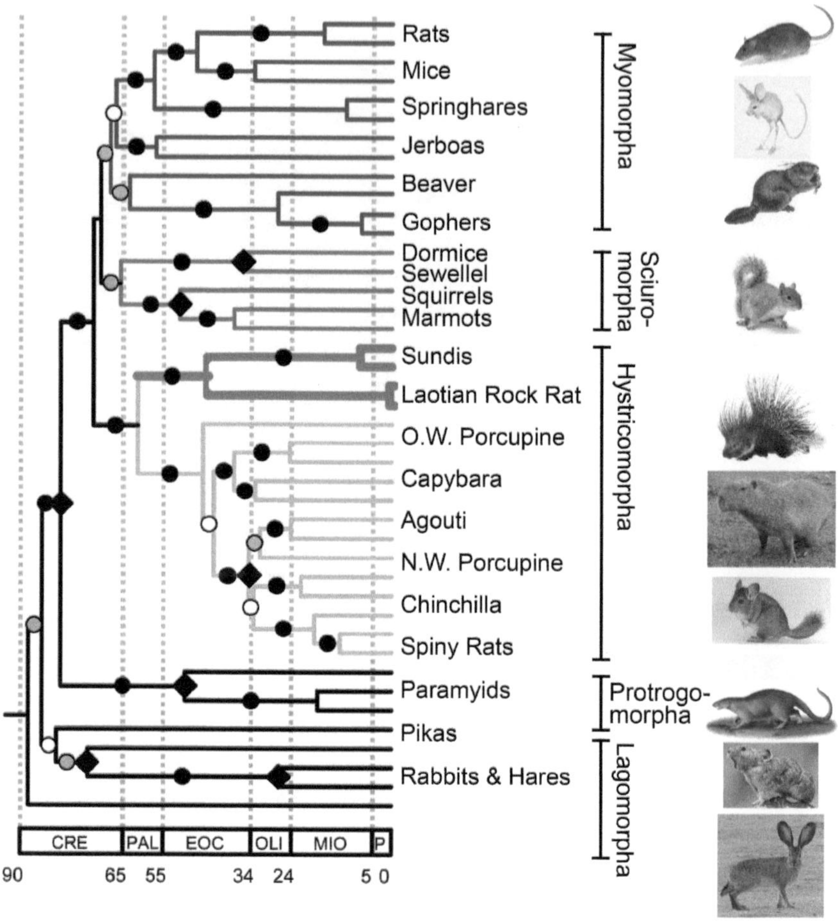

Figure 23.4 ▲

Family tree of the rodents, based mostly on molecular evidence with some anatomical evidence. (From D. R. Prothero, *Princeton Field Guide to Prehistoric Mammals* [Princeton Univerity Press, 2016].)

soft dentin with a band of hard enamel only on the leading edge, so as the teeth gnaw the enamel forms a self-sharpening edge in front of the easily-worn dentin. Rodents often sharpen their teeth by grinding them against each other, and they must continually keep these teeth sharp or they will starve. If there is a problem with occlusion, the unworn incisors can curve around and eventually pierce the skull. Behind the incisors is a

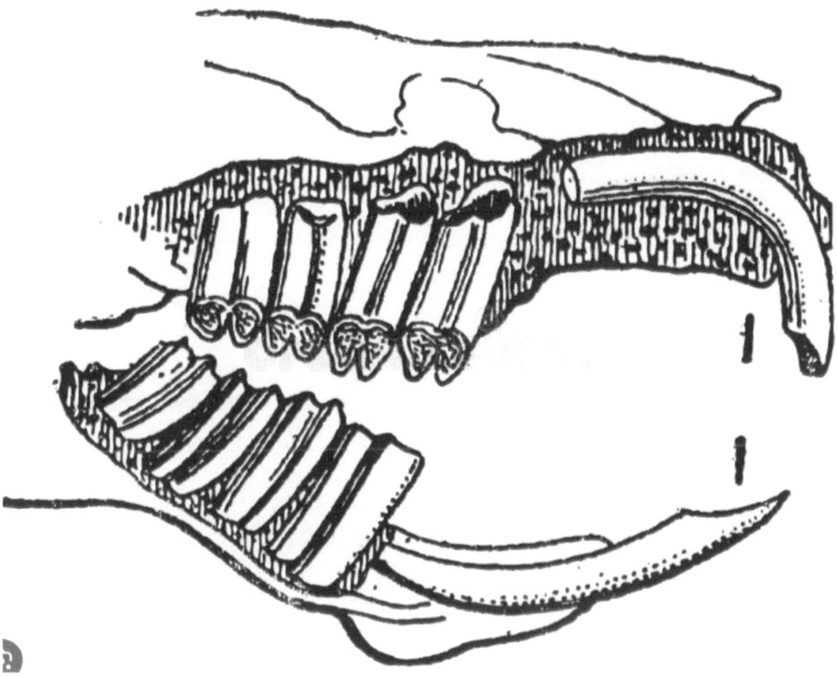

Figure 23.5 ▲

Sketch of a rodent skull, showing the ever-growing paired chisel-like incisors with open roots, the diastema behind the incisors, and the cheek teeth. (From D. R. Prothero, *Princeton Field Guide to Prehistoric Mammals* [Princeton Univerity Press, 2016].)

gap (diastema), then a small number of premolars and molars adapted for whatever the rodent eats.

In addition to gnawing incisors, there are other features of the chewing mechanism that are important to rodent classification (figure 23.6). The most primitive rodent skulls are protrogomorph with the masseter muscles that close the jaw attached to a limited area of the skull. This is the condition found in most mammals. From this protrogomorph skull, three different lineages with different jaw muscle configurations evolved. The sciuromorph (squirrel-like) rodents are just slightly more advanced in that the masseter muscles of the jaw extend up along the front of the cheekbones alongside the snout. Sciuromorph rodents include not only squirrels and chipmunks, but also woodchucks, marmots, sewellels, and beavers, including *Castoroides* and *Trogontherium*, which were previously mentioned.

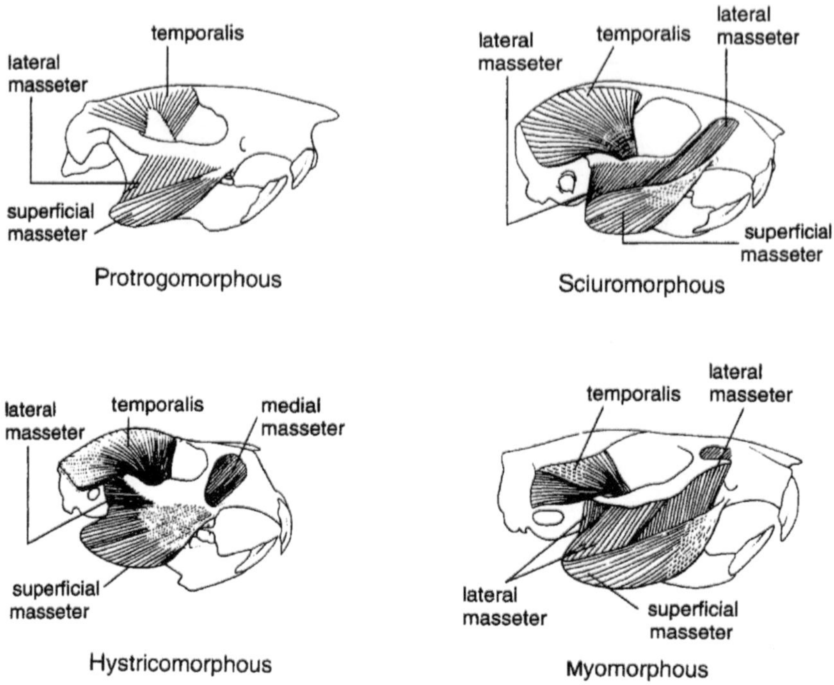

Figure 23.6 ▲

The different configurations of the jaw muscles that define the various groups of rodents. (From D. R. Prothero, *Princeton Field Guide to Prehistoric Mammals* [Princeton Univerity Press, 2016].)

Another variation is to have a large nerve opening (the infraorbital foramen) in the front of the cheekbones on either side of the snout. In the rodents known as hystricomorphs (porcupines plus the South American rodents and some African rodents), the masseter muscle passes through the infraorbital foramen to attach the jaw to the front of the snout.

Finally, in the myomorph rodents (rats, mice, and most other rodents), part of the masseter muscle passes through the infraorbital foramen (as in hystricomorphs), and part of it curves around the front (like in sciuromorphs), so it is a combination of both anatomical configurations.

Capybaras are hystricomorphs, with the masseter muscles that pass through the infraorbital foramen. Except for some Asian rodents known as gundis, all the remaining hystricomorphs also have hystricognath jaws, with large ridges that stick out sideways from the back corner of the jaw that anchor their chewing muscles.

The most primitive hystricognaths are all African forms, including a big radiation of fossils from the Eocene-Oligocene Fayûm beds of Egypt known as Phiomorpha, plus the living African porcupines, dassie rats, and cane rats. Also included are the bizarre naked mole rats, which live their entire lives in burrows underground, using their teeth to dig burrows and gnaw roots and tubers. They have a social structure much like an ant or termite colony, with one dominant female who rules the nest, and many subordinate daughters who carry out the daily tasks.

The most diverse of all the Hystricomorpha, however, is the huge radiation of South American rodents known as caviomorphs. These include fourteen families, dozens of genera, and hundreds of species, from chinchillas and pacas and agoutis and guinea pigs, to the largest living rodents of all, the capybaras discussed previously. They are all descended from an African hystricognath ancestor that must have rafted across the much narrower Atlantic Ocean during the middle Eocene. We know this because the earliest fossil rodents in South America date back to 41 Ma. Because South America had no native mammals competing for the rodent niche, the caviomorphs occupied that niche, and then underwent a huge evolutionary radiation there throughout the rest of the Cenozoic, resulting in the gigantic diversity they exhibit today. They have evolved into gopher-like forms such as the tuco tuco, tree-dwelling forms such as the porcupine and spiny rats, fast grassland runners such as the maras, and jungle runners such as the pacas and agoutis, mountain dwellers like the chinchillas, and large grazing swimming herbivores like the nutrias and capybaras (which evolved to eat grasses long before grazing hoofed mammals ever reached South America across Panama).

CAPYBARAS ON STEROIDS

A few of these caviomorph rodents successfully went northward when the Panama land bridge formed in the Pliocene. These included our North American porcupines, plus the extinct ancestors of the living capybara, known by the name *Hydrochorus holmesi*. But most impressive of all was the gigantic Ice Age capybara *Neochoerus pinckneyi*, which at 250 pounds (113 kilograms) was the size of a cow and 40 percent larger than the living

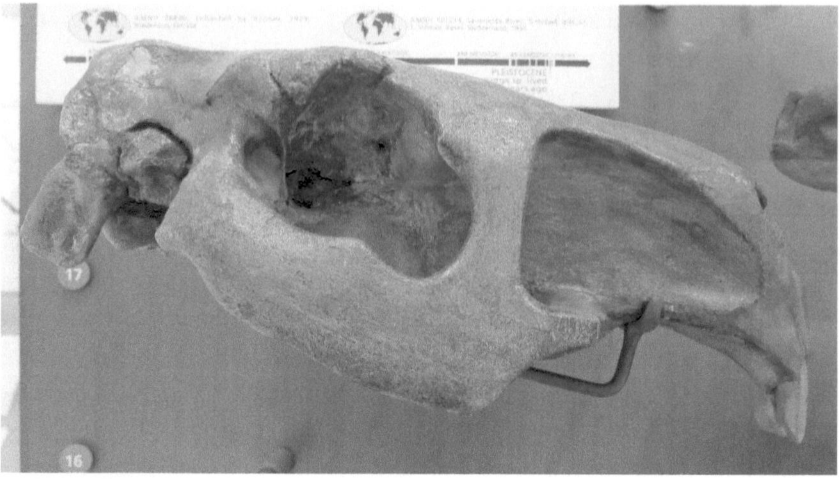

Figure 23.7 ▲
Skull of *Neochoerus pinckneyi*, the giant capybara from the Pleistocene of Florida. (Courtesy of Wikimedia Commons)

capybara (figure 23.7). That makes it larger than *Castoroides*, and only a few South American rodents discussed in this chapter were any larger. In addition to its huge size, the front of the skull is very broad and flat compared to living capybaras, and the bony bars behind the eye sockets (postorbital processes) are twice as wide as in the living species. Once *Neochoerus* arrived from South America in the late Pliocene, they flourished first in Arizona and Florida. By the Pleistocene, they had become established in most of the warmer southern states with mild winter climates, from Arizona to Texas to Georgia to South Carolina to Florida to Virginia. The first of its gigantic fossil teeth were briefly described by Leidy in 1853, but not formally named. Later specimens were referred to the genus *Hydrochoerus* with the living capybaras. Finally, the Smithsonian paleontologist Oliver P. Hay, an expert on Ice Age mammals at that time, formally gave these fossils the name *Neochoerus* in a 1926 paper about Pleistocene vertebrates from the Sinton locality near the Aransas River in southwestern Texas.

Meanwhile, South America had even larger giant rodents, including the extinct rhinoceros-sized Plio-Pleistocene pacarana, *Josephoartigasia* (figure 23.8), which was 10 feet (3 meters) long and weighed up to3,382 pounds (1,500 kilograms). The first specimens to be found were just lower

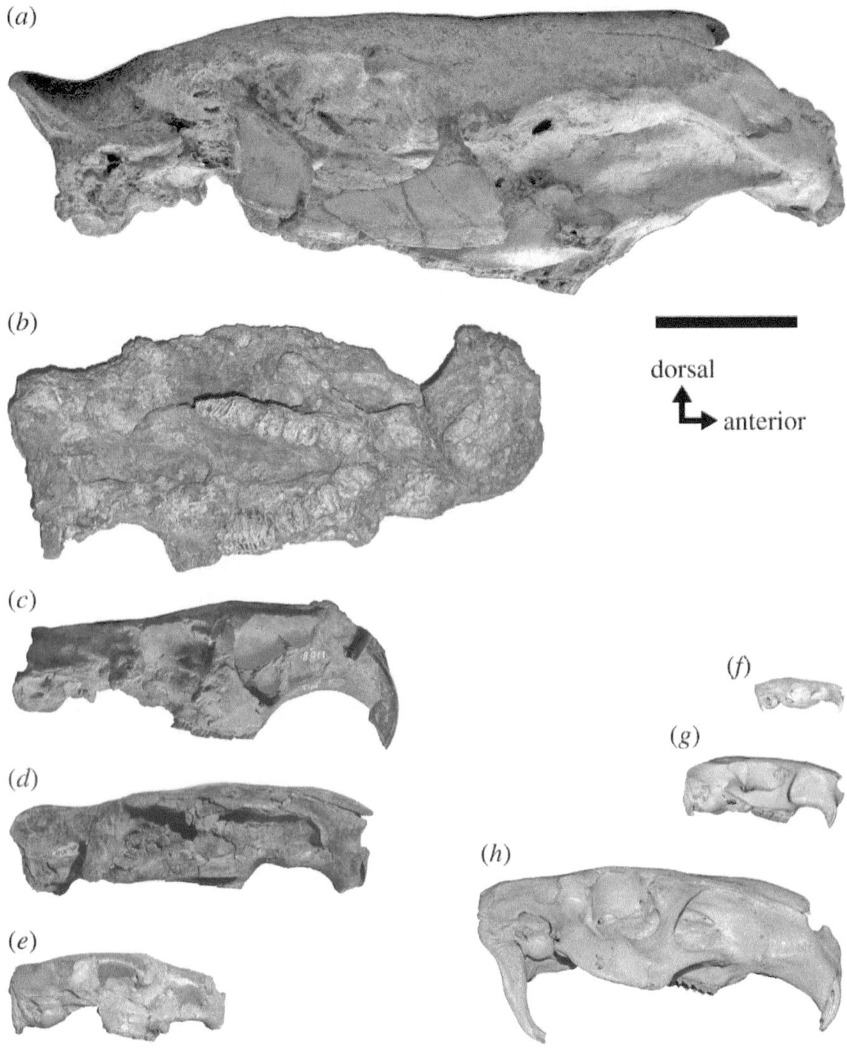

Figure 23.8 ▲

The skulls of several rodents compared side-by-side: (*A*) *Josephoartigasia monesi*, (*B*) *Phoberomys pattersoni*, (*C*) *Telicomys giganteus*, (*D*) *Neoepiblema acreensis*, (*E*) *Tetrastylus intermedius*, (*F*) the guinea pig, (*G*) the pacarana, and (*H*) the capybara. Scale = 10 cm (3.9 in). (Courtesy of Wikimedia Commons)

jaws and other fragments from sea cliffs in the Barrancas de San Gregorio, near Kiyu, in Uruguay. In 1966, they were described by the Uruguayan paleontologists Julio César Francis and Alvaro Mones as *Artigasia magna*. It was named in honor of the Uruguayan hero José Artigas. In 2007, Mones had to change the name to *Josephoartigasia* because the name *Artigasia* had already been used for a roundworm in 1934. Then in 2008, the Uruguayan paleontologist Andres Rinderknecht and the physicist Rudemar Ernesto Blanco reported on the discovery of a massive skull over 1 foot 9 inches (53 centimeters) long, also found in the Barranca de San Gregorio in 1987, but then forgotten for over twenty years. This specimen was even larger than the first specimen, so they called in *Josephoartigasia monesi*, in honor of Alvaro Mones and his work on South American rodents (figure 23.9). Thanks to its huge skull and teeth, *Josephoartigasia* would have had a bite force of about 1400 N (newtons)(= 310 lb/square inch) at the tip of the incisors, and about 5000 N (1100 lb/square inch) in its last molars. This is as strong as the biggest crocodilians, and thus its teeth were strong enough to crack nuts, excavate large burrows, dig up roots, and also fight against predators—not that there were many predators in South America that could attack a rhino-sized rodent. Geochemical analysis showed that they ate mostly leaves and fruits, and little or no grasses. They were found in deposits of a forested estuary near the coast, so they

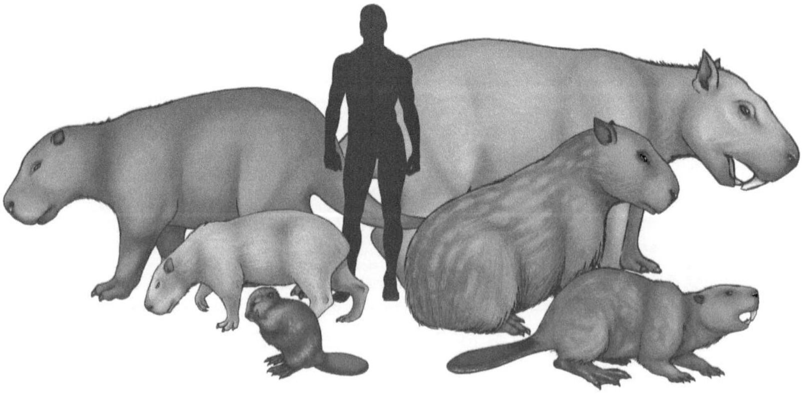

Figure 23.9 ▲

Rodents come in many shapes and sizes, and not all of them are small; some extinct rodents were huge. (Drawing by M. P. Williams).

were probably semiaquatic like capybaras and pacaranas. These same deposits also yielded fossils of ground sloths, glyptodonts, "terror birds" (Phorusrhacidae), hippo-like toxodonts, plus both the last of the marsupial saber-tooths (*Thylacosmilus*), and the first wave of scimitar-toothed saber-toothed cats, which were thought to have competed with them and driven the last thylacosmilids to extinction (see chapter 22).

Before the discovery of *Josephoartigasia*, the previous record-holders for largest rodent was the bison-sized Miocene pacarana *Phoberomys* ("terror mouse"), which was 10 feet (3 meters) long, and weighed about 1,500 pounds (700 kilograms). It was originally discovered in the upper Miocene beds from the Ituzaigó Formation of Argentina, the Solimões Formation of Brazil, and eventually in the Urumaco Formation of Venezuela and Peru. The name *Phoberomys* was coined by Lucas Kraglievich, a pioneering Argentinian paleontologist from the 1920s through the 1960s, after the originally proposed name, *Dabbenea*, was found to belong with different species from those referred to as *Phoberomys*. The best-known species is *Phoberomys pattersoni*, which was named after the legendary Harvard paleontologist Bryan Patterson who worked on a wide range of fossil mammals and is famous for his insights that many others followed later. The best fossils of *Phoberomys* occur in the upper Miocene Urumaco Formation of Venezuela, which has been studied intensively for a number of years because of its large and diverse fauna, including 21 species of sharks and rays, and 12 species of crocodilians, including the pelican-beaked crocodilian *Mourasuchus*, and the enormous narrow-snouted gharial *Gryposuchus*, which reached 33 feet (10 meters) in length. The Urumaco Formation also produces the monstrous turtle *Stupendemys geographicus*, whose shell was over 10 feet (3 meters) long, and a gigantic boid snake known only from isolated vertebrae. Among mammals, there are megatheriid, megalonychid, and mylodontid ground sloths, huge glyptodonts, and members of South America's endemic extinct hoofed mammal groups, the litopterns and notoungulates.

Finally, one more gigantic rodent from South America was the slightly smaller late Miocene-Pliocene cow-sized pacarana *Telicomys*, which was more than 7 feet (2.7 meters) long and weighed up to 1,100 pounds (500 kilograms). Telicomys means "a rodent of unusual size" in Greek, so the phrase from *The Princess Bride* is actually not original. Also named and described by Lucas Kraglievich in 1926, it has several named species, including *Telicomys giganteus* ("giant rodent of unusual size") and *Telicomys gigantissimus* ("most giant rodent of unusual size"). *Telicomys* comes from the Solimões Formation of Brazil, which yielded about eight species of mammals (mostly caviomorph rodents, plus ground sloths, glyptodonts, and a river dolphin), diverse crocodilians including the huge caiman *Purussaurus*, the gigantic gharial *Gryposuchus* previously mentioned, the pelican-beaked crocodilian *Mourasuchus* previously discussed, a gigantic mata mata turtle, and other reptiles.

In short, South America was replete with gigantic rodents through much of the late Cenozoic. It's hard to know why so many different kinds of caviomorphs became huge at different times and in different places. Perhaps it's related to the fact that caviomorph rodents occupied many niches for rodents that had no other occupants until they floated over from Africa. South America's large herbivore fauna was very different from that in the northern continents, especially since South America was dominated by large aquatic rodents, ground sloths, glyptodonts, and just a few notoungulates and litopterns mimicking the ecology of horses, rhinos, hippos, mastodonts, and other mammals from the Holarctic continents. Whatever the reason, Rodents of Unusual Size are not just a gag from *The Princess Bride* but a real phenomenon that occurred multiple times with the beavers and the caviomorphs in both the Americas and in Eurasia. Only today, with the capybara as the largest living rodent, do we no longer have rodents that are truly gigantic.

FOR FURTHER READING

Agusti, J., and M. Anton. *Mammoths, Sabertooths, and Hominids: 65 Million Years of Mammalian Evolution in Europe*. Columbia University Press, 2002.

Beck, J. C. "The Giant Beaver: A Prehistoric Memory?" *Ethnohistory* 19, no. 2 (1972): 109–122.

Blanco, R. E., A. Rinderknecht, and G. Lecuona. "The Bite Force of the Largest Fossil Rodent (Hystricognathi, Caviomorpha, Dinomyidae): Largest Rodent Bite Force." *Lethaia* 45, no. 2 (2012): 157–163.

Cox, P. G., A. Rinderknecht, and R. E. Blanco. "Predicting Bite Force and Cranial Biomechanics in the Largest Fossil Rodent Using Finite Element Analysis." *Journal of Anatomy* 226, no. 3 (2015): 215–223.

Douzery, E. J. P., F. Delsuc, M. J. Stanhope, and D. Huchon. "Local Molecular Clocks in Three Nuclear Genes: Divergence Times for Rodents and Other Mammals and Incompatibility Among Fossil Calibrations." *Journal of Molecular Evolution* 57 (2003): S201–S213.

Janis, C., G. F. Gunnell, and M. D. Uhen, eds. *Evolution of Tertiary Mammals of North America. Vol II: Small Mammals, Xenarthrans, and Marine Mammals.* Cambridge University Press, 2008.

Korth, W. W. *The Tertiary Record of Rodents in North America.* Springer, 1994.

Kurtén, B. *Before the Indians.* Columbia University Press, 1988.

——. *Pleistocene Mammals of Europe.* Columbia University Press, 1968.

Kurtén, B., and E. Anderson. *Pleistocene Mammals of North America.* Columbia University Press, 1980.

Li, C. K., R. W. Wilson, and M. R. Dawson. "The Origin of Rodents and Lagomorphs." *Current Mammalogy* 1 (1987): 97–108.

Luckett, W. P., and J.-L. Hartenberger, eds. *Evolutionary Relationships Among Rodents.* Plenum, 1985.

Martin, R. A. "Taxonomy of the Giant Pleistocene Beaver *Castoroides* from Florida." *Journal of Paleontology* 43, no. 4 (1969): 1033–1041.

Millien, Virginie. "The Largest Among the Smallest: The Body Mass of the Giant Rodent *Josephoartigasia monesi.*" *Proceedings of the Royal Society B* 275, no. 1646 (2008): 1953–1955.

Plint, T., F. J. Longstaffe, and G. Zazula. "Giant Beaver Palaeoecology Inferred from Stable Isotopes." *Scientific Reports* 9, no. 7179 (2019): 1–12.

Prothero, D. R. *The Princeton Field Guide to Prehistoric Mammals.* Princeton University Press, 2016.

Rinderknecht, A., and R. E. Blanco. "The Largest Fossil Rodent." *Proceedings of the Royal Society B* 275, no. 1637 (2008): 923–928.

Rinderknecht, A., B. T. Enrique, and M. Ubilla. "New Genus of Giant Dinomyidae (Rodentia: Hystricognathi: Caviomorpha) from the Late Miocene of Uruguay." *Journal of Mammalogy* 92, no. 1 (2011): 170, 176.

Savage, R. J. G., and M. R. Long. *Mammal Evolution: An Illustrated Guide.* Facts-on-File, 1986.

Szalay, F. S., M. J. Novacek, and M. C. McKenna, eds. *Mammal Phylogeny.* Springer-Verlag, 1993.

Turner, A., and M. Anton. *National Geographic Prehistoric Mammals.* National Geographic Society, 2004.

Wood, Albert E. "A Revised Classification of the Rodents." *Journal of Mammalogy* 36, no. 2 (1955): 165–187.

Wu, S., W. Wu, F. Zhang, J. Ye, X. Ni, J. Sun, S. V. Edwards, J. Meng, and C. L. Organ. "Molecular and Paleontological Evidence for a Post-Cretaceous Origin of Rodents." *PLOS ONE* 7, no. 10 (2012): e46445.

Xenikoudakis, G., M. Ahmed, J. C. Harris, R. Wadleigh, J. L. A. Paijmans, S. Hartmann, et al. "Ancient DNA Reveals Twenty Million Years of Aquatic Life in Beavers." *Current Biology* 30, no. 3 (2020): R110–R111.

24 APES OF CONFUSION

OREOPITHECUS AND *RAMAPITHECUS*

It is somewhat more probable that our early progenitors lived on the African continent than elsewhere. But it is useless to speculate on this subject; for two or three anthropomorphous apes, one the *Dryopithecus* of Lartet, nearly as large as a man, and closely allied to *Hylobates*, existed in Europe during the Miocene age; and since so remote a period the earth has certainly undergone many great revolutions, and there has been ample time for migration on the largest scale.

—CHARLES DARWIN, *THE DESCENT OF MAN*, 1871

DARWIN'S DILEMMA

When Charles Darwin first published *On the Origin of Species* in 1859, he deliberately avoided much discussion of humans and how evolution might affect our understanding of our place in nature, or the religious notions of humans as specially created. Darwin knew his book would be controversial enough. Darwin wrote only one enigmatic sentence, "Light will be thrown on the origin of man and his history," and that was his only mention of the topic in 1859.[1]

By the early 1870s, however, the debate had continued for more than a decade, and most of the scientific community in Europe had accepted the notion of evolution—even if they did not always accept Darwin's mechanism, natural selection. His friend and ally, Thomas Henry Huxley, had written extensively on this hot-button topic, especially with his 1863 book *Evidence as to Man's Place in Nature*, where he showed the extreme anatomical similarity of humans and great apes and monkeys. Huxley briefly mentioned the only human fossils that were known at the time, the Neanderthals, which showed enough differences to be regarded as extinct relatives of humans. So by the 1870s, Darwin could no longer avoid the topic, but needed to bolster the case for the evolution of humans.

In 1871, Darwin finally broke his silence with the publication of *The Descent of Man, and Selection in Relation to Sex*. He starts the book reviewing the enormous anatomical similarities of humans to apes and monkeys, a topic that Huxley had already documented so well. Based on his careful observations of the apes in zoos and elsewhere, Darwin discussed the remarkably human-like behaviors of many of the apes. He also commented on the evolution of human races, as they were known in the 1870s. The second half of the book deals with the topic of sexual selection, a notion that was even more controversial to sexually repressed people of the Victorian age.

But almost nowhere in the book is there much discussion of the fossil record of humans and apes, largely because almost nothing was known of them at the time. Like Huxley, he briefly commented on the first Neanderthal specimens, although these had been dismissed as the remains of "diseased Cossacks" that had died in the caves, and the specimens were not complete enough to really show how they were related to modern humans. But there was almost no other fossil record of apes or monkeys to point to at that time. The only specimens known at the time were some teeth and jaws that French paleontologist Edouard Lartet had described in 1856, three years before *On the Origin of the Species*. Lartet named them *Dryopithecus* ("oak ape" because it was thought that they had lived in Miocene oak trees), the specimens were incomplete, but definitely looked like primates, which Darwin thought were closer to gibbons (*Hylobates*) than other living apes. But *Dryopithecus* also presented a problem for Darwin's 1871 book, because Darwin reasoned that humans had evolved in Africa, since the apes closest to us (chimps and gorillas) were confined to Africa. As he wrote in 1871:

> In each great region of the world the living mammals are closely related to the extinct species of the same region. It is therefore probable that Africa was formerly inhabited by extinct apes closely allied to the gorilla and chimpanzee;

> and as these two species are now man's nearest allies, it is somewhat more probable that our early progenitors lived on the African continent than elsewhere.[2]

Yet most European scholars insisted that humans must have evolved in Europe or in Asia, a notion that did not die until more and more primitive hominids were found in Africa in the 1930s (see chapter 25). As the epigraph at the beginning of the chapter shows, Darwin dismissed the inconvenient occurrence of *Dryopithecus* in France as an artifact of the incompleteness of the fossil record at that time because almost no fossils from Africa were known in 1871.

In the following years, more and more specimens of *Dryopithecus* were found, but it was still so incomplete that there was little clarity on how it fit on the primate family tree. Eventually, additional primitive Miocene apes were found in Spain, Greece, and Hungary and in other parts of Europe. These were complemented by discoveries from the Miocene beds of the Siwalik Hills in British India (now Pakistan) and discovery of the first African ape specimens (*Proconsul* in 1933) added to the accumulation of ape-like fossils. These fossils are still being sorted out, with significant arguments as to which named apes are really valid (the early collections were taxonomically oversplit with too many invalid names) and how they are all related. But the most confusing specimens of all were *Oreopithecus*, the "mountain ape."

"MOUNTAIN APE"

During the mid-1800s, Italy was catching up to the Industrial Revolution that had swept across most of Europe and elsewhere since the beginning of the century. In particular, coal was in high demand as a fuel to burn in the boilers of steam engines, and for other industrial uses. As early as 1839, there were mines for low-grade coal (known as lignite) from the Miocene rocks of Tuscany, in the Apennines just east of Florence. Digging shaft mines into the hills using donkey power to haul the loads out of the mines, the lignite mines kept expanding, and by 1849 a railroad was built that connected the mines in Maremma, Italy, to the coast. These Miocene beds were not only full of coal seams but occasionally yielded vertebrate fossils, from bovids, giraffids, and suids, to ursid and mustelids, as well as turtles and crocodilians, all of whom inhabited Miocene swamps where the dense plant material eventually turned into coal.

The Montebamboli lignite mine was particularly rich in fossils, and both miners and local collectors kept their eyes open for more specimens. One of these was Tito Nardi, a local researcher and fossil collector. In 1862, he found a jaw of a juvenile primate, which he sold to Igino Cocchi, professor at the Istituto di Studi Superiori di Perfezionamento di Firenze and curator of the Paleontological Collection of the Regio Museo di Fisica e Storia Naturale di Firenze, today known as Museo di Geologia e Paleontologia of the Università degli Studi di Firenze. Cocchi probably wanted to study and publish this specimen (only the second fossil ape ever found in Europe), but he probably felt that mention of a fossil ape was too dangerous in Italy, where revolution and conflict had been going on since 1861 when Victor Emanuele I became king of a unified Italy. The political winds were dangerous enough without bringing in the controversial topic of evolution or declaring that Italy has a fossil of an ape-like human ancestor.

The fossil remained in that collection until Cocchi handed it over to the distinguished Paul Gervais, Chair of Comparative Anatomy at the Musée National d'Histoire Naturelle in Paris, to study. He visited Florence and recognized its importance and borrowed it. On May 6, 1872, he presented his description of the specimen at the session of the Académie des Sciences in Paris, which was published in the society's journal. As Gervais put it,

> In summary, the fossil ape of the Monte Bamboli lignites seems to constitute a separate genus which will rank at the end of the series of anthropomorphic Pithecines after the gorilla, and before the Cynocephalus [baboons] and the macaques. I will give this genus the name *Oreopithecus*, alluding to the prominent shape of the tubercles of the molar teeth, and the species which serves as the type will be *Oreopithecus bambolii*, a name taken for [the] locality where it was discovered.[3]

From that time forward, *Oreopithecus* was one of the most studied and controversial ape fossils ever found. The same year that it was first published, Charles Imanuel Forsyth Major, a Scottish doctor who grew up in Switzerland, traveled down to Florence to see it and decided it was closely related to humans. Just three years after it was first described, Ludwig Rütimeyer, Professor of Zoology and Comparative Anatomy at the Universität Basel, declared it was a fossil gibbon. But in 1878, Albert Gaudry, of the Musée National d'Histoire Naturelle in Paris (a colleague of Gervais), decided it resembled the Eocene artiodactyl *Choeropotamus*. In the British Museum, a cast of the specimen was in their displays as early as 1884, and it was put in the same case with the infamous "Piltdown man" forgery, so it was clearly regarded as a human relative by the British curators. The most common view was that of Max Schlosser, who decided it was an Old World monkey (cercopithecoid) related to the baboon and macaque, which Gervais had noted in his original description.

Meanwhile, more specimens were being found in other mines near Monte Bamboli and elsewhere in the region. In 1890, Guiseppe Ristori reported nearly a dozen new specimens, among them an upper jaw. In 1898, a left lower jaw was described by Felice Ottolenghi. In 1907, Giuseppe Merciai reported four upper jaws and a lower jaw from the Grosseto mine at Ribolla. All this new material gave a more complete picture of *Oreopithecus*, although still based entirely on teeth and jaws.

Between 1914 and 1945, two world wars and a worldwide depression occurred, and it became difficult for most foreign scientists to visit Italy and conduct paleontological research on the fossils. Consequently, little was added to the known material, particularly since the turmoil during the fascist regime of Mussolini made it difficult to conduct much research into evolution, especially in the evolution of apes and humans. Then, in 1949, the Swiss paleontologist Johannes Hürzeler of the Naturhistorisches Museum Basel took a special interest in *Oreopithecus*. Some of the more recent specimens discovered in the 1880s and 1890s had ended up in the Basel collections, along with a cast of the original lower jaw from Monte Bamboli. Hürzeler obtained permission from Giovanni Merla, Director of the Istituto di Geologia in Florence, for permission to restudy the original fossils. In 1949, he published a paper redescribing all the known specimens of *Oreopithecus*, and he pointed out that it had a short face and small canines, a feature typical of hominins and not of other apes or any kind of monkey. *Oreopithecus* then became his obsession and his life's work, leading to additional papers on it published in 1942, 1954, and 1956, all promoting his controversial notion that the short face and small canines made *Oreopithecus* a hominin, close to our ancestry, and not an ape or an Old World monkey. When Hürzeler toured the world to give a series of lectures, his views generated an enormous press coverage, often being presented as a challenge to the Darwinian idea of descent of man from apes, but from monkeys instead. Hürzeler was invited to give a lecture in New York in March 1956 at the Wenner-Gren Foundation (an organization that has funded much research in paleoanthropology). As described by Cioppi et al.:

> Thus, he started a media campaign that animated the scientific world. Contributions from the Wenner-Gren Foundation enabled him to travel to New York and Harvard University, armed with suitcases containing fossil specimens, to illustrate his ideas, and newspapers around the world covered it, rekindling the controversy between creationists and evolutionists. Media coverage of *Oreopithecus* was extensive and involve the international press, such as the New York Times, which headlined "Fossil research questions Darwin evolution theory", and Le Figaro, "Darwin s'est trompé" ("Darwin was wrong").[4]

Eventually, the Wenner-Gren Foundation arranged to finance Hürzeler's excavations in Italy, supervised by the Italian paleontologist Alberto Carlo Blanc. Hürzeler's views seemed to be confirmed on August 2, 1958, when he discovered a complete skeleton in a mine in Baccinello. In 1960 Hürzeler published yet another paper on *Oreopithecus*. The complete skeleton suggested that *Oreopithecus* might be bipedal, because its short pelvis was more like that of hominins than those of gorillas or chimps (figure 24.1A).

As Cioppi et al. explained:

> The news immediately circulated in the press all over the world, starting with articles by Andrea Barbato in *Il Messagero*, (Aug. 2, 1958: "A man who lived 12 million years ago returned a light in a Tuscan village"), *La Vanguardia Española, Le Monde*, and other international newspapers, followed by a renewed contrast between creationists and evolutionists. Several scientists followed Hürzeler's thinking by seeing in the origin of so dated for hominids an evolutionary line unique to humankind, separate from that of apes, whereas others found many shared characters with the apes. The Catholic Church also became interested in *Oreopithecus* discovery; in February 1959, Cardinal Eugène Tisserant, head of the College of Cardinals, attended a Hürzeler lecture at the University of Rome, and the following day, the Swiss paleontologist was received by Pope John XXIII. Among scientists, this was understood as an implicit acceptance by the Church of the theory of evolution.[5]

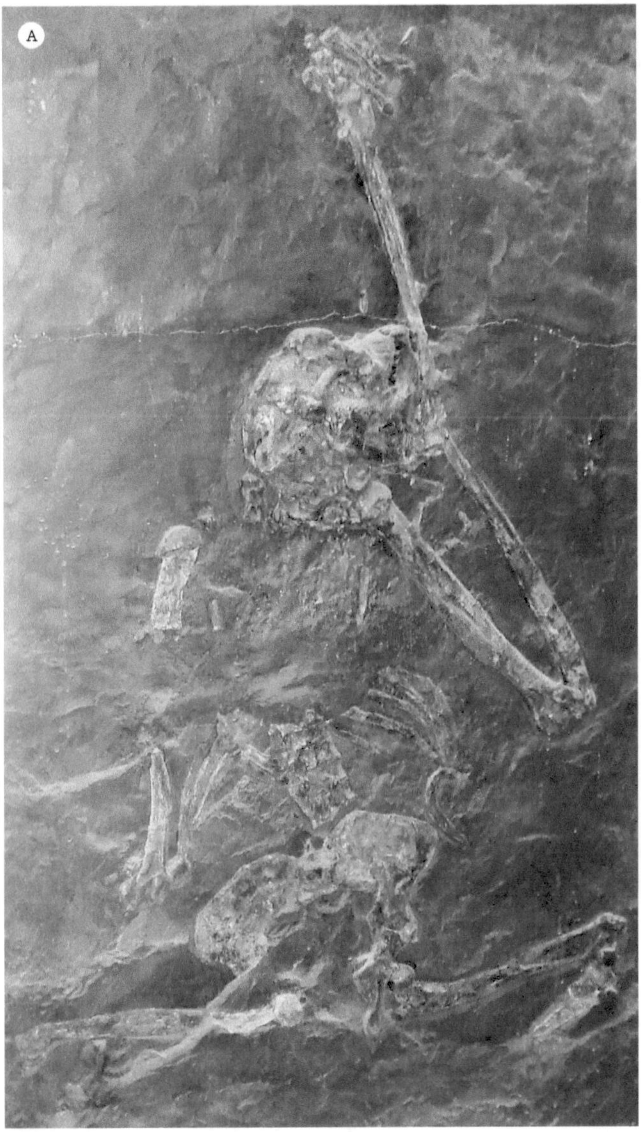

Figure 24.1 ▲ ▶

Oreopithecus bambolii. (*A*) Complete articulated skeleton embedded in lignite coal.

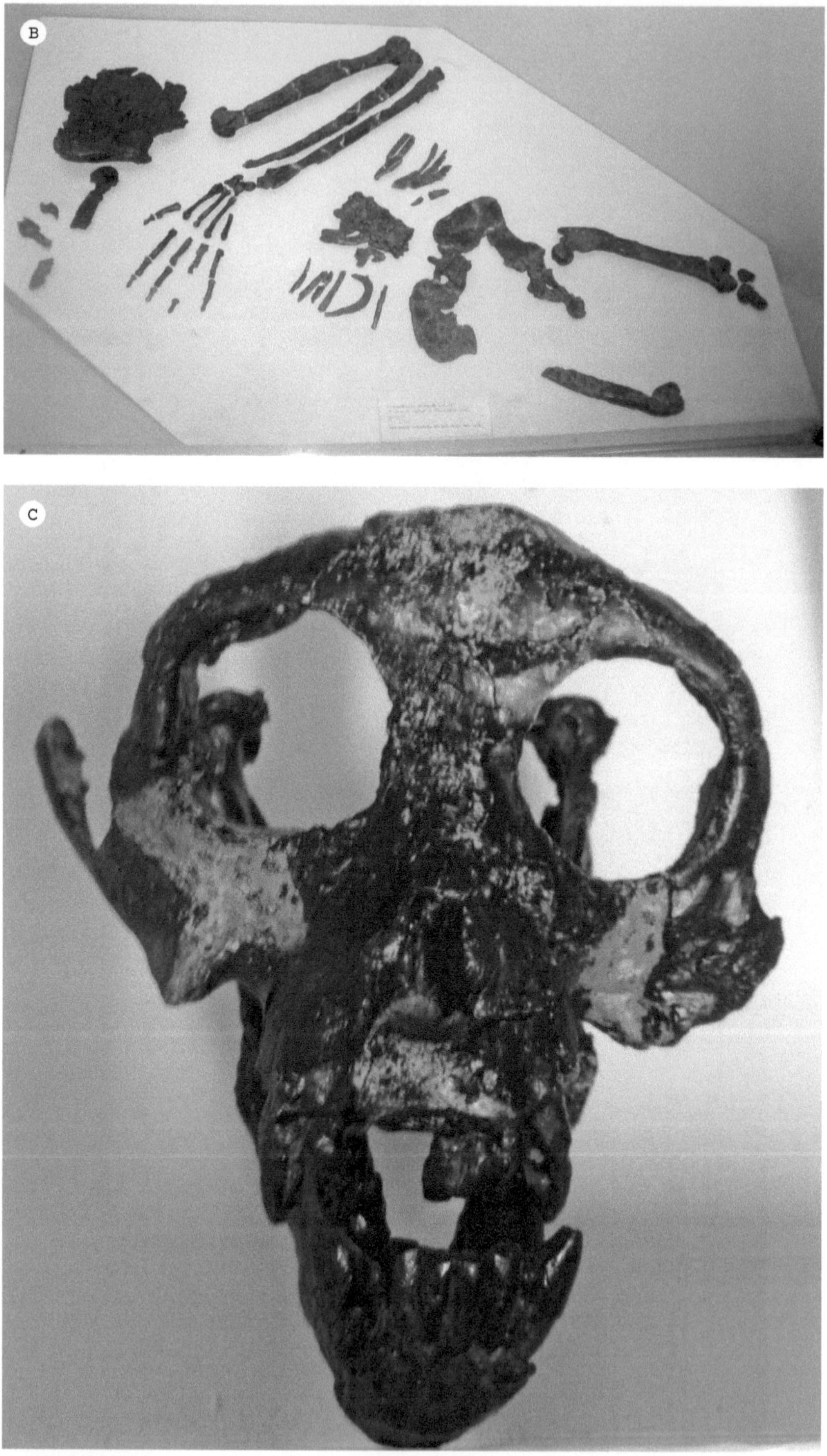

Figure 24.1 ▲

(*continued*) (*B*) Reconstruction of the individual bones removed from the coal matrix. (*C*) Facial view of the skull. (Courtesy of Wikimedia Commons)

The Italians became concerned with how the Swiss lab in Basel was preparing the fossil from the original lignite slab and called back the loan. They undertook their own preparation of the specimen, eventually getting the skull and teeth prepared out from the slab (figure 24.1B). Straus (1963) wrote that:

> The supposed dental resemblance of *Oreopithecus* to cercopithecoids will not hold water. It is true that in a few characters lower molars of *Oreopithecus* approximate those of cercopithecoids, but their overall pattern is strikingly non-cercopithecoid. In its relative length, the neck of the *Oreopithecus* femur most closely resembles those of hominoids, especially those of the great apes and man.[6]

Eventually, the flattened and distorted skull was prepared out of the slab and reconstructed in three dimensions, adding much more information to our knowledge of this controversial species. Additional specimens have been found on the island of Sardinia, far from Tuscany. However, in the Miocene, Sardinia was on the same tectonic block as Tuscany, and both were part of an isolated island in the Mediterranean, which had other unique species confined to that island.

But even with the reconstructed skull, better jaws and teeth, and nearly complete skeletons, *Oreopithecus* continues to frustrate and confuse paleoanthropologists. Alba et al. (2024) reviewed some of the more recent analyses and found a tremendous divergence of opinion, from *Oreopithecus* being a relative of gibbons, to a relative of dryopithecines, to a relative of the higher hominids (including dryopithecines), to a member of the group of African Miocene apes that included *Nyanzapithecus* and *Afropithecus* and *Proconsul*, to a close relationship with *Samburupithecus* and gibbons—and that's just between 1987 and 2022.

More than 154 years have passed since *Oreopithecus* was first discovered, and we're still no closer to consensus. It all boils down to the confusing mix of characters, from the short face and tiny canines that make it appear similar to hominins, but the skull and skeleton is much more gibbon-like—hence the conflict and confusion. In recent years, additional discoveries have shown that there was a huge diversification of apes in the late Miocene across Eurasia and Africa, where apes were far more diverse and abundant than the Old World monkeys. Most of those apes vanished, and today cercopithecoids are very diverse, with 23 genera of baboons, macaques, langurs, colobus monkeys, guenons, and mangabeys, while there are only eight genera of apes: *Homo* (humans), *Pan* (chimps), *Gorilla, Pongo* (orangutans), and four genera of gibbons.

THE *RAMAPITHECUS* BLUNDER

What about fossil apes from other continents, especially Asia? The story starts with important fossils found in the Siwalik Hills of Pakistan. This amazing sequence of rocks spans much of the Oligocene, Miocene, and Pliocene epochs of geologic history, and is incredibly fossiliferous. These deposits represent the flood of river sediments shed across southern Asia as the Himalayas slowly rose high in the sky and eroded down to form the Siwalik deposits. As we discussed in chapter 14, the Siwaliks had been studied by paleontologists and geologists since 1902, when British geologist Guy Pilgrim did pioneering research all over south Asia, which was a British Crown Colony back then.

Over the past century the Siwaliks have yielded huge collections of fossil mammals that give us a very detailed picture of evolution in south Asia during the Miocene. Thanks to the tense nature of Indian and Pakistani politics and U.S. policy toward both countries, Pakistan owed the United States millions of dollars for all the military hardware they bought from us. As a result, during the 1970s through 1990s, there was lots of grant money (especially from the Fulbright Foundation) for American scholars to go to Pakistan and produce important research. Lots of paleontologists jumped on the Fulbright opportunity, and there was a huge flood of research on the fossils and geology of the Siwalik Hills and other areas nearby in Pakistan during this time. Thanks to plenty of volcanic ashes and a technique called paleomagnetic stratigraphy, the Siwalik fossils are also extremely well dated. Today, of course, the political situation is so dangerous that few Americans can go there, and even French and other researchers from other countries with no American ties have problems with the radical Islamic tribes in many regions.

Back in 1932, the Smithsonian paleontologist G. Edward Lewis was working in the Tinau River valley in the Nepalese Siwaliks and recovered a jaw that looked very much like a primitive hominin (figure 24.2). It had relatively small canines, and the shape of the jaw was more like a broad semicircle in top view (typical of human jaws) than the "U"-shaped jaws of the apes, with

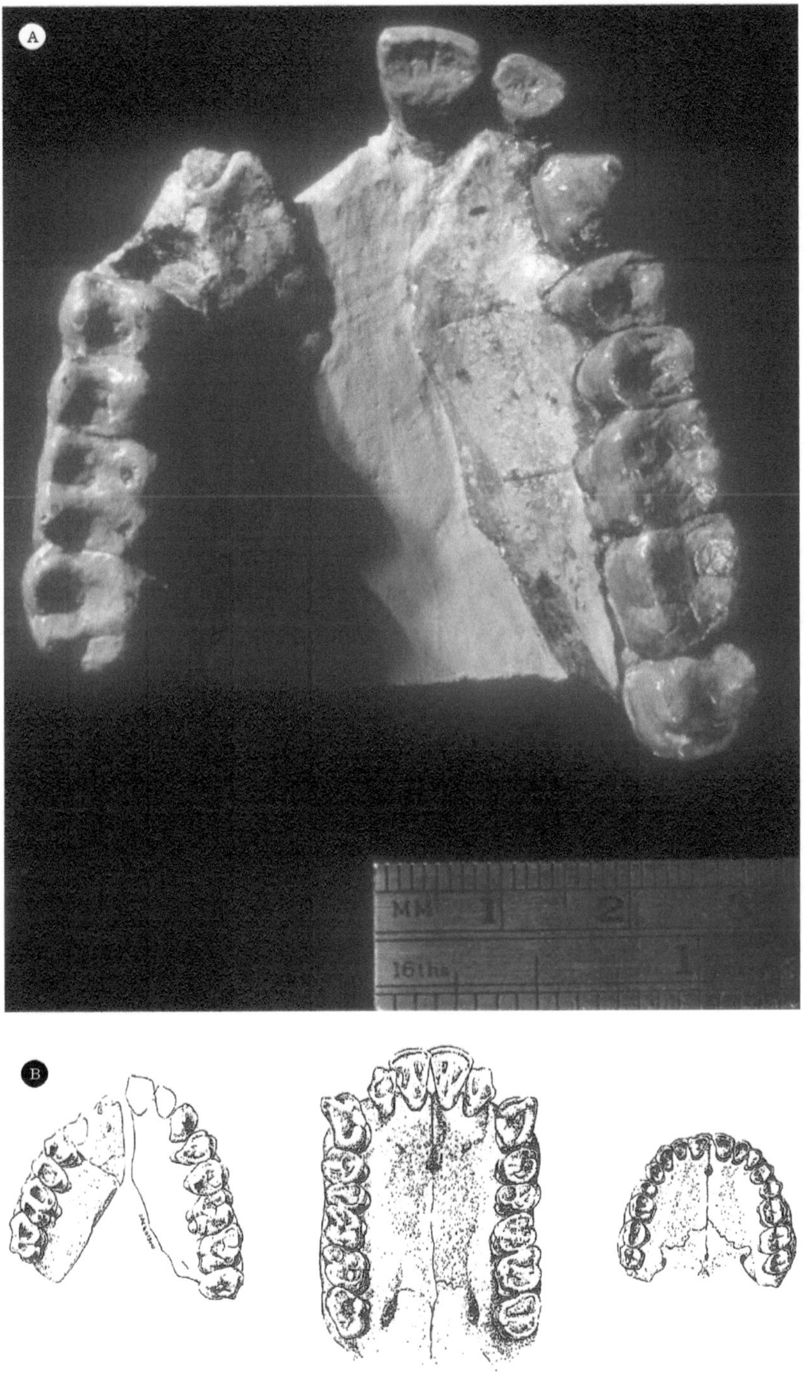

Figure 24.2 ▲

The *Ramapithecus* puzzle. (*A*) Crown view of the upper dentition of the original specimen. (*B*) Comparison of the jaw elements of *Ramapithecus* (*left*) with that of a chimpanzee (*center*) and of a human (*right*). ([*A*] Courtesy of E. Delson; [*B*] courtesy of Wikimedia Commons)

their huge canines on a flat lower chin, and long parallel back parts of the jaws. In the 1960s, the anthropologist David Pilbeam from Harvard, and the primatologist Elwyn Simons of Yale University (later Duke University), and others began to champion the view that this jaw (named *Ramapithecus* by Lewis) was the oldest known hominin fossil. (*Rama* is one of the Hindu gods, and *pithecus* is "ape" in Greek; there are also primates named after the Hindu gods Shiva and Brahma). Because some of the specimens dated back to 14 Ma in the well-calibrated Siwalik sequence, this placed the split between apes and hominins at least 14 Ma or earlier. Through the 1960s and 1970s, every student of primate evolution learned about *Ramapithecus* as the "first hominin." This was very much a part of the textbooks (and my classes) when I took anthropology and human paleontology in the early 1970s.

But there is another approach to dating the divergence time between two groups of animals: the molecular clock. As early as 1962, the legendary molecular biologists Linus Pauling (winner of two Nobel prizes) and Émile Zuckerkandl were among the first to use molecular methods to draw a tree of evolutionary relationships among organisms, the first evidence of evolution to emerge from our own cells and DNA. In their case, they noticed that the number of amino acid differences in hemoglobin molecules matched not only the branching sequence of the animals in their study, but also the number of changes was proportional to how long ago these creatures had diverged in time. A year later, another pioneer in molecular biology, Emanuel Margoliash, noted:

> It appears that the number of residue differences between cytochrome c of any two species is mostly conditioned by the time elapsed since the lines of evolution leading to these two species originally diverged. If this is correct, the cytochrome c of all mammals should be equally different from the cytochrome c of all birds. Since fish diverges from the main stem of vertebrate evolution earlier than either birds or mammals, the cytochrome c of both mammals and birds should be equally different from the cytochrome c of fish. Similarly, all vertebrate cytochrome c should be equally different from the yeast protein.[7]

All of these data suggested that molecular changes accumulated through time as different groups of animals branched apart, and that the rate of change of molecules is proportional to the time they split or diverged.

Meanwhile, the evidence that most of the DNA of any animal is "junk DNA" or at least noncoding DNA began to emerge. So much of our genome is simply never read when the genes are expressed, and thus invisible to natural selection or "adaptively neutral." Pioneering work by the Japanese biochemist Motoo Kimura established that most of the molecules in DNA are just sitting there, unread and unaffected by what happens to the organism. These adaptively invisible molecules then can spontaneously mutate, and there is no selection to weed them out or favor one version versus another. Over time these mutations keep accumulating at a regular rate, ticking like a clock. As long as natural selection can't see these changes, the ticking of the "molecular clock" is a good method of estimating divergence time in the geologic past between any two organisms. The only thing needed is calibration by using well-established divergence times of key evolutionary splits, as established in the fossil record.

Soon many molecular biologists were working hard on molecular clock estimates of the branching history and timing of divergence of many groups of animals. Again and again, work by the late Vincent Sarich and Allan Wilson at University of California Berkeley showed that the molecular clock estimate for the divergence between humans and chimps was only 5–7 Ma and no older than 8 Ma, and certainly not the 14 Ma that *Ramapithecus* suggested. Yet the paleontologists stuck by their guns. They distrusted the molecular clock method as unproven and unreliable, and indeed it gave some very strange and ridiculous results every once in a while. (This still happens today, and we don't always know why.)

As the controversy got more and more heated during the 1970s and 1980s, the major players got into shouting matches at meetings and in journals. Sarich and Wilson were convinced that their data were reliable and something must be wrong about *Ramapithecus* or its age. I knew Vince Sarich quite well, and he was a burly, towering, impressive figure with a natty beard, a loud voice, and strong opinions, who didn't mind ruffling feathers and offending people if necessary. In 1971, he said, "One no longer has the option of considering a fossil older than about eight million years as a hominid no matter what it looks like."[8] This, of course, upset people like Simons and Pilbeam, who kept insisting that *Ramapithecus* proved the molecular biologists were wrong.

The impasse was finally broken by another discovery in the Siwaliks. In 1982, David Pilbeam reported on newly discovered specimens that

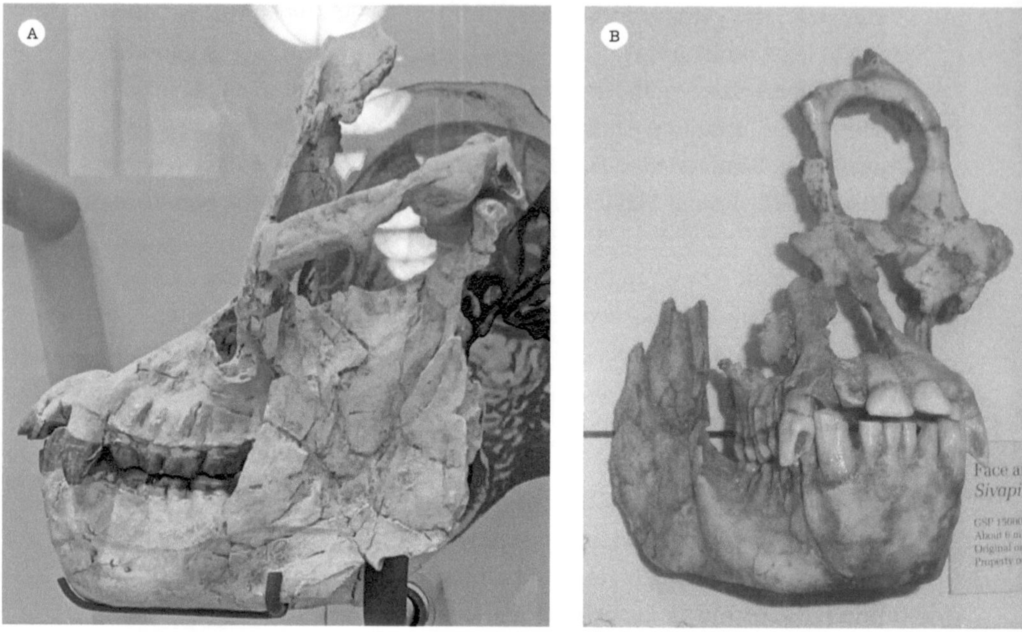

Figure 24.3 ▲
Two views of the partial skull of *Sivapithecus*: (*A* and *B*) showing the similarities with the skulls of orangutans and not hominins. (Courtesy of Wikimedia Commons)

included not only a more complete lower jaw of *Ramapithecus* but also a partial skull. With the addition of the skull, the specimen now looked much more like a fossil orangutan named *Sivapithecus* by Guy Pilgrim way back in 1910 when the Siwaliks were first collected and explored (figure 24.3A and figure 23.4B). The lower jaw named "*Ramapithecus*" was just the jaw of a fossil relative of the orangutan that happened to look like a hominin. Soon the anthropologists were forced to retreat and acknowledge their error, which ceded the victory to Sarich and Wilson and molecular biology.

NOTES

1. Charles Darwin, *On the Origin of Species* (John Murray, 1859), 502.
2. Charles Darwin, *The Descent of Man* (John Murray, 1871), 199.

3. Paul Gervais, "Sur un singe fossile, d'espèce non encore décrite, qui a été decouvert au Monte-Bamboli (Italie)," *Comptes rendus de l'Académie des sciences* 74 (1872), 1223.
4. Elisabetta Cioppi, Massimo Sozzi, and Roberta Pieraccioli, "150 Years of Discoveries, Research and Debates on *Oreopitechus bambolii* Gervais, 1872," *Bollettino della Società Paleontologica Italiana* 63, no. 2 (2024), 113.
5. Cioppi, Sozzi, and Pieraccioli, "150 years of discoveries," 113.
6. W. L. Straus Jr., "*Oreopithecus bambolii*," *Science* 126 (1957): 345–346.
7. Emanual Margoliash, "Primary Structure and Evolution of Cytochrome C," *Proceedings of the National Academy of Sciences* 50 (1963):672–679.
8. Vince Sarich, "A Molecular Approach to the Questions of Human Origins," in *Background for Man*, ed. P. Dolhinow and V. Sarich (Little Brown, 1971).

FOR FURTHER READING

Agusti, J., and M. Anton. *Mammoths, Sabertooths, and Hominids: 65 Million Years of Mammalian Evolution in Europe*. Columbia University Press, 2002.

Alba, D., A. Urciuoli, A. S. Hammond, S. Almecha, L. Rook, and C. Zanolli. "Miocene Ape Evolution: Where Does *Oreopithecus* Fit In?" Bollettino della Societa Paleontologica Italia 63, no. 2 (2024): 153–182.

Begun, D. R. "Dryopithecins, Darwin, de Bonis, and the European Origin of the African Apes and Human Clade." *Geodiversitas* 31, no. 4 (2009): 789–816.

Cioppi, E., M. Sozzi, and R. Pieraccioli. "150 Years of Discoveries, Research, and Debates on *Oreopithecus bambolii* Gervais 1872." *Bollettino della Societa Paleontologica Italia* 63, no. 2 (2024): 109–118.

Darwin, C. *The Descent of Man, and Selection in Relation to Sex*. John Murray, 1871.

Delson, E. "An Anthropoid Enigma: Historical Introduction to the Study of *Oreopithecus bambolii*." *Journal of Human Evolution* 15 (1986): 523–531.

Eiseley, L. C. "*Oreopithecus*: Homunculus or Monkey?" *Scientific American* 194, no. 6 (1956): 91–104.

Gervais, P. "Sur un singe fossile, d'espèce non encore décrite, qui a été decouvert au Monte-Bamboli (Italie)." *Comptes rendus de l'Académie des sciences* 74 (1872): 1217–1223.

Gibbons, A. *The First Human*. Doubleday, 2006.

Hürzeler, J. "Contribution à l'étude de la dentition de lait d' *Oreopithecus bambolii* Gervais." *Eclogae Geologicae Helvetiae* 44 (1952): 404–411.

——. "Neubeschreibung von *Oreopithecus bambolii* Gervais." *Schweizerische Paläontologische Abhandlungen* 66 (1949): 1–20.

——. "*Oreopithecus bambolii* Gervais: A Preliminary Report." *Verhandlungen der Naturforschenden Gesellschaft Basel* 69 (1958): 1–47.

——. "*Oreopithecus*, un point de repère pour l'histoire de l'humanité a l'ère Tertiare." In *Problèmes Actuels de Paléontologie*, 115–121. CNRS, 1956.

——. "The Significance of *Oreopithecus* in the Genealogy of Man." *Triangle* 4 (1960): 164–175.

——. "Zur systematischen Stellung von *Oreopithecus*." *Verhandlungen der Naturforschenden Gesellschaft (Basel)* 65 (1954): 88–95.

Huxley T. H. *Evidence as to Man's Place in Nature*. Williams & Norgate, 1863.

Köhler, M., and S. Moyà-Solà. "Ape-like or Hominid-like? The Positional Behavior of *Oreopithecus bambolii* Reconsidered." *PNAS* 94, no. 21 (1997): 11747–11750.

Pilbeam, D. "New Hominoid Skull Material from the Miocene of Pakistan." *Nature* 295, no. 5846 (1982): 232–234.

Prothero, D. R. *The Princeton Field Guide to Prehistoric Mammals*. Princeton University Press, 2016.

——. *Vertebrate Evolution: From Origins to Dinosaurs and Beyond*. Taylor & Francis/CRC Press, 2022.

Pugh, K. D. "Phylogenetic Analysis of Middle-Late Miocene Apes." *Journal of Human Evolution* 165, (2022): 103140.

Rook, L., L. Bondioli, M. Köhler, S. Moyà-Solà, and R. Macchiarelli. "*Oreopithecus* Was a Bipedal Ape After All: Evidence from the Iliac Cancellous Architecture." *PNAS* 96, no. 15 (1999): 8795–8799.

Szalay, F. S., and E. Delson. *Evolutionary History of the Primates*. Academic Press, 1979.

25 | THE APE'S REFLECTION

AUSTRALOPITHECUS

We must, however, acknowledge, as it seems to me, that man with all his noble qualities, still bears in his bodily frame the indelible stamp of his lowly origin.

—CHARLES DARWIN, *DESCENT OF MAN* (1871)

THE TAUNG CHILD

One summer morning in 1924, young Raymond Dart was struggling with his stiff winged collar as he was preparing to be best man and host a friend's wedding at his house. He heard the sound of two wooden crates dumped on his doorstep and went out to investigate. The first contained nothing of interest, but when he pried open the second, there was a beautiful braincase with a natural endocast of the brain, right on top! Excitedly, he rummaged around until he found the face that had been attached to the brain cast. He could already tell that the brain was much larger than that of a chimpanzee, even though the skull was about the same size. His friend, the groom, urged him to finish dressing, and during the entire ceremony Dart couldn't wait to get back to his "treasures" (figure 25.1). Over the next few months, he cleaned and prepared the specimen, and with one delicate stroke using a hammer and knitting needles, split off the matrix from the front of the face.

Dart was no amateur. He had gotten his medical degree from the University College London, then emigrated to South Africa in 1922, where he took a post in the newly established department of anatomy at the University of

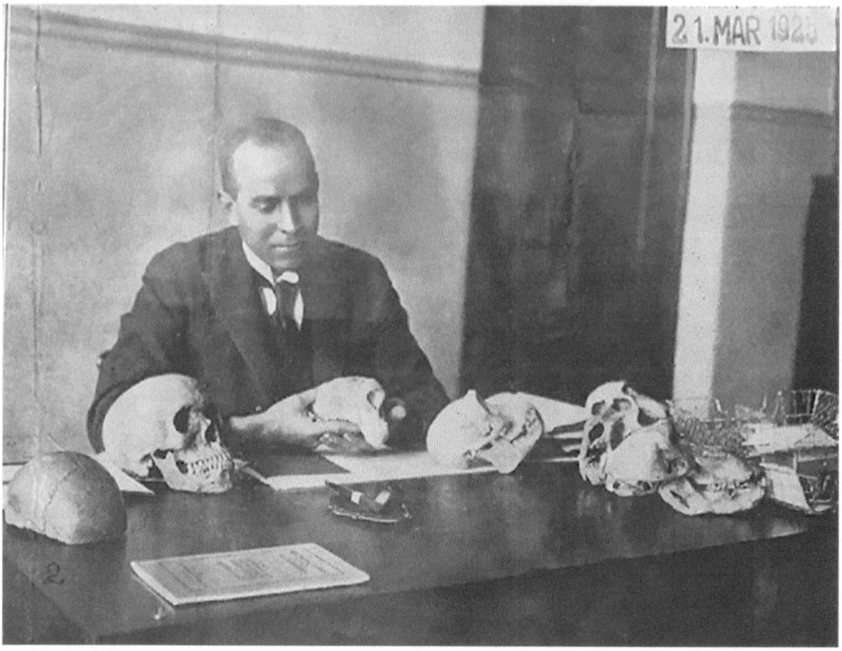

Figure 25.1 ▲
Portrait of a young Raymond Dart in 1925, examining fossil ape and human skulls. (Courtesy of Wikimedia Commons)

Witswatersrand in Johannesburg. Upon arriving, he was dismayed to find the department had no comparative collections of human and ape skulls and skeletons, which are so essential to teaching anatomy. He announced to his students that there would be a competition to see who could bring in the most interesting bones. One student, the only woman in the class, said she knew of the skull of a fossil baboon on the mantel of a friend's house. Although Dart doubted it was really a baboon (since almost no fossil primates were then known in sub-Saharan Africa), when she brought the skull in, she was right. The skull had come from the house of the director of the Northern Lime Company, turning limestone from a quarry called Taung into cement. Dart then asked him to send over any other fossils they found when blasting in the limestone caves.

Preparing the specimen yielded even more surprises. As he worked on it, the face that emerged was that of a young child of about four years, with all its baby teeth still in place (figure 25.2). The skull was about the size of

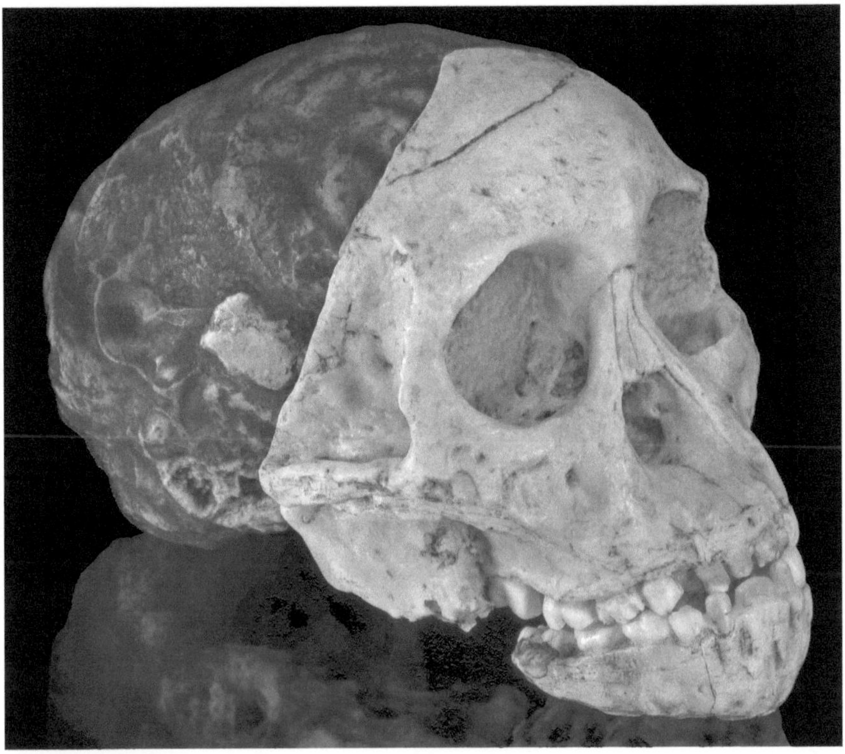

Figure 25.2 ▲

The famous Taung child skull, a young *Australopithecus africanus*, showing the complete flat face with no brow ridges, and the natural endocast. (Courtesy of Wikimedia Commons)

that of a modern chimpanzee. However, it had a number of hominin-like features, including the unusually large brain, the flat face with no snout and small brow ridges, and the reduced canine and human-like teeth arranged in a semicircle in palatal view. Most important, the hole in the base of the skull for the spinal column (foramen magnum) was directly below the brain, proving that this creature held its head up, and probably walked upright.

Dart wrote up his description and analysis and published it in *Nature*, the preeminent scientific journal in the world in 1925 (and today). He called the specimen *Australopithecus africanus* ("African southern ape" in Greek). It clearly showed that early hominins had lived in Africa, especially because it was far more primitive and ape-like than any fossil found so far. Since Dart had studied brain endocasts in medical school, he was particularly interested in the natural endocast on this specimen. It was far larger than any ape brain for a skull of that size and had a noticeably more advanced forebrain—like humans and unlike apes.

Dart thought his evidence was conclusive, and he expected to receive accolades from the scientific community. Instead he was disappointed to see all the great anthropologists in Europe dismiss his specimen as a "juvenile ape." Part of the problem is that juvenile apes do look a lot more like modern humans than they do when they grow up to become adult apes. Still, the upright posture, the hominin-like cheek teeth, the reduced canines and semicircular arrangement of teeth around the palate, and the enlarged forebrain were not artifacts of the youth of the specimen.

Another problem was that Africa was a scholarly backwater. Most African cities were sleepy colonial outposts, without major universities or museums. One of the few countries that was not a primitive outpost for science was South Africa. Thanks to its critical position for all shipping passing around the southern tip of Africa, and later the discovery of its enormous wealth in gold, diamonds, and precious metals, it had been settled and developed centuries before the rest of Africa. As a result, there had been much greater effort in developing a modern European state, both by the British colonialists, and also by the Dutch settlers, who became the Afrikaners. Cape Town, Johannesburg, Durban, Pretoria, and other cities were large and sophisticated. They had their own universities and museums, among the few in all of Africa. In addition, South Africa was the second colony in Africa to become independent of its European masters in 1910, long before most other African colonies became independent in the late 1950s and 1960s.

But the Taung fossil was running up against a wall of prejudice and false notions. British and other European anthropologists were convinced that brains evolved first, then came the teeth and upright posture in hominin evolution. They had the Piltdown skull with the large brain but ape-like teeth to prove it. But the Taung child showed just the opposite: relatively small brain but upright posture and hominin-like teeth with reduced canines. Thus it went against the basic premises of human evolution at the time and could not be accepted. Sir Arthur Keith, one of Piltdown's biggest backers, wrote: "[Dart's] claim is preposterous, the skull is that of a young anthropoid ape . . . and showing so many points of affinity with the two living African anthropoids, the gorilla and chimpanzee, that there cannot be a moment's hesitation in placing the fossil form in this living group."[1]

In addition, there were other unspoken factors: imperialism and racism. The top scholars in Europe didn't trust the conclusions of Dart, an obscure anatomist off in remote South Africa (even though he had trained in London). They dismissed him because he was not a recognized expert but a "country bumpkin" in their eyes. The original *Nature* paper was very short (as they are required to be), so they had only a brief description and a few tiny hand-drawn figures to judge the specimen by. (Dart later wrote a more detailed description, especially of the brain.) But no one had the time, money, or interest to take the long sea voyage and look at the fossil for themselves.

If Mohamed won't come to the mountain, then the mountain must come of Mohamed. Dart sailed to Britain in 1931 and brought the Taung child specimen with him, but to no avail. The prejudices of British anthropologists were just too deeply entrenched. In addition, the excitement over the skulls of "Peking man" was just reaching Europe as Davidson Black's illustrations and descriptions were published, so the poor Taung child (and Dart) were overshadowed.

THE PILTDOWN HOAX

Why was Dart's *Australopithecus* specimen rejected while European scholars focused on a specimen called "Piltdown Man"? As previously mentioned, nearly all of the anthropologists and paleontologists who sought human fossils were convinced that Eurasia was the original homeland of humanity. The idea goes all the way back to the famous German embryologist and biologist Ernst Haeckel, who forcefully argued the point (long before any fossils could test it). Even though Haeckel was Darwin's greatest protégé in Germany, he disagreed with Darwin's idea that humans came from Africa. Haeckel directly inspired Eugène Dubois who then went out to Java and found fossil hominins. As we saw, nearly all of the other pioneering anthropologists and paleontologists agreed with this idea. These scientists included not only Andersson, Zdansky, Black, Weidenreich, and Osborn, but also prominent American Museum paleontologists Walter Granger (who was the chief scientist of the Central Asiatic Expeditions), William Diller Matthew (who argued that most mammalian groups arose in Eurasia and then spread from that center of origin), and William King Gregory.

Initially, the fossil record seemed to support the notion of Asian origins of humans, first with Neanderthals, then "Java Man" and then "Peking Man." Meanwhile, an earlier discovery seemed to confirm that Eurasia was the primary center of human evolution. At a meeting of the Geological Society of London 1912, an amateur collector named Charles Dawson claimed that four years earlier a worker in a gravel pit near Piltdown in England had given him a skull fragment. The worker thought the skullcap was a fossil coconut and tried to break it up, but Dawson came back again and again to Piltdown and found more pieces. Then he showed it to Arthur Smith Woodward of the British Museum, who accompanied Dawson to the Piltdown site. Dawson supposedly found more pieces of the skullcap and a partial jaw, although Woodward found nothing.

Woodward soon produced a reconstruction of the skull and jaws, based on the few pieces that were available (figure 25.3). The specimens were very curious. The skull seemed to be very much like a modern human, with a bulging cranium and large brain and small brow ridges. However, the jaw was extremely ape-like. Crucially, the hinge of the jaw was broken and missing, as was the face and many parts of the skull, so there was no way to tell if the jaw fit properly with the skull. In August 1913, Woodward, Dawson, and the French priest and paleontologist Pierre Teilhard de Chardin went back to the Piltdown spoil piles, where Teilhard found a canine tooth that fit in the gap between the broken parts of the jaw. The canine was small and human-like, not the large fang-like canines that most apes have.

However, Dawson and Woodward's discovery and reconstruction were not unchallenged (figure 25.4). The anatomist Sir Arthur Keith disputed the reconstruction and made one that was much more human-like. The anatomist David Waterston of King's College London decided that the two specimens could not belong together, but that "Piltdown Man" was just an ape jaw attached to a human skull. This was also suggested by the French paleontologist Marcellin Boule (who had described the Neanderthals from La-Chapelle-aux-Saints), and the American zoologist Gerrit Smith Miller. In 1923, Franz Weidenreich (who described the "Peking Man" specimens) argued strongly that it was a modern human skull and an ape jaw, with the teeth filed off so the ape-like appearance of the teeth was masked.

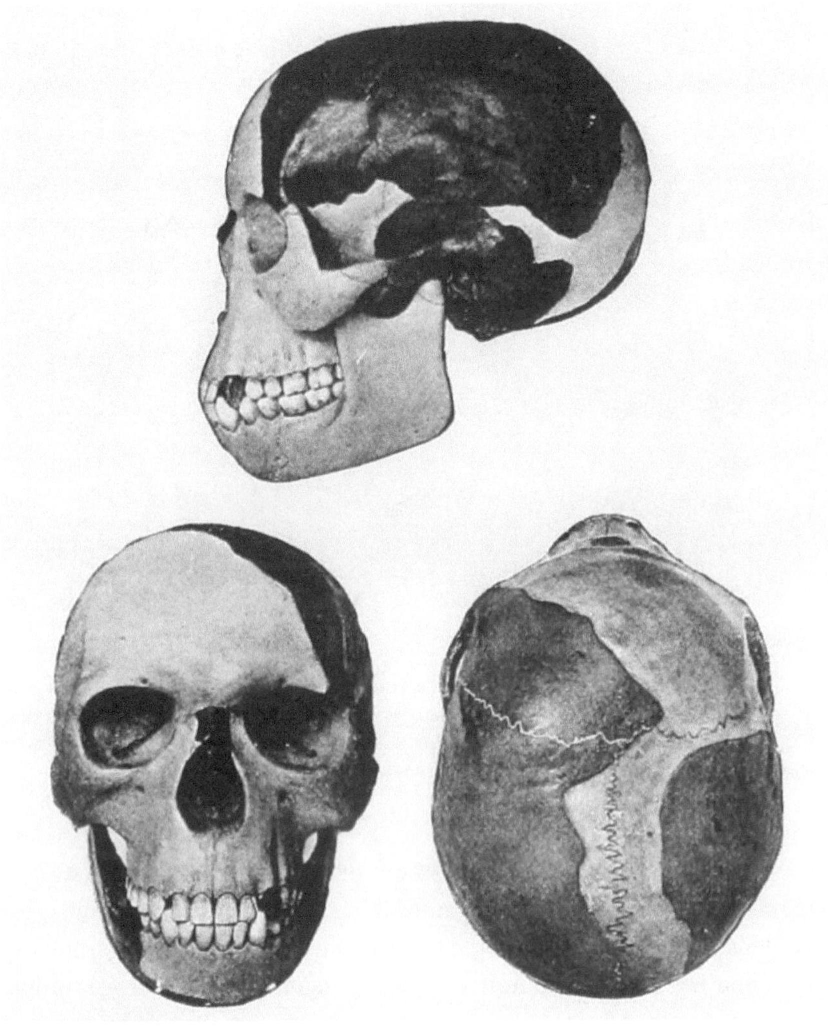

Figure 25.3 ▲
The composite skull of "Piltdown Man," now known to be a hoax with an ape's jaw and a modern human braincase. (Courtesy of Wikimedia Commons)

Although there were always critics and doubters about Piltdown in the 1920s and 1930s, the pillars of British paleontology (especially Woodward, Keith, and Grafton Eliot Smith) were firm backers. Despite the problems, it fit all of their prejudices. First of all, it seemed to suggest that human

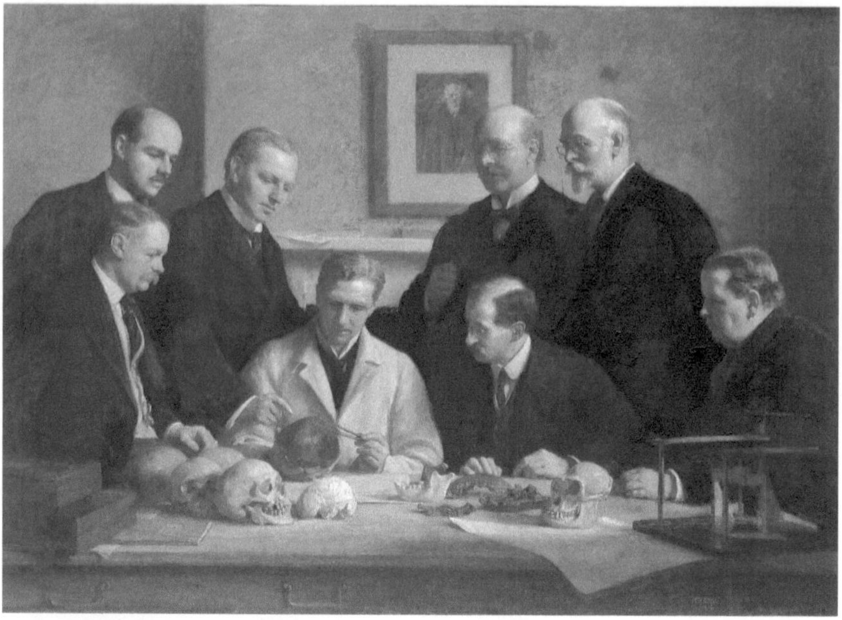

Figure 25.4 ▲
Group portrait of the Piltdown skull being examined. *Back row* (from left): F. O. Barlow, Grafton Elliot Smith, Charles Dawson, Arthur Smith Woodward. *Front row* (from left): A. S. Underwood, Arthur Keith, W. P. Pycraft, and Ray Lankester. The portrait on the wall is of Charles Darwin. Painting by John Cooke, 1915. (Courtesy of Wikimedia Commons)

evolution was driven by the enlargement of the brain, long before we lost our ape-like teeth and jaws or began walking on two legs as a bipedal creature. This was the accepted dogma of paleoanthropology at the time: our brains and intelligence came first, and intelligence is what drove human evolution. Another factor was simple chauvinism. The British were proud that the "missing link" or the "first Briton" had been found on their own soil, a creature even more primitive than "Java Man" or "Peking Man." Thus it appeared that Europe (especially the British Isles) had been the center of human evolution. Piltdown fit so perfectly with the biases and myths of anthropology of the time that the questioning soon died down and it remained an iconic specimen for forty-one years.

It wasn't until the late 1940s and early 1950s that people began to revive the old questions about the specimen, because by then it no longer fit into the fossil record that was becoming better and better known, especially in

Africa. For decades, the original specimens were kept under lock and key, and only a set of replicas was available for study, so few people saw the originals close up. Then in 1953, the chemist Kenneth Oakley, the anthropologist Wilfred E. Le Gros Clark, and Joseph Weiner examined the originals. They found that Piltdown Man was a hoax: the skull was from a modern human from a medieval grave, the jaw was from a Sarawak orangutan, and some of the teeth were chimpanzee. All of the specimens had been stained with a solution of iron and chromic acid to make them look old, and the teeth had been deliberately filed to make them look less ape-like.

The identity of all of those involved in the conspiracy is still debated. Charles Dawson, of course, was the person who "found" all the specimens, and further investigation into his past showed that he had a long history of forging artifacts and human fossils from caves, so he could have been the sole culprit. However, others have argued that he needed expert guidance from an anatomist or anthropologist to make such a successful fraud, deliberately breaking off all the parts that would demonstrate the skull and jaws didn't belong together. At various times, scholars have argued that Teilhard de Chardin, Arthur Keith, Martin A. C. Hinton, Horace de Vere Cole, and even the author of Sherlock Holmes stories, Sir Arthur Conan Doyle, were also behind it. Over a century has now passed, and all the evidence so far has been inconclusive. All we know is that Dawson was the primary (and maybe only) hoaxer and had a long track record of frauds. Whether someone helped him may never be known for sure.

GAMBLE IN JAVA

In his 1859 book *On the Origin of Species*, Darwin never discussed the fossil record of human evolution. Even in his 1871 book, *The Descent of Man*, human fossils were almost not mentioned. There was a good reason for this: there were only a few artifacts that suggested prehistoric peoples, and the first remains of Neanderthals. The first well-described Neanderthals were found in 1856 in a limestone quarry in the Neander Valley near Düsseldorf, Germany, only three years before *On the Origin of Species* was published. The remains consisted only of a skullcap and a few limb bones, and they were originally mistaken for a cave bear. Later, the fossils were widely misinterpreted as a diseased Cossack cavalryman, or other bizarre mistaken identifications. Nobody considered them anything more than an unusual modern human. The earliest complete Neanderthal skeleton from a cave near La-Chapelle-aux-Saints in France happened to be an old diseased individual with rickets, so the early reconstructions falsely showed Neanderthals as stooped and brutish, rather than upright and powerfully built, as we have learned from many better skeletons found since then.

The nineteenth century was nearly over before more primitive hominin specimens were found. In 1887, the Dutch doctor and anatomist Eugene Dubois was fascinated with Darwin's ideas and convinced that humans evolved in eastern Asia, so he volunteered for the Dutch army as a surgeon to be posted in what was then the Dutch East Indies (now Indonesia). Sure enough, he got extraordinarily lucky. After a few excavations, he hit the jackpot. It turned out that there were fossil hominins in the region, and between 1891 and 1895, he and his Javanese crews found a series of specimens, including a skullcap and a thighbone and a few teeth (figure 25.5).

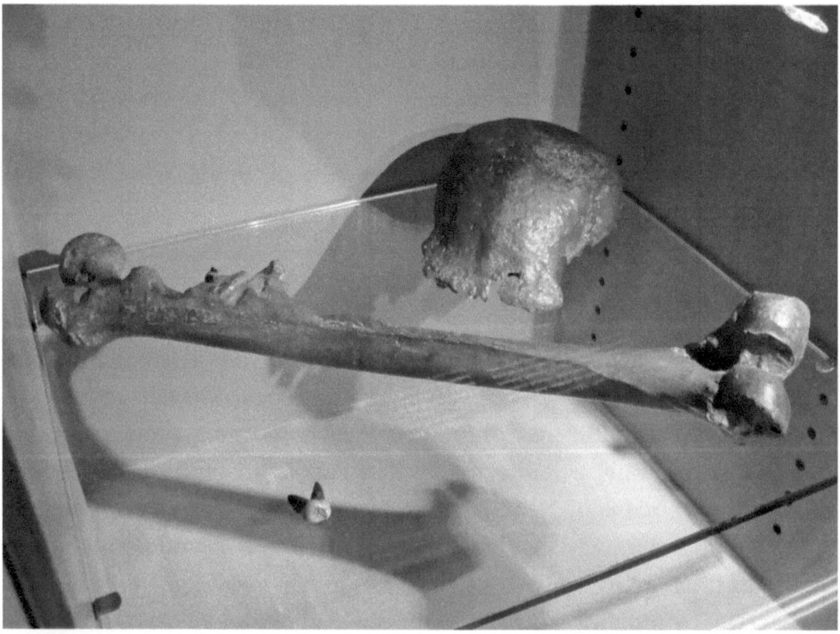

Figure 25.5 ▲

Dubois's original specimens of "Java man" (now *Homo erectus*), including a skull cap and a thighbone. (Courtesy of Wikimedia Commons).

He called these *Pithecanthropus erectus* ("upright ape-man" in Greek), but they came to be known as "Java Man" after the island on which they were found. Although the specimens were incomplete, it was clear from the thighbone that the creatures walked upright. The skullcap was very primitive, with prominent brow ridges, yet its cranial capacity was about half that of modern humans.

Dubois returned to Holland and eventually received a professorship in 1899. Unfortunately, he did not handle the normal harsh criticism from the scientific community very well. Many anthropologists were not convinced of Dubois's claims from such incomplete material and thought the fossils were from a deformed ape. As a result, Dubois withdrew from the debate, an angry and bitter man. He hid his specimens away and refused to show them to anyone or get involved in the scientific discussion. By the 1920s, opinion was turning in his favor, but he remained withdrawn and embittered, and died that way in 1940 at the age of eighty-two.

OUT OF AFRICA—OR EURASIA?

In 1871, Darwin argued that humans must have evolved from roots in Africa. His reasoning was simple: all our closest ape relatives (chimpanzees and gorillas) came from there, so it made sense that our common ancestor with them would also have originated in Africa (see epigraph). But as the twentieth century began, most anthropologists were convinced that humans originated in Eurasia, and the "out of Asia" idea was deeply entrenched in their thinking, so something from Africa could not possibly be related to advanced humans in Eurasia. Underlying this idea was a strong streak of racism. Many anthropologists of that time still regarded African peoples as sub-human and even a different sub-species from "superior" European races, so the idea that our ancestors came from the "inferior," "primitive," dark-skinned people of Africa was abhorrent to their racist notions. Clearly, modern Europeans must have been descended from an advanced, large-brained European lineage, such as Piltdown. Besides, at that point the Taung child was the only specimen from Africa, while they had Piltdown, Java Man, the Miocene ape *Dryopithecus*, and many other fossils from Eurasia.

The prominent paleontologist Henry Fairfield Osborn, president of the American Museum of Natural History (see chapter 9), organized and funded the legendary Central Asiatic Expeditions to Mongolia in the 1920s on the premise that they would find the oldest human ancestors. They didn't, but the expedition instead found very important dinosaur fossils (including the first dinosaur eggs and nests), as well as really interesting and unusual fossil mammals. Dubois's discoveries in Java helped confirm this idea.

Then in 1921, while Osborn's American Museum expeditions began to explore Mongolia, the Swedish paleontologist Johann Gunnar Andersson found a cave once called "Choukoutien" (now "Zhoukoudian" in the modern Pinyin transliteration of Mandarin) near Peking (now Beijing) in China. The Austrian paleontologist Otto Zdansky took over the excavations, which yielded an excellent fauna of Ice Age mammals, including a giant hyaena and two teeth of a hominin as well. They gave those specimens to the Canadian anatomist Davidson Black (then working at Peking Union Medical College), who published them in 1927 and called them *Sinanthropus pekingensis* ("Chinese human from Peking").

The excavations continued once funding was obtained, with only a few more teeth to show for all those years of work. Finally, in 1928 they found a lower jaw, skull fragments, and more teeth, and the primitive nature of the species was confirmed. This brought new funding, which prompted a much larger excavation with mostly Chinese workers and scientists. Soon they had more than two hundred human fossils, including six nearly complete skulls. Davidson Black died of heart failure in 1934 at age forty-nine, so the German anatomist Franz Weidenreich took over the study and description of the fossils in 1935. Although Black had published many preliminary descriptions of the fossils as they were found, it was Weidenreich's detailed monographs that gave complete documentation of the fossils. With this material, it soon became apparent that "Peking Man" was very similar to "Java Man," and today most anthropologists consider them the same species, *Homo erectus*.

As the excavations at Zhoukoudian continued, war clouds were gathering on the horizon. The Japanese Empire was expanding, and they began to attack and annex parts of China, piece by piece. In 1931, they invaded the northeastern part of China called Manchuria, and turned it into a Japanese province, Manchukuo. Japan set up a puppet government headed by Puyi, the last Qing Dynasty Emperor of China. In 1937, the second wave of Japanese invasion of China began, and Japanese annexed another large chunk of China as they fought the Nationalist army under Chiang Kai Shek, and the Communists under Mao Zedong.

Then in 1941, just before the Pearl Harbor attack, the alarmed scientists in Beijing could sense that war was coming. The crews at Zhoukoudian were afraid the specimens would fall into Japanese hands and become war souvenirs rather than specimens preserved for scientific study. They packed all the specimens at Peking Union Medical College in two large crates, loaded them on a US Marine Corps truck, and tried to smuggle them out of the country through the port of Qinhuangdao. Somewhere in the secretive scramble to avoid the Japanese invaders, the crates were lost, and no one knows where they went. Some say they had been loaded on a ship that was sunk by the Japanese. Others suggest that the specimens were secretly buried to avoid discovery, and no one knows where they are. Still others think Chinese merchants who routinely destroy fossils ("dragon bones") and grind them up for traditional "medicine" found them. Fortunately, nearly all of the original material was molded, cast, and made into accurate replicas that are found in many museums, so we know what they look like in detail. In addition, more recent excavations have found much more material, so the loss was not irreparable.

VINDICATION

For many long years, Raymond Dart stuck to his guns and insisted his Taung child was the oldest known hominin fossil. In the 1920s and 1930s, other South African scientists were convinced that Dart was right and was unfairly criticized. Among them was the Scottish doctor Robert Broom, who had already made a reputation for himself as an important paleontologist by finding spectacular specimens of Permian reptiles and the earliest relatives of mammals in the Great Karoo. With his network of collectors, he kept getting specimens sent from the many limestone caves in South Africa. Working in a cave called Kromdraai in 1938, Broom found a very robust adult skull he called *Paranthropus robustus* ("robust near-human" in Greek) (figure 25.6A). Later, in the famous cave complex at Swartkrans, he found more than 130 individuals of *P. robustus*. A recent analysis of their teeth showed than none of these robust, gorilla-like humans lived past seventeen years, and that they ate a gritty diet of nuts, seeds, and grasses.

Also in 1938 Broom obtained an endocranial cast of a fossil skull with a capacity of 485 cc, far too large to be that of an ape. He called this specimen *Plesianthropus transvaalensis* ("near ape of the Transvaal"). Then he heard word of fossils coming from a cave called Sterkfontein. On April 18, 1947, Broom and John T. Robinson found the complete skull of what was then considered to be an adult female that demonstrated hominin features, yet it was just as primitive as the Taung child. They nicknamed this specimen "Mrs. Ples," and their discovery showed that South Africa was producing many more primitive hominins than anywhere in Eurasia (figure 25.6B). Soon other fossils of the australopithecine from Sterkfontein were found, establishing the variability of the population of *Plesianthropus transvaalensis.* Later anthropologists decided that the Sterkfontein adults and the Taung child are the same species, so *Plesianthropus transvaalensis* is now lumped together in Dart's original taxon, *Australopithecus africanus.*

These discoveries in Africa—along with the complete lack of anything so primitive or ancient in Eurasia—began to shift the momentum of the debate away from the old "out of Asia" school of thought. The wide spectrum of australopithecines described by 1947 made it appear more and more likely that Darwin was right: humans originated in Africa. Not only that, but the

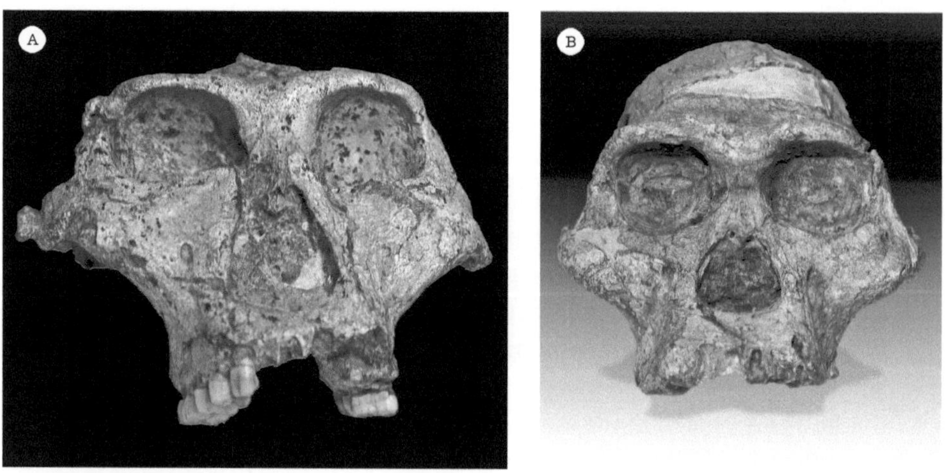

Figure 25.6 ▲

The original skull of *Paranthropus robustus.* (*B*) The famous "Mrs. Ples" skull, now thought to be a female *Paranthropus robustus.* (Courtesy of Wikimedia Commons)

idea that brains and intelligence drove human evolution, but the teeth and upright posture came later, was also being reversed (as the older generation of racist anthropologist died off as well). Every fossil found so far demonstrated that upright posture and advanced teeth came first, and much later the brain began to enlarge. By 1953, when someone finally decided to reexamine Piltdown closely, it was an embarrassment, and no longer fit the emerging picture of human evolution. The exposure of the hoax was a great relief, and removed an anomaly that flew in the face of the overwhelming trend of the data.

Dart would wait another twenty years before the European anthropological community stopped dismissing him and began to recognize the importance of his find. In 1947, Sir Arthur Keith admitted that "Dart was right and I was wrong."[2] But Dart had the last laugh. He lived until 1988, passing away at the ripe old age of ninety-five, celebrated and honored for his discoveries and for pioneering modern paleoanthropology, while most of his bitter rivals died long before him and are now forgotten.

NOTES

1. Arthur Keith, "Australopithecina or Dartians," *Nature* 159, no. 377(March 15, 1947).
2. Keith, "Australopithecinae or Dartians."

FOR FURTHER READING

Conroy, G. C. *Primate Evolution*. Norton, 1990.

Delson, E. C. *Ancestors: The Hard Evidence*. Liss, 1985.

Foley, R. A., and R. Lewin. *Principles of Human Evolution*. Wiley-Blackwell, 2003.

Harari, Y. N. *Sapiens: A Brief History of Humankind*. Harper, 2015.

Johanson, D., and M. Edey. *Lucy: The Beginnings of Humankind*. Simon & Schuster, 1981.

Johanson, D., L. Johanson, and B. Edgar. *Ancestors: In Search of Human Origins*. Villard, 1994.

Jurmain, R., L. Kilgore, D. Trevathan, and R. Ciochon. *Introduction to Physical Anthropology*. Cengage, 2014.

Larsen, C. S. *Our Origins: Discovering Physical Anthropology*. Norton, 2014.

Lewin, R. *In the Age of Mankind: A Smithsonian Book on Human Evolution*. Smithsonian Institution Press, 1988.

——. *Bones of Contention: Controversies in the Search for Human Origins*. University of Chicago Press, 1987.

Prothero, D. R. *The Princeton Field Guide to Prehistoric Mammals*. Princeton University Press, 2016.

——. *Vertebrate Evolution: From Origins to Dinosaurs and Beyond*. Taylor & Francis/CRC Press, 2022.

Roberts, A. *Evolution: The Human Story*. DK, 2018.

Sawyer, G. J., V. Deak, E. Sarmiento, and R. Milner. *The Last Human: A Guide to the Twenty-Two Species of Extinct Humans*. Yale University Press, 2007.

Stringer, C. *Lone Survivors: How We Came to Be the Only Humans on Earth*. Times, 2012.

Stringer, C., and P. Andrews. *The Complete World of Human Evolution*. Thames and Hudson, 2005.

Tattersall, I. *The Human Odyssey: Four Million Years of Human Evolution*. Prentice Hall, 1993.

——. *Masters of the Planet: The Search for Our Human Origins*. St. Martin's Griffin, 2012.

——. *The Strange Case of the Rickety Cossack and Other Cautionary Tales from Human Evolution*. St. Martin's, 2015.

Tattersall, I., and J. Schwartz. 2000. *Extinct Humans*. Westview, 2000.

Walker, A., and P. Shipman. *The Wisdom of the Bones: In Search of Human Origins*. Knopf, 1996.

INDEX

GPSR Authorized Representative: Easy Access System Europe, Mustamäe tee 50, 10621 Tallinn, Estonia, gpsr.requests@easproject.com

www.ingramcontent.com/pod-product-compliance
Ingram Content Group UK Ltd.
Pitfield, Milton Keynes, MK11 3LW, UK
UKHW040814270826
474550UK00008B/26/J
9780231218306